Compensation

Tenth Edition

George T. Milkovich
Cornell University

Jerry M. Newman
State University of New York–Buffalo

Barry Gerhart
University of Wisconsin–Madison

McGraw-Hill Irwin

**McGraw-Hill
Irwin**

COMPENSATION

Published by McGraw-Hill/Irwin, a business unit of The McGraw-Hill Companies, Inc., 1221 Avenue of the Americas, New York, NY, 10020. Copyright © 2011, 2008, 2005, 2002, 1999, 1996, 1993, 1990, 1987, 1984 by The McGraw-Hill Companies, Inc. All rights reserved. No part of this publication may be reproduced or distributed in any form or by any means, or stored in a database or retrieval system, without the prior written consent of The McGraw-Hill Companies, Inc., including, but not limited to, in any network or other electronic storage or transmission, or broadcast for distance learning.

Some ancillaries, including electronic and print components, may not be available to customers outside the United States.

This book is printed on acid-free paper.

2 3 4 5 6 7 8 9 0 DOC/DOC 1 0 9 8 7 6 5 4 3 2 1 0

ISBN   978-0-07-353049-9
MHID   0-07-353049-2

Vice president and editor-in-chief: *Brent Gordon*
Publisher: *Paul Ducham*
Director of development: *Ann Torbert*
Managing developmental editor: *Laura Hurst Spell*
Editorial coordinator: *Jane Beck*
Vice president and director of marketing: *Robin J. Zwettler*
Associate marketing manager: *Jaime Halteman*
Vice president of editing, design and production: *Sesha Bolisetty*
Project manager: *Christine A. Vaughan*
Lead production supervisor: *Michael R. McCormick*
Design coordinator: *Joanne Mennemeier*
Media project manager: *Suresh Babu, Hurix Systems Pvt. Ltd.*
Typeface: *10/12 Times Roman*
Compositor: *Aptara®, Inc.*
Printer: *R. R. Donnelley*

Library of Congress Cataloging-in-Publication Data

Milkovich, George T.
    Compensation / George T. Milkovich, Jerry M. Newman, Barry Gerhart.—10th ed.
        p. cm.
    Includes index.
    ISBN-13: 978-0-07-353049-9 (alk. paper)
    ISBN-10: 0-07-353049-2 (alk. paper)
    1. Compensation management. I. Newman, Jerry M. II. Gerhart, Barry A. III. Title.
HF5549.5.C67M54 2011
658.3'2—dc22

                                                                                                    2009042396

Table of Contents

Preface   xiii

PART ONE
INTRODUCING THE PAY MODEL AND PAY STRATEGY

Chapter 1
The Pay Model   2

Compensation: Does It Matter? (or, "So What?")   3
Compensation: Definition, Please   4
Society   4
Stockholders   6
Managers   7
Employees   8
Global Views—Vive la différence   10
Forms of Pay   10
Cash Compensation: Base   11
Cash Compensation: Merit Pay/Cost-of-Living Adjustments   12
Cash Compensation: Incentives   12
Long-Term Incentives   13
Benefits: Income Protection   13
Benefits: Work/Life Balance   13
Benefits: Allowances   14
Total Earnings Opportunities: Present Value of a Stream of Earnings   14
Relational Returns From Work   14
A Pay Model   15
Compensation Objectives   15
Four Policy Choices   19
Pay Techniques   21
Book Plan   22
Caveat Emptor—Be an Informed Consumer   22
1. Is the Research Useful?   23
2. Does the Study Separate Correlation From Causation?   23
3. Are There Alternative Explanations?   24
Your Turn: Circuit City   24

Chapter 2
Strategy: The Totality of Decisions   33

Similarities and Differences in Strategies   33
Different Strategies Within the Same Industry   35
Different Strategies Within the Same Company   36
Strategic Choices   36
Support Business Strategy   38
Support HR Strategy   40
The Pay Model Guides Strategic Pay Decisions   41
Stated Versus Unstated Strategies   42
Developing a Total Compensation Strategy: Four Steps   43
Step 1: Assess Total Compensation Implications   44
HR Strategy: Pay as a Supporting Player or Catalyst for Change?   44
Step 2: Map a Total Compensation Strategy   47
Steps 3 and 4: Implement and Reassess   50
Source of Competitive Advantage: Three Tests   50
Align   50
Differentiate   50
Add Value   51
"Best Practices" Versus "Best Fit"?   53
Guidance From the Evidence   53
Virtuous and Vicious Circles   54
Your Turn: Merrill Lynch   55
Still Your Turn: Mapping Compensation Strategies   57

PART TWO
INTERNAL ALIGNMENT: DETERMINING THE STRUCTURE

Chapter 3
Defining Internal Alignment   68

Compensation Strategy: Internal Alignment   69
Supports Organization Strategy   69

Supports Work Flow   70
Motivates Behavior   71
Structures Vary Among Organizations   71
Number of Levels   72
Differentials   72
Criteria: Content and Value   72
What Shapes Internal Structures?   75
Economic Pressures   75
Government Policies, Laws, and Regulations   76
External Stakeholders   76
Cultures and Customs   77
Organization Strategy   78
Organization Human Capital   78
Organization Work Design   78
Overall HR Policies   78
Internal Labor Markets: Combining External and
Organization Factors   79
Employee Acceptance: A Key Factor   80
Pay Structures Change   80
Strategic Choices in Designing Internal
Structures   81
Tailored Versus Loosely Coupled   81
Hierarchical Versus Egalitarian   81
Guidance From the Evidence   83
Equity Theory: Fairness   83
Tournament Theory: Motivation and
Performance   84
Institutional Model: Copy Others   85
(More) Guidance From the Evidence   85
Consequences of Structures   86
Efficiency   87
Fairness   87
Compliance   87
Your Turn: So You Want to Lead an Orchestra!   88

Chapter 4
Job Analysis   94

Structures Based on Jobs, People, or Both   95
Job-Based Approach: Most Common   97
Why Perform Job Analysis?   97
Job Analysis Procedures   98
What Information Should Be Collected?   99
Job Data: Identification   99
Job Data: Content   99

Employee Data   101
"Essential Elements" and the Americans With
Disabilities Act   104
Level of Analysis   105
How Can the Information Be Collected?   106
Conventional Methods   106
Quantitative Methods   106
Who Collects the Information?   108
Who Provides the Information?   108
What About Discrepancies?   109
Job Descriptions Summarize the Data   110
Using Generic Job Descriptions   110
Describing Managerial/Professional Jobs   110
Verify the Description   111
Job Analysis: Bedrock or Bureaucracy?   113
Job Analysis and Globalization   114
Job Analysis and Susceptibility to
Offshoring   114
Job Analysis Information and Comparability
Across Borders   116
Judging Job Analysis   116
Reliability   116
Validity   117
Acceptability   117
Currency   117
Usefulness   118
A Judgment Call   118
Your Turn: The Customer-Service Agent   119

Chapter 5
Job-Based Structures and Job
Evaluation   128

Job-Based Structures: Job Evaluation   129
Defining Job Evaluation: Content, Value, and
External Market Links   130
Content and Value   130
Linking Content With the External Market   130
"Measure for Measure" Versus "Much Ado About
Nothing"   131
"How-To": Major Decisions   131
Establish the Purpose   132
Single Versus Multiple Plans   132
Choose Among Job Evaluation
Methods   134

Job Evaluation Methods   135
  Ranking   135
  Classification   136
  Point Method   139
Who Should Be Involved?   149
  The Design Process Matters   150
The Final Result: Structure   151
Balancing Chaos and Control   152
Your Turn: Job Evaluation at Whole Foods   153

Chapter 6
Person-Based Structures   161

Person-Based Structures: Skill Plans   162
  Types of Skill Plans   162
  Purpose of the Skill-Based Structure   165
"How-To": Skill Analysis   166
  What Information to Collect?   166
  Whom to Involve?   167
  Establish Certification Methods   167
  *Outcomes of Skill-Based Pay Plans: Guidance From
  Research and Experience   169*
Person-Based Structures: Competencies   170
  Defining Competencies   171
  *Purpose of the Competency-Based
  Structure   174*
"How-To": Competency Analysis   175
  Objective   175
  What Information to Collect?   176
  Whom to Involve?   176
  Establish Certification Methods   180
  Resulting Structure   180
  *Competencies and Employee Selection and
  Training/Development   180*
  *Guidance From the Research on
  Competencies   182*
One More Time: Internal Alignment Reflected in
Structures   182
Administering the Plan   183
Evidence of Usefulness of Results   183
  Reliability of Job Evaluation Techniques   183
  Validity   183
  Acceptability   184
Bias in Internal Structures   184
  Wages Criteria Bias   185

The Perfect Structure   186
Your Turn: Climb the Legal Ladder   187

PART THREE
EXTERNAL COMPETITIVENESS: DETERMINING THE PAY LEVEL

Chapter 7
Defining Competitiveness   198

Compensation Strategy: External
Competitiveness   199
  Control Costs and Increase Revenues   199
  Attract and Retain the Right Employees   202
What Shapes External Competitiveness?   205
Labor Market Factors   205
  How Labor Markets Work   206
  Labor Demand   207
  Marginal Product   207
  Marginal Revenue   207
  Labor Supply   209
Modifications to the Demand Side   209
  Compensating Differentials   209
  Efficiency Wage   210
  Signaling   211
Modifications to the Supply Side (Only Two
More Theories to Go)   212
  Reservation Wage   213
  Human Capital   213
Product Market Factors and Ability
to Pay   213
  Product Demand   214
  Degree of Competition   214
  A Different View: What Managers Say   214
  *Segmented Supplies of Labor and (Different)
  Going Rates   215*
Organization Factors   216
  Industry and Technology   216
  Employer Size   216
  People's Preferences   217
  Organization Strategy   217
Relevant Markets   218
  Defining the Relevant Market   218
  *Globalization of Relevant Labor Markets:
  Offshoring and Outsourcing   219*

Competitive Pay Policy Alternatives   220
  *What Difference Does the Pay-Level Policy
  Make?   221*
  Pay With Competition (Match)   221
  Lead Pay-Level Policy   222
  Lag Pay-Level Policy   223
  *Different Policies for Different Employee
  Groups   223*
  Not by Pay Level Alone: Pay Mix Strategies   223
Consequences of Pay-Level and -Mix Decisions:
Guidance From the Research   227
  Efficiency   227
  Fairness   228
  Compliance   228
Your Turn: Sled Dog Software   229
Still Your Turn: Fit the Pay-Mix Policy to the
Compensation Strategy   229

Chapter 8
Designing Pay Levels, Mix, and Pay Structures   238

Major Decisions   239
Specify Competitive Pay Policy   239
The Purpose of a Survey   240
  Adjust Pay Level—How Much to Pay?   240
  Adjust Pay Mix—What Forms?   240
  Adjust Pay Structure?   240
  Study Special Situations   241
  Estimate Competitors' Labor Costs   241
Select Relevant Market Competitors   241
  Fuzzy Markets   245
Design the Survey   245
  Who Should Be Involved?   246
  How Many Employers?   246
  Which Jobs to Include?   248
  What Information to Collect?   250
Interpret Survey Results and Construct a Market
Line   253
  Verify Data   253
  Statistical Analysis   258
  Update the Survey Data   259
  Construct a Market Pay Line   261
  Setting Pay for Non-Benchmark Jobs   263
  *Combine Internal Structure and External Market
  Rates   265*

From Policy to Practice: The Pay-Policy
Line   266
  Choice of Measure   266
  Updating   266
  Policy Line as Percent of Market Line   266
From Policy to Practice: Grades and Ranges   266
  Why Bother With Grades and Ranges?   266
  Develop Grades   267
  *Establish Range Midpoints, Minimums, and
  Maximums   268*
  Overlap   268
From Policy to Practice: Broad Banding   269
  Flexibility-Control   271
Balancing Internal and External Pressures:
Adjusting the Pay Structure   272
  Reconciling Differences   272
Market Pricing   273
  *Business Strategy (More Than "Follow the
  Leader")   274*
Review   274
Your Turn: Word-of-Mouse: Dot-Com
Comparisons   275

PART FOUR
EMPLOYEE CONTRIBUTIONS: DETERMINING INDIVIDUAL PAY

Chapter 9
Pay-for-Performance: The Evidence   284

What Behaviors Do Employers Care About?
Linking Organization Strategy to Compensation
and Performance Management   285
What Does It Take to Get These Behaviors? What
Theory Says   290
What Does It Take to Get These Behaviors?
What Practitioners Say   294
Does Compensation Motivate
Behavior?   299
  Do People Join a Firm Because of Pay?   299
  *Do People Stay in a Firm (or Leave) Because
  of Pay?   300*
  *Do Employees More Readily Agree to Develop Job
  Skills Because of Pay?   301*
  *Do Employees Perform Better on Their Jobs
  Because of Pay?   301*

Designing a Pay-for-Performance Plan   305
  Efficiency   305
  Equity/Fairness   307
  Compliance   307
Your Turn: Burger Boy   308

Chapter 10
Pay-for-Performance Plans   317

What Is a Pay-for-Performance Plan?   317
Does Variable Pay Improve Performance Results?
The General Evidence   319
Specific Pay-for-Performance Plans:
Short Term   319
  Merit Pay   319
  Lump-Sum Bonuses   320
  Individual Spot Awards   321
  Individual Incentive Plans   322
  *Individual Incentive Plans: Advantages and
  Disadvantages   326*
  Individual Incentive Plans: Examples   327
Team Incentive Plans: Types   327
  *Comparing Group and Individual Incentive
  Plans   333*
  Large Group Incentive Plans   334
  Gain-Sharing Plans   334
  Profit-Sharing Plans   339
  Earnings-at-Risk Plans   340
  *Group Incentive Plans: Advantages and
  Disadvantages   341*
  Group Incentive Plans: Examples   342
Explosive Interest in Long-Term Incentive
Plans   342
  Employee Stock Ownership Plans (ESOPs)   344
  *Performance Plans (Performance Share and
  Performance Unit)   345*
  Broad-Based Option Plans (BBOPs)   345
  *Combination Plans: Mixing Individual and
  Group   346*
Your Turn: Incentives in the Clubhouse   346

Appendix
  **10-A: Gain-Sharing Plan at Dresser
         Rand   348**

  **10-B: Profit-Sharing (401K) at
         Walgreens   353**

Chapter 11
Performance Appraisals   358

The Role of Performance Appraisals in
Compensation Decisions   359
  Performance Metrics   360
Strategies for Better Understanding and
Measuring Job Performance   361
  The Balanced Scorecard Approach   361
  Strategy 1: Improve Appraisal Formats   362
  Strategy 2: Select the Right Raters   370
  *Strategy 3: Understand How Raters Process
  Information   373*
  *Common Errors in Appraising Performance:
  Criterion Contamination   373*
  *Strategy 4: Training Raters to Rate More
  Accurately   377*
Putting It All Together: The Performance
Evaluation Process   377
Equal Employment Opportunity and Performance
Evaluation   380
Tying Pay to Subjectively Appraised
Performance   382
  Competency: Customer Care   383
  Performance- and Position-Based Guidelines   384
  Designing Merit Guidelines   384
Promotional Increases as a Pay-for-Performance
Tool   386
Your Turn: Performance Appraisal at
Burger King   386

Appendix
  **11-A: Balanced Scorecard Example:
         Department of Energy (Federal Personal
         Property Management Program)   390**

  **11-B: Sample Appraisal Form for Leadership
         Dimension: Pfizer Pharmaceutical   393**

PART FIVE
EMPLOYEE BENEFITS

Chapter 12
The Benefit Determination Process   414

Why the Growth in Employee Benefits?   416
  Wage and Price Controls   416

Unions   416
Employer Impetus   416
Cost Effectiveness of Benefits   417
Government Impetus   417
The Value of Employee Benefits   417
Key Issues in Benefit Planning, Design, and Administration   419
Benefits Planning and Design Issues   419
Benefit Administration Issues   420
Components of a Benefit Plan   423
Employer Preferences   423
Employee Preferences   427
Administering the Benefit Program   429
Employee Benefit Communication   431
Claims Processing   433
Cost Containment   433
Your Turn: World Measurement   434

Chapter 13
Benefit Options   442

Legally Required Benefits   445
Workers' Compensation   446
Social Security   447
Unemployment Insurance   450
Family and Medical Leave Act (FMLA)   452
Consolidated Omnibus Budget Reconciliation Act (COBRA)   452
Health Insurance Portability and Accountability Act (HIPAA)   452
Retirement and Savings Plan Payments   452
Defined Benefit Plans   453
Defined Contribution Plans   453
Individual Retirement Accounts (IRAs)   455
Employee Retirement Income Security Act (ERISA)   455
How Much Retirement Income to Provide?   457
Life Insurance   458
Medical and Medically Related Payments   458
General Health Care   458
Health Care: Cost Control Strategies   462
Short-and Long-Term Disability   464

Dental Insurance   465
Vision Care   465
Miscellaneous Benefits   465
Paid Time Off During Working Hours   465
Payment for Time Not Worked   466
Child Care   467
Elder Care   467
Domestic Partner Benefits   467
Legal Insurance   467
Benefits for Contingent Workers   467
Your Turn: Mr. Baldy Car Wash   468

PART SIX
EXTENDING THE SYSTEM

Chapter 14
Compensation of Special Groups   477

Who Are Special Groups?   478
Compensation Strategy for Special Groups   479
Supervisors   479
Corporate Directors   480
Executives   480
What's All the Furor Over Executive Compensation? What the Critics and Press Say   486
What's All the Furor Over Executive Compensation? What Academics Say   489
Scientists and Engineers in High-Technology Industries   491
Sales Forces   494
Contingent Workers   498
Your Turn: Compensation of Special Groups   499

Chapter 15
Union Role in Wage and Salary Administration   505

The Impact of Unions in Wage Determination   506
Union Impact on General Wage Levels   506
The Structure of Wage Packages   508
Union Impact: The Spillover Effect   509
Role of Unions in Wage and Salary Policies and Practices   509

Unions and Alternative Reward Systems 513
   Lump-Sum Awards 514
   *Employee Stock Ownership Plans
   (ESOPs) 514*
   Pay-for-Knowledge Plans 514
   Gain-Sharing Plans 515
   Profit-Sharing Plans 515
Your Turn: General Technology 516

Chapter 16
International Pay Systems 521

The Global Context 523
The Social Contract 525
   *Centralized or Decentralized
   Pay-Setting 526*
   Regulation 527
Culture 530
   *Culture Matters, But So Does Cultural
   Diversity 532*
Trade Unions and Employee Involvement 534
Ownership and Financial Markets 534
Managerial Autonomy 535
Comparing Costs 536
   Labor Costs and Productivity 536
   Cost of Living and Purchasing Power 537
Comparing Systems 540
   The Total Pay Model: Strategic Choices 540
National Systems: Comparative Mind-Set 540
   Japanese Traditional National System 540
   German Traditional National System 544
   *Strategic Comparisons: Traditional Systems in
   Japan, Germany, United States 545*
   *Evolution and Change in the Traditional Japanese
   and German Models 547*
Strategic Market Mind-Set 549
   Localizer: "Think Global, Act Local" 549
   Exporter: "Headquarters Knows Best" 549
   *Globalizer: "Think and Act Globally and
   Locally" 550*
Expatriate Pay 550
   Elements of Expatriate Compensation 552
   The Balance Sheet Approach 554
   *Expatriate Systems → Objectives? Quel
   dommage! 558*

Borderless World → Borderless Pay?
Globalists 559
Your Turn: IBM's Worldwide Business and
Employment Strategies and Compensation 559

PART SEVEN
MANAGING THE SYSTEM

Chapter 17
Government and Legal Issues in
Compensation 573

Government as Part of the Employment
Relationship 575
   Demand 575
   Supply 575
Fair Labor Standards Act of 1938 578
   Minimum Wage 578
   "Living Wage" 580
   Overtime and Hours of Work 580
   Child Labor 586
Employee or Independent Contractor? 586
Prevailing Wage Laws 588
Pay Discrimination: What Is It? 589
The Equal Pay Act 591
   Definition of Equal 591
   *Definitions of Skill, Effort, Responsibility, Working
   Conditions 592*
   Factors Other Than Sex 592
   "Reverse" Discrimination 593
Title VII of the Civil Rights Act of 1964 and
Related Laws 593
   Disparate Treatment 594
   Disparate Impact 595
Executive Order 11246 595
Pay Discrimination and Dissimilar Jobs 597
   *Proof of Discrimination: Use of
   Market Data 597*
   *Proof of Discrimination: Jobs of Comparable
   Worth 598*
Earnings Gaps 599
   Sources of the Earnings Gaps 601
   *Differences in Occupations and
   Qualifications 602*

Differences in Industries and Firms 603
Union Membership 604
Presence of Discrimination 604
Gaps Are Global 605
Comparable Worth 605
The Mechanics 606
Union Developments 607
A Proactive Approach 608
Your Turn: Self-Evaluation and Pay
Discrimination 608
Still Your Turn: From Barista to Manager 609

Chapter 18
Management: Making It Work 618

Managing, Controlling (and Sometimes
Reducing) Labor Costs 619
*Number of Employees (a.k.a.: Staffing Levels or
Headcount)* 620
Hours 624
Controlling Benefits 624
Controlling Average Cash Compensation 625
Control Salary Level: Top Down 625
Current Year's Rise 626
Ability to Pay 626
Competitive Market Pressures 626
Turnover Effects 626
Cost of Living 627
Rolling It All Together 628

Control Salary Level: Bottom Up 629
Ethics: Managing or Manipulating? 631
Where Is the Compensation Professional? 631
Embedded Controls 632
Range Maximums and Minimums 632
Compa-Ratios 633
Variable Pay 633
Analyzing Costs 634
Analyzing Value Added 634
Communication: Managing the Message 636
Say What? 640
Pay as Change Agent 641
Structuring the Compensation Function 641
Centralization—Decentralization 641
*Flexibility Within Corporatewide
Principles* 642
Reengineering and Outsourcing 643
Balancing Flexibility and Control 643
Your Turn: Communication by Copier 644
Still Your Turn: Ethics in Compensation
Decisions 645

Glossary 650

Name Index 669

Subject Index 679

About the Authors

GEORGE T. MILKOVICH

George T. Milkovich is the M. P. Catherwood Emeritus Professor at the Industrial Labor Relations School, Cornell University. For more than 40 years he has studied and written about how people get paid and what difference it makes. Milkovich served on several editorial boards and received many awards for his research contributions. He received the Keystone Award for Lifetime Achievement from the WorldatWork Association and the Distinguished Career Contributions Award from the Academy of Management, and he is a Fellow in both the Academy of Management and the National Academy of Human Resources. He chaired the National Academy of Sciences Committee on Performance and Pay. Milkovich is one of the founders of the Center for Advanced HR Studies, a research and development partnership of leading corporations and Cornell's ILR School. He also advised numerous companies around the world on their compensation strategies, received three outstanding teacher awards, and was a visiting professor at several international universities in Europe and Asia. Milkovich conducted executive seminars in many countries and served on advisory boards of leading academic/research centers in the United States and China.

JERRY M. NEWMAN

Dr. Jerry Newman is a SUNY Distinguished Professor at State University of New York–Buffalo. His interests are in the area of human resource management, with particular emphasis on compensation and rewards. He is author of the book *My Secret Life on the McJob: Lessons in Leadership Guaranteed to Supersize Any Management Style (McGraw-Hill, 2007)*. This book was selected as one of the twelve "Best of 2007" by the *Wall Street Journal*. Newman is also co-author with George Milkovich of earlier editions of *Compensation*, a best-in-class-book for McGraw-Hill since 1984. He is also author of approximately 100 articles on compensation and rewards, performance management, and other HR issues. In more than 30 years of consulting, Jerry has worked with such companies as Cummins Engine, AT&T, Graphic Controls, Hewlett-Packard, RJR Nabisco, Sorrento Cheese, McDonalds, and A & W Root Beer. Dr. Newman is a recipient of nine teaching awards, including the SUNY Chancellor's Award for Excellence in teaching.

BARRY GERHART

Barry Gerhart is the Bruce R. Ellig Distinguished Chair in Pay and Organizational Effectiveness, School of Business, University of Wisconsin–Madison. Professor Gerhart received his B.S. in Psychology from Bowling Green State University and his Ph.D. in Industrial Relations from the University of Wisconsin–Madison. He serves on the editorial boards of the *Academy of Management Journal, Human Relations, Industrial and Labor Relations Review, International Journal of Human Resource Management, Journal of Applied Psychology, Management Revue,* and *Personnel Psychology*. Professor Gerhart is a past recipient of the Scholarly Achievement Award and the International Human Resource Management Scholarly Research Award, both from the Human Resources Division, Academy of Management.

Preface

A few books can change your life. This is probably not one of them. However, if you read it, you will better understand that *pay matters*. After all, you can't pick up a newspaper, power up a computer, or read a blog today without someone talking about pay. The Great Recession (our term) has had huge ramifications for pay. Some folks have had their hours cut or pay reduced. Why? Because it's a more effective way to cut costs without laying off workers. Workers still left on payroll after all the recent cost-cutting moves are the best of the best. Layoffs would mean cutting the heart of the organization. Surveys suggest workers faced with layoffs or reduction in hours almost always will choose shorter workweeks . . . at least in the short run! The recession also has focused attention on executive compensation. As the government bailed out the financial industry, newspapers were reporting huge bonuses going to the very employees who helped cause the financial disaster. For example, Merrill Lynch & Co. "secretly" moved up the date it made awards for 2008 and allotted $1 million or more to nearly 700 employees. Even our book can't explain that kind of arrogance.

Pay also matters around the globe. For example, if you are a Russian cosmonaut, you can earn a bonus of $1,000 for every space walk you take (technically known as "extravehicular activity," or EVA), up to three per space trip. A contract listing specific tasks to be done on a space mission permits you to earn up to $30,000 above the $20,000 you earn while you are on the ground. (In contrast to the Russian cosmonauts, wealthy Americans are lining up to pay $15 million [plus an additional $20 million airfare] to the Russian Space Agency for their own personal EVA.) Conclusion: *Pay matters*.

If you read this book, you will also better understand that *what you pay for matters*. Many years ago, when Green Giant discovered too many insect parts in the pea packs from one of its plants, it designed a bonus plan that paid people for finding insect parts. Green Giant got what it paid for: insect parts. Innovative Green Giant employees brought insect parts from home to add to the peas just before they removed them and collected the bonus.

The Houston public school district also got what it paid for when it promised teachers bonuses of up to $6,000 if their students' test scores exceeded targets. Unfortunately, several teachers were later fired when it was discovered that they had leaked answers to their students and adjusted test scores.

Such problems are global. A British telephone company paid a cash bonus to operators based on how quickly they completed requests for information. Some operators discovered that the fastest way to complete a request was to give out a wrong number or—even faster—just hang up on the caller. "We're actually looking at a new bonus scheme," says an insightful company spokesperson. Conclusion: *What you pay for matters*.

If you read this book, you will also learn that *how you pay matters*. Motorola trashed its old-fashioned pay system that employees said guaranteed a raise every six months if you were still breathing. The new system paid for learning new skills and working in teams. Sound good? It wasn't. Employees resented those team members who went off for six weeks of training at full pay while remaining team members picked up their work. Motorola was forced to trash its new-fashioned system, too.

Microsoft employees were also grumbling. More were leaving; top recruits were going elsewhere. The lackluster performance of Microsoft stock was depressing the value of the eye-popping stock options the company routinely doled out. What to do? Rather than stock options, Microsoft changed its pay system to give employees actual shares of stock with a value that was immediately known. This move increased the value of employees' pay and eliminated the risk they faced from the stock performance. What did Microsoft get? Happier, more expensive people. No word yet on product innovation, customer satisfaction, or even quality of new hires. Conclusion: *How you pay matters.*

We live in interesting times. Anywhere you look on the globe today, economic and social pressures are forcing managers to rethink how people get paid and what difference it makes. Traditional approaches to compensation are being questioned. But what is being achieved by all this experimentation and change? We have lots of fads and fashions, but how much of it is folderol?

In this book, we strive to cull beliefs from facts, wishful thinking from demonstrable results, and opinions from research. Yet when all is said and done, managing compensation is an art. And as with any art, not everything that can be learned can be taught.

ABOUT THIS BOOK

This book is based on the strategic choices in managing compensation. We introduce these choices, which confront managers in the United States and around the world, in the total compensation model in Chapter 1. This model provides an integrating framework that is used throughout the book. Major compensation issues are discussed in the context of current theory, research, and practice. The practices illustrate new developments as well as established approaches to compensation decisions.

Each chapter contains at least one *Cybercomp* to point you to some of the vast compensation information on the Internet. Real-life *Your Turn* cases ask you to apply the concepts and techniques discussed in each chapter. For example, the Your Turn in Chapter 6 brings you into a leading New York law firm to analyze data on salaries paid to newly graduated lawyers compared to more experienced lawyers. The Your Turn in Chapter 9 draws on Professor Newman's experience when he worked undercover for 14 months in seven fast-food restaurants. The case takes you into the gritty details of the employees' behaviors (including Professor Newman's) during rush hour, as they desperately work to satisfy the customers' orders and meet their own performance targets set by their manager. You get to recommend which rewards will improve employees' performance (including Professor Newman's) and customers' satisfaction. Chapter 13 takes you into Newman's world of car washes with a Your Turn based on his experiences working with the world's largest car wash company. Cleanse your minds and your cars.

The authors also publish *Cases in Compensation,* an integrated casebook designed to provide additional practical skills that apply the material in this book. The casebook is available directly from the authors (telephone: 310-450-5301; e-mail: gtm1@cornell.edu).

Completing the integrated case will help you develop skills readily transferable to future jobs and assignments. Instructors are invited to e-mail for more information on how *Cases in Compensation* can help translate compensation research and theory into practice and build competencies for on-the-job decisions.

But *caveat emptor!* "Congress raises the executive minimum wage to $565.15 an hour," reads the headline in the satirical newspaper *The Onion* (www.onion.com, "America's Finest News Source"). The article says that the increase will help executives meet the federal standard-of-easy-living. "Our lifestyles are expensive to maintain," complains one manager. Although the story in *The Onion* may clearly be fiction, sometimes it is more difficult to tell. One manager told us that when she searched for this textbook in her local bookstore, store personnel found the listing in their information system—under fiction!

WHAT'S NEW

We enthusiastically welcome Barry Gerhart to our author partnership. George worked closely with Barry when both were faculty at Cornell. They have collaborated on several articles on human resource issues, especially compensation. Barry has also coauthored a general HR text and is widely published on pay and performance issues. Most important, though, he is a good person who adds considerable value to our team.

All chapters have been revised. Every one includes updated comparisons of the pay strategies or practices used in specific, named companies. Some of these are well established and successful (IBM, Medtronic, Microsoft, Merrill Lynch, Toyota), some face real problems (General Motors), and others are using unique practices (Google, Whole Foods). This edition continues to emphasize the importance of total compensation and its relevance for achieving sustainable competitive advantage. It reinforces our conviction that beyond *how much* people are paid, *how* they are paid really matters. Managing pay means ensuring that the right people get the right pay for achieving objectives in the right way. Greater emphasis is given to theoretical advances and evidence from research. Throughout the book we translate this evidence into guidance for improving the management of pay.

Chapter 2 explains how to craft a total compensation strategy and how to analyze strategies used by competitors. Chapters on performance-based pay dig into all forms of variable pay such as stock options, profit sharing, gain sharing, and team-based approaches. We focus on both the effectiveness and costs of these practices. Changes in competitive market analysis caused by outsourcing and global competition are covered, as well as the increased use of market pricing and broad banding. Employee benefits, always changing and always important, are covered in two chapters. Why, for example, did McDonald's choose to launch expensive employee benefits when others are trying to limit benefits? Chapter 14 broadens its discussion of board-of-director compensation, executive compensation, and sales compensation. As always, we have used international examples in every section. We also have completely revised our chapter on global compensation. Software to aid both employees and manager decisions is covered, and we have renewed the focus on measuring the value gained from pay systems. Ethics, values, and the apparent absence of standards of conduct in compensation management, so widely reported in today's headline news and dissected in blogs, are discussed. Each chapter has links to interesting Internet sites that open up valuable information sources related to compensation and benefits.

ACKNOWLEDGMENTS

In addition to our bookstore shopper, many people have contributed to our understanding of compensation and to the preparation of this textbook. We owe a special, continuing debt of gratitude to our students. In the classroom, they motivate and challenge us, and as returning seasoned managers, they try mightily to keep our work relevant:

Kenneth Abosch
Hewitt Associates

Patrick Beall
Lockheed Martin

Joseph Bruno
Kodak

Karee Buerger
Hewitt Associates

Federico Castellanos
IBM EMEA

Joe Chaves
Subway

Cindy Cohen
Impac

Connie Colao
Taco Bell

Andrew Doyle
Oppenheimer Fund

Brian Dunn
Maclagan

Bruce Ellig
Author

Rich Floersch
McDonald's USA

Beth Florin
Clark Consulting

Richard Frings
Johnson & Johnson

Takashi Fujiwara
Mitsubishi

Yuichi Funada
Toshiba

Ted Grasela
Cognigen

Thomas Gresch
General Motors

Peter Hearl
YUM Brands (emeritus)

Lada Hruba
Bristol Meyers Squibb

Richard Ivey
KFC

Tae-Jin Kim
SK Group

Joe Kreuz
Advantage Professionals

Hiroshi Kurihara
Fuji Xerox

Christian LeBreton
IBM EMEA

Mitch Linnick
IBM

Tony Marchak
IBM EMEA

Masaki Matsuhashi
Toshiba

Randy McDonald
IBM

Matt Milkovich
Registry Nursing

Michael Milkovich
Warecorp

Sarah Milkovich
Jet Propulsion Laboratory

Sonja Milkovich
Sled Dog Software

Pat Murtha
Pizza Hut

David Ness
Medtronic

Erinn Newman
American Express

Kelly Newman
Firley Enterprises

Terrie Newman
HR Foundations

Stephen O'Byrne
Shareholder Value Advisors

Tony Ragusa
Stereo Advantage

Jaime Richardson
GE Healthcare

Lindsay Scott
Lindsay Scott & Associates

Jason Sekanina
Linear Technology

Diana Southall
HR Foundations

Cassandra Steffan
Frito-Lay

Masanori Suzuki
Google Japan

Ichiro Takemura
Toshiba

Richard Their
Xerox

Jan Tichy
Merck

Andrew Thompson
Link Group Consultants

Jose Tomas
Burger King

Karen Velkey
Northrup Grumman

Ian Ziskin
Northrop Grumman

Our universities—Cornell, Buffalo, and Wisconsin—provide forums for the interchange of ideas among students, experienced managers, and academic colleagues. We value this interchange. Other academic colleagues also provided helpful comments on this edition of the book. We particularly thank:

Timothy Brown
San Jose State University

Lisa Burke
University of Tennessee–Chattanooga

Dennis Cockrell
Washington State University–Pullman

Thomas Hall
Penn State University

Vandra Huber
University of Washington

Patrenia McAbee
Delaware County Community College

Teresa S. Nelson
Butler County Community College

Jason Shaw
University of Minnesota–Minneapolis

Tom Timmerman
Tennessee Tech University

We also thank the following colleagues for their contributions to past editions:

Tom Arnold
Westmoreland Community College

Lubica Bajzikova
Comenius University, Bratislava

Stuart Basefsky
Cornell University

Melissa Barringer
University of Massachusetts

Matt Bloom
University of Notre Dame

James T. Brakefield
Western Illinois University

Wayne Cascio
University of Colorado–Denver

Lee Dyer
Cornell University

Allen D. Engle Sr.
Eastern Kentucky University

Ingrid Fulmer
Georgia Institute of Technology

Luis Gomez-Mejia
Arizona State University

Kevin Hallock
Cornell University

Robert Heneman
Ohio State University

Greg Hundley
Purdue

Frank Krzystofiak
SUNY–Buffalo

David I. Levine
University of Califonia–Berkeley

Janet Marler
SUNY–Albany

Atul Mitra
Northern Iowa University

Michael Moore
Michigan State University

Richard Posthuma
University of Texas at El Paso

Janez Prasnikar
University of Ljubljana

Vlado Pucik
IMD

Hesan Ahmed Quazi
Nanyang Business School

Sara Rynes
University of Iowa

Dow Scott
Loyola University Chicago

Jason Shaw
University of Minnesota

Thomas Stone
Oklahoma State University

Michael Sturman
Cornell University

Ningyu Tang
Shanghai Jiao Tong University

Thomas Li-Ping Tang
Middle Tennessee State University

Charlie Trevor
University of Wisconsin

Zhong-Ming Wang
Zhejiang University

Yoshio Yanadori
University of British Columbia

Nada Zupan
University of Ljubljana

Part **One**

Introducing the Pay Model and Pay Strategy

Why do we work? If we are fortunate, our work brings meaning to our lives, challenges us in new and exciting ways, brings us recognition, and gives us the opportunity to interact with interesting people and create friendships. Oh yes—we also get a paycheck. Here in Part One of your book, we begin by talking about what we mean by "pay" and how paying people in different ways can influence them and, in turn, influence organization success. Wages and salaries, of course, are part of compensation, but so, too, for some employees are bonuses, health care benefits, stock options, and/or work-life balance programs.

Compensation is one of the most powerful tools organizations have to influence their employees. Managed well, it can play a major role in organizations successfully executing their strategies through their employees. Managed less well, as General Motors, Chrysler, and Bear Stearns, for example, learned, compensation decisions can also come back to haunt you. In Part One, we describe the compensation policies and techniques that organizations use and the multiple objectives (e.g., performance) they hope to achieve by effectively managing these compensation decisions.

Although compensation has its guiding principles, we will see that "the devil is in the details" and how any compensation program is specifically designed and implemented will help determine its success. We want you to bring a healthy skepticism when you encounter simplistic or sweeping claims about whether a particular way of managing compensation does or does not work. For example, organizations, in general, benefit from pay for performance, but there are many types of pay for performance programs and it is not always easy to design and implement a program that has the intended consequences (and avoids *unintended* consequences). So, general principles are helpful, but only to a point. Thus, in Part One, our aim is to also help you understand how compensation strategy decisions interact with the specific context of an organization (e.g., its business and human resource strategies) to influence organization success. We emphasize that good theory and research is fundamental to not only understanding compensation's likely effects, but also to developing that healthy skepticism we want you to have toward simplistic claims about what works and what does not.

Chapter One

The Pay Model

Chapter Outline

**Compensation: Does It Matter?
(or, "So What?")**

Compensation: Definition, Please
  Society
  Stockholders
  Managers
  Employees
  Global Views—Vive la différence

Forms of Pay
  Cash Compensation: Base
  *Cash Compensation: Merit Pay/
  Cost-of-Living Adjustments*
  Cash Compensation: Incentives
  Long-Term Incentives
  Benefits: Income Protection
  Benefits: Work/Life Balance

  Benefits: Allowances
  *Total Earnings Opportunities: Present
  Value of a Stream of Earnings*
  Relational Returns From Work

A Pay Model
  Compensation Objectives
  Four Policy Choices
  Pay Techniques

Book Plan

***Caveat Emptor*—Be an Informed
Consumer**
  1. Is the Research Useful?
  *2. Does the Study Separate Correlation
  From Causation?*
  3. Are There Alternative Explanations?

Your Turn: Circuit City

Money (That's What I Want)[1]

The best things in life are free
But you can keep them for the birds and bees
Chorus:

Now give me money
That's what I want
That's what I want, yeah
That's what I want

You're lovin' gives me a thrill
But you're lovin' don't pay my bills
[chorus]

Money don't get everything it's true
What it don't get, I can't use
[chorus]

COMPENSATION: DOES IT MATTER? (OR, "SO WHAT?")

Why should you care about compensation? Maybe because you and yours find that life goes more smoothly when there is at least as much money coming in as going out. (See the lyrics for "Money," above.) Maybe you would like to solve the mystery of why you or someone you know gets paid the way they do. Maybe you are curious, too, about people in the news and their pay. Why did Beyoncé earn $80 million one year, whereas Britney Spears earned $2.25 million?[2] Why did workers at General Motors get total compensation of about $60 per hour, whereas U.S. workers at Toyota received $48 per hour and the average total compensation per hour in U.S. manufacturing was $25 (and $16 in Korea, $3 in Mexico)? Why did Richard Anderson, chief executive at Delta earn $600,000, whereas Lawrence J. Ellison, chief executive at Oracle, earned about 1,000 times as much ($557 million)? Why did James Simons, a former math professor and now hedge fund manager, earn $2.5 billion? (Wow, professors can make that much money? Oh, "former" professor. OK.)

More important, does it matter how much and how these people get paid? We'll certainly talk about employee and executive pay in this book. (Maybe not so much about singers. Sorry.) Let's take a brief look at a few examples where pay does seem to have mattered.

General Motors (GM) has, for decades, paid its workers well—too well perhaps for what it received in return. So what? Well, in 1970, GM had 150 U.S. plants and 395,000 hourly workers. In sharp contrast, GM anticipates having only about 35 plants and 38,000 hourly workers in the very near future.[3] In June 2009, GM had to file for bankruptcy (avoiding it for a while thanks to loans from the U.S. government—i.e., you, the taxpayer). Not all of GM's problems were compensation related. Of course, building vehicles that consumers did not want was also a problem. But, having labor costs higher than the competition, without corresponding advantages in efficiency, quality, and customer service, does not seem to have served GM or its stakeholders well. Its stock price, which peaked at $93.62/share in April 2000, closed recently at below $1/share—about what it was during the Great Depression of the 1930s. Its market value was about $60 billion in 2000. Think of all the shareholder wealth that will be wiped out in bankruptcy. Think of the billions of dollars the U.S. taxpayer is putting into GM. Think of the hundreds of thousands of jobs that have been lost and the effects on communities that have lost those jobs.

On the other hand, Nucor Steel pays its workers very well relative to what other companies inside and outside of the steel industry pay. But Nucor also has much higher productivity than is typical in the steel industry. The result: Both the company and its workers do well.

Wall Street financial services firms and banks used **incentive** plans that rewarded people for developing "innovative" new financial investment vehicles and for taking risks to earn themselves and their firms a lot of money.[4] That is what happened—until recently. Then, the markets discovered that many such risks had gone bad. Blue Chip firms such as Lehman Brothers slid quickly into bankruptcy, whereas others like Bear Stearns and Merrill Lynch survived to varying degrees by finding other firms (J.P. Morgan and Bank of America, respectively) to buy them.

Would greater expertise in the design and execution of compensation plans have helped? Congress and the President seem to think so, because they have put into place new legislation, the Troubled Asset Relief Program (TARP), which includes restrictions on executive pay that are designed to discourage executives from taking "unnecessary and excessive risks" Another commentator agrees. In an opinion piece in the *Wall Street Journal,* entitled "How Business Schools Have Failed Business," the former Director of Corporate Finance Policy at the United States Treasury wrote that "misaligned incentive programs are at the core of what brought our financial system to its knees."[5] He says that we "should ask how many of the business schools attended by America's CEOs and directors educate their students about the best way to design managerial compensation systems." His answer: not many. Our book, we hope, can play a role in helping to better educate you, the reader, about the design of compensation systems, both for managers and for workers.

How people are paid affects their behaviors at work, which affect an organization's success.[6] For most employers, compensation is a major part of total cost, and often it is the single largest part of operating cost. These two facts together mean that well-designed compensation systems can help an organization achieve and sustain competitive advantage. On the other hand, as we have recently seen, poorly designed compensation systems can likewise play a major role in undermining organization success.

COMPENSATION: DEFINITION, PLEASE

How people view compensation affects how they behave. It does not mean the same thing to everyone. Your view probably differs, depending on whether you look at compensation from the perspective of a member of society, a stockholder, a manager, or an employee. Thus, we begin by recognizing different perspectives.

Society

Some people see pay as a measure of justice. For example, a comparison of earnings between men and women highlights what many consider inequities in pay decisions. In 2007, among full-time workers in the United States, women earned 80 percent of what men earned, up from 62 percent in 1979. If women had the same education, experience, and union coverage as men and also worked in the same industries and occupations, they would be expected to earn about 90 percent of what men earn. Society has taken an interest in such earnings differentials. One indicator of this interest is the introduction of laws and regulation aimed at eliminating the role of discrimination in causing them.[7] (See Chapter 17.)

Benefits given as part of a total compensation package may also be seen as a reflection of equity or justice in society. Individuals and businesses in the United States spend $2.2 trillion per year, or 16 percent of its economic output (gross domestic product) on health care.[8] Employers spend about 40 cents for benefits on top of every dollar paid for **wages** and **salaries**.[9] Wal-Mart reports that its health care costs have been growing faster than any other expense and that costs for care of employee spouses are far more expensive than costs for care of Wal-Mart employees. Nevertheless, roughly 46 million people in the United States (16 percent of the population) have no health insurance.[10] A major reason is that the great majority of people (who are under the age of 65 and not below the poverty line) obtain health insurance through their employers, but small employers, which account for a substantial share of employment, are much less likely than larger employers to offer health insurance to their employees. As a result, 8 in 10 of the uninsured in the United States are from working families.[11] Given that those who do have insurance typically have it through an employer, it also follows then that as the unemployment rate increases, health care coverage declines further. Some users of online dating services provide information on their employer-provided health care insurance. Dating service "shoppers" say they view health insurance coverage as a sign of how well a prospect is doing in a career.

Job losses (or gains) in a country over time are partly a function of relative labor costs (and productivity) across countries. People in the United States worry about losing manufacturing jobs to Mexico, China, and other nations. (Increasingly, white collar work in areas like finance, computer programming, and legal services is also being sent overseas.) Exhibit 1.1 reveals that the hourly wages for Mexican manufacturing

EXHIBIT 1.1   **Hourly Compensation Costs for Production Workers in Manufacturing (in U.S. Dollars)**

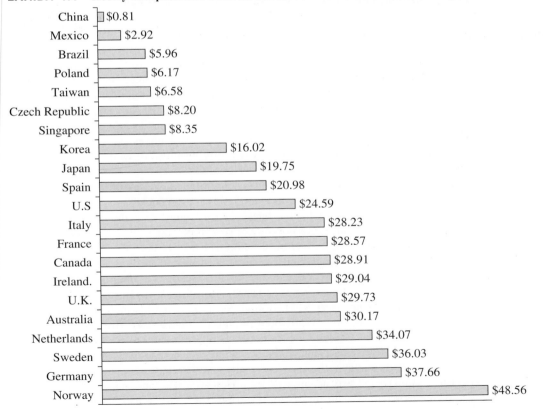

Country	Cost
China	$0.81
Mexico	$2.92
Brazil	$5.96
Poland	$6.17
Taiwan	$6.58
Czech Republic	$8.20
Singapore	$8.35
Korea	$16.02
Japan	$19.75
Spain	$20.98
U.S	$24.59
Italy	$28.23
France	$28.57
Canada	$28.91
Ireland.	$29.04
U.K.	$29.73
Australia	$30.17
Netherlands	$34.07
Sweden	$36.03
Germany	$37.66
Norway	$48.56

Source: Bureau of Labor Statistics News, March 26, 2009.

work ($2.92) are about 12 percent of those paid in the United States ($24.59). China's estimated $0.81 per hour is about 3 percent of the U.S. rate. However, the value of what is produced also needs to be considered. Productivity in China is about 6 percent of that of U.S. workers, whereas Mexican worker productivity is 22 percent of the U.S. level.[12] (We return to the topic of offshoring in Chapter 7.)

Some consumers know that pay increases often lead to price increases. They do not believe that higher labor costs benefit them. But other consumers lobby for higher wages. While partying revelers were collecting plastic beads at New Orleans' Mardi Gras, filmmakers were showing video clips of the Chinese factory that makes the beads. In the video, the plant manager describes the punishment (5 percent reduction in already low pay) that he metes out to the young workers for workplace infractions. After viewing the video, one reveler complained, "It kinda takes the fun out of it."[13]

Stockholders

Stockholders are also interested in how employees are paid. Some believe that using stock to pay employees creates a sense of ownership that will improve performance, which will, in turn, increase stockholder wealth. But others argue that granting employees too much ownership dilutes stockholder wealth. Google's stock plan cost the company $600 million in its first year of operation. So people who buy Google stock are betting that this $600 million will motivate employees to generate more than $600 million in extra revenue.[14]

Stockholders have a particular interest in executive pay. To the degree that the interests of executives are aligned with those of shareholders (e.g., by paying executives on the basis of company performance measures such as shareholder return), the hope is that company performance will be higher. There is debate, however, about whether executive pay and company performance are strongly linked in the typical U.S. company.[15] In the absence of such a linkage, concerns arise that executives can somehow use their influence to obtain high pay without necessarily performing well. Forbes compared the performance of the chief executive officer (CEO) at large U.S. firms to his/her compensation (see Exhibit 1.2). The idea, one might say, was to identify the CEOs who gave shareholders the "most (and least) bang for the buck."

Although the "best CEO for the buck" idea is interesting, the complex world of CEO pay means that things are not always so simple. Take, for example, the case of Jeffrey Bezos at Amazon, second on the Forbes list of best CEOs. Forbes reports his average annual compensation over 6 years as just over $1 million, modest for a CEO of a large firm. However, Forbes also reports that Bezos is a major shareholder, owning more than 20 percent of Amazon shares. In 2004 alone, Bezos sold 3.8 million shares, which generated over $157 million. So, to say that his income as a CEO was just over $1 million per year really does not tell the entire story. At the other extreme, Richard Fairbanks of Capital One Bank just barely missed making the Bottom Three in Exhibit 1.2. His average annual compensation over 6 years was $66.5 million. That is an awful lot of money to be sure, especially since average annual shareholder return over that same period was negative (-9%). However, Mr. Fairbanks took no base salary or bonus payments during that time period. Like Mr. Bezos, he made his money entirely through stock ownership (including by exercising options to buy stock and

EXHIBIT 1.2   Bang for the Buck: CEO Compensation and Shareholder Return

Name	Company	Firm Performance 6-Year Annual Total Shareholder Return (TSR)	Firm Performance Relative to Its Industry (Average TSR = 100)	6-Year Average CEO Compensation
Top Three				
Michael Bennett	Terra Indusries	64%	141	$3,550,000
Jeffrey Bezos	Amazon	21%	113	$1,020,000
John Wiehoff	CH Robinson Worldwide	21%	115	$4,920,000
Middle of the Pack				
Bruce Smith	Tesoro	28%	106	$15,100,000
Jerald Fishman	Analog Devices	−3%	107	$14,520,000
Ralph Lauren	Ralph Lauren Polo	4%	109	$18,770,000
Bottom Three				
Ramani Ayer	Hartford Financial	−17%	87	$13,540,000
Jeffrey Imelt	General Electric	−11%	85	$14,380,000
Kenneth Lewis	Bank of America	−16%	90	$29,670,000

Source: www.forbes.com, "CEO Compensation," April 22, 2009, extracted May 1, 2009.

then selling it). Consider that between year-end 1995 and year-end 2005, the Capital One stock price (adjusted for splits) went from $7.01/share to $81.18/share. That translated into an increase in shareholder value of roughly $20 billion. Roughly another $10 billion was created by year-end 2007. In other words, Mr. Fairbanks' "bang for the buck" depends on exactly what years are chosen for study. It is not clear that Capital One shareholders see Mr. Fairbanks as someone who has done poorly by them.

Managers

For managers, compensation influences their success in two ways. First, it is a major expense. Competitive pressures, both global and local, force managers to consider the affordability of their compensation decisions. Labor costs can account for more than 50 percent of total costs. In some industries, such as financial or professional services and in education and government, this figure is even higher. However, even within an industry, labor costs as a percent of total costs vary among individual firms. For example, small neighborhood grocery stores, with labor costs between 15 percent and 18 percent, have been driven out of business by supermarkets that delivered the same products at a lower cost of labor (9 percent to 12 percent). Supermarkets today are losing market share to the warehouse club stores such as Sam's Club and Costco, who enjoy an even lower cost of labor (4 percent to 6 percent), even though Costco pays above-average wages for the industry.

Exhibit 1.3 compares the hourly pay rate for retail workers at Costco to that at Wal-Mart and Sam's Club (which is owned by Wal-Mart). Each store tries to provide a unique shopping experience. Wal-Mart and Sam's Club compete on low prices,

EXHIBIT 1.3 Pay Rates at Retail Stores, Customer Satisfaction, Employee Turnover, and Sales per Square Foot

	Starting Pay	Pay After 4 Years	Customer Satisfaction (100 = highest)	Employee Annual Turnover	Store Size Average (sq. ft.)	Stores	Revenues	Revenue (per sq. ft.)
Costco	$11.00	$19.50	85	20%	141,000	555	$ 70,977,484,000	$907
Sam's Club	$10.00	$12.50	76	50%	133,000	602	$ 46,854,000,000	$585
Wal-Mart	$ 8.40	$10.50	68	50%	160,964	3,656	$401,244,000,000	$682

Sources: Liza Featherstone, "Wage Against the Machine," *Slate*, June 27, 2008; "Costco Outshines the Rest" and customer satisfaction data from Consumer Reports, May 2009; 2009 Costco and WalMart Annual Reports.

Notes: Separate turnover data unavailable for Sam's Club. Overall Wal-Mart turnover rate is thus used. Pay after 4 years rate unavailable for Wal-Mart. Its average pay rate is thus used.

with Sam's Club being a "warehouse store" with especially low prices on a narrower range of products, often times sold in bulk. Costco also competes on the basis of low prices, but with a mix that includes more high-end products aimed at a higher customer income segment. To compete in this segment, Costco appears to have chosen to pay higher wages, perhaps as a way to attract and retain a higher quality workforce.[16] Based on Exhibit 1.3, Costco is quite successful, relative to its competitors, in terms of employee retention, customer satisfaction, and the efficiency with which it generates sales (see revenure per square foot). So, although its labor costs are higher than those of Sam's Club and Wal-Mart, it appears that this model works for Costco because it helps gain an advantage over its competitors.

Thus, rather than treating pay only as an expense to be minimized, a manager can also use it to influence employee behaviors and to improve the organization's performance. As our Costco (versus Sam's Club and Wal-Mart) example seems to suggest, the way people are paid affects the quality of their work and their attitude toward customers.[17] It may also affect their willingness to be flexible, learn new skills, or suggest innovations. On the other hand, people may become interested in unions or legal action against their employer based on how they are paid. This potential to influence employees' behaviors, and subsequently the productivity and effectiveness of the organization, means that the study of compensation is well worth your time, don't you think?[18]

Employees

The pay individuals receive in return for the work they perform is usually the major source of their financial security. Hence, pay plays a vital role in a person's economic and social well-being. Employees may see compensation as a *return in an exchange* between their employer and themselves, as an **entitlement** for being an employee of the company, or as a *reward* for a job well done. Compensation can be all of these things.[19]

Describing pay as a reward may sound farfetched to anyone who has reluctantly rolled out of bed to go to work. Even though writers and consultants continue to use that term, no one says, "They just gave me a reward increase," or "Here is my weekly reward." Yet if people see their pay as a return for their efforts rather than as a reward, and if writers and consultants persist in trying to convince managers that pay is a reward for employees, this disconnect may mislead both employees and managers. Employees invest in education and training; they contribute their time and energy at the workplace. Compensation is their return on those investments and contributions.

Incentive and Sorting Effects of Pay on Employers' Behaviors

Pay can influence employee **motivation** and behavior in two ways. First, and perhaps most obvious, pay can affect the motivational intensity, direction, and persistence of current employees. Motivation, together with employee **ability** and work/organizational design (which can help or hinder employee performance), determines employee behaviors such as performance. We will refer to this effect of pay as an **incentive effect,** the degree to which pay influences individual and aggregate motivation among the employees we have at any point in time.

However, pay can also have an indirect, but important, influence via a **sorting effect** on the composition of the workforce.[20] That is, different types of pay strategies may cause different types of people to apply to and stay with (i.e., self-select into) an organization. In the case of pay structure/level, it may be that higher pay levels help organizations to attract more high-quality applicants, allowing them to be more selective in their hiring. Similarly, higher pay levels may improve employee retention. (In Chapter 7, we will talk about when paying more is most likely to be worth the higher costs.)

Less obvious perhaps, it is not only how much, but *how* an organization pays that can result in sorting effects.[21] Ask yourself: Would people who are highly capable and have a strong work ethic and interest in earning a lot of money prefer to work in an organization that pays employees doing the same job more or less the same amount, regardless of their performance? Or, would they prefer to work in an organization where their pay can be much higher (or lower) depending on how they perform? If you chose the latter answer, then you believe that sorting effects matter. People differ regarding which type of pay arrangement they prefer. The question for organizations is simply this: Are you using the pay policy that will attract and retain the types of employees you want?

Let's take a look at one especially informative study.[22] Individual worker productivity was measured before and after a glass installation company switched one of its plants from a salary-only (no pay for performance) system to an individual incentive plan under which each employee's pay depended on his/her own performance. An overall increase in plant productivity of 44% was observed comparing before and after. Roughly one-half of this increase was due to individual employees becoming more productive. However, the remaining one-half of the productivity gain was not explained by this fact. So, where did the other one-half of the gain come from? The answer: Less productive workers were less likely to stay under the new individual incentive system because it was less favorable to them. When they left, they tended to be replaced by more productive workers (who were happy to have the chance to make more money than they might make elsewhere). Thus, focusing only on the incentive effects of pay (on current workers) can miss the other major mechanism (sorting) by which pay decisions influence employee behaviors.

The pay model that comes later in this chapter includes compensation policies and the **objectives** (efficiency, fairness, compliance) these are meant to influence. Our point here is that compensation policies work through employee incentive and sorting effects to either achieve or not achieve those objectives.

Global Views—*Vive la différence*

In English, *compensation* means something that counterbalances, offsets, or makes up for something else. However, if we look at the origin of the word in different languages, we get a sense of the richness of the meaning, which combines entitlement, return, and reward.[23]

In China, the traditional characters for the word "compensation" are based on the symbols for logs and water; compensation provides the necessities in life. In the recent past, the state owned all enterprises and compensation was treated as an entitlement. In today's China, compensation takes on a more subtle meaning. A new word, *dai yu,* is used. It refers to how you are being treated—your wages, benefits, training opportunities, and so on. When people talk about compensation, they ask each other about the *dai yu* in their companies. Rather than assuming that everyone is entitled to the same treatment, the meaning of compensation now includes a broader sense of returns as well as entitlement.[24]

"Compensation" in Japanese is *kyuyo,* which is made up of two separate characters (*kyu* and *yo*), both meaning "giving something." *Kyu* is an honorific used to indicate that the person doing the giving is someone of high rank, such as a feudal lord, an emperor, or a samurai leader. Traditionally, compensation is thought of as something given by one's superior. Today, business consultants in Japan try to substitute the word *hou-syu,* which means "reward" and has no associations with notions of superiors. The many allowances that are part of Japanese compensation systems translate as *teate,* which means "taking care of something." *Teate* is regarded as compensation that takes care of employees' financial needs. This concept is consistent with the family, housing, and commuting allowances that are still used in many Japanese companies.[25]

These contrasting ideas about compensation—multiple views (societal, stockholder, managerial, employee, and even global) and multiple meanings (returns, rewards, entitlement)—add richness to the topic. But they can also cause confusion unless everyone is talking about the same thing. So let's define what we mean by "compensation" or "pay" (the words are used interchangeably in this book):

> **Compensation** refers to all forms of financial returns and tangible services and benefits employees receive as part of an employment relationship.

FORMS OF PAY

Exhibit 1.4 shows the variety of returns people receive from work. They are categorized as **total compensation** and **relational returns.** The relational returns (learning opportunities, status, challenging work, and so on) are psychological.[26]

EXHIBIT 1.4   Total Returns for Work

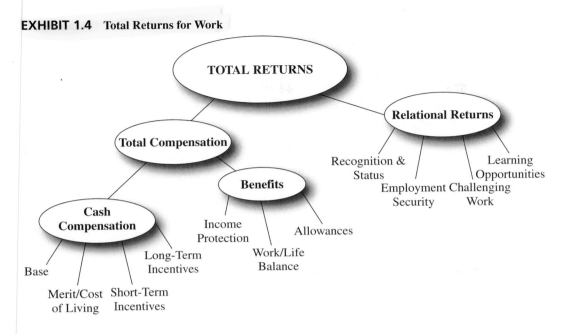

Total compensation returns are more transactional. They include pay received directly as cash (e.g., base, merit, incentives, cost-of-living adjustments) and indirectly as benefits (e.g., pensions, medical insurance, programs to help balance work and life demands, brightly colored uniforms).[27] So pay comes in different forms, and programs to pay people can be designed in a wide variety of ways. WorldatWork has a Total Rewards Model that is similar and includes compensation, benefits, work-life, performance/recognition, and development/career opportunities.[28]

Cash Compensation: Base

Base wage is the cash compensation that an employer pays for the work performed. Base wage tends to reflect the value of the work or skills and generally ignores differences attributable to individual employees. For example, the base wage for machine operators may be $20 an hour. However, some individual operators may receive more because of their experience and/or performance. Some pay systems set base wage as a function of the skill or education an employee possesses; this is common for engineers and schoolteachers.[29]

A distinction is often made in the United States between wage and salary, with **salary** referring to pay for employees who are **exempt** from regulations of the Fair Labor Standards Act (FLSA) and hence do not receive overtime pay.[30] Managers and professionals usually fit this category. Their pay is calculated at an annual or monthly rate rather than hourly, because hours worked do not need to be recorded. In contrast, workers who are covered by overtime and reporting provisions of the Fair Labor Standards Act—*nonexempts*—have their pay calculated as an hourly wage. Some organizations, such as IBM, Eaton, and Wal-Mart, label all base pay as "salary." Rather than dividing employees into separate categories of salaried and wage earners, they believe that an "all-salaried" workforce reinforces an organizational **culture** in which all employees are part of the same team. However, merely changing the terminology does not negate the need to comply with the FLSA.

Cash Compensation: Merit Pay/Cost-of-Living Adjustments

Periodic adjustments to base wages may be made on the basis of changes in what other employers are paying for the same work, changes in the overall **cost of living,** or changes in experience or skill.

Merit increases are given as increments to the base pay in recognition of *past* work behavior.[31] According to surveys, 90 percent of U.S. firms use merit pay increases.[32] Some assessment of past performance is made, with or without a formal performance evaluation program, and the size of the increase is varied with performance. Thus, outstanding performers could receive a 6 to 8 percent merit increase 8 months after their last increase, whereas an average performer may receive, say, a 3 to 4 percent increase after 12 or 15 months. In contrast to merit pay, *cost-of-living adjustments* give the same increases to everyone, regardless of performance.

Cash Compensation: Incentives

Incentives tie pay increases directly to performance.[33] However, incentives differ from merit adjustments. First, incentives do not increase the base wage, and so must be re-earned each pay period. Second, the potential size of the incentive payment will generally be known beforehand. Whereas merit pay programs evaluate past performance of an individual and then decide on the size of the increase, what must happen in order to receive the incentive payment is called out very specifically ahead of time. For example, a Toyota salesperson knows the **commission** on a Land Cruiser versus a Prius prior to making the sale. The larger commission he or she will earn by selling the Land Cruiser is the incentive to sell a customer that car rather then the Prius. Although both merit pay and incentives try to influence performance, incentives try to influence future behavior whereas merit recognizes (rewards) past behavior. The incentive-reward distinction is a matter of timing.

Incentives can be tied to the performance of an individual employee, a team of employees, a total business unit, or some combination of individual, team, and unit. The performance objective may be expense reduction, volume increases, customer satisfaction, revenue growth, return on investments, increase in stock value—the possibilities are endless. Prax Air, for example, uses return on capital (ROC). For every quarter that a 6 percent ROC target is met or exceeded, Prax Air awards bonus days of pay. An 8.6 percent ROC means 2 extra days of pay for that quarter for every employee covered by the program. An ROC of 15 percent means 8.5 extra days of pay.

Because incentives are one-time payments, they do not permanently increase labor costs. When performance declines, incentive pay automatically declines, too. Consequently, incentives are frequently referred to as **variable pay.**

Long-Term Incentives

Incentives may be short- or long-term. Long-term incentives are intended to focus employee efforts on multiyear results. Typically they are in the form of stock ownership or options to buy stock at specified, advantageous prices. The belief underlying stock ownership is that employees with a financial stake in the organization will focus on long-term financial objectives: return on investment, market share, return on net assets, and the like. Bristol-Myers Squibb grants stock to selected "Key Contributors" who make outstanding contributions to the firm's success. Stock options are often the largest component in an executive pay package. Some companies extend stock ownership beyond the ranks of managers and professionals. Sun Microsystems, Intel, Google, and Starbucks offer stock options to all their employees.[34]

Benefits: Income Protection

Exhibit 1.4 showed that benefits, including income protection, work/life services, and allowances, are also part of total compensation. Some income protection programs are legally required in the United States; employers must pay into a fund that provides income replacement for workers who become disabled or unemployed. Employers also make half the contributions to Social Security. (Employees pay the other half.) Different countries have different lists of mandatory benefits.

Medical insurance, retirement programs, life insurance, and savings plans are common benefits. They help protect employees from the financial risks inherent in daily life. Often companies can provide these protections to employees more cheaply than employees can obtain them for themselves. The cost of providing benefits has been rising. For example, in the U.S. employers pay nearly half the nation's health care bills, and health care expenditures have recently been increasing at annual rates around 15 to 20 percent. Many employers are trying to change or decrease the benefits they offer. General Motors recently bought out over 35,000 employees by paying them incentives ranging from $35,000 to $140,000 to retire and keep their pensions but drop their medical coverage.[35] GM spends so much for benefits that it has been called a pension and health care provider that also makes cars.

Benefits: Work/Life Balance

Programs that help employees better integrate their work and life responsibilities include time away from work (vacations, jury duty), access to services to meet specific needs (drug counseling, financial planning, referrals for child and elder care), and flexible work arrangements (telecommuting, nontraditional schedules, nonpaid time off). Responding to the changing demographics of the workforce (two-income families or single parents who need work-schedule flexibility so that family obligations can be met), many U.S. employers are giving a higher priority to these benefit forms. Medtronic, for example, touts its Total Well-Being Program that seeks to provide "resources for growth—mind, body, heart, and spirit" for each employee. Health and wellness, financial rewards and security, individual and family well-being, and a fulfilling work environment are part of this "total well-being."[36] Medtronic believes that this program permits employees to be "fully present" at work and less distracted by conflicts between their work and nonwork responsibilities.

Benefits: Allowances

Allowances often grow out of whatever is in short supply. In Vietnam and China, housing (dormitories and apartments) and transportation allowances are frequently part of the pay package. Sixty years after the end of World War II–induced food shortages, some Japanese companies still continue to offer a "rice allowance" based on the number of an employee's dependents. Almost all foreign companies in China discover that housing, transportation, and other allowances are expected.[37] Companies that resist these allowances must come up with other ways to attract and retain employees. In many European countries, managers assume that a car will be provided—only the make and model are negotiable.[38]

Total Earnings Opportunities: Present Value of a Stream of Earnings

Up to this point we have treated compensation as something received at a moment in time. But a fiirm's compensation decisions have a temporal effect. Say you have a job offer of $50,000. If you stay with the firm 5 years and receive an annual increase of 4 percent, in 5 years you will be earning $60,833 a year. For your employer, the five-year cost commitment of the decision to hire you turns out to be $331,649 in cash. If you add in an additional 25 percent for benefits, the decision to hire you implies a commitment of over $400,000 from your employer. Will you be worth it? You will be after this course.

A present-value perspective shifts the comparison of today's initial offers to consideration of future bonuses, merit increases, and promotions. Sometimes a company will tell applicants that its relatively low starting offers will be overcome by larger future pay increases. In effect, the company is selling the present value of the future stream of earnings. But few candidates apply that same analysis to calculate the future increases required to offset the lower initial offers. Hopefully, everyone who reads Chapter 1 will now do so.

Relational Returns From Work

Why do Google millionaires continue to show up for work every morning? Why does Andy Borowitz write the funniest satirical news site on the web (*www.borowitzreport.com*) for free? There is no doubt that nonfinancial returns from work have a substantial effect on employees' behavior.[39] Exhibit 1.4 includes such relational returns from work as recognition and status, employment security, challenging work, and opportunities to learn. Other forms of relational return might include personal satisfaction from successfully facing new challenges, teaming with great co-workers, receiving new uniforms, and the like.[40] Such factors are part of the total return, which is a broader umbrella than total compensation.

The Organization as a Network of Returns

Sometimes it is useful to think of an organization as a network of returns created by all these different forms of pay, including total compensation and relational returns. The challenge is to design this network so that it helps the organization to succeed. As in the case of rowers pulling on their oars, success is more likely if all are pulling in unison rather than working against one another. In the same way, the network of returns is more likely to be useful if bonuses, development opportunities, and promotions all work together.

So the next time you walk in an employer's door, look beyond the cash and health care offered to search for all the returns that create the network. Even though this book focuses on compensation, let's not forget that compensation is only one of many factors affecting people's decisions about work, as songwriter Roger Miller made clear in this 1960s tune:

> Got a letter just this morning, it was postmarked Omaha.
> It was typed and neatly written offering me a better job,
> Better job and higher wages, expenses paid, and a car.
> But I'm on TV here locally, and I can't quit, I'm a star.
> . . . I'm the number one attraction in every supermarket parking lot.
> I'm the king of Kansas City. No thanks, Omaha, thanks a lot.
> Kansas City Star, that's what I are . . .

Lest you think that even your parents aren't old enough to remember the 1960s, Chely Wright more recently sang,

> Oh I love what I do
> But I wonder what I do it all for
> But when I sing, they sing along . . .
> The reason why I'm standing here
> It's not the miles
> It's not the pay
> It's not the show
> It's not the fame that makes this home
> It's the song.[41]

A PAY MODEL

The pay model shown in Exhibit 1.5 serves as both a framework for examining current pay systems and a guide for most of this book. It contains three basic building blocks: (1) the compensation objectives, (2) the policies that form the foundation of the compensation system, and (3) the techniques that make up the compensation system. Because objectives drive the system, we will discuss them first.

Compensation Objectives

Pay systems are designed to achieve certain objectives. The basic objectives, shown at the right side of the model, include efficiency, fairness, ethics, and compliance with laws and regulations. *Efficiency* can be stated more specifically: (1) improving performance, increasing quality, delighting customers and stockholders, and (2) controlling labor costs.

EXHIBIT 1.5 The Pay Model

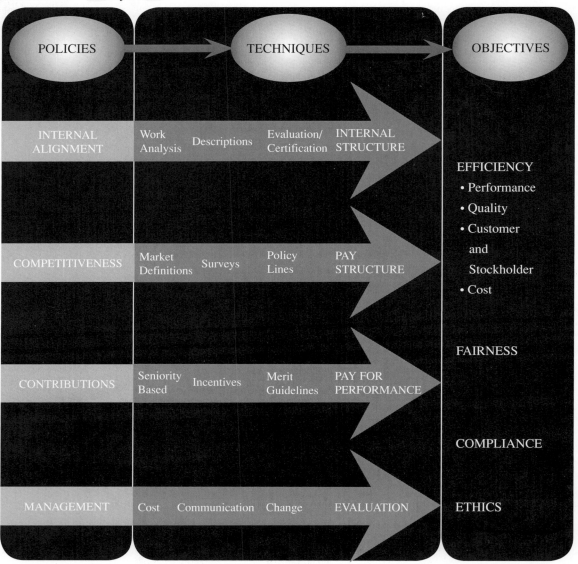

Compensation objectives at Medtronic and Whole Foods are contrasted in Exhibit 1.6 Medtronic is a medical technology company that pioneered cardiac pacemakers. Its compensation objectives emphasize performance, business success, minimizing fixed costs, and attracting and energizing top talent.

Whole Foods is the nation's largest organic- and natural-foods grocer. Its markets are a "celebration of food": bright, well-stocked, and well-staffed.[42] The company describes its

EXHIBIT 1.6   **Pay Objectives at Medtronic and Whole Foods**

Medtronic	Whole Foods
Support Medtronic mission and increased complexity of business	We are committed to increasing long-term shareholder value.
Minimize increases in fixed costs	Profits are earned every day through voluntary exchange with our customers.
Attract and engage top talent	Profits are essential to create capital for growth, prosperity, opportunity, job satisfaction, and job security.
Emphasize personal, team, and Medtronic performance	Support team member happiness and excellence
Recognize personal and family total well-being	We share together in our collective fate.
Ensure fair treatment	

commitment to offering the highest quality and least processed foods as a shared responsibility. Its first compensation objective is ". . . committed to increasing shareholder value."

Fairness is a fundamental objective of pay systems.[43] In Medtronic's objectives, fairness means "ensure fair treatment" and "recognize personal and family well-being." Whole Foods's pay objectives discuss a "shared fate." In their egalitarian work culture, pay beyond base wages is linked to team performance, and employees have some say about who is on their team.

The fairness objective calls for fair treatment for all employees by recognizing both employee contributions (e.g., higher pay for greater performance, experience, or training) and employee needs (e.g., a fair wage as well as fair procedures). *Procedural fairness* refers to the process used to make pay decisions.[44] It suggests that the way a pay decision is made may be equally as important to employees as the results of the decision.

Compliance as a pay objective means conforming to federal and state compensation laws and regulations. If laws change, pay systems may need to change, too, to ensure continued compliance. As companies go global, they must comply with the laws of all the countries in which they operate.

Ethics

Asian philosophy gives us the concept of yin and yang—complementary opposites rather than substitutes or trade-offs. It is not yin *or* yang; part of yin is in yang, and part of yang is in yin. So it is with objectives in the pay model. It is not efficiency versus fairness versus compliance. Rather, it is all three simultaneously. All three must be achieved. The tension of working toward all objectives at once creates fertile grounds for ethical dilemmas.

Ethics means the organization cares about how its results are achieved.[45] Scan the Web sites or lobby walls of corporate headquarters and you will inevitably find statements of "Key Behaviors," "Our Values," and "Codes of Conduct." One company's code of conduct is shown in Exhibit 1.7. The challenge is to put these statements into daily practice. The company in the exhibit is the formerly admired, now reviled, Enron, whose employees lost their jobs and pensions in the wake of legal and ethical misdeeds by those at the top.

Because it is so important, it is inevitable that managing pay sometimes creates ethical dilemmas. Manipulating results to ensure executive bonus payouts, misusing (or failing to understand) statistics used to measure competitors' pay rates, re-pricing or backdating stock options to increase their value, encouraging employees to invest a

EXHIBIT 1.7 Enron's Ethics Statement

Foreword

"As officers and employees of Enron Corp., its subsidiaries, and its affiliated companies, we are responsible for conducting the business affairs of the companies in accordance with all applicable laws and in a moral and honest manner. . . . We want to be proud of Enron and to know that it enjoys a reputation for fairness and honesty and that it is respected. . . . Enron's reputation finally depends on its people, on you and me. Let's keep that reputation high."

July 1, 2000
Kenneth L. Lay
Chairman and Chief Executive Officer

Values

Respect	We treat others as we would like to be treated ourselves. We do not tolerate abusive or disrespectful treatment. Ruthlessness, callousness, and arrogance don't belong here.
Integrity	We work with customers and prospects openly, honestly, and sincerely. When we say we will do something, we will do it; when we say we cannot or will not do something, then we won't do it.
Communication	We have an obligation to communicate. Here, we take the time to talk with one another . . . and to listen.
Excellence	We are satisfied with nothing less than the very best in everything we do. . . . The great fun here will be for all of us to discover just how good we can really be.

Source: *www.thesmokinggun.com.*

portion of their wages in company stock while executives are bailing out, offering just enough pay to get a new hire in the door while ignoring the relationship to co-workers' pay, and shaving the hours recorded in employees' time card—these are all too common examples of ethical lapses.

Some, but not all, compensation professionals and consultants remain silent during ethical misconduct and outright malfeasance. Absent a professional code, compensation managers must look to their own ethics—and the pay model, which calls for combining the objectives of efficiency and fair treatment of employees as well as compliance.[46]

There are probably as many statements of pay objectives as there are employers. In fact, highly diversified firms such as General Electric and Eaton, which operate in multiple lines of businesses, may have different **pay objectives** for different business units. At General Electric, each unit's objectives must meet GE overall objectives.

Objectives serve several purposes. First, they guide the design of the pay system. If an objective is to increase customer satisfaction, then incentive programs and merit pay might be used to pay for performance. Another employer's objective may be to develop innovative new products. Job design, training, and team building may be used to reach this objective. The pay system aligned with this objective may include salaries that are at least equal to those of competitors (external competitiveness) and that go up with increased skills or knowledge (internal alignment). This pay system could be very different from our first example, where the focus is on increasing customer satisfaction. Notice that policies and techniques are the means to reach the objectives.

In summary, objectives guide the design of pay systems. They also serve as the standards for judging the success of the pay system. If the objective is to attract and retain the best and the brightest skilled employees, but they are leaving for higher-paying jobs elsewhere, the system may not be performing effectively. Although there may be many nonpay reasons for such turnover, objectives provide standards for evaluating the effectiveness of a pay system.[47]

Four Policy Choices

Every employer must address the policy decisions shown on the left side of the pay model: (1) internal alignment, (2) external competitiveness, (3) employee contributions, and (4) management of the pay system. These policies are the foundation on which pay systems are built. They also serve as guidelines for managing pay in ways that accomplish the system's objectives.

Internal Alignment

Internal alignment refers to comparisons among jobs or skill levels inside a single organization. Jobs and people's skills are compared in terms of their relative contributions to the organization's business objectives. How, for example, does the work of the programmer compare with the work of the systems analyst, the software engineer, and the software architect? Does one contribute to solutions for customers and satisfied stockholders more than another? What about two marketing managers working in different business units of the same organization? Internal alignment pertains to the pay rates both for employees doing equal work and for those doing dissimilar work. In fact, determining what is an appropriate difference in pay for people performing different work is one of the key challenges facing managers. Whole Foods tries to manage differences with a salary cap that limits the **total cash** compensation (wages plus bonuses) of any executive to 19 times the average cash compensation of all full-time employees. The cap originally started at 8 times the average. However, attraction and retention problems were cited as a need for raising the cap several times since. (Note that the cap does not include stock options.)

Pay relationships within the organization affect all three compensation objectives. They affect employee decisions to stay with the organization, to become more flexible by investing in additional training, or to seek greater responsibility. By motivating employees to choose increased training and greater responsibility in dealing with customers, internal pay relationships indirectly affect the capabilities of the workforce and hence the efficiency of the entire organization. Fairness is affected through employees' comparisons of their pay to the pay of others in the organization. Compliance is affected by the basis used to make internal comparisons. Paying on the basis of race, gender, age, or national origin is illegal in the United States.

External Competitiveness

External competitiveness refers to pay comparisons with competitors. *How much* do we wish to pay in comparison to what other employers pay?

Many organizations claim their pay systems are market-driven, that is, based almost exclusively on what competitors pay. "Market driven" gets translated into practice in different ways.[48] Some employers may set their pay levels higher than their competition, hoping to attract the best applicants. Of course, this assumes that someone is able to identify and hire the "best" from the pool of applicants. And what is the appropriate market? When, for example, should international pay rates be considered? Should the pay of software engineers in New Delhi or Minsk influence pay for engineers in Silicon Valley or Boston?

External competitiveness decisions—both how much and what forms—have a two-fold effect on objectives: (1) to ensure that the pay is sufficient to attract and retain employees—if employees do not perceive their pay as competitive in comparison to what other organizations are offering for similar work, they may be more likely to leave—and (2) to control labor costs so that the organization's prices of products or services can remain competitive in a global economy.

Employee Contributions

How much emphasis should there be on paying for performance? Should one programmer be paid differently from another if one has better performance and/or greater seniority? Or should there be a **flat rate** for programmers? Should the company share any profits with employees? Share with all employees, part-time as well as full-time?

The emphasis to place on **employee contributions** (or nature of **pay mix**) is an important policy decision since it directly affects employees' attitudes and work behaviors. Eaton and Motorola use pay to support other "high-performance" practices in their workplaces.[49] Both use team-based pay and corporate profit-sharing plans. Starbucks emphasizes stock options and sharing the success of corporate performance with the employees. General Electric uses different performance-based pay programs at the individual, division, and companywide level. Performance-based pay affects fairness in that employees need to understand the basis for judging performance in order to believe that their pay is fair.

What mix of pay forms—base, incentives, stock, benefits—do our competitors use in comparison to the pay mix we use? Recall that Sam's Club's policy is to pay competitively in its market. Whole Foods combines base pay and **team incentives** to offer higher pay if team performance warrants. Medtronic sets its base pay to match its competitors but ties bonuses to performance. It offers stock to all its employees based on overall company performance.[50] Further, Medtronic believes that its benefits, particularly its emphasis on programs that balance work and life, make it a highly attractive place to work. It believes that *how* its pay is positioned and *what forms* it uses create an advantage over competitors.

The external competiveness and employee contribution decisions should be made jointly. Clearly, an above-market compensation level is most effective and sustainable when it exists together with above-market employee contributions to productivity, quality, customer service, or other important strategic objectives.

Management

A policy regarding management of the pay system is the last building block in our model. Management means ensuring that the *right people* get the *right pay* for *achieving the right objectives in the right way*. The greatest system design in the world is useless without competent management.

Managing compensation means answering the "So What" question. So what is the impact of this policy, this technique, this decision? Although it is possible to design a system that is based on internal alignment, external competitiveness, and employee contributions, what difference does it make? Does the decision help the organization achieve its objectives?[51]

The ground under compensation management has shifted. The traditional focus on how to administer various techniques is long gone, replaced by more strategic thinking—managing pay as part of the business. It goes beyond simply managing pay as an expense to better understanding and analyzing the impact of pay decisions on people's behaviors and organizations' success. The impact of pay decisions on expenses is one result that is easily measured and well understood. But other measures—such as pay's impact on attracting and retaining the right people, and engaging these people productively—are not yet widely used in the management of compensation. Efforts to do so are increasing and the perspective is shifting from "How To" toward trying to answer the "So What" question.[52] Ease of measurement is not the same as importance; costs are easy to measure (and, of course, important), so there is a tendency to focus there. Yet, the consequences of pay, although often less amenable to measurement, are nonetheless just as important.

Pay Techniques

The remaining portion of the pay model in Exhibit 1.5 shows the techniques that make up the pay system. The exhibit provides only an overview since techniques are discussed throughout the rest of the book. Techniques tie the four basic policies to the pay objectives.

Uncounted variations in **pay techniques** exist; many are examined in this book. Most consultant firms tout their surveys and techniques on their Web pages. You can obtain updated information on various practices by simply surfing the Web.

Cybercomp

World at Work (*www.worldatwork.org*) provides information on its compensation-related journals and special publications, as well as short courses aimed at practitioners. The Society of Human Resource Management (*www.shrm.org*) also offers compensation-related information as well as more general human resource management (HRM) information. The society's student services section offers guidance on finding jobs in the field of human resources. Both sites are good sources of information for people interested in careers in HRM. Information on pay trends in Europe is available from the European Industrial Relations Observatory (*www.eiro.eurofound.ie*). The International Labour Organization (www.ilo.org) maintains a database that can be browsed either by subject (conditions of employment) or country (*www.ilo.org/dyn/natlex/natlex_browse.home*). Over 2,000 articles are listed in their "wages" subheading, including such information as the minimum wage in Vanuatu. Cornell University's Industrial and Labor Relations School offers a "research portal" for articles of interest in human resource management (*www.ilr.cornell.edu/library/research/researchPortal.html*). The Employee Benefits Research Institute (EBRI) includes links to other benefits sources on its Web site (*www.ebri.org*). Every chapter in this book also mentions interesting Web sites. Use them as a starting point to search out others.

BOOK PLAN

Compensation is such a broad and compelling topic that several books are devoted to it. The focus of this book is on the design and management of compensation systems. To aid in understanding how and why pay systems work, our pay model provides the structure for much of the book. Chapter 2 discusses how to formulate and execute a compensation strategy. We analyze what it means to be strategic about how people are paid and how compensation can help achieve and sustain an organization's competitive advantage.[53]

The pay model plays a central role in formulating and implementing an organization's pay strategy. The model identifies four basic policy choices that are the core of the pay strategy. After we discuss strategy, the next sections of the book examine each of these policies in detail. Part 1 on *internal alignment* (Chapters 3 through 6) examines pay relationships within a single organization. Part 2 (Chapters 7 and 8) examines *external competitiveness*—the pay relationships among competing organizations—and analyzes the influence of market-driven forces.

Once the compensation rates and structures are established, other issues emerge. How much should we pay each individual employee? How much and how often should a person's pay be increased and on what basis—experience, seniority, or performance? Should pay increases be contingent on the organization's and/or the employee's performance? How should the organization share its success (or failure) with employees? These are questions of *employee contributions,* the third building block in the model, covered in Part 3 (Chapters 9 through 11).

In Part 4, we cover employee services and benefits (Chapters 12 and 13). How do benefits fit in the company's overall compensation package? What choices should employees have in their benefits? In Part 5, we cover systems tailored for special groups—sales representatives, executives, contract workers, unions (Chapters 14 and 15)—and we provide more detail on global compensation systems (Chapter 16). Part 6 concludes with information essential for *managing the compensation system.* The government's role in compensation is examined in Chapter 17. Chapter 18 includes understanding, communicating, budgeting, and evaluating results.

Even though the book is divided into sections that reflect the pay model, pay decisions are not discrete. All of them are interrelated. Together, they influence employee behaviors and organization performance and can create a pay system that can be a source of competitive advantage.

Throughout the book our intention is to examine alternative approaches. We believe that rarely is there a single correct approach; rather, alternative approaches exist or can be designed. The one most likely to be effective depends on the circumstances. We hope that this book will help you become better informed about these options, how to evaluate and select the most effective ones, and how to design new ones. Whether as an employee, a manager, or an interested member of society, you should be able to assess the effectiveness and fairness of pay systems.

CAVEAT EMPTOR—BE AN INFORMED CONSUMER

Most managers do not read research. They do not subscribe to research journals; they find them too full of jargon and esoterica, and they see them as impractical and irrelevant.[54] However, a study of 5,000 HR managers compared their beliefs to the research evidence in several areas and identified seven common and important misconceptions held by managers.[55] The study authors concluded that being unaware of key research findings may prove costly to organizations. For example, when it comes to motivating workers, organization efforts may be somewhat misguided if they do not know that "Money is the crucial incentive . . . no other incentive or motivational technique comes even close to money with respect to its instrumental value."[56]

So it pays to read the research. There is no question that some studies are irrelevant and poorly performed. But if you are not a reader of research literature, you become prey for the latest business self-help fad. Belief, even enthusiasm, is a poor substitute for informed judgment. Therefore, we end the chapter with a consumer's guide to research that includes three questions to help make you a critical reader—and a better-informed decision maker.

1. Is the Research Useful?

How useful are the variables in the study? How well are they measured? For example, many studies purport to measure organization performance. However, performance may be accounting measures such as return on assets or cash flow, financial measures such as earnings per share, operational measures such as scrap rates or defect indicators, or qualitative measures such as customer satisfaction. It may even be the opinions of compensation managers, as in, "How effective is your gain-sharing plan?" (Answer choices are "highly effective," "effective," "somewhat," "disappointing," "not very effective." "Disastrous" is not usually one of the choices.) The informed consumer must ask, Does this research measure anything useful?

2. Does the Study Separate Correlation From Causation?

Once we are confident that the variables are useful and accurately measured, we must be sure that they are actually related. Most often this is addressed through the use of statistical analysis. The **correlation coefficient** is a common measure of association and indicates how changes in one variable are related to changes in another. Many research studies use a statistical analysis known as *regression analysis*. One output from a regression analysis is the R^2. The R^2 is much like a correlation in that it tells us what percentage of the variation is accounted for by the variables we are using to predict or explain. For example, one study includes a regression analysis of the change in CEO pay related to change in company performance. The resulting R^2 of between 0.8 percent and 4.5 percent indicates that only a very small amount of change in CEO pay is related to changes in company performance.

But even if there is a relationship, correlation does not ensure causation. For example, just because a manufacturing plant initiates a new incentive plan and the facility's performance improves, we cannot conclude that the incentive plan caused the improved performance. Perhaps new technology, **reengineering,** improved marketing, or the general expansion of the local economy underlies the results. The two changes are associated or related, but causation is a tough link to make.

Too often, case studies, benchmarking studies of best practices, or consultant surveys are presented as studies that reveal cause and effect. They do not. Case studies are descriptive accounts whose value and limitations must be recognized. Just because the best-performing companies are using a practice does not mean the practice is causing the performance. IBM provides an example of the difficulty of deciding whether a change is a cause or an effect. Years ago, IBM pursued a no-layoff policy. History clearly reveals that the policy did not improve IBM's profitability or increase its stockholders' returns. Arguably, it was IBM's profitability that enabled its full-employment policy. However, compensation research often does attempt to answer questions of causality. How does the use of performance-based pay influence customer satisfaction, product quality, and company performance? Causality is one of the most difficult questions to answer and continues to be an important and sometimes perplexing problem for researchers.[57]

3. Are There Alternative Explanations?

Consider a hypothetical study that attempts to assess the impact of a performance-based pay program. The researchers measure performance by assessing quality, productivity, customer satisfaction, employee satisfaction, and the facility's performance. The final step is to see whether future periods' performance improves over this period's. If it does, can we safely assume that it was the incentive pay that caused performance? Or is it equally likely that the improved performance has alternative explanations, such as the fluctuation in the value of currency or perhaps a change in leadership in the facility?

In this case, causality evidence seems weak. Alternative explanations exist. If the researchers had measured the performance indicators several years prior to and after installing the plan, then the evidence of causality is only a bit stronger. Further, if the researchers repeated this process in other facilities and the results were similar, then the preponderance of evidence is stronger yet. Clearly, the organization is doing something right, and incentive pay is part of it.

The best way to establish causation is to account for competing explanations, either statistically or through control groups. The point is that alternative explanations often exist. And if they do, they need to be accounted for to establish causality. It is very difficult to disentangle the effects of pay plans to clearly establish causality. However, it is possible to look at the overall pattern of evidence to make judgments about the effects of pay.

So we encourage you to become a critical reader of all management literature, including this book. As Hogwarts' famous Professor Alaster Moody cautions, be on "constant vigilance for sloppy analysis masquerading as research."[58]

Your **Turn**   Circuit City

In 2007, Circuit City fired 3,400 of its highest-paid store employees and began to replace them with lower-paid workers in hopes of reducing labor costs. In the following quarter, Circuit City reported that the company lost money. Some commentators attributed the loss to the fact that Circuit City had gotten rid of many of its most experienced and highly trained employees, which they believed translated into a poorer customer experience and, in turn, lower revenues and profits. According to *BusinessWeek*, "In the world of pricey consumer electronics, where customer service is arguably as important as quality products, Circuit City Stores is missing the mark and further eroding its profits."

However, a company spokesman said that only a few salespeople per store were affected by the workforce reductions and that many of the employees affected worked as customer service representatives or in the warehouses. As such, he questioned whether the cuts had significantly affected the in-store customer experience and thus whether the cuts had caused the decline in the company's performance.

Eventually, the bottom fell out of Circuit City's profits and stock price and it had to liquidate, closing its over 500 stores (resulting in over 30,000 employees losing their jobs).

Thinking back to our discussion in the chapter section, *Caveat Emptor*—Be An Informed Consumer, evaluate whether the replacement of highly paid workers with lower-paid workers did or did not cause Circuit City to perform so poorly. How confident are you in your evaluation? Why?

Perhaps the following data will be helpful. You might enjoy graphing the stock prices by year. You may wish to consider whether other data or information would be helpful in assessing Circuit City's change in compensation strategy.

Year	Circuit City Year Opening Stock Price	Circuit City Customer Satisfaction (ASCI Index)	Best Buy Year Opening Stock Price	Best Buy Customer Satisfaction (ASCI Index)
2000	48.00		25.89	
2001	16.06		17.75	
2002	28.51		32.31	
2003	7.22		18.27	
2004	8.95	73	36.00	72
2005	13.63	72	36.77	72
2006	22.94	70	47.05	71
2007	19.29	69	50.00	76
2008	4.18	71	44.20	74
2009	0.14	72	28.08	74

Sources: Amy Joyce, "Circuit City's Job Cuts Backfiring, Analysts Say," *Washington Post*, (May 2, 2007), p. D1. Stock price data from www.moneycentral.com. ASCI = American Customer Satisfaction Index, http://www.theacsi.org/. David Bogoslaw, "Circuit City Gets Crushed," *BusinessWeek*, December 2, 2007.

Notes: Stock symbol for Circuit City is CCTYQ and for Best Buy is BBY. ASCI scores for Circuit City and Best Buy available from 2004 forward.

Summary

The model presented in this chapter provides a structure for understanding compensation systems. The three main components of the model are the compensation objectives, the policy decisions that guide how the objectives are going to be achieved, and the techniques that make up the pay system and link the policies to the objectives. The following sections of the book examine each of the four policy decisions—internal alignment, external competitiveness, employee performance, and management—as well as the techniques, new directions, and related research.

Two questions should constantly be in the minds of managers and readers of this text. First, why do it this way? There is rarely one correct way to design a system or pay an individual. Organizations, people, and circumstances are too varied. But a well-trained manager can select or design a suitable approach. Second, so what? What does this technique do for us? How does it help achieve our goals? If good answers to the "so-what" question are not apparent, there is no point to the technique. Adapting the pay system to meet the needs of the employees and helping to achieve the goals of the organization is what this book is all about.

The basic premise of this book is that compensation systems do have a profound impact. Yet, too often, traditional pay systems seem to have been designed in response to some historical but long-forgotten problem. The practices continue, but the logic underlying them is not always clear or even relevant. The next generation pay systems hopefully will be more flexible—designed to achieve specific objectives under changing conditions.

Review Questions

1. How do differing perspectives affect our views of compensation?

2. What is your definition of compensation? Which meaning of compensation seems most appropriate from an employee's view: return, reward, or entitlement? Compare your ideas with someone with more experience, someone from another country, someone from another field of study.

3. What is the "network of returns" that your college offers your instructor? What returns do you believe make a difference in teaching effectiveness? What "returns" would you change or add to increase the teaching effectiveness?

4. What are the four policy issues in the pay model? What purposes do the objectives in the pay model serve?

5. List all the forms of pay you receive from work. Compare your list to someone else's list. Explain any differences.

6. Answer the three questions in the *Caveat Emptor—Be An Informed Consumer* section for any study or business article that tells you how to pay people.

Endnotes

1. Written by Jenny Bradford and Berry Gordy Jr. Performed by The Beatles on *The Beatles' Second Album* (1964).

2. "What People Earn," *Parade Magazine,* April 12, 2009.

3. Bill Vlasic and Nick Bunkley. "GM's Latest Plan Envisions a Much Smaller Automaker." *New York Times,* April 28, 2008.

4. W. G. Sanders and D. C. Hambrick, "Swinging for the Fences: The Effects of CEO Stock Options on Company Risk Taking and Performance," *Academy of Management Journal* 50 (2007), pp. 1055–1078; Cynthia E Devers, Gerry McNamara, Robert M. Wiseman, and Mathias Arrfelt, "Moving Closer to the Action: Examining Compensation Design Effects on Firm Risk," *Organization Science* 19, July–August 2008, pp. 548–566.

5. Michael Jacobs, "Opinion: How Business Schools Have Failed Business," *Wall Street Journal* (April 24, 2009). For a similar view, see also Alan S. Blinder, "Crazy

Compensation and the Crisis," *Wall Street Journal,* May 28, 2009. (Mr. Blinder is a former vice chairman of the Federal Reserve Board.)

6. B. Gerhart, "Compensation," in Adrian Wilkinson, Nicholas Bacon, Tom Redman, and Scott Snell, eds., *Sage Handbook of Human Resource Management* (Thousand Oaks, CA: Thousand Oaks, CA: Sage, 2009); James H. Dulebohn and Stephen E. Werling, "Compensation Research: Past, Present, and Future," *Human Resource Management Review* 17 (2007), pp. 191–207; Steve Werner and Stephanie Ward, "Recent Compensation Research: An Eclectic Review," *Human Resource Management Review* 14 (2004), pp. 201–227; S. L. Rynes, B. Gerhart, and K. A. Minette, 2004. The Importance of Pay in Employee Motivation: Discrepancies Between What People Say and What They Do," *Human Resource Management* 43 (2004), pp. 381–394.

7. U.S. Department of Labor, Bureau of Labor Statistics, "Highlights of Women's Earnings in 2007," *Report 1008* (October 2008); Francine D. Blau and Lawrence M. Kahn, "The Gender Pay Gap: Have Women Gone as Far as They Can?" *Academy of Management Perspectives* 21, February 2007, pp. 7–23.

8. The Henry J. Kaiser Family Foundation, "Health Care Costs: A Primer," www.kff.org/insurance/upload/7670_02.pdf. Retrieved March 2009.

9. "Employer Costs for Employer Compensation," *www.bls.gov.* Retrieved March 12, 2009.

10. Carmen DeNavas-Walt, Bernadette D. Proctor, and Jessica C. Smith, *U.S. Census Bureau: Current Population Reports, P60-235: Income, Poverty, and Health Insurance Coverage in the United States: 2007* (Washington, DC: U.S. Government Printing Office, 2008).

11. The National Coalition on Health Care, "Health Insurance Coverage," *www.nchc.org/facts/coverage.shtml.* Retrieved May 22, 2009.

12. International Monetary Fund, "Gross Domestic Product Per Capita," *www.imf.org.* Retrieved April 25, 2009.

13. David Redmon, director, *Mardi Gras: Made in China, www.mardigrasmadeinchina.com/news.html;* B. Powell and D. Skarbek, "Sweatshops and Third World Living Standards: Are the Jobs Worth the Sweat?" *Journal of Labor Research,* Spring 2006, pp. 263–290.

14. L. Bebchuk and J. M. Fried, *Pay Without Performance* (Cambridge, MA: Harvard University Press, 2004); M. J. Conyon, "Executive Compensation and Incentives," *Academy of Management Perspectives* 21, February 2006, pp. 25–44; S. N. Kaplan, "Are CEOs Overpaid?" *Academy of Management Perspectives* 22(2), 2008, pp. 5–20; J. P. Walsh, 2008. "CEO Compensation: The Responsibilities of the Business Scholar to Society," *Academy of Management Perspectives,* 22(2), 2008, pp. 26–33; A. J. Nyberg, I. S. Fulmer, B. Gerhart, and M. A. Carpenter, "Agency Theory Revisited: CEO Returns and Shareholder Interest Alignment," *Academy of Management Journal,* in press; B. Gerhart, S. L. Rynes, and I. S. Fulmer. (2009). "Pay and Performance: Individuals, Groups, and Executives," *Academy of Management Annals,* 3, 251–315.

15. C. E. Devers, A. A. Cannella, G. P. Reilly, and M. E. Yoder, "Executive Compensation: A Multidisciplinary Review of Recent Developments," *Journal of Management* 33 (2007), pp. 1016–1072; I. S. Fulmer, "The Elephant in the Room: Labor Market Influences on CEO Compensation," *Personnel Psychology,* in press; A. Nyberg, I. S. Fulmer, B. Gerhart, and M. A. Carpenter, "Agency Theory Revisited: CEO Returns and Shareholder Interest Alignment," *Academy of Management Journal,* in press.

16. Wayne F. Cascio. "The High Cost of Low Wages," *Harvard Business Review* 84, December 2006, p. 23; Liza Featherstone, "Wage Against the Machine," *Slate,* June 27, 2008.

17. Jerry Newman, *My Secret Life on the McJob* (New York: McGraw-Hill, 2007); Edward Lawler III, *Treat People Right! How Organizations and Individuals Can Propel Each Other into a Virtuous Spiral of Success* (San Francisco: Jossey-Bass, 2003).

18. K. Bartol and E. Locke, "Incentives and Motivation," Chap. 4 in *Compensation in Organizations,* eds. S. Rynes and B. Gerhart (San Francisco: Jossey-Bass, 2000), pp. 104–150; B. Gerhart, S. L. Rynes, and I. S. Fulmer. (2009). "Pay and Performance: Individuals, Groups, and Executives," *Academy of Management Annals,* 3, 251–315.

19. Edward E. Lawler III, *Pay and Organizational Effectiveness: A Psychological View* (New York: McGraw-Hill, 1971); Thomas Li-Ping Tang, "Whoever Loves Money Is Never Satisfied With His or Her Income." Paper presented at the Academy of Management Meeting, Anaheim, California, August 2008.

20. E. P. Lazear, "Salaries and Piece Rates," *Journal of Business* 59, 1986, pp. 405–431; B. Gerhart and G. T. Milkovich, "Employee Compensation: Research and Practice," In eds. M. D. Dunnette and L. M. Hough, *Handbook of Industrial & Organizational Psychology,* 2nd Edition (Palo Alto, CA: Consulting Psychologists Press, 1992); B. Gerhart and S. L. Rynes, *Compensation: Theory, Evidence, and Strategic Implications* (Thousand Oaks, CA: Sage, 2003).

21. D. M. Cable and T. A. Judge, "Pay Preferences and Job Search Decisions: A Person-Organization Fit Perspective," *Personnel Psychology* 47, 2994, pp. 317–348; C. B. Cadsby, F. Song, and F. Tapon, "Sorting and Incentive Effects of Pay-for-Performance: An Experimental Investigation," *Academy of Management Journal* 50, 2007, pp. 387–405; C. Q. Trank, S. L. Rynes, and R. D. Bretz, Jr., "Attracting Applicants in the War for Talent: Differences in Work Preferences Among High Achievers," *Journal of Business and Psychology* 16, 2001, pp. 331–345; C. O. Trevor, B. Gerhart, and J. W. Boudreau, "Voluntary Turnover and Job Performance: Curvilinearity and the Moderating Influences of Salary Growth and Promotions," *Journal of Applied Psychology* 82, 1997, pp. 44–61; A. Salamin and P. W. Hom, "In Search of the Elusive U-shaped Performance-Turnover Relationship: Are High Performing Swiss Bankers More Liable to Quit?" *Journal of Applied Psychology,* 90, 2005, pp. 1204–1216; J. D. Shaw and N. Gupta, "Pay System Characteristics and Quit Patterns of Good, Average, and Poor Performers," *Personnel Psychology* 60, 2007, pp. 903–928; B. Schneider, "The people make the place," *Personnel Psychology* 40, 1987, pp. 437–453.

22. E. Lazear, "Performance Pay and Productivity," *American Economic Review* 90, 2000, pp. 1346–1361.

23. Atul Mitra, Matt Bloom, and George Milkovich, "Crossing a Raging River: Seeking Far-Reaching Solutions to Global Pay Challenges," *WorldatWork Journal* 22(2), Second Quarter 2002; Mark Fenton-O'Creevy, "HR Practice: Vive la Différence," *Financial Times,* October 2002, pp. 6–8; Mansour Javidan, Peter Dorman, Mary Sully deLuque, and Robert House, "In the Eye of the Beholder: Cross Cultural Lessons in Leadership From Project GLOBE," *Academy of Management Perspectives,* February 2006, pp. 67–90.

24. Anne Tsui and Chung-Ming Lau, *The Management of Enterprises in the People's Republic of China* (Boston: Kluwer Academic, 2002).

25. Sanford Jacoby, *The Embedded Corporation: Corporate Governance and Employment Relations in Japan and the United States* (Princeton, NJ: Princeton University Press, 2004); Yoshio Yanadori, "Minimizing Competition? Entry-Level Compensation in Japanese Firms," *Asia Pacific Journal of Management* 21, December 2004, pp. 445–467.

26. Chun Hui, Cynthia Lee, and Denise M. Rousseau, "Psychological Contract and Organizational Citizenship Behavior in China: Investigating Generalizability and Instrumentality," *Journal of Applied Psychology* 89, 2004, pp. 311–321; N. Conway

and R. Briner, *Understanding Psychological Contracts at Work: a Critical Evaluation of Theory and Research* (Oxford: Oxford University Press, 2005); WorldatWork has developed a total rewards model, described in Jean Christofferson and Bob King, "The 'It' Factor: A New Total Rewards Model Leads the Way," *Workspan,* April 2006.

27. "Brightly Colored Uniforms Boost Employee Morale," *The Onion* 36(43), November 30, 2000.

28. Jean Christofferson and Bob King, "New Total Rewards Model," *Workspan,* April 2006, pp. 1–8.

29. Allan Odden and Carolyn Kelley, *Paying Teachers for What They Know and Do: New and Smarter Compensation Strategies to Improve Schools,* 2nd ed. (Thousand Oaks, CA: Corwin Press, 2002); Ralph Blumenthal, "Houston Ties Teachers' Pay to Test Scores," *New York Times,* January 13, 2006, p. A12.

30. U.S. Department of Labor, Fair Labor Standards Act, *http://www.dol.gov/compliance/laws/comp-flsa.htm.*

31. B. Gerhart and C. O. Trevor, "Merit Pay," in A. Varma, P. S. Budhwar, and A. DeNisi, eds., *Performance Management Systems: A Global Perspective* (Oxford, U.K.: Routledge, 2008); S. L. Rynes, B. Gerhart, and L. Parks,"Personnel Psychology: Performance Evaluation and Pay for Performance," *Annual Review of Psychology* 56, 2005, pp. 571–600; R. L. Heneman, *Merit Pay: Linking Pay Increases to Performance Ratings.* (New York: Addison-Wesley, 1992); G. Milkovich and A. Wigdor, *Pay for Performance: Evaluating Performance Appraisal and Merit Pay* (Washington, DC: National Academy Press, 1991). M. C. Sturman, C. O. Trevor, J. W. Boudreau, and B. Gerhart, "Is It Worth It to Win the Talent War? Evaluating the Utility of Performance-Based Pay," *Personnel Psychology* 56, 2003, pp. 997–1035; A. Salamin and P. W. Horn, "In Search of the Elusive U-Shaped Performance-Turnover Relationship: Are High Performing Swiss Bankers More Liable to Quit?" *Journal of Applied Psychology* 90, 2005, pp. 1204–1216; Michael Sturman, "How Versus How Much You Pay: The Effects of Various Pay Components on Future Performance," working paper, Hotel School, Ithaca, NY: 2006; John J. Schaubroeck, Jason D. Shaw, and Michelle K Duffy, "An Under-Met and Over-Met Expectations Model of Employee Reactions to Merit Raises," *Journal of Applied Psychology,* 93, 2008, pp. 424–434; A. Colella, R. L. Paetzold, A. Zardkoohi, and M. J. Wesson, "Exposing Pay Secrecy," *Academy of Management Review,* 32, 2007, pp. 55–71; S. E. Scullen, P. K. Bergey, and L. Aiman-Smith, "Forced Distribution Rating Systems and the Improvement of Workforce Potential: A Baseline Simulation, *Personnel Psychology,* 58, 2005, pp. 1–32; Laura Meckler, "Obama Seeks to Expand Merit Pay for Teachers," *Wall Street Journal,* March 11, 2009; Richard Hader, Pay-for-Performance a Slippery Slope? *Nursing Management,* 39, 2008, p. 6; Karen Talley, "Wal-Mart Increases Employee Bonuses," *Wall Street Journal,* March 19, 2009.

32. WorldatWork. *2008–2009 Salary Budget Survey* (Scottsdale, AZ).

33. D. G. Jenkins, Jr., A. Mitra, N. Gupta, and J. D. Shaw, "Are Financial Incentives Related to Performance? A meta-analytic review of empirical research," *Journal of Applied Psychology* 83, 1998, pp. 777–787; Steve Kerr, "The Best Laid Incentive Plans," *Harvard Business Review,* January 2003; Michael C. Sturman and J. C. Short, "Lump Sum Bonus Satisfaction: Testing the Construct Validity of a New Pay Satisfaction Dimension," *Personnel Psychology* 53, 2000, pp. 673–700; A. D. Stajkovic and F. Luthans, "A Meta-Analysis of the Effects of Organizational Behavior Modification on Task Performance, 1975–1995," *Academy of Management Journal,* 40, 1997, pp. 1122–1149; T. M. Nisar, "Bonuses and Investment in Intangibles," *Journal of Labor Research,* Summer 2006, pp. 381–396; W. F. Whyte, *Money and Motivation: An Analysis of Incentives in*

Industry (New York: Harper Brothers, 1955); E. E. Lawler III, *Pay and Organizational Effectiveness: A Psychological View* (New York: McGraw-Hill, 1971); D. Roy, "Quota Restriction and Gold Bricking in a Machine Shop," *American Journal of Sociology,* 57, 1952, pp. 427–442; B. Gerhart and S. L. Rynes, *Compensation: Theory, Evidence, and Strategic Implications* (Thousand Oaks, CA: Sage, 2003).

34. Cory Rosen, John Case, and Martin Staubus, "Every Employee an Owner," *Harvard Business Review,* June 2005, pp. 123–130; Ben Dunford, John Boudreau, and Wendy Boswell, "Out of the Money: The Impact of Underwater Stock Options on Executive Job Search," *Personnel Psychology* 58, 2005, pp. 67–101; Bartolome Deya-Tortella, Luis R. Gomez-Mejia, Julio E. DeCastro, and Robert M. Wiseman, "Incentive Alignment or Perverse Incentives? A Behavioral View of Stock Options," *Management Research* 3(2), 2005.

35. Margaret L. Williams, Stanley B. Malos, and David K. Palmer, "Benefit System and Benefit Level Satisfaction: An Expanded Model of Antecedents and Consequences," *Journal of Management* 28(2), 2002, pp. 195–212; Carol Loomis, "The Tragedy of General Motors," *Fortune,* February 2006, *money.cnn.com/magazines/fortune/fortune_ archive/2006/02/20/8369111/index.htm.*

36. *www.medtronic.com.*

37. Mei Fong, "A Chinese Puzzle," *The Wall Street Journal,* August 16, 2004, p. B1.

38. The Web sites for the International Labour Organization (*www.ilo.org*) and the European Industrial Relations Observatory On-Line (*www.eiro.eurofound.ie*) publish news of developments in HR in Europe. Also see Paul Boselie and Jaap Paauwe, *HR Function Competencies in European Companies,* (Ithaca, NY: CAHRS Working Paper, 2005).

39. Gary P. Latham, *Work Motivation: History, Theory, Research, and Practice.* (Thousand Oaks, CA: Sage, 2007); A. H. Maslow, "A Theory of Human Motivation," *Psychological Review,* 50, 1943, pp. 370–396; F. Herzberg, B. Mausner, R. O. Peterson, and D. F. Capwell, *Job Attitudes: Review of Research and Opinion* (Piittsburgh: Psychological Service of Pittsburgh, 1957). B. Gerhart and S. L. Rynes, *Compensation: Theory, Evidence, and Strategic Implications* (Thousand Oaks, CA, 2003): R. Sage, G. Kanfer, G. Chen, and R. D. Pritchard (eds.), *Motivation: Past, Present, and Future* (New York: Taylor and Francis, 2008).

40. Austin Collins, "Pay in Theoretical Physics," *California Institute of Technology Newspaper,* May 23, 1997, p. 3; Richard P. Feynman, *The Pleasure of Finding Things Out* (Cambridge, MA: Helix Books, 1999); "Brightly Colored Uniforms Boost Employee Morale," *The Onion* 36 (43), November 30, 2000; Just Racz, *50 Jobs Worse Than Yours* (New York: Bloomsbury, 2004).

41. "Kansas City Star," words and music by Roger Miller; "It's Not the Song," written by Bonnie Baker and Katrina Elam, copyright 2005 by Painted Red Music Group, performed by Chely Wright.

42. Charles Fishman, "The Anarchist's Cookbook," *Fast Company*, July 2004, *http://www. fastcompany.com/magazine/84/wholefoods.html.* Further information on each company's philosophy and way of doing business can be deduced from their Web sites: *www .medtronic.com and www.wholefoods.com.*

43. Readers of earlier editions of this book will note that "fairness" is substituted for "equity." The word "equity" has taken on several meanings in compensation, e.g., stock ownership and pay discrimination. We decided that "fairness" better conveyed our meaning in this book.

44. Charlie O. Trevor and David L. Wazeter, "A Contingent View of Reactions to Objective Pay Conditions: Interdependence Among Pay Structure Characteristics and Pay Relative to Internal and External Referents," *Journal of Applied Psychology* 91 (2006), pp. 1260–1275. Quinetta M. Roberson and Jason A. Colquitt, "Shared and Configural Justice: A Social

Network Model of Justice in Teams," *Academy of Management Review* 30(3), 2005, pp. 595–607; Don A. Moore, Philip E. Tetlock, Lloyd Tanlu, and Max H. Bazerman, "Conflicts of Interest and the Case of Auditor Independence: Moral Seduction and Strategic Issue Cycling," *Academy of Management Review* 31(1), 2006, pp. 10–29; Maurice E. Schweitzer, Lisa Ordonez, and Bambi Douma, "Goal Setting as a Motivator of Unethical Behavior," *Academy of Management Journal* 47(3), 2004, pp. 422–432; Vikas Anand, Blake E. Ashforth, and Mahendra Joshi, "Business as Usual: The Acceptance and Perpetuation of Corruption in Organizations," *Academy of Management Executive* 19(4), 2005, pp. 9–22.

45.   John W. Budd and James G. Scoville (eds.), *The Ethics of Human Resources and Industrial Relations* (Ithaca, NY: Cornell University Press, 2004); Richard M Locke, Fei Qin, Alberto Brause, "Does Monitoring Improve Labor Standards? Lessons From Nike," *Industrial & Labor Relations Review,* 61, 2007, p. 3.

46.   "Academy of Management Code of Ethical Conduct," *Academy of Management Journal* 48(6), 2005, pp. 1188–1192; Barrie E. Litzky, Kimberly A. Eddleston, and Deborah L. Kidder, "The Good, the Bad, and the Misguided: How Managers Inadvertently Encourage Deviant Behaviors," *Academy of Management Perspectives* 20(1), February 2006, pp. 91–103; Frederic W. Cook, "Compensation Ethics: An Oxymoron or Valid Area for Debate?" Featured speech at ACA International Conference Workshop, 1999; Stuart P. Green, *Lying, Cheating, and Stealing: A Moral Theory of White-Collar Crime* (Boston: Oxford University Press, 2006); Tom Stone, "Ethics in HRM," Oklahoma State HR Conference, May 2005. See *www.shrm.org/ethics/code-of-ethics/asp*. Stone identifies an integrity test at *www.hoganassessments.com* and *www.epredix.com*. The site for the Ethics Resource Center is *www.ethics.org*. The Josephson Institute of Ethics publishes online their pamphlet *Making Ethical Decisions, www.josephsoninstitute.org*.

47.   Michael Gibbs and Wallace Hendricks, Do Formal Pay Systems Really Matter? *Industrial & Labor Relations Review,* October 2004, pp. 71–93; John Boudreau and Pete Ramstad, B*eyond Cost-Per-Hire and Time to Fill: Supply-Chain Measurement for Staffing.* Los Angeles: Center for Effective Organizations, 2006); Christopher Collins, Jeff Ericksen, and Matthew Allen, HRM Practices, Workforce Alignment, and Firm Performance (Ithaca, NY: CAHRS Working Paper, 2005).

48.   *Market Pricing: Methods to the Madness* (Scottsdale, AZ: WorldatWork, 2002).

49.   Rosemary Batt, Managing Customer Services: Human Resource Practices, Quit Rates, and Sales Growth, *Academy of Management Journal 45(3)(2002),* pp. 587–597*;* Paul Osterman, The Wage Effects of High Performance Work Organization in Manufacturing," *Industrial and Labor Relations Review,* January 2006, pp. 187–204; Patrick Wright, Timothy Gardner, Lisa Moynihan, and Mathew Allen, The Relationship Between HR Practices and Firm Performance: Examining Causal Order, *Personal Psychology,* Summer 2005, pp. 409–446. Robert D Mohr, Cindy Zoghi. (2008). High-involvement work design and job satisfaction. *Industrial & Labor Relations Review,* 61, 275. Appelbaum, Eileen, Thomas Bailey, Peter Berg, and Arne Kalleberg. 2000. *Manufacturing Advantage: Why high performance work systems pay off*. Ithaca, NY: Cornell University Press.

50.   Mary Graham, Rick Welsh, and George Mueller, "In the Land of Milk and Money: One Dairy Farm's Strategic Compensation System," *Journal of Agribusiness* 15(2), 1997, pp. 171–188.

51.   J. Paauwe. *HRM and Performance: unique approaches in order to achieve long-term viability.* (Oxford: Oxford University Press, 2004).

52.   John Boudreau and Pete Ramstad, *Beyond Cost-Per-Hire and Time to Fill: Supply-Chain Measurement for Staffing* (Los Angeles: Center for Effective Organizations, 2006); Ed

Lawler, Dave Ulrich, Jac Fitz-Enz, and James Madden, *HR Business Process Outsourcing* (San Francisco: Jossey-Bass, 2004); D. Scott, D. Morajda, T. McMullen, and R. Sperling, "Evaluating Pay Program Effectiveness," *WorldatWork Journal* 15(2) (Second Quarter 2006), pp. 50–59; S. Raza, *Optimizing Human Capital Investments for Superior Shareholder Returns* (New York: Hewitt Associates, 2006); M. Huselid and B. Becker, "Improving HR Analytical Literacy: Lessons from Moneyball," chapter 32 in M. Losey, S. Meisinger, and D. Ulrich, *The Future of Human Resource Management* (Hoboken, NJ: Wiley, 2005).

53. Y. Yanadori and J. H. Marler, "Compensation Strategy: Does Business Strategy Influence Compensation in High-Technology Firms?" *Strategic Management Journal,* 27, 2006, pp. 559–570.

54. Jeffrey Pfeffer and Robert Sutton, "Management Half-Truth and Nonsense: How to Practice Evidence-Based Management," *California Management Review,* Spring 2006; Denise Rousseau, "Is There Such a Thing as 'Evidence-Based Management'?" *Academy of Management Review* 31(2) 2006, pp. 258–269; Sara L. Rynes, Amy E. Colbert, and Kenneth G. Brown, "HR Professionals' Beliefs About Effective Human Resource Practices: Correspondence Between Research and Practice," *Human Resource Management* 41(2) Summer 2002, pp. 149–174; and Sara L. Rynes, Amy E. Colbert, and Kenneth G. Brown, "Seven Common Misconceptions About Human Resource Practices: Research Findings Versus Practitioner Beliefs," *Academy of Management Executive* 16(3) 2002, pp. 92–102.

55. Sara L. Rynes, Amy E. Colbert, and Kenneth G. Brown, "Seven Common Misconceptions About Human Resource Practices: Research Findings Versus Practitioner Beliefs," Academy of Management Executive 16(3) 2002, pp. 92–102.

56. E. A. Locke, D. B. Feren, V. M. McCaleb, et al., "The Relative Effectiveness of Four Ways of Motivating Employee Performance," in *Changes in Working Life,* K. D. Duncan, M. M. Gruenberg, and D. Walllis, eds. (New York: Wiley, 1980, pp. 363–388). See also: S. L. Rynes, B. Gerhart, and L. Parks, "Personnel Psychology: Performance Evaluation and Pay-for-Performance," *Annual Review of Psychology, 56,* 2005, pp. 571–600.

57. B. Gerhart, "Modeling Human Resource Management—Performance Linkages," in P. Boxall, J. Purcell, and P. Wright, eds., *The Oxford Handbook of Human Resource Management.* (Oxford: Oxford University Press, 2007); P. M. Wright, T. M. Gardner, L. M. Moynihan, and M. R. Allen, "The Relationship Between HR Practices and Firm Performance: Examining the Causal Order," *Personnel Psychology,* 52, 2005, pp. 409–446.

58. J. K. Rowling, *Harry Potter and the Goblet of Fire* (London: Scholastic, 2000).

Strategy: The Totality of Decisions

Chapter Outline

Similarities and Differences
in Strategies
  *Different Strategies Within the Same
  Industry*
  *Different Strategies Within the Same
  Company*
Strategic Choices
Support Business Strategy
Support HR Strategy
The Pay Model Guides Strategic
Pay Decisions
  Stated Versus Unstated Strategies
Developing a Total Compensation
Strategy: Four Steps
  *Step 1: Assess Total Compensation
  Implications*

*HR Strategy: Pay as a Supporting Player
or Catalyst for Change?*
*Step 2: Map a Total Compensation
Strategy*
Steps 3 and 4: Implement and Reassess
Source of Competitive Advantage:
Three Tests
  Align
  Differentiate
  Add Value
"Best Practices" Versus "Best Fit"?
Guidance From the Evidence
Virtuous and Vicious Circles
Your Turn: Merrill Lynch
Still Your Turn: Mapping Compensation
Strategies

You probably think you can skip this chapter. After all, what can be so challenging about a compensation strategy? How about this for a strategy: We'll let the market decide what we need to pay people! Unfortunately, a dose of reality quickly reveals that employers do not behave so simply.

SIMILARITIES AND DIFFERENCES IN STRATEGIES

In Exhibit 2.1 we compare compensation strategies at Google, Medtronic, and Merrill Lynch. Google is a popular internet search engine company. Medtronic is a pioneer in implantable medical devices such as pacemakers and stents. Merrill Lynch, now part of Bank of America, a financial services organization that has had an eventful few years, advises companies and clients worldwide. (See Your Turn: Merrill Lynch at the end of this chapter.) All three are innovators in their industry. Their decisions on the five dimensions of compensation strategy are both similar and different. All three formulate

EXHIBIT 2.1 Three Compensation Strategies

	Google	Medtronic	Merrill Lynch
Objectives	Emphasis on innovation Commitment to cost containment Recognize contributions Attract and reward the best	Focus on customers Fully present at work and in personal lives Recognize personal accomplishment and share success Attract and engage top talent Control costs	Focus on customer Attract, motivate, and retain the best talent Fair, understandable policies and practices
Internal Alignment	Minimize hierarchy Everyone wears several hats Emphasize collaboration	Reflect job responsibilities Support promotional growth opportunities Foster team culture	Pay fairly within ML Job sized on four factors: knowledge/skill, complexity, business impact, strategic value
Externally Competitive	Explore novel ideas in benefits and compensation Generous, unique benefits	Market value of jobs establishes overall pay parameters Choices in benefits	Market competitive in base and benefits Market leader in bonus and stock
Employee Contributions	Recognize individual contributions Unrivaled stock programs	Incentives directly tied to business goals Opportunity to earn above-market pay Recognition of individual and team performance	Bonus based on individual, unit, and company success Differentiate on bonuses and stock In high-profit years, top bonuses significantly larger In less-profitable years, top performers' bonuses decrease much less than poorer performers
Management	Love employees, want them to know it	Clearly understood; open Employee choice	Understandable, consistent message

their pay strategy to support their business strategy. All three emphasize outstanding employee performance and commitment. However, there are major differences.

Google positions itself as still being the feisty start-up populated by nerds and math whizzes. It offers all its employees such generous stock options that many of them have become millionaires. Its benefits are "way beyond the basics" compared to its competitors. (Yes, there is a free lunch, a gym, a grand piano, and roller hockey in the parking lot). Not surprisingly, Google was named the best company to work for by *Fortune* in 2007 and 2008 (and fourth best in 2009). Google downplays cash compensation (base plus bonus), but it does match its competitors on these pay forms.

At Medtronic, the office holiday party includes invited guests whose lives have been prolonged thanks to Medtronic medical devices. The yearly gathering brings alive to employees that what they are doing makes a real difference. So it is not surprising that Medtronic's pay strategy seeks employees' "Total Well Being"—programs designed to ensure that employees are "fully present at their work and in their personal lives" in order to focus on the customer. Additionally, there is a strong emphasis on performance-based pay that is based on individual, team, and organization accomplishments. These programs offer Medtronic employees the opportunity to earn well above what they would earn at competitors.

Merrill Lynch pay objectives are straightforward: to attract, motivate, and retain the best talent. Merrill Lynch focuses on total compensation, which includes competitive base pay, very aggressive bonuses, and equally aggressive stock awards based on each individual's accomplishments. Pay for performance is the key. Differences in total pay for top versus poor performers are significant. In good years at Merrill Lynch, total compensation for top performers is hard to beat. In lean years, the bonuses and stock awards significantly decrease, with greater reductions for poor performers than for top performers.

Merrill Lynch has recently gone through a turbulent period, having been acquired by Bank of America in a deal brokered by the U.S. Treasury Department. However, unlike its former key competitors like Lehman Brothers, which entered bankruptcy, and Bear Stearns, which appears to have lost its identity within J.P. Morgan after being acquired, Merrill Lynch has retained its separate identity and is structured as a wholly owned subsidiary of Bank of America. Its compensation approach for brokers, its key employee group, remains unchanged.[1]

The aggressive pay-for-performance approach at Merrill Lynch was traditionally seen as a key factor in generating substantial wealth both for shareholders and for many of its employees over the years. However, that same aggressive pay-for-performance approach at Merrill Lynch (and at its competitors) is now seen as a key factor in the "meltdown" in the financial industry. A widely held view is that this aggressive approach led to too much risk-taking (e.g., in areas of the business like subprime lending and currency trading) and consequently the downfall of firms in the financial industry. So, the same aggressive approach that was seen as the core of a culture that generated substantial wealth for Merrill Lynch shareholders, and many employees, subsequently was identified as the culprit in the downfall of Merrill Lynch and its peers. What about going forward? The most recent quarterly report from Bank of America showed that Merrill Lynch actually accounted for $3.7 billion of its overall $4.2 billion quarterly net income. You will have an opportunity to consider this and other issues at Merrill Lynch further in the Your Turn section at the end of this chapter.

These three companies are in very different businesses facing different conditions, serving different customers, and employing different talent. So the differences in their pay strategies may not surprise you. Pay strategies can also differ among companies competing for the same talent and similar customers.[2]

Different Strategies Within the Same Industry

Google, Microsoft, and SAS all compete for software engineers and marketing skills. In its earlier years, Microsoft adopted a very similar strategy to Google's, except its employees "put some skin in the game"; that is, they accepted less base pay to join a company whose stock value was increasing exponentially.[3] But when its stock quit performing so spectacularly, Microsoft shifted its strategy to increase base and bonus to the

65th percentile from the 45th percentile of competitors' pay. It still retained its strong emphasis on (still nonperforming) stock-related compensation, but eliminated its long-standing, broad-based stock option plan in favor of stock grants. Its benefits continue to lead the market.

SAS Institute, the world's largest privately owned software company, takes a very different approach. It emphasizes its work/life programs over cash compensation and gives only limited bonuses and no stock awards. SAS headquarters in Cary, North Carolina, include free onsite child care centers, subsidized private schools for children of employees, doctors on site for free medical care, plus recreation facilities.[4] Working more than 35 hours per week is discouraged. By removing as many of the frustrations and distractions of day-to-day life as possible, SAS, like Medtronic, believes people will focus on work when they are at work and won't burn out. SAS feels, for example, that programming code written by someone working a 35-hour week will be better than that written by tired employees. Google so far retains the excitement of a start-up, Microsoft has morphed into "the new Boeing—a solid place to work for a great salary."[5] SAS emphasizes its work/family programs and work/nonwork balance.

So, all these examples illustrate the variance in strategic perspectives among companies in different industries (Google, Medtronic, Merrill Lynch) and even among companies in the same industry (Google, Microsoft, SAS).

Different Strategies Within the Same Company

Sometimes different business units within the same corporation will have very different competitive conditions, adopt different business strategies, and thus fit different compensation strategies. The business units at United Technologies include Otis Elevator, Pratt & Whitney aircraft engines, Sikorsky Aircraft, and Carrier (air conditioning). These businesses face very different competitive conditions. The Korean company SK Holdings has even more variety in its business units. They include a gasoline retailer, a cellular phone manufacturer, and SK Construction. SK has different compensation strategies aligned to each of its very different businesses.[6]

A simple, "let the market decide our compensation" approach doesn't work internationally either. In many nations, markets do not operate as in the United States or may not even exist. People either do not—or in some cases, cannot—easily change employers. In China, central Asia, and some eastern European countries, markets for labor are just emerging. Even in some countries with highly developed economies, such as Germany and France, the labor market is highly regulated. Consequently, there is less movement of people among companies than is common in the United States, Canada, or even Korea and Singapore.[7]

The point is that a strategic perspective on compensation is more complex than it first appears. So we suggest that you continue to read this chapter.

STRATEGIC CHOICES

Strategy refers to the fundamental directions that an organization chooses.[8] An organization defines its strategy through the tradeoffs it makes in choosing what (and what not) to do. Exhibit 2.2 ties these strategic choices to the quest for competitive

EXHIBIT 2.2   Strategic Choices

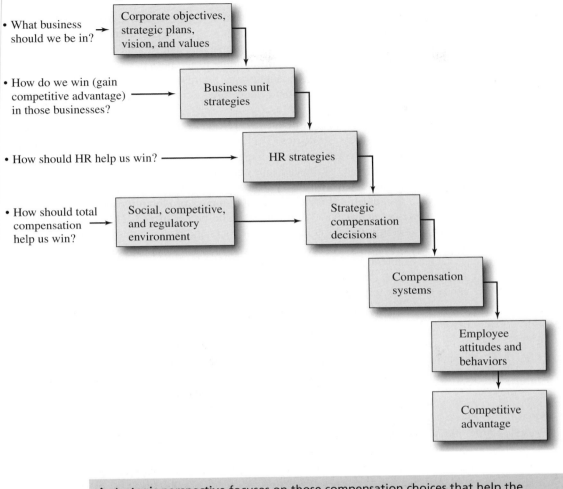

- What business should we be in? → Corporate objectives, strategic plans, vision, and values

- How do we win (gain competitive advantage) in those businesses? → Business unit strategies

- How should HR help us win? → HR strategies

- How should total compensation help us win? → Social, competitive, and regulatory environment → Strategic compensation decisions

Compensation systems

Employee attitudes and behaviors

Competitive advantage

A **strategic perspective** focuses on those compensation choices that help the organization gain and sustain competitive advantage.

advantage. At the corporate level, the fundamental strategic choice is: *What business should we be in?* At the business unit level, the choice shifts to: *How do we gain and sustain competitive advantage in this business?* At the function level the strategic choice is: *How should total compensation help this business gain and sustain competitive advantage?* The ultimate purpose—the "so what?"—is to gain and sustain competitive advantage.[9]

SUPPORT BUSINESS STRATEGY

A currently popular theory found in almost every book and consultant's report tells managers to tailor their pay systems to align with the organization's business strategy. The rationale is based on contingency notions. That is, differences in a firm's business strategy should be supported by corresponding differences in its human resource strategy, including compensation. The underlying premise is that the greater the alignment, or fit, between the organization and the compensation system, the more effective the organization.

Exhibit 2.3 gives an example of how compensation systems might be tailored to three general business strategies. The **innovator** stresses new products and short response time to market trends. A supporting compensation approach places less emphasis on evaluating skills and jobs and more emphasis on incentives designed to encourage innovations. The **cost cutter's** efficiency-focused strategy stresses doing more with less by minimizing costs, encouraging productivity increases, and specifying in greater detail exactly how jobs should be performed. The **customer-focused** business strategy stresses delighting customers and bases employee pay on how well they do this.

Other business strategy frameworks rely on similar ideas. In Michael Porter's strategy work, firms that cut costs would be said to follow a *cost leadership* strategy, while those that seek to provide a unique and/or innovative product or service at a premium price are said to follow a *differentiation* strategy. Likewise, Miles and Snow refer to

EXHIBIT 2.3 Tailor the Compensation System to the Strategy

Strategy	Business Response	HR Program Alignment	Compensation Systems
Innovator: Increase Product Complexity and Shorten Product Life Cycle	• Product Leadership • Shift to Mass Customization • Cycle Time	• Committed to Agile, Risk-Taking, Innovative People	• Reward Innovation in Products and Processes • Market-Based Pay • Flexible—Generic Job Descriptions
Cost Cutter: Focus on Efficiency	• Operational Excellence • Pursue Cost-Effective Solutions	• Do More with Less	• Focus on Competitors' Labor Costs • Increase Variable Pay • Emphasize Productivity • Focus on System Control and Work Specifications
Customer Focused: Increase Customer Expectations	• Deliver Solutions to Customers • Speed to Market	• Delight Customer, Exceed Expectations	• Customer Satisfaction Incentives • Value of Job and Skills Based on Customer Contact

defenders as those that operate in stable markets and compete on cost, whereas *prospectors* are more focused on innovation, new markets, and so forth.[10] These are known as generic strategy frameworks. Conventional wisdom would be that competing on cost requires lower compensation, whereas competing through innovation is likely to be more successful with high-powered incentives/pay for performance. Most firms, however, do not have generic strategies. Instead, as our discussion below suggests, they tend to have aspects of cost and innovation. Likewise, compensation strategies do not necessarily line up neatly with generic business strategies.[11] Lincoln Electric and Southwest Airlines rely heavily on cost leadership in their strategies, but pay their employees well above market (e.g., using stock and profit sharing plans) when firm performance is strong. SAS follows a customer and innovation strategy, but uses little in the way of pay for performance. If you think about it, if a particular business strategy automatically meant that a particular pay strategy would work best, there would not be much need for managers. These generic business strategy and pay strategy ideas are a good starting point.[12] But, to do better than its competitors, a firm must consider how to fashion its own unique way of adding value through matching its business strategy and pay strategy.[13]

How do Google, Medtronic, and Merrill Lynch fit into these generic business strategies? Look again at Exhibit 2.3. At first pass, Google might be an innovator and Merrill Lynch customer focused. Medtronic is both an innovator and customer focused. Yet managers in these companies would probably say that their company is a combination of all three descriptors. Merrill Lynch is also an innovator in financial investment derivatives and seeks to control costs; Medtronic "customers" are actually surgeons and insurance companies—no one asks patients what brand of pacemaker they prefer. So like our discussion of yin and yang in Chapter 1, the reality for each company is a unique blending of all three strategies.

It also follows that when business strategies change, pay systems should change, too. A classic example is IBM's strategic and cultural transformation. For years, IBM placed a strong emphasis on internal alignment. Its well-developed job evaluation plan, clear hierarchy for decision making, work/life balance benefits, and policy of no layoffs served well when the company dominated the market for high-profit mainframe computers. But it did not provide flexibility to adapt to competitive changes in the new century. A redesigned IBM no longer sells the PCs they popularized. Instead, IBM describes its current strategy as having a "focus on the high-growth, high-value segments of the IT industry." It notes, for example, that it "has exited commoditizing businesses like personal computers and hard disk drives." IBM describes its current global capabilities as including "services, software, hardware, fundamental research and financing" and that this "broad mix of businesses and capabilities are combined to provide business insight and solutions for the company's clients."[14] Exhibit 2.4 depicts IBM's "New Blue" approach to executing its strategy. A new business strategy meant a new compensation strategy. At IBM, this meant streamlining the organization by cutting layers of management, redesigning jobs to build in more flexibility, increasing incentive pay to more strongly differentiate on performance, and keeping a constant eye on costs. IBM changed its pay strategy and system to support its changed business strategy.

EXHIBIT 2.4   IBM's Strategic Principles and Priorities in Strategy Execution

Principles	Priorities
1. The marketplace is the driving force behind everything.	1. Delivering business value
2. At our core, we are a technology company with an overriding commitment to quality.	2. Offering world-class open infrastructure
3. Our primary measures of success are customer satisfaction and shareholder value.	3. Developing innovative leadership technology
4. We operate as an entrepreneurial organization with a minimum of bureaucracy and a never-ending focus on productivity.	4. Exploiting new profitable growth opportunities
5. We never lose sight of our strategic vision.	5. Creating brand leadership and a superior customer experience
6. We think and act with a sense of urgency.	6. Attracting, motivating, and retaining the best talent in our industry
7. Outstanding, dedicated people make it happen, particularly when they work together as a team.	
8. We are sensitive to the needs of all employees and to the communities in which we operate.	

Source: Adapted from IBM. © IBM Corporation.

SUPPORT HR STRATEGY

Although a compensation strategy that supports the business strategy implies alignment between compensation and overall HR strategies, this topic is important enough that we want to explicitly deal with it. In the literature on so-called high-performance work systems (HPWS) and HR strategy, Boxall and Purcell find an increasingly common "very basic theory of performance" being used, which they refer to as "AMO theory":

$$P = f(A,M,O)$$

P is performance, which is specified to be a function (*f*) of three factors: *A* is **ability,** *M* is motivation, and *O* is opportunity.[15] In other words, HR systems will be most effective when roles are designed to allow employees to be involved in decisions and have an opportunity to make an impact, when employee ability is developed through selective hiring and training and development, and when the compensation system motivates employees to act on their abilities and take advantage of the opportunity to make a difference. Compensation (through incentive and sorting effects) is the key to attracting, retaining, and motivating employees with the abilities necessary to execute the business strategy and handle greater decision-making responsibilities. Compensation is also the key to motivating them to fully utilize those abilities. As such, higher pay levels and pay for performance are often part of such a HPWS.

Consider alignment between compensation and other aspects of HR at SAS. Rather than being sold in a one-time transaction, SAS's software is licensed. This is part of a business strategy by which SAS gets ongoing and substantial feedback from customers regarding how products can be continually improved and also regarding what new

EXHIBIT 2.5 Fit Between HR Strategy and Compensation Strategy and Effectiveness

HR Strategy   AMO to Contribute

↓ ↑   → Horizontal Fit   →   Business Strategy Execution   →   Revenues ↗   ↘ Costs   →   **Effectiveness** Competitive Parity / Competitive Advantage / Stakeholder Satisfaction

Compensation Strategy   Vertical Fit

Horizontal Fit: Fit of Compensation Strategy with overall HR Strategy
Vertical Fit: Fit of Compensation Strategy and HR Strategy with the Business Strategy
AMO = Ability, Motivation, Opportunity

products customers would like. To support this long-term customer relationship, SAS seeks to have low employee turnover. Its heavy emphasis on benefits in compensation seems to be helpful in retaining employees. SAS also gets many job applications, which allows it to be very selective in its hiring. That no doubt helps build a highly able workforce and allows selection of those who fit SAS's emphasis on teamwork and idea sharing. The de-emphasis on pay for individual performance probably reduces the risk that competition among employees will undermine this objective. As we discuss in the next section, Whole Foods also is team-based. Unlike SAS, however, it relies heavily on pay for performance. But, it is team performance that matters. (Contrast the de-emphasis on differences in individual performance at SAS and Whole Foods with the very different approach—strong emphasis on individual pay for performance— that seems to fit the business and HR strategies of companies such as General Electric, Nucor Steel, Lincoln Electric, and Merrill Lynch.) How effective can a compensation strategy be in supporting business strategy if it is at cross-purposes with the overall HR strategy? While reading about Whole Foods below, ask yourself how well its reliance on teams and giving workers wide decision latitude would work with a different compensation strategy. Such a mismatch happens surprisingly often.[16]

Compensation strategy and HR strategy are central to successful business strategy execution. Exhibit 2.5 seeks to capture that idea, the importance of AMO and fit. It also makes the very simple, but very important, observation that all of this comes down to effects on either revenues or costs. Compensation strategy, HR strategy, and business strategy ultimately seek to decrease costs or increase revenues, relative to competitors.[17] At the same time, key stakeholders (e.g., employees, customers, shareholders) must be happy with their "deal" or relationship with the company. To the extent all of this happens, effectiveness is more likely to follow.

THE PAY MODEL GUIDES STRATEGIC PAY DECISIONS

Let us continue our discussion of Whole Foods. The competitive advantage of Whole Foods is apparent with the first visit to one of its grocery stores, described as "a mouth-watering festival of colors, smells, and textures; an homage to the appetite."[18] What started out in 1978 as a small health food store in Austin, Texas, has, through strategic decisions, grown to become the world's leading natural and organic foods supermarket whose objective is to change the way Americans eat. Along the way, Whole

Foods' managers have designed a total compensation system to support the company's phenomenal growth (from 10,000 employees and $900 million in sales in 1996 to 53,000 employees and sales of $8 billion today) while remaining true to company founder John Mackey's vision for the company.

Using our pay model, let us consider the five strategic compensation choices facing Whole Foods managers.

1. *Objectives:* How should compensation support the business strategy and be adaptive to the cultural and regulatory pressures in a global environment? (Whole Foods objectives: Increase shareholder value through profits and growth; go to extraordinary lengths to satisfy and delight customers; seek and engage employees who are going to help the company make money—every new hire must win a two-thirds vote from team members before being given a permanent position.)

2. *Internal Alignment:* How differently should the different types and levels of skills and work be paid within the organization? (Whole Foods: Store operations are organized around eight to ten self-managed teams; these teams make the types of decisions (e.g., what products to order and stock) that are often reserved for managers. Egalitarian, shared-fate philosophy means that executive salaries do not exceed 14 times the average pay of full-time employees [the ratio used to be 8 times]; all full-time employees qualify for stock options, and 94 percent of the company's options go to nonexecutive employees.)

3. *External Competitiveness:* How should total compensation be positioned against competitors? (Whole Foods: Offer a unique deal compared to competitors.) What **forms of compensation** should be used? (Whole Foods: Provide health insurance for all full-time employees and 20 hours of paid time a year to do volunteer work.)

4. *Employee Contributions:* Should pay increases be based on individual and/or team performance, on experience and/or continuous learning, on improved skills, on changes in cost of living, on personal needs (housing, transportation, health services), and/or on each business unit's performance? (Whole Foods: A shared fate—every four weeks the performance of each team is measured in terms of revenue per hour worked, which directly affects what they get paid. [This is one reason why staffers are given some say in who gets hired—co-workers want someone who will help them make money!])

5. *Management:* How open and transparent should the pay decisions be to all employees? Who should be involved in designing and managing the system? (Whole Foods: "No-secrets" management: Every store has a book listing the previous year's pay for every employee including executives; "You Decide"—employees recently voted to pick their health insurance rather than having one imposed by leadership.)

These decisions, taken together, form a pattern that becomes an organization's compensation strategy.

Stated Versus Unstated Strategies

All organizations that pay people have a compensation strategy. Some may have written compensation strategies for all to see and understand. Others may not even realize they have a compensation strategy. Ask a manager at one of these latter organizations about its compensation strategy and you may get a pragmatic response: "We do whatever it takes." Its compensation strategy is inferred from the pay decisions it has made.[19] Managers in all organizations make the five strategic decisions discussed earlier. Some do it in a rational, deliberate way, while others do it more chaotically—as ad hoc responses to pressures from the economic, sociopolitical, and regulatory context in which the organization operates. But in any organization that pays people, there is a compensation strategy at work.

DEVELOPING A TOTAL COMPENSATION STRATEGY: FOUR STEPS

Developing a compensation strategy involves four simple steps, shown in Exhibit 2.6 While the steps are simple, executing them is complex. Trial and error, experience, and insight play major roles. Research evidence can also help.[20]

EXHIBIT 2.6   **Key Steps in Formulating a Total Compensation Strategy**

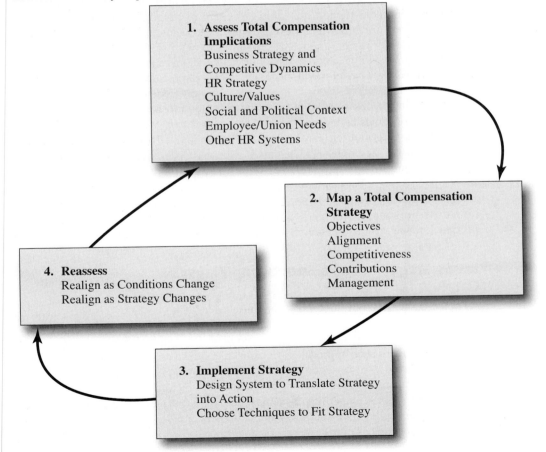

Step 1: Assess Total Compensation Implications

Think about any organization's past, present, and—most vitally—its future. What factors in its business environment have contributed to the company's success? Which of these factors are likely to become more (or less) important as the company looks ahead? Exhibit 2.6 classifies the factors as competitive dynamics, culture/values, social and political context, employee/union needs, and other HR systems.

Business Strategy and Competitive Dynamics—Understand the Business

This first step includes an understanding of the specific industry in which the organization operates and how the organization plans to compete in that industry. This corresponds with the first two decisions in Exhibit 2.2: What business should we be in, and how do we win in that business?[21] To cope with the turbulent competitive dynamics, focus on what factors in the business environment (i.e., changing customer needs, competitors' actions, changing labor market conditions, changing laws, globalization) are important today. What will be important in the future?

What is your company's strategy? How do you compete to win? How should the compensation system support that strategy? Learn to gauge the underlying dynamics in your business (or build relationships with those who can). We have already discussed aligning different compensation strategies with different business strategies using the examples of cost cutter, customer centered, and innovator (Exhibit 2.3). But be cautious: As we have already pointed out, reality is more complex and chaotic. Organizations are innovators *and* cost cutters *and* customer centered. All three, and more. The orderly image conveyed in the exhibits does not adequately capture the turbulent competitive dynamics underlying this process.[22]

Competitive dynamics can be assessed globally.[23] However, comparing pay among countries is complex. In Chapter 1, we noted differences in hourly labor costs and productivity (output per dollar of wages) among countries. But as we shall see in Chapter 16 on global pay, countries also differ on the average length of the workweek, the average number of paid holidays, the kinds of national health care and retirement programs, and even how pay is determined. Nevertheless, managers must become knowledgeable about competitive conditions both globally and locally.

HR Strategy: Pay as a Supporting Player or Catalyst for Change?

As noted earlier, the pay strategy is also influenced by how it fits with other HR systems in the organization.[24] Whatever the overall HR strategy, a decision about the prominence of pay in that HR strategy is required. Pay can be a supporting player, as in the high-performance approach, or it can take the lead and be a catalyst for change. Whatever the role, compensation is embedded in the total HR approach.[25]

So, the compensation implications of all the above factors—the organization's business strategy, global competitive dynamics, culture and values, the sociopolitical context, employee preferences, and how pay fits with other HR systems—all are necessary to formulate a compensation strategy.

Culture/Values

A pay system reflects the values that guide an employer's behavior and underlie its treatment of employees. The pay system mirrors the company's image and reputation. As we noted in Chapter 1, most companies publish a values statement on their Web sites. Medtronic publishes theirs in 24 languages. Part of it is in Exhibit 2.7. Medtronic's value #5 recognizes employees' worth by fostering "personal satisfaction in work accomplished, security, advancement opportunity, and means to share in the company's success." Its compensation strategy reflects this value by including work/life balance programs for security, incentives, and stock ownership to share the company's success.

But there are some skeptics out there. Mission statements have been described as "an assemblage of trite phrases" which impressed no one.[26] In contrast, Johnson and Johnson considers its statement its "moral compass" and "recipe for business success."[27]

Social and Political Context

Context refers to a wide range of factors, including legal and regulatory requirements, cultural differences, changing workforce demographics, expectations, and the like. These also affect compensation choices. In the case of Whole Foods, its business is very people-intensive. Consequently, Whole Foods managers may find that an increasingly diverse workforce and increasingly diverse forms of pay (child care, chemical dependency counseling, educational reimbursements, employee assistance programs) may add value and be difficult for competitors (other supermarkets) to imitate.

Because governments are major stakeholders in determining compensation, lobbying to influence laws and regulations can also be part of a compensation strategy. In the United States, employers will not sit by while Congress considers taxing employee

EXHIBIT 2.7 Medtronic Values

Written more than 30 years ago, our mission statement gives purpose to our work, describes the values we live by, and is the motivation behind every action we take.

1. To contribute to human welfare by application of biomedical engineering in the research, design, manufacture, and sale of instruments or appliances that alleviate pain, restore health, and extend life.
2. To direct our growth in the areas of biomedical engineering where we display maximum strength and ability; to gather people and facilities that tend to augment these areas; to continuously build on these areas through education and knowledge assimilation; to avoid participation in areas where we cannot make unique and worthy contributions.
3. To strive without reserve for the greatest possible reliability and quality in our products; to be the unsurpassed standard of comparison and to be recognized as a company of dedication, honesty, integrity, and service.
4. To make a fair profit on current operations to meet our obligations, sustain our growth, and reach our goals.
5. To recognize the personal worth of employees by providing an employment framework that allows personal satisfaction in work accomplished, security, advancement opportunity, and means to share in the company's success.
6. To maintain good citizenship as a company.

benefits. Similarly, the European Union's "social contract" is a matter of interest.[28] And in China, every foreign company has undoubtedly discovered that building relationships with government officials is essential. So, from a strategic perspective, managers of compensation may try to shape the sociopolitical environment as well as be shaped by it.

Employee Preferences

The simple fact that employees differ is too easily overlooked in formulating a compensation strategy. Individual employees join the organization, make investment decisions, interact with customers, design new products, assemble components, and so on. Individual employees receive the pay. A major challenge in the design of next-generation pay systems is how to better satisfy individual needs and preferences. Offering more choice is one approach. Older, highly paid workers may wish to defer taxes by putting their pay into retirement funds, while younger employees may have high cash needs to buy a house, support a family, or finance an education. Dual-career couples who have double family coverage may prefer to use more of their combined pay for child care, automobile insurance, financial counseling, or other benefits such as flexible schedules. Employees who have young children or dependent parents may desire dependent care coverage.[29] Whole Foods, in fact, as described in its 2008 Annual Report, holds an employee vote every three years to determine the nature of their benefits program.

Based on the opinions of 10,000 U.S. workers, Hudson found that:

- Nearly three out of four U.S. workers claim to be satisfied with their compensation, yet a large portion of the same sample (44%) say they would change their mix of cash and benefits if given the chance.
- When given their choice of unconventional benefits, most employees would select a more flexible work schedule (33%) or additional family benefits (22%), including parental leaves and personal days, over job training (13%) or supplemental insurance (16%).
- One in five workers say better health care benefits would make them happier with their compensation package. On the other hand, 41 percent said that the single thing that would make them happier is more money.[30]

Choice Is Good. Yes, No, Maybe?[31]

Contemporary pay systems in the United States do offer some choices. Flexible benefits and choices among health care plans and investment funds for retirement are examples. As we saw earlier, Whole Foods employees vote on the benefits they want. General Mills even allows many employees to swap several weeks' salary for stock awards. The company believes that allowing employees their choice adds value and is difficult for other companies to imitate—it is a source of competitive advantage for General Mills. Whether or not this belief is correct remains to be studied.

Some studies have found that people do not always choose well. They do not always understand the alternatives, and too many choices simply confuse them. Thus, the value added by offering choices and satisfying preferences may be offset by the expense of communicating and simply confusing people.[32]

In addition to possibly confusing employees, unlimited choice would be a challenge to design and manage. Plus, it would meet with disapproval from the U.S. Internal

Revenue Service (health benefits are not viewed by the IRS as income). Offering greater choice to employees in different nations would require meeting a bewildering maze of codes and regulations. On the other hand, the U.S. federal government, including the IRS, already offers its employees a bit of choice in their work schedules. Forty-three percent avail themselves of the option to take compensatory time off for extra hours worked. In contrast, U.S. private sector workers covered by the Fair Labor Standards Act (i.e., **nonexempt** employees) must be paid time-and-a-half overtime if they work over 40 hours in a week. A compensatory time option is not permitted.[33]

Union Preferences

Pay strategies need to take into account the nature of the union-management relationship.[34] Even though union membership among private-sector workers in the United States is now less than 10 percent of the workforce, union influence on pay decisions remains significant, especially in key sectors (e.g., manufacturing, health care, education). Union preferences for different forms of pay (e.g., protecting retirement and health care plans) and their concern with job security affect pay strategy.

Unions' interests can differ. In Denver, Colorado, a merit pay plan was developed collaboratively by the Denver Public Schools and the Denver Classroom Teachers Association, the local union affiliate. Teachers approved the agreement by a 59 to 41 percent vote, and Denver voters approved a $25 million property tax increase to pay for it. Conversely, many teachers in Springfield, Massachusetts, left for neighboring, higher-paying school districts in part because the district wanted to impose a merit pay plan.[35]

Compensation deals with unions can be costly to change. The U.S. auto companies negotiated "The Jobs Bank" program over 20 years ago with the United Auto Workers. Employees who were no longer needed to make cars continued to get paid until they were needed again. Some received up to $100,000 a year, including benefits. Their job: Do nothing but wait for a job to open. But for a number of people, those jobs never materialized. In various cities around the U.S., about 15,000 employees showed up at 6 a.m. each day and stayed until 2:30 p.m. with 45 minutes off for lunch. Some volunteered for approved community projects or took classes. Jerry Mellon claims, "They paid me like $400,000 over 6 years to learn how to deal blackjack."[36] Readers may wonder if the Jobs Bank was a compensation strategy that trumped the business strategy. No wonder GM eventually bought its way out of the Bank. No wonder GM recently found it necessary to go through bankruptcy.

Step 2: Map a Total Compensation Strategy

The compensation strategy is made up of the elements in the pay model: objectives, and the four policy choices of alignment, competitiveness, contributions, and management. Mapping these decisions is Step 2 in developing a compensation strategy.

Mapping is often used in marketing to clarify and communicate a product's identity. A strategic map offers a picture of a company's compensation strategy. It can also clarify the message that the company is trying to deliver with its compensation system.

Exhibit 2.8 maps the compensation strategies of Microsoft and SAS. The five dimensions are subdivided into a number of descriptors rated on importance. These

EXHIBIT 2.8 Contrasting Maps of Microsoft and SAS

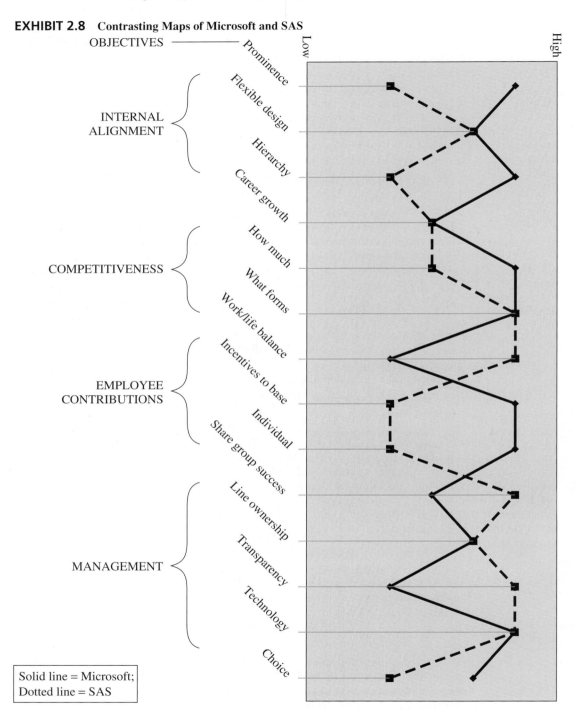

Solid line = Microsoft;
Dotted line = SAS

ratings are from your fearless (read "tenured") authors. They are not ratings assigned by managers in the companies. The descriptors used under each of the strategy dimensions can be modified as a company sees fit.

Objectives: Prominence is the measure of how important total compensation is in the overall HR strategy. Is it a catalyst, playing a lead role? Or is it less important, playing a more supporting character to other HR programs? At Microsoft, compensation is rated highly prominent, whereas at SAS it is more supportive.

Internal Alignment: This is described as the degree of internal hierarchy. For example, how much does pay differ among job levels and how well does compensation support career growth? Both SAS and Microsoft use pay to support flexible work design and promotions. But pay differences at SAS, whose philosophy is "Everyone is part of the SAS family," are smaller than at Microsoft, where differences in pay are seen as returns for superior performance.

External Competitiveness: This includes comparisons on two issues. How much are our competitors paying, and what forms of pay are they using? The importance of work/life balance achieved via benefits and services is also part of external competitiveness. According to the strategy map, Microsoft's **competitive position** is critical to its pay strategy, whereas SAS competes on work/family balance in family-oriented benefits such as private schools and doctors on the company's campus.

Employee Contributions: These two companies take a very different approach to performance-based pay. SAS uses only limited individual-based performance pay. This is consistent with its overall egalitarian approach. Microsoft is a heavy user of pay based on individual and company performance.

Management: Ownership refers to the role non-HR managers play in making pay decisions. *Transparency* refers to openness and communication about pay. As one might expect, both Microsoft and SAS rate high on the use of technology to manage the pay system, and Microsoft offers greater choices in their health care and retirement investment plans.

Each company's profile on the strategy map reflects its main message or "pay brand":

Microsoft: Total compensation is prominent, with a strong emphasis on market competitiveness, individual accomplishments, and performance-based returns.

SAS: Total compensation supports its work/life balance. Competitive market position, companywide success sharing, and egalitarianism are the hallmarks.

In contrast to the verbal description earlier in this chapter, strategic maps provide a visual reference. They are useful in analyzing a compensation strategy that can be more clearly understood by employees and managers.[37] Maps *do not* tell which strategy is "best." Rather, they provide a framework and guidance. Just like a road map, they can show where you are and where you are going.[38]

The rest of this book discusses compensation decisions in detail. It is important to realize, however, that the decisions in the pay model work in concert. It is the totality of these decisions that forms the compensation strategy.

Steps 3 and 4: Implement and Reassess

Step 3 in Exhibit 2.6 is to implement the strategy through the design and execution of the compensation system. The compensation system translates strategy into practice—and into people's bank accounts.

Step 4, Reassess and Realign, closes the loop. This step recognizes that the compensation strategy must change to fit changing conditions. Thus, periodic reassessment is needed to continuously learn, adapt, and improve. The results from using the pay system need to be assessed against the objectives we are trying to achieve.

SOURCE OF COMPETITIVE ADVANTAGE: THREE TESTS

Developing and implementing a pay strategy that is a source of sustained competitive advantage is easier said than done. Not all compensation decisions are strategic or a source of competitive advantage. Three tests determine whether a pay strategy is a source of advantage: (1) Is it aligned? (2) Does it differentiate? (3) Does it add value?

Align

Alignment of the pay strategy includes three aspects, as we have already discussed: (1) align with the business strategy, (2) align externally with the economic and socio-political conditions, and (3) align internally within the overall HR system. Alignment is probably the easiest test to pass.

Differentiate

Some believe that the only thing that really matters about a strategy is how it is different from everyone else's. If the pay system is relatively simple for any competitor to copy, then how can it possibly be a source of competitive advantage? The answer, according to the advocates of the strategic approach, is in how the pay system is managed. This rhetoric is appealing, but the evidence to support it is slim.[39]

The map profiles in Exhibit 2.8 show how Microsoft and SAS differ in their strategies. One uses pay as a strong signal; the other uses pay to support its "work/family balance" HR strategy. Both organizations claim to have organization cultures that value performance, yet their compensation strategies differ.

Are they difficult to imitate? Probably, since each strategy is woven into the fabric of the company's overall HR strategy. Copying one or another dimension of a strategy means ripping apart the overall approach and patching in a new one. So, in a sense, the alignment test (weaving the fabric) helps ensure passing the differentiation test. Microsoft's use of stock awards for all employees—often worth considerably more than people's base pay—is difficult for its competitors to copy. SAS's work-family-balance (like Medtronic's total-presence-at-the-workplace strategy) is difficult to copy. It may be relatively easy to copy any individual action a competitor takes (i.e., grant stock

Cybercomp: Compensation Consultants

Compensation consultants are major players, and practically every organization uses at least one for data and advice. So learning more about the services these consultants offer is useful. Go to the Web site of at least two of them. You can choose from the consulting firms listed below or find others.

Fred Cook *www.fredericwcook.com*
Wyatt Watson Worldwide *www.watsonwyatt.com*
Hay *www.haygroup.com*
Mercer *www.mercer.com*
Hewitt Associates *www.hewittassociates.com*
Towers Perrin *www.towersperrin.com*
Clark Consulting *www.clarkconsulting.com*
McLagan *www.mclagan.com*

1. Compare consultants. From their Web sites, construct a chart comparing their stated values and culture and their business strategies, and highlight the services offered.
2. Critically assess whether their strategies and services are unique and/or difficult to imitate. Which one would you select (based on the Web information) to help you formulate a company's total compensation strategy
3. Based on the Web information, which one would you prefer to work for? Why?
4. Be prepared to share this information with others in class.

Return on the Investment: If everyone does a great job on this Cybercomp, you will all have useful information on consultants.

For more background, see Lewis Pinault, *Consulting Demons: Inside the Unscrupulous World of Global Corporate Consulting* (New York: Harpers Business, 2000), and Fred Cook, "A Personal Perspective of the Consulting Profession," *ACA News,* October 1999, pp. 35–43.

options to more employees or offer more choice in their health insurance). But the strategic perspective implies that it is the *way* programs fit together and fit the overall organization that is hard to copy. Simply copying others by blindly benchmarking best practices amounts to trying to stay in the race, not win it.[40]

Add Value

Organizations continue to look for the return they are getting from their incentives, benefits, and even base pay. Compensation is often a company's largest controllable expense. Since consultants and a few researchers treat different forms of pay as investments, the task is to come up with ways to calculate the return on those investments (ROI). But this is a difficult proposition. As one writer put it, "It is easier to count the bottles than describe the wine."[41] Costs are easy to fit into a spreadsheet, but any value created as a result of those costs is difficult to specify, much less measure.[42] Current attempts to do so are described in Chapter 18, Management.

Trying to measure an ROI for any compensation strategy implies that people are "human capital," similar to other factors of production. Many people find this view dehumanizing. They argue that viewing pay as an investment with measurable returns diminishes the importance of treating employees fairly.[43] In Chapter 1 we discussed the need to keep all objectives, including efficiency and fairness, in mind at the same time. No doubt about it, of the three tests of strategy—align, differentiate, add value—the last is the most difficult.

It is possible to align and differentiate and still fail to add value. In the Your Turn at the end of Chapter 1, you were asked to evaluate whether changes in compensation at Circuit City in 2007 contributed to its decline and eventual liquidation in 2009. We can go back even further, to examine its earlier compensation strategy, which relied heavily on commissions. The incentive plan at consumer electronics retailer Circuit City paid off big for experienced, high-performing salespeople: At its retail stores, salespeople who moved more than $1 million a year could earn over $50,000 in salary and sales bonuses. One successful salesperson knew the products and kept up to date so well that customers would seek him out for advice before they made a purchase. Circuit City's compensation strategy aligned with its business by rewarding such experienced top performers.

The strategy also differentiated Circuit City from archrival Best Buy. Best Buy featured self-service stores with huge inventories. It hired young, less-experienced people and offered lower wages and smaller bonuses. However, Best Buy's sales and total shareholder returns soared past those of Circuit City. The compensation strategy at both companies aligned with their business strategies; they also differentiated. But Circuit City's compensation strategy no longer added value when compared to Best Buy's. This is perhaps what Circuit City concluded again in 2007, leading it to make further changes.

Circuit City laid off 3,900 top-earning salespeople in 2003 and replaced them with 2,100 less-experienced people who receive lower wages and smaller bonuses. Circuit City said it could no longer afford to pay big commissions to its sales staff while its rivals paid less.[44]

A major impetus for the Circuit City changes in both 2003 and 2007 was an attempt to be more like Best Buy by first eliminating commissions and then further reducing pay by replacing highly paid employees with lower-paid employees. The latest part of the story is that Best Buy is now trying to cut its own labor costs further by essentially demoting 8,000 senior sales associates to positions that could pay half as much. A question being asked is whether the Best Buy pay-level cuts will have the same consequences as what one person described as the "disastrous personnel moves" made at Circuit City just a few years ago.[45] Apparently, Best Buy does not see it that way.

Are there advantages to an innovative compensation strategy? We do know that in products and services, first movers (innovators) have well-recognized advantages that can offset the risks involved—high margins, market share, and mindshare (brand recognition).[46] But we do not know whether such advantages accrue to innovators in total compensation. You can evaluate for yourself what being unique versus being the same may or may not have meant for Circuit City.

What, if any, benefits accrued to Microsoft, one of the first to offer very large stock options to all employees, once its competitors did the same thing? What about General Mills, who was among the first to offer some managers a choice of more stock options for smaller base pay? Does a compensation innovator attract more and better people? Induce people to stay and contribute? Are there cost advantages? Studies are needed to find the answers.

"BEST PRACTICES" VERSUS "BEST FIT"?

The premise of any strategic perspective is that if managers align pay decisions with the organization's strategy and values, are responsive to employees and union relations, and are globally competitive, then the organization is more likely to achieve competitive advantage.[47] The challenge is to design the "fit" with the environment, business strategy, and pay plan. The better the fit, the greater the competitive advantage.

But not everyone agrees. In contrast to the notion of strategic fit, some believe that (1) a set of **best-pay practices** exists and (2) these practices can be applied universally across situations. Rather than having a better fit between business strategy and compensation plans that yields better performance, they say that best practices result in better performance with almost any business strategy.[48]

These writers believe that adopting best-pay practices allows the employer to gain preferential access to superior employees. These superior employees will in turn be the organization's source of competitive advantage. The challenge here is to select from various recommended lists which are "the" best practices.[49] Which practices truly are the best? We believe that research over the past few years is beginning to point the way to improve our choices.

GUIDANCE FROM THE EVIDENCE

There is consistent research evidence that the following practices do matter to the organization's objectives.

- *Internal alignment:* Both smaller and larger pay differences among jobs inside an organization can affect results. Smaller internal pay differences and larger internal pay differences can both be a "best" practice. Which one depends on the context; that is, the fit with business strategy, other HR practices, the organization culture, and so on.[50]
- *External competitiveness:* Paying higher than the average paid by competitors can affect results. Is higher competitive pay a "best" practice? Again, it depends on the context.
- *Employee contributions:* Performance-based pay can affect results. Are performance incentives a "best" practice? Once more, it depends on the context.[51]
- *Managing compensation:* Rather than focusing on only one dimension of the pay strategy (e.g., pay for performance or internal pay differences), all dimensions need to be considered together.[52]

- *Compensation strategy:* Finally, embedding compensation strategy within the broader HR strategy affects results. Compensation does not operate alone; it is part of the overall HR perspective.[53]

So, specific pay practices appear to be more beneficial in some contexts than in others.[54] Thus, best practice versus best fit does not appear to be a useful way to frame the question. A more useful question is, *What practices pay off best under what conditions?* Much of the rest of this book is devoted to exploring this question.

VIRTUOUS AND VICIOUS CIRCLES

A group of studies suggests specific conditions to look at when making strategic pay decisions. One study examined eight years of data from 180 U.S. companies.[55] The authors reported that while *pay levels* (external competitiveness) differed among these companies, they were not related to the companies' subsequent financial performance. However, when combined with differences in the size of bonuses and the number of people eligible for stock options, then pay levels were related to future financial success of the organizations. This study concluded that it is not only *how much* you pay but also *how* you pay that matters.[56]

Think of pay as part of a circle. Exhibit 2.9 suggests that performance-based pay works best when there is success to share. An organization whose profits or market share is increasing is able to pay larger bonuses and stock awards. And paying these bonuses fairly improves employee attitudes and work behaviors, which in turn improves their performance.[57] The circle gains upward momentum.[58] Employees receive returns that compensate for the risks they take. And they behave like owners, since they are sharing in the organization's success.

Additionally, there are several studies that analyzed pay strategies as part of the "high-performance workplace" approaches discussed earlier. This research focused on

EXHIBIT 2.9 Virtuous and Vicious Circles

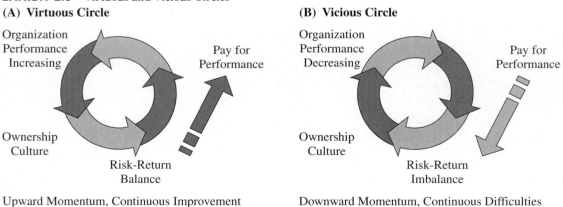

(A) Virtuous Circle

Organization Performance Increasing

Pay for Performance

Ownership Culture

Risk-Return Balance

Upward Momentum, Continuous Improvement

(B) Vicious Circle

Organization Performance Decreasing

Pay for Performance

Ownership Culture

Risk-Return Imbalance

Downward Momentum, Continuous Difficulties

specific jobs and workplaces, such as sales and service representatives in call-service centers and jobs in factories.[59] They indicate that performance-based pay that shares success with employees does improve employee attitudes, behaviors, performance—especially when coupled with the other "high-performance" practices. One study even reported that the effects of the compensation strategy equaled the impact of all the other practices [high involvement, teams, selective hiring, and training programs] combined.[60] These findings are near and dear to our hearts. So other "high-performance" HR practices also become factors that support improved performance and the virtuous circle.

It cannot have escaped your attention that circles can also gain momentum going downward to become a vicious circle. As shown in Exhibit 2.9, when organization performance declines, performance-based pay plans do not pay off; there are no bonuses, and the value of stock declines—with potentially negative effects on organization performance. Declining organization performance increases the risks facing employees—risks of still smaller bonuses, demotions, wage cuts, and even layoffs. Unless the increased risks are offset by larger returns, the risk-return imbalance will reinforce declining employee attitudes and speed the downward spiral. Unfortunately, we do not yet know what compensation practices can be used to shift an organization caught in a downward spiral into an upward one.

Perhaps we believe so strongly that pay matters and that studying it in the workplace is beneficial, that this is what we see—believing is seeing. So, caution and more evidence are required. Nevertheless, these studies do seem to indicate that performance-based pay may be a best practice, under the right circumstances. (Could performance-based pay sometimes be a "worst practice"? Yes, when incentive systems don't pay off and they alienate employees or lead to government investigation of possible stock option manipulation.) Additionally, we do not have much information about how people perceive various pay strategies. Do all managers "see" the total compensation strategy at Merrill Lynch or Google the same way? Some evidence suggests that if you ask 10 managers about their company's HR strategy, you get 10 different answers. If the link between the strategy and people's perceptions is not clear, then maybe we are using evidence to build on unstable ground.

Your **Turn**   Merrill Lynch

During the recent financial crisis, Merrill Lynch was acquired by Bank of America for $50 billion. The reason for the acquisition was that Merrill Lynch was unsure it could survive the crisis on its own. What really made headlines, however, was the disclosure that Merrill Lynch had paid out $3.6 billion in bonuses just before being taken over by Bank of America.[61] These bonuses were paid while the federal government was spending hundreds of billions of dollars to bail out financial institutions like Merrill Lynch and/or intervening to persuade firms like Bank of America to do acquisitions to save firms like Merrill Lynch. Indeed, Merrill Lynch lost $27 billion in 2008. So, the "$3.6 billion question" one might say was: WHY? President Obama saw no good answer and blasted such bonuses as "the height of irresponsibility." The U.S. House of Representatives looked for a way to get the bonus money back. It passed legislation by a 328-93 vote to impose a 90% tax on the bonuses of anyone at a bank receiving $5 billion or more from the federal government (via TARP—the Troubled Asset Relief Program) and earning more than $250,000 a year. The Administration signaled a lack of support and the legislation subsequently died in the Senate. However, TARP includes restrictions on compensation for firms that have taken a certain level of TARP money. These restrictions are designed to discourage executives from taking "unnecessary and excessive risks."

Also of interest, some employees, including some high-level, high-revenue generating employees, have begun to leave larger financial institutions like Merrill Lynch/Bank of America to go to so-called "boutique" financial services firms, which have not received TARP money and thus are not covered by TARP restrictions on compensation. Another trend seems to be an increase in base salary levels and a decrease in bonus levels, apparently in response to all of the negative publicity bonuses have received and as a way to get around TARP restrictions. One senior executive at a company receiving TARP money and now paying smaller bonuses and bigger salaries, however, questioned whether the TARP-induced greater emphasis on base pay made sense: So, "You're going to overpay them regularly, instead of just sometimes?"[62]

What do you think? Should Wall Street firms pay higher salaries and smaller bonuses? Are you outraged that firms like Merrill Lynch paid out billions in bonuses while losing billions of dollars and asking the government for help using taxpayer money? Is there any justification for paying these large bonuses? Was it the "aggressive" goal-oriented pay-for-performance system at Merrill Lynch (and its peers in the financial industry) that caused undue risk taking and all of these problems to begin with?[63] How is Merrill Lynch performing now?[64] Here are some historical data (all in millions—so, e.g., 2007 revenues were $11.25 billion). [65]

	Revenues, net of interest expense	Compensation & Benefits Expense	Net Earnings (loss)
2009 (3 months ended 3/31/2009)	$ 9,954	$ 3,142	$ 3,660
2008	($12,953)	$14,763	($27,612)
2007	$11,250	$15,903	($ 7,777)
2006	$33,781	$15,108	$ 7,499
2005	$25,277	$12,314	$ 5,116
2004	$21,500	$10,599	$ 4,436
2003	$19,548	$ 9,814	$ 3,836

Still Your **Turn** Mapping Compensation Strategies

Take any organization that you know—current employer, business school, the place you interned, a friend's employer. Look at Exhibit 2.8, "Contrasting Maps of Microsoft and SAS." Map your organization's compensation strategy then compare it to that of Microsoft and SAS.

1. Summarize the key points of your company's strategy.
2. What are the key differences compared to the strategies of Microsoft and SAS?

Or ask several managers in the *same* organization to map that organization's compensation strategy. You may need to assist them. Then compare the managers' maps.

3. Summarize the key similarities and differences.
4. Why do these similarities and differences occur?
5. How can maps be used to clarify and communicate compensation strategies to leaders? To employees?

Summary

Managing total compensation strategically means fitting the compensation system to the business and environmental conditions. We believe the best way to proceed is to start with the pay model—the objectives and four policy choices—and take the steps discussed in the chapter: (1) assess implications for the total compensation of your organization's situation; (2) map out the compensation objectives and four policy choices to achieve them (internal alignment, external competitiveness, employee contributions, and management); (3) translate these policies into the workplace via the compensation system and implement it; and (4) reassess by comparing your results against the pay objectives. And continue to learn, adapt, and improve. Sound simple? It isn't. The major challenge in managing total compensation is to understand how your pay system can add value and make the organization more successful. We believe that research is beginning to offer useful evidence-based guidance, with the promise of more to come.

Review Questions

1. Select a familiar company or analyze the approach your college uses to pay teaching assistants or faculty. Infer its compensation strategy using the five dimensions (objectives, alignment, competitiveness, employee considerations, and management). How does your company or school compare to Microsoft and Merrill Lynch? What business strategy does it seem to "fit" (i.e., cost cutter, customer centered, innovator, or something else)?

2. Contrast the essential differences between the best-fit and best-practices perspectives.

3. Reread Exhibit 2.7. Discuss how those values might be reflected in a compensation system. Are these values consistent with "Let the market decide"?

4. Three tests for any source of competitive advantage are align, differentiate, and add value. Discuss whether these tests are difficult to pass. Can compensation really be a source of competitive advantage?

5. Set up a debate over the following proposition: Nonfinancial returns (great place to work, opportunities to learn, job security, and flexible work schedules) are more important (i.e., best practice) than pay.

Endnotes

1. David Mildenbers, "Bank of America's Merrill Adds $5 Billion to Deposits in Month." *www.Bloomberg.com,* June 5, 2009. Accessed June 11, 2009.

2. Timothy M. Gardner, "Interfirm Competition for Human Resources: Evidence From the Software Industry," *Academy of Management Journal* 48(2) (2005), pp. 237–256; Yoshio Yanadori and Janet Marler, "Compensation Strategy: Does Business Strategy Influence Compensation in High Technology Firms?" *Strategic Management Journal* (June 2006), pp. 559–570.

3. An *option* is the opportunity to buy stock at a set price. If the value of shares increases, then the option has value (market price minus the set option price). Awards grant employees stock whose value is its market price. Later chapters discuss stock options and awards in detail. See Kevin F. Hallock and Craig A. Olson, "The Value of Stock Options to Non-Executive Employees," Working paper, Institute of Labor and Industrial Relations, University of Illinois Urbana/Champaign. January 2006.

4. "SAS Institute," Stanford Business School case; Also, "SAS: The Royal Treatment," *60 Minutes,* October 13, 2002.

5. Rich Karlgaard, "Microsoft's IQ Dividend," *The Wall Street Journal,* July 28, 2004, p. A13; Holman W. Jenkins Jr., "Stock Options Are Dead, Long Live Stock Options," *The Wall Street Journal,* July 16, 2003.

6. M. Treacy and F. Wiersma, *The Discipline of Market Leaders* (Reading, MA: Addison-Wesley, 1997).

7. Daniel Vaughan-Whitehead, "Wage Reform in Central and Eastern Europe," in Daniel Vaughn-Whitehead, ed., *Paying the Price* (New York: St. Martin's Press, 2000); Marshall Meyer, Yuan Lu, Hailin Lan, and Xiaohui Lu, "Decentralized Enterprise Reform: Notes on the Transformation of State-Owned Enterprises," in *The Management of Enterprises in the People's Republic of China,* Anne S. Tsui and Chung-Ming Lau, eds. (Boston: Kluwer Academic, 2002), pp. 241–274; Mei Fong, "A Chinese Puzzle," *The Wall Street Journal,* August 16, 2004, p. B1.

8. Michael Porter, "What Is Strategy?" *Harvard Business Review,* November–December 1996, pp. 61–78.

9. Deepak K. Datta, James P. Guthrie, Patrick M. Wright, "Human Resource Management and Labor Productivity: Does Industry Matter?" *Academy of Management Journal* 48(5) (2005), pp. 135–145; Yoshio Yanadori and Janet Marler, "Compensation Strategy: Does Business Strategy Influence Compensation in High Technology Firms?" *Strategic Management Journal* (June 2006), pp. 559–570; Henry Mintzberg, "Five Tips for

Strategy," in Henry Mintzberg and James Brian Quinn, eds., *The Strategy Process: Concepts and Contexts.* (Englewood Cliffs, NJ: Prentice-Hall, 1992); J. E. Delery and D. H. Doty, "Models of Theorizing in Strategic Human Resource Management," *Academy of Management Journal* 39(4) (1996), pp. 802–835; Edilberto F. Montemayor, "Congruence Between Pay Policy and Competitive Strategy in High-Performing Firms," *Journal of Management* 22(6) (1996), pp. 889–908; B. Gerhart, "Pay Strategy and Firm Performance," in S. L. Rynes and B. Gerhart, eds., *Compensation in Organizations: Current Research and Practice* (San Francisco: Jossey-Bass, 2000); Barry Gerhart and Sara Rynes, *Compensation: Theory, Evidence, and Strategic Implications* (Thousand Oaks, CA: Sage, 2003).

10. Michael E. Porter. *Competitive strategy.* (New York: Free Press, 1980); R. E. Miles and C. C. Snow. *Organizational strategy, structure, and process* (New York: McGraw-Hill, 1978).

11. George T. Milkovich, "A Strategic Perspective on Compensation," *Research in Personnel and Human Resources Management* 6 (1988), pp. 263–268. B. Gerhart and S. L. Rynes. *Compensation: Theory, Evidence, and Strategic Implications* (Thousand Oaks, CA: Sage, 2003).

12. Y. Yanadori and J. H. Marler, "Compensation Strategy: Does Business Strategy Influence Compensation in High-Technology Firms? *Strategic Management Journal* 27 (2006). pp. 559–570; N. Rajagopalan, "Strategic Orientations, Incentive Plan Adoptions, and Firm Performance: Evidence From Electrical Utility Firms," *Strategic Management Journal* 18 (1996), pp. 761–785; Luis R. Gomez-Mejia and David B. Balkin, *Compensation, Organization Strategy, and Firm Performance* (Cincinnati, OH: Southwestern Publishing, 1992); B. Gerhart, "Compensation Strategy and Organizational Performance," in S. L. Rynes and B. Gerhart, eds., *Compensation in Organizations,* Frontiers of Industrial and Organizational Psychology series (San Francisco: Jossey-Bass, 2000).

13. B. Gerhart, C. Trevor, and M. Graham "New Directions in Employee Compensation Research," in G. R. Ferris, ed., *Research in Personnel and Human Resources Management,* 1996, pp. 143–203.

14. IBM, "Our Strategy," *www.ibm.com/investor/strategy/* Retrieved May 22, 2009.

15. Peter Boxall and John Purcell. *Strategy and Human Resource Management,* 2nd ed. (Basingstoke and New York: Palgrave MacMillan, 2007); Rosemary Batt, "Managing Customer Services: Human Resource Practices, Quit Rates, and Sales Growth," *Academy of Management Journal* 45 (2002), pp. 587–597; Eileen Appelbaum, Thomas Bailey, Peter Berg, and Arne Kalleberg, *Manufacturing Advantage: Why High Performance Work Systems Pay Off* (Ithaca, NY: Cornell Universty Press, 2000); I. S. Fulmer, B. Gerhart, K. S. Scott, "Are the 100 Best Better? An Empirical Investigation of the Relationship Between Being A 'Great Place to Work' and Firm Performance." *Personnel Psychology* 56, (2003) pp. 965–993; H. C. Katz, T. A. Kochan, and M. R. Weber, "Assessing the Effects of Industrial Relations Systems and Efforts to Improve the Quality of Working Life on Organizational Effectiveness." *Academy of Management Journal* 28 (1985), pp. 509–526; Mark A. Huselid, "The Impact of Human Resource Management Practices on Turnover, Productivity, and Corporate Financial Performance." *Academy of Management Journal* 38 (1995), 635–672; John Paul Macduffie, "Human Resource Bundles and Manufacturing Performace: Organizational Logic and Flexible Production Systems in the World Auto Industry," *Industrial and Labor Relations Review* 48 (1995), 197–221. For a review, see B. Gerhart, "Horizontal and Vertical Fit in Human Resource Systems," in C. Ostroff and T. Judge, eds., *Perspectives on Organizational Fit.* SIOP Organizational Frontiers series (New York: Lawrence Erlbaum Associates, 2007).

16. P. M. Wright, G. McMahan, S. Snell, and B. Gerhart, "Comparing Line and HR Executives' Perceptions of HR Effectiveness: Services, Roles, and Contributions," *Human Resource Management* 40 (2001), pp. 111–124.

17. B. Becker, and B. Gerhart, "The Impact of Human Resource Management on Organizational Performance: Progress and Prospects." *Academy of Management Journal* 39, 1996, pp. 779–801.

18. Charles Fishman, "The Anarchist's Cookbook," *Fast Company,* July 2004, *http://www .fastcompany.com/magazine/84/wholefoods.html,* July 2004; Whole Foods Market, Inc. Annual Repor (Form 10-K), November 26, 2008, *www.sec.gov.*

19. H. Mintzberg, "Crafting Strategy," *Harvard Business Review* (July–August 1970), pp. 66–75.

20. M. Brown, M. C. Sturman, and M. Simmering, "Compensation Policy and Organizational Performance: The Efficiency, Operational, and Financial Implications of Pay Levels and Pay Structure," *Academy of Management Journal* 46 (2003), pp. 752–762; Yoshio Yanadori and Janet Marler, "Compensation Strategy: Does Business Strategy Influence Compensation in High Technology Firms?" *Strategic Management Journal* (June 2006), pp. 559–570.

21. Timothy M. Gardner, "Interfirm Competition for Human Resources: Evidence From the Software Industry," *Academy of Management Journal* 48(2) (2005), pp. 237–256; H. Mintzberg, "Crafting Strategy," *Harvard Business Review* (July–August 1970), pp. 66–75.

22. S. Chatterjee, "Core Objectives: Clarity in Designing Strategy," *California Management Review* 47(2) (2005), pp. 33–49.

23. M. Bloom and G. Milkovich, "Strategic Perspectives on International Compensation and Reward Systems," in Pat Wright, et al., eds., *Research and Theory in Strategic HRM: An Agenda for the Twenty-First Century* (Greenwich, CT: JAI Press, 1999); M. Bloom, G. Milkovich, and A. Mitra, "International Compensation: Learning From How Managers Respond to Variations in Local Host Contexts," *International Journal of Human Resource Management* (Special Issue, 2003); Allen D. Engle, Sr., and Mark Mendenhall, "Transnational Roles and Transnational Rewards: Global Integration in Executive Compensation," presentation at International HR conference, Limerick, Ireland, June 2003; Paul Evans, Vlado Pucik, and Jean-Louis Barsoux, *The Global Challenge* (New York: McGraw-Hill, 2002); *Global Rewards: A Collection of Articles From WorldatWork* (Scottsdale, AZ: WorldatWork, 2005).

24. George Milkovich and Thomas A. Mahoney, "Human Resource Planning Models: A Perspective," *Human Resource Planning* 1(1) (1978), pp. 1–18.

25. Rosemary Batt, Alexander J. S. Colvin, and Jeffrey Keefe, "Employee Voice, Human Resource Practices, and Quit Rates: Evidence From the Telecommunications Industry," *Industrial and Labor Relations Review* 55(4) (July 2002) pp. 573–594; A. Colvin, R. Batt, and H. Katz, "How High Performance HR Practices and Workforce Unionization Affect Managerial Pay," *Personnel Psychology* 54 (2001), pp. 903–934; Paul Osterman, "The Wage Effects of High Performance Work Organization in Manufacturing," *Industrial and Labor Relations Review* (January 2006), pp. 187–204.

26. Study by Christopher K. Bart cited in Steven Greenhouse, "The Nation: Mission Statements; Words That Can't Be Set to Music," *New York Times,* February 13, 2000.

27. *www.jnj.com/our_company/our_credo* in more than 50 languages!

28. See the Web site for Federation of European Employers, at *www.fedee.com.* Also, Watson Wyatt Worldwide, "Strategic Rewards: Managing through Uncertain Times," survey report (2001–2002).

29. Jason Shaw, Michelle Duffy, Atul Mitra, Daniel Lockhart, and Matthew Bowler, "Reactions to Merit Pay Increases: A Longitudinal Test of a Signal Sensitivity Perspective," *Journal*

of Applied Psychology 88 (2003), pp. 538–544; Loretta Chao, "For Gen Xers, It's Work to Live," *The Wall Street Journal,* November 29, 2005, p. B6; Eduardo Porter, "Choice is Good. Yes, No or Maybe?" *New York Times,* March 27, 2005, p. WK12; Melissa Barringer and George Milkovich, "Employee Health Insurance Decisions in a Flexible Benefit Environment," *Human Resource Management* 35 (1996), pp. 293–315; M. P. Patterson, "Health Benefit Evolutions for the 21st Century: Vouchers and Other Innovations?" *Compensation and Benefits Review* 32(4) (July/August 2000), pp. 6–14.

30. Hudson, *Rising Above the Average: Hudson's 2007 Compensation and Benefits Report.* Hudson's research also examines employee attitudes about traditional and nontraditional pay and benefit programs, including performance management, consumer-driven healthcare, and total-reward strategies. The full data set breaks down the findings by various demographics including employer type, occupational sector, age, gender, race, income, company size, managerial status, and others. *www.hudson-index.com.*

31. Eduardo Porter, "Choice Is Good. Yes, No or Maybe?" *New York Times,* March 27, 2005, p. WK12.

32. S. S. Iyengar, R. E. Wells, and B. Schwartz, "Doing Better but Feeling Worse: Looking for the 'Best' Job Undermines Satisfaction," *Psychological Science* 17(2) (2003), pp. 143–150; R. Chua, S. S. Iyengar, "Empowerment Through Choice?: A Critical Analysis of the Effects of Choice in Organizations" in B. Shaw and M. Kramer, eds., *Research on Organizational Behavior* (Oxford, UK: Elsevier, in press).

33. Karen Strossel, "Make My (Mother's) Day..." *The Wall Street Journal,* May 12, 2006, p. A13; John Deckop, Kimberly Merriman, and Gary Blau, "Impact of Variable Risk Preferences on the Effectiveness of Control by Pay," *Journal of Occupational and Organizational Psychology* 77 (2004), pp. 63–80.

34. Morris M. Kleiner, Jonathan S. Leonard, and Adam M. Pilarski, "How Industrial Relations Affects Plant Performance: The Case of Commercial Aircraft Manufacturing," *Industrial and Labor Relations Review* 55(2) (January 2002), pp. 195–218; Sean Karimi and Gangaram Singh, "Strategic Compensation: An Opportunity for Union Activism," *Compensation and Benefits Review,* March/April 2004, pp. 62–67; Henry S. Faber, "Union Success in Representation Elections: Why Does Unit Size Matter?" *Industrial and Labor Relations Review* 54(2) (2001), pp. 329–348.

35. Maria Sacchetti, "Teachers Study Merit Proposal," *Boston Globe,* August 8, 2005; Karla Dial, "Denver Voters Approve Merit Pay for Teachers," *School Reform News,* December 1, 2005.

36. Jeffrey McCracken, "Detroit's Symbol of Dysfunction: Paying Employees Not to Work," *The Wall Street Journal,* March 1, 2006, p. A1, A12; Lauren Etter, "Is General Motors Unraveling?" *The Wall Street Journal,* April 8, 2006, p. A7; "GM Offers Huge Employee Buyout," Associated Press, March 22, 2006.

37. George Milkovich and Carolyn Milkovich, *Cases in Compensation,* 9th ed. (Santa Monica, CA: Milkovich, 2004), p. 8; Aaron Chatterji and David Levine, "Breaking Down the Wall of Codes: Evaluating Non-Financial Performance Measurement," *California Management Review* 48(2) (Winter 2006), pp. 29–51.

38. W. Chan Kim and Renee Mauborgne, "Pursuing the Holy Grail of Clear Vision," *Financial Times,* August 6, 2002, p. 8; Robert S. Kaplan and David P. Norton, "Having Trouble With Your Strategy? Then Map It," *Harvard Business Review,* September–October 2000, pp. 167–176; S. Chatterjee, "Core Objectives: Clarity in Designing Strategy," *California Management Review* 47(2) (2005).

39. L. Bossidy, R. Charman, and C. Burck, *Execution: The Discipline of Getting Things Done* (New York: Crown Business Publishers, 2002); R. Preston McAffee, *Competitive Solutions: The Strategist's Toolkit* (Princeton, NJ: Princeton University Press, 2005).

40. J. Pfeffer, "When It Comes to 'Best Practices,' Why Do Smart Organizations Occasionally Do Dumb Things?" *Organizational Dynamics* 25 (1997), pp. 33–44; J. Pfeffer, *The Human Equation: Building Profits by Putting People First* (Boston: Harvard Business School Press, 1998); Barry Gerhart, Charlie Trevor, and Mary Graham, "New Directions in Employee Compensation Research," in G. R. Ferris, ed., *Research in Personnel and Human Resources Management,* Vol. 14 (Greenwich, CT: JAI Press, 1996), pp. 143–203.

41. Samir Raza, "Optimizing Human Capital Investments for Superior Shareholder Returns," *Valuation Issues,* 2006, *www.valuationissues.com;* M. Huselid and B. Becker, "Improving HR Analytical Literacy: Lessons from Moneyball," chapter 32 in M. Losey, S. Meisinger, and D. Ulrich, *The Future of Human Resource Management* (Hoboken, NJ: Wiley, 2005); Lindsay Scott, "Managing Labor Costs Using Pay-for-Performance," Lindsay Scott & Associates, Inc., *www.npktools.com,* 2006; Thomas Stewart, *Intellectual Capital: The New Wealth of Organizations* (New York: Currency, 1997); D. Scott, D. Morajda, and T. McMullen, "Evaluating Pay Program Effectiveness," *WorldatWork Journal,* First Quarter 2006; D. Scott, T. McMullen, and R. Sperling, "Evaluating Pay Program Effectiveness: A National Survey of Compensation and Human Resource Professionals," *WorldatWork Journal* 15(2) (Second Quarter 2006), pp. 50–59.

42. Richard Donkin, "Measuring the Worth of Human Capital," *Financial Times,* November 7, 2002; Peter F. Drucker, "They're Not Employees, They're People," *Harvard Business Review,* February 2002, pp. 70–77; Stephen Gates, *Value at Work: The Risks and Opportunities of Human Capital Measurement and Reporting* (New York: Conference Board, 2002).

43. John Boudreau and Pete Ramstad, "Beyond Cost-per-Hire and Time to Fill: Supply-Chain Measurement for Staffing," Working Paper T04-16 (468) (Los Angeles: Center for Effective Organizations, 2006).

44. Carlos Tejada and Gary McWilliams, "New Recipe for Cost Savings: Replace Expensive Workers," *The Wall Street Journal,* June 11, 2003, pp. 1, A12.

45. Mary Ellen Lloyd, "Best Buy's Store-Staffing Changes Draw Circuit City Comparisons," *Wall Street Journal,* April 15, 2009.

46. Connie Willis, *Bellwether* (London: Bantam Books 1996); M. Gladwell, *The Tipping Point: The Next Big Thing* (Boston: Little, Brown, 2000).

47. J. Purcell, "Best Practices and Best Fit: Chimera or Cul-de-Sac?" *Human Resources Management Journal* 9(3), pp. 26–41.

48. B. Gerhart, "Pay Strategy and Firm Performance," in S. Rynes and B. Gerhart, eds., *Compensation in Organizations: Current Research and Practice* (San Francisco: Jossey-Bass, 2000); B. Gerhart and G. Milkovich, "Employee Compensation," in M. Dunnette and L. Hough, eds., *Handbook of Industrial and Organization Psychology,* 3rd ed. (Palo Alto, CA: Consulting Psychologists Press, 1992).

49. P. K. Zingheim and J. R. Schuster, *Pay People Right!* (San Francisco: Jossey-Bass, 2000); J. Pfeffer, "Seven Practices of Successful Organizations," *California Management Review* 49(2) (1998), pp. 96–124; E. Lawler, *Rewarding Excellence* (San Francisco: Jossey-Bass, 2000).

50. Jason Shaw, Michelle Duffy, Atul Mitra, Daniel Lockhart, and Matthew Bowler, "Reactions to Merit Pay Increases: A Longitudinal Test of a Signal Sensitivity Perspective," *Journal of Applied Psychology* 88 (2003), pp. 538–544; M. Bloom and G. Milkovich, "Relationships Among Risk, Incentive Pay, and Organization Performance," *Academy of Management Journal* 41(3) (1998), pp. 283–297; Charlie O. Trevor and David L. Wazeter, "A Contingent View of Reactions to Objective Pay Conditions: Interdependence Among Pay Structure Characteristics and Pay Relative to Internal and External Referents," *Journal of Applied*

Psychology, in press; Charlie Trevor, Barry Gerhart, and Greg Reilly, "Decoupling Explained and Unexplained Pay Dispersion to Predict Organizational Performance," presentation at Academy of Management meeting Atlanta, Georgia, August 11–16, 2006; Matthew C. Bloom, "The Performance Effects of Pay Structures on Individuals and Organizations," *Academy of Management Journal* 42(1) (1999), pp. 25–40; Mark Brown, Michael C. Sturman, and Marcia Simmering, "Compensation Policy and Organizational Performance: The Efficiency, Operational, and Financial Implications of Pay Levels and Pay Structure," *Academy of Management Journal* 46 (2003), pp. 752–762; E. P. Lazear, *Personnel Economics* (Cambridge, MA: MIT Press, 1995).

51. Brian Becker and Mark Huselid, "High Performance Work Systems and Firm Performance: A Synthesis of Research and Managerial Implications," in G. R. Ferris (Ed.), *Research in Personnel and Human Resource Management* (Greenwich, CT: JAI Press, 1997); Stephen H. Wagner, Christopher P. Parker, and Neil D. Christiansen, "Employees that Think and Act Like Owners: Effects of Ownership Beliefs and Behaviors on Organizational Effectiveness," *Personnel Psychology,* Winter 2003, pp. 847–871; M. C. Sturman, C. O. Trevor, J. W. Boudreau, and B. Gerhart, "Is It Worth It to Win the Talent War? Evaluating the Utility of Performance-Based Pay," *Personnel Psychology* 56 (2003), pp. 997–1035; A. D. Stajkovic, and F. Luthans, "Differential Effects of Incentive Motivators on Work Performance," *Academy of Management Journal* (44) (2001), pp. 580–590; Jeffrey B. Arthur and Christopher L. Huntley, "Ramping Up the Organizational Learning Curve: Assessing the Impact of Deliberate Learning on Organizational Performance under Gainsharing," *Academy of Management Journal* 48(6) (2005), pp. 1159–1170.

52. Edilberto F. Montemayor, "Congruence Between Pay Policy and Competitive Strategy in High-Performing Firms," *Journal of Management* 22(6) (1996), pp. 889–908; L. R. Gomez-Mejia and D. B. Balkin, *Compensation, Organization Strategy, and Firm Performance* (Cincinnati: Southwestern, 1992); Charlie Trevor, Barry Gerhart, and Greg Reilly, "Decoupling Explained and Unexplained Pay Dispersion to Predict Organizational Performance," presentation at Academy of Management meeting, Atlanta, Georgia, August 11–16, 2006.

53. Mark A. Huselid, Brian E. Becker, and Richard W. Beatty, *The Workforce Scorecard* (Boston: Harvard Business School Press, 2005); David Ulrich and Wayne Brockbank, *The HR Value Proposition* (Boston: Harvard Business School Press, 2005); Brian Becker, Mark Huselid, and Dave Ulrich, *The HR Scorecard: Linking People, Strategy, and Performance* (Boston: Harvard Business School Press, 2001); Rosemary Batt, Virginia Doellgast, and Hyunji Kwon, *The U.S. Call Center Industry 2004: National Benchmarking Report—Strategy, HR Practices, and Performance* (Ithaca, NY: Industrial and Labor Relations School, 2005); D. Scott, D. Morajda, and T. McMullen, "Evaluating Pay Program Effectiveness," *WorldatWork Journal,* First Quarter 2006; and D. Scott, T. McMullen, and R. Sperling, "Evaluating Pay Program Effectiveness: A National Survey of Compensation and Human Resource Professionals," *WorldatWork Journal* 15(2), Second Quarter 2006, pp. 50–59; B. Becker and M. Huselid, "High Performance Work Systems and Firm Performance: A Synthesis of Research and Managerial Implications," *in Research in Personnel and Human Resources,* ed. G. Ferris (Greenwich, CT: JAI Press, 1997); Paul Osterman, "The Wage Effects of High Performance Work Organization in Manufacturing," *Industrial and Labor Relations Review,* January 2006, pp. 187–204.

54. Deepak K. Datta, James P. Guthrie and Patrick M. Wright, "Human Resource Management and Labor Productivity: Does Industry Matter?" *Academy of Management Journal* 48(5), pp. 135–145.

55. K. Murphy and M. Jensen, "It's Not How Much, You Pay, But How," *Harvard Business Review,* May–June 1990, pp. 138–149.

56. B. Gerhart and G. Milkovich, "Organization Differences in Managerial Compensation and Financial Performance," *Academy of Management Journal* 90(33), pp. 663–691.

57. Barry Gerhart and Sara Rynes. *Compensation: Theory, Evidence, and Strategic Implications.* (Thousands Oaks, CA: Sage, 2003).

58. Bartolome Deya-Tortella, Luis R. Gomez-Mejia, Julio O. DeCastro, and Robert M. Wiseman, "Incentive Alignment or Perverse Incentives?" *Management Research* 3(2) (2005); Stephane Renaud, Sylvie St-Onge, and Michel Magnan, "The Impact of Stock Purchase Plan Participation on Workers' Individual Cash Compensation," *Industrial Relations,* January 2004, pp. 120–147; Ingrid Smithey Fulmer, Barry Gerhart, and Kimberly Scott, "Are the 100 Best Better? An Empirical Investigation of the Relationship Between Being a 'Great Place to Work' and Firm Performance," *Personnel Psychology* 56 (2003), pp. 965–993; S. Werner and H. Tosi, "Other People's Money: The Effects of Ownership on Compensation Strategy," *Academy of Management Journal* 38(6), pp. 1672–1691.

59. Rosemary Batt, Virginia Doellgast, and Hyunji Kwon, *The U.S. Call Center Industry 2004: National Benchmarking Report—Strategy, HR Practices, and Performance* (Ithaca, NY: Industrial and Labor Relations School, 2005); Rosemary Batt, Alexander J. S. Colvin, and Jeffrey Keefe, "Employee Voice, Human Resource Practices, and Quit Rates: Evidence from the Telecommunications Industry," *Industrial and Labor Relations Review* 55(4) (July 2002), pp. 573–594; N. Bloom and J. Van Reenen, "Discussion Paper No. 716," *London School of Economics,* March 2006.

60. Brian Becker and Mark Huselid, "High Performance Work Systems and Firm Performance: A Synthesis of Research and Managerial Implications," in G. R. Ferris (Ed.), *Research in Personnel and Human Resource Management* (Greenwich, CT: JAI Press, 1997).

61. Susanne Craig, "Merrill's $10 million men: Top 10 Earners Made $209 Million in 2008 as Firm Foundered." *Wall Street Journal,* March 4, 2009.

62. Martha Graybow, "Wall Street Faces Pay Conundrum Amid TARP Rules." May 28, 2009. *www.reuters.com.*

63. Michael Jacobs, "Opinion: How Business Schools Have Failed Business." *Wall Street Journal,* April 24, 2009.

64. You can go to *www.SEC.gov* to find 10-K (annual) and 10-Q (quarterly) financial reports with more recent information. Choose *Search for Company Filings,* then in the box *Company or Fund Name,* enter "Merrill Lynch," or in the box *Ticker Symbol*, enter "MER." Click on first entry in the next screen. In the *Filing Type* box, enter either "10-Q" or "10-K."

65. *Merrill Lynch 2007 Factbook* at *www.ml.com/media/92209.pdf* and recent 10-Q and 10-K reports available at *www.SEC.gov.*

Internal Alignment: Determining the Structure

Nothing is routine at a *CSI* crime scene.[1] And nothing is routine during the creation of the hit TV series. Nine writers struggle to come up with a plot for the season finale that will ensure that the 20 million viewers will tune in again next season.

Ideas and dialog begin to flow. Warrick Brown will be found standing with a gun in his hand over the dead body of a gangster he has had run-ins with previously. Warrick himself will be unsure about whether he is guilty because he has partial memory loss. Grissam will investigate, find that Warrick was framed, and be able to exonerate him. Warren and the rest of the CSI team will go out to celebrate. At the end, Warrick will go to his car. But, before he can leave, Undersheriff McKean turns up and asks Warrick whether he plans to investigate the murder of the gangster. Warrick will say "Yes" and then be shot. Viewers will, of course, need to tune in next season to find out what happened.

Carol Mendelsohn, one of three executive producers and also the "show runner" (the ultimate decision maker), leads the team of creative writers and manages the cast, support crew, and production crew. In addition to the writers and actors, jobs on the series include director of photography, editor (2), story editor, executive story editor (also 2), gaffers, and special effects makeup (remember the severed head in the last episode?), among others.

What determines the pay for all the different types of work involved in creating *CSI*? Executive story editors get paid more than the editors. How much more? Does it matter? Can an editor be promoted to the executive story editor for this or some other series? Writers can become producers—Ms. Mendelsohn started her career as a writer—but can stunt coordinators become producers? Is the editor paid more than the stunt coordinator or the gaffer? And what's a gaffer, anyway?

What criteria are used to set pay—the content of the work itself, the value of what is contributed to each episode, the person's skill, experience, or reputation? Perhaps the ratings for the show? How do pay differences between jobs in the organization affect behavior? Do they support the organization's business strategy? Do they help attract and retain employees? Do they motivate employees to

EXHIBIT II.1 **The Pay Model**

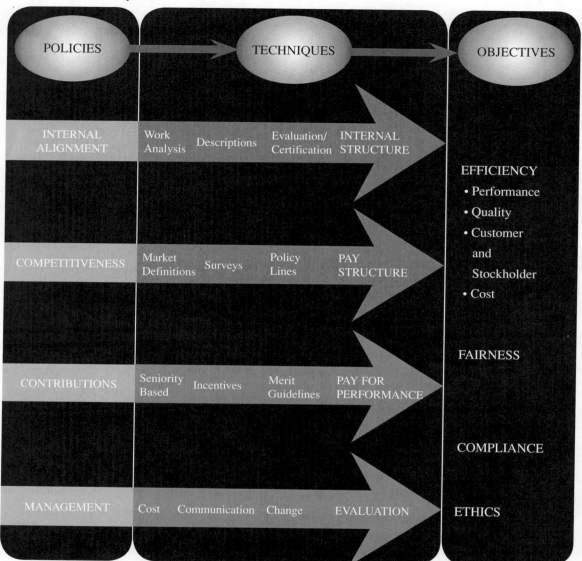

do their best work? Or are the pay procedures bureaucratic burdens that drive away creative talent?

So many questions! Two of them lie at the core of compensation management: (1) How is pay determined for the wide variety of work performed in an organization? and (2) How do the pay differences affect employees' attitudes and work behaviors? These questions are examined within the framework of the pay model introduced in Chapter 1 and shown again in Exhibit II.1. The focus in this part of the book is *within* the organization. Chapter 3 examines internal alignment, what affects it, and what is affected by it. Chapter 4 looks at how to assess the similarities and differences in work content. Chapters 5 and 6 look at various approaches to valuing those similarities and differences and using them to determine internal pay structures.

Endnote

1. Some information from Linda Myers, "Cornell Alumni Make CSI Television's Most-Watched Show," *Cornell University Chronicle Online, http://www.news.cornell.edu/,* November 3, 2005.

Defining Internal Alignment

Chapter Outline

Compensation Strategy: Internal Alignment
Supports Organization Strategy
Supports Work Flow
Motivates Behavior

Structures Vary Among Organizations
Number of Levels
Differentials
Criteria: Content and Value

What Shapes Internal Structures?
Economic Pressures
Government Policies, Laws, and Regulations
External Stakeholders
Cultures and Customs
Organization Strategy
Organization Human Capital
Organization Work Design
Overall HR Policies

Internal Labor Markets: Combining External and Organization Factors
Employee Acceptance: A Key Factor
Pay Structures Change

Strategic Choices in Designing Internal Structures
Tailored Versus Loosely Coupled
Hierarchical Versus Egalitarian

Guidance From the Evidence
Equity Theory: Fairness
Tournament Theory: Motivation and Performance
Institutional Model: Copy Others
(More) Guidance From the Evidence

Consequences of Structures
Efficiency
Fairness
Compliance

Your Turn: So You Want to Lead an Orchestra!

For the kingdom of heaven is like a householder who went out early in the morning to hire laborers for his vineyard. And having agreed with the laborers for a denarius a day, he sent them into his vineyard. And about the third hour, he went out and saw others standing . . . idle; and he said to them, "Go you also into the vineyard, and I will give you whatever is just." And again he went out about the ninth hour, and did as before . . . But about the eleventh hour he went out and found others . . . and he said to them, "Go you also into the vineyard." When evening came, the owner said to his steward, "Call the laborers, and pay them their wages, beginning from the last even to the first." When the first in their turn came . . . they also received each his denarius. . . . They began to murmur against the householder, saying, "These last have worked a single hour, and thou hast put them on a level with us, who have borne the burden of the day's heat." But answering them, he said, "Friend, I do thee no injustice; take what is thine and go."[1]

Matthew's parable raises age-old questions about internal alignment and pay structures within a single organization.[2] The laborers felt that those "who have borne the burden of the day's heat" should be paid more than those who worked fewer hours. But apparently the householder was looking at an individual's needs. He ignored (1) the content of the work, (2) the skills and knowledge required to perform it, and (3) its relative value for achieving the organization's objectives. These three are common bases for today's pay structure. And if the procedures to determine the structure are not acceptable to the parties involved, today's employees murmur, too. That murmuring translates into turnover, an unwillingness to try new technologies, even indifference to the quality of the grapes or the customer's satisfaction with them. This chapter examines internal alignment and its consequences.

COMPENSATION STRATEGY: INTERNAL ALIGNMENT

Setting objectives is our first issue in a strategic approach to pay. Our second, **internal alignment,** addresses relationships *inside* the organization. Matthew doesn't tell us how the work in the vineyard was organized. Perhaps laborers worked in teams: Some trimmed while others tied the vines. Does trimming require more judgment than tying? How do the responsibilities and pay of the trimmer relate to the responsibilities and pay of the tier, the householder's cook, or the steward? Internal alignment addresses the logic underlying these relationships. The relationships form a pay structure that should *support the organization strategy, support the work flow,* and *motivate behavior toward organization objectives.*

> **Internal alignment,** often called *internal equity,* refers to the pay relationships among different jobs/skills/competencies within a single organization.[3]

Exhibit 3.1 shows a structure for engineering work at a division of Lockheed Martin, the world's largest defense contractor. Lockheed also builds rockets, shuttles, and Martian rovers for NASA. Lockheed has the contract to build the next shuttle that will take manned flights back to the moon and on to Mars. The six levels in Lockheed's structure range from entry to consultant. You can see the relationships in the descriptions of each level. Decisions on how to pay each level create a **pay structure.**

> **Pay structure** refers to the array of pay rates for different work or skills within a single organization. The *number of levels,* the *differentials* in pay between the levels, and the *criteria* used to determine those differences describe the structure.

Supports Organization Strategy

Lockheed decided that six levels of engineering work would support the company's strategy of researching, designing, and developing advanced technology systems.

EXHIBIT 3.1 **Engineering Structure at Lockheed Martin**

Engineer
Limited use of basic principles and concepts. Develops solutions to limited problems. Closely supervised.

Senior Engineer
Full use of standard principles and concepts. Provides solutions to a variety of problems. Under general supervision.

Systems Engineer
Wide applications of principles and concepts, plus working knowledge of other related disciplines. Provides solutions to a wide variety of difficult problems. Solutions are imaginative, thorough, and practicable. Works under only very general direction.

Lead Engineer
Applies extensive expertise as a generalist or specialist. Develops solutions to complex problems that require the regular use of ingenuity and creativity. Work is performed without appreciable direction. Exercises considerable latitude in determining technical objectives of assignment.

Advisor Engineer
Applies advanced principles, theories, and concepts. Contributes to the development of new principles and concepts. Works on unusually complex problems and provides solutions that are highly innovative and ingenious. Works under consultative direction toward predetermined long-range goals. Assignments are often self-initiated.

Consultant Engineer
Exhibits an exceptional degree of ingenuity, creativity, and resourcefulness. Applies and/or develops highly advanced technologies, scientific principles, theories, and concepts. Develops information that extends the existing boundaries of knowledge in a given field. Often acts independently to uncover and resolve problems associated with the development and implementation of operational programs.

Supports Work Flow

Work flow refers to the process by which goods and services are delivered to the customer. The pay structure ought to support the efficient flow of that work and the design of the organization.[4] For example, financial service firms in the United States traditionally offer investment advice and products through client centers. At Merrill Lynch, customer associates used to take all calls from clients or new prospects and route them to financial advisors (FAs). If the caller wanted a specific transaction, such as purchasing a stock, mutual fund, or certificate of deposit, the customer associate passed the information on to an FA who was legally certified to make the purchase. No one at Merrill Lynch "owned" a client. Personal long-term relationships were not emphasized.

But Merrill Lynch recognized that its clients' investment needs varied, depending on their net worth, among other factors. Ultra-high-net-worth individuals with more than $25 million to invest were not interested in CDs or stock transactions. They wanted advice specific to their circumstances from someone they knew and trusted. And rather than waiting for calls from these people, the FAs should initiate calls to them. That would help build the long-term relationship around adding value to clients' investments.

Merrill Lynch also noticed that meeting the needs of these high-net-worth clients was very profitable (i.e., higher margins on the fees and the products).[5] So Merrill Lynch redesigned the flow of work to better reflect its clients' needs—and increase its profits.

Merrill Lynch divided its clients into five groups based on net worth: investor, emerging affluent, affluent, high net worth, and ultra high net worth (the "whales"). Then it revamped its job structure to match. The work of financial advisor now has five levels, ranging from assistant vice president, investments (AVPI), to senior vice president, investments (SVPI). These new job levels are defined by the amount of client assets the advisor manages and the expertise and knowledge the advisor possesses. Building those long-term relationships with the "whales" requires complex interactions. The "investor" clients with $250,000 or less to invest are still buying stocks, bonds, and CDs through the financial advisor centers. Newly trained and experienced FAs are now building relationships with individuals in the various client groups. In addition to the financial advisor centers, Merrill Lynch also created private banking hubs to serve clients with at least $10 million. So far over 300 of its 15,000 advisors have trained to work with the high-net-worth and the ultra-net-worth clients, with more to come.

To support the new financial advisor job structure, Merrill Lynch designed a new pay structure. Base pay ranges from $125,000 for FA1 to about $1 million for the SVPI. Aggressive bonus and stock incentives are a substantial part of the new pay structure. These incentives range from around 30 to 90 percent of total cash compensation. The pay difference between FA1s, AVPIs, and SVPIs was a major issue—just as it is for Lockheed engineers, the cast of *CSI,* and the laborers in the vineyard.

Motivates Behavior

Internal pay structures are part of the network of returns discussed in Chapter 1: pay increases for promotions, more challenging work, and greater responsibility as employees move up in the structure. The challenge is to design structures that will engage people to help achieve organization objectives. Merrill Lynch financial advisors work to meet the specific needs of their clients by building long-term relationships. Lockheed engineers work together to share knowledge with each other and with their customers. Is taking on a "bigger" job worth it? Does it pay off to take more training to get promoted? It will in a well-designed pay structure.

The structure ought to make clear the relationship between each job and the organization's objectives. This is an example of **"line-of-sight."** Employees should be able to "see" the links between their work, the work of others, and the organization's objectives. And the structure ought to be fair to employees. The vineyard owner's internal pay structure may have been aligned with his business strategy, but the employee dissatisfaction raises concerns about its fairness to employees.

STRUCTURES VARY AMONG ORGANIZATIONS

An internal pay structure can be defined by (1) the number of *levels* of work, (2) the pay *differentials* between the levels, and (3) the *criteria or bases* used to determine those levels and differentials.

EXHIBIT 3.2
Career
Bands at GE
Healthcare

Source: GE Healthcare.

GE Band	Nature of Work
Associate	Front line, administrative and secretarial
Professional	Developing professional
Lead Professional	Team leader, supervisor, or experienced Individual contributor
Senior Professional	Manager or seasoned professional
Executive	Key member of management team and/or individual contributor with major impact on business
	Driven by job scope, accountability, and skills

Number of Levels

One feature of any pay structure is its hierarchical nature: the number of levels and reporting relationships. Some are more hierarchical, with multiple levels; others are compressed, with few levels.[6] The stated goal of GE Healthcare is to provide "transformational medical technologies and services that are shaping a new age of patient care." One of their many product lines is magnetic resonance imaging (MRI). In comparison to Lockheed's six levels for engineering alone (Exhibit 3.1), GE Healthcare uses five broad levels, described in Exhibit 3.2, to cover all professional and executive work, including engineering. GE Healthcare would probably fit the Lockheed Martin structure into two or three levels.

Differentials

The pay differences among levels are referred to as **differentials.** If we assume that an organization has a compensation budget of a set amount to distribute among its employees, there are a number of ways it can do so. It can divide the budget by the number of employees to give everyone the same amount. The Moosewood Restaurant in Ithaca, New York, adopts this approach. But few organizations in the world are that egalitarian. In most, pay varies among employees.[7] Work that requires more knowledge or skills, is performed under unpleasant working conditions, or adds more value is usually paid more.[8] Exhibit 3.3 shows the percent differentials traditionally attached to Lockheed Martin's engineering structure. Northrup Grumman uses a similar six-level engineering structure with similar differentials. One intention of these differentials is to motivate people to strive for promotion to a higher-paying level. As Exhibit 3.3 shows, the same basic structure, in terms of percent differentials, can be paired with different pay level policies. For example, although a lead engineer gets paid more in the structure on the right, the percent differential between the lead engineer and systems engineer is the same in both (28 percent).

Criteria: Content and Value

Work content and its value are the most common bases for determining internal structures. **Content** refers to the work performed in a job and how it gets done (tasks, behaviors, knowledge required, etc.). **Value** refers to the worth of the work: its relative contribution to the organization objectives. A structure based on content typically ranks jobs on skills required, complexity of tasks, problem solving, and/or responsibility.

EXHIBIT 3.3   **Pay Structure at Lockheed Martin, Under Two Alternative Pay Level Policies**

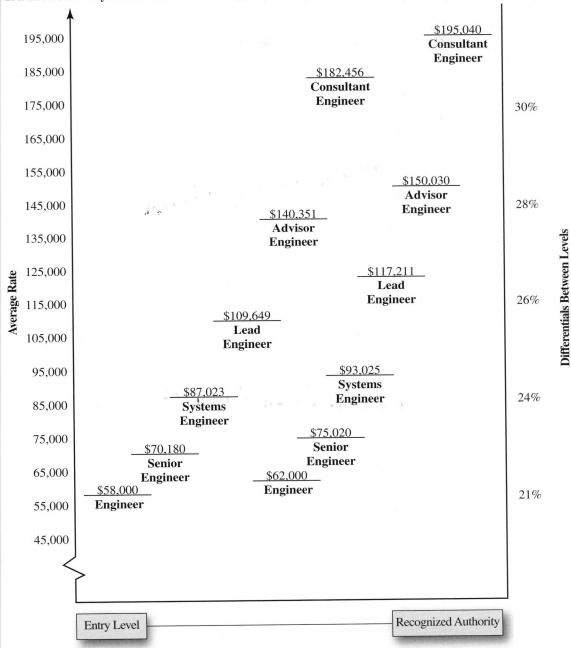

In contrast, a structure based on the value of the work focuses on the *relative contribution* of these skills, tasks, and responsibilities to the organization's goals. While the resulting structures may be the same, there are important differences. In addition to relative contribution, external market value may also be included (i.e., what competitors pay for this job). Or it may include rates agreed upon through collective bargaining, or even legislated rates (minimum wage). In centrally planned economies such as Cuba, job values in all organizations are set by a government agency. Following the now-discarded approaches of the former Soviet Union and China, Cuba's government dictates a universal structure: 8 levels for industrial workers, 16 levels for technical and engineering work, and 26 levels for government employees.

Use Value and Exchange Value

Use value reflects the value of goods or services an employee produces in a job. **Exchange value** is whatever wage the employer and employee agree on for a job. Think about IBM software engineers living in Bangalore, Kiev, and Purchase, New York. Their work content is very similar across all locations. Now think about them working together on the same project—same company, same job content, same internal job. They have the same use value. Wage rates in Bangalore and Kiev are a lot less than in Purchase, New York. The jobs' exchange value varies.[9] For promotions, IBM treats these jobs as being at the same level in the structure. But the external markets in India, the Ukraine, and the United States yield very different pay rates.

The difference between exchange value and use value also surfaces when one firm acquires another. IBM's acquisition of PricewaterhouseCoopers (PWC), where consultants were the lifeblood of the company, is a case in point. At the time, IBM was moving from being a computer company to a provider of information technology solutions whose applications were broader than the IT department. PWC consultants could help IBM's marketing teams engage with clients at a higher organization level. The use value of the PWC consultants within IBM differed from their use value within PWC (how they contributed to IBM or PWC objectives). So, similar marketing jobs in two different companies may be valued differently based on how they contribute to organization objectives. Alternatively, the same work content in the same company (IBM's software engineers) may have different exchange value based on different geographies.

Job- and Person-Based Structures

A **job-based structure** relies on the work content—tasks, behaviors, responsibilities. A **person-based structure** shifts the focus to the employee: the *skills, knowledge, or competencies* the employee possesses, whether or not they are used in the employee's particular job. The engineering structure at Lockheed Martin (Exhibit 3.1) uses the work performed as the criterion. GE Healthcare (Exhibit 3.2) uses the individual employees' competencies/knowledge required at each level of work.

In the real workplace, it is often hard to describe a job without reference to the jobholder's knowledge and skills. Conversely, it is hard to define a person's job-related knowledge or competencies without referring to work content. So rather than a job- *or* person-based structure, reality includes both job *and* person.

WHAT SHAPES INTERNAL STRUCTURES?

The major factors that shape internal structures are shown in Exhibit 3.4. We categorize them as *external* and *organization* factors, even though they are connected and interact. Exactly how they interact is not always well understood. As we discuss the factors, we will also look at various theories.[10]

Economic Pressures

Adam Smith was an early advocate of letting economic market forces influence pay structures. He was the first to ascribe both an exchange value and a use value to human resources. Smith faulted the new technologies associated with the Industrial Revolution

EXHIBIT 3.4
What Shapes Internal Structures?

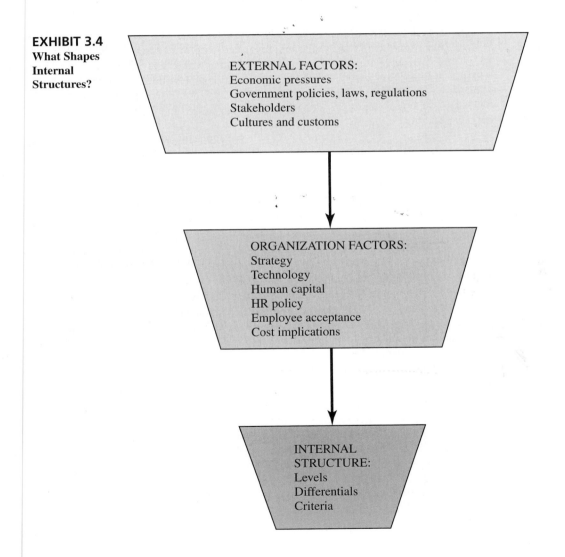

EXTERNAL FACTORS:
Economic pressures
Government policies, laws, regulations
Stakeholders
Cultures and customs

ORGANIZATION FACTORS:
Strategy
Technology
Human capital
HR policy
Employee acceptance
Cost implications

INTERNAL STRUCTURE:
Levels
Differentials
Criteria

for increasing the use value of labor without a corresponding increase in exchange value (i.e., higher wages).

Karl Marx took this criticism even further.[11] He said that employers unfairly pocketed the **surplus value** created by the difference between use and exchange value. He urged workers to overthrow capitalistic systems to become owners themselves and reap the full use value of their labor.

A countering theory put forth in the last half of the 19th century, **marginal productivity,** says that employers do in fact pay use value.[12] Unless an employee can produce a value equal to the value received in wages, it will not be worthwhile to hire that worker. One job is paid more or less than another because of differences in relative productivity of the job and/or differences in how much a consumer values the output. In the short run especially, interesting things can happen. For example, some nurses (specifically, nurse anesthetists) now earn $140,000 to $170,000 per year, more than many family practice and pediatrics doctors.[13] These nurses earn less than physician anesthesiologists ($300,000+), but can perform many of the same tasks, Not surprisingly, they are in high demand. Surgeons may be fine with the situation because it removes a possible constraint on being able to do surgery. One wonders about the views of primary care doctors. Hence, differences in productivity provide a rationale for the internal pay structure.

In addition to supply and demand for labor, supply and demand for products and services also affect internal structures.[14] Turbulent changes, either in competitors' products/services (as in the rise of the Internet for making purchases) or in customers' tastes (as in the popularity of fuel-efficient vehicles), force organizations to redesign work flow and force employees to continuously learn new skills. Unpredictable external conditions require pay structures that support agile organizations and flexible people.[15]

Government Policies, Laws, and Regulations

In the United States, equal employment legislation forbids pay systems that discriminate on the basis of gender, race, religion, or national origin. The Equal Pay Act and the Civil Rights Act require "equal pay for equal work," with work considered equal if it requires equal skill, equal effort, and equal responsibility and is performed under equal working conditions. An internal structure may contain any number of levels, with differentials of any size, as long as the criteria for setting them are not gender, race, religion, or national origin.

Much pay-related legislation attempts to regulate economic forces to achieve social welfare objectives. The most obvious place to affect an internal structure is at the minimums (minimum-wage legislation) and maximums (special reporting requirements for executive pay). But legislation also aims at the differentials. A contemporary U.S. example is the "living wage."[16] A number of U.S. cities require minimum hourly wage rates well above what federal law requires. The anticipated outcome of such legislation is a flatter, more compressed structure of wage rates in society.

External Stakeholders

Unions, stockholders, and even political groups have a stake in how internal pay structures are determined. Unions are the most obvious case. Most unions seek smaller pay differences among jobs and seniority-based promotions as a way to promote solidarity among members. In the United States, the AFL-CIO uses information on the pay differences between top executives and employees to rally support for unions and influence public opinion (see *www.afl-cio.org*).

Stockholders are also interested in the differences between what executives make compared to others within the organization. Estimates vary by what data are used, but they range from CEO pay that is 110 times to over 500 times the pay for manufacturing jobs.[17] These estimates focus on differences averaged across many companies in the U.S. economy. But *internal alignment* focuses on pay relationships *within* an organization. So Disney stockholders are interested in CEO Robert Iger's $12 million in 2005, which is about 282 times the union rates of between $20 and $27 an hour for employees who play Mickey or Minnie Mouse. (Yes, Mickey, Minnie, Pluto, and Goofy, even Snow White, are Teamsters.)[18]

The AFL-CIO website (*www.afl-cio.org*) has a tool called Executive Pay Watch that allows one to estimate how long at his or her wage it would take to match a CEO's annual pay. For example, it reports that Kenneth Lewis, CEO of Bank of America, earned $9.9 million in 2008 and that a worker paid $30,000 per year would need to work 328 years to earn as much. (Would clean living, a good diet, and exercise be enough?)

Cultures and Customs

National Public Radio host and author Garrison Keillor defines culture by what songs we know in common—camp songs, religious hymns, the big hits of the year we were fifteen. A General Mills executive says culture is the foods we eat. A more academic definition of culture is "the mental programming for processing information that people share in common."[19] Shared mind-sets may judge what size pay differential is fair. In ancient Greece, Plato declared that societies are strongest when the richest earned a maximum of four times the lowest pay. Aristotle favored a five-times limit. In 1942, President Franklin Roosevelt proposed a maximum wage: a 100 percent tax on all income above 10 times the minimum wage.

Historians note that in 14th-century western Europe, the Christian church endorsed a **"just wage" doctrine,** which supported the existing class structure. The doctrine was an effort to end the economic and social chaos resulting from the death of one-third of the population from plague. The resulting shortage of workers gave ordinary people power to demand higher wages, much to the dismay of church and state. Market forces such as skills shortages (higher exchange value) were explicitly denied as appropriate determinants of pay structures. Today, advocates of the living wage are trying to change societal judgments about what wage is just.

Even today, cultural factors play a role in shaping pay structures. Many traditional Japanese employers place heavy emphasis on experience in their internal pay structures. But pressures from global competitors plus an aging workforce have made age-based pay structures very expensive. Consequently, some Japanese employers are shifting older employees to lower-paying business units, emphasizing performance and downplaying seniority.[20] (This change is particularly irksome; as the authors have grown older, the wisdom of basing pay on age has become more and more obvious to us!)

Organization Strategy

You have already read how organization strategies influence internal pay structures. The belief is that pay structures that are not aligned with the organization strategy may become obstacles to the organization's success. However, aligned structures today may become an obstacle tomorrow. So aligned, yet adaptable, may be required.

Organization Human Capital

Human capital—the education, experience, knowledge, abilities, and skills required to perform the work—is a major influence on internal structures.[21] The greater the value added by the skills and experience, the more pay those skills will command. Lockheed's structure pays consultant engineers more than lead or senior engineers because the human capital required in the consultant engineer job brings a greater return to Lockheed. It is more crucial to Lockheed's success.

Organization Work Design

Technology used in producing goods and services influences the *organizational design,* the *work* to be performed, and the *skills/knowledge* required to perform the work. The technology required to produce precision military hardware differs from that used to develop and manufacture plastics. These differences contribute to the different structures observed at Lockheed and GE Healthcare.

Multiple structures often exist within the same organization for different types of work. For example, Northrup Grumman has supervisory, engineering, technical, administrative, and non-exempt structures, each having five to six base-pay groupings/levels.

The design of organizations is undergoing profound changes. A lot of people who work in organizations are not employees of these organizations. They may be employed by either a supplier (e.g., an IT services supplier such as IBM or Hewlett-Packard or a circuit designer such as Primarion) or perhaps a *temporary* work supplier (e.g., Accountemps, Manpower Services). Or, they may be working under a temporary contract for a limited amount of time or on a limited project. The security guards, software engineers, or accountants may be supplied by **outsourcing** specialists. Pay for these employees is based on the internal structure of their home employer (e.g., IBM or Accountemps) rather than of the workplace at which they are currently located. Another major work design change is **delayering.**[22] Entire levels of work have disappeared. Just weeks after arriving at Hewlett Packard, new CEO Mark Hurd began hearing complaints about HP's sluggish response to customer needs. He discovered that internal organization layers were delaying responses. HP cut levels of management from eleven to eight and customers immediately applauded the reduced response time.[23] Delayering can cut unnecessary, noncontributing work. It can also add work to other jobs, enlarging them. Through the use of self-managed work teams in production work, entire levels of supervisory jobs are removed and the responsibility for more decisions is delegated to the teams.[24] This will change a job's value and the job structure.

Overall HR Policies

The organization's other human resource policies also influence internal pay structures. Most organizations tie money to promotions to induce employees to apply for higher-level positions.[25] If an organization has more levels, it can offer more promotions, but there may be smaller pay differences between levels. The belief is that more frequent promotions (even without significant pay increases) offer a sense of "career progress" to employees.[26]

Internal Labor Markets: Combining External and Organization Factors

Internal labor markets combine both external and organizational factors. Internal labor markets refer to the rules and procedures that (1) determine the pay for the different jobs within a single organization and (2) allocate employees among those different jobs.[27] In the organization depicted in Exhibit 3.5, individuals are recruited only for entry-level jobs (an engineer would be hired right out of college; a senior engineer would have a few years' experience). They are later promoted or transferred to other jobs inside the organization. Because the employer competes in the external market for people to fill these **entry jobs,** their pay must be high enough to attract a pool of qualified applicants. In contrast, pay for jobs filled via transfer and promotions is buffered from external forces. External factors are dominant influences on pay for entry jobs, but the differences for nonentry jobs tend to reflect internal factors.[28]

EXHIBIT 3.5
Illustration of an Internal Labor Market

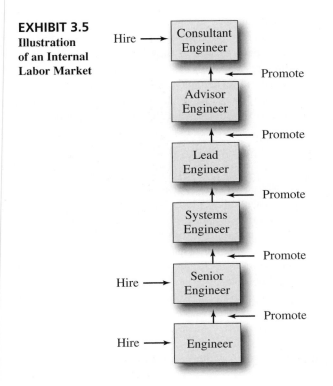

Employee Acceptance: A Key Factor

Employees judge the fairness of their pay through comparisons with the compensation paid to others for work related in some fashion to their own.[29] Accordingly, an important factor influencing the internal pay structure is its *acceptability to the employees involved.*[30] Employees make multiple pay comparisons to assess the fairness of an internal pay structure. They compare both with other jobs in the same internal structure and with the pay for their job in the external market (i.e., at competing employers).[31]

Two sources of fairness are important: the procedures for determining the pay structure, called **procedural justice;** and the results of those procedures—the pay structure itself—called **distributive justice.**

Suppose you are given a ticket for speeding. *Procedural justice* refers to the process by which a decision is reached: the right to an attorney, the right to an impartial judge, and the right to receive a copy of the arresting officer's statement. *Distributive justice* refers to the fairness of the decision: guilty. Researchers report that employees' perceptions of procedural fairness significantly influence their acceptance of the results; employees and managers are more willing to accept low pay if they believe that the way this result was obtained was fair. This research also suggests that pay procedures are more likely to be perceived as fair (1) if they are consistently applied to all employees, (2) if employees participated in the process, (3) if appeals procedures are included, and (4) if the data used are accurate. Nevertheless, a newer study raises a question about the usefulness of employee participation.[32] In a low-wage company, there was no connection between employee participation and pay fairness. It may be that employees were paid so low that no amount of participation could overcome their dissatisfaction. So rather than tossing aside the idea of participation, it may be that in extreme cases (very low wages), a pay raise may trump participation.

Applied to internal structures, procedural justice addresses how design and administration decisions are made and whether procedures are applied in a consistent manner. Distributive justice addresses whether the actual pay differences among employees are acceptable.

Pay Structures Change

Pay structures change in response to external factors such as skill shortages. Over time, distorted pay differences may become accepted as equitable and customary; efforts to change them are resisted. Thus, pay structures established for organizational and economic reasons at an earlier time may be maintained for cultural or political reasons. It may take another economic jolt to overcome the resistance. Then new norms form around the new structure. This "change-and-congeal" process does not yet support the continuous changes occurring in today's economy.[33] New norms for employee acceptance will probably need to include recognition that people must get used to constant change, even in internal pay relationships.

The pay for airport security screeners relative to other airport jobs illustrates the change-and-congeal process. Prior to 9/11, airport screeners were paid about $5.50 an hour with no benefits. Recent immigrants, some undocumented, and relatively unskilled people were hired to screen travelers and their luggage. The people working at the airport Starbucks or the newspaper shop may have been earning more than the screeners. After the 9/11 attack, the Transportation Security Administration (TSA) took over airport security and screening. Wages are now comparable to police and fire protection jobs. Entry-level pay starts at around $20 an hour plus benefits. Employees in other airport jobs have had to revise their comparisons to the security jobs.[34]

STRATEGIC CHOICES IN DESIGNING INTERNAL STRUCTURES

Aligned pay structures support the way the work gets done, fit the organization's business strategy, and are fair to employees. Greater internal alignment—fit—is more likely to lead to success. Misaligned structures become obstacles. They may still motivate employee behavior, but it may be undesirable behavior. Jeff Goldblum's mathematician character may never have stolen the dinosaur egg in *Jurassic Park* if he had been given the pay raise he felt he deserved.

But what does it mean to fit or tailor the pay structure to be internally aligned? Two strategic choices are involved: (1) how specifically tailored to the organization's design and work flow to make the structure, and (2) how to distribute pay throughout the levels in the structure.

Tailored Versus Loosely Coupled

A low-cost, customer-focused business strategy such as that followed by McDonald's or Wal-Mart may be supported by a closely tailored structure. Jobs are well defined with detailed tasks or steps to follow. You can go into a McDonald's in Cleveland, Prague, or Shanghai and find they all are very similar. Their pay structures are, too. There are seven jobs in each McDonalds (under supervisors and managers). All are very well defined in order to eliminate variance in how they are performed. Cooking french fries takes nine steps. It seems hard to make a mistake in these jobs.[35] It is also hard to be the very best french fryer in the whole company. Differences in pay among jobs are very small.

In contrast to McDonald's, 3M's business strategy requires constant product innovation and short product-design-to-market cycle times. The 3M competitive environment is turbulent and unpredictable. No steps at all are laid out. 3M engineers may work on several teams developing several products at the same time. 3M's pay structures are more loosely linked to the organization in order to provide flexibility.

Hierarchical Versus Egalitarian

Pay structures can range from hierarchical to egalitarian. Exhibit 3.6 clarifies the differences. Egalitarian structures have fewer levels and smaller differentials between adjacent levels and between the highest- and lowest-paid workers.

In Exhibit 3.7, Structure A has eight different levels, with relatively small differentials in comparison to structure B, which has only three levels. Structure A is hierarchical compared to the egalitarian structure of B; the multiple levels would include detailed descriptions of work done at each level and outline who is responsible for what. Hierarchies send the message that the organization values the differences in work content, individual skills, and contributions to the organization.[36]

EXHIBIT 3.6
Strategic Choice: Hierarchical Versus Egalitarian

	Hierarchical ←————————→	Egalitarian
Levels	Many	Fewer
Differentials	Large	Small
Criteria	Person or job	Person or job
Supports:	Close fit	Loose fit
Work Organization	Individual performers	Teams
Fairness	Performance	Equal treatment
Behaviors	Opportunities for promotion	Cooperation

EXHIBIT 3.7
Which Structure Has the Greatest Impact on Performance? On Fairness?

Structure A Layered	Structure B Delayered
Chief Engineer	Chief Engineer
Engineering Manager	
Consulting Engineer	
Senior Lead Engineer	
Lead Engineer	Consulting Engineer
Senior Engineer	
Engineer	
Engineer Trainee	Associate Engineer

Structure B can also be characterized as delayered or compressed. Several levels of work are removed so that all employees at all levels become responsible for a broader range of tasks but also have greater freedom to determine how best to accomplish what is expected of them. An egalitarian structure sends the message that all employees are valued equally. The assumption is that more equal treatment will improve employee satisfaction, support cooperation, and therefore affect workers' performance. Costco CEO James Sinegal tries to maintain his cash compensation (base plus bonus) at 8 times the average of Costco unionized employees, and John Mackey at Whole Foods maintains his at 19 times. They believe the more compressed structure better fits their emphasis on cooperative employee teams. Both CEOs are millionaires, however, due to the value of their stock options.

Yet egalitarian structures are not problem-free. For example, Ben and Jerry's Homemade, purveyors of premium ice cream, tried to maintain a ratio of only 7 to 1. (When the company started, the spread was 5 to 1.) The relatively narrow differential reflected the company's philosophy that the prosperity of its production workers and its management should be closely linked. However, it eventually became a barrier to recruiting. Ben and Jerry's was forced to abandon this policy to hire an accounting manager and a new CEO. And only when the company was acquired by Unilever did the press report the value of Ben and Jerry's stock, which netted cofounders Ben Cohen $19 million and Jerry Greenfield $42 million—far beyond the 7-to-1 ratio.

Still, it is hard to be against anything called "egalitarian." If we instead use the word "averagism," as Chinese workers do when describing the pay system under socialism's state-owned enterprises, where maximum differentials of 3 to 1 were mandated, some of the possible drawbacks of this approach become clear.[37] Equal treatment can mean that the more knowledgeable employees—the stars—feel underpaid. They may quit or simply refuse to do anything that is not specifically required of them. Their change in behavior will lower overall performance. So a case can be made for both egalitarian and hierarchical structures.

Keep in mind, though, that the choice is rarely either/or. Rather, the differences are a matter of degree: Levels can range from many to few, differentials can be large or small, and the criteria can be based on the job, the person, or some combination of the two.

GUIDANCE FROM THE EVIDENCE

Before managers recommend a pay structure for their organizations, we hope they will not only look at organization strategy, work flow, fairness, and employee motivation, but also look at the research. Both economists and psychologists have something to tell us about the effects of various structures.

Equity Theory: Fairness

As we noted earlier, employees judge the equity (fairness) of their pay by making multiple comparisons.[38] Evidence based on a study of 2,000 school teachers suggests that teachers are more likely to feel their internal pay structures are fair when they are paid relatively highly within the structure. They will also feel pay structures are fair even when they are relatively low in the internal structure if they work in a high-paying school district.

Applying these findings to Lockheed's engineers, advisors, and consultant engineers, we would assume they are more likely to say the internal structure is fair. Engineers at lower levels will think Lockheed's structure is fair only if Lockheed pays more than its aerospace defense industry competitors. What we don't know is how the lead engineer with 10 years experience will judge the pay structure if Lockheed hires new people into lead engineer jobs with only 5 years of experience. This event is unlikely to occur with unionized teachers' pay structures, but it is very common in other organizations.

So the research suggests that employees judge the fairness of their organization's internal pay structure by making multiple comparisons:

- Comparing to jobs similar to their own (internal alignment),
- Comparing their job to others at the same employer (internal alignment), and
- Comparing their jobs' pay against external pay levels (external competitiveness).

The results from these comparisons depend in part on the *accuracy* of employee knowledge of other employees' jobs, internal structures, and external pay levels.[39] Teachers' pay schedules are generally public knowledge, but this is seldom the case in private sector organizations like Lockheed. Evidence from 30-year-old research shows employees often are misinformed about their relative standing in the pay structure.[40] Equity theory could support either egalitarian or hierarchical structures, depending on the comparisons and the accuracy of information about them.

Tournament Theory: Motivation and Performance

Economists have focused more directly on the motivational effects of structures as opposed to people's perceptions of structures. Their starting point is a golf tournament where the prizes total, say, $100,000. How that $100,000 is distributed affects the performance of all players in the tournament. Compare a 3-prize schedule of $60,000, $30,000, and $10,000 with a 10-prize schedule of $19,000, $17,000, $15,000, $13,000, and so on. According to **tournament theory,** *all* players will play better in the first tournament, where the prize differentials are larger.[41] There is some evidence to support this. Raising the total prize money by $100,000 in the Professional Golf Association tournament lowered each player's score, on average, by 1.1 strokes over 72 holes.[42] And the closer the players got to the top prize, the more their scores were lowered. (Note to nongolfers: A lower score is an improvement.)

Applying these results to organization structures, the greater the differential between your salary and your boss's salary, the harder you (and everyone else but the boss) will work. If Lockheed pays its advisor engineers $125,000 and its consultant engineers $162,000, the tournament model says that increasing the consultants' pay to $200,000 will cause everyone (except the consultants) to work harder. Rather than resenting the big bucks going to the consultants, engineers at all levels will work harder to be a "winner," that is, get promoted to the next level on the way to becoming consultants themselves. Within limits, the bigger the prize for getting to the next level of the structure, the greater the motivational impact of the structure.

Several studies support tournament theory. One reported that giving larger raises with a promotion increases effort and reduces absenteeism.[43] Others find that performance improves with larger differentials at the top levels of the structure. The "winner-take-all" idea springs from these studies.[44] However, a study of the National Basketball Association revealed that once teams fail to get into the playoffs, where players would have made a lot more money, team performance drops precipitously. In fact, it can be called a "race for the bottom." Why? The poorest teams have first-draft choice for next year's new players. So, overnight, the reward goes to the worst record rather than best.[45]

Cybercomp

Salaries for all the players on the major league baseball teams are listed at *http://content.usatoday.com/sports/baseball/salaries/default.aspx.* Pick some of your favorite teams and compare the highest- and lowest-paid players on the team. Based on the differentials, which teams do the models and research discussed in this chapter predict will have the better record?

Click on the following link to check out the team standings: *http://content. usatoday.com/sports/baseball/salaries/default.aspx.* Suggestion: Don't bet your tuition on the relationship between player salary differentials on a team and the team's performance.

But most work is not a round of golf or a good jump shot. Virtually all the research that supports hierarchical structures and tournament theory is on situations where individual performance matters most (auto racing, bowling, golf tournaments) or, at best, where the demand for cooperation among a small group of individuals is relatively low (professors, stockbrokers, truck drivers).[46]

In contrast to individual performers, team sports provide a setting where both an individual player's performance as well as the cooperative efforts of the entire team make a difference.[47] Using eight years of data on major league baseball, one study found that teams with practically identical salaries did better than those with large differentials. In addition to affecting team performance, egalitarian structures had a sizable effect on individual players' performance, too. A mediocre player improved more on a team with an egalitarian structure than on a team with a hierarchical structure. It may also be that the egalitarian pay structure reflects a more flexible, supportive organization culture in which a mediocre player is given the training and support needed to improve.

Tournament theory does not directly address turnover. However, a study of executive leadership teams in 460 organizations concluded that executives were twice as likely to leave if the companies had large pay differentials among the leaders.[48] For example, the CEO of medical reconstructive products maker Biomet would hardly notice if his pay envelope was switched with someone else's on the leadership team. There is only about a 15 percent pay difference among the top five executives at Biomet. In contrast, at building materials supplier Louisiana Pacific, the CEO's salary and bonus is about three times the total of other executives on his team. True to predictions that hierarchy breeds turnover, Louisiana Pacific had 13 changes in its five-person executive team over five years, compared to only one change on the Biomet team (a retirement). Conclusion: If executives need to operate like a baseball team, then an egalitarian structure is probably a better fit.

Institutional Model: Copy Others

Sometimes internal pay structures are adopted because they have been called a "best practice."[49] Organizations simply copy others. Recent examples of such "benchmarking" behavior include the rush to outsource jobs, to emphasize teams, to de-emphasize individual contributions, and to shift to a **competency-based pay system,** often with little regard to whether any of these practices fit the organization or its employees and add value.

The institutional model predicts that very few firms are "first movers"; instead, they copy innovative practices after innovators have learned how to make the practices work. The copiers have little concern for alignment and even less for innovative pay practices.[50]

(More) Guidance From the Evidence

Exhibit 3.8 summarizes the effects attributed to internally aligned structures. The impact of internal structures depends on the context in which they operate.

- More hierarchical structures are related to greater performance when the work flow depends on individual contributors (e.g., consulting and law practices, surgical units, stockbrokers, even university researchers).

- High performers quit less under more hierarchical systems when pay is based on performance rather than seniority and when people have knowledge of the structure.

- More egalitarian structures are related to greater performance when close collaboration and sharing of knowledge are required (e.g., firefighting and rescue squads, manufacturing teams, global software design teams). The competition fostered in

EXHIBIT 3.8
Some
Consequences
of an Internally
Aligned
Structure

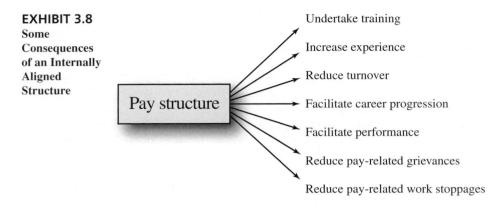

Pay structure

Undertake training

Increase experience

Reduce turnover

Facilitate career progression

Facilitate performance

Reduce pay-related grievances

Reduce pay-related work stoppages

the "winner-take-all" tournament hierarchies appears to have negative effects on performance when the work flow and organization design require teamwork.

• The impact of any internal structure on organization performance is affected by the other dimensions of the pay model; pay levels (competitiveness), employee performance (contributions), and employee knowledge of the pay structure (management).[51]

Beyond these points, much remains to be studied. There is practically no research on the optimal size of the promotional increase or its effects on behavior, satisfaction, or performance. Nor is much known about whether more frequent promotions with minimal change in the nature of the work are better (or worse) than less frequent promotions with major changes in work. Informal expectations often develop at each workplace. ("You can expect to get promoted here after about three years, and a 10 percent raise usually goes with it.") In universities, promotion from assistant to associate professor tends to occur after six years, although there is no norm on accompanying pay increases. In Japanese pay structures, promotion from associate to *kakaricho* occurs after five years in a company. Similar norms exist in the military. Little is known about how these rules of thumb develop and what their original logic was. But they do matter. Promotions sooner (or later) than expected, accompanied by a larger (or smaller) pay increase, send a powerful message.

So what should be the size of the pay differentials among the engineering levels within Lockheed? To answer this question, we would need to understand how differentials within the **career path** support Lockheed's business strategy and work flow, whether the differentials motivate engineers to contribute to Lockheed's success, and whether they are considered fair by the engineers. The next several chapters discuss how to manage these internal structures.

CONSEQUENCES OF STRUCTURES

Let's turn again to that "so-what" question and the pay model. Why worry about internal alignment at all? Why not simply pay employees whatever it takes to get them to take a job and to show up for work every day? Why not let external market forces or what competitors are paying determine internal wage differentials? Or why not let a government agency decide?

Efficiency

Research shows that an aligned structure can lead to better organization performance.[52] If the structure does not motivate employees to help achieve the organization's objectives, then it is a candidate for redesign.

Internal pay structures imply future returns. The size of the differentials between the entry level in the structure and the highest level can encourage employees to remain with the organization, increase their experience and training, cooperate with co-workers, and seek greater responsibility.[53]

Chapter 2 raised the strategy question, Do you want to be difficult to imitate? We already noted that the number of levels and titles in a career path may be rewarding beyond the pay attached to the titles. Microsoft added a "distinguished engineer" title to its structure. The consulting firm McKinsey and Company added an "associate partner." Their rationale was that employees are motivated by these more frequent steps in the career ladder. These are new titles and levels that are not yet reflected in the external market.

Fairness

Writers have long agreed that departures from an acceptable wage structure will occasion turnover, grievances, and diminished motivation.[54] But that is where the agreement ends. One group argues that if fair (i.e., sizable) differentials among jobs are not paid, individuals may harbor ill will toward the employer, resist change, change employment if possible, become depressed, and "lack that zest and enthusiasm which makes for high efficiency and personal satisfaction in work."[55] Others, including labor unions, argue for only small differentials within pay levels and for similar work, in the belief that more egalitarian structures support cooperation and commitment and improve performance.

Compliance

As with any pay decision, internal pay structures must comply with the regulations of the countries in which the organization operates.

While the research on internal alignment is very informative, there is still a lot we do not know. What about the appropriate number of levels, the size of the differentials, and the criteria for advancing employees through a structure? We believe the answers lie in understanding the factors discussed in this chapter: the organization's strategic intent, its design and work flow, human capital, and the external conditions, regulations, and customs it faces. We also believe that aligning the pay structure to fit the organization's conditions is more likely to lead to competitive advantage for the organization and a sense of fair treatment for employees. On the other hand, sometimes people take the notion of internal alignment too far. At a Houston oil company, official policy was that wall hangings were related to position in the structure. Top brass got original art, while employees at the bottom of the structure got photos of the company's oil refineries. One analyst commented, "It was so level specific that you could tell immediately upon entering an office the minimum salary level of that person."[56]

Peter Drucker calls orchestras an example of an organization design that will become increasingly popular in the 21st century, in that they employ skilled and talented people, joined together as a team to create products and services. Drucker may hear what he wants to hear. Others say orchestras are autocratic. The conductor dictates what is played and how it is played. Rather than basking in the glow of orchestral teamwork, jokes like the following are common among orchestra members: *Q. Why do so many people take an instant dislike to the viola? A. It saves time.*

Job descriptions for orchestras look simple: Play the music. *(Q. How is lightning like a keyboardist's fingers? A. Neither strikes the same place twice.)* Violins play violin parts; trumpets play trumpet parts. Yet one study reported that job satisfaction for orchestra members ranks below that of prison guards. However, orchestra members were more satisfied than operating room nurses and hockey players.

Exhibit 1 shows the pay structure for a regional chamber orchestra. *(Q. How can you make a clarinet sound like a French horn? A. Play all the wrong notes.)* The pay covers six full orchestra concerts, one Caroling by Candlelight event, three Sunday Chamber Series concerts, several Arts in Education elementary school concerts, two engagements for a flute quartet, and one Ring in the Holidays brass event as well as the regularly scheduled rehearsals. *(Q. How can you tell when a trombonist is playing out of tune? A. When the slide is moving.)* The figures do not include the 27-cents-per-mile travel pay provided to out-of-town musicians.

1. Describe the orchestra's pay structure in terms of levels, differentials, and job- or person-based approach.
2. Discuss what factors may explain the structure. Why does violinist I receive more than the oboist and trombonist? Why does the principal trumpet player earn more than the principal cellist and clarinetist but less than the principal viola and flute players? What explains these differences? Does the relative supply versus the demand for violinists compare to the supply versus the demand for trombonists? Is it that violins play more notes?
3. How well do equity and tournament models apply?

EXHIBIT 1 Orchestra Compensation Schedule

Instrument	Fee	Instrument	Fee
Violin, Concertmaster	$6,970	Violin I	$2,483
Principal Bass and Conductor	5,070	Violin I	2,483
Principal Viola	5,036	Violin I	2,483
Principal Flute	4,337	Violin II	2,483
Principal Trumpet	4,233	Violin II	2,483
Principal Cello	4,181	Viola	2,483
Principal Clarinet	4,146	Violin II	1,975
Trumpet	3,638	Viola	2,212
Principal Oboe	3,615	Oboe	2,206
Principal Violin II	3,488	Trombone	2,137
Principal Horn	3,390	Viola	2,033
Keyboard I	3,361	Violin II/Viola	1,784
Cello	3,228	Cello	1,634
Principal Percussion	3,049	Clarinet	1,548
Violin I	2,899	Horn	1,548
Cello	2,882	Flute	1,455
Principal Bassoon	2,824	Keyboard II	1,392
Violin I	2,685	Bassoon	1,265
		Violin II	1,178

Summary

This chapter discusses internal alignment and how it affects employees, managers, and employers. Internal alignment refers to the pay relationships among jobs/skills/competencies within a single organization. The potential consequences of internal pay structures are vital to organizations and individuals. Recent research plus experience offers guidance concerning the design and management of internal pay structures.

Pay structures—the array of pay rates for different jobs within an organization—are shaped by societal, economic, organizational, and other factors. Employees judge a structure to be fair by comparing to other jobs within the organization and to what competitors pay for jobs similar to theirs. Acceptance by employees of the pay differentials among jobs is a key test of an equitable pay structure. Such structures are part of the network of returns offered by organizations. They offer career paths to higher-paying jobs and a sense of achievement.

Keep the goals of the entire compensation system in mind when thinking about internal pay structures. There is widespread experience and increasing research to support the belief that differences in internal pay structures, coupled with the other dimensions of compensation systems, influence people's attitudes and work behaviors and therefore the success of organizations.

Review Questions

1. Why is internal alignment an important policy in a strategic perspective of compensation?
2. Discuss the factors that influence internal pay structures. Based on your own experience, which ones do you think are the most important? Why?
3. Internal structures are part of the incentives offered in organizations. Look into any organization: your college, workplace, or the grocery store where you shop. Describe the flow of work. How is the job structure aligned with the organization's business, the work flow, and its objectives? How do you believe it influences employee behaviors?
4. What is the "just-wage" doctrine? Can you think of any present-day applications?
5. A typical structure within colleges is instructor, assistant professor, associate professor, full professor. Is this egalitarian or hierarchical? What added information would you need to decide? What behaviors by the faculty do you believe the structure influences? Is it aligned? Difficult to copy? Does it add value?

Endnotes

1. *Matthew* 20: 1–16.
2. For a history of the different standards for pay, see Thomas Mahoney, *Compensation and Reward Perspectives* (Burr Ridge, IL: Irwin, 1979); G. Milkovich and J. Stevens, "From Pay to Rewards: 100 Years of Change," *ACA Journal* 9(1) (2000), pp. 6–18; D. F. Schloss, *Methods in Industrial Remuneration* (New York: Putnam's, 1892).
3. "Equity" could refer to stock, to some perceived balance of effort and rewards, and/or pay discrimination (gender equity). We believe "internal alignment" better reflects the meaning and importance underlying pay structures.

4. Kenneth H. Doerr, Tali Freed, Terence Mitchell, Chester Schriesheim, and Xiaohua (Tracy) Zhou, "Work Flow Policy and Within-Worker and Between-Workers Variability in Performance," *Journal of Applied Psychology* 89(5) (2004), pp. 911–921.

5. Kristen McNamara, "Push Is on to Advise the Very Wealthy," *The Wall Street Journal,* May 27, 2006, p. B4.

6. James Brian Quinn, Philip Anderson, and Sydney Finkelstein, "Leveraging Intellect," *Academy of Management Executive* 19(4) (2005), pp. 78–94.

7. Researchers use a statistic called the *gini coefficient* to describe the distribution of pay. A gini of zero means everyone is paid the identical wage. The higher the gini coefficient (maximum = 1), the greater the pay differentials among the levels.

8. Dale T. Mortensen, *Wage Dispersion: Why Are Similar Workers Paid Differently?* (Cambridge, MA: MIT Press, 2005); Barry Gerhart and Sara Rynes, *Compensation: Theory, Evidence, and Strategic Implications* (Thousand Oaks, CA: Sage, 2003); Robert Gibbons and Michael Waldman, "A Theory of Wage and Promotion Dynamics Inside Firms," *Quarterly Journal of Economics,* November 1999, pp. 1321–1358; George Baker, Michael Gibbs, and Bengt Holmstrom, "The Internal Economics of the Firm: Evidence From Personnel Data," *Quarterly Journal of Economics* (November 1994), pp. 881–919; M. Bloom and G. Milkovich, "Money, Managers, and Metamorphosis," in D. Rousseau and C. Cooper, eds., *Trends in Organizational Behavior,* 3rd ed. (New York: Wiley, 1996).

9. David Kirkpatrick, "The Net Makes It All Easier—Including Exporting U.S. Jobs," *Fortune,* May 26, 2003, p. 146.

10. Yoshio Yanadori, "Cascading Model of Compensation Management: The Determinants of Compensation of Top Executives and Employees," Vancouver, BC: Sauder School of Business working paper, January 2006.

11. C. Tucker, ed., *The Marx-Engels Reader* (New York: Norton, 1978).

12. Allan M. Carter, *Theory of Wages and Employment* (Burr Ridge, IL: Irwin, 1959).

13. Jacob Goldstein, "Some Nurses Land Higher Salaries Than Primary Care Doctors." *Wall Street Journal,* June 18, 2008.

14. Dana Matlioli, "Help-Wanted: Senior-Level Job, Junior Title, Pay." *Wall Street Journal,* April 12, 2008.

15. B. Gerhart and G. Milkovich, "Employee Compensation," in M. Dunnette and L. Hough, eds., *Handbook of Industrial and Organization Psychology, Vol. 3* (Palo Alto, CA: Consulting Psychologists Press, 1992); S. Brown and K. Eisenhardt, *Competing on the Edge: Strategy and Structured Chaos* (Boston: Harvard Business Press, 1998); George Baker, Michael Gibbs, and Bengt Holmstrom, "The Internal Economics of the Firm: Evidence From Personnel Data," *Quarterly Journal of Economics* (November 1994), pp. 881–919; Michael Gibbs, "Incentive Compensation in a Corporate Hierarchy," *Journal of Accounting and Economics* 19 (1995), pp. 247–277.

16. Scott Adams and David Neumark, "The Effects of Living Wage Laws: Evidence From Failed and Derailed Living Wage Campaigns," NBER working paper 11342, May 2005.

17. Two articles in the same issue of *Workspan,* June 2006, report ratios of 531 versus 400 percent. For a ratio of 104, see *Fortune,* July 16, 2006, p. 81; Eric Dash, "Off to the Races Again, Leaving Many Behind," *New York Times,* April 9, 2006, Section 3 (entire section on Executive Pay: A Special Report); also see "Pay for Performance? Sometimes, but Not Always," p. 6 of section.

18. Chad Terhune, "Home Depot's Critics Tear Into Firm's Practices, Conduct," *The Wall Street Journal,* May 27–28, 2006, p. B3.

19. G. Hoefstede, *Culture's Consequences: International Differences in Work Relationships and Values* (Thousand Oaks, CA: Sage, 1980); R. Donkin, "The Pecking Order's

Instinctive Appeal," *Financial Times,* August 23, 2002; A. Mitra, M. Bloom, and G. Milkovich, "Crossing a Raging River: Seeking Far-Reaching Solutions to Global Pay Challenges," *WorldatWork Journal* 11(2) (Second Quarter 2002); F. Trompenaars, *Riding the Waves of Culture: Understanding Diversity in Global Business* (Burr Ridge, IL: Irwin, 1995); J. Brockner, Y. Chen, K. Leung, and D. Skarlick, "Culture and Procedural Fairness: When the Effects of What You Do Depend on How You Do It," *Administrative Science Quarterly* 45 (2000), pp. 138–159; Thomas Li-Ping Tang, Vivenne Wai-Mei Luk, and Randy K. Chiu, "Pay Differentials in the People's Republic of China: An Examination of Internal Equity and External Competitiveness," *Compensation and Benefits Review* 32(3) (May/June 2000), pp. 43–49.

20. Yoshio Yanadori, "Minimizing Competition? Entry-Level Compensation in Japanese Firms," *Asia Pacific Journal of Management* 21 (December 2004), pp. 445–467.

21. D. Levine, D. Belman, G. Charness, et al., *The New Employment Contract: How Little Wage Structures at U.S. Employers Have Changed* (Kalamazoo, MI: Upjohn, 2001); Charlie Trevor, Barry Gerhart, and Greg Reilly, "Decoupling Explained and Unexplained Pay Dispersion to Predict Organizational Performance," Madison, WI: working paper 12507, School of Business, University of Wisconsin–Madison, May 2006.

22. Raghuram G. Rajan and Julie Wulf, "The Move From Tall to Flat: How Corporate Hierarchies Are Changing," working paper, Wharton, August 2003.

23. Pui-Wing Tam, "Hurd's Big Challenge at H-P: Overhauling Corporate Sales," *The Wall Street Journal,* April 3, 2006, pp. A1, A13.

24. Rosemary Batt, Alexander J. S. Colvin, and Jeffrey Keefe, "Employee Voice, Human Resource Practices, and Quit Rates: Evidence From the Telecommunications Industry," *Industrial and Labor Relations Review* 55(4) (July 2002), pp. 573–594; Wayne F. Cascio, "Strategies for Responsible Restructuring," *Academy of Management Executive* 19(4) (2005), pp. 39–50.

25. Paul Schumann, Dennis Ahlburg, and Christine B. Mahoney, "The Effects of Human Capital and Job Characteristics on Pay," *Journal of Human Resources* 29(2) (1994), pp. 481–503; A. Kohn, *Punished by Rewards: The Trouble With Gold Stars, Incentive Plans, A's, Praise and Other Bribes* (Boston: Houghton Mifflin, 1993); Jerald Greenberg and Suzy N. Ornstein, "High Status Job Titles as Compensation for Underpayment: A Test of Equity Theory," *Journal of Applied Psychology* 68(2) (1983), pp. 285–297.

26. Specialized studies of competitors' pay structures are conducted by some consulting firms. These are discussed in Chapter 8.

27. Thomas A. Mahoney, "Organizational Hierarchy and Position Worth," *Academy of Management Journal* (December 1979), pp. 726–737; Barry Gerhart and Sara Rynes, *Compensation: Theory, Evidence, and Strategic Implications* (Thousand Oaks, CA: Sage, 2003).

28. John Sutherland, "Wages In and Voluntary Quits From an Establishment Internal Labour Market," *Applied Economics* 34 (2002), pp. 395–400; Philip Moss, "Earnings Inequality and the Quality of Jobs," in W. Lazonick and M. O'Sullivan, eds., *Corporate Governance and Sustainable Prosperity* (New York: Macmillan, 2001); Erica L. Groshen and David I. Levine, "The Rise and Decline (?) of U.S. Internal Labor Markets," Research Paper No. 9819 (New York Federal Reserve Bank, 1998); S. Bacharach and E. Lawler, "Political Alignments in Organizations," Chapter 4 in Sam Bacharach and Stephen Mitchell, eds., *Research in the Sociology of Organizations,* Vol. IV. (Greenwich, CT: JAI Press, 1998).

29. E. Robert Livernash, "The Internal Wage Structure," in G. W. Taylor and F. C. Pierson, eds., *New Concepts in Wage Determination* (New York: McGraw-Hill, 1957), pp. 143–172.

30. T. Judge and H. G. Heneman III, "Pay Satisfaction," in S. Rynes and B. Gerhart, eds., *Compensation in Organizations: Current Research and Practice* (San Francisco: Jossey-Bass, 2000); Robert Folger and Mary Konovsky, "Effects of Procedural and Distributive Justice on Reactions to Pay Raise Decisions," *Academy of Management Journal,* March 1989, pp. 115–130; M. L. Williams, M. A. McDaniel, and N. Nguyen, "A Meta-Analysis of the Antecedents and Consequences of Pay Level Satisfaction," *Journal of Applied Psychology* 91 (2006), pp. 392–413.

31. Charlie O. Trevor and David L. Wazeter, "A Contingent View of Reactions to Objective Pay Conditions: Interdependence Among Pay Structure Characteristics and Pay Relative to Internal and External Referents," *Journal of Applied Psychology,* in press; Jason Shaw and Nina Gupta, "Pay System Characteristics and Quit Rates of Good, Average, and Poor Performers," University of Kentucky working paper, May 2006.

32. Frederick P. Morgeson, Michael A. Campion, and Carl P. Maertz, "Understanding Pay Satisfaction: The Limits of a Compensation System Implementation," *Journal of Business & Psychology* 16(1) (Fall 2001), pp. 133–163.

33. Paula England, Paul Allison, Yuxiao Wu, and Mary Ross, "Does Bad Pay Cause Occupations to Feminize, Does Feminization Reduce Pay, and How Can We Tell With Longitudinal Data?" presented at annual meeting of the American Sociological Association, August 2004, San Francisco.

34. "Federal Uniformed Police: Selected Data on Pay, Recruitment, and Retention at 13 Police Forces in the Washington, D.C. Metropolitan Area," GAO-03-658, June 13, 2003.

35. This statement does not apply to professors who work in McDonald's while on sabbatical. See Jerry Newman, *My Secret Life on the McJob* (New York: McGraw-Hill, 2007).

36. Elliot Jaques, "In Praise of Hierarchies," *Harvard Business Review,* January–February 1990, pp. 32–40; Matthew C. Bloom, "The Performance Effects of Pay Structures on Individuals and Organizations," *Academy of Management Journal* 42(1) (1999), pp. 25–40.

37. Daniel Z. Ding, Keith Goodall, and Malcolm Warner, "The End of the 'Iron Rice-Bowl': Whither Chinese Human Resource Management?" *International Journal of Human Resource Management* 11(2) (April 2000), pp. 217–236; Thomas Li-Ping Tang, Vivenne Wai-Mei Luk, and Randy K. Chiu, "Pay Differentials in the People's Republic of China: An Examination of Internal Equity and External Competitiveness," *Compensation and Benefits Review* 32(3) (May/June 2000), pp. 43–49; Li Hua Wang, "Pay Policies and Determination in China," working paper, Northwestern University, 2003.

38. E. E. Lawler, *Pay and Organizational Effectiveness: A Psychological View* (New York: McGraw-Hill, 1971); T. A. Mahoney, *Compensation and Reward Perspectives* (Homewood, IL: Irwin, 1979); Charlie O. Trevor and David L. Wazeter, "A Contingent View of Reactions to Objective Pay Conditions: Interdependence Among Pay Structure Characteristics and Pay Relative to Internal and External Referents," *Journal of Applied Psychology,* in press; E. Lawler III, *Treat People Right! How Organizations and Individuals Can Propel Each Other into a Virtuous Spiral of Success* (San Francisco: Jossey-Bass, 2003).

39. Jason Shaw and Nina Gupta, "Pay System Characteristics and Quit Rates of Good, Average, and Poor Performers," University of Kentucky working paper, May 2006.

40. George Milkovich and P. H. Anderson, "Management Compensation and Secrecy Policies," *Personnel Psychology* 25 (1972), pp. 293–302.

41. B. E. Becker and M. A. Huselid, "The Incentive Effects of Tournament Compensation Systems," *Administrative Science Quarterly* 37 (1992), pp. 336–350; E. Lazear and

S. Rosen, "Rank-Order Tournaments as Optimum Labor Contracts," *Journal of Political Economy* 89 (1981), pp. 841–864; Matthew C. Bloom, "The Performance Effects of Pay Structures on Individuals and Organizations," *Academy of Management Journal* 42(1) (1999), pp. 25–40; Michael L. Bognanno, "Corporate Tournaments," *Journal of Labor Economics* 19(2) (2001), pp. 290–315.

42. R. G. Ehrenberg and M. L. Bognanno, "The Incentive Effects of Tournaments Revisited: Evidence from the European PGA Tour," *Industrial and Labor Relations Review* 43 (1990), pp. 74S–88S; Tor Eriksson, "Executive Compensation and Tournament Theory: Empirical Tests on Danish Data," *Journal of Labor Economics,* April 1999, pp. 262–280.

43. E. P. Lazear, *Personnel Economics* (Cambridge, MA: MIT Press, 1995).

44. Robert H. Frank and Philip J. Cook, *The Winner-Take-All Society: Why the Few at the Top Get So Much More Than the Rest of Us* (New York: Penguin, 1996).

45. Beck A. Taylor and Justin G. Trogdon, "Losing to Win: Tournament Incentives in the National Basketball Association," *Journal of Labor Economics* 20(1) (2002), pp. 23–41.

46. Jason Shaw and Nina Gupta, "Pay System Characteristics and Quit Rates of Good, Average, and Poor Performers," University of Kentucky working paper, May 2006.

47. Matthew C. Bloom, "The Performance Effects of Pay Structures on Individuals and Organizations," *Academy of Management Journal* 42(1) (1999), pp. 25–40.

48. M. Bloom and J. Michel, "The Relationships Among Organizational Context, Pay Dispersion and Managerial Turnover," *Academy of Management Journal* 45(1) (2002), pp. 33–42.

49. P. S. Tolbert and L. G. Zucker, "Institutionalization of Institution Theory," in G. Glegg, C. Hardy, and W. Nord, eds., *Handbook of Organization Studies,* pp. 175–199 (London: Sage, 1996); M. Barringer and G. Milkovich, "A Theoretical Exploration of the Adoption and Design of Flexible Benefit Plans: A Case of HR Innovation," *Academy of Management Review* 23(2) (1998), pp. 305–324.

50. B. Gerhart, C. Trevor, and M. Graham, "New Directions in Employee Compensation Research," in G. R. Ferris, ed., *Research in Personnel and Human Resources Management* (Stamford, CT: JAI Press, 1996), pp. 143–203.

51. M. Brown, M. C. Sturman, and M. Simmering, "Compensation Policy and Organizational Performance: The Efficiency, Operational, and Financial Implications of Pay Levels and Pay Structure," *Academy of Management Journal* 46 (2003), pp. 752–762; Jason Shaw and Nina Gupta, "Pay System Characteristics and Quit Rates of Good, Average, and Poor Performers," University of Kentucky working paper, May 2006.

52. M. Brown, M. C. Sturman, and M. Simmering, "Compensation Policy and Organizational Performance: The Efficiency, Operational, and Financial Implications of Pay Levels and Pay Structure," *Academy of Management Journal* 46 (2003), pp. 752–762.

53. Edward Lazear, "Labor Economics and Psychology of Organization," *Journal of Economic Perspectives* 5 (1991), pp. 89–110; David Wazeter, "Determinants and Consequences of Pay Structures," Ph.D. dissertation, Cornell University, 1991.

54. E. Robert Livernash, "The Internal Wage Structure," in G. W. Taylor and F. C. Pierson, eds., *New Concepts in Wage Determination* (New York: McGraw-Hill, 1957), pp. 143–172.

55. Elliot Jaques, "In Praise of Hierarchies," *Harvard Business Review* (January–February 1990), pp. 32–46.

56. Jared Sandberg, "Apportioning Furniture by Rank Can Stir Up Anger, Envy, Rebellion," *The Wall Street Journal,* November 10, 2004, p. B1.

Job Analysis

Chapter Outline

Structures Based on Jobs, People, or Both

Job-Based Approach: Most Common
Why Perform Job Analysis?

Job Analysis Procedures

What Information Should Be Collected?
Job Data: Identification
Job Data: Content
Employee Data
"Essential Elements" and the Americans With Disabilities Act
Level of Analysis

How Can the Information Be Collected?
Conventional Methods
Quantitative Methods
Who Collects the Information?
Who Provides the Information?
What About Discrepancies?

Job Descriptions Summarize the Data
Using Generic Job Descriptions
Describing Managerial/Professional Jobs
Verify the Description

Job Analysis: Bedrock or Bureaucracy?

Job Analysis and Globalization
Job Analysis and Susceptibility to Offshoring
Job Analysis Information and Comparability Across Borders

Judging Job Analysis
Reliability
Validity
Acceptability
Currency
Usefulness
A Judgment Call

Your Turn: The Customer-Service Agent

Three people sit in front of their keyboards scanning their monitors. One is a customer representative in Ohio, checking the progress of an order for four dozen web-enabled cell phones from a retailer in Texas, who just placed the four dozen into his shopping cart on the company's Web site. A second is an engineer logging in to the project design software for the next generation of these phones. Colleagues in China working on the same project last night (day in China) sent some suggestions for changes in the new design; the team in the United States will work on the project today and have their work waiting for their Chinese colleagues when they come to work in the morning. A third employee, in Ireland, is using the business software recently installed worldwide to analyze the latest sales reports. In today's workplace, people working for the same company no longer need to be down the hallway from one another. They can be on-site and overseas. Networks and business software link them all. Yet all their jobs are part of the organization's internal structure.

If pay is to be based on work performed, some way is needed to discover and describe the differences and similarities among these jobs—observation alone is not enough. **Job analysis** is that systematic method.

STRUCTURES BASED ON JOBS, PEOPLE, OR BOTH

Exhibit 4.1 outlines the process for constructing a work-related internal structure. No matter the approach, the process begins by looking at people at work. Job-based structures look at what people are doing and the expected outcomes; skill- and competency-based structures look at the person. However, the underlying purpose of each phase of the process, called out in the left-hand side of the exhibit, remains the same for both

EXHIBIT 4.1   **Many Ways to Create Internal Structure**

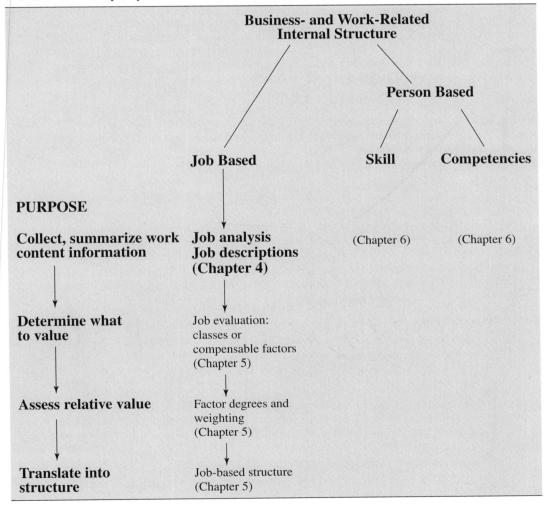

job- and person-based structures: (1) collect and summarize work content information that identifies similarities and differences, (2) determine what to value, (3) assess the relative value, and (4) translate the relative value into an internal structure. (The blank areas in the person-based structure will be filled in when we get to Chapter 6.) This chapter and the next focus on the job-based structure.[1]

Exhibit 4.2 is part of a job description for a registered nurse. The job summary section provides an overview of the job. The section on relationships to other jobs demonstrates where the job fits in the organization structure: which jobs are supervised

EXHIBIT 4.2 **Contemporary Job Description for Registered Nurse**

Job Title: Registered Nurse
Job Summary
Accountable for the complete spectrum of patient care from admission through transfer or discharge through the nursing process of assessment, planning, implementation, and evaluation. Each R.N. has primary authority to fulfill responsibility of the nursing process on the assigned shift and for projecting future needs of the patient/family. Directs and guides patient teaching and activities for ancillary personnel while maintaining standard of professional nursing.
Relationships
Reports to: Head Nurse or Charge Nurse.   Supervises: Responsible for the care delivered by L.P.N.s, nursing assistants, orderlies, and transcribers.   Works with: Ancillary Care Departments.   External relationships: Physicians, patients, patients' families.
Qualifications

Education: Graduate of an accredited school of nursing.
 Work experience: Critical care requires one year of recent medical/surgical experience (special care nursing preferred), medical/surgical experience (new graduates may be considered for noncharge positions).
 License or registration requirements: Current R.N. license or permit in the State of Minnesota.
 Physical requirements: A. Ability to bend, reach, or assist to transfer up to 50 pounds.
                 B. Ability to stand and/or walk 80 percent of 8-hour shift.
                 C. Visual and hearing acuity to perform job-related functions.

Essential Responsibilities

1. Assess physical, emotional, and psychosocial dimensions of patients.
    Standard: Provides a written assessment of patient within one hour of admission and at least once a shift. Communicates this assessment to other patient care providers in accordance with hospital policies.
 	
 2. Formulates a written plan of care for patients from admission through discharge.
    Standard: Develops short-and long-term goals within 24 hours of admission. Reviews and updates care plans each shift based on ongoing assessment.
 	
 3. Implements plan of care.
    Standard: Demonstrates skill in performing common nursing procedures in accordance with but not limited to the established written R.N. skills inventory specific to assigned area.

Note: Additional responsibilities omitted from exhibit.

by this jobholder, which job supervises this jobholder, and the nature of any internal and external relationships.

The section on essential responsibilities elaborates on the summary: "Provides a written assessment of patient within one hour of admission and at least once a shift." Collecting information on these essential responsibilities is the heart of job analysis.

JOB-BASED APPROACH: MOST COMMON

Exhibit 4.3 shows how job analysis and the resulting job description fit into the process of creating an internal structure. Job analysis provides the underlying information. It identifies the content of the job. This content serves as input for describing and valuing work.

> **Job analysis** is the systematic process of collecting information that identifies similarities and differences in the work.

Exhibit 4.3 also lists the major decisions in designing a job analysis: (1) Why are we performing job analysis? (2) What information do we need? (3) How should we collect it? (4) Who should be involved? (5) How useful are the results?

Why Perform Job Analysis?

Potential uses for job analysis have been suggested for every major personnel function. Often the type of job analysis data needed varies by function. For example, identifying the skills and experience required to perform the work clarifies hiring and promotion standards and identifies training needs. In performance evaluation, both employees and supervisors look to the required behaviors and results expected in a job to help assess performance. IBM recently identified every role (490 in all) performed by its 300,000-plus workers, managers, and executives. For example, IBM's vice president for learning has the roles of learning leader and manager. IBM also measures and monitors 4,000 skill sets.[2]

An internal structure based on job-related information provides both managers and employees a work-related rationale for pay differences. Employees who understand

EXHIBIT 4.3   **Determining the Internal Job Structure**

Internal work relationships within the organization	$\rightarrow$	Job analysis The systematic process of collecting information that identifies similarities and differences in the work	$\rightarrow$	Job descriptions Summary reports that identify, define, and describe the job as it is actually performed	$\rightarrow$	Job evaluation Comparison of jobs within an organization	$\rightarrow$	Job structure An ordering of jobs based on their content or relative value

Some Major Decisions in Job Analysis

- Why perform job analysis?
- What information is needed?
- How to collect information?
- Who to involve?
- How useful are the results?

this rationale can see where their work fits into the bigger picture and can direct their behavior toward organization objectives. Job analysis data also help managers defend their decisions when challenged.

In compensation, job analysis has two critical uses: (1) It establishes similarities and differences in the work contents of the jobs, and (2) it helps establish an internally fair and aligned job structure. If jobs have equal content, then in all likelihood the pay established for them will be equal (unless they are in different geographies). If, on the other hand, the job content differs, then the differences, along with the market rates paid by competitors, are part of the rationale for paying jobs differently.

The key issue for compensation decision makers is still to ensure that the data collected are useful and acceptable to the employees and managers involved. As the arrows in Exhibit 4.3 indicate, collecting job information is only an interim step, not an end in itself.

JOB ANALYSIS PROCEDURES

Exhibit 4.4 summarizes some job analysis terms and their relationship to each other. Job analysis usually collects information about specific tasks or behaviors.[3] A group of tasks performed by one person makes up a *position*. Identical positions make a *job,* and broadly similar jobs combine into a **job family.**[4]

EXHIBIT 4.4   **Job Analysis Terminology**

JOB FAMILY

Grouping of related jobs with broadly similar content; e.g., marketing, engineering, office support, technical.

JOB

Group of tasks performed by one person that make up the total work assignment of that person; e.g., customer support representative.

TASK

Smallest unit of analysis, a specific statement of what a person does; e.g., answers the telephone.
Similar tasks can be grouped into a task dimension; e.g., responsible for ensuring that accurate information is provided to customer.

The U.S. federal government, one of the biggest users of job analysis data, has developed a step-by-step approach to conducting **conventional job analysis.**[5] The government's procedures, shown in Exhibit 4.5, include developing preliminary information, interviewing jobholders and supervisors, and then using the information to create and verify job descriptions. The picture that emerges from reading the steps in the exhibit is of a very stable workplace where the division from one job to the next is clear, with little overlap.

In this workplace, jobs follow a steady progression in a hierarchy of increasing responsibility, and the relationship between jobs is clear. So is how to qualify for promotion into a higher-level job. While some argue that such a traditional, stable structure is a shrinking part of the workplace landscape, such structures nevertheless persist, in varying degrees, in many large organizations.[6] Thus, the federal Department of Labor's description of conventional job analysis provides a useful "how-to" guide.

WHAT INFORMATION SHOULD BE COLLECTED?

As Exhibit 4.5 suggests, a typical analysis starts with a review of information already collected in order to develop a framework for further analysis. Job titles, major duties, task dimensions, and work flow information may already exist. However, it may no longer be accurate. So the analyst must clarify existing information, too.

Generally, a good job analysis collects sufficient information to adequately identify, define, and describe a job. Exhibit 4.6 lists some of the information that is usually collected. The information is categorized as "related to the job" and "related to the employee."

Job Data: Identification

Job titles, departments, the number of people who hold the job, and whether it is exempt from the Fair Labor Standards Act are all examples of information that identifies a job.

While a job title may seem pretty straightforward, it may not be. An observer of the U.S. banking system commented that "every employee over 25 seems to be a vice president." A study accuses the U.S. government of creating more new job titles in a recent 6-year period than in the preceding 30 years.[7] Some of the newer positions include deputy to the deputy secretary, principal assistant deputy undersecretary, and associate principal deputy assistant secretary. Most of these titles were created at the highest levels of government service, often to attract a specific person with unique skills. Our personal favorite is at the Jet Propulsion Laboratory in Pasadena, California, where the head of the Interplanetary Network Directorate is, naturally, the director of the Directorate.[8] On the other hand, your tax dollars are paying the wages of 484 deputy assistant secretaries, 148 associate assistant secretaries, 220 assistant assistant secretaries, and 82 deputy assistant assistant secretaries.

Job Data: Content

This is the heart of job analysis. Job content data involve the elemental tasks or units of work, with emphasis on the purpose of each task. An excerpt from a job analysis questionnaire that collects task data is shown in Exhibit 4.7 The inventory describes the job

EXHIBIT 4.5   **Conventional Job Analysis Procedures**

Step	Things to Remember or Do
1. Develop preliminary job information	a. Review existing documents in order to develop an initial "big-picture" familiarity with the job: its main mission, its major duties or functions, work flow patterns. b. Prepare a preliminary list of duties that will serve as a framework for conducting the interviews. c. Make a note of major items that are unclear or ambiguous or that need to be clarified during the data-gathering process.
2. Conduct initial tour of work site	a. The initial tour is designed to familiarize the job analyst with the work layout, the tools and equipment that are used, the general conditions of the workplace, and the mechanics associated with the end-to-end performance of major duties b. The initial tour is particularly helpful in those jobs where a firsthand view of a complicated or unfamiliar piece of equipment saves the interviewee the thousand words required to describe the unfamiliar or technical. c. For continuity, it is recommended that the first-level supervisor-interviewee be designated the guide for the job-site observations
3. Conduct interviews	a. It is recommended that the first interview be conducted with the first-level supervisor, who is considered to be in a better position than the jobholders to provide an overview of the job and how the major duties fit together. b. For scheduling purposes, it is recommended that no more than two interviews be conducted per day, each interview lasting no more than three hours.
Notes on selection of interviewees	a. The interviewees are considered subject-matter experts by virtue of the fact that they perform the job (in the case of job incumbents) or are responsible for getting the job done (in the case of first-level supervisors). b. The job incumbent to be interviewed should represent the *typical*/employee who is knowledgeable about the job (*not* the trainee who is just learning the ropes *or* the outstanding member of the work unit). c. Whenever feasible, the interviewees should be selected with a view toward obtaining an appropriate race/sex mix.
4. Conduct second tour of work site	a. The second tour of the work site is designed to clarify, confirm, and otherwise refine the information developed in the interviews. b. As in the initial tour, it is recommended that the same first-level supervisor-interviewee conduct the second walk-through.
5. Consolidate job information	a. The consolidation phase of the job study involves piecing together into one coherent and comprehensive job description the data obtained from several sources: supervisor, jobholders, on-site tours, and written materials about the job. b. Past experience indicates that one minute of consolidation is required for every minute of interviewing. For planning purposes, at least five hours should be set aside for the consolidation phase. c. A subject-matter expert should be accessible as a resource person to the job analyst during the consolidation phase. The supervisor-interviewee fills this role. d. The job analyst should check the initial preliminary list of duties and questions—all must be answered or confirmed.
6. Verify job description	a. The verification phase involves bringing all the interviewees together for the purpose of determining if the consolidated job description is accurate and complete. b. The verification process is conducted in a group setting. Typed or legibly written copies of the job description (narrative description of the work setting *and* list of task statements) are distributed to the first-level supervisor and the job incumbent interviewees. c. Line by line, the job analyst goes through the entire job description and makes notes of any omissions, ambiguities, or needed clarifications. d. The job analyst collects all materials at the end of the verification meeting.

EXHIBIT 4.6
Typical Data
Collected for
Job Analysis

Data Related to Job	
Job Identification	**Job Content**
Title	Tasks
Department in which job is located	Activities
Number of people who hold job	Constraints on actions
	Performance criteria
	Critical incidents
	Conflicting demands
	Working conditions
	Roles (e.g., negotiator, monitor, leader)

Data Related to Employee		
Employee Characteristics	**Internal Relationships**	**External Relationships**
Professional/technical knowledge	Boss and other superiors	Suppliers
Manual skills		Customers
Verbal skills	Peers	Regulatory
Written skills	Subordinates	Professional industry
Quantitative skills		Community
Mechanical skills		Union/employee groups
Conceptual skills		
Managerial skills		
Leadership skills		
Interpersonal skills		

aspect of communication in terms of actual tasks, such as "read technical publications" and "consult with co-workers." The inventory takes eight items to cover "obtain technical information" and another seven for "exchange technical information." In fact, the task inventory from which the exhibit is excerpted contains 250 items and covers only systems and analyst jobs. New task-based questions need to be designed for each new set of jobs.

In addition to the emphasis on the task, the other distinguishing characteristic of the inventory in the exhibit is the emphasis on the objective of the task, for example, "read technical publications to keep current on industry" and "consult with co-workers to exchange ideas and techniques." **Task data** reveal the actual work performed and its purpose or outcome.

Employee Data

We can look at the kinds of behaviors that will result in the outcomes. Exhibit 4.6 categorizes employee data as employee characteristics, internal relationships, and external relationships. Exhibit 4.8 shows how communication can be described with verbs (e.g., negotiating, persuading). The verbs chosen are related to the employee characteristic being identified (e.g., bargaining skills, interpersonal skills). The rest of the statement helps identify whether the behavior involves an internal or external relationship. So both Exhibit 4.7 and Exhibit 4.8 focus on communication, but they come at it with different approaches.

EXHIBIT 4.7 **Communication: Task-Based Data**

	Do This	Very small amount	Much below average	Below average	Slightly below average	About average	Slightly above average	Above average	Much above average	Very large amount

1. Mark the circle in the "Do This" column for tasks that you currently perform.

Time spent in current position

2. At the end of the task list, write in any unlisted tasks that you currently perform.

3. Rate each task that you perform for relative time spent by marking the appropriate circle in the "Time Spent" column.

Please use a No. 2 pencil and fill all circles completely.

PERFORM COMMUNICATION ACTIVITIES	
Obtain technical information	
421. Read technical publications about competitive products.	○ ①②③④⑤⑥⑦⑧⑨
422. Read technical publications to keep current on industry.	○ ①②③④⑤⑥⑦⑧⑨
423. Attend required, recommended, or job-related courses and/or seminars.	○ ①②③④⑤⑥⑦⑧⑨
424. Study existing operating systems/programs to gain/maintain familiarity with them.	○ ①②③④⑤⑥⑦⑧⑨
425. Perform literature searches necessary to the development of products.	○ ①②③④⑤⑥⑦⑧⑨
426. Communicate with system software group to see how their recent changes impact current projects.	○ ①②③④⑤⑥⑦⑧⑨
427. Study and evaluate state-of-the-art techniques to remain competitive and/or lead the field.	○ ①②③④⑤⑥⑦⑧⑨
428. Attend industry standards meetings.	○ ①②③④⑤⑥⑦⑧⑨
Exchange technical information	
429. Interface with coders to verify that the software design is being implemented as specified.	○ ①②③④⑤⑥⑦⑧⑨
430. Consult with co-workers to exchange ideas and techniques.	○ ①②③④⑤⑥⑦⑧⑨
431. Consult with members of other technical groups within the company to exchange new ideas and techniques.	○ ①②③④⑤⑥⑦⑧⑨
432. Interface with support consultants or organizations to clarify software design or courseware content.	○ ①②③④⑤⑥⑦⑧⑨

Source: Excerpted from Control Data Corporation's Quantitative Job Analysis. Used by permission.

The excerpt in Exhibit 4.8 is from the **Position Analysis Questionnaire (PAQ)**, which groups work information into seven basic factors: information input, mental processes, work output, relationships with other persons, job context, other job characteristics, and general dimensions. Similarities and differences among jobs are described in terms of these seven factors, rather than in terms of specific aspects unique to each job.[9] The communication behavior in this exhibit is part of the relationships-with-other-persons factor.

The entire PAQ consists of 194 items. Its developers claim that these items are sufficient to analyze any job. However, you can see by the exhibit that the reading level is quite high. A large proportion of employees need help to get through the whole thing.

EXHIBIT 4.8   Communication: Behavioral-Based Data

Section 4 Relationships with Others	Code Importance to This job (1)
This section deals with different aspects of interaction between people involved in various kinds of work.	N Does not apply 1 Very minor 2 Low 3 Average 4 High 5 Extreme

4.1 Communication

Rate the following in terms of how important the activity is to the completion of the job. Some jobs may involve several or all of the items in this section.

4.1.1 Oral (communicating by speaking)

99 _____ Advising (dealing with individuals in order to counsel and/or guide them with regard to problems that may be resolved by legal, financial, scientific, technical, clinical, spiritual, and/or professional principles)

100 _____ Negotiating (dealing with others in order to reach an agreement on solution, for example, labor bargaining, diplomatic relations, etc.)

101 _____ Persuading (dealing with others in order to influence them toward some action or point of view, for example, selling, political campaigning, etc.)

102 _____ Instructing (the teaching of knowledge or skills, in either an informal or a formal manner, to others, for example, a public school teacher, a machinist teaching an apprentice, etc.)

103 _____ Interviewing (conducting interviews directed toward some specific objective, for example, interviewing job applicants, census taking, etc.)

104 _____ Routine information exchange job related (the giving and/or receiving of *job-related* information of a routine nature, for example, ticket agent, taxicab dispatcher, receptionist, etc.)

105 _____ Nonroutine information exchange (the giving and/or receiving of *job-related* information of a nonroutine or unusual nature, for example, professional committee meetings, engineers discussing new product design, etc.)

106 _____ Public speaking (making speeches or formal presentations before relatively large audiences, for example, political addresses, radio/TV broadcasting, delivering a sermon, etc.)

4.1.2 Written (communicating by written/printed material)

107 _____ Writing (for example, writing or dictating letters, reports, etc., writing copy for ads, writing newspaper articles, etc.; do *not* include transcribing activities described in item 4.3 but only activities in which the incumbent creates the written material)

Source: E. J. McConnick, P. R., Jeanneret, and R. C. Mecham, *Position Analysis Questionnaire*, copyright © 1969 by Purdue Research Foundation, West Lafayette, IN 47907. Reprinted with permission.

Another, more nuanced view of "communication" focuses on the nature of the interactions required plus knowledge underlying them. Interactions are defined as the knowledge and behaviors involved in searching, monitoring, and coordinating required to do the work. Some interactions are transactional—routine; "do it by the book." The nine steps of a McFry job, shown in Exhibit 4.9, seem transactional to us. Other interactions are more tacit—complex and ambiguous. Work content that involves more tacit interactions is believed to add greater value than more transactional tasks.[10]

The content of communications that occurs between the Merrill Lynch financial advisor and a client to complete a stock transaction differs substantively from that between a Merrill Lynch senior vice president investor and client who aims to build a long-term relationship to manage a client's $10 million in assets. Communication in both settings includes interactions with clients, but "building long-term relationships" versus "complete transactions" reveals substantive differences in content.

However appealing it may be to rationalize job analysis as the foundation of all HR decisions, collecting all of this information for so many different purposes is very expensive. In addition, the resulting information may be too generalized for any single purpose, including compensation. If the information is to be used for multiple purposes, the analyst must be sure that the information collected is accurate and sufficient for each use. Trying to be all things to all people often results in being nothing to everyone.

"Essential Elements" and the Americans With Disabilities Act

In addition to the job description having sections that identify, describe, and define the job, the **Americans With Disabilities Act (ADA)** requires that **essential elements** of a job—those that cannot be reassigned to other workers—must be specified for jobs covered by the legislation. If a job applicant can perform these essential elements, it is assumed that the applicant can perform the job. After that, reasonable accommodations must be made to enable an otherwise-qualified handicapped person to perform those elements.[11]

EXHIBIT 4.9
The McFry Nine-Step Program

Source: Jerry Newman, *My Secret Life on the McJob*, (New York: McGraw-Hill, 2007).

1. Open a bag of fries.
2. Fill basket about half full (at McDonald's, a machine does this step because we humans might make a mistake. At most places, the task is manual.)
3. Place basket in deep fryer.
4. Push timer button to track cooking time.
5. Play Pavlov's dog—remove basket from fryer when buzzer rings and tip so fries go into holding tray. Be careful; this takes two hands, and hot grease can be flying about. Don't spill even a drop of grease on the floor or you will be skating—not walking—in it for the rest of the day.
6. Salt fries.
7. Push another button that signals when 7 minutes are up, the "suggested holding time" for fries.
8. Check screen for size fries requested on next order.
9. Fill the corresponding fry container with fries and place in holding bin.

ADA regulations state that "essential functions refers to the fundamental job duties of the employment position the individual with a disability holds or desires." The difficulty of specifying essential elements varies with the discretion in the job and with the stability of the job. Technology changes tend to make some tasks easier for all people, including those with disabilities, by reducing the physical strength or mobility required to do them. Unfortunately, employment rates for people with disabilities are still low.

The law does not make any allowances for special pay rates or special benefits for people with disabilities. Say a company subsidizes paid parking for its employees. An employee who does not drive because of a disability requests that the employer provide the cash equivalent of the parking subsidy as a reasonable accommodation so that the money can be used to pay for alternative transportation.

While the law does not require any particular kind of analysis, many employers have modified the format of their job descriptions to specifically call out the essential elements. A lack of compliance places an organization at risk and ignores one of the objectives of the pay model.

Level of Analysis

The job analysis terms defined in Exhibit 4.4 are arranged in a hierarchy. The level at which an analysis begins influences whether the work is similar or dissimilar. The three jobs described in the beginning of the chapter—customer representative, engineer, account analyst—all involve use of computers, but a closer look showed that the jobs are very different. At the job-family level bookkeepers, tellers, and accounting clerks may be considered to be similar jobs, yet at the job level they are very different. An analogy might be looking at two grains of salt under a microscope versus looking at them as part of a serving of french fries. If job data suggest that jobs are similar, the jobs must be paid equally; if jobs are different, they can be paid differently.[12]

> **Cybercomp**
> Many companies post a sample of job openings on their Web sites. Compare the job postings from several companies. How complete are the job descriptions included with the postings? Are "essential elements" listed? Are job titles specific or generic? Can you get any sense of a company's culture from its job postings?
>
> Links to fast-growing small private companies can be found via the Inc 500 link at *www.inc.com/resources/inc500/*. Are there any differences in job postings between large and small companies?

Does this mean that the microscopic approach is best? Not necessarily. Many employers find it difficult to justify the time and expense of collecting task-level information, particularly for flexible jobs with frequently changing tasks. They may collect just enough job-level data to make comparisons in the external market for setting wages. However, the ADA's essential-elements requirement for hiring and promotion decisions seems to require more detail than what is required for pay decisions. Designing career paths, staffing, and legal compliance may also require more detailed, finely grained information.

Using broad, generic descriptions that cover a large number of related tasks closer to the job-family level in Exhibit 4.4 is one way to increase flexibility. Two employees working in the same broadly defined jobs may be doing entirely different sets of related tasks. But for pay purposes, they may be doing work of equal value. Employees in these broadly defined jobs can switch to other tasks that fall within the same broad range without the bureaucratic burden of making job transfer requests and wage adjustments. Thus, employees can more easily be matched to changes in the work flow. Recruiter, compensation analyst, and training specialist could each be analyzed as a separate, distinct job, or could all be combined more broadly in the category "HR associate."

Still, a countervailing view deserves consideration. A promotion to a new job title is part of the organization's network of returns. Reducing the number of titles may reduce the opportunities to reinforce positive employee behavior. E*Trade experienced an increase in turnover after it retitled jobs. It reduced its vice presidents and directors to 85, down from around 170 before the retitling.[13] Moving from the federal government job of assistant secretary to that of associate assistant secretary (or reverse) may be far more meaningful than people outside Washington, DC, imagine.

HOW CAN THE INFORMATION BE COLLECTED?

Conventional Methods

The most common way to collect job information is to ask the people who are doing a job to fill out a questionnaire. Sometimes an analyst will interview the jobholders and their supervisors to be sure they understand the questions and that the information is correct. Or the analyst may observe the person at work and take notes on what is being done.

Exhibit 4.10 shows part of a job analysis questionnaire. Questions range from "Give an example of a particularly difficult problem that you face in your work. Why does it occur? How often does it occur? What special skills and/or resources are needed to solve this difficult problem?" to "What is the nature of any contact you have with individuals or companies in countries other than the United States?" These examples are drawn from the Complexity of Duties section of a job analysis questionnaire used by 3M. Other sections of the questionnaire are Skills/Knowledge Applied (19 to choose from), Impact This Job Has on 3M's Business, and Working Conditions. It concludes by asking respondents how well they feel the questionnaire has captured their particular job.

The advantage of conventional questionnaires and interviews is that the involvement of employees increases their understanding of the process. However, the results are only as good as the people involved. If important aspects of a job are omitted, or if the jobholders themselves either do not realize or are unable to express the importance of certain aspects, the resulting job descriptions will be faulty. If you look at the number of jobs in an organization, you can see the difficulty in expecting a single analyst to understand all the different types of work and the importance of certain job aspects. Different people have different perceptions, which may result in differences in interpretation or emphasis. The whole process is open to bias and favoritism.[14] As a result of this potential subjectivity, as well as the huge amount of time the process takes, conventional methods have given way to more quantitative (and systematic) data collection.

Quantitative Methods

Increasingly, employees are directed to a Web site where they complete a questionnaire online.[15] Such an approach is characterized as **quantitative job analysis (QJA),** since

EXHIBIT 4.10 **3M's Structured Interview Questionnaire**

I. Job Overview

Job Summary	What is the main purpose of your job? (Why does it exist and what does the work contribute to 3M?)
	  Examples: To provide secretarial support in our department by performing office and administrative duties.
	  To purchase goods and services that meet specifications at the least cost.
	  To perform systems analysis involved in the development, installation, and maintenance of computer applications.
	
	Hint: It may help to list the duties first before answering this question.

Duties and Responsibilities	What are your job's main duties and responsibilities? (These are the major work activities that usually take up a significant amount of your work time and occur regularly as you perform your work.) In the spaces below, list your job's five most important or most frequent duties. Then, in the boxes, estimate the percentage of the time you spend on each duty each day.	Percentage of Time Spent (Total may be less than but not more than 100%)
	1.	

II. Skills/Knowledge Applied

Formal Training or Education	What is the level of formal training/education that is needed to start doing your job?
	  Example: High School, 2 Year Vo-Tech in Data Processing. Bachelor of Science in Chemistry.
	In some jobs, a combination of education and job-related experience can substitute for academic degrees.
	  Example: Bachelor's Degree in Accounting or completion of 2 years of general business plus 3–4 years' work experience in an accounting field.

Experience	Months: Years: None
Skills/ Competencies	What important skills, competencies, or abilities are needed to do the work that you do? (Please give examples for each skill that you identify.) **A. Coordinating Skills** (such as scheduling activities, organizing/maintaining records) Are coordinating skills required? ☐ Yes ☐ No If yes, give examples of specific skills needed Example **B. Administrative Skills** (such as m...

III. Complexity of Duties

Structure and Variation of Work	How processes and tasks within your work are determined, and how you do them are important to understanding your work at 3M. Describe the work flow in your job. Think of the major focus of your job or think of the work activities on which you spend the most time. 1. From whom/where (title, not person) do you receive work? 2. What processes or tasks do you perform to complete it?
Problem Solving and Analysis	3. Give an example of a particularly difficult problem that you face in your work. Why does it occur? How often does it occur? What special skills and/or resources are needed to solve this difficult problem?

VI. General Comments

General Comments	What percentage of your job duties do you feel was captured in this questionnaire? ☐ 0–25% ☐ 26–50% ☐ 51–75% ☐ 76–100% What aspect of your job was not covered adequately by this questionnaire?

statistical analysis of the results is possible. Exhibits 4.7 and 4.8 are excerpts from quantitative questionnaires. In addition to facilitating statistical analysis of the results, quantitative data collection allows more data to be collected faster.

A questionnaire typically asks jobholders to assess each item in terms of whether or not that particular item is part of their job. If it is, they are asked to rate how important it is and the amount of job time spent on it. The responses can be machine-scored, similar to the process for a multiple-choice test (only there are no wrong answers), and the results can be used to develop a profile of the job. Questions are grouped around five compensable factors (discussed in Chapter 5): knowledge, accountability, reasoning, communication, and working conditions. Knowledge is further subcategorized as range of depth, qualifications, experience, occupational skills, management skills, and learning time. Assistance is given in the form of prompting questions and a list of jobs whose holders have answered each question in a similar way. Results can be used to prepare a job profile based on the compensable factors. If more than one person is doing a particular job, results of several people in the job can be compared or averaged to develop the profile. Profiles can be compared across jobholders in both the same and different jobs.

Some consulting firms have developed quantitative inventories that can be tailored to the needs of a specific organization or to a specific family of jobs, such as data/information processing jobs.[16] Many organizations find it practical and cost-effective to modify these existing inventories rather than to develop their own analysis from ground zero. But, remember, as we have said, the results depend on the quality of the inputs. Here, the items on the questionnaire matter. If important aspects of a job are omitted or if the jobholders themselves do not realize the importance of certain aspects, the resulting job descriptions will be faulty. In one study, the responses of high-performing stockbrokers on amounts of time spent on some tasks differed from those of low performers. The implication is that any analysis needs to include good performers to ensure that the work is usefully analyzed.[17]

Who Collects the Information?

Collecting job analysis information through one-on-one interviews can be a thankless task. No matter how good a job you do, some people will not be happy with the resulting job descriptions. In the past, organizations often assigned the task to a new employee, saying it would help the new employee become familiar with the jobs of the company. Today, if job analysis is performed at all, human resource generalists and supervisors do it. The analysis is best done by someone thoroughly familiar with the organization and its jobs and trained in how to do the analysis properly.[18]

Who Provides the Information?

The decision on the source of the data (jobholders, supervisors, and/or analysts) hinges on how to ensure consistent, accurate, useful, and acceptable data. Expertise about the work resides with the jobholders and the supervisors; hence, they are the principal sources. For key managerial/professional jobs, supervisors "two levels above" have also been suggested as valuable sources since they may have a more strategic view of how jobs fit in the overall organization. In other instances, subordinates and employees in other jobs that interface with the job under study are also involved.

The number of incumbents per job from which to collect data probably varies with the stability of the job, as well as the ease of collecting the information. An ill-defined or changing job will require either the involvement of more respondents or a more careful selection of respondents. Obviously, the more people involved, the more time-consuming and expensive the process, although computerization helps mitigate these drawbacks.

Whether through a conventional analysis or a quantitative approach, completing a questionnaire requires considerable involvement by employees and supervisors. Involvement can increase their understanding of the process, thereby increasing the likelihood that the results of the analysis will be acceptable.[19] But it also is expensive.

What About Discrepancies?

What happens if the supervisor and the employees present different pictures of the jobs? While supervisors, in theory, ought to know the jobs well, they may not, particularly if jobs are changing. People actually working in a job may change it. They may find ways to do things more efficiently, or they may not have realized that certain tasks were supposed to be part of their jobs.

3M had an interesting problem when it collected job information from a group of engineers. The engineers listed a number of responsibilities that they viewed as part of their jobs; however, the manager realized that those responsibilities actually belonged to a higher level of work. The engineers had enlarged their jobs beyond what they were being paid to do. No one wanted to tell these highly productive employees to slack off. Instead, 3M looked for additional ways to reward these engineers rather than bureaucratize them.

What should the manager do if employees and their supervisors do not agree on what is part of the job? Differences in job data may arise among the jobholders as well. Some may see the job one way, some another. The best answer is to collect more data. Enough data are required to ensure consistent, accurate, useful, and acceptable results. Holding a meeting of multiple jobholders and supervisors in a focus group to discuss discrepancies and then asking both employees and supervisors to sign off on the revised results helps ensure agreement on, or at least understanding of, the results. Disagreements can be an opportunity to clarify expectations, learn about better ways to do the job, and document how the job is actually performed. Discrepancies among employees may even reveal that more than one job has been lumped under the same job title.

Top Management (and Union) Support Is Critical

In addition to involvement by analysts, jobholders, and their supervisors, support of top management is absolutely essential. Support of union officials in a unionized workforce is as well. They know (hopefully) what is strategically relevant. They must be alerted to the cost of a thorough job analysis, its time-consuming nature, and the fact that changes will be involved. For example, jobs may be combined; pay rates may be adjusted. If top managers (and unions) are not willing to seriously consider any changes suggested by job analysis, the process is probably not worth the bother and expense.

JOB DESCRIPTIONS SUMMARIZE THE DATA

So now the job information has been collected, maybe even organized. But it still must be summarized and documented in a way that will be useful for HR decisions, including job evaluation (Chapter 5). That summary of the job is the **job description.** The job description provides a "word picture" of the job. Let us return to Exhibit 4.2, our job description for a registered nurse. It contains information on the tasks, people, and things included. Trace the connection between different parts of the description and the job analysis data collected. The job is identified by its title and its relationships to other jobs in the structure. A job summary provides an overview of the job. The section on essential responsibilities elaborates on the summary. It includes the tasks. Related tasks may be grouped into task dimensions.

This particular job description also includes very specific standards for judging whether an essential responsibility has been met—for example, "Provides a written assessment of patient within one hour of admission and at least once a shift." A final section lists the qualifications necessary in order to be hired for the job. These are the **job specifications** that can be used as a basis for hiring—the knowledge, skills, and abilities required to adequately perform the tasks. But keep in mind that the summary needs to be relevant for pay decisions and thus must focus on similarities and differences in content.

Using Generic Job Descriptions

To avoid starting from scratch (if writing a job description for the first time) or as a way to cross-check externally, it can be useful to refer to generic job descriptions that have not yet been tailored to a specific organization. One readily accessble source is the Occupational Information Network, or O*NET (*www.onetcenter.org*). Exhibit 4.11 shows the information O*NET provides using the job of computer programmer as an example.

Cybercomp

Use O*NET to find the knowledge, skills, and other characteristics needed to be a computer programmer (or an occupation of your choice).
Go to *http://online.onetcenter.org/*
Choose: Find Occupations
Enter the occupation name into space under "Keyword or O*NET-SOC code"
Click on "go"
Then click on the name of the occupation to see the knowledge, skills, etc. required.
Would this information from O*NET be useful to you if you needed to write job descriptions in your organizations?

Describing Managerial/Professional Jobs

Descriptions of managerial/professional jobs often include more-detailed information on the nature of the job, its scope, and accountability. One challenge is that an individual manager will influence the job content.[20] Professional/managerial job descriptions must capture the relationship between the job, the person performing it, and the organization objectives—how the job fits into the organization, the results expected, and what the person performing it brings to the job. Someone with strong information

EXHIBIT 4.11 O*NET Code Connector

Computer Programmers – 15-1021.00

O*NET–SOC Description

Convert project specifications and statements of problems and procedures to detailed logical flow charts for coding into computer language. Develop and write computer programs to store, locate, and retrieve specific documents, data, and information. May program web sites.

Sample of Reported Job Titles

- Programmer Analyst
- Programmer
- Computer Programmer
- Software Developer
- Internet Programmer
- Web Programmer

SOC Occupation Groups

15-0000	Computer and Mathematical Occupations
15-1000	Computer Specialists
15-1020	Computer Programmers
15-1021.00	**Computer Programmers**

Related Occupations

5 of 8 displayed

11-3021.00	Computer and Information Systems Managers
15-1041.00	Computer Support Specialists
15-1051.00	Computer Systems Analysts
15-2031.00	Operations Research Analysts
25-1021.00	Computer Science Teachers, Postsecondary

Tasks

5 of 15 displayed

- Assign, coordinate, and review work and activities of programming personnel.
- Collaborate with computer manufacturers and other users to develop new programming methods.
- Compile and write documentation of program development and subsequent revisions, inserting comments in the coded instructions so others can understand the program.
- Conduct trial runs of programs and software applications to be sure they will produce the desired information and that the instructions are correct.
- Consult with and assist computer operators or system analysts to define and resolve problems in running computer programs.

Detailed Work Activities

5 of 63 displayed

- adjust computer operation system
- analyze workflow
- assist co-workers with software problems
- communicate technical information
- configure computers in industrial or manufacturing setting

Military Crosswalk Titles

4 of 11 displayed

- Classic Wizard Configuration Maintenance Analyst (Navy – Enlisted)
- Communications – Computer Systems Programming Apprentice (Air Force – Enlisted)
- Entry Level Programmer/Analyst (Navy – Enlisted)
- Information Systems Technician (Army – Warrant Officer only)

Apprenticeship Crosswalk Titles

- Computer Programmer
- Programmer, Engineering and Scientific

DOT Crosswalk Titles

- Chief, Computer Programmer
- Computer Programmer
- Programmer, Engineering and Scientific

Source: National Center for O*NET Development, U.S. Department of Labor, Employment and Training Administration, *http://www.onetcodeconnector.org/ccreport/15-1021.00*

systems and finance expertise performing the compensation manager's job will probably shape it differently, based on this expertise, than someone with strong negotiation and/or counseling expertise.

Exhibit 4.12 excerpts this scope and accountability information for a nurse manager. Rather than emphasizing the tasks to be done, this description focuses on the accountabilities (e.g., "responsible for the coordination, direction, implementation, evaluation, and management of personnel and services; provides leadership; participates in strategic planning and defining future direction").

Verify the Description

The final step in the job analysis process is to verify the accuracy of the resulting job descriptions (step 6 in Exhibit 4.5). Verification often involves the jobholders as well as their supervisors to determine whether the proposed job description is accurate and complete. The description is discussed, line by line, with the analyst, who makes notes of any omissions, ambiguities, or needed clarifications (an often excruciating and thankless task). It would have been interesting to hear the discussion between our nurse from 100 years ago, whose job is described in Exhibit 4.13, and her supervisor.

EXHIBIT 4.12
Job
Description for
a Manager

Title: Nurse Manager

Department: ICU

Position Description:

Under the direction of the Vice President of Patient Care Services and Directors of Patient Care Services, the Nurse Manager assumes 24-hour accountability and responsibility for the operations of defined patient specialty services. The Nurse Manager is administratively responsible for the coordination, direction, implementation, evaluation, and management of personnel and services. The Nurse Manager provides leadership in a manner consistent with the corporate mission, values, and philosophy and adheres to policies and procedures established by Saint Joseph's Hospital and the Division of Patient Care Services. The Nurse Manager participates in strategic planning and defining future direction for the assigned areas of responsibility and the organization.

Qualification:

Education: Graduate of accredited school of nursing. A bachelor's degree in Nursing or related field required. Master's degree preferred. Current license in State of Wisconsin as a Registered Nurse, Experience: A minimum of three years' clinical nursing is required. Minimum of two years' management experience or equivalent preferred.

EXHIBIT 4.13
Job
Description
for Nurse
100 Years
Ago

In addition to caring for your 50 patients each nurse will follow these regulations:

1. Daily sweep and mop the floors of your ward, dust the patient's furniture and window sills.
2. Maintain an even temperature in your ward by bringing in a scuttle of coal for the day's business.
3. Light is important to observe the patient's condition. Therefore, each day, fill kerosene lamps, clean chimneys, and trim wicks. Wash the windows once a week.
4. The nurse's notes are important in aiding the physician's work. Make your pens carefully, you may whittle nibs to your individual taste.
5. Each nurse on the day duty will report every day at 7 a.m. and leave at 8 p.m. except on the Sabbath on which day you will be off from 12:00 noon to 2:00 p.m.
6. Graduate nurses in good standing with the director of nurses will be given an evening off each week for courting purposes, or two evenings a week if you go regularly to church.
7. Each nurse should lay aside from each pay day a goodly sum of her earnings for her benefit during her declining years, so that she will not become a burden. For example, if you earn $30 a month you should set aside $15.
8. Any nurse who smokes, uses liquor in any form, gets her hair done at a beauty shop, or frequents dance halls will give the director good reason to suspect her worth, intentions, and integrity.
9. The nurse who performs her labors and serves her patients and doctors faithfully and without fault for a period of five years will be given an increase by the hospital administration of five cents a day, provided there are no hospital debts that are outstanding.

The job description paints a vivid picture of expectations at that time, although we suspect the nurse probably did not have much opportunity for input regarding the accuracy of the job description.

JOB ANALYSIS: BEDROCK OR BUREAUCRACY?

HRNet, an Internet discussion group related to HR issues, provoked one of its largest responses ever with the query, "What good is job analysis?" Some felt that managers have no basis for making defensible, work-related decisions without it. Others called the process a bureaucratic boondoggle. Yet job analysts are an endangered species. Many employers, as part of their drive to contain expenses, no longer have job analysts. The unknown costs involved are too difficult to justify.

One expert writes, "Whenever I visit a human resources department, I ask whether they have any [job analysis]. I have not had a positive answer in several years, except in government organizations."[21] Yet if job analysis is the cornerstone of human resource decisions, what are such decisions based on if work information is no longer rigorously collected?

This disagreement centers on the issue of flexibility. Many organizations today are using fewer employees to do a wider variety of tasks in order to increase productivity and reduce costs. Reducing the number of different jobs and cross-training employees can make work content more fluid and employees more flexible.[22]

Generic job descriptions that cover a larger number of related tasks (e.g., "associate") can provide flexibility in moving people among tasks without adjusting pay. Employees may be more easily matched to changes in the work flow; the importance of flexibility in behavior is made clear to employees.

Traditional job analysis that makes fine distinctions among levels of jobs has been accused of reinforcing rigidity in the organization. Employees may refuse to do certain tasks that are not specifically called out in their job descriptions. It should be noted, however, that this problem mainly arises where employee relations are already poor. In unionized settings, union members may "work to the rules" (i.e., not do anything that is not specifically listed in their job descriptions) as a technique for putting pressure on management.

In some organizations, analyzing work content is now conducted as part of work flow and supply chain analysis. **Supply chain analysis** looks at how an organization does its work: activities pursued to accomplish specific objectives for specific customers. A "customer" can be internal or external to the organization. So Starbucks, in its continuous quest for improved service, frets over "average wait time." If the time to put that Venti Double Chocolate Chip Frappuccino Blended Creme in your hand is increased because customers in front of you are musing over the new CD for sale at the register, you may decide that the Dunkin' Donuts across the street might be a better choice. Starbucks shaved 20 seconds off its wait time by redesigning the barista job to include "floating." Floaters walk the queue, take your order, mark the cup, and hand the cup to the barista who will actually fill your order—all before you get to the cash register. Floaters also "communicate" with the customers to make the experience enjoyable. Notice that as part of a work flow study, job analysis is conducted to understand the work and how it adds value. Is the barista job content now different with the floating tasks? Yes. We will face the issue of whether to pay floaters differently in later chapters.[23]

JOB ANALYSIS AND GLOBALIZATION

Job Analysis and Susceptibility to Offshoring

Offshoring refers to the movement of jobs to locations beyond a country's borders. Historically, manual, low-skill jobs were most susceptible to offshoring. As we saw in Chapter 1, there are substantial differences in hourly compensation costs across countries for manufacturing workers; this has played an important role in companies' decisions about where to locate production operations. Similar differences in cost in other low-skill occupations (e.g., in call centers) have had similar ramifications. (So, when you call for an airline reservation or help with your printer, you may well reach someone in another country.) Of course, as we also noted, labor cost is only part of the story. There are productivity differences across countries as well, meaning that lower labor costs may in some cases be offset by lower productivity. Availability of workers with needed education and skills is another potential constraint. Proximity to customers is yet another issue. Sometimes that argues for moving offshore, sometimes it does not.

Increasingly, susceptibility to offshoring is no longer limited to low-skill jobs. White-collar jobs are also increasingly at risk. Is there a way to systematically measure which jobs are most susceptible to offshoring? The U.S. Bureau of Labor Statistics has attempted to do just this with respect to service-providing occupations. Exhibit 4.14 shows the list of occupations it found to have the highest and lowest susceptibility to offshoring. The offshoring susceptibility scores are based on the sum of scores on the four items shown. So, jobs are most susceptible to outsourcing when inputs and outputs can easily be transmitted electronically, little interaction with other workers is required, little local knowledge is required, and the work can be routinized.

Interestingly, highly susceptible jobs include not only those that require little education and training, such as data entry keyers and telemarketers, but also computer programmers and tax preparers. Turning to jobs with low susceptibility to outsourcing, we see various managerial positions and also positions where local knowledge is required (e.g., marketing managers presumably need to know consumer preferences in particular regions of the world) or where being "on the ground" (literally, in the case of landscape architects) is necessary.

To our knowledge, the system for assessing susceptibility to offshoring has not been rigorously validated to see how it well it predicts actual offshoring of occupations. Nevertheless, as Exhibit 4.14 indicates, growth rates (in the United States) for jobs on the highly susceptible list are generally small or negative, while jobs on the low susceptibility list have shown strong growth. Unless the two sets of jobs have different growth rates across countries, the differential growth rates seem consistent with the possibility that jobs on the highly susceptible list have lower growth rates, at least in part because they have experienced greater offshoring. Also, there are certainly numerous examples of jobs on the highly susceptible list (e.g., data entry keyers, telemarketers, and computer programmers) being offshored. In Chapter 7, we return to the topic of offshoring to discuss labor cost and effectiveness ramifications.

EXHIBIT 4.14 Susceptibility of Occupations to Offshoring and Projected Employment Growth

Susceptibility Score	Occupation	Projected 10-Year Employment Growth
	Highest Susceptibility to Offshoring	
16	Computer programmers	−4%
16	Pharmacy technicians	32%
16	Parts salespersons	−2%
16	Telephone operators	−4.9%
16	Billing and posting clerks and machine operators	−39%
16	Computer operators	4%
16	Data entry keyers	−25%
16	Word processors and typists	−5%
15	Tax preparers	−11%
15	Medical transcriptionists	−9%
15	Telemarketers	14%
15	Payroll and timekeeping clerks	−10%
15	Proofreaders and copy markers	6%
	Lowest Susceptibility to Offshoring	
6	Chief executives	2%
6	General and operations managers	1%
6	Administrative services managers	12%
6	Computer and information systems managers	16%
6	Wholesale and retail buyers, except farm products	0%
6	Computer systems analysts	29%
6	Landscape architects	16%
6	Industrial engineers	21%
6	Animal scientists	9%
6	Advertising sales agents	21%
5	Advertising and promotions managers	6%
5	Marketing managers	15%
5	Sales managers	10%
5	Public relations managers	17%
5	Engineering managers	7%
5	Natural science managers	12%
5	Management analysts	22%
5	Civil engineers	18%
5	Art directors	9%
4	Environmental engineers	26%

Offshoring susceptibility questions (maximum score = 16, minimum score = 4)?

1. To what degree can the inputs and outputs of the occupation be transmitted electronically?

   | Very low degree (1 point) | Low degree (2 points) | High degree (3 points) | Very high degree (4 points) |

2. To what degree do the duties of this occupation require interaction with other types of workers?

   | Very low degree (1 point) | Low degree (2 points) | High degree (3 points) | Very high degree (4 points) |

3. To what degree is knowledge of social and cultural idiosyncrasies, or other local knowledge, needed to carry out the tasks of this occupation?

   | Very low degree (4 point) | Low degree (3 points) | High degree (2 points) | Very high degree (1 points) |

4. To what degree can the work of the occupation be routinized or handled by following a script?

   | Very low degree (1 point) | Low degree (2 points) | High degree (3 points) | Very high degree (4 points) |

Source: Roger J. Moncarz, Michael G. Wolf, and Benjamin Wright, "Service-Providing Occupations, Offshoring and The Labor Market." *Monthly Labor Review*, December 2008, pp. 71–86.

EXHIBIT 4.15 **Updated Job Descriptions**

How many jobs in your organization have up-to-date position, job, or role descriptions in place?

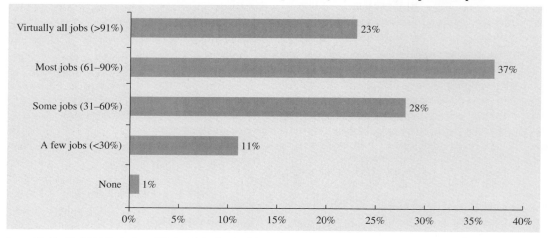

Source: *World at Work,* "Job Evaluation and Market-Pricing Practices," *http://www.worldatwork.org/waw/adimLink?id=31378,* 2009.

Job Analysis Information and Comparability Across Borders

As firms spread work across multiple countries, there is an increasing need to analyze jobs to either maintain consistency in job content or else be able to measure the ways in which jobs are similar and different. For example, for a software development team to work equally effectively with programmers in the United States and India, the job descriptions and job specifications need to be measured and understood. One potential challenge is that norms or perceptions regarding what is and what is not part of a particular job may vary across countries. However, a study of three different jobs (first-line supervisor, general office clerk, and computer programmer) in the United States, China, Hong Kong, and New Zealand found that ratings of the importance and amount of work activities and job requirements were "quite similar" across countries, suggesting that job analysis information "is likely to transport quite well across countries."[24]

JUDGING JOB ANALYSIS

Beyond beliefs about its usefulness—or lack thereof—for satisfying both employees and employers, there are several ways to judge job analysis.

Reliability

If you measure something tomorrow and get the same results you got today, or if I measure and get the same result you did, the measurement is considered to be reliable. This doesn't mean it is right—only that repeated measures give the same result. **Reliability** is a measure of the consistency of results among various analysts, various methods, various sources of data, or over time. Reliability is a necessary, but not sufficient, condition for **validity.**

Research on employee and supervisor agreement on the reliability of job analysis information is mixed.[25] For instance, experience may change an employee's perceptions about a job since the employee may have found new ways to do it or added new tasks to the job. The supervisor may not realize the extent of change. In such cases, the job the employee is actually doing may not be the same as the job originally assigned by the supervisor. Differences in performance seem to influence reliability. Other research finds that reliability is lower for jobs that are more interdependent with other jobs, and have more autonomy/are less routine.[26] To date, no studies have found that gender and race differences affect reliability.[27] Obviously, the way to increase reliability in a job analysis is to understand and reduce sources of difference. Quantitative job analysis helps do this. But we need to be sure that we do not eliminate the richness of responses while eliminating the differences. Sometimes there really may be more than one job. Training can also improve reliability.[28]

Validity

Does the analysis create an accurate portrait of the work? There is almost no way of showing statistically the extent to which an analysis is accurate, particularly for complex jobs. No gold standard exists; how can we know? Consequently, *validity* examines the convergence of results among sources of data and methods. If several job incumbents, supervisors, and peers respond in similar ways to questionnaires, then it is more likely that the information is valid. However, a sign-off on the results does not guarantee the information's validity.[29] It may mean only that all involved were sick to death of the process and wanted to get rid of the analyst so they could get back to work.

Acceptability

If job holders and managers are dissatisfied with the initial data collected and the process, they are not likely to buy into the resulting job structure or the pay rates attached to that structure. An analyst collecting information through one-on-one interviews or observation is not always accepted because of the potential for subjectivity and favoritism. One writer says, "We all know the classic procedures. One [worker] watched and noted the actions of another . . . at work on [the] job. The actions of both are biased and the resulting information varied with the wind, especially the political wind."[30] However, quantitative computer-assisted approaches may also run into difficulty, especially if they give in to the temptation to collect too much information for too many purposes. After four years in development, one application ran into such severe problems due to its unwieldy size and incomprehensible questions that managers simply refused to use it.

Currency

To be valid, acceptable, and useful (see below), job information must be up to date. Some jobs stay relatively stable over time, while others may change in important ways, even over short time periods. As Exhibit 4.15 shows, most organizations report that they have up-to-date job information, but a substantial portion report that job information is not up to date. That can not only hinder compensation practice and decision-making, but also employee selection, training, and development. Most organizations do not engage in any regular (e.g., annual or biannual) updating of job analysis information, instead being more likely to update job information when the significant changes are believed to have occurred or when the job is being re-evaluated for compensation purposes.[31] It may be useful to develop a systematic protocol for evaluating when job information needs to be updated.[32]

Usefulness

Usefulness refers to the practicality of the information collected. For pay purposes, job analysis provides work-related information to help determine how much to pay for a job—it helps determine whether the job is similar to or different from other jobs. If job analysis does this in a reliable, valid, and acceptable way and can be used to make pay decisions, then it is useful.[33]

As we have noted, some see job analysis information as useful for multiple purposes, such as hiring and training. But multiple purposes may require more information than is required for pay decisions. The practicality of all-encompassing quantitative job analysis plans, with their relatively complex procedures and analysis, remains in doubt. Some advocates get so taken with their statistics and computers that they ignore the role that judgment must continue to play in job analysis. Dunnette's point, made more than 25 years ago, still holds true today: "I wish to emphasize the central role played in all these procedures by human judgment. I know of no methodology, statistical technique or objective measurements that can negate the importance of, nor supplement, rational judgment."[34]

A Judgment Call

In the face of all the difficulties, time, expense, and dissatisfaction, why on earth would you as a manager bother with job analysis? Because work-related information is needed to determine pay, and differences in work determine pay differences. There is no satisfactory substitute that can ensure the resulting pay structure will be work-related or will provide reliable, accurate data for making and explaining pay decisions.

If work information is required, then the real issue should be, How much detail is needed to make these pay decisions? The answer is, Enough to help set individual employees' pay, encourage continuous learning, increase the experience and skill of the work force, and minimize the risk of pay-related grievances. Omitting this detail and contributing to an incorrect and costly decision by uninformed managers can lead to unhappy employees who drive away customers with their poor service, file lawsuits, or complain about management's inability to justify their decisions. The response to inadequate analysis ought not to be to dump the analysis; rather, the response should be to obtain a more useful analysis.

Your **Turn**   The Customer-Service Agent

Read the accompanying article on a day in the work life of Bill Ryan. Then write a job description for the job of customer service agent. Use the exhibits in this chapter to guide you in deciding what information in the story is relevant for job analysis.

1. Does the day diary include sufficient information?
2. Identify the specific information in the article that you found useful.
3. What additional information do you require? How would that information help you?

Pick a teammate (or the instructor will assign one) and exchange job descriptions with your teammate.

1. How similar/different are the two descriptions? You and your teammate started with exactly the same information. What might explain any differences?
2. What process would you go through to understand and minimize the differences?
3. What are some of the relational returns of the job?

Bill Ryan often deals with difficult people. It's what he gets paid for. He's one of 30 customer-service agents at Half.com, an online marketplace owned by eBay Inc., the Internet auction company. Like eBay, Half.com attempts to match buyers and sellers in a vast flea market featuring millions of products ranging from trading cards to camcorders. But unlike eBay, there's no bidding. Half.com lists items only at fixed prices. If you see something you like, pay the price and it's yours.

The other big difference with eBay is that for most of the products listed on Half.com, there's no way for buyers and sellers to interact directly. Usually there's no need to. To make a purchase, buyers use their credit cards or checking accounts to pay Half.com, which then automatically credits the amount to the seller's card or account—minus a transaction fee. Once the payment is made, the seller ships the product.

Despite a well-oiled system, however, questions arise. Things can go wrong. A purchased item doesn't arrive, or isn't in the condition the buyer expected. Or maybe an interesting product is listed but its description isn't clear.

And that's where Mr. Ryan and his colleagues come in, handling the buckets of e-mail and intermittent phone calls from curious, addled, and upset users. They pass information between buyers and sellers, answer questions, and resolve the occasional dispute. Half.com says that fewer than 1 percent of the site's transactions require customer service's involvement. But with more than 15 million items for sale—well, you do the math.

In fact, the customer-service department receives about 1,500 to 2,000 e-mails a day, of which nearly a third are complaints about transactions. The rest are mostly questions about the goods and how the site works. Mr. Ryan himself on a typical day fields between 60 and 100 e-mails and half a dozen phone calls. The calls are the most stressful. "People panic and they want answers," Mr. Ryan says. "If they are calling, they are not happy."

For Half.com—as well as most other e-commerce companies—customer-service agents like Mr. Ryan are the crucial link between the faceless Web site and the consumer. And how they deal with the public can make or break a business. As Half.com's vice president for operations, says, "It costs too much to get a new customer only to fumble the relationship away." Half.com wouldn't discuss salaries. But Mr. Ryan and his colleagues, who are split into two shifts covering 8 a.m. to midnight, seven days a week, say they're satisfied with their wages, which include quarterly bonuses.

What he likes about the work, Mr. Ryan says, is the kind of customer problem that requires research and deep digging to find the resolution. What he sometimes doesn't like about his work are the routine questions that generate stock responses. Here's a day in Mr. Ryan's work life:

THE ANSWER MAN

8 AM Mr. Ryan strolls into the Half.com office in Plymouth Meeting, Pa., a short drive from his home. The company's single-story gray building is a former tire factory in this colonial-era industrial town on the outskirts of Philadelphia. Mr. Ryan works in a low-slung, black cubicle toward the back of the office, his space sparsely decorated.

The atmosphere at Half.com is decidedly young and casual. Jeans are the uniform. Mr. Ryan certainly fits in, though at 32 he's a few years older than most of his cubicle mates.

He started doing strictly customer service, answering customer e-mails. Now he also does what the company calls "trust and safety work": investigating fraud and looking for things on the site that are "funky." For instance, when Half.com receives a complaint from a buyer about a seller, it's Mr. Ryan's job to contact both parties and make sure there is no fraud occurring.

This day, because the site has received a high volume of e-mails, he's on regular customer service duty. After checking the few internal e-mail messages he receives each day, he gets right to work. Mr. Ryan downloads his first batch of 10 e-mails for the day. He says it usually takes him about an hour to get through 10 messages.

8:10 AM The first e-mail is from a woman interested in buying an audio book on CD that she saw listed on the site. She wants to know whether the CD will work on her DVD player. But since she doesn't specify the exact listing, Mr. Ryan is stuck. He can't search for it among all the listings or contact the seller. The best he can do is suggest that she send him an item number so he can contact the seller with her question.

8:15 AM The next e-mail comes from a user who sold the Diana Krall CD "When I Look in Your Eyes," but lost the buyer's shipping information. The seller is concerned that a delay in her shipment will give the buyer reason to give her a negative rating on the site. After each purchase is made, the buyer gets a chance to rate the seller's performance on a scale from 1 to 5—"poor" to "excellent." Every rating sellers collect is displayed along with their user name next to subsequent items they list. Just one negative rating can ruin a seller's reputation, depending on how many sales he or she has made overall.

Mr. Ryan tracks down the details on this particular transaction in the Half.com user database. He identifies the buyer and writes an e-mail to explain that the seller lost the shipping address and "wants to let you know they are sorry for the inconvenience." He then e-mails the buyer's shipping address to the seller.

Mr. Ryan says he doesn't find the e-mails tedious. "There is such a variety of topics to respond to," he says. "I never get 50 of the same questions in a row." But, a few e-mails later, he shrugs with disapproval. The user's question could easily have been answered by going to the help section of the Web site: "Do I include shipping in the sale price or is it added later?"

Says Mr. Ryan, "It's a general question. I like the detailed research questions." Mr. Ryan pastes in an answer from a database of stock responses the customer-service team has put together. He then tacks onto the end of the e-mail a salutation that he draws from a list of suggested message closers provided by Half.com. The list, the company says, makes it easier for the agents to write so many e-mails. For this message, Mr. Ryan chooses, "It was my pleasure to assist you."

GOT JUICE

9:30 AM After answering a few more messages, it's time for a coffee break. Mr. Ryan says he drinks two cups of coffee a day, a habit he picked up since starting at Half.com.

"A year ago I wouldn't have touched the stuff," he says. He heads to the kitchen, which is just down the hall from his desk. The well-lit room is stocked with free cappuccino, juice, soda, fruit, cereal, cookies, and other munchies. The cafeteria also doubles as a lounge with a satellite television playing ESPN, a Foosball table, and a ping-pong table. This early in the morning, however, most people are interested in the coffee.

9:48 AM An e-mail arrives from a Half.com colleague in charge of the stock-answer database. He writes that a response Mr. Ryan submitted on how users can sign up for direct deposit—linking their Half.com transactions with their checking accounts—would be included in the database. "There are so many things we don't have responses to," Mr. Ryan says. "It makes everyone's life easier to have the [database]."

9:50 AM The first 10 e-mails are done. Mr. Ryan downloads 10 more. One is from a father who several days earlier ordered the latest Sony PlayStation for his son's birthday and is concerned because it hasn't arrived yet. Half.com's policy is that if a buyer hasn't received an item within 30 days of the purchase, he or she can lodge an official complaint. The PlayStation seller is thus a long way from the delivery deadline. Nevertheless, as a courtesy, Mr. Ryan sends the seller an e-mail asking whether he can provide a shipping date and tracking number that Mr. Ryan can pass on to the restless father.

Half.com believes that help like this—beyond the requirements of its own rules—separates its customer-service approach from that of other companies. When the company was starting out, says Training Supervisor Ed Miller, customer service tried to respond to as many messages as it could, as fast as possible. What the company learned, however, is that "customers don't mind if you take a little more time to answer their specific question." Instead of just firing off e-mails, Half.com now sees it as important to personalize each message. Even with the personalization, Half.com says it responds to most messages within 24 hours.

Communications with customers have a consistent and pleasant tone. E-mail messages should conform to the "grandmother rule." Each message should "make sense to my grandmother."

10:10 AM Bathroom break.

10:15 AM "All right," Mr. Ryan says eagerly, returning to his desk. He cracks his knuckles and starts typing.

A buyer who purchased a video game two months ago but never received it writes to thank Half.com for "hounding" the seller to send him the item. But he wants a refund. Mr. Ryan verifies the buyer's version of events in Half.com's records, then refunds the buyer's money and charges the seller's account for the amount of the sale. Mr. Ryan sends e-mails to both parties informing them of his action. Half.com's rules say that when an official complaint has been lodged the other party has five days in which to respond. In this case, the seller didn't respond, so the buyer won the dispute by default.

10:25 AM Snack time. Mr. Ryan breaks into a high-energy Balance bar—a little nourishment to get him ready for what comes next.

WRECKING CREW

10:30 AM Time to knock down some walls. Lively human-resources worker Alicia DiCiacco invites Mr. Ryan and his colleagues to pick up sledge-hammers and knock through a wall at the end of the office. Half.com's staff has doubled in the past year, and the company is expanding into adjacent space in the old tire factory. Everyone in the office takes turns whacking at the wall. Some of the younger males dish out screams of "I'm not going to take it any more!" and "Where's the Pink Floyd?!"—a reference to the 1970s rock album "The Wall" by Pink Floyd.

Mr. Ryan eats up the office energy. "It's exciting to work here," he says. "We're growing. We had the second launch of the site. [Half.com expanded its product line in April]. We're doing construction. It's good to come to work when the company is doing well."

11:15 AM Finished with another batch of 10 e-mails, he downloads 10 more, including two separate queries from customers who can't redeem special introductory coupons Half.com offers to new users.

11:47 AM Mr. Ryan gets an e-mail from a seller responding to a message from Half.com. A potential buyer has asked Half.com whether the seller's 75-cent copy of Carolyn Davidson's Harlequin romance "The Midwife" is a paperback or hardcover. Half.com forwarded the question to the seller, who now is writing back to say it's a paperback.

Mr. Ryan sends two e-mails: one to the buyer, answering his question, and one to the seller, thanking him for the information.

12:10 PM Lunch. Mr. Ryan eats his turkey wrap in the company cafeteria with some colleagues and heads back to his desk by 1 p.m.

1:06 PM E-mail from a user who can't find the new Stephen King novel on Half.com. The site is supposed to list all new books from major publishers, even if no one is selling them. That

way, if a user is interested, he or she can put it on a wish list and the site will automatically e-mail him or her when a copy has been posted for sale.

Mr. Ryan searches for the book meticulously, checking by title, author and publisher's ISBN number. Once he's sure the book isn't listed, he e-mails Matt Walsh, who is in charge of fixing catalog errors. Mr. Ryan then e-mails the user and instructs him to check back at the site soon.

1:21 PM First phone call of the day. Because Half.com prefers to conduct customer service on e-mail, to keep its costs down, it doesn't display its phone number on its Web site. Still, persistent users get the number through directory assistance or other sources.

This caller, an agitated buyer of the video "Valley Girl," a 1983 comedy starring Nicolas Cage, says she received a damaged tape. She has lodged an official complaint against the seller on the Web site, but the seller hasn't responded. Mr. Ryan tells her that the five days the seller has to respond aren't up yet. He assures her that if the seller doesn't respond within the allotted time, he will refund her money and charge the seller's account. Until then, there's nothing Mr. Ryan can do except comfort the caller with apologies and explanations.

In the event that the seller disputes the buyer's claim about the tape, Half.com is still likely to grant a refund, especially on such an inexpensive item. Half.com makes it clear, however, that its customer-service team keeps a close watch on users' complaints, looking out for fraudulent refund requests. If Half.com suspects foul play, it doesn't grant refunds so easily.

2:02 PM A seller of the video "I Know What You Did Last Summer" got the package returned, marked address unknown. Mr. Ryan looks up the buyer's information in the user database and e-mails him, asking for an updated address to forward to the seller. He then e-mails the seller, telling him the address should be on its way shortly.

2:21 PM He downloads 10 more e-mails.

HOME STRETCH

2:30 PM The day is starting to get long, at least to an observer. But Mr. Ryan says sitting still all day doesn't cramp his style. "Sometimes it's tough to work at a desk, but it doesn't really bother me," he says. "I work out after work, and that really loosens things up."

3 PM Bathroom break.

3:15 PM With the clock ticking toward quitting time, Mr. Ryan hunkers down to finish his last batch of e-mails. It's more of the same: a user unsure how Half.com works; a seller who wants to list a 1976 edition of "The Grapes of Wrath" but can't figure out where to put it on the site; a buyer who wants a book shipped second-day air, even though the order was already placed.

3:30 PM A call from a buyer interrupts Mr. Ryan's streak of dispensing e-mails. The buyer felt the quality of a book she bought was not up to snuff. The book, a $2 copy of Danielle Steel's "Secrets," apparently had a torn cover.

The buyer is upset, but Mr. Ryan remains calm, calling on skills he learned in a one-day seminar called "Dealing With Difficult People." In the class, which he took before coming to Half.com, he learned to paraphrase what the customer is saying to make sure he understands the complaint. Mr. Ryan also takes care to speak clearly with a strong sense of empathy. At one point he says, "I understand your frustration." When he explains that the buyer will have to wait some time for a final resolution of the matter, he makes sure to preface it with a heartfelt "I'm sorry to let you know . . ." An observer listening to Mr. Ryan gets the sense that he is not acting.

"If you don't understand what they are saying, then you have a problem," he says. Though he can't satisfy this customer then and there, he promises to talk to his supervisor and to call her back tomorrow with more information.

4 PM The day is done. Mr. Ryan finishes his last e-mail, closes up his desk and shoves on home. A new shift of workers picks up where Mr. Ryan left off, toiling from 4 p.m. to 12 a.m. When they finish, the customer-service staff in eBay's facility in Salt Lake City will take over. Tomorrow, Mr. Ryan will be back on duty at 8 a.m., downloading his first 10 e-mails.

Source: Alex Frangos, *The Wall Street Journal*, July 16, 2001.

Summary

Encouraging employee behaviors that help achieve an organization's objectives and fostering a sense of fairness among employees are two hallmarks of a useful internal pay structure. One of the first strategic pay decisions is how much to align a pay structure internally compared to aligning it to external market forces. Do not be misled. The issue is *not* achieving internal alignment versus alignment with external market forces. Rather, the strategic decision focuses on sustaining the optimal balance of internally aligned and externally responsive pay structures that helps the organization achieve its mission. *Both are required.* This part of the book focuses on one of the first decisions managers face in designing pay systems: how much to emphasize pay structures that are internally aligned with the work performed, the organization's structure, and its strategies. Whatever the choice, the decision needs to support (and be supported by) the organization's overall human resource strategy.

Next, managers must decide whether job and/or individual employee characteristics will be the basic unit of analysis supporting the pay structure. This is followed by deciding what data will be collected, what method(s) will be used to collect the information, and who should be involved in the process.

A key test of an effective and fair pay structure is acceptance of results by managers and employees. The best way to ensure acceptance of job analysis results is to involve employees as well as supervisors in the process. At the minimum, all employees should be informed of the purpose and progress of the activity.

If almost everyone agrees about the importance of job analysis, does that mean everyone does it? Of course not. Unfortunately, job analysis can be tedious and time-consuming. Often the job is given to newly hired compensation analysts, ostensibly to help them learn the organization, but perhaps there's also a hint of "rites of passage" in such assignments.

Alternatives to job-based structures such as **skill-based** or **competency-based systems** are being experimented with in many firms. The premise is that basing structures on these other criteria will encourage employees to become more flexible, and thus fewer workers will be required for the same level of output. This may be the argument, but as experience increases with the alternatives, managers are discovering that they can be as time consuming and bureaucratic as job analysis. Bear in mind, job content remains the conventional criterion for structures.

Review Questions

1. Job analysis has been considered the cornerstone of human resource management. Precisely how does it support managers making pay decisions?
2. What does job analysis have to do with internal alignment?
3. Describe the major decisions involved in job analysis.
4. Distinguish between task data and behavioral data.
5. What is the critical advantage of quantitative approaches over conventional approaches to job analysis?
6. How would you decide whether to use job-based or person-based structures?
7. Why do many managers say that job analysis is a colossal waste of their time and the time of their employees? Are they right?

Endnotes

1. Stanley Bing, *100 Bullshit Jobs . . . And How to Get Them* (New York: HarperColllins, 2006); Justin Racz, *50 Jobs Worse Than Yours* (New York: Bloomsbury, 2004). Our personal favorite is the ride operator at the "It's a Small World" ride at Disney.
2. Robert J. Grossman, "IBM's HR takes a risk," *HR Magazine*, April 2007.
3. Michael T. Brannick, Edward L. Levine, Frederick P. Morgeson, *Job and Work Analysis: Methods, Research, and Applications for Human Resource Management*, 2nd edition (Los Angeles: Sage, 2007).
4. E. J. McCormick, "Job and Task Analysis," in M. D. Dunnette, ed., *Handbook of Industrial and Organizational Psychology* (Chicago: Rand McNally, 1976), pp. 651–696; Robert J. Harvey, "Job Analysis," in M. D. Dunnette and L. Hough, eds., *Handbook of Industrial*

and Organizational Psychology, Vol. 2 (Palo Alto, CA: Consulting Psychologists Press, 1991), pp. 72–157.

5. Particularly valuable sources of information on job analysis definitions and methods are U.S. Department of Labor, Manpower Administration, *Revised Handbook for Analyzing Jobs* (Washington, DC: U.S. Government Printing Office, 1992); Robert J. Harvey, "Job Analysis," in M. D. Dunnette and L. Hough, eds., *Handbook of Industrial and Organizational Psychology,* Vol. 2, (Palo Alto, CA: Consulting Psychologists Press, 1991), pp. 72–157; Brenda Lister, *Evaluating Job Content* (Scottsdale, AZ: WorldatWork, 2006).

6. Wayne Cascio, "Strategies for Responsible Restructuring," *Academy of Management Executive* 19(4) (2005), pp. 39–50; Janet Marler, Melissa Barringer, and George Milkovich, "Boundaryless and Traditional Contingent Employees: Worlds Apart," *Journal of Organizational Behavior* 23 (2002), pp. 425–453.

7. Paul C. Light, *The True Size of Government* (Washington, DC: Brookings Institute, 1999); Candice Prendergast, "The Role of Promotion in Inducing Specific Human Capital Acquisition," *Quarterly Journal of Economics* (May 1993), pp. 523–534.

8. Dan Neil, "All Rays Lead to Pasadena," *Los Angeles Times,* February 5, 2006.

9. Much of the developmental work and early applications of the PAQ was done in the 1960s and 1970s. See, for example, E. J. McCormick, "Job and Task Analysis," in M. D. Dunnette, ed., *Handbook of Industrial and Organizational Psychology* (Chicago: Rand McNally, 1976), pp. 651–696; E. J. McCormick et al., "A Study of Job Characteristics and Job Dimensions As Based on the Position Analysis Questionnaire," Occupational Research Center, Purdue University, West Lafayette, IN, 1969. The PAQ is distributed by PAQ Services, *www.paq.com;* see PAQ's Web site and newsletters for recent discussions.

10. Thomas H. Davenport, "The Coming Commoditization of Processes," *Harvard Business Review,* June 2005, p. 101–108.

11. *Benefits Compliance: An Overview for the HR Professional* (Scottsdale, AZ: WorldatWork, 2006).

12. V. L. Huber and S. R. Crandall, "Job Measurement: A Social-Cognitive Decision Perspective," in Gerald R. Ferris, ed., *Research in Personnel and Human Resources Management,* Vol. 12, (Greenwich, CT: JAI Press, 1994), pp. 223–269; Juan I. Sanchez, I. Prager, A. Wilson, and C. Viswesvaran, "Understanding Within-Job Title Variance in Job-Analytic Ratings," *Journal of Business and Psychology* 12 (1998), pp. 407–419.

13. Susanne Craig, "E*Trade Lowers Corporate Titles, In Move That Could Spur Departures," *The Wall Street Journal,* September 6, 2001, pp. C1, C14.

14. Theresa M. Glomb, John D. Kammeyer-Mueller, and Maria Rotundo, "Emotional Labor Demands and Compensating Wage Differentials," *Journal of Applied Psychology* 89(4) (2004), pp. 700–714; Juan I. Sanchez and Edward L. Levine, "Is Job Analysis Dead, Misunderstood, or Both? New Forms of Work Analysis and Design," in A. I. Kraut and A. K. Korman, eds., *Evolving Practices in Human Resource Management: Responses to a Changing World of Work* (San Francisco: Jossey-Bass, 1999), pp. 43–68.

15. R. Reiter-Palmon, M. Brown, D. Sandall, C. Buboltz, and T. Nimps, "Development of an O*NET Web-Based Job Analysis and Its Implementation in the U.S. Navy: Lessons Learned," *Human Resources Management Review* 16 (2006) pp. 294–309.

16. Towers Perrin has done a lot of research on this issue. See its Web site at *www.towers.com;* "Joint Compensation Study: Technical Occupational Analysis Questionnaire," Control Data Business Advisors, Minneapolis, 1985.

17. Juan I. Sanchez and Edward L. Levine, "Accuracy or Consequential Validity: Which Is the Better Standard for Job Analysis Data?" *Journal of Organizational Behavior* 21 (2000), pp. 809–818; W. C. Borman, D. Dorsey, and L. Ackerman, "Time-Spent Responses and

Time Allocation Strategies: Relations with Sales Performance in a Stockbroker Sample," *Personnel Psychology* 45 (1992), pp. 763–777.

18. Richard Arvey, Emily M. Passino, and John W. Lounsbury, "Job Analysis Results as Influenced by Sex of Incumbent and Sex of Analyst," *Journal of Applied Psychology* 62(4) (1977), pp. 411–416.

19. V. L. Huber and S. R. Crandall, "Job Measurement: A Social-Cognitive Decision Perspective," in Gerald R. Ferris, ed., *Research in Personnel and Human Resources Management,* Vol. 12 (Greenwich, CT: JAI Press, 1994), pp. 223–269.

20. David Levine, Dale Belman, Gary Charness, Erica Groshen, and K. C. O'Shaughnessy, *Changes in Careers and Wage Structures at Large American Employers* (Kalamazoo, MI: Upjohn Institute, 2003).

21. See commentary by Charlie Fay in "The Future of Salary Management," *Compensation and Benefits Review,* July/August 2001, p. 10.

22. Allen I. Kraut, Patricia R. Pedigo, D. Douglas McKenna, and Marvin D. Dunnette, "The Role of the Manager: What's Really Important in Different Management Jobs," *Academy of Management Executive* 19(4) (2005), pp. 122–129; Lee Dyer and Richard A. Shafer, "From HR Strategy to Organizational Effectiveness," in Patrick M. Wright, Lee D. Dyer, John W. Boudreau, and George T. Milkovich, eds., *Strategic Human Resources Management in the Twenty-First Century,* Suppl. 4, (Stamford, CT: JAI Press, 1999).

23. S. Steven Gray, "Coffee on the Double," *The Wall Street Journal,* April 12, 2005, pp. B1–B7; Kenneth H. Doerr, Tali Freed, Terence Mitchell, Chester Schriesheim, and Xiaohua (Tracy) Zhou, "Work Flow Policy and Within-Worker and Between-Workers Variability in Performance," *Journal of Applied Psychology* (October 2004), pp. 911–921.

24. Paul Taylor, Wen-Dong Li, Kan Shi, and Walter Borman, "The Transportability of Job Information Across Countries," *Personnel Psychology* 61 (2008), pp. 69–111.

25. Juan I. Sanchez and E. L. Levine, "The Impact of Raters' Cognition on Judgment Accuracy: An Extension to the Job Analysis Domain," *Journal of Business and Psychology* 9 (1994), pp. 47–57; Juan I. Sanchez and Edward L. Levine, "Accuracy or Consequential Validity: Which Is the Better Standard for Job Analysis Data?" *Journal of Organizational Behavior* 21 (2000), pp. 809–818; Frederick P. Morgeson and Michael A. Campion, "Accuracy in Job Analysis: Toward an Inference-Based Model," *Journal of Organizational Behavior* 21 (2000) pp. 819–827; Erich Dierdorff and Mark Wilson, "A Meta-Analysis of Job Analysis Reliability," *Journal of Applied Psychology* (August 2003), pp. 635–646.

26. Erich C. Dierdorff and Frederick Morgeson, "Consensus in Role Requirements: The Influence of Discrete Occupational Context on Role Expectations," *Journal of Applied Psychology* 92 (2007), pp. 1228–1241.

27. Richard Arvey, Emily M. Passino, and John W. Lounsbury, "Job Analysis Results as Influenced by Sex of Incumbent and Sex of Analyst," *Journal of Applied Psychology* 62(4) (1977), pp. 411–416; Sara L. Rynes, Caroline L. Weber, and George T. Milkovich, "Effects of Market Survey Rates, Job Evaluation, and Job Gender on Job Pay," *Journal of Applied Psychology* 74(1) (1989), pp. 114–123.

28. Filip Lievens and Juan I. Sanchez, "Can Training Improve the Quality of Inferences Made by Raters in Competency Modeling? A Quasi-Experiment," *Journal of Applied Psychology* 92 (2008), pp. 812–819.

29. Juan I. Sanchez and E. L. Levine, "The Impact of Raters' Cognition on Judgment Accuracy: An Extension to the Job Analysis Domain," *Journal of Business and Psychology* 9 (1994), pp. 47–57; Juan I. Sanchez and Edward L. Levine, "Accuracy or Consequential

Validity: Which Is the Better Standard for Job Analysis Data?" *Journal of Organizational Behavior* 21 (2000), pp. 809–818; Frederick P. Morgeson and Michael A. Campion, "Accuracy in Job Analysis: Toward an Inference-Based Model," *Journal of Organizational Behavior* 21 (2000), pp. 819–827.

30. E. M. Ramras, "Discussion," in *Proceedings of Division of Military Psychology Symposium: Collecting, Analyzing, and Reporting Information Describing Jobs and Occupations,* 77th Annual Convention of the American Psychological Association, Lackland Air Force Base, TX, September 1969, pp. 75–76; Tony Simons and Quinetta Roberson, "Why Managers Should Care About Fairness: The Effects of Aggregate Justice Perceptions on Organizational Outcomes," *Journal of Applied Psychology* (June 2003), pp. 432–443.

31. World at Work, "Job Evaluation and Market-Pricing Practices," *http://www.worldatwork. org/waw/adimLink?id=31378,* 2009.

32. P. Bobko, P. L. Roth, M. A. Buster, "A Systematic Approach for Assessing the Currency ('Up-To-Dateness') of Job-Analytic Information," *Public Personnel Management* 37 (2008), pp. 261–277.

33. Edward L. Levine, Ronald A. Ash, Hardy Hall, and Frank Sistrunk, "Evaluation of Job Analysis Methods by Experienced Job Analysts," *Academy of Management Journal* 26(2) (1983), pp. 339–348.

34. M. D. Dunnette, L. M. Hough, and R. L. Rosse, "Task and Job Taxonomies as a Basis for Identifying Labor Supply Sources and Evaluating Employment Qualifications," in George T. Milkovich and Lee Dyer, eds., *Affirmative Action Planning* (New York: Human Resource Planning Society, 1979), pp. 37–51.

Job-Based Structures and Job Evaluation

Chapter Outline

Job-Based Structures: Job Evaluation

Defining Job Evaluation: Content, Value, and External Market Links
- *Content and Value*
- *Linking Content With the External Market*
- *"Measure for Measure" Versus "Much Ado About Nothing"*

"How-to": Major Decisions
- *Establish the Purpose*
- *Single Versus Multiple Plans*
- *Choose Among Job Evaluation Methods*

Job Evaluation Methods
- *Ranking*
- *Classification*
- *Point Method*

Who Should Be Involved?
- *The Design Process Matters*

The Final Result: Structure

Balancing Chaos and Control

Your Turn: Job Evaluation at Whole Foods

As soon as my daughter turned 14, she absolutely refused to go shopping with me. At first I thought it was because I like to hum along with the mall music. But she says it is because I embarrass her when I interrogate assistant store managers about how they are paid—more precisely, how their pay compares to that of the stock clerks, managers, and regional managers in the same company. My daughter claims I do this everywhere I go. *Compensationitis,* she calls it. And I know it's contagious, because a colleague grills his seatmates on airplanes. He's learned the pay rates for American Airlines captains who pilot Boeing 737s versus those who pilot the A330 Airbus.

How does any organization go about valuing work? The next time you go to the supermarket, check out the different types of work there: store manager, produce manager, front-end manager, deli workers, butchers, stock clerks, checkout people, bakers—the list is long, and the work surprisingly diverse. If you managed a supermarket, how would you value work? But be careful—*compensationitis* is contagious, and it can embarrass your friends.

This chapter and the next one discuss techniques used to value work. Both chapters focus on "how-to"—the specific steps involved. Job evaluation techniques are discussed in this chapter. Person-based techniques, both skill-based and competency-based, are discussed in Chapter 6. All these techniques are used to design pay structures that will influence employee behavior and help the organization sustain its competitive advantage.

JOB-BASED STRUCTURES: JOB EVALUATION

Exhibit 5.1 is a variation on Exhibit 4.1 in the previous chapter. It orients us to the process used to build a job-based internal structure. Our job analysis and job descriptions (Chapter 4) collected and summarized work information. In this chapter, the focus is on what to value in the jobs, how to assess that value, and how to translate it into a **job-based structure.** Job evaluation is a process for determining **relative value.**

> **Job evaluation** is the process of systematically determining the relative worth of jobs to create a job structure for the organization. The evaluation is based on a combination of job content, skills required, value to the organization,

EXHIBIT 5.1   **Many Ways to Create Internal Structure**

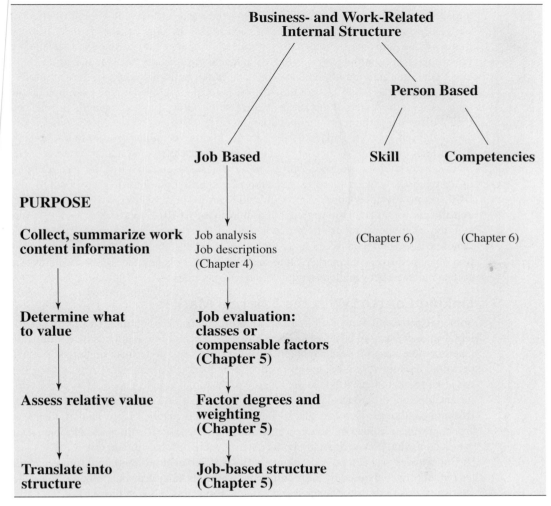

organizational culture, and the external market. This potential to blend organizational forces and external market forces is both a strength and a challenge of job evaluation.

DEFINING JOB EVALUATION: CONTENT, VALUE, AND EXTERNAL MARKET LINKS

Content and Value

We noted in Chapter 3 that **content** refers to what work is performed and how it gets done. Perspectives differ on whether job evaluation is based on **job content** or job value. Internal alignment based on content orders jobs on the basis of the skills required for the jobs and the duties and responsibilities associated with the jobs. A structure based on job value orders jobs on the basis of the relative contribution of the skills, duties, and responsibilities of each job to the organization's goals. But can this structure translate directly into pay rates, without regard to the external market, government regulations, or any individual negotiation process? Most people think not. Recall that internal alignment is just one of the building blocks of the pay model. Job content matters, but it is not the only basis for pay. Job value may also include the job's value in the external market (*exchange value*). Plus, pay rates may be influenced by collective bargaining or other negotiations.

In addition, the value added by the same work may be more (or less) in one organization than in another. We observed in Chapter 3 that the value added by consultants in Pricewaterhouse, where earnings were generated directly by consultants, may differ from the value added by the same consultants now that they are merged into IBM, where revenues come through a wide variety of services. At Pricewaterhouse, consultants were critical to organization objectives. At IBM, they are less so. As a result, those who remain with IBM may have their base pay frozen but are getting larger bonuses. So, while we talk about internal job value based on contributions to organization objectives, external market value may differ. There is not necessarily a one-to-one correspondence between internal job value and pay rates.

Linking Content With the External Market

Some see job evaluation as a process for linking job content and internal value with external market rates. Aspects of job content (e.g., skills required and customer contacts) take on value based on their relationship to market wages. Because higher skill levels or willingness to work more closely with customers usually commands higher wages in the labor market, then skill level and nature of customer contacts become useful criteria for establishing differences among jobs. If some aspect of job content, such as stressful working conditions, is not related to wages paid in the external labor market, then that aspect may be excluded in the job evaluation. In this perspective, the value of job content is based on what it can command in the external market; it has no intrinsic value.[1]

But not everyone agrees. A developer of the **Hay job evaluation system** (probably still the plan most widely used by large corporations) claims that job evaluation establishes the relative value of jobs based on their content, independent of a link to the market.

EXHIBIT 5.2
Assumptions
Underlying
Different
Views of Job
Evaluation

Aspect of Job Evaluation	Assumption
Assessment of job content	Content has intrinsic value outside external market.
Assessment of relative value	Stakeholders can reach consensus on value.
External market link	Value cannot be determined without external market.
Measurement	Honing instruments will provide objective measures.
Negotiation	Negotiating brings rationality to a social/political process; establishes rules of the game and invites participation.

"Measure for Measure" Versus "Much Ado About Nothing"

Researchers, too, have their own perspective on job evaluation. Some say that if job evaluation takes on the trappings of measurement (objective, numerical, generalizable, documented, and reliable), then it can be judged according to technical standards. Just as with employment tests, the reliability, validity, and usefulness of job evaluation plans can be compared.

As you might expect, those actually making pay decisions hold different views. They see job evaluation as a process that helps gain acceptance of pay differences among jobs—an administrative procedure through which the parties become involved and committed. Its statistical validity is not an issue. Its usefulness is that it provides a framework for give-and-take—an exchange of views. Employees, union representatives, and managers haggle over "the rules of the game" for determining the relative value of work. If all participants agree that skills, effort, responsibilities, and working conditions are important, then work is evaluated based on these factors. As in sports and games, we are more willing to accept the results if we accept the rules and believe they are applied fairly.[2] This interpretation is consistent with the history of job evaluation, which began as a way to bring peace and order to an often-chaotic and dispute-riven wage-setting process between labor and management.[3]

Exhibit 5.2 summarizes the assumptions that underlie the perspectives on job evaluation. Some say the content of jobs has intrinsic value that the evaluation will uncover; others say the only fair measure of job value is found in the external market. Some say contemporary job evaluation practices are just and fair; others say they are just fair. "Beneath the superficial orderliness of job evaluation techniques and findings, there is much that smacks of chaos."[4] We try to capture all these perspectives in this chapter.

"HOW-TO": MAJOR DECISIONS

Exhibit 5.3 shows job evaluation's role in determining the internal structure. You already know that the process begins with job analysis, in which the information on jobs is collected, and that job descriptions summarize the information and serve as input for the evaluation. The exhibit calls out some of the major decisions in the job evaluation process. They are (1) establish the purpose(s), (2) decide on single versus multiple plans, (3) choose among alternative methods, (4) obtain involvement of relevant stakeholders, and (5) evaluate the usefulness of the results.

EXHIBIT 5.3
Determining
an Internally
Aligned Job
Structure

**Internal Alignment: Work Relationships Within the
Organization** → **Job Analysis** → **Job Description** → **Job Evaluation** →
Job Structure

Some Major Decisions in Job Evaluation

- Establish purpose of evaluation.
- Decide whether to use single or multiple plans.
- Choose among alternative approaches.
- Obtain involvement of relevant stakeholders.
- Evaluate plan's usefulness.

Establish the Purpose

Job evaluation is part of the process for establishing an internally aligned pay structure. Recall from Chapter 2 that a structure is aligned if it supports the organization strategy, fits the work flow, is fair to employees, and motivates their behavior toward organization objectives.

- *Supports organization strategy:* Job evaluation aligns with the organization's strategy by including what it is about work that adds value—that contributes to pursuing the organization's strategy and achieving its objectives. Job evaluation helps answer, How does this job add value?[5]

- *Supports work flow:* Job evaluation supports work flow in two ways. It integrates each job's pay with its relative contributions to the organization, and it helps set pay for new, unique, or changing jobs.

- *Is fair to employees:* Job evaluation can reduce disputes and grievances over pay differences among jobs by establishing a workable, agreed-upon structure that reduces the role of chance, favoritism, and bias in setting pay.

- *Motivates behavior toward organization objectives:* Job evaluation calls out to employees what it is about their work that the organization values, what supports the organization's strategy and its success. It can also help employees adapt to organization changes by improving their understanding of what is valued in their new assignments and why that value may have changed. Thus, job evaluation helps create the network of rewards (promotions, challenging work) that motivates employees.

If the purpose of the evaluation is not called out, it becomes too easy to get lost in complex procedures, negotiations, and bureaucracy. The job evaluation process becomes the end in itself instead of a way to achieve an objective. Establishing its purpose can help ensure that the evaluation actually is a useful systematic process.

Single Versus Multiple Plans

Rarely do employers evaluate all jobs in the organization at one time. More typically, a related group of jobs, for example, manufacturing, technical, or administrative, will be the focus. As we saw in Chapter 3, for example, Northrup Grumman has four different structures. Many employers design different evaluation plans for different types of work. They do so because they believe that the work content is too diverse to be usefully evaluated by one plan. For example, production jobs may vary in terms of manipulative skills, knowledge of statistical quality control, and working conditions. But these tasks and skills may not be relevant to engineering and finance jobs. Rather, the nature of the contacts with customers may be relevant. Consequently, a single, universal plan may not be acceptable to employees or useful to managers if the work covered is highly diverse. Even so, there are some plans that have been successfully applied across a wide breadth and depth of work. The most prominent examples include the Hay plan (more on this later) and the **position analysis questionnaire** (discussed in Chapter 4).

Benchmark Jobs—A Sample

To be sure that all relevant aspects of work are included in the evaluation, an organization may start with a sample of **benchmark (key) jobs.** In Exhibit 5.4, benchmark jobs would be identified for as many of the levels in the structure and groups of related jobs (administrative, manufacturing, technical) as possible. The heavy shading in the exhibit marks the benchmark jobs.

A benchmark job has the following characteristics:

- Its contents are well known and relatively stable over time.
- The job is common across a number of different employers. It is not unique to a particular employer.
- A reasonable proportion of the work force is employed in this job.

A representative sample of benchmark jobs will include the entire domain of work being evaluated—administrative, manufacturing, technical, and so on—and capture the diversity of the work within that domain.

EXHIBIT 5.4 **Benchmark Jobs**

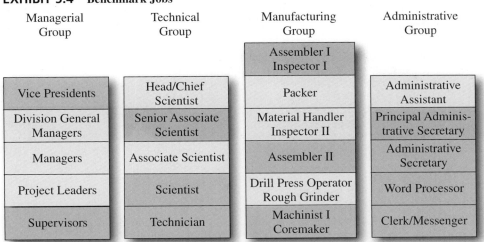

Managerial Group	Technical Group	Manufacturing Group	Administrative Group
		Assembler I / Inspector I	
Vice Presidents	Head/Chief Scientist	Packer	Administrative Assistant
Division General Managers	Senior Associate Scientist	Material Handler / Inspector II	Principal Administrative Secretary
Managers	Associate Scientist	Assembler II	Administrative Secretary
Project Leaders	Scientist	Drill Press Operator / Rough Grinder	Word Processor
Supervisors	Technician	Machinist I / Coremaker	Clerk/Messenger

Note: More heavily shaded jobs have been selected as benchmarks.

Diversity in the work can be thought of in terms of depth (vertically) and breadth (horizontally). The *depth of work* in most organizations probably ranges from strategic leadership jobs (CEOs, general directors) to the filing and mail distribution tasks in entry-level office jobs. Horizontally, the *breadth of work* depends on the nature of business. Relatively similar work can be found in specialty consulting firms (e.g., compensation or executive search firms). The breadth of work performed in some multinational conglomerates such as General Electric mirrors the occupations in the entire nation. GE includes jobs in businesses spanning financial services, entertainment (NBC), aircraft engines, medical instruments, power systems, and home appliances.

Typically, a job evaluation plan is developed using benchmark jobs, and then the plan is applied to the remaining nonbenchmark jobs. Selecting benchmark jobs from each level ensures coverage of the entire work domain, thus helping to ensure the accuracy of the decisions based on the job evaluation.

The number of job evaluation plans used hinges on how detailed an evaluation is required to make pay decisions and how much it will cost. There is no ready answer to the question of "one plan versus many." Current practice (not always the best answer for the future, since practice is based on the past) is to use separate plans for major domains of work: top-executive/leadership jobs, managerial/professional jobs, operational/technical jobs, and office/administrative jobs. Open the door on some organizations and you will find additional plans for sales, legal, engineers/scientists, and skilled trades.

The costs associated with all these plans (including time) give impetus to the push to simplify job structures (reduce titles and levels). Some employers, notably Hewlett-Packard, simplify by using a single plan with a core set of common factors for all jobs and additional factors specific to particular occupational or functional areas (finance, manufacturing, software and systems, sales).

Choose Among Job Evaluation Methods

Ranking, classification, and **point method** are the most common job evaluation methods, though uncounted variations exist. Research over 40 years consistently finds that different job evaluation plans generate different pay structures. So the method you choose matters.

Exhibit 5.5 compares the methods. They all begin by assuming that a useful job analysis has been translated into job descriptions methods.

EXHIBIT 5.5
Comparison of Job Evaluation Methods

	Advantage	Disadvantage
Ranking	Fast, simple, easy to explain.	Cumbersome as number of jobs increases. Basis for comparisons is not called out.
Classification	Can group a wide range of work together in one system.	Descriptions may leave too much room for manipulation.
Point	Compensable factors call out basis for comparisons. Compensable factors communicate what is valued.	Can become bureaucratic and rule-bound.

JOB EVALUATION METHODS

A survey of roughly 1,000 members of WorldatWork, the association for compensation professionals, asked the primary job evaluation method used in their organizations. As Exhibit 5.6 indicates, the most common response was—"Well, not really any job evaluation method." Rather, **market pricing** was overwhelmingly chosen (67 to 75%, depending on the job level) as the primary method of job evaluation. What is market pricing? We will return to this topic in more detail later, especially in Chapter 8. For now, think of market pricing as directly matching as many of your own organization's jobs as possible to jobs described in the external pay surveys you use. To the extent that such matches can be made, the pay rate for your job will be based on the survey data. Internal equity is greatly de-emphasized (as is the organization's strategy—more on this in Chapter 8).

Note that Exhibit 5.6 does indicate that somewhere between 1 in 3 and 1 in 4 organizations continue to use traditional job evaluation approaches as their *primary* methods. Further, it is likely that job evaluation is also used widely even in organizations that rely primarily on market pricing because it is usually not possible to directly match all jobs to market survey jobs. Thus, job evaluation is still needed and we now discuss three job evaluation methods, with most of our attention given to point or point factor approaches.

Ranking

Ranking simply orders the job descriptions from highest to lowest based on a global definition of relative value or contribution to the organization's success. Ranking is simple, fast, and easy to understand and explain to employees; it is also the least expensive method, at least initially. However, it can create problems that require difficult and potentially expensive solutions because it doesn't tell employees and managers what it is about their jobs that is important.

Two ways of ranking are common: **alternation ranking** and **paired comparison.** *Alternation ranking* orders job descriptions alternately at each extreme. Agreement is reached among evaluators on which jobs are the most and least valuable (i.e., which is a 10, which is a 1), then the next most and least valued (i.e., which is a 9, which is a 2), and so on, until all the jobs have been ordered. The *paired comparison* method uses a matrix to compare all possible pairs of jobs. Exhibit 5.7 shows that the higher-ranked job is entered in the cell of the matrix. When all comparisons have been completed, the job most frequently judged "more valuable" becomes the highest-ranked job, and so on.

EXHIBIT 5.6
Primary
Method of Job
Evaluation

Source: WorldatWork,
"Job Evaluation and
Market-Princing
Practices," February
2009.

	What is the *primary* method of job evaluation used by your organization?		
	Market Pricing	**Point Factor**	**All Other**
Senior Management	75%	14%	11%
Middle Management	70%	18%	12%
Professional	69%	18%	13%
Sales	72%	16%	12%
Administrative	67%	19%	14%
Production	68%	17%	15%

Note: "All Other" includes ranking, paired-comparison, and job component methods. Number of respondents ranged from 947 to 1,120 organizations.

EXHIBIT 5.7
Paired Comparison Ranking

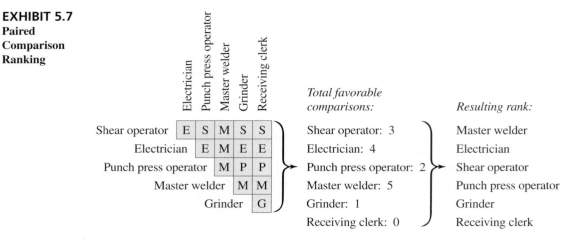

Alternation-ranking and paired-comparison methods may be more reliable (produce similar results consistently) than simple ranking. Nevertheless, ranking has drawbacks. The criteria on which the jobs are ranked are usually so poorly defined, if they are specified at all, that the evaluations become subjective opinions that are impossible to justify in strategic and work-related terms. Further, evaluators using this method must be knowledgeable about every single job under study. The numbers alone turn what should be a simple task into a formidable one—50 jobs require 1,225 comparisons—and as organizations change, it is difficult to remain knowledgeable about all jobs. Some organizations try to overcome this difficulty by ranking jobs within single departments and merging the results. However, even though the ranking appears simple, fast, and inexpensive, in the long run the results are difficult to defend and costly solutions may be required to overcome the problems created.

Classification

Picture a bookcase with many shelves. Each shelf is labeled with a paragraph describing the kinds of books on that shelf and, perhaps, one or two representative titles. This same approach describes the **classification method of job evaluation.** A series of classes covers the range of jobs. Class descriptions are the labels. A job description is compared to the class descriptions to decide which class is the best fit for that job. Each class is described in such a way that the "label" captures sufficient work detail yet is general enough to cause little difficulty in slotting a job description onto its appropriate "shelf" or class. The classes may be described further by including titles of benchmark jobs that fall into each class.

Determining the number of classes and writing class descriptions to define the boundaries between each class (e.g., how many bookshelves and what distinguishes each from the other—fiction, nonfiction, mysteries, biographies, etc.) are something of an art form. One way to begin is to find the natural breaks or changes in the work content. At Lockheed, the engineering work discussed in previous chapters has obvious natural breaks between engineers (individual contributors) and lead engineers (responsible for overall projects). But how many classes within each of these make sense? Exhibit 5.8

EXHIBIT 5.8 Classifications for Engineering Work Used by Clark Consulting

137

Engineer 1	Engineer 2	Engineer 3	Engineer 4	Engineer 5	Eng Mgr 1	Eng Mgr 2	Eng Mgr 3
Participates in development, testing, and documentation of software programs. Performs design and analysis tasks as a project team member. Typical minimum requirements are a bachelor's degree in a scientific or technical field or the equivalent and up to two years of experience.	Develops, tests, and documents software programs of a more difficult nature. Assists in the development of assignments and schedules. Typical minimum requirements are a bachelor's degree in a scientific or technical field and two years to four years of experience or a master's degree and up to two years of experience.	Develops project plans, functional specifications, and schedules. Designs and performs analysis on complex programs and systems. Assists in determining product needs and enhancements. Typical minimum requirements are a bachelor's degree in engineering, computer science, or related technical field and four to six years of experience or a master's degree and two to four years of experience.	Acts as project engineer for complex programs in design, development, and analysis. Proposes new ideas and products and guides their implementation. Provides technical direction in area of specialty on major products. Typical minimum requirements are a bachelor's degree in engineering, computer science, or a related technical field and six or more years of experience or a master's degree and four to six years of experience.	Provides technical direction and advice to management in long-range planning for new areas of technological research. Designs, researches, and develops new systems while providing guidance to support staff. Typical minimum requirements are a bachelor's degree in engineering, computer science, or a related technical field and ten or more years of experience or a master's degree and six years or more of experience.	Supervises the design and development of software products or systems and related schedules and costs. Participates in developing management policies for software group. Typically manages up to 10 employees performing similar tasks. First level of management with human resource responsibilities.	Establishes work environment for development or implementation of complete products and programs. Develops long-range plans, schedules, and cost objectives. Typically manages 10 to 25 employees, including first-level managers. (May be from multiple disciplines.)	Develops long-range strategy for a product family including positioning, marketing, and pricing. Manages engineering product group to ensure timely delivery of high-quality products. Typically manages over 25 employees from multiple disciplines.

Source: 2008 Clark Consulting. All Rights Reserved.

shows classifications used by Clark Consulting to conduct salary surveys of engineering salaries at many different employers. Managerial work includes three classes, while there are five classes of individual contributors. Information to guide the writing of class descriptions can come from managers, job incumbents, job descriptions, and career progression considerations.

Writing class descriptions can be troublesome when jobs from several job families are covered by a single plan. Although greater specificity of the class definition improves the reliability of evaluation, it also limits the variety of jobs that can easily be classified. For example, class definitions written with sales jobs in mind may make it difficult to slot office or administrative jobs and vice versa. Exhibit 5.9 gives some of the class definitions from the U.S. federal government's 15-class **General Schedule.** These classes correspond to 15 levels in the government's internal structure plus five more levels on the Executive Schedule. The vagueness of the descriptions seems to leave a lot of room for "judgment."[6] Including titles of benchmark jobs for each class helps make the descriptions more concrete.

EXHIBIT 5.9   Federal Government's Job Classification Method, General Schedule Descriptions

Grade-General Schedule 1 includes all classes of positions the duties of which are to be performed, under immediate supervision, with little or no latitude for the exercise of independent judgment (1) the simplest routine work in office, business, or fiscal operations, or (2) elementary work of a subordinate technical character in a professional, scientific, or technical field.

Grade-General Schedule 9 includes all classes of positions the duties of which are (1) to perform, under general supervision, very difficult and responsible work along lines requiring special technical, supervisory, or administrative experience which has (A) demonstrated capacity for sound independent work, (B) thorough and fundamental knowledge of a special and complex subject matter, or of the profession, art, or science involved, and (C) considerable latitude for the exercise of independent judgment; (2) with considerable latitude for the exercise of independent judgment, to perform moderately difficult and responsible work, requiring (A) professional, scientific, or technical training equivalent to that represented by graduation from a college or university of recognized standing, and (B) considerable additional professional, scientific, or technical training or experience which has demonstrated capacity for sound independent work; or (3) to perform other work of equal importance, difficulty, and responsibility, and requiring comparable qualifications.

Grade-General Schedule 13 includes all classes of positions the duties of which are (1) to perform, under administrative direction, with wide latitude for the exercise of independent judgment work of unusual difficulty and responsibility along special technical, supervisory, or administrative lines, requiring extended specialized, supervisory, or administrative training and experience which has demonstrated leadership and marked attainments; (2) to serve as assistant head of a major organization involving work of comparable level within a bureau; (3) to perform, under administrative direction, with wide latitude for the exercise of independent judgment, work of unusual difficulty and responsibility requiring extended professional, scientific, or technical training and experience which has demonstrated leadership and marked attainments in professional, scientific, or technical research, practice, or administration; or (4) to perform other work of equal importance, difficulty, and responsibility, and requiring comparable qualification.

Source: U.S. Office of Personnel Management (*www.opm.gov*).

In practice, with a classification method, the job descriptions not only are compared to the class descriptions and benchmark jobs but also can be compared to each other to be sure that jobs within each class are more similar to each other than to jobs in adjacent classes.

The end result is a job structure made up of a series of classes with a number of jobs in each. All these comparisons are used to ensure that this structure is based on the organization strategy and work flow, is fair, and focuses behaviors on desired results. The jobs within each class are considered to be equal (similar) work and will be paid equally. Jobs in different classes should be dissimilar and may have different pay rates.

The Wall Street Journal once compiled a list of the 10 most unusual U.S. government jobs. It included Smokey Bear's manager, a Supreme Court seamstress (job responsibility: keeping the Supremes in stitches), a gold stacker, condom tester, currency reconstructor, and Air Force art curator. The Office of Personnel Management publishes the complete General Schedule and Executive Schedule on its Web site (*www.opm.gov*). Visit the site to discover the level of detail in the government's approach. Contrast that with "Big Blue" (IBM), which puts its complete classification plan on a single page.

Point Method

Point methods have three common characteristics: (1) compensable factors, with (2) factor degrees numerically scaled, and (3) weights reflecting the relative importance of each factor.[7] Each job's relative value, and hence its location in the pay structure, is determined by the total points assigned to it.

Point plans are the most commonly used job evaluation approach in the United States and Europe. They represent a significant change from ranking and classification methods in that they make explicit the criteria for evaluating jobs: *compensable factors.*[8]

Compensable factors are based on the strategic direction of the business and how the work contributes to these objectives and strategy. The factors are scaled to reflect the degree to which they are present in each job and weighted to reflect their overall importance to the organization. Points are then attached to each **factor weight.** The total points for each job determine its position in the job structure.

There are six steps in the design of a point plan.

1. Conduct job analysis.
2. Determine compensable factors.
3. Scale the factors.
4. Weight the factors according to importance.
5. Communicate the plan and train users; prepare manual.
6. Apply to nonbenchmark jobs.

1. Conduct Job Analysis

Just as with ranking and classification, point plans begin with job analysis. Typically a representative sample of jobs, that is, benchmark jobs, is drawn for analysis. The content of these jobs is the basis for defining, **scaling,** and weighting the compensable factors.

2. Determine Compensable Factors

Compensable factors play a pivotal role in the point plan. These factors reflect how work adds value to the organization. They flow from the work itself and the strategic direction of the business.

> **Compensable factors** are those characteristics in the work that the organization values, that help it pursue its strategy and achieve its objectives.

To select compensable factors, an organization asks itself, What is it about the work that adds value? One company chose decision making as a compensable factor. As shown in Exhibit 5.10, the definition of *decision making* is three-dimensional: (1) the risk and complexity (hence the availability of guidelines to assist in making the decisions), (2) the impact of the decisions, and (3) the time that must pass before the impact is evident.

In effect, this firm determined that its competitive advantage depends on decisions employees make in their work. And the relative value of the decisions depends on their risk, their complexity, and their impact on the company. Hence, this firm is signaling to all employees that jobs will be valued based on the nature of the decisions required by employees in those jobs. Jobs that require riskier decisions with greater impact have a higher relative worth than jobs that require fewer decisions with less consequence.

To be useful, compensable factors should be

- Based on the strategy and values of the organization.
- Based on the work performed.
- Acceptable to the stakeholders affected by the resulting pay structure.

Based on the Strategy and Values of the Organization

The leadership of any organization is the best source of information on where the business should be going and how it is going to get there. Clearly, the leaders' input into factor selection is crucial. If the business strategy involves providing innovative, high-quality products and services designed in collaboration with customers and suppliers, then jobs with greater responsibilities for product innovation and customer contacts should be valued higher. Or if the business strategy is more Wal-Mart-like, "providing goods and services to delight customers at the lowest cost and greatest convenience possible," then compensable factors might include impact on **cost containment,** customer relations, and so on.

Compensable factors reinforce the organization's culture and values as well as its business direction and the nature of the work. If the direction changes, then the compensable factors may also change. For example, strategic plans at many companies call for increased globalization. Proctor & Gamble and 3M include a "multinational responsibilities" factor similar to the one in Exhibit 5.11 in their managerial job evaluation plan. In this example, multinational responsibilities are defined in terms of the type of responsibility, the percent of time devoted to international issues, and the number of countries covered. Do you suppose that managers at 3M or P&G got raises when Czechoslovakia, Yugoslavia, and the Soviet Union rearranged themselves into a greater number of smaller, independent countries?

EXHIBIT 5.10 Compensable Factor Definition: Decision Making

Compensable Factor Definition:	Evaluates the extent of required decision making and the beneficial or detrimental effect such decisions would have on the profitability of the organization.

Consideration is given to the:

- *Risk* and *complexity* of required decision making
- *Impact* such action would have on the company

What type of guidelines are available for making decisions?

_____ 1. Few decisions are required; work is performed according to standard procedures and/or detailed instructions.

_____ 2. Decisions are made within an established framework of clearly defined procedures. Incumbent is only required to recognize and follow the prescribed course of action.

_____ 3. Guidelines are available in the form of clearly defined procedures and standard practices. Incumbent must exercise some judgment in selecting the appropriate procedure.

_____ 4. Guidelines are available in the form of some standard practices, well-established precedent, and reference materials and company policy. Decisions require a moderate level of judgment and analysis of the appropriate course of action.

_____ 5. Some guidelines are available in the form of broad precedent, related practices, and general methods of the field. Decisions require a high level of judgment and/or modification of a standard course of action to address the issue at hand.

_____ 6. Few guidelines are available. The incumbent may consult with technical experts and review relevant professional publications. Decisions require innovation and creativity. The only limitation on course of action is company strategy and policy.

What is the impact of decisions made by the position?

_____ 1. Inappropriate decisions, recommendations, or errors would normally cause minor delays and cost increments. Deficiencies will not affect the completion of programs or projects important to the organization.

_____ 2. Inappropriate decisions, recommendations, or errors will normally cause moderate delays and additional allocation of funds and resources within the immediate work unit. Deficiencies will not affect the attainment of the organization's objectives.

_____ 3. Inappropriate decisions, recommendations, or errors would normally cause considerable delays and reallocation of funds and resources. Deficiencies will affect scheduling and project completion in other work units and, unless adjustments are made, could affect attainment of objectives of a major business segment of the company.

_____ 4. Inappropriate decisions, recommendations, or errors would normally affect critical programs or attainment of short-term goals for a major business segment of the company.

_____ 5. Inappropriate decisions, recommendations, or errors would affect attainment of objectives for the company and would normally affect long-term growth and public image.

The effectiveness of the majority of the position's decisions can be measured within:

_____ 1. One day.

_____ 2. One week.

_____ 3. One month.

_____ 4. Six months.

_____ 5. One year.

_____ 6. More than a year.

Source: Jill Kanin-Lovers, "The Role of Computers in Job Evaluations: A Case in Point," *Journal of Compensation and Benefits*, 1985. Reprinted by permission of Thomson Reuters.

EXHIBIT 5.11
Compensable
Factor
Definition:
Multinational
Responsibilities

Source: 3M. Used by
permission.

This factor concerns the multinational scope of the job. Multinational responsibilities are defined as line or functional managerial activities in one or several countries.

1. **The multinational responsibilities of the job can best be described as:**

    A. Approving major policy and strategic plans.

    B. Formulating, proposing, and monitoring implementation of policy and plans.

    C. Acting as a consultant in project design and implementation phases.

    D. Not applicable.

2. **Indicate the percentage of time spent on multinational issues:**

    A. >50%

    B. 25–49%

    C. 10–24%

    D. <10%

3. **The number of countries (other than your unit location) for which the position currently has operational or functional responsibility:**

    A. More than 10 countries

    B. 5 to 10 countries

    C. 1 to 4 countries

    D. Not applicable

Factors may also be eliminated if they no longer support the business strategy. The railway company Burlington Northern revised its job evaluation plan to omit the factor "number of subordinates supervised." It decided that a factor that values increases to staff runs counter to the organization's objective of reducing bureaucracy and increasing efficiency. Major shifts in the business strategy are not daily occurrences, but when they do occur, compensable factors should be reexamined to ensure they are consistent with the new directions.[9]

Based on the Work Itself

Employees and supervisors are experts in the work actually done in any organization. Hence, it is important to seek their answers to what should be valued in the work itself. Some form of documentation (i.e., job descriptions, job analysis, employee and/or supervisory focus groups) must support the choice of factors. Work-related documentation helps gain acceptance by employees and managers, is easier to understand, and can withstand a variety of challenges to the pay structure. For example, managers may argue that the salaries of their employees are too low in comparison to those of other employees or that the salary offered a job candidate is too low. Union leaders may wonder why one job is paid differently from another. Allegations of **pay discrimination** may be raised. Employees, line managers, union leaders, and compensation managers must understand and be able to explain why work is paid differently or the same. Differences in factors that are obviously based on the work itself provide that rationale or even diminish the likelihood of the challenges arising.

Acceptable to the Stakeholders

Acceptance of the compensable factors used to slot jobs into the pay structure may depend, at least in part, on tradition. For example, people who work in hospitals, nursing homes, and child care centers make the point that responsibility for people is used less often as a compensable factor, and valued lower, than responsibility for property.[10] This omission may be a carryover from the days when nursing and child care service were provided by family members, usually women, without reimbursement. People now doing these jobs for pay say that properly valuing a factor for people responsibility would raise their wages. So the question is, acceptable to whom? The answer ought to be the stakeholders.

Adapting Factors From Existing Plans

Although a wide variety of factors are used in standard existing plans, the factors tend to fall into four generic groups: skills required, effort required, responsibility, and working conditions. These four were used more than 60 years ago in the **National Electrical Manufacturers Association (NEMA) plan** and are also included in the Equal Pay Act (1963) to define equal work. Many of these early point plans, such as those of the **National Metal Trades Association (NMTA)** and NEMA, and the Steel Plan, were developed for manufacturing and/or office jobs. Since then, point plans have also been applied to managerial and professional jobs. The *Hay Guide Chart-Profile Method*, used by 5,000 employers worldwide (including 130 of the 500 largest U.S. corporations), is perhaps the most widely used. The three Hay factors—know-how, problem solving, and accountability—use guide charts to quantify the factors in more detail. Exhibit 5.12 summarizes the basic definitions of the three Hay factors. A fourth factor, working conditions, is used when applied to nonmanagerial work. In Exhibit 5.13, the

EXHIBIT 5.12
Factors in Hay Plan

Know-how—the sum total of what a person must have the capability to do to be effective

- Technical, specialized depth and breadth
- Managerial requirements to plan, organize, staff, direct, and control resources for results
- Human relations skills to influence, motivate, change behavior, and build relationships

Problem solving—the requirement for and ability to use know-how effectively to develop solutions that improve effectiveness

- Environment—the context of the job and its focus
- Challenge—the availability of guides and complexity of analyses required

Accountability—the requirement for and ability to achieve desired results

- Freedom to act—focus on decision-making authority vested in the position to achieve results
- Scope—focus on the magnitude of the results expected relative to the enterprise
- Impact—focus on the impact the position has on the relevant scope measure for the position

EXHIBIT 5.13   Hay Guide Chart—Profile Method of Job Evaluation

KNOW-HOW DEFINITIONS

DEFINITION: Know-How is the sum total to every kind of skill however acquired, required for acceptable job performance. This sum total which comprises the overall savvy has 3 dimensions–the requirements for:

1 Practical procedures, specialized techniques, and scientific disciplines.

2 Know-How of integrating and harmonizing the diversified functions involved in managerial situations occurring in operating, supporting, and administrative fields. This Know-How may be exercised consultatively (about management) as well as executive and involves in some combination the areas of organizing, planning, executing, controlling and evaluating.

3 Active, practicing, face-to-face skills in the area of human relationships (as defined at right).

MEASURING KNOW-HOW: Know-How has both scope (variety) and depth (thoroughness). Thus, a job may require some knowledge about a lot of things, or a lot of knowledge about a few things. The total Know-How is the combination of scope and depth. This concept makes practical the comparison and weighing of the total Know-How content of different jobs in terms of: "How much knowledge about how many things."

2 HUMAN RELATIONS SKILLS

1. **BASIC:** Ordinary courtesy and effectiveness in dealing with others.

2. **IMPORTANT:** Understanding, influencing, and/or serving people are important, but not critical considerations.

3. **CRITICAL:** Alternative or combined skills in understanding, selecting, developing and motivating people are important in the highest degree.

KNOW-HOW 1

	MANAGERIAL KNOW-HOW											
	I. MINIMAL			II. RELATED			III. DIVERSE			IV. BROAD		
	1	2	3	1	2	3	1	2	3	1	2	3
A. PRIMARY	50	57	66	66	76	87	87	100	115	115	132	152
	57	66	76	76	87	100	100	115	132	132	152	175
	66	76	87	87	100	115	115	132	152	152	175	200
B. ELEMENTARY VOCATIONAL	66	76	87	87	100	115	115	132	152	152	175	200
	76	87	100	100	115	132	132	152	175	175	200	230
	87	100	115	115	132	152	152	175	200	200	230	264
C. VOCATIONAL	87	100	115	115	132	152	152	175	200	200	230	264
	100	115	132	132	152	175	175	200	230	230	264	304
	115	132	152	152	175	200	200	230	264	264	304	350
D. ADVANCED VOCATIONAL	115	132	(152)	152	175	200	200	230	264	264	304	350
	132	152	175	175	200	230	230	264	304	304	350	400
	152	175	200	200	230	264	264	304	350	350	400	460
E. BASIC TECHNICAL-SPECIALIZED	152	175	200	200	230	264	264	304	350	350	400	460
	175	200	230	230	264	304	304	350	400	400	460	528
	200	230	264	264	304	350	350	400	460	460	528	608
F. SEASONED TECHNICAL-SPECIALIZED	200	230	264	264	304	350	350	400	460	460	528	608
	230	264	304	304	350	400	400	460	528	528	608	700
	264	304	350	350	400	460	460	528	608	608	700	800
G. TECHNICAL-SPECIALIZED MASTERY	264	304	350	350	400	460	460	528	608	608	700	800
	(304)	350	400	400	460	528	528	608	(700)	700	800	920
	350	400	460	460	528	608	608	700	800	800	920	1056
H. PROFESSIONAL MASTERY	350	400	460	460	528	608	608	700	800	800	920	1056
	400	460	528	528	608	700	700	800	920	920	1056	1216
	460	528	608	608	700	800	800	920	1056	1056	1216	1400

KH	PS	AC	TOTAL
152			

SUPERVISOR

KH	PS	AC	TOTAL
304			

ACTUARIAL SPECIALIST RESEARCH ASSOCIATE

KH	PS	AC	TOTAL
700			

AREA MANAGER

Source: Hay Group, "The Hay Guide Chart-Profile Method of Job Evaluation: An Overview," http://www.haygroup.com/ww/services/index.aspx?ID=1529.

Hay factor know-how is first measured on two dimensions: scope (practical procedures, specialized techniques, or scientific disciplines); and depth (minimal, related, diverse, or broad). After that, the degree of human relations skills required (basic, important, or critical) is judged. The cell that corresponds to the right level of all three dimensions for the job being evaluated is located in the guide chart. The cell gives the points for this factor. In the exhibit, the supervisor position gets 152 points for know-how.

How Many Factors?

A remaining issue to consider is how many factors should be included in the plan. Some factors may have overlapping definitions or may fail to account for anything unique in the criterion chosen. In fact, the NEMA plan explicitly states that the compensable factor experience should be correlated with education. One writer calls this the "illusion of validity"—we want to believe that the factors are capturing divergent aspects of the job and that both are important.[11] It has long been recognized that factors overlap or are highly correlated, raising the concern about double counting the value of a factor. Indeed, in the Hay plan, problem solving is defined as a percentage of know-how. So by definition, they overlap.

Another challenge is called "small numbers." If even one job in our benchmark sample has a certain characteristic, we tend to use that factor for the entire work domain. Unpleasant working conditions are a common example. If even one job is performed in unpleasant working conditions, it is tempting to make those conditions a compensable factor and apply it to all jobs. Once a factor is part of the system, other workers are likely to say their jobs have it, too. For example, office staff may feel that ringing telephones or leaky toner cartridges constitute stressful or hazardous conditions.

In one plan, a senior manager refused to accept a job evaluation plan unless the factor working conditions was included. The plan's designer, a recent college graduate, showed through statistical analysis that working conditions did not vary enough among 90 percent of the jobs to have a meaningful effect on the resulting pay structure. Nevertheless, the manager pointed out that the recent grad had never worked in the plant's foundry, where working conditions were extremely meaningful. In order to get the plan accepted by the foundry workers, the working-conditions factor was included.

This situation is not unusual. In one study, a 21-factor plan produced the same rank order of jobs that could be generated using only 7 of the factors. Further, the jobs could be correctly slotted into pay classes using only 3 factors. Yet the company decided to keep the 21-factor plan because it was "accepted and doing the job." Research as far back as the 1940s demonstrates that the skills dimension explains 90 percent or more of the variance in job evaluation results; three factors generally account for 98 to 99 percent of the variance.[12]

3. Scale the Factors

Once the factors are determined, scales reflecting the different degrees within each factor are constructed. Each degree may also be anchored by the typical skills, tasks, and behaviors taken from the benchmark jobs that illustrate each factor degree. Exhibit 5.14 shows NMTA's scaling for the factor of knowledge.

EXHIBIT 5.14
Factor
Scaling—
National
Metal Trades
Association

1. Knowledge

This factor measures the knowledge or equivalent training required to perform the position duties.

1st Degree

Use of reading and writing, adding and subtracting of whole numbers; following of instructions; use of fixed gauges, direct reading instruments, and similar devices; where interpretation is not required.

2nd Degree

Use of addition, subtraction, multiplication, and division of numbers including decimals and fractions; simple use of formulas, charts, tables, drawings, specifications, schedules, wiring diagrams; use of adjustable measuring instruments; checking of reports, forms, records, and comparable data; where interpretation is required.

3rd Degree

Use of mathematics together with the use of complicated drawings, specifications, charts, tables; various types of precision measuring instruments. Equivalent to 1 to 3 years' applied trades training in a particular or specialized occupation.

4th Degree

Use of advanced trades mathematics, together with the use of complicated drawings, specifications, charts, tables, handbook formulas; all varieties of precision measuring instruments. Equivalent to complete accredited apprenticeship in a recognized trade, craft, or occupation; or equivalent to a 2-year technical college education.

5th Degree

Use of higher mathematics involved in the application of engineering principles and the performance of related practical operations, together with a comprehensive knowledge of the theories and practices of mechanical, electrical, chemical, civil, or like engineering field. Equivalent to completing 4 years of technical college or university education.

Most **factor scales** consist of four to eight degrees. In practice, many evaluators use extra, undefined degrees such as plus and minus around a scale number. So what starts as a 5-degree scale—1, 2, 3, 4, 5—ends up as a 15-degree scale, with −1, 1, 1+, −2, 2, 2+, and so on. The reason for adding plus/minus is that users of the plan believe more degrees are required to adequately differentiate among jobs. If we are trying to design 15 levels into the job structure but the factors use only three or five degrees, such users may be right.[13] However, all too often inserting pluses and minuses gives the illusion of accuracy of measurement that is simply not the case.

Another major issue in determining degrees is whether to make each degree equidistant from the adjacent degrees (**interval scaling**). For example, the difference between the first and second degrees in Exhibit 5.14 should approximate the difference between the fourth and fifth degrees, since the differences in points will be the same. In contrast, the intervals in the U.S. government plan range from 150 to 200 points.

The following criteria for scaling factors have been suggested: (1) Ensure that the number of degrees is necessary to distinguish among jobs, (2) use understandable terminology, (3) anchor degree definitions with benchmark-job titles and/or work behaviors, and (4) make it apparent how the degree applies to the job.

4. Weight the Factors According to Importance

Once the degrees have been assigned, the factor weights can be determined. Factor weights reflect the relative importance of each factor to the overall value of the job. Different weights reflect differences in importance attached to each factor by the employer. For example, the National Electrical Manufacturers Association plan weights education at 17.5 percent; another employer's association weights it at 10.6 percent; a consultant's plan recommends 15.0 percent; and a trade association weights education at 10.1 percent.

Weights are often determined through an advisory committee that allocates 100 percent of the value among the factors.[14] In the illustration in Exhibit 5.15, a committee allocated 40 percent of the value to skill, 30 percent to effort, 20 percent to responsibility, and 10 percent to working conditions. Each factor has two subfactors, with five degrees each. In the example for the bookstore manager, the subfactor mental skill gets half the 40 percent given to skill and the subfactor experience gets the other half: 4 degrees of mental skill times 20 equals 80 points, and 3 degrees of experience times 20 equals another 60 points.[15]

EXHIBIT 5.15   **Job Evaluation Form**

Compensable Factors	Degree	x	Weight	=	Total
Skill: (40%)	1 2 3 4 5				
Mental	[4] X		20%		80
Experience	[2] X		20%		60
Effort: (30%)					
Physical	[1] X		15%		30
Mental	[4] X		15%		60
Responsibility: (20%)					
Effect of Error	[4] X		10%		40
Inventiveness/ Innovation	[2] X		10%		30
Working Conditions: (10%)					
Environment	[1] X		5%		5
Hazards	[1] X		5%		5
					(310)

Job *bookstore manager*
Check one: ☒ Administrative
              ☐ Technical

Select Criterion Pay Structure

Contemporary job evaluation often supplements committee judgment for determining weights with statistical analysis.[16] The committee members recommend the ***criterion pay structure,*** that is, a pay structure they wish to duplicate with the point plan. The criterion structure may be the current rates paid for benchmark jobs, market rates for benchmark jobs, rates for jobs held predominantly by males (in an attempt to eliminate gender bias), or union-negotiated rates.[17] Once a criterion structure is agreed on, statistical modeling techniques are used to determine the weight for each factor and the factor scales that will reproduce, as closely as possible, the chosen structure. The statistical approach is often labeled **policy capturing** to differentiate it from the **committee a priori judgment** approach. Not only do the weights reflect the relative importance of each factor, but research clearly demonstrates that the weights influence the resulting pay structure.[18] Thus, selecting the appropriate pay rates to use as the criteria is critical. The job evaluation and its results are based on it.[19]

Perhaps the clearest illustration can be found in municipalities. Rather than using market rates for firefighters, some unions have successfully negotiated a link between firefighters' pay and police rates. So the criterion structure for firefighters becomes some percentage of whatever wage structure is used for police.

5. Communicate the Plan and Train Users

Once the job evaluation plan is designed, a manual is prepared so that other people can apply the plan. The manual describes the method, defines the compensable factors, and provides enough information to permit users to distinguish varying degrees of each factor. The point of the manual is to allow users who were not involved in the plan's development to apply the plan as its developers intended. Users will also require training on how to apply the plan and background information on how the plan fits into the organization's total pay system. An **appeals process** may also be included so that employees who feel their jobs are unfairly evaluated have some recourse. Employee acceptance of the process is crucial if the organization is to have any hope that employees will accept the resulting pay as fair. In order to build this acceptance, communication to all employees whose jobs are part of the process used to build the structure is required. This communication may be done through informational meetings, Web sites, or other methods.

6. Apply to Nonbenchmark Jobs

Recall that the compensable factors and weights were derived using a sample of benchmark jobs. The final step is to apply the plan to the remaining jobs. This can be done by people who were not necessarily involved in the design process but have been given adequate training in applying the plan. Increasingly, once the plan is developed and accepted, it becomes a tool for managers and HR specialists. They evaluate new positions that may be created or reevaluate jobs whose work content has changed. They may also be part of panels that hear appeals from murmuring employees.

7. Develop Online Software Support

Online job evaluation is widely used in larger organizations. It becomes part of a Total Compensation Service Center for managers and HR generalists to use. The U.S. State Department, with more than 50,000 employees in 180 countries, uses the "Link. Evaluate" systems. Accessed online by over 400 users worldwide, the time to process an evaluation has been cut from three months to 48 hours.[20]

WHO SHOULD BE INVOLVED?

If the internal structure's purpose is to aid managers—and if ensuring high involvement and commitment from employees is important—those managers and employees with a stake in the results should be involved in the process of designing it. A common approach is to use committees, task forces, or teams that include representatives from key operating functions, including nonmanagerial employees. In some cases, the group's role is only advisory; in others, the group designs the evaluation approach, chooses compensable factors, and approves all major changes. Organizations with unions often find that including union representatives helps gain acceptance of the results. Union-management task forces participated in the design of a new evaluation system for the federal government. However, other union leaders believe that philosophical differences prevent their active participation. They take the position that collective bargaining yields more equitable results. So the extent of union participation varies. No single perspective exists on the value of active participation in the process, just as no single management perspective exists.

Exhibit 5.16 shows further results from the survey of WorldatWork members discussed earlier. We see that compensation professionals (i.e., usually compensation analysts, sometimes also those at a higher levels such as the compensation manager) are primarily responsible for most job evaluations for most jobs. Although that holds true for senior management jobs as well, we see that the higher level compensation manager is more likely to be charged with the job evaluation in this case and that consultants also play a much larger role here.

EXHIBIT 5.16   **Who Typically Conducts the Job Evaluation?**

	Compensation Analyst	Compensation Manager	Consultant	Senior Management	Employee Committee
Senior Management	22%	45%	33%	13%	3%
Middle Management, Professional, Sales, Administrative, Production	64%	27%	3%	2%	4%

Source: "Job Evaluation and Market-Pricing Practices," *WorldatWork*, February 2009.

Note: Number of respondents ranged from 911 to 1,119 organizations.

> **Cybercomp**
>
> O*Net, the Occupational Information Network, is the U.S. Department of Labor's database that identifies and describes occupations; worker knowledge, skills, and abilities; and workplace requirements for jobs across the country in all sectors of the economy. For more information, visit O*Net's Web site: *www.onetcenter.org*.
>
> How can public sector agencies use this information? Go to an occupation that is of interest to you. Compare the information offered by the Department of Labor to the job-opening descriptions you looked at for specific companies (Chapter 4's Cybercomp).
>
> Why are they different? What purpose does each serve?

The Design Process Matters

Research suggests that attending to the fairness of the design process and the approach chosen (job evaluation, skill/competency-based plan, and market pricing), rather than focusing solely on the results (the internal pay structure), is likely to achieve employee and management commitment, trust, and acceptance of the results. The absence of participation may make it easier for employees and managers to imagine ways the structure might have been rearranged to their personal liking. Two researchers note, "If people do not participate in decisions, there is little to prevent them from assuming that things would have been better, 'if I'd been in charge.'"[21]

Additional research is needed to ascertain whether the payoffs from increased participation offset potential costs (time involved to reach consensus, potential problems caused by disrupting current perceptions, etc.). We noted earlier that no amount of participation overcomes low wages. In multinational organizations the involvement of both corporate compensation and country managers raises the potential for conflict due to their differing perspectives. Country managers may wish to focus on the particular business needs in their markets, whereas corporate managers may want a system that operates equally well (or poorly) across all countries. The country manager has operating objectives, does not want to lose key individuals, and views compensation as a mechanism to help accomplish these goals; corporate adopts a worldwide perspective and focuses on ensuring that decisions are consistent with the overall global strategy.

Appeals/Review Procedures

No matter what the technique, no job evaluation plan anticipates all situations. It is inevitable that some jobs will be incorrectly evaluated—or at least employees and managers may suspect that they were. Consequently, review procedures for handling such cases and helping to ensure procedural fairness are required. In the past, the compensation manager handled reviews, but increasingly teams of managers and even peers are used. Sometimes these reviews take on the trappings of formal grievance procedures (e.g., documented complaints and responses and levels of approval). Problems may also be handled by managers and the employee relations generalists through informal discussions.[22]

When the evaluations are completed, approval by higher levels of management is usually required. An approval process helps ensure that any changes that result from evaluating work are consistent with the organization's operations and directions.

"I Know I Speak for All of Us When I Say I Speak for All of Us"

A recent study found that more powerful departments in a university were more successful in using the appeals process to change the pay or the classification of a job than were weaker departments.[23] This is consistent with other research that showed that a powerful member of a **job evaluation committee** could sway the results.[24] Consequently, procedures should be judged for their susceptibility to political influences. "It is the decision-making process, rather than the instrument itself, that seems to have the greatest influence on pay outcomes," writes one researcher.[25]

THE FINAL RESULT: STRUCTURE

The final result of the job analysis–job description–job evaluation process is a *structure,* a **hierarchy** of work. As shown in Exhibit 5.3 at the beginning of this chapter, this hierarchy translates the employer's internal alignment policy into practice. Exhibit 5.17 shows four hypothetical job structures within a single organization. These structures were obtained via different approaches to evaluating work. The jobs are arrayed within four basic functions: managerial, technical, manufacturing, and administrative. The managerial and administrative structures were obtained via a point job evaluation plan; the technical and manufacturing structures, via two different person-based plans

EXHIBIT 5.17   Resulting Internal Structures—Job, Skill, and Competency Based

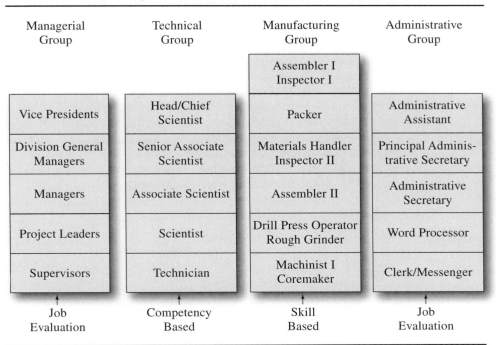

(Chapter 6). The manufacturing plan was negotiated with the union. The exhibit illustrates the results of evaluating work: structures that support a policy of internal alignment.

Organizations commonly have multiple structures derived through multiple approaches that apply to different functional groups or units. Although some employees in one structure may wish to compare the procedures used in another structure with their own, the underlying premise in practice is that internal alignment is most influenced by fair and equitable treatment of employees doing similar work in the same skill/knowledge group.

BALANCING CHAOS AND CONTROL

Looking back at the material we have covered in the past three chapters (determining internal alignment, job analysis, job evaluation), you may be thinking that we have spent a lot of time and a lot of our organization's money to develop techniques. But we have yet to pay a single employee a single dollar. Why bother with all this? Why not just pay whatever it takes and get on with it?

Prior to the widespread use of job evaluation, employers in the 1930s and 1940s did just that, and got irrational pay structures—the legacy of decentralized and uncoordinated wage-setting practices. Pay differences were a major source of unrest among workers. American Steel and Wire, for example, had more than 100,000 pay rates. Employment and wage records were rarely kept; only the foreman knew with any accuracy how many workers were employed in his department and the rates they received. Foremen were thus "free to manage," but they used wage information to vary the day rate for favored workers or assign them to jobs where piece rates were loose.

Job evaluation, with its specified procedures and documented results, helped change that. The technique provided work-related and business-related order and logic. However, over time, complex procedures and creeping bureaucracy can cause users to lose sight of the objectives, focusing instead on "how-to" rather than "so what does this do to help accomplish our objectives." Too often we become so enamored with our techniques that we slip into knowing more and more about less and less.

At the same time, the world of work is changing. The work of many people now requires that they figure out what to do in a given situation (tacit knowledge) instead of simply invoking a canned routine (transactional work). They must identify problems and opportunities, make decisions, plan courses of action, marshal support, and, in general, design their own work methods, techniques, and tools. The challenge is to ensure that job evaluation plans afford flexibility to adapt to changing conditions.

Generic factors and vague descriptions such as "associates" or "technicians" may be very attractive to managers coping with increased competitive pressures and the need to restructure work and reduce costs. This flexibility avoids bureaucracy and leaves managers "free to manage"—just like the American Steel and Wire foremen. But it also reduces control and guidelines, and this in turn may make it harder to ensure that people are treated fairly. Some balance between chaos and control is required. History suggests that when flexibility without guidelines exists, chaotic and irrational pay rates too frequently result. Removing inefficient bureaucracy is important, but balanced guidelines are necessary to ensure that employees are treated fairly and that pay decisions help the organization achieve its objectives.

Your **Turn** 　　　　　 Job Evaluation at Whole Foods

Rather than wait until you are next in a supermarket to check out the different types of work, we brought some of the jobs at Whole Foods Market to you. Now that you have some background in job evaluation, it is time to try it out. As a first step, Whole Foods has done job analysis and prepared job descriptions. The results are shown below. Now a job structure is needed. The manager has assigned this job to you.

1. Divide into teams of four to six each. Each team should evaluate the jobs and prepare a job structure based on its evaluation. Assign titles to each job, and show your structure by title and job letter. A broad hint: Recall from our discussion of Whole Foods' business and pay strategy that teams play an important role.

2. Your team should describe the process it went through to arrive at that job structure. The job evaluation techniques and compensable factors used should be described, and the reasons for selecting them should be stated.

3. Each team should give each job a title and put its job structure on the board. Comparisons can then be made among job structures of the various teams. Does the job evaluation method used appear to affect the results? Do the compensable factors chosen affect the results? Does the process affect the results?

4. Evaluate the job descriptions. What parts of them were most useful? How could they be improved?

JOB A

Kind of Work

Provide excellent customer service. Follow and comply with all applicable health and sanitation procedures. Prepare food items: sandwiches, slice deli meats and cheeses. Prepare items on station assignment list and as predetermined. Stock and rotate products, stock supplies and paper goods in a timely basis; keep all utensils stocked. Check dates on all products in stock to ensure freshness and rotate when necessary. Use waste sheets properly, as directed. Operate and sanitize all equipment in a safe and proper manner. Comply with and follow Whole Foods Market Safety Procedures. Follow established Weights and Measures procedures (tares). Answer the phone and pages to department quickly and with appropriate phone etiquette. Practice proper use of knives, slicer, trash compactor, baler (must be 18 years of age or older), and all other equipment used during food preparation and cleanup. Perform other duties as assigned, and follow through on supervisor requests in a timely manner.

Requirements

- Some deli experience preferred.
- Clear and effective communicator.
- Patient and enjoys working and mentoring people.
- Ability to perform physical requirements of position.
- Ability to learn proper use of knives, slicer, baler (must be 18 years of age or older) and all other equipment used during food preparation and cleanup.
- Ability to work well with others as a team.
- Knowledge of all relevant Whole Foods Market policies and standards.
- Understands and can communicate quality goals to customers.

JOB B

Kind of Work

Assist and focus on customers during entire checkout process. Perform all cash register functions according to established procedures. Maintain a positive company image by providing courteous, friendly, and efficient customer service. Check out customer groceries efficiently and accurately. Pass entry-level PLU code test. Maintain a professional demeanor at all times. Stock registers with supplies as needed. Follow proper check-receiving procedure. Clean, stock, and detail front-end area with special attention to own register. Change journal tapes and ribbon as needed. Walk produce department at the beginning of every shift to identify and learn new produce codes. Comply with all posted state health and safety codes.

Requirements

- Excellent communication skills necessary for good customer and team relations.
- Ability to work well with others.
- Ability to learn proper use of baler (must be 18 or older).
- Desire to learn and grow.
- Ability to work in a fast-paced environment, with a sense of urgency.
- Understanding the importance of working as a team.
- Good math skills.
- Patience.

JOB C

Kind of Work

Reports to store team leader and to associate store team leader. Provides overall management and supervision of the Prepared Foods Department. Responsible for team member hiring, development, and terminations. Also responsible for profitability, expense control, buying/merchandising, regulatory compliance, and special projects as assigned. Complete accountability for all aspects of department operations. Consistently communicate and model Whole Foods vision and goal. Interview, select, train, develop, and counsel team members in a manner that builds and sustains a high-performing team and minimizes turnover. Make hiring and termination decisions with guidance of store team leader. Establish and maintain a positive work environment. Manage inventory to achieve targeted gross profit margin. Manage the ordering process to meet Whole Foods Market quality standards. Maintain competitive pricing and achieve targeted sales. Establish and maintain positive and productive vendor relationships. Develop and maintain creative store layout and product merchandising in support of regional and national vision. Establish and maintain collaborative and productive working relationships. Model and cultivate effective inter-department and inter-store communication. Provide accurate, complete information in daily, weekly, monthly, annual, and "ad hoc" management reports. Maintain comprehensive knowledge of, and ensure compliance with, relevant regulatory rules and standards.

Requirements

- Two years relevant experience as a team leader, assistant team leader, supervisor, or buyer.
- Thorough knowledge of products, buying, pricing, merchandising, and inventory management.
- Excellent verbal and written communication skills.
- Strong organizational skills.
- Knowledge of all relevant Whole Foods Market policies and standards.
- Computer skills.

JOB D

Kind of Work

Perform all duties and responsibilities of Prepared Foods Team Member. Provide excellent customer service. Assist team leader in nightly team operations. Report all actions of team members that violate policies or standards to the team leader or associate team leader. Mentor and train team members. Maintain quality standards in production and counter display. Comply with all applicable health and safety codes. Help implement and support all regional programs

Requirements

- Minimum 6 months' retail food production experience, or equivalent.
- Overall knowledge of both front and back of the house operations.
- Comprehensive product knowledge.
- Comprehensive knowledge of quality standards.
- Excellent organizational skills.
- Excellent interpersonal skills, and ability to train others.
- Demonstrated decision-making ability, and leadership skills.
- Ability to perform physical requirements of position.
- Able to work a flexible schedule based on the needs of the store.

JOB E

Kind of Work

Performs all duties related to dishwashing: unloading kitchen deliveries and cleaning all dishes, utensils, pots, and pans. May be prep work. Maintain food quality and sanitation in kitchen. Maintain a positive company image by being courteous, friendly, and efficient. Wash and sanitize all dishes, utensils, and containers. Assist with proper storage of all deliveries. Rotate and organize products. Perform prep work as directed. Provide proper ongoing maintenance of equipment. Maintain health department standards when cleaning and handling food. Perform deep-cleaning tasks on a regular basis. Take out all of the garbage and recycling materials. Sweep and wash floors as needed.

Requirements

- Entry-level position.
- Able to perform physical requirements of job.
- Practices safe and proper knife skills.
- Ability to work box baler (must 18 years of age or older).
- Works well with others and participates as part of a team.

JOB F

Kind of Work

Performs all functions related to breaking down deliveries and moving back stock to floor. Assists in organizing and developing promotional displays; maintains back room, training entry-level grocery clerks. Trained and capable of operating any of the subdepartments as needed. Maintains and ensures retail standards during their shift. Responsible for implementing team's break schedule. Performs all duties and responsibilities of grocery team member. Builds displays and requests appropriate signage. Supervises shift to ensure standards are maintained. Implements break schedule for shift. Responsible for problem solving in team leader or associate team leader's absence. Fully responsible for completion of all opening or closing checklists. Responsible for checking in deliveries.

Requirements

- Minimum one-year retail grocery experience, or equivalent.
- Proficient in math skills (addition, subtraction, multiplication, and division).
- Ability to perform physical requirements of position.
- Ability to properly use baler (must be 18 years of age or older).
- Able to direct team members and implement break schedule.
- Ability to work well with others.

JOB G

Kind of Work

Reports directly to Prepared Foods Team Leader. Assists in overall management and supervision of the Prepared Foods Department. Can be responsible for team member hiring, development, and terminations. Also responsible for profitability, expense control, buying/merchandising, regulatory compliance, and special projects as assigned. Complete accountability for all assigned aspects of department operations. Consistently communicate and model Whole Foods vision and goals. Assist in the interview, selection, training, development, and counseling of team members in a manner that builds and sustains a high-performing team and minimizes turnover. Discuss hiring and termination decisions with guidance of others. Establish and maintain a positive work environment. Manage inventory to achieve targeted gross profit margin. Manage the ordering process to meet Whole Foods Market quality standards, maintain competitive pricing, and achieve targeted sales. Develop and maintain creative store layout and product merchandising in support of regional and national vision. Establish and maintain collaborative and productive working relationships. Model and cultivate effective inter-department and inter-store communication. Provide accurate, complete information in daily, weekly, monthly, annual, and "ad hoc" management reports. Maintain comprehensive knowledge of, and ensure compliance with, relevant regulatory rules and standards.

Requirements

- One to two years of department experience, or industry equivalent.
- Analytical ability and proficiency in math needed to calculate margins, monitor profitability, and manage inventory.
- Clear and effective communicator.
- Patient and enjoys working and mentoring people.

- Strong organizational skills.
- Knowledge of all relevant Whole Foods Market policies and standards.
- Computer skills.

JOB H

Kind of Work

Rotate among stores. Assist and support the store team leader with all store functions. Interview, select, evaluate, counsel, and terminate team members. Coordinate and supervise all store products and personnel. Follow through on all customer and team member questions and requests. Evaluate customer service and resolve complaints. Operate the store in an efficient and profitable manner. Have a firm understanding of store financials and labor budgets. Establish and achieve sales, labor, and contribution goals. Review department schedules and research productivity improvements. Order store equipment and supplies in a timely manner. Enforce established food safety, cleaning, and maintenance procedures. Inspect store; ensure cleanliness; visit off-hours for consistency. Maintain accurate retail pricing and signage. Ensure that product is cross-merchandised in other departments. Coordinate, supervise, and report physical inventory. Analyze product transfers, waste, and spoilage. Manage expenses to maximize the bottom line. Provide, maintain, and safety-train team members on all equipment and tools. Resolve safety violations and hazards immediately. Maintain store security and ensure that opening and closing procedures are followed. Show EVA improvement over a designated period. Leverage sales growth to improve store profitability. Assist in handling liability claims and minimize their occurrence. Establish and maintain good community relations. Create a friendly, productive, and professional working environment. Communicate company goals and information to team members. Ensure and support team member development and training. Evaluate team member duties, dialogues, raises, and promotions. Keep regional leadership informed of all major events that affect the store. Ensure store policies and procedures are followed. Visit the competition on a regular basis and react to current industry trends.

Requirements

- A passion for retailing.
- Complete understanding of Whole Foods Market retail operations.
- Strong leadership and creative ability.
- Management and business skills with financial expertise.
- Well organized with excellent follow through.
- Detail oriented with a vision and eye for the big picture.
- Self-motivated and solution oriented.
- Excellent merchandising skills and eye for detail.
- Ability to delegate effectively and use available talent to the best advantage.
- Strong communicator/motivator; able to work well with others and convey enthusiasm.
- Ability to maintain good relationships with vendors and the community.
- Can train and inspire team members to excellence in all aspects of the store.
- Ability to make tough decisions.
- Love and knowledge of natural foods.
- Strong computer skills.

JOB I

Kind of Work

Performs all functions related to breaking down deliveries and moving back stock to floor. May assist in organizing and developing promotional displays; maintains back room. Stock and clean grocery shelves, bulk bins, frozen and dairy case. Maintain back stock in good order. Sweep floors and face shelves throughout the store. Comply with all applicable health and safety codes. Provide excellent customer service. Log and expedite customers' special orders. Retrieve special orders for customers by request and offer service out to car. Respond to all grocery pages quickly and efficiently. Build displays and request appropriate signage.

Requirements

- Retail grocery or natural foods experience a plus.
- Proficient in math skills (addition, subtraction, multiplication, and division).
- Ability to learn basic knowledge of all products carried in department.
- Ability to perform physical requirements of position.
- Proper and safe use of box cutter, baler (must be 18 years of age or older), and all equipment.
- Ability to work well with others.

Summary   The differences in the rates paid for different jobs and skills affect the ability of managers to achieve their business objectives. Differences in pay matter. They matter to employees, because their willingness to take on more responsibility and training, to focus on adding value for customers and improving quality of products, and to be flexible enough to adapt to change all depend at least in part on how pay is structured for different levels of work. Differences in the rates paid for different jobs and skills also influence how fairly employees believe they are being treated. Unfair treatment is ultimately counterproductive.

So far, we have examined the most common approach to designing pay differences for different work: job evaluation. In the next chapter, we will examine several alternative approaches. However, any approach needs to be evaluated for how useful it is.

Job evaluation has evolved into many different forms and methods. Consequently, wide variations exist in its use and how it is perceived. This chapter discussed some of the many perceptions of the role of job evaluation and reviewed the criticisms leveled at it. No matter how job evaluation is designed, its ultimate use is to help design and manage a work-related, business-focused, and agreed-upon pay structure.

Review Questions

1. How does job evaluation translate internal alignment policies (loosely coupled versus tight fitting) into practice? What does (a) organization strategy and objectives, (b) flow of work, (c) fairness, and (d) motivating people's behaviors toward organization objectives have to do with job evaluation?

2. Why are there different approaches to job evaluation? Think of several employers in your area (the college, hospital, retailer, 7-Eleven, etc.). What approach would you expect them to use? Why?

3. What are the advantages and disadvantages of using more than one job evaluation plan in any single organization?

4. Why bother with job evaluation? Why not simply market-price? How can job evaluation link internal alignment and external market pressures?

5. Consider your college or school. What are the compensable factors required for your college to evaluate jobs? How would you go about identifying these factors? Should the school's educational mission be reflected in your factors? Or are the more generic factors used in the Hay plan okay? Discuss.

6. You are the manager of 10 people in a large organization. All of them become very suspicious and upset when they receive a memo from the HR department saying their jobs are going to be evaluated. How do you try to reassure them?

Endnotes

1. Maeve Quaid, *Job Evaluation: The Myth of Equitable Assessment* (Toronto: University of Toronto Press, 1993); David W. Belcher, *Wage and Salary Administration* (New York: Prentice-Hall, 1955); *Job Evaluation: Methods to the Process* (Scottsdale, AZ: WorldatWork, 2006); Donald P. Schwab, "Job Evaluation and Pay Setting: Concepts and Practices," in E. Robert Livernash, ed., *Comparable Worth: Issues and Alternatives* (Washington, DC: Equal Employment Advisory Council, 1980), pp. 49–77.

2. M. A. Konovsky, "Understanding Procedural Justice and Its Impact on Business Organizations," *Journal of Management* 26(3) (2000), pp. 489–511; B. H. Sheppard, R. J. Lewicki, and J. W. Minton, *Organizational Justice: The Search for Fairness in the Workplace* (New York: Macmillan, 1992); Frederick P. Morgeson, Michael A. Campion, and Carl P. Maertz, "Understanding Pay Satisfaction: The Limits of a Compensation System Implementation," *Journal of Business and Psychology* 16(1), (Fall 2001).

3. E. Robert Livernash, "Internal Wage Structure," in George W. Taylor and Frank C. Pierson, eds., *New Concepts in Wage Determination* (New York: McGraw-Hill, 1957).

4. M. S. Viteles, "A Psychologist Looks at Job Evaluation," *Personnel* 17 (1941), pp. 165–176.

5. Robert L. Heneman and Peter V. LeBlanc, "Developing a More Relevant and Competitive Approach for Valuing Knowledge Work," *Compensation and Benefits Review,* July/August 2002, pp. 43–47; Robert L. Heneman and Peter V. LeBlanc, "Work Valuation Addresses Shortcomings of Both Job Evaluation and Market Pricing," *Compensation and Benefits Review,* January/February 2003, pp. 7–11.

6. Howard Risher and Charles Fay, *New Strategies for Public Pay* (Saratoga Springs, NY: AMACOM, 2000). The Office of Personnel Management (OPM) does special studies on the Federal Civil Service. They are on the OPM's Web site at *www.opm.gov/studies/index.htm.*

7. Factor comparison, another method of job evaluation, bears some similarities to the point method in that compensable factors are clearly defined and the external market is linked to the job evaluation results. However, factor comparison is used by less than 10 percent of employers that use job evaluation. The method's complexity makes it difficult to explain to employees and managers, thus limiting its usefulness.

8. John Kilgour, "Job Evaluation Revisited: The Point Factor Method," *Compensations Benefits Review,* June/July 2008, 37–46.

9. Robert L. Heneman, "Job and Work Evaluation: A Literature Review," *Public Personnel Management,* Spring 2003; Robert L. Heneman and Peter V. LeBlanc, "Work Valuation Addresses Shortcomings of Both Job Evaluation and Market Pricing," *Compensation and Benefits Review,* January/February 2003, pp. 7–11; C. Ellis, R. Laymon, and P. LeBlanc, "Improving Pay Productivity With Strategic Work Valuation," *WorldatWork,* Second Quarter 2004, pp. 56–65.

10. M. K. Mount and R. A. Ellis, "Investigation of Bias in Job Evaluation Ratings of Comparable Worth Study Participants," *Personnel Psychology* 40 (1987), pp. 85–96; Morley Gunderson, "The Evolution and Mechanics of Pay Equity in Ontario," *Canadian Public Policy* Vol. XXVIII, Supplement 1, 2002, pp. S117–S131.

11. D. F. Harding, J. M. Madden, and K. Colson, "Analysis of a Job Evaluation System," *Journal of Applied Psychology* 44 (1960), pp. 354–357.

12. See a series of studies conducted by C. H. Lawshe and his colleagues published in the *Journal of Applied Psychology* from 1944 to 1947. For example, C. H. Lawshe, "Studies in Job Evaluation: II. The Adequacy of Abbreviated Point Ratings for Hourly Paid Jobs in Three Industrial Plans," *Journal of Applied Psychology* 29 (1945), pp. 177–184. Also see Theresa M. Welbourne and Charlie O. Trevor, "The Roles of Departmental and Position Power in Job Evaluation," *Academy of Management Journal* 43 (2000), pp. 761–771.

13. Tjarda Van Sliedregt, Olga F. Voskuijl, and Henk Thierry, "Job Evaluation Systems and Pay Grade Structures: Do They Match?" *International Journal of Human Resource Management* 12(8) (December 2001), pp. 1313–1324; R. M. Madigan and D. J. Hoover, "Effects of Alternative Job Evaluation Methods on Decisions Involving Pay Equity," *Academy of Management Journal* (March 1986), pp. 84–100.

14. John R. Doyle, Rodney H. Green, and Paul A. Bottomley, "Judging Relative Importance: Direct Rating and Point Allocation Are Not Equivalent," *Organizational Behavior and Human Decision Processes* 70(1) (April 1997), pp. 65–72.

15. Some contemporary job evaluation plans include the factor weight directly in each factor scale. So rather than a one-to-five scale for each factor, each factor has a unique scale. An illustration: The weight or relative importance of skill/knowledge is 40 percent; each degree on a 1–5 scale is worth 40 points. The point range is 40 to 200. In practice, statistically modeling values for factor scales often yields more results.

16. Paul M. Edwards, "Statistical Methods in Job Evaluation," *Advanced Management* (December 1948), pp. 158–163.

17. Paula England, "The Case for Comparable Worth," *Quarterly Review of Economics and Finance* 39 (1999), pp. 743–755; N. Elizabeth Fried and John H. Davis, *Developing Statistical Job-Evaluation Models* (Scottsdale, AZ: WorldatWork, 2004); M. Gunderson, "The Evolution and Mechanics of Pay Equity in Ontario," *Canadian Public Policy* Vol. XXVIII, Supplement 1 (2002), pp. S117–S131.

18. M. K. Mount and R. A. Ellis, "Investigation of Bias in Job Evaluation Ratings of Comparable Worth Study Participants," *Personnel Psychology* 40 (1987); Tjarda Van Sliedregt, Olga F. Voskuijl, and Henk Thierry, "Job Evaluation Systems and Pay Grade Structures: Do They Match?" *International Journal of Human Resource Management* 12(8), (December 2001), pp. 1313–1324; Judith M. Collins and Paul M. Muchinsky, "An Assessment of the Construct Validity of Three Job Evaluation Methods: A Field Experiment," *Academy of Management Journal* 36(4) (1993), pp. 895–904; Robert M. Madigan and David J. Hoover, "Effects of Alternative Job Evaluation Methods on Decisions Involving Pay Equity," *Academy of Management Journal* 29 (1986), pp. 84–100.

19. The importance of appropriate criterion pay structure is particularly relevant in "pay equity studies" to assess gender bias. (*Canadian Telephone Employees Association et al. v. Bell Canada; Canada Equal Wages Guidelines,* 1986).

20. See *www.link.hrsystems.com.* Also see *www.npktools.com.*

21. Carl F. Frost, John W. Wakely, and Robert A. Ruh, *The Scanlon Plan for Organization Development: Identity, Participation, and Equity* (East Lansing, MI: Michigan State Press, 1974); E. A. Locke and D. M. Schweiger, "Participation in Decision Making: One More Look," *Research in Organization Behavior* (Greenwich, CT: JAI Press, 1979); G. J. Jenkins, Jr., and E. E. Lawler III, "Impact of Employee Participation in Pay Plan Development," *Organizational Behavior and Human Performance* 28 (1981), pp. 111–128; Frederick P. Morgeson, Michael A. Campion, and Carl P. Maertz, "Understanding Pay Satisfaction: The Limits of a Compensation System Implementation," *Journal of Business and Psychology* 16(1) (Fall 2001); R. Crepanzano, *Justice in the Workplace: Vol. 2. From Theory to Practice* (Mahwah, NJ: Lawrence Erlbaum Associates, 2000); R. Folger and R. Crepanzano, *Organizational Justice and Human Resource Management* (Thousand Oaks, CA: Sage, 1998).

22. B. Carver and A. A. Vondra, "Alternative Dispute Resolution: Why It Doesn't Work and Why It Does," *Harvard Business Review,* May–June 1994, pp. 120–129.

23. Theresa M. Welbourne and Charlie O. Trevor, "The Roles of Departmental and Position Power in Job Evaluation," *Academy of Management Journal* 43 (2000), pp. 761–771.

24. N. Gupta and G. D. Jenkins, Jr., "The Politics of Pay," paper presented at the annual meeting of the Society for Industrial and Organizational Psychology, Montreal, 1992.

25. Vandra Huber and S. Crandall, "Job Measurement: A Social-Cognitive Decision Perspective," in Gerald R. Ferris, *Research in Personnel and Human Resources Management*, Vol. 12, (Greenwich, CT: JAI Press, 1994).

Person-Based Structures

Chapter Outline

Person-Based Structures: Skill Plans
    Types of Skill Plans
    Purpose of the Skill-Based Structure
"How-to": Skill Analysis
    What Information to Collect?
    Whom to Involve?
    Establish Certification Methods
    Outcomes of Skill-Based Pay Plans:
    Guidance From Research and Experience
Person-Based Structures: Competencies
    Defining Competencies
    Purpose of the Competency-Based Structure
"How-to": Competency Analysis
    Objective
    What Information to Collect?
    Whom to Involve?
    Establish Certification Methods

    Resulting Structure
    Competencies and Employee Selection
    and Training/Development
    Guidance From the Research on
    Competencies
One More Time: Internal Alignment
Reflected in Structures
Administering the Plan
Evidence of Usefulness of Results
    Reliability of Job Evaluation Techniques
    Validity
    Acceptability
Bias in Internal Structures
    Wages Criteria Bias
The Perfect Structure
Your Turn: Climb the Legal Ladder

History buffs tell us that some form of job evaluation was in use when the pharaohs built the pyramids. Chinese emperors managed the Great Wall construction with the assistance of job evaluation. In the United States, job evaluation in the public sector came into use in the 1880s, when Chicago reformers were trying to put an end to patronage in government hiring and pay practices. To set pay based not on your connections but instead on the work you did was a revolutionary old idea.

The logic underlying job-based pay structures flows from scientific management, championed by Frederick Taylor in the early 20th century. Work was broken into a series of steps and analyzed so that the "one best way," the most efficient way to perform every element of the job (right down to how to shovel coal), could be specified. Strategically, Taylor's approach fit with mass production technologies that were beginning to revolutionize the way work was done.

Taylorism still pervades our lives. Not only are jobs analyzed and evaluated in terms of the "best way" (i.e., McFry's nine steps, Exhibit 4.9), but cookbooks and software manuals specify the methods for baking a cake or using a program as a series of simple, basic steps. Golf is analyzed as a series of basic tasks that can be combined successfully to lower one's handicap. At work, at play, in all daily life, "Taylor's thinking so permeates the soil of modern life we no longer realize it is there."[1]

In today's organizations, the work is also analyzed with an eye toward increasing competitiveness and success. Routine work **(transactional work)** is separated from more complex work **(tacit work).** Investment bankers can isolate routine transactions—even routine analysis of financial statements—from more complex analysis and problem solving required to make sound investment recommendations to clients. Legal work such as patent searches, entering documents into readable databases, even vetting simple contracts can be broken out from more complex client relationships. The more routine work generates lower revenues and requires less knowledge. People doing this work are likely paid less than people doing the more complex work that yields greater profits.

Once fragmented, work processes can be rebundled into new, different jobs.[2] Pay structures based on each person's skills/knowledge/experience offer flexibility to align talent with continuously redesigned workplaces. A few years ago, machine operators on Eaton's assembly line needed to know how to operate one machine; now, as part of a manufacturing cell, they are members of self-managing teams. Eaton assembly lines now require people to be multiskilled, continuously learning, flexible, and possess problem-solving and negotiating skills. The search is on for pay systems that support the fragmented and rebundled work flows. Routine work may even be outsourced, though outsourcing a McFryer is not on the horizon.

More complex work requires pay systems that support continuous learning, improvement, and flexibility. Person-based structures hold out that promise. Person-based approaches are the topic of this chapter. At the end of this chapter, we shall discuss the usefulness of the various job-based and approaches for determining internal structures.

Exhibit 6.1 points out the similarities in the logic underlying job-based versus people-based approaches. No matter the basis for the structure, a way is needed to (1) collect and summarize information about the work, (2) determine what is of value to the organization, (3) quantify that value, and (4) translate that value into an internal structure.

PERSON-BASED STRUCTURES: SKILL PLANS

The majority of applications of **skill-based pay** have been in manufacturing, where the work often involves teams, multiskills, and flexibility. An advantage of a skill-based plan is that people can be deployed in a way that better matches the flow of work, thus avoiding bottlenecks as well as idle hands.[3]

Types of Skill Plans

Skill plans can focus on *depth* (specialists in corporate law, finance, or welding and hydraulic maintenance) and/or *breadth* (generalists with knowledge in all phases of operations including marketing, manufacturing, finance, and human resources).

Specialist: Depth

The pay structures for your elementary or high school teachers were likely based on their knowledge as measured by education level. A typical teacher's contract specifies

EXHIBIT 6.1   **Many Ways to Create Internal Structure**

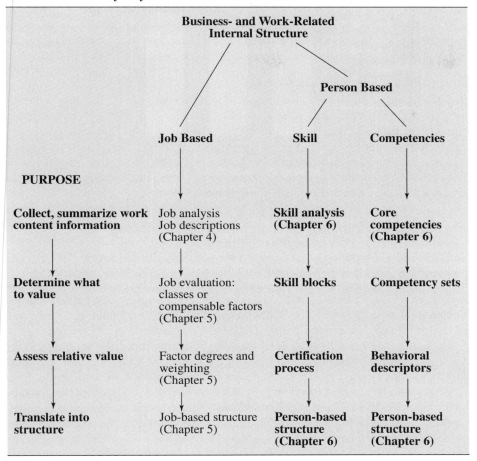

Skill-based structures link pay to the depth or breadth of the skills, abilities, and knowledge a person acquires that are relevant to the work. Structures based on skill pay individuals for all the skills for which they have been certified regardless of whether the work they are doing requires all or just a few of those particular skills. The wage attaches to the person. In contrast, a job-based plan pays employees for the job to which they are assigned, regardless of the skills they possess.

a series of steps, with each step corresponding to a level of education. A bachelor's degree in education is step 1 and is the minimum required for hiring. To advance a step to higher pay requires additional education. Each year of seniority also is associated with a pay increase. The result can be that two teachers may receive different pay rates for doing essentially the same job—teaching English to high school juniors. The pay is based on the knowledge of the individual doing the job (measured by number of college credits and years of teaching experience) rather than on job content or output (performance of students).[4] The presumption is that teachers with more knowledge are more effective and more flexible (able to teach seniors, too).

Generalist/Multiskill Based: Breadth

As with teachers, employees in a **multiskill system** earn pay increases by acquiring new knowledge, but the knowledge is specific to a range of related jobs. Pay increases come with certification of new skills, rather than with job assignments. Employees can then be assigned to any of the jobs for which they are certified, based on the flow of work. An example from Balzer Tool Coating makes the point. This company coats cutting tools by bombarding them with metal ions. The coating keeps the edge sharper longer. Originally, eight different jobs were involved in the coating process. Everyone started at the same rate, no matter the job to which the person was assigned. Employees received cross-training in a variety of jobs, but without a specific training path or level. Different locations started new people in different jobs. In order to put some order into its system and make better use of its employees, Balzer moved to a skill-based plan for all its hourly workers, including administrative and sales employees. Its new structure includes four different levels, from fundamental to advanced. Exhibit 6.2 shows the new structure and the skill blocks in each level. New employees are hired into the fundamental level. Fundamental skills include familiarity with company forms and procedures, basic product knowledge, safety, basic computer usage, and so on.

Once they have been certified in all the skills at the fundamental level, they receive a pay increase of $.50 an hour and move to the basic skill level. For each additional skill-block certification at this level, pay is increased by $.50 an hour. Basic-level employees can be assigned to any of the tasks for which they are certified; they will be paid whatever is their highest certification rate. The same approach is used at the intermediate and advanced levels. A person certified at the very top of the structure, earning at least $10.50 an hour, could be assigned to any of the tasks in the structure. The advantage to Balzer is workforce flexibility and, hence, staffing assignments that can

EXHIBIT 6.2
Skill Ladder at Balzer Tool Coating

Grade	Administration	Sales	Tool	Machine
Advanced ($10.50–$13.50)	Office administration	Inside sales	Incoming inspection	Service Arc technology
Intermediate ($9.50–$12.50)	Blueprint expediting	Customer service pricing–B	Outgoing inspection shipping	Evaporation technology coating
Basic ($7.50–$11.50)	Software pricing file/ route general office	Van driver licensing packing courier	Receiving racking packing fixturing	Degas stripping cleaning blasting
Fundamental ($7.00–$7.50)	Fundamental	Fundamental	Fundamental	Fundamental

be better matched to the work flow.[5] The advantage to employees is that the more they learn, the more they earn.

The system at Balzer differs from the system for teachers in that the responsibilities assigned at Balzer can change drastically over a short period of time, whereas teachers' basic responsibilities do not vary on a day-to-day basis. Additionally, Balzer's system is designed to ensure that all the skills are clearly work-related. Training improves skills that the company values. In contrast, a school district has no guarantee that courses taken improve teaching skills (or students' knowledge and performance).

Purpose of the Skill-Based Structure

Skill-based structures can be evaluated using the objectives already specified for an internally aligned structure: supports the organization strategy, supports work flow, is fair to employees, and directs their behavior toward organization objectives.

Supports the Strategy and Objectives

The skills on which to base a structure need to be directly related to the organization's objectives and strategy. In practice, however, the "line of sight" between changes in the specific work skills (fundamental to advanced) required to operate the Balzer coaters and increased shareholder returns is difficult to make clear. In some cosmic sense, we know that these operating skills matter, but the link to the plant's performance is clearer than the link to corporate goals.

Supports Work Flow

The link here is more clear. One of the main advantages of a skill-based plan is that it facilitates matching people to a changing work flow.[6] For example, one national hotel chain moves many of its people to the hotel's front desk between 4 p.m. and 7 p.m., when the majority of guests check in. After 7 p.m., these same employees move to the food and beverage service area to match the demand for room service and dining room service. By ensuring that guests will not have to wait long to check in or to eat, the hotel believes it can provide a high level of service with fewer staff. (We, too, wondered about the tastiness of food prepared by the check-in staff—which makes the point that skill-based systems focus on inputs, not results.)

Is Fair to Employees

Employees like the potential of higher pay that comes with learning. And by encouraging employees to take charge of their own development, skill-based plans may give them more control over their work lives.

However, favoritism and bias may play a role in determining who gets first crack at the training necessary to become certified at higher-paying skill levels. Employees complain that they are forced to pick up the slack for those who are out for training. Additionally, the courts have not yet been asked to rule on the legality of having two people do the same task but for different (skill-based) pay.

Motivates Behavior Toward Organization Objectives

Person-based plans have the potential to clarify new standards and behavioral expectations. The fluid work assignments that skill-based plans permit encourage employees to take responsibility for the complete work process and its results, with less direction from supervisors.[7] If less direction from supervisors is needed, then fewer supervisors may likewise be needed. Indeed, research at nine manufacturing plants concluded that the number of managers in plants under skill-based pay was as much as 50 percent lower compared to traditional plants.[8] Having fewer supervisors can result in substantial labor cost savings, but, of course, supervisors can see this potential consequence as well, which can certainly dampen their enthusiasm for skill-based pay and the often related practice of using teams and moving some decision responsibility from supervisors to workers.[9]

"HOW TO": SKILL ANALYSIS

Exhibit 6.3 depicts the process for determining a skill-based structure. It begins with an analysis of skills, which is similar to the task statements in a job analysis. Related skills can be grouped into a **skill block;** skill blocks can be arranged by levels into a skill structure. To build the structure, a process is needed to describe, certify, and value the skills.

Exhibit 6.3 also identifies the major **skill analysis** decisions: (1) What is the objective of the plan? (2) What information should be collected? (3) What methods should be used? (4) Who should be involved? (5) How useful are the results for pay purposes? These are exactly the same decisions as in job analysis.

> **Skill analysis** is a systematic process of identifying and collecting information about skills required to perform work in an organization.

What Information to Collect?

There is far less uniformity in the use of terms in person-based plans than there is in job-based plans. Equipment manufacturer FMC assigns points and groups skills as

EXHIBIT 6.3   **Determining the Internal Skill-Based Structure**

Internal Alignment: Work Relationships Within the Organization	→	Skill Analysis	→	Skill Blocks	→	Skill Certification	→	Skill-Based Structure
Basic Decisions								
• What is the objective of the plan?								
• What information should be collected?								
• What methods should be used to determine and certify skills?								
• Who should be involved?								
• How useful are the results for pay purposes?								

foundation, core electives, and optional electives. Its plan for technicians is more fully developed in Exhibit 6.4.

- Foundation skills include a quality seminar, videos on materials handling and hazardous materials, a three-day safety workshop, and a half-day orientation. All foundation skills are mandatory and must be certified to reach the Technician I rate ($11).
- Core electives are necessary to the facility's operations (e.g., fabrication, welding, painting, finishing, assembly, inspection). Each skill is assigned a point value.
- Optional electives are additional specialized competencies ranging from computer applications to team leadership and consensus building.

To reach Technician I ($12 per hour), 40 core elective points (of 370) must be certified, in addition to the foundation competencies. To reach Technician II, an additional 100 points of core electives must be certified, plus one optional elective.

A fully qualified Technician IV (certified in the foundations, 365 points of core electives, and 5 optional electives) is able to perform all work in any cell at the facility. Technician IVs earn $17.00 per hour no matter what task they are doing. FMC's approach should look familiar to any college student: required courses, required credits chosen among specific categories, and optional electives. There is a minor difference, of course—FMC employees get paid for passing these courses, whereas college students pay to take courses!

The FMC plan illustrates the kind of information that underpins skill-based plans: very specific information on every aspect of the production process. This makes the plans particularly suited for continuous-flow technologies where employees work in teams.

Whom to Involve?

Employee involvement is almost built into skill-based plans. Employees and managers are the source of information on defining the skills, arranging them into a hierarchy, bundling them into skill blocks, and certifying whether a person actually possesses the skills. At Balzer and FMC, a committee consisting of managers from several sites developed the skill listing and certification process for each of the four skill ladders, with input from employees.

Establish Certification Methods

Organizations may use peer review, on-the-job demonstrations, or tests to certify that employees possess skills and are able to apply them. Honeywell evaluates employees during the six months after they have learned the skills. Leaders and peers are used in the certification process. Still other companies require successful completion of formal courses. However, we do not need to point out to students that sitting in the classroom doesn't guarantee that anything is learned. School districts address this issue in a variety of ways. Some will certify for any courses; others only for courses in the teacher's subject area. However, no districts require evidence that the course makes any difference on results.

Newer skill-based applications appear to be moving away from an on-demand review and toward scheduling fixed review points in the year. Scheduling makes it easier to

EXHIBIT 6.4 FMC's Technician Skill-Based Structure

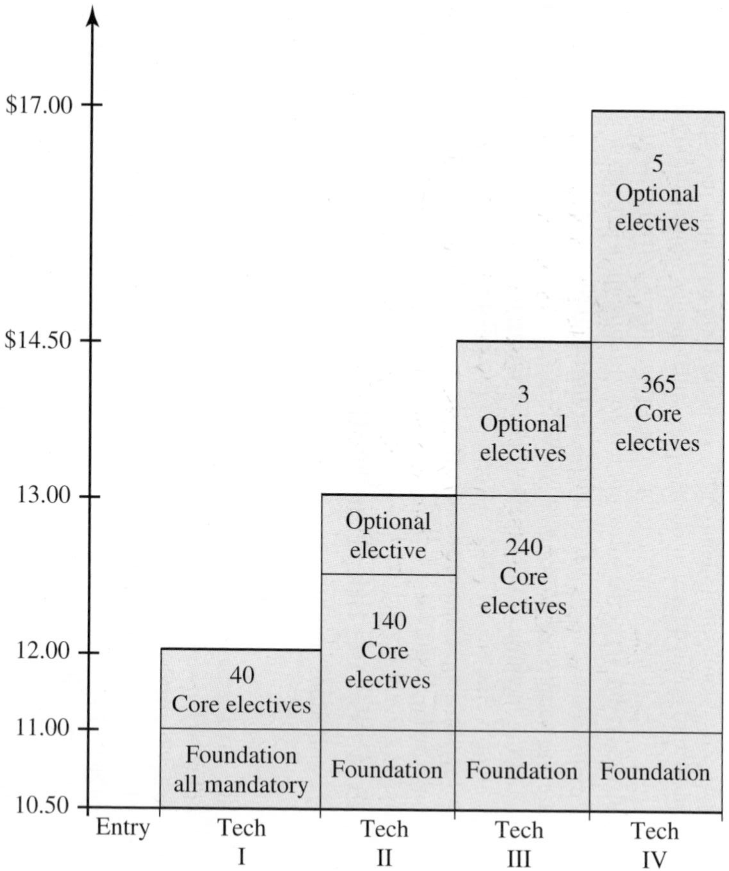

Foundations

Quality course
Shop floor control
Materials handling
Hazardous materials video
Safety workshop
Orientation workshop

Core Electives

Skills	Points	Skills	Points
Longeron Fabrication	10	Leak Check/Patch Weld	5
Panel Fabrication	15	Final Acceptance Test	10
Shell Fabrication	15	Welding Inspection	15
End Casting Welding	20	Flame Spraying	15
Finishing—Paint	20	Assembly Inspection	5
Finishing—Ablative/Autoclave	20	Safe % Arm Assembly	15
Finishing—Surface Prep	10	MK 13 Machining	25
MK 13 Assembly	15	MK 14 Machining	25
MK 14 Assembly	15	Tool Setup	10
Finishing Inspection	5	NC1 Inspection	30
Machining Inspection	20	Degrease	10
Pad Welding	15	Guide Rail Assembly	5
		Receiving Inspection	5

Optional Electives

Maintenance	Career Development
Logistics—JIT	Group Decision Making
Plant First Aid	Public Relations
Geometric Tolerancing	Group Facilitator
Computer—Lotus	Training
Computer—dBASE III	Group Problem Solving
Computer—Word Processing	Administration
Assessment Center	Plant Security
Consensus Building	

Wage scale: $17.00 — $14.50 — 13.00 — 12.00 — 11.00 — 10.50

Entry | Tech I | Tech II | Tech III | Tech IV

Tech I: 40 Core electives; Foundation all mandatory
Tech II: Optional elective; 140 Core electives; Foundation
Tech III: 3 Optional electives; 240 Core electives; Foundation
Tech IV: 5 Optional electives; 365 Core electives; Foundation

budget and control payroll increases. Other changes include ongoing recertification, which replaces the traditional one-time certification process and helps ensure skills are kept fresh, and removal of certification (and accompanying pay) when a particular skill is deemed obsolete.[10] However, it can be difficult to change certification procedures once a system is in place. TRW Automotive faced this problem in regard to using formal classes for its Mesa, Arizona, airbag facility. TRW felt that some employees were only putting in "seat time." Yet no one was willing to take the responsibility for refusing to certify, since an extra sign-off beyond classroom attendance had not been part of the original system design.

Many plans require that employees be recertified, since the skills may get rusty if they are not used frequently. At its Ome facility in Tokyo, where Toshiba manufactures laptops, all team members are required to recertify their skills every 24 months. Those who fail have the opportunity to retrain and attempt to recertify before their pay rate is reduced. However, the pressure to keep up to date and avoid obsolescence is intense.

Outcomes of Skill-Based Pay Plans: Guidance From Research and Experience

Skill-based plans are generally well accepted by employees because it is easy to see the connection between the plan, the work, and the size of the paycheck. Consequently, the plans provide strong motivation for individuals to increase their skills.[11] "Learn to earn" is a popular slogan used with these plans. One study connected the ease of communication and understanding of skill-based plans to employees' general perceptions of being treated fairly by the employer.[12] The design of the certification process is crucial in this perception of fairness. Two studies related use of a skills system to productivity. One found positive results; the other did not.[13] Another study found that younger, more educated employees with strong growth needs, organizational commitment, and a positive attitude toward workplace innovations were more successful in acquiring new skills.[14] Nevertheless, for reasons not made clear, the study's authors recommend allocating training opportunities by seniority.

Skill-based plans become increasingly expensive as the majority of employees become certified at the highest pay levels. As a result, the employer may have an average wage higher than competitors who are not using skill-based plans. Unless the increased flexibility permits leaner staffing, the employer may experience higher labor costs. Some employers are combating this by requiring that employees stay at a rate a certain amount of time before they can take the training to move to a higher rate. Motorola abandoned its skill-based plan because at the end of three years, everyone had topped out (by accumulating the necessary skill blocks). TRW, too, found that after a few years, people at two airbag manufacturing plants on skill-based systems had all **topped out.** They were flexible and well trained. So now what? What happens in the next years? Does everybody automatically receive a pay increase? Do the work processes get redesigned? In a firm with labor-intensive products, the increased labor costs under skill-based plans may become a source of competitive disadvantage.

So what kind of workplace seems best suited for a skill-based plan? Early researchers on skill-based plans found that about 60 percent of the companies in their original sample were still using skill-based plans seven years later. One of the key factors that determined a plan's success was how well it was aligned with the organization's strategy. Plans were more viable in organizations that follow a cost-cutter strategy (see Chapter 2)—doing more with less. The reduced numbers of highly trained, flexible employees that skill-based pay promises fit this strategy very well.[15]

On the other hand, it has also been argued that the higher labor costs under skill-based pay (estimated as between 10 and 15 percent) mean that it may be a better fit to companies in industries where labor costs are a small share of total costs, such as paper and forest products, chemicals, and food processing. If labor costs are 15 percent of total costs and skill-based pay translates into labor costs higher by 10 percent, then total costs would be higher by 1.5% due to skill-based pay.[16] The question then is whether this increase in labor costs is more than offset by gains in productivity, quality, customer responsiveness, flexibility, or worker retention, for example.

A final question is whether a multiskilled "jack-of-all-trades" might really be the master of none. Some research suggests that the greatest impact on results occurs immediately after just a small amount of increased flexibility.[17] Greater increments in flexibility achieve fewer improvements. There may be an optimal number of skills for any individual to possess. Beyond that number, productivity returns are less than the pay increases. Additionally, some employees may not be interested in giving up the job they are doing. Such a "camper" creates a bottleneck for rotating other employees into that position to acquire those skills. Organizations should decide in advance whether they are willing to design a plan to work around campers or whether they will force campers into the system.

The bottom line is that skill-based approaches may be only short-term initiatives for specific settings. Unfortunately, the longitudinal study of survival rates discussed above does not address the 40 percent of cases where skill-based pay did not survive beyond six years.

PERSON-BASED STRUCTURES: COMPETENCIES

As with job evaluation, there are several perspectives on what **competencies** are and what they are supposed to accomplish. Are they a skill that can be learned and developed, or are they a trait that includes attitudes and motives? Do competencies focus on the minimum requirements that the organization needs to stay in business, or do they focus on outstanding performance? Are they characteristics of the organization or of the employee? Unfortunately, the answer to all of these questions is "yes."[18] A lack of consensus means that competencies can be a number of things; consequently, they stand in danger of becoming nothing.

By now you should be able to draw the next exhibit (Exhibit 6.5) yourself. The top part shows the process of using competencies to address the need for internal alignment by creating a **competency-based structure.** All approaches to creating a structure begin by looking at the work performed in the organization. While **skill-** and **job-based systems** hone in on information about specific tasks, competencies take the opposite approach. They try to abstract the underlying, broadly applicable knowledge, skills, and behaviors that form the foundation for success at any level or job in the organization. These are the *core competencies.* Core competencies are often linked to mission statements that express an organization's philosophy, values, business strategies, and plans.

EXHIBIT 6.5   Determining the Internal Competency-Based Structure

Internal Alignment: Work Relationships Within the Organization	→	Core Competencies	→	Competency Sets	→	Behavioral Descriptors	→	Competency-Based Structure

Basic Decisions

- What is objective of plan?
- What information to collect?
- Methods used to determine and certify competencies?
- Who is involved?
- How useful for pay purposes?

Competency sets translate each core competency into action. For the core competency of *business awareness,* for example, competency sets might be related to organizational understanding, cost management, third-party relationships, and ability to identify business opportunities.

Competency indicators are the observable behaviors that indicate the level of competency within each set. These indicators may be used for staffing and evaluation as well as for pay purposes.

TRW's competency model for its human resource management department, shown in Exhibit 6.6, includes the four core competencies considered critical to the success of the business.[19] All HR employees are expected to demonstrate varying degrees of these competencies. However, not all individuals would be expected to reach the highest level in all competencies. Rather, the HR function should possess all levels of mastery of all the core competencies within the HRM group. Employees would use the model as a guide to what capacities the organization wants people to develop.

The *competency indicators* anchor the degree of a competency required at each level of complexity of the work. Exhibit 6.7 shows five levels of competency indicators for the competency *impact and influence.* These behavioral anchors make the competency more concrete. The levels range from "uses direct persuasion" at level 1 to "uses experts or other third parties to influence" at level 5. Sometimes the behavioral anchors might include scales of the intensity of action, the degree of impact of the action, its complexity, and/or the amount of effort expended. Scaled competency indicators are similar to job analysis questionnaires and degrees of compensable factors, discussed in previous chapters.

Defining Competencies

As supporters of planet Pluto have discovered, definitions matter. Because competencies are trying to get at what underlies work behaviors, there is a lot of fuzziness in defining them. Early conceptions of competencies focused on five areas:

1. Skills (demonstration of expertise)
2. Knowledge (accumulated information)
3. Self-concepts (attitudes, values, self-image)

EXHIBIT 6.6 **TRW Human Resources Competencies**

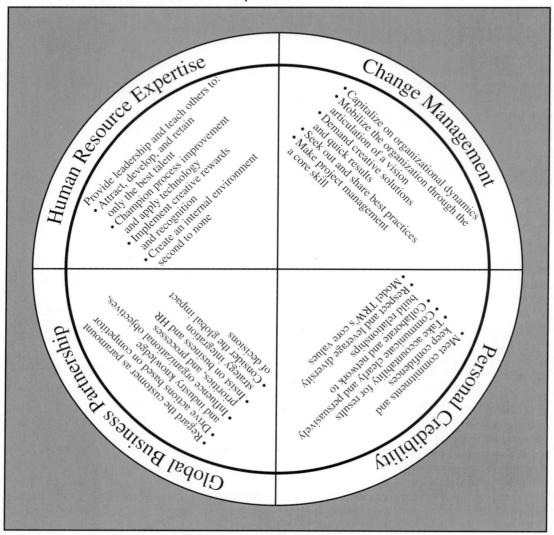

4. Traits (general disposition to behave in a certain way)
5. Motives (recurrent thoughts that drive behaviors)[20]

As experience with competencies has grown, organizations seem to be moving away from the vagueness of self-concepts, traits, and motives. Instead, they are placing greater emphasis on business-related descriptions of behaviors "that excellent performers exhibit much more consistently than average performers." Competencies are becoming "a collection of observable behaviors (not a single behavior) that require no

EXHIBIT 6.7   Sample Behavioral Competency Indicators

Impact and Influence: The intention to persuade, convince, or influence to have a specific impact. It includes the ability to anticipate and respond to the needs and concerns of others. *"Impact and Influence" is one of the competencies considered "most critical."*

Level	Behaviors
0: Not shown	• Lets things happen • Quotes policy and issues instruction
1: Direct persuasion	• Uses direct persuasion in a discussion or presentation • Appeals to reason; uses data or concrete examples • Does not adapt presentation to the interest and level of the audience • Reiterates the same points when confronted with opposition
2: Multiple attempts to persuade	• Tries different tactics when attempting to persuade without necessarily making an effort to adapt to the level or interest of an audience (e.g., making two or more different arguments or points in a discussion)
3: Builds trust and fosters win-win mentality (expected performance level)	• Tailors presentations or discussions to appeal to the interest and level of others • Looks for the "win-win" opportunities • Demonstrates sensitivity and understanding of others in detecting underlying concerns, interests, or emotions, and uses that understanding to develop effective responses to objections
4: Multiple actions to influence	• Takes more than one action to influence, with each action adapted to the specific audience (e.g., a group meeting to present the situation, followed by individual meetings) • May include taking a well-thought-out unusual action to have a specific impact
5: Influences through others	• Uses experts or other third parties to influence • Develops and maintains a planned network of relationships with customers, internal peers, and industry colleagues • When required, assembles "behind the scenes" support for ideas regarding opportunities and/or solving problems

Source: Reprinted from *Raising the Bar: Using Competencies to Enhance Employee Performance* with permission from the American Compensation Association (ACA), 14040 N. Northsight Blvd., Scottsdale, AZ USA 85260; telephone (602) 483-8352. © ACA.

inference, assumption or interpretation."[21] Exhibit 6.7 shows behavioral anchors for the competency: Impact and Influence. Comparison with compensable factors used in job evaluation—Decision Making (Exhibit 5.9) and Knowledge (Exhibit 5.10)—reveal the greater behavioral orientation of competencies. However, differences can be rather small. For example, "consults" and "uses experts" anchor both the sixth level of the compensable factor and fifth level of the competency.

Purpose of the Competency-Based Structure

Do competencies help support an internally aligned structure? Using our by-now familiar yardstick, how well do competencies support the organization strategy and work flow, treat employees fairly, and motivate their behavior toward organization objectives?

Organization Strategy

The main appeal of competencies is the direct link to the organization's strategy. The process of identifying competencies starts with the company leadership deciding what will spell success for the company. It resembles identifying compensable factors as part of job evaluation.

Frito-Lay, which has used competency-based structures for over 10 years, lists four competencies for managerial work, shown in Exhibit 6.8. Frito-Lay believes four are required in managerial work: leading for results, building work-force effectiveness, leveraging technical and business systems, and doing it the right way. The top of the exhibit shows the levels. At the first level, exhibiting the competency affects the team. At the next level, it has an impact across teams. And at the highest level, it has an impact on the entire location.

Work Flow

As you can judge from reading the previous exhibits, competencies are chosen to ensure that all the critical needs of the organization are met. For example, it is common practice to note: "These skills are considered important for all professionals but the weighting of importance and the level of proficiency varies for different positions, organizations, and business conditions."[22] So while the skills-based plans are tightly

EXHIBIT 6.8   **Frito-Lay Managerial Competencies**

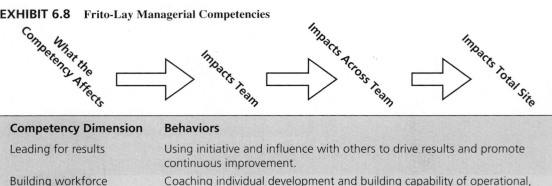

Competency Dimension	Behaviors
Leading for results	Using initiative and influence with others to drive results and promote continuous improvement.
Building workforce effectiveness	Coaching individual development and building capability of operational, project, or cross-functional teams to achieve business results.
Leveraging technical and business systems	Acquiring and applying a depth and/or breadth of knowledge, skills, and experience to achieve functional excellence.
Doing it the right way	Modeling, teaching, and coaching company values.

Source: Nancy Jagmin, "Assessing and Rewarding Competencies: The Ten-Year Tune-up at Frito-Lay," presentation for Center for Organization Effectiveness, April 2003, Marina del Rey, CA.

coupled to today's work, competencies more loosely apply to work requiring more tacit knowledge such as in managerial and professional work.

Fair to Employees

Advocates of competencies say they can empower employees to take charge of their own development. By focusing on optimum performance rather than average performance, competencies can help employees maintain their marketability.[23] However, critics of competencies worry that the field is going back to the middle of the last century, when basing pay on personal characteristics was standard practice.[24] Basing pay on race or gender seems appalling today, yet it was standard practice at one time. Basing pay on someone's judgment of another person's integrity raises a similar flag. Trying to justify pay differences based on inferred personal competencies creates risks that need to be managed.

Cybercomp Look again at the Your Turn at the end of Chapter 4. How much do you think Bill Ryan, the customer service representative, is paid? Go to *www.salary.com* and search on the Salary Wizard—Basic Report for some information. How does your job description for Mr. Ryan's job compare to those on salary.com? Does it matter?

Motivate Behavior Toward Organization Objectives

Competencies in effect provide guidelines for behavior and keep people focused. They can also provide a common basis for communicating and working together. This latter possibility has become increasingly important as organizations go global, and as employees with widely differing viewpoints and experiences fill leadership positions in these global organizations.

"HOW-TO": COMPETENCY ANALYSIS

The bottom part of Exhibit 6.5 shows the basic decisions in creating a competency-based structure. The first decision, and by far the most important, is to clarify the objective of the plan.

Objective

We have already pointed out that one of the pitfalls of competency systems is trying to do too many things with ill-suited systems. Competencies may have value for personal development and communicating organization direction. However, the vagueness and subjectivity (what exactly *are* this person's motives?) make competencies a "risky foundation for a pay system."[25] The competency structure may exist on paper by virtue of the competency sets and scaled behavioral indicators but bear little connection to the work employees do. In contrast, companies like Frito-Lay have been using theirs for 10 years. Perhaps paying for competencies is the only way to get people to pay attention to them.

What Information to Collect?

A number of schemes for classifying competencies have been proposed.[26] One of them uses three groups:

1. *Personal characteristics:* These have the aura of the Boy Scouts about them: trustworthy, loyal, courteous. In business settings, the relevant characteristics might be personal integrity, maturity of judgment, flexibility, and respect for others. Employees are expected to come in the door with these characteristics and then develop and demonstrate them in increasingly complex and ambiguous job situations.

2. *Visionary:* These are the highest-level competencies. They might be expressed as possessing a global perspective, taking the initiative in moving the organization in new directions, and able to articulate the implications for the organization of trends in the marketplace, in world events, in the local community.

3. *Organization specific:* Between the above two groups are the competencies that are tied specifically to the particular organization and to the particular function where they are being applied. They generally include leadership, customer orientation, functional expertise (e.g., able to leap tall buildings and explain the difference between competencies and compensable factors), and developing others—whatever reflects the company values, culture, and strategic intent.

Exhibit 6.9 shows the leadership competencies that 3M developed internally for its global executives.[27] Behavioral anchors are used to rate an executive on each of these competencies. Exhibit 6.10 shows the behavioral anchors for the global-perspective competency. Executives' ratings on these competencies are used to assess and develop executives worldwide. Because 3M relies heavily on promotion from within, competency ratings help develop executive talent for succession planning. Again, the link to development is clear; the link to pay is less clear.

Because they stem from each organization's mission statement or its strategy to achieve competitive advantage, you might conclude that the core competencies would be unique for each company. In fact, they are not. One analysis showed that most organizations appear to choose from the same list of 20 core competencies (Exhibit 6.11).[28] What does appear to differ among organizations is how they apply competencies. This parallels an issue in the strategy chapter (Chapter 2): There may be only slight differences in the words, but the actions differ. It is the actions that are the source of competitive advantage.

Whom to Involve?

Like compensable factors, competencies are derived from the executive leadership's beliefs about the organization and its strategic intent. However, anecdotal evidence indicates that not all employees understand that connection. Employees at one bank insisted that processing student tuition loans was a different competency from processing auto loans. The law department at Polaroid generated a list of over 1,000 competencies it felt were unique to the law department and that created value for the organization.

Exhibit 6.12 shows part of the competencies used by a major toy company. This is one of eight competencies for the marketing department. Other departments have

EXHIBIT 6.9   3M Leadership Competencies

Fundamental

- **Ethics and integrity**

  Exhibits uncompromising integrity and commitment to 3M's corporate values, human resource principles, and business conduct policies. Builds trust and instills self-confidence through mutually respectful, ongoing communication.

- **Intellectual capacity**

  Assimilates and synthesizes information rapidly, recognizes the complexity in issues, challenges assumptions, and faces up to reality. Capable of handling multiple, complex, and paradoxical situations. Communicates clearly, concisely, and with appropriate simplicity.

- **Maturity and judgment**

  Demonstrates resiliency and sound judgment in dealing with business and corporate challenges. Recognizes when a decision must be made and acts in a considered and timely manner. Deals effectively with ambiguity and learns from success and failure.

Essential

- **Customer orientation**

  Works constantly to provide superior value to the 3M customer, making each interaction a positive one.

- **Developing people**

  Selects and retains an excellent work force within an environment that values diversity and respects individuality. Promotes continuous learning and the development of self and others to achieve maximum potential. Gives and seeks open and authentic feedback.

- **Inspiring others**

  Positively affects the behavior of others, motivating them to achieve personal satisfaction and high performance through a sense of purpose and spirit of cooperation. Leads by example.

- **Business health and results**

  Identifies and successfully generates product, market, and geographic growth opportunities, while consistently delivering positive short-term business results. Continually searches for ways to add value and position the organization for future success.

Visionary

- **Global perspective**

  Operates from an awareness of 3M's global markets, capabilities, and resources. Exerts global leadership and works respectfully in multicultural environments to 3M's advantage.

- **Vision and strategy**

  Creates and communicates a customer-focused vision, corporately aligned and engaging all employees in pursuit of a common goal.

- **Nurturing innovation**

  Creates and sustains an environment that supports experimentation, rewards risk taking, reinforces curiosity, and challenges the status quo through freedom and openness without judgment. Influences the future to 3M's advantage.

- **Building alliances**

  Builds and leverages mutually beneficial relationships and networks, both internal and external, which generate multiple opportunities for 3M.

- **Organizational agility**

  Knows, respects, and leverages 3M culture and assets. Leads integrated change within a business unit to achieve sustainable competitive advantage. Utilizes teams intentionally and appropriately.

Source: Margaret E. Allredge and Kevin J. Nilan, "3M's Leadership Competency Model: An Internally Developed Solution," *Human Resource Management* 39 (Summer/Fall 2000), pp. 133–145. Reprinted by permission of John Wiley & Sons, Inc.

EXHIBIT 6.10 Behavioral Anchors for Global-Perspective Competency

Global Perspective: Behaviors
• Respects, values, and leverages other customs, cultures, and values. Uses a global management team to better understand and grow the total business. Able to leverage the benefits from working in multicultural environments.
• Optimizes and integrates resources on a global basis, including manufacturing, research, and businesses across countries, and functions to increase 3M's growth and profitability.
• Satisfies global customers and markets from anywhere in the world.
• Actively stays current on world economies, trade issues, international market trends and opportunities.

Source: Margaret E. Allredge and Kevin J. Nilan, "3M's Leadership Competency Model: An Internally Developed Solution," *Human Resource Management* 39 (Summer/Fall 2000), pp. 133–145. Reprinted by permission of John Wiley & Sons, Inc.

EXHIBIT 6.11
The Top 20
Competencies

Achievement orientation
Concern of quality
Initiative
Interpersonal understanding
Customer service orientation
Influence and impact
Organization awareness
Networking
Directiveness
Teamwork and cooperation
Developing others
Team leadership
Technical expertise
Information seeking
Analytical thinking
Conceptual thinking
Self-control
Self-confidence
Business orientation
Flexibility

separate competencies. Notice the mind-numbing level of detail. While this approach may be useful for career development, it is doubtful that all this information is useful, much less necessary, for compensation purposes. The initial promise of simplicity and flexibility in person-based systems remains unfulfilled.

EXHIBIT 6.12 Product Development Competency for Marketing Department at a Toy Company

Manages the product development process by:

- Analyzing and evaluating marketplace to identify niches/opportunities
- Evaluating product/concepts
- Developing marketing strategies
- Coordinating and evaluating research/testing
- Generating product recommendations and obtaining management support
- Driving product schedules/activities

Phase I: Baseline Expectation

- Analyzes market/competitive data (e.g., TRST, NPD) and provides top-line trend analysis, with supervision
- Evaluates products/concepts (see Toy Viability competency)
- Contributes to product brainstorming sessions
- Oversees market research activities and ensures timely completion
- Obtains Account Management input to the product development effort
- Develops and implements marketing strategy, with supervision: product, positioning, pricing/financial, promotion, packaging, merchandising, and advertising
- Facilitates cost reductions to achieve price/profit goals; ensures execution of cost meeting next steps
- Ensures adherence to product schedules
- Coordinates licensor approval of product concept/models

Phase II: Competent/Proficient

- Monitors and analyzes market/competitive data (e.g., TRST, NPD) with minimal supervision, and provides recommendations for product development opportunities
- Makes substantial contributions in product brainstorming sessions
- Analyzes market research results and makes appropriate product recommendations
- Partners with Account Management group to obtain their buy-in to the product development effort
- Develops and implements marketing strategy, with minimal supervision
- Drives cost reductions to achieve price/profit goals
- Drives product schedules and resolves product scheduling issues (late delivery, late debug)
- Negotiates with licensors to obtain product approvals

Phase III: Advanced/Coach

- Independently monitors and analyzes market/competitive data (e.g., TRST, NPD), provides recommendations for product development opportunities, and coaches others to do so
- Leads and facilitates formal product brainstorming sessions
- Coaches others in analyzing market research results and making product recommendations
- Develops innovative marketing plans (e.g., new channels of distribution, niche markets)
- Independently develops and implements marketing strategy, and coaches others to do so
- Identifies/evaluates cost reduction opportunities, and coaches others to do so
- Identifies and implements product schedule improvement tactics
- Coaches others to manage product schedules
- Shares product ideas/strategies with other teams/categories

Phase IV: Expert/Mentor

- Reviews/approves recommendations for product development opportunities
- Provides short- and long-term vision and goals for developing the corporate product portfolio across categories or brands
- Reviews/approves marketing strategy, and proactively adjusts strategy in response to internal/external changes
- Approves cost reduction recommendations
- Anticipates critical issues that may impact product schedules and develops alternate plans
- Ensures on-strategy delivery

179

Establish Certification Methods

The heart of the person-based plan is that employees get paid for the relevant skills or competencies they possess, whether or not those skills are used. Skill-based plans assume that possessing these skills will make it easier to match work flow with staffing levels, so whether or not an individual is *using* a particular skill on a particular day is not an issue. Competency-based plans assume—what? That all competencies are used all the time? The assumptions are not clear. What is clear, however, is the requirement that if people are to be paid based on their competencies, then there must be some way to demonstrate or certify to all concerned that a person possesses that level of competency. Although consultants discuss competencies as compatible with 360-degree feedback and personal development, they are silent on objectively certifying whether a person possesses a competency.

Resulting Structure

Recall that internal structures are described in terms of number of levels, pay differentials, and criterion on which the job structure is based. In practice, competency-based structures generally are designed with relatively few levels—four to six—and relatively wide differentials for increased flexibility. Exhibit 6.13 depicts the toy company's structures based on the four phases (levels) shown in Exhibit 6.12. Such a generic structure could be applied to almost any professional work, even the work of a university faculty.

Competencies and Employee Selection and Training/Development

In Chapter 2, we noted that human resource strategies can be thought of as influencing effectiveness through their impact on workforce ability, motivation, and ability to contribute (AMO). In the case of competencies, there is clear evidence that ability (broadly defined to include personality traits) is related to general competencies. Like Exhibit 6.11, Exhibit 6.14 shows a set of generic competencies, called the Great Eight, that seem to capture in an efficient way the themes found in the array of competency frameworks available. What Exhibit 6.14 adds are hypotheses regarding how these competencies relate to the individual characteristics of personality ("Big Five"), motivation, and ability. So, for example, based on Exhibit 6.14, if we wish to have managers who are competent in leading and deciding, we need to select or train and develop people high in need for power, need for control, and who have extroverted personalities. Failure to adequately screen employees on these individual characteristics would not only put more pressure on training and development, but also potentially de-motivate employees who are seeking

EXHIBIT 6.13	Level	Phase	Title
Toy Company's			
Structure	4	Expert	Visionary; Champion; Executive
Based on	3	Advanced	Coach; Leader
Competencies	2	Resource	Contributor; Professional
	1	Proficient	Associate

EXHIBIT 6.14   Titles and High-Level Definitions of the Great Eight Competencies™

Factor	Competency Domain Title	Competency Domain Definition	Hypothesized Big Five, Motivation, and Ability Relationships[a]
1	Leading and deciding	Takes control and exercises leadership. Initiates action, gives direction, and takes responsibility.	Need for power and control, extroversion
2	Supporting and cooperating	Supports others and shows respect and positive regard for them in social situations. Put people first, working effectively with individuals and tams, clients, and staff. Behaves consistently with clear personal values that complement those of the organization.	Agreeableness
3	Interacting and presenting	Communicates and networks effectively. Successfully persuades and influences these. Relates to others in a confident, relaxed manner.	Extroversion, general mental ability
4	Analyzing and interpreting	Shows evidence of clear analytical thinking. Gets to the heart of complex problems and issues. Applies own expertise effectively. Quickly takes on new technology. Communicates well in writing.	General mental ability, openness to new experience
5	Creating and conceptualizing	Works well in situations requiring openness to new ideas and experiences. Seeks out learning opportunities. Handles situations and problems with innovation and creativity. Thinks broadly and strategically. Supports and drives organizational change.	Openness to new experience, general mental ability
6	Organizing and executing	Plans ahead and works in a systematic and organized way. Follows directions and procedures. Focuses on customer satisfaction and delivers a quality service or product to the agreed standards.	Conscientiousness, general mental ability
7	Adapting and coping	Adapts and responds well to change. Manages pressure effectively and cops well with setbacks.	Emotional stability
8	Enterprising and performing	Focuses on results and achieving personal work objectives. Works best when work is related closely to results and the impact of personal efforts is obvious. Shows an understanding of business, commerce, and finance. Seeks opportunities for self-development and career advancement.	Need for achievement, negative agreeableness

[a] Where more than one predictor is shown, the second is expected to be of lesser importance than the first. The competency titles and definitions are taken from the SHL Universal Competency Framework™ Profiler and Designer Cards (copyright © 2004 by SHL Group plc, reproduced with permission of the copyright holder). These titles may be freely used for research purposes subject to due acknowledgment of the copyright holder.

Source: Dave Bartram, SHL Group, "The Great Eight Competencies: a Criterion-Centric Approach to Validation," *Journal of Applied Psychology* 2005. Vol. 90, No. 6, pp. 1185–1203.

Note. More detailed definitions of each of he Great Eight are provided by the competency component level of the SHL Universal Competency Framework™ (see Appendix).

to acquire and demonstrate these competencies, but who may not be well-suited to do so. Competency-based pay would be less likely to succeed in this situation.

Guidance From the Research on Competencies

While the notion of competencies may have value in identifying what distinguishes typical from truly outstanding performance, there is debate on whether competencies can be translated into a measurable, objective basis for pay. Competencies often morph into compensable factors. So it is not surprising that little empirical research exists. Only one study has analyzed the competencies/performance relationship for managers. Managers' competencies are related to their performance ratings, but there is no relationship to unit-level performance.[29]

An area of research with potential application to competencies deals with human capital and knowledge management.[30] Viewing the competencies of employees as a portfolio similar to a diversified investment portfolio highlights the fact that some competencies deliver greater returns than others. The focus then changes to managing existing competencies and developing new ones in ways that maximize the overall returns to the organization.[31] As organizations globalize, they may rebalance their values and perspectives to allow a global strategy to function.[32] They seek the right balance among the range and depth of cultural, functional, and product competencies in the global organization. But this is speculative and remains to be translated into pay practices.

The basic question remains: Is it appropriate to pay you for what I believe you are *capable of doing* versus what you are doing? Isn't it likely to be more effective, for pay purposes, to focus on what is easily measurable and directly related to organizational success (i.e., knowledge and skills that are job/performance related)?

ONE MORE TIME: INTERNAL ALIGNMENT REFLECTED IN STRUCTURES

Now that we have spent three chapters examining all the trees, let's look again at the forest. The purpose of job- and person-based procedures is really very simple—to design and manage an internal pay structure that helps the organization succeed.

As with job-based evaluation, the final result of the person-based plan is an internal structure of work in the organization. This structure should reflect the organization's internal alignment policy (loosely versus tightly linked, egalitarian versus hierarchical) and support its business operations. Further, managers must ensure that the structure *remains* internally aligned by reassessing work/skills/competencies when necessary. Failure to do so risks pay structures that open the door to bias and potentially unethical and misdirected behavior.

In practice, when evaluating higher-value, nonroutine work, the distinction between job- versus person-based approaches blurs. The focus is on what factors (*both* job and person) create value for the organization. The person influences the job content in managerial and professional work. Skill-based fits more easily with manufacturing work.[33] Yet caution is advised: Much of the work required in contemporary manufacturing cells requires tacit, nonroutine knowledge (problem solving, interacting, negotiating).

ADMINISTERING THE PLAN

Whatever plan is designed, a crucial issue is the fairness of its administration. Just as with job evaluation, sufficient information should be available to apply the plan, such as definitions of compensable factors, degrees, or details of skill blocks, competencies, and certification methods. Increasingly, online tools are available for managers to learn about these plans and apply them.[34]

We have already mentioned the issue of employee understanding and acceptance. Communication and employee involvement are crucial for acceptance of the resulting pay structures. See Chapter 18 for more discussion of pay communication.

EVIDENCE OF USEFULNESS OF RESULTS

There is vast research literature on job evaluation compared to person-based structures. Most of it focuses on the procedures used rather than the resulting structure's usefulness in motivating employee behaviors or achieving organization objectives. In virtually all the studies, job-based evaluation is treated as a measurement device; the research assesses its reliability, validity, costs, and its compliance with laws and regulations. Any value added by job evaluation (e.g., reducing pay dissatisfaction, improving employees' understanding of how their pay is determined) has been largely ignored.[35] In contrast, research on person-based structures tends to focus on their effects on behaviors and organization objectives and ignores questions of reliability and validity.

Reliability of Job Evaluation Techniques

A reliable evaluation would be one where different evaluators produce the same results. Most studies report high agreement when different people rank-order jobs—correlations between .85 and .96.[36] This is important because in practice, several different people usually evaluate jobs. The results should not depend on which person did the evaluation. Reliability can be improved by using evaluators who are familiar with the work and trained in the job evaluation process. Some organizations use group consensus to increase reliability. Each evaluator makes a preliminary independent evaluation. Then, they discuss their results until consensus emerges. Consensus certainly appears to make the results more acceptable. However, some studies report that results obtained through consensus were not significantly different from those obtained either by independent evaluators or by averaging individual evaluators' results. Others report that a forceful or experienced person on the committee can sway the results. So can knowledge about the job's present salary level.[37]

As part of efforts to reduce costs, job evaluation committees are disappearing. Instead, managers do the evaluations online as part of the organization's "HR Toolkit" or "shared services." The reliability and validity of the results obtained this way have not been studied.

Validity

Validity refers to the degree to which the evaluation assesses what it is supposed to—the relative worth of jobs to the organization. Validity of job evaluation has been measured in two ways: (1) the degree of agreement between rankings that resulted from the job evaluation with an agreed-upon *ranking of benchmarks* used as the criterion, and (2) by **"hit rates"**—the degree to which the job evaluation plan matches (hits) an agreed-upon *pay structure for benchmark jobs*. In both cases, the predetermined, agreed-upon ranking or pay structure is for benchmark jobs. It can be established by organization leadership or be based on external market data, negotiations with unions, or the market rates for benchmarks held predominantly by men (to try to eliminate any gender discrimination reflected in the market), or some combination of these.

Many studies report that when different job evaluation plans are compared to each other, they generate *very similar rankings* of jobs but *very low hit rates*—they disagree on how much to pay the jobs.[38] One study that looked at three different job evaluation plans applied to the same set of jobs reported similar rank order among evaluators using each plan but substantial differences in the resulting pay.[39] Some studies have found pay differences of up to $427 per month ($750/per month in today's dollars, or $9,000 a year) depending on the method used.

So it is clear that the definition of validity needs to be broadened to include impact on pay decisions. How the results are judged depends on the standards used. For managing compensation the correct standard is the pay structure—what jobholders get paid—rather than simply the jobs' rank order.

Studies of the degree to which different job evaluation plans produce the same results start with the assumption that if different approaches produce the same results, then those results must be "correct," that is, valid. But in one study, three plans all gave the same result (they were reliable) but all three ranked a police officer higher than a detective. They were not valid.[40] TV fans of *Law and Order* know that in U.S. police departments, the detectives outrank the uniforms. What accounts for the reliability of invalid plans? Either the compensable factors did not pick up something deemed important in the detectives' jobs or the detectives have more power to negotiate higher wages. So while these three plans gave the same results, they would have little acceptance among detectives.

You may wonder why any manager or employee cares about such details? Is this an example of compensation specialists inventing work for themselves? Not if your organization is facing challenges by dissatisfied employees or their lawyers. To miss this point is to place your organization at risk.[41]

Acceptability

Several methods are used to assess and improve employee acceptability. An obvious one is to include a *formal appeals process*. Employees who believe their jobs are evaluated incorrectly should be able to request reanalysis and/or skills reevaluation. Most firms respond to such requests from managers, but few extend the process to all employees unless it is part of a union-negotiated grievance process.[42] *Employee attitude surveys* can assess perceptions of how useful evaluation is as a management tool. Ask employees whether their pay is related to their job and how well they understand what is expected in their job.[43]

BIAS IN INTERNAL STRUCTURES

The continuing differences in jobs held by men, women, and people of color, and the accompanying pay differences, have focused attention on internal structures as a possible source of discrimination. Much of this attention has been directed at job evaluation as both a potential source of bias against women and a mechanism to reduce bias.[44] It has been widely speculated that job evaluation is susceptible to gender bias—jobs held predominantly by women are undervalued simply because of the jobholder's gender. But evidence does not support this proposition.[45] Additionally, there is no evidence that the job *evaluator's* gender affects the results.

In contrast to the gender of the jobholder or the evaluator, the evidence on compensable factors and bias is less clear. One study found that compensable factors related to job content (such as contact with others and judgment) did reflect bias against work done predominantly by women, but factors pertaining to employee requirements (such as education and experience) did not.[46]

Wages Criteria Bias

The second potential source of bias affects job evaluation indirectly, through the current wages paid for jobs. If job evaluation is based on the current wages paid and the jobs held predominantly by women are underpaid, then the results simply mirror bias in the current pay rates.[47] Since many job evaluation plans are purposely structured to mirror the existing pay structure, it is not surprising that current wages influence the results of job evaluation. One study of 400 compensation specialists revealed that market data had a substantially larger effect on pay decisions than did job evaluations or current pay data.[48] This study is a unique look at several factors that may affect pay structures.

Several recommendations seek to ensure that job evaluation plans are bias-free, including the following:

1. Define the compensable factors and scales to include the content of jobs held predominantly by women. For example, working conditions may include the noise and stress of office machines and the repetitive movements associated with the use of computers.
2. Ensure that factor weights are not consistently biased against jobs held predominantly by women. Are factors usually associated with these jobs always given less weight?
3. Apply the plan in as bias-free a manner as feasible. Ensure that the job descriptions are bias-free, exclude incumbent names from the job evaluation process, and train diverse evaluators.

At the risk of pointing out the obvious, all issues concerning job evaluation also apply to skill-based and competency-based plans. For example, the acceptability of the results of skill-based plans can be studied from the perspective of measurement (reliability and validity) and administration (costs, simplicity). The various points in skill certification at which errors and biases may enter into judgment (e.g., different views of skill-block definitions, potential favoritism toward team members, defining and assessing skill obsolescence) and whether skill-block points and evaluators make a difference all need to be studied. In light of the detailed bureaucracy that has grown up around job evaluation, we confidently predict a growth of bureaucratic procedures around person-based plans, too. In addition to bureaucracy to manage costs, the whole approach to certification may be fraught with potential legal vulnerabilities if employees who fail to be certified challenge the process. Unfortunately, no studies of gender effects in skill-based or competency-based plans exist. Little attention has been paid to assessor training or validating the certification process. Just as employment tests used for hiring and promotion decisions must be demonstrably free of illegal bias, it seems logical that certification procedures used to determine pay structures would face the same requirement.

THE PERFECT STRUCTURE

Exhibit 6.15 contrasts job-, skill-, and competency-based approaches. Pay increases are gained via promotions to more responsible jobs under job-based structures or via the acquisition of more-valued skills/competencies under the person-based structures. Logically, employees will focus on how to get promoted (experience, performance) or on how to acquire the required skills or competencies (training, learning).

Managers whose employers use job-based plans focus on placing the right people in the right job. A switch to skill-/competency-based plans reverses this procedure. Now, managers must assign the right work to the right people, that is, those with the right skills and competencies. A job-based approach controls costs by paying only as much as the work performed is worth, regardless of any greater skills the employee may possess. So, as Exhibit 6.15 suggests, costs are controlled via job rates or work assignments and budgets.

In contrast, skill-/competency-based plans pay employees for the highest level of skill/competency they have achieved *regardless of the work they perform*. This maximizes flexibility. But it also encourages all employees to become certified at top rates. Unless an employer can either control the rate at which employees can certify skill/competency mastery or employ fewer people, the organization may experience higher

EXHIBIT 6.15   Contrasting Approaches

	Job Based	Skill Based	Competency Based
What is valued	Compensable factors	Skill blocks	Competencies
Quantify the value	Factor degree weights	Skill levels	Competency levels
Mechanisms to translate into pay	Assign points that reflect criterion pay structure	Certification and price skills in external market	Certification and price competencies in external market
Pay structure	Based on job performed/market	Based on skills certified/market	Based on competency developed/market
Pay increases	Promotion	Skill acquisition	Competency development
Managers' focus	Link employees to work promotion and placement cost control via pay for job and budget increase	Utilize skills efficiently provide training control costs via training, certification, and work assignments	Be sure competencies add value provide competency-developing opportunities control costs via certification and assignments
Employee focus	Seek promotions to earn more pay	Acquire skills	Acquire competencies
Procedures	Job analysis job evaluation	Skill analysis skill certification	Competency analysis competency certification
Advantages	Clear expectations sense of progress pay based on value of work performed	Continuous learning flexibility reduced work force	Continuous learning flexibility lateral movement
Limitations	Potential bureaucracy potential inflexibility	Potential bureaucracy requires cost controls	Potential bureaucracy requires cost controls

labor costs than do competitors using job-based approaches. The key is to offset the higher rates with greater productivity. One consulting firm claims that an average company switching to a skill-based system experiences a 15 to 20 percent increase in wage rates, a 20 to 25 percent increase in training and development costs, and initial *increases* in head count to allow people to cross-train and move around.[49] Another study found costs were no higher.[50]

In addition to having potentially higher rates and higher training costs, skill/competency plans may become as complex and burdensome as job-based plans. Additionally, questions still remain about a skill/competency system's compliance with the U.S. Equal Pay Act.

So where does all this come out? What is the best approach to pay structures, and how will we know it when we see it? The answer is, it depends. The best approach may be to provide sufficient ambiguity (loosely linked internal alignment) to afford flexibility to adapt to changing conditions. Too generic an approach may not provide sufficient detail to make a clear link between pay, work, and results; too detailed an approach may become rigid. Bases for pay that are too vaguely defined will have no credibility with employees, will fail to signal what is really important for success, and may lead to suspicions of favoritism and bias.

This chapter concludes our section on internal alignment. Before we move on to external considerations, let's once again address the issue of, So what? Why bother with a pay structure? The answer should be, because it supports improved organization performance. An internally aligned pay structure, whether strategically loosely linked or tightly fitting, can be designed to (1) help determine pay for the wide variety of work in the organization, and (2) ensure that pay influences peoples' attitudes and work behaviors and directs them toward organization objectives.

Your **Turn**   Climb the Legal Ladder

Sullivan & Cromwell, a large New York law firm with offices around the world, recently raised its starting salary for law school graduates to $160,000, up from $145,000 the previous year. But, at Sullivan & Cromwell, like at many firms, starting salaries have not increased since. Indeed, some firms are cutting salaries and/or jobs. Most large firms use pay structures with six to eight levels from associate to partner. The associate's level is typically based on experience plus performance (see Exhibit 1). In the world of associate attorneys, performance is measured as billable hours. So the associates who meet or exceed the expected billable hours advance to the next level each year. Similar to the tenure process in academic settings, after six to eight years associates are expected to become partners or "find opportunities elsewhere." The likelihood of making partner differs among firms, but the norm seems to be less than one-third of the associates make it. Associates are expected to bill around 2,200 hours per year. That works out to six hours a day 365 days per year. Sullivan & Cromwell partners reportedly earn an average of over $2 million a year.

Clients are billed about $250/hour for each associate. (Some partners' billing rates in New York firms have now hit $1,000 per hour.) So if associates hit or exceed their targets, they generate $550,000 annually ($250 times 2,200 hours). Many firms also use performance bonuses for associates, capped at around $60,000.

1. Think about the research evidence discussed in the book. Would you expect the Sullivan & Cromwell associates to feel their pay structure is fair? What comparisons would they likely make? What work behaviors would you expect Sullivan & Cromwell's pay structure to motivate? Explain.

2. What about associates who joined the firm four years ago? If the salaries for new associates increased by $20,000, what would you recommend for other levels in the structure? Explain.

EXHIBIT 1	Associate Base Salary		Bonus Range		Bonus
Pay Structure at a Law Firm	**Year**		**Low**	**High**	**Discretionary**
	1st	$160,000	$0	$30,000	Yes
	2nd	170,000	0	35,000	Yes
	3rd	185,000	0	40,000	Yes
	4th	210,000	0	45,000	Yes
	5th	230,000	0	50,000	Yes
	6th	250,000	0	55,000	Yes
	7th	265,000	0	60,000	Yes
	8th	275,000	0	65,000	Yes

3. Partners make around 10 times the highest-paid associates. A *Wall Street Journal* writer laments that law firms form "giant pyramids . . . (in which) associates at the bottom funnel money to partners at the top." What is missing from the writer's analysis? Hint: Speculate about the likely differences in content and value of the work performed by partners compared to associates. Any parallels to Merrill Lynch's FAs and SVPIs?

4. Sullivan & Cromwell announced that year-end bonuses will be cut in half, with a maximum of $17,500 for early-career associates and $32,500 for eighth-year associates. It will, however, issue another bonus payment later in the year, which will depend on the firm's performance. How will this change to bonuses affect the pay structure and its impact on employees? Should Sullivan & Cromwell be concerned about difficulties in recruiting or retention?

Sources: *www.infirmation.com, www.sullcrom.com;* Lindsey Fortado, "Linklaters Becomes Latest Law Firm to Cut Starting Lawyer Pay," *Bloomberg.com,* April 30, 2009; "The American Lawyer," *The AmLaw* 100, April 2009; Susan Beck, "Are Blue-Chip New York Firms Losing Their Balance?" *Law.com,* April 30, 2009; "Heavy Lies the Crown: Associate Cuts Were the Story in 2008. Are Partners Next? *American Lawyer,* February 2009; "Sullivan & Cromwell Halves Associate Bonuses," *JD Journal,* December 19, 2008.

Summary

This section of the book examines pay structures within an organization. The premise underlying internal alignment is that internal pay structures need to be aligned with the organization's business strategy and objectives, the design of the work flow, a concern for the fair treatment of employees, and the intent of motivating employees. The work relationships within a single organization are an important part of internal alignment. The structures are part of the web of incentives within organizations. They affect satisfaction with pay, the willingness to seek and accept promotions to more responsible jobs, the effort to keep learning and undertake additional training, and the propensity to remain with the employer. They also reduce the incidence of pay-related grievances.

The techniques for establishing internally aligned structures include job analysis, job evaluation, and person-based approaches for skill-/competency-based plans. But, in practice, aspects of both jobs and people are used. Although viewed by some as bureaucratic burdens, these techniques can aid in achieving the objectives of the pay system when they are properly designed and managed. Without them, our pay objectives of improving competitiveness and fairness are more difficult to achieve.

We have now finished the first part of the book. We discussed the techniques used to establish internal alignment as well as its effects on compensation objectives. The next part of the book focuses on the next strategic issue in our pay model: external competitiveness.

Review Questions

1. What are the pros and cons of having employees involved in compensation decisions? What forms can employee involvement take?

2. Why does the process used in the design of the internal pay structure matter? Distinguish between the processes used to design and administer a person-based and a job-based approach.

3. If you were managing employee compensation, how would you recommend that your company evaluate the usefulness of its job evaluation or person-based plans?

4. Based on the research on job evaluation, what are the sources of possible gender bias in skill-/competency-based plans?

5. How can a manager ensure that job evaluation or skill-/competency-based plans support a customer-centered strategy?

Endnotes

1. Robert Kanigel, *The One Best Way* (New York: Viking, 1997).

2. M. Marchington, D. Grimshaw, J. Rubery, and H. Willmott, eds., *Fragmenting Work: Blurring Organizational Boundaries and Disordering Hierarchies* (New York: Oxford University Press, 2004).

3. N. Gupta and J. D. Shaw, "Successful Skill-Based Pay Plans," in C. Fay, D. Knight, and M. A. Thompson, eds., *The Executive Handbook of Compensation: Linking Strategic Rewards to Business* (New York: Free Press, 2001); Laurie Bienstock and Sandra McLellan, "Job Leveling in a Changing Environment," *WorldatWork Journal,* Fourth Quarter 2002, pp. 37–44.

4. The Consortium for Public Research in Education at the University of Wisconsin (*www.wcer.wisc.edu/cpre/tcomp/research*) publishes research on teachers' pay and analysis of emerging issues; see A. Milanowski, "The Varieties of Knowledge and Skill-Based Pay Design: A Comparison of Seven New Pay Systems for K–12 Teachers," Working Paper TC-01-2, University of Wisconsin, Wisconsin Center for Education Research, Consortium for Policy Research in Education, Madison, 2001; Steve Farkas, Jean Johnson, Ann Duffett, et al., *Stand by Me: What Teachers Really Think About Unions, Merit Pay, and Other Professional Matters* (New York: Public Agenda, 2003).

5. Diana Southall and Jerry Newman, *Skill-Based Pay Development* (Buffalo, NY: HR Foundations, 2000).

6. G. Douglas Jenkins Jr., Gerald E. Ledford Jr., Nina Gupta, and D. Harold Doty, *Skill-Based Pay* (Scottsdale, AZ: American Compensation Association, 1992).

7. B. Murray and B. Gerhart, "An Empirical Analysis of a Skill-Based Pay Program and Plant Performance Outcomes," *Academy of Management Journal* 41 (1998), pp. 68–78.

8. Gerald Ledford, "Factors Affecting the Long-Term Success of Skill-Based Pay," *WorldatWork Journal*, First Quarter, 2008, pp. 6–18; Judy Canavan, "Overcoming the Challenge of Aligning Skill-Based Pay Levels to the External Market," *WorldatWork Journal*, First Quarter (2008), pp. 18–24.

9. Rosemary Batt, "Who Benefits From Teams? Comparing Workers, Supervisors, and Managers," *Industrial Relations*, 43 (2004), pp. 183–212.

10. Gerald E. Ledford, Jr., "Three Case Studies of Skill-Based Pay: An Overview," *Compensation and Benefits Review*, March/April 1991, pp. 11–23; Gerald Ledford, "Factors Affecting the Long-Term Success of Skill-Based Pay," *WorldatWork Journal*, First Quarter (2008), pp. 6–18.

11. Erich C. Dierdorff and Eric A. Surface, "If You Pay for Skills, Will They Learn? Skill Change and Maintenance Under a Skill-Based Pay System," *Journal of Management* 34 (2008), pp. 721–743.

12. Cynthia Lee, Kenneth S. Law, and Philip Bobko, "The Importance of Justice Perceptions on Pay Effectiveness: A Two-Year Study of a Skill-Based Pay Plan," *Journal of Management* 25(6) (1999), pp. 851–873.

13. K. Parrent and C. Weber, "Case Study: Does Paying for Knowledge Pay Off?" *Compensation and Benefits Review*, September–October 1994, pp. 44–50; B. Murray and B. Gerhart, "An Empirical Analysis of a Skill-Based Pay Program and Plant Performance Outcomes," *Academy of Management Journal* 41 (1998), pp. 68–78.

14. Kenneth Mericle and Dong-One Kim, "Determinants of Skill Acquisition and Pay Satisfaction Under Pay-for-Knowledge Systems," Working Paper Series, Institute of Industrial Relations, University of California, Berkeley, *www.iir.berkeley.edu/ncw/*, 1996; Steve Farkas, Jean Johnson, Ann Duffett, et al., *Stand by Me: What Teachers Really Think About Unions, Merit Pay, and Other Professional Matters* (New York: Public Agenda, 2003), *www.publicagenda.org*.

15. Jason D. Shaw, Nina Gupta, Atul Mitra, and Gerald E. Ledford Jr., "Success and Survival of Skill-Based Pay Plans," *Journal of Management*, February 2005, pp. 28–49.

16. Gerald Ledford, "Factors Affecting the Long-Term Success of Skill-Based Pay," *WorldatWork Journal*, First Quarter (2008), pp. 6–18.

17. N. Fredric Crandall and Marc J. Wallace Jr., "Paying Employees to Develop New Skills," in Howard Risher, ed., *Aligning Pay and Results* (New York: American Management Association, 1999).

18. Patricia Zingheim, Gerald E. Ledford Jr., and Jay R. Schuster, "Competencies and Competency Models: Does One Size Fit All?" *ACA Journal*, Spring 1996, pp. 56–65.

19. TRW Corporate Competency Model.

20. Lyle M. Spencer Jr. and Signe M. Spencer, *Competence at Work* (New York: Wiley, 1993).

21. William M. Mercer, *Competencies, Performance and Pay* (New York: William M. Mercer, 1995).

22. TRW Corporate Competency Model.

23. James T. Kochanski and Howard Risher, "Paying for Competencies: Rewarding Knowledge, Skills, and Behaviors," in Howard Risher, ed., *Aligning Pay and Results* (New York: American Management Association, 1999).

24. C. A. Bartlett and Sumantra Ghoshal, "The Myth of the Generic Manager: New Personal Competencies for New Management Roles," *California Management Review* 40(1) (1997), pp. 92–105.

25. Edward E. Lawler III, "From Job-Based to Competency-Based Organizations," *Journal of Organizational Behavior* 15 (1994), pp. 3–15.

26. Patricia K. Zingheim and Jay R. Schuster, "Reassessing the Value of Skill-Based Pay: Getting the Runaway Train Back on Track," *WorldatWork Journal* 11(3), Third Quarter, 2002.

27. Margaret E. Allredge and Kevin J. Nilan, "3M's Leadership Competency Model: An Internally Developed Solution," *Human Resource Management* 39, Summer/Fall 2000, pp. 133–145.

28. Patricia Zingheim, Gerald E. Ledford, Jr., and Jay R. Schuster, "Competencies and Competency Models," in Ameican Compensation Association, Raising *the Bar: Using Competencies to Enhance Employee Performance* (Scottsdale, AZ: American Compensation Association, 1996).

29. A. R. Levenson, W. A. Van der Stede, and S. G. Cohen, "Measuring the Relationship Between Managerial Competencies and Performance," *Journal of Management* 32(3) (2006), pp. 360–380.

30. Scott A. Snell, David P. Lepak, and Mark A. Youndt, "Managing the Architecture of Intellectual Capital," in Patrick M. Wright, Lee E. Dyer, John W. Bodreau, and George T. Milkovich, eds., *Strategic Human Resources Management in the Twenty-First Century,* Suppl. 4 (Stamford, CT: JAI Press, 1999).

31. Robert L. Heneman and Peter V. Leblanc, "Developing a More Relevant and Competitive Approach for Valuing Knowledge Work," *Compensation and Benefits Review,* July/August 2002, pp. 43–47; James R. Bowers, "Valuing Work—An Integrated Approach," Chapter 16 in Charles H. Fay, Michael A. Thompson, and Damien Knight, eds., *The Executive Handbook on Compensation—Linking Strategic Rewards to Business Performance* (New York: Free Press, 2001).

32. Allen D. Engle Sr. and Mark E. Mendenhall, "Spinning the Global Competency Cube: Toward a Timely Transnational Human Resource Decision Support System," working paper, Eastern Kentucky University, Richmond, KY, 2000.

33. Jason D. Shaw, Nina Gupta, Atul Mitra, and Gerald E. Ledford Jr., "Success and Survival of Skill-Based Pay Plans," *Journal of Management,* February 2005, pp. 28–49.

34. *HRJob Evaluation Software, Online Job Classification, Web. NPKTools* (part of CompXpert compensation analysis suite), *www.npktools.com.*

35. An exception is the study cited in A. R. Levenson, W. A. Van der Stede, and S. G. Cohen, "Measuring the Relationship Between Managerial Competencies and Performance," *Journal of Management* 32(3) (2006), pp. 360–380.

36. Tjarda van Sliedregt, Olga F. Voskuijl, and Henk Thierry, "Job Evaluation Systems and Pay Grade Structures: Do They Match?" *International Journal of Human Resource Management* 12(8) (December 2001), pp. 1313–1324.

37. Erich C. Dierdorff and Mark A. Wilson, "A Meta-Analysis of Job Analysis Reliability," *Journal of Applied Psychology,* August 2003, pp. 635–646; Vandra Huber and S. Crandall, "Job Measurement: A Social-Cognitive Decision Perspective," in Gerald R. Ferris, ed., *Research in Personnel and Human Resources Management,* Vol. 12 (Greenwich, CT: JAI Press, 1994), pp. 223–269; Sheila M. Rutt and Dennis Doverspike, "Salary and Organizational Level Effects on Job Evaluation Ratings," *Journal of Business and Psychology,* Spring 1999, pp. 379–385.

38. R. M. Madigan and D. J. Hoover, "Effects of Alternative Job Evaluation Methods on Decisions Involving Pay Equity," *Academy of Management Journal,* March 1986, pp. 84–100.

39. D. Doverspike and G. Barrett, "An Internal Bias Analysis of a Job Evaluation Instrument," *Journal of Applied Psychology* 69 (1984), pp. 648–662; Kermit Davis, Jr., and William

Sauser, Jr., "Effects of Alternative Weighting Methods in a Policy-Capturing Approach to Job Evaluation: A Review and Empirical Investigation," *Personnel Psychology* 44 (1991), pp. 85–127.

40. Judith Collins and Paul M. Muchinsky, "An Assessment of the Construct Validity of Three Job Evaluation Methods: A Field Experiment," *Academy of Management Journal* 36(4) (1993), pp. 895–904; Todd J. Maurer and Stuart A. Tross, "SME Committee vs. Field Job Analysis Ratings: Convergence, Cautions, and a Call," *Journal of Business and Psychology* 14(3), Spring 2000, pp. 489–499.

41. Examples abound. A recent one one is the pay equity settlement by Bell Canada, discussed in Chapter 17. See Pay Equity Information Centre at *www.equityic.ca* and "CEP Reaches $104 million pay Equity Settlement at Bell," *www.cep.ca/human_rights/equity/bell/equityrelease_e.pdf.*

42. D. Lipsky and R. Seeber, "In Search of Control: The Corporate Embrace of Alternative Dispute Resolution," *Journal of Labor and Employment Law* 1(1) (Spring 1998), pp. 133–157.

43. Hudson Employment Index, *www.hudson-index.com/node.asp?SID56755.*

44. D. J. Treiman and H. I. Hartmann, eds., *Women, Work and Wages: Equal Pay for Jobs of Equal Value* (Washington, DC: National Academy of Sciences, 1981); H. Remick, *Comparable Worth and Wage Discrimination* (Philadelphia: Temple University Press, 1984); Morley Gunderson, "The Evolution and Mechanics of Pay Equity in Ontario," *Canadian Public Policy* 28(1) (2002), pp. S117–S126; Deborah M. Figart, "Equal Pay for Equal Work: The Role of Job Evaluation in an Evolving Social Norm," *Journal of Economic Issues,* March 2000, pp. 1–19.

45. D. Schwab and R. Grams, "Sex-Related Errors in Job Evaluation: A 'Real-World' Test," *Journal of Applied Psychology* 70(3) (1985), pp. 533–559; Richard D. Arvey, Emily M. Passino, and John W. Lounsbury, "Job Analysis Results as Influenced by Sex of Incumbent and Sex of Analyst," *Journal of Applied Psychology* 62(4) (1977), pp. 411–416.

46. Michael K. Mount and Rebecca A. Ellis, "Investigation of Bias in Job Evaluation Ratings of Comparable Worth Study Participants," *Personnel Psychology,* Spring 1987, pp. 85–96.

47. D. Schwab and R. Grams, "Sex-Related Errors in Job Evaluation: A 'Real-World' Test," *Journal of Applied Psychology* 70(3) (1985), pp. 533–559.

48. S. Rynes, C. Weber, and G. Milkovich, "The Effects of Market Survey Rates, Job Evaluation, and Job Gender on Job Pay," *Journal of Applied Psychology* 74 (1989), pp. 114–123.

49. N. Fredric Crandall and Marc J. Wallace Jr., "Paying Employees to Develop New Skills," in Howard Risher, ed., *Aligning Pay and Results* (New York: American Management Association, 1999); B. Murray and B. Gerhart, "An Empirical Analysis of a Skill-Based Pay Program and Plant Performance Outcomes," *Academy of Management Journal* 41 (1998), pp. 68–78.

50. Howard Risher, ed., *Aligning Pay and Results* (New York: American Management Association, 1999).

External Competitiveness: Determining the Pay Level

If you are a star, you can make a pretty good living. *Forbes* magazine recently reported the earnings of some well-known people. One of them was Tiger Woods. Tiger's accomplishments on the golf course are legendary. So are his earnings. Last year, he made $110 million, despite being laid up for about 8 months because of knee surgery. Lucky (if that is really the right word for somebody that good, smart, and hard-working) for Tiger, he makes most of his money off the golf course. David Letterman made $45 million last year goofing around on television at night. Harder to quantify perhaps is the pleasure he may be feeling at the thought of outlasting rival Jay Leno and not having to compete with him any more. (We'll have to see how Conan does.) While we're talking about late night, let's not forget Jon Stewart. Despite doing what seems to be multiple jobs (news anchor and comedian), Jon earned $14 million last year, less than David Letterman. (However, he claims that he gets a discount at Red Lobster. So, it all comes out even—sort of.) Why does Letterman earn more than Stewart? Perhaps it is because Letterman's show brings more viewers (and thus more advertising revenue)? There are many more examples of great success stories and the "pot of gold" that comes with this success. Beyonce Knowles earned somewhere in the neighborhood of $80 million last year. Soccer player Ronaldinho, baseball player Derek Jeter, and basketball player Kevin Garnett all earned about $30 million last year. Not quite as glamorous perhaps, but not too shabby either, *Human Resource Executive* reported that the top–paid HR executive of last year, Jon D. Walton of Alleghany Technologies, made $9.7 million last year. (We have not been able to verify as of yet whether he used our compensation book when he was in college, or if he feels what he learned from our book was the key to his success. But, we are willing to assume that all of this is true. Unfortunately, we probably can't take much credit for the others we have discussed. Oh well, "baby steps.")

The recent earnings for Mr. Woods and some others are shown in **Exhibit III.1**. For some of you, these examples may confirm what you have always suspected: Pay is determined without apparent reason or justice. Nevertheless, there is also logic, at least in many cases. The celebrities on the list generally drive some pretty big dollars in revenues. Executives, hedge fund managers, and others making big

EXHIBIT III.1 Who Makes How Much?

Name	Age	Occupation	Location	Earnings
Ann Sin	34	Math teacher	Clovis, CA	$66,000
Chesley Sullenberger	58	Airline pilot	Danville, CA	$100,000
Kathleen Mason	44	Realtor	Midland, GA	$38,400
Josh Bacott	31	Sports blogger	St. Louis, MO	$10,700
Alex Rodriguez	33	Baseball player	New York, NY	$34,000,000
Jimmy Jamie	26	Home-health-care CEO	Charleston, WV	$2,200,000
Deborah Blakeney	47	Letter carrier	Charlotte, NC	$53,700
Britney Spears	27	Singer	Los Angeles, CA	$2,250,000
John Benes	35	Plumber	Gonzales, TX	$39,300
Jennifer Aniston	40	Actress	Los Angeles, CA	$27,000,000
Mark Chandler	53	Library messenger	Evansville, IN	$19,700
Susan Meisner	44	Port-of-entry inspector	Lenore, ID	$30,000
Michael Bloomberg	67	Mayor of New York City	New York, NY	$1
Christine Kenseth	52	Aerobics instructor	Janesville, WI	$78,000
Laurie Metoyer	37	MRI technician	Baton Rouge, LA	$48,000
Joshua Gropper	43	Trial attorney	New York, NY	$400,000
Theodore Jones	65	Court of Appeals judge	Albany, NY	$151,200
Brian Davis	39	Pharmaceutical sales rep	Katy, TX	$90,000
Tina Fey	38	Actress/comedian	New York, NY	$4,600,000
Sarah Palin	45	Governor of Alaska	Wasilla, AK	$125,000
Ronald Curell	57	Carpenter	Maryville, MI	$35,500
John Arnold	35	Hedge-fund manager	Houston, TX	$1,500,000,000
Steven Walsh	48	Air-traffic controller	East Falmouth, MA	$128,000
Aubrey Carter	24	Social worker	Southhaven, MS	$45,800
Jace Scribner	40	Electrical contractor	Woodinville, WA	$165,000
Beyonce	27	Singer	New York, NY	$80,000,000
Jay-Z	39	Rapper	New York, NY	$82,000,000
Eileen Coleman	35	Website manager	Port Republic, MD	$86,300
Aaron Vrooman	36	Truck driver	Lancaster, SC	$54,000
Michael Olson	44	Probation officer	Flagstaff, AZ	$58,000
John Grisham	54	Author	Charlottesville, VA	$25,000,000
Pradeep Das	58	Library director	Ellenwood, GA	$41,500
Julie Sorenson	45	Certified nurse's aide	Glenwood, UT	$20,200
Darin Anstine	44	Fire chief	Fountain, CO	$102,000
Tammy Toussin	37	Pet sitter/dog walker	St. Louis, MO	$100,000

Name	Age	Occupation	Location	Earnings
Rick Sandoval	46	Auto salesperson	Abingdon, IL	$48,200
Danica Patrick	27	Racecar driver	Phoenix, AZ	$7,000,000
Tyler Perry	39	Actor/director	Atlanta, GA	$125,000,000
Roseanne Gentry	55	Registered nurse	Big Horn, WY	$68,500
Rush Limbaugh	58	Radio host	Palm Beach, FL	$38,000,000
Jose Alexio	48	Solar-energy worker	Dacula, GA	$70,000
Phylecia Roas	31	Computer scientist	La Mesa, CA	$89,000
Kevin Wright	45	Pastor	Getzville, NY	$41,500
Alex Hatt	40	Auto technician	Edmonds, WA	$48,000
Ken Lewis	62	CEO, Bank of America	Charlotte, NC	$10,000,000
Cindy Hing	31	Actress	Miami, FL	$2,000
David Borst	66	Gambling counselor	Syracuse, NY	$30,000
Karen Carter	41	Insurance agent	Oklahoma, OK	$27,000
Linda Tillman	53	School principal	Wichita, KS	$102,800
Tiger Woods	33	Pro golfer	Orlando, FL	$110,000,000
Bret Collins	43	Golf-course keeper	Kirkland, IL	$72,000
Gloria Gomez	53	Courtroom clerk	Waterford, CA	$47,000
Janice O'Connell	57	Finance director	Weare, NH	$76,000
David Chmielewski	62	School bus driver	Land O'Lakes, FL	$18,700
Carolyn Murphy	33	Supermodel	Los Angeles, CA	$4,500,000
Tabitha Roberts	33	Bookkeeper	Huntsville, AL	$26,900
Will Ferrell	41	Actor/comedian	Los Angeles, CA	$31,000,000
Venitra Taylor	27	Asst. retail manager	Upper Marlboro, MD	$36,500
Edwin Tanedo	35	Special-ed assistant	Beaverton, OR	$18,000
Taylor Swift	19	Singer	Hendersonville, TN	$5,500,000
Angela McIver	30	Claims assistant	Fayetteville, AR	$33,100
Ron Gettelfinger	64	President UAW	Detroit, MI	$155,000
Kathleen Douthat	50	College counselor	Knoxville, TN	$45,000

Source: "What People Earn," *Parade Magazine*, April 12, 2009.

bucks (no, the $1.5 billion for hedge fund manager John Arnold is not a typo) show what can happen if you work hard, take advantage of opportunities (in this case, to get to a position where a lot of people trust you with their money), and maybe have some good luck along the way. There are also some "real" people on the list too: an airline pilot hero who safely landed a disabled plane on the Hudson River, and less famous people in everyday jobs like plumber, realtor, letter carrier, carpenter, truck driver, certified nurse's aid, computer programmer, and others. It's kind of interesting to think about why these people get paid what they do. Why don't they get paid more? Why not less? What would they do if they were paid more or paid less? How well would their employers do if they raised or lowered pay for these people and others in their jobs or other jobs? These are the kinds of questions we will now address.

External competitiveness is the term we use to describe the "how much to pay" and "*how* to pay" questions. It is the next strategic decision in the total pay model, as shown in **Exhibit III.2.** Two aspects of pay translate external competitiveness into practice: (1) how much to pay relative to competitors—whether to pay more than competitors, to match what they pay, or to pay less—and (2) what mix of base, bonus, stock options, and benefits to pay relative to the pay mix of competitors. In a sense, "what forms" to pay (base, bonus, benefits) are the pieces of the pie. "How much" is the size of the pie. External competitiveness includes both questions.

As we shall see in the next two chapters, a variety of answers exist. Chapter 7 discusses choosing the external competitiveness policy, the impact of that choice, and related theories and research. Chapter 8 has two parts: First, it discusses how to translate competitiveness policy into pay level and forms. Second, it discusses how to integrate information on pay levels and forms with the internal structure from Part One.

EXHIBIT III.2   **The Pay Model**

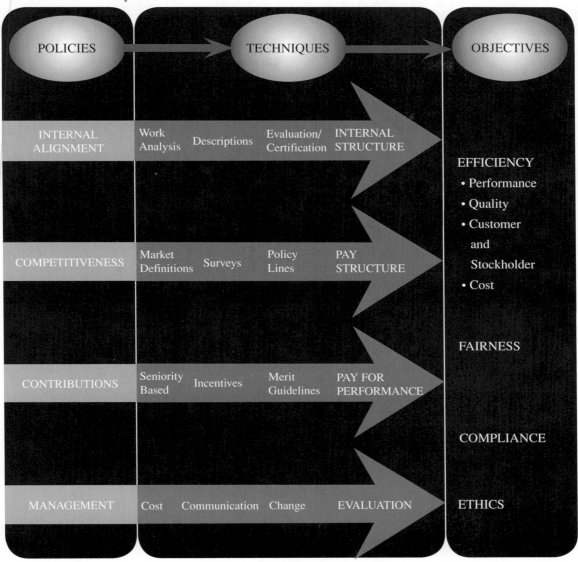

Defining Competitiveness

Chapter Outline

Compensation Strategy: External Competitiveness
  Control Costs and Increase Revenues
  Attract and Retain the Right Employees

What Shapes External Competitiveness?

Labor Market Factors
  How Labor Markets Work
  Labor Demand
  Marginal Product
  Marginal Revenue
  Labor Supply

Modifications to the Demand Side
  Compensating Differentials
  Efficiency Wage
  Signaling

Modifications to the Supply Side (Only Two More Theories to Go)
  Reservation Wage
  Human Capital

Product Market Factors and Ability to Pay
  Product Demand
  Degree of Competition
  A Different View: What Managers Say
  Segmented Supplies of Labor and (Different) Going Rates

Organization Factors
  Industry and Technology
  Employer Size
  People's Preferences
  Organization Strategy

Relevant Markets
  Defining the Relevant Market
  Globalization of Relevant Labor Markets: Offshoring and Outsourcing

Competitive Pay Policy Alternatives
  What Difference Does the Pay-Level Policy Make?
  Pay With Competition (Match)
  Lead Pay-Level Policy
  Lag Pay-Level Policy
  Different Policies for Different Employee Groups
  Not by Pay Level Alone: Pay-Mix Strategies

Consequences of Pay-Level and -Mix Decisions: Guidance From the Research
  Efficiency
  Fairness
  Compliance

Your Turn: Sled Dog Software

Still Your Turn: Fit the Pay-Mix Policy to the Compensation Strategy

January is always a good month for travel agents in Ithaca, New York. In addition to the permanent population eager to flee Ithaca's leaden skies (our computer has a screen saver whose color is titled "Ithaca"; it consists of 256 shades of gray), graduating students from Ithaca's two colleges are traveling to job interviews with employers across the country—at company expense, full fare, no Saturday-night stayovers required. When they return from these trips, students compare notes and find that even for people receiving the same degree in the same field from the same college, the offers vary from company to company. What explains the differences? Location has an effect: Firms in San Francisco and New York City make higher offers. The work also has an effect: Jobs in employment pay a little less than jobs in compensation and employee relations. (Now aren't you glad you didn't drop this course?) And the industry to which the different firms belong has an effect: Pharmaceuticals, brokerage houses, and petroleum firms tend to offer more than consumer products, insurance, and heavy-manufacturing firms.[1]

Students would like to attribute these differences to themselves: differences in grades, courses taken, interviewing skills, and so on. But the same company makes the identical offer to most of its candidates at the school. So it is hard to make the case that an individual's qualifications totally explain the offers. Why would companies extend identical offers to most candidates? And why would different companies extend different offers? This chapter discusses these choices and what difference they make for the organization.

The sheer number of economic theories related to compensation can make this chapter heavy going. Another difficulty is that the reality of pay decisions doesn't necessarily match the theories. The key to this chapter is to always ask, So what? How will this information help me? So grab a box of Krispy Kremes and let's find out.

COMPENSATION STRATEGY: EXTERNAL COMPETITIVENESS

In Part One, we looked at comparisons *inside* the organization. In **external competitiveness,** our second pay policy, we look at comparisons *outside* the organization—comparisons with other employers that hire people with the same skills. A major strategic decision is whether to mirror what competitors are paying or to design a pay package that may differ from competitors but better fits the business strategy.

External competitiveness is expressed in practice by (1) setting a pay level that is above, below, or equal to that of competitors; and (2) determining the mix of pay forms relative to those of competitors.

> **External competitiveness** refers to the pay relationships among organizations—the organization's pay relative to its competitors.
>
> **Pay level** refers to the *average* of the array of rates paid by an employer:
>
> (base + bonuses + benefits + value of stock holdings) / number of employees
>
> **Pay forms** are the various types of payments, or pay mix, that make up total compensation.

Both pay level and pay mix decisions focus on two objectives: (1) control costs and increase revenues and (2) attract and retain employees.

Control Costs and Increase Revenues

Pay level decisions have a significant impact on expenses. Other things being equal, the higher the pay level, the higher the labor costs:

> Labor costs = (pay level) times (number of employees)

Furthermore, the higher the pay level relative to what competitors pay, the greater the relative costs to provide similar products or services. So you might think that all organizations would pay the same job the same rate. However, they do not. A national survey of over 1,200 entry-level software engineers employed by high-tech companies found an average base salary of $54,300, with a range from $36,500 to $94,000. Why would Microsoft pay more (or less) than Google? What would any company pay above whatever minimum amount is required to hire engineers or other employees?

Paying employees above market can be an effective or ineffective strategy. It all depends on what the organization gets in return. Let's look at a few examples. Exhibit 7.1 compares labor costs at the U.S. Big Three automakers with those at three Japanese automakers (Toyota, Honda, Nissan) in the United States. It also compares what the companies get in return. As of 2007, U.S. automakers had higher labor costs, but lower reliability and lower road test performance ratings on average. GM and Chrysler subsequently went through bankruptcy. One might infer that the Big Three's pay level strategy has not worked for it. (In Chapter 1, we also noted the huge drop in employment among U.S. producers like GM.) As part of that process and also as a result of government involvement, agreements have been reached with the United Auto Workers that are expected to reduce labor costs to make them competitive with Japanese producers. The harder question to answer is whether the quality and performance of the cars will also become more competitive.

Exhibit 7.2 pertains to two airline companies, Southwest and USAir. In 2000, USAir trailed Southwest in terms of efficiency, with overall operating costs of 14 cents per available seat mile (ASM), almost double that of Southwest at 7.7 cents per ASM.

EXHIBIT 7.1
Comparing the Big Three Automakers in U.S. and Japan

Sources: Oliver Wyman, "The Harbour Report™, North America 2008," www.liverwyman.com; *Consumer Reports,* April 2009; David Leonhardt, "$73 an Hour: Adding It Up," *New York Times,* December 10, 2008.

	2007		2011 (Projected)	
	Ford GM Chrysler	**Toyota Nissan Honda**	**Ford GM Chrysler**	**Toyota Nissan Honda**
Total Labor Hours per Vehicle	32.2	31.2	*	*
Hourly Total Compensation	$73	$48	$54	$47
Hourly Total Compensation (without legacy costs)	$59	$48	$54	$47
Hourly Wages	$29	$26	$29**	$26**
Labor Cost/Vehicle	$1,650	$1,040	$1,080	$980
Consumer Reports				
Reliability (100 = best)	41	71	*	*
Road-Test Performance (100 = best)	58	76	*	*

Notes: Hourly Total Compensation includes wages and benefits, as well as legacy costs: health care and pension payments to retirees. Total Labor Hours is hours for assembly, stamping, engine, and transmission.

*Not available.

**Hourly wages (and Hourly Total Compensation) projections must consider at least three factors: (1) The Big Three have negotiated two-tier wage structures with the United Auto Workers, which have newly hired workers starting at a wage of roughly $14/hour, and (2) The Japanese producers also have a lower starting wage. Thus, wage and total compensation costs will depend on how many new versus experienced hires are employed in the future. (3) Legacy costs for the Big Three will be taken "off the books" through an agreement with the United Auto Workers (UAW), under which the UAW are given a lump sum payment and assume responsibility for pension and retiree health care obligations.

EXHIBIT 7.2   Revenues, Capacity, Operating Costs, and Labor Costs of USAir and Southwest Airlines

Source: 2001 and 2009 10-K statements, available at www.sec.gov; www.theacsi.org/index.php; http//airconsumer.ost.dot.gov/www.airlinepilotcentral.com; MIT Airline Data Project, http://web.mit.edu/airlinedata/www/default.html

	2000 US Airways	2000 Southwest	2008 US Airways	2008 Southwest
Revenues	$9,269,000,000	$5,649,560,000	$12,118,000,000	$11,023,000,000
Operating Costs	$9,322,000,000	$4,628,415,000	$13,918,000,000	$10,574,000,000
Labor Costs	$9,637,000,000	$1,683,470,017	$2,231,000,000	$3,340,000,000
Employees	43,467	29,274	32,671	35,499
Labor Costs/ Revenues	39.24%	29.80%	18.41%	30.30%
Labor Costs/ Employees	$83,672.67	$57,507.34	$68,286.86	$94,087,16
Available Seat Miles (ASM)	66,506,000,000	59,909,965,000	74,151,000,000	102,271,343,000
Operating Costs/ASM	$0.140	$0.077	$0.188	$0.103
Labor Costs/ASM	$0.055	$0.028	$0.030	$0.28
Pilot Annual Pay*	$138,301.50	$111,430.00	$85,396.00	$130,954,00
Pilot Hourly Rate**			$99	$157
Net Income (Loss)	−$269,000,000	$625,224,000	−$2,210,000,000	$178,000,000
Customer Complaints (per 100,000)***	2.1	0.4	1.8	0.2
American Customer Satisfaction Index™	62	70	54	79

*For 2000, used average of 2000 and 2001 data because of large fluctuation in USAir data.

**Average of hourly rate for first officer, 5 years experience and captain, 10 years experience, large narrowbody aircraft.

***Average of October and July reports for each year.

Likewise, USAir had labor costs per ASM roughly double (5.5 cents versus 2.8 cents) that of Southwest Airlines. Part of the cost disadvantage for USAir in 2000 was its higher pay (e.g., for pilots). USAir and other so-called legacy airlines realized that they needed to move their costs lower to compete with Southwest. By 2008, USAir seems to have made considerable progress, at least with respect to labor costs, which dropped from 5.5 cents per ASM in 2000 to 3 cents per ASM in 2008, almost the same as at Southwest. (Part of USAir's success in reducing labor costs is due to it going through bankruptcy and using that as an opportunity to reduce pay and benefits costs.) However, there remains a difference not only in overall operating cost, but also in the passenger experience. In both years, Southwest had many fewer customer complaints and higher customer satisfaction. If anything, Southwest's advantage in customer satisfaction seems to have increased. So, Southwest continues to outperform USAir. It is not necessarily how much it pays that is the key. Rather, it can be argued that it is its ability to pay competitively and get a great deal in return from its employees. Southwest has been widely studied for its total compensation strategy, which includes employee profit sharing and stock, but also having fun at work and strong employee relations. However, there is growing concern that Southwest's labor costs may become a problem. As Exhibit 7.2 shows, it now pays its pilots much more than USAir pays theirs. For the first time in many, many years, Southwest has recently reported losing money.[2] It will be interesting to see what the future brings in the airline industry for companies using different compensation and human resource approaches.

Attract and Retain the Right Employees

One company may pay more because it believes its higher-paid engineers are more productive than those at other companies. Their engineers may be better trained; maybe they are more innovative in dreaming up new applications. Maybe they are less likely to quit, thus saving the company recruiting and training costs. Another company may pay less because it is differentiating itself on nonfinancial returns—more challenging and interesting projects, possibility of international assignments, superior training, more rapid promotions, or even greater job security. Different employers set different pay levels; that is, they deliberately choose to pay above or below what others are paying for the same work. That is why there is no single "going rate" in the labor market for a specific job.[3]

Not only do the rates paid for similar jobs vary among employers, but a single company may set a different pay level for different job families.[4] The company in Exhibit 7.3 illustrates the point. The *top chart* shows that this particular company pays about 2 percent above the market for its entry-level engineer. (Market is set at zero in the exhibit.) However, it pays 13 percent above the market for most of its marketing jobs and over 25 percent above the market for marketing managers. Office personnel and technicians are paid below the market. So this company uses very different pay levels for different job families.

These data are based on comparisons of **base wage.** When we look at **total compensation** in the bottom of the exhibit, a different pattern emerges. The company still has a different pay level for different job families. But when bonuses, stock options, and benefits are included, only marketing managers remain above the market. Every other job family is now substantially below the market. Engineering managers take the deepest plunge, from only 2 percent below the market to over 30 percent below.[5]

EXHIBIT 7.3 **A Single Company's Market Position May Differ Depending on Whether Comparing Base Pay or Total Compensation**

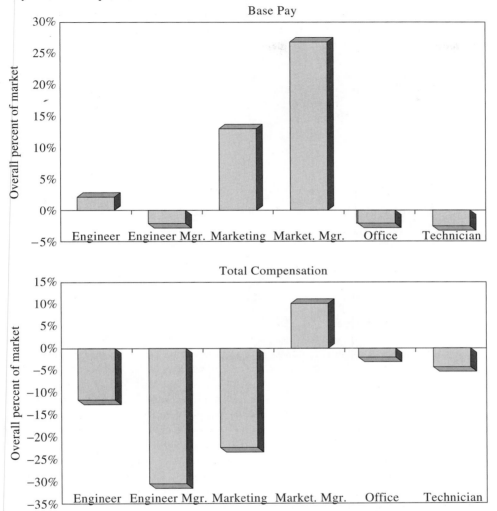

The exhibit, based on actual company data, makes two points. First, companies often set different pay-level policies for different job families. Second, how a company compares to the market depends on what competitors it compares to and what pay forms are included. It is not clear whether the company in the exhibit deliberately chose to emphasize marketing managers and deemphasize engineering in its pay plan or if it is paying the price for not hiring one of you readers to design its plan.[6] Either way, the point is, people love to talk about "the market rate" as if a single rate exists for any job, with the implication that organizations are constrained to pay that same rate to their own employees in that job. Nevertheless, Exhibit 7.4 instead shows that

EXHIBIT 7.4
Two Companies: Same Total Compensation, Different Mixes

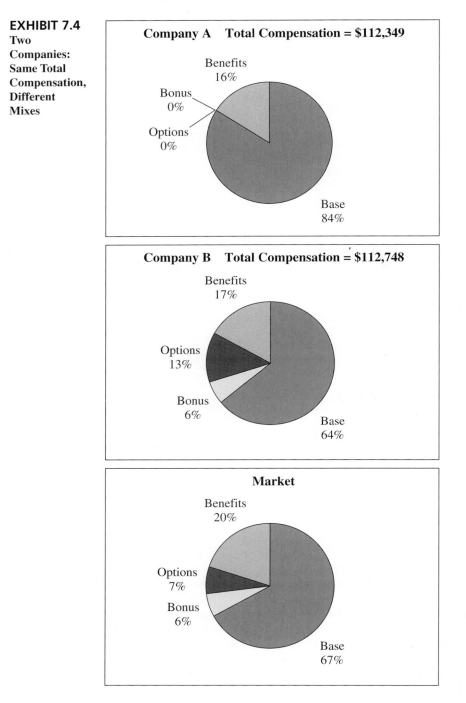

Company A   Total Compensation = $112,349

Benefits
16%

Bonus
0%

Options
0%

Base
84%

Company B   Total Compensation = $112,748

Benefits
17%

Options
13%

Bonus
6%

Base
64%

Market

Benefits
20%

Options
7%

Bonus
6%

Base
67%

EXHIBIT 7.5   **What Shapes External Competitiveness?**

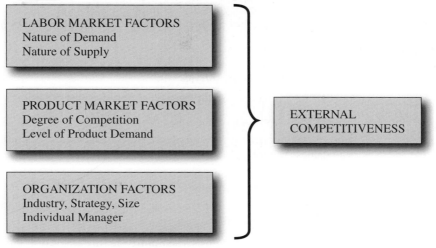

organizations can and do vary in how closely they match the "going rate." There is no single "going mix" of pay forms, either. Exhibit 7.4 compares the pay mix for the same job (software marketing manager) at two companies in the same geographic area. Both companies offer about the same total compensation. Yet the percentages allocated to base, bonuses, benefits, and options are very different.

WHAT SHAPES EXTERNAL COMPETITIVENESS?

Exhibit 7.5 shows the factors that affect decisions on pay level and mix. The factors include (1) competition in the *labor market* for people with various skills; (2) competition in the *product and service markets,* which affects the financial condition of the organization; and (3) characteristics unique to each organization and its employees, such as its business strategy, technology, and the productivity and experience of its work force. These factors act in concert to influence pay-level and pay-mix decisions.

LABOR MARKET FACTORS

Economists describe two basic types of markets: the **quoted price** and the **bourse.** Stores that label each item's price or ads that list a job opening's starting wage are examples of quoted-price markets. You cannot name your own price when you order from Amazon, but Priceline says you can. However, Priceline does not guarantee that your price will be accepted, whereas an Amazon order arrives in a matter of days. In contrast with Amazon's quoted price, eBay allows haggling over the terms and conditions until an agreement is reached; eBay is a *bourse*. Graduating students usually find themselves in a quoted-labor market, though minor haggling may occur.[7] In both the bourse and the quoted market, employers are the buyers and the potential employees are the sellers. If the inducements (total compensation) offered by the employer and the skills offered by the employee are mutually acceptable, a deal is struck. It may be formal contracts negotiated by unions, professional athletes, and executives, or it may be a brief letter or maybe only the implied understanding of a handshake. All this activity makes up the labor market; the result is that people and jobs match up at specified pay rates.

How Labor Markets Work

Theories of labor markets usually begin with four basic assumptions:

1. Employers always seek to maximize profits.
2. People are homogeneous and therefore interchangeable; a business school graduate is a business school graduate is a business school graduate.
3. The pay rates reflect all costs associated with employment (e.g., base wage, bonuses, holidays, benefits, even training).
4. The markets faced by employers are competitive, so there is no advantage for a single employer to pay above or below the market rate.

Although these assumptions oversimplify reality, they provide a framework for understanding labor markets. As we shall see later, as reality forces us to change our assumptions, our theories change too.

Organizations often claim to be "market-driven"; that is, they pay competitively with the market or even are market leaders. Understanding how markets work requires analysis of the demand and supply of labor. The demand side focuses on the actions of the employers: how many new hires they seek and what they are willing and able to pay new employees. The supply side looks at potential employees: their qualifications and the pay they are willing to accept in exchange for their services.

Exhibit 7.6 shows a simple illustration of demand and supply for business school graduates. The vertical axis represents pay rates from $25,000 to $80,000 a year. The horizontal axis depicts the number of business school graduates in the market. The

EXHIBIT 7.6
Supply and Demand for Business School Graduates in the Short Run

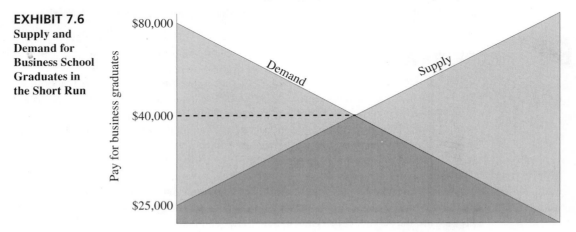

Number of business graduates available

line labeled "Demand" is the sum of *all* employers' hiring preferences for business graduates at various pay levels. At $80,000, only a small number of business graduates will be hired because only a few firms are able to afford them. At $25,000, companies can afford to hire a large number of business graduates. However, as we look at the line labeled "Supply," we see that there aren't enough business graduates willing to be hired at $25,000. In fact, only a small number are willing to work for $25,000. As pay rates rise, more graduates become interested in working, so the labor supply line slopes upward. *The market rate is where the lines for labor demand and labor supply cross.* In this illustration, the interaction among all employers and all business graduates determines the $40,000 market rate. Because any single employer can hire all the business graduates it wants at $40,000 and all business graduates are of equal quality (i.e., assumption 2 above), there is no reason for any wage other than $40,000 to be paid.

Labor Demand

If $40,000 is the market-determined rate for business graduates, how many business graduates will a specific employer hire? The answer requires an analysis of **labor demand.** In the short term, an employer cannot change any other factor of production (i.e., technology, capital, or natural resources). Thus, its level of production can change only if it changes the level of human resources. Under such conditions, a single employer's demand for labor coincides with the **marginal product of labor.**

> The **marginal product of labor** is the additional output associated with the employment of one additional person, with other production factors held constant.
>
> The **marginal revenue of labor** is the additional revenue generated when the firm employs one additional person, with other production factors held constant.

Marginal Product

Assume that two business graduates form a consulting firm that provides services to 10 clients. The firm hires a third person, who brings in four more clients. The marginal product (the change in output associated with the additional unit of labor) of the third person is four clients. But adding a fourth employee generates only two new clients. This diminishing marginal productivity results from the fact that each additional employee has a progressively smaller share of the other factors of production with which to work. In the short term, these other factors of production (e.g., office space, number of computers, telephone lines, hours of clerical support) are fixed. Until these other factors are changed, each new hire produces less than the previous hire. The amount each hire produces is the marginal product.

Marginal Revenue

Now let's look at marginal revenue. Marginal revenue is the money generated by the sale of the marginal product, the additional output from the employment of one additional person. In the case of the consulting firm, it's the revenues generated by each additional hire. If each new client generates $25,000 in revenue, then the third employee's four clients will generate $100,000. But the fourth employee's two clients will generate only $40,000. This $40,000 is exactly the wage that must be paid that fourth employee. So the consulting firm will break even on the fourth person but will lose money if it hires beyond that. Recall that our first labor market theory assumption is that employers seek to maximize profits. Therefore, the employer will continue to hire until the marginal revenue generated by the last hire is equal to the costs associated with employing that person. Because other potential costs will not change in the short run, the level of demand that maximizes profits is that level at which the marginal revenue of the last hire is equal to the wage rate for that hire.

Exhibit 7.7 shows the connection between the labor market model and the conditions facing a single employer. On the left is the *market level* supply and demand model from Exhibit 7.6, showing that pay level ($40,000) is determined by the interaction of *all employers'* demands for business graduates. The right side of the exhibit shows supply and demand for an *individual employer.* At the market-determined rate ($40,000), the individual employer can hire as many business graduates as it wants. Therefore, supply is now an unlimited horizontal line. However, the demand line still slopes downward. The two lines intersect at 4. For this employer, the market-determined wage rate ($40,000) equals the marginal revenue of the fourth hire. The marginal revenue of the fifth graduate is less than $40,000 and so will not add enough revenue to cover costs. The point on the graph at which the incremental income generated by an additional employee equals the wage rate is the *marginal revenue product.*

A manager using the marginal revenue product model must do only two things: (1) Determine the pay level set by market forces, and (2) determine the marginal revenue generated by each new hire. This will tell the manager how many people to hire. Simple? Of course not.

The model provides a valuable analytical framework, but it oversimplifies the real world. In most organizations, it is almost impossible to quantify the goods or services produced by an individual employee, since most production is through joint efforts of employees with a variety of skills. Even in settings that use piece rates (i.e., 50 cents

EXHIBIT 7.7 Supply and Demand at the Market and Individual Employer Level

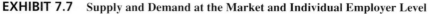

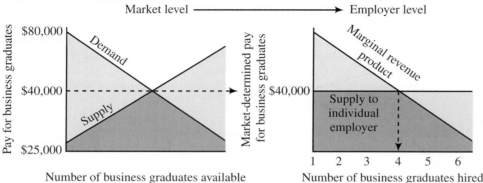

for each soccer ball sewn), it is hard to separate the contributions of labor from those of other resources (efficient machines, sturdy materials, good lighting, and ventilation).

So neither the marginal product nor the marginal revenue is directly measurable. However, managers do need some measure that reflects value. In the last two chapters, we discussed compensable factors, skill blocks, and competencies. If compensable factors define what organizations value, then job evaluation reflects the job's contribution and may be viewed as a proxy for marginal revenue product. However, compensable factors are usually defined as input (skills required, problem solving required, responsibilities) rather than value of output. This same logic applies to skills and competencies.

Labor Supply

Now let us look more closely at the assumptions about the behavior of potential employees. This model assumes that many people are seeking jobs, that they possess accurate information about all job openings, and that no barriers to mobility (discrimination, licensing provisions, or union membership requirements) exist.[8]

Just as with the analysis of labor demand, these assumptions greatly simplify the real world. As the assumptions change, so does the supply. For example, the upward sloping supply assumes that as pay increases, more people are willing to take a job. But if unemployment rates are low, offers of higher pay may not increase supply— everyone who wants to work is already working. If competitors quickly match a higher offer, the employer may face a higher pay level but no increase in supply. For example, when Giant Foods raised its hourly pay $1 above the minimum wage in the Chicago area, Wendy's and Burger King quickly followed suit. The result was that the supermarket was paying more for the employees it already had but was still shorthanded. Although some firms find lowering the job requirements and hiring less-skilled workers a better choice than raising wages, this choice incurs increased training costs (which were included in assumption 3).

MODIFICATIONS TO THE DEMAND SIDE

The story is told of the economics professor and the student who were strolling through campus. "Look," the student cried, "there's a $100 bill on the path!"

"No, that cannot be," the wiser head replied. "If there were a $100 bill, someone would have picked it up."

The point of the story is that economic theories must frequently be revised to account for reality. When we change our focus from *all* the employers in an economy to a *particular* employer, models must be modified to help us understand what actually occurs. A particularly troublesome issue for economists is why an employer would pay more than what theory states is the market-determined rate. Exhibit 7.8 looks at three modifications to the model that address this phenomenon: compensating differentials, efficiency wage, and signaling.

Compensating Differentials

More than 200 years ago, Adam Smith argued that individuals consider the "whole of the advantages and disadvantages of different employments" and make decisions based

EXHIBIT 7.8
Labor Demand Theories and Implications

Theory	Prediction	So What?
Compensating differentials	Work with negative characteristics requires higher pay to attract workers.	Job evaluation and compensable factors must capture these negative characteristics.
Efficiency wage	Above-market wages will improve efficiency by attracting workers who will perform better and be less willing to leave.	Staffing programs must have the capability of selecting the best employees; work must be structured to take advantage of employees' greater efforts.
Signaling	Pay policies signal the kinds of behavior the employer seeks.	Pay practices must recognize desired behaviors with more pay, larger bonuses, and other forms of compensation.

on the alternative with the greatest "net advantage."[9] If a job has negative characteristics—that is, if the necessary training is very expensive (medical school), job security is tenuous (stockbrokers, CEOs), working conditions are disagreeable (highway construction), or chances of success are low (professional sports)—then employers must offer higher wages to compensate for these negative features.

Such **compensating differentials** explain the presence of various pay rates in the market. Although the notion is appealing, it is hard to document, due to the difficulties in measuring and controlling all the factors that go into a net-advantage calculation.

Efficiency Wage

According to **efficiency-wage theory,** high wages may increase efficiency and actually lower labor costs if they:

1. Attract higher-quality applicants.
2. Lower turnover.
3. Increase worker effort.
4. Reduce **"shirking"** (what economists say when they mean "screwing around"). The higher the wage, the less likely it is that an employee would be able to find another job that pays as well. Also, the risk of losing one's high-paying job depends on how likely it is that you can be replaced. One indicator is the unemployment rate. (Karl Marx referred to the unemployed as a "reserve army" that employers can use to replace current workers.) Thus, efficiency wage predicts that high effort will be most likely and shirking likely to the degree that the wage premium is high and the unemployment rate is high.
5. Reduce the need to supervise employees (academics say "monitoring").

So, basically, efficiency increases by hiring better employees or motivating present employees to work smarter or harder. The underlying assumption is that pay level determines effort—again, an appealing notion that is difficult to document. Later in this chapter (see the Appendix), we show how something called **utility theory** can help compare the costs and benefits of different pay level policies. We will also discuss how business strategy plays a role in pay level choice.

There is some research on efficiency-wage theory, however.[10] One study looked at shirking behavior by examining employee discipline and wages in several auto plants. Higher wages were associated with lower shirking, measured as the number of disciplinary layoffs. However, the authors of the study were unable to say whether it was cut enough to offset the costs of the higher wage.[11]

Research shows that higher wages actually do attract more qualified applicants.[12] But higher wages also attract more unqualified applicants. Few companies evaluate their recruiting programs well enough to show whether they do in fact choose only superior applicants from the larger pool. So an above-market wage does not guarantee a more productive work force.

Does an above-market wage allow an organization to operate with fewer supervisors? Some research evidence says yes. A study of hospitals found that those that paid high wages to staff nurses employed fewer nurse supervisors.[13] The researchers did not speculate on whether the higher wages attracted better nurses or caused average nurses to work harder. They also did not say whether the hospital was able to reduce its overall nursing costs.

An organization's **ability to pay** is related to the efficiency wage model. Firms with greater profits than competitors are able to share this success with employees. This could be done via "leading" competitors' pay levels and/or via bonuses that vary with profitability. Academics see this as "rent sharing." **Rent** is a return (profits) received from activities that are in excess of the minimum (pay level) needed to attract people to those activities.[14] Pay levels at more profitable firms were about 15 percent greater than at firms with lower profits, according to one study.[15]

Notice that the discussion so far has dealt with pay level only. What forms to pay—the mix question—is virtually ignored in these theories. The simplifying assumption is that the pay level includes the value of different forms. Abstracted away is the distinct possibility that some people find more performance-based bonus pay or better health insurance more attractive. Signaling theory is more useful in understanding pay mix.

Signaling

Signaling theory holds that employers deliberately design pay levels and mix as part of a strategy that signals to both prospective and current employees the kinds of behaviors that are sought.[16] Viewed through a marketing lens, how much to pay and what pay forms are offered establishes a "brand" that sends a message to prospective employees, just like brands of competing products and services.[17]

A policy of paying below the market for **base pay** yet offering generous bonuses or training opportunities sends a different signal, and presumably attracts different people, than does a policy of matching the market wage and offering no performance-based pay. An employer that combines lower base pay with high bonuses may be signaling that it wants employees who are risk takers. Its pay policy helps communicate expectations.

Check out Exhibit 7.4 again. It shows a breakdown of forms of pay for two competitors, as well as their relationship to the market. The pay mix at company A emphasizes base pay (84 percent) more than does the mix at company B (64 percent) or the market average (67 percent). Company A pays no bonuses, no stock options, and somewhat lighter benefits. Company B's mix is closer to the market average. What is the message that A's pay mix is communicating? Which message appeals to you, A's or B's? The astute reader will note that at A, you can earn the $112,349 with very little apparent link to performance. Maybe just showing up is enough. At B, earning the $112,748 requires performance bonuses and stock options as well. Riskier? Why would anyone work at B without extra returns for the riskier pay? Without a premium, how will B attract and retain employees? Perhaps with more interesting projects, flexible schedules, or more opportunity for promotions—all part of B's "total pay brand."

A study of college students approaching graduation found that both pay level and mix affected their job decisions.[18] Students wanted jobs that offered high pay, but they also showed a preference for individual-based (rather than team-based) pay, fixed (rather than variable) pay, job-based (rather than skill-based) pay, and flexible benefits. Job seekers were rated on various personal dimensions—materialism, confidence in their abilities, and risk aversion—that were related to pay preferences. Pay level was most important to materialists and less important to those who were risk-averse. So applicants appear to select among job opportunities based on the perceived match between their personal dispositions and the nature of the organization, as signaled by the pay system. Both pay level and pay mix send a signal.

Signaling works on the supply side of the model, too, as suppliers of labor signal to potential employers. People who are better trained, have higher grades in relevant courses, and/or have related work experience signal to prospective employers that they are likely to be better performers. (Presumably they signal with the same degree of accuracy as employers.) So both characteristics of the applicants (degrees, grades, experience) and organization decisions about pay level (lead, match, lag) and mix (higher bonuses, benefit choices) act as signals that help communicate.

MODIFICATIONS TO THE SUPPLY SIDE (ONLY TWO MORE THEORIES TO GO)

Two theories shown in Exhibit 7.9—**reservation wage** and **human capital**—focus on understanding employee behavior: the supply side of the model.

EXHIBIT 7.9
Supply Side Theories and Implications

Theory	Prediction	So What?
Reservation wage	Job seekers will not accept jobs with pay below a certain wage, no matter how attractive other job aspects.	Pay level will affect ability to recruit.
Human capital	The value of an individual's skills and abilities is a function of the time and expense required to acquire them.	Higher pay is required to induce people to train for more difficult jobs.

Reservation Wage

Economists are renowned for their great sense of humor. So it is not surprising that they describe pay as "noncompensatory." What they mean is that job seekers have a reservation wage level below which they will not accept a job offer, no matter how attractive the other job attributes. If pay level does not meet their minimum standard, no other job attributes can make up (i.e., compensate) for this inadequacy. Other theorists go a step further and say that some job seekers—satisfiers—take the first job offer they get where the pay meets their reservation wage. A reservation wage may be above or below the market wage. The theory seeks to explain differences in workers' responses to offers. Reservation levels likely exist for pay forms, too, particularly for health insurance. A young high school graduate recently told us, "If I can't find a job that includes health insurance, I will probably go to college."

Human Capital

The theory of human capital, perhaps the most influential economic theory for explaining pay-level differences, is based on the premise that higher earnings flow to those who improve their potential productivity by investing in themselves (through additional education, training, and experience).[19] The theory assumes that people are in fact paid at the value of their marginal product. Improving productive abilities by investing in training or even in one's physical health will increase one's marginal product. In general, the value of an individual's skills and abilities is a function of the time, expense, and effort to acquire them. Consequently, jobs that require long and expensive training (engineering, physicians) should receive higher pay than jobs that require less investment (clerical work, elementary school teaching).[20] As pay level increases, the number of people willing to make that investment increases, thereby creating an upward-sloping supply. In fact, different types of education do get different levels of pay. In the United Kingdom, new graduates with a degree in math, law, or economics will earn around 25 percent more than job seekers their age who do not have a college degree. An extra year of education adds about $4,200 per year.

A number of additional factors affect the supply of labor.[21] Geographic barriers to mobility among jobs, union requirements, lack of information about job openings, the degree of risk involved, and the degree of unemployment also influence labor markets. Also, nonmonetary aspects of jobs (e.g., time flexibility) may be important aspects of the return on investment.

PRODUCT MARKET FACTORS AND ABILITY TO PAY

The supply and demand for labor are major determinants of an employer's pay level. However, any organization must, over time, generate enough revenue to cover expenses, including compensation. It follows that an employer's pay level is constrained by its ability to compete in the product/service market. So product market conditions to a large extent determine what the organization can afford to pay.

Product demand and the degree of competition are the two key product market factors. Both affect the ability of the organization to change what it charges for its products and services. If prices cannot be changed without decreasing sales, then the ability of the employer to set a higher pay level is constrained.

Product Demand

Although labor market conditions (and legal requirements) put a floor on the pay level required to attract sufficient employees, the product market puts a lid on the maximum pay level that an employer can set. If the employer pays above the maximum, it must either pass on to consumers the higher pay level through price increases or hold prices fixed and allocate a greater share of total revenues to cover labor costs.

Degree of Competition

Employers in highly competitive markets, such as manufacturers of automobiles or generic drugs, are less able to raise prices without loss of revenues. At the other extreme, single sellers of a Lamborghini or a breakthrough cancer treatment are able to set whatever price they choose. However, too high a price often invites the eye of government regulators.

Other factors besides product market conditions affect pay level. Some of these have already been discussed. The productivity of labor, the technology employed, the level of production relative to plant capacity available—all affect compensation decisions. These factors vary more across than within industries. The technologies employed and consumer preferences may vary among auto manufacturers, but the differences are relatively small compared to the differences between the technology and product demand of auto manufacturers versus those of the oil or financial industry.

A Different View: What Managers Say

Discussions with managers provide insight into how all of these economic factors translate into actual pay decisions. In one study, a number of scenarios were presented in which unemployment, profitability, and labor market conditions varied.[22] Managers were asked to make wage adjustment recommendations for several positions. Level of unemployment made almost no difference. One manager was incredulous at the suggestion that high unemployment should lead to cutting salaries: "You mean take advantage of the fact that there are a lot of people out of work?" The company's profitability was considered a factor for higher management in setting the overall pay budget but not something managers consider for individual pay adjustments. What it boiled down to was "whatever the chief financial officer says we can afford!" They thought it shortsighted to pay less, even though market conditions would have permitted lower pay. In direct contradiction to efficiency-wage theory, managers believed that problems attracting and keeping people were the result of poor management rather than inadequate compensation. They offered the opinion that, "Supervisors try to solve with money their difficulties with managing people."[23]

Of course, what managers say that they would do in a hypothetical situation is not necessarily what they would do when they actually experience a situation. Nor are their views or decisions necessarily the same as those of managers in other companies that do things differently. In this same vein, what managers think is not always what their employees think. As we write this, the unemployment rate is higher than it has been in two decades and companies are indeed making pay cuts, either outright or by requiring employees to take days off (often called furloughs) without pay. Another common cut is reducing contributions to 401k retirement plans. Other companies are imposing pay freezes.[24] With respect to employee retention, a national survey found that pay was the most often cited reason (51 percent) among high-performing employees for leaving, whereas relationship with supervisor was cited only 1 percent of the time by such employees. Employers, however, somewhat underestimated the role of pay (with 45 percent citing its role versus 51 percent of employees) and they very much overestimated the role of relationship with supervisor (with 31 percent citing its role versus 1 percent of employees).[25]

Segmented Supplies of Labor and (Different) Going Rates

However, faced with significant competition, a number of employers have cut pay. As we saw earlier, the U.S. airline industry is a notable example. Significant differences in wages paid around the world and the ease of offshoring work have also led many companies to consider this action.[26] Other options to reduce labor costs include segmenting the source of labor.

People Flow to the Work

St. Luke's, a 100-bed hospital in the Phoenix, Arizona, area, staffs between 15 and 20 registered nurses each shift, depending on patient loads. The nurse manager staffs from four different sources:

- Regular nurses (St. Luke's full-time employees paid for 35 hours per week).
- Pool nurses (not St. Luke full-time regulars).
- "Registry" nurses (employees of temporary-help agencies specializing in nursing—on call for any hospital in the Phoenix area).
- "Travelers" (nurses from outside the Phoenix area, employed by agencies that send them to hospitals around the country for extended periods (e.g., six months).

St. Luke's faces a **segmented labor supply.** This means it uses multiple sources of nurses, from multiple locations, with multiple employment relationships. The level and mix of cash and benefits paid each nurse depends on the source. Regulars earn about $22 per hour plus benefits. Pool nurses earn about $29 per hour but no benefits. Registry nurses get $33 plus benefits, paid to them by the agency. Travelers get $33 plus benefits and expenses, including rent, paid by the contracting agencies. St. Luke's pays a fee to the registry and traveler agencies in addition to the nurses' compensation. The segmented supply results in nurses working the same jobs side by side on the same shift but earning significantly different pay.

This is a case of people flowing to the work. St. Luke's patients are in Phoenix. The hospital cannot send its nursing work to other cities or other nations.[27]

Work Flows to the People—On-Site, Off-Site, Offshore

Apriso, a Long Beach, California, company, designs and installs computer-assisted manufacturing software that is used in factories around the world. When Apriso competes for a project, the bid is structured in part on the compensation paid to people in different locations. Apriso can staff the project with employees who are on-site (in Long Beach), off-site (contract employees from throughout the United States), or off-shore. Design engineers in Long Beach earn about twice as much as those in Krakow,

Poland. Apriso can "mix and match" its people from different sources. Which source Apriso includes in its bid depends on many factors: customer preferences, time schedules, the nature of the project. To put together its bids, Apriso managers need to know pay levels and mix of forms not only in the market in Long Beach but also in other locations, including Krakow, Shanghai, Vancouver, and Bangalore. (We return to this topic later in this chapter.)

There are three points ("so whats?") to take with you from this discussion:

1. Reality is complex and theories abstract. It is not that our theories are useless. They simply abstract away the detail, clarifying the underlying factors that help us understand how reality works. Theories of market dynamics, the interaction of supply and demand, form a useful foundation.

2. The segmented sources of labor means that determining pay levels and mix increasingly requires understanding market conditions in different, even worldwide, locations.

3. Managers also need to know the jobs required to do the work, the tasks to be performed, and the knowledge and behaviors required to perform them (sound like job analysis?) so that they can bundle the various tasks to send to different locations.

ORGANIZATION FACTORS

Although product and labor market conditions create a range of possibilities within which managers create a policy on external competitiveness, organizational factors influence pay level and mix decisions, too.[28]

Industry and Technology

The industry in which an organization competes influences the technologies used. Labor-intensive industries such as education and health care tend to pay lower than technology-intensive industries such as petroleum or pharmaceuticals, whereas professional services such as consulting firms pay high. In addition to differences in technology across industries affecting compensation, the introduction of new technology *within an industry* influences pay levels. The next time you are waiting in line at the supermarket, think about the pay the checkout person gets. The use of universal product codes, scanners, scales built into the counter, even do-it-yourself checkout lanes have reduced the skills required of checkers. As a result, their average pay has declined over time.[29]

Qualifications and experience tailored to particular technologies is important in the analysis of labor markets. Machinists and millwrights who build General Electric diesel locomotives in Erie, Pennsylvania, have very different qualifications from machinists and millwrights who build Boeing airplanes in St. Louis.[30]

Employer Size

There is consistent evidence that large organizations tend to pay more than small ones. A study of manufacturing firms found that firms with 100 to 500 workers paid 6 percent higher wages than did smaller firms; firms of more than 500 workers paid 12 percent more than did the smallest firms.[31] This relationship between organization size, ability to pay, and pay level is consistent with economic theory that says that talented individuals have a higher marginal value in a larger organization because they can influence more people and decisions, thereby leading to more profits. Compare the advertising revenue that David Letterman can bring to CBS versus the potential revenue to station WBNS if his late-night show was only seen in Athens, Ohio. No matter how cool he is in Athens, WBNS could not generate enough revenue to be able to afford to pay Mr. Letterman his multimillion dollar salary; CBS can. However, theories are less useful in explaining why practically everyone at bigger companies such as CBS, including janitors and compensation managers, is paid more. It seems unlikely that everyone has Letterman's impact on revenues.

People's Preferences

What pay forms (health insurance, eye care, bonuses, pensions) do employees really value? Better understanding of employee preferences is increasingly important in determining external competitiveness. Markets, after all, involve both employers' and employees' choices.[32] However, there are substantial difficulties in reliably measuring preferences. In response to the survey question "What do you value most in your work?" who among us would be so crass as to (publicly) rank money over cordial co-workers or challenging assignments? Researchers find that people place more importance on pay than they are willing to admit.[33]

Organization Strategy

A variety of pay-level and mix strategies exist. Some employers adopt a low-wage, no-services strategy; they compete by producing goods and services with the lowest total compensation possible. Nike and Reebok reportedly do this. Both rely heavily on outsourcing to manufacture their products. Nike, for example, outsources 99 percent of its footwear production to independent contract suppliers in China, Vietnam, Indonesia, and Thailand, all of which have much lower labor costs than found in the United States. Others select a low-wage, high-services strategy. Marriott offers its low-wage room cleaners a hotline to social workers who assist with child care and transportation crises. English and citizenship courses are available for recent immigrants. Seminars cover how to manage one's paycheck and one's life. Still other employers use a high-wage, high-services approach. Medtronic's "fully present at work" approach, discussed in Chapter 2, is an example of high wage, high services. Obviously, these are extremes on a continuum of possibilities. One study found that like the company in Exhibit 7.3, a variety of pay-level strategies exist within some organizations. Pay levels that lead competition are used in jobs that most directly impact the organization's success (research and development and marketing in pharmacy companies). In jobs with less impact (human resource management and manufacturing), pay levels reflect a "meet competition" policy.

As noted earlier, efficiency wage argues that some firms, for a variety of reasons (e.g., their technology depends more heavily on having higher-quality workers or it is more difficult to monitor employee performance) do indeed have efficiency reasons to pay higher wages. Higher pay levels, either for the organization as a whole or for critical jobs, may be well-suited to particular strategies, such as higher value-added customer segments.[34] (Recall our example of Costco from Chapter 1.) Similarly, evidence suggests that organizations making greater use of so-called high-performance work practices (teams, quality circles, total quality management, job rotation) and computer-based technology and having higher-skilled workers also pay higher wages.[35] This is consistent with our discussion in Chapter 2 about the need for human resources practices designed to encourage ability, motivation, and opportunity to contribute (AMO) to reinforce each other. The observable benefits of higher wages may include: higher **pay satisfaction,** improved attraction and retention of employees, and higher quality, effort, and/or performance.[36] Ultimately, higher wages must bring something in return (e.g., higher productivity, quality, and/or innovation). Otherwise, a firm's ability to compete and survive is in question. (See our discussion of General Motors and the U.S. automobile industry in Chapter 1 and elswhere in this chapter.) Evidence shows that in manufacturing, productivity (defined as sales value of production divided by employee hours worked) is positively correlated ($r = .45$) with hourly wage level.[37] Thus, the relationship, while far from perfect, is meaningful in manufacturing.

RELEVANT MARKETS

Economists take "the market" for granted—as in "The market determines wages." But managers at St. Luke's and Apriso realize that defining the **relevant markets** is a big part of figuring out how and how much to pay.

Although the notion of a single homogeneous labor market may be a useful analytical device, each organization operates in many labor markets, each with unique demand and supply. Some, as in the case of hospitals, face segmented supplies for the same skills in the same market. Others, such as Apriso, think more broadly about which markets to use as sources of talent. They seek to answer the question, What is the right pay to get the right people to do the right things?

Consequently, managers must define the markets that are relevant for pay purposes and establish the appropriate competitive positions in these markets. The three factors usually used to determine the relevant labor markets are the occupation (skill/knowledge required), geography (willingness to relocate, commute, or become virtual employees), and competitors (other employers in the same product/service and labor markets).

Defining the Relevant Market

How do employers choose their relevant markets? Surprisingly little research has been done on this issue. But if the markets are incorrectly defined, the estimates of competitors' pay rates will be incorrect and the pay level and mix inappropriately established.

Cybercomp
Select several companies that you believe might be labor market competitors (e.g., Microsoft, Oracle, IBM; or Johnson & Johnson, Merck, Pfizer). Compare their job postings on their Web sites. Do any of the companies list salaries for their jobs? Do they quote a single salary? Do they allow room for haggling?

Two studies do shed some light on this issue.[38] They conclude that managers look at both *competitors*—their products, location, and size—and the *jobs*—the skills and knowledge required and their importance to the organization's success (e.g., lawyers in law firms, software engineers at Microsoft). So depending on its location and size, a company may be deemed a relevant comparison even if it is not a product market competitor. We will see an example in Chapter 8 when we look at how Google and Microsoft define their relevant markets for paying executives.

The data from product market competitors (as opposed to labor market competitors) are likely to receive greater weight when:

1. Employee skills are specific to the product market (recall the differences in Boeing millwrights versus GE Locomotive millwrights).

2. Labor costs are a large share of total costs.

3. Product demand is responsive to price changes. That is, people won't pay $4 for a bottle of Leinenkugel; instead, they'll go to Trader Joe's for a bottle of Charles Shaw wine, a.k.a. "two-buck Chuck" (the best $2 wine we have ever tasted).[39]

4. The supply of labor is not responsive to changes in pay (recall the earlier low-wage, low-skill example).

Globalization of Relevant Labor Markets: Offshoring and Outsourcing

Work flowing to lower wage locations is not new. Historically, clothing (needle trades) and furniture jobs flowed from New England to southern states. Nor is work flowing across national borders new. First, it was low-skill and low-wage jobs (clothing and Mardi Gras beads) from the U.S. to China and Central America; then higher-paid blue collar jobs (electronics, appliances); now it is service and professional jobs (accounting, legal, engineering, radiology). Vastly improved communication and software connectivity have accelerated these trends. For example, programming code and radiographic images can now be transported in an instant across the world.

In Chapter 4, we discussed characteristics of jobs (e.g., easily routinized, inputs/outputs easily transmitted electronically, little need for interaction with other workers, little need for local knowledge such as unique social and cultural factors) that are thought to increase susceptibility to offshoring (i.e., moving jobs to other countries). Here, we discuss why firms use offshoring, as well as challenges in doing so.

Several years ago, IBM found that a computer programmer (one of the occupations reported in Chapter 4 to be most susceptible to offshoring) in the United States with three to five years of experience cost $56 per hour in total compensation. In China, a similarly qualified programmer cost $12.50 per hour.[40] Based on these data, IBM estimated that it could save $168 million per year by shifting some of these programmer jobs to countries like China, India, and Brazil. That sort of savings is difficult to ignore, especially when competing firms are either based in lower labor cost countries (e.g., Infosys in India) or are offshoring or expanding operations there.

As noted, offshoring is also happening to lawyers and financial services jobs. In Mumbai, India, Pangea3 LLC employs Indian lawyers to do legal work for Wall Street banks. Whereas starting associates in the United States might bill more than $200 per hour, similar lawyers in India might bill something closer to $75 to $100 per hour. One estimate is that 35,000 U.S. legal jobs will be moved offshore by 2010 and another 79,000 will move by 2015.[41] In financial services, Copal Partners of India has seen large increases in its business as Wall Street firms not only outsource or offshore "back office" work (e.g., processing of transactions), but increasingly also production of research reports, trading recommendations, and so forth. Citigroup now employs over 20,000 people in India and Deutsche Bank has about 6,000. According to one observer, "There's a huge amount of grunt work that has been done by $250,000-a-year Wharton M.B.A.s" but "some of that stuff, it's natural to outsource it."[42] It is possible that more sophisticated jobs will increasingly follow.

While large differences in labor costs cannot simply be ignored, there are other factors to consider in deciding where jobs will be.[43] First, as we saw in Chapter 1, countries with lower average labor costs also tend to have lower average productivity. So, a company must assure itself that labor costs savings will not be neutralized by lower productivity. There may also be other risks. For example, going back to the case of manufacturing, consulting firm AMR Research found that, in the case of China, theft of intellectual property and product quality were major concerns and higher in China than any other country. In fact, China was ranked the riskiest country on 9 of 15 risk factors.[44] AMR observes that while some the potential costs of these risks are difficult to quantify, they can be of great potential harm, for example, if they affect the value of brands and corporate reputation. Second, agency theory, which we discuss later, tells us that companies must devote resources to systems that monitor worker effort or output. This, as well as coordination of efforts, can be more difficult and more costly when geographic or cultural distance is great (and time zones different), even with advances in technology.[45] Third, customers' reactions must be considered. For example, Delta Air Lines Inc. decided to stop using call centers in India to handle sales and reservations, despite the fact that call-center workers in India earn roughly $500 a month (about one-sixth of U.S.–based call center workers). Delta said that customers had trouble communicating with India-based representatives. Delta's CEO explained that "Customer acceptance of call centers in foreign countries is low" and that "Our customers are not shy about letting us have that feedback."[46] Fourth, if labor costs are the driving force behind placing jobs, one must ask for how long the labor cost advantage at a significantly lower wage even will hold and whether sufficiently qualified employees will continue to be available as other companies also tap into this pool of labor.

COMPETITIVE PAY POLICY ALTERNATIVES

Compensation theories offer some help in understanding the variations in pay levels we observe among employers. They are less helpful in understanding differences in the mix of pay forms. Relevant markets are shaped by pressures from the labor and product markets and the organization. But so what? How, in fact, do managers set pay-level and pay-mix policy, and what difference does it make? In the remainder of this chapter, we will discuss those two issues.

Recall that pay level is the average of the array of rates inside an organization. There are three conventional pay-level policies: to lead, to meet, or to follow competition.

Newer policies emphasize flexibility: among policies for different employee groups, among pay forms for individual employees, and among elements of the employee relationship that the company wishes to emphasize in its external competitiveness policy.

What Difference Does the Pay-Level Policy Make?

The basic premise is that the competitiveness of pay will affect the organization's ability to achieve its compensation objectives, and this in turn will affect its performance.[47] The probable effects of alternative policies are shown in Exhibit 7.10 and discussed in more detail below. The problem with much pay-level research is that it focuses on base pay and ignores bonuses, incentives, options, employment security, benefits, or other forms of pay. Yet the exhibits and discussion in this chapter should have convinced you that base pay represents only a portion of compensation. Comparisons on base alone can mislead. In fact, many managers believe they get more bang for the buck by allocating dollars away from base pay and into variable forms that more effectively shape employee behavior.[48]

General Mills, for example, seeks to pay at the 50th percentile of base salary (among consumer packaged goods companies) but at the 75th percentile for total cash (base salary variable pay) for managers if they have superior perfromance.[49] As Exhibit 7.11 shows, this seems to be a common strategy.

Pay With Competition (Match)

Given the choice to match, lead, or lag, the most common policy is to match rates paid by competitors.[50] Managers historically justify this policy by saying that failure to match competitors' rates would cause murmuring among present employees and limit the organization's ability to recruit. Many non-unionized companies tend to match or even lead competition in order to discourage unions. A **pay-with-competition policy** tries to ensure that an organization's wage costs are approximately equal to those of its product competitors and that its ability to attract applicants will be approximately equal to its labor market competitors.

Classical economic models predict that employers meet competitive wages. While this avoids placing an employer at a disadvantage in pricing products, it may not provide a competitive advantage in its labor markets.

EXHIBIT 7.10 **Probable Relationships Between External Pay Policies and Objectives**

Policy	Compensation Objectives				
	Ability to Attract	Ability to Retain	Contain Labor Costs	Reduce Pay Dissatisfaction	Increase Productivity
Pay above market (lead)	+	+	?	+	?
Pay with market (match)	=	=	=	=	?
Pay below market (lag)	−	?	+	−	?
Hybrid policy	?	?	+	?	+
Employer of choice	+	+	+	−	?

EXHIBIT 7.11   Competitive Pay Policy Objectives, Base Salary, and Total Cash

Base Salary Target

What Is Your Organization's *Base Salary* Target (or Goal) Compared to the Relevant Labor Market?

	<25th Percentile	25th–40th Percentile	40th–60th Percentile	60th–75th Percentile	>75th Percentile	Varies/Do Not Have a Target
Senior Management (n = 1,034)	0%	1%	73%	14%	3%	9%
Middle Management (n = 1,045)	0%	1%	85%	7%	2%	5%
Professional (n = 1,042)	1%	1%	86%	6%	2%	4%
Sales (n = 1,037)	1%	1%	85%	6%	1%	7%
Administrative (n = 1,037)	1%	2%	86%	6%	1%	5%
Production (n = 835)	0%	3%	84%	6%	1%	6%

Total Cash Target

What Is Your Organization's *Total Cash* Target (or Goal) Compared to the Relevant Labor Market?

	<25th Percentile	25th–40th Percentile	40th–60th Percentile	60th–75th Percentile	>75th Percentile	Varies/Do Not Have a Target
Senior Management (n = 1,037)	0%	1%	50%	24%	5%	20%
Middle Management (n = 1,041)	0%	1%	61%	18%	3%	18%
Professional (n = 1,035)	0%	1%	64%	14%	2%	18%
Sales (n = 1,896)	0%	1%	63%	15%	3%	18%
Administrative (n = 1,033)	0%	2%	65%	13%	2%	18%
Production (n = 837)	0%	3%	63%	12%	2%	20%

Source: "Job Evaluation and Market-Pricing Practices," WorldatWork, 2009, http://www.worldatwork.org/waw/adimLink?id=31378.

Lead Pay-Level Policy

A **lead pay-level policy** maximizes the ability to attract and retain quality employees and minimizes employee dissatisfaction with pay. It may also offset less attractive features of the work, à la Adam Smith's "net advantage." Combat pay premiums paid to military personnel offset some of the risk of being fired upon.[51] The higher pay offered by brokerage firms offsets the risk of being fired when the market tanks.

As noted earlier, sometimes an entire industry can pass high pay rates on to consumers if pay is a relatively low proportion of total operating expenses or if the industry is highly regulated. But what about specific firms within a high-pay industry? For example, Merrill Lynch adheres to a pay leadership position for financial analysts *in its industry*. Do any advantages actually accrue to Merrill Lynch? If all firms in the industry have similar operating expenses, then the lead policy must provide some competitive advantage to Merrill Lynch that offsets the higher costs.

A number of researchers have linked high wages to ease of attraction, reduced vacancy rates and training time, and better-quality employees.[52] Research also suggests that high pay levels reduce turnover and absenteeism.[53] Several studies found that the use of variable pay (bonuses and long-term incentives) is related to an organization's improved financial performance but that pay level is not.[54] To make things more complex, it appears that in hospitals, competitive pay levels interact with internal pay structures to impact patient recovery time and quality of care.[55]

A lead policy can also have negative effects. It may force the employer to increase wages of current employees too, to avoid internal misalignment and murmuring. Additionally, a lead policy may mask negative job attributes that contribute to high turnover later on (e.g., boring assignments or hostile colleagues). Remember the managers' view mentioned earlier that high turnover was more likely to be a managerial problem than a compensation problem.[56]

Lag Pay-Level Policy

A policy of paying below-market rates may hinder a firm's ability to attract potential employees. But if a **lag pay-level policy** is coupled with the promise of higher future returns (e.g., stock ownership in a high-tech start-up firm), this combination may increase employee commitment and foster teamwork, which may increase productivity. How long this promise works, in the face of flat or declining stock markets, is unknown. Unmet expectations probably have negative effects. Additionally, it is possible to lag competition on pay level but to lead on other returns from work (e.g., hot assignments, desirable location, outstanding colleagues, cool tools, work/life balance).

Different Policies for Different Employee Groups

In practice, many employers go beyond a single choice among the three policy options. They may vary the policy for different occupational families, as did the company in Exhibit 7.3. They may vary the policy for different forms of pay, as did the companies in Exhibit 7.4. They may also adopt different policies for different business units that face very different competitive conditions.

Not by Pay Level Alone: Pay-Mix Strategies

Thus far, we have devoted limited attention to pay-mix policies. Some obvious alternatives include *performance driven, market match, work/life balance,* and *security.* Exhibit 7.12 illustrates these four alternatives. Compared to the other three, incentives and stock ownership make up a greater percent of total compensation in *performance-driven* policies. The *market match* simply mimics the pay mix competitors are paying. How managers actually make these mix decisions is a ripe issue for more research.

EXHIBIT 7.12 Pay-Mix Policy Alternatives

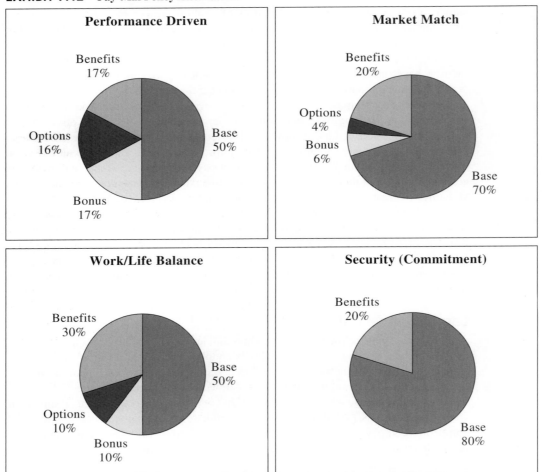

How managers position their organization's pay against competitors is changing. Some alternatives that are emerging focus on total returns from work (beyond financial returns) and offering people choices among these returns. Rather than "flexible," perhaps a better term would be "fuzzy" policies.

Such pay-mix policy alternatives exist among enterprises in other countries, too. Apache Footware, located in Quingyuan, China, offers base plus bonus, which matches local practice. It also offers benefits that include a new medical clinic, housing for married couples, a school, sports facilities, and a shopping mall. Steve Chen, Apache's chief executive, states, "It's not just about pay, it's about lifestyle. We're building a community so people will stay." (Reminiscent of SAS, whose strategy was discussed in Chapter 2?) In contrast, Top Form Undergarment Wear, located in the same region, phased out its employee housing. It opted to pay employees over 20 percent higher base pay than local practice. Top Form executive Charles Lee says, "Workers need to have a life of their own. They are not children. We pay them more and let each worker decide what is best for them."[57]

Employer of Choice/Shared Choice

Some companies compete based on their overall reputation as a place to work, beyond pay level and mix. For example, IBM compares within the information technology marketplace and positions its pay "among the best" in this group. Further, it claims to "strongly differentiate based on business and individual results." It leads the market with its strong emphasis on performance. IBM also offers extensive training opportunities, challenging work assignments, and the like. In a sense, **"employer of choice"** corresponds to the brand or image the company projects as an employer.

Shared choice begins with the traditional alternatives of lead, meet, or lag. But it then adds a second part, which is to *offer employees choices* (within limits) in the pay mix. This "employee-as-customer" perspective is not all that revolutionary, at least in the United States. Many employers offer choices on health insurance (individual versus dependent coverage), retirement investments (growth or value), and so on. (See flexible benefits in Chapter 13.) More advanced software is making the employee-as-customer approach more feasible. Mass customization—being able to select among a variety of features—is routine when purchasing a new laptop or auto. It is now possible with total compensation, too. Does offering people choices matter? One risk is that employees will make "wrong" choices that will jeopardize their financial well-being (e.g., inadequate health insurance). Another is the "24 jars of jam" dilemma. Supermarket studies report that offering consumers a taste of just a few different jams increases sales. But offering a taste of 24 different jams decreases sales. Consumers feel overwhelmed by too many choices and simply walk away. Perhaps offering employees too many choices of different kinds of pay will lead to confusion, mistakes, and dissatisfaction.[58]

Pitfalls of Pies

The pie charts in Exhibit 7.12 contrast various pay mix policies. However, thinking about the mix of pay forms as pieces in a pie chart has limitations. These are particularly clear when the value of stock is volatile. The pie charts in Exhibit 7.13 show how a well-known software company's mix changed after a major stock market decline (stock prices plummeted 50 percent within a month). Base pay went from 47 to 55 percent of total compensation, whereas the value of stock options fell from 28 to 16 percent. (The reverse has happened in this company, too.) The mix changed even though the company made no overt decision to change its pay strategy. But wait, it can get worse. One technology company was forced to disclose that three-quarters of all its stock options were "under water," that is, exercisable at prices higher than the market price. Due to stock market volatility, the options had become worthless to employees. So what is the message to employees? To competitors? The company's intended strategy has not changed, but in reality the mix has changed. So the possible volatility in the value of different pay forms needs to be anticipated.

EXHIBIT 7.13   Volatility of Stock Value Changes Total Pay Mix

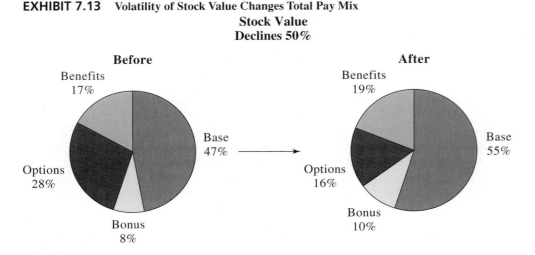

Stock Value
Declines 50%

Some companies prefer to report the mix of pay forms using a "dashboard," as depicted in Exhibit 7.14. The dashboard changes the focus from emphasizing the relative importance of each form within a single company to comparing each form by itself to the market (many companies). In the example, the value of stock options is 79 percent of competitors' median, base pay is at 95 percent of competitors' median, and overall total compensation is 102 percent of (or 2 percent above) the market median. Pies, dashboards—different focus, both recognizing the importance of the mix of pay forms.

Keep in mind that the mix employees receive differs at different levels in the internal job structure. Exhibit 7.15 shows the different mix of base, cash incentives, and stock programs Merrill Lynch pays at different organization levels. Executive leadership positions receive less than 10 percent in base, about 20 percent in stock, and the rest in annual incentives. This compares to 50 percent in base, 40 percent in annual

EXHIBIT 7.14
Dashboard:
Total Pay Mix
Breakdown vs.
Competitors*

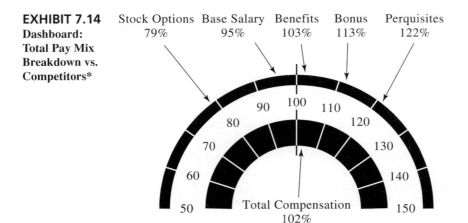

*100 = Chosen market position, e.g., market median

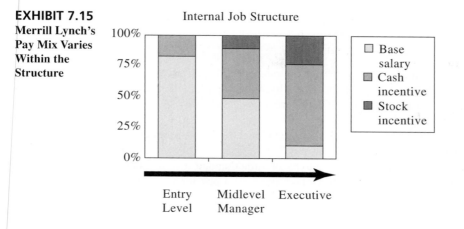

EXHIBIT 7.15
Merrill Lynch's Pay Mix Varies Within the Structure

incentives, and 10 percent in stock for midlevel manager/professional positions, and 80 percent base, 20 percent incentives, and no stock for entry- and lower-level jobs. While the percentages vary among organizations, greater emphasis on performance (through incentives and stock) at higher levels is common practice. This is based on the belief that jobs at higher levels in the organization have greater opportunity to influence organization performance.

CONSEQUENCES OF PAY-LEVEL AND -MIX DECISIONS: GUIDANCE FROM THE RESEARCH

Earlier we noted that external competitiveness has two major consequences: It affects (1) operating expenses and (2) employee attitudes and work behaviors. Exhibit 7.16 summarizes these consequences, which have been discussed throughout this chapter.

Efficiency

A variety of theories make assumptions about the effects of relative pay levels on an organization's efficiency. Some recommend lead policies to diminish shirking and permit hiring better-qualified applicants. Others—such as marginal productivity theory—recommend

EXHIBIT 7.16
Some Consequences of Pay Levels

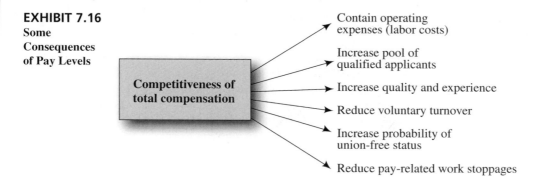

matching. A utility model even supports a lag policy.[59] No research suggests under what circumstances managers should choose which pay-mix alternative.

Which Policy Achieves Competitive Advantage?

Research on the effect of pay-level policies is difficult because companies' stated policies often do not correspond to reality. For example, HR managers at 124 companies were asked to define their firm's target pay level. All 124 of them reported that their companies paid above the median![60]

Beyond opinions, there is little evidence of the consequences of different policy alternatives. We do know that pay level affects costs; we do not know whether any effects it might have on productivity or attracting and retaining employees are sufficient to offset costs. Nor is it known how much of a pay-level variation makes a difference to employees; will 5 percent, 10 percent, or 15 percent be a noticeable difference? Although lagging competitive pay could have a noticeable reduction in short-term labor costs, it is not known whether this savings is accompanied by a reduction in the quality and performance of the work force. It may be that an employer's pay level will not gain any competitive *advantage;* however, the wrong pay level may put the organization at a serious *disadvantage.* Similarly, we simply do not know the effects of the different pay-mix alternatives or the financial results of shifting the responsibility for choosing the mix to employees. Perhaps it is the message communicated by pay mix and levels that is the key to achieving competitive advantage.

So where does this leave the manager? In the absence of convincing evidence, the least-risk approach may be to set both pay level and pay mix to match competition. An organization may adopt a lead policy for skills that are critical to its success, a match policy for less-critical skills, and a lag policy for jobs that are easily filled in the local labor market. An obvious concern with flexible policies is to achieve some degree of business alignment and fair treatment for employees among the choices. (The Appendix to this chapter shows how utility analysis can help evaluate pay level strategies.)

Fairness

Satisfaction with pay is diretly related to the pay level: More is better.[61] But employees' sense of fairness is also related to how others are paid. A friend at Stanford claims that if all but one of the faculty in their business school got $1,000,000 and one person received $1,000,001, the others would all be lined up at the dean's office demanding an explanation. Employers have many choices about how and where to invest their resources. Even if the decision is made to invest in improving people's feelings about fairness of their pay, there is little research to tell us this will improve employees' overall feeling about fair treatment in the workplace.[62]

Compliance

It's not enough to say that an employer must pay at or above the legal minimum wage. Provisions of prevailing wage laws and equal rights legislation must also be met. In fact, we will return to the subject of market wages again when we discuss pay discrimination and the concept of "living wage." In addition to pay level, various pay forms are also regulated. Pensions and health care are considered part of every citizen's economic security and are regulated to some degree in most countries. This is discussed again when we look at international practices and benefits. Employers must also exercise caution when sharing salary information to avoid antitrust violations.[63]

No matter the competitive pay policy, it needs to be translated into practice. The starting point is measuring the market through use of a salary survey. For this, we turn to the next chapter.

Your **Turn** Sled Dog Software

Software engineers directly affect the success of many start-up companies. Suppose you are facing a clean slate: A group of investors is about to create a new start-up, a specialty software company based in Laramie, Wyoming. These investors have hired you to help them determine the marketing manager's pay. What would you advise? Consider the information in Exhibits 7.3, Exhibits 7.4, and Exhibits 7.14 in making your recommendation.

1. What policy regarding external competitiveness would you advise? List the options and the pros and cons of each policy option. Offer the rationale for your recommendation.
2. What forms of pay and in what percentages would you recommend? Again, offer your rationales.
3. Consider the theories and research presented in this chapter. Which ones did you use to support your recommendation?
4. List three pieces of additional information you would like to have to refine your recommendation. Explain how this information would help you.
5. Finally, would you physically locate all the actual software development in Laramie? What, if any, other options would you consider?

Still Your **Turn** Fit the Pay-Mix Policy to the Compensation Strategy

Take another look at Exhibit 7.11, the maps of SAS and Microsoft compensation strategy. Then compare it to the alternative mix of pay forms policies shown in Exhibit 7.9.

1. Based on SAS and Microsoft's business and compensation strategies, which *pay-mix policy* would you recommend these employers adopt?
2. What results do you anticipate? Don't forget efficiency, including costs, fairness, and compliance.
3. Pick a couple of theories discussed in this chapter (e.g., signaling, efficiency wage). How, if at all, do these theories help you anticipate what the results of your recommendations will be?

Summary

One reviewer of this book told us that "There are three important contributions of this chapter: (1) that there is no 'going rate' and so managers make conscious pay level and mix decisions influenced by several factors; (2) that there are both product market and labor market competitors that impact the pay level and mix decisions; and (3) that alternative pay level and mix decisions have different consequences." That is a great summary of the key points.

The pay model used throughout this book emphasizes strategic policy issues: objectives, alignment, competitiveness, contributions, and management. Policies need to be designed to achieve specific pay objectives. This part of the book is concerned with external competitiveness, or pay comparisons among organizations. Does Apple Computer pay its accountants the same wage that Florida Power pays its accountants? Probably not. Different companies pay different rates; the average of the overall array of rates in an organization constitutes the pay level. Different companies also use different forms of pay. To achieve the objectives stipulated for the pay system, both the pay level and the pay mix must be properly positioned relative to competitors. Each integrated job structure or career path within the organization may have its own competitive position in the market. The next chapter considers the decisions involved and the variety of techniques available to implement those decisions.

Before we proceed, let us reemphasize that the major reason we are interested in the external competitiveness policy—pay level and mix of pay forms—is that it has profound consequences on the organization's objectives. Theories and practical experience support this belief. But as we have also noted, more research is needed to guide us in making decisions. We have clearly established that differences among organizations' competitive policies and their pay levels and forms exist. We have examined the factors that determine these differences. What remains to be better understood is the potential effects of various policies.

Review Questions

1. Distinguish policies on external competitiveness from policies on internal alignment. Why is external competitiveness so important?

2. What factors shape an organization's external competitiveness?

3. What does marginal revenue product have to do with pay?

4. What pay level does the efficiency wage predict? Does the theory accurately predict organization behavior? Why or why not?

5. What is a relevant market? What difference does it make when determining people's pay?

6. Can you think of any companies that follow a lag and/or lead policy? Why do they believe it pays to pay differently? Can you think of any companies that follow performance driven and/or work/life balance policies?

Appendix **7-A**

Utility Analysis

One way to quantify and think about the effects of a compensation program is to use utility analysis. We define *utility* as the dollar value created by increasing revenues and/ or decreasing costs by changing one or more human resource practices.[64] Utility analysis has most typically been used to analyze the payoff to making more valid employee hiring/selection decisions. Compensation plays a major role here because a higher pay level may increase an organization's ability to hire and keep the best talent. In addition, as our discussion of sorting effects in Chapter 1 suggested, differences in pay mix may also have major effects. For example, a pay mix that emphasizes performance-based pay may also have an impact by being especially attractive to high performers. In the broader picture, compensation decisions can be analyzed by modeling the cost and value created by different pay level and pay mix strategies. What does each strategy cost and what does it do for revenues via attraction, selection, and retention of a workforce that has a particular level of ability and motivation? Here, we will use a very basic form of utility analysis, which focuses only on the quality of the workforce initially hired.

To estimate utility in this basic approach, we model it as a function of several parameters:

$$u = r \times SDy \times Z - C/SR$$

where:

u = utility (revenue − cost) per hire per year

r = validity coefficient, the correlation between criterion, y, and one or more pre-employment assessments used to make hiring decisions. It is the accuracy of our predictions regarding which applicants will perform well as employees.

SDy = standard deviation of the dollar value of different employee performance levels. In essence, this parameter measures the value of high performance versus average or low performance in a job. (This parameter would be higher for jobs like CEO, actors, athletes, attorneys, real estate brokers, and consultants where star performers can generate much more profit than weaker performers and lower for most lower-skill or highly structured jobs, where performance differences are less consequential.) Although accuracy of utility estimates depends on accurate estimation of SDy, we will use a very rough rule of thumb here to keep things more manageable: SDy equals 40% of salary.

Z = mean standard score (z distribution, mean = 0, SD =1) of those hired on the predictor used to select/hire employees

C = cost per applicant. Note that in the utility formula, C is divided by the selection ratio. Thus, C/SR becomes large (and drives the utility estimate lower) as either cost per applicant increases or our selectivity increases (i.e., SR decreases). For example, a cost per applicant of $200 and a selection ratio of

.5 yields $200/.5 = 400, but a cost per applicant of $200 and a selection ratio of .05 yields $200/.05 = $4,000$. Thus, there is a trade-off between the gains from increasing average hire quality (Z) and the cost of being more selective in hiring to achieve this higher quality.

SR = selection ratio, which is hires/applicants.

It is important to note how Z changes as we become more selective (lower SR) in our hiring. Based on the standard normal distribution function:

SR	Z
5%	2.06
10%	1.75
20%	1.40
50%	0.80
80%	0.35
100%	0.00

In other words, if we hire all (100%) of applicants, our average z (Z) score would be .00, indicating that the average quality of our hires would be the same as the average quality of the applicant pool. However, if we are more selective and hire only 20% of our applicants, then our average quality will be much higher, 1.40. At a still higher selectivity of 5%, our applicant pool would be 2.06 standard deviations above the mean.

Let us assume we are filling a position that will cost us a salary of $100,000 under our new selective hiring approach (versus $90,000 under the old system). If we are able to increase the quality of our hires to $Z = 2.06$ through selective hiring, what would the impact be on utility? Assume that the average cost per applicant is $200. (Some applicants can be screened out quickly and cheaply, while other applicants will require higher costs to do more intensive screening.)

Old Selection Strategy

$SR = .50$ ($Z = .80$), $r = .40$, $SD = $50,000$, $cost = 200
$u = .40 \times $50,000 \times .80 - $200/.50 = $15,600$/hire

New Selection Strategy

$SR = .05$ ($Z = 2.06$), $r = .40$, $SD = $50,000$, $cost = 100
$u = .40 \times $50,000 \times 2.06 - $200/.05 = $37,200$/hire

In other words, our new, more selective hiring approach yields a utility gain of $37,200 - $15,600 = $21,500$ per hire.

But hold on. We are paying a $10,000 higher salary to enable us to be more selective in our hiring in the new approach. Thus, the utility gain is instead $21,500 - $10,000 = $11,500$. Further, benefits, on average, add about another $40 cents on top of every dollar of direct pay. So, perhaps we should use $1.4 \times $10,000 = $14,000$ as the incremental compensation cost of the new selection strategy. The incremental utility would then be $21,500 - $14,000 = $7,500$ per hire.[65]

Of course, our conclusion depends entirely on the estimates and assumptions we put into the model. Paying more will, of course, not always generate higher utility. It really depends on the situation and the organization's strategy. More accurate estimates of utility of compensation can be obtained by following more complex models that have been developed.[66] Estimates obtained with these models would very likely change and be more accurate because they more fully recognize sorting effects (including retention patterns of high and low performers) and gains and losses to compensation decisions that accumulate over time. We have tried to keep things simpler here in the interest of introducing some basic ideas and logic.

Endnotes

1. Erica Groshen, "Five Reasons, Why Wages Vary Among Employers," *Industrial Relations* 30 (1991), pp. 350–381; B. Gerhart and S. Rynes, *Compensation: Theory, Evidence and Strategic Implications* (Thousand Oaks, CA: Sage, 2003); B. Gerhart and G. Milkovich, "Organization Differences in Managerial Compersation and Financial Performance," *Academy of Management Journal* 33 (1990), pp. 663–691.

2. Mike Esterl, "Will Southwest Lose Some of the LUV?" *Wall Street Journal,* April 17, 2009, http://blogs.wsj.com/middleseat/2009/04/17/will-southwest-lose-some-of-the-luv/.

3. The National Association of Colleges and Employers, Bethlehem, PA, publishes a quarterly survey of starting-salary offers to college graduates; data are reported by curriculum, by functional area, and by degree at *www.naceweb.org.* It is one of several sources employers may use to establish the offers they extend to new graduates.

4. Adapted from our analysis of CHiPS data set, by arrangement with Clark Consulting, Boston.

5. C. Trevor and M. Graham, "Deriving the Market Wage: Three Decision Areas in the Compensation Survey Process," *WorldatWork* 9(4) (2000), pp. 69–77.

6. Barry Gerhart and George Milkovich, "Employee Compensation: Research and Practice," in M. D. Dunnette and L. M. Hought, eds., *Handbook of Industrial and Organizational Psychology,* 2nd ed. (Palo Alto, CA: Consulting Psychologists Press, 1992).

7. Barry Gerhart and Sara Rynes, "Determinants and Consequences of Salary Negotiations by Male and Female MBA Graduates," *Journal of Applied Psychology* 76(2) (1991), pp. 256–262.

8. Morris M. Kleiner, *Licensing Occupations: Ensuring Quality or Restricting Competition?* (Kalamazoo, MI: Upjohn Institute, 2006).

9. Thomas A. Mahoney, *Compensation and Reward Perspective* (Burr Ridge, IL: Irwin, 1979), p. 123.

10. David Levine, Dale Belman, Gary Charness, et al., *Changes in Careers and Wage Structures at Large American Employers* (Kalamazoo, MI: Upjohn Institute, 2001); David I. Levine, D. Belman, et al., *The New Employment Contract: Evidence About How Little Wage Structures Have Changed* (Kalamazoo, MI: Upjohn Institute, 2001); Edward P. Lazear, *Personnel Economics* (New York: Wiley, 1998); Carl M. Campbell III, "Do Firms Pay Efficiency Wages? Evidence With Data at the Firm Level," *Journal of Labor Economics* 11(3) (1993), pp. 442–469.

11. Peter Cappelli and Keith Chauvin, "An Interplant Test of the Efficiency Wage Hypothesis," *Quarterly Journal of Economics,* August 1991, pp. 769–787.

12. L. Rynes and J. W. Boudreau, "College Recruiting in Large Organizations: Practice, Evaluation, and Research Implications," *Personnel Psychology* 39 (1986), pp. 729–757.

13. E. Groshen and A. B. Krueger, "The Structure of Supervision and Pay in Hospitals," *Industrial and Labor Relations Review,* February 1990, pp. 134S–146S.

14. P. Milgrom and J. Roberts, *Economics, Organizations, and Management* (Englewood Cliffs, NJ Prentice-Hall, 1992).

15. A. K. G. Hildreth and A. Oswald, "Rentsharing and Wages: Evidence From Company and Establishment Panels," *Journal of Labor Economics* 15 (1997), pp. 318–337.

16. C. O. L. H. Porter, D. E. Conlon, and Allison Barber, "The Dynamics of Salary Negotiations: Effects on Applicants' Justice Perceptions and Recruitment Decisions," *The International Journal of Conflict Management* 15(3) (2005), pp. 273–303; A. VanVinnen, "Person-Organization Fit: The Match Between Newcomers' and Recruiters' Preferences for Organization Cultures," *Personnel Psychology* 53 (2000), pp. 115–125.

17. Christopher J. Collins and Jian Han, "Exploring Applicant Pool Quantity and Quality: The Effects of Early Recruitment Practice Strategies, Corporate Advertising, and Firm Reputation," *Personnel Psychology,* Autumn 2004, pp. 685–717.

18. Daniel M. Cable and Timothy A. Judge, "Pay Preferences and Job Search Decisions: A Person-Organization Fit Perspective," *Personnel Psychology,* Summer 1994, pp. 317–348.

19. Gary S. Becker, *Human Capital* (Chicago: University of Chicago Press, 1975); Barry Gerhart, "Gender Differences in Current and Starting Salaries: The Role of Performance, College Major, and Job Title," *Industrial and Labor Relations Review* 43 (1990), pp. 418–433; Robert Bretz, C. Quinn Trank, and S. L. Rynes, "Attracting Applicants in the War for Talent: Differences in Work Preferences Among High Achievers," *Journal of Business and Psychology* 16 (2002), pp. 331–345.

20. Occupational earnings information for the United States is available at www.bls.govloes/curent/os_nat.htm. Earnings by education level is availale at www.bls.gov/cps/earnings.htm#demographic.

21. George F. Dreher and Taylor Cox, Jr., "Labor Market Mobility and Cash Compensation: The Moderating Effects of Race and Gender," *Academy of Management Journal* 43(5) (2000), pp. 890–900.

22. Peter Drucker, "They're Not Employees, They're People," *Harvard Business Review,* February 2002, pp. 70–77; David I. Levine, "Fairness, Markets, and Ability to Pay: Evidence From Compensation Executives," *American Economic Review,* December 1993, pp. 1241–1259; B. Klaas, "Containing Compensation Costs: Why Firms Differ in Their Willingness to Reduce Pay," *Journal of Management* 25(6) (1999), pp. 829–850.

23. David I. Levine, "Fairness, Markets, and Ability to Pay: Evidence From Compensation Executives," *American Economic Review,* December 1993, p. 1250.

24. Dana Mattioli, "Salary Cuts: Ugly, But It Could Be Worse," *Wall Street Journal,* April 9, 2009; Matthew Quinn, "Survey: One in Four Companies Has Frozen Salaries," *Workforce Management,* February 9, 2009.

25. Watson Wyatt, "Aligning Rewards With the Changing Employment Deal," *WorldatWork,* 2007, www.watsonwyatt.com.

26. "National Wages Council Recommends the Restructuring of Wage System for Competitiveness—Ministers and Top Civil Servants to Lead With Wage Cuts," *Singapore Straits,* May 22, 2003; Marek Szwejczewski and Sri Srikanthan, "The Risks of Outsourcing: Unexpected Consequences," *Financial Times,* April 14, 2006, p. 8; Thomas Friedman, *The World Is Flat* (New York: Farrar, Straus and Giroux, 2006); "CEO's Marital Duties Outsourced to Mexican Groundskeeper," *The Onion* 39(48), December 10, 2003, p. 1.

27. Dinah Wisenberg Brin, "Staffing Agencies May See Pickup in Demand for Traveling Nurses," *The Wall Street Journal,* June 22, 2005, p. B2A.

28. Erica L. Groshen and David Levine, *The Rise and Decline (?) of Employer Wage Structures* (New York: Federal Reserve Bank, 2000).

29. John W. Budd and Brian P. McCall, "The Grocery Stores Wage Distribution: A Semi-Parametric Analysis of the Role of Retailing and Labor Market Institutions," *Industrial and Labor Relations Review* 54(2A) (2001), pp. 484–501.

30. D. M. Raff, "The Puzzling Profusion of Compensation Systems in the Interwar Automobile Industry," working paper, NBER, 1998. Raff attributes the fantastic diversity of compensation programs for blue-collar employees (firm-based, piece rate, companywide, team-based) to differences in technology employed among competitors.

31. Walter Oi and Todd L. Idson, "Firm Size and Wages," in O. Ashenfelter and D. Card, eds., *Handbook of Labor Economics* (Amsterdam: North Holland, 1999), pp. 2165–2214.

32. H. Heneman and T. Judge, "Pay and Employee Satisfaction," in S. L. Rynes and B. Gerhart, eds., *Compensation in Organizations: Current Research and Practice* (San Francisco: Jossey-Bass, 2000); T. R. Mitchell and A. E. Mickel, "The Meaning of Money: An Individual Differences Perspective," *Academy of Management Review* 24 (1999), pp. 568–578; Watson Wyatt, Playing *to Win: Strategic Rewards in the War for Talent* (New York: Watson Wyatt, 2001); Hudson Employment Index, *Transforming Pay Plans: 2006 Compensation and Benefits Report, www.hudson-index.com/node.asp?SID=6755.*

33. Sara L. Rynes, Amy E. Colbert, and Kenneth G. Brown, "HR Professionals' Beliefs About Effective Human Resource Practices: Correspondence Between Research and Practice," *Human Resource Management* 41(2) (Summer 2002), pp. 149–174; Sara L. Rynes, Amy E. Colbert, and Kenneth G. Brown, "Seven Common Misconceptions About Human Resource Practices: Research Findings Versus Practitioner Beliefs," *Academy of Management Executive* 16(3) (2002), pp. 92–102.

34. Larry W. Hunter, "What Determines Job Quality in Nursing Homes?" *Industrial 8 Labor Relations Review* 53, (2000) pp. 463–481; Rosemary Batt, "Explaining Intra-Occupational Wage Inequality in Telecommunications Services: Customer Segmentation, Human Resource Practices, and Union Decline." *Industrial and Labor Relations Review* 54 (2A) (2001) pp. 425–449.

35. P. Osterman, "The Wage Effects of High Performance Work Organization in Manufacturing," *Industrial and Labor Relations Review* 59 (2006), pp. 187–204.

36. A. E. Barber and R. D. Bretz Jr., "Compensation, Attraction and Retention," in S. L. Rynes and B. Gerhart eds., *Compensation in Organizations* (San Francisco, CA: Jossey-Bass, 2000) pp. 32–60; S. C. Currall, A. J. Towler, T. A. Judge, and L. Kohn, "Pay Satisfaction and Organizational Outcomes," *Personnel Psychology*, 58 (2005) pp. 613–640; H. G. Heneman III, and T. A. Judge, "Compensation Attitudes," in S. L. Rynes and B. Gerhart, eds., *Compensation in Organizations* (San Franciscso: Jossey-Bass, 2000); M. L. Williams, M. A. McDaniel, and N. T. Nguyen, "A Meta-Analysis of the Antecedents and Consequences of Pay Level Satisfaction," *Journal of Applied Psychology,* 91, (2006), pp. 392–413; B. Gerhart and S. L. Rynes, *Compensation: Theory, Evidence, and Strategic Implications,* (Thousand Oaks, CA: Sage, 2003); B. S. Klaas and J. A. McCledon, "To Lead, Lag, or Match: Estimating the Financial Impact of Pay Level Policies," *Personnel Psychology* 49 (1996), pp. 121–141.

37. Mark C. Long, Kristin M. Dziczek, Daniel D. Luria, and Edith A. Wiarda, "Wage and Productivity Stability in U. S. Manufactuing Plants," *Monthly Labor Review* 131(5) (2008), pp. 24–36.

38. Charlie Trevor and M. E. Graham, "Deriving the Market Wage: Three Decision Areas in the Compensation Survey Process," *WorldatWork Journal* 9(4) (2000), pp. 69–77.

39. Trader's Joe's, *http://www.traderjoes.com/product_categories.html#Booze,* August 31, 2009.

40. William M. Bulkeley, "IBM Documents Give Rare Look at Sensitive Plans on 'Offshoring,'" *Wall Street Journal,* January 19, 2004.

41. Nira Sheth and Nathan Koppel, "With Times Tight, Even Lawyers Get Outsourced," *Wall Street Journal,* November 26, 2008.

42. Heather Timmons, "Cost-Cutting in New York, But a Boom in India," *New York Times,* August 12, 2008.

43. P. J. Dowling, M. Festing, and A. D. Engle, Sr., *International Human Resource Management,* 5th ed. (London: Thomson Learning, 2008).

44. Peter Engardio, "China Losing Luster With U.S. Manufacturers," *BusinessWeek,* November 26, 2008.

45. Kendall Roth and Sharon O'Donnell, "Foreign Subsidiary Compensation Strategy: An Agency Theory Perspective," *Academy of Management Journal* 39 (1996), pp. 678–703.

46. Paulo Prada and Niraj Shethapril, "Delta Air Ends Use of India Call Centers," *Wall Street Journal,* April 18, 2009.

47. Margaret Williams, Michael McDaniels, and Njung Nguyen, "A Meta-Analysis of the Antecedents and Consequences of Pay Level Satisfaction," *Journal of Applied Psychology,* March 2006, pp. 392–413; David I. Levine, "Fairness, Markets, and Ability to Pay: Evidence From Compensation Executives," *American Economic Review,* December 1993, pp. 1241–1259.

48. See, for example, any of the surveys conducted by leading consulting firms: Hewitt, *www.hewitt.com;* Wyatt Watson, *www.watsonwyatt.com;* Hay, *www.haygroup.com;* Mercer, *www.mercer.com;* Towers Perrin, *www.towersperrin.com;* Executive Alliance, *www.executivealliance.com.*

49. Laura Johnson and Darrll Cira, "Taking the Best Path to Implementing a Global Pay Structure: The General Mill's Experience," paper at WorldatWork Conference, Seattle, WA, June 1, 2009.

50. Brian S. Klaas and John A. McClendon, "To Lead, Lag, or Match: Estimating the Financial Impact of Pay Level Policies," *Personnel Psychology* 49 (1996), pp. 121–140.

51. Robert Kaplan, *Imperial Grunts* (New York: Random House. 2005).

52. B. Gerhart and S. Rynes, *Compensation: Theory, Evidence and Strategic Implications* (Thousand Oaks, CA: Sage, 2003).

53. Robert Bretz, J. W. Boudreau, W. R. Boswell, and T. A. Judge, "Personality and Cognitive Ability as Predictors of Job Search Among Employed Managers," *Personnel Psychology* 54 (2001), pp. 25–50; Charlie Trevor, Barry Gerhart, and John Boudreau, "Voluntary Turnover and Job Performance: Curvilinearity and the Moderating Influences of Salary Growth and Promotions," *Journal of Applied Psychology* 82 (1997), pp. 44–61.

54. B. Gerhart and G. Milkovich, "Organizational Differences in Managerial Compensation and Financial Performance," *Academy of Management Journal* 33 (1990), pp. 663–691; M. Bloom and J. Michel, "The Relationships Among Organization Context, Pay, and Managerial Turnover," *Academy of Management Journal* 45 (2002), pp. 33–42; M. Bloom and G. Milkovich, "Relationships Among Risk, Incentive Pay, and Organization Performance," *Academy of Management Journal* 41(3) (1998), pp. 283–297; B. Hall and J. Liebman, "Are CEOs Really Paid Like Bureaucrats?" *Quarterly Journal of Economics,* August 1998, pp. 653–691. Variable pay is discussed in Chapters 9 through 11. "Variable" indicates that the pay increase (bonus) is not added to base pay; hence, it is not part of fixed costs but is variable, since the amount may vary next year.

55. Michael Sturman, "'How' Versus 'How Much' You Pay: The Effects of Various Pay Components on Future Performance," Ithaca, NY: working paper, Hotel School, 2006.

56. David I. Levine, "Fairness, Markets, and Ability to Pay: Evidence From Compensation Executives," *American Economic Review,* December 1993, pp. 1241–1259.

57. Mei Fong, "A Chinese Puzzle," *The Wall Street Journal,* August 16, 2005, p. B1.

58. L. Gaughan and J. Kasparek, "Employees as Customers: Using Market Research to Manage Compensation and Benefits," *Workspan* (9) (2000), pp. 31–38; M. Sturman, G. Milkovich, and J. Hannon, "Expert Systems' Effect on Employee Decisions and Satisfaction," *Personnel Psychology* (1997), pp. 21–34; J. Shaw and S. Schaubrock, "The Role of Spending Behavior Patterns in Monetary Rewards," Working Paper, University of Kentucky, 2001; S. Dubner, "Calculating the Irrational in Economics," *New York Times,* June 28, 2003.

59. Brian Klaas and John A. McClendon, "To Lead, Lag, or Match: Estimating the Financial Impact of Pay Level Policies," *Personnel Psychology* 49 (1996), pp. 121–140.

60. Barry Gerhart and George Milkovich, "Employee Compensation: Research and Practice," in M. D. Dunnette and L. M. Hough, eds., *Handbook of Industrial and Organizational Psychology,* 2nd ed., eds. (Palo Alto, CA: Consulting Psychologists Press, 1992).

61. H. Heneman and T. Judge, "Pay and Employee Satisfaction," in S. Rynes and B. Gerhart, eds., *Compensation in Organizations: Current Research and Practice* (San Francisco: Jossey-Bass, 2000).

62. B. Gerhart and S. Rynes, *Compensation Theory, Evidence and Strategic Implications* (Thousand Oaks, CA: Sage, 2003).

63. Kris Maher, "Nurses Win Setlement Over Wages," *Wall Street Journal,* March 9, 2009, p. A6.

64. Wayne F. Cascio and John W. Boudreau, "Investing in People: Financial Impact of Human Resource Initiatives," (Upper Saddle River, NJ: Financial Times Press, 2008); H. E. Brogden, "When Testing Pays Off," *Personnel Psychology* 2 (1949), pp. 171–185; J. W. Boudreau, and C. J. Berger, "Decision-Theoretic Utility Analysis Applied to Employee Separations and Acquisitions," *Journal of Applied Psychology* [monograph] 73 (1985), pp. 467–481; J. W. Boudreau, "Utility Analysis for Decisions in Human Resource Management, in M. D. Dunnette and L. M. Hough, eds., *Handbook of Industrial and Organizational Psychology,* 2nd ed. (Palo Alto, CA: Consulting Psychologists Press, 1991).

65. The accuracy of utility estimates depends on whether higher quality applicants actually accept job offers. To the degree they do not, the Z parameter estimate will be biased upward, biasing utility estimates upward as well. Kevin R. Murphy, "When Your Top Choice Turns You Down: Effect of Rejected Offers on the Utility of Selection Tests," *Psychological Bulletin* 99 (1986), pp. 133–138. Compensation level is one way to increase the probability of job offer acceptance.

66. B. S. Klaas and J. A. McCledon, "To Lead, Lag, or Match: Estimating the Financial Impact of Pay Level Policies," *Personnel Psychology* 49 (1996), pp. 121–141; M. C. Sturman, C. O. Trevor, J. W. Boudreau, and B. Gerhart, "Is It Worth It to Win the Talent War? Evaluating the Utility of Performance-Based Pay," *Personnel Psychology* 56 (2003), pp. 997–1035.

Designing Pay Levels, Mix, and Pay Structures

Chapter Outline

Major Decisions

Specify Competitive Pay Policy

The Purpose of a Survey
- *Adjust Pay Level—How Much to Pay?*
- *Adjust Pay Mix—What Forms?*
- *Adjust Pay Structure?*
- *Study Special Situations*
- *Estimate Competitors' Labor Costs*

Select Relevant Market Competitors
- *Fuzzy Markets*

Design the Survey
- *Who Should Be Involved?*
- *How Many Employers?*
- *Which Jobs to Include?*
- *What Information to Collect?*

Interpret Survey Results and Construct a Market Line
- *Verify Data*
- *Statistical Analysis*
- *Update the Survey Data*
- *Construct a Market Pay Line*
- *Setting Pay for Non-Benchmark Jobs*
- *Combine Internal Structure and External Market Rates*

From Policy to Practice: The Pay-Policy Line
- *Choice of Measure*
- *Updating*
- *Policy Line as Percent of Market Line*

From Policy to Practice: Grades and Ranges
- *Why Bother With Grades and Ranges?*
- *Develop Grades*
- *Establish Range Midpoints, Minimums, and Maximums*
- *Overlap*

From Policy to Practice: Broad Banding
- *Flexibility-Control*

Balancing Internal and External Pressures: Adjusting the Pay Structure
- *Reconciling Differences*

Market Pricing
- *Business Strategy (More Than "Follow the Leader")*

Review

Your Turn: Word-of-Mouse: Dot-Com Comparisons

Average pay of benchmark jobs set to average pay of similar jobs in comparable companies.—3M

Pay among the leaders. Base pay will be fully comparable (50th percentile of competitors). Total compensation, including benefits and performance incentives, will bring our compensation to the 75th percentile of competitors.—Colgate

Our competitive strategy will deliver rewards at the market competitive median for median performance, at the 75th percentile for 75th percentile performance, and so on. We emphasize work-life balance; our benefits insure that every person is fully present and focused when they are at work.—Medtronic[1]

These are statements of different organizations' external competitiveness policies—comparisons of an employer's pay relative to its competitors. In the last chapter, we discussed market and organization factors that influence these policies. Now we examine how managers use these factors to determine pay levels, mix of forms, and structures.

MAJOR DECISIONS

The major decisions in setting externally competitive pay and designing the corresponding pay structures are shown in Exhibit 8.1. They include (1) specify the employer's competitive pay policy, (2) define the purpose of the survey, (3) select relevant market competitors, (4) design the survey, (5) interpret survey results and construct the market line, (6) construct a pay policy line that reflects external pay policy, and (7) balance competitiveness with internal alignment through the use of **ranges,** flat rates, and/or bands. This is a lengthy list. Think of Exhibit 8.1 as a road map through this chapter. The guideposts are the major decisions you face in designing a pay structure. Don't forget to end with, So what? "So what" means ensuring that pay structures both support business success and treat employees fairly.

SPECIFY COMPETITIVE PAY POLICY

The first decision, determining the external competitive pay policy, was covered in the previous chapter. Translating any external pay policy into practice requires information on the external market. Surveys provide the data for translating that policy into pay levels, pay mix, and structures.

A **survey** is the systematic process of collecting and making judgments about the compensation paid by other employers.

EXHIBIT 8.1   Determining Externally Competitive Pay Levels and Structures

External Competitiveness: Pay Relationships Among Organizations →	Specify Policy →	Select Market →	Design Survey →	Draw Policy Lines →	Merge Internal & External Pressures →	Competitive Pay Levels, Mix, and Structures

Some Major Decisions in Pay-Level Determination

- Specify pay-level policy.
- Define purpose of survey.
- Specify relevant market.
- Design and conduct survey.
- Interpret and apply result.
- Design grades and ranges or bands.

THE PURPOSE OF A SURVEY

An employer conducts or participates in a survey for a number of reasons: (1) to adjust the pay level in response to changing rates paid by competitors, (2) to set the mix of pay forms relative to that paid by competitors, (3) to establish or price a pay structure, (4) to analyze pay-related problems, or (5) to estimate the labor costs of product/service market competitors.

Adjust Pay Level—How Much to Pay?

Most organizations make adjustments to employees' pay on a regular basis. Such adjustments can be based on the overall movement of pay rates caused by the competition for people in the market. Adjustments may also be based on performance, ability to pay, or terms specified in a contract.

Adjust Pay Mix—What Forms?

Adjustments to the different forms of pay competitors use (base, bonus, stock, benefits) and the relative importance they place on each form occur less frequently than adjustments to overall pay level. It is not clear (without good research) why changes to the pay mix occur less frequently than changes in the pay level. Perhaps the high costs of redesigning a different mix create a barrier. Perhaps inertia prevails. More likely, insufficient attention has been devoted to mix decisions. That is, the mix organizations use may have been based on external pressures such as health-care costs, stock values, government regulations, union demands, and what others did. Yet some pay forms may affect employee behavior more than others. So good information on total compensation, the mix of pay competitors use, and costs of various pay forms is increasingly important.

Adjust Pay Structure?

Many employers use market surveys to validate their own job evaluation results. For example, job evaluation may place purchasing assistant jobs at the same level in the job structure as some secretarial jobs. But if the market shows vastly different pay rates for the two types of work, most employers will recheck their evaluation process to see whether the jobs have been properly evaluated. Some may even establish a separate structure for different types of work. IBM sets pay according to market conditions for each separate occupation (finance, engineering, law). Thus, the job structure that results from internal job evaluation may not match competitors' pay structures in the external market. Reconciling these two pay structures is a major issue.

Rather than integrating an internal and external structure, some employers go straight to market surveys to establish their internal structures. Such "market pricing" mimics competitors' pay structures. Accurate market data is increasingly important as organizations move to more generic work descriptions (associate, leader) that focus on the person's skill as well as the job. Former relationships between job evaluation points and dollars may no longer hold. Accurate information and informed judgment are vital for making all these decisions.

Study Special Situations

Information from specialized surveys can shed light on specific pay-related problems. A special study may focus on a targeted group such as patent attorneys, retail sales managers, secretaries, or software engineers. Unusual increases in an employer's turnover in specific jobs may require focused market surveys to find out if market changes are occurring.[2]

Estimate Competitors' Labor Costs

Survey data are used as part of employers' broader efforts to gather **"competitive intelligence."**[3] To better understand how competitors achieve their market share and price their products/services, companies seek to examine (i.e., benchmark) practices costs, and so forth against competitors, including in the area of compensation. One source of publicly available labor cost data is the Employment Cost Index (ECI), one of four types of salary surveys published regularly by the Department of Labor on its Web site at *www.bls.gov/ncs/*.[4] The ECI measures quarterly changes in employer costs for compensation. The index allows a firm to compare changes in its average costs to an all-industry or specific-industry average. However, this comparison may have limited value because industry averages may not reflect relevant competitors.[5]

SELECT RELEVANT MARKET COMPETITORS

We are up to the third of our major decisions shown in Exhibit 8.1: Specify relevant markets. To make decisions about pay level, mix, and structures, a relevant labor market must be defined that includes employers who compete in one or more of the following areas:

1. The same occupations or skills
2. Employees within the same geographic area
3. The same products and services[6]

Exhibit 8.2 shows how Microsoft and Google select relevant market competitors in establishing executive compensation. Both explicitly include product market ("technology") and labor market competitors. The geographic level is national or international.

Exhibit 8.3 shows how qualifications interact with geography to define the scope of relevant labor markets. As the importance and the complexity of the qualifications increase, the geographic limits also increase.[7] Competition tends to be national or international for managerial and professional skills (as in Exhibit 8.2) but local or regional for clerical and production skills.

However, these generalizations do not always hold true. In areas with high concentrations of scientists, engineers, and managers (e.g., Boston, Austin, or Palo Alto), the primary market comparison may be regional, with national data used only secondarily. As Exhibit 8.4 shows, pay differentials vary among localities. A job that averages $73,470 nationally can pay from $51,610 in Jackson, Mississippi to $81,910 in Boston, Massachusetts. However, some larger firms ignore local market conditions.[8] Instead, they emphasize internal alignment across geographic areas to facilitate the use of virtual

EXHIBIT 8.2 External Competitiveness Strategy for Top Executives, Microsoft and Google

MICROSOFT
Peer Group

Technology Peer Group. These are companies operating in the information technology industry that focus on producing software or hardware or providing online services, and that employ work forces with skill sets and professional backgrounds similar to those of our work force.

Dow 30 Peer Group. Generally, these are large, diversified companies with significant international operations. As an industry and worldwide business leader, they compete for senior executive talent with top companies across a variety of other industries, not just those in the information technology industry.

Technology Peer Group

Accenture	IBM	3M
Adobe Systems	Intel	Alcoa
Apple	Oracle	American Express
Cisco Systems	SAP	American International Group
Dell Computer	Sun Microsystems	ATT
EDS	Symantec	Bank of America
Google	Time Warner	Boeing
Hewlett Packard		Caterpillar
		Chevron Group

Dow 30 Peer Group*

Citigroup	Merck
Coca-Cola	Pfizer
DuPont	Procter & Gamble
ExxonMobil	United Technologies
General Electric	Verizon
General Motors	Wal-Mart
Home Depot	Walt Disney
JPMorgan Chase	MCDonald's
Johnson and Johnson	

Market Position Target

Cash compensation target	"below median"
Equity award target	"above median"

GOOGLE
Peer Group

Peers were considered to be companies that met at least three of the following criteria:
Key labor market competitor (e.g., Microsoft, Yahoo, Amazon, eBay).
High-growth, with a minimum of 25% revenue and/or headcount growth over the previous two-year period.
$10 billion or more in annual revenues.
$50 billion or more in market capitalization.

Amazon.com	EMC	Oracle
Apple	Hewlett Packard	Qualcomm
Cisco	IBM	Sun Microsystems
Dell	Intel	Yahoo
eBay	Microsoft	

Market Position Target

Element of Compensation	Percentile
Base Salary	50th to 70th
Target Total Cash	75th
Target Equity	90th

Source: Microsoft 2008 Proxy Statement, *www.sec.gov,* April 26, 2009; 2008 Google Proxy Statement, *www.sec.gov,* April 26, 2009.

*Hewlett Packard, IBM, and Intel are members of the Dow 30, but are excluded because they are members of the Technology Peer Group. Microsoft is also a Dow 30 member but is excluded from this review.

EXHIBIT 8.3 Relevant Labor Markets by Geographic and Employee Groups

Geographic Scope	Production	Office and Clerical	Technicians	Scientists and Engineers	Managerial Professional	Executive
Local: Within relatively small areas such as cities or Metropolitan Statistical Areas (e.g., Dallas metropolitan area)	Most likely	Most likely	Most likely			
Regional: Within a particular area of the state or several states (e.g., oil-producing region of southwestern United States)	Only if in short supply or critical	Only if in short supply or critical	Most likely	Likely	Most Likely	
National: Across the country				Most likely	Most likely	Most likely
International: Across several countries				Only for critical skills or those in very short supply	Only for critical skills or those in very short supply	Sometimes

243

EXHIBIT 8.4   **Pay Differences by Location: Annual Wage by Metro Area, Computer Programmer**

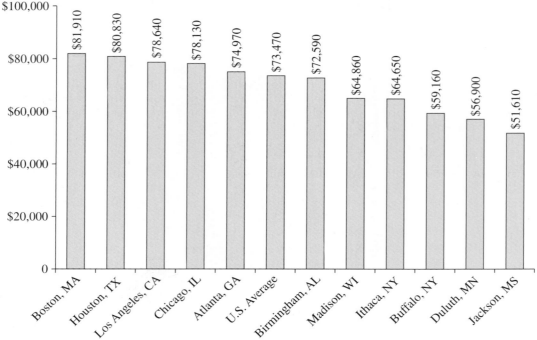

Source: U.S. Bureau of Labor Statistics. www.bls.sov/bls/blswage.htm

teams. But it turns out that team members in different locations compare their pay. What a surprise.

Some writers argue that if the skills are tied to a particular industry—as underwriters, actuaries, and claims representatives are to insurance, for example—it makes sense to define the market on an industry basis, and some research agrees.[9] If accounting, sales, or clerical skills are not limited to one particular industry, then industry considerations are less important. From the perspective of cost control and ability to pay, including competitors in the product/service market is crucial.[10] However, this becomes a problem when the major competitors are based in countries with far lower pay rates, such as China or Mexico. But a segmented labor supply (see Chapter 7) requires multiple country comparisons.[11] Legal regulations, tax policies, and customs vary among countries. Because of tax laws, managers in Korea and Spain receive company credit cards to use for personal expenses (groceries, clothing). In the United States, these purchases count as taxable income, but they do not in Korea and Spain.

While the quantity of data available for international comparisons is improving, using the data to adjust pay still requires a lot of judgment. Labor markets are just emerging in some regions (China, Russia). Historically, state planning agencies set nationwide wage rates, so there was no need for surveys.[12] Japanese companies share information among themselves but not with outsiders, so no surveys are available.[13]

But even with good international survey data, judgment is still required. For example, while salaries at international companies in developing economies are low by U.S., Western European, and Japanese standards, they are often very high compared to salaries at domestic companies in those countries. Pay practices of foreign companies can disrupt emerging local markets in developing economies.[14] IBM software engineers in India told us that while they are paid very well by Indian standards, they feel underpaid compared to IBM engineers in the United States who work on the same projects.[15]

Fuzzy Markets

Walk through a bay of cubicles (plastered with *Dilbert* cartoons) at Yahoo and you are likely to find former kindergarten teachers, software engineers, and sales representatives all collaborating on a single team. Yahoo combines technology, media, and commerce into one company. What is the relevant labor market? Which firms should be included in Yahoo's surveys?

Even within traditional companies, unique talent is required for unique jobs. West Publishing, a provider of legal information to law firms, designed the position of Senior Director of Future Vision Services. The holder of this mouthful title is responsible for ensuring that West's customers (litigious lawyers) increase their purchases over the Web plus increase their satisfaction with West's services. The job was filled by a software engineer with e-commerce, marketing, and theater experience. Try finding that job in the market. These new organizations and jobs fuse together diverse knowledge and experience, so "relevant" markets appear more like "fuzzy" markets.[16] Organizations with unique jobs and structures face the double bind of finding it hard to get comparable market data at the same time they are placing more emphasis on external market data.

DESIGN THE SURVEY

Consulting firms offer a wide choice of ongoing surveys covering almost every job family and industry group imaginable. Their surveys are getting better and better.[17] While we would like to attribute this to the fact that our textbook has improved the sophistication of compensation education (the first edition of our book was published in 1985, and at least some of those early readers ought to be in power positions by now), it is more likely that the improvement is the result of technological advances. Increasingly, consultants offer clients the option of electronically accessing the consultants' survey databases. Clients then do whatever special analysis they need. General Electric conducts most of its market analysis in this manner. Hay PayNet permits organizations to tie into Hay's vast survey data 24/7.[18]

Designing a survey requires answering the following questions: (1) Who should be involved in the survey design? (2) How many employers should be included? (3) Which jobs should be included? and (4) What information should be collected?

Who Should Be Involved?

In most organizations, the responsibility for managing the survey lies with the compensation manager. But since compensation expenses have a powerful effect on profitability, including managers and employees on the task forces makes sense.

Outside consulting firms are typically used as third-party protection from possible "price-fixing" lawsuits. Suits have been filed alleging that the direct exchange of survey data violates Section 1 of the Sherman Act, which outlaws conspiracies in restraint of trade. Survey participants may be guilty of price fixing if the overall effect of the information exchange is to *interfere with competitive prices* and *artificially hold down wages*. Identifying participants' data by company name is considered price fixing.[19]

How Many Employers?

There are no firm rules on how many employers to include in a survey. Large firms with a lead policy may exchange data with only a few (6 to 10) top-paying competitors.[20] Merrill Lynch aims for the 75th percentile among 11 peer financial firms. A small organization in an area dominated by two or three employers may decide to survey only smaller competitors. National surveys conducted by consulting firms often include more than 100 employers. Clients of these consultants often stipulate special analyses that report pay rates by selected industry groups, geographic region, and/or pay levels (e.g., top 10 percent).

Publicly Available Data

In the United States, the **Bureau of Labor Statistics (BLS)** is the major source of publicly available compensation (cash, bonus, and benefits but not stock ownership) data. The BLS publishes extensive information on various occupations (very broadly defined—e.g., professional, executive, sales, and administrative support are the categories for white-collar occupations) in different geographic areas. According to the BLS, administrative support in Birmingham, Alabama, pays $12.48 an hour in the private sector and $13.78 in government. In Iowa City, the comparable rates are $12.38 and $17.98. Public sector employers use BLS data more often than do private sector employers—especially those in Iowa![21]

While some private firms may track the rate of change in BLS data as a cross-check on other surveys, the data are often not specific enough to be used alone. Tailoring analysis to specific industry segments, select companies, and specific job content is not feasible.

"Word of Mouse"

Once upon a time (about 15 years ago) individual employees had a hard time comparing their salaries to others'. Information was gathered haphazardly, via word of mouth. Today, a click of the mouse makes a wealth of data available to everyone. Employees are comparing their compensation to data from the BLS or Salary.com or occupation-specific Web sites.[22] This ease of access means that managers must be able to explain (defend?) the salaries paid to employees compared to those a mouse click away. Whole Foods confronted this issue via an "open book" list of last year's pay of all employees.[23] Unfortunately, the quality of much salary data on the Web is highly suspect. Few of the sites (except the BLS, of course) offer any information on how the data

EXHIBIT 8.5
Free Salary
Survey Data
on the Web for
Programmer
From U.S.
Bureau
of Labor
Statistics, and
Salary.com

	Percentile		
	25th	50th	75th
Bureau of Labor Statistics			
National			
Computer Programmer (code 15-1021)	$52,640	$ 69,620	$ 89,720
Birmingham, Alabama			
Computer Programmer (code 15-1021)	$56,700	$ 72,960	$ 86,660
Salary.com			
National			
Programmer I	$47,039	$ 53,445	$ 61,063
Programmer III	$69,246	$ 77,382	$ 85,920
Programmer V	$92,313	$100,170	$111,644
Birmingham, Alabama			
Programmer I	$44,122	$ 50,131	$ 57,277
Programmer III	$64,875	$ 72,584	$ 80,496
Programmer V	$86,589	$ 93,959	$104,722

were collected, what pay forms are included, and so on. Most are based on information volunteered by site users. Some popular Web sites even misuse the cost-of-living
index when making geographic salary comparisons.[24] On the other hand, Salary.com
includes a compensation glossary, identifies where the site's information comes from,
and explains what the statistics mean. Put in programmer for Birmingham, Alabama,
and you will be asked to choose from 37 job descriptions. Exhibit 8.5 shows the
Salary.com results for just three of those programmer jobs, both at the national level
and in Birmingham. By comparison, all programmer positions are included in a single
category in the BLS survey, making it all but impossible to get a good match.

Many Surveys (But Few That Are Validated)

Opinions about the value of consultant surveys are rampant; research is not. Do Hay,
Mercer, Towers Perrin, Radford, and Clark Consulting surveys yield significantly different results? The fact that companies typically use three or more surveys (for all job
types) suggsts that different surveys do, in fact, imply diferent pay levels.[25] Many

Cybercomp 1
For a demonstration of online surveys, go to *www.haypaynet.com* or *www.
salary.com* or *www.bls.gov/bls/blswage.htm* How do the sites compare? Do they
give information on which employers are included and which ones are not?
Where do their data come from? Do the sites tell you? Which would you use to
design a pay system? Explain.

firms select one survey as their primary source and use others to cross-check or "validate" the results. Some employers routinely combine the results of several surveys and weight each survey in this composite according to somebody's judgment of the quality of the data reported.[26] No systematic study of the effects of differences in market definition, participating firms, types of data collected, quality of data, analysis performed, and/ or results is available. Issues of sample design and statistical inference are seldom considered. For staffing decisions, employment test designers report the test's performance against a set of standards (reliability, validity, etc.). Job evaluation's reliability and validity (or lack of) has been much studied and debated. Yet for market surveys and analysis, similar standards do not exist.[27] Without reliability and validity metrics, survey data is open to challenge.

Which Jobs to Include?

A general guideline is to select as few employers and jobs as necessary to accomplish the purpose. The more complex the survey, the less likely other employers will participate. There are several approaches to selecting jobs for inclusion.

Benchmark-Job Approach

In Chapter 5 we noted that benchmark jobs have stable job content, are common across different employers, and include sizable numbers of employees. If the purpose of the survey is to price the entire structure, then benchmark jobs can be selected to include the entire job structure—all key functions and all levels, just as in job evaluation. In Exhibit 8.6, the more heavily shaded jobs in the structures are benchmark jobs. Benchmark jobs are chosen from as many levels in each of these structures as can be matched with the descriptions of the benchmark jobs that are included in the survey. Exhibit 8.7 indicates that about one in three organizations are able to match over 80 percent of jobs to salary survey jobs, with the remaining organizations report less success in matching.

EXHIBIT 8.6 **Benchmarks**

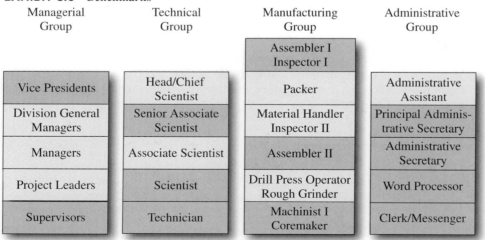

Managerial Group	Technical Group	Manufacturing Group	Administrative Group
		Assembler I / Inspector I	
Vice Presidents	Head/Chief Scientist	Packer	Administrative Assistant
Division General Managers	Senior Associate Scientist	Material Handler / Inspector II	Principal Administrative Secretary
Managers	Associate Scientist	Assembler II	Administrative Secretary
Project Leaders	Scientist	Drill Press Operator / Rough Grinder	Word Processor
Supervisors	Technician	Machinist I / Coremaker	Clerk/Messenger

EXHIBIT 8.7
Percentage
of Jobs in
Organizations
That Match to
Salary Survey
Jobs

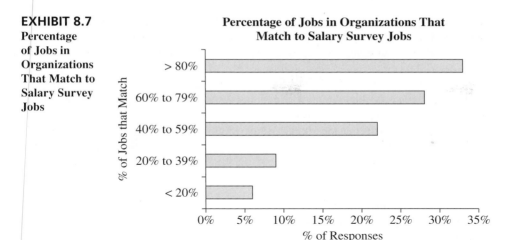

**Percentage of Jobs in Organizations That
Match to Salary Survey Jobs**

The degree of match between the survey's benchmark jobs and each company's benchmark jobs is assessed by various means. The Hay Group, for example, has installed the same job evaluation plan in many companies that participate in its surveys. Consequently, jobs in different organizations can be compared on their job evaluation points and the distribution of points among the compensable factors. Other surveys simply ask participants to check the degree of match (e.g., my company's job is of moderately less value, slightly less value, equal value, etc.). A good survey will include this information in its results. A consultant friend insists that when the compensation manager of a company changes, the job matches change, too.

Low-High Approach

If an organization is using skill-competency-based structures or generic job descriptions, it may not have benchmark jobs to match with jobs at competitors who use a traditional job-based approach. Market data must be converted to fit the skill or competency structure. The simplest way to do this is to identify the lowest- and highest-paid benchmark jobs for the relevant skills in the relevant market and to use the wages for these jobs as anchors for the skill-based structures. Work at various levels within the structure can then be slotted between the anchors. For example, if the entry market rate for operator A is $12 per hour and the rate for a team leader is $42 per hour, then the rate for operator B can be somewhere between $12 and $42 per hour.[28]

The usefulness of this approach depends on how well the extreme benchmark jobs match the organization's work and whether they really do tap the entire range of skills. Hanging a pay system on two pieces of market data raises the stakes on the accuracy of those data.

Benchmark Conversion/Survey Leveling

In cases where the content (e.g., job description) of an organization's jobs does not sufficiently match that of jobs in the salary survey, an effort can be made to quantify the difference via **benchmark conversion.** If an organization uses job evaluation, then its job evaluation system can be applied to the survey jobs. The magnitude of difference be-tween job evaluation points for internal jobs and survey jobs provides an estimate of their relative value and thus guidance for adjusting the market data. (Again, a judgment.)

What Information to Collect?

Three basic types of data typically are requested: (1) information about the organiza-tion, (2) information about the total compensation system, and (3) specific pay data on each incumbent in the jobs under study. Exhibit 8.8 lists the basic data elements and the logic for including them. No survey includes all the data that will be dis-cussed. Rather, the data collected depend on the purpose of the survey and the jobs and skills included.

Organization Data

This information reflects the similarities and differences among organizations in the survey. Surveys of executive and upper-level positions include financial and reporting relationships data, since compensation for these jobs is more directly related to the or-ganization's financial performance. Typically, financial data are simply used to group firms by size, expressed in terms of sales or revenues, rather than to analyze competi-tors' performance. These data are used descriptively to report pay levels and mix by company size. The competitors' data have not been used to compare competitors' pro-ductivity (revenues to compensation) or labor costs.

But this is changing. The increased gathering of "competitive intelligence" is changing the type of organization data collected and the way it gets used. Metrics of organization performance such as turnover and revenues are being collected. Some surveys such as Clark and Radford collect turnover data. Other outcomes such as earn-ings per share, market share, customer satisfaction, employee pay satisfaction, and recruiting yield ratios are not included. Financial data are gathered from other, often publicly available sources (e.g., Google Financial, Thompson Financial). Examples include metrics on organization success (revenues, net income, customer satisfaction), turnover (voluntary quit rates), and recruiting (yield ratios).[29]

Total Compensation Data

Information on all types of pay forms is required to assess the total pay package and competitors' practices.[30] The list shown in Exhibit 8.8 reveals the range of forms that could be included in each company's definition of total compensation. As a practical matter, it can be hard to include *all* the pay forms. Too much detail on benefits, such as medical coverage deductibles and flexible work schedules, can make a survey too cumbersome. Alternatives range from a brief description of a benchmark benefit pack-age to including only the most expensive and variable benefits to an estimate of total benefit expenses as a percentage of total labor costs. Three alternatives—base pay, total cash (base, profit sharing, bonuses), and total compensation (total cash plus benefits and **perquisites**)—are the most commonly used measures of compensation. Exhibit 8.9 draws the distinction between these three alternatives and highlights the usefulness and limitations of each. Exhibit 8.10 shows some results of conducting a pay survey that includes these three measures on a sample of engineers.

EXHIBIT 8.8 Possible Survey Data Elements and Rationale

Basic Elements	Examples	Rationale
Nature of Organization		
Identification	Company, name, address, contact person	Further contacts
Financial performance	Assets, sales, profits, cash flow	Indicates nature of product/service markets, ability to pay, size, and financials
Size	Profit centers, product lines	Importance of specific job groups
	Total number of employees	Impact on labor market
Structure	Organizational charts	Indicates how business is organized
	Percent of employees at each level	Indicates staffing patttern
Nature of Total Compensation System		
Cash forms used	Base pay, pay-increase schedules, **long-** and **short-term incentives,** bonuses, cost-of-living adjustments, overtime and shift differentials	Indicate the mix of compensation offered; used to establish a comparable base
Noncash forms used	Benefits and services, particularly coverage and contributions to medical and health insurance and pensions	
Incumbent and Job		
Date	Date survey data in effect	Update to current date
Job	Match generic job description	Indicates degree of similarity with survey's key jobs
	Reporting levels	Scope of responsibilities
Individual	Years since degree, education, date of hire	Indicates training tenure
Pay	Actual rates paid to each individual, total earnings, last increase, bonuses, incentives	
HR Outcomes		
Productivity	Revenues/employee Revenues/labor costs	Reflect organization performance and efficiency
Total labor costs	Number of employees × (averages wages + benefits)	Major expense
Attraction	Yield ratio: Number accepting offers/Number of job offers	Reveals recruiting success, a compensation objective
Retention	Turnover rate: Number of high or low performers who leave/ Number of employees	Reveals outflow of people, which is related to a compensation objective
Employee views	Total pay satisfaction	Reveals what employees think about their pay

EXHIBIT 8.9 Advantages and Disadvantages of Measures of Compensation

Base pay	Tells how competitors are valuing the work in similar jobs	Fails to include performance incentives and other forms, so will not give true picture if competitors offer low base but high incentives.
Total cash (base + bonus)	Tells how competitors are valuing work; also tells the cash pay for performance opportunity in the job	All employees may not receive incentives, so it may overstate the competitors' pay; plus, it does not include long-term incentives.
Total compensation (base + bonus + stock options + benefits)	Tells the total value competitors place on this work	All employees may not receive all the forms. Be careful: Don't set base equal to competitors' total compensation. Risks high fixed costs.

EXHIBIT 8.10 Pay Survey Results for Different Measures of Compensation

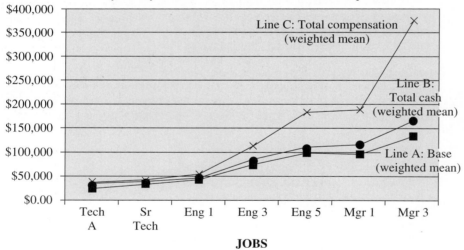

Survey Job	A: Base, Wtd Mean	B: Cash, Wtd Mean	C: Total Comp, Wtd Mean
Tech A	$ 22,989	$ 24,554	$ 30,831
Sr Tech	$ 37,748	$ 42,510	$ 51,482
Eng 1	$ 46,085	$ 48,289	$ 56,917
Eng 3	$ 73,134	$ 81,285	$ 112,805
Eng 5	$ 102,415	$ 112,587	$ 179,449
Mgr 1	$ 95,260	$ 115,304	$ 188,509
Mgr 3	$ 134,173	$ 171,030	$ 378,276

A: *Base pay.* This is the amount of *cash* the competitors decided *each job and incumbent* is worth. A company might use this information for its initial observations of how "good" the data appear to fit a range of jobs. The market line A is based on base pay.

B: *Total cash.* This is base plus bonus—line B in the exhibit. Total cash measures reveal competitors' use of performance-based cash payments.

C: *Total compensation.* This includes total cash plus stock options and benefits. Total compensation reflects the total overall value of the employee (performance, experience, skills, etc.) plus the value of the work itself.

It is no surprise that for all seven jobs, total compensation is higher than base pay alone or base plus bonus. However, the variability and magnitude of the difference may be a surprise: from $7,842 (34 percent) for the job of technician A, to $244,103.38 (182 percent) for the job of manager 3. Base pay is, on average, only 35 percent of total compensation for the manager 3s in this survey. So the measure of compensation is an important decision. Misinterpreting competitors' pay practices can lead to costly mispricing of pay levels and structures.

INTERPRET SURVEY RESULTS AND CONSTRUCT A MARKET LINE

Survey data today are typically exchanged online. Technology has made processing data and spitting out reports easy. The greatest challenge of total compensation surveys is to understand how to evaluate the information. In the best total compensation projects, each firm sees the survey as a customizable database project where they can specify the characteristics of the employers and jobs to analyze.

After the survey data are all collected, the next step is to analyze the results and use statistics to construct a **market pay line.** More than twenty years ago, Belcher interviewed compensation professionals to discover how survey data are actually analyzed. He reported:

> Every organization uses its own methods of distilling information from the survey; uses different surveys for different purposes; and uses different methods for company surveys. I could find no commonality in these methods of analysis by industry, by firm size, or by union presence. For example, some did nothing except read the entire survey, some emphasized industry data, others geographic competitors (commuting distances), some made comparisons with less than five competitors, some emphasized only large firms, others threw out the data from large firms.[31]

His conclusion still holds today. We hope this diversity reflects flexibility in dealing with a variety of circumstances and the use of improved compensation software. We worry that it reflects expediency and a lack of business- and work-related logic.

Verify Data

A common first step is to check the *accuracy* of the job matches, and then check for anomalies (i.e., an employer whose data are substantially out of line from data of others), age of data, and the nature of the organizations (e.g., industry, size—State Farm Insurance versus Google). Exhibit 8.11 is an excerpt from the survey used to prepare

EXHIBIT 8.11 Survey Data

A. Job Description: Engineer 1

Participates in development, testing, and documentation of software programs. Performs design and analysis tasks as a project team member. Typical minimum requirements are a bachelor's degree in a scientific or technical field or the equivalent and up to two years of experience.

B. Individual Salary Data (partial data; for illustration only)

Job	Base	Bonus	Total Cash	Stock Option	Benefits	Total Comp
Engineer 1					JE Points:	50
					Number of Incumbents:	585
Company 1						
Engineer 1	$79,000	$500	$79,500	$0	$8,251	$87,751
Engineer 1	$65,500	$2,500	$68,000	$0	$8,251	$76,251
Engineer 1	$65,000	$0	$65,000	$0	$8,251	$73,251
Engineer 1	$58,000	$4,000	$62,000	$0	$8,251	$70,251
Engineer 1	$57,930	$3,000	$60,930	$0	$8,251	$69,181
Engineer 1	$57,200	$2,000	$59,200	$0	$8,251	$67,451
Engineer 1	$56,000	$1,100	$57,100	$0	$8,251	$65,351
Engineer 1	$54,000	$0	$54,000	$0	$8,251	$62,251
Engineer 1	$52,500	$0	$52,500	$0	$8,251	$60,751
Engineer 1	$51,500	$1,500	$53,000	$0	$8,251	$61,251
Engineer 1	$49,000	$3,300	$52,300	$0	$8,251	$60,551
Engineer 1	$48,500	$0	$48,500	$0	$8,251	$56,751
Engineer 1	$36,500	$0	$36,500	$0	$8,251	$44,751
Company 2						
Engineer 1	$57,598	$0	$57,598	$28,889	$8,518	$95,004
Engineer 1	$57,000	$0	$57,000	$31,815	$8,518	$97,332
Engineer 1	$55,000	$0	$55,000	$20,110	$8,518	$83,628

C. Company Data (partial data; for illustration only)

	# Incumbents		Base	Short Term	Total Cash	LTI	Benefits	Total Comp
Company 1	13	Avg.	56,202.31	1,376.92	57,579.23	0.00	8,250.89	65,830.12
		Min.	36,500.00	0.00	36,500.00	0.00	8,250.89	44,750.89
		Max.	79,000.00	4,000.00	79,500.00	0.00	8,250.89	87,750.89
Company 2	13	Avg.	52,764.80	1,473.56	54,238.36	21,068.91	8,517.56	83,824.83
		Min.	47,376.20	0.00	50,038.33	4,878.98	8,517.56	65,416.54
		Max.	57,598.21	3,716.89	58,494.01	31,814.83	8,517.56	97,332.39
Company 4	2	Avg.	56,004.00	0.00	56,004.00	0.00	9,692.56	65,696.56
			55,016.00	0.00	55,016.00	0.00	9,692.56	64,708.56
		Avg.	55,510.00	0.00	55,510.00	0.00	9,692.56	65,202.56
Company 8	14	Avg.	54,246.00	4,247.21	58,493.21	0.00	7,204.50	65,697.71
		Min.	45,000.00	860.00	48,448.00	0.00	7,204.50	55,363.50
		Max.	62,000.00	8,394.00	68,200.00	0.00	7,204.50	75,404.50
Company 12	35	Avg.	50,459.34	1,123.26	51,582.60	1,760.05	7,693.11	61,035.76
		Min.	42,000.00	0.00	43,092.00	0.00	7,693.11	52,606.26
		Max.	64,265.00	1,670.89	65,935.89	9,076.52	7,693.11	73,629.00
Company 13	5	Avg.	48,700.80	400.00	49,100.80	2,050.00	8,001.00	59,152.20
		Min.	45,456.00	0.00	45,456.00	0.00	8,001.00	53,458.00
		Max.	54,912.00	2,000.00	54,912.00	8,506.00	8,001.00	66,507.00
Company 14	10	Avg.	44,462.40	863.43	45,325.83	0.00	7,337.00	52,662.83
		Min.	37,440.00	372.95	37,812.95	0.00	7,337.00	45,149.95
		Max.	47,832.00	1,197.12	49,029.12	0.00	7,337.00	56,366.12

EXHIBIT 8.11 (Continued)

Company 15

n	Stat	Base Salary		Total Cash		Stock Options	Total Compensation
71	Avg.	49,685.92	8,253.61	57,939.52	1,762.97	8,404.00	68,106.48
	Min.	44,900.00	0.00	49,022.00	0.00	8,404.00	57,426.00
	Max.	57,300.00	14,132.00	68,357.00	63,639.00	8,404.00	125,471.00

Company 51

n	Stat	Base Salary		Total Cash		Stock Options	Total Compensation
4	Avg.	46,193.88	1,399.75	47,593.63	41,954.39	7,640.89	97,188.90
	Min.	42,375.06	0.00	44,988.75	20,518.14	7,640.89	75,159.23
	Max.	48,400.04	2,985.31	51,385.35	74,453.00	7,640.89	133,479.24

Company 57

n	Stat	Base Salary		Total Cash		Stock Options	Total Compensation
226	Avg.	44,091.57	1,262.43	45,354.00	0.00	6,812.00	52,166.00
	Min.	38,064.00	0.00	39,372.00	0.00	6,812.00	46,184.00
	Max.	60,476.00	2,179.00	62,655.00	0.00	6,812.00	69,467.00

Company 58

n	Stat	Base Salary		Total Cash		Stock Options	Total Compensation
107	Avg.	44,107.18	1,367.04	45,474.21	0.00	6,770.00	52,244.21
	Min.	36,156.00	0.00	37,569.00	0.00	6,770.00	44,339.00
	Max.	57,600.00	2,147.00	58,913.00	0.00	6,770.00	65,683.00

Company 59

n	Stat	Base Salary		Total Cash		Stock Options	Total Compensation
71	Avg.	44,913.63	1,152.85	46,066.48	0.00	6,812.00	52,878.48
	Min.	39,156.00	407.00	40,473.00	0.00	6,812.00	47,285.00
	Max.	57,000.00	1,639.00	57,407.00	0.00	6,812.00	64,219.00

D. Summary Data for Engineer 1

	Base Salary	Total Cash	Total Compensation	Bonuses	Stock Options
Wtd Mean:	$46,085.21	$48,289.66	$56,917.08	Avg: 2,370.59	Avg: 16,920.18
Mean:	$49,092.71	$50,940.53	$65,524.22	As a %. of Base:	As a % of Base:
50th:	$45,000.00	$46,422.00	$53,271.00	5.18%	33.96%
25th:	$42,600.00	$43,769.00	$50,593.11	% who Receive:	% who Receive:
75th:	$48,500.00	$51,854.04	$60,750.89	92.99%	8.38%

Exhibit 8.12   Frequency Distributions

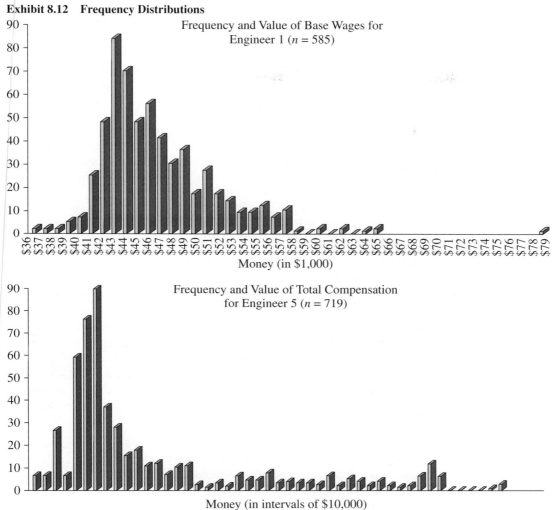

Exhibit 8.12. The survey was conducted at the behest of FastCat, a small start-up familiar to many readers. While there were a number of jobs included in the survey, we use information for just one job—engineer 1—to illustrate. As you can see, surveys do not make light reading. However, they contain a wealth of information. To extract that information, step through the portal . . . to being the FastCat analyst.[32]

Accuracy of Match

Part A of the survey contains the description of the survey job. If the company job is similar but not identical, some companies use the benchmark conversion/survey leveling approach discussed earlier in this chapter; that is, they multiply the survey data by some factor that the analyst judges to be the difference between the company job and the survey job.[33] Leveling is another example of judgment entering survey analysis. It clearly leaves the objectivity of the decisions open to challenge.

Anomalies

Part B of the survey shows actual engineer 1 salaries. Perusal of salary data gives the analyst a sense of the quality of the data and helps identify any areas for additional consideration. For example, Part B of Exhibit 8.11 shows that no engineer 1 at company 1 receives stock options, and five receive no bonuses. The bonuses range from $500 to $4,000. (Because there are 585 engineer 1s in this survey, we have not included all their salary information.) Individual-level data provide a wealth of information about specific practices. Understanding minimums, maximums, and what percent actually receive bonuses and/or options is essential. Unfortunately, many surveys provide only summary information such as company averages.

Part C of Exhibit 8.11 provides company data. Again, the first step is to look for anomalies:

1. *Does any one company dominate?* If so (i.e., company 57), a separate analysis of the largest company's data will isolate that employer's pay practices and clarify the nature of its influence.

2. *Do all employers show similar patterns?* Probably not. In our survey, base pay at company 1 ranges from $36,500 to $79,000 for a single job. This raises the possibility that this company might use broad bands (discussed later in this chapter). While seven of the companies have a bonus-to-base-pay ratio of around 2 to 3 percent, company 15 pays an average bonus of $8,254 for a bonus-to-base ratio of over 6 percent.

3. **Outliers?** Company 51 gives one of its engineers options valued at $74,453 on top of base pay. An analyst may consider dropping a company with such an atypical pay practice. The question is, What difference will it make if certain companies are dropped? What difference will it make if they are included?

The best way to answer questions on anomalies is to do an analysis of them alone. They may have deliberately differentiated themselves with pay as part of their strategy. Learning more about competitors that differentiate can offer valuable insights. Combining outliers' pay data with their financials may reveal that the most successful competitors also use larger bonuses for their engineers.

Part D at the bottom of Exhibit 8.11 contains summary data: five different measures of base pay, cash, and total compensation, as well as the percent of engineers who receive bonuses and options. The data suggest that most of FastCat's competitors use bonuses but are less likely to use options for this particular job. Summary data help abstract the survey information into a smaller number of measures for further statistical analysis. Statistics help FastCat get from pages of raw data (Exhibit 8.11) to graphs of actual salaries (Exhibit 8.12) and from there to a market line that reflects its competitive pay policy.

Statistical Analysis

While the statistics necessary to analyze survey data, including **regression,** are covered in basic statistics classes, a number of Web sites are probably more fun. Our favorite lets us click anywhere we want on a graph to see how adding that new data point (the mouse click) changes a regression line.[34] A useful first step in our analysis is to look at a frequency distribution of the pay rates.

Frequency Distribution

Exhibit 8.12 shows two frequency distributions created from the data in the Exhibit 8.11 survey. The top one shows the distribution of the base wages for the 585 engineer 1s in increments of $1,000. The second one shows the *total compensation* for 719 engineer 5s in increments of $10,000. (The wide range of dollars—from under $90,000 to over $900,000—is the reason that many surveys switch to logs of dollars for higher-level positions.) Frequency distributions help visualize information and may highlight anomalies. For example, the base wage above $79,000 may be considered an outlier. Is this a unique person? Or an error in reporting the data? A phone call (or e-mail) to the survey provider may answer the question.

Shapes of frequency distributions can vary. Unusual shapes may reflect problems with job matches, widely dispersed pay rates, or employers with widely divergent pay policies. If the data look reasonable at this point, one wag has suggested that it is probably the result of two large errors that offset one another.

Central Tendency

A measure of **central tendency** reduces a large amount of data into a single number. Exhibit 8.13 defines commonly used measures. The distinction between "mean" and "weighted mean" is important. If only company averages are reported in the survey, a *mean* may be calculated by adding each company's base wage and dividing by the number of companies. While use of the mean is common, it may not accurately reflect actual labor market conditions, since the base wage of the largest employer is given the same weight as that of the smallest employer. *Weighted mean* is calculated by adding the base wages for all 585 engineers in the survey and then dividing by 585 ($46,085). A weighted mean gives equal weight to *each individual employee's* wage.

Variation

The distribution of rates around a measure of central tendency is called *variation*. The two frequency distributions in Exhibit 8.12 show very different patterns of variation. Variation tells us how the rates are spread out in the market. *Standard deviation* is probably the most common statistical measure of variation, although its use in salary surveys is rare.

Quartiles and *percentiles* are more common measures in salary survey analysis. Recall from the chapter introduction that someone's policy was "to be in the 75th percentile nationally." This means that 75 percent of all pay rates are *at or below* that point and 25 percent are *above*. Quartiles (25th and 75th percentiles) are often used to set pay ranges. More on pay ranges later.

Update the Survey Data

Because they reflect decisions of employers, employees, unions, and government agencies, wages paid by competitors are constantly changing. Additionally, competitors

EXHIBIT 8.13   **Statistical Measures to Analyze Survey Data**

Measure	What Does It Tell Us?	Advantage/Disadvantage
Central Tendency		
Mode	Most commonly occurring rate.	Must draw frequency distribution to calculate it.
Mean	Sum all rates and divide by number of rates. If have only company (rather than individual) data, wage of largest employer given same weight as smallest employer.	Commonly understood (also called the "average"). However, if have only company data, will not accurately reflect actual labor market conditions.
Median	Order all data points from highest to lowest; the one in the middle is the median.	Minimizes distortion caused by outliers.
Weighted mean	If have only companywide measures (rather than individual measures), the rate for each company is multiplied by the number of employees in that company. Total of all rates is divided by total number of employees.	Gives equal weight to each individual's wage. Captures size of supply and demand in market.
Variation		
Standard deviation	How tightly all the rates are clustered around the mean.	Tells how similar or dissimilar the market rates are from each other. A small SD means they are tightly bunched at center; a large SD means rates are more spread out.
Quartiles and percentiles	Order all data points from lowest to highest, then convert to percentages.	Common in salary surveys; frequently used to set pay ranges or zones.

adjust their wages at different times. Universities typically adjust to match the academic year. Unionized employers adjust on dates negotiated in labor agreements. Some employers operating in competitive locations (e.g., Minsk, Shanghai) update every quarter or even every month. Many employers adjust each employee's pay on the anniversary of the employee's date of hire. Even though these changes do not occur smoothly and uniformly throughout the year, as a practical matter we assume that they do. Therefore, a survey that requires three months to collect and analyze is probably outdated before it is available. The pay data are usually updated (a process often called *aging* or *trending*) to forecast the competitive rates for the future date when the pay decisions will be implemented.

The amount to update is based on several factors, including historical trends in the labor market, prospects for the economy in which the employer operates, and the manager's judgment, among others. Some recommend using the **Consumer Price Index (CPI).** We do not. The CPI measures the rate of change in prices for goods and services in the product market, not wage changes in labor markets. Chapter 18 has more information on this distinction.

EXHIBIT 8.14   Choices for Updating Survey Data Reflect Pay Policy

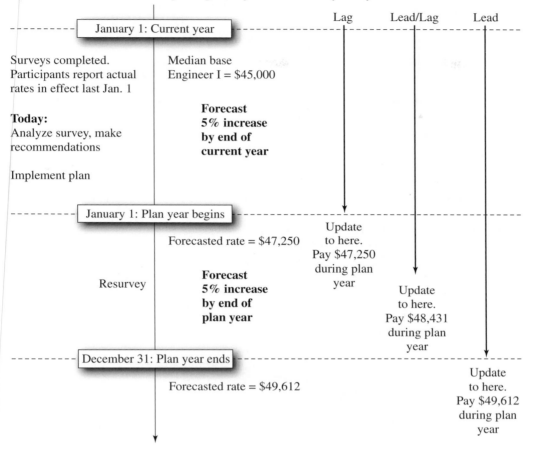

Exhibit 8.14 illustrates updating. In the example, the base pay rate of $45,000 collected in the survey was in effect at January 1 of the current year—already in the past. The compensation manager will use this information for pay decisions that go into effect on January 1 of the plan year. So if base pay has been increasing by approximately 5 percent annually, and we assume that the future will be like the past, the rate is multiplied by 105 percent to account for the change expected by the end of the current year (to $47,250) and then by an additional percentage to estimate pay rates for the plan year.

Construct a Market Pay Line

Look again at Exhibit 8.10. It shows the results of the FastCat analyst's decisions on which salary survey jobs to include that are judged to closely match internal benchmark jobs (the seven jobs on the *x* [horizontal] axis), which companies to include, and which measures of pay to use. For each of the compensation metrics, a line has been drawn connecting the pay for the seven jobs. Jobs are ordered on the horizontal axis according to their position (i.e., number of job evaluation points) in the internal structure. Thus, the line trends upward to create a market line.

> A **market line** links a company's benchmark jobs on the horizontal axis (internal structure) with market rates paid by competitors (market survey) on the vertical axis. It summarizes the distribution of going rates paid by competitors in the market.

A market line may be drawn freehand by connecting the data points, as was done in Exhibit 8.10, or statistical techniques such as regression analysis may be used. Regression generates a straight line that best fits the data by minimizing the variance around the line. Exhibit 8.15 shows the regression lines that use the pay survey data in Exhibit 8.10 as the dependent variable(s) and the job evaluation points of matched

EXHIBIT 8.15   **From Regression Results to a Market Line**

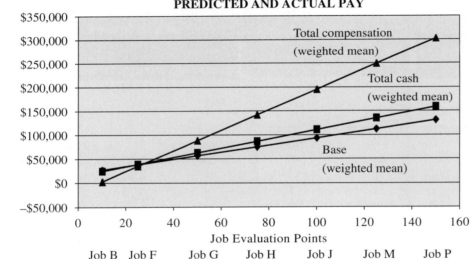

Survey Job	Matching FastCat Job*	FastCat JEPts	Predicted Base, Wtd Mean	Predicted Cash, Wtd Mean	Predicted Total Comp
Tech A	B	10	$23,057	$20,543	–$1,330
Sr Tech	F	25	$34,361	$35,116	$31,172
Eng 1	G	50	$53,199	$59,404	$85,343
Eng 3	H	75	$72,038	$83,692	$139,514
Eng 5	J	100	$90,876	$107,980	$193,685
Mgr 1	M	125	$109,715	$132,268	$247,856
Mgr 3	P	150	$128,553	$156,556	$302,027*

*We thought it best to leave it to an expert (you) to decide which FastCat job/jobtitle is a good match for each survey job, if you are using *Cases in Compensation* with your textbook.

EXHIBIT 8.16   **Understanding Regression**

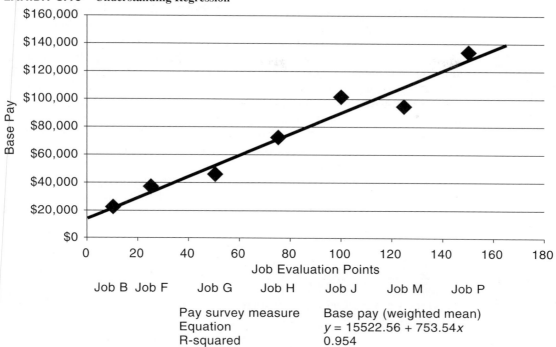

Pay survey measure	Base pay (weighted mean)
Equation	$y = 15522.56 + 753.54x$
R-squared	0.954

FastCat jobs as the independent variable. Compare the data tables in Exhibit 8.10 and Exhibit 8.15. Exhibit 8.10 shows the market rates for survey jobs. Exhibit 8.15 shows the job evaluation points for the FastCat jobs that match these survey jobs plus the regression's statistical "prediction" of each pay measure for each job. The actual base pay for the survey job Tech A is $22,989 (Exhibit 8.10); the "predicted" base pay for the job is $23,058 (Exhibit 8.15).

In Exhibit 8.16, we focus in on the regression results that use base pay from the survey as the dependent variable. The diamonds are the actual results of the survey and the solid line is the regression result. Regression smoothes large amounts of data while minimizing variations. As the number of jobs in the survey increases, the advantage of the straight line that regression provides becomes clear.

Setting Pay for Non-Benchmark Jobs

The market pay lines in Exhibit 8.15 are especially useful for helping set pay for non-benchmark jobs (i.e., those jobs for which there is no good match among jobs included in the pay survey). For example, take a job, Job Z, that has no match, but for which we have assigned a job evaluation points score of 110. How might we estimate its base pay? From Exhibit 8.15, we know that FastCat Job J has 100 job evaluation points and matches a survey job, Eng 5, that has a base pay of $90,876. So, one approach is to pay Job Z 110/100 × $90,876 = $99,964. Or, we can use the market survey line regression equation shown in Exhibit 8.16. The predicted base pay = $15,522.56 + $753.54 (110 job evaluation points) = $98,412. The results are close, but not identical. (Remember, the regression line smoothes the relationship, resulting in a small difference in predicted base pay.) So, our market line is very valuable. Even though only benchmark jobs in our company can be directly matched to the survey, the market line allows us to estimate the market pay for non-benchmark jobs. (See also our earlier discussion of survey leveling.)

Before we leave survey data analysis, we must emphasize that not all survey results look like our examples and that not all companies use these statistical and analytical techniques. There is no one "right way" to analyze survey data. It has been our intent to provide some insight into the kinds of calculations that are useful and the assumptions that underlie salary surveys.

We are now beyond the halfway point of this long chapter. May we suggest that it might be a good time to consider resorting to the Puking Pastilles, one of the Weasleys' Wizarding Wheezes described in the fifth Harry Potter book? The Puking Pastilles

---

Cybercomp 2
Calculating a Market Line Using Regression Analysis
Regression analysis uses the mathematical formula for a straight line,
$y = a + bx$, where

y = dollars

x = job evaluation points

a = the y value (in dollars) at which $x = 0$ (i.e., the straight line crosses the y axis)

b = the slope of the regression line

Using the dollars from the market survey data and the job evaluation points from the internal structure, replicate our Exhibit 8.15 and 8.16 results.
The market line can be written as

Pay for job A = a + (b × job evaluation points for job A)
Pay for job B = a + (b × job evaluation points for job B)

and so on.
Regression estimates the values of a and b in an efficient manner, so errors of prediction are minimized.

For a demonstration of regression that is a lot of fun, go to *www.math.csusb.edu/faculty/stanton/m262/regress/regress.html*. Click on points and the program immediately draws the new regression line. A site that does the regression and also shows the correlation coefficient is *www.stat.uiuc.edu/stat100/java/guess/PPApplet.html*. Play around with both these sites until you have an understanding of what a regression line tells you. Then use the sites to analyze data. You might even study the relationship between the height of your classmates and what they expect to be earning when they graduate.

make you just ill enough to convince your professor to give you an extension on an assignment before you magically recover to enjoy your illicit time off.[35]

Combine Internal Structure and External Market Rates

At this point, two parts of the total pay model have merged. Their relationship to each other can be seen in Exhibit 8.17.[36]

- The *internally aligned structure* (developed in Chapters 3–6) is shown on the horizontal (x) axis. For this illustration, our structure consists of jobs A through P. Jobs B, F, G, H, J, M, and P are the seven benchmark jobs that have been matched in the survey. Jobs A, C, D, E, I, K, L, N, and O have no direct matching jobs in the salary survey.
- The salaries paid by relevant competitors for those benchmark jobs, as measured by the survey—*the external competitive data*—are shown on the vertical (y) axis.

These two components—internal alignment and external competitiveness—come together in the pay structure. The pay structure has two aspects: the *pay-policy line* and *pay ranges*.

EXHIBIT 8.17
Develop Pay Grades

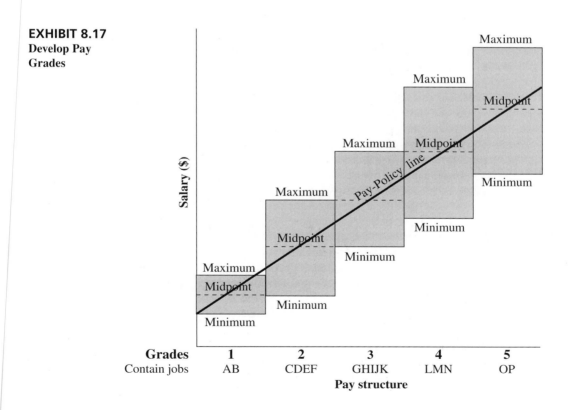

Grades	1	2	3	4	5
Contain jobs	AB	CDEF	GHIJK	LMN	OP

Pay structure

FROM POLICY TO PRACTICE: THE PAY-POLICY LINE

There are several ways to translate external competitive policy into practice. You have already made some of the choices that help you do this.

Choice of Measure

If Colgate practices what it claims at the beginning of the chapter, then we would expect Colgate to use the 50th percentile for base pay and the 75th percentile for total compensation as compensation measures in its regression.

Updating

Look again at Exhibit 8.14. The arrows on the right side of the exhibit show how updating survey data reflects policy. If the company chooses a "match" policy but then updates survey data to the end of the current year/start of the plan year and keeps this rate in effect throughout the plan year, the company will actually be lagging the market. It will match its desired market pay level only at the beginning of the plan year. The market rates continue to rise throughout the year; the company's rates do not.

Aging the market data to a point halfway through the plan year (middle arrow in Exhibit 8.14) is called *lead/lag*. The original survey rates are updated to the end of the current year plus half the projected amount for the plan year ($48,431). An employer who wants to lead the market may age data to the *end* of the plan year ($49,612) and pay at this rate throughout the plan year.

Policy Line as Percent of Market Line

Another way to translate pay-level policy into practice is to simply *specify a percent* above or below the regression line (market line) that an employer intends to match and then draw a new line at this higher (or lower) level. This **pay-policy line** would carry out a policy statement of, "We lead the market by 10 percent." Other possibilities exist. An employer might lead by including only a few top-paying competitors in the analysis and then matching them ("pay among the leaders") or lead for some job families and lag for others. The point is that there are alternatives among competitive pay policies, and there are alternative ways to translate policy into practice. If the practice does not match the policy (e.g., we say one thing but do another), then employees receive the wrong message.

FROM POLICY TO PRACTICE: GRADES AND RANGES

The next step is to design **pay grades** and **pay ranges.** These analyses are usually done with base pay data, since base pay reflects the basic value of the work rather than performance levels of employees (see Exhibit 8.9 for a comparison of metrics).

Why Bother With Grades and Ranges?

Grades and ranges offer flexibility to deal with pressures from external markets and differences among organizations. These include:

1. *Differences in quality (skills, abilities, experience) among individuals applying for work* (e.g., Microsoft may have stricter hiring requirements for engineers than does FastCat, even though job descriptions appear identical).

2. *Differences in the productivity or value of these quality variations* (e.g., The value of the results from a software engineer at Microsoft probably differs from that of the results of a software engineer at Best Buy).

3. *Differences in the mix of pay forms competitors use* (e.g., Oracle uses more stock options and lower base compared to IBM).

In addition to offering flexibility to deal with these external differences, an organization may use differences in rates paid to employees on the same job. *A pay range exists whenever two or more rates are paid to employees in the same job.* Hence, ranges provide managers the opportunity to:

1. Recognize individual performance differences with pay.

2. Meet employees' expectations that their pay will increase over time, even in the same job.

3. Encourage employees to remain with the organization.

From an internal alignment perspective, the range reflects the differences in performance or experience that an employer wishes to recognize with pay. From an external competitiveness perspective, the range is a control device. A range maximum sets the lid on what the employer is willing to pay for that work; the range minimum sets the floor.

In Chapter 11, we will see that many organizations use a merit increase grid or salary increase matrix, which uses two factors, employee performace rating and position in the salary range, to guide pay increases. The goal is to continually adjust employee pay so that it is appropriately positioned relative to the market. Thus, an employee with consistently high performance ratings should move above the market median and **range midpoint,** whereas an employee with consistently average performance shoud be near the range midpoint.

Develop Grades

The first step in building flexibility into the pay structure is to group different jobs that are considered substantially equal for pay purposes into a grade. Grades enhance an organization's ability to move people among jobs with no change in pay. In Exhibit 8.17, the jobs are grouped into five grades on the horizontal axis.

The question of which jobs are substantially equal and therefore slotted into one grade requires the analyst to reconsider the original job evaluation results. Each grade will have its own pay range, and *all the jobs within a single grade will have the same pay range.* Jobs in different grades (e.g., jobs C, D, E, and F in grade 2) should be dissimilar from those in other grades (grade 1 jobs A and B) and will have a different pay range.

Although grades permit flexibility, they are challenging to design. The objective is for all jobs that are similar for pay purposes to be placed within the same grade. If jobs with relatively close job evaluation point totals fall on either side of grade boundaries, the magnitude of difference in the salary treatment may be out of proportion to the magnitude of difference in the value of the job content. Resolving such dilemmas requires an understanding of the specific jobs, career paths, and work flow in the organization, as well as considerable judgment.

EXHIBIT 8.18

Range
Midpoint,
Minimum, and
Maximum

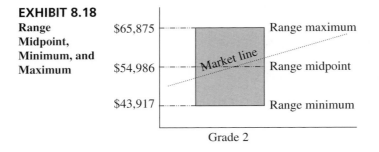

Grade 2

Establish Range Midpoints, Minimums, and Maximums

Grades group job evaluation data on the horizontal axis; ranges group salary data on the vertical axis. Ranges set upper and lower pay limits for all jobs in each grade. A range has three salient features: a midpoint, a minimum, and a maximum. Exhibit 8.18 is an enlargement of grade 2 in Exhibit 8.17, which contains the engineer 1 job. The midpoint is $54,896. This is the point where the pay-policy line crosses the center of the grade. The range for this grade has been set at 20 percent above and 20 percent below the midpoint. Thus, all FastCat engineer 1s are supposed to receive a salary higher than $43,917 but lower than $65,875.[37]

What Size Should the Range Be?

The size of the range is based on some judgment about how the ranges support career paths, promotions, and other organization systems. Top-level management positions commonly have ranges of 30 to 60 percent above and below the midpoint; entry to midlevel professional and managerial positions, between 15 and 30 percent; office and production work, 5 to 15 percent. Larger ranges in the managerial jobs reflect the greater opportunity for individual discretion and performance variations in the work.

Some compensation managers use the actual survey rates, particularly the 75th and 25th percentiles, as maximums and minimums. Others ensure that the proposed range includes at least 75 percent of the rates in the survey data. Still others establish the minimum and maximum separately, with the amount between the minimum and the midpoint a function of how long it takes a new employee to become fully competent. Short training time may translate to minimums much closer to the midpoints. The maximum becomes the amount above the midpoint that the company is willing to pay for sustained performance on the job. In the end, the size of the range is based on judgment that weighs all these factors.

Overlap

Exhibit 8.19 shows two extremes in overlap between adjacent grades. The high degree of overlap and low midpoint differentials in Exhibit 8.19(a) indicate small differences in the value of jobs in the adjoining grades. Being promoted from one grade to another may include a title change but not much change in pay. The smaller ranges in Exhibit 8.19(b) create less overlap, which permits the manager to reinforce a

EXHIBIT 8.19
Range Overlap

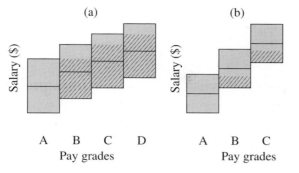

promotion into a new grade with a larger pay increase. The downside is that there may be fewer opportunities for promotion.

Promotion Increases Matter

The size of differentials between grades should support career movement through the structure. A managerial job would typically be at least one grade higher than the jobs it supervises. Although a 15 percent pay differential between manager and employee has been offered as a rule of thumb, large overlap and possible overtime in some jobs but not in managerial jobs can make it difficult to maintain manager–employee differentials. We are cautious about such rules of thumb. They are often ways to avoid thinking about what makes sense.

What is the optimal overlap between grades? It ought to be large enough to induce employees to seek promotion into a higher grade. However, there is virtually no research to indicate how much of a differential is necessary to influence employees to do so. Tracing how an employee might move through a career path in the structure (e.g., from engineer 1 to engineer 2 . . . to manager 3) and what size pay increases will accompany that movement will help answer that question.

Not all employers use grades and ranges. Skill-based plans establish single *flat rates* for each skill level regardless of performance or seniority. And many collective bargaining contracts establish single flat rates for each job (i.e., all senior machinists II receive $17.50 per hour regardless of performance or seniority). This flat rate often corresponds to some midpoint on a survey of that job. And increasingly, *broad bands* (think "really fat ranges") are being adopted for even greater flexibility.

FROM POLICY TO PRACTICE: BROAD BANDING

Exhibit 8.20 collapses salary grades into only a few broad bands, each with a sizable range. This technique, known as **broad banding,** consolidates as many as four or five traditional grades into a single band with one minimum and one maximum. Because the band encompasses so many jobs of differing values, a range midpoint is usually not used.[38]

Contrasts between ranges and broad bands are highlighted in Exhibit 8.21. Supporters of broad bands list several advantages over traditional approaches. First,

EXHIBIT 8.20
From Grades to Bands

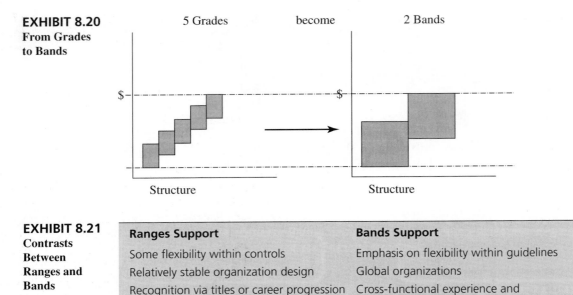

EXHIBIT 8.21
Contrasts Between Ranges and Bands

Ranges Support	Bands Support
Some flexibility within controls	Emphasis on flexibility within guidelines
Relatively stable organization design	Global organizations
Recognition via titles or career progression	Cross-functional experience and lateralprogression
Midpoint controls, comparatives	Reference market rates, shadow ranges
Controls designed into system	Controls in budget, few in system
Give managers "freedom with guidelines"	Give managers "freedom to manage" pay
To 150 percent range-spread	100–400 percent spread

broad bands provide flexibility to define job responsibilities more broadly. They support redesigned, downsized, or boundaryless organizations that have eliminated layers of managerial jobs. They foster cross-functional growth and development in these new organizations. Employees can move laterally across functions within a band in order to gain depth of experience. Companies with global operations such as 3M and Medtronic use bands to move managers among worldwide assignments. The emphasis on lateral movement with no pay adjustments helps manage the reality of fewer promotion opportunities in flattened organization structures. The flexibility of banding eases mergers and acquisitions since there are not a lot of levels to argue over.[39]

Broad bands are often combined with more traditional salary administration practices by using midpoints, **"zones,"** or other control points within bands.[40] Perhaps the most important difference between the grades-and-ranges and broad-banding approaches is the location of the controls. The grade-and-range approach has guidelines and controls designed right into the pay system. Range minimums, maximums, and midpoints ensure consistency across managers. Managers using bands have only a total salary budget limiting them. But as experience with bands has advanced, guidelines and structure are increasingly designed into them (e.g., reference market rates or shadow ranges).

Bands may add flexibility: Less time will be spent judging fine distinctions among jobs. But perhaps the time avoided judging jobs will now be spent judging individuals, a prospect managers already try to avoid. How will an organization avoid the appearance of salary treatment based on personality and politics rather than objective criteria? Ideally, with a well-thought-out performance management system.

Banding takes two steps:

1. *Set the number of bands.* Merck uses six bands for its entire pay structure. Band titles range from "contributor" to "executive." A unit of General Electric replaced 24 levels of work with 5 bands. Usually bands are established at the major "breaks," or differences, in work or skill/competency requirements. Titles used to label each band reflect these major breaks, such as "associate" (entry-level individual contributor), "professional" (experienced, knowledgeable team member), "leader" (project or group supervisor), "director," "coach," or even "visionary." The challenge is how much to pay people who are in the same band but in different functions performing different work.

2. *Price the bands: reference market rates.* The four bands in Exhibit 8.22 (associates, professionals, lead professionals, senior professionals) include multiple job families within each band, for example, finance, purchasing, engineering, marketing, and so on. It is unlikely that General Electric pays associates and professionals with business degrees the same as associates and professionals with engineering degrees. Usually external market differences exist, so the different functions or groups within bands are priced differently. As the pop-out in Exhibit 8.22 depicts, the three job families (purchasing, finance, and engineering) in the professional band have different *reference rates,* drawn from survey data.

You might say that this is beginning to look a lot like grades and ranges within each band. You would be correct. The difference is that ranges traditionally serve as controls, whereas reference rates act as guides. Today's guides grow to tomorrow's bureaucracy.

Flexibility-Control

Broad banding encourages employees to seek growth and development by moving cross-functionally (e.g., from purchasing to finance). The assumption is that this cross-fertilization of ideas will benefit the organization. Hence, career moves within bands are more common than between bands. According to supporters, the principal payoff of broad banding is this flexibility. But flexibility is one side of the coin; chaos and favoritism is the other. Banding presumes that managers will manage employee pay to accomplish the organization's objectives (and not their own) and treat employees fairly. Historically, this is not the first time managers have sought greater flexibility. Indeed, the rationale for using grades and ranges was to reduce inconsistencies and favoritism in previous generations. The challenge today is to take advantage of flexibility without increasing labor costs or leaving the organization vulnerable to charges of inconsistent or illegal practices.

EXHIBIT 8.22   **Reference Rates Within Bands**

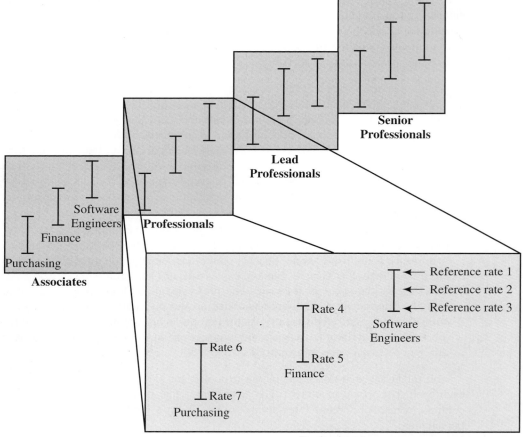

BALANCING INTERNAL AND EXTERNAL PRESSURES: ADJUSTING THE PAY STRUCTURE

Up until now, we have made a distinction between the job structure and the pay structure. A **job structure** orders jobs on the basis of internal factors (reflected in job evaluation or skill certification). The **pay structure,** on the other hand, is anchored by the organization's external competitive position and reflected in its pay-policy line.

Reconciling Differences

The problem with using two standards (internal and external) to create a structure is that they are likely to result in two different structures. The order in which jobs are ranked on internal versus external factors may not agree. Differences between market structures and rates and job evaluation rankings warrant a review of the basic decisions in evaluating and pricing a particular job. This may entail a review of the job analysis, the evaluation of the job, or the market data for the job in question. Often this reanalysis solves the problem. Sometimes, however, discrepancies persist. Survey data may be discarded, or benchmark-job matches may be changed.

One study of how differences are actually reconciled found that managers weigh external market data more heavily than internal job evaluation data. In light of all the judgments that go into internal evaluation, market data are often considered to be more objective.[41] Yet this chapter and research show that market data are also based on judgment.

Sometimes differences arise because a shortage of a particular skill has driven up the market rate. But reclassifying such a job into a higher salary grade, where it will remain long after the supply/demand imbalance has been corrected, creates additional problems. Creating a special range that is clearly designated as *market responsive* may be a better approach. Decisions made on the basis of expediency may undermine the integrity of the pay decisions.

MARKET PRICING

Some organizations adopt pay strategies that emphasize external competitiveness and deemphasize internal alignment. In fact, we saw in Chapter 4 that this approach is now quite common. Indeed, it has been said that "the core change" in compensation in recent years "is the diminished concern with internal salary relationships."[42] Called *market pricing,* this approach sets pay structures almost exclusively on external market rates.[43] Market pricers match a large percentage of their jobs with market data and collect as much market data as possible. The competitive rates for jobs for which external market data are available are calculated; then the remaining (nonbenchmark) jobs are blended into the pay hierarchy created by the external rates ("rank to market"). Pfizer, for example, begins with job analysis and job descriptions. This is immediately followed by market analysis and pricing for as many jobs as possible. After that, the few remaining jobs are blended in and the internal job relationships are reviewed to be sure they are *"reasonable in light of organization work flow and other uniqueness."* The final step is pricing the nonbenchmark jobs. This is done by comparing the value of these jobs to the Pfizer jobs already priced in the market.

Market pricing goes beyond using benchmark jobs and slotting nonbenchmarks. The objective of market pricing is to base most, if not all, of the internal pay structure on external rates, breaking down the boundaries between the internal organization and the external market forces. Some companies even match all forms of pay for each job to its competitors in the market. For example, if the average rate for a controller job is $150,000, then the company pays $150,000. If 60 percent of the $150,000 is base pay, 20 percent is annual bonus, 5 percent is stock options, and 15 percent is benefits, the company matches not only the amount but also this mix of pay forms. Another $150,000 job, say, director of marketing, may have a different pattern among market competitors, which is also matched.

Business Strategy (More Than "Follow the Leader")

Pure market pricing carried to this extreme ignores internal alignment completely. Gone is any attempt to align internal pay structures with the business strategy and the work performed. Rather, the internal pay structure is aligned with competitors' decisions as reflected in the market. In a very real sense, the decisions of its competitors determine an organization's pay.

Why should competitors' pay decisions be the sole or even primary determinant of another company's pay structure? If they are, then *how much or what mix of forms* a company pays is no longer a potential source of competitive advantage. It is not unique, nor is it difficult to imitate. The implied assumption is that little value is added through internal alignment.

Any unique or difficult-to-imitate aspects of the organization's pay structure, which may have been based on unique technology or the way work is organized, are de-emphasized by market pricers. Fairness is presumed to be reflected by market rates; employee behavior is presumed to be reinforced by totally market-priced structures, which are the very same as those of competitors.

In contrast, an organization may choose to differentiate its pay strategy from that of its competitors to better execute its own strategy.[44] We saw earlier that organizations may choose different overall pay levels, depending on their business strategy. We also saw earlier that an organizations may choose to pay some of its jobs above market, but other jobs at or below market. For example, according to resource dependence theory, employees who are more central to strategy execution in terms of their criticality in obtaining resources from the environment would be expected to be paid better relative to the market than would other employees. For example, in a study of universities, it was found that private universities, which rely more on private fundraising to operate, paid their chief development (fundraising) officers more than did public universities, which rely more on state funds. On the other hand, public universities, which typically rely more heavily on athletic programs to build alumni relations, paid their athletic directors more than did private universities.[45] Other evidence shows that in capital intensive and highly diversified firms, where finance expertise is especially important, compensation for managers in finance jobs was higher relative to market than for other jobs on average. Likewise, managers in marketing were paid more in firms with large expenditures on marketing and advertising, and managers in research in development were paid more relative to market than other managers in firms focusing on product innovation.[46]

In sum, the process of balancing internal and external pressures is a matter of judgment, made with an eye on the pay system objectives. De-emphasizing internal alignment may lead to unfair treatment among employees and inconsistency with the strategy and fundamental culture of the organization. Neglecting external competitive pay practices, however, will affect both the ability to attract applicants and the ability to retain valued employees. External pay relationships also directly impact labor costs and hence the ability to compete in the product/service market.

REVIEW

The end of Part Two of the textbook is a logical spot for a midterm exam. Exhibit 8.23 has been designed to help you review.

EXHIBIT 8.23
Open-Book
Midterm Exam

Answer true or false to the following questions:

You know you are spending too much time working on compensation when you

- Use "pay mix" and "external competitiveness" when you e-mail home for money.
- Think that paying for lunch requires a strategic approach.
- Ask your date to specify his or her competencies.
- Think that copying your classmate's answers on this exam is "gathering competitive intelligence."
- Can explain the difference between traditional pay grades and ranges and new broad bands with shadow ranges.
- Believe your answer to the above.
- Would cross the street to listen to economists and psychologists discuss the "likely effects of alternative external competitiveness policies."
- Consider your Phase II assignment a wonderful opportunity to increase your human capital.
- Think adding points to your project grade creates a "balanced scorecard."
- Are willing to pay your instructor to teach any other course.
- Are surprised to learn that some people think a COLA is a soft drink.
- Turn your head to listen rather than roll your eyes when someone talks about being "incentivized" with pay.
- Believe that instead of your mom, "the market" knows best.

How did you do? Good. Now let's move on to the next chapters.

Your Turn   Word-of-Mouse: Dot-Com Comparisons

More compensation information is available than ever before. Click on the Web site *www.salary. com.* This site provides pay data on hundreds of jobs in cities all over the United States in many different industries. Identify several jobs of interest to you, such as accountant, financial analyst, product manager, or stockbroker. Select specific cities or use the U.S. national average. Obtain the median, the 25th and 75th percentile base wage, and total cash compensation rates for each job. Then consider the following questions:

1. Which jobs are paid more or less? Is this what you would have expected? Why or why not? What factors could explain the differences in the salaries?
2. Do the jobs have different bonuses as a percentage of their base salaries? What could explain these differences?
3. Do the data include the value of stock options? What are the implications of this?

4. Read the job descriptions. Are they accurate descriptions for jobs that you would be applying for? Why or why not? Are there jobs for which you cannot find an appropriate match? Why do you think this is the case?

5. Check out pay levels for these types of jobs in your school's career office. How does the pay for jobs advertised in your career office differ from the pay levels on salary.com? Why do you think these differences exist?

6. How could you use this information while negotiating your salary in your job after graduation? What data would you provide to support your "asking price"? What factors will influence whether or not you get what you ask for?

7. What is the relevant labor market for these jobs? How big are the differences between salaries in different locations?

8. For each job, compare the median salary to the low and high averages. How much variation exists? What factors might explain this variation in pay rates for the same job?

9. Look for a description of how these salary data are developed. Do you think it provides enough information? Why or why not? Discuss some of the factors that might impair the accuracy of these data. What are the implications of using inaccurate salary data for individuals or companies?

10. With this information available for free, why would you bother with consultants' surveys?

11. If you were a manager, how would you justify paying one of your employees either higher or lower than the results shown on this Web site?

Summary

This chapter has detailed the decisions and techniques that go into setting pay levels and mix and designing pay structures. Most organizations survey other employers' pay practices to determine the rates competitors pay. An employer using the survey results considers how it wishes to position its total compensation in the market: to lead, to match, or to follow competition. This policy decision may be different for different business units and even for different job groups within a single organization. The policy on competitive position is translated into practice by setting pay-policy lines; these serve as reference points around which pay grades and ranges or bands are designed.

The use of grades and ranges or bands recognizes both external and internal pressures on pay decisions. No single "going rate" for a job exists in the market; instead, an array of rates exists. This array results from conditions of demand and supply, variations in the quality of employees, and differences in employer policies and practices. It also reflects the fact that employers differ in the values they attach to the jobs and people. And, very importantly, it reflects differences in the mix of pay forms among companies.

Internally, the use of ranges is consistent with variations in the discretion in jobs. Some employees will perform better than others; some employees are more experienced than others. Pay ranges permit employers to recognize these differences with pay.

Managers are increasingly interested in broad banding, which offers even greater flexibility than grades and ranges to deal with the continuously changing work assignments required in many successful organizations. Broad banding offers freedom to adapt to changes without requiring approvals. However, it risks self-serving and potentially inequitable decisions on the part of the manager. Recently, the trend has been toward approaches with greater flexibility to adapt to changing conditions. Such flexibility also makes mergers and acquisitions easier and global alignment possible.

Let us step back for a moment to review what has been discussed and preview what is coming. We have examined two strategic components of the total pay model. A concern for internal alignment means that analysis and perhaps descriptions and evaluation are important for achieving a competitive advantage and fair treatment. A concern for external competitiveness requires competitive positioning, survey design and analysis, setting the pay-policy line (how much and what forms), and designing grades and ranges or broad bands. The next part of the book is concerned with employee contributions—paying the people who perform the work. This is perhaps the most important part of the book. All that has gone before is a prelude, setting up the pay levels, mix, and structures by which people are to be paid. It is now time to pay the people.

Review Questions

1. Which competitive pay policy would you recommend to an employer? Why? Does it depend on circumstances faced by the employer? Which ones?

2. How would you design a survey for setting pay for welders? How would you design a survey for setting pay for financial managers? Do the issues differ? Will the techniques used and the data collected differ? Why or why not?

3. What factors determine the relevant market for a survey? Why is the definition of the relevant market so important?

4. What do surveys have to do with pay discrimination?

5. Contrast pay ranges and grades with bands. Why would you use either? Does their use assist or hinder the achievement of internal alignment? External competitiveness?

Endnotes

1. Adapted from each company's compensation strategy statements.

2. Consulting firms' Web sites list their specialized surveys. See, for example, Clark Consulting's Total Compensation Survey of the computer and semiconductor industries, *www.clarkconsulting.com;* Hewitt, *www.hewitt.com;* Towers Perrin, *www.towers.com/ towers/services_products/TowersPerrin/online.htm;* Hay, *www.haypaynet.com;* Radford's "Total Compensation Survey and Overall Practices Report," *www.radford.com/rbss/index. html;* Wyatt Watson, *www.watsonwyatt.com;* Mercer, *www.mercer.com;* or McLagan Partners executive compensation surveys at *www.mclagan.com.*

3. Donna Cavallini and Sabrina Pacifici, "Competitive Intelligence: A Selective Resource Guide," *www.llrx.com/features/ciguide.htm,* 2006; "Analyze This: The Evolution of Competitive Intelligence Products for the Legal Profession," *www.llrx.com/features/ analyzethis.htm,* 2006.

4. Joseph R. Meisenheimer II, "Real Compensation, 1979 to 2003: Analysis from Several Data Sources," *Monthly Labor Review,* May 2005, pp. 3–22; National Compensation Survey: *Guide for Evaluating Your Firm's Jobs and Pay,* www.bls.gov/ncs/ocs/sp/ncbr0004.pdf, 2005.

5. Sara L. Rynes and G. T. Milkovich, "Wage Surveys: Dispelling Some Myths About the 'Market Wage,'" Personnel Psychology, Spring 1986, pp. 71–90; B. Gerhart and

S. Rynes, Compensation: Theory, Evidence, and Strategic Implications (Thousand Oaks, CA: Sage, 2003).

6. Charlie Trevor and Mary E. Graham, "Deriving the Market Wage Derivatives: Three Decision Areas in the Compensation Survey Process," *WorldatWork Journal* 9(4) (2000), pp. 69–77; Brian Klaas and John A. McClendon, "To Lead, Lag, or Match: Estimating the Financial Impact of Pay Level Policies," *Personnel Psychology* 49 (1996), pp. 121–140.

7. F. Theodore Malm, "Recruiting Patterns and the Functioning of the Labor Markets," *Industrial and Labor Relations Review* 7 (1954), pp. 507–525; "Job Evaluation and Market Pricing Practices," *WorldatWork*, February 2009.

8. Andrew Klein, David G. Blanchflower, and Lisa M. Ruggiero, "Pay Differentials Hit Employees Where They Live," *Workspan*, June 2002, pp. 36–40; Stephen Ohlemacher, "Highest Wages in East, Lowest in South," U.S. Census Bureau: *www.census.gov/hhes/www/saipe/index.html,* 2005.

9. Charlie Trevor and Mary E. Graham, "Deriving the Market Wage Derivatives: Three Decision Areas in the Compensation Survey Process," *WorldatWork Journal* 9(4) (2000), pp. 69–77.

10. Barry Gerhart and George Milkovich, "Employee Compensation," in M. D. Dunnette and L. M. Hough, eds., *Handbook of Industrial and Organizational Psychology*, 2d ed. (Palo Alto, CA: Consulting Psychologists Press, 1992); B. Gerhart and S. Rynes, *Compensation: Theory, Evidence, and Strategic Implications* (Thousand Oaks, CA: Sage, 2003).

11. Beyond the U.S. consultants, international organizations also do surveys. See Income Data Services' Web site (*www.incomesdata.co.uk*). Also see William M. Mercer's "International Compensation Guidelines 2006" (information on 61 nations) or their European Total Rewards Survey 2006 at *www.mercerhr.com/totalrewardseurope;* Towers Perrin's "Global Surveys," and Organization Resource Counselors online survey for positions in countries ranging from Azerbaijan to Yugoslavia (*www.orcinc.com*). The Mercer and Towers Perrin Web site addresses are provided in footnote 2.

12. M. Bloom, G. Milkovich, and A. Mitra, "International Compensation: Learning from How Managers Respond to Variations in Local-Host Conditions," *International Journal of Human Resource Management,* December 2003, pp. 1350–1367.

13. Yoshio Yanadori, "Minimizing Competition? Entry-Level Compensation in Japanese Firms," *Asia Pacific Journal of Management* 21 (2004), pp. 445–467.

14. Daniel Vaughn-Whitehead, *Paying the Price: The Wage Crisis in Central and Eastern Europe* (Handmill Hampshire, UK: McMillin Press Ltd., 1998).

15. M. Bloom, G. Milkovich, and A. Mitra, "International Compensation: Learning From How Managers Respond to Variations in Local-Host Conditions," *International Journal of Human Resource Management,* December 2003, pp. 1350–1367.

16. Michael Wanderer, "Dot-Comp: A 'Traditional' Pay Plan with a Cutting Edge," *WorldatWork Journal,* Fourth Quarter 2000, pp. 15–24.

17. For consultants' Web sites, see footnotes 2 and 11 in this chapter. Also see WorldatWork's *2006–2007 Survey Handbook and Directory* (Scottsdale, AZ: WorldatWork, 2006).

18. Hay PayNet is at *www.haypaynet.com.*

19. In response to a lawsuit, the Boston Survey Group agreed to publish only aggregated (rather than individual employee) information and not categorize information by industry. Eight hospitals in Utah made the mistake of exchanging information on their *intentions* to increase starting pay offers. They were charged with keeping entry-level wages for registered nurses in the Salt Lake City area artificially low. As part of the legal settlement, no health-care facility in Utah can design, develop, or conduct a wage survey. They can respond in writing (only) to a written request for information for wage survey purposes

from a third party, but only after the third party provides written assurance that the survey will be conducted with particular safeguards. *District of Utah U.S. District Court v. Utah Society for Healthcare Human Resources Administration, et al.,* 59 Fed. Reg. 14,203 (March 25, 1994). The resulting guidelines may buy legal protection, but they also give up control over the decisions that determine the quality and usefulness of the data. Prohibiting exchange of industry data eliminates the ability to make industry or product market comparisons. This might not be important in nursing or clerical jobs, but industry groups are important in comparisons among competitors.

20.   Chockalingam Viswesvaran and Murray Barrick, "Decision-Making Effects on Compensation Surveys: Implications for Market Wages," *Journal of Applied Psychology* 77(5) (1992), pp. 588–597.

21.   John E. Buckley, "Comparing a Firm's Occupational Wage Patterns With National Wage Patterns," Bureau of Labor Statistics, September 29, 2006, *www.bls.gov/opub/cwc/ cm20060922ar01p1.htm.*

22.   John A. Menefee, "The Value of Pay Data on the Web," *Workspan,* September 2000, pp. 25–28.

23.   Charles Fishman, "The Anarchist's Cookbook," *Fast Company,* July 2004, Issue 84.

24.   Some Web sites treat the federal government's Consumer Price Index as a measure of the cost of living in an area. It is not. The Consumer Price Index measures the rate of *change* in the cost of living in an area. So it can be used to compare how quickly prices are rising in one area versus another, but it cannot be used to compare living costs between two different areas.

25.   "Job Evaluation and Market-Pricing Practices," *WorldatWork* report, February 2009.

26.   Sara L. Rynes and G. T. Milkovich, "Wage Surveys: Dispelling Some Myths About the 'Market Wage,'" *Personnel Psychology,* Spring 1986, pp. 71–90; Frederic Cook, "Compensation Surveys Are Biased," *Compensation and Benefits Review,* September– October 1994, pp. 19–22.

27.   Samir Raza, "Optimizing Human Capital Investments for Superior Shareholder Returns," *Valuation Issues* 2006 (*www.valuationissues.com*); M. Huselid and B. Becker, "Improving HR Analytical Literacy: Lessons from Moneyball," Chap. 32 in M. Losey, S. Meisinger, and D. Ulrich, *The Future of Human Resource Management* (Hoboken, NJ: Wiley, 2005); Lindsay Scott, "Managing Labor Costs Using Pay-for-Performance," *Lindsay Scott 8 Associates, Inc.,* www.npktools.com, 2006; J. Fitzens, *How to Measure HRM* (New York: McGraw-Hill, 2002). Also see the Web site of the Saratoga Institute: *www.pwcservices. com/saratoga-institute/default.htm* and *www.hudson-index.com/node.asp?SID=6755.*

28.   Years-since-degree (YSD) or maturity curves, commonly used for scientists, are discussed in Chapter 14, Special Groups.

29.   Donna Cavallini and Sabrina Pacifici, "Competitive Intelligence: A Selective Resource Guide," *www.llrx.com/features/ciguide.htm,* 2006; "Analyze This: The Evolution of Competitive Intelligence Products for the Legal Profession," *www.llrx.com/features/ analyzethis.htm,* 2006. Additional information is available through the Sarasota Institute, *www.pwcservices.com/saratoga-institute/default.htm,* and the Society of HR Management, *www.shrm.org.*

30.   Joseph R. Rich and Carol Caretta Phalen, "A Framework for the Design of Total Compensation Surveys," *ACA Journal,* Winter 1992–1993, pp. 18–29.

31.   Letter from D. W. Belcher to G. T. Milkovich, in reference to D. W. Belcher, N. Bruce Ferris, and John O'Neill, "How Wage Surveys Are Being Used," *Compensation and Benefits Review,* September–October 1985, pp. 34–51.

32.   Users of Milkovich and Milkovich's *Cases in Compensation,* 9th ed. (Santa Monica, CA: Milkovich, 2004) will recognize the software company FastCat. The casebook offers the opportunity for hands-on experience. For more information, contact the authors at gtm1@ cornell.edu (contains the number 1, not the letter L).

33. Margaret A. Coil, "Salary Surveys in a Blended-Role World," in *2003–2004 Survey Handbook and Directory* (Scottsdale, AZ: WorldatWork, 2002), pp. 57–64.

34. For an online tutorial in statistics, go to *www.robertniles.com;* for reading on the bus, try Larry Gonick and Woollcott Smith, *Cartoon Guide to Statistics* (New York: Harper Perennial, 1993); for the fun stuff, see Cybercomp 2 in this chapter.

35. J. K. Rowling, *Harry Potter and the Order of the Phoenix* (New York: Scholastic, 2003).

36. Brian Hinchcliffe, "Juggling Act: Internal Equity and Market Pricing," *Workspan,* February 2003, pp. 42–45.

37. An alternative formula for calculating minimum is midpoint / [100% + (1/2 range)] and for calculating maximum is minimum +1 (range × minimum). This approach gives a different result than does adding 20 percent above and below the midpoint. The important points are to be consistent in whatever approach you choose and to be sure other users of the survey are apprised of how range minimums and maximums are calculated.

38. Charles Fay, Eric Schulz, Steven Gross, and David VanDeVoort, "Broadbanding, Pay Ranges and Labor Costs," *WorldatWork Journal,* Second Quarter 2004, pp. 8–24; Gene Baker and Joe Duggan, "Global Banding Program and a Consultant's Critique," *WorldatWork Journal,* Second Quarter 2004, pp. 24–35; and Kenan S. Abosch and Beverly Hmurovic, "A Traveler's Guide to Global Broadbanding," *ACA Journal,* Summer 1998, pp. 38–47.

39. "Life with Broadbands," ACA Research Project, 1998; "Broad Banding Case Study: General Electric," *WorldatWork Journal,* Third Quarter 2000, p. 43.

40. Kenan S. Abosch and Janice S. Hand, *Broadbanding Models* (Scottsdale, AZ: American Compensation Association, 1994); Charles Fay, Eric Schulz, Steven Gross, and David VanDeVoort, "Broadbanding, Pay Ranges and Labor Costs," *WorldatWork Journal,* Second Quarter 2004, pp. 8–24; Gene Baker and Joe Duggan, " Global Banding Program and a Consultant's Critique," *WorldatWork Journal,* Second Quarter 2004, pp. 24–35.

41. S. Rynes, C. Weber, and G. Milkovich, "Effects of Market Survey Rates on Job Evaluation, and Job Gender on Job Pay," *Journal of Applied Psychology* 74 (1989), pp. 114–123.

42. Howard Risher, "Second Generation Banded Salary Systems," *Wordatwork Journal* 16(1), 2007, p. 20.

43. *Market Pricing: Methods to the Madness* (Scottsdale, AZ: WorldatWork, 2002). "Job Evaluation and Market-Pricing Practices," *www.worldatwork.com,* accessed February 2009.

44. B. Gerhart and S. L. Rynes, *Compensation: Theory, Evidence, and Strategic Implications* (Thousand Oaks, CA: Sage, 2003); B. Gerhart, C. Trevor, and M. Graham, "New Directions in Employee Compensation Research," in G. R. Ferris, ed., *Research in Personnel and Human Resources Management,* (Greenwich, CT: JAI Press, 1996, pp. 143–203).

45. Jeffrey Pfeffer and Alison Davis-Blake, "Understanding Organizational Wage Structures: A Resource Dependence Approach," *Academy of Management Journal* 30 (1987), pp. 437–455.

46. Mason Carpenter and James Wade, "Micro-Level Opportunity Structures As Determinants of Non-CEO Executive Pay," *Academy of Management Journal,* 45 (2002), pp. 1085–1103.

Employee Contributions: Determining Individual Pay

The first two sections of the pay model outlined in **Exhibit IV.1** essentially deal with fairness. Alignment, covered in Part Two, is all about internal fairness: describing jobs and determining their worth relative to each other based on content of the jobs and impact on the organization's objectives. Part Three extended fairness to the external market. It's not enough that jobs within a company are treated fairly in comparison to each other; we also need to look at external competitiveness with similar jobs in other companies. This raises questions of conducting salary surveys, setting pay policies, and arriving at competitive pay levels and equitable pay structures. This fourth part of the book finally brings people into the pay equation. How do we design a pay system so that individual contributors are rewarded according to their value to the organization? Let's hope the following example isn't a role model for today's practices:

> Another 4th dynasty tomb, beautifully carved and painted with vibrantly colored scenes, belonging to a priest of the royal cult and senior scribe named Kay. A fascinating glimpse into an ancient economic exchange is offered by the inscription at the entrance to this tomb, which reads: It is the tomb makers, the draftsmen, the craftsmen, and the sculptors who made my tomb. I paid them in bread and beer and made them take an oath that they were satisfied.
>
> ———Zahi Hawass, *Mountains of the Pharaohs: The Untold Story of the Pyramid Builders* (Cairo: American University in Cairo Press, 2006, p. 136)

How much should one employee be paid relative to another when they both hold the same jobs in the same organization? If this question is not answered satisfactorily, all prior efforts to evaluate and price jobs may have been in vain. For example, the compensation manager determines that all customer service representatives (CSRs) should be paid between $28,000 and $43,000.

EXHIBIT IV.1 The Pay Model

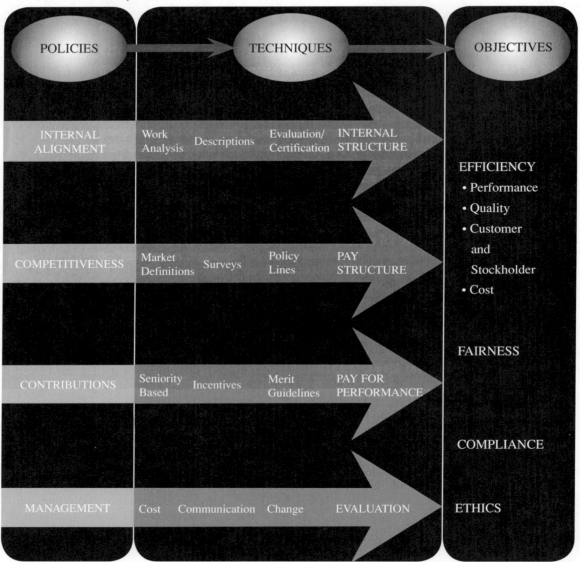

But where in that range is each individual paid? Should a good CSR be paid more than a poor one? If the answer is yes, how should performance be measured and what should be the differential reward? Similarly, should the CSR with more years of experience (i.e., higher seniority) be paid more than one with less time on the job? Again, if the answer is yes, what is the tradeoff between seniority and performance in assigning pay raises? Should Wesley, the compensation manager's son-in-law, be paid more simply because he is family? What are the legitimate factors to consider in the reward equation? As Exhibit IV.1 suggests, all of these questions involve the concept of employee contribution. For the next three chapters, we will be discussing different facets of employee contribution.

Chapter 9 asks whether companies should invest in pay-for-performance plans. In other words, does paying for performance result in higher performance? The answer may seem obvious, but there are many ways to complicate this elegant notion.

Chapter 10 looks at actual pay-for-performance plans. The compensation arena is full of programs that promise to link pay and performance. We identify these plans and discuss their relative advantages and disadvantages.

Chapter 11 acknowledges that performance can't always be measured objectively. What do we do to ensure that subjective appraisal procedures are as free from error as possible? Much progress has been made here, and we provide a tour of the different strategies for measuring performance.

Pay-for-Performance: The Evidence

Chapter Outline

What Behaviors Do Employers Care About? Linking Organization Strategy to Compensation and Performance Management

What Does It Take to Get These Behaviors? What Theory Says

What Does It Take to Get These Behaviors? What Practitioners Say

Does Compensation Motivate Behavior?

   Do People Join a Firm Because of Pay?
   Do People Stay in a Firm (or Leave) Because of Pay?

Do Employees More Readily Agree to Develop Job Skills Because of Pay?
Do Employees Perform Better on Their Jobs Because of Pay?

Designing a Pay-for-Performance Plan
   Efficiency
   Equity/Fairness
   Compliance

Your Turn: Burger Boy

The primary focus of Part Three was on determining the worth of jobs, independent of who performed those jobs. **Job analysis, job evaluation,** and **job pricing** all have a common theme. They are techniques to identify the value a firm places on its jobs. Now we introduce people into the equation. Now we declare that different people performing the same job may add different value to the organization. Wesley is a better programmer than Kelly. Erinn knows more programming languages than Ian. Who should get what?

Entering people into the compensation equation greatly complicates the compensation process. People don't behave like robots. We can't simply tighten a bolt here, oil a joint there (Do robots have joints? Do they need oil?), and walk away secure in the knowledge that people will behave in ways that support organizational objectives. Indeed, there is growing evidence that the way we design HR practices, like performance management, strongly affects the way employees perceive the company. And this directly affects corporate performance.[1] The simple (or not so simple, as we will discuss) process of implementing a performance appraisal system that employees find acceptable goes a long way toward increasing trust for top management.[2] Alternatively, implementing a new compensation system can affect recruitment and selection. In Chapter 2, we talked about sorting effects. Not everyone "appreciates" an incentive system or even a merit-based pay system. People who prefer less performance-based pay systems will "sort themselves" out of organizations with these pay practices and philosophies. Either they won't respond to recruitment ads, or, if already employed, may go so far as to seek employment elsewhere.[3] So as we discuss pay and performance in Chapters 9 to 11, remember that there are other important outcomes that also depend on building good performance measurement tools.

In Chapter 1, we talked about compensation objectives complementing overall human resource objectives and both of these helping an organization achieve its overall strategic objectives. But this begs the question, "How does an organization achieve its overall strategic objectives?" In this part of the book, we argue that organizational success ultimately depends on human behavior. Our compensation decisions and practices should be designed to increase the likelihood that employees will behave in ways that help the organization achieve its strategic objectives. This chapter is organized around employee behaviors. First, we identify the four kinds of behaviors organizations are interested in. Then we note what theories say about our ability to motivate these behaviors. And, finally, we talk about our success, and sometimes lack thereof, in designing compensation systems to elicit these behaviors.

WHAT BEHAVIORS DO EMPLOYERS CARE ABOUT? LINKING ORGANIZATION STRATEGY TO COMPENSATION AND PERFORMANCE MANAGEMENT

The simple answer is that employers want employees to perform in ways that lead to better organizational performance. Exhibit 9.1 shows how organizational strategy is the guiding force that determines what kinds of employee behaviors are needed.

As an illustration, Nordstrom's department stores are known for extremely good quality merchandise and high levels of customer satisfaction—this is the organization strategy they use to differentiate themselves from competitors. Nordstrom's success isn't

EXHIBIT 9.1 The Cascading Link Between Organization Strategy and Employee Behavior

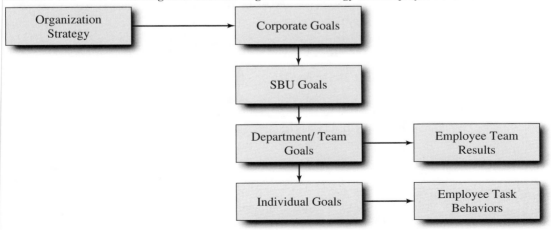

a fluke. You can bet that some of their corporate goals, strategic business unit goals (SBU goals, where a strategic business unit might be a store), department-level goals, and indeed individual employee goals are linked to pleasing customers and selling high-quality products. The job of Human Resources is to devise policies and practices (and compensation falls in this mix) that lead employees (the last box in Exhibit 9.1) to behave in ways that ultimately support corporate goals. Walk into a Nordstrom, you see employees politely greeting you, helping without suffocating, and generally making the shopping experience a pleasant one. These are behaviors that support Nordstrom's strategic plan. Every organization, whether they realize it or not, has Human Resource practices that can either work together, or conflict with each other, in trying to generate positive employee behaviors. One way of looking at this process is evident from Exhibit 9.2.

Let's use an example from baseball to illustrate the equation in Exhibit 9.2. When Manny Ramirez attempts to hit a baseball, his performance depends on three things: (1) his physical abilities and skills (including vision) to master a pitch coming at approximately 90 mph, (2) his motivation to do well, and (3) the absence of environmental obstacles (e.g., Is the sun shining in his eyes when he tries to watch the ball leave the pitcher's hands; does he get randomly drug-tested for steroid use?).[4] Wanting to succeed isn't enough. Having the ability but not the motivation also isn't enough. Many a player with lots of talent doesn't have the motivation to endure thousands of hours of repetitive drills, or to endure weight training and general physical conditioning. Even with both ability and motivation, a player's work environment (both physical and political) must be free of obstacles. A home run hitter drafted by a team with an enormous ball park (home run fences set back much farther from home plate) might never reach

EXHIBIT 9.2
The Big Picture, or Compensation Can't Do It Alone!

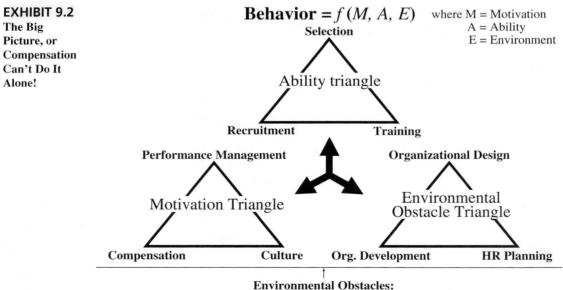

$$\textbf{Behavior} = f\,(M,\,A,\,E)$$

where M = Motivation
A = Ability
E = Environment

Selection

Ability triangle

Recruitment   Training

Performance Management   Organizational Design

Motivation Triangle   Environmental Obstacle Triangle

Compensation   Culture   Org. Development   HR Planning

Environmental Obstacles:
Unions, Economic Conditions, Public Policy/Legislation

his full potential. The same thing is true in more traditional jobs. Success depends on finding people with ability—that's the primary job of recruitment, selection, and training. Once good people are hired, they need to be motivated to behave in ways that help the organization. (Note, part of selection is also to hire motivated people, so the triangles interact with each other, as denoted by the three-pronged arrow in the center of Exhibit 9.2.) This is where compensation enters the picture. Pay and other rewards should reinforce desired behaviors. But so, too, should performance management, by making sure that what is expected of employees, and what is measured in regular performance reviews, is consistent with what the compensation practices are doing. And perhaps most important of all, the culture of the organization (i.e., the informal rules and expectations that are evident in any company) should point in the same direction. Finally, HR needs to establish policies and practices that minimize the chances that outside "distractors" hinder performance.

In the 1980s, Nabisco was slow to recognize customer demand for "soft batch" cookies. Why? They had a centralized organization structure that took a long time to get sales information up to the top decision makers. No matter how much ability or motivation the sales staff has, it's hard to sell cookies the public doesn't want. What did Nabisco do? They decentralized (organization design) the company, creating divisions responsible for different product lines. Now when sales people say consumer preferences are changing, response is much more rapid. Similarly, if we don't recognize changing **skill requirements** (human resource planning), it's hard to set up revised training programs or develop compensation packages to reward these new skills instantly. Knowing in advance about needed changes makes timely completion easier. Similarly, if we have inefficient processes (e.g., too many steps in getting approval for change), organization development (process to change the way a company operates) can free up motivated workers to use their skills.

The key lesson from Exhibit 9.2 is an important one: Compensation can't do it all alone. Try changing behavior by developing a compensation system to reward that behavior. If you haven't selected the right people, if they don't have the necessary training, if you aren't measuring performance, and if it's not part of the culture to do things that way, you're destined for failure.

So, what behaviors does compensation need to reinforce? First, our compensation should be sufficiently attractive to make recruiting and hiring good potential employees possible (attraction).[5] Second, we need to make sure the good employees stay with the company (retention). The recession of 2008–2010 is severely testing companies on these two behaviors. Many organizations claim they are much leaner than in prior recessions.[6] Lean organizations don't want to resort to layoffs, the traditional recessionary strategy. Cutting employees now means letting go stars or potential stars. Instead companies are keeping costs down by cutting salaries. Caterpillar, FedEx, Black and Decker, The New York Times, and the State of Pennsylvania all decided to trim salaries of their current workforce rather than resort to layoffs.[7] If we can succeed at these first two things, we can then concentrate on building further knowledge and skills (develop skills). And, finally, we need to find ways to motivate employees to perform well on their jobs—to take their knowledge and abilities and apply them in ways that contribute to organizational performance.

The oil that lubricates this compensation engine (E-mail the authors if you agree this is a horrible metaphor!) is performance measurement and performance management. We need to accurately measure performance to tell if our compensation efforts are working. We can't tell if our compensation system helps recruit and select good employees if we don't know how to measure what constitutes *good*. We can't tell if employees are building the kinds of knowledge base they need if we can't measure knowledge accumulation. We can't reward performance if we can't measure it! As a simple example, think about companies where piece-rate systems are used to pay people. Why do many sales jobs use commissions (a form of piece rate) as the primary compensation vehicle? Conventional wisdom has always been that it is relatively easy to measure performance in sales jobs—just measure the dollar sales generated by salespeople if you want to know how well each of them is doing. There is little ambiguity in the measure of performance, and this makes it easy to create a strong link between units of performance and amount of compensation. One of the biggest recent advances in compensation strategy has been to document and extend this link between ease of measuring performance and the type of compensation system that works best.

Let's take a minute to talk about each of the cells in Exhibit 9.3. They help explain why incentives work in some situations and not in others.[8] The columns in Exhibit 9.3 divide companies into those with widely variable performance from year to year and those with much more stable performance across time. What might cause wide swings in corporate performance? Often this occurs when something in the corporation's external environment (we call these environmental obstacles in Exhibit 9.2) fluctuates widely, too (e.g., gas prices). It probably wouldn't be fair, and employees would certainly object, if a large part of pay were incentive-based in this kind of environment. Employees building SUVs at Ford today are screaming because their bonuses, based loosely on number of vehicles sold, are impossible to attain. Is it the workers' fault? Of course not! Who buys an Explorer that gets 17 mpg when gas costs $3/gallon? (Except, of course, a dumb second author! By the way, it's a really pretty red!) HR can't control these types of environmental

EXHIBIT 9.3   **Performance Measurement Relates to Compensation Strategy**

		Variability in Organizational Performance	
		Low variability: Few swings in overall corporate performance	High variability: Regular and large swings in overall corporate performance
Variability/ ease of measurement in individual performance	Unstable, unclear, and changing objectives	Cell A—provide wide range of rewards beyond just money. Include significant incentive component.	Cell B—provide wide range of rewards beyond just money. Emphasize base pay with low-incentive portion.
	Stable and easily measured objectives	Cell C—emphasize monetary rewards with large-incentive component.	Cell D—emphasize monetary rewards: large base pay with low-incentive portion.

obstacles, after all. Things the employees don't control (in the external environment) would be dictating a big part of pay. Lack of employee control translates into perceptions of unfair treatment if pay is tied to these uncontrollable things. Cells B and D both suggest that a low-incentive component is appropriate in organizations with highly variable annual performance. Conversely, as cells A and C indicate, larger-incentive components are appropriate in companies with stable annual performance.

The rows in Exhibit 9.3 note that individual employee performance also can vary. Some jobs are fairly stable, with expectations fairly consistent across time. What I do today is basically the same thing I did yesterday. And tomorrow looks like a repeat too! In other jobs, though, there might be high fluctuation in the kinds of things expected of employees, and employees willing to be flexible and adjust to changing demand are much in demand for these jobs. Here, using incentive pay exclusively might not work. Incentive systems are notorious for getting people to do exactly what is being incentivized. Pay me big money to sell suits, and that's just what I'm going to do. You want me to handle customer returns, too? No way, not unless the compensation system rewards a broader array of duties. Evidence suggests that companies are best able to get employees to adjust, be flexible, and show commitment when a broader array of rewards, rather than just money, is part of the compensation package.[9] For example, why does Lincoln Electric (a major producer of welding machines) out-produce other companies in the same industry year after year? Normally we think it's because the company has a well-designed incentive system that links to level of production. Certainly this is a big factor! But when you talk to people at Lincoln Electric, they suggest that part of the success comes from other forms of reward, including the strong commitment to job security—downsizing simply isn't part of the vocabulary there—that reinforces a willingness to try new technologies and new work processes (a culture that supports innovation). Cell A describes the kind of reward package that fits these job and organizational performance characteristics.

When we distill all of this, what can we conclude? We think the answer depends on how we respond to the following four questions:

1. How do we attract good employment prospects to *join* our company?
2. How do we *retain* these good employees once they join?
3. How do we get employees to *develop skills* for current and future jobs?
4. How do we get employees to *perform well* while they are here?

First, how do we get good people to join our company? How did Nike get Tiger Woods to serve as a corporate spokesperson? Part of the answer is rumored to be cold hard cash, estimated to be $110 million in 2009 (over multiple years).[10] Even when the decision doesn't involve millions of dollars, the long-run success of any company depends on getting good people to accept employment. And the compensation challenge is to figure out what components of our compensation package are likely to influence this decision to join.

Second, the obvious complement to the decision to join is the decision to stay. How do we retain employees? It doesn't do much good to attract exceptional employees to our company only to lose them a short time later. Once our compensation practices get a good employee in the door, we need to figure out ways to ensure it's not a revolving door. Ben Wallace, four-time defensive player of the year, recently left the Detroit Pistons for the Chicago Bulls. Why? Some people argue it's the $50 million offered for a four-year contract. Is that what it takes to retain key people? Money! Or are other rewards important? And does their absence lead us to use money as the great neutralizer?

Third, we also must recognize that what we need employees to do today may change. Literally, overnight! A fast-changing world requires employees who can adjust more quickly. How do we get employees, traditionally resistant to change, to willingly develop skills that may not be vital on the current job but are forecast to be critical as the company's strategic plan adjusts to change? Another compensation challenge!

Finally, we want employees to do well on their current jobs. This means performing—and performing well—tasks that support our strategic objectives. What motivates employees to succeed? The compensation challenge is to design rewards that enhance job performance.

WHAT DOES IT TAKE TO GET THESE BEHAVIORS? WHAT THEORY SAYS

Another way of phrasing these same questions is to ask, "What motivates employees?" If you know the right answer, you're way ahead of the so-called experts. In the simplest sense, *motivation* involves three elements: (1) what's important to a person, and (2) offering it in exchange for some (3) desired behavior. As to the first element, what's important to employees, data suggest employees prefer pay systems that are influenced by individual performance, changes in cost of living, seniority, and the market rate, to name the most important factors.[11] To narrow down specific employee preferences, though, there has been some work on what's called **cafeteria-style** or **flexible compensation**—a takeoff on cafeteria-style benefits, to be described further when we talk about employee benefits in Chapters 12 and 13. Cafeteria-style compensation is based on the idea that only the individual employee knows what package of rewards would best suit personal needs. Employees who hate risk could opt for more base pay and less incentive pay. Tradeoffs between pay and benefits could also be selected. The key ingredient in this new concept is careful cost analysis to make sure the dollar cost of the package an employee selects meets employer budgetary limits.[12]

In Exhibit 9.4 we briefly summarize some of the important motivation theories.[13] They try to answer the three questions we posed above: what's important, how do we offer it, and how does it help deliver desired behaviors. Pay particular attention to the "So What?" column, in which we talk about the ways theory suggests employee behavior is delivered.

Some of the theories in Exhibit 9.4 focus on content—identifying what is important to people. Maslow's and Herzberg's theories, for example, both fall in this category. People have certain needs, such as physiological, security, and self-esteem, that influence behavior. Although neither theory is clear on how these needs are offered and how they help deliver behavior, presumably if we offer rewards that satisfy one or more needs, employees will behave in desired ways. These theories often drive compensation decisions about the breadth and depth of compensation offerings. Flexible compensation, with employees choosing from a menu of pay and benefit choices, clearly is driven by the issue of needs. Who best knows what satisfies needs? The employee! So let employees choose, within limits, what they want in their reward package.

EXHIBIT 9.4   Motivation Theories

Theory	Essential Features	Predictions About Performance-Based Pay	So What?
Maslow's need hierarchy	People are motivated by inner needs. Needs form a hierarchy from most basic (food and shelter) to higher-order (e.g., self-esteem, love, self-actualization). Needs are never fully met; they operate cyclically. Higher-order needs become motivating after lower-order needs have been met. When needs are not met, they become frustrating.	1. Base pay must be set high enough to provide individuals with the economic means to meet their basic living needs. 2. An at-risk program will not be motivating since it restricts employees' ability to meet lower-order needs. 3. Success-sharing plans may be motivating to the extent they help employees pursue higher-order needs.	A. Performance-based pay may be de-motivating if it impinges upon employees' capacity to meet daily living needs. B. Incentive pay is motivating to the extent it is attached to achievement, recognition, or approval.
Herzberg's two-factor theory	Employees are motivated by two types of motivators: hygiene factors and satisfiers. Hygiene, or maintenance, factors in their absence prevent behaviors, but in their presence cannot motivate performance. They are related to basic living needs, security, and fair treatment. Satisfiers, such as recognition, promotion, and achievement, motivate performance.	1. Base pay must be set high enough to provide individuals with the economic means to meet hygiene needs, but it cannot motivate performance. 2. Performance is obtained through rewards—payments in excess of that required to meet basic needs. 3. Performance-based pay is motivating to the extent it is connected with meeting employees' needs for recognition, pleasure attainment, achievement, and the like. 4. Other factors such as interpersonal atmosphere, responsibility, type of work, and working conditions influence the efficacy of performance-based pay.	A. Pay level is important—must meet minimum requirements before performance-based pay can operate as motivator. B. Security plans will induce minimum, but not extra, performance. Success-sharing plans will be motivating. At-risk plans will be demotivating. C. Other conditions in the working relationship influence the effectiveness of performance-based pay.

EXHIBIT 9.4 *(Continued)*

Theory	Essential Features	Predictions about Performance-Based Pay	So What?
Expectancy	Motivation is the product of three perceptions: expectancy, instrumentality, and valence.	1. Job tasks and responsibilities should be clearly defined.	A. Larger incentive payments are better than smaller ones.
	Expectancy is employees' assessment of their ability to perform required job tasks.	2. The pay-performance link is critical.	B. Line of sight is critical—employees must believe they can influence performance targets.
	Instrumentality is employees' beliefs that requisite job performance will be rewarded by the organization.	3. Performance-based pay returns must be large enough to be seen as rewards.	C. Employee assessments of their own ability are important—organizations should be aware of training and resource needs required to perform at target levels.
	Valence is the value employees attach to the organization rewards offered for satisfactory job performance.	4. People choose the behavior that leads to the greatest reward.	
Equity	Employees are motivated when perceived outputs (i.e., pay) are equal to perceived inputs (e.g., effort, work behaviors).	1. The pay-performance link is critical; increases in performance must be matched by commensurate increases in pay.	A. Performance measures must be clearly defined, and employee must be able to affect them through work behaviors.
	A disequilibrium in the output-to-input balance causes discomfort.	2. Performance inputs and expected outputs must be clearly defined and identified.	B. If payouts do not match expectations, employees will react negatively.
	If employees perceive that others are paid more for the same effort, they will react negatively (e.g., shirk) to correct the output-to-input balance.	3. Employees evaluate the adequacy of their pay via comparisons with other employees.	C. Fairness and consistency of performance-based pay across employees in an organization is important.
			D. Since employees evaluate their pay-effort balance in comparison to other employees, relative pay matters.

Theory	Essential Features	Predictions about Performance-Based Pay	So What?
Reinforcement	Rewards reinforce (i.e., motivate and sustain) performance. Rewards must follow directly after behaviors to be reinforcing. Behaviors that are not rewarded will be discontinued.	1. Performance-based payments must follow closely behind performance. 2. Rewards must be tightly coupled to desired performance objectives. 3. Withholding payouts can be a way to discourage unwanted behaviors.	A. Timing of payouts is very important.
Goal setting	Challenging performance goals influence greater intensity and duration in employee performance. Goals serve as feedback standards to which employees can compare their performance. Individuals are motivated to the extent that goal achievement is combined with receiving valued rewards.	1. Performance-based pay must be contingent upon achievement of important performance goals. 2. Performance goals should be challenging and specific. 3. The amount of the incentive reward should match the goal difficulty.	A. Line-of-sight is important; employees must believe they can influence performance targets. B. Performance targets should be communicated in terms of specific, difficult goals. C. Feedback about performance is important. D. Performance-based payouts should be contingent upon goal achievement.
Agency	Pay directs and motivates employee performance. Employees prefer static wages (e.g., a salary) to performance-based pay. If performance can be accurately monitored, payments should be based upon satisfactory completion of work duties. If performance cannot be monitored, pay should be aligned with achieving organizational objectives.	1. Performance-based pay must be tightly linked to organizational objectives. 2. Employees dislike risky pay and will demand a wage premium (e.g., higher total pay) in exchange for accepting performance-based pay. 3. Performance-based pay can be used to direct and induce employee performance.	A. Performance-based pay is the optimal compensation choice for more complex jobs where monitoring employees' work is difficult. B. Performance targets should be tied to organizational goals. C. Use of performance-based pay will require higher total pay opportunity.

A second set of theories, best exemplified by expectancy theory, equity theory, and agency theory, focus less on need states and more on the second element of motivation—the nature of the exchange- company rewards in exchange for desired employee behaviors.[14] Many of our compensation practices recognize the importance of a fair exchange. We evaluate jobs using a common set of compensable factors (Chapter 5) in part to let employees know that an explicit set of rules governs the evaluation process. We collect salary survey data (Chapter 8) because we want the exchange to be fair compared to external standards. We design incentive systems (Chapter 10) to align employee behavior with the needs (desired behaviors) of the organization. All of these pay decisions, and more, owe much to understanding how the employment exchange affects employee motivation.

Expectancy theory argues that people behave as if they cognitively evaluate what behaviors are possible (e.g., the probability that they can complete the task) in relation to the value of rewards offered in exchange. According to this theory, we choose behaviors that yield the most satisfactory exchange. Equity theory also focuses on what goes on inside an employee's head. Not surprisingly, equity theory argues that people are highly concerned about equity, or fairness of the exchange process. Employees look at the exchange as a ratio between what is expected and what is received. Some theorists say we judge transactions as fair when others around us don't have a more (or less) favorable balance between the give and get of an exchange.[15] Even greater focus on the exchange process occurs in the last of this second set of theories, agency theory.[16] Here, employees are depicted as agents who enter an exchange with principals—the owners or their designated managers. It is assumed that both sides to the exchange seek the most favorable exchange possible and will act opportunistically if given a chance (e.g., try to "get by" with doing as little as possible to satisfy the contract). Compensation is a major element in this theory, because it is used to keep employees in line: Employers identify important behaviors and important outcomes and pay specifically for achieving desired levels of each. Such incentive systems penalize employees who try to shirk their duties by giving proportionately lower rewards.

Finally, at least one of the theories summarized in Exhibit 9.4 focuses on the third element of motivation: desired behavior. Identifying desired behaviors—and goals expected to flow from these behaviors—is the emphasis of a large body of goal-setting research. Most of this research says that how we set goals (the process of goal setting, the level and difficulty of goals, etc.) can influence the performance levels of employees.[17] For example, workers assigned "hard" goals consistently do better than workers told to "do your best."[18]

WHAT DOES IT TAKE TO GET THESE BEHAVIORS? WHAT PRACTITIONERS SAY

In the past, compensation people didn't ask this question very often. Employees learned what behaviors were important as part of the socialization process or as part of the performance management process.[19] If it was part of the culture to work long hours, you quickly learned this. One of our daughters worked as a business consultant for Accenture, a very large consulting company. She learned quickly that 70–80 hour work weeks were fairly common. Sure, she had very good wages for someone with a bachelor's degree in biology and no prior business experience, but it didn't take long to burn out when weeks of long hours turned into months. If your performance appraisal at the end of the year stressed certain types of behaviors, or if your boss said certain things were important to her, then the signals were pretty clear: Do these things! Compensation might have rewarded people for meeting these expectations, but usually the compensation package wasn't designed to be one of the signals about expected performance. Not true today![20] Now compensation people talk about pay in terms of a neon arrow flashing "Do these things." Progressive companies ask, "What do we want our compensation package to do? How, for example, do we get our product engineers to take more risks?" Compensation is then designed to support this risk-taking behavior. Compensation people will also tell you, though, that money isn't everything.

> **Cybercomp**
> The International Society for Performance Improvement has Web information on performance journals, strategies for improving performance, and conferences covering the latest research on performance improvement techniques. Go to the society's Web site, *www.ispi.org*.

In fact, compensation is but one of many rewards that influence employee behavior. Sometimes this important point is missed by compensation experts. Going back at least to Henry Ford, we tend to look at money as the great equalizer. Job boring? No room for advancement? Throw money at the problem! Depending on the survey you consult, workers highly value such other job rewards as empowerment, recognition, and opportunities for advancement.[21] And there is growing sentiment for letting workers choose their own "blend" of rewards from the thirteen we note in Exhibit 9.5. We may be overpaying in cash *and* missing the opportunity to let employees construct both a more satisfying and less-expensive reward package. Known as cafeteria compensation, this idea introduced earlier is based on the notion of different rewards having different

EXHIBIT 9.5   **Components of a Total Reward System**

1. Compensation	Wages, commissions, and bonuses
2. Benefits	Vacations, health insurance
3. Social interaction	Friendly workplace
4. Security	Stable, consistent position and rewards
5. Status/recognition	Respect, prominence due to work
6. Work variety	Opportunity to experience different things
7. Workload	Right amount of work (not too much, not too little)
8. Work importance	Work is valued by society
9. Authority/control/autonomy	Ability to influence others; control own destiny
10. Advancement	Chance to get ahead
11. Feedback	Receive information helping to improve performance
12. Work conditions	Hazard free
13. Development opportunity	Formal and informal training to learn new knowledge skills/abilities

dollar costs associated with them. Armed with a fixed sum of money, employees move down the line, buying more or less of the 13 rewards as their needs dictate.[22] While widespread use of this type of system may be a long time in the future, the cafeteria approach still underscores the need for integration of rewards in compensation design.

If we don't think about the presence or absence of rewards other than money in an organization, we may find the compensation process producing unintended consequences. Consider the following three examples, which show how compensation decisions have to be integrated with total reward system decisions:

Example 1: This example asks you to think about team-based work environments like Xerox where the culture of the organization strongly supports empowerment of workers. Empowerment is a form of reward. In Exhibit 9.5, we identify the dimensions of empowerment (see item 9) as *authority* to make decisions, some *control* over factors that influence outcomes, and the *autonomy* to carry out decisions without overregulation by upper management. Some people find empowerment a very positive inducement, making coming to work each day a pleasure. However, others may view empowerment as just added responsibility—legitimizing demands for more pay. In the first case, adding extra compensation may not be necessary. Some have even argued it can lessen motivation.[23] In the second case, extra compensation may be a necessity. Is it any wonder that companies are having trouble finding *one* right answer to the team compensation question.

Example 2: This example comes from airline industry leader Southwest Airlines.[24] Southwest Airlines promotes a business culture of fun and encourages employees to find ways to make their jobs more interesting and relevant to them personally. All this is accomplished without using incentives as a major source of competitive advantage. Indeed, pay at Southwest isn't any higher than for competitor airlines, yet it's much easier to recruit top people there. Fun, a good social environment, is a reward!

Example 3: Consider the relationship between the different forms of compensation and another of the general rewards listed in Exhibit 9.5: security. Normally, we think of security in terms of job security. Drastic reductions in middle-management layers during the downsizing decade of the 1980s increased employee concerns about job security and probably elevated the importance of this reward to employees today. Maybe that's why new millenial workers are concerend not only about employment risk but also about compensation at risk. There is evidence that compensation at risk (pay based on incentives rather than base pay that is secure) leaves many employees less satisfied both with their pay level and with the process used to determine pay.[25] Security as an issue, it appears, is creeping into the domain of compensation. It used to be fairly well established that employees would make more this year than they did last year, and employees counted on such *security* to plan their purchases and other economic decisions. The trend today is toward less stable and less secure compensation packages. The very design of compensation systems today contributes to instability and insecurity. Exhibit 9.6 outlines the different types of wage components.

Notice that Exhibit 9.6 generally orders compensation components from least risky to most risky for employees. We define risky in terms of stability of income, or the ability

EXHIBIT 9.6   **Wage Components**

Wage Component	Definition	Level of Risk to Employee
Base pay	The guaranteed portion of an employee's wage package.	As long as employment continues, this is the secure portion of wages.
Across-the-board increase	Wage increase granted to all employees, regardless of performance. Size related to some subjective assessment of employer about ability to pay. Typically an add-on to base pay in subsequent years.	Some risk to employee since at discretion of employer. But not tied to performance differences, so risk lower in that respect.
Cost-of-living increase	Same as across-the-board increase, except magnitude based on change in cost of living (e.g., as measured by the Consumer Price Index [CPI]).	Same as-across-the-board increases.
Merit pay	Wage increase granted to employee as function of some assessment of employee performance. Adds on to base pay in subsequent years.	Two types of risk faced by employees. Size of total merit pool at discretion of employer (risk element), and individual portion of pool depends on performance, which also is not totally predictable.
Lump-sum bonus	As with merit pay, granted for individual performance. Does not add into base pay, but is distributed as a one-time bonus.	Three types of risks faced here. Both types mentioned under merit pay, plus not added into base—requires annually "re-earning" the added pay.
Individual incentive	Sometimes this variable pay is an add-on to a fixed base pay. The incentive component ties increments in compensation directly to extra individual production (e.g., commission systems, piece rate). While measures of performance are typically subjective with merit and lump-sump components, this form of variable pay differs because measures of performance are objective (e.g., sales volume).	Most risk compensation component if sole element of pay, but often combined with a base pay. No or low fixed-base pay means each year employee is dependent upon number of units of performance to determine pay.
Success-sharing plans	A generic category of pay add-on (variable pay) which is tied to some measure of group performance, not individual performance. Not added into base pay. Distinguished from risk-sharing plans, below, because employees share in any success—performance above standard—but are not penalized for performance below standard.	All success-sharing plans have risks noted in above pay components plus the risk associated with group performance measures. Now individual worker is also dependent upon the performance of others included in the group.

(continued)

EXHIBIT 9.6 *(continued)*

Wage Component	Definition	Level of Risk to Employee
• Gain sharing	Differs from profit sharing in that goal to exceed is not financial performance of organization but some cost index (e.g., labor cost is most common, might also include scrap costs, utility costs).	Less risk to individual than profit sharing because performance measure is more controllable.
• Profit sharing	Add-on linked to group performance (team, division, total company) relative to exceeding some financial goal.	Profit measures are influenced by factors beyond employee control (e.g., economic climate, accounting write-offs). Less control means more risk.
Risk sharing plans	Generic category of pay add-on (variable pay) that differs from success sharing in that employee not only shares in the successes but also is penalized during poor performance years. Penalty is in form of lower total compensation in poor corporate performance years. Reward, though, is typically higher than that for success-sharing programs in high performance years.	Greater risk than success-sharing plans. Typically, employees absorb a "temporary" cut in base pay. If performance targets are met, this cut is neutralized by one component of variable pay. Risk to employee is increased, though because even base pay is no longer totally predictable.

to accurately predict income level from year to year. Base pay is, at least as far as there are any guarantees, the guaranteed portion of income, as long as employees remain employed. There have been very few years since the Depression when base wages did not rise, or at least stay the same.[26] Across the board increases, cost-of-living increases and merit increases all help the base pay component increase on a regular basis. Of course, there always has to be an exception to the rule—and the Great Recession of 2008–2010 has spawned many corporate base wage cuts. The next seven components are distinguished by increasing levels of uncertainty for employees. In fact, risk-sharing plans actually include a provision for cuts in base pay that are only recaptured in years when the organization meets performance objectives.

All of this discussion of risk is only an exercise in intellectual gymnastics unless we add one further observation: Over the last several decades, companies have been moving more toward compensation programs higher on the risk continuum. New forms of pay are less entitlement-oriented and more linked to the uncertainties of individual, group, and corporate performance.[27] Employees increasingly are expected to bear a share of the risks that businesses have solely born in the past. It's not entirely clear what impact this shifting of risk will have in the long run, but some authors are already voicing concerns that efforts to build employee loyalty and commitment may be an early casualty of these new pay systems.[28] Some research suggests that employees may need a risk premium (higher pay) to stay and perform in a company with pay at risk.[29] Even a premium might not work for employees who are particularly risk-averse. Security-driven employees actually might accept lower wages if they come in a package that is more stable.[30] To explore what impact these new forms of pay have, the remainder of this chapter summarizes what we know about the ability of different compensation components to motivate the four general behaviors we noted earlier.

> **Cybercomps**
> IOMA is the Institute of Management and Administration. It specializes in finding studies from a wide variety of places that discuss different aspects of pay for performance. The index for IOMA's Web site is at *www.ioma.com.*

DOES COMPENSATION MOTIVATE BEHAVIOR?

Now let's look at the role of compensation in motivating the four types of behavior outlined earlier: the decision to join, to stay, to develop skills, and to perform well.

Do People Join a Firm Because of Pay?

Level of pay and pay system characteristics influence a job candidate's decision to join a firm, but this shouldn't be too surprising.[31] Pay is one of the more visible rewards in the whole recruitment process. Job offers spell out the level of compensation and may even include discussions about the kind of pay such as bonuses and profit-sharing participation. Less common are statements such as "You'll get plenty of work variety," or "Don't worry about empowerment," or "The workload isn't too heavy." These other rewards are subjective and tend to require actual time on the job before we can decide if they are positive or negative features of the job. Not so for pay. Being perceived as more objective, it's more easily communicated in the employment offer.

Recent research suggests job candidates look for organizations with reward systems that fit their personalities.[32] Below we outline some of the ways that "fit" is important.

Person Characteristics	Preferred Reward Characteristics
Materialistic	Relatively more concerned about pay level[33]
Low self-esteem	Want large, decentralized organization with little pay for performance[34]
Risk takers	Want more pay based on performance[35]
Risk-averse	Want less performance-based pay[36]
Individualists ("I control my destiny")	Want pay plans based on individual performance, not group performance[37]

None of these relationships is particularly surprising. People are attracted to organizations that fit their personalities. Evidence suggests talented employees are attracted to companies that have strong links between pay and performance.[38]

It's not a big jump, then, to suggest organizations should design their reward systems to attract people with desired personalities and values. For example, if we need risk takers, maybe we should design reward systems that have elements of risk built into them.

Do People Stay in a Firm (or Leave) Because of Pay?

There is clear evidence that poor performers are more likely to leave an organization than are good performers.[39] How does pay affect this relationship? Much of the equity theory research in the 1970s documented that workers who feel unfairly treated in pay react by leaving the firm for greener pastures.[40] This is particularly true under incentive conditions. Turnover is much higher for poor performers when pay is based on individual performance (a good outcome!). Conversely, group incentive plans may lead to more turnover of better performers—clearly an undesirable outcome. When AT&T shifted from individual to team-based incentives a number of years ago, star performers either reduced their output or quit. Out of 208 above-average performers, only one continued to report performance increases under the group incentive plan. The rest felt cheated because the incentives for higher individual performance were now spread across all group members.[41]

Clearly, pay can be a factor in decisions to stay or leave. Data suggest dissatisfaction with pay can be a key factor in turnovers.[42] Too little pay triggers feelings of unfair treatment. Result? Turnover. Supporting this, pay that employees find reasonable can help reduce turnover.[43] Even the way we pay has an impact on turnover. Evidence suggests that some employees are uncomfortable with pay systems that put any substantial future earnings at risk or pay systems that link less to personal effort and more to group effort.[44] Another recent study found superior performing employees were less likely to leave if they received bonuses. No such positive result was found with pay increases (thus changing base pay).[45] We need to make sure, as one critic has noted, that we don't let our design of new reward systems rupture our relationships with existing employees.[46] Recent efforts to use different types of compensation as a tool for retaining workers have focused on what is called *scarce talent*. For example, information technology employees have been scarce for much of the past decade, at least. One way to retain these workers is to develop a variable-pay component for each project. For example, reports of variable pay linked to individual length of stay on a project, to peer ratings, and to project results suggest that this pay-for-performance combination may appeal to scarce talent.[47]

The next time you go into an Applebee's restaurant, think about how the company uses compensation to reduce turnover. In an industry where manager turnover hovers around 50 percent, Applebee's allows general managers to earn as much as $30,000 above base salary for hitting sales, profitability, and customer satisfaction targets. To discourage turnover, this extra compensation is deferred for two years.[48]

Besides money, other rewards also influence the decision to stay (retention) in a firm. According to one recent study, the rewards that "work" to help retain employees in the tough economic times we face heading into the middle of this decade are as follows:[49]

Type of Reward	Percent Who Think It's Important in Retention
1. Work variety and challenge	50
2. Development opportunity	38
3. Social	40
4. Status recognition	23
5. Work importance	20
6. Benefits	22

In the early 2000s, we experienced another form of turnover problem: Key employees left companies because the firms appeared financially troubled. The airline industry, in particular, was hurt badly by 9/11, increased terrorism in general, and rising fuel prices. How does a company keep key personnel when the dangers of job loss are very real? One answer is to adopt "stay bonuses." These are generally lump-sum or installment bonuses designed specifically to retain key employees during and after a Chapter 11 restructuring. These bonuses can be as large as 50 to 75 percent of salary for CEOs, dropping down to 25 percent for middle-level managers and below.[50]

Do Employees More Readily Agree to Develop Job Skills Because of Pay?

We don't know the answer to this question. Skill-based pay (Chapter 6) is intended, at least partially, to pay employees for learning new skills—skills that hopefully will help employees perform better on current jobs and adjust more rapidly to demands on future jobs. For example, the U.S. Army pays ROTC cadets in college to learn new languages. Hot spots like the Mideast command monthly premiums of $100 to $250 per month.[51] Anyone know Farsi (spoken in Iran)?

We do know that one complaint about skill-based pay centers on cost implications. More employees request training, spurred by the promise of skill-based increments. Poorly administered plans, allowing more people to acquire certification in a skill than are actually required, creates cost inefficiencies. This leads to plan abandonment. So is the net result positive? Whether the promise of skill-based pay is fulfilled is unclear. Evidence is starting to accumulate that pay for skill may not increase productivity, but it does focus people on believing in the importance of quality and in turning out significantly higher quality products.[52]

Do Employees Perform Better on Their Jobs Because of Pay?

We'll be the first to admit that no matter what stand you take on this question, someone is going to disagree with you. Pfeffer reports that hundreds of studies and dozens of systematic reviews show that rewards motivate performance.[53] A well-designed plan linking pay to behaviors of employees generally results in better individual and organizational performance.[54] One particularly good study looked at the HR practices of over 3,000 companies.[55] One set of questions asked: (1) Did the company have a formal appraisal process, (2) Was the appraisal tied to the size of pay increases, and (3) Did performance influence who would be promoted? Organizations significantly above the mean (by one standard deviation) on these and other "high-performance work practices" had annual sales that averaged $27,000 more per employee. So rewarding employees for performance pays off.

In another comprehensive review, Heneman reports that 40 of 42 studies looking at merit pay show performance increases when pay is tied to performance.[56] One study of 841 union and nonunion companies found gain-sharing and profit-sharing plans (both designed to link pay to performance) increased individual and team performance 18 to 20 percent.[57] How, though, does this translate into corporate performance? A review of 26 studies gives high marks to profit-sharing plans: Organizations with such plans had 3.5 to 5 percent higher annual performance.[58] Gerhart and Milkovich took the performance-based pay question one step further. Across 200 companies they found a 1.5-percent increase in return on assets for every 10-percent increase in the size of a bonus.[59] Further, they found that the variable portion of pay had a stronger impact on individual and corporate performance than did the level of base pay.

Conversely, numerous critics, led by Alfie Kohn, argue that incentives are both morally and practically wrong.[60] The moral argument suggests that incentives are flawed because they involve one person controlling another. The counterargument to this notes that employment is a reciprocal arrangement. In periods of low unemployment especially, workers can choose whether they want to work under compensation systems with strong pay-for-performance linkages (as in the case of incentive systems). We do know that applicants aren't totally risk-averse. There are circumstances when they will prefer an incentive component to compensation rather than a totally fixed salary. Generally, if the incentive depends on individual performance, applicants find the company more attractive. Team-based incentives, in contrast, are less attractive.

Kohn also suggests that incentive systems can actually harm productivity, a decidedly negative practical outcome. His rationale is based on citations mostly from laboratory studies where subjects work in isolation on a task for either pay or no pay. His conclusion, based heavily on the work of Deci and colleagues, is that rewarding a person for performing a task reduces interest in that task—**extrinsic rewards** (money) reduce intrinsic rewards (enjoyment of the task for its own sake).[61] Critics of this interpretation point out at least two important flaws in Kohn's conclusions.[62] First, the pragmatics of business demand that some jobs be performed—indeed, many jobs— that aren't the most intrinsically interesting. Although Target may be a great store at which to shop, spending day after day stocking shelves with towels and other nonbreakables falls far down the intrinsic-interest scale.[63] If incentives are required for real-world jobs to be completed and thus to create value for an organization and its consumers, so be it. This may simply be one of the costs of doing business. Second, Kohn's studies frequently looked at people in isolation. In the real world people interact with each other, know who is performing and who isn't, and react to this when rewards are allocated. Without any link to performance, the less-motivated employees will eventually recognize that harder work isn't necessary. It quickly becomes evident that some workers are being paid the same for doing less. Think, for example, of the last time you completed a group project. Were you happy with the team member who did less but received the same grade? Did you think it fairer when you had a teacher who asked for evaluations of all group members' performance and used these data to assign individualized grades (rewards tied to performance)? The same situation arises in industry and makes the question "Should we tie rewards to performance?" at least worthy of further examination.

The first part of this examination perhaps should focus on an obvious but often overlooked question: Do employees think any link at all should be made between pay and performance? Substantial evidence indicates that management and workers alike believe pay should be tied to performance. Dyer and colleagues asked 180 managers from 72 different companies to rate nine possible factors in terms of the importance they should receive in determining the size of salary increases.[64] This group believed the most important factor for salary increases should be job performance. Following close behind is a factor that presumably would be picked up in job evaluation (nature of job) and a motivational variable (amount of effort expended).

Other research supports these findings.[65] Both college students and a second group of managers ranked job performance as the most important variable in allocating pay raises. Another way to make the pay-for-performance argument is to look at the ways HR professionals try to cut costs. At the top of the list: Create greater distinction between high and low performers![66] In other words, really pay for performance! Once we move away from the managerial ranks, though, other groups express a different view of the pay-performance link. The role that performance levels should assume in determining pay increases is less clear-cut for blue-collar workers.[67] As an illustration, consider the frequent opposition to compensation plans that are based on performance (i.e., incentive piece-rate systems). Unionized workers prefer seniority rather than performance as a basis for pay increases.[68] Part of this preference may stem from a distrust of subjective performance measurement systems. Unions ask, "Can management be counted on to be fair?" In contrast, seniority is an objective index for calculating increases. Some evidence also suggests that women might prefer allocation methods not based on performance.[69]

It's probably a good thing that, in general, workers believe pay should be tied to performance, because the research we've reported suggests this link makes a difference.[70] And the difference may translate into bottom-line results! In a study of over 3,000 companies, convincing evidence showed that linking pay to performance has a positive impact on the bottom line. Over a five-year period such practices can increase per-employee sales by as much as $100,000.[71]

How does this performance improvement occur? One view suggests that linking pay to performance occurs through two mechanisms, an incentive effect and a sorting effect.[72] Incentive effect means pay can motivate people to perform better. Sorting effect means people sort themselves by what is important to them. So if Company X pays for performance, and you don't want to play by those rules (i.e., work harder or smarter to perform better) you sort yourself out, most easily by leaving Company X and finding another company with different rules for getting rewards.

Many meta-analyses (reviews of pay for performance research that use statistical tools to estimate the magnitude of pays impact on performance) demonstrate the incentive effect of pay. Strong evidence suggests that linking pay to performance does increase motivation of workers and lead to improved performance. Locke and colleagues analyzed studies where individual incentives were introduced into actual work settings. Productivity increased on average 30 percent![73] A host of other meta-analyses draw similar conclusions—money does motivate performance.

Choice of pay systems (pay increases based on performance or some other attribute like seniority) also influence productivity through the sorting effect—people sort themselves into or out of organizations based on a preference for being paid based on personal performance or some something else.[74] Of course, the most obvious sorting factor is ability. Higher ability individuals are attracted to companies that will pay for performance, thus recognizing their greater contribution.[75] High performers will also leave firms that don't reward their performance (pay for something like seniority rather than performance) and go to those that do.[76]

EXHIBIT 9.7
Examples of Group Incentive Plans

Company	Pay Component
Corning	Competitive base pay. Group bonus based on meeting certain quality measures, customer satisfaction measures, and production targets.
Nucor	Plant manager base pay 25 percent below market. Five percent of excess over target goes to bonus. Bonus often equals base pay in amount.
PepsiCo	Competitive base pay. All employees get stock options equal to 10 percent of base pay. Employees share in corporate triumphs and failures as stock prices rise or fall.

When we look at pay and group performance (instead of individual performance), the evidence is mixed. In general, though, we think group pay (whether the group is a team or an entire organization) leads to small (relative to individual pay for performance) productivity increases. On average, that productivity increase is about 4–5 percent.

Companies like Corning, Nucor Steel, and PepsiCo all strongly support variable pay based on group performance (usually the group is all employees in the organization, or some subset).[77] The reasons are quite compelling. First, organizations are moving to job structures and production systems that require team effort. This quite naturally leads to team-based and organization-wide incentives. Second, firms that ignore the interaction needed to boost quality and quantity sometimes find units competing against each other rather than cooperating.

Exhibit 9.7 describes elements of the variable-pay plans at these companies. Most well-controlled studies on companies that link part of pay to some measure of corporate or division performance report increases in performance of about 4 to 6 percent per year.[78] In one typical study, a utility company placed one division on an experimental group incentive plan and left the other division with no pay changes (the control group).[79] The goal in the experimental division was to lower the unit cost of electricity. The utility set performance goals for such things as operating expenses, maintenance expenses, and absenteeism. If these goals were exceeded, employees would receive a bonus that grew as the goals were exceeded by a larger amount. After the utility implemented this variable pay plan (or group incentive plan), the experimental group's performance improved significantly over that of the control group on 11 of 12 objective performance measures. As an example, unit production costs fell 6 percent.

Compensation experts estimate that every dollar spent on any performance-based pay plan yields $2.34 more in organizational earnings.[80] Put differently, there is further documented evidence that every 10 percent increase in the bonus paid to employees yields a 1.5 percent increase in ROA (return on assets) to the firm.[81]

Before we rush out and develop a variable-pay component to the compensation package, though, we should recognize that such plans can, and do, fail. Sometimes the failure arises, ironically, because the incentive works too well, leading employees to exhibit rewarded behaviors to the exclusion of other desired behaviors. Exhibit 9.8 documents one such embarrassing incident that haunted Sears for much of the early 1990s.[82]

Apparently the Sears example is no fluke. Other companies have found poorly implemented incentive pay plans can hurt rather than help. Green Giant, for example,

EXHIBIT 9.8
**Sears Makes
a Mistake**

Strategic Goal	Supporting Compensation Component as Translated for Tire and Auto Centers	Unintended Consequence
Cut costs by $600 million, provide facelift to stores, cut prices, make every employee focus on profits.	Set high quotas for generating dollars from repairs and back up with commissions.	The California Consumer Affairs Division went undercover posing as customers. On 34 of 38 undercover runs, Sears charged an average of $235 for unnecessary repairs.

used to pay a bonus based on insect parts screened in its pea-packing process. The goal, of course, was to cut the number of insect parts making their way into the final product (anyone planning on vegetables for dinner tonight?). Employees found a way to make this incentive system work for them. By bringing insect parts from home, inserting, and inspecting, their incentive dollars rose. Clearly, the program didn't work as intended. Experts contend this is evidence that the process wasn't managed well. What does this mean in terms of design?

DESIGNING A PAY-FOR-PERFORMANCE PLAN

A recent survey of HR professionals offers the following opinions about different reward systems and their effectiveness for motivating high performing employees (see Exhibit 9.9). As the pay model suggests, this effectiveness is dependent on three things: efficiency, equity, and compliance in designing a pay system.

Efficiency

Efficiency involves three general areas of concern.

Strategy

Does the pay-for-performance plan support corporate objectives? For example, is the plan cost-effective, or are we making payouts that bear no relation to improved performance on the bottom line? Similarly, does the plan help us improve quality of service? Some pay-for-performance plans are so focused on quantity of performance as a measure

EXHIBIT 9.9
**Overall
Prevalence
of Short- and
Long-Term
Incentive Plans
for Alternative
Reward Plans**

	Prevalence in Private Companies
Short-term incentives (STI)	79%
Bonus	95% (of those with STI)
Individual incentive	35%
Team/unit/small group	17%
Long-term incentives	35%

Source: WorldatWork and Vivien Consulting, "Private company incentive pay practices," 2007.

that we forget about quality. Defect rates rise. Customers must search for someone to handle a merchandise return. A number of things happen that aren't consistent with the emphasis on quality that top organizations insist upon.

The plan also should link well with HR strategy and objectives. If other elements of our total HR plan are geared to select, reinforce, and nurture risk-taking behavior, we don't want a compensation component that rewards the status quo.

Finally, we address the most difficult question of all—how much of an increase makes a difference? What does it take to motivate an employee? Is 4 percent, the recent average of pay increases, really enough to motivate higher performance?[83] While there are few hard data on this question, most experts agree that employees don't begin to notice payouts unless they are at least 10 percent, with 15 to 20 percent more likely to evoke the desired response.[84]

Structure

Is the structure of the organization sufficiently decentralized to allow different operating units to create flexible variations on a general pay-for-performance plan? For example, IBM adapted performance reviews to the different needs of different units, and the managers in them, resulting in a very flexible system. In this new system, midpoints for pay grades don't exist. Managers get a budget, some training on how to conduct reviews, and a philosophical mandate: Differentiate pay for stars relative to average performers, or risk losing stars. Managers are given a number of performance dimensions. Determining which dimensions to use for which employees is totally a personal decision. Indeed, managers who don't like reviews at all can input merit increases directly, anchored only by a brief explanation for the reason.[85] Different operating units may have different competencies and different competitive advantages. We don't want a rigid pay-for-performance system that detracts from these advantages, all in the name of consistency across divisions.

Standards

Operationally, the key to designing a pay-for-performance system rests on standards. Specifically, we need to be concerned about the following:

Objectives: Are they specific yet flexible? Can employees see that their behavior influences their ability to achieve objectives (called the "line-of-sight" issue in industry)?

Measures: Do employees know what measures (individual appraisals, peer reviews of team performance, corporate financial measures, etc.) will be used to assess whether performance is sufficiently good to merit a payout?

Eligibility: How far down the organization will the plan run? Companies like PepsiCo and Starbucks believe all employees should be included. Others think only top management can see how their decisions affect the bottom line.

Funding: Will you fund the program out of extra revenue generated above and beyond some preset standard? If so, what happens in a bad year? Many employees become disillusioned when they feel they have worked harder but economic conditions or poor management decisions conspire to cut or eliminate bonuses.

Equity/Fairness

Our second design objective is to ensure that the system is fair to employees. Two types of fairness are concerns for employees. The first type is fairness in the *amount* that is distributed to employees. Not surprisingly, this type of fairness is labeled *distributive justice*.[86] Does an employee view the amount of compensation received as fair? As we discussed earlier in the section on equity theory, perceptions of fairness here depend on the amount of compensation actually received relative to input (e.g., productivity) compared against some relevant standard. Notice that several of the components of this equity equation are frustratingly removed from the control of the typical supervisor or manager working with employees. A manager has little influence over the size of an employee's paycheck. It is influenced more by external market conditions, pay-policy decisions of the organization, and the occupational choice made by the employee. Indeed, recent research suggests that employees may look at the relative distribution of pay. For example, some major league baseball teams have met with mixed success in trying to buy stars via the free-agent market. Some speculate that this creates feelings of inequity among other players. Some evidence suggests that narrower ranges for pay differences may actually have positive impacts on overall organizational performance.[87]

Managers have somewhat more control over the second type of equity. Employees are also concerned about the fairness of the *procedures* used to determine the amount of rewards they receive. Employees expect *procedural justice*.[88] Evidence suggests that organizations using fair procedures and having supervisors who are viewed as fair in the means they use to allocate rewards are perceived as more trustworthy and command higher levels of commitment.[89] Some research even suggests that employee satisfaction with pay may depend more on the procedures used to determine pay than on the actual level distributed.[90]

A key element in fairness is communications. Employees want to know in advance what is expected of them. They want the opportunity to provide input into the standards or expectations. And, if performance is judged lacking relative to these standards, they want a mechanism for appeals. In a union environment, this is the grievance procedure. Something similar needs to be set up in a nonunion environment.[91] As evidence, only 15 percent of employees who feel well informed indicate they are considering leaving their company. This jumps to 41 percent who think about leaving if they feel poorly informed about the way the pay system operates.[92]

Compliance

Finally, our pay-for-performance system should comply with existing laws. We want a reward system that maintains and enhances the reputation of our firm. Think about the companies that visit a college campus. For some of these companies, students naturally gravitate to interview opportunities—the interview schedule fills very quickly indeed. Why? Because of reputation.[93] We tend to undervalue the reward value of a good reputation. To guard this reputation, we need to make sure we comply with compensation laws.

Your **Turn**

Burger Boy

This is a true case. Jerry Newman (second author of this book) spent 14 months working in seven fast-food restaurants (two McDonald's, two Burger Kings, one each of Wendy's, Arby's, and Krystal (a southern chain similar to White Castle). He wrote about his experiences in the book *My Secret Life on the McJob* (McGraw-Hill, 2007). This is a description of events in one store . . . labeled here Burger Boy.

Person	Job Title	Base Salary	Other Wage Information	Avg Hrs/Wk
Otis	Assistant Store Manager	34k	Exempt (no overtime pay)	55
Leon	Shift Supervisor	23k	Nonexempt	55
Marge	Crew Member (fries)	$6.25/hr	Nonexempt	30
Me	Cook	$6.50/hr	Nonexempt	20
Chuck	Drive-thru Window	$7.00/hr	Nonexempt	30
Lucy	Sandwich Assembler	$7.00/hr	Nonexempt	35

It's a hot Friday in Florida, and lunch rush is just beginning. Chuck is working the pay window and is beginning to grouse about the low staffing for what is traditionally the busiest day of the week. "Where the heck is LaVerne?" he yells to no one. Chuck has only worked here for six weeks, but has prior experience at another Burger Boy. Marge, typically working the fries station (the easiest job at this Burger Boy), has been pressed into service on the front drive-thru window because 2 of 10 scheduled workers have called in sick. She can handle the job when business is slow, but she clearly is getting flustered as more cars enter the drive-thru line. I'm cooking, my third day on the job, but my first one alone. I've worked the grill for 10 years as a volunteer at Aunt Rosie's Womens Fastpitch Softball Tournament, but nothing prepared me for the volume of business we will do today. By 11:30 I've got the grill full of burgers. Lucy is going full speed trying to keep up with sandwich assembly and wrapping. She's the best assembler the place has, and would be a supervisor if she could just keep from self-destructing. Yesterday she lit a can of vegetable spray with a lighter and danced around the floor, an arc of flame shooting out from the can. She thinks this is funny. Everyone else thinks she's nuts. But she's rumored to be a friend of the manager, Nancy, so everyone keeps quiet.

"Marge, you've got to get moving girl. The line's getting longer. Move girl, move," shouts Otis, unfazed by the fact that Marge really isn't good enough to work the window, and clearly is showing signs of heavy stress. "I'll help her," chimes in Chuck. "I can work the pay window, then run up front to help Marge when she gets way behind." Otis says nothing and goes back to the office where he begins to count the morning receipts for the breakfast rush.

My job as cook also includes cooking baked potatoes in the oven and cooking chicken in the pressure cooker, so I have little time to do anything besides stay on top of my job. Finally, at noon, in comes Leon. He will replace Otis at three, but for now he is a sorely needed pair of hands on the second sandwich assembly board. Leon looks over at me and shouts above the din, "Good job, Jerry. Keeping up with Friday rush on your third cooking day. Good job." That's the first compliment I've received in the two weeks I've worked here, so I smile at the unexpected recognition. By 12:30 we're clearly all frazzled. Even with Chuck's help, Marge falls farther behind. She is now making mistakes on orders in efforts to get food out the drive-thru window quickly. Otis comes barreling up front from the office and shouts for everyone to hear: "We're averaging 3:05 (minutes) on drive time. Someone's in trouble if we don't get a move on." He says this while staring directly at Marge. Everyone knows that drive times (the amount of time from an order being placed until the customer receives it) should be about 2:30 (two minutes, thirty seconds). In my head I do some mental math. The normal staffing for a Friday is 13 people (including management). Because of absenteeism we're working with eight, including Otis and Leon. By noon Marge is crying, but she stays at it. And finally things begin to slow at 1 p.m. We know rush is officially over when Lucy tells Leon she's "going to the can." This starts a string of requests for rest breaks that are interrupted by Otis, "All right, for God's sake. Here's the order of breaks." He points to people in turn, with me being next to last, and Marge going last. After Lucy, Chuck is second, and the others fill in the gap ahead of me. When my turn finally comes I resolve to break quickly, taking only 6 minutes instead of the allotted 10. When I return Otis sneers at me and chides, "What was that, about a half hour?" I snap, I'm angry, and let him know it. "If I could tell time, would I be working fast food?" Now I realize I've done the unforgivable, sassing my boss. But I'm upset, and I don't care. My only care is I've just claimed fast food is work for dummies, and I absolutely don't believe this. But as I said, I was mad. Otis looks me over, staring at my face, and finally decides to let out a huge bellow, "You're ok, Newman. Good line!"

It's now 2:10 and Marge has told Otis twice that she has to leave. Her agreement with the store manager at the time of hire was that she would leave no later than 2:30 every day. Her daughter gets off the school bus at 2:45, and she must meet her at that time. Otis ignores her first request, and is nowhere to be seen when, at 2:25, Marge looks around frantically and pleads to no one in particular, "What should I do? I have to leave." I look at her and declare, "Go. I will tell Otis when he comes out again." Marge leaves. Ten minutes later we have a mini-surge of customers. Leon yells, "Where the hell is Marge? That's it; she's out of here tomorrow. No more chances for her." When he's done ranting, I explain the details of Marge's plight. Angrily Leon stomps back to the manager's office and confronts Otis. The yelling quickly reaches audible levels. Everyone in the store, customers included, hear what is quickly broadening into confrontations about other unresolved issues:

Leon: "I'm sick of coming in here and finding nothing stocked. Otis, it's your job to make sure the lunch shift (roughly 10 a.m.–2 p.m.) stocks items in their spare time. It never happens and I'm sick of it. Now you tell me you're leaving and sticking me with a huge stocking job."

Otis: "I'm sick of your whining, Leon. I work 50–60 hours a week. I'm sick of working 10–12 hours a day for crappy wages. You want things stocked . . . you do it. I'm going home and try to forget this place."

With that Otis drops what he has in his hands, a printout of today's receipts so far, and walks out the door. Leon swears, picks up the spreadsheet, and storms back to the office. I finish my shift, and happily go home. No more Burger Boy for this burger boy.

1. What appear to be the problems at this Burger Boy?
2. How many of these problems could be explained by compensation issues?
3. How many other problems could be lessened with diligent use of rewards other than pay?
4. Are hours of work a reward? What might explain why I was happy to be working 20 hours per week, but Chuck was unhappy with 30 hours per week? How might schedules be used as a reward?

Summary   Why not admit it? We don't know what makes people tick! Reading this chapter should prove that we have more questions unanswered than we have supposed truths. We know that employee performance depends upon some blend of skill, knowledge, and motivation. If any of these three ingredients is missing, performance is likely to be suboptimal. This chapter concentrates on the motivation component of this performance triangle. Rewards must help organizations attract and retain employees; they must make high performance an attractive option for employees; they must encourage employees to build new skills and gradually foster commitment to the organization. A tall order, you say! The problem is especially big because we are just starting to realize all the different things that can serve as rewards (or punishments) for employees. This chapter outlines 13 rewards and makes a strong case that fair administration of these rewards can lead a company to higher performance levels.

Review Questions

1. A father decides to put his two sons to work landscaping. The business involves going to a customer's home and providing landscaping services (cut grass, edge sidewalk, pull weeds in flower beds, prune bushes and trees, rake leaves). Rather than paying a flat wage, the father decides to pay an incentive according to the following schedule (average across all lawns).

Task	Piece Rate Incentive per Person	Physical Effort	Time to Complete per Person	Charge to Customer
Cut grass	$4	Easy	.4 hr	$30
Edge sidewalk	$1	Easy	.1 hr	$ 5
Pull weeds	$6	Very Hard	.5 hr	$40
Prune bushes, etc.	$5	Hard	.5 hr	$30
Rake leaves	$5	Hard	.5	$25

At the end of the second week under this arrangement the boys are quarreling with each other and not happy with their dad. All of the disagreements revolve around the incentive system. What might be the problems?

2. Father Michael's Wraps (pitas, wraps, flat breads) is experiencing turnover in the range of 100 percent. Most of this occurs in the first 18 months of employment. How would you determine if this turnover rate is high? How would you justify to your boss that lower turnover is strategically important? What would you look at in both pay and other forms of rewards to identify ways of reducing turnover? Justify your choices based on your reading of this chapter.

3. Restco Products makes pillows and blankets specifically for passengers on airliners. For the past 15 years, profits in the airline industry have been hugely variable, partially because of labor unrest, gas prices, 9/11, and so on. Restco has been tinkering with other kinds of "nap" opportunities tailored to rest homes and senior citizens in general. This experimentation makes current strategic objectives and goals quite ambiguous. What would you suggest would be a good compensation mix given this constellation of factors?

4. Companies focus heavily on cost-saving strategies to be competitive today. Identify both monetary and nonmonetary ways of cost saving that would be relevant to a compensation person's job.

5. You supervise in a company that is a low payer relative to competitors. What things do you have control over to increase the likelihood that workers will feel fairly treated?

Endnotes

1. Ingrid Smithey Fulmer, Barry Gerhart, and Kimberly Scott, "Are the 100 Best Better? An Empirical Investigation of the Relationship Between Being a Great Place to Work and Firm Performance," *Personnel Psychology* 56 (2003), pp. 965–993.

2. Bonnie G. Mani, "Performance Appraisal Systems, Productivity, and Motivation: A Case Study," *Public Personnel Management* 31(2) (2000), pp. 141–159; R. Mayer and J. Davis, "The Effect of the Performance Appraisal System on Trust for Management," *Journal of Applied Psychology* 84(1) (1999), pp. 123–136.

3. Barry Gerhart, Sara L. Rynes, and Ingrid Smithey Fulmer, "Pay and Performance: Individuals, Groups and Executives," in A. P. Brief and J. P. Walsh, *Academy of Management Annals,* Vol. 3. (Mahwah, NJ: Lawrence Erlbaum, forthcoming).

4. Bill Shaikin and Dylan Hern, "Manny Ramirez Suspended 50 Games for Positive Drug Test" *Los Angeles Times,* May 8, 2009, p. 1.

5. Sara L. Rynes, Kenneth G. Brown, and Amy E. Colbert, "Seven Common Misconceptions About Human Resource Practices: Research Findings Versus Practitioner Beliefs," *Academy of Management Executive* 16(3) (2002), pp. 92–102; Brian Becker and Barry Gerhart, "The Impact of Human Resource Management on Organizational Performance: Progress and Prospects," *Academy of Management Journal 39*(4) (1996), pp. 779–801.

6. Towers Perrin, "Towers Perrin Survey Finds That the Economy Is Forcing Companies to Evaluate Compensation and Incentive Plans," www.towersperrin.com/tp/showdctmdoc.jsp?country=global&url=Master_Brand_2/USA/Press_Releases/2008/20081107/2008_11_07.htm., June 27, 2009.

7. Sue Kirchoff and Del Jones, "Caterpillar Joins Other Companies Cutting Pay," Reuters, December 23, 2008, p. B1; Jena McGregor, "Cutting Salaries Instead of Jobs." *BusinessWeek,* June 8, 2009, pp. O46–O48.

8. This table extrapolates the findings from two studies: Matthew C. Bloom and George T. Milkovich, "The Relationship Among Risk, Incentive Pay, and Organizational Performance," *Academy of Management Journal* 14(3) (1998), pp. 283–297, and Anne Tsui, Jone L. Pearce, Lyman W. Porter, and Angela M. Tripoli, "Alternative Approaches to the Employee-Organization Relationship: Does Investment in Employees Pay Off?" *Academy of Management Journal* 40(5) (1997), pp. 1089–1121.

9. Anne Tsui, Jone L. Pearce, Lyman W. Porter, and Angela M. Tripoli, "Alternative Approaches to the Employee-Organization Relationship: Does Investment in Employees Pay Off?" *Academy of Management Journal* 40(5) (1997), pp. 1089–1121.

10. Kurt Badenhausen, "The World's Highest-Paid Athletes," *www.Forbes.com,* June 18, 2009.

11. A. Mamman, M. Sulaiman, and A. Fadel, "Attitude to Pay Systems: An Exploratory Study Within and Across Cultures," *International Journal of Human Resource Management* 7(1) (1996), pp. 101–121.

12. IOMA, "Are You Ready to Serve Cafeteria Style Comp?" *Pay for Performance Report,* June 2000, pp. 1, 13.

13. For an excellent discussion of recent developments in motivation theory, see the special topic forum, including the following articles in the 2004 [29(2)] issue of *Academy of*

Management Review: R. Steers, R. Mowday, and D. Shapiro, "The Future of Work Motivation," pp. 379–387; E. Locke and G. Latham, "What Should We Do about Motivation Theory? Six Recommendations for the Twenty-First Century," pp. 388–403; Y. Fried and L. H. Slowik, "Enriching Goal-Setting Theory With Time: An Integrated Approach," pp. 404–422; and M. Seo, L. Barrett, and J. Bartunek, "The Role of Affective Experience in Work Motivation," pp. 423–438.

14. Barry Gerhart, Sara L. Rynes, and Ingrid Smithey Fulmer, "Pay and Performance: Individuals, Groups and Executives," in A. P. Brief and J. P. Walsh, *Academy of Management Annals*, Vol. 3 (Mahwah, NJ: Lawrence Erlbaum, 2009).

15. J. S. Adams, "Toward an Understanding of Inequity," *Journal of Abnormal and Social Psychology* 67 (1963), pp. 422–436; J. S. Adams, "Injustice in Social Exchange," in L. Berkowitz, ed., *Advances in Experimental Social Psychology,* Vol. 2. (New York: Academic Press, 1965); R. Cosier and D. Dalton, "Equity Theory and Time: A Reformulation," *Academy of Management Review* 8 (1983), pp. 311–319.

16. B. Oviatt, "Agency and Transaction Cost Perspectives on the Manager-Shareholder Relationship: Incentives for Congruent Interests," *Academy of Management Review* 13 (1988), pp. 214–225.

17. D. Knight, C. Durham, E. A. Locke, "The Relationship of Team Goals, Incentives, and Efficacy to Strategic Risk, Tactical Implementation, and Performance," *Academy of Management Journal* 44(2) (2001), pp. 326–338.

18. E. A. Locke, K. N. Shaw, L. M. Saari, and G. P. Latham, "Goal Setting and Task Performance: 1969–1980," *Psychological Bulletin* 90 (1981), pp. 125–152.

19. M. R. Louis, B. Z. Posner, and G. N. Powell, "The Availability and Helpfulness of Socialization Practices," *Personnel Psychology* 36 (1983), pp. 857–866; E. H. Schein, "Organizational Socialization and the Profession of Management," *Industrial Management Review* 9 (1968), pp. 1–16.

20. P. Zingheim and J. Schuster, "Creating a High-Performance Culture by Really Paying for Performance," in IOMA, *Complete Guide to Best Practices in Pay for Performance,* 2005, pp 1.17–1.22.

21. E. L. Kersten, *The Art of Demotivation* (Austin, TX: Despair, 2005); IOMA, "Pay for Performance Report," *Pay for Performance Report,* January 1998, p. 8; P. Stang and B. Laird, "Working Women's Motivators," reported in *USA Today,* February 9, 1999, p. B1, for Nationwide Insurance/*Working WomenMagazine* Survey.

22. J. Tropman, *The Compensation Solution: How to Develop an Employee-Driven Rewards System* (Jossey-Bass: San Francisco, 2001).

23. E. L. Deci and R. M. Ryan, *Intrinsic Motivation and Self-Determination in Human Behavior* (New York: Plenum Press, 1985). Note, however, that the evidence is not very strong.

24. N. Stein, "America's Most Admired Companies," *Fortune,* March 3, 2003, pp. 81–87; J. Pfeffer, "Six Dangerous Myths about Pay," *Harvard Business Review,* May–June 1998, pp. 109–119.

25. K. Brown and V. Huber, "Lowering Floors and Raising Ceilings: A Longitudinal Assessment of the Effects of an Earnings-at-Risk Plan on Pay Satisfaction," *Personnel Psychology* 45 (1992), pp. 279–311.

26. Please note, though, most of the declines experienced in base pay have occurred since 1980.

27. IOMA, *Complete Guide to Best Practices in Pay for Performance* (Newark, NJ: BNA Subsidiaries, 2005), pp. 1.8–1.10; J. R. Schuster and P. K. Zingheim, *The New Pay: Linking Employee and Organizational Performance* (New York: Lexington Books, 1992).

28. E. J. Conlon and J. M. Parks, "Effects of Monitoring and Tradition on Compensation Arrangements: An Experiment With Principal-Agent Dyads," *Academy of Management Journal* 33 (1990), pp. 603–622.

29. Ibid.

30. D. M. Cable and T. A. Judge, "Pay Preferences and Job Search Decisions: A Person-Organization Fit Perspective," *Personnel Psychology* 47 (1994), pp. 317–348.

31. S. L. Rynes, K. G. Brown, and A. E. Colbert, "Seven Common Misconceptions About Human Resource Practices: Research Findings Versus Practitioner Beliefs," *Academy of Management Executive* 16(2) (2002), pp. 92–103; E. E. Lawler, *Pay and Organizational Effectiveness: A Psychological View* (New York: McGraw-Hill, 1971); E. E. Lawler and G. D. Jenkins, "Strategic Reward Systems" in M. D. Dunnette and L. M. Hough, eds., *Handbook of Industrial and Organizational Psychology* (Palo Alto, CA: Consulting Psychologist Press, 1992), pp. 1009–1055; W. Mobley, *Employee Turnover: Causes, Consequences and Control* (Reading, MA: Addison-Wesley, 1982).

32. D. M. Cable and T. A. Judge, "Pay Preferences and Job Search Decisions: A Person-Organization Fit Perspective," *Personnel Psychology* 47 (1994), pp. 317–348.

33. Ibid.

34. D. B. Turban and T. L. Keon, "Organizational Attractiveness: An Interactionist Perspective," *Journal of Applied Psychology* 78 (1993), pp. 184–193.

35. D. M. Cable and T. A. Judge, "Pay Preferences and Job Search Decisions: A Person-Organization Fit Perspective," *Personnel Psychology* 47 (1994), pp. 317–348; A. Kohn, *Punished by Rewards: The Trouble With Gold Stars, Incentive Plans, A's, Praise and Other Bribes* (Boston: Houghton-Mifflin, 1993).

36. Cable & Judge, ibid.

37. Cable and Judge, ibid.

38. T. R. Zenger, "Why Do Employers Only Reward Extreme Performance? Examining the Relationships Among Performance Pay and Turnover," *Administrative Science Quarterly* 37 (1992), pp. 198–219.

39. Chi-Sum Wong and Kenneth Law, "The Effects of Leader and Follower Emotional Intelligence on Performance and Attitude: An Exploratory Study," *Leadership Quarterly* 13(3) (2002), pp. 243–274; David A. Harrison, Meghna Virick, and Sonja William, "Working Without a Net: Time, Performance, and Turnover Under Maximally Contingent Rewards," *Journal of Applied Psychology* 81(4) (1996), pp. 331–345.

40. M. R. Carrell and J. E. Dettrich, "Employee Perceptions of Fair Treatment," *Personnel Journal* 55 (1976), pp. 523–524.

41. A. Weiss, "Incentives and Worker Behavior: Some Evidence," in H. R. Nalbantian, ed., *Incentives, Cooperation and Risk Sharing* (Totowa, NJ: Rowan & Littlefield, 1987), pp. 137–150.

42. Susan Warren, "The Transient Workers," *The Wall Street Journal,* October 28, 2002, p. R4; R. Heneman and T. Judge, "Compensation Attitudes: A Review and Recommendations for Future Research," in S. l. Rynes and B. Gerhart, eds., *Compensation in Organizations: Progress and Prospects* (San Francisco: New Lexington Press, 1999).

43. P. W. Hom and R. W. Griffeth, *Employee Turnover* (Cincinnati, OH: Southwestern, 1995); M. Kim, "Where the Grass Is Greener: Voluntary Turnover and Wage Premiums," *Industrial Relations* 38 (October 1999), p. 584.

44. D. M. Cable and T. A. Judge, "Pay Preferences and Job Search Decisions: A Person-Organization Fit Perspective," *Personnel Psychology* 47 (1994), pp. 317–348.

45. S. Salamin, P. Hom, "In Search of the Elusive U-Shaped Performance-Turnover Relationship: Are High Performing Swiss Bankers More Liable to Quit? *Journal of Applied Psychology* 90(6) (2005), pp. 1–9.

46. A. Kohn, *Punished by Rewards: The Trouble With Gold Stars, Incentive Plans, A's, Praise and Other Bribes* (Boston: Houghton-Mifflin, 1993).

47. P. Zingheim and J. R. Shuster, *Pay People Right* (San Francisco: Jossey-Bass, 2000); J. Boudreau, M. Sturman, C. Trevor, and B. Gerhart, "Is It Worth It to Win the Talent War? Using Turnover Research to Evaluate the Utility of Performance-Based Pay," Working Paper 99–06, Center for Advanced Human Resource Studies, Cornell University, 2000.

48. Allison Perlik, "Payback Time," *Restaurants and Institutions,* Chicago, January 15, 2003, pp. 22–29.

49. IOMA, "Top-Notch Retention Strategies for These Tight-Money Times," *Pay for Performance Report* (Newark, NJ: BNA Subidiaries, 2002), p. 2.

50. Claudia Z. Poster, "Retaining Key People in Troubled Companies," *Compensation and Benefits Review,* January–February 2002, pp. 7–11.

51. AAmer Madhani, "ROTC Recruits Paid to Command New Languages." *USA Today,* December 23, 2008, p. B1.

52. IOMA, "Report on Salary Surveys," BNA Subsidiaries, Newark: NJ, May 1997, p. 14; Kevin J. Parent and Caroline L. Weber, "Does Paying for Knowledge Pay Off?" *Compensation and Benefits Review,* September 1994, pp. 44–50.

53. J. Pfeffer, *The Human Equation: Building Profits by Putting People First.* (Boston: Harvard Business School Press, 1998).

54. R. L. Heneman, *Strategic Reward Management: Design, Implementation, and Evaluation* (Greenwich, CT: Information Age Publishing, 2002); W. N. Cooke, "Employee Participation Programs, Group Based Incentives, and Company Performance," *Industrial and Labor Relations Review* 47 (1994), pp. 594–610; G. W. Florkowski, "The Organizational Impact of Profit Sharing," *Academy of Management Review* 12 (1987), pp. 622–636; R. Heneman, *Merit Pay: Linking Pay Increases to Performance Ratings* (Reading, MA: Addison-Wesley, 1992); J. L. McAdams and E. J. Hawk, *Organizational Performance and Rewards* (Phoenix, AZ: American Compensation Association, 1994); D. McDonaly and A. Smith, "A Proven Connection: Performance Management and Business Results," *Compensation and Benefits Review,* January–February 1995, pp. 59–64; G. T. Milkovich, "Does Performance-Based Pay Really Work? Conclusions Based on the Scientific Research," unpublished document for 3M, 1994; G. Milkovich and C. Milkovich, "Strengthening the Pay Performance Relationship: The Research," *Compensation and Benefits Review,* May–June 1992, pp. 53–62.

55. Mark A. Huselid, "The Impact of Human Resource Management Practices on Turnover, Productivity, and Corporate Financial Performance," *Academy of Management Journal* 38(3) (1995), pp. 635–672.

56. *Merit Pay: Linking Pay Increases to Performance Ratings* (Reading, MA: Addison-Wesley, 1992).

57. W. N. Cooke, "Employee Participation Programs, Group Based Incentives and Company Performance: A Union–Non Union Comparison," *Industrial and Labor Relations Review* 47(4) (1994), pp. 594–610.

58. D. L. Kruse, *Profit Sharing: Does It Make a Difference?* (Kalamazoo, MI: Upjohn Institute, 1993).

59. B. Gerhart and G. Milkovich, "Organizational Differences in Managerial Compensation and Financial Performance," *Academy of Management Journal* 33 (1990), pp. 663–690.

60. A. Kohn, *Punished by Rewards. The Trouble with Gold Stars, Incentive Plans, A's, Praise and Other Bribes* (Boston: Houghton-Mifflin, 1993).

61. E. Deci, R. Ryan, and R. Koestner, "A Meta-Analytic Review of Experiments Examining the Effects of Extrinsic Rewards on Intrinsic Motivation," *Psychological Bulletin,* 125(6) (1999), pp. 627–668.

62. R. McKensie and D. Lee, *Managing Through Incentives* (New York: Oxford University Press, 1998); R. Eisenberger and J. Cameron, "Detrimental Effects of Rewards," *American Psychologist,* November 1996, pp. 1153–1156.

63. The second author knows this all too well, based on the daily venting of his daughter, a short-term Target employee.

64. L. Dyer, D. P. Schwab, and R. D. Theriault, "Managerial Perceptions Regarding Salary Increase Criteria," *Personnel Psychology* 29 (1976), pp. 233–242.

65. J. Fossum and M. Fitch, "The Effects of Individual and Contextual Attributes on the Sizes of Recommended Salary Increases," *Personnel Psychology* 38 (1985), pp. 587–603.

66. IOMA, *Complete Guide to Best Practices in Pay for Performance,* (Newark, NJ: BNA Subsidiaries, 2005), pp. 1–5.

67. L. V. Jones and T. E. Jeffrey, "A Quantitative Analysis of Expressed Preferences for Compensation Plans," *Journal of Applied Psychology* 48 (1963), pp. 201–210; Opinion Research Corporation, *Wage Incentives* (Princeton, NJ: Opinion Research Corporation, 1946); Opinion Research Corporation, *Productivity from the Worker's Standpoint* (Princeton, NJ: Opinion Research Corporation, 1949).

68. D. Koys, T. Keaveny, and R. Allen, "Employment Demographics and Attitudes That Predict Preferences for Alternative Pay Increase Policies," *Journal of Business and Psychology* 4 (1989), pp. 27–47.

69. B. Major, "Gender, Justice and the Psychology of Entitlement," *Review of Personality and Social Psychology* 7 (1988), pp. 124–148.

70. IOMA, "Incentive Pay Programs and Results: An Overview," (Newark, NJ: Institute of Management and Administration, May 1996), p. 11; G. Green, "Instrumentality Theory of Work Motivation," *Journal of Applied Psychology* 53 (1965), pp. 1–25; R. D. Pritchard, D. W. Leonard, C. W. Von Bergen, Jr., and R. J. Kirk, "The Effects of Varying Schedules of Reinforcement on Human Task Performance," *Organizational Behavior and Human Performance* 16 (1976), pp. 205–230; D. P. Schwab and L. Dyer, "The Motivational Impact of a Compensation System on Employee Performance," *Organizational Behavior and Human Performance* 9 (1973), pp. 215–225; D. Schwab, "Impact of Alternative Compensation Systems on Pay Valence and Instrumentality Perceptions," *Journal of Applied Psychology* 58 (1973), pp. 308–312.

71. Mark A. Huselid, "The Impact of Human Resource Management Practices on Turnover, Productivity, and Corporate Financial Performance," *Academy of Management Journal* 38(3) (1995), pp. 635–673.

72. Barry Gerhart, Sara L. Rynes, and Ingrid Smithey Fullmer, "Pay and Performance: Individuals, Groups and Executives," in A. P. Brief and J. P. Walsh, *Academy of Management Annals,* Vol. 3 (Newark, NJ: Lawrence Erlbaum, 2009).

73. E. A. Locke, D. B. Feren, V. M. McCaleb, K. N. Shaw, and A. T. Denny, "The Relative Effectiveness of Four Methods of Motivating Employee Performance" in K. D. Duncan, M. M. Gruenberg, and D. Wallis, eds., *Changes in Working Life* (New York: Wiley, 1980), pp. 363–388.

74. B. Gerhart and G. T. Milkovich, "Employee Compensation: Research and Practice," in M. D. Dunnette and L. M. Hough, eds., *Handbook of Industrial & Organizational Psychology,* 2nd ed. (Palo Alto, CA: Consulting Psychologists Press, 1992).

75. C. Q. Trank, S. L. Rynes, and R. D. Bretz, Jr., "Attracting Applicants in the War for Talent: Differences in Work Preferences Among High Achievers," *Journal of Business and Psychology* 16 (2001), pp. 331–345.

76. A. J. Nyberg, I. S. Fulmer, B. Gerhart, and M. A. Carpenter, "The Future of Agency Theory in Executive Compensation Research: Separating Fact from Fiction," unpublished working paper, 2008.

77. Mason Carpenter and W. M. Gerard Sanders, "Top Management Team Compensation: The Missing Link Between CEO Pay and Firm Performance?" *Strategic Management Journal* 23(4) (April 2002), pp. 367–375; Barry Gerhart, "Pay Strategy and Firm Performance," in S. Rynes and B. Gerhart, eds., *Compensation in Organizations: Progress and Prospects.* (San Francisco: New Lexington Press, 1999).

78. W. N. Cooke, "Employee Participation Programs, Group-Based Incentives and Company Performance: A Union–Non Union Comparison," *Industrial and Labor Relations Review* 47(4) (1994), pp. 594–610; D. L. Kruse, *Profit Sharing: Does It Make a Difference?* (Kalamazoo, MI: Upjohn Institute, 1993); G. T. Milkovich, "Does Performance-Based Pay Really Work?"*Journal of Human Resources,* 27(2), 1998, pp. 23–31; M. M. Petty, B. Singleton, and D. W. Connell, "An Experimental Evaluation of an Organizational Incentive Plan in the Electric Utility Industry," *Journal of Applied Psychology* 77 (1992), pp. 427–436; J. R. Schuster, "The Scanlon Plan: A Longitudinal Analysis," *Journal of Applied Behavioral Science* 20 (1984), pp. 23–28.

79. M. M. Petty, B. Singleton, and D. W. Connell, "An Experimental Evaluation of an Organizational Incentive Plan in the Electric Utility Industry," *Journal of Applied Psychology* 77 (1992), pp. 427–436; M. M. Petty, B. Singleton, and D. W. Connell, "An Experimental Evaluation of an Organizational Incentive Plan in the Electric Utility Industry," *Journal of Applied Psychology* 77 (1992), pp. 427–436.

80. J. McAdams and E. Hawk, "Organizational Performance and Rewards," *ACA Journal* 3(3) (1994), pp. 28–34.

81. B. Gerhart and G. Milkovich, "Organizational Differences in Managerial Compensation and Financial Performance," *Academy of Management Journal* 33 (1990), pp. 663–690.

82. K. Kelly and E. Schine, "How Did Sears Blow This Gasket?" *BusinessWeek,* June 29, 1992, p. 38.

83. Richard Metcalf, "A Modest Raise," *Albuquerque Tribune,* October 6, 2002, p. C1.

84. IOMA, "When Are Bonuses High Enough to Improve Performance?" *IOMA* (Newark, NJ: Institute of Management and Administration, November 1996), p. 12.

85. A. Richter, "Paying the People in Black at Big Blue," *Compensation and Benefits Review,* May/June 1998, pp. 51–59.

86. John Thibaut and Laurens Walker, *Procedural Justice: A Psychological View* (Hillsdale, NJ: Wiley, 1975).

87. M. Bloom, "The Performance Effects of Pay Dispersion on Individuals and Organizations," *Academy of Management Journal* 4(1) (1999), pp. 25–40.

88. Joel Brockner, "Making Sense of Procedural Fairness: How High Procedural Fairness Can Reduce or Heighten the Influence of Outcome Favorability," *Academy of Management Review* 27(1) (2002), pp. 58–76.

89. Robert Folger and Mary Konovsky, "Effects of Procedural and Distributive Justice on Reactions to Pay Raise Decisions," *Academy of Management Journal* 32(1) (March 1989), pp. 155–130.

90. S. Alexander and M. Ruderman, "The Role of Procedural and Distributive Justice in Organizational Behavior," *Social Justice Research* 1 (1987), pp. 177–198.

91. G. S. Leventhal, J. Karuza, and W. R. Fry, "Beyond Fairness: A Theory of Allocation Preferences," in G. Mikula, ed., *Justice and Social Interaction* (New York: Springer Verlag, 1980), pp. 167–218.

92. IOMA, *Complete Guide to Best Practices in Pay for Performance* (Newark: NJ: Institute of Management and Administration, 2005).

93. K. B. Stone, B. A. Backhaus, and K. Heiner, "Exploring the Relationship Between Corporate Social Performance and Employer Attractiveness," *Business and Society,* September 2002, pp. 28–41.

Pay-for-Performance Plans

Chapter Outline

What Is a Pay-for-Performance Plan?

Does Variable Pay Improve Performance Results? The General Evidence

Specific Pay-for-Performance Plans: Short Term

    Merit Pay

    Lump-Sum Bonuses

    Individual Spot Awards

    Individual Incentive Plans

    Individual Incentive Plans: Advantages and Disadvantages

    Individual Incentive Plans: Examples

Team Incentive Plans: Types

    Comparing Group and Individual Incentive Plans

    Large Group Incentive Plans

    Gain-Sharing Plans

    Profit-Sharing Plans

    Earnings-at-Risk Plans

    Group Incentive Plans: Advantages and Disadvantages

    Group Incentive Plans: Examples

Explosive Interest in Long-Term Incentive Plans

    Employee Stock Ownership Plans (ESOPs)

    Performance Plans (Performance Share and Performance Unit)

    Broad-Based Option Plans (BBOPs)

    Combination Plans: Mixing Individual and Group

Your Turn: Incentives in the Clubhouse

Appendix 10-A: Gain-Sharing Plan at Dresser Rand

Appendix 10-B: Profit-Sharing (401k) at Walgreens

WHAT IS A PAY-FOR-PERFORMANCE PLAN?

Good question! Many different compensation practices are lumped under the name **pay-for-performance.** Listen long enough and you will hear about **incentive plans, variable pay plans, compensation at risk, earnings at risk, success sharing, risk sharing,** and others. Sometimes these names are used interchangeably. They shouldn't be. The major thing all these names have in common is a shift in thinking about compensation. We used to think of pay as primarily an entitlement. If you went to work and did well enough to avoid being fired, you were entitled to the same size check as everyone else doing the same job as you. Pay-for-performance plans signal a movement away from entitlement . . . sometimes a very *slow* movement toward pay that varies with some measure of individual or organizational performance. Of the pay components we discussed in Chapter 9, only base pay and across-the-board increases don't fit the pay-for-performance category. Curiously, though, many of the surveys on pay for performance tend to omit the grandfather of all these plans, **merit pay.**

317

EXHIBIT 10.1   Use of Different Variable Pay Plan Types

Type of Plan	Percent of Companies With Plan				
	1996	1998	1999	2002	2007
Special-recognition plans	44	51	59	34	72
Stock option plans	21	46	43	40	
Individual incentive plans	17	35	39	38	49
Cash profit sharing	22	22	23	18	16
Gainsharing plans	16	20	18	11	10
Team awards	13	17	15	8	32

Source: 2007 data are from US Compensation Planning Survey, Mercer Human Resource Consulting; 2005 data are from *www.hewitt.com* as reported in IOMA, *Complete Guide to Best Practices in Pay for Performance,* 2005, pp. 1–8; 2002 data are from IOMA, "Latest Data—What's Hot and What's Not in PFP," *Pay for Performance Report,* May 2002, p. 11, and IOMA, "Variable Pay Popularity," *Pay for Performance Report,* January 2003, p. 8; 1996–1999 data are from IOMA, "The Goods and Evils of Variable-Based Pay," *Pay for Performance Report,* July 2000, p. 12.

Despite this omission, merit pay is still a pay-for-performance plan used for more than three-quarters of all exempt, clerical, and administrative employees.[1] In comparison, variable pay of some form (individual or group incentive pay) is offered by 78 percent of all companies, up from 51 percent in 1991 (see Exhibit 10.1 for other forms of variable pay).[2]

Exhibit 10.1 illustrates the wide variety of variable-pay plans in use today. What used to be primarily a compensation tool for top management is gradually becoming more prevalent for lower-level employees, too. Exhibit 10.2 indicates that variable pay is commanding a larger share of total compensation for all employee groups.

The greater interest in variable pay probably can be traced to two trends. First, the increasing competition from foreign producers forces American firms to cut costs and/or increase productivity. Well-designed variable-pay plans have a proven track record in motivating better performance and helping cut costs. Plus, variable pay is, by definition, a variable cost. No profits, or poor profits, means no extra pay beyond base pay—when times are bad, compensation is lower.[3] Second, today's fast-paced business environment means that workers must be willing to adjust what they do and how they do it. There are new technologies, new work processes, and new work relationships. All these require workers to adapt in new ways and with a speed that is unparalleled. Failure to move quickly means market share goes to competitors. If this happens, workers face possible layoffs and terminations. To avoid this scenario, compensation experts are focusing on ways to design reward systems so that workers will be able—and willing—to move quickly into new jobs and new ways of performing old jobs. The

EXHIBIT 10.2
Base Versus Variable Pay

	Percent of Total Compensation Today		
	2004	2005	2009 (projected)
Variable pay as percentage of payroll	9.5%	11.4%	11.3%

Sources: 2009 data are from *Report on Salary Surveys,* IOMA, July 2008; 2005 data are from *www.hewitt.com* survey as reported in IOMA.

ability and incentive to do this come partially from reward systems that more closely link worker interests with the objectives of the company.[4]

DOES VARIABLE PAY IMPROVE PERFORMANCE RESULTS? THE GENERAL EVIDENCE

As the evidence pointed out in Chapter 9, pay-for-performance plans, those that introduce variability into the level of pay you receive, seem to have a positive impact on performance if designed well. Notice that we have qualified our statement that variable-pay plans can be effective *if they are designed well*. In the next sections, we talk about issues in design and the impacts they can have.

SPECIFIC PAY-FOR-PERFORMANCE PLANS: SHORT TERM

Merit Pay

A **merit pay** system links increases in base pay (called *merit increases*) to how highly employees are rated on a performance evaluation. Chapter 11 covers performance evaluation, but as a simple illustration consider the following typical merit pay setup:

	Well Above Average	Above Average	Average	Below Average	Well Below Average
Performance rating	1	2	3	4	5
Merit pay increase	5%	4%	3%	1%	0%

At the end of a performance year, the employee is evaluated, usually by the direct supervisor. The performance rating, 1 to 5 in the above example, determines the size of the increase added into base pay. This last point is important. In effect, what you do this year in terms of performance is rewarded *every year* you remain with your employer. By building into base pay, the dollar amount, just like the Energizer bunny, keeps on going! With compounding, this can amount to tens of thousands of dollars over an employee's work career.[5]

Increasingly, merit pay is under attack. Not only is it expensive, but many argue it doesn't achieve the desired goal: improving employee and corporate performance.[6] In a thorough review of merit pay literature, though, Heneman concludes that merit pay does have a small, but significant, impact on performance.[7] High performance ratings are nearly always statistically related to high merit increases and the reverse holds too. Departments and strategic business units with better merit pay programs have higher subsequent performance.[8] And removal of merit pay appears to result in lower subsequent performance, as well as lower satisfaction among top performers. A final argument for merit pay centers on the sorting effect we discuss throughout our sections on variable pay impacts. People who don't want to have their pay tied to performance don't accept jobs at such companies or leave when pay for performance is implemented. This sorting leaves a residual workforce that is more productive and more responsive to merit rewards.[9]

Interestingly, some of the most exciting experiments with merit pay are taking place in the public sector. The Office of Personnel Management (OPM), a huge federal bureaucracy, proposed some years ago to introduce pay for performance into the white-collar pay system.[10] Flash forward in time, though, and it appears some of the problems OPM is experiencing with pay for performance are very similar to the experiences in the private sector. Over 95 percent of employees were being rated as average or better. In the senior employee ranks, 84 percent were rated at the highest level. The OPM is now monitoring rankings, and that figure has fallen to 59 percent.[11] While it will take a near miracle to change the culture and management processes needed to facilitate merit pay (e.g., a performance management system that is accepted as fair), the OPM seems intent on shaking up the system. Meanwhile, at the state level, public schools in Minnesota, Cincinnati, Denver, and Philadelphia are leading the way to merit pay for teachers.[12] In Cincinnati, for example, teachers are held accountable for things they control: good professional practices. Teachers argue they should be held to standards similar to doctors: not a promise of a long healthy life but a promise that the highest professional standards will be followed. To assess teacher professional practices, in Cincinnati six evaluations are conducted over the school year, four by a trained teacher evaluator (essentially a trained teacher) and two by a building administrator. The size of pay increases is directly linked to performance during these observational reviews.[13] Maybe because of these pioneers, governors in 20 other states have recently announced changes in the way teachers are paid, including much better links of pay to teacher performance.[14] In another vein, the public sector is also experimenting with bonuses for better student test scores. Teachers who show improved student scores can receive up to $8,000 in annual bonuses in Chicago and up to $15,000 in Nashville.[15]

If we want merit pay to live up to its potential, it needs to be managed better.[16] This requires a complete overhaul of the way we allocate raises: improving the accuracy of performance ratings, allocating enough merit money to truly reward performance, and making sure the size of the merit increase differentiates across performance levels. To illustrate the latter point, consider the employee who works hard all year, earns a 5 percent increase as our guidelines above indicate, and compares herself with the average performer who coasts to a 3 percent increase. First we take out taxes on that extra 2 percent. Then we spread the raise out over 52 paychecks. It's only a slight exaggeration to suggest that the extra money won't pay for a good cup of coffee. Unless we make the reward difference larger for every increment in performance, many employees are going to say, "Why bother?"

Lump-Sum Bonuses

Lump-sum bonuses (or awards) are thought to be a substitute for merit pay. Based on employee or company performance, employees receive an end-of-year bonus that does not build into base pay. Because employees must earn this increase every year, it is viewed as less of an entitlement than merit pay. As Exhibit 10.3 indicates, lump-sum bonuses can be considerably less expensive than merit pay over the long run.

Notice how quickly base pay rises under a merit pay plan. After just five years, base pay is almost $14,000 higher than it is under a lump-sum bonus plan. It should be no surprise that cost-conscious firms report switching to lump-sum pay. It also should be

EXHIBIT 10.3
Relative Cost Comparisons

	Merit Pay		Lump-Sum Bonus
Base pay	$50,000		$50,000
Year 1 payout 5%	(2,500)	5%	(2,500)
New base pay	52,500		50,000
Extra cost total	2,500		2,500
Year 2 payout 5%	($2,625 = .05 × 52,500)	5%	(2,500 =.05 × 50,000)
New base pay	55,125 (52,500 + 2,625)		50,000
Extra cost total	5,125		5,000
After 5 years:			
Year 5 payout	3,039		2,500
New base pay	63,814		50,000

no surprise that employees aren't particularly fond of lump-sum bonuses. After all, the intent of lump-sum bonuses is to cause shock waves in an entitlement culture. By giving lump-sum bonuses for several years, a company is essentially freezing base pay. Gradually this results in a repositioning relative to competitors. The message becomes loud and clear: "Don't expect to receive increases in base pay year after year—new rewards must be earned each year." Consider the bonus system developed by Prometric Thomson Learning call centers, which register candidates for computerized tests. The centers have very clear targets that yield specific employee bonuses, as shown in Exhibit 10.4. At Prometric, each day is a new day when it comes to earning bonuses.

Individual Spot Awards

Technically, **spot awards** should fall under pay-for-performance plans. About 35 percent of all companies use spot awards.[17] And an impressive 74 percent of companies in one survey reported that these awards were either highly or moderately effective.[18] Usually these payouts are awarded for exceptional performance, often on special projects or for performance that so exceeds expectations as to be deserving of an add-on bonus. The mechanics are simple: After the fact, someone in the organization alerts top management to the exceptional performance. If the company is large, there may be

EXHIBIT 10.4 **Customer Service Bonus Scheme at Prometric Thomson Learning Call Centers**

Performance Measure	Minimum Performance	Bonus	Target Performance	Bonus	Superior Performance	Bonus
Average call wait	<32 min/day	0.5%	<28 min/day	1%	<20 min/day	1.75%
Average talk time	3 min 50 sec	.5	<3 min 20 sec	1	3 min	1.75
Attendance	2 occurrences	.5	1 occurrence	1	0 occurrence	1.75
Quality	As monitored	.5	As monitored	1	As monitored	0.75
Total Bonus		2%		4%		7%

a formal mechanism for this recognition, and perhaps some guidelines on the size of the spot award (so named because it is supposed to be awarded "on the spot"). Smaller companies may be more casual about recognition and more subjective about deciding the size of the award. The University of California at San Francisco's Pharmacy School has a pretty typical spot award program. Awards of up to $225 are given for such behaviors as "effectively resolved a complaint situation," or "went beyond the expected by staying late to get a grant out on time."[19]

Individual Incentive Plans

These plans differ from the merit and lump sum payments because they offer a promise of pay for some objective, preestablished level of performance. For example, Cellular One pays its car phone installers on a very simple individual-based incentive system. Every customer complaint costs $10. Damage a car during installation and expect to lose $20. When this **reverse incentive plan** (penalty for poor performance rather than reward for good) was first implemented, vehicle damage dropped 70 percent. This is but one of many studies showing pretty conclusive evidence that individual incentive plans increase performance substantially.[20]

All incentive plans have one common feature: an established standard against which worker performance is compared to determine the magnitude of the incentive pay. For individual incentive systems, this standard is compared against individual worker performance. Because it's often difficult to find good, objective individual measures, individual incentive plans don't work for every job. How, for example, would you come up with an incentive plan for construction laborers. Maybe if they did the same thing all day the task wouldn't be difficult: Your goal is to dig 5 feet of trench, 2 feet wide by 18 inches deep, every hour. But construction laborers aren't limited to shovel jobs. They also help pour concrete, assist carpenters and masons framing buildings, etc. The job is too complex for an individual incentive plan. Even a repetitive job like working on an assembly line isn't well-suited to individual incentives. One of us (Newman) used to work on a Ford Assembly line building Lincolns. Even if we wanted to build faster to make more money, the line went by with a new car frame every 55 seconds. No room for individual differences here, we would argue.

Despite this constraint, a number of different individual incentive plans exist. Their differences can be reduced to variation along two dimensions and can be classified into one of four cells, as illustrated in Exhibit 10.5.

The first dimension on which incentive systems vary is in the **method of rate determination.** Plans set up a rate based either on units of production per time period or on time period per unit of production. On the surface, this distinction may appear trivial, but, in fact, the deviations arise because tasks have different cycles of operation.[21] Short-cycle tasks, those that are completed in a relatively short period of time, typically have as a standard a designated number of units to be produced in a given time period. For example, a book distributor we worked with had an incentive plan for packers. Number of books packed is a short cycle task, with only seconds taken to get a book from a supply stack and place in a shipping box. For long-cycle tasks, this would not be appropriate. It is entirely possible that only one task or some portion of it may be completed in a day. Consequently, for longer-cycle tasks, the standard is typically set

EXHIBIT 10.5
Individual
Incentive Plans

		Method of Rate Determination	
		Units of production per time period	Time period per unit of production
Relationship Between Production Level and Pay	Pay constant function of production level	(1) Straight piecework plan	(2) Standard hour plan
	Pay varies as function of production level	(3) Taylor differential piece-rate system Merrick multiple piece rate system	(4) Halsey 50-50 method Rowan plan Gantt plan

in terms of time required to complete one unit of production. Individual incentives are based on whether or not workers complete the task in the designated time period. Auto mechanics work off a blue book that tells how long, for example, a fuel injection system should take to replace. Finish faster than the allotted time and the full pay is awarded.

The second dimension on which individual incentive systems vary is the *specified relationship between production level and wages.* The first alternative is to tie wages to output on a one-to-one basis, so that wages are some constant function of production. In contrast, some plans vary wages as a function of production level. For example, one common alternative is to provide higher dollar rates for production above the standard than for production below the standard.

Each of the plans discussed in this section has as a foundation a standard level of performance determined by some form of time study or job analysis completed by an industrial engineer or trained personnel administrator. (Exhibit 10.6 provides an illustration of a time study.) The variations in these plans occur in either the way the standard is set or the way wages are tied to output. As in Exhibit 10.5, there are four general categories of plans:

1. *Cell 1:* The most frequently implemented incentive system is a **straight piece-work system** (see Exhibit 10.7). Rate determination is based on units of production per time period, and wages vary directly as a function of production level. The major advantages of this type of system are that it is easily understood by workers and, perhaps consequently, is more readily accepted than some of the other incentive systems.

2. *Cell 2:* Two relatively common plans set standards based on time per unit and tie incentives directly to level of output: (1) **standard hour plans** and (2) **Bedeaux plans.** A standard hour plan is a generic term for plans setting the incentive rate based on completion of a task in some expected time period. A common example we introduced earlier can be found in any neighborhood gasoline station or automobile repair shop. Let us assume that you need a new transmission. The estimate you receive for labor costs is based on the mechanic's hourly rate of pay, multiplied by a time estimate for

EXHIBIT 10.6 A Time Study

Task: Drilling Operation. Elements:

1. Move part from box to jig.
2. Position part in jig.
3. Drill hole in part.
4. Remove jig and drop part in chute.

Notes and Remarks	Observation Number	Elements			
		(1)	**(2)**	**(3)**	**(4)**
	1	.17	.22	.26	.29
	2	.17	.22	.27	.34
	3	.16	.21	.28	.39
	4	.18	.21	.29	.29
	5	.19	.20	.30	.36
	6	.25	.21	.31	.31
	7	.17	.23	.29	.33
Observed time		.17 (mode)	.21 (mode)	.29 (median)	.33 (mean)
Effort rating	(130%)	1.30	1.30	1.30	1.30
Corrected time		.2210	.2730	.3370	.4290
Total corrected time					1.2600
Allowances:					
Fatigue	5%				
Personal needs	5%				
Contingencies	10%				
Total	20% (of total corrected time of 1.2600)				.2520
Total allotted time for task					1.5120

Source: From Stephen J. Carroll and Craig E. Schneider, *Performance Appraisal and Review Systems* (Glenview, IL: Scott, Foresman, 1982). Copyright 1982 by Scott, Foresman and Company. Reprinted by permission.

job completion derived from a book listing average time estimates for a wide variety of jobs. If the mechanic receives $40 per hour and a transmission is listed as requiring four hours to be removed and replaced, the labor cost would be $160. All this is determined in advance of any actual work. Of course, if the mechanic is highly experienced and fast, the job may be completed in considerably less time than indicated in the

EXHIBIT 10.7
A Straight Piece Rate Plan

Piece rate standard (e.g., determined from time study): 10 units/hour
Guaranteed minimum wage (if standard is not met): $5/hour
Incentive rate (for each unit over 10 units): $.50/unit

Worker Output	Wage
10 units or less	$5.00/hour (as guaranteed)
20 units	20 × $.50 = $10/hour
30 units	30 × $.50 = $15/hour

book. However, the job is still charged as if it took the quoted time to complete. The "surplus" money is split between the employee and the service station. Standard hour plans are more practical than straight piecework plans for long-cycle operations and jobs that are nonrepetitive and require numerous skills for completion.[22]

3. A *Bedeaux* plan provides a variation on straight piecework and standard hour plans. Instead of timing an entire task, a Bedeaux plan requires division of a task into simple actions and determination of the time required by an average skilled worker to complete each action. After the more detailed time analysis of tasks, the Bedeaux system functions similarly to a standard hour plan.

4. *Cell 3:* The two plans included in cell 3 provide for variable incentives as a function of units of production per time period. Both the **Taylor plan** and the **Merrick plan** provide different piece rates, depending on the level of production relative to the standard. The Taylor plan establishes two piecework rates. One rate goes into effect when a worker exceeds the published standard for a given time period. This rate is set higher than the regular wage incentive level. A second rate is established for production below standard, and this rate is lower than the regular wage.

   The Merrick system operates in the same way, except that three piecework rates are set: (1) high for production exceeding 100 percent of standard; (2) medium for production between 83 and 100 percent of standard; and (3) low for production less than 83 percent of standard. Exhibit 10.8 compares these two plans.

5. *Cell 4:* The three plans included in cell 4 provide for variable incentives linked to a standard expressed as a time period per unit of production. The three plans include the Halsey 50–50 method, the Rowan plan, and the Gantt plan.

The **Halsey 50–50 method** derives its name from the shared split between worker and employer of any savings in direct cost. An allowed time for a task is determined via time study. The savings from completion of a task in less than the standard time are allocated 50–50 (most frequent division) between the worker and the company.

The **Rowan plan** is similar to the Halsey plan in that an employer and employee both share in savings resulting from work completed in less than standard time. The major distinction in this plan, however, is that a worker's bonus increases as the time required to complete the task decreases. For example, if the standard time to complete

EXHIBIT 10.8
The Taylor and Merrick Plans

- Piece rate standard: 10 units/hour
- Standard wage: $5/hour
- Piecework rate:

Output (Units/hour)	Taylor Rate per Unit	Taylor Wage	Merrick Rate per Unit	Merrick Wage
7	$.50	$3.50	$.50	$3.50
8	$.50	$4.00	$.50	$4.00
9	$.50	$4.50	$.60	$5.40
10	$.50	$5.00	$.60	$6.00
11	$.70	$7.70	$.70	$7.70
12 +	Calculations at same rate as for 11 units.			

a task is 10 hours and it is completed in 7 hours, the worker receives a 30 percent bonus. Completion of the same task in 6 hours would result in a 40 percent bonus above the hourly wage for each of the 6 hours.

The **Gantt plan** differs from both the Halsey and the Rowan plans in that the standard time for a task is purposely set at a level requiring high effort to complete. Any worker who fails to complete the task in the standard time is guaranteed a preestablished wage. However, for any task completed in standard time or less, earnings are pegged at 120 percent of the time saved. Consequently, workers' earnings increase faster than production whenever standard time is met or exceeded.

Individual Incentive Plans: Advantages and Disadvantages

We already mentioned that incentive plans can lead to unexpected, and undesired, behaviors. Certainly Sears, our example in Chapter 9, did not want the public relations nightmare of having mechanics sell unnecessary repairs, but the incentive program encouraged that type of behavior. This is a common problem with incentive plans: Employees and managers end up in conflict because the incentive system often focuses only on one small part of what it takes for the company to be successful.[23] Employees, being rational, do more of what the incentive system pays for. Exhibit 10.9 outlines some of the other problems, as well as advantages, with individual incentive plans.

EXHIBIT 10.9   Advantages and Disadvantages of Individualized Incentive Plans

Advantages

1. Substantial impact that raises productivity, lowers production costs, and increases earnings of workers.
2. Less direct supervision is required to maintain reasonable levels of output than under payment by time.
3. In most cases, systems of payment by results, if accompanied by improved organizational and work measurement, enable labor costs to be estimated more accurately than under payment by time. This helps costing and budgetary control.

Disadvantages

1. Greater conflict may emerge between employees seeking to maximize output and managers concerned about deteriorating quality levels.
2. Attempts to introduce new technology may be resisted by employees concerned about the impact on production standards.
3. Reduced willingness of employees to suggest new production methods for fear of subsequent increases in production standards.
4. Increased complaints that equipment is poorly maintained, hindering employee efforts to earn larger incentives.
5. Increased turnover among new employees discouraged by the unwillingness of experienced workers to cooperate in on-the-job training.
6. Elevated levels of mistrust between workers and management.

Source: Michael Coates, *Psychology and Organizations, Heineman Themes in Psychology* (Heineman: Boston, 2001); T. Wilson, "Is It Time to Eliminate the Piece Rate Incentive System?" *Compensation and Benefits Review* 24(2) (1992), pp. 43–49; Pinhas Schwinger, *Wage Incentive Systems* (New York: Halsted, 1975).

EXHIBIT 10.10   Lincoln Electric's Compensation System

Description of culture	Reservoir of trust. Long history of employment stability even during severe economic downturns. Employees with 3+ years' seniority are guaranteed (on 1 year renewable basis) at least 75 percent full-time work for that year. In exchange, employees agree to flexible assignment across jobs.
Base wages	Market rate determined. Time study department sets piece rate so that average worker can earn market rate.
Bonus (short term)	Board of directors sets year-end bonus pool as function of company performance. Employee's share in pool is function of semiannual performance review (see below).
Incentive (long term)	Employees share in long-term company successes/failures in form of **employee stock ownership plan (ESOP).** Employees now own 28 percent of outstanding stock shares.
Performance review	Employees rated on four factors: (1) dependability, (2) quality, (3) output, (4) ideas and cooperation in comparison to others in department. To ensure against rating inflation, the average score in department cannot exceed 100.

Individual Incentive Plans: Examples

Even though incentive systems are less popular than they used to be, there are still notable successes. Of course, most sales positions have some part of pay based on commissions, a form of individual incentive. Perhaps the longest-running success with individual incentives, going back to before World War I, belongs to a company called Lincoln Electric. In Exhibit 10.10, the compensation package for factory jobs at Lincoln Electiric is described. Notice how the different pieces fit together. This isn't a case of an incentive plan operating in a vacuum. All the pieces of the compensation and reward package fit together. Lincoln Electric's success is so striking that it's the subject of many case analyses.[24]

TEAM INCENTIVE PLANS: TYPES

When we move away from individual incentive systems and start focusing on people working together, we shift to **group incentive plans.** The group might be a work team. It might be a department. Or we might focus on a division or the whole company. The basic concept is still the same, though. A standard is established against which worker performance (in this case, team performance) is compared to determine the magnitude of the incentive pay. With the focus on groups, now we are concerned about group performance in comparison against some standard, or level, of expected performance. The standard might be an expected level of operating income for a division. Or the measure might be more unusual, as at Litton Industries (now a part of Northrop Grumman Corp). One division has a team variable-pay measure that is based on whether customers would be willing to act as a reference when Litton solicits other business. The more customers willing to do this, the larger the team's variable pay.[25] Another study, which tracked six retail stores, found team incentive plans improved customer satisfaction indices, raised sales performance, and lowered turnover rates.[26]

Despite an explosion of interest in teams and team compensation, many of the reports from the front lines are not encouraging.[27] Companies report they generally are not satisfied with the way their team compensation systems work. There is almost no research outside of lab studies on team incentives, and even those studies are not overly optimistic.[28] Failures of team incentive schemes can be attributed to at least five causes.[29] First, one of the problems with team compensation is that teams come in many varieties. There are full-time teams (work group organized as a team). There are part-time teams that cut across functional departments (experts from different departments pulled together to improve customer relations). There are even full-time teams that are temporary (e.g., cross-functional teams pulled together to help ease the transition into a partnership or joint venture).

With so many varieties of teams, it's hard to argue for one consistent type of compensation plan. Unfortunately, we still seem to be at the stage of trying to find the one best way. Maybe the answer is to look at different compensation approaches for different types of teams. Perhaps the best illustration of this differential approach for different teams comes from Xerox.

Xerox has a **gain-sharing plan** that pays off for teams defined at a very broad level, usually at the level of a strategic business unit. For smaller teams, primarily intact work teams (e.g., all people in a department or function), there are group rewards based on supervisory judgments of performance. Units that opt to have their performance judged as teams (it is also possible to declare that a unit wouldn't be fairly judged if team measures were used) have managers who judge the amount to be allocated to each team based on the team's specific performance results. For new teams, the manager might also decide how much of the total will go to each individual on the team. More mature teams do individual allocations on their own. In Xerox's experience, these teams start out allocating equal shares, but as they evolve the teams allocate based on each worker's performance. Out of about 2,000 work teams worldwide at Xerox, perhaps 100 have evolved to this level of sophistication. For problem-solving teams and other temporary teams, Xerox has a reward component called the Xerox Achievement Award. Teams must be nominated for exceptional performance. A committee decides which teams meet a set of predetermined absolute standards. Even contributors outside the core team can share in the award. If nominated by team members, extended members who provide crucial added value are given cash bonuses equal to those of team members.

A second problem with rewarding teams is called the "level problem." If we define teams at the very broad level—the whole organization being an extreme example—much of the motivational impact of incentives can be lost. As a member of a 1,000-person team, I'm unlikely to be at all convinced that my extra effort will significantly affect our team's overall performance. Why, then, should I try hard? Conversely, if we let teams get too small, other problems arise. TRW found that small work teams competing for a fixed piece of incentive awards tend to gravitate to behaviors that are clearly unhealthy for overall corporate success. Teams hoard star performers, refusing to allow transfers even for the greater good of the company. Teams are reluctant to take on new employees for fear that time lost to training will hurt the team—even when the added employees are essential to long-run success. Finally, bickering arises when awards are given. Because teams have different performance objectives, it is difficult to equalize for difficulty when assigning rewards. Inevitably, complaints arise.[30]

The last three major problems with team compensation involve the three Cs: *complexity, control,* and *communications.* Some plans are simply too complex. Xerox's Houston facility had a gain-sharing plan for teams that required understanding a three-dimensional performance matrix. Employees (and these authors!) threw their hands up in dismay when they tried to understand the "easy-to-follow directions." In contrast, Xerox's San Diego unit has had great success with a simple program called "bet the boss." Employees come to the boss with a performance-saving idea and bet their hard effort against the boss's incentive that they can deliver. Such plans have a simplicity that encourages employee buy-in.

The second C is control. Praxair, a worldwide provider of gases (including oxygen) extracted from the atmosphere, works hard to make sure all its team pay comes from performance measures under the control of the team. If mother nature ravages a construction site, causing delays and skyrocketing costs, workers aren't penalized with reduced team payouts. Such uncontrollable elements are factored into the process of setting performance standards. Indeed, experts assert that this ability to foretell sources of problems and adjust for them is a key element in building a team pay plan.[31] Key to the control issue is the whole question of fairness. Are the rewards fair given our ability to produce results? Recent research suggests that this perception of fairness is crucial.[32] With it, employees feel it is appropriate to monitor all members of the group—slackers beware! Without fairness, employees seem to have less sense of responsibility for the team's outcomes.[33]

The final C is a familiar factor in compensation successes and failures: communication. Team-based pay plans simply are not well communicated. Employees asked to explain their plans often flounder because more effort has been devoted to designing the plan than to deciding how to explain it.

Although there is much pessimism about team-based compensation, many companies still seek ways to reward groups of employees for their interdependent work efforts. Companies that do use team incentives typically set team performance standards based on productivity improvements (38 percent of plans), customer satisfaction measures (37 percent), financial performance (34 percent), or quality of goods and services (28 percent).[34] For example, Kraft Foods uses a combination of financial measures (e.g., income from operations and cash flow) combined with measures designed to gauge success in developing managers, building diversity, and adding to market share.[35] Exhibit 10.11 summarizes some of these measures.

As Exhibit 10.11 suggests, the range of performance measures for different types of corporate objectives is indeed impressive.[36] For example, if the corporate objective is to reward short term performance, the measures outlined in Exhibit 10.12 could be used.

Historically, financial measures have been the most widely used performance indicator for large group incentive plans. Increasingly, though, top executives express concern that these measures do a better job of communicating performance to stock analysts than to managers trying to figure out how to improve operating effectiveness.[37]

Whatever our thinking is about appropriate performance measures, the central point is still that we are now concerned about group performance. This presents both problems and opportunities. As Exhibit 10.13 illustrates, we need to decide which type of group

EXHIBIT 10.11   A Sampling of Performance Measures

Customer-Focused Measures	Financially Focused Measures
Time-to-Market Measures	**Value Creation**
• On-time delivery	• Revenue growth
• Cycle time	• Resource yields
• New product introductions	• Profit margins
	• Economic value added
Customer Satisfaction Measures	**Shareholder Return**
• Market share	• Return on invested capital
• Customer satisfaction	• Return on sales/earnings
• Customer growth and retention	• Earnings per share
• Account penetration	• Growth in profitability
Capability-Focused Measures	**Internal Process-Focused Measures**
Human Resource Capabilities	**Resource Utilization**
• Employee satisfaction	• Budget-to-actual expenses
• Turnover rates	• Cost-allocation ratios
• Total recruitment costs	• Reliability/rework
• Rate of progress on developmental plans	• Accuracy/error rates
• Promotability index	• Safety rates
• Staffing mix/head-count ratio	
Other Asset Capabilities	**Change Effectiveness**
• Patents/copyrights/regulations	• Program implementation
• Distribution systems	• Teamwork effectiveness
• Technological capabilities	• Service/quality index

EXHIBIT 10.12   Private Company Bonus Performance Measures

Measure	Percent of Companies Using
Sales	49
Operating Income	44
Net Income (EPS)	34
Service Quality	25
Customer Satisfaction	24
Returns	15
Other	23

Source: WorldatWork and Vivien Consulting, "Private Company Incentive Pay Practices," *http://www.worldatwork.org/waw/Content/research/html/research-home.jsp*, 2007.

EXHIBIT 10.13 Types of Variable-Pay Plans: Advantages and Disadvantages

Plan Type	What Is It?	Advantages	Disadvantages	Why?
Cash profit sharing	• Award based on organizational profitability • Shares a percentage of profits (typically above a target level of profitability) • Usually an annual payout • Can be cash or deferred 401(k)	• Simple, easily understood • Low administrative costs	• Profit influenced by many factors beyond employee control • May be viewed as an entitlement • Limited motivational impact	• To educate employees about business operations • To foster teamwork or "one-for-all" environment
Stock ownership or options	• Award of stock shares or options	• Option awards have minimal impact on the financial statements of the company at the time they are granted • If properly communicated, can have powerful impact on employee behavior • Tax deferral to employee	• Indirect pay/performance link • Employees may be required to put up money to exercise grants	• To recruit top-quality employees when organization has highly uncertain future (i.e., start-ups, high-tech, or biotech industries) • To address employee retention concerns
Balanced scorecard	• Awards that combine financial and operating measures for organization, business unit, and/or individual performance • Award pool based on achieving performance targets	• Communicates organizational priorities	• Performance criteria may be met, but if financial targets are not met, there may be a reduced payout or no payout at all • Can be complex	• To focus employees on need to increase shareholder value • To focus employees on organization, division, and/or individual goals • To link payouts to a specific financial and/or operational target

(Continued)

EXHIBIT 10.13 *(Continued)*

Plan Type	What Is It?	Advantages	Disadvantages	Why?
	• Multiple performance measures may include: 1. Nonfinancial/ operating: quality improvements, productivity gains, customer service improvements 2. Financial: EPS, ROE, ROA, revenues			
Productivity/ gain sharing	• Awards that share economic benefits of improved productivity, quality, or other measurable results • Focus on group, plant, department, or division results • Designed to capitalize on untapped knowledge of employees	• Clear performance–reward links • Productivity and quality improvements • Employee's knowledge of business increases • Fosters teamwork, cooperation	• Can be administratively complicated • Unintended effects, like drop-off in quality • Management must "open the books" • Payouts can occur even if company's financial performance is poor	• To support a major productivity/ quality initiative (such as TQM or reengineering) • To foster teamwork environment • To reward employees for improvements in activities that they control
Team/group incentives	• Awards determined based on team/group performance goals or objectives • Payout can be more frequent than annual and can also extend beyond the life of the team • Payout may be uniform for team/group members	• Reinforces teamwork and team identity/ results • Effective in stimulating ideas and problem-solving • Minimizes distinctions between team members • May better reflect how work is performed	• May be difficult to isolate impact of team • Not all employees can be placed on a team • Can be administratively complex • May create team competition • Difficult to set equitable targets for all teams	• To demonstrate an organizational commitment to teams • To reinforce the need for employees to work together to achieve results

Source: Kenan S. Abosch, "Variable Pay: Do We Have the Basics in Place?" *Compensation and Benefits Review*, 30(4) 1998, pp. 12–22.

incentive plan best fits our objectives. Indeed, we should even ask if an incentive plan is appropriate. Recent evidence, for example, suggests that firms high on business risk and those with uncertain outcomes, are better off not having incentive plans at all—corporate performance is higher.[38]

Comparing Group and Individual Incentive Plans

In this era of heightened concern about productivity, we frequently are asked if setting up incentive plans really boosts performance. As we noted in Chapter 9, the answer is yes. And individual—rather than group—incentives win the productivity "medal." We also are asked, though, which is better in a specific situation—group or individual incentive plans. Often this is a misleading question. Individual incentives yield higher productivity gains, but group incentives often are right in situations where team coordination is the issue. One study found that changing from individual incentives to gain sharing resulted in a decrease in grievances and a fairly dramatic increase in product quality (defects per 1000 products shipped declined from 20.93 to 2.31).[39]

As we noted in Exhibit 10.8, things like the type of task, the organizational commitment to teams, and the type of work environment may preclude one or the other type of incentive plan. Exhibit 10.14 provides a guide for when to choose group or individual plans. When forced to choose the type of plan with greater productivity "pep," experts agree that individual incentive plans have better potential for—and probably better track records in—delivering higher productivity. Group plans suffer from what is called the *free-rider problem*. See if this sounds familiar: You are a team member on a school

EXHIBIT 10.14   The Choice Between Individual and Group Plans

Characteristic	Choose an Individual Plan when . . .	Choose a Group Plan when . . .
Performance measurement	Good measures of individual performance exist. Task accomplishment not dependent on performance of others.	Output is group collaborative effort. Individual contributions to output cannot be assessed.
Organizational adaptability	Individual performance standards are stable. Production methods and labor mix relatively constant.	Performance standards for individuals change to meet environmental pressures on relatively constant organizational objectives. Production methods and labor mix must adapt to meet changing pressures.
Organizational commitment	Commitment strongest to individual's profession or superior. Supervisor viewed as unbiased and performance standards readily apparent.	High commitment to organization built upon sound communication of organizational objectives and performance standards.
Union status	Nonunion; unions promote equal treatment. Competition between individuals inhibits "fraternal" spirit.	Union or nonunion; unions less opposed to plans that foster cohesiveness of bargaining unit and which distribute rewards evenly across group.

project and at least one person doesn't carry his or her share of the load. Yet, when it comes time to divide the rewards, they are typically shared equally. Problems like this caused AT&T to phase out many of its team reward packages. Top-performing employees quickly grew disenchanted with having to carry free riders. End result—turnover of the very group that is most costly to lose.

Research on free riders suggests that the problem can be lessened through use of good performance measurement techniques. Specifically, free riders have a harder time loafing when there are clear performance standards. Rather than being given instructions to "do your best," poorer performers who were asked to deliver specific levels of performance at a specific time actually showed the most performance improvement.[40]

Large Group Incentive Plans

When we get beyond a small work team and try to incentivize large groups, there are generally two types of plans. Gain-sharing plans use operating measures to gauge performance. Profit sharing plans use financial measures.

Gain-Sharing Plans

Our discussion of team-based compensation often mentioned gain-sharing plans as a common component. As the name suggests, employees share in the gains in these types of group incentive plans. With profit-sharing plans (surprise) the sharing involves some form of profits. Realistically, though, most employees feel as if little they can do will affect profits; that's something top-management decisions influence more. So gain sharing looks at cost components of the income ledger and identifies savings over which employees have more impact (e.g., reduced scrap, lower labor costs, reduced utility costs). It was just this type of thinking that led the United States Post Office to an annual cost avoidance of $497 million under its gain-sharing plan.[41] Other studies of gain sharing report similar positive results. Indeed, the empirical evidence on gain sharing appears to be quite favorable.[42] One study of 1600 employees in an auto parts company showed gain sharing over five years reduced labor, material, tool purchase, scrap, rework and supply costs. The total savings were $15 million over the five-year period. Absenteeism (20 percent) and grievances (50 percent) also decreased.[43]

In a particularly good study of a major retailer, stores with gain-sharing incentives had 4.9 percent higher sales, 3.4 percent higher customer satisfaction, and 4.4 percent higher profit than stores without the incentive plan. In our experience these effects are pretty typical of gain-sharing plans—improvements in the 4–5 percent range. Keep in mind, though, gain-sharing plans can lead to the sorting effect we talked about in Chapter 9. Good employees want to be rewarded for their individual effort and performance. Changes to group plans, like gain-sharing, can lead to turnover. Just ask AT&T. They found that very high and very low performing individuals had much higher turnover rates under gain-sharing than other employees.[44] The following issues are key elements in designing a gain-sharing plan:[45]

1. *Strength of reinforcement:* What role should base pay assume relative to incentive pay? Incentive pay tends to encourage only those behaviors that are rewarded. For

example, try returning an unwanted birthday present to a store that pays its sales force solely for new sales. Tasks carrying no rewards are only reluctantly performed (if at all).

2. *Productivity standards:* What standard will be used to calculate whether employees will receive an incentive payout? Almost all group incentive plans use a historical standard. A historical standard involves choice of a prior year's performance to use for comparison with current performance. But which baseline year should be used? If too good (or too bad) a comparison year is used, the standard will be too hard (or easy) to achieve, with obvious motivational and cost effects. One possible compromise is to use a moving average of several years (e.g., the average for the past five years, with the five-year block changing by one year on an annual basis).

   One of the major problems with historical standards is that changing environmental conditions can render a standard ineffective. For example, consider the company that sets a target of 6 percent return on investment based on historical standards. When this level is reached, it triggers an incentive for eligible employees. Yet, in a product market where the average for that year is 15 percent return on investment, it is apparent that no incentive is appropriate for our underachiever.[46] Such problems are particularly insidious during economic swings and for organizations facing volatile economic climates. Care must be taken to ensure that the link between performance and rewards is sustained. This means that environmental influences on performance, which are not controllable by plan participants, should be factored out when identifying incentive levels.

3. *Sharing the gains split between management and workers:* Part of the plan must address the relative cuts between management and workers of any profit or savings generated. This also includes discussion of whether an emergency reserve (gains withheld from distribution in case of future emergencies) will be established in advance of any sharing of profits.

4. *Scope of the formula:* Formulas can vary in the scope of inclusions for both the labor inputs in the numerator and the productivity outcomes in the denominator.[47] Recent innovations in gain-sharing plans largely address broadening the types of productivity standards considered appropriate. Given that organizations are complex and require more complex measures, performance measures have expanded beyond traditional financial measures. For example, with the push for greater quality management, we could measure retention of customers or some other measure of customer satisfaction. Similarly, other measures include delivery performance, safety, absenteeism, turnaround time, and number of suggestions submitted. Four specific examples are:[48]

What Is Rewarded	Goal	Bonus per Month
Productivity	38,500 lb/month	
Cost	.009 lb below standard	
Product damage	15 per 10,000 cases	
Customer complaints	14 per million lbs	

5. Great care must be exercised with such alternative measures, though, to ensure that the behaviors reinforced actually affect the desired bottom-line goal. Getting workers to expend more effort, for example, might not always be the desired behavior. Increased effort may bring unacceptable levels of accidents. It may be preferable to encourage cooperative planning behaviors that result in more efficient work.

6. *Perceived fairness of the formula:* One way to ensure the plan is perceived as fair is to let employees vote on whether implementation should go forward. This and union participation in program design are two elements in plan success.[49]

7. *Ease of administration:* Sophisticated plans with involved calculations of profits or costs can become too complex for existing company information systems. Increased complexities also require more effective communications and higher levels of trust among participants.

8. *Production variability:* One of the major sources of problems in group incentive plans is failure to set targets properly. At times the problem can be traced to volatility in sales. Large swings in sales and profits, not due to any actions by workers, can cause both elation (in good times) and anger (in bad times). As stated above, a good plan ensures that environmental influences on performance, which are not controllable by plan participants, should be factored out when identifying incentive levels. The second author once worked with an ice cream producer that experienced huge unexpected increases in milk costs. End result? The original profit goal was unattainable. To their credit, the company adjusted the profit target to reflect the uncontrollable cost change. One alternative would be to set standards that are relative to industry performance. To the extent data are available, a company could trigger gain sharing when performance exceeds some industry norm. The obvious advantage of this strategy is that economic and other external factors hit all firms in the industry equally hard. If our company performs better, relatively, it means we are doing something as employees to help achieve success.

Exhibit 10.15 illustrates three different formulas that can be used as the basis for gain-sharing plans. The numerator, or input factor, is always some labor cost variable, expressed in either dollars or actual hours worked; the denominator is some output measure such as net sales or value added. Each of the plans determines employees' incentives based on the difference between the current value of the ratio and the ratio in some agreed-upon base year. The more favorable the current ratio relative to the historical

EXHIBIT 10.15 Three Gain-Sharing Formulas

	Scanlon Plan (Single Ratio Volume)	Rucker Plan	Improshare
Numerator of ratio (input factor)	Payroll costs	Labor cost	Actual hours worked
Denominator of ratio (output factor)	Net sales (plus or minus inventories)	Value added	Total standard value hours

Source: Adapted from M. Bazerman and B. Graham-Moore, "PG. Formulas: Developing a Reward Structure to Achieve Organizational Goals," in B. Graham-Moore and T. Ross, eds., *Productivity Gainsharing* (Englewood Cliffs, NJ: Prentice-Hall, 1983).

EXHIBIT 10.16   Examples of a Scanlon Plan

2005 Data (base year) for Alton, Ltd.		
Sales Value of Production (SVOP)	=	$10,000,000
Total wage bill	=	4,000,000
Total wage bill/SVOP	=	4,000,000/10,000,000 = .40 = 40%
Operating Month, March 2006		
SVOP	=	$950,000
Allowable wage bill	=	.40 ($950,000) = $380,000
Actual wage bill (August)	=	$330,000
Savings	=	$ 50,000
50,000 available for distribution as a bonus.		

standard, the larger the incentive award.[50] The three primary types of gain-sharing plans, differentiated by their focus on either cost savings (the numerator of the equation) or some measure of revenue (the denominator of the equation), are noted below.

Scanlon Plan

Scanlon plans are designed to lower labor costs without lowering the level of a firm's activity. Incentives are derived as a function of the ratio between labor costs and **sales value of production (SVOP)**.[51] The SVOP includes sales revenue and the value of goods in inventory. To understand how these two figures are used to derive incentives under a Scanlon plan, see Exhibit 10.16

In practice, the $50,000 bonus in Exhibit 10.16 is not all distributed to the work force. Rather, 25 percent is distributed to the company, 75 percent of the remainder is distributed as bonuses, and 25 percent of the remainder is withheld and placed in an emergency fund to reimburse the company for any future months when a "negative bonus" is earned (i.e., when the actual wage bill is greater than the allowable wage bill). The excess remaining in the emergency pool is distributed to workers at the end of the year. Appendix 10-A illustrates a variant of the Scanlon plan adopted at Dresser Rand's Painted Post facility.

To look at the impact of Scanlon plans, consider the retail chain that adopted a Scanlon plan in six of its stores and compared results against six control stores chosen for their similarity.[52] Presence of a Scanlon plan led to stores having higher customer satisfaction, higher sales, and lower turnover.

> **Cybercomp**
> HR Guide provides information about gain-sharing plans, including critiques of plans and statistical studies. The Web site is at *www.hr-guide.com\data\G443.htm*.

Rucker Plan

The **Rucker plan** involves a somewhat more complex formula than a Scanlon plan for determining worker incentive bonuses. Essentially, a ratio is calculated that expresses the value of production required for each dollar of total wage bill. Consider the following illustration:[53]

1. Assume accounting records show that the company expended $.60 worth of electricity, materials, supplies, and so on, to produce $1.00 worth of product. The value added is $.40 for each $1.00 of sales value. Assume also that 45 percent of the value added was attributable to labor; a productivity ratio (PR) can be allocated from the formula in item 2.

2. *PR* (labor) $\times$ .40 $\times$ .45 = 1.00. Solving yields *PR* = 5.56.

3. If the wage bill equals $100,000, the *expected* production value is the wage bill ($100,000) $\times$ *PR* (5.56) = $555,556.

4. If *actual* production value equals $650,000, then the savings (actual production value minus expected production value) is $94,444.

5. Since the labor contribution to value added is 45 percent, the bonus to the work force should be .45 $\times$ $94,444 = $42,500.

6. The savings are distributed as an incentive bonus according to a formula similar to the Scanlon formula—75 percent of the bonus is distributed to workers immediately and 25 percent is kept as an emergency fund to cover poor months. Any excess in the emergency fund at the end of the year is then distributed to workers.

Implementation of the Scanlon/Rucker Plans

Two major components are vital to the implementation and success of a Rucker or Scanlon plan: (1) a productivity norm and (2) effective worker committees. Development of a productivity norm requires both effective measurement of base-year data and acceptance by workers and management of this standard for calculating bonus incentives. Effective measurement requires that an organization keep extensive records of historical cost relationships and make them available to workers or union representatives to verify cost accounting figures. Acceptance of these figures, assuming they are accurate, requires that the organization choose a base year that is neither a "boom" nor a "bust" year. The logic is apparent. A boom year would reduce opportunities for workers to collect bonus incentives. A bust year would lead to excessive bonus costs for the firm. The base year chosen also should be fairly recent, allaying worker fears that changes in technology or other factors would make the base year unrepresentative of a given operational year.

The second ingredient of Scanlon/Rucker plans is a series of worker committees (also known as productivity committees or bonus committees). The primary function of these committees is to evaluate employee and management suggestions for ways to improve productivity and/or cut costs. Operating on a plantwide basis in smaller firms, or a departmental basis in larger firms, these committees have been highly successful in eliciting suggestions from employees. It is not uncommon for the suggestion rate to be above that found in companies with standard suggestion incentive plans.[54]

Scanlon/Rucker plans foster this type of climate, and that is perhaps the most vital element of their success. Numerous authorities have pointed out that these plans have the best chance for success in companies with competent supervision, cooperative union-management attitudes, strong top-management interest and participation in the development of the program, and management open to criticism and willing to discuss different operating strategies. It is beyond the scope of this discussion to outline specific strategies adopted by companies to achieve this climate, but the key element is a belief that workers should play a vital role in the decision-making process.

Similarities and Contrasts Between Scanlon and Rucker Plans

Scanlon and Rucker plans differ from individual incentive plans in their primary focus. Individual incentive plans focus primarily on using wage incentives to motivate higher performance through increased effort. While this is certainly a goal of the Scanlon/Rucker plans, it is not the major focus of attention. Rather, given that increased output is a function of group effort, more attention is focused on organizational behavior variables. The key is to promote faster, more intelligent, and more acceptable decisions through participation. This participation is won by developing a group unity in achieving cost savings—a goal that is not stressed, and is often stymied, in individual incentive plans.

Even though Scanlon and Rucker plans share this common attention to groups and committees through participation as a linking pin, there are two important differences between the two plans. First, Rucker plans tie incentives to a wide variety of savings, not just the labor savings focused on in Scanlon plans.[55] Second, this greater flexibility may help explain why Rucker plans are more amenable to linkages with individual incentive plans.

Improshare

Improshare (Improved Productivity through Sharing) is a gain-sharing plan that has proved easy to administer and to communicate.[56] First, a standard is developed that identifies the expected hours required to produce an acceptable level of output. This standard comes either from time-and-motion studies conducted by industrial engineers or from a base-period measurement of the performance factor. Any savings arising from production of the agreed-upon output in fewer than the expected hours is shared by the firm and by the workers.[57] For example, if 100 workers can produce 50,000 units over 50 weeks, this translates into 200,000 hours (40 hours × 50 weeks) for 50,000 units, or 4 hours per unit. If we implement an Improshare plan, any gains resulting in less than 4 hours per unit are shared 50–50 between employees and management (wages times number of hours saved).[58]

One survey of 104 companies with an Improshare plan found a mean increase in productivity during the first year of 12.5 percent.[59] By the third year the productivity gain rose to 22 percent. A significant portion of this productivity gain was traced to reduced defect rates and downtime (e.g., repair time).

Profit-Sharing Plans

If you were to read most books or articles on variable-pay today, you would see less discussion of profit-sharing plans and much energy devoted to gain-sharing plans or related variants. An erroneous conclusion to draw from this is that profit sharing is dead. In fact, profit sharing seems to have a pretty consistent impact on productivity about equal to that of gain sharing. One study of 6 million employees across 275 firms found

3.5–5.0 percent higher profits in companies that used profit sharing than in those that didn't.[60] Productivity was much higher in plans where payouts were that year than in plans were payment was deferred (as in profit sharing used for a pension program). Also, these plans worked much better in smaller (less than 775 employees) companies.

Even in companies that don't have profit sharing plans, many variable-pay plans still require a designated profit target to be met before any payouts occur. Our experience with chief executive officers is that they have a hard time giving employees extra compensation if the company isn't also profiting. Thus, many variable-pay plans have some form of profit "trigger" linked to revenue growth or profit margins or some measure of shareholder return such as earnings per share or return on capital. Profit sharing continues to be popular because the focus is on the measure that matters most to the most people: a predetermined index of profitability. When payoffs are linked to such measures, employees spend more time learning about financial measures and the business factors that influence them.

On the downside, most employees don't feel their jobs have a direct impact on profits. A small cog in a big wheel is difficult to motivate very well. For example, before the big crunch in the auto industry Ford Motor announced its annual profit-sharing check to employees would average $600, compared to $186 for the same type of workers at General Motors.[61] You can bet the GM employees felt they deserved more than one-third the payout. Complaints centered on GMs continuing sales problems. Today, though, we don't hear many complaints about profit sharing in the auto industry. GM's declaration of bankruptcy and the ill-health of the industry in general has led to wage concessions and complete chaos in wage programs and HR practices.[62] Expect the entire industry to emerge leaner and more receptive to variable compensation instead of very high base compensation. We live in unusual times!

The trend in recent variable-pay design is to combine the best of gain-sharing and profit-sharing plans.[63] The company will specify a funding formula for any variable payout that is linked to some profit measure. As experts say, the plan must be self-funding. Dollars going to workers are generated by additional profits gained from operational efficiency. Along with having the financial incentive, employees feel they have a measure of control. For example, an airline might give an incentive for reductions in lost baggage, with the size of the payout dependent on hitting profit targets. Such a program combines the need for fiscal responsibility with the chance for workers to affect something they can control.

Earnings-at-Risk Plans

We probably shouldn't separate **earnings-at-risk plans** as a distinct category. In fact, any incentive plan could be an at-risk plan. Think of incentive plans as falling into one of two categories: success sharing or risk sharing. In success-sharing plans, employee base wages are constant and variable pay adds on during *successful years*. If the company does well, you receive a predetermined amount of variable pay. If the company does poorly, you simply forgo any variable pay—there is no reduction in your base pay, though. In a risk-sharing plan, base pay is reduced by some amount relative to the level that would be offered in a success-sharing plan. AmeriSteel's at-risk plan is typical of risk-sharing plans. Base pay was reduced 15 percent across the board in year 1. That 15 percent was replaced with a .5 percent increase in base pay for every 1 percent increase in productivity beyond 70 percent of the prior year's productivity. This figure would leave workers whole (no decline in base pay) if they only matched the prior year's productivity. Each additional percent improvement in productivity yielded a 1.5 percent increase in base wages. Everyone in AmeriSteel, from the CEO on down, is in this type of plan and the result has been an 8 percent improvement in productivity.[64]

Clearly, at-risk plans shift part of the risk of doing business from the company to the employee. The company hedges against the devastating effects of a bad year by mortgaging part of the profits that would have accrued during a good year. Companies like DuPont and Saturn report mixed results. DuPont terminated its plan in the second year because of lackluster performance and the expectation of no payout. Much of the concern can be traced to employee dissatisfaction with the plan at DuPont. At-risk plans appear to be met with decreases in satisfaction with both pay in general and the process used to set pay.[65] In turn, this can result in higher turnover.[66]

Group Incentive Plans: Advantages and Disadvantages

Clearly, group pay-for-performance plans are gaining popularity while individual plans are stable or declining in interest. Why? One explanation with intriguing implications suggests that group-based plans, particularly gain-sharing plans, cause organizations to evolve into learning organizations.[67] Apparently the suggestions employees are encouraged to make (how to do things better in the company) gradually evolve from first-order learning experiences of a more routine variety (maintenance of existing ways of doing things) into suggestions that exhibit second-order learning characteristics— suggestions that help the organization break out of existing patterns of behavior and explore different ways of thinking and behaving.[68]

Exhibit 10.17 outlines some of the general positive and negative features of group pay-for-performance plans.[69]

EXHIBIT 10.17   Group Incentive Plans: Advantages and Disadvantages

Advantages

1. Positive impact on organization and individual performance of about 5 to 10 percent per year.
2. Easier to develop performance measures than it is for individual plans.
3. Signals that cooperation, both within and across groups, is a desired behavior.
4. Teamwork meets with enthusiastic support from most employees.
5. May increase participation of employees in decision-making process.

Disadvantages

1. Line-of-sight may be lessened, that is employees may find it more difficult to see how their individual performance affects their incentive payouts.
2. May lead to increased turnover among top individual performers who are discouraged because they must share with lesser contributors.
3. Increases compensation risk to employees because of lower income stability. May influence some applicants to apply for jobs in firms where base pay is a larger compensation component.

EXHIBIT 10.18 Corporate Examples of Group Incentive Plans

GE Information systems	A team-based incentive that also links to individual payouts. Team and individual performance goals are set. If the team hits its goals, the team members earn their incentive only if they also hit their individual goals. The team incentive is 12 to 15 percent of monthly base pay.
Corning Glass	A gain-sharing program (goal sharing) where 75 percent of the payout is based on unit objectives such as quality measures, customer satisfaction measures, and production targets. The remainder is based on Corning's return on equity.
3M	Operates with an earnings-at-risk plan. Base pay is fixed at 80 percent of market. Employees have a set of objectives to meet for pay to move to 100 percent of market. Additionally, there is a modest profit-sharing component.
Saturn	Earnings-at-risk plan where base pay is 93 percent of market. Employees meet individual objectives to capture at-risk component. All team members must meet objectives for any to get at-risk money. A profit-sharing component is based on corporate profits.
DuPont Fibers	Earnings-at-risk plan where employees receive reduced pay increases over 5 years resulting in 6 percent lower base pay. If department meets annual profit goal, employees collect all 6 percent. Variable payout ranges from 0 (reach less than 80 percent of goal) to 12 percent (150 percent of goal).

Group Incentive Plans: Examples

All incentive plans, as we noted earlier, can be described by common features: (1) the size of the group that participates in the plan, (2) the standard against which performance is compared, and (3) the payout schedule. Exhibit 10.18 illustrates some of the more interesting components of plans for leading companies.

EXPLOSIVE INTEREST IN LONG-TERM INCENTIVE PLANS

All of the individual and group plans we have discussed thus far focus on short time horizons for performance and payouts. Usually the time horizon is a year or less. Now we shift to variable pay plans where the time horizon is longer than a year. Such programs force executives to think long term, and develop strategic plans that don't sacrifice tomorrow's riches for today's small gains.

Exhibit 10.19 shows different types of **long-term incentives** and their definitions. These plans are also grouped by the level of risk faced by employees having these incentives, as well as the expected rewards that might come from them.

Long-term incentives (LTIs) focus on performance beyond the one-year time line used as the cutoff for short-term incentive plans. Recent explosive growth in long-term plans appears to be spurred in part by a desire to motivate longer-term value creation.[70] One analysis of over 200 empirical studies of the relation between stock ownership and financial performance casts a gloomy pallor indeed. There is very little empirical evidence that stock ownership by management leads to better corporate performance.[71] There is some evidence, though, that stock ownership is likely to increase internal growth, rather than more rapid external diversification.[72]

EXHIBIT 10.19 Long-Term Incentives and Their Risk/Reward Tradeoffs

Level One: Low Risk/Reward

1. *Time-based restricted stock:* An award of shares that actually are received only after the completion of a predefined service period. Employees who terminate employment before the restriction lapses must return their shares to the company.

2. *Performance-accelerated restricted stock:* Restricted stock granted only after attainment of specified performance objectives.

3. *Stock purchase plan:* Opportunity to buy shares of company stock either at prices below market price or with favorable financing.

Level Two: Medium Risk/Reward

4. *Time-vested stock option:* This is what most stock options are—the right to purchase stock at a specified price for a fixed time period.

5. *Performance-vested restricted stock:* This is a grant of stock to employees upon attainment of defined performance objective(s).

6. *Performance-accelerated stock option:* An option with a vesting schedule that can be shortened if specific performance criteria are met.

Level Three: High Risk/Reward

7. *Premium-priced stock option:* A stock option that has an exercise price about market value at the time of grant. This creates an incentive for employees to create value for the company, see the stock price rise, and thus be eligible to purchase the stock.

8. *Indexed stock option:* An option whose exercise price depends on what peer companies' experiences are with stock prices. If industry stock prices are generally rising, it would be difficult to attribute any similar rise in specific improvements beyond general industry improvement.

9. *Performance-vested stock option:* One that vests only upon the attainment of a predetermined performance objective.

Source: IOMA, "PFP News Brief," *Pay for Performance Report,* June 2000, p. 8.

All this talk about stock options neglects the biggest change in recent memory. As of June 2005 companies were required to report stock options as an expense.[73] Prior to this date, generally accepted accounting rules didn't require options to be reported as an overhead cost. They were (wrongly) viewed as a free good under old accounting rules.[74] Think about the executive issued 500,000 shares with a vesting period of five years (the shares can be bought in five years). After five years, the CEO can purchase the stock at the initial-offer price (if the market price is now lower than that, the stock option is said to be "underwater" and is not exercised).[75] If the executive bought the shares, they were typically issued from a pool of unissued shares. The money paid by the CEO was treated like money paid by any investor . . . found money? Not really. Options diluted the per-share earnings because they increase the denominator applied to net profits used to figure per-share earnings. (OK, OK we promise, no more accounting terms!) Cases like Enron, which did not expense options, gave an unrealistic picture of profits and helped to elevate stock prices. The publicity from this case increased pressure to change accounting rules and led to the changes that began affecting most companies in 2006.[76] This dampens popularity of options, but tech firms like Cisco still report options accounting for 13 percent of profits this year, versus nontech firms like Pfizer (3 percent of profits) and General Electric (1 percent of profits). Under the new accounting rules Cisco now reports profits of 22 cents per share, 4 cents per share lower than before option expensing was required. Some estimates suggest the ruling will lower earnings by 4 percent across the spectrum of companies with stock options.[77] As a direct result of the changing rules, some companies, like Dell Inc., Aetna Inc., Pfizer Inc., McDonald's Corp., Time Warner Inc., ExxonMobil Corp., and Microsoft Corp either stopped granting options or only grant them to executives.[78] It's still too early to tell if other companies will also follow, but clearly options are less attractive than they used to be.

Employee Stock Ownership Plans (ESOPs)

Some companies believe that employees can be linked to the success or failure of a company in yet another way—through employee stock ownership plans.[79] At places like PepsiCo, Lincoln Electric, DuPont, Coca-Cola, and others, the goal is to increase employee involvement in the organization, and hopefully this will influence performance. Toward this end, employees own 28 percent of the stock at Lincoln Electric. At Worthington Industries, an oft-praised performer in the steel industry, the typical employee owns $45,000 in stock.[80]

Despite these high-profile adoptions, ESOPs don't make sense as an incentive. First, the effects are generally long-term. How I perform today won't have much of an impact on the stock price at the time I exercise my option.[81] Nor does my working harder mean more for me. Indeed, we can't predict very well what makes stock prices rise and this is the central ingredient in the reward component of ESOPs. So if the performance measure is too complex to figure out, how can we control our own destiny? Sounds like ESOPs do poorly on two of the three Cs we mentioned earlier as causing incentive plans to fail. Why then do about 9,500 companies have ESOPs covering more than 10 million employees with holdings of over $600 billion in the stock's of their companies?[82] The answer may well be that ESOPs foster employee willingness to participate in the decision-making process.[83] And a company that takes advantage of that willingness can harness a considerable resource—the creative energy of its workforce.

If we just look at the impact of ESOPs on productivity or financial outcomes, leaving aside the positive effect on employee participation, the results are very modest. ESOPs have little impact on productivity or profit.[84] Critics of ESOP argue that companies don't use these programs effectively. If more firms would combine ESOPs with high goal setting, improved employee communication with management, and greater participation in decision making by employees, maybe ESOPs would have more positive results.[85]

Beware of stock options in declining markets though. After Microsoft stock was battered by the company's antitrust battle in 2000, employee morale plummeted. Many of the options granted to employees had exercise prices higher than the current market value, in effect making the options all but worthless. In mid-2000 Microsoft issued 70 million shares of stock at $66.25, the then closing stock price. This price was considerably below that of many options issued in the past and was intended to motivate workers to help drive stock prices back up.[86] And, of course, today's market has made ESOPs a compensation tool with little motivation power. When the market is playing like a yo-yo, few employees are interested in owning more stock.

Performance Plans (Performance Share and Performance Unit)

Performance plans typically feature corporate performance objectives for a time three years in the future. They are driven by financial earnings or return measures, and they pay out for meeting or exceeding specific goals.

Broad-Based Option Plans (BBOPs)

The latest trend in long-term incentives, and probably the component of compensation generating the most discussion in recent years, is **broad-based option plans.** BBOPs are stock grants: The company gives employees shares of stock over a designated time period. The strength of BBOPs is their versatility. Depending on the way they are distributed to employees, they can either reinforce a strong emphasis on performance (performance culture) or inspire greater commitment and retention (ownership culture) of employees. Some of the best-known companies in the country offer stock grants to employees at all levels: Southwest Airlines, Chase Manhattan, DuPont, General Mills, Procter & Gamble, PepsiCo, Merck, Eli Lilly, Kimberly-Clark, Microsoft, and Amazon. com.[87] For example, Starbucks has a stock grant program called Beanstock, and all employees who work at least 500 hours per year, up to the level of vice president, are eligible (broad-based participation).[88] If company performance goals are reached, all employees receive equal stock grants worth somewhere between 10 and 14 percent of their earnings. The grants vest 20 percent each year, and the option expires 10 years after the grant date. This program exists to send the clear signal that all employees, especially the two-thirds who are part-timers, are business partners. This effort to create a culture of ownership is viewed as the primary reason Starbucks has turnover that is only a fraction of the usually high turnover in the retail industry.

Microsoft's program shares one common feature with Starbucks. The stock grant program, again, is broad-based. By rewarding all employees, Microsoft hopes to send a strong signal to its employees that reinforces its culture: Take reasoned risks that have long-run potential for contributing to the company. Microsoft's BBOP is targeted at all permanent employees. Unlike Starbucks' plan, though, the size of the stock grant is linked to individual performance and estimated long-run contribution to the company. Starting 12 months after the stock grant date, 12.5 percent is vested every 6 months.

Kodak provides a third example. Only nonmanagement employees are eligible, and grants are given only to the small percentage of employees who are recognized for extraordinary accomplishments based on recommendations by an individual's or team's manager. Kodak prides itself on giving immediate grant options for outstanding contributions.

Finally, Paychex, a payroll processing firm, offers broad-based options both to create a sense of ownership and to attract and retain employees. The first grants were made in

1996. They vested 50 percent in 1999 and 100 percent in 2001. Grant amounts depend on pay grade level, with lower grades granted 100 shares and upper grades receiving 200 shares.[89]

Combination Plans: Mixing Individual and Group

It's not uncommon for companies to use both individual and group incentives. The goal is to both motivate individual behavior and to insure that employees work together, where needed, to promote team and corporate goals. These combination programs start with standard individual (e.g., performance appraisal, quantity of output) and group measures (e.g., profit, operating income). Variable pay level depends on how well individuals perform and how well the company (or division/strategic business unit) does on its macro (e.g., profit) measures. A typical plan might call for a 75–25 split. Seventy-five percent of the payout is based on how well the individual worker does, the other portion is dependent on corporate performance. An alternative might be a completely **self-funding plan,** often favored by CEOs who don't like to make payouts when the company loses money. These plans specify that payouts only occur after the company reaches a certain profit target. Then variable payouts for individual, team, and company performance are triggered.

Your **Turn**   Incentives in the Clubhouse

Gone are the days when attendants—or "clubbies" in dugout lingo—did little more than shine shoes and pass out towels in exchange for the occasional dollar. Nowadays, their jobs are more like those of Hollywood personal assistants: When they aren't sorting socks, they're arranging dinner reservations and programming player iPods.

In most sports, junior locker-room attendants are paid roughly $7–8 an hour by the team, while more senior managers, who sometimes double as travel coordinators, can earn salaries of up to $80,000 before bonuses or tips.

Bonuses work as follows:

1. Among players, it's understood that unusual requests should be rewarded and that wealthier players should be more generous. During the season players often reward clubbies with tips of as much as $300 for (errands).

2. Players and coaches also are expected to add gratuities to the daily "dues" they pay to clubhouse managers at home and on the road. (The dues cover food and drinks, which clubhouse managers pay for out of their own pockets).

3. By custom, team members meet privately at the end of the regular season to vote on how the postseason "shares" will be allocated. When the Anaheim Angels won the title in 2002, Clubhouse Manager Ken Higdon was awarded a full share that came out to $279,000.

Questions

1. Which part of the compensation for "clubbies" is similar to what happens in any organization?
2. Does the compensation for Ken Higdon seem excessive? Is he like a highly paid executive?
3. How is compensation different in baseball? And how does this affect clubby pay?
4. From the information provided above, what part of the total package is base pay? What kind of incentive rewards are the rest of the forms of compensation? Does there appear to be any merit pay in this package?

Source: Much of this comes from Jon Weinbach, "The Windfall Classic," *The Wall Street Journal,* October 21, 2005. pp. W1, W4.

Summary   Pay-for-performance plans can work. But as this chapter demonstrates, the design and effective administration of these plans is key to their success. Having a good idea is not enough. The good idea must be followed up by sound practices that recognize rewards can, if used properly, shape employee behavior.

Review Questions

1. As VP of HR at Pilsner Roofing, the eleventh largest roofing company in the world, you are experiencing turnover problems with the employees who actually install roofs (roofers) General Manager Roy Cranston has asked you to fix the problem. While your primary emphasis might be on having a competitive base pay, you need to decide if there is anything you can do in the incentive department. Before you can make this decision, what information would you like about (a) pay (base + incentive) at major competitors, (b) the nature of the turnover, and (c) next year's labor budget?

2. How is an earnings-at-risk plan different from an ordinary gain-sharing or profit-sharing plan? How might earnings-at-risk plans affect attraction and retention of employees? How does the 2008–2010 recession affect the viability of earnings at risk plans?

3. You own Falzer's Tool Coating Company, a high-tech firm specializing in the coating of cutting tools (e.g., drill bits, cutting blades) to provide longer life before resharpening is needed. You are concerned that the competition continues to develop new coating methods and new applications of coating in different industries. You want to create a work environment where employees offer more new product ideas and suggest new industries where these ideas might be applied. What type of compensation plan will you recommend? What are some of the problems you need to be aware of?

4. Why do the new accounting standards make stock options less popular?

5. When might you use a group incentive plan rather than an individual plan?

Gain-Sharing Plan at Dresser Rand

KEY FEATURES OF THE PAINTED POST FACILITIES (DRESSER RAND) GAIN-SHARING PLAN

1. A productivity, quality, and cost reduction formula to recognize employees for their efforts. Employees can earn a bonus by:

   - Increasing productivity
   - Improving quality
   - Saving on shop supplies

   This element of the plan gives employees a triple opportunity to be productive and, at the same time, be conscious of quality, material, and shop supplies.

2. An expansion of the Employee Involvement Teams (EITs) to provide employees with an opportunity to solve problems in a way that can increase productivity and quality while reducing the costs of material and shop supplies.

3. A Bonus Committee composed of four union and four management representatives responsible for the overall administration of the program.

4. The program recognizes Painted Post employees for performance efforts that exceed the plant's [baseline year] levels.

5. Teamwork and employee participation are the key ingredients of the plan. Both require your support and commitment in order for the program to be successful.

The Employee Involvement Teams

The success of the Painted Post Gain-Sharing Plan will largely be determined by the extent to which all employees, hourly and salary, get involved in making Painted Post a successful business once again. The vehicle for doing this is an expanded and modified process of employee involvement. *All employees must get involved if we are to make this gain-sharing plan a success.*

You know more about your work operations than anyone else. You know best how they can be improved, what shortcuts can be taken, how materials can be saved and scrap minimized, and how work can be performed more efficiently.

The best suggestions are those which recognize the problem and propose a solution.

There will be Employee Involvement Teams (EITs) in each department of the plant, and where possible on the second shift as well. The primary purpose of the EITs should be in the areas of cost reduction, quality, and productivity. The teams will have the option of seeking their own projects. The Steering Committee will also form task forces, task teams, and project teams to work on specific projects, which, in the view of the Steering Committee, might contribute to reducing costs, increasing quality, or reducing production inefficiencies and bottlenecks. Based on results at other companies, expansion of the EITs will allow us to:

- Use our creative powers in our daily tasks to make suggestions which will improve productivity and quality and result in better earnings and bonuses.
- Communicate clearly with each other—management to employees and employees to management.
- Join fully and cooperatively in the common effort to increase productivity, quality, and earnings.
- Keep an open-minded attitude to change.

When an EIT team has developed a solution to a problem and the supervisor agrees with the solution, it may be implemented immediately if the cost of the solution is less than $200 and it does not impact on another department. The reason for this is that we want all employees to take greater responsibility for the success of the business.

If, after discussion and analysis, the employees feel the idea is still a good one and the supervisor or area manager does not, the employees may ask for a review by the EIT Steering Committee. The reason for this is that no one employee, hourly or salaried, can be permitted to stand in the way of a good idea being heard.

The only bad idea is one that is not suggested. You may think your suggestion is not important enough to bring up. Wrong. It may prove to be the catalyst needed by your fellow employees, to trigger another idea.

There will be an Employee Involvement Steering Committee which will coordinate all employee involvement activities. The EIT Steering Committee will have the following functions:

- Oversee the operation of the EIT teams.
- Encourage the teams to take on significant projects.
- Review ideas that have been rejected by supervisors or managers.
- Coordinate review of ideas that cut across more than one department.
- Provide regular communications on the activities of the EITs.
- Act as a mechanism that will create greater trust, confidence, and teamwork.

The Bonus Committee

The Bonus Committee is made up of four union and four company representatives. It is one of the most effective means of communication between employees and management. The committee meets once each quarter to review the bonus computation for the previous quarter and analyze why it was, or was not, favorable. Accurate minutes will be kept by the Bonus Committee.

The Gain-Sharing Bonus

The productivity bonus is paid to recognize employees for their efforts. The bonus is not a gift. It will be paid when it has been earned by exceeding [baseline year] performance levels for labor costs, quality, and shop supplies.

The program utilizes three measurement points when calculating the bonus payout:

- Productivity (as measured in labor costs)
- Quality (as measured by spoilage, scrap, and reclamations)
- Shop supplies

The Painted Post Gain-Sharing Plan permits gains in productivity to be enhanced by savings in scrap and reclamation expenses and shop supplies. Thus, a bonus is determined by the following formula:

$$\text{Gain-sharing bonus} = \text{productivity (labor costs)}$$
$$\pm \text{ quality (spoilage, scrap, \& reclamation)} \pm \text{shop supplies}$$

However, if quality falls below the stated target, it will reduce the bonus earned from a productivity gain. Conversely, if productivity falls below the stated target, it will reduce a bonus that could have been earned from a quality improvement.

Thus, employees are required to focus on three very important indicators of plant performance. This measurement system ensures that productivity gains are not achieved at the expense of quality and prudent shop supply usage. At Painted Post, the dual importance of productivity and quality must be recognized by all employees.

The Role of Quality

Maintaining and increasing the quality of Painted Post products is achieved with this measurement formula in two ways:

- First, only "good product" is to be recognized in accounting for sales.
- Second, "bad product" will be scrapped and will adversely affect spoilage, scrap, and reclamation, as well as labor costs.
- Thus, there is a double benefit for employees to produce good-quality products and a severe penalty for failure to do so.

Calculation of the Gain-Sharing Bonus

Employees will receive a bonus when they exceed their own levels of performance in [baseline year]. Bonuses from the Painted Post Gain-Sharing Plan are not based upon management or employee opinion of how much work should be done and of what quality. Instead, the bonus is based upon improvements in how the workforce actually performed in [baseline year]. The following is an example of how the gain-sharing bonus will be calculated:

Painted Post Gain-Sharing Calculation Example

Net sales	$9,000,000
Inventory change sales value	+1,000,000
Sales value of production	10,000,000

Labor Bonus Pool

Target labor and fringe (16.23%)	1,623,000
Actual labor and fringe	1,573,000
Labor/fringe savings bonus	50,000
Actual percent of sales value	15.73%

Waste Savings Bonus Pool

Target spoiled and reclamation (3.34)	$334,000
Actual spoiled and reclamation	294,000
Waste savings bonus	40,000
Actual percent of sales value	2.94%

Operating Supplies Bonus Pool

Target operating supplies (4.00%)	$400,000
Actual operating supplies	370,000
Operating supplies savings bonus	30,000
Actual percent of sales value	3.70%

Distribution

Total all savings bonus pools	$120,000
Less: Current quarter reserve provision	40,000
Apply to prior quarter loss	-0-
Available for distribution	80,000
Employee share (65%)	52,000
Participating payroll	1,000,000
Employee share—percentage of participating payroll	5.20%
Reserve balance	$40,000

The reserve is established in order to safeguard the Company against any quarters with lower-than-normal output. At the end of each plan year, whatever is left in the reserve will be paid out with 65 percent going to the employees and 35 percent to the Company.

On the next several pages we examine the bonus formula in detail. Please read this information carefully. It is very important for every employee to understand how we arrive at a bonus.

QUESTIONS AND ANSWERS

- *Q:* What should an employee do if he or she has a question about the plan or an idea that might increase the bonus?
- *A:* Questions or ideas should be referred to the employee's supervisor, the EIT Steering Committee, the Plant Personnel office, or the Gain-Sharing Committee.
- *Q:* Will being absent or tardy affect my bonus?
- *A:* Employees will receive a bonus only for actual hours worked. The employee who has lost time will not be paid a bonus for that period of absences.
- *Q:* What about other pay-for-time-not-worked benefits?
- *A:* Bonuses will be excluded from all pay-for-time-not-worked benefits, such as vacations, holidays, death in family, jury duty, and so forth.

- *Q:* What if there is ever a question as to the accuracy of the calculation of the bonus formula?
- *A:* If there is ever a question as to the accuracy of the information, the Company has agreed to permit PriceWaterhouseCoopers to conduct an audit.
- *Q:* How long will the program last?
- *A:* The Gain-Sharing Plan will exist for the life of the present collective bargaining agreement. Since the plan is an annual plan, each year the nature of the plan will be reviewed. The Union and the Company will have the right to meet to review the plan if either becomes dissatisfied with it.

Profit-Sharing (401k) at Walgreens[90]

Many of our employees say Walgreens 401(k) plan, called the Walgreens Profit-Sharing Plan, is the No. 1 benefit Walgreens offers. That's because you benefit from the company's success through an annual match that is one of the highest match rates in American business.

Here's how it works: After you have 90 days of service with the company and have worked an average of 20 hours per week, you have the opportunity to contribute up to 50 percent of your annual salary to the Profit-Sharing Plan, up to the IRS limit. The company matches the first 2 percent of your contributions with a guaranteed match of $2 for every $1 you contribute. There's also the possibility of an additional match based on company profits for the year. The great thing about our plan is that as long as the company's profits grow, so does your retirement account.

Endnotes

1. American Management Association, "Merit Raises Remain Popular Among Fortune 1000," *Compflash* (December 1994), p. 6.

2. Data are from a *www.hewitt.com* survey as reported in IOMA, *Complete Guide to Best Practices in Pay for Performance* (Newark, NJ: Institute of Management & Administration, 2005), pp. 1–8.

3. Kenan S. Abosch, "Rationalizing Variable Pay Plans," in Lance A. Berger and Dorothy Berger, *The Compensation Handbook* (New York: McGraw-Hill, 2008), pp. 227–238.

4. Jeffrey Arthur and Lynda Aiman-Smith, "Gainsharing and Organizational Learning: An Analysis of Employee Suggestions Over Time," *Academy of Management Journal* 44(4) (2001), pp. 737–754.

5. Jerry M. Newman and Daniel J. Fisher, "Strategic Impact Merit Pay," *Compensation and Benefits Review* (July/August 1992), pp. 38–45.

6. Jonathan Day, Paul Mang, Ansgar Richter, and John Roberts, "Has Pay for Performance Had Its Day?" *McKinsey Quarterly* 25(2) (2002), pp. 6–54.

7. Robert Heneman, *Merit Pay: Linking Pay Increases to Performance Ratings* (Reading, MA: Addison-Wesley, 1992).

8. R. E. Kopelman and L. Reinharth, "Research Results: The Effect of Merit-Pay Practices on White Collar Performance." *Compensation Review,* 1982, 14(4), pp 30–40.

9. S. L. Rynes, B. Gerhart, and L. Parks, "Personnel Psychology: Performance Evaluation and Pay for Performance," *Annual Review of Psychology* 56 (2005) 56, pp. 571–600.

10. Howard Risher, "Pay-for-Performance: The Keys to Making It Work," *Public Personnel Management* 31(3) (2002), pp. 317–332.

11. D. Wills, "I'm OK, You're Outstanding," *Government Executive* (July 1, 2006), pp. 23–26.

12. Sam Dillon, "Long Reviled, Merit Pay Gains Among Teachers." *New York Times,* June 18, 2007, *www.NYTimes.com,* accessed June 29, 2009.

13. Cincinnati Federation of Teachers, "Teacher Quality Update," *www.cft-aft.org/prof/tqa_comp3.html,* August 2000.

14. R. Tomsho, "More Districts Pay Teachers for Performance," *The Wall Street Journal,* March 23, 2006, pp. B1, B5.

15. Greg Toppo, "Teachers Take Test Scores to Bank," *USA Today,* October 22, 2008, p. A1.

16. Myrna Hellerman and James Kochanski, "Merit Pay," in Lance A. Berger and Dorothy Berger, *The Compensation Handbook,* 5th ed. (New York: McGraw-Hill, 2008), pp. 85–93; D. Eskew and R. L. Heneman, "A Survey of Merit Pay Plan Effectiveness: End of the Line for Merit Pay or Hope for Improvement," in R. L. Heneman, *Strategic Reward Management,* (Greenwich, CT: Information Age Publishing, 2002).

17. IOMA, "Incentives Are Gaining Ground," *Complete Guide to Best Practices in Pay for Performance* (Newark NJ: Institute of Management & Administration, 2005), pp. 1–8.

18. IOMA, *2002 Incentive Pay Programs and Results* (Newark NJ: Institute of Management and Administration, May 2002), p. 13.

19. UCSF School of Pharmacy, Office of the Associate Dean for Administration Personnel Unit, "Spot Awards," *http://pharmacy.ucsf.edu/personnel/spot.html,* July 6, 2009.

20. E. A. Locke, D. B. Feren, V. M. McCaleb, K. N. Shaw, and A. T. Denny, "The Relative Effectiveness of Four Methods of Motivating Employee Performance," in K. D. Duncan, M. M. Gruenberg, and D. Wallis, eds., *Changes in Working Life* (New York: Wiley, 1980), pp. 363–388; R. A. Guzzo, R. D. Jette, and R. A. Katzell, "The Effects of Psychologically Based Intervention Programs on Worker Productivity: A Meta-Analysis," *Personnel Psychology* 38 (1985), pp. 275–291.

21. E. A. Locke, D. B. Feren, V. M. McCaleb, et al., "The Relative Effectiveness of Four Methods of Motivating Employee Performance," in K. D. Duncan, M. M. Gruenberg, and D. Wallis, eds., *Changes in Working Life* (New York: Wiley, 1980), pp. 363–388; R. A. Guzzo, R. D. Jette, and R. A. Katzell, "The Effects of Psychologically Based Intervention Programs on Worker Productivity: A Meta-Analysis," *Personnel Psychology* 38 (1985), pp. 275–291.

22. Thomas Patten, *Pay, Employee Compensation, and Incentive Plans* (New York: Macmillan, 1977).

23. Thomas Wilson, "Is It Time to Eliminate the Piece Rate Incentive System?" *Compensation and Benefits Review,* March–April 1992, pp. 43–49.

24. Daniel Eisenberg, "Where People Are Never Let Go," *Time,* June 18, 2001, p. 40; Kenneth Chilton, "Lincoln Electric's Incentive System: A Reservoir of Trust," *Compensation and Benefits Review* (November–December 1994), pp. 29–34.

25. Jon Katzenbach and Douglas Smith, *The Wisdom of Teams* (New York: HarperCollins, 1993).

26. P. Zingheim and J. R. Shuster, *Pay People Right* (San Francisco: Jossey-Bass, 2000).

27. K. Dow Scott, Jane Floyd, Philip G. Benson, and James W. Bishop, "The Impact of the Scanlon Plan on Retail Store Performance," *WorldatWork* 11(3) (2002), pp. 18–27.

28. Ibid.

29. Barry Gerhart, Sara L. Rynes, and Ingrid Smithey Fullmer, "Pay and Performance: Individuals, Groups and Executives," in A. P. Brief and J. P. Walsh, *Academy of Management Annals,* Vol. 3 (Newark NJ: Lawrence Erlbaum, forthcoming).

30. Conversation with Thomas Ruddy, manager of research, Xerox Corporation, 1997.

31. John G. Belcher, *Results Oriented Variable Pay System* (New York: AMACOM, 1996); Steven E. Gross, *Compensation for Teams* (New York: AMACOM, 1995).

32. Theresa M. Welbourne, David B. Balkin, and Luis R. Gomez-Mejia, "Gainsharing and Mutual Monitoring: A Combined Agency-Organizational Justice Interpretation," *Academy of Management Journal* 38(3) (1995), pp. 881–899.

33. D. Terpstra and A. Honoree, "The Relative Importance of External, Internal, Individual, and Procedural Equity to Pay Satisfaction," *Compensation and Benefits Review,* November–December 2003, pp. 67–78.

34. American Management Association, "Team-Based Pay: Approaches Vary, But Produce No Magic Formulas," *Compflash* (April 1994), p. 4.

35. Conversation with Sharon Knight, director of compensation, and Martha Kimber, manager of compensation, both at Kraft Foods, 1997.

36. John G. Belcher, *Results Oriented Variable Pay System* (New York: AMACOM, 1996).

37. F. McKenzie and M. Shilling, "Ensuring Effective Incentive Design and Implementation," *Compensation and Benefits Review,* May–June 1998, pp. 57–65.

38. Ibid.

39. M. Bloom and G. Milkovich, "Relationships Among Risk, Incentive Pay, and Organizational Performance," *Academy of Management Journal* 11(3) (1998), pp. 283–297.

40. L. Hatcher, T. L. Ross, "From Individual Incentives to an Organization-Wide Gain-Sharing Plan: Effects on Teamwork and Product Quality," *Journal of Organizational Behavior* 12 (1991), pp. 169–183.

41. American Management Association, "Team-Based Pay: Approaches Vary, But Produce No Magic Formulas," *Compflash,* April 1994, p. 4.

42. G. K. Shives and K. D. Scott, "Gainsharing and EVA: The US Postal Experience," *WorldatWork Journal,* First Quarter 2003, pp. 1–30.

43. B. Gerhart and G. Milkovich, "Employee Compensation: Research and Practice," in M. D. Dunnette and L. M. Hough, eds., *Handbook of Industrial & Organizational Psychology,* 2nd Edition, 1992, Palo Alto, CA: Consulting Psychologists Press, Inc.; T. M. Welbourne, & L. Gomez-Mejia, "Gain sharing: A critical review and a future research agenda," *Journal of Management* 21 (1995), pp. 559–609.

44. J. B. Arthur and G. S. Jelf, "The Effects of Gain Sharing on Grievance Rates and Absenteeism Over Time," *Journal of Labor Research* 20 (1999), pp. 133–145.

45. A. Weiss, "Incentives and Worker Behavior: Some Evidence," in H. R. Nalbantian, ed., *Incentives, Cooperation and Risk Taking* (Lanham, MD: Rowman & Littlefield, 1987).

46. Some of these issues are addressed at *www.hr-guide.com/data/G443.htm,* retrieved July 17, 2006.

47. Robert Masternak, "How to Make Gainsharing Successful: The Collective Experience of 17 Facilities," *Compensation and Benefits Review,* September–October 1997, pp. 43–52.

48. John G. Belcher, "Gainsharing and Variable Pay: The State of the Art," *Compensation and Benefits Review,* May/June 1994, pp. 50–60.

49. John Belcher, "Design Options for Gain Sharing," unpublished paper, American Productivity Center, 1987.

50. D. Kim, "Determinants of the Survival of Gainsharing Programs," *Industrial and Labor Relations Review* 53(1) 1999, pp. 21–42.

51. A. J. Geare, "Productivity From Scanlon Type Plans," *Academy of Management Review* 1(3) (1976), pp. 99–108.

52. Ibid.

53. K. D. Scott, J. Floyd, and P. Benson, "The Impact of the Scanlon Plan on Retail Store Performance," *WorldatWork Journal* 11(3), 2002, pp. 4–13.

54. T. H. Patten, *Pay: Employee Compensation and Incentive Plans* (New York: Free Press, 1977); P. Schwinger, *Wage Incentive Systems* (New York: Halsted, 1975).

55. B. Graham-Moore and T. Ross, *Productivity Gainsharing* (Englewood Cliffs, NJ: Prentice-Hall, 1983).

56. J. Newman, "Selecting Incentive Plans to Complement Organizational Strategy," in L. Gomez-Mejia and D. Balkin, eds., *Current Trends in Compensation Research and Practice,* ed. L. Gomez-Mejia and D. Balkin (Englewood Cliffs, NJ: Prentice-Hall, 1987).

57. Marhsall Fein, "Improshare: A Technique for Sharing Productivity Gains With Employees," M. L. Rock and L. A. Berger, eds., *The Compensation Handbook* (New York: McGraw-Hill, 1993), pp. 158–175.

58. R. Kaufman, "The Effects of Improshare on Productivity," *Industrial and Labor Relations Review* 45(2) (1992), pp. 311–322.

59. Darlene O'Neill, "Blending the Best of Profit Sharing and Gainsharing," *HR Magazine,* March 1994, pp. 66–69.

60. Ibid.

61. D. L. Kruse, *Profit Sharing: Does It Make a Difference?* (Kalamazoo, MI: Upjohn Institute for Employment Research, 1993).

62. Ford data appears at *www.chryslerforum.com/m_346/mpage_1/key_/tm.htm* and GM data appears at *search.yahoo.com/search?ei=utf-8˜fr=slv8-˜p=GM%20profit%20sharing%20 payout%202005,* July 18, 2006.

63 "GM Files for Bankruptcy," *Chicago Tribune, http://www.chicagobreakingnews. com/2009/06/gm-files-for-bankruptcy.html,* June 1, 2009.

64. K. Brown and V. Huber, "Lowering Floors and Raising Ceilings: A Longitudinal Assessment of the Effects of an Earnings-at-Risk Plan on Pay Satisfaction," *Personnel Psychology* 45 (1992), pp. 279–311.

65. S. E. Gross and D. Duncan, "Gainsharing Plan Spurs Record Productivity and Payouts at AmeriSteel," *Compensation and Benefits Review,* November–December 1998, pp. 46–50.

66. These observations are drawn from a variety of sources, including K. Brown and V. Huber, "Lowering Floors and Raising Ceilings: A Longitudinal Assessment of the Effects of an Earnings-at-Risk Plan on Pay Satisfaction," *Personnel Psychology* 45 (1992), pp. 279–311; D. Collins, L. Hatcher and T. Ross, "The Decision to Implement Gainsharing: The Role of Work Climate, Expected Outcomes and Union Status," *Personnel Psychology* 46 (1993), pp. 77–103; American Management Association, "Team-Based Pay: Approaches Vary but Produce No Magic Formulas," *Compflash,* April 1994, p. 4; W. N. Cooke, "Employee Participation Programs, Group Based Incentives and Company Performance," *Industrial and Labor Relations Review* 47 (1994), pp. 594–610; G. W. Florowski, "The Organizational Impact of Profit Sharing," *Academy of Management Review* 12(4) (1987), pp. 622–636.

67. R. Renn and W. K. Barksdale, "Earnings-at-Risk Incentive Plans: A Performance, Satisfaction, and Turnover Dilemma," *Compensation and Benefits Review,* July–August 2001, pp. 68–73.

68. P. M. Senge, *The Fifth Discipline:* The Art and Practice of *the Learning Organization* (New York: Doubleday, 1990).

69. Jeffrey Arthur and Lynda Aiman-Smith, "Gainsharing and Organizational Learning An Analysis of Employee Suggestions Over Time," *Academy of Management Journal* 44(4) (2001), pp. 737–754.

70. T. H. Hammer and R. N. Stern, "Employee Ownership: Implications for the Organizational Distribution of Power," *Academy of Management Journal* 23 (1980), pp. 78–100.

71. B. J. Hall, "What You Need to Know About Stock Options," *Harvard Business Review,* March–April 2000, pp. 121–129.

72. D. R. Dalton, S. T. Certo, and R. Roengpitya, "Meta-Analyses of Financial Performance and Equity: Fusion or Confusion?" *Academy of Management Journal* 46(1) (2003), pp. 13–26.

73. Barry Gerhart, "Pay Strategy and Firm Performance," in S. Rynes and B. Gerhart, eds., *Compensation in Organizations:* Progress and Prospects (San Francisco: New Lexington Press, 1999).

74. Wikipedia, "Employee Stock Option," *en.wikipedia.org/wiki/Employee_stock_option,* retrieved July 24, 2006.

75. W. Zellner, "An Insider's Tale of Enron's Toxic Culture," *BusinessWeek,* March 31, 2003, pp. 16.

76.   T. Buyniski and B. Harsen, "The Cancel and Regrant: A Roadmap for Addressing Underwater Options," *Compensation and Benefits Review,* January–February 2002, pp. 28–32.

77.   PFP News Brief, "Expensing Stock Options Is Only a Matter of Time," *Pay for Performance Report,* November 2002, p. 8.

78.   T. McCoy, " Emerging Option to Stock Options." *Pay for Performance Report* (Newark, NJ: Institute of Management & Administration, June 2001), p. 2.

79.   "Expensing Stock *Options: The Rule Is Final—Or Is it?," http://accounting.smartpros. com/x49842.xml, July 24, 2006.*

80.   K. W. Chilton, "Lincoln Electric's Incentive System: A Reservoir of Trust," *Compensation & Benefits Review* 26(6) (1994), pp. 29–34; Howard Rudnitsky, "You Have to Trust the Workforce," *Forbes,* July 19, 1993, pp. 78–81.

81.   IOMA, "Stock Options Motivate." *Pay for Performance Report,* May 1996, p. 3.

82.   IOMA, "Another Pan of Stock Option Plans," *Pay for Performance Report,* January 1999, p. 11.

83.   Staff, "An *ESOP* to the Workers," Economist, April 14, 2007, pp. 26–28.

84.   Ibid.

85.   J. Blasi, M. Conte, and D. Kruse, "Employee Stock Ownership and Corporate Performance Among Public Companies," *Industrial and Labor Relations Review* 50 (1996), pp. 60–66.

86.   J. Blasi, D. Kruse, J. Sesil, and M. Kroumova, "An Assessment of Employee Ownership in the United States With Implications for the EU," *International Journal of Human Resource Management* 14 (2003), pp. 893–919.

87.   R. Buckman, "Microsoft Uses Stock Options to Lift Morale," *The Wall Street Journal,* April 26, 2000, p. A3.

88.   P. Singh, "Strategic Reward Systems at Southwest Airlines," *Compensation and Benefits Review,* March/April 2002, pp. 28–33; P. Zingheim and J. Schuster, *Pay People Right!* (San Francisco: Jossey-Bass, 2000).

89.   Workforce Management, "Starbucks Is Pleasing Employees and Pouring Profits," *http:// www.workforce.com/section/02/feature/23/52/96/,* June 30, 2009.

90.   S. Burzawa, "Broad-Based Stock Options Are Used to Attract, Retain, and Motivate Employees," *Employee Benefit Plan Review,* July 1998, pp. 46–50.

Performance Appraisals

Chapter Outline

The Role of Performance Appraisals
in Compensation Decisions
  Performance Metrics

Strategies for Better Understanding
and Measuring Job Performance
  The Balanced Scorecard Approach
  Strategy 1: Improve Appraisal Formats
  Strategy 2: Select the Right Raters
  *Strategy 3: Understand How Raters
  Process Information*
  *Common Errors in Appraising
  Performance: Criterion Contamination*
  *Strategy 4: Training Raters to Rate
  More Accurately*

Putting It All Together: The
Performance Evaluation Process

Equal Employment Opportunity and
Performance Evaluation

Tying Pay to Subjectively Appraised
Performance
  Competency: Customer Care
  *Performance- and Position-Based
  Guidelines*
  Designing Merit Guidelines

Promotional Increases as a
Pay-for-Performance Tool

Your Turn: Performance Appraisal at
Burger King

Appendix 11-A: Balanced Scorecard
Example: Department of Energy
(Federal Personal Property
Management Program)

Appendix 11-B: Sample Appraisal
Form for Leadership Dimension:
Pfizer Pharmaceutical

Here's What Performance Appraisals Are Really Like:

Attention: Human Resources—submission of performance review for Joe Smith

Joe Smith, my assistant programmer, can always be found
hard at work in his cubicle. Joe works independently, without
wasting company time talking to colleagues. Joe never
thinks twice about assisting fellow employees, and he always
finishes given assignments on time. Often Joe takes extended
measures to complete his work, sometimes skipping
coffee breaks. Joe is an individual who has absolutely no
vanity in spite of his high accomplishments and profound
knowledge in his field. I firmly believe that Joe can be

classed as a high-caliber employee, the type which cannot be dispensed with. Regards,

Project Leader

---

e-mail to Attention: Human Resources

Joe Smith was reading over my shoulder while I wrote the report sent to you earlier today. Kindly read only the odd numbered lines [1, 3, 5, etc.] for my true assessment of his ability.

Regards,
Project Leader

Chapters 9 and 10 covered the merits of pay-for-performance plans. A key element of these plans is some measure of performance. Sometimes these measures are subjective and yield ratings that don't represent employee performance, as in the example above; sometimes this measure is objective and quantifiable. Blue Cross–Blue Shield of New Jersey, for example, uses data from insurance claims (number of tests ordered, treatments administered, drugs prescribed) to compare doctors with their peers.[1] Certainly, when we are measuring performance for a group incentive plan, objective financial measures may be readily available. As we move down to the level of the individual and the team, these "hard" measures are not as readily available. Despite this, some organizations are guilty of "criterion deficiency"—using objective measures that don't truly represent all of the key dimensions of the job. A secretary who is measured solely on words per minute in word processing would complain, legitimately, that he or she does other things that are far more vital to job performance. This chapter discusses in more detail the difficulties of measuring performance, particularly when we use subjective procedures.

THE ROLE OF PERFORMANCE APPRAISALS IN COMPENSATION DECISIONS

The first use of merit ratings apparently took place in a Scottish cotton mill around 1800. Wooden cubes, indicating different levels of performance, were hung above worker stations as a visible signal of who was doing well.[2] Some 200 years later, the Iraqi national soccer team reports that bad performance frequently led to torture of players during the Saddam Hussein reign. While performance reviews don't usually lead to such questionable outcomes, they are used for a wide variety of decisions in organizations—only one of which is to guide the allocation of merit increases. Unfortunately, as we will discover, the link between performance ratings and these outcomes is not always as strong as we would like. In fact, it's common to make a distinction between performance judgments and performance ratings.[3] Performance ratings—the things we enter into an employee's permanent record—are influenced by a host of factors besides the employee behaviors observed by raters. Such things as organization values (e.g., valuing technical skills or interpersonal skills more highly), competition among departments, differences in status between departments, economic conditions (labor shortages which make for less willingness to terminate employees for poor performance)—all influence the way raters rate employees. There is even some evidence that much of job performance ratings can be attributed to a general performance factor (after accounting for error) that is present across a wide variety of jobs and situations.[4] Is it any wonder then that employees often voice frustration about the appraisal process? A survey of 2,600 employees nationwide yielded the following rather disheartening conclusions:

39 percent felt their performance goals weren't clearly defined.

39 percent felt they didn't know how their performance was evaluated.

45 percent didn't believe their last performance review guided them on how to improve.

45 percent didn't think the reviews could differentiate among good, average, and poor performers.

48 percent didn't think doing a good job was recognized.[5]

This dissatisfaction makes a difference. Employees unhappy with the appraisal process were less satisfied with their firms, less satisfied with their pay, less committed, and more likely to turn over.[6] Perhaps the biggest complaint of all from employees (and managers too) is that appraisals are too subjective. And lurking behind subjectivity, always, is the possibility of unfair treatment by a supervisor. Is it any surprise that the subject of **performance metrics** is one of the hottest areas of study in both academic and business organizations? Critics of subjective measures want performance measures (metrics) that are fair to employees and reflect value for the organization.

Performance Metrics

At times, measurement of performance can be quantified. Indeed, some reliable estimates suggest that between 13 percent of the time (hourly workers) and 70 percent of the time (managerial employees), employee performance is tied to quantifiable measures.[7] Just because something is quantifiable, though, doesn't mean it is an objective measure of performance. As any accounting student knows, financial measures are arrived at through a process that involves some subjective decision making (can we spell "Enron"?). Which year we choose to take write-offs for plant closings, for example, affects the bottom line reported to the public. Such potential for subjectivity has led some experts to warn that so-called objective data can be deficient (**criterion deficient**) and may not tell the whole story.[8] Even with external audits, supposedly solid financial performance indicators can be misrepresented for extended periods. Just ask the folks at HealthSouth, who overstated earnings for almost 15 years without being caught by their auditor, Ernst and Young.[9] Despite these concerns, most HR professionals probably would prefer to work with quantitative data. Sometimes, though, performance isn't easily quantified. Either job output is not readily quantifiable or the components that are quantifiable do not reflect important job dimensions. As we noted earlier, a secretarial job could be reduced to words per minute and errors per page of keyboarding. But many secretaries, and their supervisors, would argue this captures only a small portion of the job. Courtesy in greeting clients and in answering phones, initiative in solving problems without running to the boss, dependability under deadlines—all of these intangible qualities can make the difference between a good secretary and a poor one. Such subjective goals are less easily measured. The end result, all too often, is a performance appraisal process that is plagued by errors.

Perhaps the biggest attack against appraisals in general, and subjective appraisals in particular, comes from top names in the total-quality-management area. Edward Deming, the grandfather of the quality movement here and in Japan, launched an attack on appraisals because, he contended, the work situation (not the individual) is the major determinant of performance.[10] Variation in performance arises many times because employees don't have the necessary information, technology, or control to adequately perform their jobs.[11] Further, Deming argued, individual work standards and performance ratings rob employees of pride and self-esteem.

Some experts argue that rather than throwing out the entire performance appraisal process, we should apply total-quality-management principles to improving it.[12] A first way to improve performance appraisals, then, would be to recognize that part of performance is influenced more by the work environment and system than by employee behaviors. For example, sometimes when a student says "The dog ate my paper" (latest version: "The computer ate my flash drive"), it really happened. When we tell teachers, or other raters, that the system sometimes does affect performance, raters are more sympathetic and rate higher.[13]

A second way to improve performance appraisal, one that involves most of the remainder of this chapter, concerns identifying strategies for understanding and measuring job performance better. This may help us reduce the number and types of rating errors illustrated in the next section.

STRATEGIES FOR BETTER UNDERSTANDING AND MEASURING JOB PERFORMANCE

Efforts to improve the performance rating process take several forms.[14] First, researchers and compensation people alike devote considerable energy to defining job performance: What exactly should be measured when we evaluate employees? Managers can be grouped into one of three categories, based on the types of employee behaviors they focus on. One group looks strictly at task performance, how the employees perform the responsibilities of their jobs. A second group looks primarily at counterproductive performance, evaluating based on the negative behaviors employees show. The final group looks at both these types of behavior.[15] Studies that examine more specific factors focus on such performance dimensions as planning and organizing, training, coaching, developing subordinates, and technical proficiency.[16] As we noted earlier, one particularly good mega study found that much of performance can be accounted for by one general performance factor. Perhaps breaking performance ratings down into component performance dimensions may not be fruitful.[17] Countering this argument is the large amount of research and heavy adoption by industry of balanced scorecards.

The Balanced Scorecard Approach

A **balanced scorecard approach** is a way to look at what contributes value in an organization. Too often we just look at the bottom line, as measured by financial goals. The balanced scorecard acknowledges that bottom line success doesn't just happen. It depends on satisfied customers buying products and services from effective and satisfied employees who both serve the customers *and* produce goods in the most operationally efficient way possible. If this is true, then we need to measure all four of the following dimensions and be prepared to say that success depends on high scores for each: customer satisfaction, employee internal growth and commitment, operational efficiency in internal processes, and financial measures. Besides the widespread enthusiasm in industry for this approach, there is data that suggest implementation of a balanced scorecard can have positive impacts on the bottom line.[18] Appendix 11-A shows a balanced scorecard used by the Department of Energy.

A second direction for performance research notes that the definition of performance and its components is expanding. Jobs are becoming more dynamic, and the need for employees to adapt and grow is increasingly stressed. This focus on individual characteristics, or personal competencies, is consistent with the whole trend toward measuring job competency.[19] Pizza Hut, for example, has five competencies that store managers must master: 1) Sets High Standards, 2) Communicates Well, 3) Executes Processes and Routines, 4) Holds Self and Others Accountable, and 5) Celebrates Successes. Each of these competencies has specific behaviors a Pizza Hut general manager must show at three different levels of mastery.[20]

A third direction for improving the quality of performance ratings centers on identifying the best appraisal format. If only the ideal format could be found, so the argument goes, raters would use it to measure job performance better, that is, make more accurate ratings. As you might expect, there is little evidence that an ideal format exists.

Recent attention has focused less on the rating format and more on the raters themselves. This fourth direction identifies possible groups of raters (supervisor, peers, subordinates, customers, self) and examines whether a given group provides more or less accurate ratings. The fifth direction attempts to identify how raters process information about job performance and translate it into performance ratings. Such information, including an understanding of the role irrelevant information plays in the evaluation of employees, may yield strategies for reducing the flaws in the total process. Finally, data also suggest that raters can be trained to increase the accuracy of their ratings. The following sections focus on these last four approaches to better understanding and measuring performance: improving the format, selecting the right raters, understanding the way raters process information, and training raters to improve rating skills.

Strategy 1: Improve Appraisal Formats

Types of Formats

Evaluation formats can be divided into two general categories: **ranking** and **rating.**[21] **Ranking formats** require that the rater compare employees against each other to determine the relative ordering of the group on some performance measure (usually some measure of overall performance). Exhibit 11.1 illustrates three different methods of ranking employees:

- The **straight ranking** procedure is just that: employees are ranked relative to each other.
- **Alternation ranking** recognizes that raters are better at ranking people at extreme ends of the distribution. Raters are asked to indicate the best employee and then the worst employee. Working at the two extremes permits a rater to get more practice prior to making the harder distinctions in the vast middle ground of employees.

EXHIBIT 11.1
Three Ranking Formats

Straight Ranking Method	
Rank	**Employee's Name**
Best	1. _____
Next Best	2. _____
Next Best	3. _____
Etc.	

Alternation Ranking*	
Rank	**Employee's Name**
Best performer	1. _____
Next best	2. _____
Next best	3. _____
Etc.	4. _____
Next worst	3. _____
Next worst	2. _____
Worst performer	1. _____

Paired Comparison Ranking Method+					
	John	**Pete**	**Sam**	**Tom**	**Ranked Higher**
Bill	X	X	X	X	4
John		X	X	X	3
Pete			X	X	2
Sam				X	1

- The **paired-comparison ranking** method simplifies the ranking process by forcing raters to make ranking judgments about discrete pairs of people. Each individual is compared separately with all others in the work group. The person who "wins" the most paired comparisons is ranked top in the group, and so on. Unfortunately, when the size of the work group goes above 10 to 15 employees, the number of paired comparisons becomes unmanageable.

The second category of appraisal formats—ratings—is generally more popular than ranking systems. This popularity, though, is not accompanied by any evidence that rating formats are particularly valid.[22] Their use, especially when nonbehavioral anchors are employed (see Exhibit 11.3, for example), is more an issue of convenience than credibility.

The various **rating formats** have two elements in common. First, in contrast to ranking formats, rating formats require raters to evaluate employees on some absolute standard rather than relative to other employees. Second, each performance standard is measured on a scale whereby appraisers can check the point that best represents the employee's performance. In this way, performance variation is described along a continuum from good to bad. It is the types of descriptors used in anchoring this continuum that provide the major difference in rating scales.

These descriptors may be adjectives, behaviors, or outcomes. When adjectives are used as anchors, the format is called a **standard rating scale.** Exhibit 11.2 shows a

EXHIBIT 11.2
Rating Scale Using Absolute Standards

Standard Rating Scale With Adjective Anchors					
Communications Skills	Written and oral ability to clearly and convincingly express thoughts, ideas, or facts in individual or group situations				
Circle the number that best describes the level of employee performance	1 well above average	2 above average	3 average	4 below average	5 well below average

typical rating scale with adjectives as anchors ("well above average" to "well below average"). **Behaviorally anchored rating scales (BARS)** seem to be the most common format using behaviors as descriptors. By anchoring scales with concrete behaviors, firms adopting a BARS format hope to make evaluations less subjective. When raters try to decide on a rating, they have a common definition (in the form of a behavioral example) for each of the performance levels. Consider, as an example, the following behaviors as recorded on a fictitious officer fitness reports for the British Royal Navy. They are easily identifiable and, hopefully, humorous:

"This Officer reminds me very much of a gyroscope—always spinning around at a frantic pace, but not really going anywhere."

"He would be out of his depth in a car park puddle."

"Works well when under constant supervision and cornered like a rat in a trap."

"This man is depriving a village somewhere of an idiot."

"Only occasionally wets himself under pressure."[23]

A more serious behavioral scale for a similar occupation was developed by the Royal Canadian Mounted Police.[24] On the leadership dimension, the top and bottom ratings a mountie could get have behavioral descriptors that look like this:

Bottom rating—Ignores advice and views of other members: does not accept responsibility for own views and actions; blames others for own failures; provides others with incorrect information on policies and procedures.

Top rating—Takes charge of situations; consulted by other members for advice on operational and/or administrative policies and procedures.

This rating format directly addresses a major criticism of standard adjective rating scales: Different raters carry with them into the rating situation different definitions of the scale levels (e.g., different raters have different ideas about what "average work" is). Exhibit 11.3 illustrates a complete behaviorally anchored rating scale for teamwork.

In both the standard rating scale and the BARS, overall performance is calculated as some weighted average (weighted by the importance the organization attaches to each dimension) of the ratings on all dimensions. One way to derive an overall evaluation from the dimensional ratings appears in Exhibit 11.4. The employee evaluated in Exhibit 11.4 is rated slightly above average. An alternative method for obtaining the overall rating would be to allow the rater discretion not only in rating performance on the individual dimensions but also in assigning the overall evaluation. The weights

EXHIBIT 11.3 **Standard Rating Scale With Behavioral Scale Anchors**

Teamwork:	Ability to contribute to group performance, to draw out the best from others, to foster activities building group morale, even under high-pressure situations.	
Exceeds Standards	1	Seeks out or is regularly requested for group assignments. Groups this person works with inevitably have high performance and high morale. Employee makes strong personal contribution and is able to identify strengths of many different types of group members and foster their participation. Wards off personality conflicts by positive attitude and ability to mediate unhealthy conflicts, sometimes even before they arise. Will make special effort to ensure credit for group performance is shared by all.
	2	Seen as a positive contributor in group assignments. Works well with all types of people and personalities, occasionally elevating group performance of others. Good ability to resolve unhealthy group conflicts that flare up. Will make special effort to ensure strong performers receive credit due them.
Meets Standards	3	Seen as a positive personal contributor in group assignments. Works well with most types of people and personalities. Is never a source of unhealthy group conflict and will encourage the same behavior in others.
	4	When group mission requires skill this person is strong in, employee seen as strong contributor. On other occasions will not hinder performance of others. Works well with most types of people and personalities and will not be the initiator of unhealthy group conflict. Will not participate in such conflict unless provoked on multiple occasions.
	5	Depending on the match of personal skill and group mission, this person will be seen as a positive contributor. Will not be a hindrance to performance of others and avoids unhealthy conflict unless provoked.
Does Not Meet Standards	6	Unlikely to be chosen for assignments requiring teamwork except on occasions where personal expertise is vital to group mission. Not responsive to group goals, but can be enticed to help when personal appeals are made. May not get along with other members and either withdraw or generate unhealthy conflict. Seeks personal recognition for team performance and/or may downplay efforts of others.
	7	Has reputation for noncontribution and for creating conflicts in groups. Cares little about group goals and is very hard to motivate towards and goal completion unless personal rewards are guaranteed. May undermine group performance to further personal aims. Known to seek personal recognition and/or downplay efforts of others.
Rating:	Documentation of Rating (optional except for 6 and 7):	

(shown in the far–right column of Exhibit 11.4) would not be used, and the overall evaluation would be based on a subjective and internal assessment by the rater.

Appendix 11-B for this chapter gives an example of the rating scale and appraisal form used by Pfizer Pharmaceutical to assess leadership, one of the competencies tracked by Pfizer. Pay attention to how long and involved Pfizer's form

EXHIBIT 11.4
An Example of Employee Appraisal

Employee: Kelsey T. Mahoney
Job Title: Supervisor, Shipping and Receiving

Performance Dimension	Dimension Rating					Dimension Weight
	Well Below Average **1**	*Below Average* **2**	*Average* **3**	*Above Average* **4**	*Well Above Average* **5**	
Leadership Ability				×		0.2 (× 4) = 0.8
Job Knowledge					×	0.1 (× 5) = 0.5
Work Output				×		0.3 (× 4) = 1.2
Attendance			×			0.2 (× 3) = 0.6
Initiative			×			0.2 (× 3) = 0.6

Sum of Rating × Weight = 3.7
Overall Rating = 3.7

is—and this only covers one of four competencies. Considerable money went into its development.

In addition to adjectives and behaviors, outcomes also are used as a standard. The most common form is **management by objectives (MBO).**[25] Management by objectives is both a planning and an appraisal tool that has many different variations across firms.[26] As a first step, organization objectives are identified from the strategic plan of the company. Each successively lower level in the organizational hierarchy is charged with identifying work objectives that will support attainment of organizational goals. Exhibit 11.5 illustrates a common MBO objective. Notice that the emphasis is on outcomes achieved by employees. At the beginning of a performance review period, the employee and supervisor discuss performance objectives (column 1).[27] Months later, at the end of the review period, the two again meet to record results formally (of course, multiple informal discussions should have occurred before this time). Results are then compared against objectives, and a performance rating is determined based on how well the objectives were met.

Merck, the pharmaceutical giant, combines an MBO approach focusing on outcomes with a set of measures designed to assess how those outcomes were achieved—Merck calls

EXHIBIT 11.5
Example of MBO Objective For Communications Skill

1. Performance Objective	2. Results
By July 1 of this year, Bill will complete a report summarizing employee reactions to the new performance appraisal system. An oral presentation will be prepared and delivered to all nonexempt employees in groups of 15–20. All oral presentations will be completed by August 31, and reactions of employees to this presentation will average at least 3.0 on a 5-point scale.	Written report completed by July 1. All but one oral presentation completed by August 31. Last report not completed until September 15 because of unavoidable conflicts in vacation schedules. Average rating of employees (reaction to oral presentation) was 3.4, exceeding minimum expectations.

EXHIBIT 11.6
Components of a Successful MBO Program

Source: Mark L. McConkie, "A Clarification of the Goal Setting and Appraisal Process in MBO," *Academy of Management Review* 4(1) (1979), pp. 29–40. © 1979, Academy of Management Review.

	Total No. of Responses*	Percent of Authorities in Agreement
1. Goals and objectives should be specific.	37	97
2. Goals and objectives should be defined in terms of measurable results.	37	97
3. Individual goals should be linked to overall organization goals.	37	97
4. Objectives should be reviewed "periodically."	31	82
5. The time period for goal accomplishment should be specified.	27	71
6. Wherever possible, the indicator of the results should be quantifiable; otherwise, it should be at least verifiable.	26	68
7. Objectives should be flexible; changed as conditions warrant.	26	68
8. Objectives should include a plan of action for accomplishing the results.	21	55
9. Objectives should be assigned priorities of weights.	19	50

*In this table the total number of responses actually represents the total number of authorities responding; thus, percentages also represent the percent of authorities in agreement with the statements made.

this its multidimensional view of performance. The MBO portion of a performance review is regularly updated to ensure that individual objectives are aligned with corporate and department goals. At the end of the year, employees are reviewed both on goal performance and on five other measures: quality of work, resource utilization, timeliness of completing objectives, innovation, and leadership. Ratings on these latter measures must be accompanied by examples of behaviors shown by employees that justify particular ratings.

A review of firms using MBO indicates generally positive improvements in performance both for individuals and for the organization. This performance increase is accompanied by managerial attitudes toward MBO that become more positive over time, particularly when the system is revised periodically to reflect feedback of participants. Managers are especially pleased with the way MBO provides direction to work units, improves the planning process, and increases superior/subordinate communication. On the negative side, MBO appears to require more paperwork and to increase both performance pressure and stress.[28]

Exhibit 11.6 shows some of the common components of an MBO format and the percentage of experts who judge this component vital to a successful evaluation effort.

A final type of appraisal format does not easily fall into any of the categories yet discussed. In an **essay format,** supervisors answer open-ended questions, in essay form, describing employee performance. Since the descriptors used could range from comparisons with other employees to the use of adjectives describing performance, types of behaviors, and goal accomplishments, the essay format can take on characteristics of all the formats discussed previously. Exhibit 11.7 illustrates the relative popularity of these formats in industry.

EXHIBIT 11.7 An Evaluation of Performance Appraisal Formats

	Employee Development Criterion	Administration Criterion	Personnel Research Criterion	Economic Criterion	Validity Criterion
Ranking	Poor—ranks typically based on overall performance, with little thought given to feedback on specific performance dimensions.	Poor—comparisons of ranks across work units to determine merit raises are meaningless. Other administrative actions similarly hindered.	Average—validation studies can be completed with rankings of performance.	Good—inexpensive source of performance data. Easy to develop and use in small organizations and in small units.	Average—good reliability but poor on rating errors, especially halo.
Standard rating scales	Average—general problem areas identified. Some information on extent of developmental need is available, but no feedback on necessary behaviors/outcomes.	Average—ratings valuable for merit increase decisions and others. Not easily defended if contested.	Average—validation studies can be completed, but level of measurement contamination unknown.	Good—inexpensive to develop and easy to use.	Average—content validity is suspect. Rating errors and reliability are average.
Behaviorally anchored rating scales	Good—extent of problem and behavioral needs are identified.	Good—BARS good for making administrative decisions. Useful for legal defense because job-relevant.	Good—validation studies can be completed and measurement problems on BARS less than many other criterion measures.	Average—expensive to develop but easy to use.	Good—high content validity. Some evidence of **interrater reliability** and reduced rating errors.
Management by objectives	Excellent—extent of problem and outcome deficiencies are identified.	Poor—MBO not suited to merit income decisions. Level of completion and difficulty of objectives hard to compare across employees.	Poor—nonstandard objectives across employees and no overall measures of performance make validity studies difficult.	Poor—expensive to develop and time-consuming to use.	Excellent—high content validity. Low rating errors.
Essay	Unknown—depends on guidelines or inclusions in essay as developed by organization or supervisors.	Poor—essays not comparable across different employees considered for merit or other administrative actions.	Poor—no quantitative indices to compare performance against employee test scores in validation studies.	Average—easy to develop but time-consuming to use.	Unknown—unstructured format makes studies of essay method difficult.

Evaluating Performance Appraisal Formats

What makes for a good appraisal format? Good ones score well on five dimensions: (1) employee development potential (amount of feedback about performance that the format offers), (2) administrative ease, (3) personnel research potential, (4) cost, and (5) validity. Admittedly, different organizations will attach different weights to these dimensions. For example, a small organization in its formative years is likely to be very cost-conscious. A large organization with pressing affirmative action commitments might place relatively high weight on validity and nondiscrimination and show less concern about cost issues. A progressive firm concerned with employee development might demand a format allowing substantial employee feedback. For example, 10 years ago Dow Chemical Company did away with performance ratings but kept performance reviews; stress was placed on using reviews to help develop employee skills. The five main criteria are explained below:[29]

1. *Employee development criterion:* Does the method communicate the goals and objectives of the organization? Is feedback to employees a natural outgrowth of the evaluation format, so that employee developmental needs are identified and can be attended to readily? We know that feedback has a positive impact on job performance.[30] There is also evidence that different kinds of feedback have different effects. Critical feedback that attacks the individual rather than focusing on the task has negative effects. Employees respond better to feedback that tells them what went wrong on the task and how to improve.[31] Keep in mind, though, that the desire for feedback doesn't extend across all cultures. Lucent Technologies found that certain cultures are very reluctant to give feedback, either positive or negative. In most Asian cultures feedback is viewed with great suspicion, and only the most reckless executive would jeopardize his reputation by giving feedback, particularly in public.

2. *Administrative criterion:* How easily can evaluation results be used for administrative decisions concerning wage increases, promotions, demotions, terminations, and transfers? Comparisons among individuals for personnel action require some common denominator. Typically this is a numerical rating of performance. Evaluation forms that do not produce numerical ratings cause administrative headaches. So, for example, an essay format (solely a written explanation of what the employee did well and not so well), with no numerical evaluation, is difficult to evaluate relative to other essays. Who did better is an important question when giving out merit increases.

3. *Personnel research criterion:* Does the instrument lend itself well to validating employment tests? Can applicants predicted to perform well be monitored through performance evaluation? Similarly, can the success of various employees and organizational development programs be traced to impacts on employee performance? As with the administrative criterion, evaluations typically need to be quantitative to permit the statistical tests so common in personnel research.

4. *Cost criterion:* Does the evaluation form initially require a long time to be developed? Is it time-consuming for supervisors to use the form in rating their employees? Is it expensive to use? All of these factors increase the format cost.

5. *Validity criterion:* By far the most research on formats in recent years has focused on reducing error and improving accuracy. Success in this pursuit would mean that

decisions based on performance ratings (e.g., promotions, merit increases) could be made with increased confidence. In general, the search for the perfect format to eliminate rating errors and improve accuracy has been unsuccessful. The high acclaim, for example, accompanying the introduction of BARS has not been supported by research.[32]

Exhibit 11.7 provides a report card on the five most common rating formats relative to the criteria just discussed.

Which of these appraisal formats is the best? Unfortunately, the answer is a murky "It depends." Keeley suggests that the choice of an appraisal format is dependent on the type of tasks being performed.[33] He argues that tasks can be ordered along a continuum from those that are very routine to those for which the appropriate behavior for goal accomplishment is very uncertain. In Keeley's view, different appraisal formats require assumptions about the extent to which correct behavior for task accomplishment can be specified. The choice of an appraisal format requires a matching of formats with tasks that meet the assumptions for that format. At one extreme of the continuum are behavior-based evaluation procedures that define specific performance expectations against which employee performance is evaluated. Keeley argues that behaviorally anchored rating scales fall into this category. The behavioral anchors specify performance expectations representing the different levels of performance possible by an employee. Only for highly routine, mechanistic tasks is it appropriate to specify behavioral expectations. For these routine tasks it is possible to identify the single sequence of appropriate behaviors for accomplishing a goal. Consequently, it is possible to identify behavioral anchors for a performance scale that illustrate varying levels of attainment of the proper sequence of activities.

However, when tasks are less routine, it is more difficult to specify a single sequence of procedures that must be followed to accomplish a goal. Rather, multiple strategies are both feasible and appropriate to reach a final goal. Under these circumstances, the appraisal format should focus on evaluating the extent to which the final goal can be specified.[34] Thus, for less certain tasks an MBO strategy would be appropriate. As long as the final goal can be specified, performance can be evaluated in relation to that goal without specifying or evaluating the behavior used to reach that goal. The focus is exclusively on the degree of goal accomplishment.

At the other extreme of the continuum are tasks that are highly uncertain in nature. A relatively low consensus exists about the characteristics of successful performance. Moreover, the nature of the task is so uncertain that it may be difficult to specify expected goals. For this type of task, Keeley argues that judgment-based evaluation procedures—as exemplified by standard rating scales—may be the most appropriate. Raters make subjective estimates about the levels of employee performance on tasks for which neither the appropriate behavior nor the final goal is well specified. The extent of this uncertainty makes this type of appraisal very subjective and may well explain why trait rating scales are openly criticized for the number of errors that occur in performance evaluations.

Strategy 2: Select the Right Raters

A second way that firms have tried to improve the accuracy of performance ratings is by focusing on who might conduct the ratings and which of these sources is more likely to be accurate. For example, recent evidence indicates raters who are not particularly conscientious and raters who are too agreeable tend to give artificially high evaluations of employees.[35] To lessen the impact of one reviewer, and to increase participation in the process, a method known as **360-degree feedback** has grown more popular in recent years. Generally, this system is used in conjunction with supervisory reviews.[36] The method assesses employee performance from five points of view: supervisor, peer, self, customer, and subordinate. The flexibility of the process makes it appealing to employees at all levels within an organization; most companies using the system report that their employees are satisfied with its results.[37] They feel that the 360-degree system has outperformed their old systems in improving employee understanding and self-awareness, promoting communication between supervisors and staff, and promoting better performance and results.[38] Hershey Foods, for example, uses a 360-degree process that identifies areas for leadership training, and employees have voiced support for continuation of the program.[39]

Regardless of the positive responses from those who have implemented the 360-degree feedback system, today most companies still use it only for evaluation of their top-level personnel and for employee development rather than for appraisal or pay decisions.[40] Some companies report frustration with the number of evaluation surveys each rater has to complete and the time necessary to complete the entire process.[41] Let's take a closer look at the role and benefit of each of the raters.

Supervisors as Raters

Who rates employees? Some estimates indicate that more than 80 percent of the input for performance ratings comes from supervisors.[42] There are good reasons why supervisors play such a dominant role. Supervisors assign (or jointly determine) what work employees are to perform. This makes a supervisor knowledgeable about the job and the dimensions to be rated. Also, supervisors frequently have considerable prior experience in rating employees, thus giving them some pretty firm ideas about what level of performance is required for any given level of performance rating.[43] Supervisor ratings also tend to be more reliable than those from other sources.[44] On the negative side, though, supervisors are particularly prone to halo and leniency errors.[45]

Peers as Raters

One of the major strengths of using peers as raters is that they work more closely with the ratee and probably have an undistorted perspective of typical performance, particularly in group assignments (as opposed to what a supervisor might observe in a casual stroll around the work area). Balanced against this positive are at least two powerful negatives. First, peers may have little or no experience in conducting appraisals, leading to rather mixed evidence about the reliability of this rating source. Second, in a situation where teamwork is promoted, placing the burden of rating peers on co-workers can either create group tensions (in the case of low evaluations) or yield ratings second only to self-ratings in level of leniency.[46] One exception to this leniency effect comes from top performers, who it seems give the most objective evaluations of peers.[47] However, Motorola, one of the leaders in the use of teams and in peer ratings, reports that peer ratings help team members exert pressure on co-workers to perform better.[48]

Self as Rater

Some organizations have experimented with self-ratings. Obviously self-ratings are done by someone who has the most complete knowledge about the ratee's performance. Unfortunately, though, self-ratings are generally more lenient and possibly more unreliable than ratings from other sources.[49] One compromise in the use of self-ratings is to use them for developmental rather than administrative purposes. In addition, increasingly firms are asking employees to rate themselves as the first step in the appraisal process.[50] Forcing employees to think about their performance before they go into the formal appraisal with their boss may lead to more realistic assessments, ones that are also more in tune with a supervisor's own perceptions.

Customer as Rater

This is the era of the customer. The drive for quality means more companies are recognizing the importance of customers. One logical outcome of this increased interest is ratings from customers. For example, McDonald's surveys its customers, sets up 800 numbers to get feedback, and hires mystery customers to order food and report back on the service and treatment they receive. In a more personal example, Newman is a mystery shopper for the car wash company discussed several times in the book. He goes for a car wash, writes down the names of employees who do things out of the ordinary (either good or bad) and reports back to headquarters with a written report. For example, one time he asked for a new type of wax finish advertised on bill boards—the employee had no idea about this wash and "bluffed" that no such option was available. Bad boy! In exchange for regular reports on performance, Newman gets car washes and oil changes for free. Yes, he's incredibly cheap!

Increasingly we can expect the boundaries between organizations and the outside world to fade. Although much of the customer rating movement is directed at performance of business units, we can expect some of this to distill down to individual workers. As another example, Home Depot prints its Web address on receipts and encourages feedback about specific employees. Great feedback can result in a $2000 bonus.[51]

Subordinate as Rater

Historically, upward feedback has been viewed as countercultural, but the culture within organizations has undergone a revolution in the past 10 years and views are everchanging.[52] The notion of subordinates as raters is appealing since most superiors want to be successful with the people who report to them. Hearing how they are viewed by their subordinates gives them the chance to both see their strengths and their weaknesses as a leader and to modify their behavior.[53] The difficulty with this type of rating is in attaining candid reviews and also in counseling the ratee on how to deal with the feedback. Research shows that subordinates prefer, not surprisingly, to give their feedback to managers anonymously. If their identity is known, subordinates give artificially inflated ratings of their supervisors.[54]

Cybercomp

The American Compensation Association has an extensive Web site, including a bookstore. Go to *www.worldatwork.org/bookstore/* if you want information about other books on performance measurement, including books that talk about the advantages and disadvantages of using multiple raters.

Strategy 3: Understand How Raters Process Information

A third way to improve job performance ratings is to understand how raters think. When we observe and evaluate performance, what else influences ratings besides an employee's performance?[55] We know, for example, that feelings, attitudes, and moods influence raters. If your supervisor likes you, then regardless of how well you perform, you are likely to get better ratings.[56] Your boss's general mood also influences performance ratings. Hope for a rater who is generally cheerful rather than grumpy; it could influence how you are evaluated![57]

Researchers continue to explore how raters process information about the performance of the people they rate. In general, we think the following kinds of processes occur:

1. The rater observes the behavior of a ratee.
2. The rater encodes this behavior as part of a total picture of the ratee (i.e., the rater forms stereotypes).
3. The rater stores this information in memory, which is subject to both short- and long-term decay. Simply put, raters forget things.
4. When it comes time to evaluate a ratee, the rater reviews the performance dimensions and retrieves stored observations/impressions to determine their relevance to the performance dimensions.
5. The information is reconsidered and integrated with other available information as the rater decides on the final ratings.[58]

Quite unintentionally, this process can produce errors, and they can occur at any stage.

Errors in the Rating Process

Ideally raters should notice only performance-related factors when they observe employee behavior. In fact, all of the processing stages should be guided by performance relevancy. Unless a behavior (or personality trait) affects performance, it should not influence performance ratings. Fortunately, studies show that performance actually does play an important role, perhaps the major role, in determining how a supervisor rates a subordinate.[59] Employees who are technically proficient and who do not create problems on the job tend to receive higher ratings than these who are weaker on these dimensions.[60] Indeed, political skill (amongst other things, your ability to ingratiate yourself—get in good—with your boss), pays off in a number of ways in performance ratings.[61] On the negative side, though, performance-irrelevant factors appear to influence ratings, and they can cause errors in the evaluation process.[62]

Common Errors in Appraising Performance: Criterion Contamination

Suppose you supervise 1,000 employees. How many would you expect to rate at the highest level? How many would be average or below? If you're tempted to argue that the distribution should look something like a normal curve, you might get an A in statistics but fail Reality 101. One of the authors had a consulting project once with a county department of social services. Part of the project required collecting performance ratings for the prior 10 years. With more than 10,000 performance reviews, guess how many times

EXHIBIT 11.8
Ratings of
Managers

Rating	Percent of Managers Receiving Rating
Above average	46.4
Average	49.0
Below average	4.6

people were rated "average" or "below average"? Three times! Do you think that's just an aberration? **Criterion contamination,** or allowing non-performance factors to affect performance scores, occurs in every company and every job, and probably affects each of us at sometime during our careers. Sound a bit over the top? Consider the following: One survey of 1,816 organizations reported that only 4.6 percent of the managers were rated below average. See Exhibit 11.8; it looks like we all live in Lake Wobegone.

Now, we might argue that people who get to the managerial level do so because they are better-than-average performers.[63] So, of course, most of them rate average or better in their jobs. But the truth is that as raters we tend to make mistakes. Our ratings differ from those that would occur if we could somehow, in a moment of clarity, divine (and report!) the truth. We make errors in ratings. Recognizing and understanding the errors, such as those noted in Exhibit 11.9, are the first steps to communicating and building a more effective appraisal process.

EXHIBIT 11.9
Common
Errors in the
Appraisal
Process

Halo error	An appraiser giving favorable ratings to all job duties based on impressive performance in just one job function. For example, a rater who hates tardiness rates a prompt subordinate high across all performance dimensions exclusively because of this one characteristic.
Horn error	The opposite of a halo error. Downgrading an employee across all performance dimensions exclusively because of poor performance on one dimension.
First impression error	Developing a negative or positive opinion of an employee early in the review period and allowing that to negatively or positively influence all later perceptions of performance.
Recency error	The opposite of first impression error. Allowing performance, either good or bad, at the end of the review period to play too large a role in determining an employee's rating for the entire period.
Leniency error	Consistently rating someone higher than is deserved.
Severity error	The opposite of leniency error. Rating individuals consistently lower than is deserved.
Central tendency error	Avoiding extremes in ratings across employees.
Clone error	Giving better ratings to individuals who are like the rater in behavior and/or personality.
Spillover error	Continuing to downgrade an employee for performance errors in prior rating periods.

Not surprisingly, the potential for errors causes employees to lose faith in the performance appraisal process. Employees, quite naturally, will be reluctant to have pay systems tied to such error-ridden performance ratings. At the very least, charges that the evaluation process is political will abound.[64] There are several factors that lead raters to give inaccurate appraisals: (1) guilt, (2) embarrassment about giving praise, (3) taking things for granted, (4) not noticing good or poor performance, (5) the halo effect (seeing one good attribute and leaping to positive impressions on remaining attributes), (6) dislike of confrontation, and (7) spending too little time on preparation of the appraisal.[65] To counter such problems, companies and researchers alike have expended considerable time and money to identify ways job performance can be measured better.

Errors in Observation (Attention)

Generally, researchers have varied three types of input information to see what raters pay attention to when they are collecting information for performance appraisals. First, it appears that raters are influenced by general appearance characteristics of the ratees. Males are rated higher than females (other things being equal). A female ratee is observed not as a ratee but as a female ratee. A rater may form impressions based on stereotypic beliefs about women rather than the reality of the work situation and quite apart from any performance information. Females are rated less accurately when the rater has a traditional view of women's "proper" role; raters without traditional stereotypes of women are not prone to such errors.[66] Race also matters in performance ratings. Both in layoff decisions and in performance ratings, blacks are more likely to do worse than whites.[67]

Researchers also look at change in performance over time to see if this influences performance ratings. Both the pattern of performance (performance gets better versus worse over time) and the variability of performance (consistent versus erratic) influence performance ratings, even when the overall level (average) of performance is controlled.[68] Workers who start out high in performance and then get worse are rated lower than workers who remain consistently low.[69] Not surprisingly, workers whose performance improves over time are seen as more motivated, while those who are more variable in their performance are tagged as lower in motivation. All of us have seen examples of workers and students who intuitively recognize this type of error and use it to their advantage. The big surge of work at the end of an appraisal period is often designed to "color" a rater's perceptions.

Errors in Storage and Recall

Research suggests that raters store information in the form of traits.[70] More importantly, they tend to recall information in the form of trait categories. For example, a rater observes a specific behavior such as an employee resting during work hours. The rater stores this information not as the specific behavior but rather in the form of a trait, such as "That worker is lazy." Specific instructions to recall information about the ratee, as for a performance review, elicit the trait—lazy. Further, in the process of recalling information, a rater may remember events that didn't actually occur, simply because they are consistent with the trait category.[71] The entire rating process, then, may be heavily influenced by the trait categories that the rater adopts, regardless of their accuracy.

Errors in storage and recall also appear to arise from memory decay. At least one study indicates that rating accuracy is a function of the delay between performance and subsequent rating. The longer the delay, the less accurate the ratings.[72] Some research suggests that memory decay can be avoided if raters keep a diary and record information about employee performance as it occurs.[73] And should you ever have to go into court to defend your performance rating of an employee (e.g., discrimination charges sometimes come down to this), the judiciary likes witnesses who keep diaries documenting employee performance.

Errors in the Actual Evaluation

The context of the actual evaluation process also can influence evaluations.[74] Several researchers indicate that the purpose of an evaluation affects the rating process.[75] For example, performance appraisals sometimes serve a political end.[76] Supervisors have been known to deflate performance to send a signal to an employee—"You're not wanted here."[77] Supervisors also tend to weigh negative attributes more heavily than positive attributes: You are more likely to receive a much lower score if you do one task badly than you are to receive a proportionally higher score if you perform one task particularly well.[78]

If the purpose of evaluation is to divide up a fixed pot of merit increases, ratings also tend to be less accurate. Supervisors who know ratings will be used to determine merit increases are less likely to differentiate among subordinates than they are when the ratings will be used for other purposes.[79]

Rank and Yank: Good Idea or Bad?

Jack Welch, a hugely popular and successful former CEO of General Electric, popularized what came to be called **"rank and yank."** Rank and yank requires managers to force-rank employees according to some preset distribution. McDonald's, GE, and Sun Microsystems, for example, use a 20–70–10 distribution (top 20 percent,[80] vital 70 percent, bottom 10 percent). Employees in the bottom 10 percent are given a chance to improve. Failure to move into the middle 70 percent usually results in termination. *Workforce* magazine figures that one in five large companies use some version of this forced ranking.[81] Some consultants and academics view forced ranking as the cure for inflated ratings and poor appraisal processes.[82] As a result, these supporters claim, company performance improves.[83] Some managers wonder, though, if there is a limit to this yank strategy. After awhile, people ask, "Haven't you rid yourself of the deadwood?" and then you start cutting good employees. One simulation study, asking just this question, suggested as much as 16 percent average improvement over the first four years of rank and yank, but that benefits fall off dramatically after that.[84] This suggests the method has strong short-term benefits.

Also, being required to provide feedback to subordinates about their ratings yields less accuracy than a secrecy policy.[85] Presumably, anticipation of an unpleasant confrontation with the angry ratee persuades the rater to avoid confrontation by giving a rating higher than is justified. However, when raters must justify their scoring of subordinates in writing, the rating is more accurate.[86]

Strategy 4: Training Raters to Rate More Accurately

Although there is some evidence that training is not effective[87] or is less important in reducing errors than are other factors,[88] most research indicates rater training is an effective method for reducing appraisal errors.[89] Rater training programs can be divided into three distinct categories:[90] (1) **rater-error training,** in which the goal is to reduce psychometric errors (e.g., leniency, severity, central tendency, halo) by familiarizing raters with their existence; (2) **performance-dimension training,** which exposes supervisors to the performance dimensions to be used in rating (e.g., quality of work, job knowledge), thus making sure everyone is on the same page when thinking about a specific performance dimension; and (3) **performance-standard training,** which provides raters with a standard of comparison or frame of reference for making appraisals (what constitutes good, average, and bad). Several generalizations about ways to improve rater training can be summarized from this research:

1. Straightforward lecturing to ratees (the kind we professors are notorious for) about ways to improve the quality of their ratings generally is ineffective.
2. Individualized or small-group discussion sections are more effective in conveying proper rating procedures.
3. When these sessions are combined with extensive practice and feedback sessions, rating accuracy significantly improves.
4. Longer training programs (more than two hours) generally are more successful than shorter programs.
5. **Performance-dimension training** and **performance-standard training** generally work better than rater-error training, particularly when they are combined.
6. The greatest success has come from efforts to reduce halo errors and improve accuracy.

Leniency errors are the most difficult form of error to eliminate. This shouldn't be surprising. Think about the consequences to a supervisor of giving inflated ratings versus those of giving accurate or even deflated ratings. The latter two courses are certain to result in more complaints and possibly reduced employee morale. The easy way out is to artificially inflate ratings.[91] Unfortunately, this positive outcome for supervisors may come back to haunt them: With everyone receiving relatively high ratings there is less distinction between truly good and poor performers. Obviously, it is also harder to pay for real performance differences.

PUTTING IT ALL TOGETHER: THE PERFORMANCE EVALUATION PROCESS

A good performance evaluation doesn't begin on the day of the performance interview.[92] We outline here some of the key elements in the total process that from day one make for a good appraisal outcome.[93] First, we need a sound basis for establishing the performance appraisal dimensions and the scales associated with each dimension. Performance dimensions should be relevant to the strategic plan of the company. If innovation of new products is key to success, we'd better have something in our performance dimensions that assesses that component of individual performance. Performance dimensions also should reflect what employees are expected to do in their jobs, that is, their job descriptions.[94] If the job descriptions include nothing on quality (admittedly an unlikely event), the appraisal should not measure quality. Unclear job expectations are one of the most significant barriers to good performance. If employees don't know what you expect of them, how can they possibly please you?[95]

Second, we need to involve employees in every stage of developing performance dimensions and building scales to measure how well they perform on these dimensions. In cases where this occurs, employees have more positive reactions to ratings, regardless of how well they do. They are happier with the system's fairness and the appraisal accuracy. They give better evaluations of managers and indicate intentions to stay with their organization. Managers also respond well to this type of "due process" system. They feel they have a greater ability to resolve work problems. They have higher job satisfaction and less reason to distort appraisal results to further their own interests.[96] Employees also provide a unique perspective on what will or won't work. Consider the performance appraisal system developed by Lucent Technologies for its overseas operations. A performance dimension that worked well in Lucent's U.S. operations was translated in local cultures as "obsession with serving our customers." It turns out that the word *obsession* in Saudi Arabia, Thailand, the Caribbean, and Latin America has very, very erotic and negative connotations. The problem was discovered only when managers reported employees speaking with one voice: "I don't care how important the customer is— I'm not doing this!"[97]

Third, we need to make sure raters are trained in use of the appraisal system and that all employees understand how the system operates and what it will be used for. Fourth, we need to make sure raters are motivated to rate accurately. One way to achieve this is to ensure that managers are rated on how well they utilize and develop human resources. A big part of this would be evaluation and feedback to employees. Less than one-half of managers report that they provide feedback, and of those who do give feedback, most admit they are unsure if their feedback is worthwhile.[98] Almost one-half of employees agreed with this assessment, feeling performance reviews did little to guide performance.[99] Regardless of the quality of feedback one receives, don't assume that every review will improve performance![100]

Fifth, raters should maintain a diary of employee performance, both as documentation and to jog the memory.[101] This will help ensure that supervisors are knowledgeable about subordinates' performance and serve as an objective exhibit in any court-based allegation of discrimination..[102] Sixth, raters should attempt a performance diagnosis to determine in advance if performance problems arise because of motivation, skill deficiency, or external environmental constraints;[103] this process in turn tells the supervisor whether the problem requires motivation building, training, or efforts to remove external constraints. Exhibit 11.10 recaps the important steps in the appraisal process.[104]

EXHIBIT 11.10

Tips on
Appraising
Employee
Performance

Preparation for the Performance Interview

1. Keep a weekly log of individual's performance. Why?
   A. It makes the task of writing up the evaluation simpler. The rater does not have to strain to remember six months or a year ago.
   B. It reduces the chances of some rating errors (e.g., regency, halo).
   C. It gives support/backup to the rating.

2. Preparation for the interview should not begin a week or two before it takes place. There should be continual feedback to the employee on his or her performance so that (a) problems can be corrected before they get out of hand, (b) improvements can be made sooner, and (c) encouragement and support are ongoing.

3. Allow sufficient time to write up the evaluation. A well-thought-out evaluation will be more objective and equitable. Sufficient time includes (a) the actual time necessary to think out and write up the evaluation, (b) time away from the evaluation, and (c) time to review and possibly revise.

4. Have employees fill out an appraisal form prior to the interview. This prepares employees for what will take place in the interview and allows them to come prepared with future goal suggestions, areas they wish to pursue, and suggestions concerning their jobs or the company.

5. Set up an agreed-upon, convenient time to hold the interview (at least one week in advance). Be sure to pick a nonthreatening day.

6. Be prepared!
   A. Know what you are going to say. Prepare an outline (which includes the evaluation and future goal suggestions).
   B. Decide on developmental opportunities before the interview. Be sure you know of possible resources and contacts.
   C. Review performance interview steps.

7. Arrange the room in such a way as to encourage discussion.
   A. Do not have barriers between yourself and the employee (such as a large desk).
   B. Arrange with your secretary that there be no phone calls or interruptions.

Performance Appraisal Interview (Steps)

1. Set the subordinate at ease. Begin by stating the purpose of the discussion. Let the individual know that it will be a two-way process. Neither the superior nor the subordinate should dominate the discussion.

2. Give a general, overall impression of the evaluation.

3. Discuss each dimension separately. Ask the employee to give an impression on his or her own performance first. Then explain your position. If there is a problem on some dimensions, try together to determine the cause. When exploring causes, urge the subordinate to identify three or four causes. Then, jointly determine the most important ones. Identifying causes is important because it points out action plans which might be taken.

4. Together, develop action plans to correct problem areas. These plans will flow naturally from the consideration of the causes. Be specific about the who, what, and when. Be sure to provide for some kind of follow-up or report back.

5. Close the interview on an optimistic note.

(Continued)

EXHIBIT 11.10 *(Continued)*

Communication Technique Suggestions

1. Do not control the interview—make it two-way. Do this by asking open-ended questions rather than submitting your own solutions. For example, rather than saying, "Jim, I'd like you to do these reports over again," it would be better to say, "Jim, what sort of things might we do here?" Avoid questions that lead to one-word answers.

2. Stress behaviors and results rather than personal traits. Say, "I've noticed that your weekly report has been one to two days late in the last six weeks," rather than, "You tend to be a tardy, lazy person."

3. Show interest and concern. Instead of saying, "Too bad, but we all go through that," say, "I think I know what you're feeling. I remember a similar experience."

4. Allow the subordinate to finish a sentence or thought. This includes being receptive to the subordinate's own ideas and suggestions. For example, rather than saying, "You may have something there, but let's go back to the real problem," say, "I'm not certain I understand how that relates to this problem. Why don't you fill me in on it a bit more?"

These last four suggestions emphasize problem analysis rather than appraisal. Of course, appraisal of past performance is a part of the problem analysis, but these suggestions should lead to a more participative and less defensive subordinate role. These suggestions will also help improve creativity in problem solving. The subordinate will have a clearer understanding of why and how he or she needs to change work behavior. There should be a growth of a climate of cooperation, which increases motivation to achieve performance goals.

EQUAL EMPLOYMENT OPPORTUNITY AND PERFORMANCE EVALUATION

Equal employment opportunity (EEO) and **affirmative action** have influenced HR decision making for 40 years now. While there are certainly critics of these programs, at least one important trend can be traced to the civil rights vigil in the workplace. Specifically, EEO has forced organizations to document decisions and to ensure they are firmly tied to performance or expected performance. This may well be the legacy of EEO. While it doesn't directly reduce segregation in the workforce, research shows that EEO affects HR practices and legal practices of companies that have been found guilty, and this in turn yields gradual positive changes in practices.[105] Nowhere is this more apparent than in the performance appraisal area. Just ask folks at the Social Security Administration, who settled an $8 million class action suit brought by blacks who successfully argued there was bias in the performance appraisal process.[106] Performance appraisals are subject to the same scrutiny as employment tests. Consider the use of performance ratings in making decisions about promotions. In this context, a performance appraisal takes on all the characteristics of a test used to make an initial employment decision. If employees pass the test—are rated highly in the performance evaluation process—they are predicted to do well at higher-level jobs. This interpretation of performance evaluation as a test, subject to validation requirements, was made in ***Brito v. Zia Company.***[107] In this case, Zia Company used performance evaluations based on a rating format to lay off employees. The layoffs resulted in a disproportionate number of minorities being discharged. The court held that:

> Zia, a government contractor, had failed to comply with the testing guidelines issued by the Secretary of Labor, and that Zia had not developed job-related criteria for evaluating employees' work performance to be used in determining employment promotion and discharges which is required to protect minority group applicants and employees from the discriminatory effects of such failure.[108]

Since the *Brito* case there has been growing evidence that the courts have very specific standards and requirements for performance appraisal.[109] The courts stress six issues in setting up a performance appraisal system.[110]

1. Courts are favorably disposed to appraisal systems that give specific written instructions on how to complete the appraisal. Presumably, more extensive training in other facets of evaluation would also be viewed favorably by the courts.

2. Organizations tend to be able to support their cases better when the appraisal system incorporates clear criteria for evaluating performance. Performance dimensions and scale levels that are written, objective, and clear tend to be viewed positively by courts in discrimination suits.[111] In part, this probably arises because behaviorally oriented appraisals have more potential to provide workers feedback about developmental needs.

3. As pointed out by every basic personnel book ever printed—and reinforced by this text—the presence of adequately developed job descriptions provides a rational foundation for personnel decisions. The courts reinforce this by ruling more consistently for defendants (companies) when their appraisal systems are based on sound job descriptions.

4. Courts also approve of appraisal systems that require supervisors to provide feedback about appraisal results to the employees affected. Absence of secrecy permits employees to identify weaknesses and to challenge undeserved appraisals.

5. The courts seem to like evaluation systems that incorporate a review of any performance rating by a higher-level supervisor.

6. Perhaps most importantly, the courts consistently suggest that the key to fair appraisals depends on consistent treatment across raters, regardless of race, color, religion, sex, or national origin.

The focal question then becomes: Are similarly situated individuals treated similarly? This standard is particularly evident in a court case involving performance appraisal and merit pay.[112] A black male filed suit against General Motors, claiming race discrimination in both the timing and the amount of a merit increase. The court found this case without merit. General Motors was able to show that the same set of rules was applied equally to all individuals. There also has been a recent jump in lawsuits challenging as discriminatory the practice of "rank and yank." Employees are arguing they've been "ranked and yanked" not because of performance, but because of age.[113] As a result, there has been a noticeable drop in the number of companies using this method.

A final word of caution about the role of equal employment and performance appraisal: Experts note that firms approaching performance appraisal primarily as a way to defend against discrimination claims may actually create more claims. Documentation of performance to discourage such claims only causes poor employee relations, and it can lead to solid employees feeling like plaintiffs themselves.[114] A better strategy is to follow the guidelines we developed earlier. They permit both good performance reviews and a strong foundation in case legal issues arise.

TYING PAY TO SUBJECTIVELY APPRAISED PERFORMANCE

Think, for a moment, about what it really means to give employees merit increases. Bill Peterson makes $40,000 per year. He gets a merit increase of 3 percent, the approximate average increase over the past several decades. Bill's take-home increase (adjusted for taxes) is a measly $16 per week more than he used to make. Before we console Bill, though, consider Jane Krefting, who is a better performer than Bill and receives a 6 percent merit increase. Should she be thrilled by this pay-for-performance differential and be motivated to continue as a high achiever? Probably not. After taxes, her paycheck (assuming a base salary similar to Bill's) is only $15 dollars per week more than Bill's check.

The central issue involving merit pay is, "How do we get employees to view raises as a reward for performance?" Chapter 9 illustrated this difficulty in theoretical terms. Now it is addressed from a pragmatic perspective. Very simply, organizations frequently grant increases that are not designed or communicated to be related to performance. Perhaps the central reason for this is the way merit pay is managed. Many companies view raises not as motivational tools to shape behavior but as budgetary line items to control costs.[115] Frequently this results in **pay increase guidelines** with little motivational impact. Three pay increase guidelines that particularly fit the low-motivation scenario will be discussed briefly below before we outline standards that attempts to link pay to performance.

Two types of pay increase guidelines with low-motivation potential provide equal increases to all employees regardless of performance. The first type, a general increase, typically is found in unionized firms. A contract is negotiated that specifies an across-the-board, equal increase for each year of the contract. Similarly, in the second type, across-the-board increases often are linked to cost-of-living changes. When the Consumer Price Index (CPI) rises, some companies adjust base pay for all employees to reflect the rising costs. (This is discussed in more detail in Chapter 17.) The third form of guideline comes somewhat closer to tying pay to performance. **Seniority increases** tie pay increases to a preset progression pattern based on seniority. For example, a pay grade might be divided into 10 equal steps, with employees moving to higher steps based on seniority. To the extent that performance improves with time on the job, this method has the rudiments of paying for performance.

In practice, tying pay to performance requires three things. First, we need some definition of performance. One set of subjective measures, as we discussed in Chapter 6, involves the competencies that people possess or acquire. Increasingly companies assert that corporate performance depends on having employees who possess key competencies. Xerox identifies 17 core competencies. As a company with strong strategic objectives

EXHIBIT 11.11 Performance-Based Guideline

	Performance Level				
	1	2	3	4	5
	Outstanding	Very Satisfactory	Satisfactory	Marginally Unsatisfactory	Unsatisfactory
Merit Increase	6–8%	5–7%	4–6%	2–4%	0%

linked to customer satisfaction and quality, it's not surprising to find that Xerox values such competencies as quality orientation, customer care, dependability, and teamwork. Recent trends in compensation center on finding ways to build competencies in employees. Merit increases may be linked to employee ability and willingness to demonstrate key competencies. For example, showing more of the following behaviors might be tied to higher merit increases:

Competency: Customer Care

1. Follows through on commitments to customers in a timely manner
2. Defines and communicates customer requirements
3. Resolves customer issues in a timely manner
4. Demonstrates empathy for customer feelings
5. Presents a positive image to the customer
6. Displays a professional image at all times
7. Communicates a positive image of the company and individuals to customers

Whether we measure performance by behaviors, competencies, or traits, there must be agreement that higher levels of performance will have positive impacts on corporate strategic objectives. Second, we need some continuum that describes different levels from low to high on the performance measure. Third, we need to decide how much of a merit increase will be given for different levels of performance. Decisions about these three questions lead to some form of merit pay guide. In its simplest form a guideline specifies pay increases permissible for different levels of performance (see Exhibit 11.11).

A more complex guideline ties pay not only to performance but also to position in the pay range. Exhibit 11.12 illustrates such a system for a food market firm. The percentages in the cells of Exhibit 11.12 are changed yearly to reflect changing economic conditions. Two patterns are evident in this merit guideline. First, as would be expected in a pay-for-performance system, lower performance is tied to lower pay increases. In fact, in many organizations the poorest performers receive no merit increases. The second relationship is that pay increases at a decreasing rate as employees move through a pay range. For the same level of performance, employees low in the range receive higher percentage increases than employees who have progressed further through the range. In part this is designed to forestall the time when employees reach the salary maximum and have their salaries frozen. In part, though,

EXHIBIT 11.12 Performance Rating Salary Increase Matrix

	Performance Rating				
Position in Range	**Not Satisfactory**	**Needs Improvement**	**Competent**	**Commendable**	**Superior**
Fourth quartile	0%	0%	4%	5%	6%
Third quartile	0	0	5	6	7
Second quartile	0	0	6	7	8
First quartile	0	2	7	8	9
Below minimum of range	0	3	8	9	10

it is also a cost-control mechanism tied to budgeting procedures, as discussed in Chapter 18.

Performance- and Position-Based Guidelines

Given a salary increase matrix, merit increases are relatively easy to determine. As Exhibit 11.12 indicates, an employee at the top of his or her pay grade who receives a "competent" rating would receive a 4 percent increase in base salary. A new trainee starting out below the minimum of a pay grade would receive a 10 percent increase for a "superior" performance rating.

Designing Merit Guidelines

Designing merit guidelines involves answering four questions. First, what should the poorest performer be paid as an increase? Notice that this figure is seldom negative. Base wages are, unfortunately, considered an entitlement. Wage cuts tied to poor performance are very rare. Most organizations, though, are willing to give no increases to very poor performers, perhaps as a prelude to termination if no improvements are shown.

The second question involves average performers: How much should they be paid as an increase? Most organizations try to ensure that average performers are kept whole (wages will still have the same purchasing power) relative to cost of living. This dictates that the midpoint of the merit guidelines equal the percentage change in the local or national consumer price index. Following this guideline, the 6 percent increase for an average performer in the second quartile of Exhibit 11.11 would reflect the change in CPI for that area. In a year with lower inflation, all the percentages in the matrix probably would be lower.

Third, how much should the top performers be paid? In part, budgetary considerations (Chapter 18) answer this question. But there is also growing evidence that employees do not agree on the size of increases that they consider meaningful (Chapter 8). Continuation of this research may help determine the approximate size of increases that is needed to make a difference in employee performance.

Finally, matrixes can differ in the size of the differential between different levels of performance. Exhibit 11.11 basically rewards successive levels of performance

EXHIBIT 11.13   Merit Grids

Merit grids combine three variables: level of performance, distribution of employees within their job's pay range, and merit increase percentages.

Example

1. Assume a performance rating scale of A through D: 30 percent of employees get A, 35 percent get B, 20 percent get C, and 15 percent get D. Change the percents to decimals.

A	B	C	D
.30	.35	.20	.15

2. Assume a range distribution as follows: 10 percent of all employees are in the top (fourth) quartile of the pay range for their job, 35 percent in the third quartile, 30 percent in second quartile, and 25 percent in the lowest quartile. Change the percents to decimals.

1	.10
2	.35
3	.30
4	.25

3. Multiply the performance distribution by the range distribution to obtain the percent of employees in each cell. Cell entries = performance 3 range.

	A	B	C	D
1	.30 × .10 = .03	.35 × .20 = .037	.30 × .10 = .03	.15 × .10 = .015
2	.30 × .35 = .105	.35 × .35 = .1225	.20 × .35 = .07	.15 × .35 = .0525
3	.30 × .30 = .09	.35 × .30 = .105	.20 × .30 = .06	.15 × .30 = .045
4	.30 × .25 = .075	.35 × .25 = .1225	.20 × .25 = .05	.15 × .25 = .0375

Cell entries tell us that 3 percent of employees are in the top quartile of pay range *and* received an A performance rating, 10.5 percent of employees are in the second quartile of pay range *and* received an A performance rating, etc.

4. Distribute increase percentage among cells, varying the percentages according to performance and range distribution, for example, 6 percent to those employees in cell A1, 5 percent to those employees in B1.

5. Multiply increase percentages by the employee distribution for each cell. The sum of all cells should equal the total merit increase percentage.

    Example: 6% × cell A1 = .06 × .03 = .0018
                5% × cell B1 = .05 × .035 = .00175
                            Etc.   _____
                Targeted merit increase percentage = Sum

6. Adjust increase percentages among cells if needed in order to stay within budgeted increase.

with 1 percent increases (at least in the portion of the matrix in which any increase is granted). A larger jump between levels would signal a stronger commitment to recognizing performance with higher pay increases. Most companies balance this, though, against cost considerations. Larger differentials cost more. When money is tight, this option is less attractive. Exhibit 11.13 shows how a merit grid is constructed when cost constraints (merit budget) are known.

PROMOTIONAL INCREASES AS A PAY-FOR-PERFORMANCE TOOL

Let's not forget that firms have methods of rewarding good performance other than by giving raises. One of the most effective is a promotion accompanied by a salary increase, generally reported as being in the 8 to 12 percent range. This method of linking pay to performance has at least two characteristics that distinguish it from traditional annual merit pay increases. First, the very size of the increment is approximately double a normal merit increase. A clearer message is sent to employees, in the forms of both money and promotion, that good performance is valued and tangibly rewarded. Second, promotion increases represent, in a sense, a reward to employees for commitment and exemplary performance over a sustained period of time. Promotions are not generally annual events. They complement annual merit rewards by showing employees that there are benefits to both single-year productivity and continuation of such desirable behavior.

Your **Turn**   Performance Appraisal at Burger King

Crew members at Burger King are evaluated using the form in Exhibit 1.[116] Compare this form with the one illustrated in Exhibit 11.4. Years ago Burger King used a form like the one in Exhibit 11.4. Why do you think they made the change?

One of their restaurants found that ratings on two of the dimensions on the new form were considerably lower than on the other four. On the dimensions Executes Against Priorities and Delivers Excellent Service, ratings averaged about 3.1. On the other four dimensions ratings averaged 4.4. We don't have data for other restaurants, so comparisons can't be made. Do you think a problem exists? Are crew members simply worse on execution and service? Without any data, speculate on why rating differences exist, assuming some type of error is occurring. What three questions would you like to ask crew members and/or the restaurant general manager to identify the source of the problem. If corporate headquarters were to see this same pattern across stores, what might be their reaction?

Team Member
Performance Review Form

FY'09

It's Performance Review and Merit Increase time again, so let's get ready to share our thoughts about what we've done since our last review. The ratings focus on our Keys to the Kingdom and describe the behaviors needed to deliver an excellent experience for the guest, every time! The sections below contain the process steps for you to follow.

STEP #1: Fill in your information.

Employee Name:_____Date:_____

Supervisor's Name: _____Restaurant #:_____

STEP #2: Complete the self-rating of your performance for each Key to the Kingdom. Complete the SELF portion and your Manager will complete the MGR portion. Use ratings guide below and the Keys to the Kingdom "Tips from the King" for help in completing this section.

KEYS TO THE KINGDOM

	SELF	MGR

EXECUTES AGAINST PRIORITIES
- Achieves restaurant goals on a daily basis
- Consistently follows through on responsibilities and tasks ahead of schedule
- Organized, prepared and ensures work stations are always in order

DEMONSTRATES ETHICS & HIGH STANDARDS
- Exhibits passion and enthusiasm for the job and Burger King as a brand
- Promotes BKC values and ethics within the team while serving as a role model to others
- Consistently executes company policies and promotes organizational messages

DELIVERS EXCELLENT SERVICE
- Greets each guest promptly with a smile and a friendly, positive attitude
- Respects guests' opinions and responds to complaints immediately and thoroughly
- Makes a difference by personalizing service to exceed each guest's expectations

TAKES INITIATIVE
- Willing to take on additional tasks when necessary
- Recognizes and takes ownership of mistakes
- Uses "down time" to stay ahead

EXHIBITS OPTIMISM
- Approaches work in an energetic manner
- Maintains and upbeat attitude and is accepting of others
- Agrees to help when asked

TREATS PEOPLE WITH DIGNITY AND RESPECT
- Accepting of others with different backgrounds and experiences
- Cooperates well with others and responds to requests for help
- Receptive to feedback and suggestions

5 – SIGNIFICANTLY ABOVE EXPECTATIONS
Consistently displays the behavior beyond what is expected for the role.
Sets an example for others.

4 – ABOVE EXPECTATIONS
At times displays the behavior above what is expected for the role.

3 – MEETS EXPECTATIONS
Displays the behavior as expected for the role.

2 – BELOW EXPECTATIONS
At times does not exhibit the behavior as expected for the role.

1 – SIGNIFICANTLY BELOW EXPECTATIONS
Consistently does not exhibit the behavior as expected for the role.

U – UNABLE TO ASSESS
New to this role and still developing or learning results expected. Does not apply to this person.

(continued on next page)

387

Team Member
Performance Review Form

FY'09

STEP #3: SELF - Use this space to record any additional information. Provide some supporting comments for your self-ratings. Talk about the great things that happened this year. Celebrate the good stuff. We want details.

STEP #4: MANAGER – Here's where you provide overall supporting comments describing the employee's performance. Please note any extremely high or low ratings given. Highlight what went well and why, and what could have been better and why.

STEP #5: MANAGER – Assign an overall rating. Use whole numbers only please.

PERFORMANCE RATING:
5 – Significantly Above Expectations
4 – Above Expectations
3 – Meets Expectations
2 – Below Expectations
1 – Significantly Below Expectations

STEP #6: OK…last step. All we need now is some signatures and dates.

_____
Employee's Signature

_____
General Manager's Signature

_____
Wage Action Amount

_____
Date

_____
Date

Source: The BURGER KING® trademarks and forms are used with permission from Burger King Corporation.

388

Summary

The process of appraising employee performance can be both time-consuming and stressful. These difficulties are compounded if the appraisal system is poorly developed or if a supervisor lacks the appropriate training to collect and evaluate performance data. Development of sound appraisal systems requires an understanding of organizational objectives balanced against the relative merits of each type of appraisal system. For example, despite its inherent weaknesses, an appraisal system based on ranking of employee performance may be appropriate in small organizations that, for a variety of reasons, choose not to tie pay to performance; a sophisticated MBO appraisal system may not be appropriate for such a company.

Training supervisors effectively to appraise performance requires an understanding of organizational objectives. We know relatively little about the ways raters process information and evaluate employee performance. However, a thorough understanding of organizational objectives combined with a knowledge of common errors in evaluation can make a significant difference in the quality of appraisals.

Review Questions

1. We talked in depth about four ways to improve performance ratings. Pick one that you think shows the most promise and defend your position.

2. You own a nonunion company with 93 nonexempt employees. All of these employees pack books into boxes for shipment to customers throughout the United States. Because of wide differences in performance, you have decided to try performance appraisal, something never done before. Until now, you have given every worker the same size increase. Now you want to measure performance and reward the best performers with bigger increases. Without any further information, which of the five types of appraisal formats do you think would be most appropriate? Justify your answer. Do you anticipate any complaints, or other comments, from employees after you implement your new system?

3. Think about the last group project you worked on. Describe that project and identify three performance criteria you think would be appropriate for evaluating the team members. Should every team member be able to rate one another on all these dimensions? Should the team-member ratings be used for feedback only or for feedback and part of the overall grade (with teacher approval, of course)? Should the teacher rate each team member on performance (all three criteria) in the group assignment? How are these questions relevant to setting up a 360° performance review?

4. Angela Lacy, an African American employee in your accounts receivable department, has filed a charge of discrimination, alleging she was unfairly passed over for promotion and regularly receives smaller pay increases than do employees who perform less well (she alleges). You have to go to your boss, the VP of HR, and explain what elements of your HR system can be used in your legal defense. What things do you hope you did in setting up and administering your systems to counter this discrimination charge?

Balanced Scorecard Example: Department of Energy (Federal Personal Property Management Program)

THE BSC PERSPECTIVES

Customer Perspective

The Customer Perspective enables organizations to align the core measure (customer satisfaction) to targeted customers. For this perspective, the primary objectives are to provide effective service to and establish effective partnerships with external and internal customers. Effective service and partnerships are key ingredients in assessing the health of any federal personal property management program.

Internal Business Processes Perspective

The objectives in the Internal Business Processes Perspective collectively assure that an effective federal personal property management program is established to (1) support customer needs; (2) provide efficient life cycle management (accountability, utilization and disposition) of direct operations personal property; and (3) maintain oversight of entities that have federal personal property management program responsibilities. Key processes in the federal personal property management program must be monitored to ensure that the outcomes satisfy program objectives. This perspective is important because it not only addresses the internal business processes that must be developed and maintained to meet customer and stakeholder requirements and expectations, but also the process results that lead to financial success and satisfied customers. Within any personal property management organization, there are a number of internal business processes that require focused management attention to ensure requirements and expectations are met as effectively as possible, while accommodating cost efficiency issues addressed in the Financial Perspective.

Learning and Growth

The two objectives under the Learning and Growth Perspective promote organizational and individual growth that will provide long-term benefits to the federal personal property management program. These objectives must be achieved if program performance is going to improve over time. While the objectives in the other perspectives identify where the program must excel to achieve breakthrough performance, the Learning and Growth objectives provide the infrastructure needed to enable the objectives in the other perspectives to be achieved. The Learning and Growth objectives are the drivers for achieving excellence in the other perspectives.

This perspective is important because it promotes individual and organizational growth—factors that are crucial to future success. Support for this perspective equates to recognition of the link between top-level strategic objectives and activities needed to re-skill and motivate employees; supply information; and align individuals, teams, and organizational units with the Department's strategy and long-term objectives. An analysis of the cause-and-effect relationships of the measures in this perspective clearly shows that employee satisfaction, employee alignment, and information availability are vital contributors to meeting the objectives stated in the other perspectives.

Financial Perspective

The objective of the Financial Perspective is to strive for optimum efficiency in the federal personal property management program. To achieve that, processes need to be analyzed to determine (1) cost and performance trends over time and (2) process changes that can be implemented to produce optimum efficiencies. Success for entities charged with federal personal property management program responsibilities should be measured by how effectively and efficiently these entities meet the needs of their constituencies. This perspective is important because optimizing the cost efficiency of the federal personal property management program ensures that the maximum amount of funds are available for accomplishing the primary missions of the Department and its field organizations. Managers must ensure that federal personal property management program operating costs are optimized in order to meet the challenge of creating business programs that work better and cost less.

OBJECTIVES, MEASURES, AND TARGETS

General

Each federal personal Property BSC should contain both national and local performance objectives, measures, and targets. The national elements of the BSC are developed by the Department in support of the Departmental mission, vision, and strategy. The local elements of the BSC are developed locally, based on site-specific missions and needs.

National (Core) Measures

The core measures contained in the federal personal property BSC are measures that the Department expects all entities charged with federal personal property management program responsibilities to implement where applicable. The formulae and measuring methods should be maintained as standard as practicable from self assessment to self assessment. Some core measures may contain core and optional elements. Core elements are aspects of the federal personal property management program that the Department expects all entities to take into consideration, where applicable, when measuring. Optional elements are aspects of the federal personal property management program that the Department suggests, but does not require, for measurement where applicable.

Local Measures

The federal personal property BSC should also include local measures to track performance in areas of importance to the local site. The following measures are provided as examples of local measures that are currently in use throughout the DOE complex:

1. Customer Perspective

- Percent accuracy of key property data elements (e.g., property control number, nomenclature, part/model number, and serial number) where customers maintain or update databases.

2. *Internal Business Processes Perspective*

- Number of property system processes re-engineered during period.
- Percent and/or value (acquisition cost) of personal property items lost, damaged, destroyed, and/or stolen during the period.
- Value (acquisition cost) of personal property items found during the period.
- Percent of scheduled property management reviews conducted during period.
- Percent of scheduled management walk-throughs completed during period.
- Percent of excess or surplus property shipped within XX days of receipt of requisitions or transfer orders.
- Percent of usable property with sale value sold within XX days after completion of required screening.
- Extent to which reliable property, administrative, and financial systems are in place and integrated.
- Percent of government equipment issues resolved in a timely (defined locally) fashion.

3. *Learning and Growth*

- Number of classes/training sessions, supporting BSC objectives, provided to personal property custodians/representatives during the period.
- Percent of personal property custodians/representatives who attended the classes that were provided during the period in support of BSC objectives.
- Percent of personal property custodians/representatives who have been trained regarding their property management responsibilities.
- Percent of professional personal property employees who have attended a basic property administration course.
- Percent of professional personal property employees who have attended property management related training (e.g., demilitarization, high risk, NPMA).
- Number of employee suggestions, supporting BSC objectives, that were adopted during the period.
- Percent of personal property professional staff with professional certifications related to BSC objectives.

4. *Financial Perspective*

- Net proceeds from the sale of surplus assets as a percent of asset acquisition cost. Dollar value of site-generated excess property reutilized internally at the site.
- Dollar value of externally generated excess property (i.e., by other DOE sites and other Federal agencies) utilized by the site.
- Reutilization screening transactions (number and dollar value) completed during period.

Sample Appraisal Form for Leadership Dimension:
Pfizer Pharmaceutical

PERFORMING FOR RESULTS

Reaching for the Future

*District Manager/Regional Manager
Capabilities*

District Manager Baseline Capability Assessment

Employee Name:			Self Assessment:	[ ]	
Title:					(Select one)
			Manager Assessment:	[ ]	
District:			Manager's Name:		

I. Strategic Capability Assessment	Unacceptable/ Needs Improvement	Stage I	Stage II	Stage III	Stage IV	Comments
1. Leadership						
2. Recruiting and Selection						
3. People Development						
4. Strategic Perspective						

Capabilities Cross-Reference Table

II. Core Behaviors Assessment	U	NI	S	RO	A	Comments
1. Planning & Organizing						
2. Impact						
3. Job Knowledge						
4. Problem Analysis						
5. Communication Ability						
6. Facilitation Skills						
7. Judgment						

8. Flexibility						
9. Political Savvy/Protocol						
10. Sensitivity						
11. Teamwork						

III. Employee Comments

Employee Signature:	Date:
Supervisor Signature:	Date:

	Key
U	"Unacceptable"
NI	"Needs Improvement"
S	"Sometimes"
RO	"Routinely"
A	"Always"

District Manager Strategic Capabilities

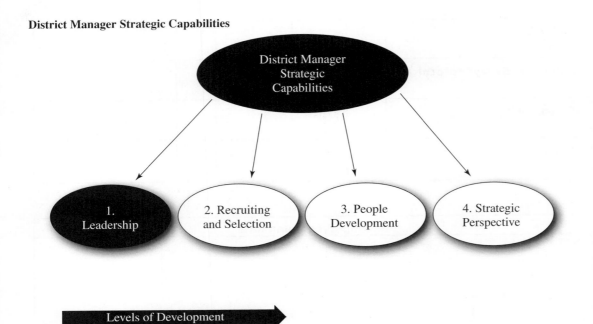

District Manager Strategic Capabilities (*Continued*)

Outlined below are four strategic capabilities for the District Manager (DM) role.

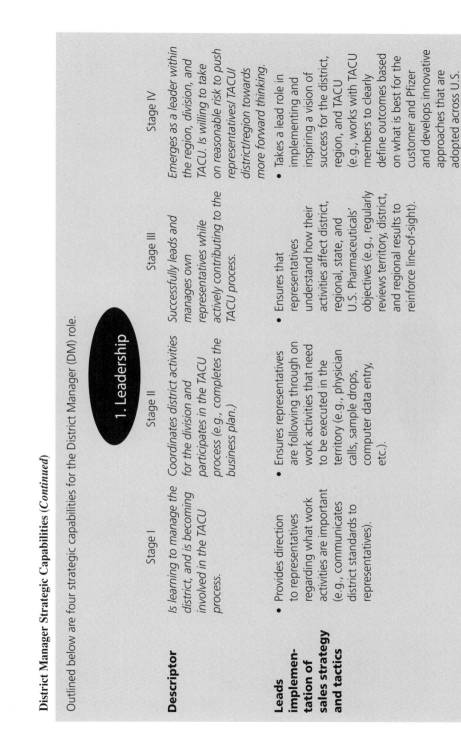

1. Leadership

	Stage I	Stage II	Stage III	Stage IV
Descriptor	*Is learning to manage the district, and is becoming involved in the TACU process.*	*Coordinates district activities for the division and participates in the TACU process (e.g., completes the business plan.)*	*Successfully leads and manages own representatives while actively contributing to the TACU process.*	*Emerges as a leader within the region, division, and TACU. Is willing to take on reasonable risk to push representatives/TACU/ district/region towards more forward thinking.*
Leads implementation of sales strategy and tactics	• Provides direction to representatives regarding what work activities are important (e.g., communicates district standards to representatives).	• Ensures representatives are following through on work activities that need to be executed in the territory (e.g., physician calls, sample drops, computer data entry, etc.).	• Ensures that representatives understand how their activities affect district, regional, state, and U.S. Pharmaceuticals' objectives (e.g., regularly reviews territory, district, and regional results to reinforce line-of-sight).	• Takes a lead role in implementing and inspiring a vision of success for the district, region, and TACU (e.g., works with TACU members to clearly define outcomes based on what is best for the customer and Pfizer and develops innovative approaches that are adopted across U.S. Pharmaceuticals lines).

District Manager Strategic Capabilities (*Continued*)

Outlined below are four strategic capabilities for the District Manager (DM) role.

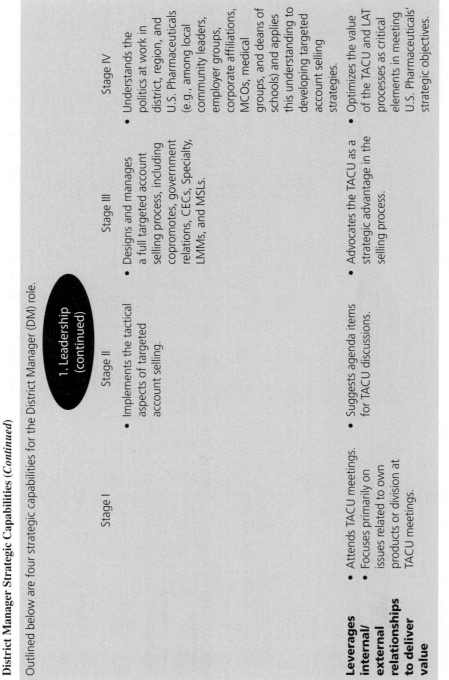

1. Leadership (continued)

	Stage I	Stage II	Stage III	Stage IV
		• Implements the tactical aspects of targeted account selling.	• Designs and manages a full targeted account selling process, including copromotes, government relations, CECs, Specialty, LMMs, and MSLs.	• Understands the politics at work in district, region, and U.S. Pharmaceuticals (e.g., among local community leaders, employer groups, corporate affiliations, MCOs, medical groups, and deans of schools) and applies this understanding to developing targeted account selling strategies.
Leverages internal/ external relationships to deliver value	• Attends TACU meetings. • Focuses primarily on issues related to own products or division at TACU meetings.	• Suggests agenda items for TACU discussions.	• Advocates the TACU as a strategic advantage in the selling process.	• Optimizes the value of the TACU and LAT processes as critical elements in meeting U.S. Pharmaceuticals' strategic objectives.

District Manager Strategic Capabilities (*Continued*)

Outlined below are four strategic capabilities for the District Manager (DM) role.

1. Leadership (continued)

Stage I

- Pays attention to other DMs' successes to learn management and leadership techniques and approaches.
- Discourages or confronts the exchange of negative disrespectful comments.

- Often focuses on individual contributors but is beginning to encourage a team approach (e.g., encourages representatives to coordinate business plan, goals, speakers, and call cycles).

Stage II

- Actively networks with DMs from other districts to learn from their successes.

- Recognizes and encourages a team approach to achieving results (e.g., acknowledges a representative's support of a priority copromote selling effort).

Stage III

- Works seamlessly with copromote partners. Regularly engages in activities to strengthen copromote relationships to maximize their benefits (e.g., openly shares resources, knowledge, and experience to facilitate representative/ DM mastery of market issues).

- Focuses on growing Pfizer's market share and profitability [e.g., adopts a customer-focused (versus division-focused) selling approach].

Stage IV

- Encourages and facilitates collaborating with CECs, MSLs, MSMs, Headquarters, and other field force members (e.g., identifies opportunities where a pooling of resources will increase the likelihood of success, matches up field force members who would benefit from collaboration).

District Manager Strategic Capabilities (*Continued*)

Outlined below are four strategic capabilities for the District Manager (DM) role.

1. Leadership (continued)

	Stage I	Stage II	Stage III	Stage IV
Raises performance in the field and develops high-performing teams	• Holds self to the same standards as representatives (e.g., is always punctual, files reports on time, willingly performs details, etc.). • Closely manages representative activities.	• Leads by example—personally demonstrates the core behaviors, skills, knowledge, and traits that representatives need to be successful. • Understands the principles of situational leadership and how it can improve performance (e.g., acknowledges individual differences but tends to rely on one preferred leadership style/approach). • Imparts a sense of responsibility among team members (e.g., requires representatives to assess their contributions and impact on district results, does not micro-manage or under manage representatives, etc.).	• Raises performance of representatives by setting high performance standards that are perceived by representatives as being challenging but achievable. • Applies the principles of situational leadership (e.g., uses multiple leadership styles and adapts approach to individual needs/circumstances).	• Raises performance of the field beyond division, TACU, district, and regional lines. • Sought out by peers for advice on developing high-performing teams. • Recognized by representatives, peers, RM, and Sales VP as a situational leadership role model as measured by IMDI, EQ, 360 Degrees, and Situational Leadership surveys.

District Manager Strategic Capabilities (*Continued*)

Outlined below are four strategic capabilities for the District Manager (DM) role.

1. Leadership (continued)

	Stage I	Stage II	Stage III	Stage IV
Manages conflicts and makes tough decisions to position the district for success	• Learning to surface and manage conflicts when dealing with individual representatives and at the TACU level (e.g., points out when representatives are making excuses).	• Does not wait until problems arise before addressing performance issues (e.g., addresses significant work activity performance shortfalls early).	• Recognizes opportunities to improve policies and/or practices and takes action to do so. • Makes tough decisions within an appropriate time frame and with the appropriate documentation (e.g., places a representative on final probation after several performance discussions and demonstrates to the representative how to correct his/her behaviors).	• Sought out by peers, Headquarters, and sales leadership for advice, counsel, and assistance regarding business, customer, market, and people issues (e.g., is recommended by RM or Sales VP for various advisory panels).

District Manager Strategic Capabilities (*Continued*)

Outlined below are four strategic capabilities for the District Manager (DM) role.

1. Leadership (continued)

	Stage I	Stage II	Stage III	Stage IV
Capitalizes on the benefits of diversity (field force and customers)	• Understands that representatives and customers have individual needs and styles and respects these differences.	• Helps representatives respect and understand individual differences. • Hires diverse candidates to complement the current field force (e.g., works with minority recruiters to select top talent).	• Adapts management style to respond to individual and customer needs/styles. • Utilizes a diverse set of skills and perspectives to enhance the overall effectiveness of the team.	• Recognizes and draws on individual backgrounds, experiences, and strengths to optimize district performance. • Is considered to be a role model by representatives, peers, and RM for his/her commitment to using diversity to increase effectiveness (e.g., helps others develop relationships with minority recruiting centers). • Assesses individuals' backgrounds and strengths and matches them to specific initiatives to optimize district performance.

Note: DMs will be expected to maintain demonstration/mastery of behaviors from prior stages.

Endnotes

1. L. Landro, "Pay for Performance Reaches Out to Specialists," *The Wall Street Journal,* December 15, 2004, p. D3.
2. R. Heilbroner, *The Worldly Philosophers* (New York: Simon & Schuster, 1953).
3. K. Murphy and J. Cleveland, *Understanding Performance Appraisal* (Thousand Oaks, CA: Sage, 1995).
4. C. Viswesvaran, F. L. Schmidt, and D. Ones, "Is There a General Factor in Ratings of Job Performance? A Meta-Analytic Frame Disentangling Substantive and Error Influences," *Journal of Applied Psychology* 90(1) (2005), pp. 108–131.
5. Mercer homepage, *www.mercerhr.com,* April 24, 2003.
6. M. J. Ducharme, P. Singh, and M. Podolsky, "Exploring the Links Between Performance Appraisals and Pay Satisfaction," *Compensation and Benefits Review,* September–October 2005, pp. 46–52; K. Murphy and J. Cleveland, *Understanding Performance Appraisal* (Thousand Oaks, CA: Sage, 1995).
7. Susan E. Jackson, Randall S. Schuler, and J. Carlos Rivero, "Organizational Characteristics as Predictors of Personnel Practices," *Personnel Psychology* 42 (1989), pp. 727–786.
8. Robert L. Cardy and Gregory H. Dobbins, *Performance Appraisal: Alternative Perspectives* (Cincinnati, OH: Southwestern, 1994).
9. J. Weil, "HealthSouth Becomes Subject of a Congressional Probe," *The Wall Street Journal,* April 23, 2003, p. C1.
10. W. E. Deming, *Out of the Crisis* (Cambridge, MA: MIT Press, 1986).
11. David Waldman, "The Contributions of Total Quality Management to a Theory of Work Performance," *Academy of Management Review* 19 (1994), pp. 510–536.
12. David Antonioni, "Improve the Performance Management Process Before Discontinuing Performance Appraisals," *Compensation and Benefits Review,* May–June 1994, pp. 29–37.
13. R. L. Cardy, C. L. Sutton, K. P. Carson, and G. H. Dobbins, "Degree of Responsibility: An Empirical Examination of Person and System Effects on Performance Ratings," paper presented at the national meeting of the Academy of Management, San Francisco, 1990.
14. R. Arvey and K. Murphy, "Performance Evaluation in Work Settings," *Annual Review of Psychology* 49 (1998), pp. 141–168.
15. P. Gwynne, "How Consistent Are Performance Review Criteria," *MIT Sloan Management Review,* Summer 2002, pp. 15–22.
16. W. Borman and D. Brush, "More Progress Towards a Taxonomy of Managerial Performance Requirements," *Human Performance* 6(1) (1993), pp. 1–21.
17. C. Viswesvaran, F. L. Schmidt, and D. Ones, "Is There a General Factor in Ratings of Job Performance? A Meta-Analytic Frame Disentangling Substantive and Error Influences," *Journal of Applied Psychology* 90(1) (2005), pp. 108–131.
18. Rachael Griffith and Andrew Neely, "Performance Pay and Managerial Experience in Multitask Teams: Evidence from within a Firm," *Journal of Labor Economics* 27(1) (2009), pp. 49–82.
19. D. Coleman, *Working With Emotional Intelligence* (New York: Bantam Books, 1998).
20. Based on a personal visit to Pizza Hut headquarters, March 2009.
21. Daniel Ilgen and Jack Feldman, "Performance Appraisal: A Process Focus," *Research in Organizational Behavior* 5 (1983), pp. 141–197.
22. Barry Gerhart, Sara L. Rynes, and Ingrid Smithey Fulmer, "Pay and Performance: Individuals, Groups and Executives," in A.P. Brief and J. P. Walsh, *Academy of Management Annals,* Vol. 3 (Newark, NJ: Lawrence Erlbaum, 2009).
23. Royal Navy and Marines fitness reports. Technical Report S206. Royal Navy Publications, 2004.

24. Victor M. Catano, Wendy Darr, and Catherine A. Campbell, "Performance Appraisal of Behavior Based Competencies." *Personnel Psychology* 60 (2007), pp. 201–230.

25. H. Levinson, "Management by Whose Objectives," *Harvard Business Review,* January 2003, pp. 1007–1016.

26. Mark L. McConkie, "A Clarification of the Goal Setting and Appraisal Processes in MBO," *Academy of Management Review* 4(1) (1979), pp. 29–40.

27. Ibid.

28. J. S. Hodgson, "Management by Objectives: The Experiences of a Federal Government Department," *Canadian Public Administration* 16(4) (1973), pp. 422–431.

29. Bruce McAfee and Blake Green, "Selecting a Performance Appraisal Method," *Personnel Administrator* 22(5) (1977), pp. 61–65.

30. Abraham N. Kluger and Angelo DeNisi, "The Effects of Feedback Interventions on Performance: A Historical Review, A Meta-Analysis and A Preliminary Feedback Intervention Theory," *Psychological Bulletin* 119(2) (1996), pp. 254–284.

31. Ibid.

32. H. John Bernardin, "Behavioral Expectation Scales v. Summated Ratings: A Fairer Comparison," *Journal of Applied Psychology* 62 (1977), pp. 422–427; H. John Bernardin, Kim Alvares, and C. J. Cranny, "A Recomparison of Behavioral Expectation Scales to Summated Scales," *Journal of Applied Psychology* 61 (1976), pp. 284–291; C. A. Schriesheim and U. E. Gattiker, "A Study of the Abstract Desirability of Behavior-Based v. Trait-Oriented Performance Rating," *Proceedings of the Academy of Management* 43 (1982), pp. 307–311; F. S. Landy and J. L. Farr, "Performance Rating," *Psychological Bulletin* 87 (1980), pp. 72–107.

33. Michael Keeley, "A Contingency Framework for Performance Evaluation," *Academy of Management Review* 3 (1978), pp. 428–438.

34. H. Risher, "Refocusing Performance Management for High Performance," *Compensation and Benefits Review,* September–October 2003, pp. 20–30.

35. H. J. Bernardin, K. Cooke, and P. Villanova, "Conscientiousness and Agreeableness as Predictors of Rating Leniency," *Journal of Applied Psychology* 85(2) (2000), pp. 232–234.

36. Mark R. Edwards and Ann J. Ewen, *360 Degree Feedback: The Powerful New Model for Employee Assessment and Performance Improvement* (Toronto: American Management Association, 1996).

37. Ibid.

38. Ibid.

39. IOMA, "Perils and Payoffs of Multi-Rater Feedback Programs," *Pay for Performance Report,* May 2003, p. 2.

40. Mark R. Edwards and Ann J. Ewen, *360 Degree Feedback: The Powerful New Model for Employee Assessment and Performance Improvement* (Toronto: American Management Association, 1996).

41. IOMA, "Perils and Payoffs of Multi-Rater Feedback Programs" (Newark, NJ: BNA Subsidiaries, 2007); D. Waldman, L. Atwater, and D. Antonioni, "Has 360 Degree Feedback Gone Amok?," *Academy of Management Executive* 12(2) (1998), pp. 86–94.

42. Susan E. Jackson, Randall S. Schuller, and J. Carlos Rivero, "Organizational Characteristics as Predictors of Personnel Practices," *Personnel Psychology* 42 (1989), pp. 727–786.

43. E. Pulakos and W. Borman, *Developing the Basic Criterion Scores for Army-Wide and MOS-Specific Ratings* (Alexandria, VA: U.S. Army Research Institute, 1983).

44. Deniz S. Ones, Frank L. Schmidt, and Chockalingam Viswesvaran, "Comparative Analysis of the Reliability of Job Performance Ratings," *Journal of Applied Psychology* 81(5) (1996), pp. 557–574.

45. F. S. Landy and J. L. Farr, "Performance Rating," *Psychological Bulletin* 87 (1980), pp. 72–107.

46. M. M. Harris and J. Schaubroeck, "A Meta Analysis of Self-Supervisor, Self-Peer, and Peer-Supervisor Ratings," *Personnel Psychology* 4 (1988), pp. 43–62.

47. R. Saavedra and S. Kwun, "Peer Evaluation in Self Managing Work Groups," *Journal of Applied Psychology* 78(3) (1993), pp. 450–462.

48. Conference on Performance Management, Center for Effective Organizations, April 23 2003.

49. M. M. Harris and J. Schaubroeck, "A Meta Analysis of Self-Supervisor, Self-Peer, and Peer-Supervisor Ratings," *Personnel Psychology* 41(1) (1988), pp. 43–62.

50. C. Longenecker and L. Fink, "On Employee Self-Appraisals: Benefits and Opportunities," *Journal of Compensation and Benefits* 22(3) (2006), pp. 12–16.

51. Patti Bond, "Home Depot Uses Customer Ratings for Employee Incentives," Cox News Service. Wednesday, June 21, 2006. Visited July 7, 2009 *http://www.statesman.com/news/content/shared/money/stories/coxnews/HOME_DEPOT_0621_COX.html*

52. Mark R. Edwards and Ann J. Ewen, *360 Degree Feedback: The Powerful New Model for Employee Assessment and Performance Improvement* (Toronto: American Management Association, 1996).

53. William L. Bearly and John E. Jones, *360 Degree Feedback: Strategies, Tactics, and Techniques for Developing Leaders* (Amherst, MA: HRD Press, 1996).

54. D. Antonioni, "The Effects of Feedback Accountability on Upward Appraisal Ratings," *Personnel Psychology* 47 (1994), pp. 349–356.

55. J. Schaubroeck and S. Lam, "How Similarity to Peers and Supervisor Influences Organizational Advancement in Different Cultures," *Academy of Management Journal,* 45(6) (2002), pp. 1125–1136; K. Murphy and J. Cleveland, *Understanding Performance Appraisal* (Thousand Oaks, CA: Sage, 1995).

56. J. Lefkowitz, "The Role of Interpersonal Affective Regard in Supervisory Performance Ratings: A Literature Review and Proposed Causal Model," *Journal of Occupational and Organizational Psychology* 73(1) (2000), pp. 61–85; R. L. Cardy and G. H. Dobbins, "Affect and Appraisal Accuracy: Liking as an Integral Dimension in Evaluating Performance," *Journal of Applied Psychology* 71 (1986), pp. 672–678; Robert C. Liden and Sandy J. Wayne, "Effect of Impression Management on Performance Ratings: A Longitudinal Study," *Academy of Management Journal* 38(1) (1995), pp. 232–260; Angelo S. Denisi, Lawrence H. Peters, and Arup Varma, "Interpersonal Affect and Performance Appraisal: A Field Study," *Personnel Psychology* 49 (1996), pp. 341–360.

57. G. Alliger and K. J. Williams, "Affective Congruence and the Employment Interview," in J. R. Meindl, R. L. Cardy, and S. M. Puffer, eds., *Advances in Information Processing in Organizations,* Vol. 4, (Greenwich, CT: JAI Press, 1986).

58. F. S. Landy and J. L. Farr, "Performance Rating," *Psychological Bulletin* 87 (1980), pp. 72–107; A. S. Denisi, T. P. Cafferty, and B. M. Meglino, "A Cognitive View of the Performance Appraisal Process: A Model and Research Propositions," *Organizational Behavior and Human Performance* 33 (1984), pp. 360–396; Jack M. Feldman, "Beyond Attribution Theory: Cognitive Processes in Performance Appraisal," *Journal of Applied Psychology* 66(2) (1981), pp. 127–148; W. H. Cooper, "Ubiquitous Halo,"*Psychological Bulletin* 90 (1981), pp. 218–244.

59. Angelo Denisi and George Stevens, "Profiles of Performance, Performance Evaluations, and Personnel Decisions," *Academy of Management* 24(3) (1981), pp. 592–602; Wayne Cascio and Enzo Valtenzi, "Relations Among Criteria of Police Performance," *Journal of Applied Psychology* 63(1) (1978), pp. 22–28; William Bigoness, "Effects of Applicant's Sex, Race, and Performance on Employer Performance Ratings: Some Additional Findings,"

Journal of Applied Psychology 61(1) (1976), pp. 80–84; Dorothy P. Moore, "Evaluating In-Role and Out-of-Role Performers," *Academy of Management Journal* 27(3) (1984), pp. 603–618; W. Borman, L. White, E. Pulakos, and S. Oppler, "Models of Supervisory Job Performance Ratings," *Journal of Applied Psychology* 76(6) (1991), pp. 863–872.

60. W. Borman, L. White, E. Pulakos, and S. Oppler, "Models of Supervisory Job Performance Ratings," *Journal of Applied Psychology* 76(6) (1991), pp. 863–872.

61. Darren C Treadway, Gerald R. Ferris, Allison B. Duke, et al., "The Moderating Role of Subordinate Political Skill on Supervisors' Impressions of Subordinate Ingratiation and Ratings of Subordinate Interpersonal Facilitation," *Journal of Applied Psychology* 92(3) (2007), pp. 848–855.

62. H. J. Bernardin and Richard Beatty, *Performance Appraisal: Assessing Human Behavior at Work* (Boston: Kent, 1984).

63. American Management Association, "Top Performers? Most Managers Rated Average or Better," Compflash, September 1992, p. 3.

64. Clinton Longnecker, Henry Sims, and Dennis Gioia, "Behind the Mask: The Politics of Employee Appraisal," *Academy of Management Executive* 1(3) (1987), pp. 183–193.

65. Timothy D. Schellhardt, "Annual Agony," *The Wall Street Journal,* November 19, 1996, p. A1.

66. G. Dobbins, R. Cardy, and D. Truxillo, "The Effects of Purpose of Appraisal and Individual Differences in Stereotypes of Women on Sex Differences in Performance Ratings: A Laboratory and Field Study," *Journal of Applied Psychology* 73(3) (1988), pp. 551–558.

67. M. Elvira and C. Zatzick, "Who's Displaced First? The Role of Race in Layoff Decisions," *Industrial Relations* 49(2) (2002), pp. 329–361.

68. A. S. Denisi and G. E. Stevens, "Profiles of Performance, Performance Evaluations, and Personnel Decisions," *Academy of Management Journal* 24(3) (September, 1981), pp. 592–602; William Scott and Clay Hamner, "The Influence of Variations in Performance Profiles on the Performance Evaluation Process: An Examination of the Validity of the Criterion," *Organizational Behavior and Human Performance* 14 (1975), pp. 360–370; Edward Jones, Leslie Rock, Kelly Shaver, George Goethals, and Laurence Ward, "Pattern of Performance and Ability Attributions: An Unexpected Primacy Effect," *Journal of Personality and Social Psychology* 10(4) (1968), pp. 317–340.

69. B. Gaugler and A. Rudolph, "The Influence of Assessee Performance Variation on Assessor's Judgments," *Personnel Psychology* 45 (1992), pp. 77–98.

70. F. J. Landy and J. L. Farr, "Performance Rating," *Psychological Bulletin* 87 (1980), pp. 72–107; H. J. Bernardin and R. W. Beatty, *Performance Appraisal: Assessing Human Behavior at Work* (Dallas: Scott, Foresman, 1984).

71. N. Cantor and W. Mischel, "Traits v. Prototypes: The Effects on Recognition and Memory," *Journal of Personality and Social Psychology* 35 (1977), pp. 38–48; R. J. Spiro, "Remembering Information From Text: The 'State of Schema' Approach," in R. C. Anderson, R. J. Spiro, and W. E. Montatague, eds., *Schooling and the Acquisition of Knowledge* (Hillsdale, CA: Erlbaum, 1977); T. K. Srull and R. S. Wyer, "Category Accessibility and Social Perception: Some Implications for the Study of Person Memory and Interpersonal Judgments," *Journal of Personality and Social Psychology* 38 (1980), pp. 841–856.

72. Robert Heneman and Kenneth Wexley, "The Effects of Time Delay in Rating and Amount of Information Observed on Performance Rating Accuracy," *Academy of Management Journal* 26(4) (1983), pp. 677–686.

73. B. P. Maroney and R. M. Buckley, "Does Research in Performance Appraisal Influence the Practice of Performance Appraisal? Regretfully Not," *Public Personnel Management* 21 (1992), pp. 185–196.

74. Robert Liden and Terence Mitchell, "The Effects of Group Interdependence on Supervisor Performance Evaluations,"*Personnel Psychology* 36(2) (1983), pp. 289–299.

75. Dick Grote, *Forced Ranking: Making Performance Management Work* (Boston, MA: Harvard Business School Press, 2005); G. H. Dobbins, R. L. Cardy, and D. M. Truxillo, "The Effects of Purpose of Appraisal and Individual Differences in Stereotypes of Women on Sex Differences in Performance Ratings: A Laboratory and Field Study," *Journal of Applied Psychology* 73(33) (1986), pp. 551–558.

76. Samuel Y. Todd, Kenneth J. Harris, Ranida B. Harris, and Anthony R. Wheeler. "Career Success Implications of Political Skill." *Journal of Social Psychology* 149(3) (June 2009), pp. 179–204.

77. G. R. Ferris and T. A. Judge, "Personnel/Human Resource Management: A Political Influence Perspective," *Journal of Management* 17 (1991), pp. 1–42.

78. Yoav Ganzach, "Negativity (and Positivity) in Performance Evaluation: Three Field Studies," *Journal of Applied Psychology* 80(4) (1995), pp. 491–499.

79. D. Winstanley, "How Accurate Are Performance Appraisals?" *Personnel Administrator* 25(8) (1980), pp. 55–58; F. S. Landy and J. L. Farr, "Performance Rating," Psychological Bulletin 87 (1980), pp. 72–107; R. L. Heneman and K. N. Wexley, "The Effects of Time Delay in Rating and Amount of Information Observed on Performance Rating Accuracy," *Academy of Management Journal* 26 (1983), pp. 677–686.

80. Conversation between Jerry Newman and Lisa Emerson, VP Global Total Compensation, McDonalds, Fall 2008.

81. D. Jones, "Study: Thinning Herd From Bottom Helps," *USA Today,* March 14, 2005, p. B1.

82. D. Grote, *Forced Ranking: Making Performance Management Work* (Boston, MA: Harvard Business School Press, 2005).

83. Ibid.

84. S. Scullen, P. Bergey, and L. Aiman-Smith, "Forced Distribution Rating Systems and the Improvement of Workforce Potential: A Baseline Simulation," *Personnel Psychology* 58(1) (2005), pp. 1–33.

85. L. Cummings and D. Schwab, *Performance in Organization* (Glenview, IL: Scott Foresman, 1973).

86. Neal P. Mero and Stephan J. Motowidlo, "Effects of Rater Accountability on the Accuracy and the Favorability of Performance Ratings," *Journal of Applied Psychology* 80(4) (1995), pp. 517–524.

87. H. J. Bernardin and E. C. Pence, "Effects of Rater Training: Creating New Response Sets and Decreasing Accuracy," *Journal of Applied Psychology* 6 (1980), pp. 60–66.

88. Sheldon Zedeck and Wayne Cascio, "Performance Appraisal Decision as a Function of Rater Training and Purpose of the Appraisal," *Journal of Applied Psychology* 67(6) (1982), pp. 752–758.

89. E. Rogers, C. Rogers, and W. Metlay, "Improving the Payoff From 360-Degree Feedback," *Human Resource Planning,* 25(3) (2002), pp. 44–54; H. J. Bernardin and M. R. Buckley, "Strategies in Rater Training," *Academy of Management Review* 6(2) (1981), pp. 205–212; D. Smith, "Training Programs for Performance Appraisal: A Review," *Academy of Management Review* 11(1) (1986), pp. 22–40; B. Davis and M. Mount, "Effectiveness of Performance Appraisal Training Using Computer Assisted Instruction and Behavioral Modeling," *Personnel Psychology* 3 (1984), pp. 439–452; H. J. Bernardin, "Effects of Rater Training on Leniency and Halo Errors in Student Ratings of Instructors," *Journal of Applied Psychology* 63(3) (1978), pp. 301–308; J. M. Ivancevich, "Longitudinal Study of the Effects of Rater Training on Psychometric Error in Ratings," *Journal of Applied Psychology* 64(5) (1979), pp. 502–508.

90. H. J. Bernardin and M. R. Buckley, "Strategies in Rater Training," *Academy of Management Review* 6 (1981), pp. 205–221.

91. C. O. Longnecker, H. P. Sims Jr., and D. A. Gioia, "Behind the Mask: The Politics of Employee Appraisal," *Academy of Management Executive* 1(3) (August, 1987), pp. 183–193.

92. S. Waugh, "Solid Performance Reviews," *Supervision* 67(5) (2006), pp. 16–17.

93. Robert Heneman, *Merit Pay: Linking Pay Increases to Performance Ratings* (Reading, MA: Addison-Wesley, 1992).

94. S. Waugh, "Solid Performance Reviews," *Supervision* 67(5) (2006), pp. 16–17.

95. Ann Podolske, "Creating a Review System That Works," *Pay for Performance Report,* March 1996, pp. 2–4.

96. Stephen J. Carroll, J. Kline Harrison, Monika K. Renard, et al., "Due Process in Performance Appraisal: A Quasi-Experiment in Procedural Justice," *Administrative Science Quarterly* 40 (1995), pp. 495–523.

97. IOMA, *Pay for Performance Report* (Newark, NJ: BNA Subsidiaries, January 2002, p. 13).

98. Ann Podolske, "Creating a Review System That Works," *Pay for Performance Report,* March 1996, pp. 2–4.

99. Mercer homepage, *www.mercerhr.com,* April 24, 2003.

100. Avraham N. Kluger, and Angelo DeNisi, "The Effects of Feedback Interventions on Performance: A Historical Review, a Meta-Analysis, and a Preliminary Feedback Intervention Theory," *Psychological Bulletin* 119(2) (1996), pp. 254–284.

101. A. DeNisi, T. Robbins, and T. Cafferty, "Organization of Information Used for Performance Appraisals: Role of Diary-Keeping," *Journal of Applied Psychology* 74(1) (1989), pp. 124–129.

102. Angelo S. Denisi, Lawrence H. Peters, and Arup Varma, "Interpersonal Affect and Performance Appraisal: A Field Study," *Personnel Psychology* 49 (1996), pp. 341–360; F. J. Landy, J. L. Barnes, and K. R. Murphy, "Correlates of Perceived Fairness and Accuracy of Performance Evaluations," *Journal of Applied Psychology* 63 (1978), pp. 751–754.

103. S. Snell and K. Wexley, "Performance Diagnosis: Identifying the Causes of Poor Performance," *Personnel Administrator,* April 1985, pp. 117–127.

104. Ann Podolske, "Creating a Review System That Works," *Pay for Performance Report,* March 1996, pp. 2–4.

105. Elizabeth C. Hirsh, "The Strength of Weak Enforcement: The Impact of Discrimination Charges, Legal Environments, and Organizational Conditions on Workplace Segregation." *American Sociological Review* 74(2) (2009), pp. 245–271.

106. LRP Publications, "Black SSA Employees Get 7.75 Million Settlement," *Federal Human Resources Week* 8(39) (2002), pp. 1, 3.

107. *Brito v. Zia Company,* 478 F.2d 1200 (1973).

108. Ibid.

109. G. L. Lubben, D. E. Thompson, and C. R. Klasson, "Performance Appraisal: The Legal Implications of Title VII," *Personnel* 57(3) (1980), pp. 11–21; H. Feild and W. Halley, "The Relationship of Performance Appraisal System Characteristics to Verdicts in Selected Employment Discrimination Cases," *Academy of Management Journal* 25(2) (1982), pp. 392–406; *Albermarle Paper Company v. Moody,* U.S. Supreme Court, no. 74–389 and 74–428, 10 FEP Cases 1181 (1975); *Moody v. Albermarle Paper Company,* 474 F.3d. 134.

110. H. S. Feild and W. H. Holley, "The Relationship of Performance Appraisal System Characteristics to Verdicts in Selected Employment Discrimination Cases," *Academy of Management Journal* 25(2) (1982), pp. 392–406; Gerald Barrett and Mary Kernan, "Performance Appraisal and Terminations: A Review of Court Decisions Since *Brito*

v. Zia With Implications for Personnel Practices," *Personnel Psychology* 40 (1987), pp. 489–503.

111. D. Martin and K. Bartol, "The Legal Ramifications of Performance Appraisal: An Update," *Employee Relations* 17(2) (1991), pp. 286–293.
112. *Payne v. General Motors,* 53 FEP Cases 471 (D. C. Kan. 1990).
113. J. McGregor, "The Struggle to Measure Performance," *BusinessWeek,* January 9, 2006, p. 26.
114. C. Wood, "Measuring Progress, Avoiding Liability in Evaluating Employees," *Employment Law Weekly,* December 1999, pp. 1–9.
115. George Milkovich and Carolyn Milkovich, "Strengthening the Pay-Performance Relationship: The Research," *Compensation and Benefits Review,* November–December 1992, pp. 22–31.
116. My deepest thanks to Christine Stewart for graciously giving time for an interview (2009) and for putting together material for this exhibit.

Employee Benefits

Dig two holes in the ground. In the first, bury $7.93. In the second, put $13.41. Now every hour, Monday through Friday, 8 a.m. until 4 p.m., dig up those holes and add the corresponding amount.[1] Leave the money in these holes as very expensive fertilizer for your geraniums. Why these amounts, you ask? Why bury them in the backyard, you ask? Well, those dollar amounts are the cost of a full-time employee's benefits each hour of every workweek in, respectively, a private sector firm and in a state or local government job. Burying the money in the backyard is our way of saying it's not clear the money is any worse off in the ground than invested in employee benefits. A bit harsh? An exaggeration, you say! Most executives would agree with you. A recent survey shows 89 percent of executives think employee benefits are extremely important factors in attracting and retaining good employees.[2] But stop and think about what we know that is fact—not faith—in the benefits area. Which of the issues covered in the pay model (see Exhibit V.1), for example, can we answer with respect to benefits? Does effective employee benefit management facilitate organization performance? The answer is unclear. We do know that benefit costs can be cut, and this affects the bottom line (admittedly an important measure of organization performance). But what about other alignment and management efforts? Do benefits complement organization strategy and performance? We don't know. Or do employee benefits impact an organization's ability to attract, retain, and motivate employees? Conventional wisdom, as the executives in our survey indicated, says employee benefits can affect retention, but there is no definitive research to support this conclusion. A similar lack of research surrounds each of the other potential payoffs to a sound benefits program.

The only absolute reality is this: Employee benefits cost about $5 trillion per year. Maybe it's time we found out if this is a good way to spend corporate funds. Not surprisingly, firms are increasingly paying attention to this reward component. It represents a labor cost with no apparent returns.

Compounding this concern is the ever-present entitlement problem. Employees perceive benefits as a right, independent of how well they or the company performs. Efforts to reduce benefit levels or eliminate parts of the package altogether would meet with employee resistance and dissatisfaction. Just ask workers and retirees at GM, Ford, or Chrysler.[3] In an effort to stop the competitive bleeding, the auto industry is cutting benefits for both current and retired employees.

EXHIBIT V.1 The Pay Model

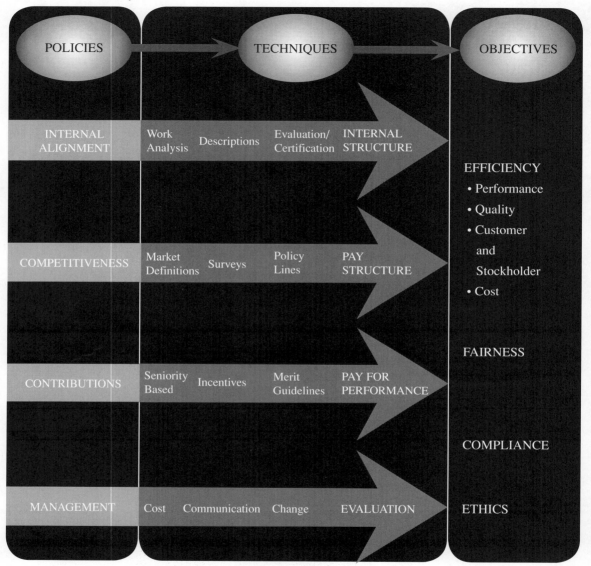

Assuming that organizations must find ways to control the costs of benefits wherever possible, this section of the book focuses on identifying ways to maximize the returns from benefit expenditures. As a first step in this direction, Chapter 12 identifies issues organizations should face in developing and maintaining a benefit program. A model of the benefit determination process is also presented, to provide a structure for thinking about employee benefits. Chapter 13 provides a summary of the state of employee benefits today. Hopefully this will provide the groundwork for the innovative and effective benefit packages of tomorrow.

Endnotes

1. Bureau of Labor Statistics, *www.data.bls.gov/cgi-bin/surveymost,* June 21, 2006.
2. The *McKinsey Quarterly* Chart Focus Newsletter, June 2006, Member Edition.
3. I. Watson, "GM Puts Salaried Staff in Firing Line," *Knight Ridder Tribune Business News,* March 26, 2006, p. 1.

The Benefit
Determination Process

Chapter Outline

Why the Growth in Employee Benefits?
Wage and Price Controls
Unions
Employer Impetus
Cost Effectiveness of Benefits
Government Impetus

The Value of Employee Benefits

Key Issues in Benefit Planning, Design, and Administration
Benefit Planning and Design Issues
Benefit Administration Issues

Components of a Benefit Plan
Employer Preferences
Employee Preferences

Administering the Benefit Program
Employee Benefit Communication
Claims Processing
Cost Containment

Your Turn: World Measurement

What can you do with four trillion dollars?[1] Help balance the budget? Buy four new copies of this book? Well, the answer is, you can cover the cost of all employee benefits in the United States today. It's hard to believe that employee benefits cost this much. This is particularly hard to believe when we take a look at what used to pass as benefits in the not-too-distant past:

- A carriage shop published a set of rules for employees in 1880 that stated, in part: "Working hours shall be from 7 a.m. to 9 p.m. every day except the Sabbath. . . . After an employee has been with this firm for five years he shall receive an added payment of five cents per day, provided the firm has prospered in a manner to make it possible. . . . It is the bounden duty of each employee to put away at least 10 percent of his monthly wages for his declining years so he will not become a burden upon his betters."

- In 1915, employees in the iron and steel industry worked a standard 60 to 64 hours per week. By 1930 that schedule had been reduced to 54 hours.

- It was not until 1929 that the Blue Cross concept of prepaid medical costs was introduced.

- Prior to 1935, only one state (Wisconsin) had a program of unemployment compensation benefits for workers who lost their jobs through no fault of their own.

- Before World War II, very few companies paid hourly employees for holidays. In most companies, employees were told not to report for work on holidays and to enjoy the time off, but their paychecks were smaller the following week.[2]

414

EXHIBIT 12.1
Changes in Benefit Costs Over Time

Source: U.S. Chamber of Commerce, Annual Benefit Surveys, *www. uschamber.com*, June 22, 2008.

	1959	1969	1990	1998	2008
Percentage of Payroll	24.7	31.1	38.4	37.2	42.7

In comparison to these "benefits" from the past, today's reality seems staggering. Consider the kinds of things that are common in companies that made the *Fortune* magazine list of "100 Best Companies to Work For in America." These companies recognize the importance of taking care of employees' needs as a key factor in attracting and retaining the best employees. A first-class benefit plan includes some mix of the following benefits: education reimbursement and employee training; on-site child care services, financial counseling, and concierge services; and retirement benefits.[3] Just consider some of the extra benefits beyond the norm at this year's number-1 rated company to work at: NetApp, a data storage, management, and protection company. Want to help Habitat for Humanity build homes in a hurricane ravaged coastal area? No problem. At NetApp you get five paid days for volunteer work. Want to adopt a child? NetApp gives you $11,390 adoption aid. NetApp is so family centered that it even has coverage for autistic children. Since 2006, 43 employees have tapped into this benefit at a cost of $242,452.[4]

Clearly NetApp would argue that these extra services are important benefits of employment, perhaps making attraction, retention, and motivation of employees just that much easier. But the truth is, we don't know if even ordinary benefits have positive payoffs. We do know that employees consistently rate benefits a key factor in job satisfaction.[5] Unfortunately, though, there is a mismatch between cost to employer and perceived value to employee: the cost is much higher than employees estimate.[6]

Until we can clearly identify the advantages of employee benefits, we need to find ways to control their costs or at least slow their growth. Exhibit 12.1 illustrates the rapid rise in employee benefit costs, moving from about 25 percent of payroll costs in 1959 to more than 40 percent by some calculations today.[7]

As Exhibit 12.1 illustrates, **employee benefits** can no longer realistically be called "fringe benefits." As an example, visualize a $20,000 car rolling down the assembly line at General Motors. A cost accountant would tell you that $1,200 of this cost is due to worker health insurance alone. Compare it to the cost of all the steel for the same car—$500—and the impact is evident. Now compare it to health insurance costs as low as $100 for foreign automakers in their U.S. factories (with their younger, healthier workers and hardly any retirees), and the global implications of benefit costs are all too frightening.[8]

Over one 20-year period (1955–1975), employee benefit costs rose at a rate almost four times greater than employee wages or the consumer price index.[9] A similar

Employee benefits are that part of the total compensation package, other than pay for time worked, provided to employees in whole or in part by employer payments (e.g., life insurance, pension, workers' compensation, vacation).

comparison for the period 1963–1987 showed that the rate of growth had slowed (benefit costs rose twice as fast as wage costs). And a still later comparison, for the period 1993–1999, the cost of benefits actually stabilized at about $14,700 per full-time employee. Recently, though, benefit costs have begun to heat up again—with survey results from 2008 showing the average cost at $18,496.[10] Health care costs alone increased an average of 5.0 percent last year, only slightly less than the 5.9 percentage trend for the past 15 years.[11] That translates into health care costs that have more than doubled since 1990 (an increase of 123 percent), and that are expected to hit 4.3 trillion dollars by 2017. Pension costs also are an area of concern. Just ask Delta Airlines or Sara Lee. Both companies face huge unfunded pension liabilities. When you are behind hundreds of millions in pension funding, it's difficult to interest anyone in buying your stock.[12] And problems may even be worse in the public sector, where state governments have regularly underfunded **pension plans.** With looming retirements of baby boomers, this could spell catastrophe for already burdened state budgets.[13]

WHY THE GROWTH IN EMPLOYEE BENEFITS?

Wage and Price Controls

During both World War II and the Korean War, the federal government instituted strict **wage and price controls.** The compliance agency charged with enforcing these controls was relatively lenient in permitting reasonable increases in benefits. With strict limitations on the size of wage increases, both unions and employers sought new and improved benefits to satisfy worker demands. This was the catalyst for growth in pensions, health care coverage, time off, and the broad spectrum of benefits virtually unthinkable before 1950.

Unions

The climate fostered by wage and price controls created a perfect opportunity for unions to flex the muscles they had acquired under the Wagner Act of 1935. Several National Labor Relations Board rulings during the 1940s freed unions to negotiate over employee benefits. With little freedom to raise wages during the war, unions fought for the introduction of new benefits and the improvement of existing benefits. Success on this front during the war years led to further postwar demands. Largely through the efforts of unions, most notably the autoworkers and steelworkers, several benefits common today were given their initial impetus: pattern pension plans, supplementary unemployment compensation, extended vacation plans, and guaranteed annual wage plans.[14]

Employer Impetus

Many of the benefits in existence today were provided at employer initiative. Much of this initiative can be traced to pragmatic concerns about employee satisfaction and productivity. Rest breaks often were implemented in the belief that fatigue increased accidents and lowered productivity. Savings and profit sharing plans were implemented (e.g., Procter & Gamble's profit sharing plan was initiated in 1885) to improve performance and provide increased security for worker retirement years. Indeed, many employer-initiated benefits were designed to create a climate in which employees perceived that management was genuinely concerned for their welfare. Notice, though, these supposed benefits were taken on faith. But their costs were quite real: Without hard data about payoffs, employee benefits slowly became a costly entitlement of the American workforce.

Cost Effectiveness of Benefits

Another important and sound impetus for the growth of employee benefits is their cost effectiveness in two situations. The first cost advantage is that most employee benefits are not taxable. Provision of a benefit rather than an equivalent increase in wages avoids payment of federal and state personal income tax. Remember, though, recurrent tax reform proposals continue to threaten the favorable tax status granted to many benefits.

A second cost-effectiveness component of benefits arises because many group-based benefits (e.g., life, health, and legal insurance) can be obtained at a lower rate than could be obtained by employees acting on their own. Group insurance also has relatively easy qualification standards, giving security to a set of employees who might not otherwise qualify.

Government Impetus

Obviously the government has played an important role in the growth of employee benefits. Three employee benefits are mandated by either the state or federal government: **workers' compensation** (state), **unemployment insurance** (federal), and **social security** (federal). In addition, most other employee benefits are affected by such laws as the **Employee Retirement Income Security Act** (ERISA affects pension administration) and various sections of the Internal Revenue Code.

THE VALUE OF EMPLOYEE BENEFITS

Exhibit 12.2 shows the relative importance employees attached to different types of benefits across five different studies.[15]

In general, the five studies reported in Exhibit 12.2 show remarkably consistent results over the past two decades. For example, medical payments regularly are listed as one of the most important benefits employees receive. These rankings have added significance when we note that over the past two decades health care costs are the most rapidly growing and the most difficult to control of all the benefit options offered by employers.[16] In 2008, health care costs alone were $4,256 for the typical employer.[17]

The four trillion dollars employers spend on benefits each year would not seem nearly so outrageous if we had evidence that employees place high value on the benefits they receive. Unfortunately, there is evidence that employees frequently are not even aware of, or undervalue, the benefits provided by their organization. For example, in one study employees were asked to recall the benefits they received. The typical employee could recall less than 15 percent of them. In another study, MBA students were asked to rank the importance attached to various factors influencing job selection.[18]

EXHIBIT 12.2
Ranking of Employee Benefits

Note: × = indicates a benefit that was not rated in this study.

	Study				
	1	2	3	4	5
Medical	1	1	3	1	1
Pension	2	3	8	3	2
Paid vacations and holidays	3	2	×	2	3
Sickness	4	×	5	8	×
Dental	5	×	6	6	×
Long-term disability	7	×	7	9	6
Life insurance	8	×	4	×	5

Presumably the large percentage of labor costs allocated to payment of employee benefits would be easier to justify if benefits turned out to be an important factor in attracting good MBA candidates. Of the six factors ranked, employee benefits received the lowest ranking. Opportunity for advancement (#1), salary (#2), and geographic location (#3) all ranked considerably higher than benefits as factors influencing job selection. Compounding this problem, these students also were asked to estimate the percentage of payroll spent on employee benefits. Slightly less than one-half (46 percent) of the students thought that benefits comprised 15 percent or less of payroll, and 9 out of 10 students (89 percent) thought benefits accounted for less than 30 percent of payroll. Only 1 in 10 students had a reasonably accurate (39 percent of payroll) or inflated perception of the magnitude of employee benefits.[19]

For the past 20 years, we've argued here that benefits are taken for granted. Given their cost, that's not a good thing. Now, though, with companies cutting back benefits, or shifting costs to employees (or retirees!), the air of entitlement may be disappearing. A recent study by the Society of Human Resource Management indicates both employees and HR professionals see benefits as the top factor driving job satisfaction.[20]

One possible direction out of this money pit comes from recent reports of employees looking not necessarily for more benefits, but rather for greater choice in the benefits they receive.[21] In fact, up to 70 percent of employees in one study indicated they would be willing to pay more out of pocket for benefits if they were granted greater choice in designing their own benefit package. We do know, in support of this, that the perceived value of benefits rises when employers introduce choice through a flexible benefit package.[22] Maybe better benefit planning, design, and administration offer an opportunity to improve benefit effectiveness. Indeed, preliminary evidence indicates employers are making serious efforts to educate employees about benefits, with an outcome of increased employee awareness.[23] For example, the simple act of stating in an employment ad that benefits are generous leads to applicants' focusing on this characteristic and relying more heavily on it in job choice. Some experts speculate that a key element in reward attractiveness (and benefits in this example) may be their visibility. Not only do we have to plan and design effective benefit programs; we also need to communicate their value to employees.

KEY ISSUES IN BENEFIT PLANNING, DESIGN, AND ADMINISTRATION

Benefits Planning and Design Issues

What do you want—or expect—the role of benefits to be in your overall compensation package?[24] For example, if a major compensation objective is to attract good employees, we need to ask, "What is the best way to achieve this?" The answer is not always, or even frequently, "Let's add another benefit."

Put yourself in the following situation as the benefits manager. Recently, a casino opened up in the Niagara Falls area. The Seneca Indians own this casino, and they needed to fill thousands of entry-level jobs. The wages for a blackjack dealer were $4 per hour plus tips. The combination of the two exceeds minimum wage, but not by much. How do we attract more dealers, and other applicants, given these low wages? One temptation might be to set up a day care center to attract more mothers of preschool children. Certainly this is a popular response today, judging from all the press business-sponsored day care centers are receiving. A more prudent compensation policy would ask the question: "Is day care the most effective way to achieve my compensation objective?" Sure, day care may be popular with working mothers, but can the necessary workers be attracted to the casino using some other compensation tool that better meets needs? If we went to compensation experts in the gaming industry, they might say (and we would be impressed if you said this along with them): "We target recruitment of young females for our entry-level jobs. Surveys of this group indicate day care is an extremely important factor in the decision to accept a job."

If you used this kind of logic in your arguments as benefits manager, we think you're well on the way to a successful career. As a second example, how do we deal with undesirable turnover? Rich Floersch, Sr. Vice President of HR at McDonald's, faced this very question. After looking at other alternatives to reduce turnover, Rich decided that the best strategy was to design a benefit package that improved progressively with seniority, thus providing a reward for continuing service. Keep in mind, though, Rich only made this decision after evaluating the effectiveness of other compensation tools (e.g., increasing wages, introducing incentive compensation).

In addition to integrating benefits with other compensation components, the planning process also should include strategies for ensuring external competitiveness and adequacy of benefits.[25] Competitiveness requires an understanding of what other firms in your product and labor markets offer as benefits. Firms conduct benefit surveys much as they conduct salary surveys. Either our firm must have a package comparable to that of survey participants or there should be a sound justification of why deviation makes sense for the firm.

In contrast, ensuring that benefits are adequate is a somewhat more difficult task. Most organizations evaluating adequacy consider the financial liability of employees with and without a particular benefit (e.g., employee medical expenses with and without medical expense benefits). There is no magic formula for defining benefit adequacy.[26] In part, the answer may lie in the relationship between benefit adequacy and the third plan objective: cost of effectiveness. More organizations need to consider whether employee benefits are cost justified. All sorts of ethical questions arise when we start asking this question. How far should we go with elder care? Can we justify paying for a $250,000 surgical procedure that will likely buy only a few more months of life? Companies face these impossible questions when designing a benefit system. And more frequently than ever before, companies are saying no to absorbing the cost increases of benefits. A recent survey shows that 59 percent of employers are shifting increased benefit costs to employees through higher deductibles and copays, for example.[27]

> **Cybercomp**
> Benefitslink, at *www.benefitslink.com/index.shtml,* provides a wealth of information about types of benefits, a message board for interacting in discussions with others interested in benefits, and an "Ask the Expert" question-and-answer column.

Benefit Administration Issues

Four major administration issues arise in setting up a benefit package: (1) Who should be protected or benefited?; (2) How much choice should employees have among an array of benefits?; (3) How should benefits be financed?[28]; and (4) Are your benefits legally defensible?[29]

The first issue—who should be covered—ought to be an easy question. The answer is *employees,* of course. But every organization has a variety of employees with different employment statuses. Should these individuals be treated equally with respect to benefits coverage? Exhibit 12.3 illustrates that companies do indeed differentiate treatment based on employment status. Across the board, far fewer part-time workers are eligible for the benefits regularly given to full-time employees.

As a second example, should retired automobile executives be permitted to continue purchasing cars at a discount price, a benefit that could be reserved solely for current employees or—given the state of the auto industry—perhaps eliminated entirely? In fact, a whole series of questions need to be answered:

1. What probationary periods (for eligibility of benefits) should be used for various types of benefits? Does the employer want to cover employees and their dependents immediately upon employment or provide such coverage only for employees who

EXHIBIT 12.3
Contingent-Worker Benefits Compared to Full-Time Workers

Source: "National Compensation Survey 2005," Bureau of Labor Statistics, *www.bls.gov,* June 27, 2006.

	Full Time	Part Time
Holidays	89%	37%
Vacations	90	36
Short-Term Disability	48	14
Long-Term Disability	38	5
Life Insurance	64	12
Retirement	69	27
Medical	85	22
Dental	56	14
Vision	35	9

have established more or less permanent employment with the employer? Is there a rationale for different probationary periods with different benefits?

2. Which dependents of active employees should be covered?

3. Should retirees (as well as their spouses and perhaps other dependents) be covered, and for which benefits?

4. Should survivors of deceased employees (and/or retirees) be covered? If so, for which benefits? Are benefits for surviving spouses appropriate?

5. What coverage, if any, should be extended to employees who are suffering from disabilities?

6. What coverage, if any, should be extended to employees during layoffs, leaves of absence, strikes, and so forth?

7. Should coverage be limited to full-time employees?[30]

The answers to these questions depend on the policy decisions regarding adequacy, competition, and cost effectiveness discussed in the last section.

The second administrative issue concerns choice (flexibility) in plan coverage. In the standard benefit package, employees typically have not been offered a choice among employee benefits. Rather, a package is designed with the average employee in mind, and any deviations in needs simply go unsatisfied. The other extreme (discussed in greater detail later) is represented by "cafeteria-style," or flexible, benefit plans. Under this concept employees are permitted great flexibility in choosing the benefit options of greatest value to them. Picture an individual allotted x dollars walking down a cafeteria line and choosing menu items (benefits) according to their attractiveness and cost. The flexibility in this type of plan is apparent. Exhibit 12.4 illustrates a typical choice among packages offered to employees under a flexible benefit system. Imagine an employee whose spouse works and already has family coverage for health, dental, and vision. The temptation might be to select package A. An employee with retirement in mind might select option B with its contributions to a **401(k)** pension plan. Exhibit 12.5 summarizes some of the major advantages and disadvantages of flexible benefits.

Even companies that are not considering a flexible benefit program are offering greater flexibility and choice. Such plans might provide, for example, (1) optional levels of group term life insurance; (2) the availability of death or disability benefits under pension or profit-sharing plans; (3) choices of covering dependents under group

EXHIBIT 12.4
Possible Options in a Flexible Benefit Package

* AE = average earnings.

	Package			
	A	**B**	**C**	**D**
Health	No	No	Yes	Yes
Dental	No	No	No	Yes
Vision	No	Yes	Yes	Yes
Life insurance	$1 \times AE$*	$2 \times AE$	$2 \times AE$	$3 \times AE$
Dependent care	Yes	No	No	No
401(k) savings	No	Yes	No	No
Cash back	Yes	No	No	No

EXHIBIT 12.5
Advantages
and
Disadvantages
of Flexible
Benefit
Programs

Advantages

1. Employees choose packages that best satisfy their unique needs.
2. Flexible benefits help firms meet the changing needs of a changing workforce.
3. Increased involvement of employees and families improves understanding of benefits.
4. Flexible plans make introduction of new benefits less costly. Any new option is added merely as one among a wide variety of elements from which to choose.
5. Cost containment: Organization sets dollar maximum; employee chooses within that constraint.

Disadvantages

1. Employees make bad choices and find themselves not covered for predictable emergencies.
2. Administrative burdens and expenses increase.
3. Adverse selection: Employees pick only benefits they will use; the subsequent high-benefit utilization increases its cost.
4. Flexible benefit plans are subject to nondiscrimination requirements in Section 125 of the Internal Revenue Code.

medical expense coverage; and (4) a variety of participation, cash distribution, and investment options under profit-sharing, thrift, and capital accumulation plans.[31]

The level at which an organization finally chooses to operate on this choice/flexibility dimension really depends on its evaluation of the relative advantages and disadvantages of flexible plans, noted in Exhibit 12.5.[32] Many companies cite the cost savings from flexible benefits as a primary motivation. Companies also offer flexible plans in response to cost pressures related to the increasing diversity of the workforce. Flexible benefit plans, it is argued, increase employee awareness of the true costs of benefits and, therefore, increase employee recognition of benefit value.[33]

Another way to increase employee awareness, and probably the biggest trend today in health care, is to offer **market-based,** or **customer-driven,** health care. Although there are many variants on **consumer-driven health care,** here are the basic choices:[34]

- **Full-Defined Contribution**—The employee is responsible for finding and purchasing individual medical coverage. The employer provides funding through either **direct compensation** or a voucher.
- **Tiered Networks**—The employer offers employees a choice of medical plans, which include medical systems of varying costs.
- **Menu-Driven**—Employers provide online information to help employees customize their own benefit plan by selecting co-pays, deductibles, and so forth.
- **Managed Competition**—The employer provides a subsidized basic medical plan with buy-up options. Plans can be from the same or multiple insurers.
- **Health Savings Accounts**—A fund is created by the employer, employee, or jointly that is used to pay the first x dollars of health care expenses.

Each of the alternatives creates a motivation for employees to think about what option fits their budget and particular health characteristics. The third administrative issue involves the question of how to finance benefit plans. Alternatives include:

1. Noncontributory (Employer pays total costs.)
2. Contributory (Costs are shared between employer and employee.)
3. Employee financed (Employee pays total costs for some benefits—by law the organization must bear the cost for certain benefits.)

In general, organizations prefer to make benefit options contributory, reasoning that a "free good," no matter how valuable, is less valuable to an employee. Furthermore, employees have no personal interest in controlling the cost of a free good. And with the cost of benefits rising considerably more than other goods and services, employers are increasingly turning to ways for cutting their costs.[35]

Finally, benefits have to comply with hundreds of arcane sections of the tax code and other "devils" designed to turn any benefit administrator's hair gray. Because there are so many rules and regulations, benefit administrators should develop a compliance checklist and regularly conduct audits to ensure that they are complying with the avalanche of new and existing requirements.[36]

COMPONENTS OF A BENEFIT PLAN

Exhibit 12.6 outlines a model of the factors influencing benefit choice, from both the employer's and the employee's perspective. The remainder of this chapter briefly examines each of these factors.

Employer Preferences

As Exhibit 12.6 indicates, a number of factors affect employer preference in determining desirable components of a benefit package.

Relationship to Total Compensation Costs

A good compensation manager considers employee benefit costs as part of a total package of compensation costs. Frequently employees think that just because an employee benefit is attractive, the company should provide it. A good compensation manager thinks somewhat differently: "Is there a better use for this money? Could we put the money into some other compensation component and achieve better results?" Benefit costs are only one part of a total compensation package. Decisions about outlays have to be considered from this perspective.

Costs Relative to Benefits

A major reason for the proliferating cost of benefit programs is the narrow focus of benefit administrators. Too frequently the costs/advantages of a particular benefit inclusion are viewed in isolation, without reference to total package costs or forecasts of rising costs in future years. To control spiraling benefit costs, administrators should adopt a broader, cost-centered approach. As a first step, this approach would require

EXHIBIT 12.6
Factors
Influencing
Choice of
Benefit
Package

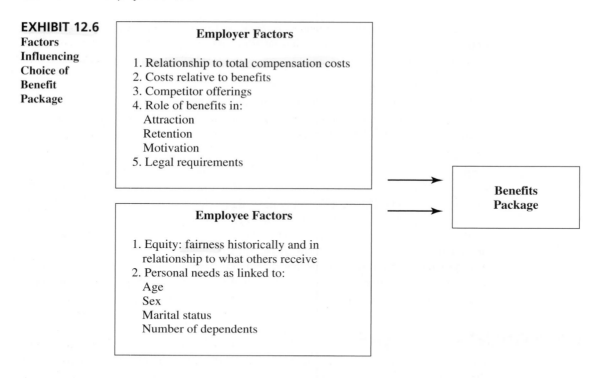

Employer Factors

1. Relationship to total compensation costs
2. Costs relative to benefits
3. Competitor offerings
4. Role of benefits in:
   Attraction
   Retention
   Motivation
5. Legal requirements

Employee Factors

1. Equity: fairness historically and in relationship to what others receive
2. Personal needs as linked to:
   Age
   Sex
   Marital status
   Number of dependents

Benefits Package

policy decisions on the level of benefit expenditures acceptable both in the short and the long runs. Historically, benefit managers negotiated or provided benefits on a package basis rather than a cost basis. The current cost of a benefit would be identified, and if the cost seemed reasonable, the benefit would be provided for or negotiated with employees. This failed to recognize that rising costs of this benefit were expected to be born by the employer. The classic example of this phenomenon is health care coverage. An employer considering a community-based medical plan like Blue Cross during the early 1960s no doubt agreed to pay all or most of the costs of one of the Blue Cross options. As costs of this plan skyrocketed between the 1960s and the 1990s, the employer was expected to continue coverage at the historical level. In effect, the employer became locked into a level of coverage rather than negotiating a level of cost. In subsequent years, then, the spiraling costs were essentially out of the control of the benefit manager.

A cost-centered approach would require that benefit administrators, in cooperation with insurance carriers and armed with published forecasts of anticipated costs for particular benefits, determine the cost commitments for the existing benefit package. Budget dollars not already earmarked may then be allocated to new benefits that best satisfy organizational goals. Factors affecting this decision include an evaluation of benefits offered by other firms and the competitiveness of the existing package. Also important is compliance with various legal requirements as they change over time (Chapter 13). Finally, the actual benefit of a new option must be explored in relation to employee preferences. The benefits that top the list of employee preferences should be evaluated in relation to current and future costs. Because future cost estimates may be difficult to project, it is imperative that benefit administrators reduce uncertainty.

If a benefit forecast suggests future cost containment may be difficult, the benefit should be offered to employees only on a cost-sharing basis. Management determines what percentage of cost it can afford to bear within budget projections, and the option is offered to employees on a cost-sharing basis, with projected increases in both employer and employee costs communicated openly. In the negotiation process, then, employees or union representatives can evaluate their preference for the option against the forecasted cost burden. In effect, this approach defines in advance the contribution an employer is willing to make. And it avoids the constraints of a defined-benefit strategy that burdens the employer with continued provision of that defined-benefit level despite rapidly spiraling costs.

Competitor Offerings

Benefits must be externally equitable, too. This begs the question, what is the absolute level of benefit payments relative to important product and labor market competitors? A policy decision must be made about the position (market lead, market lag, or competitive) the organization wants to maintain in its absolute level of benefits relative to the competition. One of the best strategies for determining external equity is to conduct a benefit survey. Alternatively, many consulting organizations, professional associations, and interest groups collect benefit data that can be purchased. Perhaps the most widely used of these surveys is the annual benefit survey conducted by the U.S. Chamber of Commerce.[37]

Role of Benefits in Attraction, Retention, and Motivation

Given the rapid growth in benefits and the staggering cost implications, it seems only logical that employers would expect to derive a fair return on this investment. In fact, there is at best only anecdotal evidence that employee benefits are cost-justified.[38] This evidence falls into three categories.[39] First, employee benefits are widely claimed to help in the retention of workers. Benefit schedules are specifically designed to favor longer-term employees. For example, retirement benefits increase with years of service, and most plans do not provide for full employee eligibility until a specified number of years of service have been reached. Equally, the amount of vacation time increases with years of service, and employees' savings plans, profit-sharing plans, and stock purchase plans frequently provide for increased participation or benefits as seniority increases. By tying these benefits to seniority, it is assumed that workers are more reluctant to change jobs.

There is also some research to support this common assumption that benefits increase retention. Two studies found that higher benefits reduced mobility.[40] More detailed follow-up studies, though, found that only two specific benefits curtailed employee turnover: pensions and medical coverage.[41] Virtually no other employee benefit had a significant impact on turnover.

We've been assuming here that turnover is bad and stability is good. In fact, there are times when turnover may be good—something we may not want to discourage. For example, at one time or another 3 Americans in 10 have stayed in a job they wanted to leave simply because they could not give up their health care coverage.[42] This "job lock" probably is not a desirable outcome for employers.

Employee benefits also might be valued if we could prove they increase employee satisfaction. Unfortunately, today only 32 percent of workers are satisfied with their benefits.[43] This is down from 83 percent in the early 1980s.[44] Why have satisfaction ratings fallen? One view holds that benefit satisfaction falls as cost-cutting companies attempt to reduce coverage and also shift more of the costs to employees.[45] A second view is more pessimistic, arguing that benefit plans fail to meet either employer or employee needs. In this view, simply pumping more money into benefits is inappropriate. Rather, employers must make fundamental changes in the way they approach the benefit planning process. Companies must realize that declining satisfaction with benefits is a result of long-term changes in the workforce. Ever-increasing numbers of women in the labor force, coupled with increasing numbers of dual-career families and higher educational attainments, suggest changing values of employees.[46] Changing values, in turn, necessitate a reevaluation of benefit packages.

Finally, employee benefits also are valued because they may have an impact on the bottom line. Although supporting evidence is slim, there are some glimmers of potential. For example, employee stock ownership plans used for pensions (Chapter 10), according to some reports, improve company productivity.[47] Presumably, owning stock motivates employees to be more productive. After all, part of the reward returns to them in the form of dividends and increased stock value. Similar productivity improvements are reported for employee assistance programs (e.g., alcohol and drug treatment programs for employees), with reports of up to 25 percent jumps in productivity after their implementation.[48] This finding suggests there may be some payoff to so-called work/life benefits, those that increase employee perceptions of a company's caring attitude. Things like day care, elder care, on-site fitness centers, and weight-loss programs foster a perception that the company cares about its employees. And in one well-constructed research study, this caring attitude led to greater worker involvement in suggesting ways to improve productivity and in helping others with their work.[49] Maybe benefits can pay off; we just need to document this better.

Legal Requirements

Employers obviously want a benefit package that complies with all aspects of the law. Exhibit 12.7 shows part of the increasingly complex web of legislation in the benefit area. Greater details on the three legally mandated benefits (workers' compensation, social security, and unemployment insurance) are provided in Chapter 13.

Absolute and Relative Compensation Costs

Any evaluation of employee benefits must be placed in the context of total compensation costs. Cost competitiveness means the total package must be competitive—not just

EXHIBIT 12.7   Impact of Legislation on Selected Benefits

Legislation	Impact on Employee Benefits
Fair Labor Standards Act 1938	Created time-and-a-half overtime pay. Benefits linked to pay (e.g., social security) increase correspondingly with those overtime hours.
Employee Retirement Income Security Act 1974	If an employer decides to provide a pension (it is not mandated), specific rules must be followed. Plan must vest (employee has right to both personal and company contributions into pension) after five years' employment. Pension Benefit Guaranty Corporation, as set up by this law, provides worker some financial coverage when a company and its pension plan go bankrupt.
Tax reforms—1982, 1986	Permit individual retirement accounts (IRAs) for eligible employees. Established 401(k) programs, a matched-contribution saving plan (employer matches part or all of employee contribution) that frequently serves as part of a retirement package.
Health Maintenance Act 1973	Required employers to offer alternative health coverage (e.g., **health maintenance organizations**) options to employees.
Discrimination legislation (Age Discrimination in Employment Act, Civil Rights Act, Pregnancy Disability Act, various state laws)	Benefits must be administered in a manner that does not discriminate against protected groups (on basis of race, color, religion, sex, national origin, age, pregnancy).
Consolidated Omnibus Budget Reconciliation Act (COBRA) 1984	Employees who resign or are laid off through no fault of their own are eligible to continue receiving health coverage under employer's plan at a cost borne by the employee.
Family Medical Leave Act (1993)	Mandates 12 weeks of leave for all workers at companies that employ 50 or more people.

specific segments. Consequently, decisions on whether to adopt certain options must be considered in light of the impact on total costs and in relationship to expenditures of competitors (as determined in benefit surveys such as the Chamber of Commerce survey mentioned earlier in this chapter).

Employee Preferences

Employee preferences for various benefit options are determined by individual needs. The benefits perceived to best satisfy individual needs are the most highly desired. In part, these needs arise out of feelings of perceived equity or inequity.

Equity

To illustrate the impact of equity, consider the example of government employees working in the same neighborhood as autoworkers. Imagine the dissatisfaction with government holidays that arises when government employees leave for work every morning, knowing that the autoworkers are home in bed for the whole week between Christmas and New Year's Day. The perceived unfairness of this difference need not be rational. But it is, nevertheless, a factor that must be considered in determining employee needs. Occasionally this comparison process leads to a "bandwagon" effect, in which new benefits offered by a competitor are adopted without careful consideration, simply because the employer wants to avoid hard feelings. This phenomenon is particularly apparent for employers with strong commitments to maintaining a totally or partially nonunion work force. Benefits obtained by a unionized competitor or a unionized segment of the firm's workforce are frequently passed along to nonunion employees. While the effectiveness of this strategy in thwarting unionization efforts has not been demonstrated, many nonunion firms would prefer to provide the benefit as a safety measure.

Personal Needs of Employees

One way to gauge employee preferences is to look at demographic differences. The demographic approach assumes that demographic groups (e.g., young versus old, married versus unmarried) can be identified for which benefit preferences are fairly consistent across members of the group. Furthermore, it assumes that meaningful differences exist between groups in terms of benefit preferences.

There is some evidence that these assumptions are only partially correct. In an extensive review of employee preference literature, Glueck traced patterns of group preferences for particular benefits.[50] As one might expect, older workers showed stronger preferences than younger workers for pension plans.[51] Also, families with dependents had stronger preferences for health/medical coverage than families with no dependents.[52] The big surprise in all these studies, though, is that many of the other demographic group breakdowns fail to result in differential benefit preferences. Traditionally, it has been assumed that benefit preferences ought to differ among males versus females, blue collar versus white collar, and married versus single. Few of these expectations have been born out by these studies. Rather, the studies have tended to be more valuable in showing preference trends that are characteristic of all employees. Among the benefits available, health/medical and stock plans are highly preferred benefits, while such options as early retirement, profit sharing, shorter hours, and counseling services rank among the least-preferred options. Beyond these conclusions, most preference studies have shown wide variation in individuals with respect to benefits desired.

The weakness of this demographic approach has led some organizations to undertake a second and more expensive empirical method of determining employee preference: surveying individuals about needs. One way of accomplishing this requires development of a questionnaire on which employees evaluate various benefits. For example, Exhibit 12.8 illustrates a questionnaire format.

A third empirical method of identifying individual employee preferences is commonly known as a **flexible benefit plan** (also called a **cafeteria-style plan** or a **supermarket plan**). As previously noted, employees are allotted a fixed amount of money and permitted to spend that amount in the purchase of benefit options. From a theoretical perspective, this approach to benefit packaging is ideal. Employees directly identify

EXHIBIT 12.8   Questionnaire Format for Benefit Surveys

Employee Benefit Questionnaire

1. In the space provided in front of the benefits listed below indicate how important each benefit is to you and your family. Indicate this by placing a "1" for the most important, and "2" for the next most important, etc. Therefore, if life insurance is the most important benefit to you and your family, place a "1" in front of it.

Importance		Improvement
_____	Dental insurance	_____
_____	Disability (pay while sick)	_____
_____	Educational assistance	_____
_____	Holidays	_____
_____	Life insurance	_____
_____	Medical insurance	_____
_____	Retirement annuity plan	_____
_____	Savings plan	_____
_____	Vacations	_____
_____	_____	_____
_____	_____	_____

Now, go back and in the space provided after each benefit, indicate the priority for improvement. For example, if the savings plan is the benefit you would most like to see improved, give it a "1," the next a priority "2," etc. Use the blank lines to add any benefits not listed.

2. Would you be willing to contribute a portion of your earnings for new or improved benefits beyond the level already provided by the Company?

   ❏ Yes   ❏ No

   If yes, please indicate below in which area(s):

   ❏ Dental insurance   ❏ Medical insurance

   ❏ Disability benefits   ❏ Retirement annuity plan

   ❏ Life insurance   ❏ Savings plan

the benefits of greatest value to them, and by constraining the dollars employees have to spend, benefit managers are able to control benefit costs. NCR has adopted a variant on flexible benefits that is part of its "customer-oriented" benefit push. Employees who wish can actually exchange some of their base salary for greater coverage on desired benefits, as illustrated in Exhibit 12.9.

ADMINISTERING THE BENEFIT PROGRAM

The job description for an employee benefit manager at Warner Brothers, shown in Exhibit 12.10, indicates that administrative time is spent on three functions requiring further discussion: (1) communicating about the benefits program, (2) claims processing, and (3) cost containment.[53]

EXHIBIT 12.9 Administering the Benefits Program

A. Costs. Please modify this "base" benefit package into another which you would most prefer, bearing in mind that selecting different levels will impact your cash pay (see box to right).

Base Benefit Package	$11,460
Chosen Benefit Package	$11,460
Change in cash pay	$0

ALTERNATIVE LEVELS

FEATURE					
Medical Plan	Opt Out −$4,800	Traditional-Basic Current A Base	**HMO** −$800	Traditional-Enhanced +$1,000	PPO +$1,300
Long-Term Disability Plan	Opt Out −$840	50% of Your Salary Current A Base	60% of Your Salary +$240	70% of Your Salary +$480	
Life Insurance	None A Base	1 Times Your Salary +$240	2 Times Your Salary Current +$480	3 Times Your Salary +$720	4 Times Your Salary +$960
401(k) Plan	None −$1,800	3% Match 5-Year Vesting +$1,200	6% Match 5-Year Vesting Current A Base	6% Match 1-Year Vesting $900	10% Match No Vesting $2,400
Paid Parental/ Family Leave	None Current −$180	3-Day Leave A Base	12-Week Leave 1/2 Salary +$540	12-Week Leave Full Salary +$1,800	

Source: Lynn Gaughan and Jorg Kasparek, "Employee a Customer" NCR Corp., and Jeff Hagens and Jeff Young, *Workspan*, September 2000, pp. 31–37.

EXHIBIT 12.10
Entertainment Inc. Seeks an Employee Benefits Manager for the Compensation and Benefits Department.

- General responsibility for health, welfare, and retirement questions from employees.
- Oversees Executive Health, Medical Reimbursement, and Flexible Spending Account Programs.
- Liaison for Appeals Committee and the Emergency Allocations Committee.
- Will assume leadership role in special projects such as intranet communications system.
- Charged with identification and maintenance of benefits' communications programs coming from a variety of different media (intranet, newsletter, computer-generated individual benefit accounts).
- Performs and completes benefit surveys as required.
- Evaluates performance of vendors and processes/facilitates employee complaints about delivery systems.
- Resolves benefits administration problems emanating from MIS, finance, accounting, and legal departments.
- Serves on committees to improve policies and processes in benefits strategy development and implementation.
- Assists in Development of Strategic Benefits Survey, including identification of sample groups.
- Provides input into design of benefits satisfaction survey and suggests format and conclusions for final report.
- Attends benefits conferences to network with other benefits professionals.
- Maintains working knowledge of new benefits studies, research, and practices.
- Leads committee to evaluate benefits costs and reduction strategies.
- Incorporates into benefits program relevant changes in state/federal law.

Employee Benefit Communication

Benefits communications revolves around four issues: What is communicated, to whom, how it's communicated, and how frequently. Much of the effort to achieve benefit goals today focuses on identifying methods (how) of communication. The most frequent method for communicating employee benefits today is probably still the employee benefit handbook.[54] A typical handbook contains a description of all benefits, including levels of coverage and eligibility requirements. To be most effective, the benefit manual should be accompanied by group meetings and videotapes.[55] While some organizations may supplement this initial benefit discussion with periodic refreshers (e.g., once per year), a more typical approach involves one-on-one discussions between the benefit administrator and an employee seeking information on a particular benefit. In recent years the dominance of the benefit handbook is being challenged by personalized benefit statements generated by computer software programs specially designed for that purpose. These tailor-made reports provide a breakdown of package components and list selected cost information about the options.

Despite these and other innovative plans to communicate employee benefit packages, failure to understand benefit components and their value is still one of the root causes of employee dissatisfaction with a benefit package.[56] One study of 500 employees in seven Canadian organizations found that perceived fairness of a plan was significantly higher

EXHIBIT 12.11   **Employees Happy With Their Benefits Versus Employees Happy With Communication About Their Benefits**

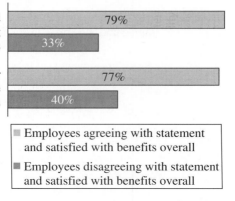

My organization does a good job communicating about benefits programs — 79% / 33%

I am satisfied with the customer service I receive when I have questions about my benefits — 77% / 40%

■ Employees agreeing with statement and satisfied with benefits overall
■ Employees disagreeing with statement and satisfied with benefits overall

*Multiple responses permitted

Source: "Rx for Rewards in the Downturn: Insights From Towers Perrin's Total Rewards Study," (New York: Towers Perrin, March 2009).

when there was extensive communications and employee participation in plan design.[57] We believe an effective communications package must have two elements. First, an organization must spell out its benefit objectives and it must ensure that any communications achieve these objectives. Exhibit 12.11 shows that employees who think company communications about benefits are effective are in turn more satisfied with those same benefits.

Second, an effective communications package should match the message with the appropriate medium. Technological advances have made tremendous improvements in employee benefit communication. In the last several years, a new medium has emerged for communicating benefits—the intranet. In today's corporations, benefit administrators are aiming to maintain communication with employees in a timely, consistent, and accurate manner, and many are selecting an intranet as their chosen avenue of communication.[58]

An intranet is an internal organizational online Web through which all forms of communication within the organization can be streamlined. Advantages of an intranet include employee access to benefit information 24 hours a day, 7 days a week without added cost; employee's ability to directly post changes to their accounts without completing lengthy paperwork; and an increased ease of updating information.[59]

Employers are increasingly posting their employee benefit handbook components on their intranets.[60] This change is beneficial to employers because of the decreased cost and increased ease of making revisions in the employee benefit handbook components. More than 100,000 employees at IBM get benefit communications and enrollment data through the intranet, at savings estimated as $1 million per year. Joining IBM in this intranet-based enrollment process are such organizations as Lucent and Continental Airlines. Experts say **"e-benefits"** are a huge trend waiting to reinvent human resource practices.[61]

Benefit administration over the Internet is also growing at a rapid pace. One report suggests that perhaps as many as 80 percent of the Fortune 1000 companies will utilize at least some form of Internet-based employee benefit application.[62] A wide range of applications will be offered, from online benefit information to annual benefit enrollment processing, personal data changes, 401(k) changes, and complete employee self-service.[63]

The Cedar Group estimates that the cost of a single hands-on HR-based benefits transaction is $35.65. The same transaction over the Internet or intranet is just $16.38.[64]

Another example of the recent advances in benefit communication is the streamlined call center operation that Kellogg Company launched in 1999 and that still operates today.[65] The call center decreased costs by as much as $105 million while improving service levels and maintaining close employee interaction. At a cost equal to approximately one-fifth of its paper-based predecessor, which required that specialists be located at every Kellogg's facility in the United States and Canada, the call center allows users to access benefit plan information, download and print documents, and retrieve basic information regarding Kellogg's benefit vendors. Annual cost savings of this system equal $500,000. Kellogg's anticipates that the future technological initiatives will include setting up kiosks, which will be Web-enabled personal computers that allow employees to access the information they presently access over the telephone and to contact specialists over the Internet in live chat rooms.

Claims Processing

As noted by one expert, **claims processing** arises when an employee asserts that a specific event (e.g., disability, hospitalization, unemployment) has occurred and demands that the employer fulfill a promise of payment.[66] As such, a claims processor must first determine whether the act has, in fact, occurred. If the answer is yes, the second step involves determining if the employee is eligible for the benefit. If payment is not denied at this stage, the claims processor calculates the payment level. It is particularly important at this stage to ensure coordination of benefits. If multiple insurance companies are liable for payment (e.g., working spouses covered by different insurers), a good claims processor can save from 10 to 15 percent of a claims cost by ensuring that the liability is jointly paid.[67]

Cost Containment

Increasingly, employers are auditing their benefit options for **cost containment** opportunities. The most prevalent practices include:

1. **Probationary periods**—excluding new employees from benefit coverage until some term of employment (e.g., 3 months) is completed.
2. **Benefit limitations**—it is not uncommon to limit disability income payments to some maximum percentage of income and to limit medical/dental coverage for specific procedures to a certain fixed amount.
3. **Copay**—requiring that employees pay a fixed or percentage amount for coverage.
4. **Administrative cost containment**—controlling costs through policies such as seeking competitive bids for program delivery.

So prevalent is the cost issue today that the terminology of cost containment is becoming a part of every employee's vocabulary. Exhibit 12.12 provides definitions of some common cost containment terms.

Probably the biggest cost-containment strategy in recent years is the movement to **outsourcing.** By hiring vendors to administer their benefits programs, many companies, such as GTE and Tenneco, claim greater centralization, consistency, and control of costs and benefits.[68] Other companies, like Digital Equipment Corporation, outsource so that they may focus on their core businesses, "leaving benefits to the benefits experts."[69]

EXHIBIT 12.12   Basic Primer of Cost Containment Terminology

Deductibles: An employee claim for insurance coverage is preceded by the requirement that the first $x be paid by the claimant.

Coinsurance: A proportion of insurance premiums are paid by the employee.

Benefit cutbacks: Corresponding to wage concessions, some employers are negotiating with employees to eliminate employer contributions or reduce them to selected options.

Defined contribution plans: Employers establish the limits of their responsibility for employee benefits in terms of a dollar contribution maximum.

Defined benefit plans: Employers establish the limits of their responsibility for employee benefits in terms of a specific benefit and the options included. As the cost of these options rises in future years, the employer is obligated to provide the benefit as negotiated, despite its increased cost.

Dual coverage: In families where both spouses work there is frequently coverage of specific claims from each employer's benefit package. Employers cut costs by specifying payment limitations under such conditions.

Benefit ceiling: Employers establish a maximum payout for specific claims (e.g., limiting liability for extended hospital stays to $150,000).

Your **Turn**   World Measurement

World Measurement is the global leader in product testing for safety. The recent problem with Chinese-made toy products (for example, Mattel recalled 19 million toys with evidence of lead paint) combined with the global recession has caused a 7 percent decline in sales and a 12 percent decline in net profits. The president of the company, Lewis Jacobs, is convinced that he must get concessions from the workers if World Measurement is to compete effectively with increasing foreign competition. In particular, Jacobs is displeased with the cost of employee benefits. He doesn't mind conceding a competitive wage increase (maximum 3 percent), but he wants the total compensation package to cost 3 percent less. The current costs are shown in Exhibit 1.

Your assistant has surveyed other companies that are obtaining concessions from employees. You also have data from a consulting firm that indicates employee preferences for different forms of benefits (Exhibit 2). Based on all this information, you have two possible concession packages that you can propose, labeled "Option 1" and "Option 2" (Exhibit 3).

1. Cost out these packages given the data in Exhibits 1 and the information obtained from various insurance carriers and other information sources (Exhibit 4).

2. Which package should you recommend to Jacobs? Why?

3. Which of the strategies do you think will require less input from employees in terms of their reactions?

EXHIBIT 1 Current Compensation Costs

Average yearly wage	$26,769
Average hourly wage	$13.12
Dollar value of yearly benefits, per employee	$8,923
Total compensation (wages plus benefits)	$35,692
Daily average number of hours paid	8.0

Benefits (by Category)	Dollar Cost/Employee/Year
1. Legally required payments (employer's share only)	$2,141.00
a. Old-age, survivors, disability, and health insurance (FICA) taxes	$1,509.00
b. Unemployment compensation	$ 292.00
c. Workers' compensation (including estimated cost of self-insured)	$ 311.00
d. Railroad retirement tax, railroad unemployment and cash sickness insurance, state sickness benefits insurance, etc.	$ 29.00
2. Pension, insurance, and other agreed-upon payments (employer's share only)	$3,124.00
a. Pension plan premiums and pension payments not covered by insurance-type plan (net)	$1,460.00
b. Life insurance premiums; death benefits; hospital, surgical, medical, and major medical insurance premiums; etc. (net)	$1,427.00
c. Short-term disability	$ 83.00
d. Salary continuation or long-term disability	$ 57.00
e. Dental insurance premiums	$ 51.00
f. Discounts on goods and services purchased from company by employees	$ 27.00
g. Employee meals furnished by company	$ 0
h. Miscellaneous payments (compensation payments in excess of legal requirements, separation or termination pay allowances, moving expenses, etc.)	$ 24.00
3. Paid rest periods, lunch periods, wash-up time, travel time, clothes-change time, get-ready time, etc. (60 minutes)	$ 727.00
4. Payments for time not worked	$2,769.00
a. Paid vacations and payments in lieu of vacation (16 days average)	$1,558.00
b. Payments for holidays not worked (9 days)	$ 973.00
c. Paid sick leave (10 days maximum)	$ 172.00
d. Payments for state or national guard duty; jury, witness, and voting pay allowances; payments for time lost due to death in family or other personal reasons, etc.	$ 66.00
5. Other items	$ 157.00
a. Profit-sharing payments	$ 0
b. Contributions to employee thrift plans	$ 71.00
c. Christmas or other special bonuses, service awards, suggestion awards, etc.	$ 0
d. Employee education expenditures (tuition refunds, etc.)	$ 40.00
e. Special wage payments ordered by courts, payments to union stewards, etc.	$ 46.00
Total	$8,923.00

EXHIBIT 2 Benefit Preferences

Benefit Type or Method of Administering	Importance to Workers	Benefit Type or Method of Administering	Importance to Workers
Pensions	87	Paid rest periods, lunch periods, etc.	55
Hospitalization	86	Dental insurance	51
Life insurance	79	Christmas bonus	31
Paid vacation	82	Profit sharing	21
Holidays	82	Education expenditures	15
Long-term disability	72	Contributions to thrift plans	15
Short-term disability	69	Discount on goods	5
Paid sick leave	70	Fair treatment in administration	100

Note: 0 = unimportant; 100 = extremely important.

EXHIBIT 3
Two Possible Packages for Cutting Benefit Costs

Option 1

Implement Copay for Benefit	Amount of Copay
Pension	$300.00
Hospital, surgical, medical, and major medical premiums	350.00
Dental insurance premiums	75.00

Reduction of Benefit

Eliminate 10-minute paid break (workers leave work 10 minutes earlier)
Eliminate one paid holiday per year
Coordination with **legally required benefit;** social security coordinated with Lightning Industries pension plan

Option 2

Improved claims processing:
  Unemployment compensation
  Workers' compensation
  Long-term disability
Require probationary period (one year) before eligible for:
  Discounts on goods
  Employee meal paid by company
  Contributions to employee thrift plans
Deductible ($100 per incident):
  Life insurance, death benefits, hospital, etc.
  Dental insurance

Copay	Amount of Copay
Hospital, surgical, medical and major medical premiums	$350.00

EXHIBIT 4
Analysis
of Cost
Implications
for Different
Cost-Cutting
Strategies:
Lightning
Industries

Cost-Saving Strategy	Savings as Percent of Benefit-Type Cost
Copay	Dollar-for-dollar savings equal to amount of copay
Deductible ($100 per incident):	
Life insurance premiums, death benefits, hospital, etc.	10%
Dental insurance	15
Require probationary period before eligible (one year):	
Discount on goods and services	10
Employee meals furnished by company	15
Contributions to employee thrift plans	10
Improved claims processing:	
Unemployment compensation	8
Workers' compensation	3
Long-term disability	1
Coordination with legally required benefits:	
Coordinate social security with Lightning pension plan	15

Summary

Given the rapid escalation in the cost of employee benefits over the past 15 years, organizations would do well to evaluate the effectiveness of their benefit adoption, retention, and termination procedures. Specifically, how do organizations go about selecting appropriate employee benefits? Are the decisions based on sound evaluation of employee preferences balanced against organizational goals of legal compliance and competitiveness? Do the benefits chosen serve to attract, retain, and/or motivate employees? Or are organizations paying billions of dollars of **indirect compensation** without any tangible benefit? This chapter has outlined a benefit determination process that identifies major issues in selecting and evaluating particular benefit choices. The next chapter catalogs the various benefits available and discusses some of the decisions confronting a benefit administrator.

Review Questions

1. Early in this chapter, we identified five reasons for the historical growth in the size of benefits packages. Which of these reasons still affect the growth of employee benefits today? Which actually might be current reasons for declines in the size of benefit packages?

2. Erinn Kelly, VP of Human Resources at Lawson Chemical, just purchased a local salary survey that has employee benefits data. She was shocked to see that Lawson has a larger benefits bill (38 percent of payroll) than the average in the community (31 percent). In a memo to you, she demands an explanation for why our package is significantly bigger. What sound reasons might save you from getting fired?

3. You are the benefits manager in a firm metaphorically described as part of the rust belt, in Syracuse, NY. The average age of your 600-person workforce is 43. Eighty-eight percent of your workforce is male, and there is hardly any turnover. Not much is happening on the job front. How do these facts influence your decisions about designing an employee benefit program?

4. As HR director at Crangle Fixtures, your bonus this year is based on your ability to cut employee benefit costs. Your boss has said that it's okay to shift some of the costs over to employees (right now they pay nothing for their benefits) but that he doesn't want you to overdo it. In other words, at least one-half of your suggestions should not hurt the employee's pocket book. What alternatives do you want to explore, and why?

5. Describe how a benefits program might increase worker attraction, retention, and motivation.

Endnotes

1. U.S. Department of Labor, Bureau of Labor Statistics, "Employee Benefits in the United States, March, 2009," *http://www.bls.gov/news.release/ebs2.nr0.htm,* June 22, 2009.

2. R. McCaffery, *Managing the Employee Benefits Program* (New York: American Management Association, 1972), pp. 1–2.

3. S. Bates, "Benefit Packages Nearing 40 Percent of Payroll," *HRMagazine,* March 2003, pp. 36–38.

4. NetApp, *www.NetApp.com,* June 22, 2009; *Fortune,* "100 Best Companies to Work For 2009," *http://money.cnn.com/magazines/fortune/bestcompanies/2009/snapshots/1.html,* June 22, 2009.

5. Stephen Miller, "Survey: Employees Undervalue Benefits," *HR Magazine* 52(8) (2008), p. 7.

6. Ibid.

7. S. Bates, "Benefit Packages Nearing 40 Percent of Payroll," *HRMagazine,* March 2003, pp. 17–22.

8. Rebecca Blumenstein, "Seeking a Cure: Auto Makers Attack High Health-Care Bills With a New Approach," *The Wall Street Journal,* December 9, 1996, p. A1.

9. John Hanna, "Can the Challenge of Escalating Benefits Costs Be Met?" *Personnel Administration* 27(9) (1977), pp. 50–57.

10. *U.S. Chamber of Commerce 2008 Employee Benefits Survey* (Washington, DC: US Chamber of Commerce, 2008).

11. National Coalition on Health Care, *www.nchc.org,* June 22, 2009.

12. J. Jargon, *Chicago Business,* March 2, 2006, *www.chicagobusiness.com,* June 26, 2006.

13. Gov Benefits.gov, *http://www.govbenefits.gov/govbenefits_en.portal?_nfpb=true&_pageLabel=gbcc_page_locate_state*

14. R. McCaffery, *Managing the Employee Benefits Program* (New York: American Management Association, 1983).

15. Exhibit 12.2 was compiled from five different sources. Some of the reward components rated in some of the studies were not traditional employee benefits and have been deleted from the rankings here. The five sources were: Employee Benefits Research Institute and Matthew Greenwald and Associates, "Worker Ranking of Employee Benefits," *www.ebri.org/pdf/publications/facts/fastfacts/fastfact062905.pdf,* June 26, 2006; "Employees Value Basic Benefits Most" (Aon survey), *Best's Review* 103(4) (2002), pp. 1527–1591; "The Future Look of Employee Benefits" (Hewitt Associates

survey), *The Wall Street Journal,* September 8, 1988, p. 23; Kermit Davis, William Giles, and Hubert Feild, *How Young Professionals Rank Employee Benefits: Two Studies* (Brookfield, WI: International Foundation of Employee Benefit Plans, 1988); Kenneth Shapiro and Jesse Sherman, "Employee Attitude Benefit Plan Designs," *Personnel Journal,* July 1987, pp. 49–58.

16. Mary Fruen and Henry DiPrete, *Health Care in the Future* (Boston: John Hancock, 1986); Conference Board, "Health Plan Increases" (HRM update), New York, May 1988; H. J. Kintner and E. B. Smith, "General Motors Provides Health Care Benefits to Millions," *American Demographics,* May 1987, pp. 44–45; Health Research Institute, *1985 Health Care Cost Containment Survey,* (Walnut Creek, CA: Health Research Institute, 1985); North West National Life Insurance Co., "Ten Ways to Cut Employee Benefit Costs," (Milwaukee, WI: North West National Life 1988).

17. "Benefits Marketplace 2009," *www.benefitsnews.com,* June 23, 2009.

18. M. L. Williams and E. Newman, "Employees' Definitions of and Knowledge of Employer-Provided Benefits, paper presented at Academy of Management meetings, Atlanta, GA, 1993; Richard Huseman, John Hatfield, and Richard Robinson, "The MBA and Fringe Benefits," *Personnel* Administration 23(7) (1978), pp. 57–60.

19. Ibid.

20. 2008 Job Satisfaction Survey, *www.shrm.org.*

21. Employee Benefit Research Institute, *America in Transition: Benefits for the Future* (Washington, DC: EBRI, 1987).

22. D. M. Cable and T. A. Judge, "Pay Preferences and Job Search Decisions: A Person-Organization Fit Perspective," *Personnel Psychology* 47 (1994), pp. 317–348.

23. Carol Danehower and John Lust, "How Aware Are Employees of Their Benefits?" *Benefits Quarterly* 12(4) (1996), pp. 57–61.

24. Burton Beam, Jr., and John J. McFadden, *Employee* Benefits (Chicago: Dearborn Financial, 1996).

25. Joseph J. Martocchio, *Employee Benefits: A Primer for Human Resource Professionals.* (New York: McGraw-Hill, 2006).

26. Ibid.

27. Mercer, "Health Benefit Cost Growth Predicted to Ease Slightly in 2009 as Employers Shift Cost," *http://www.mercer.com/summary.htm?idContent=1319885,* June 23, 2009.

28. Ibid.

29. E. Parmenter, "Employee Benefit Compliance Checklist," *Compensation and Benefits Review,* May/June 2002, pp. 29–39.

30. Ibid.

31. Karen Lee, "Full Plate: Employers Are Offering a Soup to Nuts Array of Non-Traditional Benefits to Increase Flexibility and Choice for Their Workers," *Employee Benefit News,* October 2000; Kenneth Shapiro, "Flexibility in Benefit Plans," *1983 Hay Compensation Conference Proceedings* (Philadelphia: Hay Management Consultants, 1983).

32. Melissa W. Barringer and George T. Milkovich, "A Theoretical Exploration of the Adoption and Design of Flexible Benefit Plans: A Case of Human Resource Innovation," *Academy of Management Review* 23 (1998), pp. 306–308; Commerce Clearing House, "Flexible Benefits" (Chicago: Commerce Clearing House, 1983); American Can Company, "Do It Your Way" (Greenwich, CT: American Can Co., 1978); L. M. Baytos, "The Employee Benefit Smorgasbord: Its Potential and Limitations," *Compensation Review,* First Quarter 1970, pp. 86–90; "Flexible Benefit Plans Become More Popular," *The Wall Street Journal,* December 16, 1986, p. 1; Richard Johnson, *Flexible Benefits: A How-to Guide* (Brookfield, WI: International Foundation of Employee Benefit Plans, 1986).

33. EBRI, *Employee Benefits Research Institute Databook on Employee Benefits* (Washington, DC: Employee Benefits Research Institute, 1995).

34. "Consumer-Driven Healthcare—The Wave of the Future, But Still in Its Infancy," *www. amacombooks.org/editorial/healthcare_brief.htm,* June 27, 2006.

35. F. Hansen, "The Cutting Edge of Benefit Cost Control," *Workforce,* March 2003, pp. 36–42.

36. E. Parmenter, "Employee Benefit Compliance Checklist," *Compensation and Benefits Review* 34(3) (2002), pp. 29–39.

37. U.S. Chamber of Commerce, *Employee Benefits Annual Surveys, www. chamberofcommerce.com,* July 8, 2009.

38. Kim Glinsky, "Go Green: Three R's of Conservation Apply to HR Benefits." *Employee Benefits News* 22(13), (2008), pp. 15–16.

39. Donald P. Crane, *The Management of Human Resources,* 2nd ed. (Belmont, CA: Wadsworth, 1979); J. Foegen, "Are Escalating Employee Benefits Self-Defeating?" *Pension World* 14(9) (September 1978), pp. 83–84, 86.

40. Olivia Mitchell, "Fringe Benefits and Labor Mobility," *Journal of Human Resources* 17(2) (1982), pp. 286–298; Bradley Schiller and Randal Weiss, "The Impact of Private Pensions on Firm Attachment," *Review of Economics and Statistics* 61(3) (1979), pp. 369–380.

41. W. Even and D. Macpherson, "Employer Size and Labor Turnover: The Role of Pensions," *Industrial and Labor Relations Review* 49(4) (1996), pp. 707–729; Olivia Mitchell, "Fringe Benefits and the Cost of Changing Jobs," *Industrial and Labor Relations Review* 37(1) (1983), pp. 70–78.

42. *New York Times* and CBS poll, as reported in *Human Resource Management News* (Chicago: Remy Publishing, 1991).

43. S. Bates, "Employees Not As Happy With Benefits As Employers Believe," *HRMagazine* 49(2) (February 2004), p. 12.

44. Christopher Conte, "Flexible Benefit Plans Grow More Popular as Companies Seek to Cut Costs," *The Wall Street Journal,* March 19, 1991, p. A1.

45. George Dreher, Ronald Ash, and Robert Bretz, "Benefit Coverage and Employee Cost: Critical Factors in Explaining Compensation Satisfaction," *Personnel Psychology* 41 (1988), pp. 237–254.

46. Ibid.

47. "Employee Stock Ownership Plans," in *Fundamentals of Employee Benefit Programs*, 2009, *www.EBRI.org.* pp. 93–100.

48. Lynn Densford, "Bringing Employees Back to Health," *Employee Benefit News* 2 (February 1988), p. 19.

49. S. Lambert, "Added Benefits: The Link between Work-Life Benefits and Organizational Citizenship Behavior," *Academy of Management Journal* 43(5) (2000), pp. 801–815.

50. William F. Glueck, *Personnel: A Diagnostic Approach* (Plano, TX: Business Publications, 1978).

51. Ludwig Wagner and Theodore Bakerman, "Wage Earners' Opinions of Insurance Fringe Benefits," *Journal of Insurance,* June 1960, pp. 17–28; Brad Chapman and Robert Otterman, "Employee Preference for Various Compensation and Benefits Options," *Personnel Administrator* 25 (November 1975), pp. 31–36.

52. Stanley Nealy, "Pay and Benefit Preferences," *Industrial Relations,* October 1963, pp. 17–28.

53. Robert M. McCaffery, *Managing the Employee Benefits Program,* rev. ed. (New York: American Management Association, 1983).

54. See "Towers Perrin Survey Finds Dramatic Increase in Companies Utilizing the Web for HR Transactions: Two- to Threefold Increase Compared to 1999 Survey," *www.towers.*

com/towers/news, October 20, 2000; Towers, Perrin, Forster, and Crosby, "Corporate Benefit Communication . . . Today and Tomorrow," (New York: Towers, Perrin, Forster, and Crosby, 1988).

55. Ibid.

56. "Yoder-Heneman Creativity Award Supplement," *Personnel Administration* 26(11) (1981), pp. 49–67.

57. N. Cole and D. Flint, "Opportunity Knocks: Perceptions of Fairness in Employee Benefits," *Compensation and Benefits Review* 37(2) (2004), pp. 55–62.

58. S. Smith, "New Trends in Health Care Cost Control," *Compensation and Benefits Review,* January/February 2002, pp. 38–44; B. Ambrose, "Leveraging Technology via Knowledge Portals," *Compensation and Benefits Review,* May/June 2001, pp. 43–46; Frank E. Kuzmits, "Communicating Benefits: A Double-Click Away," *Compensation and Benefits Review* 61 (September/October 1998).

59. Ibid.

60. Jonathan A. Segal, "Don't Let the Transmission of Bits of Data Bite You in Court," *HRMagazine* 45 (June 2000), pp. 1–10.

61. Stephanie Armour, "Workers Just Click to Enroll for Benefits," *USA Today,* November 8, 2000, p. B1.

62. Scott Carver, "Making Internet Benefits Enrollment Work for You," *Employee Benefits Journal* 24(4) (December 1999), pp. 40–42.

63. S. Simon and W. Mattle, "Rethinking Online Benefits," *Compensation and Benefits Review,* March/April 2002, pp. 80–84; "Towers Perrin Survey Finds Dramatic Increase in Companies Utilizing the Web for HR Transactions: Two- to Threefold Increase Compared to 1999 Survey," *www.towers.com/towers/news,* October 20, 2000.

64. T. Clifford, "Recognizing Maximum Return on Benefits Administration and Compensation Planning Technology Investments," *Employee Benefit Plan Review* 58(10) (2004), pp. 11–14.

65. Judith N. Mottl, "Cereal Killer," *Human Resources Executive,* May 2000, pp. 74–75.

66. Bennet Shaver, "The Claims Process," in H. Wayne Snider, ed., *Employee Benefit Management* (New York: Warren, Gorham and Lamont. 1997), pp. 141–152.

67. Thomas Fannin and Theresa Fannin, "Coordination of Benefits: Uncovering Buried Treasure," *Personnel Journal,* May 1983, pp. 386–391.

68. G. McWilliams, "ACS Finds Profits in Business Outsourcing," *The Wall Street Journal,* May 3, 2001, p. B5; E. Scott Peterson, "From Those Who've Been There . . . Outsourcing Leaders Talk About Their Experiences," *Benefits Quarterly* 6(1) (First Quarter 1997), pp. 6–13.

69. Ibid.

Benefit Options

Chapter Outline

Legally Required Benefits
Workers' Compensation
Social Security
Unemployment Insurance
Family and Medical Leave Act (FMLA)
Consolidated Omnibus Budget Reconciliation Act (COBRA)
Health Insurance Portability and Accountability Act (HIPAA)

Retirement and Savings Plan Payments
Defined Benefit Plans
Defined Contribution Plans
Individual Retirement Accounts (IRAs)
Employee Retirement Income Security Act (ERISA)
How Much Retirement Income to Provide?

Life Insurance

Medical and Medically Related Payments
General Health Care
Health Care: Cost Control Strategies
Short- and Long-Term Disability
Dental Insurance
Vision Care

Miscellaneous Benefits
Paid Time Off During Working Hours
Payment for Time Not Worked
Child Care
Elder Care
Domestic Partner Benefits
Legal Insurance

Benefits for Contingent Workers
Your Turn: Mr. Baldy Car Wash

An Historical Perspective

The idea of employee benefits in the United States dates back to colonial days. Plymouth Colony settlers established a retirement program in 1636 for the military. American Express began the first private pension plan in 1875. Montgomery Ward, a now defunct competitor of JC Penneys, started the first group health and life insurance programs in 1910. In 1915, employees in the iron and steel industry worked a standard 60 to 64 hours per week. By 1930 that schedule had been reduced to 54 hours. It was not until 1929 that the Blue Cross concept of prepaid medical costs was introduced. And prior to 1935 only one state (Wisconsin) had a program of unemployment compensation benefits for workers who lost their jobs through no fault of their own. Before World War II very few companies paid hourly employees for holidays. In most companies employees were told not to report for work on holidays and to enjoy the time off, but their paychecks were smaller the following week.[1]

The biggest early push for benefits, though, came from Uncle Sam. In 1935 the federal government mandated retirement income protection under Social Security. Coverage for the disabled and elderly followed in the 1950s and 60s.

Fast forward 50 years and companies are now reeling from the high cost of benefits, especially health-care costs. And some of the measures to cut these costs are attracting public attention. For example, companies like PepsiCo, General Mills, and Northwest Airlines charge $20–50 a month extra for smokers.[2] The argument runs, if you're going to continue habits that raise our health insurance costs, we're going to charge you. Going even one giant step further, Wal-Mart distributed an internal memo to the Board of Directors proposing that health-care costs could be cut dramatically by discouraging unhealthy people from applying.[3] Illegal, you cry in dismay? What if Wal-Mart, as suggested in the same internal memo, includes as a task in every job description that employees must take their turn at rounding up shopping carts in the parking lot.[4] If even a few unhealthy applicants are discouraged, Wal-Mart could save untold millions. After all, health-care provider WellPoint Inc says just 7 percent of its 29 million customers account for 63 percent of its medical costs. Add to these snippets of reality the explosion of ongoing research on the human genome, and we aren't very far away from a time when a company could test applicants for a disposition to contract fatal diseases—*years in the future!* Employers intent on reducing health-care costs need only refuse to hire these future insurance risks.

All of these scenarios make the study of employee benefits far more interesting. Desperate to even slow the ever-growing cost of employee health insurance and other benefits, companies are experimenting with different, and sometimes radical, methods to entice, bribe, and even threaten. At the very least, this makes the study of benefits more exciting. Happy reading!

For years we've asked our students and HR professionals to rate different kinds of rewards in terms of importance. Usually, at least in the past, employee benefits lagged behind such rewards as pay, advancement opportunity, job security and recognition. Recently, though, we've noticed a dramatic shift in this admittedly unscientific poll. As benefits costs, especially health care, have skyrocketed, so has their popularity. A recent survey listed the top five rewards contributing to employee satisfaction. In order, they are compensation, benefits, job security, work/life balance, and communication between employees and senior management.[5]

With this increased popularity comes a need for HR professionals to understand what benefits are important to employees. Just ask Rich Floersch, the Executive Vice President for Human Resources at McDonald's Corporation. As we noted in Chapter 12, about a year ago, McDonald's unveiled a new benefits program for crew members. When we asked Rich why McDonald's was modifying its health-care package as part of a total benefits upgrade, he cited the rising value of benefits to workers and the strategic importance of its 400,000 plus workers. Look at it from another perspective: The population (and your two favorite authors) are aging. This alone changes the pattern of preferences. We're not sure all companies are as attuned to changing preferences as McDonald's. For example, a McKinsey Survey reports 89% of CEOs think benefits are extremely or very important to attracting and retaining employees. However, less than one-half of these executives thought they understood what benefits employees wanted. Moreover, almost 60 percent of these executives admitted they never assessed whether benefits were helping the company achieve its strategic

EXHIBIT 13.1 Costs of Benefits for Government and Private Sectors

Benefit Type	Private Sector Average ($)	State and Local Government Average ($)
Paid Leave	1.81 (6.7%)	3.25 (8.2%)
Insurance (including health)	2.07 (7.7%)	3.55 (12.4%) to 4.89 (10.1%) range depending on occupation.
Retirement	.97 (3.6%)	3.09 (7.9%)
Social Security, Unemployment Insurance, and Workers Compensation	$2.26 (8.3%)	2.33 (5.9%)

Source: Bureau of Labor Statistics, "Employer Costs for Employee Compensation Summary" http://www.bls.gov/news.release/ecec.nr0.htm, February 4, 2009.

goals.[6] Is it any wonder that daily news reports bring new alarms about the rising cost of benefits?

Our goal in this chapter is to give you a clearer appreciation of employee benefits. Let's start by comparing wages to benefits. In 2008 private industry wages averaged $19.14 per hour (70.7 percent). Benefits averaged $7.93 (29.3 percent). Comparable figures for state and local government employees were $25.77 per hour wages (65.8 percent) and benefits costs of $13.41 (34.2 percent). Both wages and benefits are higher in the state and local government sector.[7] A breakdown of benefits in Exhibit 13.1 shows the relative costs.

A close look at Exhibit 13.1 shows one seemingly odd figure. Notice how the retirement benefit for the private sector is smaller than the other benefits listed, and smaller than the same retirement component in the state and local government figures. Why? Doesn't everyone get a retirement package? The answer is No! Many Americans work in jobs with no paid retirement. The same thing is true for health coverage. The insurance figures in this exhibit would be much higher if more organizations provided health-care insurance. The other thing to note: It pays to work in a government job. Both wages and benefits tend to be higher.

One way to get your attention is to show the dramatic increase in costs of benefits. Back about the time the first McDonalds opened (mid-1950s), benefits cost $18 billion. Today that figure is $4 trillion and change! If for no other reason than cost escalation, we need to understand the world of employee benefits. Let's begin by looking at a widely accepted categorization of employee benefits (Exhibit 13.2). The U.S. Chamber of Commerce issues an annual update of benefit expenditures.[8] This report identifies seven categories of benefits in a breakdown that is highly familiar to benefit plan administrators. These seven categories will be used to organize this chapter and illustrate important principles affecting strategic and administrative concerns for each benefit type.

Exhibit 13.3 shows employee participation in selected benefit programs. In virtually every category the percentages are higher in large- and medium-size companies.[9] Moral one of this story: If benefits are important to you, find a job in a larger company. Moral two of this story: If you're an entrepreneur starting your own company, remember in general your competitors aren't providing lavish benefits. If you want to be competitive, pay attention to this.

EXHIBIT 13.2   Categorization of Employee Benefits

Type of Benefit

1. Legally required payments (employers' share only)
   a. Old-age, survivors, disability, and health insurance (employer FICA taxes) and railroad retirement tax
   b. Unemployment compensation
   c. Workers' compensation (including estimated cost of self-insured)
   d. State sickness benefit insurance

2. Retirement and savings plan payments (employers' share only)
   a. Defined benefit pension plan contributions (401(k) type)
   b. Defined contribution plan payments
   c. Profit sharing
   d. Stock bonus and employee stock ownership plans (ESOPs)
   e. Pension plan premiums (net) under insurance and annuity contracts (insured and trusted)
   f. Administrative and other costs

3. Life insurance and death benefits (employers' share only)

4. Medical and medical-related benefit payments (employers' share only)
   a. Hospital, surgical, medical, and major medical insurance premiums (net)
   b. Retiree hospital, surgical, medical, and major medical insurance premiums (net)
   c. Short-term disability, sickness, or accident insurance (company plan or insured plan)
   d. Long-term disability or wage continuation (insured, self-administered, or trust)
   e. Dental insurance premiums
   f. Other (vision care, physical and mental fitness benefits for former employees)

5. Paid rest periods, coffee breaks, lunch periods, wash-up time, travel time, clothes-change time, get-ready time, etc.

6. Payments for time not worked
   a. Payments for or in lieu of vacations
   b. Payments for or in lieu of holidays
   c. **Sick leave pay**
   d. Parental leave (maternity and paternity leave payments)
   e. Other

7. Miscellaneous benefit payments
   a. Discounts on goods and services purchased from company by employees
   b. Employee meals furnished by company
   c. Employee education expenditures
   d. Child care
   e. Other

Source: U.S. Chamber of Commerce, "Employee Benefits Study," 2008, http://www.uschamber.com/research/benefits.htm.

LEGALLY REQUIRED BENEFITS

Virtually every employee benefit is somehow affected by statutory or common law (many of the limitations are imposed by tax laws). In this section the primary focus is on benefits that are required by statutory law: workers' compensation, Social Security, and unemployment compensation.

EXHIBIT 13.3
Participation in Selected Benefits, 2005

Source: 2005 National Compensation Survey, U.S. Department of Labor, Bureau of Labor Statistics.

Benefit	Small Firms	Medium and Large Firms
Paid holiday	68%	87%
Paid vacation	70	87
Paid sick leave	49	70
Long-term disability	17	43
Health insurance	61	96
Life insurance	34	67
Retirement	37	67
Defined benefit plan	9	36
Defined contribution plan	32	5

Workers' Compensation

What costs employers $55 billion a year and is a major cost of doing business? Answer: workers' compensation.[10] Of this total, $26.5 billion was for medical care and the remainder was paid as cash benefits.[11]

As a form of no-fault insurance (employees are eligible even if their actions caused the accident), workers' compensation covers injuries and diseases that arise out of, and while in the course of, employment. Benefits are given for:[12]

1. Medical care for work-related injuries, beginning right after the accident.
2. Temporary disability benefits after a 3–7 day waiting period.
3. Permanent partial and permanent total disability benefits for lasting consequences of disabilities on the job.
4. Survivor benefits.
5. Rehabilitation and training in most states, for those unable to return to their prior career.

Workers compensation costs vary over time. During the early years of this century, the costs rose. But as recently as 2005, the dollar costs began to decline. In 2006, worker's compensation cost $.99 for every $100 of wages. This is the lowest figure in the past 18 years. Experts believe part of this stabilization relates to employer safety programs, with far fewer fatal accidents occurring and somewhat higher incidents of minor, less costly accidents.

States vary in the size of the payout for claims. New York State, for example, has a payout formula for totally or partially disabled that is based on his/her average weekly wage for the previous year. The following formula is used to calculate benefits:

$$2/3 \times \text{average weekly wage} \times \% \text{ of disability} = \text{weekly benefit}$$

Therefore, a claimant who was earning $400 per week and is totally (100%) disabled would receive $266.67 per week. A partially disabled claimant (50%) would receive $133.34 per week.[13]

Some states provide "second-injury funds." These funds relieve an employer's liability when a pre-employment injury combines with a work-related injury to produce

EXHIBIT 13.4   Commonalities in State Workers' Compensation Laws

Issue	Most Common State Provision
Type of law	Compulsory (in 47 states)
	Elective (in 3 states)
Self-insurance coverage	Self-insurance permitted (in 48 states)
	All industrial employment
	Farm labor, domestic servants, and casual employees usually exempted
	Compulsory for all or most public sector employees (in 47 states)
Occupational diseases	Coverage for all diseases arising out of and in the course of employment
	No compensation for "ordinary diseases of life"

Source: *www.ncci.com*

a disability greater than that caused by the latter alone. For example, if a person with a known heart condition is hired and then breaks an arm in a fall triggered by a heart attack, medical treatments for the heart condition would not be paid from workers' compensation insurance; treatment for the broken arm would be compensated.

Workers' compensation is covered by state, not federal, laws. For details on each state's laws, go to the Cybercomp Web site below.

> **Cybercomp**
> Each state differs in its workers' compensation law. If you're a glutton for punishment, visit *www.comp.state.nc.us/ncic/pages/all50.htm* (visited February 6, 2009).

In the past decade, more than 30 states passed significant workers' compensation reforms, most of which target safety concerns.[14] As Exhibit 13.4 shows, in general the states have fairly similar coverage, with differences occurring primarily in benefit levels and costs.

> **Cybercomp**
> This Web site from the Department of Labor provides extensive information about legally required benefits and specific requirements for compliance: *www.dol.gov/dol/regs/main.htm*.

Social Security

When Social Security was introduced in 1937, only about 60 percent of all workers were eligible.[15] Today, nearly every American worker (96%) is covered.[16] Whether a worker retires, becomes disabled, or dies, Social Security benefits are paid to replace part of the lost family earnings. About 69 percent of benefits go to retirees and their dependents, 16 percent to disabled workers and their dependents, and 16 percent to survivors of deceased beneficiaries.[17] Indeed, ever since its passage, the Social Security Act has been designed and amended to provide a foundation of basic security for American workers and their families. Exhibit 13.5 outlines the initial provisions of the law and its subsequent broadening over the years.[18]

EXHIBIT 13.5   Changes in Social Security Over the Years

1939	Survivor's insurance was added to provide monthly life insurance payments to the widow and dependent children of deceased workers.
1950–1954	Old-age and survivor's insurance was broadened.
1956	Disability insurance benefits were provided to workers and dependents of such employees.
1965	Medical insurance protection was provided for the aged, and later (1973) for the disabled under age 65 (Medicare).
1972	Cost-of-living escalator was tied to the consumer price index—guaranteed higher future benefits for all beneficiaries.
1974	Existing state programs of financial assistance to the aged, blind, and disabled were replaced by SSI (supplemental security income) administered by the Social Security Administration.
1983	Effective 1984, all new civilian federal employees were covered. All federal employees covered for purpose of Medicare.
1985	Social Security Administration (SSA) became an independent agency administered by a commissioner and a bipartisan advisory board.
1994	Amendments were enacted imposing severe restrictions on benefits paid to drug abusers and alcoholics (together with treatment requirements and a 36-month cap on the payment of benefits).
1996	Contract with America Advancement Act of 1996 (CWAAA) was enacted, eliminating substance abuse as a disabling impairment. Substance abuse may no longer be the basis for a finding of disability.
2000	Depression-era limits on amount of money that workers age 65 to 69 may earn without having their Social Security benefits reduced were eliminated—retroactive to January 1, 2000. The rules governing individuals who take early retirement at age 62 and the status of workers age 70 and over were not changed by the new law.
2003	**The Medicare Prescription Drug, Improvement and Modernization Act of 2003** (P.L.108-173) archive. Seniors must choose from among a variety of plans written in bureaucratic hieroglyphics.

Source: http://www.ssa.gov/OP_Home/handbook/handbook.01/handbook-toc01.html, June 10, 2009.

The money to pay these benefits comes from the Social Security contributions made by employees, their employers, and self-employed people during working years. As contributions are paid in each year, they are immediately used to pay for the benefits to current beneficiaries. Herein lies a major problem with Social Security. While the number of retired workers continues to rise (because of earlier retirement and longer life spans), no corresponding increase in the number of contributors to Social Security has offset the costs. Combine the increase in beneficiaries with other cost stimulants (e.g., liberal cost-of-living adjustments) and the outcome is not surprising. To maintain solvency, there has been a dramatic increase in both the maximum earnings base and the rate at which that base is taxed. Exhibit 13.6 illustrates the trends in tax rate, maximum earnings base, and maximum tax for Social Security.

Several points immediately jump out from this exhibit. First, with the rapid rise in taxable earnings, you should get used to paying some amount of Social Security tax on every dollar you earn. This wasn't always true. Notice that in 1980 the maximum taxable earnings were $25,900. Every dollar earned over that amount was free of Social

EXHIBIT 13.6   Trends in Social Security Taxes 1980–2009

	OASI (All But Health)			Health Component		Total Contribution	
Year	Maximum Taxable Earnings	% OASI (Old Age Survivors)	% DI (Disability)	Maximum Taxable Earnings	% Health	%	$
1980	$25,900	4.52	0.56	$25,900	1.05	6.13	1,587.67
1990	51,300	5.6	0.6	51,300	1.45	7.65	3,924.45
1995	61,200	5.26	0.94	No max	1.45	7.65	No max because of uncapped health care
1997–1999	Increases with market wage movement	5.35	0.85	No max	1.45	7.65	No max, uncapped health
2000+	Increases with market wage movement— $90,000 in 2005 and $106,800 in 2009	5.3	0.9	No max	1.45	7.65	No max, uncapped health

Source: U.S. Social Security Administration Office of Retirement and Disability Policy, Program Highlight 2008–2009, *www.ssa.gov/policy/docs/quickfacts/ prog_highlights/index.html,* June 10, 2009.

Security tax. Now the maximum is over $106,000, and for one part of Social Security (Medicare) there is no earnings maximum.[19] If Tiger Woods makes $30 million this year, he will pay 7.65 percent social security tax on the first $106,800 and 1.45 percent (the health/Medicare portion) on all the rest of his income. For the super rich (even with royalties, textbook authors need not apply), this elimination of the cap is costly.

Second, remember that for every dollar deducted as an employees' share of social security, there is a matching amount paid by employers. For an employee with income in the $70,000 range, this means an employer contribution of just under $6,000. Because Social Security is retirement income to employees, employers should decrease private pension payouts by a corresponding amount.

Current funding levels produced a massive surplus throughout the 1990s. There is still, at least in accounting terms, a huge surplus (perhaps over two trillion dollars today. Unfortunately the suplus is something of a myth. The federal government doesn't put your contributions in a savings bank in anticipation of your retirement. Rather, they've continually used the fund to finance government spending. Baby boomers have reached their peak earnings potential, and their Social Security payments subsidize a much smaller generation born during the 1930s. There are now almost 3.5 workers paying into the system for each person collecting benefits. Within the next 40 years this ratio will drop to about 2 to 1.[20] Many experts believe this statistic foreshadows the collapse of Social Security as we know it.

Look at the following questions and answers from the Social Security Administration to see just how unclear your social security future is.

Q: I am retired and receiving a monthly check from Social Security. Are my monthly payments going to be cut?

A: No, there are no plans to cut benefits for current retirees. In fact, benefits will continue to be increased each year with inflation. Even without any changes, current benefits are expected to be fully payable on a timely basis until 2041.

Q: I'm 35 years old in 2007. If nothing is done to change Social Security, what can I expect to receive in retirement benefits from the program?

A: Unless changes are made, at age 69 in 2041 your scheduled benefits could be reduced by 22 percent and could continue to be reduced every year thereafter from presently scheduled levels.[21]

Now don't let your anxiety level get too high. The government won't let the Social Security safety net vanish. In the next few years we expect the uncertainty of funding to be resolved.

Benefits Under Social Security

The majority of benefits under Social Security fall into four categories: (1) old age or disability benefits, (2) benefits for dependents of retired or disabled workers, (3) benefits for surviving family members of a deceased worker, and (4) lump-sum death payments. To qualify for these benefits, a worker must work in covered employment and earn a specified amount of money (about $780 today) for each quarter-year of coverage. Forty quarters of coverage will insure any worker for life. The amount received under the four benefit categories noted above varies, but in general it is tied to the amount contributed during eligibility quarters. For example, a person who had maximum-taxable earnings in each year since age 22, and who retires at age 62 in 2009, would receive a reduced benefit (because of early retirement) of $2,346.30.[22]

Unemployment Insurance

The earliest union efforts to cushion the effects of unemployment for their members (c. 1830s) were part of benevolent programs of self-help. Working members made contributions to their unemployed brethren. With passage of the unemployment insurance law (as part of the Social Security Act of 1935), this floor of security for unemployed workers became less dependent upon the philanthropy of co-workers (129 million workers are covered today). Since unemployment insurance laws vary by state, this review will cover some of the major characteristics of different state programs.

Financing

In the majority of states, unemployment compensation paid out to eligible workers is financed exclusively by employers that pay federal and state unemployment insurance tax. The federal tax amounts to 6.2 percent of the first $7,000 earned by each worker.[23] In addition, states impose a tax above the $7,000 figure. The extra amount a company pays depends on its **experience rating**—lower percentages are charged to employers who have terminated fewer employees. The tax rate may fall to almost 0 percent in some states for employers that have had no recent experience (hence the term "experience rating") with downsizing and may rise to 10 percent for organizations with large numbers of layoffs.

Coverage

All workers except a few agricultural and domestic workers are currently covered by unemployment insurance (UI) laws. These covered workers (97 percent of the work-force), though, must still meet eligibility requirements to receive benefits:

1. You must meet the state requirements for wages earned or time worked during an established (one year) period of time referred to as a "base period." [In most states, this is usually the first four out of the last five completed calendar quarters prior to the time that your claim is filed.]

2. You must be determined to be unemployed through no fault of your own [determined under state law], and meet other eligibility requirements of state law.[24]

Duration

Until 1958, the maximum number of weeks any claimant could collect UI was 26 weeks. However, the 1958 and 1960–61 recessions yielded large numbers of claimants who exhausted their benefits, leading many states temporarily to revise upward the maximum benefit duration. During the recession of 2008–2010, the rise in unemployment was staggering. Several prominent employers announced huge layoffs: Caterpillar (20,000 layoffs), Alcoa (15,000), Boeing (10,000), Pfizer (8,300), and tens of thousands more. The number of jobs lost in the U.S. during the first year of the recession was nearly three million.[25] In 2002, a new add-on law was passed, the Job Creation and Worker Assistance Act of 2002, that gave individuals as much as 1.5 years of coverage, depending on the state in which they lived.[26]

Weekly Benefit Amount

In general, benefits are based on a percentage of an individual's earnings over a recent 52-week period—up to the state maximum amount.[27] For example, in many states, the compensation will be half your earnings, up to a maximum amount. New York State residents are eligible to collect up to a maximum of $405, which is half the state's average weekly wage. In contrast, in Arizona the highest benefit rate is $205.[28]

Controlling Unemployment Taxes

Every unemployed worker's **unemployment benefits** are "charged" against the firm or firms most recently employing that currently unemployed worker. The more money paid out on behalf of a firm, the higher is the unemployment insurance rate for that firm. Efforts to control these costs quite logically should begin with a well-designed **human resource planning system.** Realistic estimates of human resource needs will reduce the pattern of hasty hiring followed by morale-breaking terminations. Additionally, a benefit administrator should attempt to audit pre-layoff behavior (e.g., lateness, gross misconduct, absenteeism, illness, leaves of absence) and compliance with UI requirements after termination (e.g., job refusals can disqualify an unemployed worker). The government can also play an important part in reducing unemployment expenses by decreasing the number of weeks that people are unemployed. Recent research has shown that unemployment duration decreases by three weeks simply by stepping up enforcement of sanctions against fraudulent claims.[29]

Family and Medical Leave Act (FMLA)

The 1993 **Family and Medical Leave Act** applies to all employers having 50 or more employees and entitles all eligible employees to receive unpaid leave up to 12 weeks per year for specified family or medical reasons.[30] To be eligible, an employee must have worked at least 1,250 hours for the employer in the previous year. Common reasons for leave under FMLA include caring for an ill family member or adopting a child. More state legislatures are now moving toward some form of paid family and medical leave for workers. California has signed a bill enacting an employee-paid disability benefit that would provide six weeks of paid leave to care for a sick family member or a new baby.[31]

Consolidated Omnibus Budget Reconciliation Act (COBRA)

In 1985 Congress enacted this law to provide current and former employees and their spouses and dependents with a temporary extension of group health insurance when coverage is lost due to qualifying events (e.g., layoffs). All employers with 20 or more employees must comply with COBRA. An employer may charge individuals up to 102 percent of the premium for coverage (100 percent premium plus 2 percent administration fee), which can extend up to 36 months (standard 18 months), depending on the category of the qualifying event.[32] The rising costs of the health insurance premiums (12.7 percent in 2002) cause major financing problems for the unemployed, with only one in every four workers who get laid off being able to afford the continued health insurance through COBRA.

Health Insurance Portability and Accountability Act (HIPAA)

The 1996 HIPAA is designed to (1) lessen an employer's ability to deny coverage for a preexisting condition and (2) prohibit discrimination on the basis of health-related status.[33] Perhaps the most significant element of HIPAA began in 2002, when stringent new privacy provisions added considerable compliance problems for both the HR people charged with enforcement and the information technology people delegated the task of building secure health information systems.

RETIREMENT AND SAVINGS PLAN PAYMENTS

Pensions have been around for a long, long time. The first plan was established in 1759 to protect widows and children of Presbyterian ministers. After decades of steady growth in private pension plan coverage, today only 43 percent of workers are covered by their employer.[34]

Blame competitive pressures from globalization, the recession, and paltry growth in productivity, but the reality is that more than half of the population will depend on Social Security for retirement income. That represents a problem because employees tend to rank pensions as one of the more important benefits.[35] Let's face it, baby boomers are a huge part of the working population now. They look a few years ahead and dream of retirement. Pensions play a big role in this dream. The importance of employer-provided retirement plans is evidenced by a study showing that employees with employer-provided retirement plans are more likely to have sufficient savings for a comfortable retirement than those who do not have these plans.[36] Two generic types of pension plans are discussed below: **defined benefit plans** and **defined contribution plans.** As you read their descriptions, keep in mind that defined benefit plans may be a dying breed.[37] Prominent companies such as IBM, Verizon, and Sears have frozen their traditional defined benefit pension payouts. Workers still get their pensions, but there isn't any growth in the amount as a function of additional time on the job. Rather, many companies are shifting to 401(k) plans where the dollar contribution is known and controllable.[38] Today 48 percent of employers offer a defined contribution plan, compared to only 33 percent (some employers offer both during transition periods) for defined benefit plans.[39] To understand why this rapid change is occurring, we have to explain the cost saving distinctions between the two types of plans.

Defined Benefit Plans

In a defined benefit plan an employer agrees to provide a specific level of retirement pension, which is expressed as either a fixed dollar or a percentage-of-earnings amount that may vary (increase) with years of seniority in the company. The firm finances this obligation by following an actuarially determined benefit formula and making current payments that will yield the future pension benefit for a retiring employee.[40]

The majority of defined benefit plans calculate average earnings over the last 3 to 5 years of service for a prospective retiree and offer a pension that is about one-half this amount (varying from 30 to 80 percent) adjusted for years of seniority.

So what is it about defined benefit (DB) plans that make them prime targets for cost cutting? The major complaints by chief financial officers (CFOs) center on funding. If I've got to pay Jim $40,000 a year at retirement, I have to start investing now to have that cash available. How much should I invest though? Given how volatile the stock market is, it's hard to predict how much is needed. CFOs report this is a drag on corporate financial health and a distraction from running the core business. Other major reasons for the decline in DB plans include disproportionate cost increases and unfavorable accounting rules.[41]

Defined Contribution Plans

In a defined contribution (DC) plan the employer makes provisions for contributions to an account set up for each participating employee. Years later when employees retire, the pension is based on their contributions, employer contributions, and any gains (or should we say losses these days) in stock investments. There are three popular forms of defined contribution plans. A **401(k) plan,** so named for the section of the Internal Revenue Code describing the requirements, is a savings plan in which employees are allowed to defer pretax income. Employers typically match employee savings at a rate of 50 cents on the dollar.[42] Defined contribution plans are more popular than defined benefit plans in both small and large companies. Expect this disparity to only grow with time! The number of traditional plans is dropping about 1.5 percent a year.[43]

Interestingly, for younger employees this shift may be one of those rare win-win situations. Historically these plans are faster to vest (the companies matched share of the contribution permanently shifts over to employee ownership, and they are more portable—job hopping employees can take their pension accruals along to the next job). On the negative side, the recession of 2008–2010 destroyed many 401(k) portfolios. Poor investment decisions, either by employees or by a chosen financial advisor, reduced many retirement funds by half or more. Further, these plans have been plagued by low contribution rates. About 40 percent of all employees don't contribute enough to get the full employer match.[44]

The second type of plan is an **employee stock ownership plan (ESOP).** In a basic ESOP a company makes a tax-deductible contribution of stock shares or cash to a trust. The trust then allocates company stock (or stock bought with cash contributions) to participating employee accounts. The amount allocated is based on employee earnings. When an ESOP is used as a pension vehicle (as opposed to an incentive program), the employees receive cash at retirement based upon the stock value at that time. ESOPs have one major disadvantage, which limits their utility for pension accumulations. Many employees are reluctant to "bet" most of their future retirement income on just one investment source. If the company's stock takes a downturn, the result can be catastrophic for employees approaching retirement age. A classic example of this comes from Enron . . . yes, the same Enron linked to all the ethics problems. Under Enron's 401(k), employees could elect to defer a portion of their salaries. The employees were given 19 different investment choices, one of which was Enron common stock. Enron matched contributions, up to 6 percent of an employee's compensation. Enron's contributions were made in Enron stock and had to be held until the employee was at least age 50. This feature resulted in 60 percent of the total plan value being in Enron stock in 2001. Guess what? When Enron's shares went through the floor in 2001–2002, thousands of employees saw their retirement nest eggs destroyed. Recently 401(k) contributions have shifted away from company stock. The majority (53%) of companies allow less than 10 percent of assets in company stock.[45]

Finally, a *profit sharing* **plan** can be considered a defined contribution pension plan if the distribution of profits is delayed until retirement. Chapter 10 explains the basics of profit sharing.

Not surprisingly, both DB and DC compensation plans are subject to stringent tax laws. For **deferred compensation** to be exempt from current taxation, specific requirements must be met. To qualify, an employer cannot freely choose who will participate in the plan (hence it is labeled a **"qualified" deferred compensation plan**). This requirement eliminated the common practice of building tax-friendly, extravagant pension packages for executives and other highly compensated employees. The major advantage of a qualified plan is that the employer receives an income tax deduction for contributions made to the plan even though employees may not yet have received any benefits. The disadvantage arises in recruitment of high-talent executives. A plan will not qualify for tax exemptions if an employer pays high levels of deferred compensation to entice executives to the firm unless proportionate contributions also are made to lower-level employees.

A hybrid of defined benefit and defined contribution plans has emerged in recent years. **Cash balance plans** are defined benefit plans that look like a defined contribution plan. Employees have a hypothetical account (like a 401[k]) into which is deposited what is typically a percentage of annual compensation. The dollar amount grows both from contributions by the employer and from some predetermined interest rate (e.g., often set equal to the rate given on 30-year treasury certificates). Because the Internal Revenue Service isn't convinced conversions fairly impact older workers, many companies are reluctant to adopt this platform.[46]

In 2009, 401(k) contributions were suspended by many companies in the wake of the suffering U.S. economy. General Motors, FedEx, Sears Holdings, and Eastman Kodak are among companies who suspended contributions. Twelve percent of 245 large companies surveyed by Watson Wyatt Worldwide have cut 401(k) or 403(b) contribution plans while an additional 12% planned to do so by 2010.[47] About half of the companies with suspended plans expect to reinstate 401(k)s when the economy picks up, but under a reduced formula. Most plans now match 50 cents for every employee dollar up to 6 percent of payroll. The most common new formula will vary as a function of profits, creating greater flexibility in another economic downturn.[48]

Individual Retirement Accounts (IRAs)

An **individual retirement account (IRA)** is a tax-favored retirement savings plan that individuals can establish themselves. That's right, unlike the other pension options, IRAs don't require an employer to set them up. Even people not in the workforce can establish an IRA. Currently, IRAs are used mostly to store wealth accumulated in other retirement vehicles, rather than as a way to build new wealth.[49]

Employee Retirement Income Security Act (ERISA)

The early 1970s were a public relations and economic disaster for private pension plans. Many people who thought they were covered were the victims of complicated rules, insufficient funding, irresponsible financial management, and employer bankruptcies. Some pension funds, including both employer-managed and union-managed funds, were mismanaged; other pension plans required long vesting periods. The result was a pension system that left far too many lifelong workers poverty stricken. Enter the Employee Retirement Income Security Act in 1974 as a response to these problems.

ERISA does not require that employers offer a pension plan. But if a company decides to have one, it is rigidly controlled by ERISA provisions.[50] These provisions were designed to achieve two goals: (1) to protect the interest of approximately 100 million active participants,[51] and (2) to stimulate the growth of such plans. The actual success of ERISA in achieving these goals has been mixed at best. In the first two full years of operation (1975 and 1976) more than 13,000 pension plans were terminated. A major factor in these terminations, along with the recession, was ERISA. Employers complained about the excessive costs and paperwork of living under ERISA. Some disgruntled employers even claimed ERISA was an acronym for "Every Ridiculous Idea Since Adam." To examine the merits of these claims, let us take a closer look at the major requirements of ERISA.

General Requirements

ERISA requires that employees be eligible for pension plans beginning at age 21. Employers may require 12 months of service as a precondition for participation. The service requirement may be extended to three years if the pension plan offers full and immediate vesting.

Vesting and Portability

These two concepts are sometimes confused but have very different meanings in practice. **Vesting** refers to the length of time an employee must work for an employer before he or she is entitled to employer payments made into the pension plan. The vesting concept has two components. First, any contributions made by the employee to a pension fund are immediately and irrevocably vested. The vesting right becomes questionable only with respect to the employer's contributions. The Economic Growth and Tax Relief Reconciliation Act of 2001 states that the employer's contribution must vest at least as quickly as one of the following two formulas: (1) full vesting after three years (down from five years previously) or (2) 20 percent after two years (down from three years) and 20 percent each year thereafter, resulting in full vesting after six years (down from seven years).

The vesting schedule an employer uses is often a function of the demographic makeup of the workforce. An employer who experiences high turnover may wish to use the three-year service schedule. By so doing, any employee with less than three years' service at time of termination receives no vested benefits. Or the employer may use the second schedule in the hopes that earlier benefit accrual will reduce undesired turnover. The strategy adopted is, therefore, dependent on organizational goals and workforce characteristics.

Portability of pension benefits becomes an issue for employees moving to new organizations. Should pension assets accompany the transferring employee in some fashion?[52] ERISA does not require mandatory portability of private pensions. On a voluntary basis, though, the employer may agree to let an employee's pension benefits transfer to the new employer. For an employer to permit portability, of course, the pension rights must be vested.

Pension Benefit Guaranty Corporation

Despite the wealth of constraints imposed by ERISA, the potential still exists for an organization to go bankrupt or in some way fail to meet its vested pension obligations. We guarantee you, there are many General Motors employees who lose sleep over this issue! To protect individuals confronted by this problem, employers are required to pay insurance premiums to the **Pension Benefit Guaranty Corporation (PBGC)** established by ERISA. In turn, the PBGC guarantees payment of vested benefits to employees formerly covered by terminated pension plans. Over 40 million people depend on the PBGC to protect 1.5 trillion dollars in pension benefits. In 2008 the PBGC had deficits of 11.2 billion dollars.[53] The recent Bernard Madoff Ponzi scheme undoubtedly will result in many more bankruptcies and create further deficits.[54]

The Pension Protection Act of 2006 (PPA)

You remember Enron? Maybe you didn't know that many Enron employees lost more than their jobs. Many employees had pension funds allocated to Enron stock. When the stock went through the floor, so did many retirement dreams. The PPA was passed by Congress in the wake of Enron and WorldCom. Its purpose was to protect employees' retirement income as well as transfer some responsibility for retirement savings from the employer to the employee. A key provision of the law allows employees in publicly traded companies the freedom to sell off any employer stock purchased through deferrals or after-tax contributions. We expect this provision will motivate employees toward investing in defined contribution plans and reduce some of the burden on employers. The law also aims at employers who fail to set aside enough reserves to cover current and future pension obligations by defining plans less than 70% funded as 'at risk' plans.

How Much Retirement Income to Provide?

The level of pension a company chooses to offer depends on the answers to five questions. First, what level of retirement compensation would a company like to set as a target, expressed in relation to pre-retirement earnings? Second, should Social Security payments be factored in when considering the level of income an employee should have during retirement? One integration approach reduces normal benefits by a percentage (usually 50 percent) of Social Security benefits.[55] Another feature employs a more liberal benefit formula on earnings that exceed the maximum income taxed by Social Security. Regardless of the formula used, about one-half of U.S. companies do not employ the cost-cutting strategy. Once a company has targeted the level of income it wants to provide employees in retirement, it makes sense to design a system that integrates private pension and social security to achieve that goal. Any other strategy is not cost-effective.

Third, should other postretirement income sources (e.g., savings plans that are partially funded by employer contributions) be integrated with the pension payment? Fourth, a company must decide how to factor seniority into the payout formula. The larger the role played by seniority, the more important pensions will be in retaining employees. Most companies believe that the maximum pension payout for a particular level of earnings should be achieved only by employees who have spent an entire career with the company (e.g., 30 to 35 years). As Exhibit 13.7 vividly illustrates, job hoppers are hurt financially by this type of strategy. In our example—a very plausible scenario—job hopping cuts final pension amounts in half.

Finally, companies must decide what they can afford. In the past year the press has printed dozens of stories about companies having a hard time funding their pension plans. Because many of these plans are financed with company stock, and because stock prices have been weak through the beginning of this decade, companies are in trouble.

Similar problems are on the public sector horizon. Between 2000 and 2004 average state and local benefit amounts grew 37 percent to $19,875. States also are allowing their employees to retire younger, often as early as 55. Estimates suggest federal, state, and local governments have promised pension (and medical) benefits for retirees that, to be funded for the next 75 years, need an investment today of $5 trillion.[56] Don't count on your taxes being cut any time soon!

EXHIBIT 13.7 The High Cost of Job Hopping*

Career History	Years in Company	Percent of Salary for Pension		Salary at Company (Final)	Annual Pension
Sam					
Job 1	10	10%		$ 35,817	= $ 3,582
Job 2	10	10%	×	$ 64,143	= 6,414
Job 3	10	10%	×	$114,870	= 11,487
Job 4	10	10%	×	$205,714	= 20,571
Total pension					$42,054
Ann					
Job 1	40		×	$205,714	= $82,286
Total pension					$82,286

*Assumptions: (1) Starting Salary of $20,000 with 6 percent annual inflation rate. (2) Both employees receive annual increases equal to inflation rate. (3) Pensions based on 1 percentage point (of salary) for each year of service multiplied by final salary at time of exit from company.

Source: Federal Reserve Bank of Boston.

LIFE INSURANCE

Roughly three-fourths of all employees have access to paid life insurance, and this figure is about the same in both the private and public sectors.[57] Typical coverage would be a group term insurance policy with a face value of one to two times the employee's annual salary.[58] Most plan premiums are paid completely by the employer.[59] Slightly over 30 percent include retiree coverage. To discourage turnover, almost all companies make this benefit forfeitable at the time of departure from the company.

Life insurance is one of the benefits heavily affected by movement to a flexible benefit program. Flexibility is introduced by providing a core of basic life coverage (e.g., $25,000). The option then exists to choose greater coverage (usually in increments of $10,000 to $25,000) as part of the optional package.

MEDICAL AND MEDICALLY RELATED PAYMENTS

General Health Care

Health-care costs continue to increase. Exhibit 13.8 shows the dollar increase over time. More costly technology, the increased number of elderly people, and a system that does not encourage cost savings have all contributed to the rapidly rising costs of medical insurance. In the past 15 years, though, employers have battled these rises. Despite these efforts, companies like GM figure about $1,500 toward the price of every car they manufacture comes from health-care costs. Comparatively, steel in the same cars costs less! Is it any wonder that Delphi and other major manufacturers are taking the publicly painful step of cutting retiree health-care benefits?[60] About 15,000 Delphi

EXHIBIT 13.8
**Health Care
Costs per
Employee
2005–2008**

Source: U.S.
Department of Labor,
Bureau of Labor
Statistics, www.bls.gov.

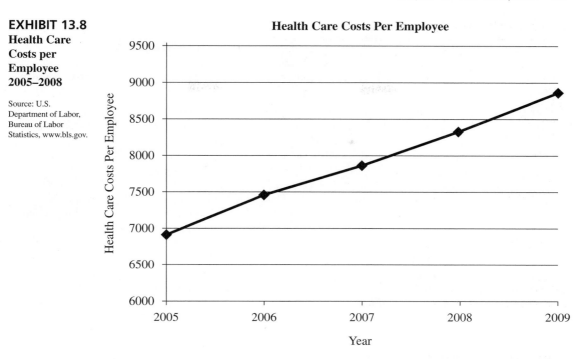

Health Care Costs Per Employee

salaried employees could lose their health-care benefits. After a discussion of the types of health-care systems, these cost-cutting strategies will be discussed. Exhibit 13.9 provides a brief overview of the four most common health-care options.

An employer's share of health-care costs is contributed into one of six health-care systems: (1) a community-based system, such as Blue Cross, (2) a commercial insurance plan, (3) self-insurance, (4) a health maintenance organization (HMO), (5) a preferred provider organization (PPO), or (6) a point-of-service plan (POS).

Of these six, plans 1 through 3 (labeled "Traditional Coverage" in Exhibit 13.9) operate in a similar fashion. Two major distinctions exist, however. The first distinction is in the manner payments are made. With Blue Cross, the employer-paid premiums guarantee employees a direct service, including room, board, and necessary health services covered by the plan. Coverage under a commercial insurance plan guarantees fixed payment to the insured for hospital service, and the insured in turn reimburses the hospital. A self-insurance plan implies that the employer provides coverage out of its own assets, assuming the risks itself within state legal guidelines. To protect against catastrophic loss, the most common strategy for self-insurers is to have stop-loss coverage, with an insurance policy covering costs in excess of some predetermined level (e.g., $50,000).

The second distinction is in the way costs of medical benefits are determined. Blue Cross uses the concept of **community rating.** In effect, insurance rates are based on the medical experience of the entire community. Higher use of medical facilities and

EXHIBIT 13.9 How Health Insurance Options Differ on Key Dimensions*

Issue	Traditional Coverage	Health Maintenance Organization (HMO)	Preferred Provider Organization (PPO)	Point-of-Service Plan (POS)
Who is eligible?	May live anywhere	May be required to live in HMO-designated service area	May live anywhere	May live anywhere
Who provides health care?	May use doctor and health-care facility of patient's choice	Must use doctors and facilities designated by HMO	May use doctors and facilities associated with PPO; if not, may pay additional copayment/ deductible	Must choose HMO or PPO doctor at time service is needed
How much coverage on routine, preventive level?	Does not cover regular checkups and other preventive services; diagnostic tests may be covered	Covers regular checkups, diagnostic tests, other preventive services with low or no fee per visit	Same as with HMO if doctor and facility are on approved list; copayments and deductibles are assessed at much higher rate for those not on list	Same as HMO/ PPO if network physicians used
Hospital care	Covers doctors and hospital bills	Covers doctors and hospital bills if HMO-approved hospital	Covers doctors and hospitals if PPO-approved	Same as HMO/ PPO if network physicians used; deductible otherwise

*Overview of the four most common health-care options.

services results in higher premiums. In contrast, insurance companies use a narrower, **experience rating** base, preferring to charge each employer separately according to its medical facility usage. Under a self-insurance program, the cost of medical coverage is directly related to usage level, with employer payments going directly to medical care providers rather than to secondary sources in the form of premiums.

As a fourth delivery system, **health maintenance organizations (HMO)** provide comprehensive benefits for a fixed fee. Health maintenance organizations offer routine medical services at a specific site. Employees make prepayments in exchange for guaranteed health-care services on demand. By law, employers of more than 25 employees are required to provide employees the option of joining a federally qualified HMO. If the employee opts for HMO coverage, the employer is required to pay the HMO premium or an amount equal to the premium for previous health coverage, whichever is less.

Preferred provider organizations (PPO) represent a variation on health-care delivery in which there is a direct contractual relationship between and among employers, health-care providers, and third-party payers.[61] An employer is able to select certain providers who agree to provide price discounts and submit to strict utilization controls (e.g., strict standards on number of diagnostic tests that can be ordered). In turn, the employer influences employees to use the preferred providers through financial incentives. Doctors benefit by increased patient flow. Employers benefit through increased cost savings. And employees benefit through a wider choice of doctors than might be available under an HMO.

Finally, a **point-of-service plan (POS)** is a hybrid plan combining HMO and PPO benefits. The POS plan permits an individual to choose which plan to seek treatment from at the time that services are needed. POS plans, therefore, provide the economic benefits of the HMO with the freedom of the PPO. The HMO component of the POS plan requires office visits to an assigned primary care physician, with the alternative of receiving treatment through the PPO component. The PPO component does not require the individual to first contact the primary care physician but does require that in-network physicians be used. When POS plan participants receive all of their care from physicians in the network, they are fully covered, as they would be under a traditional HMO. Point-of service plans also allow individuals to see a doctor outside the network, for which payment of an annual deductible ranging between $100 and $5,000 is required.[62] Costs of the different types of plans can be seen in Exhibit 13.10.

Consumer Directed Health Care Gains Ground!

A recent development in controlling health-care costs links consumer choice of more or less expensive options to higher or lower individual costs. Opt for the best plan, you pay more. Opt for less, pay less. (This choice is the reason the name is "consumer directed.") Three variants on these **consumer directed health-care plans** exist:

Health reimbursement arrangements (HRAs)—the employer sets up an account for a specified amount. When an employee has qualified medical costs, they're submitted for reimbursement until the account is depleted. Anything left over at the end of the year rolls over to the next year. These HRAs usually are coupled with a high-deductible (for example, $2,000 annually) insurance product.

Customized plans—the employee chooses among a menu of health-care products each with different prices (broader networks, better coverage . . . higher cost). The employer subsidizes part of the premium for the choice made by the employee.

"Design your own" products—employees select their own providers and benefit features and the employer subsidizes up to a set level.

Health savings accounts (HSAs) represent a second direction taken by Consumer Directed Health Plans (CDHP). An HSA is a tax-exempt account built up through contributions of the employee, employer, or both that can be used to pay for health care

EXHIBIT 13.10 Cost of Different Health Care Options

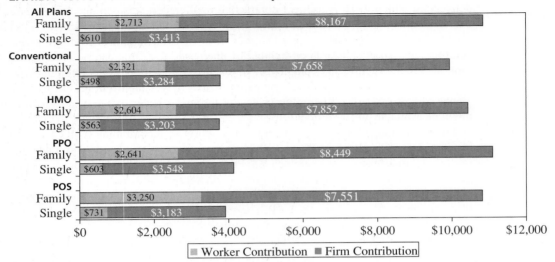

Source: "Employer Health Benefits 2005 Annual Survey—Full Report" (#7315). The Henry J. Kaiser Family Foundation and HRET, September 2005.

expenses.[63] Keep in mind, CDHPs are getting considerable coverage in the press, but more traditional plans like POS (58 percent of covered workers), HMO (20 percent), and POS (12 percent) considerably outnumbered CDHPs (5 percent) in 2008.[64]

Health Care: Cost Control Strategies

There are three general strategies available to benefit managers for controlling the rapidly escalating costs of health care.[65] First, organizations can motivate employees to change their demand for health care, through changes in either the design or the administration of health insurance policies. Included in this category of control strategies are (1) deductibles, or the first x dollars of health-care cost are paid by the employee (at the extreme the state of Georgia recently told employees that certain name brand drugs will require a $100 copay, clearly signaling that enough is enough[66]); (2) coinsurance rates (premium payments are shared by the company and employee); (3) maximum benefits (defining a maximum payout schedule for specific health problems); (4) coordination of benefits (ensure no double payment when coverage exists under the employee's plan and a spouse's plan); (5) auditing of hospital charges for accuracy; (6) requiring preauthorization for selected visits to health-care facilities; (7) mandatory second opinion whenever surgery is recommended; (8) using intranet technology to allow employees access to online benefit information, saving some of the cost of benefit specialists.[67] The more questions answered online, the fewer specialists needed. A final example in this category is the formation **of personal care accounts (PCA).** This is a tool used by employers to salvage some control over health-care costs while still providing health security to workers. Under a PCA an employer establishes a high deductible, say $2,000. Normally it would be a great hardship if the first $2,000 of an illness had to be borne by the employee. To lessen this impact, the employer sets up

EXHIBIT 13.11 **Why Companies Don't Provide Health Coverage**

Reasons for Not Offering	Very Important	Somewhat Important	Not Too Important	Not At All Important	Don't Know
High premiums	73%	13%	5%	9%	<1%
Employees covered elsewhere	33	26	13	25	3
High turnover	16	13	23	49	0
Obtain good employees without offering a health plan	22	32	18	27	2
Administrative hassle	14	29	25	28	3
Firm too newly established	2	9	9	80	0
Firm is too small	52	21	9	19	0
Firm has seriously ill employee	4	6	5	82	3

Source: "Employer Health Benefits 2005 Annual Survey—Summary of Findings" (#7316). The Henry J. Kaiser Family Foundation and HRET, September 2005.

a PCA with $1,000 in it. Now the liability for the employee is only $1,000. Any money not used by the employee in a year can be rolled over to the next year, lessening further the size of the deductible coming out of the employee's pocket. Clearly this type of account creates an incentive to build a PCA "nest egg," benefiting both the company (lower health costs) and the employee.[68]

The second general cost control strategy involves changing the structure of health-care delivery systems and participating in business coalitions (for data collection and dissemination). At the extreme are companies that simply decline to provide any health-care coverage whatsoever. Exhibit 13.11 shows the reasons companies opt for this extreme choice.

Less extreme are choices like HMOs, PPOs, POSs, and consumer-directed health-care plans. Even under more traditional delivery systems, there is more negotiation of rates with hospitals and other health-care providers. Indeed, one trend involves direct contracting, which allows self-insured companies or employer associations to buy health-care services directly from physicians or provider-sponsored networks. Some experts contend that direct contracting can save 30 to 60 percent over fee-for-service systems.[69]

A final category of cost control strategies links incentives to healthy behaviors. We know that preventable illnesses account for 70 percent of all health-care costs.[70] Obesity, for example, is preventable. Dieting, however, is not a favorite pastime. How, then, do we get people to lose weight? The answer may be health incentives. Positive incentives include things like discounts on gym memberships as noted in Exhibit 13.12.

EXHIBIT 13.12
Types of Incentive Rewards Offered

Source: "WORKING WELL: A Global Survey of Health Promotion and Workplace Wellness Strategies," October 2008, Buck Consultants, LLC.

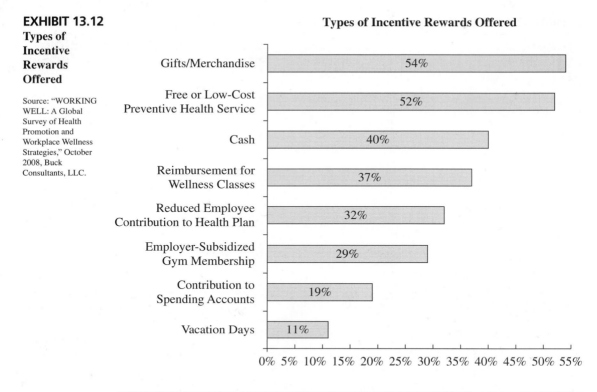

Types of Incentive Rewards Offered

Gifts/Merchandise	54%
Free or Low-Cost Preventive Health Service	52%
Cash	40%
Reimbursement for Wellness Classes	37%
Reduced Employee Contribution to Health Plan	32%
Employer-Subsidized Gym Membership	29%
Contribution to Spending Accounts	19%
Vacation Days	11%

0% 5% 10% 15% 20% 25% 30% 35% 40% 45% 50% 55%

Cybercomp
The Health Insurance Association of America provides research about a wide variety of specific health-related issues at its Web site, www.hiaa.org/pubs/.

Short- and Long-Term Disability

A number of benefit options provide some form of protection for disability. For example, workers' compensation covers disabilities that are work-related. Even Social Security has provisions for disability income to those who qualify. Beyond these two legally required sources, there are two private sources of disability income: employee **salary continuation plans** and **long-term disability plans**.[71]

Many companies have some form of salary continuation plan that pays out varying levels of income depending on duration of illness (see Exhibit 13.13).

At one extreme is short-term illness covered by sick leave policy and typically reimbursed at a level equal to 100 percent of salary.[72] The most prevalent practice these days is to give paid time off (PTO) rather than sick days. This reduces the need for companies to "police" whether employees are indeed sick, and allows employees more flexibility in life planning. After such benefits run out, disability benefits become operative. **Short-term disability (STD)** pays a percentage of your salary (about 60 percent on average) for temporary disability because of sickness or injury (on-the-job injuries

EXHIBIT 13.13   Access to Leave Programs

Characteristic	2000	2005	2008
Percent of all workers with access to paid holidays	77	77	76
Percent of all workers participating in short-term disability benefits	34	39	41
Percent of all workers with access to paid sick leave	N/A	58	N/A
Percent of all workers with access to paid vacation	80	77	75

Source: U.S. Department of Labor, Bureau of Labor Statistics, *http://www.bls.gov.*

are covered by workers' compensation). Only about 30 percent of all employers provide this insurance after sick leave.[73] **Long-term disability plans (LTD),** if available, typically kick in after the short-term plan expires. Long-term disability is usually underwritten by insurance firms and provides 60 to 70 percent of pre-disability pay for a period varying between two years and life.[74] Estimates indicate that only about 30 percent of all U.S. businesses provide long-term disability insurance.[75]

Dental Insurance

A rarity 30 years ago, dental insurance is now much more prevalent, with about 90 percent of all employers with more than 500 employees providing some level of coverage.[76] In many respects dental care coverage follows the model originated in health-care plans. The dental equivalent of HMOs and PPOs is the standard delivery system. For example, a dental HMO enlists a group of dentists who agree to treat company employees in return for a fixed monthly fee per employee.

At the start of the century, the typical cost for employee dental coverage was $219.[77] Annual cost increases now, though, are beginning to heat up. Employers battle these increases by requiring employee contributions—94 percent of employers require cost sharing now.[78] The relatively modest increase in dental care costs can be traced to stringent cost control strategies (e.g., plan maximum payouts are typically $1,000 or less per year) and an excess supply of dentists. As the excess turns into a predicted shortage in the coming years, we may expect dental benefit costs to grow at a faster rate.[79]

Vision Care

Vision care dates back only to the 1976 contract between the United States Auto Workers and the Big Three automakers. Since then, this benefit has spread to other auto-related industries and parts of the public sector. Seventy-eight percent of large employers offer a vision plan.[80] Most plans are noncontributory and usually cover partial costs of eye examination, lenses, and frames. Sixty-five thousand GM auto workers are likely to lose both vision and dental care as part of the bankruptcy plan currently being negotiated. This may signal a growing reluctance across industries to provide these two forms of health care.[81]

MISCELLANEOUS BENEFITS

Paid Time Off During Working Hours

Paid rest periods, lunch periods, wash-up time, travel time, clothes-change time, and get-ready time benefits are self-explanatory.

Payment for Time Not Worked

Included within this category are several self-explanatory benefits:

1. Paid vacations and payments in lieu of vacation
2. Payments for holidays not worked
3. Paid sick leave
4. Other (payments for National Guard, Army, or other reserve duty; jury duty and voting pay allowances; payments for time lost due to death in the family or other personal reasons).

Exhibit 13.14 shows what you can look forward to for vacations after you graduate. Stay in school!

Twenty years ago it was relatively rare to grant time off for anything but vacations, holidays, and sick leave. Now many organizations have a policy of ensuring payments for civic responsibilities and other obligations. Any outside pay for such civic duties (e.g., jury duty) is usually nominal, so companies often supplement this pay, frequently to the level of 100 percent of wages lost. There is also increasing coverage for parental leaves. Maternity and, to a lesser extent, paternity leaves are much more common than they were 25 years ago. Indeed, passage of the Family and Medical Leave Act in 1993 provides up to 12 weeks of unpaid leave (with guaranteed job protection) for the birth or adoption of a child or for the care of a family member with a serious illness. The following sick policy, taken from Motley Fool's employee manual, shows just how far such policies have come:

> Unlike other companies, The Motley Fool doesn't make you wait for six months before accruing vacation or sick time. Heck, if you're infected with some disgusting virus—stay home! We like you, but don't really want to share in your personal anguish. In other words, if you're bleeding out your eyes and coughing up a lung—don't be a hero! Stay home. Out of simple Foolish courtesy, we expect you to call your supervisor and let him or her know you won't be in. And yes, you will get paid. So, pop quiz: You're feeling like you're going to snap any moment if you don't take some personal time off, you've made a small deposit on an M-16 rifle and are scoping out local clock towers, BUT you've only been a paid Fool for a short time . . . what do you do, what do you do?[82]

Interestingly, paid time off is one area where firms are trying to cut employee benefits. In 1980, every medium- and large-sized private employer offered at least one paid holiday per year. In 2008, however, the number of companies offering paid holidays was down 10 percent.

EXHIBIT 13.14 **Employees Receiving Leave Time Benefits**

Employee Benefit—Paid Time Off	All Full-Time Employees	Professional, Technical, and Related Employees	Office and Administrative Employees	Blue-Collar and Service Employees
Holidays	76%	80%	88%	71%
Vacations	75	74	86	79
Personal leave	41	58	44	8
Funeral leave	71	86	79	42

Source: Bureau of Labor Statistics, *www.bls.gov*, visited February 6, 2009.

Many companies are switching from **traditional time-off plans (TTO),** as described above, to **paid-time-off (PTO) plans.** These lump all time off together into one total allotment and deduct any day missed from this bank. Not only is this administratively easier for companies to track, but it also eliminates the need for employees to lie and say they're sick when the reality is, for example, a scheduled dentist appointment.[83]

Child Care

Relatively few companies directly provide child care. However, it's becoming quite common for employers (96 percent) to offer flexible spending accounts with child care expenditures as a legitimate expense.[84] The employee, employer, or both pay into an account with pre-tax monies, and individuals can then use these funds to pay local child care providers.

Elder Care

With longer life expectancy than ever before and the aging of the baby-boom generation, one benefit that will become increasingly important is elder care assistance. Almost one-half of the companies offering child care assistance to employees also offer elder care assistance.[85]

Domestic Partner Benefits

Domestic partner benefits are benefits that are voluntarily offered by employers to an employee's unmarried partner, whether of the same or opposite sex. The major reasons motivating U.S. corporations to provide domestic partner benefits include fairness to all employees regardless of their sexual orientation or marital status and the market competition and diversity that are evident in today's tight labor market. One study found that 18 percent of U.S. employees were employed by corporations that offered health benefits for domestic partners; 11 percent, by corporations that offered these benefits to same-sex couples; and 12 percent, by corporations that offered these benefits to unmarried partners of the opposite sex.[86] In designing these offerings, an employer must first identify what constitutes a domestic partner and whether the plan will be available to same-sex partners, opposite-sex partners, or both.[87]

Legal Insurance

Prior to the 1970s, prepaid legal insurance was practically nonexistent. Even though such coverage was offered only by approximately 7 percent of all employers in 1997, that percentage has more than tripled in the past decade (24 percent).[88] A majority of plans provide routine legal services (e.g., divorce, real estate matters, wills, traffic violations) but exclude provisions covering felony crimes, largely because of the expense and potential for bad publicity. Keep in mind, though, that most legal insurance premiums are paid by the employee, not the employer. Technically, then, this doesn't qualify as a traditional employee benefit.

BENEFITS FOR CONTINGENT WORKERS

Depending on what definition we use, **contingent workers** represent between 5 and 35 percent of the workforce. Ninety percent of all employers use some contingent workers.[89] Contingent work relationships include working through a temporary help agency, working

EXHIBIT 13.15 Benefits Received: Full-Time Versus Contingent Employees

Benefit	Small Companies		Medium Companies		Large Companies	
	Full-Time	Contingent	Full-Time	Contingent	Full-Time	Contingent
Vacation	98%	40%	100%	79%	100%	80%
Health insurance	96	21	100	56	100	67
Holidays	97	48	100	77	100	67
Life insurance	85	21	100	47	100	58
Pension	89	43	98	91	100	71
Sick leave	70	26	83	53	96	58

Source: U.S. Bureau of Labor Statistics, 2006, http://www.bls.gov/news.release/empsit.t06.htm.

for a contract company, working on call, and working as an independent contractor. Both to reduce costs and to permit easier expansion and contraction of production/services, contracting offers a viable way to meet rapidly changing environmental conditions.

Contingent workers cost less primarily because the benefits offered are lower than those for regular employees. As Exhibit 13.15 shows, contingent workers regularly receive fewer benefits. This "benefit penalty" is less prominent in larger organizations.[90]

Your **Turn**
Mr. Baldy Car Wash

Mr. Baldy Car Wash has seven locations in the greater Buffalo, New York, area. Demand for car washes is highly dependent on the weather. During the winter months (November–March), the number of washes per day is roughly four times greater than during the summer months. Also during the winter months, the variability is almost exclusively a function of the pavement. Dry pavement means increased demand. Wet pavement means almost zero demand. On a busy day, Mr. Baldy can process 180 cars per hour, about 10 percent higher than industry standards. To wash 180 cars per hour requires a workforce of 20 to 22 employees at each site. On a wet day, 8 employees can cover the total operation, and on an average day, 15 employees are needed. This variability is the source of many problems for site supervisors. Just listen to Jim Jenkins, site supervisor at the Niagara Falls Boulevard wash:

Every winter day I have to listen to weather reports. If the prediction is for a dry and sunny day, I've got to call up 22 employees. When I wake up in the morning, I check the streets. If it snowed, I've got to call more than half of those employees and tell them not to come in. If this happens for several days, I start to hear grumbling. Too many non-wash days and my turnover starts to rise. How can I keep my employees happy, even when they might not have work for several days?

Two of the more vocal site supervisors have approached George Newman, HR Director for Mr. Baldy, and asked him to review the compensation package and hiring arrangements. The company-wide numbers presented in Exhibit 1 focus exclusively on operational employees (car wash people and their supervisors) and leave out staff and executives. Every wash employee gets the same wages because Mr. Baldy feels they're all doing the same job. The only difference is between full- and part-timers.

EXHIBIT 1   Wages and Benefits at Mr. Baldy Car Wash

	Supervisors	Assistant Supervisors	Associates: Full-time	Associates: Part-time
Hourly wages	$18.50	$14.00	$9.00	$7.35
Tips per hour (average)			3.00	6.00
Benefits cost per hour (total)	6.22	4.30	2.50	1.60
Legally required benefits*	2.88	2.08	1.33	1.33
401K (employer portion)	.99	.79	0	0
Health care	1.86	1.06	1.00	0
Paid time off	.27	.27	.17	0
Other	.22	.05	0	.27**

*All benefits are presented as cost per hour.

**Part time associates receive "on-call pay" of .27 (cents) per hour worked, as compensation for periods of not being called in (see "other" column).

At Mr. Baldy, all of the workforce flexibility comes through part-timers. Full-timers are guaranteed 40 hours per week over the course of a seven-day Monday–Sunday work schedule. Part-timers have no hours guaranteed, but do have two features that make their jobs more attractive. First, for every hour worked, an extra 27 cents goes to wages as "on-call pay"—a form of compensation to make up for the fact that they are always "on call," depending on road conditions. Second, these workers are disproportionately assigned the job of car dryer. At the end of the line, each car is inspected and dried by a Mr. Baldy employee. About 45 percent of all customers tip these dryers, with the average tip being $1.00. This shows up in the table as tip money. See below for more information:

	Full-Time	Part-Time, Contingent
Average Performance Rating (1–5, 1 = great)	2.8	2.3
Overall Job Satisfaction (1–5, 1 = high)	2.1	4.1
Number of customer complaints per 100 car washes	.3	1.3
Voluntary turnover per year	77%	180%
Average age	29	17

Jerry Newman has extracted from the recent satisfaction survey some of the more frequently mentioned open-ended comments. They are broken down by supervisory, full-time, and part-time contingent.

SUPERVISORY

1. I'm sick of having to call the evening before a "dry day" and begging for the contingents to come in. Why can't we have more full-timers?
2. My full timers complain that the high tip jobs all go to the part-timers, which doesn't seem fair.

FULL-TIMERS

1. This is a back-breaking job and I get 9 bucks an hour. That's the same as someone who just started yesterday. That's not fair.
2. I've worked here 3 years, yet the choice jobs (dryer) go to the temps. That sucks.

3. Baldy claims this is a job that we can advance in, make a life out of it. I'm 33 and have nothing in my pension. How can I make a life that way?

PART-TIMERS

1. I'm sick of working my tail off, 14 hours a day, for two sunny days, then nothing for a week. I need more stability in my pay.

Mr. Baldy's strategic plan calls for being the best car wash in town, at a fair price. His only competition is the laser washes (automated wash centers where you pay a machine and your car is laser measured and robotically washed) and U-wash centers. This focus on excellence and the reputation of Mr. Baldy's washes makes new recruiting not difficult. But it's still estimated that each new hire costs roughly $800 dollars (in recruitment and training costs).

What do you think should be done? This isn't necessarily just a benefits case. Remember, compensation and benefits are but two parts of the overall job experience.

Summary

Since the 1940s, employee benefits have been the most volatile area in the compensation field. From 1940 to 1980, dramatic changes came in the form of more and better types of employee benefits. The result should not have been unexpected. Employee benefits are now a major, and many believe prohibitive, component of doing business. Look for this century to be dominated by cost-saving efforts to improve the competitive position of American industry. A part of these cost savings will come from tighter administrative controls on existing benefit packages. But another part, as already seen in the auto industry, may come from a reduction in existing benefit packages. If this does evolve as a trend, benefit administrators will need to develop a mechanism for identifying employee preferences (in this case "least preferences") and use them as a guideline to meet agreed upon savings targets.

Review Questions

1. James A. Klingon has a mandate from his boss to cut employee benefit costs. In a company expanding by 10 percent in employees every year, Jim decides to control costs through his selection strategy. Is he crazy? Or crazy like a fox? Explain.

2. Explain the concept of experience rating using examples from unemployment insurance. Would the same concept apply to workers' compensation? Using the Internet, find out if experience rating plays a role in insurance coverage.

3. The CEO of Krinkle Forms Inc says there is a serious problem with turnover, with data for her observation provided below.

Seniority	Turnover Rate
0–2 yrs	61%
2–5 yrs	21%
5+ yrs	9%

The CEO wants to use employee benefits to lessen this problem. Before agreeing to look at this as the solution, what should run through your mind as a trained professional? What might you do, specifically, in the areas of pension vesting, vacation and holiday allocation, and life insurance coverage in the effort to reduce turnover?

4. Why are defined contribution pension plans gaining in popularity in the United States and defined benefit plans losing popularity?

5. Some experts argue that consumer-directed health care is, amongst other things, a great communications tool for employee benefits. Defend this position.

Endnotes

1. R. McCaffery, *Managing the Employee Benefits Program* (New York: American Management Association, 1972), pp. 1–2.
2. Lisa Cornwell, "Some Employers Charge Smokers More for Health Insurance." *Buffalo News,* February 17, 2006, pp. D1, 8.
3. Ann Zimmerman, Robert Matthews, and Kris Hudson, "Can Employers Alter Hiring Policies to Cut Health Costs?" *The Wall Street Journal,* October 17, 2005, p. B1.
4. Ibid.
5. Stephen Miller, "HR, Employees Vary on Job Satisfaction," *HR Magazine* 52(8), August 2007, pp. 23–27.
6. Lydell Bridgeford, "CEOs in the Dark on Employees' Benefits Preferences," *Employee Benefits News,* September 1, 2006, pp. 12, 17.
7. Bureau of Labor Statistics, "Employer Costs for Employee Compensation Summary," *http://www.bls.gov/news.release/ecec.nr0.htm,* February 4, 2009.
8. U.S. Chamber of Commerce, *Employee Benefits,* 2008 edition (Washington, DC: Chamber of Commerce, 2008).
9. U.S. Department of Labor, "Employee Benefits Survey," *data.bls.gov/labjava/outside.jsp?survey=eb,* September 23, 2008.
10. National Academy of Social Insurance, *Workers' Compensation: Benefits, Coverage and Costs* (Washington, DC: National Academy of Social Insurance, July 2005), p. 1.
11. Employee Benefits Research Institute, *Fundamentals of Employee Benefit Programs* (Washington, DC: EBRI-ERF, 2009).
12. Ibid.
13. New York State Workers Compensation Board, *http://www.wcb.state.ny.us/content/main/onthejob/CashBenefits.jsp,* February 4, 2009.
14. Ruth Gastel, "Workers' Compensation." *Insurance Institution Information* (1997), pp. 20–37.
15. Employee Benefit Research Institute, *Fundamentals of Employee Benefit Programs* (Washington, DC: EBRI, 2009).
16. Ibid.
17. Joseph Martocchio, *Employee Benefits* (New York: McGraw-Hill, 2006).
18. William J. Cohen, "The Evolution and Growth of Social Security," in J. P. Goldberg, E. Ahern, W. Haber, and R. A. Oswald, eds., *Federal Policies and Worker Status Since the Thirties* (Madison, WI: Industrial Relations Research Association, 1976), p. 62.
19. Social Security (Old-Age, Survivors, and Disability Insurance), *www.ssa.gov/policy/docs/statcomps/supplement/2002/oasdi.pdf,* May 15, 2003.
20. Thomas H. Paine, "Alternative Ways to Fix Social Security," *Benefits Quarterly,* Third Quarter 1997, pp. 14–18.
21. *http://www.ssa.gov,* February 5, 2009.
22. Social Security Online: Automatic Increases, *http://www.ssa.gov/OACT/COLA/Benefits.html,* February 5, 2009.

23. Employee Benefit Research Institute, *Fundamentals of Employee Benefit Programs* (Washington, DC: EBRI, 2009).

24. U.S. Department of Labor, Employment & Training Administration, *http://workforcesecurity. doleta.gov/unemploy/uitaxtopic.asp,* February 5, 2009.

25. Jennifer Reingold, "Voices of the Recession: The New Jobless," *Fortune* 159(3) (2009), p. 27.

26. U.S. Department of Labor, *www.workforcesecurity.doleta.gov/uitaxtopic.asp,* visited May 15, 2003.

27. Ibid.

28. *http://jobsearch.about.com/cs/unemployment/a/unemployment.htm,* visited February 5, 2009.

29. "The Effect of Benefit Sanctions on the Duration of Unemployment," Center for Economic Policy Research Report #469, April 2002.

30. Employee Benefit Research Institute, *Fundamentals of Employee Benefit Programs* (Washington, DC: EBRI, 2009).

31. *Employee Benefit News,* November 2002, *web.lexis-nexis.com/universe/document?_m=f0b 98fa6d631a36028b211b198777688&_docnum=28wchp=dGLbVlb-1S1A1&_md5=cf85df 0d5da0a29b169777139041cec0.*

32. U.S. Department of Labor, Employee Benefits Security Administration, *www.dol.gov/ebsa,* August 18, 2009.

33. U.S. Department of Health and Human Services, *http://www.hhs.gov/ocr/privacy/index. html,* February 5, 2009.

34. Sylvia Nasar, "Pensions Covering Lower Percentage of U.S. Work Force", *New York Times,* February 5, 2009, p. B1.

35. Aon survey, "Employees Value Basic Benefits Most," *Best's Review,* 103(4) (2002), pp. 1527–1534.

36. IOMA, "Managing 401(k) Plans," Institute of Management & Administration (Newark, NJ: BNA Subsidiaries, August 2000).

37. Gordon Clark and Ashby Monk, "Conceptualizing the Defined Benefit Pension Promise," *Benefits Quarterly,* July 2007, pp. 7–26.

38. Ellen E. Schultz and Theo Francis, "How Safe Is Your Pension," *The Wall Street Journal,* January 12, 2006, pp. B1, B3.

39. "Employee Benefits News," *Benefits Marketplace* 22(16), (2009), pp. 19–22.

40. Employee Benefit Research Institute, *Fundamentals of Employee Benefit Programs* (Washington, DC: EBRI, 1997), pp. 69–73.

41. Gordon Clark and Ashby Monk, "Conceptualizing the Defined Benefit Pension Promise," *Benefits Quarterly,* July 2007, pp. 7–26.

42. "Employee Benefits News," *Benefits Marketplace* 22(16), (2009), pp. 19–22.

43. Jim Morris, "The Changing Pension Landscape," *Compensation & Benefits Review* 37(5) (2005), pp. 30–35.

44. "Employee Benefits News," *Benefits Marketplace* 22(16) (2009), pp. 19–22.

45. Ibid.

46. Employee Benefit Research Institute, Fundamentals of Employee Benefit Programs (Washington, DC: EBRI, 2009).

47. Watson Wyatt Worldwide, *http://www.watsonwyatt.com/research/reports.asp,* October 2, 2009.

48. Sandra Block, "Companies Rethink 401(k) Matches," *USA Today,* June 25, 2009, p. B1.

49. Employee Benefit Research Institute, "EBRI Research Highlights: Retirement Benefit," Special Report SR-42 (Washington, DC: EBRI, June 2003).

50. In 2001, the Economic Growth and Tax Relief Reconciliation Act of 2001 was passed. This act replaced some of the aspects of the original ERISA and came into effect for plans starting after December. 31, 2001.

51. Employee Benefit Research Institute, *Fundamentals of Employee Benefit Programs* (Washington, DC: EBRI, 2009).

52. Stuart Dorsey, "Pension Portability and Labor Market Efficiency: A Survey of the Literature," *Industrial and Labor Relations Review,* January 1, 1995, pp. 43–58.

53. Amir Efrati and Jeffrey McCracken, "PBGC Stakes Claim in Bankruptcy Case," *Wall Street Journal* 253(11), January 14, 2009, p. C3.

54. Ibid.

55. Burton T. Beam and John J. McFadden, *Employee Benefit 5* (Chicago, IL: Dearborn Financial Publishing, 1992).

56. Department of Labor, Bureau of Labor Statistics, *data.bls.gov/labjava/outside.jsp?survey=eb,* June 5, 2006.

57. U.S. Department of Labor, Bureau of Labor Statistics, "Table 5: Life Insurance Benefits: Access, Participation, and Take-Up Rates," *http://www.bls.gov/news.release/ebs2.t05.htm,* February 6, 2009.

58. Ibid.

59. Employee Benefit Research Institute, Fundamentals of Employee Benefit Programs (Washington, DC: EBRI, 2009).

60. Jewel Gowani, "Delphi Seeks Permission to Eliminate Retiree Health Care" *Detroit Free Press,* February 5, 2009, *http://www.freep.com/article/20090205/BUSINESS01/90205096/1002/rss02,* February 6, 2009.

61. Milt Freudenheim, "H.M.O. Costs Spur Employers to Shift Plans," *New York Times,* September 9, 2000, p. A1; Craig Gunsauley, "Health Plan Almanac—Sellers' Market: Health Plans Struggle for Profitability as Underlying Costs Increase and Patients Demand Greater Access to Providers and Services," *Employee Benefit News,* April 15, 2000.

62. Catherine Siskos, "Don't Get Sick," *Kiplinger's Personal Finance Magazine* 54 (July 2000), p. 80; Diana Twadell, "Employee Benefits Made Simple," *San Diego Business Journal,* June 12, 2000, p. b1.

63. Employee Benefit Research Institute, *Fundamentals of Employee Benefit Programs* (Washington, DC: EBRI, 2009).

64. "Employee Benefits News," *Benefits Marketplace* 22(16) (2009), pp. 19–22.

65. S. Smith, "New Trends in Health Care Cost Control," *Compensation and Benefits Review,* January 2002, pp. 38–44; Regina Herzlinger and Jeffrey Schwartz, "How Companies Tackle Health Care Costs: Part I," *Harvard Business Review,* July–August 1985, pp. 69–81.

66. Tracey Walker, "Benefit Designs Continue to Evolve," *Managed Healthcare Executive* 15(9) (2005), p. 9.

67. "GE Workers Plan Strike over Benefit Cost-Shifting," *Business Insurance,* January 6, 2003, pp. 23–26.

68. P. Fronstin, "Can Consumerism Slow the Rate of Health Benefit Cost Increase," EBRI Issue Brief No. 246 (Washington, DC: EBRI, July 2002).

69. "Business & Health, March 1997," *Compensation and Benefits Review,* July/August 1997, p. 12.

70. Barry Hall, "Health Incentives: The Science and Art of Motivating Healthy Behaviors," *Benefits Quarterly,* 2008 (second quarter), pp. 12–22.

71. The Health Insurance Association of America provides research about a wide variety of specific health-related issues at its Web site, *www.hiaa.org/pubs/.*

72. Employee Benefit Research Institute, *Fundamentals of Employee Benefit Programs* (Washington, D.C.: EBRI, 2009).

73. U.S. Department of Labor, *http://www.dol.gov/,* February 6, 2009.

74. Ibid.

75. U.S. Department of Labor, 2008, *http://www.dol.gov/* visited February 6, 2009.

76. Mercer Human Resources Consulting. *National Survey of Employer-Sponsored Health Plans: 2005 Survey Report* (New York: Mercer Human Resources Consulting, 2006).

77. U.S. Chamber of Commerce, "1999 Employee Benefits Survey," (2000), p. 10.

78. Hewitt Associates LLC. *Salaried Employee Benefits Provided by Major U.S. Employers 2005–2006* (Lincolnshire, Il: Hewitt Associates LLC, 2006).

79. T. Dolatowski, "Buying Dental Benefits," Delta Dental, *www.deltadental.com,* August 18, 2009.

80. Ibid.

81. HR Focus, "How Does Your PTO Bank Measure Up?" *HR Focus,* May 2009, p. 3.

82. The Motley Fool, "The Fool Rules! A Global Guide to Foolish Behavior," *Motley Fool Employees Manual* (Alexandria, VA: The Motley Fool, 1997), p. 14.

83. *www.cbsnews.com/stories/2009/05/28/eveningnews.*

84. Hewitt Associates LLC. *Spec.Summary: United States Salaried 2007–2008* (Lincolnshire, Il: Hewitt Associates LLC, 2008).

85. Ibid.

86. Employee Benefits Research Institute, "Domestic Partner Benefits," *Facts From EBRI,* (Washington, D.C.: Employee Benefit Research Institute, 2009).

87. Employee Benefit Research Institute, *Fundamentals of Employee Benefit Programs, 2009* (Washington. D.C.: EBRI, 2009).

88. David Schlaifer, "Legal Benefit Plans Help Attract and Retain Employees," *HR Focus,* December 1999, pp. S7–S8.

89. P. Allan, "The Contingent Workforce: Challenges and New Directions," *American Business Review,* June 2002, pp. 103–110.

90. IOMA, "What Benefits Are Being Offered to Attract and Retain P/T Personnel?" *Managing Benefit Plans,* August 2002, p. 3.

Extending the System

You've now read about three strategic policies in the pay model. The first, which focused on determining the structure of pay, dealt with internal alignment. The second examined determining pay level based on external competitiveness, and the third dealt with determining the pay for employees according to their performance. Strategic decisions regarding alignment, competitiveness, and performance are directed at achieving the objectives of the pay system. Specific objectives vary among organizations; helping achieve competitive advantage and treating employees fairly are basic ones.

We now extend the basic pay model to the strategic issue of execution. A number of employee groups require, because of their importance to strategic success, special consideration in the way we design their compensation packages. In fact, Chapter 14 is titled just that: "Compensation of Special Groups." Here we talk about employee groups that don't quite fit our basic model. Their special employment status, for reasons we will discuss in a moment, dictates the design of compensation administration programs that sometimes differ from the more traditional designs covered in Parts Two through Five.

In Chapter 15 we look at compensation in unionized firms. Although less than 15 percent of the work force in the United States is unionized, the role of unions in wage determination extends far beyond the size of this small group. Firms looking to remain nonunion often pay considerable attention to the way rewards are distributed to union employees. As we shall see, the role of a compensation person in a unionized organization is, indeed, different.

Our final extension of the system focuses on international employees. Different cultures, different laws, and different economies all can lead to different strategic and administrative decisions for international employees. If we are truly to embrace the globalization of business, the globalization of compensation must be a key ingredient.

EXHIBIT VI.1 The Pay Model

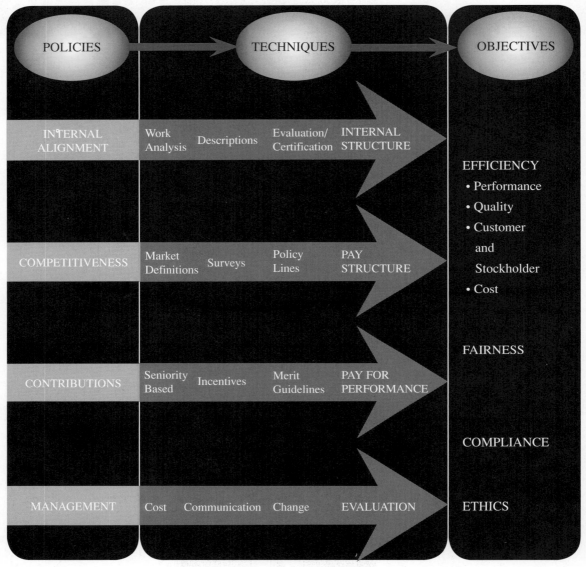

Compensation of Special Groups

Chapter Outline

Who Are Special Groups?

Compensation Strategy for Special Groups

   Supervisors

   Corporate Directors

   Executives

   What's All the Furor Over Executive Compensation? What the Critics and Press Say

   What's All the Furor Over Executive Compensation? What Academics Say

   Scientists and Engineers in High-Technology Industries

   Sales Forces

   Contingent Workers

Your Turn: Compensation of Special Groups

Congress Raises Executive Minimum Wage To $565.15/Hr

WASHINGTON, DC—Congress approved a bill to increase the executive minimum wage from $515.15 to $565.15 an hour, House Majority Leader Tom DeLay (R-TX) announced Monday. The move marks the first increase in the wage since 1997.

"This is good news for all Americans who work in the upper levels of commerce," DeLay said. "Almost a third of America's hard-working executives toil at corporations day after day, yet still live below the luxury line. It was about time we gave a boost to the American white-collar worker."

The wage was calculated to help executives meet the federal standard-of-easy-living mark of $1.1 million a year. DeLay said that, although his goal is to ultimately reach an executive minimum wage of $800 per hour, he was satisfied with what he characterized as a "stop-gap measure."

"Many of the thousands of Americans overseeing the nation's factories, restaurant chains, and retailers can't even afford a jet," DeLay said. "It's our long-term goal to ensure that no one who sees to it that others work hard for a living will have to go without the basic necessities of the good life."

—*The Onion* 44(39), November 12, 2003

This satirical article is a reflection of our worst fears about pay: We fall farther and farther behind as executives get richer. This chapter takes a look at groups that, for reasons we will discuss, receive compensation that is anything but common. Our goal is to show the logic, or illogic, of compensation practices for these special groups.

So far we have described compensation programs as if they were fairly uniform across all jobs in an organization: Jobs are analyzed; then job evaluation determines a job's internal worth; salary surveys give an indication of what other competitors pay for the job; discrepancies are reconciled; and provisions are made to recognize that variation in performance across individuals in the same job should be recognized with compensation differences. Not all jobs follow all these stages, though. Indeed, all we have to do is open a newspaper to see that some jobs and some people are singled out for special compensation treatment in an organization. Why did Tiger Woods earn $117 million in 2008?[1] And why was Intel CEO Paul Otellini's compensation doubled in 2007, increasing to over $12 million (with approximately $6.2 million added to his previous compensation of $5.9 in 2006)[2] and a base salary of $770,000?[3] He must have had a great year for Intel, you suggest? Well if that's your best answer, it's wrong. Intel's stock fell from $34 per share to $25 during the same period, and the company's earnings growth and market share both also declined. Explaining Tiger Woods might be easier. He won the U.S. Open with a broken leg and messed up (yes, that's the technical term) knee. The drama alone made for great television and great value-added by Tiger. Explaining Paul Otellini is a bit harder. Is the value of these jobs determined in the same way that compensation is determined for other jobs in a company? The answer is probably No. But why? To answer this question, it is useful to work backward. What jobs get special compensation treatment in a company? Are they basically the same kinds of jobs across companies? If they are the same kinds of jobs, are there any common characteristics the jobs share that would cause companies to devise special compensation packages?

WHO ARE SPECIAL GROUPS?

When we look at company practices with these questions in mind, a pattern begins to emerge. Special treatment, either in the form of add-on packages not received by other employees or in the form of compensation components entirely unique in the organization, tends to focus on a few specific groups. This chapter argues that special groups share two characteristics. First, special groups tend to be strategically important to the company. If they don't succeed at their jobs, success for the whole organization is in jeopardy. Second, their positions tend to have built-in conflict, conflict that arises because different factions place incompatible demands on members of the group.

As the first characteristic explains, the work these employees perform is central to the strategic success of the company. As an example, consider the contrast in compensation treatment for engineers in two different organizations. One is a high-technology firm with a strong research and development component. The other organization employs a few engineers, but their role is not central to the mission of the organization. A survey of this type of difference in employee composition and organizational strategy found that research and development organizations with heavy concentrations of engineers had evolved unique compensation systems that were responsive to the special needs of the engineering contingent. Organizations with a different focus and with fewer engineers merged this group's compensation with the standard package offered to other employees.

EXHIBIT 14.1   Conflicts Faced by Special Groups

Special Group	Type of Conflict Faced
Supervisors	Caught between upper management and employees. Must balance need to achieve organization's objectives with importance of helping employees satisfy personal needs. If unsuccessful, either corporate profit or employee morale suffers.
Top management	Stockholders want healthy return on investment. Government wants compliance with laws. Executives must decide between strategies that maximize short-run gains at expense of long run versus directions that focus on long run.
Boards of directors	Face possibility that disgruntled stockholders may sue over corporate strategies that don't "pan out."
Professional employees	May be torn between goals, objectives, and ethical standards of their profession (e.g., should an engineer leak information about a product flaw, even though that information may hurt corporate profits) and demands of an employer concerned more with the profit motive.
Sales staff	Often go for extended periods in the field with little supervision. Challenge is to stay motivated and continue making sales calls even in the face of limited contact or scrutiny from manager. Conflict is inevitable between customers who want product now and production facilities that can't deliver that quickly.
Contingent workers	Play an important "safety valve" role for companies. When demand is high, more are hired; when demand drops, they are the first workers downsized. Employment status is highly insecure and challenge is to find low-cost ways to motivate.

Exhibit 14.1 describes the nature of the conflicts faced by such special groups as supervisors, top management, boards of directors, scientists and engineers, sales personnel, and contingent workers. When both of these characteristics are present, we tend to find distinctive compensation practices adopted to meet the needs of these special groups.

COMPENSATION STRATEGY FOR SPECIAL GROUPS

Supervisors

Remember, supervisors are caught between the demands of upper management to meet production goals and the needs of employees to receive rewards, reinforcements, and general counseling.[4] The major challenge in compensating supervisors centers on equity. Some incentive must be provided to entice nonexempt employees to accept the challenges of being a supervisor. Supervisor jobs often are classified as exempt, meaning they are exempt from overtime pay. If the job requires more than forty hours of work per week (a very common occurrence), every extra hour is paid at straight time rather than time and a half. Picture a "recently promoted" supervisor working alongside a team member who collects overtime—and the financial incentive to be a supervisor quickly disappears. More recently, organizations have devised several strategies to attract workers into supervisory jobs. The most popular method is to key the base salary of supervisors to some amount exceeding the top-paid subordinate in the unit (5 to 30 percent represents the typical size of the differential).

Another method for maintaining equitable differentials is simply to pay supervisors for scheduled overtime. Companies that do pay overtime are about evenly split between paying straight time and paying time-and-one-half for overtime hours.

The biggest trend in supervisory compensation centers on increased use of variable pay. Slightly more than half of all companies now have a variable pay component for supervisors, up from 16 percent in prior years.[5]

Corporate Directors

A typical board of directors comprises 10 outside (the company) and 3 inside directors, each having a term averaging three years. Historically, directors frequently were given the role of "rubber stamping" decisions made by top management. Such boards were stacked with people affiliated in some way with the organization (e.g., retired corporate officers, suppliers, attorneys). Modern corporate boards have changed considerably. Approximately two-thirds of boards now include more outside directors than inside directors; and wow, has their job changed! The "rubber stamp" days have been replaced by serious attention to the executive compensation complaints so evident in every newspaper and blog we read. Stockholders are angry about what they perceive to be excessively high executive compensation, and a big part of the blame falls on the corporate directors, especially those who serve on the compensation subcommittee. As an early reaction to these complaints, directors are much more active in decision making and somewhat less prone to grant huge salaries to the CEO. Along with this shift in duties, pay is moving more towards pay for performance. While oversight of corporate activity—corporate governance—is still vital, the bottom line is increasingly important.[6]

As evidence, five years ago cash compensation was about equal to incentives in the mix of pay for board members. Today, stock awards and options are about sixty percent of total compensation, with cash retainers (28%) and meeting fees (11%) representing the remainder.[7] Total compensation for board members in leading companies averages around $250,000.[8]

Burger King is a classic example of a company that follows these compensation standards. Outside directors are paid $50,000 for service, payable at their option either 100 percent in cash or 100 percent in stock options.[9] In addition, $85,000 in deferred shares and a $10,000 fee (cash or options) are part of the package. Deferred shares are paid when a director leaves the board. More unusual is Coca-Cola's compensation package for directors. Coke announced a plan tying all pay to meeting earnings targets. Directors would get $175,000 in equity each year, but couldn't exercise the stocks until 2009, and then only if the company met annual earnings per share growth targets (8 percent compounded annually). Although only a small number of companies tie pay to stock performance (2 percent), maybe Coke is leading the way.[10]

Executives

Every spring the major business publications (e.g., *BusinessWeek, The Wall Street Journal*) announce the top-paid executives in the country. Without fail this sparks a flurry of articles detailing stockholder disgust with CEO pay and vitriolic demands that something be done. How can anyone be worth tens of millions of dollars, they demand? Especially infuriating, stockholders argue, is a reward package worth millions when, by all financial measures, the company is doing poorly. Today there are the same complaints, only now the complaints are backed by reams of data suggesting executive compensation is badly in need of repair. Part of the global economy meltdown can be traced directly to executive compensation. Some chief executives, such as Dick Fuld at Lehman Brothers and Jimmy Cayne at Bear Stearns, let their firms take huge risks and then paid the price when the value of their shareholdings evaporated. Who else paid the price? Yes, the shareholders took huge losses, but so also did the government, and ultimately the tax payers. The public is understandably looking for someone to blame, and executive compensation is one legitimate target. Let's talk for a minute about standard executive compensation and then figure out what went wrong.

Components of an Executive Compensation Package

There are five basic elements of most executive compensation packages: (1) **base salary,** (2) short-term (annual) incentives or bonuses, (3) long-term incentives and capital appreciation plans, (4) employee benefits, and (5) perquisites.[11] Because of the changing nature of tax legislation, each of these at one time or another has received considerable attention in designing executive compensation packages. Exhibit 14.2 traces the trend in these components over time. Exhibit 14.3 shows overall compensation for the top 10 executives in 2008.

One obvious trend is apparent from these data. Companies are placing more and more emphasis on incentives at the expense of base salary. Such a change in emphasis signals the growing importance attached to making decisions that ensure profitability and survival of a company.

Base Salary   Although formalized job evaluation still plays an occasional role in determining executive **base pay,** other sources are much more important. Particularly important is the opinion of a compensation committee, composed usually of the company's board of directors or a subset of the board.[12] Frequently the compensation committee will take over some of the data analysis tasks previously performed by the chief personnel officer, even going so far as to analyze salary survey data and performance records for executives of comparably sized firms.[13] One empirical study

EXHIBIT 14.2   Breakdown of Executive Compensation Components

Compensation Component	1970s	1980s	1990s	Today
Base salary	60%	40%	33%	19%
Benefits	*	15	*	*
Perks	*	5	*	*
Short–term bonus	25	20	27	17
Long–term incentives	15	20	40	66

Source: "Mercer Issues Study of U.S. CEO Compensation Trends," http://www.mercer.com/summary.htm?siteLanguage=100˜idContent=1307260, March 23, 2009. IOMA, *Pay for Performance Report,* June 2006, p. 12, and May 1998, p. 11; various issues of *The Wall Street Journal;* Data from Towers, Perrin, Wyatt Co.; M. Bishko, "Compensating Your Overseas Executive, Part 1: Strategies for the 1990s," *Compensation and Benefits Review,* May–June 1990, pp. 22–30.

*Unreported.

EXHIBIT 14.3
Overall Compensation for the Top 10 of 2008

Source: The Huffington Post, "Highest-Paid CEOs For 2008: AP's Top 10 List," *The Associated Press*, http://www.huffingtonpost.com/2009/05/02/highestpaid-ceos-for-2008_n_195183.html, May 2, 2009.

1. Aubrey McClendon, Chesapeake Energy Corp., $112.5 million
2. Sanjay Jha, Motorola Inc., $104.4 million
3. Robert Iger, Walt Disney Co., $51.1 million
4. Lloyd Blankfein, Goldman Sachs Group Inc., $42.9 million
5. Kenneth Chenault, American Express Co., $42.9 million
6. Vikram Pandit, Citigroup Inc., $38.2 million
7. Steven Farris, Apache Corp., $37.2 million
8. Louis Camilleri, Philip Morris International Inc., $36.9 million
9. Kevin Johnson, Juniper Networks Inc., $36.1 million
10. Jamie Dimon, JPMorgan Chase & Co., $35.7 million

suggests the most common approach (60 percent of the cases) of executive compensation committees is to identify major competitors and set the CEO's compensation at a level between the best and worst of these comparison groups.[14]

Let's just pull one of these companies out, largely because its CEO tends to be in the top paid group regularly. Robert Iger, the CEO at Disney (in earlier years, Michael Eisner's name regularly appeared on the highest paid list representing Disney), had total compensation of $51 million and change in 2008. Only $2 million of this was base pay. Another $14 millon was bonus. Gee, how do we get to $51 million? A whopping $34 million was paid out for stock and option awards exercised.[15] Is it any wonder that stock options are getting close scrutiny?

Bonuses   Annual bonuses often play a major role in executive compensation and are primarily designed to motivate better short-term performance. Only 20 years ago, just 36 percent of companies gave annual bonuses. Today bonuses are given to 90 percent of executives. As Exhibit 14.4 shows, though, the portion of executive compensation allotted to bonuses is smaller this decade than in the past (16 percent of total, down from 27 percent in the 1990s). Part of the explanation can be traced to the motivational impact of bonuses. They pay for good short-term results. This caused CEOs to approve decisions with great short-term payouts, but clear long-term dire consequences. Less of this motivation is better, critics agreed. A second reason for lower interest in bonuses is their subjectivity. Yes, when companies file information about compensation to the SEC, they include bonus information. But good luck in trying to figure out precisely what performance objectives are used to decide bonus size. Bonus targets tend to be vague, with a laundry list of goals such as sales earnings, stock price, and cash flow considered by the board in setting bonuses. Try to figure out how or even which of these measures are used . . . that's the challenge. Company officials claim vagueness is essential; otherwise competitors might glean corporate secrets.[16] Some experts argue, perhaps as a result of such vague rules, that bonuses are on a recent upswing that seems abusive. Consider American Airlines, whose shares have jumped to over $20 per share from slightly over $1, largely because of employee givebacks. The latest executive bonuses are as high as $2 million, even though AMR, the parent company, has debt in the billions of dollars. Or note the $1.38 million bonus Raymond Gilmartin got from the Merck board. Oh, did we mention he got this bonus in the year Vioxx was pulled from the shelves?[17] Balanced against these seemingly irresponsible bonus allocations is a move toward linking executive bonuses to customer satisfaction. Companies like Motorola

EXHIBIT 14.4
The Declining Trend in Use of Stock Options

1996	1999	2002	2005
68%	78%	76%	52%

Source: Mercer Consulting, *http://www.mercer.com/shopbroker.htm?siteLanguage=100*, October 7, 2009.

and Ford link bonuses to performance on customer surveys or scorecards filled out by customers.[18] Part of the longer run move to bonuses reflects a strong economy and buoyed corporate profits. Another part can be linked to increasing incidents of companies reporting stock options as expenses, making them far less attractive as a compensation tool.[19] In fact, let's take a look at this and other long term incentives.

Long-Term Incentive and Capital Appreciation Plans   Bucking a trend toward ever-rising long-term incentives (e.g., stock options), both the dollar allocation and the portion of dollars allocated to long-term incentives has been declining recently (see Exhibit 14.4).

So why the recent declines? Part of the reason is the furor over stock options' tax advantages. In just the last few years companies increasingly have been pressured to expense stock options in their annual reports, showing stockholders the real cost of options. Previously they received accounting treatment as if they were a free good. No more, say stockholders. So companies like Coca-Cola are increasingly volunteering to show the present cost of future stock options exercised. A second factor is stockholder dismay at the ease with which options are granted and exercised. We've just gone through one of the toughest stock market years in history, yet many executives in underperforming firms lined up for huge incentive payouts. Only public outcry and government intervention prevented this injustice. The complaint, of course, is that stock options don't really link to performance of the executive. Consider a rising stock market. If everyone's stock is going up, as often happens in a bull market, should CEOs be excessively rewarded because their stock also rises? It happens every day in boom markets. In a stock market that is rising on all fronts, executives can exercise options at much higher prices than the initial grant price—and the payouts are more appropriately attributed to general market increases than to any specific action by the executive. In a falling market stock options are underwater—the market price is below the exercise price. If I can exercise options at $23 per share, but they're valued at $18, I would be a fool to exercise. Unless the company issues options at a new (and lower!) price, there is evidence CEOs will turn over.[20] That's not a bad thing, though, if the CEO is underperforming.

Companies are showing clear signs that the free lunch is over. Executives now are subjected to external performance standards—meet performance goals and you can exercise your options, or be given stock (stock grant) straight out! About 40 percent of 300 corporations with more than $1 billion of revenues in a recent Hay Group survey link stock payouts to things like net income, total shareholder return, growth, and earnings per share.[21] A good example of this model is Tyson, the giant meatpacker. CEO John Tyson got 150,000 performance shares, so called because the shares are only granted if Mr. Tyson meets specific performance goals. Half of the shares depend on how Tyson stock performs against 12 other food companies. The more companies he beats, the more shares he keeps. Unless Mr. Tyson beats half the companies, he forfeits half the shares. The other half also evaporate unless Tyson's return on invested capital hits 13.25 percent.[22]

A third reason why traditional stock options may be declining in favor is linked to recent illegal backdating allegations. United Health Group and Caremark Rx, two large national health care companies, have been accused of backdating the granting of stock options to coincide with dates when share prices were particularly low.[23] When prices rebound, executives profit greatly. We think the decline in popularity masks an important reality. Executive decisions have an important impact on corporate success. Responsibly linking executive compensation to stock price is a very effective way to make sure executives are motivated to seek corporate successes. In comparison, **base wages** seem like an entitlement. As long as the executive doesn't get fired, wages are guaranteed. Bonuses also are flawed. They pay off for good short-term performance. What's good in the short run isn't necessarily responsible in the long term. Stock options, which typically are vested (meaning they can't be exercised for a specified length of time, often three years), have a built–in incentive for executives to strive for long-term success. Exhibit 14.5 describes and comments on long-term incentives for executives.

Executive Benefits Since many benefits are tied to income level (e.g., life insurance, disability insurance, pension plans), executives typically receive higher benefits than most other exempt employees. Beyond the typical benefits outlined in Chapter 13, however, many executives also receive additional life insurance, exclusions from deductibles for health–related costs, and supplementary pension income exceeding the maximum limits permissible under ERISA guidelines for qualified (eligible for tax deductions) pension plans.

Of course, various sections of ERISA and the tax code restrict employers' ability to provide benefits for executives that are too far above those of other workers. The assorted

EXHIBIT 14.5 **Description of Long-Term Incentives for Executives**

Type	Description	Comments
Incentive stock options	Purchase of stock at a stipulated price, conforming with Internal Revenue Code (Section 422A).	No taxes at grant. Company may not deduct as expense.
Nonqualified stock options	Purchase of stock at a stipulated price, not conforming with Internal Revenue Code.	Excess over fair market value taxed as ordinary income. Company may deduct.
Phantom stock plans	Cash or stock award determined by increase in stock price at a fixed future date.	Taxed as ordinary income. Does not require executive financing.
Stock appreciation rights	Cash or stock award determined by increase in stock price during any time chosen (by the executive) in the option period.	Taxed as ordinary income. Does not require executive financing.
Restricted stock plans	Grant of stock at a reduced price with the condition that it may not be sold before a specified date.	Excess over fair market value taxed as ordinary income.
Performance share/unit plans	Cash or stock award earned through achieving specific goals.	Taxed as ordinary income. Does not require executive financing.

Source: B. Ellig, *The Complete Guide to Executive Compensation* (New York: McGraw-Hill, 2002).

clauses require that a particular benefit plan (1) cover a broad cross–section of employees (generally 80 percent), (2) provide definitely determinable benefits, and (3) meet specific vesting (see Chapter 13) and nondiscrimination requirements. The nondiscrimination requirement specifies that the average value of benefits for low-paid employees must be at least 75 percent of the average value of those for highly paid employees.[24]

Executive Perquisites   Perquisites, or "perks," probably have the same genesis as the expression "rank has its privileges." Indeed, life at the top has its rewards, designed to satisfy unique needs and preferences. Since 1978, various tax and regulatory agency rulings have slowly been requiring companies to place a value on perks.[25] Despite this obstacle perks rose in value seven percent last year. Examples of interesting perks are the following:[26]

1. The most interesting perk pays for an executive's death. If the CEO of the Shaw group, James Bernhard, should die, the company will pay his family $18 million for him (the deceased) to not compete in Shaw's industry for two years. Is executive compensation insane, or what?

2. Robert Ulrich, retired CEO of Target, is the founder and Chairman of the Musical Instrument Museum that opens in 2010 in Phoenix. Target will offer free service of its employees and office space to help design the museum.

3. FTI Consulting paid $1.1 million dollars for a country club membership for top executives.

4. William Weldom, CEO of Johnson & Johnson, got $154,000 of company jet use and $26,000 for a car and driver.

Exhibit 14.6 illustrates different types of perks and the percentage of companies that offer them.

EXHIBIT 14.6
Popular Perks Offered to Executives

Source: Hewitt Associates, "Executive Compensation and Perks" (Lincolnshire, IL: Hewitt Associates, 1990).

Perk	Companies Offering Perk
Physical examination	91%
Company car	68%
Financial counseling	64%
Company plane	63%
Income tax preparation	63%
First-class air travel	62%
Country club membership	55%
Luncheon club membership	55%
Estate planning	52%
Personal liability insurance	50%
Spouse travel	47%
Chauffeur service	40%
Reserved parking	32%
Executive dining room	30%
Home security system	25%
Car phone	22%
Financial seminars	11%
Loans at low or no interest	9%
Legal counseling	6%

What's All the Furor Over Executive Compensation? What the Critics and Press Say

Let's first look at empirical data on executive compensation. If we average the CEO compensation of the 100 biggest companies, it amounts to $18 million per year.[27] Now, let's assume you accept that anyone can be worth that much money, will you grant that they should earn it? Our guess is that about 25% of the furor over executive compensation is from people who don't think anyone is worth $18 million per year. Many critics fall in this category—that this level of compensation can't be justified under any circumstances. Part of the argument includes comparisons to other countries. Wages in the European Union, for example, are much lower. Wages plus incentives for French CEOs, the highest–paid EU executives, average about $2 million in a sample of the 300 largest European companies. U.K. salaries for CEOs are about one–half that of their American counterparts, and other European executives fall even farther behind.[28] The remainder of the furor, though, is over the rest of us who need to be convinced that someone is worth double-digit millions of dollars. Think about the job of the compensation directors sitting on an executive pay committee. How do they convince shareholders they are acting prudently? One argument could be that executive compensation is simply a reflection of changes in the market. Yes, executive compensation has risen dramatically since 1900, but so has the pay of other groups. Hedge fund, private equity, and venture capital investors have had fee increases multiply by a factor of 5–10 times what they were in the period 1994–2005.[29] "The top 20 hedge fund managers earned more in 2005 than all 500 CEOs in the S&O 500"[30] Top professional ball players (football, baseball and basketball) making more than $5 million from 1994 to 2005 increased by a factor of 10. During the same period, the salaries of top lawyers increased by a factor of 2.5. Compare this, the supporters of executive pay, say, to the increase in CEO pay during the same period—a multiplier of 4–5.[31] Even if you don't buy these arguments—and many critics don't[32]—we can still fall back on a pay-for-performance argument. Maybe executives earn their increases. Increasingly boards are trying to make this very argument by linking pay to performance. Large pay can then be explained by great company performance. A typical argument would be as follows: If the company performance exceeds industry standards, big bonuses and stock payouts follow. Poor financial performance means much smaller pay packages. NCR (maker of automated teller machines, amongst other things) typifies this trend. CEO William Nuti was hired in 2005 and given $1 million in salary and $500,000 guaranteed bonus for that year. He also was granted 650,000 shares of stock provided he met undisclosed net operating profits by the end of 2008. Failure to meet these targets meant a loss of 400,000 of those shares.[33] Examples of other companies with at least 40 percent of executive compensation tied to performance targets include Briggs and Stratton, ConAgra Foods, and Intuit Inc.[34] Before the linkage to performance targets, executives were reaping huge payouts unrelated to their decision making and leadership skills. In a rising stock market, executives with stock options see an increase in their stock's value, even when their company might be lagging in financial performance. Stockholders rightly cry foul!

How did salaries get so high? Exhibit 14.7 gives a brief history of the path executive compensation took to reach these incredible heights. Pay attention to the way the granting of stock options has gradually played a bigger role in executive compensation.

EXHIBIT 14.7   **Brief History of Executive Compensation: The Key Event**

1974	Michael Bergerac cracks the $1 million mark when recruited to Revlon.
1979	Chrysler's Lee Iacocca takes $1 million plus 400,000 option shares.
1983	William Bendix of Bendix becomes the first executive to collect a huge golden parachute (contract clause for payment in a takeover leading to termination) of $3.9 million over five years.
1984	Congress tries to limit excessive golden parachutes but gives rise to unintended consequences—the rules actually lead to larger amounts.
1986	New law gives favorable tax treatment to stock option awards. Sizes increase.
1987	Lee Iacocca receives first mega-grant of stock options: 820,000 option shares worth 15.3 times his salary and bonus that year.
1987	Junk bond expert Michael Milkin explodes through the $5 million mark in salary and bonus.
1987	Leon Hirsch of U.S. Surgical gets even larger megastock option award, worth 126 times his salary and bonus.
1992	Securities and Exchange Commission rules CEO salaries must be disclosed more often in proxy statements. Easier availability of peer compensation data serves to drive up the standard.
1992	Michael Eisner of Walt Disney exercises low–cost stock options for pretax profit of $126 million.
1993	New tax law sets upper limit on tax–deductible executive compensation at $1 million but has unintended effect of raising bar to that level.
2000	Charles Wang, Computer Associates Intl. executive, cracks two-thirds of billion-dollar mark.
2006	Steve Jobs lost the top-paid CEO position to Oracle's Lawrence J. Ellison, who was compensated $192.92 million in 2007.
2009	Aubrey McClendon, Chesapeake Energy Corp., is top paid executive for 2009. This is a drop of $36 million dollars over the 2006 "winner," leading to speculation that furor over CEO pay is finally having an impact.

Source: *BusinessWeek*, April 17, 2000, p. 100, April 23, 2003; *The Wall Street Journal*, April 10, 2006, pp. R1–R4; "Executive Pay," *BusinessWeek*, April 17, 2009, pp. 23–31.

Perhaps you can take small comfort in the fact that executives are sharing our pain. They too are seeing drops in compensation. Trying to lessen the public relations disaster trifecta of bankruptcy, record unemployment, *and* excessive executive compensation, many companies are making very public announcements about the cuts they are making in their top pay structure (Exhibit 14.8).[35]

While these percentages aren't huge, at least symbolically they have important meaning. Wages don't usually fall for employees, especially executives.[36]

EXHIBIT 14.8
Public
Announcements
About the
Cuts in Top
Pay Structure

Company	Executive Pay Action
AMD	Slashed salaries 15% for vice-presidents and above
Saks 5th Ave	Cut salaried employee salaries 3–7%
Black & Decker	10% cut for executives
Hewlett Packard	CEO Mark Hurd cut his own salary 20%
Gymboree	Senior executive pay cut 10–15%

Source: *money.cnn.com/2009/02/04/news/economy/*, October 7, 2009.

So far we've overwhelmed you with information about executive compensation in the private sector. The world of compensation is very different in not-for-profit organizations. Top officers in charities make about $160,000 per year. Yes, you're right, if you want to get rich, don't work in a not-for-profit! Further, a large fraction of total compensation in the not-for-profit arena—much more than in the private sector—is allocated to expense accounts and employee benefits.[37]

Some experts today argue that executive compensation could be reined in by making sure the board of directors has explicit knowledge of how much CEOs receive each year. Sounds strange, doesn't it—why wouldn't the board know how much their CEO makes? Isn't that their job? Yes, but figuring out the worth of a compensation package in any given year isn't exactly easy. How do you value stock options that haven't been exercised yet? What's the value of unlimited use of a corporate jet? Only recently have companies begun to capture the true value of an entire compensation package, using a simple (at least in theory) tool called a **tally sheet.**[38] A tally sheet gives a comprehensive view on the true value of executive compensation. It's a simple concept that surprisingly only now is making its way into the executive board room: Tally up the value of base salary, annual incentives, long-term incentives, benefits, and perks. Part of this process includes estimating the current value of stock options (using something called the Black–Scholes model), stock appreciation rights, vested and unvested pensions, and payouts upon termination.[39] Experts argue that a tally sheet gives board members a single figure that they can then debate over: Is this competitive? Does performance justify this amount?

An alternative way to rein in executive compensation is to increase government regulation. In 1992 the Securities and Exchange Commission entered the controversy.[40] Stockholders are now permitted to propose and vote on limits to executive compensation. And it appears these votes make a difference. The larger the portion of stockholders voting "No," the more likely the board is to respond by limiting CEO salary growth. Don't go out and celebrate this victory too quickly, though. CEO salaries don't fall, they just rise more slowly when attacked by stockholders.[41] On another front, the 1993 Revenue Reconciliation Act limited employer deductions for executive compensation to $1 million and capped the amount of executive compensation used in computing contributions to and benefits from qualified retirement plans. Ironically, this very law may be contributing to the growth of executive compensation. The $1 million mark now serves as a new standard: Many executives who had been making less than $1 million are finding their pay quickly rising to this amount.

Although the 2008-2010 economic crisis brought many cries for more government controls on executive compensation, thus far President Obama has resisted popular pressure. His experts rightly point to history: Wage and price controls usually don't work effectively.

Cybercomp

For a union view of CEO wages, visit *www.aflcio.org/paywatch/.* This site is maintained by the AFL–CIO and is designed to monitor executive compensation. The union view is that CEOs are overpaid and that monitoring is the first step to curbing excess.

Are the critics right? Is CEO compensation excessive? A second way to answer the question is to look at the different ways executive compensation is determined and ask, "Does this seem reasonable?"

What's All the Furor Over Executive Compensation? What Academics Say

Over the past 50 years behavioral scientists have tried to explain executive compensation excesses. One explanation for the extreme pay of executives involves *social comparisons*.[42] In this view, executive salaries bear a consistent relative relationship to compensation of lower–level employees. When salaries of lower-level employees rise in response to market forces, top executive salaries also rise to maintain the same relative relationship. In general, managers who are in the second level of a company earn about two-thirds of a CEO's salary, while the next level down earns slightly more than half of a CEO's salary.[43] Much of the criticism of this theory—and an important source of criticism about executive compensation in general—is the gradual increase in the spread between executives' compensation and the average salaries of the people they employ. In 1980, CEOs received about 42 times the average pay of lower-level workers. Now top executives are paid more than 364 times the pay of the average worker.[44] As a point of reference, the corresponding differential in Japan is 11.[45] Both these pieces of information suggest that a social comparison explanation is not sufficient to explain why executive wages are as high as they are.

A second approach to understanding executive compensation focuses less on the difference in wages between executive and other jobs and more on explaining the level of executive wages.[46] The premise in this economic approach is that the worth of CEOs, or their subordinates, should correspond closely to some measure of company success, such as profitability or sales or firm size. Intuitively, this explanation makes sense. There is also empirical support. Numerous studies over the past 30 years have demonstrated that executive pay bears some relationship to company success.[47] A recent article analyzing the results from over 100 executive pay studies found empirical evidence that firm size (sales or number of employees) is by far the best predictor of CEO compensation. Size variables are nine times better at explaining executive compensation than are performance measures. How big the firm is explains what the boss gets paid better than does how well he performs![48]

Some evidence contradicts this, though. Research of pay packages at 702 publicly traded U.S. companies (1995–2004) showed a 1 percent increase in company value led to a 0.43 percent increase in compensation of senior executives. So far, so good. But what was troubling was the huge variations across the sample. Executive compensation in some firms was highly related to company value, while at others there was no relationship whatsoever. Worse yet, the present value of future compensation (mostly stock options, which account for about 75 percent of executive pay packages) shows very little sensitivity to company value.[49] Apparently a pure economic explanation for executive compensation isn't very successful. A variant on this argues that we should take into account environmental performance when measuring company value. One interesting study found that environmental performance (e.g., pollution prevention) is an important determinant of CEO pay in polluting industries. This suggests that CEOs are rewarded for setting and working towards environmental goals. Remember it's still difficult to determine if these green goals have tangible benefits; they are not measured in typical bottom-line accounting.[50] Two other studies combined both social comparison and economic explanations to try to better understand CEO salaries.[51] Both of these explanations turned out to be significant. Size and profitability affected level of compensation, but so did social comparisons. In one study, the social comparison was between wages of CEOs and those of the board of directors. It seems that CEO salaries rose, on average, 51 percent for every $100,000 more that was earned by directors on the board.[52] Recognizing this, CEOs sometimes lobby to get a board loaded with directors who are highly paid in their primary jobs.

A third view of CEO salaries, called **agency theory,** incorporates the political motivations that are an inevitable part of the corporate world.[53] Sometimes, this argument runs, CEOs make decisions that aren't in the economic best interest of the firm and its shareholders. One variant on this view suggests that the normal behavior of a CEO is self–protective. CEOs will make decisions to solidify their positions and to maximize the rewards they personally receive.[54] As evidence of this self-motivated behavior, consider the following description of how executives ensure themselves high compensation.[55] The description comes from the experience of a well-known executive compensation consultant, now turned critic, who specialized for years in the design of executive compensation packages:

1. *If the CEO is truly underpaid:* A compensation consultant is hired to survey actual competitors of the company. The consultant reports to the board of directors that the CEO is truly underpaid. Salary is increased to a competitive or higher level.

2. *If the CEO is not underpaid and the company is doing well:* A compensation consultant is hired. Specific companies are recommended to the consultant as appropriate for surveying. The companies tend to be selected because they are on the top end in terms of executive compensation. The consultant reports back to the board that its CEO appears to be underpaid. Salary is increased.

3. *If the CEO is not underpaid and the company is doing poorly:* A compensation consultant is hired. The CEO laments with the consultant that wages are so low for top management that there is a fear that good people will start leaving the company and going to competitors. Of course, no one ever asks why the company is underperforming if it has such a good management team. Anyway, the result is that the consultant recommends a wage increase to avoid future turnover.

In each of these scenarios CEO wages rise. Is it any surprise that executive compensation is under close scrutiny by an outraged public and, more importantly, angry stockholders?[56]

Despite this jaundiced view of the compensation determination process, agency theory argues that executive compensation should be designed to ensure that executives have the best interests of stockholders in mind when they make decisions.[57] The outcome has been to use some form of long-term incentive plan, most commonly stock options. A *Wall Street Journal*/Mercer survey of 350 firms found 265 (75 percent) gave long-term incentives to CEOs.[58] In the simplest form, an executive is given the option to purchase shares of the company stock at some future date for an amount equal to the fair market price at the time the option is granted. There is a built-in incentive for an executive to increase the value of the firm. Stock prices rise. The executive exercises the option to buy the stock at the agreed-upon price. Because the stock price has risen in the interim, the executive profits from the stock sale.

Although this sounds like an effective tool for motivating executives, there are still many critics.[59] As we noted earlier, one major complaint is that stock options don't have a downside risk. If stock prices rise, the stock options are exercised. If stocks don't improve, or even decline, as was the case for much of the past four years, the executive suffers no out-of-pocket losses. Another complaint is that stocks can rise simply because the general market is rising, not because of some exceptional behavior by the CEO. To counter this argument about 30 percent of companies force CEOs to meet some financial performance target before they can exercise their options.[60] Some argue that executive compensation should move more toward requiring that executives own stock, rather than just have options to buy it.[61] With the threat of possible financial loss and the hope of possible substantial gains, motivation may be higher. Others advocate linking stock options to executive performance. For example, if an executive doesn't lead his or her company to outperform other companies in the same industry, no stock options are granted.[62] Finally, there is growing recognition that the linkage between performance and pay is much more complex for executives than was previously thought. Current work focuses on firm risk, stock ownership versus stock options, and type of industry as possible additional factors explaining executive pay.[63]

Scientists and Engineers in High-Technology Industries

Scientists and engineers are classified as **professionals.** According to the Fair Labor Standards Act, this category includes any person who has received special training of a scientific or intellectual nature and whose job does not entail more than a 20 percent time allocation for lower-level duties. If you take a look at firms hiring scientists and engineers, they struggle to figure out what pay should be. Some experts argue that salaries are beginning to lag compared to common comparisons like pharmacists, and this is causing drops in demand for engineering training.[64] To restore our lead in the generation of scientific knowledge, more attention needs to be paid to knowledge workers who should be paid for their special scientific or intellectual training. Here, though, lies one of the special compensation problems that scientists and engineers face. Consider the freshly minted electrical engineer who graduates with all the latest knowledge in the field. For the first few years after graduation this knowledge is a valuable resource on engineering projects where new applications of the latest theories are a primary objective. Gradually, though, this engineer's knowledge starts to become obsolete, and team leaders begin to look to newer graduates for fresh ideas. If you track the salaries of engineers and scientists, you will see a close parallel between pay increases and knowledge obsolescence (Exhibit 14.9). Early years bring larger–than–average increases (relative to employees in other occupations). After 10 years, increases drop below average, and they become downright puny in 15 to 20 years.

EXHIBIT 14.9
**Maturity
Curve: Years
Since Last
Degree Relative
to Salary**

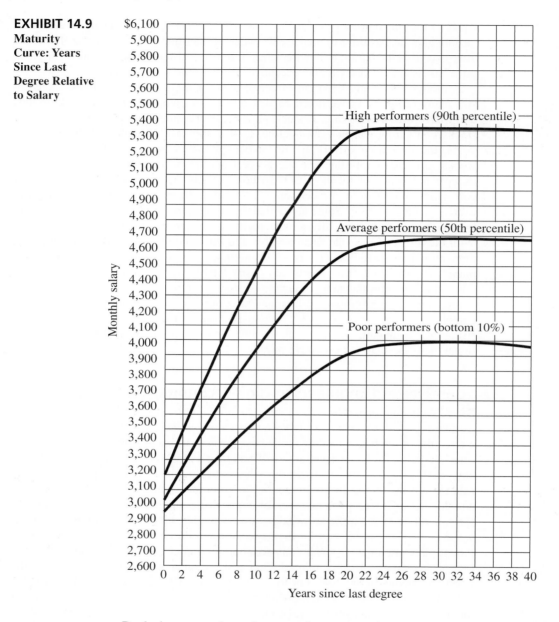

Partly because salary plateaus arise, many scientists and engineers make career changes such as moving into management or temporarily leaving business to update their technical knowledge. In recent years some firms have tried to deal with the plateau effect and also accommodate the different career motivations of mature scientists and engineers. The answer is something called **a dual-career ladder.** Exhibit 14.10 shows a typical dual career ladder.

EXHIBIT 14.10
IBM Dual
Ladders

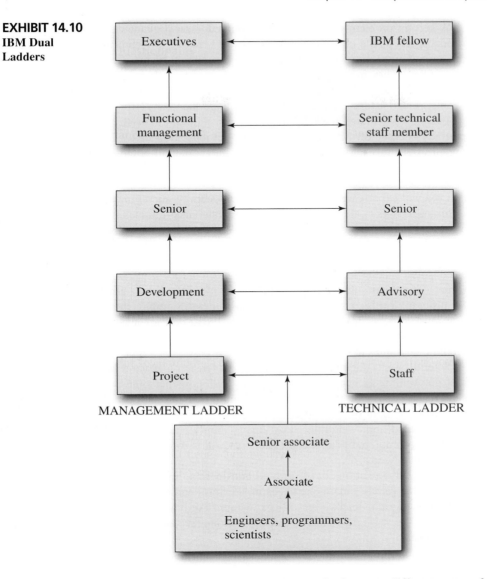

Notice that dual ladders provide exactly that: two different ways of progressing in an organization, each reflecting different types of contributions to the organization's mission. The managerial ladder offers a promotion path with increasing responsibility for management of people. The professional track rises with increasing technical responsibility. At some point in a scientist's career, the choice to opt for one or the other track arises. The idea is that talented technical people shouldn't feel that they have to take management jobs in order to advance in their careers, that they can advance through the excellence of their technical work. The titles are different in each ladder, but pay and perquisites are supposed to be comparable across the rungs.[65]

A second problem in designing the compensation package of scientists and engineers centers on the question of equity. The very nature of technical knowledge and its dissemination requires the relatively close association of these employees across organizations. They mingle at trade association meetings. They keep in touch and cross-fertilize knowledge by discussing recent developments in the field. Perhaps because of this, scientists and engineers tend to compare themselves for equity purposes with graduates who entered the labor market when they did. Partially because of this and partially because of the volatile nature of both jobs and salaries in these occupations, organizations rely very heavily on external market data in pricing scientists' and engineers' base pay.[66] The result is the use of something called **maturity curves.**

Maturity curves reflect the relationship between scientist/engineer compensation and years of experience in the labor market. Generally, surveying organizations ask for information about salaries as a function of years since the incumbent(s) last received a degree. This is intended to measure the half-life of technical obsolescence. In fact, a plot of this data, with appropriate smoothing to eliminate aberrations, typically shows curves that are steep for the first 5 to 7 years and then rise more gradually as technical obsolescence erodes the value of jobs. Exhibit 14.9 illustrates such a graph with somewhat greater sophistication built into it, in that different graphs are constructed for different levels of performance. To construct such graphs, the surveying organization must also ask for data broken down by broad performance levels. Notice in the illustration that the high performers begin with somewhat higher salaries and the differential continues to broaden over the first few years.

Scientists and engineers also receive compensation beyond base pay. More than half get a bonus either linked to company profits or personal performance. The incentives, though, tend to be small, averaging less than 5 percent of pay. Other incentives link payment of specific cash amounts to completion of specific projects on or before agreed-upon deadlines. Post-hiring bonuses are also paid for such achievements as patents, publications, elections to professional societies, and attainment of professional licenses.[67]

Finally, organizations have devoted considerable creative energy to development of perks that satisfy the unique needs of scientists and engineers. These perks include flexible work schedules, large offices, campuslike environments, and lavish athletic facilities. The strategic importance of these groups dictates that both mind and body be kept active.

Sales Forces

The sales staff spans the all-important boundary between the organization and consumers of the organization's goods or services. Besides the sales function—or even as part of selling—the sales staff must be sensitive to changing consumer tastes and provide rapid feedback to appropriate departments. Indeed, there is a growing trend toward linking **sales compensation** to customer satisfaction measures, with about one-third of all companies reporting use of such quality-based measures.[68] The role of interacting in the field with customers requires individuals with high initiative who can work under low supervision for extended periods of time. The standard compensation

EXHIBIT 14.11   Sales Compensation Components

	Average Salary for Sales Employees					
Level	Base Salary		Bonus Plus Commission		Total Compensation	
	2002	2005	2002	2005	2002	2005
Executive	$87,178	$95,170	$35,721	$49,483	$122,899	$144,653
Top-level sales representative	78,483	87,342	60,976	66,075	139,459	153,417
Midlevel sales representative	49,144	58,546	28,035	33,791	77,179	92,337
Low-level sales representative	37,698	44,248	14,294	19,486	51,992	63,775
Average of all representatives	54,452	70,588	25,571	40,547	80,023	111,135

Source: IOMA, *Report on Salary Surveys 2006 Yearbook* (New York: IOMA, 2006), pp. 10–15, and C. Galea, "2002 Salary Survey," *Sales and Marketing Management*, May 1, 2003.

system is not designed for this type of job. As you might expect, there is much more reliance on incentive payments tied to individual performance. Thus, even when salespeople are in the field—and relatively unsupervised—there is always a motivation to perform. As you might expect though, sales compensation in the recessionary economy of 2008–2010 has not set any records. In fact, sales compensation over the past two years has been flat.[69] Exhibit 14.11 shows that sales employees at every organization level have some component of pay (usually a large one) that is incentive-based. For top-level sales representatives, the incentive-based pay can be over 40 percent of total compensation.

Designing a Sales Compensation Plan

Six major factors influence the design of sales compensation packages: (1) the nature of people who enter the sales profession, (2) organizational strategy, (3) market maturity, (4) competitor practices, (5) economic environment, and (6) product to be sold.

The Nature of the People   Popular stereotypes of salespeople characterize them as being heavily motivated by financial compensation.[70] One study supports this perception, with salespeople ranking pay significantly higher than five other forms of reward. In the study, 78 percent of the salespeople ranked money as the number-one motivator, with recognition and appreciation being ranked as the number-two motivator.[71] Promotional opportunities, sense of accomplishment, personal growth, and job security were all less highly regarded. These values almost dictate that the primary focus of sales compensation should be on direct financial rewards (base pay plus incentives).

Organizational Strategy   A sales compensation plan should link desired behaviors of salespeople to organizational strategy.[72] This is particularly true in the Internet age. As more sales dollars are tied to computer-based transactions, the role of sales personnel

EXHIBIT 14.12 Sales Strategy Matrix

		Sales Strategy Mix	
		Conversion Selling	*New Concept Selling*
	Prospects	**(grow base)**	**(develop markets)**
Buyers			
		Retention Selling	*Penetration Selling*
	Customers	(protect base)	(penetrate accounts)
		Existing	**New/Additional In-Line**
		Prospects	

Source: Jerome A. Colletti and Mary S. Fiss, "Sales Compensation," in Lance A. Berger and Dorothy R. Berger, eds., *The Compensation Handbook* (New York: McGraw-Hill, 2008), pp. 239–257.

will change.[73] Salespeople must know when to stress customer service and when to stress volume sales. And when volume sales are the goal, which products should be pushed hardest? Strategic plans signal which behaviors are important. For example, emphasis on customer service to build market share or movement into geographic areas with low potential may limit sales volume (see cell labeled New Concept Selling). Ordinarily, sales representatives under an incentive system will view customer service as an imposition, taking away from money-making sales opportunities. And woe be to the sales supervisor who assigns a commission-based salesperson to a market with low sales potential. Salespeople who are asked to forgo incentive income for low-sales tasks should be covered under a compensation system with a high base pay and small incentive component. Exhibit 14.12 outlines the strategy as a function of type of buyers.

Alternatively, an organization may want to motivate aggressive sales behavior. A straight commission-based incentive plan will focus sales efforts in this direction, to the possible exclusion of supportive tasks such as processing customer returns. Such incentive plans include both a statement about the size of the incentive and a discussion of the performance objective necessary to achieve the incentive. Typical performance measures include overall territory volume, market share, number of product placements in retail stores, number of new accounts, gross profit, percentage of list-price attainment (relative to other salespeople in the organization), consistency of sales results, expense control, productivity per square foot (especially popular in retail stores), and bad debt generated by sales.[74] Each measure, of course, corresponds to a different business goal. For example, an organization might use a volume measure such as number of units, orders, invoices, or cash received if the business goal is to increase sales growth. Alternatively, if the goal is profit improvement, the appropriate measurement would be gross margin on sales or price per unit. Percentage account erosion would be stressed if improved account retention became a major focus of attention, while customer satisfaction indices are increasingly popular because of greater emphasis on quality.

Market Maturity   As the market of a product matures, the sales pattern for that product will change, and companies need to adapt the compensation for their sales force accordingly. A recent study showed that with maturing markets, companies move toward a more conservative sales pattern, focusing even more on customer satisfaction and retention. This leads companies to employ more conservative, rather than aggressive, salespeople, who can comply with the companies' customer retention plans. In maturing markets, companies focus both on performance-based pay tied to customer satisfaction and on greater base salaries to retain conservative salespeople.[75]

Competitor Practices   In selecting an appropriate pay level, organizations should recognize that external competitiveness is essential. The very nature of sales positions means that competitors will cross paths, at least in their quest for potential customers. This provides the opportunity to chat about relative compensation packages, an opportunity which salespeople will frequently take. To ensure that the comparison is favorable, the organization should identify a compensation strategy that explicitly indicates target salaries for different sales groups and performance levels.

Economic Environment   The economic environment also affects the way a compensation package is structured. In good economic climates with roaring sales, companies can afford to hire mid- and low-level sales personnel to capture the extra sales. In a recession environment, however, companies need to react to the decreasing level of sales by focusing more on the top-level performers and rewarding those that achieve high levels of sales despite the economic downturn. In the downturn of 2001, mid- and low-level performers' total compensation was down about 10 percent from the year before, while top performers increased their total compensation by an average of 9.3 percent.

. ***Product To Be Sold***   The nature of the product or service to be sold may influence the design of a compensation system. For a product that, by its very technical nature, is difficult to understand, it will take time to fully develop an effective sales presentation. Such products are said to have high barriers to entry, meaning considerable training is needed to become effective in the field. Compensation in this situation usually includes a large base-pay component, thus minimizing the risk a sales representative will face, and an encouraging entry into the necessary training program. At the opposite extreme are products with lower barriers to entry, where the knowledge needed to make an effective sales presentation is relatively easy to acquire. These product lines are sold more often using a higher incentive component, thus paying more for actual sales than for taking the time to learn the necessary skills.

Products or services that sell themselves, where sales ability isn't as crucial, inspire different compensation packages than do opportunities where the salesperson is more prominent. Base compensation tends to be more important with easily sold products. Not surprisingly, incentives become more important when willingness to work hard may make the difference between success and failure. One recent study argues convincingly that setting sales targets or quotas is the most important, and most difficult, part of sales compensation. Several factors can help you determine whether your quotas are reasonable: (1) Can the sales force tell you explicitly how the quotas are set?[76] (2) In periods when the company hits its performance target does 60 to 70 percent of the sales force hit quota? (3) Do high performers hit their target consistently? (4) Do low performers show improvement over time?[77]

Most jobs do not fit the ideal specifications for either of the two extremes represented by straight salary or straight commission plans. A combination plan is intended to capture the best of both these plans. A guaranteed straight salary can be linked to performance of nonsales functions such as customer service, while a commission for sales volume yields the incentive to sell. A plan combining these two features signals the intent of the organization to ensure that both types of activities occur in the organization.

Contingent Workers

Ninety percent of all U.S. employers hire **contingent workers.**[78] Let's define a contingent worker as anyone hired through a temporary-help agency, on an on-call basis, or as an independent contractor. Workers in the first two of these categories typically earn less than workers in traditional arrangements; those in the latter category earn more. For example, working through a temporary-help agency usually means low pay in administrative or day labor positions. In contrast, the wages for an independent contractor might be higher than those for a more permanently employed counterpart. Indeed, independent contractors often are people who have been downsized and then reemployed by the company. DuPont cut its work force by 47,000 during the 1990s. About 14,000 of these workers were subsequently hired as vendors or contractors.[79] Because the employment status of contingent workers is temporary and employee benefits are less or nonexistent, wages at times tend to compensate by being somewhat higher.

Why the move to contingent workers? Part of the answer may be cost savings. Employee benefit costs are about 50 percent less for contingent workers.[80] This may quickly change, though, if *Vizcaino v. Microsoft Corporation*[81] is upheld. In this case the United States Court of Appeals in San Francisco decided that as many as 15,000 temp agency workers assigned to Microsoft in specified positions are "presumptively" common law employees of Microsoft and, therefore, "presumptively" entitled to receive retroactive benefits. Although the case is still being appealed, there is growing concern that "temporary workers" may be entitled to corporate benefits. If the courts agree with this position, some of the reduced benefit costs of contingent workers would be lessened.[82] The main reason for contingent workers may be the added flexibility such employment offers the employer. In today's fast-paced marketplace, lean and flexible are desirable characteristics, and contingent workers offer these options.

A major compensation challenge for contingent workers, as with all our special-group employees, is identifying ways to deal with equity problems. Contingent workers may work alongside permanent workers yet often receive lower wages and benefits for the same work. Employers deal with this potential source of inequity on two fronts, one traditional and one that challenges the very way we think about employment and careers. One company response is to view contingent workers as a pool of candidates for more permanent hiring status. High performers may be moved off contingent status and afforded more employment stability. Cummins Engine, for example, is famous for its hiring of top-performing contingent workers. The traditional reward of a possible "promotion," then, becomes a motivation to perform.

A second way to look at contingent workers is to champion the idea of boundaryless careers.[83] At least for high-skilled contingent workers, it is increasingly popular to view careers as a series of opportunities to acquire valuable increments in knowledge and skills. In this framework, contingent status isn't a penalty or cause of dissatisfaction. Rather, employees who accept the idea of boundaryless careers may view contingent status as part of a fast-track developmental sequence. Lower wages are offset by opportunities for rapid development of skills—opportunities that might not be so readily available in more traditional employment arrangements. Companies like General Electric that promote this reward—enhanced employability status through acquisition of highly demanded skills—may actually have tapped an underutilized reward dimension.

Your **Turn** Compensation of Special Groups

You are the plant manager for Harlow Romance Novels, a distribution company for romance novels from a major publisher. You have both an internet site (40 percent) and a traditional brick-and-mortar business with phone sales representing 40 percent of your business. A declining 20 percent of the business comes from mail-in orders. All three types of orders are processed in the plant located in Amherst, NY. Twenty-five percent of your production employees are temps hired from Robert Raft Agency, a specialist in temporary employees. The major production jobs and their wages are listed below.

Title	% Temp	Wage per Hour	Turnover %
Forklift Driver	2	18.00	14
Inspector	8	12.00	15
Expediter	12	10.00	33
Packer	38	9.00	50

Drivers get books stored on pallets from their warehouse location and move them to location for packing. Packers take books from boxes as needed to complete orders. Expediters fill special rush orders and get single copies of books needed by packers to complete orders. Inspectors check packing slips against actual hard copies of books to make sure orders are complete and accurate. Employees begin as packers and move up the career path through expediter and inspector to forklift operator. Packer is the physically most demanding job, with expediter having the greatest pressure (usually they are filling orders with strict time deadlines).

Although only 25 percent of your production staff are temps, they represent 38 percent of the packers. By contract these workers make 20 percent less wages than those posted above, and they are aware of the differential between them and corporate workers. In recent months you have heard grumblings about the lack of fairness in this wage differential. After all, the temps say, they're doing exactly the same job for less money. Moreover, they argue, their jobs are far less secure. And this is true: if layoffs occur, they're in the temp ranks.

You're starting to see signs of sabotage—mostly books with pages ripped out—and this isn't caught by the inspectors. You think it might be temps acting out their anger, but it could be nontemps seeking to cause friction. Temps also have a 6 percent higher turnover rate across all job titles. You're reluctant to stop hiring temps altogether because you save about 8 percent in total labor costs. What would you recommend doing?

Summary
Special groups are portrayed here as sharing two common characteristics: They all have jobs with high potential for conflict, and resolution of this conflict is central to the goals of the organization. Probably because of these characteristics, special groups receive compensation treatment that differs from the approach for other employees. Unfortunately, most of this compensation differentiation is prescriptive in nature (i.e., all we have is opinion to guide us, not hard data), and little is known about the specific roles assumed by special groups and the functions compensation should assume in motivating appropriate performance. Future practice and research should focus on answering these questions.

Review Questions

1. We read an article the other day that said it's getting harder to find good people willing to serve on a corporate board of directors. Given what you learned in this chapter, speculate on why it's hard to attract good people to this job.

2. What makes professional/scientist jobs different, such that they qualify for special group status in many companies? Why is the compensation of knowledge workers so frequently linked to the amount of time these workers have been out of school?

3. The differential between the salary of top executives and the lowest paid workers in the same country is quite small in Japan, at least in comparison to the United States. The same is true in unions (president of union versus union workers). Explain why the differential might be small in Japan and in U.S. unions but much larger in private U.S. corporations.

4. Romance Novels, Inc, located in Cheektowaga, NY, has gradually increased the number of contingent workers (full-time, temporary) from 10 percent of the workforce to about 28 percent today. Why might they do this? Also, what equity problems can arise from hiring contingent workers, especially when they work alongside regular employees?

5. Why is it easier to explain a $2 million payout to Tiger Woods for working 4 days to win a Masters Championship than it is to explain why William Clay Ford made $30 million as CEO of Ford Motor Company?

Endnotes
1. "Golf Digest GD50." *http://www.golfdigest.com/magazine/2008/02/gd50?currentPage=4.* Retrieved February 23, 2009.

2. "Intel's Otellini, Paid Double in 2007," *http://news.softpedia.com/news/Intel-039-s-Otellini-Paid-Double-in-2007-82482.shtml,* February 23, 2009.

3. "Paul S. Otellini," *Forbes.com, http://wpeople.forbes.com/profile/paul-s-otellini/377777,* February 23, 2009.

4. P. Frost, "Handling the Pain of Others: The Hidden Role of Supervisors," *Canadian HR Reporter,* April 7, 2003, pp. 7–8.

5. IOMA, *Pay for Performance Report,* May 2000, p. 6.

6. Jack Dolmat-Connell and Gerry Miller, "What Should We Pay Board Members For?" *Directors and Boards,* Fourth Quarter, 2008, pp. 34–35.

7. Lance A. Berger and Dorothy R. Berger, "Board Compensation," in Peter Meyer and Nora McCord, eds., *The Compensation Handbook* (New York: McGraw-Hill, 2008), pp. 423–432.

8. Ibid.

9. Taken from S1 filed by Burger King, as required by the SEC whenever an IPO is announced, 2006.

10. Chad Terhune and Joann Lublin, "In Unusual Move, Coke Ties All Pay for Directors to Earnings Targets," *The Wall Street Journal,* April 6, 2006, p. A1.

11. Joann S. Lublin, "Boards Tie CEO Pay More Tightly to Performance," *The Wall Street Journal,* February 11, 2006, p. A1.

12. Ibid. Based on an analysis done by Mercer Human Resource Consulting.

13. Gary Strauss and Barbar Hansen, "Median Pay for CEOs of 100 Largest Companies Rose 25%," *USA Today,* April 10, 2006, p. B1.

14. Ibid.

15. Del Jones and Barbara Hansen, "CEO Pay Packages Sink With Economy," *USA Today,* May 4, 2009, pp B1–B2.

16. Joanna L. Ossinger, "Poorer Relations: When It Comes to CEO Pay, Why Are the British So Different?", *The Wall Street Journal,* April 10, 2006, p. R6.

17. Kevin F. Hallock, "Managerial Pay and Governance in American Nonprofits," *Industrial Relations* 41(3) (July 2002), pp. 377–406.

18. Hay Group, "Tally Sheets," *The Executive Edition,* (1) (2006), p. 7.

19. Floyd Norris, "G.E. Is Latest to Reconfigure Stock Options," *New York Times,* August 1, 2002, *http://www.nytimes.com/2002/08/01/business/01PLAC.html,* October 7, 2009.

20. Benjamin B. Dunford, Derek K. Oler and John W. Boudreau, "Underwater Stock Options and Voluntary Executive Turnover: A Multidisciplinary Perspective Integrating Behavioral and Exonomic Theories," *Personnnel Psychology* 61 (2008), pp. 687–726.

21. M. Langley, "Big Companies Get Low Marks for Lavish Executive Pay," *The Wall Street Journal,* June 9, 2003, p. C1; Graef S. Crystal, *In Search of Excess* (New York: Norton, 1991).

22. P. Betts, "France Has the Fattest Cats," *Financial Times,* June 23, 2003.

23. A. Henderson and J. Fredrickson, "Top Management Team Coordination Needs and the CEO Pay Gap: A Competitive Test of Economic and Behavioral Views," *Academy of Management Journal* 44(1) (2001), pp. 96–107; A. Simon, *Administrative Behavior,* 2nd ed. (New York: Macmillan, 1957); Conference Board, *Top Executive Compensation* (New York: Conference Board, 1996).

24. *United for a Fair Economy,* "Executive Excess 2007," 14th Annual Compensation Survey, *http://www.faireconomy.org/files/pdf/ExecutiveExcess2007.pdf,* Aug. 29, 2007.

25. "Politics and Economy: Executive Pay," *http://www.pbs.org/now/politics/executivepay06. html.* This comparison needs to be interpreted with some caution. One counterargument (the Hay Group, *Compflash,* April 1992, p. 3) notes that American companies are generally much larger than their foreign counterparts. When compared to like–size companies in other countries, the U.S. multiple is comparable to the international average.

26. Del Jones and Barbara Hansen, "Companies Get Creative to Boost CEOs' Pay. *USA Today,* May 4, 2009. p. 4B.

27. S. O'Byrne, and S. D. Young, "Why Executive Pay Is Failing," *Harvard Business Review* 84(6) (2006), p. 28; A. Henderson and J. Fredrickson, "Top Management Team Coordination Needs and the CEO Pay Gap: A Competitive Test of Economic and Behavioral Views," *Academy of Management Journal* 44(1) (2001), pp. 96–107.

28. Ibid.; Marc J. Wallace, "Type of Control, Industrial Concentration, and Executive Pay," *Academy of Management Proceedings* (1977), pp. 284–288; W. Lewellan and B. Huntsman,

"Managerial Pay and Corporate Performance," *American Economic Review* 60 (1977), pp. 710–720.

29. S. Kaplan and J. Rauh, "Wall Street and Main Street: What Contributes to The Rise in The Highest Incomes?" working paper, University of Chicago, 2008.

30. Steven N. Kaplan, "Are U.S. CEOs Overpaid? *The Academy of Management Perspectives* 22(2) (2008), pp. 5–19.

31. Ibid.

32. John C. Bogle, "Reflections on CEO Compensation, *Academy of Management Perspectives* 22(2) (2008), pp. 21–25.

33. H. L. Tosi, S. Werner, J. Katz, and L. Gomez–Mejia, "A Meta Analysis of CEO Pay Studies," *Journal of Management* 26(2) (2000), pp. 301–339.

34. Stephen F. O'Byrne and S. David Young, "Why Executive Pay Is Failing," *Harvard Business Review* 84(6) (June 2006), p. 28.

35. "ADP CEO Received 22 Percent Less in 2009," *BusinessWeek,* June 8, 2009, p. D48.

36. A. Henderson and J. Fredrickson, "Top Management Team Coordination Needs and the CEO Pay Gap: A Competitive Test of Economic and Behavioral Views," *Academy of Management Journal* 44(1) (2001), pp. 96–107; Charles O'Reilly, Brian Main, and Graef Crystal, "CEO Compensation as Tournament and Social Comparison: A Tale of Two Theories," *Administrative Science Quarterly* 33 (1988), pp. 257–274.

37. Charles O'Reilly, Brian Main, and Graef Crystal, "CEO Compensation as Tournament and Social Comparison: A Tale of Two Theories," *Administrative Science Quarterly* 33 (1988), pp. 257–274.

38. For an excellent review identifying factors affecting executive compensation see Martin J. Canyon, "Executive Compensation and Incentives," *Academy of Management Perspectives,* February 2006, pp. 25–44.

39. B. Deyá–Tortella, L. Gomez–Mejía, J. De Castro, and R. M. Wiseman, "Incentive Alignment or Perverse Incentives? *A Behavioral View of Stock Options Management Research*" 3(2) (2005), pp. 33–48; K. M. Eisenhardt, "Agency Theory: An Assessment and Review," *Academy of Management Review* 14 (1989), pp. 57–74.

40. Graef S. Crystal, *In Search of Excess: The Overcompensation of American Executives* (Hopewell, NJ: Ecco Press, 1991); L. Bebchuk and J. Fried, "Pay Without Performance," *Academy of Management Perspective,* February 2006, pp. 5–24.

41. William E. Gillis and James G. Combs, "How Much Is Too Much? Board of Director Responses to Shareholder Concerns About CEO Stock Options." *Academy of Management Perspectives* 20(2), May 2006, pp. 70-72.

42. Mark Maremont, "Latest Twist in Corporate Pay: Tax–Free Income for Executives," *The Wall Street Journal,* December 22, 2005, p. A1; M. Langley, "Big Companies Get Low Marks for Lavish Executive Pay," *The Wall Street Journal,* June 9, 2003, p. C1.

43. IOMA, "A New Look at Long-Term Incentive Plans for Execs," *Pay for Performance Report,* June 2003, pp. 1, 11.

44. Nancy C. Pratt, "CEOs Reap Unprecedented Riches While Employees' Pay Stagnates," *Compensation and Benefits Review,* September/October 1996, p. 20.

45. J. Lublin, "Boards Tie CEO Pay More Tightly to Performance," *The Wall Street Journal,* February 21, 2006, p. B1.

46. Ira T. Kay, "Beyond Stock Options: Emerging Practices in Executive Incentive Programs," *Compensation and Benefits Review* 23(6) (1991), pp. 18–29.

47. IOMA, "Here's the Latest Thinking on How Organizations Can Solve the CEO Pay Problem," *Pay for Performance Report,* April 2003, pp. 1, 13.

48. Martin J. Canyon, "Executive Compensation and Incentives," *Academy of Management Perspectives,* February 2006, pp. 25–44.

49. M. Makri, P. J. Lane, and L. R. Gomez–Mejia, "CEO Incentives, Innovation, and Performance in Technology–Intensive Firms: A Reconciliation of Outcome and Behavior–Based Incentive Schemes, working paper, 2006.

50. Pascual Berone and Luis R. Gomez-Mejia, "Environmental Performance and Executive Compensation: An Interated Agency-Institutional Perspective," *Academy of Management Journal* 52(9) (2009), pp. 103–126.

51. Del Jones and Barbara Hansen, "Companies Get Creative to Boost CEOs' pay," *USA Today,* May 4, 2009, p. 4B.

52. C. Daly, J. Johnson, A. Ellstrand, and D. Dalton, "Compensation Committee Composition as a Determinant of CEO Compensation," *Academy of Management Journal* 41(2) (1998), pp. 209–220.

53. B. Ellig, *The Complete Guide to Executive Compensation* (New York: McGraw–Hill, 2002).

54. Daniel J. Miller, "CEO Salary Increases May Be Rational After All: Referents and Contracts in CEO Pay," *Academy of Management Journal* 38(5) (1995), pp. 1361–1385.

55. Gretchen Morgenson, "Big Bonuses Still Flow, Even if Bosses Miss Goals," *New York Times,* June 1, 2006.

56. Eric Dash. "A Bad Year for the Chief (But Not for the Bonus)," *New York Times,* April 3, 2005, pp. 3, 13.

57. B. Murti, "Customer Satisfaction Figures into Some Executives' Bonuses," *The Wall Street Journal,* September 28, 2005, pp. B3C.

58. E. Dash, "A Bad Year for the Chief (But Not for the Bonus)," *New York Times.* April 3. 2005, pp. 3, 13.

59. Hay Group, "2005 Executive Compensation Survey," *The Executive Edition* 5 (2006).

60. J. S. Lublin, "Boards Tie CEO Pay More Tightly to Performance," *The Wall Street Journal,* February 11, 2006, p. A1.

61. M. Taylor, "Stock Options Probe Grows," *Modern Healthcare* 36(21), May 22, 2006, p. 9.

62. Dennis Blair and Mark Kimble, "Walking Through the Discrimination Testing Wage for Welfare Plans," *Benefits Quarterly* 3(2) (1987), pp. 18–26.

63. Michael F. Klein, "Executive Perquisites," *Compensation Review* 12 (Fourth Quarter, 1979), pp. 46–50.

64. Leland Teschler, "How to Get More Engineers? Pay Them! *Machine Design,* 78(20) (2006), pp. 10–13.

65. J. Ostrowski, "Executives' Perks Soar," *Knight Ridder Tribune Business News,* Washington, June 4, 2006.

66. L. VanKirk and L. S. Schenger, "Executive Compensation: The Trend Is Back to Cash," *Financial Executive,* May 1978, pp. 83–91.

67. Ibid.

68. Richard Demers, "Dual Career Ladders," *www.cincomsmalltalk.com/userblogs/rademers/blogView?showComments=true¯entry=3253517059,* June 16, 2006.

69. IOMA, "Three Surveys Find Sales Comp in Holding Pattern," *Report on Salary Surveys,* 9(4), April 2009, p. 1.

70. Jo C. Kail, "Compensating Scientists and Engineers," in David B. Balkin and Luis R. Gomez-Mejia, eds., *New Perspectives on Compensation* (Englewood Cliffs, NJ: Prentice–Hall, 1987), pp. 247–281.

71. George T. Milkovich, "Compensation Systems in High Technology Companies," in David B. Balkin and Luis Gomez-Mejia, eds., *New Perspectives on Compensation* (Englewood Cliffs, NJ: Prentice-Hall, 1987), pp. 269–277.

72. "Sales Compensation Is Increasingly Tied to Quality," *Compflash,* July 1995, p. 1.

73. B. Davenport, "Now Is the Time to Redesign Your Sales Comp Plan," *Report on Salary Surveys 2006 Yearbook* (New York: IOMA, 2006), p. 10–12.

74. Charles Warner, "Recognition and Appreciation Is Vital for Salespeople," *www. charleswarner.us/recogsls.html,* April 10, 2003.

75. Bill O'Connell, "Dead Solid Perfect: Achieving Sales Compensation Alignment," *Compensation and Benefits Review,* March/April 1996, pp. 41–48.

76. B. Weeks, "Setting Sales Force Compensation in the Internet Age," *Compensation and Benefits Review,* March/April 2000, pp. 25–34.

77. John K. Moynahan, *The Sales Compensation Handbook* (New York: AMACOM, 1991).

78. "Where Is Sales Compensation Heading?" *Workspan,* January 1, 2003.

79. B. Davenport, "Now Is the Time to Redesign Your Sales Comp Plan," *Report on Salary Surveys 2006 Yearbook,* (New York: IOMA, 2006), p. 10–12.

80. S. Sands, "Ineffective Quotas: The Hidden Threat to Sales Compensation Plans," *Compensation and Benefits Review,* March/April 2000, pp. 35–42.

81. P. Allan, "The Contingent Workforce: Challenges and New Directions," *American Business Review* 20(2) (2002), pp. 103–110.

82. Kim Clark, "Manufacturing's Hidden Asset: Temp Workers," *Fortune,* November 10, 1997, pp. 28–29.

83. Ibid.

Union Role in Wage and Salary Administration

Chapter Outline

The Impact of Unions in Wage Determination

Union Impact on General Wage Levels

The Structure of Wage Packages

Union Impact: The Spillover Effect

Role of Unions in Wage and Salary Policies and Practices

Unions and Alternative Reward Systems

Lump-Sum Awards

Employee Stock Ownership Plans (ESOPs)

Pay-for-Knowledge Plans

Gain-Sharing Plans

Profit-Sharing Plans

Your Turn: General Technology

Many experts believe that unions are facing their most critical challenge of the last 50 years.[1] From 1988 to 2008, union membership fell from 19 percent to 13.7 percent.[2] The number of certification elections attempting to unionize a firm fell two-thirds, from a high of 8,799 in 1973 to 1,700 in 2004. The win rate in these elections was almost 75 percent in the 1950s but has stabilized now at 56 percent.[3] Today collective bargaining, except in the public sector, is not a major force. A recent study indicates unions peaked in the 1950s and 1960s and may well be no better off now than in their early days of struggle in the 1920s.[4] While 37 percent of firms in the public sector are unionized, the figure is only 7.8 percent in the private sector, and most of this concentration is in declining industries such as manufacturing.[5]

Four popular explanations are usually offered for this decline: (1) The structure of American industry is changing, and declining industries are most heavily unionized, while growing industries are less so. (While this is true, research suggests this isn't a primary explanation for union decline.) (2) Unionization may be declining because workers don't view unions as a solution to their problems. (3) There has been reduced intensity of union organizing efforts (frequently cited as a reason why several large and powerful unions, including the Teamsters, broke off from the AFL-CIO in 2005). and (4) Management is taking an increasingly hard stance against unions in general and union demands in particular.[6] A large portion of this management opposition to unions is spurred by increasing pressure from both domestic and international competitors. Management more frequently resists wage increases that would give nonunion competitors, both domestic and foreign, a competitive price advantage. The end result of these competitive pressures is a declining union-nonunion wage differential. In fact, one study shows that a 10 percent rise in import share (a popular measure of international competition) has the effect of lowering the union wage differential (the difference between union and nonunion wages) by approximately 2 percent.[7]

Such competitive pressures, starting in the 1980s and continuing today, have triggered lower-than-normal wage increases in unionized firms and even some wage concessions. You can't open a newspaper today without seeing articles about beleaguered UAW employees agreeing to concessions with GM or Chrysler. Even Ford, arguably the healthiest of the auto firms, has reduced substantially several key employee benefits. Although the statistics indicate a decline in unionism, some of the issues that are important cornerstones of unionization continue to be important for workers. Fully 63 percent of employees say they want to have more influence in workday decisions. If need be, 40 percent of workers would vote union to achieve their needs. When workplace relations are bad, when management is not trustworthy, when workers feel they have little influence over decisions affecting them, the workers show strong interest in joining a union. You want to invite a unionization effort? Show little concern for employees' welfare and be unwilling to share power—over 70 percent of workers who see management acting this way claim they would vote for a union.[8] Just ask the physicians, nuclear engineers, psychologists, and judges who recently decided to unionize. Unions may be down but not out. The percentage supporting unionization today is comparable to a figure reported 15 years earlier in a similar survey, and it suggests antiunion support may have bottomed out.[9]

THE IMPACT OF UNIONS IN WAGE DETERMINATION

Despite strong management efforts to lessen the impact of unions, they still have an important effect on wages. Even in a nonunion firm, compensation managers will adjust rewards (usually upward) when there is a hint of nearby union activity. This section outlines four specific areas of union impact: (1) impact on general wage and benefit levels, (2) impact on the structure of wages, (3) impact on nonunion firms (also known as **spillover effect**), and (4) impact on wage and salary policies and practices in unionized firms. The chapter's concluding section focuses on union response to the changing economic environment of the 1980s and the alternative compensation systems that have evolved in response to these changes.

> **Cybercomp**
> This site gives detailed information about dozens of unions, including specifics of union contracts: *www.iir.berkeley.edu/library/contracts/* (choose union or state).

Union Impact on General Wage Levels

Do unions raise wages? Are unionized employees better off than they would be if they were nonunion? Unfortunately, comparing "what is" to "what might have been" is no easy chore. Several measurement problems are difficult to overcome. The ideal situation would compare numerous organizations that were identical except for the presence or absence of a union.[10] Any wage differences among these organizations could then be attributed to unionization (a union wage premium). Unfortunately, few such situations exist. One alternative strategy that has been adopted is to identify organizations within the same industry that differ in level of unionization. For example, consider company A, which is unionized, and company B, which is not. Although they are in the same industry, it is still difficult to argue with assurance that wage differences between the two firms are attributable to the presence or absence of a union. First, the fact that the union has not organized the entire industry weakens its power base (strike efforts to shut down the entire industry could be thwarted by nonunion firms). Consequently, any union impact in this example might underestimate the role of unions in an industry where the percentage of unionization is greater. A second problem in measuring union impact is apparent from this example. What if company B grants concessions to employees as a strategy to avoid unionization? These concessions, indirectly attributable to the presence of a union, would lead to underestimation of union impact on wages.

Another strategy in estimating union impact on wages is to compare two different industries that vary dramatically in the level of unionization.[11] This strategy suffers because nonunionized industries (e.g., agriculture, service) are markedly different from unionized industries in the types of labor employed and their general availability. Such differences have a major impact on wages independent of the level of unionization and make any statements about union impact difficult to substantiate.

One source of continuing data on unionized and nonunionized firms is the Bureau of Labor Statistics. From 1969 to 1985, the union wage premium more than doubled, from 17.6 to 35.6 percent.[12] In 2003, the union wage premium declined a substantial amount to 24.5 percent.[13] In 2005, workers represented by unions had median weekly earnings of $801 compared to nonunion wages of $622, a 29 percent difference (32 percent difference in 1999).[14] Historically, union wages have experienced multiple-year upswings followed by multiple-year downswings. The 1950s were characterized by a widening of the union wage premium, followed by a constriction in the 1960s, an enlargement from 1969 to 1983, and in general a constriction from 1983 into the new millennium.[15] Since 1983, the nonunion sector has been securing larger wage increases than the unionized sector, partially due to unions' acceptance of lump-sum payments in lieu of increases in base wage.[16] Of course, these differentials differ by industry. Some of the traditional union strongholds, such as construction (52 percent) and transportation/warehousing (32 percent), enjoy much larger union-nonunion differentials than do less-unionized segments such as utilities (3 percent).[17]

Perhaps the best conclusion about union versus nonunion wage differences comes from a summary analysis of 114 different studies.[18] Two important points emerged:

1. *Unions do make a difference in wages, across all studies and all time periods.* Union workers earn between 8.9 and 12.4 percent more than their nonunion counterparts.

2. *The size of the gap varies from year to year.* During periods of higher unemployment, the impact of unions is larger. During strong economies the union-nonunion gap is smaller. Part of the explanation for this time-based phenomenon is related to union resistance to wage cuts during recessions and the relatively slow response of unions to wage increases during inflationary periods (because it's hard to respond quickly when a union is tied to a multiyear labor contract).

Cybercomp

These sites provide union employment and wage information: *www.unionstats. com http://stats.bls.gov/news.release/union2.nr0.htm*

Similar studies of union-nonunion wage differentials exist for employees in the public sector.[19] Union employees in the public sector earn, on average, about 22 percent more than their nonunion counterparts.[20] However, historically, this figure masks some large variations across unions, depending on the occupation(s) they represent. The largest gains for public sector employees are reported for firefighters. At the other extreme, however, teachers' unions (primarily affiliates of the National Education Association and the American Federation of Teachers) have not fared as well, with reported impacts generally in the range of 1 to 4 percent.[21]

In recent years, wage concessions have become more prominent. Some experts claim these concessions are more common in unionized firms and that this reduces the advantage union workers hold in wages, particularly during downturns in the economy. For example, in 1908 the glass-bottle blowers accepted a 20 percent wage cut in the hopes of fighting automation. During the 1930s, concessions were a regular feature in the construction, printing, and shoe industries. Concessions were also made in the apparel and textile industries during the 1950s. Continuing today, terrorism and gas prices have deeply affected wages in several industries, most notably the airline industry. In recent years, reservation agents for American Airlines announced wage concessions of 12.9 percent to help keep troubled AMR, the parent company, afloat.[22] In the auto industry, Delphi got the UAW to agree all new employees will be hired in at $14 per hour, substantially below the $25 wage for seasoned veterans.[23]

The Structure of Wage Packages

The second compensation issue involves the structuring of wage packages. One dimension of this issue concerns the division between direct wages and employee benefits. In unionized firms, voluntary benefits (other than those legally required) amount to 36.9 percent of the total compensation package and 27.8 percent for nonunion employees.[24] So not only is the pie bigger in unionized companies, the share devoted to benefits is bigger too.[25] Research indicates that the presence of a union adds about 30 to 40 percent to employee benefits. Whether because of reduced management control, strong union-worker preference for benefits, or other reasons, unionized employees also have a greater percentage of their total wage bill allocated to employee benefits. The most recent statistics show that benefits accounted for 37.9 percent of the total compensation package for union workers and 27.8 percent for nonunion employees.[26] Typically the higher costs show up in the form of higher pension expenditures or higher insurance benefits. One particularly well-controlled study found unionization associated with a 213 percent higher level of pension expenditures and 136 percent higher insurance expenditures.[27]

A second dimension of the wage structure issue is the evolution of **two-tier pay plans.** Basically a phenomenon of the union sector, two-tier wage structures differentiate pay based upon hiring date. A contract is negotiated which specifies that employees hired after a given target date will receive lower wages than their higher-seniority peers working on the same or similar jobs. In 2008, the UAW and GM agreed to a two-tier wage system, with wages for 16,000 positions being cut to $14 dollars per hour.[28] Three years earlier, the United Auto Workers, ratified a new contract with Caterpillar

Inc. to established a two-tier pay system for the next six years. New employees make $10 to $15 per hour upon hire whereas their veteran counterparts make about $20–22 an hour.[29] From management's perspective, wage tiers represent a viable alternative compensation strategy. Tiers can be used as a cost control strategy to allow expansion or investment or as a cost-cutting device to allow economic survival.[30] Two-tier pay plans initially spread because unions viewed them as less painful than wage freezes and staff cuts among existing employees. The tradeoff, however, was a bargaining away of equivalent wage treatment for future employees. Remember, this is a radical departure from the most basic precepts of unionization. Unions evolved and continue to endure, in part based on the belief that all members are equal. Two-tier plans are obviously at odds with this principle. Lower-tier employees, those hired after the contract is ratified, receive wages 50 to 80 percent lower than employees in the higher tier.[31] The contract may specify that the wage differential may be permanent, or the lower tier may be scheduled ultimately to catch up with the upper tier. Eventually the inequity from receiving different pay for the same level may cause employee dissatisfaction.[32] Consider the Roman emperor who implemented a two-tier system for his army in AD 217.[33] He was assassinated by his disgruntled troops shortly thereafter. Although such expressions of dissatisfaction are unlikely today, unions are much more reluctant to accept a two-tier structure and may view it as a strategy of last resort.

A third dimension of the wage structure issue involves the relationship between worker wages and what their supervisors are paid in union and nonunion environments. The gap between workers and their managers is 27 percent smaller in unionized firms.[34] Interestingly, this narrowing doesn't occur at the expense of lower or even constant wages for managers combined with higher union wages. Rather, managers in union firms receive higher wages than nonunion managers, perhaps as a bid to maintain internal equity. Apparently then, the narrowing of the gap arises because worker wages go up faster than manager wages in unionized firms.[35]

Union Impact: The Spillover Effect

Although union wage settlements have declined in recent years, the impact of unions in general would be understated if we did not account for what is termed the *spillover effect*. Specifically, employers seek to avoid unionization by offering workers the wages, benefits, and working conditions won in rival unionized firms. The nonunion management continues to enjoy the freedom from union "interference" in decision making, and the workers receive the spillover of rewards already obtained by their unionized counterparts. Several studies document the existence of this phenomenon, although smaller as union power diminishes, providing further evidence of the continuing role played by unions in wage determination.[36]

Role of Unions in Wage and Salary Policies and Practices

Perhaps of greatest interest to current and future compensation administrators is the role unions play in administering wages. The role of unions in administering compensation is outlined primarily in the contract. The following illustrations of this role are taken from major collective bargaining agreements.

Basis of Pay

The vast majority of contracts specify that one or more jobs are to be compensated on an hourly basis and that overtime pay will be paid beyond a certain number of hours. Notice the specificity of the language in the following contract clause:

A. Overtime pay is to be paid at the rate of one and one-half (1 1/2) times the basic hourly straight-time rate.

B. Overtime shall be paid to employees for work performed only after eight (8) hours on duty in any one service day or forty (40) hours in any one service week. Nothing in this Section shall be construed by the parties or any reviewing authority to deny the payment of overtime to employees for time worked outside of their regularly scheduled work week at the request of the Employer.

C. Penalty overtime pay is to be paid at the rate of two (2) times the basic hourly straight-time rate. Penalty overtime pay will not be paid for any hours worked in the month of December.

D. Excluding December, part-time flexible employees will receive penalty overtime pay for all work in excess of ten (10) hours in a service day or fifty-six (56) hours in a service week.

(Bargaining agreement between American Postal Workers Union, AFL-CIO, and U.S. Postal Service, contract approved 2007. Source: *http://www.apwu.org/issues–contract/ index.htm.*)

Further, many contracts specify a premium be paid above the worker's base wage for working nonstandard shifts:

Employees regularly employed on the second or third shift shall receive in addition to their regular pay for the pay period five (5) percent and ten (10) percent, respectively, additional compensation. (DaimlerChrysler and Auto Workers, contract approved 2006)

Alternatively, agreements may specify a fixed daily, weekly, biweekly, or monthly rate. In addition, agreements often indicate a specific day of the week as payday and sometimes require payment on or before a certain hour.

Much less frequently, contracts specify some form of incentive system as the basis for pay. The vast majority of clauses specifying incentive pay occur in manufacturing (as opposed to nonmanufacturing) industries:

Section 7. Establishment of Labor Standards. The Company and the Union, being firmly committed to the principle that high wages can result only from high productivity, agree that the Company will establish Labor Standards that:

a. Are fair and equitable to both the Company and the workers; and

b. Are based on the working capacity of a normally qualified worker properly motivated and working at an incentive pace; and

c. Give due consideration to the quality of workmanship and product required; and

d. Provide proper allowances for fatigue, personal time, and normal delays, and

e. Provide for payment of incentive workers based on the earned hours produced onstandard (except when such Employees are working on a Preliminary Estimate, etc.), and for each one per cent (1%) increase in acceptable production over standard, such workers shall receive a one per cent (1%) increase in pay over the applicable incentive rate.

The Company will, at its discretion as to the time and as to jobs to be placed on or removed from incentive, continue the earned-hour incentive system now in effect, and extend it to jobs in such other job classifications which, in the opinion of the Company, can properly be placed on incentive, with the objective of increasing productivity and providing an opportunity for workers to enjoy higher earnings thus made possible. The plan shall be maintained in accordance with the following principles.

(Source: Maytag, Maytag and Admiral Products, and Auto Workers, 2008 contract approved)

Occupation-Wage Differentials

Most contracts recognize that different occupations should receive different wage rates. Within occupations, though, a single wage rate prevails:

Occupation	Hourly Wage
Clerk typists	$ 7.30
Computer operators	10.05
Maintenance mechanics	12.30

Source: Negotiated agreement between District School Board of St. Johns County and St. Johns School Support Association, contract approved 2005.

Although rare, there are some contracts that do not recognize occupational/skill differentials. These contracts specify a single standard rate for all jobs covered by the agreements. Usually such contracts cover a narrow range of skilled groups.

Experience/Merit Differentials

Single rates are usually specified for workers within a particular job classification. Single-rate agreements do not differentiate wages on the basis of either seniority or merit. Workers with varying years of experience and output receive the same single rate. Alternatively, agreements may specify wage ranges. The following example is fairly typical:

Job Title	Years of Experience							
	None	1	2	3	4	6	8	12
Computer operators	$10.05	$10.30	$10.55	$10.80	$11.05	$11.55	$12.30	$14.05
QC inspectors	$12.30	$12.55	$12.80	$13.05	$13.30	$13.80	14.30	$16.30

Source: Negotiated agreement between District School Board of St. Johns County and St. Johns School Support Association, contract approved 2006.

The vast majority of contracts, as in the example above, specify seniority as the basis for movement through the range. *Automatic progression* is an appropriate name for this type of movement through the wage range, with the contract frequently specifying the time interval between movements. This type of progression is most appropriate when the necessary job skills are within the grasp of most employees. Denial of a raise is rare and frequently is accompanied by the right of the union to grieve the decision.

A second, and far less common, strategy for moving employees through wage ranges is based exclusively on merit. Employees who are evaluated more highly receive larger or more rapid increments than average or poor performers. Within these contracts, it is common to specify that disputed merit appraisals may be submitted to grievance. If the right to grieve is not explicitly excluded, the union also has the implicit right to grieve.

The third method for movement through a range combines automatic and merit progression in some manner. A frequent strategy is to grant automatic increases up to the midpoint of the range and permit subsequent increases only when merited on the basis of performance appraisal.

Other Differentials

There are a number of remaining contractual provisions that deal with differentials for reasons not yet covered. A first example deals with different pay to unionized employees who are employed by a firm in different geographic areas. Very few contracts provide for different wages under these circumstances, despite the problems that can arise in paying uniform wages across regions with markedly different costs of living.

A second category where differentials are mentioned in contracts deals with part-time and temporary employees. Few contracts specify special rates for these employees. Those that do, however, are about equally split between giving part-time and temporary employees wages above full-time workers (because they have been excluded from the employee benefit program) or below full-time workers.

Vacations and Holidays

Vacation and holiday entitlements are among the clauses frequently found in labor contracts. They, too, use very specific language, as the following example illustrates:

26.01 Observance
The following holidays will be observed:
New Year's Day—First Day in January;
Martin Luther King, Jr.'s Birthday—Third Monday in January;
President's Day—Third Monday in February;
Memorial Day—Last Monday in May;
Independence Day—Fourth day of July;
Labor Day—First Monday in September;
Columbus Day—Second Monday in October;
Veterans' Day—Eleventh day of November;
Thanksgiving Day—Fourth Thursday in November;
Christmas Day—Twenty-fifth day of December;
Any other day proclaimed by the Governor of the State of Ohio or the President of the United States.

When a holiday falls on a Sunday, the holiday is observed on the following Monday. When a holiday falls on a Saturday, the holiday is observed on the preceding Friday. For employees whose work assignment is to a seven (7) day operation, the holiday shall be celebrated on the day it actually falls. A holiday shall start at 12:01 A.M. or with the work shift that includes 12:01 A.M.

26.02 Work on Holidays
Employees required to work on a holiday will be compensated at their discretion either at the rate of one and one-half (1 1/2) times their regular rate of pay, or granted compensatory time at the rate of one and one-half (1 1/2) 57 times, plus straight-time pay for the holiday. The choice of compensatory time or wages will be made by the employee. Holiday work beyond regularly scheduled work shall be distributed among employees by the provisions covered in Article 13. No employees' posted regular schedule or days off

shall be changed to avoid holiday premium pay. Once posted, the employee's schedule shall not be changed, except that an employee who is scheduled to work on the holiday may be directed not to report to work on the holiday. The Agency reserves the right to determine the number of employees needed to work the holiday.

(Source: State of Ohio and Ohio Civil Service Employees Association (OCSEA) collective bargaining agreement, 2006–2009.)

Wage Adjustment Provisions

Frequently in multiyear contracts some provision is made for wage adjustment during the term of the contract. There are three major ways these adjustments might be specified: (1) deferred wage increases, (2) **reopener clauses,** and (3) **cost-of-living adjustments (COLAs)** or escalator clauses. A *deferred wage increase* is negotiated at the time of initial contract negotiations with the timing and amount specified in the contract. A *reopener clause* specifies that wages, and sometimes such nonwage items as pension and benefits, will be renegotiated at a specified time or under certain conditions. Finally, a *COLA clause,* as noted earlier, involves periodic adjustments based typically on changes in the consumer price index:

Section 4. Cost of Living Adjustment

A. Definitions

    1. "Consumer Price Index" refers to the "National Consumer Price Index for Urban Wage Earners and Clerical Workers," published by the Bureau of Labor (1967 = 100) and referred to herein as the "Index."

    2. "Consumer Price Index Base" refers to the Consumer Price Index for the month of October 2001 and is referred to herein as the "Base Index."

B. Effective Dates of Adjustment

    Each employee covered by this Agreement shall receive cost-of-living adjustments, upward, in accordance with the formula in Section 4.C, below, effective on the following dates:

    —the second full pay period after the release of the January 2002 Index

    —the second full pay period after the release of the July 2002 Index

    —the second full pay period after the release of the January 2003 Index

    —the second full pay period after the release of the July 2003 Index

C. The basic salary schedules provided for in this Agreement shall be increased 1 cent per hour for each full 0.4 of a point increase in the applicable Index above the Base Index. For example, if the increase in the Index from October 2001 to January 2002 is 1.2 points, all pay scales for employees covered by this Agreement will be increased by 3 cents per hour. In no event will a decline in the Index below the Base Index result in a decrease in the pay scales provided for in this Agreement.

    (Bargaining agreement between American Postal Workers Union, AFL-CIO, and U.S. Postal Service, contract approved 2007)

UNIONS AND ALTERNATIVE REWARD SYSTEMS

International competition causes a fundamental problem for unions. If a unionized company settles a contract and raises prices to cover increased wage costs, there is always the threat that an overseas competitor with lower labor costs will capture market share.

Eventually, enough market share erosion means the unionized company is out of business. To keep this from happening, unions have become much more receptive in recent years to alternative reward systems that link pay to performance. After all, if worker productivity rises, product prices can remain relatively stable even with wage increases.

About 20 percent of all U.S. collective bargaining agreements permit some alternative reward system (e.g., lump sum, piece rate, gain sharing, profit sharing, skill-based pay).[37] Willingness to try such plans is higher when the firm faces extreme competitive pressure.[38] In the unionized firms that do experiment with these alternative reward systems, though, the union usually insists on safeguards that protect both the union and its workers. The union insists on group-based performance measures with equal payouts to members. This equality principle cuts down strife and internal quarrels among the members and reinforces the principles of equity that are at the very foundation of union beliefs. To minimize bias by the company, performance measures more often tend to be objective in unionized companies. Most frequently the measures rely on past performance as a gauge of realistic targets rather than on some time study or other engineering standard that might appear more susceptible to tampering.[39] Below we offer specific feedback about union attitudes toward alternative reward concepts.

Lump-Sum Awards

As discussed in Chapter 10, **lump-sum awards** are one-time cash payments to employees that are not added to an employee's base wages. These awards are typically given in lieu of merit increases, which are more costly to the employer. This higher cost results both because merit increases are added on to base wages and because several employee benefits (e.g., life insurance and vacation pay) are figured as a percentage of base wages. Lump-sum payments are a reality of union contracts. For the past 10 years, a stable one-third of all major collective bargaining agreements in the private sector have contained a provision for lump-sum payouts. Lump-sum awards can also be given as an incentive for workers to retire. As an example, Delphi Corporation recently filed for bankruptcy protection. As part of its plan to emerge from bankruptcy, the company offered eligible employees a $35,000 lump-sum payment as incentive to retire.[40]

Employee Stock Ownership Plans (ESOPs)

An alternative strategy for organizations hurt by intense competition is to control base wages in exchange for giving employees part ownership in the company. For example, Southwest Airlines readily grants employee stock options as a key feature of its wage control strategy.[41]

Pay-for-Knowledge Plans

Pay-for-knowledge plans do just that: pay employees more for learning a variety of different jobs or skills. For example, the UAW negotiates provisions giving hourly-wage increases for learning new skills on different parts of the assembly process. By coupling this new wage system with drastic cuts in the number of job classifications, organizations have greater flexibility in moving employees quickly into high-demand areas. Unions also may favor pay-for-knowledge plans because they make each individual worker more valuable, and less expendable, to the firm. In turn, this also lessens the probability that work can be subcontracted out to nonunion organizations.

EXHIBIT 15.1   Union Perceptions of Gain Sharing

The Top Nine Reasons for Unions Favoring Gain Sharing:	The Top Nine Reasons for Unions Opposing Gain Sharing:
1. Increased recognition	1. Management may try to substitute it for wages
2. Better job security	2. Management cannot be trusted
3. Increased involvement with job activities	3. Peer pressure to perform may increase
4. More money	4. Bonus calculations are not understood or
5. Increased feeling of achievement or contributing to the organization	trusted
6. Increased influence of union	5. Union influence is undermined
7. Greater contributions to the nation's productivity	6. Increased productivity may reduce need for jobs
8. Compatibility with union goals	7. Grievances may go unprocessed
9. Fewer grievances	8. Gains haring is incompatible with union goals
	9. Employees really do not want more involvement

Source: http://www.bovino-consulting.com

Gain-Sharing Plans

Gain-sharing plans are designed to align workers and management in efforts to streamline operations and cut costs. Any cost savings resulting from employees' working more efficiently are split, according to some formula, between the organization and the workers. Some reports indicate gain sharing is more common in unionized than nonunionized firms.[42] In our experience, success is dependent on a willingness to include union members in designing the plan. Openness in sharing financial and production data, key elements of putting a gain-sharing plan in place, are important in building trust between the two parties.

While unions aren't always enthusiastic about gain sharing, they rarely directly oppose it, at least initially. Rather, the most common union strategy is to delay taking a stand until real costs and benefits are more apparent.[43] Politically, this may be the wisest choice for a union leader. As Exhibit 15.1 illustrates, there are numerous possible costs and benefits to union members for agreeing to a gain-sharing plan. Until the plan is actually implemented, though, it is unclear what the impact will be in any particular firm.

Profit-Sharing Plans

Unions have debated the advantages of profit-sharing plans for at least 80 years.[44] Walter Reuther, president of the CIO in 1948 (which became the AFL-CIO in 1955) championed the cause of profit sharing in the auto industry. The goal of unions is to secure sound, stable income levels for the membership. When this is achieved, subsequent introduction of a profit-sharing plan allows union members to share the wealth with more profitable firms while still maintaining employment levels in marginal organizations. Introduction of a profit-sharing plan is particularly effective when union members participate in plan development.[45] We should note, though, that not all unions favor profit-sharing plans. As indicated by recent grumblings of employees at General Motors, inequality in profits among firms in the same industry can lead to wage differentials for workers performing the same work. Witness the 2006 profit-sharing payout to GM and Ford employees— ZERO. In contrast, Toyota and Honda employees are expecting to receive awards in the thousands-of-dollars range. Most General Motors and Ford employees would argue that the difference in payout cannot be traced to harder work by Toyota and Honda employees. In fact, the difference in profitability, the UAW argues, is due to management decision making. Therefore, the argument runs, workers should not be penalized for factors beyond their control. The 2006 DaimlerChrysler payout supports this argument. Profit-sharing checks dropped from $1,500 in 2005 to $650 in 2006. Why? The company says the drop is due to increases in retiree pension as well as health-care expenses.[46]

Your **Turn**   General Technology

THE COMPANY

General Technology (GT) produces burglar alarm systems. To crack the international market, GT must comply with quality standards as set by the International Organization for Standardization (ISO). Compliance requires that all products and processes pass a series of 17 strict criteria, the so-called ISO 9000 audit.

THE UNION

The Technology Workers of America (TWA) organized GT's Buffalo division in 1979. In the last contract, both parties agreed to have a three-person panel listen to all disputes between union and management concerning the proper classification of jobs.

YOUR ROLE

You are the neutral third-party hired to hear the dispute described below. The union representative has voted in the union's favor, and the management representative has sided with management's position. You will break the tie. How do you vote and why? Some experts would argue that not enough evidence is presented here for you to make a decision. See if you can figure out what the logic was that led to this conclusion. Further, list what other information you would like to have and how that might influence your decision.

THE GRIEVANCE

A job titled "technical review analyst I" with responsibility for ISO 9000 audits is slotted as a tier 3 job.* The union believes that this job should be evaluated as a tier 4 job. Management contends that both this job and its counterpart in tier 4 (senior technical review analyst) should be graded in tier 3.

SUMMARY OF IMPORTANT POINTS IN THE UNION CASE

The union asserts, and management agrees, that the only difference historically between auditors classified as technical review analysts I (tier 3) and those classified as senior technical review analysts (tier 4) was the presence or absence of one task. That task was the performance of systems

*Tier 1 is the low end and tier 5 is the highest for all skilled craft jobs. Different evaluation systems are used for management and for clerical employees.

tests. Only tier 4 personnel performed this work, and this yielded the higher-tier classification. With the introduction of ISO 9000 audits, the systems test component of the tier 4 job was eventually phased out and both tier 3 and tier 4 auditors were asked to perform the ISO 9000 audit. The union and management agree that the systems test work previously performed by tier 4 employees was easier (and less valuable to the company) than the new ISO 9000 work now being performed. However, the union maintains that the added responsibility from the ISO 9000 audit, which involves about 150 hours of training, is sufficiently complex to warrant tier 4 classification. As partial support, the union provided a list of attendees to one ISO 9000 training session and noted that many of the attendees from other companies are managers and engineers, asserting this as evidence of the complexity involved in the audit material and the importance attached to this job by other firms.

The union also presented evidence to support the assertion that tier 3 personnel performing ISO 9000 audits are doing work of substantially the same value as the old grade 310 work.[†] This grade, as agreed by both the union and the company, is equivalent to the new tier 4.

SUMMARY OF IMPORTANT POINTS IN MANAGEMENT CASE

Management's case includes four major points. First, management argues that a technical review analyst performing ISO 9000 audits has a job that is similar in complexity, responsibility, and types of duties to jobs previously classified as grades 308 and 309. Jobs in these old grades are now slotted into tier 3, per the contract.

Second, management presented evidence that many of the duties performed in the ISO 9000 audits were performed in a series of prior audits, variously labeled "Eastcore MPA," "QSA 1981," and "QPS 1982." This long and varied history of similar duties, management contends, is evidence that ISO 9000 does not involve higher-level or substantially different (and hence no more valuable) duties than have been performed historically.

Fourth, management provided evidence that these jobs at other facilities, with other local contract provisions and conditions, were all classified into tier 3.[‡]

[†]The former job evaluation system broke jobs down into many more grades. As of the last contract, jobs are now classified into one of five tiers or grades.

[‡]The union strongly contests the introduction of this information. In the past, management has vehemently argued that conditions at other facilities should not be introduced because local contracts were negotiated, with different tradeoffs being made by the different parties. The union believes that this same logic should now apply if a consistent set of rules is to evolve.

Summary

Other countries continue to make inroads in product areas traditionally the sole domain of American companies. The impact of this increased competition has been most pronounced in the compensation area. Labor costs must be cut to improve our competitive stance. Alternative compensation systems to achieve this end are regularly being devised. Unions face a difficult situation. How should they respond to these attacks on traditional compensation systems? Many unions believe that the crisis demands changing attitudes from both management and unions. Labor and management identify compensation packages that both parties can abide. Sometimes these packages include cuts in traditional forms of wages in exchange for compensation tied more closely to the success of the firm. We expect the beginning of the 21st century to be dominated by more innovation in compensation design and increased exploration between unions and management for ways to improve the competitive stance of American business.

Review Questions

1. What is spillover? How does it lead to underestimation of the impact unions have on wages?

2. Why don't many public sector unions have the right to strike, a weapon almost universally guaranteed in the private sector? Make your explanation based on compensation.

3. If merit pay is supposed to increase individual equity and unions are very concerned about equity, why do unions frequently oppose merit pay for their membership?

4. It is probably true that, if given a choice, unions would prefer to implement a skill-based pay system rather than some form of gain-sharing plan. Why?

Endnotes

1. Jack Fiorito, "Human Resource Management Practices and Worker Desires for Union Representation," *Journal of Labor Research* 22(2) (Spring 2001), pp. 335–354; Thomas A. Kochan, Harry C. Katz, and Robert B. McKersie, *The Transformation of American Industrial Relations* (New York: Basic Books, 1986), pp. 221–223.

2. Barry T. Hirsch and David A. Macpherson, Union Membership and Coverage Database From the Census Population Survey, *www.unionstats.com,* May 4, 2009.

3. The Labor Research Association, "Union Elections: Certification Elections (1990–2004)." *www.laborresearch.org/charts.php?id=48,* June 3, 2006.

4. John Pencavel, "How Successful Have Trade Unions Been? A Utility-Based Indicator of Union Well-Being." *Industrial & Labor Relations Review* 62(2), January 2009, pp. 147–156.

5. The Labor Research Association, "Union Elections: Certification Elections (1990–2004)." *www.laborresearch.org/charts.php?id=48,* retrieved on June 3, 2006.

6. *www.bls.gov/opub/ted/2008/feb/wk2/art01.htm,* retrieved on September 9, 2008.

7. Robert J. Flanagan, "Has Management Strangled U.S. Unions?" *Journal of Labor Research,* 26(1) (2005), pp. 33–98; Gail McCallion, "Union Membership Decline: Competing Theories and Economic Implications," *CRS report for Congress,* August 23, 1993, p. 13.

8. David A. Macpherson and James B. Steward, "The Effect of International Competition on Union and Non-Union Wages," *Industrial and Labor Relations Review* 43(4) (1990), pp. 434–446.

9. R. Wayne Mondy and Shane Preameaux, "The Labor Management Power Relationship Revised," *Personnel Administrator,* May 1985, pp. 51–54.

10. Allan M. Carter and F. Ray Marshall, *Labor Economics* (Homewood, IL: Irwin, 1982).

11. Ibid.

12. David A. Macpherson and James B. Steward, "The Effect of International Competition on Union and Non-Union Wages," *Industrial and Labor Relations Review* 43(4) (1990), pp. 434–446.

13. Lawrence Mishel and Matthew Walters, "How Unions Help All Workers," Economic Policy Institute, *www.epinet.org/content.cfm/briefingpapers_bp143,* June 2, 2006.

14. The Labor Research Association, "Union v. Non-Union: Median Weekly Earnings in 2004," *www.laborresearch.org/charts.php?id=34,* June 3, 2006.

15. Fehmida Sleemi, "Collective Bargaining Outlook for 1995," *Compensation and Working Conditions* 47(1) (January 1995), pp. 19–39.

16. Ibid.

17. The Labor Research Association, "Union v. Non-Union: Median Weekly Earnings in 2004," *www.laborresearch.org/charts.php?id=34,* June 3, 2006.

18. Stephen B. Jarrell and T. D. Stanley, "A Meta-Analysis of the Union–Non-Union Wage Gap," *Industrial and Labor Relations Review* 44(1) (1990), pp. 54–67.

19. David Lewin, "Public Sector Labor Relations: A Review Essay," in David Lewin, Peter Feuille, and Thomas Kochan, eds., *Public Sector Labor Relations: Analysis and Readings* (Glen Ridge, NJ: Thomas Horton and Daughters, 1977), pp. 116–144.

20. The Labor Research Association, "Union v. Non-Union: Median Weekly Earnings in 2004," *www.laborresearch.org/charts.php?id=34,* June 3, 2006.

21. For a discussion on the reasons for this smaller public sector union impact, see Lewin et al., *Public Sector Labor Relations: Analysis and Readings* (Glen Ridge, N.J.: Thomas Horton and Daughters, 1977).

22. Kris Maher, "Unions Struggle to Retain Strength," *The Wall Street Journal,* September 16, 2005, p. A6.

23. Joseph Szczesny, "Delphi, Visteon Get UAW Concessions," *www.thecarconnection.com/index.asp?article=7099,* June 7, 2006.

24. Bureau of Labor Statistics, "Employer Costs for Employee Compensation Summary," Table 7: Private industry, by region and bargaining status," *stats.bls.gov/news.release/ecec.nr0.htm,* March 28, 2006.

25. Bureau of Labor Statistics, "Employer Costs for Employee Compensation Summary, Table 7: Private industry, by major occupational group and bargaining status," December 2008, *http://www.bls.gov/news.release/ecec.nr0.htm,* retrieved on January 29, 2009; Bureau of Labor Statistics, "Employer Costs for Employee Compensation Summary, Table 5: Private industry, by major occupational group and bargaining status," December 2008, *http://www.bls.gov/news.release/ecec.nr0.htm,* January 29, 2009.

26. Ibid.

27. Loren Solnick, "Unionism and Fringe Benefits Expenditures," *Industrial Relations* 17(1) (1978), pp. 102–107.

28. Robert Snell, "Buyouts at GM Open Door for Hiring at Lower Wages," *Detroit News,* March 27, 2009, p. A1.

29. The Labor Research Association, "Two-Tier and Lump Sum Contracts Reappear," *www.laborresearch.org/page_src.php?id=372˜src=Two%20tier,* June 5, 2006.

30. James E. Martin and Thomas D. Heetderks, *Two Tier Compensation Structures: Their Impact on Unions, Employers and Employees* (Kalamazoo, MI: Upjohn Institute for Employment Research, 1990).

31. Mollie Bowers and Roger Roderick, "Two-Tier Pay Systems: The Good, the Bad, and the Debatable," *Personnel Administrator* 32(6) (1987), pp. 101–112.

32. James Martin and Melanie Peterson, "Two-Tier Wage Structures: Implications for Equity Theory," *Academy of Management Journal* 30(2) (1987), pp. 297–315.

33. Ann C. Foster, "Union-nonunion Wage Differences, 1997," *Compensation and Working Conditions,* 2006, p. 46.

34. Alexander J. Colvin, Rosemary Batt, and Harry Katz, "How High Performance Human Resource Practices and Workforce Unionization Affect Managerial Pay," *Personnel Psychology* 54(4) (2001), pp. 903–927.

35. Ibid.

36. Richard B. Freeman and Joel Rogers, *What Workers Want* (Ithaca, NY: ILR Press, 1999); David Neumark and Michael L. Wachter, "Union Effects on Nonunion Wages: Evidence from Panel Data on Industries and Cities," *Industrial and Labor Relations Review* 31(1) (1978), pp. 205–216.

37. J. L. McAdams and E. J. Hawk, *Organizational Performance and Reward: 663 Experiences in Making the Link* (Scottsdale, AZ: American Compensation Association, 1994).

38. L. B. Cardinal and I. B. Helbrun, "Union Versus Nonunion Attitudes Toward Share Agreements," in *Proceedings of the 39th Annual Meeting of the Industrial Relations Research Association* (Madison, WI: IRRA, 1987), pp. 167–173.

39. R. L. Heneman, C. von Hippel, D. E. Eskew, and D. B. Greenberger, "Alternative Rewards in Union Environments," *ACA Journal,* Summer 1997, pp. 42–55.

40. Paulette Chu, "Court Says Delphi Can Offer Employees $35,000 to Retire," *The Associated Press State & Local Wire,* April 7, 2006, *www.ap.org/pages/indnews,* June 1, 2006.

41. "Southwest Air, Agents' Union Reach an Accord," *The Wall Street Journal,* December 26, 2002.

42. R. L. Heneman and C. von Hippel, "Alternative Rewards in Unionized Environments," *ACA Journal* 6 (1995), pp. 42–55.

43. T. Ross and R. Ross, "Gainsharing and Unions: Current Trends," in B. Graham-Moore and T. Ross, eds., *Gainsharing: Plans for Improving Performance* (Washington, DC: Bureau of National Affairs), pp. 200–213.

44. J. Zalusky, "Labor's Collective Bargaining Experience with Gainsharing and Profit Sharing," paper presented at the 39th Annual Meeting of the Industrial Relations Research Association, December 1986, pp. 175–182; William Shaw, "Can Labor Be Capitalized?" *American Federationist* 17 (June 1910), p. 517.

45. Dong-One Kim, "Determinants of the Survival of Gainsharing Programs," *Industrial and Labor Relations Review* 53(1) (1999), pp. 21–42.

46. "Chrysler Workers to Get Profit-Sharing Checks Averaging $650," *The Associated Press State & Local Wire,* February 16, 2006, *www.ap.org/pages/indnews,* June 3, 2006.

International Pay Systems

Chapter Outline

The Global Context

The Social Contract
  Centralized or Decentralized Pay-Setting
  Regulation

Culture
  Culture Matters, But So Does Cultural
  Diversity

Trade Unions and Employee
Involvement

Ownership and Financial Markets

Managerial Autonomy

Comparing Costs
  Labor Costs and Productivity
  Cost of Living and Purchasing Power

Comparing Systems
  The Total Pay Model: Strategic Choices

National Systems: Comparative
Mind-Set

Japanese Traditional National System
German Traditional National System
Strategic Comparisons: Traditional
Systems in Japan, Germany, United States
Evolution and Change in the Traditional
Japanese and German Models

Strategic Market Mind-Set
  Localizer: "Think Global, Act Local"
  Exporter: "Headquarters Knows Best"
  Globalizer: "Think and Act Globally and
  Locally"

Expatriate Pay
  Elements of Expatriate Compensation
  The Balance Sheet Approach
  Expatriate Systems → Objectives? Quel
  dommage!

Borderless World → Borderless Pay?
Globalists

Your Turn: IBM's Worldwide
Business Employment Strategies and
Compensation

All around the world, decentralized pay-setting competitive forces have changed the way people work and how they get paid.[1] Toyota and other Japanese companies have dismantled their seniority-based pay systems for managers and replaced them with merit-based systems.[2] Toshiba offers stock awards, which were not even legal in Japan only a few years ago.[3] Deutsche Bank, Nokia, Seimens, and other European companies are shifting to variable pay and performance-based (rather than personality-based) appraisal in their search for ways to improve productivity and control labor costs.[4]

Global acquisitions of former competitors change pay systems. As part of its takeover and restructuring of Tungsram Electric in Poland, General Electric changed from a rigid seniority-based pay system to broad bands, market-based wage rates, and performance bonuses. India's leading software companies such as Tata Consulting Services, Wipro, and Infosystems all use performance-based bonus plans for their software engineers. Prior to Daimler's acquisition of Chrysler in 1998, the pay for Chrysler's CEO was equal to the combined total pay of the top 10 Daimler executives.

As little as 25 percent of Chrysler managers' total compensation was in the form of base pay, whereas Daimler managers' base pay accounted for up to 60 percent of their total compensation. The merged DaimlerChrysler adopted a Chrysler-like approach to executive compensation. Some have even claimed that the attractive pay was the reason Daimler executives were eager to acquire Chrysler![5]

This merger, described by some as a "marriage made in hell," ended unhappily after 10 years (but presumably Daimler executives got to keep the "engagement ring" of higher pay).[6] One might also say that Daimler in particular had "hell to pay" to get out of the marriage. Daimler paid $36 billion for Chrysler in 1998, but received only $7.4 billion in 2006 when it sold 80.1 percent of Chrysler to Cerberus Capital Management.[7] As part of Chrysler's recent bankruptcy, Daimler appears to have received nothing for its remaining stake. Rather, it had to write off $1.5 billion in loans it made to Chrysler in 2008 and also had to make a payment of $600 million to Chrysler's pension plan.[8] Daimler will not be having bouts of nostalgia looking back at its marriage with Chrysler. Perhaps Daimler and Chrysler underestimated the challenges posed by the differences in contextual factors of the sort we highlight in this chapter. Any merger or acquisition, even between companies in the same country, has challenges. Adding an international component adds another layer of challenges.[9] Nevertheless, another suitor has burst onto the scene. Now, the Italian carmaker, Fiat, has acquired 20 to 35 percent ownership in Chrysler. Although Fiat is more similar (basic vehicles) than Daimler (high-end vehicles) to Chrysler in some ways, it is more similar to Daimler in its experience on a number of the other factors we will discuss in this chapter (ownership structure, regulation, trade union experience, social contract).[10] It will be very interesting to see whether things work out better the second time around for a Chrysler merger with a European company that is used to operating in a different context.[11]

Sometimes changes in pay are directly tied to cataclysmic sociopolitical change, as in China, Russia, and eastern Europe, where government authorities had long dictated pay rates.[12] Now companies in these countries face the challenge of devising pay systems responsive to business and market pressures while maintaining a sense of social justice among the people. In China, the only hope for profitability in many state-owned enterprises is to cut the massively bloated head count. Yet an army of unemployed people without social support is a threat to government survival.[13] Some state-owned enterprises, such as Baogang, the country's largest steelmaker, have moved to more "market- and performance-based" systems, even though labor markets are just emerging in many regions in China. Shanghai Shenyingwanguo Security Company and Shanghai Bank have implemented job-based structures to help them retain key employees and increase pay satisfaction. Most surprising of all is that some town-owned enterprises are using stock ownership as part of their employee compensation.[14] China may still be striving to become a worker's paradise, but the experimentation with compensation approaches might already qualify it as a pay pundit's paradise.

However, too much change and experimentation can have a dark side that threats to create social unrest. Following the breakup of the USSR, workers in some of the formerly socialist countries reported going unpaid for months. At one point over half the Russian workers said they were owed back wages, with the average wait to be paid at 4.8 months.[15] A friend in Russia maintains that "the most effective pay delivery system is a brown bag under the table."

So it is a time of unprecedented global change. Or is it? Let's step back to gain some historical perspective:

There is hardly a village or town anywhere on the globe whose wages are not influenced by distant foreign markets, whose infrastructure is not financed by foreign capital, whose engineering, manufacturing, and even business skills are not imported from abroad, or whose labor markets are not influenced by the absence of those who had emigrated or by the presence of strangers who had immigrated.[16] This is not a description of the 21st century. Rather, it is from 100 years ago. In the late 1800s, trade barriers were being reduced, free trade was being promoted, and mass migration of people was underway. Thanks to transoceanic telegraphic cables, the speed of communication had increased dramatically, and investment capital flowed among nations. Yet by 1917 these global links had been replaced with a global war. Citizens desired security rather than face the greater risks and uncertainty of globalization. Nations began to raise tariffs to protect domestic companies hurt by foreign competitors. Immigrants were accused of "robbing jobs." Historians conclude that "globalization is neither unique nor irreversible; it has and can again sow seeds of its own destruction."[17]

THE GLOBAL CONTEXT

Understanding international compensation begins with recognizing differences and similarities and figuring out how best to manage them. How people get paid around the world depends on variations shown in Exhibit 16.1— *economic, institutional, organizational,* and *employee characteristics.* These factors have been discussed throughout the book; now they can be applied globally. But once we shift from a domestic to an international perspective, the discussion must necessarily broaden.

Organizations must first determine the degree to which each of these contextual factors constrain their compensation decisions and practices. Some constraints are regulatory (i.e., laws), while others may be more normative (national culture, the social contract).[18] In some cases (e.g., laws/regulations), there may be little room to exercise strategy.[19] On the other hand, in the case of other contextual factors (e.g., national culture), the constraint may be less than often believed.[20] So, to be sure, there are differences, on average, between organizations, depending on the country.[21] However, there is also evidence that different management approaches are used within the same country.[22] To the degree that strategy can be exercised, an organization must decide the degree to which it will choose compensation practices similar to those used by other organizations and the degree to which it will be different. Being the same is perhaps less risky, but, by necessity, following the pack means there is little chance to stand out from the pack and thus little chance to achieve anything better than average performance.[23] Also, in the international context, it is not always simple to follow the pack. A multinational enterprise (MNE) having the United States as its home country may see a typical way of doing things there, but may see a different typical way of doing things in another country where it operates. If they want to play follow the pack or follow the leader, which do they follow? (There seem to be a lot of metaphors available here! Bonus points for you if you can name the group that sang "Leader of the Pack." Double bonus points if you can name the most well-known sound effect in the song's performance and in which country the song was banned from the airwaves.) Evidence

EXHIBIT 16.1 **The International Context of Compensation**

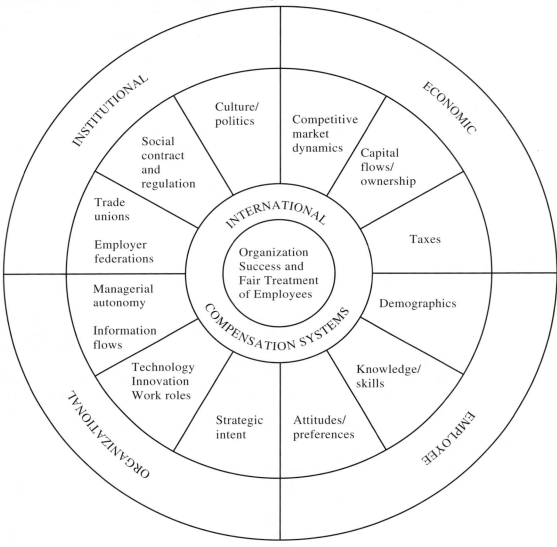

Source: © George T. Milkovich.

indicates that MNCs are influenced by both the institutional pressures in their home country and in the local context.[24] To follow the (leader, pack, herd, lemmings, you choose), companies must balance pressures toward localization ("when in Rome . . .")— where compensation practice is tailored to each country—and standardization (where consistency, not with the local context, but instead with the organization's business strategy, is the objective).[25]

In the following discussion, we highlight five specific, contextual factors we feel are especially relevant in international compensation. These are variations in (1) social contracts, including the legal framework and regulation; (2) cultures; (3) trade unions; (4) ownership and financial markets; and (5) managers' autonomy. Although we separate the factors to clarify our discussion, they do not separate so easily in reality. Instead, they overlap and interact.

THE SOCIAL CONTRACT

Viewed as part of the social contract, the employment relationship is more than an exchange between an individual and an employer. It includes the government, all enterprise owners (sometimes acting individually and sometimes collectively through owner associations), and all employees (sometimes acting individually and sometimes in trade unions). The relationships and expectations of these parties form the social contract. As you think about how people get paid around the world, it will be clear that different people in differnt countries hold differing beliefs about the role of government, employees, unions, and employers. Understanding how to manage employee compensation in any country requires an understanding of the social contract in that country. Changing employee compensation systems—for example, to make them more responsive to customers, encourage innovative and quality service, or control costs— require changing the expectations of parties to the social contract.

The social contract evolves over time, sometimes very quickly. One need look no further than the United States for recent examples. Compared to many countries (e.g., those in the European Union), government has traditionally played a relatively modest role in the employment relationship. However, that role has recently greatly expanded, at least in two key sectors of the U.S. economy: automobiles and financial services. Consider that Chrysler and General Motors (GM) have recently gone through bankruptcy and when they exit, their major shareholders will be the United Automobile Workers (UAW) union and the U.S. government (in return for the many billions in funds it has provided to stave off liquidation). At the new GM, the U.S. government will have a 60 percent ownership stake, the UAW 17.5 percent, and the Canadian government, 12 percent. In the case of Chrysler, the UAW will have a 55 percent ownership stake, the U.S. government 8 percent, and the Canadian government 2 percent. Finally, as noted earlier, Fiat, the Italian car maker, will have a 20 to 35 percent ownership stake. (Fiat hopes to have more success with its ownership stake in Chrysler than did Daimler-Benz, the German carmaker.) In the financial services industry, the U.S. government also played a major role recently in saving firms, either by providing funds (e.g., Citibank, Goldman Sachs, Capital One, and many others) under the Troubled Assets Relief Program (TARP) or by actively facilitating mergers and acquisitions (e.g., Bank of America's acquisition of Merrill Lynch). The TARP program in the United States provided $700 billion (in return for warrants enabling the U.S. government to buy stock in the companies), an amount roughly the same as the total economic output (gross domestic product) of Turkey, the 17th largest economy in the world. As one of the "strings attached" to the TARP funds, the U.S. Treasury Department has issued special executive compensation regulations for firms while they have TARP funding (see Chapter 17). In summary, the social contract in the United States, known for the small role of government and the lack of a tripartite relationship between government, employees (and their representatives), and employers, has done a rapid "about face," at least in two of its major industries. While this government involvement and tripartism is seen as temporary, the question is whether this model will become the norm in the United States for handling future crises of this sort.

Centralized or Decentralized Pay-Setting

Perhaps the most striking example of the social contract's effects on pay systems is in Exhibit 16.2, which contrasts the degree of centralization of pay setting among countries.[26] Companies in the United States, United Kingdom, and some central European countries use highly decentralized approaches with little government involvement. In contrast, in western and northern European countries, wage bargaining is more likely to be centralized, taking place primarily at the industry or national level, with government involvement being typical in national-level bargaining countries.

Although understanding differences in wage bargaining levels is important, it should also be understood that things continue to evolve.[27] For example, not so long ago, countries like the Czech Republic and Sweden would have been placed in the national level bargaining group in Exhibit 16.2. Japan, not included in Exhibit 16.2, has become more decentralized in its wage bargaining.[28] Also, even where bargaining is primarily centralized, there is also typically bargaining at other levels.[29] Likewise, there may be exceptions, under particular circumstances, that permit companies to deviate from the centralized agreement. Thus, differences across countries in the degree of pay-setting centralization translate, but not perfectly, into differences in wage flexibility. Such flexibility is generally desirable to employers who do not want to be "locked in" to a particular wage level when product market conditions (i.e., level and

EXHIBIT 16.2
The Social Contracts and Primary Bargaining Level in Selected European Union Countries and the United States

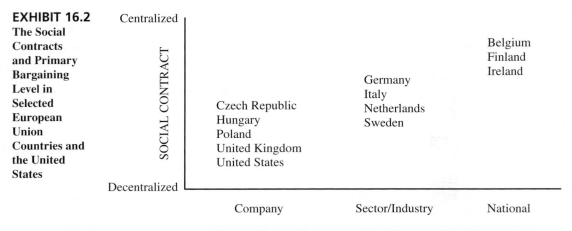

Source: European Industrial Relations Observatory Online, "Changes in National Collective Bargaining Systems Since 1990," 2005, http://www.eurofound.europa.eu/eiro/, June 30, 2009.

EXHIBIT 16.3   **Flexibility of Wage Determination**

7 = up to each individual company,
1 = set by a centralized bargaining process

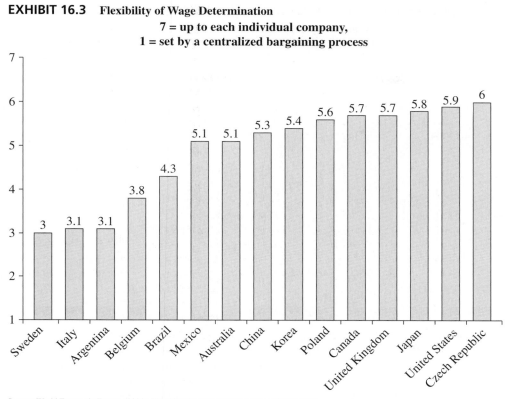

Source: World Economic Forum. (2008). The Global Competitiveness Report 2008-2009.

growth of sales and profits) are in flux. Exhibit 16.3 shows judgments of wage flexibility gathered from an international sample of executives. We can see that countries with more centralized bargaining levels (e.g., Belgium, Germany, Sweden, Italy) generally have less wage flexibility, while countries with more decentralized bargaining (e.g., Poland, Czech Republic, United States) generally have higher wage flexibility, as do the Asian countries included.

Regulation

The social compact also relates to the legal/regulatory environment for human resource decisions in each country. The country differences in wage flexibility relate not only to degree of bargaining centralization, but also to regulatory restrictions such as maximum hours of work. The European Union Working Time Directive limits the workweek to no more than 48 hours. Currently, the United Kingdom continues to successfully have an opt-out exception to the Directive. Other countries such as France have gone the opposite direction, experimenting with a 35-hour workweek, which was

EXHIBIT 16.4 **Legal Restrictions on Hiring and Firing Workers**

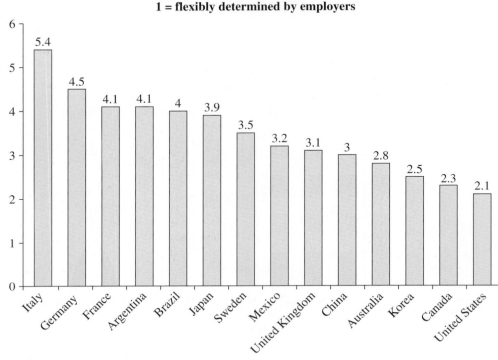

7 = impeded by regulations,
1 = flexibly determined by employers

Source: World Economics Forum, *The Global Competitiveness Report 2008-2009©*, 2008.

in effect from 1998 until 2008.[30] In contrast, in countries like Japan, the United States, and the United Kingdom, there is no maximum work week and, as we saw, wage flexibility is high. In fact, Britain, requires no overtime premium and has also has no works council requirement.

Another indicator of employment regulation (i.e., restriction on flexibility) is the degree of legal restriction in hiring and firing workers. As shown in Exhibit 16.4, employers in the United States have more flexibility than employers in the European Union, South America, and Japan. Interestingly, Korea and China are not so different from the United States. As a final example of how the legal framework comes into play and affects employer flexibility, consider the role of works councils and co-determination in a European country like Germany.[31] A works council may be formed by employees in any business unit having five or more permanent employees. It operates separately from the trade union and collective bargaining process (although works council members are often union members) and may not, for example, call a strike. In general, the German works council deals with issues of a collective nature (i.e., that affect two or more employees). It has rights to information and consultation in these matters. In the area of compensation, consider that:

> the employer must obtain the consent of the Works Council on collective rules regarding criteria to be applied for determining wages and salaries of all employees, the implementation of systems that classify wages according to performance or time spent (e.g., bonus schemes), the mode of payment, and the method of determining criteria for pension rights.[32]

An employer must consult the Works Council and give it an opportunity to respond prior to taking actions in the area of compensation as well as in a wide range of other human resource and operational areas. The Works Council has "veto-rights and rights of consent" including "the right to block management decisions until an agreement is reached or a decision by the labour court is taken overruling the veto."[33]

In addition, the co-determination law in Germany requires that in companies with 500 to 2000 employees, one-third of the supervisory board (akin to the board of directors in a United States company) must be employee representatives. In companies with over 2000 employees, one-half of the board must be composed of employee representatives. However, there is not true parity here because shareholders elect the chairperson, who has the power to cast a tie-breaking vote.[34] By way of contrast, neither works councils or co-determination are legally required in the United States and are quite rare. Clearly, an employer from the United States that becomes an employer in Germany will find that things work very differently.

In Europe, like in the United States, laws can also vary within countries. Further, there are also, as we have seen, directives that apply across countries such as that dealing with working time in the European Union (EU). Another EU directive gives employees the right to information and consultation on company decisions in companies having 1,000 or more employees, including 150 or more in at least two member countries through the establishment of a European works council. Thus, a company operating in multiple EU countries might have consultation obligations with a works council in each country as well as a European works council. The EU has a goal of providing common labor standards in all its member countries. The purpose of standards is to avoid "social dumping," or the relocation of a business in a country with lower standards and labor costs. At present, average hourly labor costs vary substantially among the EU countries, sometimes in countries right next door, such as Germany, which, as we saw in Chapter 1, has much higher labor costs than Poland.

Finally, the social compact in Europe, with its regulatory and institutional limits on employer flexibility and protection of workers, comes at a cost. A longstanding literature seeks to determine whether more generous worker protection (e.g., unemployment benefits) undermines incentives for workers to put forth effort on the job (as efficiency wage theory would suggest) and look for work (thus resulting in higher unemployment rates and higher public expenditures). Here, we will simply look at how expenditures vary across countries, as well as how taxes, which of course are needed to fund such expenditure, also vary. Exhibit 16.5 shows that the tax burden in countries like Germany and France is about 70 percent higher than in the United States, Canada,

EXHIBIT 16.5   Combined Employer-Employee Tax Rate on Wages

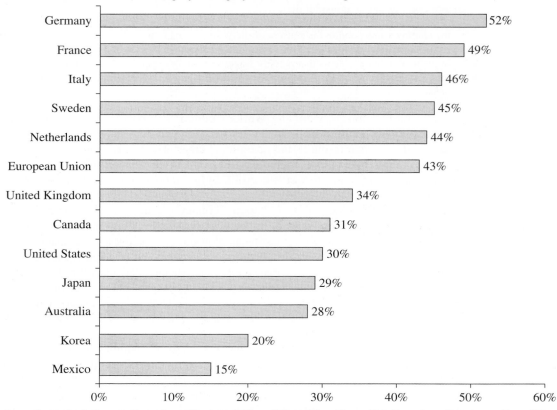

Source: Organization for Economic Cooperation and Development; Marcus Walker and Roger Thurow, "U.S., Europe Are an Ocean Apart on Human Toll of Joblessness," *Wall Street Journal*, May 7, 2009; Includes personal income tax, and unemployment disability, and health insurance, using income level of average worker.

Australia, and Japan. One purpose of these higher taxes is to help insulate workers from income losses due to unemployment. As Exhibit 16.6 indicates, Germany, as well as some other EU countries, spends nearly 10 times as much as the United States on unemployment benefits. Consider that the gross domestic product of the United States in recent years has been around $14 trillion. Spending 0.24 percent of that on unemployment benefits works out to roughly $34 billion per year. If, however, it spent 2.16 percent, as in Germany, it would be about $306 billion per year.

CULTURE

Culture is defined as shared mental programming which is rooted in the values, beliefs, and assumptions held in common by a group of people and which influences how information is processed.[35] The assumption that pay systems must be designed to fit different *national cultures* is based on the belief that most of a country's inhabitants share

EXHIBIT 16.6   **Expenditures on Unemployment Benefits as a Percent of Gross Domestic Product**

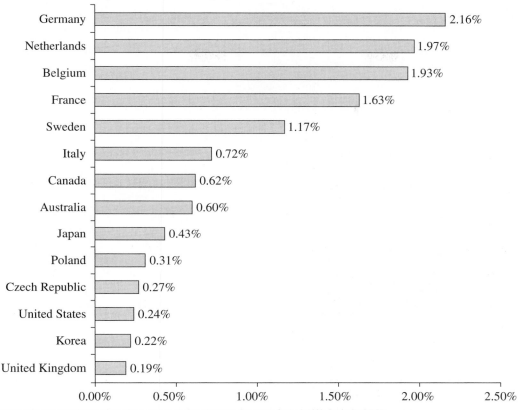

Source: Organisation for Economic Co-operation and Development. Economic Outlook 2007. Brussels: OECD.

a national character. The job of the global manager, according to this assumption, is to define the national characteristics that influence pay systems. Typical of this thinking is the widely used list of national cultural attributes proposed by Hofstede (power distance, individualism–collectivism, uncertainty avoidance, and masculinity–femininity).[36] (See Exhibit 16.7.) Advocates of this view believe that "it is crucial that companies adjust their compensation practices to the cultural specifics of a particular host country."[37] Accordingly, in Malaysia and Mexico, where the culture is alleged to emphasize respect for status and hierarchy (high power distance), hierarchical pay structures are appropriate. In low-power-distance nations such as Australia and the Netherlands, egalitarianism is a better approach.[38]

Advice can get even more specific. Companies operating in nations with supposedly "collectivistic" cultures, such as Singapore, Japan, Israel, and Korea, should use egalitarian pay structures, equal pay increases, and group-based rather than individual-based

EXHIBIT 16.7   Hofstede's National Culture Dimensions and Scores for Four Countries

Hofstede Culture Dimensions	United States	Germany	China	Japan
Power Distance The extent to which the less powerful members of organizations and institutions accept and expect that power is distributed unequally.	Low (40)	Low (35)	High (80)	Medium (54)
Uncertainty Avoidance The extent to which a culture programs its members to feel either uncomfortable or comfortable in unstructured situations. Unstructured situations are unknown, surprising, different from usual and societies differ in the degree to which they try to control the uncontrollable.	Low (46)	Medium (65)	Medium (60)	High (92)
Individualism On the one side versus its opposite, collectivism, it is the degree to which individuals are supposed to look after themselves or remain integrated into groups, usually around the family.	High (91)	High (67)	Low (20)	Medium (47)
Masculinity versus Femininity This refers to the distribution of emotional roles between the genders; it opposes 'tough' masculine to 'tender' feminine societies. Masculine societies emphasize assertiveness, performance, and competition.	High (62)	High (66)	Medium (50)	High (95)
Long-Term versus Short-term Orientation This refers to the extent to which a culture programs its members to accept delayed gratification of their material, social, and emotional needs.	Low (29)	Medium (31)	High (118)	High (80)

Source: G. Hofstede, "Cultural Constraints in Management Theories," *Academy of Management Executive,* 7 (1993) pp. 81–94; G. Hofstede, G., *Culture's Consequences: Comparing Values, Behaviors, Institutions, and Organizations Across Nations,* 2nd edition (Thousand Oaks, CA: Sage, 2001), pp. xix–xx.

performance incentives. Employers in the more "individualistic" national cultures, such as the United States, United Kingdom, and Hong Kong, should use individual-based pay and performance-based increases.[39]

But such thinking risks stereotyping.[40] The question is not, What are the cultural differences among nations? Rather, the question is, Which culture matters?[41] Any group of people may exhibit a shared set of beliefs. Look around your college or workplace; engineers, lawyers, accountants, and technicians may each share some beliefs and values. Employees of organizations may, too. Your school's culture probably differs from Microsoft's, Toshiba's, or the London Symphony Orchestra's. You may even have chosen your school because of its culture. However, you are likely part of many cultures. You are not only part of your university but also part of your family, your social/political/interest groups, your region of the state or country, and so on. Cultures may be similar or different among all these categories.

Culture Matters, But So Does Cultural Diversity

Culture classifiers consider the United States a country of risk takers who rank high on the individualistic (rather than collectivistic) scale. In contrast, the country of Slovenia has been classified as more collectivistic and security-conscious (as opposed to risk taking).[42] Slovenia was the first country to break off from the former Yugoslavia. (How is that for taking a risk?) It has a population of less than 3 million and by most standards would be

EXHIBIT 16.8
Understanding the "Full House" of Variation Within a Culture

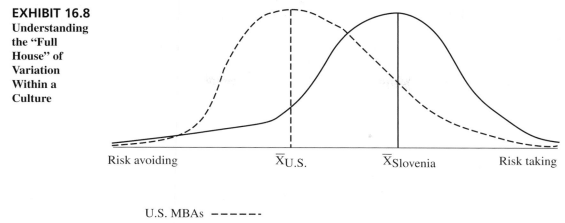

Risk avoiding $\overline{X}_{U.S.}$ $\overline{X}_{Slovenia}$ Risk taking

U.S. MBAs   − − − − − ·
Slovenian MBAs   ————

considered very homogeneous. So you might expect Slovenian managers to be very different from U.S. managers. However, a study found that Slovenian managers tended, on average, to be more risk taking and individualistic than U.S. managers. The most striking finding, as shown in Exhibit 16.8, was that the degree of variation among managers on cultural dimensions was virtually the same in both the Slovenian and the U.S. data. Thus, one can find risk-averse collectivists and risk-taking individualists in both nations.[43]

Indeed, re-analysis of data from Hofstede's seminal work on national differences in culture finds that the variance between individuals within countries is far larger than the variance between countries.[44] In other words, knowing what country someone is from tells us much less than the national culture literature seems to suggest.

So how useful is the notion of a *national* culture when managing international pay? In the absence of better data on variations such as those in Exhibit 16.8, it may offer a starting point. However, *it is only a starting point.* National culture can be thought of as the "average" in Exhibit 16.8. It provides some information about what kinds of pay attitudes and beliefs you are likely to find in an area. But overreliance on the "average" can seriously mislead. This point is critical for managing international pay.

To claim that all organizations and people within Germany or within China share a certain mind-set ignores variations and differences within each nation, and reviews of empirical work bear out the fact that differences in worker preferences across countries (including China and the United States) for the use of performance-based pay, for example, tend to be small in practical terms.[45] Again, country is just too rough of a proxy to use in making compensation decisions. Considerable diversity among companies and people within any country exists. The Chinese computer company Lenovo, which purchased IBM's PC division, illustrates the point. Throughout its short history, Lenovo has relied heavily upon government support. Yet Lenovo's approach to compensating employees does not reflect widely held beliefs about Chinese national culture. (Go to *geert-hofstede.international-business-center.com/* for Hofstede's description of Chinese national culture.) For example, the CEO uses 20 percent of the company's profits to award high-performing employees with "special merit" bonuses. Pay differentials among jobs, which in 1990 were 2 to 1, are now up to 30 to 1. Most amazing is a benefits plan in which individual employees select the specific benefits that best meet their personal preferences. All this diversity in a company in which the Chinese government still owns controlling interest!

So keep in mind our basic premise in this chapter: The interplay among economic, institutional, organizational, and individual conditions within each nation or region, taken as a whole, forms distinct contexts for determining compensation. Understanding these factors in the global guide is useful for managing employee compensation. However, do not assume uniformity (the average) within a country. Understanding the full range of individuals within nations is even more important.[46]

So how may understanding cultural diversity within a nation matter to global pay? Perhaps with an eye to attracting and motivating those risk-taking, entrepreneurial Slovenians, a multinational firm may use performance bonuses, stock awards, and hierarchical pay structures rather than simply matching the "average" Slovenian culture.

TRADE UNIONS AND EMPLOYEE INVOLVEMENT

Europe remains highly unionized: In Sweden, 71 percent of the workforce belongs to unions; in the United Kingdom, 28 percent; and in Italy, 33 percent. Asia is less heavily unionized. Japan's unionization rate is 18 percent, and South Korea's is around 10 percent. In some countries, workers' pay is set by collective agreements even though the workers may not be union members. In France, for example, more than 90 percent of workers are covered by collective agreements, even though fewer than 10 percent are union members.[47] In addition to having higher rates of unionization, as we have seen, workers in countries like Germany have the right to establish works councils, which must be involved in any changes to a pay plan.[48]

OWNERSHIP AND FINANCIAL MARKETS

Ownership and financing of companies differ widely around the world. These differences are important to international pay. In the United States, corporate ownership and access to capital is far less concentrated than in most other countries. Fifty percent of American households own stock in companies either directly or indirectly through mutual funds and pension funds.[49] Direct stock ownership is only a few mouse clicks away. In Korea, six conglomerates control a significant portion of the Korean economy, and the six are closely linked with specific families. In Germany, the national Bundesbank and a small number of other influential banks have ownership interests in most major companies. These patterns of ownership make certain types of pay systems almost nonsensical because ownership in the companies is not readily available for individual investors. For example, linking performance bonuses to increased shareholder value or offering stock options to employees makes little sense in the large conglomerates in Germany, Korea, and Japan. However, ownership in small start-ups in the nations is outside the traditional channels, so these firms do offer stock options to attract new employees.[50] Recent tax law changes in many countries have made stock options more attractive, but limited ownership of many companies remains the rule.

The most vivid illustrations of the importance of ownership occur in China and in eastern Europe (Poland, Hungary, Slovenia, Czech Republic, and Slovakia), where a variety of forms are emerging. While state-owned enterprises still employ two-thirds of all workers in China, township enterprises, wholly privately owned enterprises, joint ventures with foreign companies, and wholly owned foreign enterprises (WOFEs) account for 50 percent of the profits. Chinese employees switching from government-owned enterprises to these newer organizations find that both the pay and the employer expectations (i.e., the social contract) are substantially different.[51] Individuals attracted to work in these various enterprises have different values and expectations. One study found that those working for local or town-owned enterprises prefer more performance-based pay than those working in federal-owned enterprises.[52] Many families find it makes sense to have one wage earner working at a safe but low-paying government enterprise and another wage earner working at a private enterprise where expectations and pay are high. So it is clear that ownership differences may influence what forms of pay make sense. It is very misleading to assume that every place is like home.

MANAGERIAL AUTONOMY

Managerial autonomy, an organizational factor in the global guide in Exhibit 16.1, refers to the degree of discretion managers have to make total compensation a strategic tool. It is inversely related to the degree of centralization and regulatory intensity discussed earlier. Thus, most U.S.- and U.K.-based organizations have relatively greater freedom to relative change employee pay practices or to hire and downsize than do most European companies. As already noted, the centralized pay setting found in European Union countries limits organizations' autonomy to align pay to business strategies and changing market conditions.[53] Volkswagen AG, which is trying to reduce labor costs to better compete with Toyota and others, must negotiate changes with both IG Metall, a powerful trade union, and also with a federal labor agency.[54] Works councils also have information and consultation rights. In contrast, in Singapore the National Wage Council issues guidelines that are voluntary (e.g., "Wage freezes for most companies," "Emphasize variable and performance-based pay"). Most government organizations adhere to these guides, but private organizations do so to varying degrees.[55]

> **Cybercomp**
> A good source of free information on labor laws throughout the world is the NATLEX database produced by the International Labor Organization (ILO): *natlex.ilo.org.*

Governments and trade unions are not the only institutions to limit managerial autonomy. Corporate policies often do so as well. Compensation decisions made in the home-country corporate offices and exported to subunits around the world may align with the corporate strategy but discount local economic and social conditions. While IBM corporate in Armonk, New York, expects all its worldwide operations to "differentiate people on performance" with total compensation, some IBM units in Tokyo remain convinced that Japanese IBMers in Japan prefer more egalitarian practices.[56] Nevertheless, managers are expected to comply with Armonk.

In sum, as the global guide depicts, international compensation is influenced by economic, institutional, organizational, and individual conditions. Globalization really means that these conditions are changing—hence international pay systems are changing as well.

COMPARING COSTS

In Chapter 8, we discussed the importance of obtaining accurate information on what competitors pay in domestic markets. Similar comparisons of total compensation among nations can be very misleading. Even if wage rates appear the same, expenses for health care, living costs, and other employer-provided allowances complicate the picture. Outside the United States, many nations offer some form of national health care. An organization may pay for it indirectly through payroll taxes, but since all people in a nation share similar coverage, its value as part of total compensation is diminished.

Comparisons between a specific U.S. firm and a specific foreign competitor may be even more misleading. Accurate data are usually difficult to obtain. While consulting firms are improving their global data collection, much of their data is still from U.S. companies' operations in global locations. Other foreign and local-national companies' data are often not available. Thus, international data may be biased toward U.S. companies' practices.[57]

Labor Costs and Productivity

Nevertheless, substantial differences in (average) labor costs do exist and companies may find that it makes sense to move or grow employment in lower cost countries if productivity can be maintained at a workable level. In Chapter 1, for example, we saw that hourly wages for Mexican manufacturing work ($2.92) are about 12 percent of those paid in the United States ($24.59). China's estimated $0.81 per hour is about 3 percent of the U.S. rate. Productivity in China is about 6 percent of that of U.S. workers, while Mexican worker productivity is 22 percent of the U.S. level. Based on those numbers, the average loss in productivity is more than offset by the labor cost savings. Of course, most companies are not average and so each has to do its own analysis of the pros and cons of where to locate employment, as we discussed in Chapter 7. Also, while differences in labor costs are often the impetus to do the analysis, many other factors must be considered.

Consider the case of a small custom software company in the midwest that provides high end web applications to meet clients' core business needs (e.g., online registration or customer service). It sets up longstanding web development teams to provide client support on an ongoing basis. The engineering work (software coding, architecture, testing, graphics production, database) is all done in a former Soviet Bloc country in Eastern Europe. Some employees work in teams that write HTML code (which tells web browsers how to present a page). New college graduates are hired at a rate of about $6,000 per year, with more senior team leads earning up to $15,000 per year. (We suspect that many readers of this book expect to make considerably more than that upon graduating from college.) Other employees, software engineers, with 2 to 4 years of experience, and writing applications in more complex languages, earn $10,000 per year, with the more senior and most highly skilled engineers earning $22,000 to $30,000 per year. You may wish to compare these salaries to those we saw in Chapter 8 for engineers (and programmers). There, we saw that an engineer fresh out of college could expect about $60,000 per year and more senior engineers could advance to earning well over $100,000 per year. Thus, the labor cost savings for this midwest customer software company were too large to ignore. Of course, it is not quite that simple. In a global market, some of the very best engineering talent from Eastern Europe migrates to where it can command higher pay and be at the epicenter of the most exciting work being done (e.g., Silicon Valley in California). Thus, the productivity of the company's engineers in Eastern Europe is not as high. That is not necessarily a problem if the work to be done is relatively routine and not oriented toward innovation. What about setting up a team several time zones and a 16- to 20-hour roundtrip away? This company's experience has been that it can take 6 months to a year to get off the ground and fine tune. Other differences are harder to quantify. Former Soviet Bloc countries do not have the same consumer/marketing oriented culture as in the United States—until recently, you did not have multiple options when it came to toothpaste, apartments, cars, and so forth. So the underlying shared experiences and knowledge that you might find among U.S. engineers may not exist. Think of someone who has never had a credit card. How would a software engineer go about designing an online shopping experience without an inherent understanding of credit cards and comparison shopping?

Cost of Living and Purchasing Power

If comparing total compensation is difficult, comparing living costs and standards across borders is even more complex. (Recall our discussion of the limitations of the CPI for wage setting in Chapter 8.) However, companies need such data to adjust pay for employees who transfer among countries. The objective is to maintain the same level of *purchasing* power.[58] Exhibit 16.9, provides several types of relevant data for this purpose. In the first two columns are cost of living indices (based on the cost of a basket of goods and services), with the cost of rent either excluded or included. With the cost of rent included, Jakarta's cost of living is 45.9 percent of New York, whereas London is 20.2 percent more expensive than New York. Thus, to maintain the purchasing power of an expatriate from New York moving to London, additional compensation must be provided beyond that paid in New York. In contrast, a move to Jakarta from New York at New York pay levels would provide an economic windfall. The third column, purchasing power, divides average hourly earnings by the cost of living in each city and then standardizes that as a percentage of New York. Purchasing power in Jakarta is 18.1 percent of that in New York, while in London it is 91.5 percent of New York. Thus, paying the prevailing local compensation to an expatriate in these cities would result in a decline in their cost of living relative to what it would be getting paid the prevailing rate of pay in New York. So, again, using the example of an expatriate moving from New York to London, paying the person at the local London level of compensation would result in a decrease in purchasing power. Paying a New York–based expatriate in Jakarta at the local level would result in a

EXHIBIT 16.9   Cost of Living, Domestic Purchasing Power, and Minutes of Working Time Required to Buy a Big Mac, Bread, and Rice

Source: UBS, "Prices and Earnings" May 2008, www.ubs.org

City	Cost of Living* (w/o rent) (New York = 100)	Cost of Living* (w/ rent) (New York = 100)	Domestic Purchasing Power** (New York = 100)	Minutes of Working Time Required to Buy:		
				Big Mac***	1 kg of bread***	1 kg of bread***
Amsterdam	104	86	101	19	10	9
Athens	89	70	85	26	10	20
Auckland	88	72	122	14	13	5
Bangkok	64	47	27	67	49	22
Barcelona	99	80	102	21	16	10
Beijing	55	43	30	44	42	29
Berlin	98	76	129	17	10	17
Bogota	67	49	32	97	59	25
Bratislava	68	54	50	55	21	20
Brussels	106	82	114	20	12	12
Bucharest	64	54	30	69	31	25
Budapest	78	62	41	48	14	24
Buenos Aires	45	34	57	56	18	24
Caracas	82	69	33	85	76	13
Chicago	92	82	115	12	18	10
Copenhagen	130	103	111	18	12	6
Dehli	51	41	23	59	22	36
Dubai	82	73	88	25	11	12
Dublin	123	105	126	15	7	9
Frankfurt	103	83	124	16	9	17
Geneva	115	96	136	16	10	7
Helsinki	117	93	117	19	17	9
Hong Kong	81	72	49	17	26	11
Istambul	95	77	41	48	14	36
Jakarta	52	46	18	86	47	36
Johanesburg	58	46	78	30	12	11
Kiev	57	48	27	55	19	21
Kuala Lumpur	41	31	69	33	21	9
Lima	54	39	46	86	37	19
Lisbon	87	75	62	32	20	10
Ljubljana	80	60	60	35	37	30
London	126	120	92	16	5	5
Los Angeles	92	81	120	11	18	10
Luxembourg	112	92	131	17	14	12
Lyon	104	79	106	24	15	15
Madrid	98	81	98	19	15	8
Manama	64	55	70	24	28	22
Manila	58	43	23	81	64	29
Mexico City	61	49	29	82	53	22

City	Cost of Living* (w/o rent) (New York = 100)	Cost of Living* (w/rent) (New York = 100)	Domestic Purchasing Power** (New York = 100)	Minutes of Working Time Required to Buy:		
				Big Mac***	1 kg of bread***	1 kg of bread***
Miami	89	73	102	12	20	11
Milan	99	81	87	20	17	15
Montreal	99	80	110	17	17	9
Moscow	82	71	44	25	12	12
Mumbai	46	50	22	70	14	32
Munich	105	85	120	17	11	15
Nairobi	57	46	28	91	32	33
New York	100	100	100	13	16	8
Nicosia	89	79	105	19	19	8
Oslo	144	112	117	18	14	6
Paris	114	93	88	21	16	13
Prague	71	56	62	39	14	14
Riga	72	55	38	28	24	23
Rio de Janeiro	78	67	39	53	40	19
Rome	97	81	73	25	23	19
Santiago de Chil	69	60	44	56	32	21
Sao Paolo	79	65	55	38	30	11
Seoul	88	76	67	29	28	13
Shanghai	55	43	36	38	35	23
Singapore	86	71	64	22	26	10
Sofia	66	53	25	69	19	31
Stockholm	118	91	102	21	18	15
Sydney	96	82	117	14	15	5
Taipei	68	56	77	20	18	11
Tallinn	80	63	46	39	24	21
Tel Aviv	81	65	—	—	—	—
Tokyo	108	94	95	10	16	12
Toronto	100	80	114	14	10	6
Vienna	113	88	111	16	13	10
Vilnius	63	48	42	43	18	24
Warsaw	82	64	39	43	17	18
Zurich	120	98	144	15	10	5

*Cost of standard basket of 122 goods and services without rent and with rent included.
**Hourly wage for 14 professions divided by cost of standard basket of 122 goods and services.
***Price of product divided by hourly wage for 14 professions.

serious decline in living standard. The final three columns take a slightly different approach to comparing purchasing power by estimating the amount of work time it takes, given the prevailing rate of pay and cost of living, to buy three different "staples." In the case of a Big Mac, a New Yorker must work 13 minutes. In sharp contrast, a person in Jakarta would have to work 86 minutes.

COMPARING SYSTEMS

We have made the points that pay systems differ around the globe and that the differences relate to variations in economic pressures, sociopolitical institutions, and the diversity of organizations and employees. In this section we compare several compensation systems. The caution about stereotyping raised earlier applies here as well. Even in nations described by some as homogeneous, pay systems differ from business to business. For example, two well-known Japanese companies, Toyota and Toshiba, have designed different pay systems. Toyota places greater emphasis on external market rates, uses far fewer levels in its structure, and places greater emphasis on individual-based merit and performance pay than does Toshiba. So as we discuss "typical" national systems, remember that differences exist and that change in these systems is occurring everywhere.

The Total Pay Model: Strategic Choices

The total pay model used throughout the book guides our discussion of pay systems in different countries. You will recognize the basic choices, which seem universal:

- Objectives of pay systems
- External competitiveness
- Internal alignment
- Employee contributions
- Management

While the choices may be universal, the results are not.

NATIONAL SYSTEMS: COMPARATIVE MIND-SET

A national system mind-set assumes that most employers in a country adopt similar pay practices. Understanding and managing international compensation then consists mainly of comparing the Japanese to the German to the U.S. or other national systems. This method may be useful in nations with centralized approaches (see Exhibit 16.8). Some even apply it to regional systems, as in the "European Way," the "Asian Way," or the "North American Way."[59] We describe the Japanese and German national systems below. But we cannot say this often enough: The national or regional mind-set overlooks variations among organizations within each nation. Thus, we refer to the national systems below as the "traditional" systems, to emphasize that this is one country model in each but not the only one.

Japanese Traditional National System

Traditionally, Japan's employment relationships were supported by "three pillars":

1. Lifetime security within the company.
2. Seniority-based pay and promotion systems.
3. Enterprise unions (decentralized unions that represent workers within a single company).

Japanese pay systems tend to emphasize the person rather than the job; seniority and skills possessed rather than job or work performed; promotions based on a combination of supervisory evaluation of trainability, skill/ability levels, and performance rather than on performance alone; internal alignment over competitors' market rates; and employment security based on the performance of the organization and the individual (formerly lifetime security). Japanese pay systems can be described in terms of three basic components: base pay, bonuses, and allowances/benefits.[60]

Base Pay

Base pay accounts for 60 to 80 percent of an employee's monthly pay, depending on the individual's rank in the organization. Base pay is not based on job evaluation or market pricing (as predominates in North America), nor is it attached to specific job titles. Rather, it is based on a combination of employee characteristics: career category, years of service, and skill/performance level.

Career   Five career categories prevail in Japan: (1) general administration, (2) engineer/scientific, (3) secretary/office, (4) technician/blue-collar job, and (5) contingent.

Years of Service   Seniority remains a major factor in determining base pay. Management creates a matrix of pay and years of service for each career category. Exhibit 16.10 shows a matrix for general administration work. Companies meet periodically to compare their matrixes, a practice that accounts for the similarity among companies. In general, salary increases with age until workers are 50 years old, when it is reduced. Employees can expect annual increases no matter what their performance level until age 50, although the amount of increase varies according to individual skills and performance.

Skills and Performance   Each skill is defined by its class (usually 7 to 13) and rank (1 to 9) within the class. Exhibit 16.11 illustrates a skill salary chart for the general administration career category. Classes 1 and 2 typically include associate (entry) and senior associate work; 2, 3, and 4, supervisor and managerial; 5, 6, and 7, managerial, general director, and so on. Employees advance in rank as a result of their supervisor's evaluation of their:

- Effort (e.g., enthusiasm, participation, responsiveness).
- Skills required for the work (e.g., analytical, decision making, leadership, planning, process improvement, teamwork).
- Performance (typical MBO-style ratings).

EXHIBIT 16.10
Salary and Age Matrix for General Administration Work in a Japanese Company

Age*	Salary†	Age	Salary	Age	Salary	Age	Salary
		31	$1,900	41	$2,900	51	$3,800
22	$1,000	32	2,000	42	3,000	52	3,700
23	1,100	33	2,100	43	3,100	53	3,600
24	1,200	34	2,200	44	3,200	54	3,500
25	1,300	35	2,300	45	3,300	55	3,400
26	1,400	36	2,400	46	3,400	56	3,300
27	1,500	37	2,500	47	3,500	57	3,200
28	1,600	38	2,600	48	3,600	58	3,100
29	1,700	39	2,700	49	3,700	59	3,000
30	1,800	40	2,800	50	3,800	60	2,900

*Age 22 is typical entry with college degree.
†Monthly salary, converted to dollars.

EXHIBIT 16.11   **Skill Chart for General Administration Work in Japan**

	Associate	Senior Associate	Supervisor		Manager	General Director	
	Class 1	Class 2	Class 3	Class 4	Class 5	Class 6	Class 7
Rank 1	$ 600	$1,600	$2,600	$3,100	$3,600	$4,500	$5,500
Rank 2	700	1,700	2,650	3,150	3,750	4,700	6,000
Rank 3	800	1,800	2,700	3,200	3,800	4,900	
Rank 4	900	1,900	2,750	3,250	3,900	5,100	
Rank 5	1,000	2,000	2,800	3,300	4,000		
Rank 6	1,100	2,100	2,850	3,350	4,100		
Rank 7	1,200	2,200	2,900	3,400			
Rank 8	1,300	2,300	2,950	3,450			
Rank 9	1,400	2,400	3,000	3,500			

To illustrate how the system works, say you are a graduate fresh from college who enters at class 1, rank 1. After one year, you and all those hired at the same time are evaluated by your supervisors on their effort, abilities, and performance. Early in your career (the first three years) effort is more important; in later years abilities and performance receive more emphasis. The number of ranks you move each year (and therefore your increase in base pay) depends on this supervisory rating (e.g., receiving an A on an appraisal form lets you move up three ranks within the class, a B moves you two ranks, and so on).

Theoretically, a person with an A rating could move up three ranks in class each year and shift to the next class in three years. However, most companies require both minimum and maximum years of service within each class. So even if you receive four A ratings, you would still remain in class 1 for the minimum of six years. Conversely, if you receive four straight D grades, you would still get promoted to the next skill class after spending the maximum number of years in class 1. Setting a minimum time in each class helps ensure that the employee knows the work and returns value to the company. However, the system slows the progress of high-potential performers. Additionally, even the weakest performers eventually get to the top of the pay structure, though they do not get the accompanying job titles or responsibility. The system reflects the traditional Japanese saying, "A nail that is standing too high will be pounded down." An individual employee will not want to stand out. Employees work to advance the performance of the group or team rather than themselves.

Under the traditional Japanese system, increases in annual base pay are a bit smaller (7 percent in our example of superior performance, compared to 8 to 10 percent for star performers in many U.S. merit systems), although they compound over time, just like conventional merit and across-the-board increases in the United States. However, since the Japanese system is so seniority-based, labor costs increase as the average age of the workforce increases. In fact, a continuing problem facing Japanese employers is the increasing labor costs caused by the cumulative effects of annual increases and lifetime employment security. Early retirement incentives and "new jobs" with lower salaries are being used to contain these costs.[61]

Bonuses

Bonuses account for between 20 and 40 percent of annual salary, depending on the level in the organization. Generally, the higher up you are, the larger the percent of annual salary received as bonus. Typical Japanese companies pay bonuses twice a year (July and December). The bonuses are an *expectable* additional payment to be made twice a year, even in bad financial times. They are not necessarily related to performance.

> **Cybercomp**
> U.S. consulting firms are entering the Japanese market to provide HR consulting services for firms in Japan. For example, the Unifi Tokyo office has an English Web site *(www.unifinetwork.co.jp/html/index_eng.htm)*. Go to this Web site to see how it describes Japanese pay systems.

The amount of bonuses is calculated by multiplying employees' monthly base pay by a multiplier. The size of the multiplier is determined by collective bargaining between employers and unions in each company. Sometimes the multiplier may also vary according to an employee's performance evaluation. In a recent year, the average multiplier was 4.8 (2.3 in summer and 2.5 in winter) for white-collar workers. So an individual whose monthly base pay is $4,500 would receive a bonus of $10,350 in July and $11,250 in December.

According to the Japan Institute of Labour, for most employees (other than managers) bonuses are in reality variable pay that helps control the employer's cash flow and labor costs but are not intended to act as a motivator or to support improved corporate performance. Japanese labor laws encourage the use of bonuses to achieve cost savings by omitting bonuses from calculations of many other benefit costs (i.e., pension plan, overtime pay, severance pay, and early retirement allowances).

The timing of the bonuses is very important. In Japan both the summer festival and the new year are traditional gift-giving times; in addition, consumers tend to make major purchases during these periods. Employees use their bonuses to cover these expenses. Thus, the tradition of the bonus system is deeply rooted in Japanese life and is today considered an indispensable form of pay.

Benefits and Allowances

The third characteristic of Japanese pay systems, the allowance, comes in a variety of forms: family allowances, commuting allowances, housing and geographic differential allowances, and so on. Company housing in the form of dormitories for single employees or rent or mortgage subsidies is a substantial amount. Life-passage payments are made when an employee marries or experiences a death in the immediate family. Commuting allowances are also important. One survey reported that employees who took public transportation received about 9,000 yen (approximately $90) per month for commuting.

Family allowances vary with number of dependents. Toyota provides about 17,500 to 18,000 yen ($175 to $180) a month for the first dependent and about 4,500 to 5,500 yen ($45 to $55) for additional dependents. Some employers even provide matchmaking allowances for those who tire of life in company dorms.

Legally Mandated Benefits   Legally mandated benefits in Japan include social security, unemployment, and workers' compensation. Although these three are similar to the benefits in the United States, Japanese employers also pay premiums for mandated health insurance, preschool child support, and employment of the handicapped.

German Traditional National System

Traditional German pay systems are embedded in a social partnership between business, labor, and government that creates a generous *vater staat,* or "nanny state."[62] *Vergutung* is the most common German word for "compensation." Pay decisions are highly regulated; over 90 different laws apply. Different **tariff agreements** (pay rates and structures) are negotiated for each industrial sector (e.g., banking, chemicals, metals, manufacturing) by the major employers and unions. Thus, the pay rates at Adam Opel AG, a major car company, are quite similar to those at Daimler, Volkswagen, and any other German car company. Methods for job evaluation and career progression are included in the tariff agreements. However, these agreements do not apply to managerial jobs. Even small organizations that are not legally bound by tariffs tend to use them as guidelines.

Base Pay

Base pay accounts for 70 to 80 percent of German employees' total compensation depending on their job level. Base pay is based on job descriptions, job evaluations, and employee age. The tariff agreement applicable to Adam Opel AG, for example, sets the following *tariff groups* (akin to job families and grades):

Wage earners	8 levels (L2–L9)
Salary earners	6 administrative levels (K1–K6)
	6 technical levels (T1–T6)
	4 supervisory levels (M1–M4)

Generally, a rate will be negotiated for one of the levels, for example, K2 and the other levels in that group will be calculated as a percentage of the negotiated rate.

Cybercomp

A number of Web locations offer currency conversions to change euros into U.S. dollars, Canadian dollars, Hong Kong dollars, and any number of other currencies. Try *www.xe.com* or *www.globaldevelopment.org* over a period of several weeks to appreciate the complexity that currency conversion adds to managing compensation.

Bonuses

While there is a trend toward performance-based bonuses, they have not been part of a traditional German pay system for unionized workers. However, Adam Opel AG's tariff agreement stipulates that an average of 13 percent of the total base wages must be paid as "efficiency allowances." Systems for measuring this efficiency are negotiated with the works councils for each location. In reality, the efficiency allowances become expected annual bonuses. Performance bonuses for managerial positions not included in tariffs are based on company earnings and other company objectives. Currently only about one-third of top executives receive stock options.

Allowances and Benefits

As discussed, Germany's social contract includes generous social benefits.[63] These nationally mandated benefits, paid by taxes levied on employers and employees, include liberal social security, unemployment protection, health care, nursing care, and other programs. Employer and employee contributions to the social security system can add up to more than one-third of wages. Additionally, companies commonly provide other benefits and services such as pension plans, savings plans, building loans, and life insurance. Company cars are always popular. The make and model of the car and whether or not the company provides a cell phone are viewed as signs of status in an organization. German workers also receive 30 days of vacation plus about 13 national holidays annually (compared to an average of 11 holidays in the United States).

Strategic Comparisons: Traditional Systems in Japan, Germany, United States

As we have emphasized, speaking of *the* German, Japanese, or U.S. system is too simplistic, as there are important variations between firms within each country. Nevertheless, in looking at the average firm in each country. Japanese and German traditional systems reflect different approaches compared to U.S. pay systems. Exhibit 16.12 uses the basic choices outlined in the total pay model—objectives, internal alignment, competitiveness, and contributions—as a basis for comparisons. Both the Japanese and the German sociopolitical and culture systems constrain organizations' use of pay as a strategic tool. German companies face pay rates, job evaluation methods, and bonuses identical to those of their competitors, set by negotiated tariff agreements. The basic strategic premise, that competitive advantage is sustained by aligning with business strategy, is limited by laws and unions. Japanese companies do not face pay rates fixed industrywide; rather, they voluntarily meet to exchange detailed pay information. However, the end result appears to be the same: similar pay structures across companies competing within an industry. In contrast, managers in U.S. companies possess considerable flexibility to align pay systems with business strategies. As a result, greater variability exists among companies within and across industries.

The pay objectives in traditional German systems include mutual long-term commitment, security, egalitarian pay structures, and cost control through tariff agreements, which apply to competitors' labor costs too. Japanese organizations set pay objectives that focus on the long term (age and security), support high commitment (seniority-based/ability-based), are also more egalitarian, signal the importance of company and individual performance, and encourage flexible workers (person-based pay). U.S. companies, in contrast, focus on the shorter term (less job security); are market-sensitive (competitive total pay); emphasize cost control (variable pay based on performance); reward performance improvement, meritocracy, and innovation (individual bonuses and stock, etc.); and encourage flexibility.

EXHIBIT 16.12 Strategic Similarities and Differences: An Illustrated Comparison

	Japan	United States	Germany
Objectives	Long-term focus High commitment Egalitarian—internal fairness Flexible work force Control cash flow with bonuses	Short/intermediate focus High commitment Peformance—market—meritocratic Flexible work force Cost control; varies with performance	Long-term focus High commitment Egalitarian—fairness Highly trained Cost control through tariff negotiations
Internal alignment	Person based: age, ability, performance determines base pay Many levels Small pay differences	Work based: jobs, skills, accountabilities Fewer levels Larger pay differences	Work based: jobs and experience Many levels Small pay differences
External competitiveness	Monitor age-pay charts Consistent with competitors	Market determined Compete on variable and performance-based pay	Tariff based Same as competitors
Employee contribution	Bonuses vary with performance only at higher levels in organization Performance appraisal influences promotions and small portion of pay increases	Bonuses an increasing percentage of total pay Increases based on individual, unit, and corporate performance	Tariff negotiated bonuses Smaller performance bonuses for managers
Advantages	Supports commitment and security Greater predictability for companies and employees Flexibility—person based	Supports performance—competitor focus Costs vary with performance Focus on short-term payoffs (speed to market)	Supports commitment and security Greater predictability for companies and employees Companies do not compete with pay
Disadvantages	High cost of aging work-force Discourages unique contributors Discourages women and younger employees	Skeptical workers, less security Fosters "What's in it for me?" No reward for investing in long-term projects	Inflexible; bureaucratic High social and benefit costs Not a strategic tool

In Japan, person-based factors (seniority, ability, and performance) are used to set base pay. Market comparisons are monitored in Japan, but internal alignment based on seniority remains far more important. Job-based factors (job evaluation) and seniority are also used in Germany. Labor markets in Germany remain highly regulated, and tariff agreements set pay for union workers. So, like the Japanese system, the German system places much greater emphasis on internal alignment than on external markets.

Each approach has advantages and disadvantages. Clearly, the Japanese approach is consistent with low turnover/high commitment and high security, greater acceptance of change, and the need to be flexible. U.S. firms face higher turnover and greater skepticism about change. U.S. firms encourage innovation; they also recognize the contributions to be tapped from workforce diversity. German traditional systems tend to be more bureaucratic and rule-bound. Hence, they are more inflexible. However, they also offer more stability. Both the Japanese and the German national systems face challenges from the high costs associated with an aging workforce. Japan has taken very limited advantage of women's capabilities. The U.S. challenges include the impact of increased uncertainty that employees face, the system's short-term focus, and employees' skepticism about continuous change.

> **Cybercomp**
> Discussing national systems in other countries in the same detail as we do here for the Japanese and German systems would require another textbook. More information on these and other countries can be found easily on the Web. Some useful Web sites for starting your search are provided by:
> > Economist Intelligence Unit (EIU):
> > *countrydata.bvdep.com/ip* (EIU country reports)
> > *www.ebusinessforum.co* (Ebusiness Forum)
> > Federation of European Employers:
> > *www.euen.co.uk/condits.html* (Report on Pay and Working Conditions across Europe)
> > Trak-it-Down: *www.trak-it-down.com/InterHR.htm* (list of international HR sites, updated regularly)

Evolution and Change in the Traditional Japanese and German Models

The slow economic growth that Japan has experienced combined with the emphasis in its traditional model on seniority-based pay creates a challenge in controlling labor costs. At the same time, cheaper labor in emerging Asian countries (e.g., China) puts further pressure on controlling labor costs and/or increasing productivity. Faced with these pressures, many companies are trying to maintain *long-time employment* (rather than **lifetime employment**) and are looking for other ways to reward less senior employees. These younger employees, who have been paid relatively poorly under the seniority-based pay system, are increasingly finding alternative job opportunities in non-Japanese firms operating in Japan, which have in the past rewarded individual ability and performance

EXHIBIT 16.13

Use of Performance (Versus Seniority) in Compensation Decisions

Source: Markus Pudelko, "The Seniority Principle in Japanese Companies: A Relic of the Past?" *Asia Pacific Journal of Human Resources* 44, pp. 276–294.

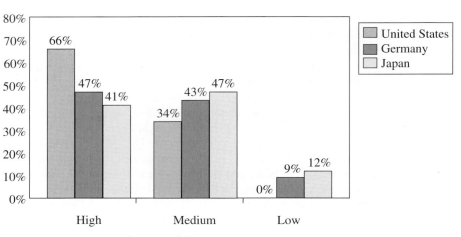

Emphasis on Performance (Versus Seniority)

more strongly.[64] To compete, companies such as Toyota, Toshiba, and Mitsubishi are increasingly using performance-based pay. As a result, more variation in pay systems has emerged among traditional Japanese companies.[65] As Exhibit 16.13 shows, 41 percent of Japanese companies now report that they place a high emphasis on performance in compensation decisions.[66] Only 12 percent report that performance receives a low emphasis. Other evidence reports that 57 percent of Japanese firms now use merit pay and 21 percent have "eliminated" seniority-based pay and many more report that they "plan" to reduce its importance.[67] Likewise, Exhibit 16.14 shows that Japan is similar to other countries such as the United States in its degree of performance-based differentiation in the merit increase process. Thus, the Japanese model has moved closer to the U.S. model in some key ways.[68]

Turning to Germany, it is no longer all traditional manufacturing, machine tools, and BMW. It has over half of the top Internet companies in Europe. And nearly one in five German adults own stock—double the rate in the late 1990s. Many of the changes are the result of global competitive pressures and technological changes. Like many advanced economies, Germany, along with a number of other Western European countries, faces serious challenges. An aging population, low birth rates, earlier retirement ages, and high pension and unemployment benefits are pushing up the costs of the social support system. A relatively inflexible labor market means that employers are finding it easier to move to (or expand in) other EU countries (e.g., just across the border to countries like Poland where labor costs are much lower) as well as to China and India. All these factors are causing a rethinking of the traditional German social contract and the resulting total compensation systems. Companies are asking for greater autonomy in negotiating tariff agreements to better reflect each company's economic conditions, the use of performance-based pay, and ways to link job security to company performance.

A number of studies report substantial changes in the traditional German model, including greater use of pay for performance, similar to the shifts seen in Japan. Again, foreign multinationals have played some part.[69] As Exhibit 16.13 indicates,

EXHIBIT 16.14   Merit Pay Increase for Top Performer Versus Average Performer, by Country

Country	Number of Companies	Type of Employee	Top Performer	Average Performer	Top/Average Ratio[a]
United Kingdom	152	Professional/Technical	8.2%	4.1%	2.0
China	332	Junior Manager/ Supervisor/Professional	17.8%	8.6%	2.1
Japan	115	Professional/Technical	6.4%	4.3%	1.5
Germany	127	Professional/Technical	8.3%	3.6%	2.3
United States	774	All Employees			1.0 to 1.5

Source: Hewitt Associates, Salary Increase Survey 2008 and 2009 for each country shown.

[a]Merit increase for top performers divided by merit increase for average performers for all countries but United States. For United States, merit increases not reported separately by performance. Instead, companies reported most typical ratio of merit increases for top and average performers.

47 percent of German companies now report that performance is highly emphasized in compensation decisions and only 9 percent report that it receives little emphasis. Exhibit 16.13 shows that performance is one of the most important factors in promotion decisions as well. Exhibit 16.4 demonstrates further that the magnitude of merit pay increases for top versus average performers is similar in Germany, China, the United States, and the United Kingdom, with Japan being somewhat different. Finally, the use of stock options in Germany has gone from near zero in 1990 (prior to the lifting of legal restrictions in 1998) to being commonplace in large firms.[70]

STRATEGIC MARKET MIND-SET

A global study of pay systems used by companies with worldwide operations identifies three general compensation strategies: (1) localizer, (2) exporter, and (3) globalizer.[71] These approaches reflect the company's business strategy.[72]

Localizer: "Think Global, Act Local"

If a localizer operates in 150 countries, it may have 150 different systems. The company's business strategy is to seek competitive advantage by providing products and services tailored to local customers. Localizers operate independently of the corporate headquarters. One manager compared his company's pay system this way: "It's as if McDonald's used a different recipe for hamburgers in every country. So, too, for our pay system." Another says, "We seek to be a good citizen in each nation in which we operate. So should our pay system." The pay system is consistent with local conditions.

Exporter: "Headquarters Knows Best"

Exporters are virtual opposites of localizers. Exporters design a total pay system at headquarters and "export" it worldwide for implementation at all locations. Exporting a basic system (with some adjustments for national laws and regulations) makes it easier to move managers and professionals among locations or countries without having to change how they are paid. It also communicates consistent corporatewide objectives. Managers say that "one plan from headquarters gives all managers around the world a common vocabulary and a clear message about what the leadership values." Common software used to support compensation decisions and deployed around the world makes uniform policies and practices feasible. However, not everyone likes the idea of simply implementing what others have designed. One manager complained that headquarters rarely consulted managers in the field: "There is no notion that ideas can go both ways. It's a one-way bridge."

Globalizer: "Think and Act Globally and Locally"

Similar to exporters, globalizers seek a common system that can be used as part of the "glue" to support consistency across all global locations. But headquarters and the operating units are heavily networked to share ideas and knowledge. Managers in these companies said:

> "No one has a corner on good ideas about how to pay people. We need to get them from all our locations."

> "'Home country' begins to lose its meaning; performance is measured where it makes sense for the business, and pay structures are designed to support the business."

> "Compensation policy depends more on tax policies and the dynamics of our business than it does on 'national' culture. The culture argument is something politicians hide behind."

Cybercomp

Go to the Organization Resources Counselors' International Web site, *www.orcin.com,* to observe a state-of-the-art global market site. ORCI collects data from Azerbaijan, Belarus, and other central and eastern European locations as well as Latin America. How useful do you think its data would be for making pay decisions? What limitations exist? Compare the ORCI Web site with another consulting company's Web site. Critique each site.

Some believe the globalizer is the business model for the 21st century. IBM, for example, calls itself a "globally integrated enterprise." The aim is for all its operations, from production to marketing to R&D to be integrated around the world.[73] They continue to compete as multinationals. The point is that rather than emphasizing national pay systems as the key to international compensation, the three strategic **global approaches** focus first on the global business strategy and then adapt to local conditions. The upcoming "Your Turn" contrasts different perspectives on global corporations.

EXPATRIATE PAY

Multinationals operate, by definition, in many nations. Employees temporarily working and living in a foreign country are called **expatriates** (or "expats"). One key decision for companies is the degree of reliance on expatriates relative to local employees.[74]

- Expatriates who are citizens of the employer's parent or home country and living and working in another country (e.g., a Japanese citizen working for Toshiba in Toronto) are called parent-country nationals (PCNs).

- Expatriates who are citizens of neither the employer's parent country nor the foreign country where they are living and working (e.g., a German citizen working for Toshiba in Toronto) are called third-country nationals (TCNs).
- **Local country nationals (LCNs)** are citizens of a foreign country where the parent employer operates (e.g., a Canadian citizen working for Toshiba in Toronto).

Hiring LCNs has advantages. LCNs know local conditions and have relationships with local customers, suppliers, and government regulators. The company saves relocation expenses and the other often substantial expenses associated with the use of expatriates. It also avoids concerns about employees adapting to the local culture. Employment of LCNs satisfies nationalistic demands for hiring locals. Only rarely do organizations decide that hiring LCNs is inappropriate.

However, expats or TCNs may be brought in for a number of reasons.[75] The foreign assignment may represent an opportunity for selected employees to develop an international perspective; the position may be sufficiently confidential that information is entrusted only to a proven domestic veteran; or the particular skills required for a position may not be readily available in the local labor pool. Exhibit 16.15 catalogs a number of reasons for asking employees to take work assignments in another country.

EXHIBIT 16.15   **Why Expatriates Are Selected**

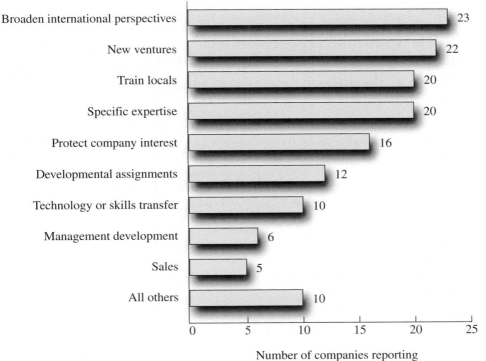

Number of companies reporting
(44 companies surveyed)

Designing expatriate pay is a challenge. A company that sends a U.S. employee (base salary of $80,000) with a spouse and two children to London for three years can expect to spend $800,000 to $1,000,000. Obviously, the high cost of expatriate assignments must be offset by the value of the employee's contributions.

Elements of Expatriate Compensation

"(W)e are becalmed. There has been little real innovation in the expatriate compensation field in years," according to a leading consultant.[76] We would add, "So much money, going to so many people, with so little evidence of added value." Exhibit 16.16 is a shopping list of items that can make up expatriate compensation. The list includes everything from household furnishing allowances to language and culture training, spousal employment assistance, and rest and relaxation leaves for longer-term assignments. Usually such lists are organized into four major components: salary, taxes, housing, and allowances and premiums.[77]

Salary

The base salary plus incentives (merit, eligibility for profit sharing, bonus plans, etc.) for expatriate jobs is usually determined via job evaluation or some system of "job leveling."[78] 3M applies a global job evaluation plan for its international assignments. Common factors describe different 3M jobs around the world. With this system, the work of a general manager in Brussels can be compared to the work of a manager in Austin, Texas, or in Singapore. General Mills has recently implemented a similar system.[79]

EXHIBIT 16.16   **Common Allowances in Expatriate Pay Packages**

Financial Allowances	Social Adjustment Assistance
Reimbursement for tax return preparation	Emergency leave
Tax equalization	Home leave
Housing differential	Company car/driver
Children's education allowance	Assistance with locating new home
Temporary living allowance	Access to western health care
Goods and services differential	Club membership
Transportation differential	General personal services (e.g., translation)
Foreign service premium	Personal security (manager and family)
Household furnishing allowance	General culture-transition training (manager)
Currency protection	Social events
Hardship premium	Career development and repatriation planning
Completion bonus	Training for local-culture customs (manager)
Family Support	Orientation to community (manager and family)
	Counseling services
Language training	Rest and relaxation leave
Assistance locating schools for children	Domestic staff (excluding child care)
Training for local culture's customs (family)	Use of company-owned vacation facilities
Child care providers	
Assistance locating spousal employment	

Beyond salaries and incentives, the intent of the other components is to help keep expatriate employees financially whole and minimize the disruptions of the move. This means maintaining a standard of living about equal to their peers in their home or base country. This is a broad standard that often results in very costly packages.

Taxes

Income earned in foreign countries has two potential sources of income tax liability.[80] With few exceptions (Saudi Arabia is one), foreign tax liabilities are incurred on income earned in foreign countries. For example, money earned in Japan is subject to Japanese income tax, whether earned by a Japanese or a Korean citizen. The other potential liability is the tax owed in the employee's home country. The United States has the dubious distinction of being the only developed country that taxes its citizens for income earned in another country, even though that income is taxed by the country in which it was earned. Most employers pay whatever income taxes are due to the host country and/or the home country via **tax equalization.**[81] Taxes are deducted from employees' earnings up to the same amount of taxes they would pay had they remained in their home country.

This allowance can be substantial. For example, the marginal tax rates in Belgium, the Netherlands, and Sweden can run between 70 and 90 percent. So if a Swedish expatriate is sent to a lower-tax country, say, Great Britain, the company keeps the difference. If a British expatriate goes to Sweden, the company makes up the difference in taxes. The logic here is that if the employee kept the windfall from being assigned to a low-tax country, then getting this person to accept assignments elsewhere would become difficult.

Housing

Appropriate housing has a major impact on an expatriate's success. Most international companies pay housing allowances or provide company-owned housing. **Expatriate colonies** often grow up in sections of major cities where many different international companies group their expatriates.

Allowances and Premiums

A friend in Moscow cautions that when we take the famed Moscow subway, we should pay the fare at the beginning of the ride. Inflation is so high there that if we wait to pay until the end of the ride, we won't be able to afford to get off! Cost-of-living allowances, club memberships, transportation assistance, child care and education, spousal employment, local culture training, and personal security are some of the many service allowances and premiums expatriates receive. The logic supporting these allowances is that foreign assignments require that the expatriate (1) work with less direct supervision than a domestic counterpart, (2) often live and work in strange and sometimes uncongenial surroundings, and (3) represent the employer in the host country. The size of the premium is a function of both the expected hardship and hazards in the host country and the type of job. An assignment in London will probably yield fewer allowances than one in Tehran, where Death to Americans Day is still a national holiday.

The Balance Sheet Approach

Most North American, European, and Japanese global firms combine these elements of pay in a **balance sheet approach.**[82] The name stems from accounting, where credits and debits must balance. It is based on the premise that employees on overseas assignments should have the same spending power as they would in their home country. Therefore, the home country is the standard for all payments. The objective is to:

1. Ensure mobility of people to global assignments as cost-effectively as feasible.
2. Ensure that expatriates neither gain nor lose financially.
3. Minimize adjustments required of expatriates and their dependents.

Notice that none of these objectives link (explicitly) to performance.

Exhibit 16.17 depicts the traditional balance sheet approach. Home-country salary is the first column. A person's salary (based on job evaluation, market surveys, merit, and incentives) must cover taxes, housing, and goods and services, plus other financial obligations (a "reserve").

The proportions set for each of the components in the exhibit are *norms* (i.e., assumed to be "normal" for the typical expatriate) set to reflect consumption patterns in the home country for a person at that salary level with that particular family pattern. They are not actual expenditures. These norms are based on surveys conducted

EXHIBIT 16.17
Balance Sheet
Approach

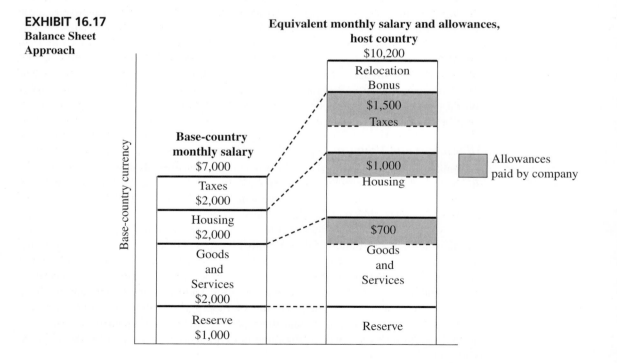

by consulting firms. Using the norms is supposed to avoid negotiating with each individual, although substantial negotiation still occurs.

Let us assume that the norms suggest that a typical manager with a spouse and one child, earning $84,000 ($7,000 per month) in the United States, will spend $2,000 per month on housing, $2,000 on taxes, and $2,000 on goods and services and put away a reserve of $1,000 per month. The next building block is the equivalent costs in the host country where the assignment is located. For example, if similar housing costs $3,000 in the host country, the expatriate is expected to pay the same $2,000 paid in the United States and the company pays the employee the difference; in our example, an extra $1,000 per month. In the illustration, the taxes, housing, and goods and services components are all greater in the host country than in the home country. The expatriate bears the same level of costs (white area of right-hand column) as at home. The employer is responsible for the additional costs (shaded area). (Changing exchange rates among currencies complicates these allowance calculations.)

However, equalizing pay may not motivate an employee to move to another country, particularly if the new location has less personal appeal. Therefore, many employers also offer some form of financial incentive or bonus to encourage the move. The right-hand column in Exhibit 16.17 includes a relocation bonus. Most U.S. multinational corporations pay relocation bonuses to induce people to take expatriate assignments.

If gaining international experience is really one of the future competencies required by organizations, then the need for such bonuses ought to be reduced, since the expatriate experience should increase the likelihood of future promotions. Either the experience expatriates obtain is unique to each situation and therefore not transferable or companies simply do not know how to value it. Whatever the reason, research reveals that **U.S. expatriates** feel their U.S. organizations still do not value their international expertise.[83] So the rhetoric of the value of global competencies has yet to match the reality—hence the need for relocation incentives. Another way to look at it is that the employee takes a risk going overseas. Near-term promotion opportunities may be lost. While international experience could have a handsome payoff in later promotions for some, this payoff is not certain and not true for all. Moreover, a nontrivial share of expatriate assignments are cut short, due either to performance problems or family-related problems (e.g., spouse and/or children having difficulties adapting).[84] Thus, consistent with our earlier discussion of agency theory, a compensating differential for risk may be required.

Alternatives to Balance Sheet Approach

Employers continue to explore alternatives to the balance sheet, due primarily to the cost. Although in Exhibit 16.10, the expatriate premium was 46 percent ($10,200/$7,000 − 1), that premium can be much higher. For example, Exhibit 16.18 shows survey data on the cost of a manager (married plus one child/dependent) with a U.S. salary of $116,000 posted to Singapore. The balance sheet approach cost ranged from a "budget package" cost of $260,000 to a "premium package" cost of $393,000,

EXHIBIT 16.18 Manager Working in Singapore or United States ("Married Plus One" Situation)

Type of Employee	Type of Approach	Net Pay (After taxes)	Percent Premium Relative to Pay in United States
Expatriate in Singapore	Balance Sheet Approach		
	Premium Package	$393,000	239%
	Standard Package	$312,000	169%
	Budget Package	$260,000	124%
Expatriate in Singapore	Local Plus Package	$247,000	113%
Local Employee in Singapore		$135,000	16%
Employee in United States		$116,000	

Source: Carole Mestre, Anne Rossier-Renaud, and Madeline Berger, "Better Benchmarks for Global Mobility." *Workspan*, April 2009.

or a 239 percent premium. The "standard package" was $312,000, a 169 percent premium and had the following components:

Home Net Base Salary	$115,500
Cost of Living Adjustment	$ 16,570
Mobility Premium	$ 16,570
Accommodation/Housing	$115,500
Car Benefit	$ 14,400
Education Benefit	$ 33,600
Total	$312,140

Negotiation simply means the employer and employee find a mutually agreeable package. The arrangements tend to be relatively costly (or generous, depending on your point of view), create comparability problems when other employees are asked to locate overseas ("but Mike and Sarah got . . ."), and need to be renegotiated with each transfer.

Another alternative, *localization,* or *local plus,* ties salary to the host country's salary scales and provides some cost-of-living allowances for taxes, housing, and dependents. The allowances tend to be similar to those under the balance sheet, but the salary can vary with the location. As Exhibit 16.18 shows, in the case of Singapore, the localization approach would, on average, result in a cost of $247,000, a 113 percent premium, in contrast to the premium of as much as 239 percent for the balance sheet approach.

While the balance sheet approach ties salary to the home country, the *modified balance sheet* ties salary to a region (Asia-Pacific, Europe, North America, Central America, or South America). The logic is that if an employee of a global business who relocates from San Diego, California, to Portland, Maine, receives only a moving allowance, why should all the extras be paid for international moves of far less distance (e.g., from Germany to Spain)? In Europe, many companies no longer view European managers who work outside their home country as expats. Instead, they are Europeans running their European businesses. And the use of a common currency, the euro, makes this easier. In this vein, a study compared the over-base pay allowance provided by 17 multinational companies to an employee earning 100,000 euros being transferred from Frankfurt, Germany to Paris, France.[85] The median premium was 23,000 euros, or 13 percent and the range was from as little as 5,000 euros, a 5 percent premium, to 45,000 euros, a 45 percent premium. Thus, in all 17 companies, the premium was modest relative to what we have seen.

Another common modification is to decrease allowances over time. The logic is that the longer the employee is in the host country, the closer the standard of living should come to that of a local employee. For example, if Americans eat a $10 pizza twice a week in the United States, should they eat a $30 pizza twice a week in Tokyo, at the employer's expense? More typically, after a couple of months, the expatriate will probably learn where the nationals find cheaper pizza or will switch to sushi. We had a friend posted to London by a U.S. company. The expatriate and spouse ate dinner out each night, leased a nice apartment in an upscale centrally located neighborhood, had a car, and the spouse went back to school. All this was paid for by the company, so the couple's entire paycheck went into the bank and investments. They were living in London with all expenses paid! When they had to eventually return to the United States, at the behest of the company, it was with great reluctance and after running out of extensions to the assignment.

The *lump-sum/cafeteria approach* offers expats more choices. This approach sets salaries according to the home-country system and simply offers employees lump sums of money to offset differences in standards of living. For example, a company will still calculate differences in cost of living, but instead of allocating them housing, transportation, goods and services, and so on, it simply gives the employee a total allowance. Perhaps one employee will trade less spacious housing for private schooling and tutors for the children; another employee will make different choices. We know of one expatriate who purchased a winery in Italy with his lump-sum allowance. He has been reassigned to Chicago but still owns and operates his winery.

Finally, a company can consider using fewer expatriates and more *local country nationals.* As we stated at the beginning of our discussion of expatriate pay, such a strategy has many advantages, including lower cost, and greater familiarity with the aspects of the business environment unique to that country. Another advantage is that such a strategy can be combined with a strategy of greater integration of talent into the career planning and development system. An increasing number of companies have foreign-born managers and executives in key posts. Some of these key people would not be where they are now making important contributions if they had not had the opportunity at some point to gain experience in key jobs in their home countries and then build on that to progress through the company's ranks.[86] Along these same lines, greater use of **third-country nationals (TCNs)** can also fit this strategy. In addition, TCNs can be less expensive if they come from countries having lower compensation levels. For example, whereas we saw in our earlier example that a U.S. expatriate earning $116,000 at home and posted to Singapore would cost $312,000, a comparable TCN from India posted to Singapore would cost $209,000.[87] In addition, given that the Indian TCN would earn $49,000 in India, the premium he or she would realize would be quite substantial and thus perhaps the assignment would have higher value than it would to a comparable expatriate from the United States.

Expatriate Systems → Objectives? *Quel dommage!*

Talk to experts in international compensation, and you soon get into complexities of taxes, exchange rates, housing differences, and the like. What you do not hear is how the expatriate pay system affects competitive advantage, customer satisfaction, quality, or other performance concerns. It does emphasize maintaining employee purchasing power and minimizing disruptions and inequities. But the lack of attention to aligning expatriate pay with organization objectives is glaring. Sadly, the major innovation in expat pay over the past decade seems to have been to relabel expats and TCNs as "international assignees."

Expatriate compensation systems are forever trying to be like Goldilocks' porridge: not too high, not too low, but just right. The expatriate pay must be sufficient to encourage the employee to take the assignment yet not be so attractive that local nationals will feel unfairly treated or that the expatriate will refuse any future reassignments. These systems also presume that expats will be repatriated to their home country. However, the relevant standard for judging fairness may not be home-country treatment. It may be the pay of other expats, that is, the expat community, or it may be local nationals. And how do local nationals feel about the allowances and pay levels of their expat co-workers? Very little research tells us how expats and those around them judge the fairness of expat pay.

Employee Preferences

Beyond work objectives, costs, and fairness, an additional consideration is employees' preferences for international assignments. For many Europeans, working in another country is just part of a career. Yet for many U.S. employees, leaving the United States means leaving the action. They may worry that expatriate experience sidetracks rather than enhances a career. Employees undoubtedly differ in their preferences for overseas jobs, and preferences can vary over time. Having children in high school or elderly parents to care for, divorce, working spouses, and other life factors exert a strong influence on whether an offer to work overseas is a positive or negative opportunity. Research does inform us of the following:

- 68 percent of expatriates do not know what their jobs will be when they return home.
- 54 percent return to lower-level jobs. Only 11 percent are promoted.
- Only 5 percent believe their company values overseas experience.
- 77 percent have less disposable income when they return home.
- Only 13 percent of U.S. expatriates are women. (Yet 49 percent of all U.S. managers and professionals are women.)
- More than half of returning expatriates leave their company within one year.[88] Unfortunately, while research does highlight the problem, it does not offer much guidance for designers of expat pay systems. Consequently, we are at the mercy of conjecture and beliefs.[89]

We should emphasize that, of course, some companies do a much better job of managing expatriates. Also, there is disagreement over what the evidence actually says on rates of success and failure of expatriates, especially those from the United States.[90]

BORDERLESS WORLD → BORDERLESS PAY? GLOBALISTS

Some corporations, particularly those attempting to become "globally integrated enterprises," are creating cadres of globalists: managers who operate anywhere in the world in a borderless manner. They expect that during their career, they will be located in and travel from country to country. According to a former CEO of General Electric, "The aim in a global business is to get the best ideas from everyone, everywhere." To support this global flow of ideas and people some companies are also designing borderless, or at least regionalized, pay systems. One testing ground for this approach is the European Union. As our global guide points out, one difficulty with borderless pay is that base pay levels and the other components depend too much on differences in each nation's laws and customs.

Focusing on expatriate compensation may blind companies to the issue of appropriate pay for employees who seek global career opportunities. Ignoring these employees causes them to focus only on the local operations, their home country pay, and devote less attention to integrating operations in global firms. It is naive to expect commitment to a long-term global strategy in which local managers have little input and receive limited benefits. Paradoxically, attempts to localize top management in subsidiaries may reinforce the differences in focus between local and global management.

Your **Turn** — IBM's Worldwide Business and Employment Strategies and Compensation

Read the description of IBM's worldwide business strategy in Exhibit 1. Next, in Exhibit 2, read the description of IBM's geographic breakdown of revenues and growth and its offer to North American employees being laid off to keep a job with IBM by moving overseas. Then, answer the following questions:

1. Think back to our discussion in Chapter 7 and in the current chapter regarding the labor cost difference between employing programmers in the United States versus overseas in locations like India and Eastern Europe. Is IBM's growth in employment in such countries inevitable given labor cost differences? How does this relate to Mr. Palmisano's comments in Exhibit 1?

2. Is the IBM offer typical of that offered to expatriates?

3. What is your reaction to the critical comments made by the Alliance@IBM spokesman, including the comment about asking employees to "offshore their citizenship"?

4. Review Exhibit 16.9 earlier in this chapter—The Cost of Living, Domestic Purchasing Power, and Minutes of Working Time Required to Buy a Big Mac, Bread, and Rice? How do the numbers for Indian cities like Dehli and Mumbai compare to those for U.S. cities like Chicago, Los Angeles, and New York? What are the implications of such differences?

5. Exhibit 2 gives examples of people who seem to enjoy living and working in India and also reports the opinion of an academic that this sort of move will become much more common. Do you believe that is likely? Why or why not?

EXHIBIT 1   **Palmisano: Multinationals Have Been Superseded**

Everyone, it seems, has a strongly felt position on globalization. . . . The emerging business model of the 21st century is not, in fact, "multinational." This new kind of organization—at IBM we call it "the globally integrated enterprise"—is very different in its structure and operations. Many parties to the globalization debate mistakenly project the 20th-century multinational on to 21st century global reality. . . .

In a multinational model, companies built local production capacity within key markets, while performing other tasks on a global basis. . . . As an example, American multinationals such as General Motors, Ford, and IBM built plants and established local workforce policies in Europe and Asia, but kept research and development and product design principally in the "home country."

The globally integrated enterprise, in contrast, fashions its strategy, management, and operations to integrate production—and deliver value to clients—worldwide. That has been made possible by shared technologies and shared business standards, built on top of a global information technology and communications infrastructure. . . .

These decisions are not simply a matter of offloading non-core activities, nor are they mere labor arbitrage—that is, shifting work to low-wage regions. Rather, they are about actively managing different operations, expertise, and capabilities to open the enterprise up in multiple ways, allowing it to connect more intimately with partners, suppliers, and customers and, most importantly, enabling it to engage in multifaceted, collaborative innovation.

This kind of innovation is much more than the creation of new products. It is also how services are delivered: three-quarters of most employment is in services. . . . Today, innovation is inherently global.

I believe the globally integrated enterprise is a better and more profitable way to organize business activities—and it can deliver enormous economic benefits to developed and developing nations. For example, integration of the workforce in developing countries into global production systems is already raising living standards, improving working conditions and creating more jobs in those countries. . . .

Source: Samuel Palmisano, "Multinationals Have Been Superseded," *Financial Times*, June 11, 2006.

EXHIBIT 2   **IBM's Global Employment and Compensation**

The majority of IBM's roughly 400,000 employees (71 percent) are now outside of the United States, with over 70,000 of those in India. Likewise, as the following information from IBM's recent annual report shows, most of its revenue (and its fastest revenue growth) has been outside of the Americas as well:

Revenues (in millions)	2008	2007	Year-to-Year Change
Geographies:	$100,938	$95,322	5.9%
Americas	42,807	41,122	4.1
Europe/Middle East/Africa	37,020	34,699	6.7
Asia Pacific	21,111	19,501	8.3

One result of this shifting emphasis to overseas markets is that IBM employees who are being laid off in North America now have an alternative to joining the growing ranks of the unemployed— work for the company abroad. IBM is offering laid-off workers in the United States and Canada a chance to take an IBM job in India, Nigeria, Russia, or other countries, including Argentina, Brazil, China, Czech Republic, Hungary, Mexico, Poland, Romania, Slovakia, Slovenia, South Africa, Turkey, and United Arab Emirates.

(Continued)

Source: Karina Frayter, "IBM to Laid-Off: Want a Job in India? Employees Who Would Otherwise Face Layoffs From Their North American Jobs at IBM Are Being Given the Chance to Work Abroad Through 'Project Match,'" *CNN.com*, February 5. 2009, retrieved 7/5/2009; William M. Bulkeley, "IBM to Cut U.S. Jobs, Expand in India: International Business Machines Corp. Plans to Lay Off About 5,000 U.S. Employees, With Many of the Jobs Being Transferred to India, According to People Familiar With the Situation," *Wall Street Journal*, March 26, 2009; Ben Arnoldy. "For Laid-Off IBM Workers, A Job in India? An IBM Program Offers Some Incentive to Relocate. Americans Who Have Migrated Overseas Find Less Pay—But a Good Lifestyle," *Christian Science Monitor*, March 26, 2009.

EXHIBIT 2   (*Continued*)

The company also will help with moving costs and provide visa assistance, it says. Only "satisfactory performers" who are "willing to work on local terms and conditions" should pursue the jobs, the document says. IBM would not immediately confirm if it means that the workers would be paid local wages and would be subject to local labor laws.

Some of the jobs are being eliminated because customers have ended contracts or the company has automated tasks. But employees say in many cases, they have been training IBM workers from India to do work that will now be moved overseas.

A spokesman for Alliance@IBM, a workers' group that is affiliated with the Communications Workers of America but does not have official union status at IBM, slammed the initiative: "IBM not only is offshoring its work to low-cost countries, now IBM wants employees to offshore themselves. At a time of rising unemployment IBM should be looking to keep both the work and the workers in the United States." And, "It [is] like people [are] not only [seeing] their jobs offshored but their citizenship offshored."

IBM's latest round of cuts show that even companies that have so far navigated the global recession profitably are continuing to slash costs. The IBM offer hints at a future where it's not just skilled Indians who might have to travel halfway around the globe for a job. It's likely that more American job seekers will have to think globally, say analysts, and the experiences of Americans who have taken jobs with companies here say it's not something to fear.

"I was making six figures when I left the States. I'm making six figures here – in rupees," laughs Jeanne Heydecker, a marketing executive now living outside of Delhi and working at her third Indian company. The salary for this single mother actually translates to roughly $50,000 a year. But it would be a mistake to suppose her quality of life has gone down. Most everything she could want is available in Delhi. The healthcare, she says, has been top-notch and bottom-dollar. And like most Westerners and wealthy Indians here, she is able to hire people to cook, clean, and drive for her. "You can come home from work and focus on your family, not on maintaining the car and the housework," she says. She left Chicago in 2007 after realizing that she was bored at work and didn't see companies nearby that were hiring "new people to do new things." Through the social-networking site Linkedin.com and Skype, Ms. Heydecker talked with the head of a Calcutta technology company who eventually hired her sight unseen.

Hers is not yet a well-worn path. But in the coming decades, it will be, says Arvind Panagariya, an expert on the Indian economy at Columbia University in New York. "Does the average American [worker] think globally? No. I don't think we're at that stage yet. But it will happen," he says. "Such a massive technological revolution will cause the borders to blur, if not disappear."

So far, there isn't much evidence of Americans expanding their search beyond places less like Peoria and more like Pune. In IBM's case, fewer than 20 people have taken up the offer for help in locating a new IBM job overseas, estimated company spokesman Doug Shelton. But the jobs in places like India are worth considering, Mr. Shelton suggested, saying that the cost of living is lower and international experience is highly prized in a global marketplace.

Moving beyond the IBM situation, in one of the new office high-rises, Mindcrest, a legal outsourcing firm, has recently hired three Americans—and has plans to hire more Westerners in the coming year. Like Heydecker in Delhi, the three women are mid-career and weren't sent here on a temporary foreign rotation by a multinational firm back home. Ms. Vega and her American counterparts Deirdre Byrne and Rana Rosen help the Indian attorneys understand what the Western clients want. None of them believe their work takes away American jobs, but say it instead frees young lawyers in the US from some early-career drudgery. Over lunch, the three women laugh about stashing pine nuts, manila folders, and lint-remover rolling pins in their luggage when they come back from visits home. There are other challenges: power cuts, the bureaucracy of setting up basic services like a cellphone, and the more pervasive scenes of deep poverty on the street here.

(*Continued*)

EXHIBIT 2 (*Continued*)

But Ms. Byrne, who has worked as a high-powered Manhattan attorney and a realtor for Sotheby's in the Hamptons, sums up the consensus: "We have a very nice life, and for a fraction of the costs at home"—even with smaller salaries. She stresses that the work is demanding "on the scale of a New York law firm," but comes with a "bonhomie" generally absent from Big Apple offices.

As for why more Americans are not considering work abroad, expatriates here admit it grows more complicated for those with more family ties. Heydecker's teenage son had to give up friends and skateboarding but has adjusted well, she says. She adds that the advantages to working abroad are often not communicated well.

"I don't think companies like IBM are getting people in touch with those who are out here doing it, and showcasing those success stories," says Heydecker. "It can be isolating in the beginning, but eventually, your life is pretty sweet. It all depends on how open your mind is."

Summary

Studying employee compensation only in your neighborhood, city, or country is like being a horse with blinders. Removing the blinders by adopting an international perspective deepens your understanding of local issues. Anyone interested in compensation must adopt a worldwide perspective. The globalization of businesses, financial markets, trade agreements, and even labor markets is affecting every workplace and every employment relationship. And employee compensation, so central to the workplace, is embedded in the different political-socioeconomic arrangements found around the world. Examining employee compensation with the factors in the global pay model offers insights into managing total compensation internationally.

The basic premise of this book is that compensation systems have a profound impact on individual behavior, organization success, and social well-being. We believe this holds true within and across all national boundaries.

Review Questions

1. Rank the factors in the global guide according to your belief in their importance for understanding and managing compensation. How does your ranking differ from those of your peers? From those of international peers? Discuss how the rankings may change over time.

2. Distinguish between nationwide and industrywide pay determination. How do they compare to a business strategy–market approach?

3. Develop arguments for and against "typical" Japanese-style, "typical" German-style, and "typical" U.S.-style approaches to pay. Using the global guide, what factors are causing each approach to change?

4. Distinguish between global workers, expatriates, local nationals, and third-country nationals.

5. In the balance sheet approach to paying expats, most of total compensation is linked to costs of living. Some argue that expatriate pay resembles a traditional Japanese pay system. Evaluate this argument.

Endnotes

1. Ken Abosch, Jill Schermerhorn, and Lori Wisper, "Broad-Based Variable Pay Goes Global," *Workspan,* May 2008, pp. 57–62; Jie Shen, "HRM in Chinese Privately Owned Enterprises," *Thunderbird International Business Review* 50(2) (2008), pp. 91–101.

2. Hiroko Tabuchi, "Slacker Nation? Young Japanese Shun Promotions. 'Hodo-Hodo' Favor Humdrum Jobs Even as Recession Looms," *Wall Street Journal,* November 1, 2008; Mitsuo Ishida, Akiko Ono, Naoki Mitani, Yoshinori Tomita, and Anja Kirsch, "The Automotive Industry in Japan," in Russell D. Lansbury, Nick Wailes, Jim Kitay, and Anja Kirsch, eds., *Globalization and Employment Relations in the Auto Assembly Industry. Bulletin of Comparative Labor Relations. Volume 64.* (Alphen aan den Rijn, Netherlands: Wolters Kluwer, 2008); Markus Pudelko, "The Seniority Principle in Japanese Companies: A Relic of the Past?" *Asia Pacific Journal of Human Resources* 44 (2006), pp. 276–294; T. Kono and S. Clegg, *Trends in Japanese Management: Continuing Strengths, Current Problems and Changing Priorities* (New York: Palgrave-Macmillan, 2001).

3. Interviews with Toshiba managers, included in M. Bloom, G. Milkovich, and A. Mitra, "Managing the Chaos of Global Pay Systems," *International Journal of Human Resource Management* 14 (2003), pp.1350–1367.

4. Geraldine Fabrikant, "U.S.-Style Pay Packages Are All the Rage in Europe," *New York Times,* June 16, 2006; "New Equity Incentive Programs Gain Favor With Employers Around the World," *Towers Perrin Monitor,* July 22, 2005; *European Total Rewards Survey 2005, www.merhr.com/totalrewardseurope.*

5. Geraldine Fabrikant, "U.S. Style Pay Packages Are All the Rage in Europe," *New York Times,* June 16, 2006; Thomas Li Ping Tang, Toto Sutarso, Adebowale Akande, et al., "The Love of Money and Pay Level Satisfaction: Measurement and Functional Equivalence in 29 Geopolitical Entities Around the World," paper presented at the Annual Meeting of the Academy of Management, August 11–16 2006, Atlanta, GA.

6. "Marriages Made in Hell," *The Economist,* May 20, 2009, *www.economist.com,* August 2009.

7. "Costs of Chrysler Sale Blamed in Daimler Loss," *New York Times,* October 25, 2007, *www.nytimes.com,* August 2009.

8. Parmy Olson, "The Carmaker Finally Rids Itself of 19.9% Stake," *Forbes,* April 28, 2009, *www.forbes.com,* August 2009.

9. Torsten Kühlmann and Peter J. Dowling, "DaimlerChrysler: A Case Study of a Cross Border Merger," in Günther Stahl and Mark E. Mendenhall, eds., *Mergers and Acquisitions: Managing Cultures and Human Resources* (Stanford, California: Stanford Business Books, 2005).

10. Carmelo Cennamo, "Shareholders' Value Maximization and Stakeholders' Interest," in Luis R. Gomez-Mejia and Steve Werner eds., *Global Compensation: Foundations and Perspectives* (London: Routledge, 2008). See especially Table 8.1.

11. Mike Ramsey, "Chrysler Installs Fiat Production System Before Plants Restart," *www.bloomberg.com,* 6/29/2009; "The Italian Solution: Fiat's Ambitions," *The Economist,* May 9, 2009, *www.economist.com,* August 2009; Serena Saitto, "Detroit Suburbs Beckon Fiat Executives With $1,595 Sandals," *www.bloomberg.com,* 6/29/2009.

12. S. Basu, S. Estrin, and J. Svejnar, "Employment Determination in Enterprises Under Communism and in Transition: Evidence From Central University," *Industrial and Labor Relations Review,* April 2005, pp. 353–369; J. Banister, "Manufacturing Compensation in China," *Monthly Labor Review,* November 2005, pp. 22–40; *Overview of the Chinese Economy,* Report by the Joint Economic Committee of United States Congress, July 2005; N. Zupan, "HRM in Slovenian Transitional Companies," presentation at CAHRS International Conference, Berlin, June 2002.

13. D. Dong, K. Goodall, and M. Warner, "The End of the Iron Rice Bowl," *International Journal of Human Resource Management,* April 2, 2000, pp. 217–236; Hesan A. Quazi, *Compensation and Benefits Practices in Selected Asian Countries* (Singapore: McGraw Hill, 2004).

14. Zhong-Ming Wang, presentation to Cornell University Global HRM Distance Learning seminar, Shanghai, China, March 2000; comments by Ningyu Tang, instructor in Shanghai for Global HRM Distance Learning seminar; Jing Zhou and J. J. Martocchio, "Chinese and American Managers' Compensation Award Decisions," *Personnel Psychology* 54 (Spring 2001), pp. 115–145; Mei Fong, "A Chinese Puzzle," *The Wall Street Journal,* August 16, 2005, p. B1; Zaohui Zhao, "Earnings Differentials Between State and Non-State Enterprises in Urban China," *Pacific Economic Review* 7(1) (2002), pp. 181–197.

15. *Doing Business in the Russian Federation,* PricewaterhouseCoopers, April 2004; John S. Earle and Klara Sabirianova Peter, "Complementarity and Custom in Wage Contract Violation," Upjohn Institute Staff Working Paper 06-129, July 2006.

16. Kevin O'Rourke and J. G. Williamson, *Globalization and History: The Evolution of a 19th Century Atlantic Economy* (Cambridge, MA: MIT Press, 1999), p. 2.

17. Kevin O'Rourke and J. G. Williamson, *Globalization and History: The Evolution of a 19th Century Atlantic Economy* (Cambridge, MA: MIT Press, 1999), chap. 14. Also see W. Keller, L. Pauly, and S. Reich, *The Myth of the Global Corporation* (Princeton, NJ: Princeton University Press, 1998); B. Kogut, "What Makes a Company Global?" *Harvard Business Review,* January–February 1999, pp. 165–170.

18. T. Kostova, "Transnational Transfer of Strategic Organizational Practices: A Contextual Perspective," *Academy of Management Review,* 24 (1999), pp. 308–324; W. R. Scott, *Institutions and Organizations* (Thousand Oaks, CA: Sage Publications, 2000); T. Kostova and K. Roth, "Adoption of Organizational Practice by Subsidiaries of Multinational Corporations: Institutional and Relational Effects,:" *Academy of Management Journal,* 45 (2002), pp. 215–233; R. Whitley, *Divergent Capitalisms: The Social Structuring and Change of Business Systems* (Oxford: Oxford University Press, 1999); Peter Hall and David Soskice, eds., *Varieties of Capitalism: The Institutional Foundations of Comparative Advantage* (New York: Oxford University Press, 2001); Tony Edwards and Sarosh Kuruvilla. "International HRM: National Business Systems, Organizational Politics and the International Division of Labour in MNCs," *International Journal of Human Resource Management,* 16 (2005), pp. 1–21; Luis R. Gomez-Mejia and Steve Werner, eds., *Global Compensation: Foundations and Perspectives* (London: Routledge, 2008); P. J. Dowling, M. Festing, and A. D. Engle, Sr., *International Human Resource Management,* 5th ed. (London: Thomson Learning, 2008): P. Evans, V. Pucik, and J. L. Barsoux, 2002. *The Global Challenge: International Human Resource Management* (New York: McGraw-Hill/Irwin, 2002); Gregory Jackson and Richard Deeg, "Comparing Capitalisms: Understanding Institutional Diversity and Its Implications for International Business," *Journal of International Business Studies,* 39 (2008), pp. 540–561; Chris Brewster, "Different Paradigms in Strategic HRM: Questions Raised by Comparative Research," in Patrick Wright, Lee Dyer, John Boudreau, and George T. Milkovich, eds., *Research in Personnel and Human Resources Management,* Supplement 4 (Greenwich, CT: JAI Press,1999).

19. C. Oliver, "Strategic Responses to Institutional Processes," *Academy of Management Review,* 16 (1991), pp. 145–179.

20. K. Y. Au, "Intra-Cultural Variation: Evidence and Implications for International Business," *Journal of International Business Studies,* 30 (1991), pp. 799–812; M. Bloom and G. T. Milkovich, "A SHRM Perspective on International Compensation and Rewards," in P. M. Wright, L. Dyer, J. W. Boudreau, and G. T. Milkovich, *Research in Personnel and Human Resources Management,* Supplement 4, (Stamford, CT: JAI Press, 1999), pp. 283–303; Barry Gerhart, "How Much Does National Culture Constrain Organization Culture?" *Management*

and Organization Review, 5 (2009), pp. 244–259; Barry Gerhart, "Cross-Cultural Management Research: Assumptions, Evidence, and Suggested Directions," *International Journal of Cross Cultural Management,* 8 (2008), pp. 259–274; Barry Gerhart. and Meiyu Fang, "National Culture and Human Resource Management: Assumptions and Evidence," *International Journal of Human Resource Management,* 16 (2005), pp. 975–990; R. Nelson and S. Gopalan, "Do Organizational Cultures Replicate National Cultures? Isomorphism, Rejection, and Reciprocal Opposition in the Corporate Values of Three Countries," *Organization Studies,* 24 (2003), pp. 1115–1151; B. Gerhart, "Compensation and National Culture," in S. Werner and L. R. Gomez-Mejia, eds., *Global Compensation: Foundations and Perspectives* (London, U.K.: Routledge, 2008); Barry Gerhart, "Does National Culture Constrain Organization Culture and Human Resource Strategy? The Role of Individual Mechanisms and Implications for Employee Selection," *Research in Personnel and Human Resources Management* (forthcoming).

21. Russell D. Lansbury, Nick Wailes, Jim Kitay, and Anja Kirsch, eds., *Globalization and Employment Relations in the Auto Assembly Industry,* Bulletin of Comparative Labor Relations, Vol. 64 (Alphen aan den Rijn, Netherlands: Wolters Kluwer, 2008).

22. H. C. Katz and O. Darbishire, *Converging Divergences: Worldwide Changes in Employment Systems* (Ithaca, NY: ILR Press/Cornell University Press, 2000).

23. J. B. Barney, "Organizational Culture: Can It Be a Source of Sustained Competitive Advantage?" *Academy of Management Review,* 11 (1986), pp. 656–665; J. B. Barney, "Firm Resources and Sustained Competitive Advantage. *Journal of Management,* 17 (1991), pp. 99–120.

24. M. Pudelko, A. W. K. Harzing, "The Golden Triangle for MNCs: Standardization Towards Headquarters Practices, Standardization Towards Global Best Practices and Localization," *Organizational Dynamics,* 37 (4) (2008), pp. 394–404; M. Pudelko and A. W. K. Harzing, "How European Is Management in Europe? An Analysis of Past, Present and Future Management Practices in Europe," *European Journal of International Management,* 1 (3) (2007), pp. 206–224; M. Pudelko, A. W. K. Harzing, "Country-of-Origin, Localization or Dominance Effect? An Empirical Investigation of HRM Practices in Foreign Subsidiaries," *Human Resource Management,* 46 (2007), pp. 535–559; Anthony Ferner, "Country of Origin Effects and HRM in Multinational Companies. Human Resource Management Journal, 7(1) (1997), pp. 19–37; Anthony Ferner and Javier Quintanilla, "Multinationals, National Business Systems and HRM: The Enduring Influence of National Identity or a Process of 'Anglo-Saxonization.'" *International Journal of Human Resource Management,* 9(4) (1998), pp. 710–731; Ingmar Björkman, Carl F Fey, and Hyeon Jeong Park, "Institutional Theory and MNC Subsidiary HRM Practices: Evidence From a Three-Country Study," *Journal of International Business Studies,* 38 (2007), pp. 430–446.

25. Marion Festing, Judith Eidems, and Susanne Royer, "Strategic Issues and Local Constraints in Transnational Compensation Strategies: An Analysis of Cultural, Institutional and Political Processes," *European Management Journal* 25, (2007), pp. 118–131; Allen D. Engle, Sr., Peter J. Dowling, and Marion Festing, "State of Origin: Research in Global Performance Management: A Proposed Research Domain and Emerging Implications," *European Journal of International Management,* 2 (2008), pp. 153–169; C.A. Bartlett and S, Ghoshal, *Managing Across Borders: The Transnational Solution* (Boston: Harvard Business School Press, 1989); Matt Bloom, George T. Milkovich, and Atul Mitra, "International Compensation: Learning From How Managers Respond to Variations in Local Host Contexts," *International Journal of Human Resource Management,* 14 (2008) pp. 1350–1367.

26. Fran Blau and Lawrence Kahn, *At Home and Abroad: U.S. Labor Market Performance in International Perspective* (New York: Russell Sage Foundation, 2002).

27. Harry C. Katz, Wonduck Lee, and Joohee Lee, eds., "The New Structure of Labor Relations," *Tripartism and Decentralization.* (Ithaca, NY: Cornell University Press, 2004).

28. *World of Work Report* (Geneva, Switzerland: International Labour Organization, 2008). See especially Table 3.3.

29. Matthew M. C. Allen, Heinz-Joseph Tuselmann, Hamed El-Sa'id, and Paul Windrum, "Sectoral Collective Agreements: Remuneration Straitjackets for German Workplaces?" *Personnel Review,* 36 (2006) pp. 963–967; European Industrial Relations Observatory Online. (2005). "Changes in National Collective Bargaining Systems Since 1990," *http:// www.eurofound.europa.eu/eiro/* retrieved 6/30/2009.

30. Bruce Crumley, "Goodbye to France's 35-Hour Week," *Time,* July 24, 2008.

31. Baker & McKenzie LLP. (2009). "Worldwide Guide to Trade Unions and Works Councils," *www.gurn.info/en/,* June 30, 2009.

32. Ibid., p. 105.

33. Ibid., p. 104.

34. John W. Budd, *Labor Relations: Striking a Balance,* 2nd edition (New York: McGraw-Hill/ Irwin, 2008).

35. G. Hofstede, *Culture's Consequences: International Differences in Work-Related Values.* (Beverly Hills, CA: Sage, 1980); G. Hofstede, *Culture's Consequences: Comparing Values, Behaviors, Institutions, and Organizations Across Nations,* 2nd edition (Thousand Oaks, CA: Sage, 2001); R. J. House, P. J. Hanges, M. Javidan, P. W. Dorfman, and V. Gupta, *Culture, Leadership, and Organizations: The Globe Study of 62 Societies* (Thousand Oaks, CA: Sage Publications, 2004);. Trompenaars, *Riding the Waves of Culture: Understanding Diversity in Global Business* (Burr Ridge, IL: Irwin, 1995); H. C. Triandis, "Cross-Cultural Industrial and Organizational Psychology," in M. D. Dunnette and L. M. Hough, eds., *Handbook of Industrial and Organizational Psychology* (Palo Alto, CA: Consulting Psychologists Press, 1994), pp. 103–172.

36. G. Hofstede, "The Cultural Relativity of Organizational Practices and Theories," *Journal of International Business Studies,* 14 (1983) pp. 75–89; G. Hofstede, "Cultural Constraints in Management Theories," *Academy of Management Executive,* 7 (1993) pp. 81–94; G. Hofstede, *Culture's Consequences: International Differences in Work-Related Values.* (Beverly Hills, CA: Sage, 1980); G. Hofstede, *Culture's Consequences: Comparing Values, Behaviors, Institutions, and Organizations Across Nations,* 2nd edition (Thousand Oaks, CA: Sage, 2001).

37. R. Schuler and N. Rogovsky, "Understanding Compensation Practice Variations cross Firms: The Impact of National Culture," *Journal of International Business Studies* 29 (1998), pp. 159–178.

38. L. R. Gomez-Mejia and T. Welbourne, "Compensation Strategies in a Global Context," *Human Resource Planning* 14 (1994), pp. 29–41; Sunny C. L. Fong and Margaret A. Shaffer, "The Dimensionality and Determinants of Pay Satisfaction: A Cross-Cultural Investigation of a Group Incentive Plan," *International Journal of Human Resource Management* 14(4), (June 2003), pp. 559–580.

39. P. C. Early and M. Erez, *The Transplanted Executive: Why You Need to Understand How Workers in Other Countries See the World Differently* (New York: Oxford University Press, 1997).

40. G. Milkovich and M. Bloom, "Rethinking International Compensation: From Expatriates and National Cultures to Strategic Flexibility," *Compensation and Benefits Review,* April 1998; L. Markoczy, "Us and Them," *Across the Board,* February 1998, pp. 44–48; Brendan McSweeney, "Hofstede's Model of National Cultural Differences and Their Consequences: A Triumph of Faith, A Failure of Analysis," *Human Relations,* January 2002, pp. 89–118; Paul Gooderham and Odd Nordhaug, "Are Cultural Differences in Europe on the Decline?" *geert-hofstede.international-business-center.com.*

41. M. Bloom, G. Milkovich, and A. Mitra, "International Compensation: Learning from How Managers Respond to Variations in Local Host Contexts," *International Journal of Human*

Resource Management special issue, 2003; Allen D. Engle, Sr., and Mark Mendenhall, "Transnational Roles and Transnational Rewards: Global Integration in Executive Compensation," presentation at international HR conference, Limerick, Ireland, June 2003; Paul Evans, Vlado Pucik, and Jean-Louis Barsoux, *The Global Challenge* (New York: McGraw-Hill, 2002); G. Hundley and J. Kim, "National Culture and the Factors Affecting Perceptions of Pay Fairness in Korea and the U.S.," *International Journal of Organization Analysis* 5(4) (October 1997), pp. 325–341; David Landes, *Culture Matters: How Values Shape Human Progress* (New York: Basic Books, 2001).

42. M. Bloom, G. Milkovich, and N. Zupan, "Contrasting Slovenian and U.S. Employment Relations: The Links between Social Contracts and Psychological Contracts," *CEMS Business Review,* No. 2 (1997), pp. S95–S109; Chun Hui, Cynthia Lee, and Denise Rousseau, "Psychological Contract and Organizational Citizenship Behavior in China: Investigating Generalizability and Instrumentality," *Journal of Applied Psychology* 89(2) (2004), pp. 311–321.

43. M. Bloom and G. T. Milkovich, "A SHRM Perspective on International Compensation and Rewards" in P.M. Wright, L. Dyer, J.W. Boudreau, and G.T. Milkovich, *Research in Personnel and Human Resources Management,* Supplement 4 (Stamford, CT: JAI Press, 1999), pp. 283–303; Barry Gerhart, "Does National Culture Constrain Organization Culture and Human Resource Strategy? The Role of Individual Mechanisms and Implications for Employee Selection," *Research in Personnel and Human Resources Management,* forthcoming; K. Y. Au, "Intra-Cultural Variation: Evidence and Implications for International Business. *Journal of International Business Studies,* 30 (1999), pp. 799–812.

44. Barry Gerhart, "Cross-Cultural Management Research: Assumptions, Evidence, and Suggested Directions," *International Journal of Cross Cultural Management,* 8 (2008), pp. 259–274; Barry Gerhart. and Meiyu Fang, "National Culture and Human Resource Management: Assumptions and Evidence," *International Journal of Human Resource Management,* 16 (2005), pp. 975–990.

45. R. Fischer, P. Smith, "Reward Allocation and Culture: A Meta-Analysis," *Journal of Cross-cultural Psychology,* 34 (2003), pp. 251–268; B. Gerhart, "Compensation and National Culture," in S. Werner and L. Gomez-Mejia, eds., *Global Compensation* (London, UK: Routledge, 2008).

46. Zhijun Ling and Martha Avery, *The Lenovo Affair: The Growth of China's Computer Giant and Its Takeover of IBM-PC* (New York: John Wiley & Sons, 2006). See especially pp. 266–273. Also see D. Z. Ding, S. Akhtar, and G. L. Ge, "Organizational Differences in Managerial Compensation and Benefits in Chinese Firms," *International Journal of Human Resource Management* 17(4) (April 2006), pp. 693–715; and Wan Lixin, "The Student Job Crunch," *China International Business,* June 2006, pp. 18–25.

47. Organisation for Economic Co-operation and Development, "Trade Union Density, 1960–2007," *www.oecd.org/dataoecd/25/42/39891561.xls,* retrieved 6/29/2009; Jelle Visser, "Union Membership Statistics in 24 Countries," *Monthly Labor Review,* January 2006, pp. 38–49.

48. Baker & McKenzie LLP, "Worldwide Guide to Trade Unions and Works Councils," *www.gurn.info/en/,* 6/29/2009.

49. The Web site of the National Center for Employee Ownership (NCEO) has information and referrals concerning employee stock ownership plans (ESOPs) and other forms of employee ownership: *www.esop.org.* Worker ownership around the world is discussed at *www.activistnet.org.*

50. Lowell Turner, ed., *Negotiating the New Germany: Can Social Partnership Survive?* (Ithaca, NY: Cornell University Press, 1998); Wolfgang Streeck, *Social Institutions and Economic Performance: Studies of Industrial Relations in Advanced Capitalist Economies* (London: Sage, 1992).

51. Wei He, Chao C. Chen, and Lihua Zhang, "Rewards Allocation Preferences in Chinese State-Owned Enterprises: A Revisit after a Decade's Radical Reform," in Anne S. Tsui and Chung-Ming Lau, eds., *The Management of Enterprises in the People's Republic of China* (Boston: Kluwer Academic, 2002); Marshall Meyer, Yuan Lu, Hailin Lan, and Xiaohui Lu, "Decentralized Enterprise Reform: Notes on the Transformation of State-Owned Enterprises," in Anne S. Tsui and Shung-Ming Lau, eds., *The Management of Enterprises in the People's Republic of China* (Boston: Kluwer Academic, 2002); Chun Hui, Cynthia Lee, and Denise Rousseau, "Psychological Contract and Organizational Citizenship Behavior in China: Investigating Generalizability and Instrumentality," *Journal of Applied Psychology* 89(2) (April 2004), pp. 311–321.

52. Jing Zhou and J. J. Martocchio, "Chinese and American Managers' Compensation Award Decisions," *Personnel Psychology* 54 (Spring 2001), pp. 115–145.

53. The European Trade Union Institute's Web site is at *www.etuc.org/etui/default.cf.*

54. Stephen Power and Guy Chazan, "Europe Auto Relations Get Testy," *The Wall Street Journal,* June 15, 2006, p. A8.

55. Hesan Ahmed Quazi, *Compensation and Benefits Practices in Selected Asian Countries* (Singapore: McGraw Hill, 2004).

56. Samuel Palmisano, "Multinationals Have Been Superseded," *Financial Times,* June 11, 2006.

57. Mercer Human Resource Consulting, *2006 Worldwide Pay Survey* (London: October 3, 2005); Marie-Claire Guillard, "A Visual Essay: International Labor Market Comparisons," *Monthly Labor Review,* April 2006, pp. 33–37; Nic Paton, "Performance-Related Pay Becoming a Global Phenomenon," *www.management-issues.com,* accessed January 13, 2006; Chris Giles, "Moscow Is Now World's Costliest City for Expatriates," *Financial Times,* June 26, 2006, p. 2.

58. W. Lane and M. Schmidt, "Comparing U.S. and European COI and the HICP," *Monthly Labor Review* 129(5) (May 2006), pp. 20–27; J. Abowd and M. Bognanno, "International Differences in Executive and Managerial Compensation," in R. B. Freeman and L. Katz, eds., *Differences and Changes in Wage Structures* (Chicago: NBER, 1995), pp. 67–103; "Big Mac Index," *The Economist,* February 4, 2009, *www.economist.com.*

59. Duncan Brown, "The Third Way: The Future of Pay and Rewards in Europe," *WorldatWork,* Second Quarter 2000, pp. 15–25.

60. S. Jacoby, *The Embedded Corporation* (Princeton: Princeton University Press, 2005); J. Abegglen, *Twenty-First Century Japanese Management: New System, Lasting Values* (New York: Palgrave-Macmillan, 2006); Toyo Keizai, *Japan Company Handbook* (Tokyo: Japan Labour Bureau, Summer 2001).

61. T. Kato, "The End of Lifetime Employment in Japan? Evidence from National Surveys and Field Research," *Journal of the Japanese and International Economies* 15 (2002), pp. 489–514; T. Kato and M. Rockell, "Experiences, Credentials, and Compensation in the Japanese and U.S. Managerial Labor Markets: Evidence from New Micro Data," *Journal of the Japanese and International Economies* 6 (1992), pp. 30–51; P. Evans, V. Pucik, and J. Barsoux, *The Global Challenge: Frameworks for International Human Resource Management* (New York: McGraw-Hill/Irwin, 2002).

62. We thank Thomas Gresch and Elke Stadelmann, whose manuscript, *Traditional Pay System in Germany* (Ruesselsheim, Germany: Adam Opel AG, 2001), is the basis for this section of the chapter; Geoff Dyer, "A Tale of Two Corporate Cultures," *Financial Times,* May 23, 2006, p. 8; Paul DeGrauwe, "Germany's Pay Policy Points to a Eurozone Design Flaw," *Financial Times,* May 5, 2006, p. 13.

63. Bertrand Benoit, "Benefit Check: Why Germany is Confronted with a Welfare State Fiasco," *Financial Times,* June 26, 2006.

64. Hiroshi Ono, "Careers in Foreign-Owned Firms in Japan," *American Sociological Review,* 72 (2007), pp. 267–290.

65. See S. Jacoby, *The Embedded Corporation* (Princeton: Princeton University Press, 2005), especially pp. 75–77; S. Strom, "In Japan, from Lifetime Job to No Job at All," *New York Times* Online, February 3, 1999; M. Bloom, G. Milkovich, and A. Mitra, "International Compensation: Learning From How Managers Respond to Variations in Local Host Contexts," *International Journal of Human Resource Management,* special issue, 2003; T. Kato, "The End of Lifetime Employment in Japan? Evidence from National Surveys and Field Research," *Journal of Japanese and International Economies* 15 (2002), pp. 489–514; T. Kato and M. Rockell, "Experiences, Credentials, and Compensation in the Japanese and U.S. Managerial Labor Markets: Evidence from New Micro Data," *Journal of the Japanese and International Economies* 6 (1992), pp. 30–51; Hiromichi Shibata, "Wage and Performance Appraisal Systems in Flux: Japan-U.S. Comparison," *Industrial Relations* 41(4) (2002), pp. 629–652; National Personnel Authority, *Current Status of Private Firms' Remuneration Systems* (Tokyo: Japan Labour Bureau, 2006) ; D. Raj Adhikari, *National Factors in Employment Relations in Japan* (Tokyo: Japan Institute of Labor Policy, 2005).

66. Markus Pudelko, "The Seniority Principle in Japanese Companies: A Relic of the Past?" *Asia Pacific Journal of Human Resources,* 44 (2006), pp. 276–294.

67. Gregory Jackson, "Employment Adjustment and Distributional Conflict in Japanese Firms," in M. Aoki, G. Jackson, and H. Miyajima, eds., *Corporate Governance in Japan: Institutional Change and Organizational Diversity* (Oxford: Oxford University Press, 2007).

68. "JapAnglo-Saxon Capitalism," *The Economist,* December 1, 2007.

69. Antje Kurdelbusch, "Multinationals and the Rise of Variable Pay in Germany," *European Journal of Industrial Relations,* 8 (2002), pp. 324–349; James Arrowsmith, Heidi Nicolaisen, Barbara Bechter, and Rosa Nonell, "The Management of Variable Pay in Banking: Forms and Rationale in Four European Countries," in Roger Blanplain and Linda Dickens, eds., *Challenges of European Employment Relations and Employment Regulation* (The Netherlands: Kluwer Law International, 2008); Matthias Schmitt and Dieter Sadowski," A Cost-Minimization Approach to the International Transfer of HRM/IR Practices: Anglo-Saxon Multinationals in the Federal Republic of Germany," *International Journal of Human Resource Management,* 14 (2003), pp. 409–430.

70. William Gerard Sanders and Anja Tuschke, "The Adoption of Institutionally Contested Organizational Practices: The Emergence of Stock Option Pay in Germany," *Academy of Management Journal* 50 (2007), pp. 33–56.

71. M. Bloom, G. Milkovich, and A. Mitra, "International Compensation: Learning From How Managers Respond to Variations in Local Host Contexts," *International Journal of Human Resource Management,* special issue, 2003. See also N. Napier and Van Tuan Vu, "International HRM in Developing and Transitional Economy Context," *Human Resource Management Review* 8(1) (1998), pp. 39–71.

72. Thomas Friedman, *The World Is Flat: A Brief History of the Twenty-First Century* (New York: Farrar, Straus and Giroux, 2006); J. W. Walker, "Are We Global Yet?" *Human Resource Planning* (First Quarter 2000), pp. 7–8; R. Locke and K. Thelen, "Apples and Oranges Revisited: Contextualized Comparisons and Comparative Labor Policies," *Politics and Society* 23(2), (1996), pp. 337–367; M. Mendenhall and Gary Oddou, *Readings and Cases in International Human Resource Management* (Cincinnati: Southwestern, 2000).

73. Samuel Palmisano, "The Globally Integrated Enterprise," *Foreign Affairs,* May/June 2006.

74. P. J. Dowling, M. Festing, and A. D. Engle, Sr., *International Human Resource Management,* 5th ed. (London: Thomson Learning, 2008).

75. G. Latta, "The Future of Expatriate Compensation," *WorldatWork* (Second Quarter 2006), pp. 42–49; Geoffrey Latta, "Expatriate Policy and Practice: A 10-Year Comparison of Trends," *Compensation and Benefits Review* 31(4) (1999), pp. 35–39; C. Reynolds, "Global Compensation and Benefits in Transition," *Compensation and Benefits Review*

32(1), (January/February 2000), pp. 27–37; J. Stewart Black and Hal B. Gregerson, "The Right Way to Manage Expats," *Harvard Business Review* (March–April 1999), pp. 52–62; Roger Heron, "The Cardinal Sins of Expatriate Policies," *Organization Resources Counselors: Innovations in International HR,* Fall 2001.

76. G. Latta, "The Future of Expatriate Compensation," *WorldatWork* (Second Quarter 2006), pp. 42–49; Cris Prystay and Tom Herman, "Tax Hike Hits Home for Americans Abroad," *The Wall Street Journal,* July 19, 2006, pp. D1, D5.

77. Runzheimer International, *www.runzheimer.com,* publishes monthly newsletters on the costs of relocation.

78. Bobby W. Watson, Jr., and Gangaram Singh, "Global Pay Systems: Compensation in Support of a Multinational Strategy," *Compensation and Benefits Review* 37(1), (January/February 2005), pp. 33–36; Sherrie Webster Brown, "Spanning the Globe for Quality Pay Data," in *2003–2004 Survey Handbook and Directory* (Scottsdale, AZ: WorldatWork, 2002), pp. 95–100; Margaret A. Coil, "Salary Surveys in a Blended-Role World," in *2003–2004 Survey Handbook and Directory* (Scottsdale, AZ: WorldatWork, 2002), pp. 57–64.

79. Laura Johnson and Darrell Cira, "Taking the Best Path to Implementing a Global Pay Structure: The General Mill's Experience," World at Work Conference, Seattle, Washington, June 1, 2009.

80. W. Lane and M. Schmidt, "Comparing U.S. and European COI and the HICP," *Monthly Labor Review* (May 2006), pp. 20–27.

81. C. Reynolds, "Expatriate Compensation in Historical Perspective," *International Human Resource Journal* (Summer 1997), pp. 118–131.

82. *Global Rewards: A Collection of Articles From WorldatWork* (Scottsdale, AZ: WorldatWork, 2005); Cal Reynolds, "International Compensation," in William A. Caldwell, ed., *Compensation Guide* (Boston: Warren, Gorham and Lamont, 1998).

83. Chun Hui, Cynthia Lee, and Denise Rousseau, "Psychological Contract and Organizational Citizenship Behavior in China: Investigating Generalizability and Instrumentality," *Journal of Applied Psychology* 89(2) (April 2004), pp. 311–321; Richard A. Guzzo, Katherine A. Noonan, and Efrat Elron, "Expatriate Managers and the Psychological Contract," *Journal of Applied Psychology* 7(4) (1994), pp. 617–626; Steve Gross and Per Wingerup, "Global Pay? Maybe Not Yet!" *Compensation Benefits Review* 31 (1999), pp. 25–34.

84. P. J. Dowling, M. Festing, and A. D. Engle, Sr., *International Human Resource Management,* 5th ed. (London: Thomson Learning, 2008).

85. Carole Mestre, Anne Rossier-Renaud, and Madeline Berger, "Better Benchmarks for Global Mobility," *Workspan,* April 2009.

86. P. J. Dowling, M. Festing, and A. D. Engle, Sr., *International Human Resource Management,* 5th ed. (London: Thomson Learning, 2008).

87. Carole Mestre, Anne Rossier-Renaud, and Madeline Berger, "Better Benchmarks for Global Mobility," *Workspan,* April 2009.

88. Garry M. Wederspahn, "Costing Failures in Expatriate Human Resource Management," *Human Resource Planning* 15(3), pp. 27–35; Soo Min Toh and Angelo S. DeNissi, "Host Country National Reactions to Expatriate Pay Policies: A Model and Implications," *Academy of Management Review,* 28(4) (2003), pp. 606–621.

89. Paul Evans, Vlado Pucik, and Jean-Louis Barsoux, *The Global Challenge* (New York: McGraw-Hill, 2002); Allen D. Engle, Sr. and Peter Dowing, "Global Rewards: Strategic Patterns in Complexity," presentation at international HR conference, Ljubljana, Slovenia, June 2004.

90. For a very helpful review and analysis of this issue, see P. J. Dowling, M. Festing, and A. D. Engle, Sr., *International Human Resource Management,* 5th ed. (London: Thomson Learning, 2008). Also, see Claus Christensen and Anne-Wil Harzing, "Expatriate Failure: Time to Abandon the Concept?" *Career Development International* 9 (2004), pp. 616–626.

Managing the System

The last part of our total pay model is management. This means ensuring that the right people get the right pay for achieving the right objectives in the right way. We have touched on aspects of management already—the use of budgets in merit increase programs; the "message" that employees receive from their variable pay bonuses, communication, and cost control in benefits; and the importance of employee involvement in designing the total compensation system.

Several important issues remain. The first, already noted in Chapter 16's global guide, is the significant role that government plays in managing compensation. Laws and regulations are the most obvious government intervention. In the United States, minimum-wage legislation, the Equal Pay Act, and Title VII of the Civil Rights Act, among others, regulate pay decisions. Legal issues in compensation in the United States are covered in Chapter 17.

Government is more than a source of laws and regulations, however. As a major employer, as a consumer of goods and services, and through its fiscal and monetary policies, government affects the supply of and the demand for labor.

Chapter 18 covers several aspects of managing compensation: costs and added value, communication, and change. One of the key reasons for being systematic about pay decisions is to manage the costs associated with those decisions. As Chapter 18 will show, a total compensation system is really a device for allocating money in a way that is consistent with the organization's objectives. Recent developments in how to evaluate the value gained from compensation programs are discussed.

Communication and change are linked. What is to be communicated to whom is an important, ongoing issue. Compensation itself communicates. A pay increase tells people how they are doing. Changes in the pay system also communicate; they may signal change in business direction or even reinforce restructuring of the organization. Any system will founder if it is ineffectively communicated and managed.

Chapter 18 also discusses enterprise software that holds out the promise of helping users make pay decisions faster and smarter. Perhaps most critical of all, we return to look at ethics and the increasing importance of personal standards when no professional standards exist.

EXHIBIT VII.1 **The Pay Model**

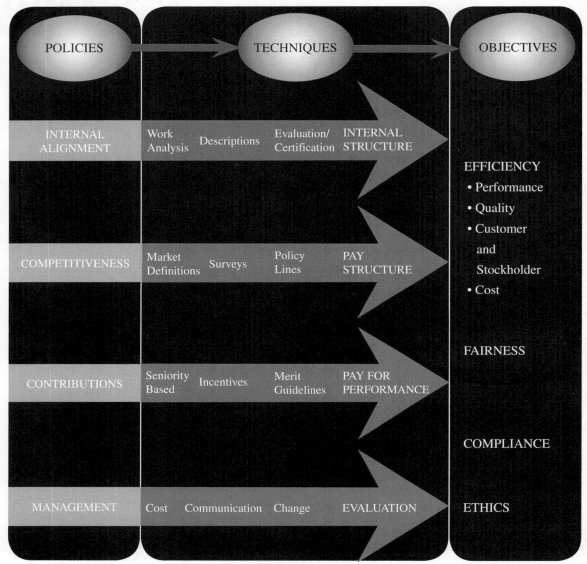

Government and Legal Issues in Compensation

Chapter Outline

Government as Part of the
Employment Relationship
   Demand
   Supply
Fair Labor Standards Act of 1938
   Minimum Wage
   "Living Wage"
   Overtime and Hours of Work
   Child Labor
Employee or Independent Contractor?
Prevailing Wage Laws
Pay Discrimination: What Is It?
The Equal Pay Act
   Definition of Equal
   Definitions of Skill, Effort, Responsibility,
   Working Conditions
   Factors Other Than Sex
   "Reverse" Discrimination
Title VII of the Civil Rights Act of 1964
and Related Laws
   Disparate Treatment
   Disparate Impact

Executive Order 11246
Pay Discrimination and Dissimilar Jobs
   Proof of Discrimination: Use of
   Market Data
   Proof of Discrimination: Jobs of
   Comparable Worth
Earnings Gaps
   Sources of the Earnings Gaps
   Differences in Occupations and
   Qualifications
   Differences in Industries and Firms
   Union Membership
   Presence of Discrimination
   Gaps Are Global
Comparable Worth
   The Mechanics
   Union Developments
   A Proactive Approach
Your Turn: Self-Evaluation and Pay
Discrimination
Still Your Turn: From Barista to Manager

A 1939 pay policy handbook for a major U.S. corporation outlines this justification for paying different wages to men and women working on the same jobs:[1]

> The . . . wage curve . . . is not the same for women as for men because of the more transient character of the former, the relative shortness of their activity in industry, the differences in environment required, the extra services that must be provided, overtime limitations, extra help needed for the occasional heavy work, and the general sociological factors not requiring discussion herein. Basically then we have another wage curve . . . for women below and not parallel with the men's curve.

The presumption that people should be paid different wages based on "general sociological factors" was still evident in the United States in the 1960s, in newspaper help-wanted ads that specified "perky gal Fridays" and in whites-only local unions. The 1960s civil rights movement and subsequent legislation were intended to end such practices.

Are you thinking you have stumbled into a history class by mistake? Not so. These historical practices and subsequent legislation still affect pay decisions. However, legislation does not always achieve what it intends nor intend what it achieves. Consequently, *compliance* and *fairness* are continuing compensation objectives.

In democratic societies, the legislative process begins when a problem is identified (not all citizens are receiving fair treatment in the workplace) and corrective legislation is proposed (the Civil Rights Act). If enough support develops, often as a result of compromises and tradeoffs, the proposed legislation becomes law. Employers, along with other stakeholders, attempt to influence the form any legislation will take.

Once passed, laws are enforced by agencies through rulings, regulations, inspections, and investigations. Companies respond to legislation by auditing and perhaps altering their practices, perhaps defending their practices before courts and agencies, and perhaps lobbying for still further legislative change. The laws and regulations issued by governmental agencies created to enforce the laws are a significant influence on compensation decisions throughout the world.

In the United States, there are three branches of *federal* government and each plays a role in the legal and regulatory framework in which employers work toward compliance objectives. The *legislative* branch (Congress) passes laws (or statutes). The *executive* branch, headed by the President, enforces laws through agencies and its other bodies (e.g., the Department of Labor), and the *judicial* branch interprets laws and considers their constitutionality. Over time, the legislative branch may change existing laws or pass new ones. The way that the judicial branch interprets laws can also change. The great interest in Supreme Court justice appointments and the difficulty sometimes encountered in gaining their confirmation is based on the belief that who the justices are will matter. Finally, enforcement priorities and intensity can vary from one presidential administration to the next. Compliance efforts by employers must take that fact into account.

Of course, the regulatory environment is also a function of *state and local* laws, which often cover employers not covered by federal laws and/or include requirements that go beyond federal laws. For example, Title VII of the (federal) Civil Rights Act, which prohibits employment (including pay) discrimination on the basis of race, color, religion, sex, or national origin, covers employers with 15 or more employees. But, under the Wisconsin Fair Employment Act, all employers are covered and discrimination on the basis of some characteristics (e.g., sexual orientation) not included in Title VII is prohibited. As another example, in our discussion of minimum wage laws later in this chapter, we will see that some states have minimums greater than the federal minimum. We will also see that some cities have living wage laws. Finally, of course, as we saw in Chapter 16, laws differ by country.[2]

Our objective in this chapter is to help you become more familiar with the legal and regulatory framework of compensation. Importantly, however, you will not be an attorney after reading this chapter. Compliance will require legal advice.

GOVERNMENT AS PART OF THE EMPLOYMENT RELATIONSHIP

People differ in their view of what role government should play in the contemporary workplace. Some call for organizations and the government to act in concert to carry out a public policy that protects the interests of employees.[3] Others believe that the best opportunities for employees are created by the constant change and reconfiguring that is inherent in market-based economies; the economy ought to be allowed to adapt and transform, undistorted by government actions.[4] All countries throughout the world must address these issues. However, different countries and cultures have different perspectives.

Governments' usual interests in compensation decisions are whether procedures for determining pay are fair (e.g., pay discrimination), safety nets for the unemployed and disadvantaged are sufficient (e.g., minimum wage, unemployment compensation), and employees are protected from exploitation (e.g., overtime pay, child labor restrictions). Consequently, company pay practices set the context for national debates on the minimum wage, health care, the security and portability of pensions, and even immigration, the quality of public education, and the availability of training.

In addition to being a party to all employment relationships, government units are also employers and purchasers. Consequently, government decisions also affect conditions in the labor market.

Demand

The U.S. federal government employs 1.75 million people; state and local governments employ many times that. Government employment is growing faster than population growth; plus, governments tend to pay more than the private sector.[5] Overall, government employment is 18 percent of the U.S. labor force.

In addition to being a big employer, government also indirectly affects labor demand through its purchases (military aircraft, computer systems, paper clips) as well as its financial policy decisions. For example, lowering interest rates generally boosts manufacturing of everything from condoms to condominiums. Increased business activity translates into increased demand for labor and upward pressure on wages.

Supply

In addition to being an employer, government affects labor supply through legislation. Laws aimed at protecting specific groups also tend to restrict those groups' participation in the labor market. Compulsory schooling laws restrict the supply of children available to sell hamburgers or to assemble soccer balls. Licensing requirements for certain occupations (plumbers, cosmetologists, psychologists) restrict the number of people who can legally offer a service.[6]

Immigration policy and how rigorously it is enforced is an increasingly important factor in labor supply. Economists estimate that immigration depresses wages for low-skill workers by approximately 5 percent, with previous immigrants being hit the hardest.[7]

To see how regulations reflect a society, Exhibit 17.1 shows how the compensation issues have changed over time. An early emphasis was basic protection: Child labor was prohibited and overtime wage provisions were specified in the Fair Labor Standards

EXHIBIT 17.1   U.S. Federal Pay Regulations

1931	**Davis-Bacon Act**	Requires that mechanics and laborers on public construction projects be paid the "prevailing wage" in an area.
1934	**Securities Exchange Act**	Created the Securities and Exchange Commission (SEC). Currently, the SEC requires companies that have more than $10 million in assets and whose securities are publicly traded and held by more than 500 owners to periodically report information, which is available to the public. This includes disclosure of compensation received by the CEO, CFO, and three other highest paid executives.
1936	**Walsh-Healey Public Contracts Act**	Extends prevailing-wage concept to manufacturers or suppliers of goods for government contracts.
1938	**Fair Labor Standards Act**	Sets minimum wage, hours of work, overtime premiums; prohibits child labor.
1963	**Equal Pay Act**	Equal pay required for men and women doing "substantially similar" work in terms of skill, effort, responsibility, and working conditions.
1964	**Title VII of Civil Rights Act of 1964**	Prohibits discrimination in all employment practices on basis of race, sex, color, religion, or national origin.
1965	**Executive Order 11246**	Prohibits discrimination by federal contractors and subcontractors in all employment practices on basis of race, sex, color, religion, or national origin.
1967	**Age Discrimination in Employment Act (ADEA)**	Protects employees age 40 and over against age discrimination.
1978	**Pregnancy Discrimination Act**	Pregnancy must be covered to same extent that other medical conditions are covered.
1990	**Americans With Disabilities Act**	Requires that "essential elements" of a job be called out. If a person with a disability can perform these essential elements, reasonable accommodation must be provided.
1991	**Civil Rights Act of 1991**	Increases border of proof on employers to rebut some discrimination claims. Stronger remedies available in cases of international discrimination
1993	**Family and Medical Leave Act**	Requires employers to provide up to 12 weeks' unpaid leave for family and medical emergencies.
1997	**Mental Health Act**	Mental illness must be covered to same extent that other medical conditions are covered.
2000	**Worker Economic Opportunity Act**	Income from most stock plans need not be included in calculating overtime pay.
2002	**Sarbanes-Oxley Act**	Executives cannot retain bonuses or profits from selling company stock if they mislead the public about the financial health of the company.

2004	Financial Accounting Standards Board Statement 123 R	Value of all employee stock options must be expensed at estimates of fair value on financial statements.
2006	Securities and Exchange Commission (SEC) rule change on executive compensation disclosure	Adopts enhanced executive compensation disclosure requirements. For example, the Compensation Discussion and Analysis in the proxy statement must address the objectives and implementation of executive compensation programs.
2009	Lilly Ledbetter Fair Pay Act	Employers can be liable for current pay differences that are a result of discrimination (as defined under existing laws such as Title VII of the Civil Rights Act) that occurred many years earlier.
2009	Troubled Asset Relief Program (TARP), American Recovery and Reinvestment Act of 2009 (ARRA)	Financial institutions receiving funds from TARP have restrictions on compensation. Prohibits use of several compensation programs, including, but not limited to bonuses, retention awards, and incentive pay, except where part of a preexisting employment contract, during the period TARP funds are received. Restricted stock is permitted if one-third or less of annual compensation. In firms receiving the largest TARP assistance, restrictions cover senior executives and next 20 highest paid employees.
Ongoing	SEC, Internal Revenue Service (IRS)/U.S. Treasury Department, Financial Accounting Standards Board (FASB)	Each engages in ongoing rule-making and/or interpretation of statutes that affects, respectively, public disclosure of executive compensation, tax treatment of executive and employee compensation, and accounting treatment of executive and employee compensation.
Ongoing	Department of Labor (DOL) Equal Employment Opportunity Commission (EEOC), and DOL Office of Federal Contract Compliance Programs (OFCCP)	DOL monitors compliance with Fair Labor Standards Act. EEOC and OFCCP monitor compliance with Title VII of the Civil Rights Act and Executive Order 11246, respectively.

Act. Prevailing-wage laws (Davis-Bacon and Walsh-Healey) specified government's obligations as an employer. The minimum wage has been periodically increased ever since its initial passage, and additional prevailing wage legislation continues to be passed. However, the main thrust of legislation shifted in the 1960s to emphasize civil rights. Since then we have continued to increase the scope of that legislation.

More recently, legislation has dealt with issues in the changing contemporary workplace. The Worker Economic Opportunity Act exempts stock options from the calculation for overtime pay. However, new accounting rules require that options be expensed on financial statements. The Sarbanes-Oxley Act stiffens requirements for reporting executive pay and other information to the Securities and Exchange Commission of the federal government. As Exhibit 17.1 shows, executive pay has continued to receive a good deal of attention.

This chapter will examine the most important U.S. regulations concerning wages. Because our society continues to wrestle with the issue of discrimination, we will go into some depth on how pay discrimination has been defined and the continuing earnings gaps between men and women and among racial/ethnic groups.

FAIR LABOR STANDARDS ACT OF 1938

The **Fair Labor Standards Act of 1938 (FLSA)** covers all employees (with some exceptions, discussed later) of companies engaged in interstate commerce or in the production of goods for interstate commerce. In spite of its age, this law remains a cornerstone of pay regulation in the United States. The FLSA's major provisions are:

1. Minimum wage
2. Hours of work
3. Child labor

An additional provision requires that records be kept of employees, their hours worked, and their pay.

Minimum Wage

Minimum-wage legislation is intended to provide an income floor for workers in society's least productive jobs. When first enacted in 1938, the minimum wage was 25 cents an hour. It has been raised periodically; in 2009, it was raised to $7.25.

Forty-four states plus the District of Columbia have their own minimum wages to cover jobs omitted from federal legislation.[8] If state and federal laws cover the same job, the higher rate prevails. Several states have minimums higher than the federal rate, with Washington being the highest at $8.55.

Exhibit 17.2 shows the purchasing power of the federal minimum wage over time, adjusted for inflation. The decline in real purchasing power (especially prior to the recent increase in the minimum wage) could be used to argue for indexing the minimum wage to changes in the consumer price index.

Estimates from the U.S. Bureau of Labor Statistics indicate that approximately 1.7 million U.S. workers are paid at or below the minimum wage. Nearly three-quarters of those earning minimum wage or less are in service occupations, mostly food service, where tips supplement hourly wages for many workers. The proportion of hourly paid workers earning minimum wage or less has trended downward since 1979 when data first began to be collected systematically. In 1979, 13.4 percent of hourly workers (7.7 percent of men and 20.2 percent of women) earned at or below minimum. More recently, the figures are 2.3 percent of hourly workers (1.4 percent of men and 3.1 percent of women). As a percentage of all wage and salary workers, those earning at or below minimum wage has declined from 7.9 percent in 1979 to 1.3 percent more recently.[9] An important reason for the decline in those directly affected is that the federal minimum wage stayed unchanged at $5.15 from 1997 to 2007.

With recent increases (to $7.25 as of July 2009), the number of workers affected is expected to increase. One study estimates that with the increase of the federal

EXHIBIT 17.2
Real (Inflation-Adjusted) Value of the Minimum Wage, by Year

Source: Kai Filion, "Minimum Wage Issue Guide" (Figure A), Economic Policy Institute, July 21, 2009, http://epi.3cdn.net/ 9f5a60cec02393cbe4_ a4m6b5t1v.pdf.

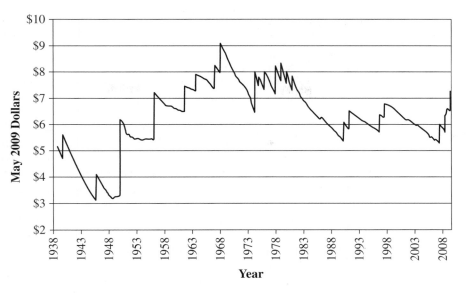

minimum wage to $7.25 in 2009, 12.5 million workers, or almost 10 percent of the workforce will be affected[10] Of the 12.5 million, 5.3 million would be directly affected (because their current wage is between any state minimum wage and $7.25). Another 7.2 million are expected to be indirectly affected by spillover effects. In other words, the effect of raising the minimum wage goes beyond the number of people who actually are paid the minimum. As legislation forces pay rates at the lowest end of the scale to move up, pay rates above the minimum often increase in order to maintain differentials. This shift in pay structure does not affect all industries equally. The lowest rates paid in the software, chemical, oil, and pharmaceutical industries are already well above minimum; any legislative change has little direct impact on them. In contrast, retailing and hospitality firms tend to pay at or near minimum wage to many clerks, sales persons, and cleaning people.

Why would anyone be opposed to a mandated minimum wage or making increases to it? The concern is that the resulting higher labor costs for affected firms may lead them to decrease their demand for workers and/or their hours worked. (See our discussion of supply and demand curves in Chapter 7.) In other words, a higher minimum wage, which is intended to help low wage workers, runs the risk of reducing employment opportunities for these very workers it is intended to help. So, whether a minimum wage "works" or not depends on whether the gains through higher wages are greater than the losses of jobs and/or hours.[11] Another consideration in evaluating minimum wage law effectiveness is whether wage gains go primarily to workers from low income families rather than going to workers from families with higher incomes.[12] Employers certainly have a stake in minimum wage public policy and thus may seek to influence it over time. In the shorter run, employers must be in compliance and will need to consider how changes to the minimum wage will affect their labor costs, to what degree they can pass the higher costs on to customers, and to what degree they will need to take some other action to control or offset higher labor costs.

"Living Wage"

Although living wage provisions are not part of the FLSA, we cover the topic here because of its similarity to FLSA minimum wage provisions.

Rather than push for changes in the FLSA, an alternative approach in recent years has been to push for a "living wage" at local levels that provides a minimum wage tailored to living costs in an area.[13] Generally, the amount specified is up to two times the federal minimum wage. Sometimes the laws cover only city employees; other times they cover employers that do business with the city. Sometimes they cover only base wages, but more frequently they require health insurance, vacations, sick pay, job security, and provide incentives to unionize.

Recently, Maryland became the first to adopt a statewide **living wage** ordinance, effective in 2009. More than 140 ordinances have been put into effect in the United States by cities, counties, universities, and other public entities. California has the most; it is followed by Michigan, New York, and Wisconsin.[14]

Los Angeles's law covers 9,000 people whose employers receive benefits from tax abatements (e.g., restaurant workers in an area redeveloped with public funds), through service contracts (e.g., janitors who clean public buildings), or through leases at the Los Angeles airport (e.g., baggage handlers, wheelchair attendants). The law mandates wages of $10.03 an hour if no benefits are offered, or $8.78 with benefits equal to $1.25/hour.

A study of the Los Angeles law's effects found that 7,735 of the covered employees got an average wage increase of 20 percent.[15] Another 149 noncovered employees got increases in order to maintain pay differentials. Employers adjusted to the law by making only very minor adjustments in employment—an estimated 112 jobs, or 1 percent of covered jobs, were lost. Fringes were cut for less than 5 percent of affected jobs, including cuts in health benefits, merit pay, bonuses, and employer-provided meals. Training for new hires stayed the same, but nonaffected firms were increasing their training. Firms benefited via reduced turnover and absenteeism. New hires tended to be better qualified, with higher levels of education and training than those hired before the law was passed. The new hires also included a higher proportion of males: 56 percent, compared to 45 percent of hires before the living wage. The study also found that 70 percent of the benefit of the law went to low-income families.

Living wage laws are increasingly popular. Coalitions of union members and church groups often support them. Because they are so narrowly tailored, there is some speculation that their real intention is to reduce any cost savings a municipality might receive from outsourcing. Reduced outsourcing means more government jobs, which generally translates into more union members.[16]

Overtime and Hours of Work

The overtime provision of the FLSA requires payment at one-and-a-half times the standard for working more than 40 hours per week. The law's objective is to share available work by making the hiring of additional workers a less costly option than the scheduling of overtime for current employees. However, the conditions that inspired the legislation have changed since the law was passed. Contemporary employers face (1) an increasingly skilled workforce with higher training costs per employee and (2) higher benefits costs, the bulk of which are fixed per employee. These factors have lowered the break-even point at which it pays employers to schedule longer hours and pay the overtime premium, rather than hire, train, and pay benefits for more employees.

Again, state laws sometimes go beyond the FLSA. California, for example, requires time and a half pay for working more than 8 hours in a day and double time for working more than 12 hours in a day. It also requires premium pay for working a seventh day during a week.

Exemptions

The Wage and Hour Division of the Department of Labor, which is charged with enforcement of the FLSA, provides strict criteria that must be met in order for jobs to be **exempt** from minimum-wage and overtime provisions. These are summarized in Exhibit 17.3.

Unscrupulous employers sometimes try to get around the overtime requirement by classifying employees as executives, even though the work of these "executives" differs only slightly from that of their co-workers. However, in the eyes of the Department of Labor, the job title is not relevant. Rather, it is the actual nature of the work that matters.

Merrill Lynch reached a $37 million settlement with financial analysts in California regarding overtime pay. A Merrill Lynch financial analyst argued that because his salary was entirely from commissions, he did not meet the "salary basis" test for the administrative exemption. The plaintiff also successfully argued that he did not exercise sufficient discretion and independent judgement. Instead, the financial analyst's work was considered "production," Merrill Lynch's practices were standard in the financial industry, and the impact of this ruling rippled through other financial service companies and brought changes to Merrill Lynch's pay system for analysts.[17]

Subsequently, Citigroup's Smith Barney brokerage unit settled an FLSA overtime lawsuit for $98 million, with UBS Financial Services and Morgan Stanley both also making substantial payments to settle similar suits. Insurance claims adjustors settled overtime lawsuits against Farmers Insurance for as much as $210 million and against State Farm Insurance for $135 million. Both of these lawsuits were brought under California law, under which it was more difficult than under federal law (i.e., the FLSA) to meet the administrative employee exemption. Indeed, similar lawsuits brought under FLSA have not succeeded.

Another challenge in compliance is that "in an evolving, always-on workplace where employees routinely put in extra hours and shoot off e-mails late at night from mobile devices, when the workday begins and ends has become an issue for employers."[18] For example, writers at ABC News asked that they be paid overtime for using their BlackBerrys for work purposes after business hours. As a result, ABC News asked writers to sign an agreement waiving rights to overtime for such activity. Writers who declined to sign had their BlackBerrys taken away.[19]

EXHIBIT 17.3   Fact Sheet #17A: Exemption for Executive, Administrative, Professional, Computer & Outside Sales Employees Under the Fair Labor Standards Act

Executive Exemption

To qualify for the executive employee exemption, all of the following tests must be met:

- The employee must be compensated on a salary basis (as defined in the regulations) at a rate not less than $455 per week;
- The employee's primary duty must be managing the enterprise, or managing a customarily recognized department or subdivision of the enterprise;
- The employee must customarily and regularly direct the work of at least two or more other full-time employees or their equivalent; and
- The employee must have the authority to hire or fire other employees, or the employee's suggestions and recommendations as to the hiring, firing, advancement, promotion or any other change of status of other employees must be given particular weight.

Administrative Exemptions

To qualify for the administrative employee exemption, all of the following tests must be met:

- The employee must be compensated on a salary or fee basis (as defined in the regulations) at a rate not less than $455 per week;
- The employee's primary duty must be the performance of office or non-manual work directly related to the management or general business operations of the employer or the employer's customers; and
- The employee's primary duty includes the exercise of discretion and independent judgment with respect to matters of significance.

Professional Exemption

To qualify for the learned professional employee exemption, all of the following tests must be met:

- The employee must be compensated on a salary or fee basis (as defined in the regulations) at a rate not less than $455 per week;
- The employee's primary duty must be the performance of work requiring advanced knowledge, defined as work which is predominantly intellectual in character and which includes work requiring the consistent exercise of discretion and judgment;
- The advanced knowledge must be in a field of science or learning; and
- The advanced knowledge must be customarily acquired by a prolonged course of specialized intellectual instruction.

To qualify for the creative professional employee exemption, all of the following tests must be met:

- The employee must be compensated on a salary or fee basis (as defined in the regulations) at a rate not less than $455 per week;
- The employee's primary duty must be the performance of work requiring invention, imagination, originality or talent in a recognized field of artistic or creative endeavor.

Computer Employee Exemption

To qualify for the computer employee exemption, the following tests must be met:

- The employee must be compensated either on a salary or fee basis (as defined in the regulations) at a rate not less than $455 per week or, if compensated on an hourly basis, at a rate not less than $27.63 an hour;
- The employee must be employed as a computer systems analyst, computer programmer, software engineer or other similarly skilled worker in the computer field performing the duties described below;
- The employee's primary duty must consist of:
  1. The application of systems analysis techniques and procedures, including consulting with users, to determine hardware, software or system functional specifications;
  2. The design, development, documentation, analysis, creation, testing or modification of computer systems or programs, including prototypes, based on and related to user or system design specifications;
  3. The design, documentation, testing, creation or modification of computer programs related to machine operating systems; or
  4. A combination of the aforementioned duties, the performance of which requires the same level of skills.

Outside Sales Exemption

To qualify for the outside sales employee exemption, all of the following tests must be met:

- The employee's primary duty must be making sales (as defined in the FLSA), or obtaining orders or contracts for services or for the use of facilities for which a consideration will be paid by the client or customer; and
- The employee must be customarily and regularly engaged away from the employer's place or places of business.

Highly Compensated Employees

Highly compensated employees performing office or non-manual work and paid total annual compensation of $100,000 or more (which must include at least $455 per week paid on a salary or fee basis) are exempt from the FLSA if they customarily and regularly perform at least one of the duties of an exempt executive, administrative or professional employee identified in the standard tests for exemption.

NOT Exempt

Blue-collar workers
Police, fire fighters, paramedics, and other first responders
These employee groups are not exempt, but rather are covered by the FLSA.

State Laws

When the state laws differ from the federal FLSA, an employer must comply with the standard most protective to employees.

Source: Excerpts from U.S. Department of Labor, Employment Standards Administration, Wage and Hour Division, http://www.dol.gov/esa/whd/regs/compliance/fairpay/, June 20, 2009.

The impact of FLSA and other laws depends importantly on the degree to which they are enforced. A Government Accountability Office (GAO) report found that the Labor Department's Wage and Hour Division "mishandled" 9 of 10 cases brought by GAO undercover agents posing as workers who had experienced FLSA violations.[20] As one example, an agent posing as a dishwasher called four times to complain that he had not been paid overtime for almost five months. His calls were not returned until 4 months later and he was then told it would take another 8 to 10 months to begin an investigation. GAO also investigated existing files. In another case, an undercover agent posing as an employer who had violated the law appeared to escape any penalty by simply saying that business was bad, so he could not afford to pay anything. The Department of Labor investigator was quoted as saying "OK, so you're not in a position where you can pay?" and when the undercover agent said that was correct, the investigator seemed to give up and said that he would let the worker know that he could pursue the case on his own (i.e., need to hire an attorney). In response, the Department of Labor noted that it had recently secured back pay for more than 300,000 workers per year. However, the new Secretary of Labor, Hilda Solis, said enforcement should be improved and accordingly she planned to increase the staff at the Wage and Hour Division by a third through hiring 250 additional investigators.

In Japan, unpaid overtime is a major issue. The Japanese Trade Union Confederation reports that two-thirds of men work more than 20 hours of unpaid overtime each month.[21] Only in 2008 did Toyota begin to pay factory workers for participating in quality control programs that were held outside of normal work hours. Some large companies have introduced "no overtime" days on which employees are to leave at 5:30 p.m. However, the concern is that many employees just take the work home, which is referred to as *furoshiki,* or "cloaked overtime."[22] "Death by overwork" (*karoshi*) has resulted in lawsuits against companies in Japan.

What Time Is Covered?

Sometimes counting the hours of work becomes a contest. Exhibit 17.4 details what we mean. WalMart settled 64 separate lawsuits at a cost of $640 million that included similar issues: workers stating they were not allowed to take bathroom breaks and not getting paid for hours worked (including overtime).[23] Occupational Safety and Health Administration legislation specifies the number of breaks that must be provided in an eight-hour workday. The Portal-to-Portal Act provides that time spent on activities before beginning the "principal activity" is generally not compensable. The original issue that inspired the act was the time that miners were forced to spend traveling to and from the actual underground site where the mining was occurring. The meat processing industry has been the source of several cases defining time spent at work. Time spent sharpening knives and cutting tools is compensable time, as is the time spent donning protective gear and walking in this "integral" gear to the production area.[24]

The law is also relevant to "on-call employees" who must be available to respond outside the usual workday. Firefighters and emergency personnel are traditional examples. Today, telecommunications and software services personnel who must respond quickly to problems outside their regularly scheduled workday are newer categories of employees eligible for "beeper pay." (See also our ABC News example earlier.) In

EXHIBIT 17.4
There's No
Such Thing as
a Free . . .

Gainers Workers Must Pay to Use Bathroom
EDMONTON—Employees at Gainers Inc. are now docked pay for every bathroom break visit made outside of breaks and lunch hour under regulations brought in last week by company owner Burns Meats Ltd.

A notice posted in the meat-packing plant tells employees that abusing washroom visits has lowered productivity. If employees need to use the bathroom outside of breaks, they must report to a supervisor, who records the time of departure and return. The time is tabulated at the end of the week and pay cheques are deducted based on an employee's hourly wage.

"How can they charge you for going to the washroom?" asked one angry employee. The man said one worker at the plant had a kidney transplant and has to use the washroom often.

"Because of this system, he had to hold it in [between breaks] for a whole week. He went once for three minutes and was charged 43 cents." . . .

Such washroom rules are rare but there is nothing in the Alberta employment standards code that requires a person to be paid when they don't work, said Kathy Lazowski, a public affairs officer with Alberta Labour. . . .

Source: Sid Shniad, "There's No Such Thing as a Free . . . Gainers Workers Must Pay to Use Bathroom," *Canadian Press,* September 22, 1994.

general, if employees can use this "on-call" time for their own purposes, there is no legal requirement to pay employees for such time, even if they are required to carry a beeper or must let their employer know where they can be reached. However, if they are required to stay on the employer's premises while on call, then they must be compensated for that time. Sometimes a flat rate is paid for the added inconvenience of being on call. These payments must be included when computing overtime pay.[25]

What Income Is Covered?

FLSA specifies one and a half times pay for overtime, but one and a half of what? As more employees became eligible for bonuses, there was an argument over whether bonus, gain-sharing, and stock option payments needed to be included for calculating overtime pay. A 1999 advisory from the Wage and Hour Division said they did. But the extra bookkeeping and calculations provided enough of a burden that employers simply did not offer these forms of pay to **nonexempt** employees. The Worker Economic Opportunity Act, a 2000 amendment to FLSA, allows stock options and bonuses to be exempt from inclusion in overtime pay calculations. Gifts or special-occasion bonuses have never needed to be included, because they are at the employer's discretion rather than a pay form promised to employees if certain conditions are met.

Compensatory Time Off

The changing nature of the workplace and of pay systems has led to calls to reform FLSA to allow for more flexible scheduling and easier administration of variable pay plans.

Federal legislation has been proposed (but not yet passed) that would give employees and employers the option of trading overtime pay for time off. Rather than being paid overtime after 8 hours for a 10-hour workday, an employee would have the option of taking 2 or more hours off at another time. Or, a 50-hour workweek could be banked against a future 30-hour workweek.[26] The employee would get more scheduling flexibility to attend to personal matters, and the employer would save money. This kind of change has a lot of appeal for employees who are also raising children and/or caring for elderly parents. One poll reported that 81 percent of women would prefer compensatory time off in lieu of overtime wages.[27]

Child Labor

Generally, persons under 18 cannot work in hazardous jobs such as meat packing and logging; persons under 16 cannot be employed in jobs involving interstate commerce except for nonhazardous work for a parent or guardian. Additional exceptions and limitations also exist.[28]

The union movement in the United States has taken a leading role in publicizing the extent of the use of child labor outside the United States to produce goods destined for U.S. consumers. A Your Turn exercise at the end of this chapter explores some of the issues surrounding child labor outside the United States. Government guidelines help importers monitor the employment practices of subcontractors producing goods for the U.S. market. A recent International Labour Organization report finds that globally, child labor is declining, particularly in Latin America. Brazil and Mexico, where half the children in Latin America live, have made the greatest strides, which the study attributed to increased political will, awareness, poverty reduction, and education. The steepest declines were among children 14 and younger, and among hazardous occupations. The highest rates of child labor are in sub-Saharan Africa, where high population growth, grinding poverty, and the HIV/AIDS epidemic have left a lot of families in need of the income that children can provide.[29]

EMPLOYEE OR INDEPENDENT CONTRACTOR?

As we saw in Chapter 12, U.S. employers are legally obligated to pay Social Security, unemployment compensation, and workers compensation taxes on wages and salaries on behalf of their employees. In 2009, the average total compensation per employee was $29.39 per hour, with $20.49 of that being in the form of wages and salaries and the remaining $8.90 being for benefits. Of the $8.90, $2.28 was for the legally required benefits just mentioned. However, in the case of a worker who is an independent contractor rather than an employee, the employer is not obligated to pay the legally required benefits. In addition, independent contractors would also typically not receive other benefits. Thus, whether a worker is classified as an employee or an independent contractor can have substantial cost implications for an employer, which of course increases with the number of workers involved.

As with the FLSA exceptions discussed a few pages earlier, the decision of whether to classify a worker as an employee or independent contractor requires careful attention to compliance issues. Both tax law—enforced by the Internal Revenue Service (IRS)—and the Employee Retirement Income Security Act (ERISA)—enforced by the Department of Labor—are relevant. The most widely used classification criteria are provided by the IRS and shown in Exhibit 17.5. Two general criteria have to do with behavioral and financial control. The more control a firm is able to exercise, the more

EXHIBIT 17.5   **Employee or Independent Contractor: Internal Revenue Service Tests**

Behavioral control. Facts that show whether the business has a right to direct and control how the worker does the task for which the worker is hired include the type and degree of:

Instructions that the business gives to the worker. An employee is generally subject to the business' instructions about when, where, and how to work. Even if no instructions are given, sufficient behavioral control may exist if the employer has the right to control how the work results are achieved. Examples of types of instructions include: when and where to do the work, what tools or equipment to use, what workers to hire or to assist with the work, where to purchase supplies and services, what work must be performed by a specified individual, what order or sequence to follow.

Training that the business gives to the worker. An employee may be trained to perform services in a particular manner. Independent contractors ordinarily use their own methods.

Financial control. Facts that show whether the business has a right to control the business aspects of the worker's job include:

The extent to which the worker has unreimbursed business expenses. Independent contractors are more likely to have unreimbursed expenses than are employees.

The extent of the worker's investment. An independent contractor often has a significant investment in the facilities he or she uses in performing services for someone else.

The extent to which the worker makes his or her services available to the relevant market. An independent contractor is generally free to seek out business opportunities. Independent contractors often advertise, maintain a visible business location, and are available to work in the relevant market.

How the business pays the worker. An employee is generally guaranteed a regular wage amount for an hourly, weekly, or other period of time. An independent contractor is usually paid by a flat fee for the job. However, it is common in some professions, such as law, to pay independent contractors hourly.

The extent to which the worker can realize a profit or loss. An independent contractor can make a profit or loss.

Type of relationship. Facts that show the parties' type of relationship include:

Written contracts describing the relationship the parties intended to create.

Whether or not the business provides the worker with employee-type benefits, such as insurance, a pension plan, vacation pay, or sick pay.

The permanency of the relationship. If you engage a worker with the expectation that the relationship will continue indefinitely, rather than for a specific project or period, this is generally considered evidence that your intent was to create an employer-employee relationship.

The extent to which services performed by the worker are a key aspect of the regular business of the company. If a worker provides services that are a key aspect of your regular business activity, it is more likely that you will have the right to direct and control his or her activities. For example, if a law firm hires an attorney, it is likely that it will present the attorney's work as its own and would have the right to control or direct that work. This would indicate an employer-employee relationship.

Source: Adapted from *Publication 15-A (2009)*, Internal Revenue Service, Department of U.S. Treasury. http://www.irs.gov/publications/p15a/ar02.html#en_US_publink100052199

likely it is that the IRS will see the worker as an employee rather than an independent contractor. The IRS also considers the type of relationship, including its permanence. The Supreme Court, in *Nationwide v. Darden*, has applied similar criteria in deciding whether a worker is an employee under ERISA.[30]

Microsoft hired workers as independent contractors. It had these workers sign agreements acknowledging their independent contractor status. However, after an audit by the IRS concluded that these workers were actually employees, Microsoft agreed to begin paying legally required taxes (see above). Microsoft had used the workers on projects, often working on teams with regular employees, doing similar work, working similar hours, and being supervised by the same managers. Microsoft also required them to work onsite and they were given office equipment and supplies.[31]

Next, two separate suits *(Vizcaino v. Microsoft* and *Hughes v. Microsoft)* were filed against Microsoft to compel it to retroactively provide other benefits (e.g., a discounted stock purchase program) that it provided to its (other) employees. Some of the workers had been at Microsoft for several years with a few being there as long as 10 years. Microsoft eventually settled these suits for $97 million, which after attorneys fees, will be divided between 8,000 and 12,000 people employed at Microsoft for at least 9 months during a several-year period.[32] Microsoft implemented new rules, including limiting independent contractor assignments to 12 months with at least 100 days between assignments. More recently, FedEx was ordered to pay $27 million to 203 drivers in California who were ruled *(Estrada v. FedEx Ground Package System, Inc.)* to have been wrongly classified as independent contractors.[33] And, that may not be the end of the compliance issue for FedEx. It announced that the IRS, upon tentatively deciding that FedEx has misclassified workers as contractors, was considering $319 million in tax and penalties for one year and that it was in the process of looking at other years also.[34]

PREVAILING WAGE LAWS

Prevailing wage laws set pay for work done to produce goods and services contracted by the federal government. A *government-defined prevailing wage* is the minimum wage that must be paid for work done on covered government projects or purchases. Consider, for example, "The Big Dig," Boston's $15 billion taxpayer-financed project to put its freeways underground.[35] A construction project of such magnitude attracts workers from a very wide area and distorts the labor market. Prevailing-wage laws prevent contractors from using their size to drive down wages. The law was passed in response to conditions on projects such as the construction of the Hoover Dam during the Depression. Workers who collapsed from the July heat in Nevada or were killed in accidents were quickly replaced from a pool of unemployed men who were already camping near the job site.

To comply with the law, contractors must determine the "going rate" for construction labor in an area. As a practical matter, the "union rate" for labor becomes the going rate. That rate then becomes the mandated minimum wage on the government-financed project. One effect is to distort market wages and drive up the cost of government-financed projects. For example, the market wage for plumbers in Kentucky is $18.15 an hour, according to the Bureau of Labor Statistics. Yet a wage survey for Owsley

County, Kentucky, requires that plumbers on public projects receive $23.75 an hour, more than 30 percent above the government's own market wage.[36]

A number of laws contain prevailing-wage provisions. They vary on the government expenditures they target for coverage. The main prevailing-wage laws include the Davis-Bacon Act, the Walsh-Healey Public Contracts Act, the Service Contract Act, and the National Foundation for the Arts and Humanities Act. A spate of new laws extends prevailing-wage coverage to new immigrants to the United States and to noncitizens who are working in the United States under special provisions. For example, the Nursing Relief for Disadvantaged Areas Act of 1999 allows qualified hospitals to employ temporary foreign workers as registered nurses for up to three years under a special visa program. The prevailing wage for registered nurses must be paid to these foreign workers. Similar acts target legal immigrants and farm workers.

Much of the legislation discussed so far was originally passed in the 1930s and 1940s in response to social issues of that time. While this legislation has continued to be extended up to the present, the Equal Rights movement in the 1960s pushed different social problems to the forefront. The Equal Pay Act and the Civil Rights Act were passed. Because of their substantial impact on human resource management and compensation, they are discussed at length below.

PAY DISCRIMINATION: WHAT IS IT?

Before we look at specific federal pay discrimination laws, which are summarized in Exhibit 17.6, let us address the more general question of how to legally define discrimination. The law recognizes two types of discrimination: access discrimination and valuation discrimination. The charges of discrimination and reverse discrimination that most often make the news involve **access discrimination:** the denial of particular jobs, promotions, or training opportunities to qualified women or minorities. The University of Michigan, for example, was accused of access discrimination for using differential standards among different racial groups to determine who is "qualified" for admission. Being a member of a minority group counted for 20 points, whereas the quality of the admission essay counted for 3 points. (Being an athlete also counted for 20 points.) In 2003, the Supreme Court ruled that while schools can take race into account for admission, this 20-point differential was illegal because it was applied in a mechanical way.[37] However, the admission process for Michigan's law school was upheld because it was narrowly tailored and more flexible. Minority candidates for the law school were interviewed and their entire record was examined, in contrast to the routine addition of 20 points that the undergraduate school used. (The court did not address the issue of the preferred treatment for athletes or children of alumni or big donors.)[38]

A second legally recognized interpretation of discrimination is **valuation discrimination,** which looks at the pay women and minorities receive for the jobs they perform. This is the more salient definition for our purposes. The Equal Pay Act makes it clear that it is discriminatory to pay women less than males when they are performing equal work (i.e., working side by side, in the same plant, doing the same work, producing the same results). This definition of pay discrimination hinges on the standard of *equal pay for equal work.*

EXHIBIT 17.6 Federal Pay Discrimination Law and Enforcement

	Equal Pay Act	Title VII, Civil Rights Act	Executive Order 11246
Year	1963	1964	1965
Discrimination Prohibited on Basis of:	Sex	Race, color, religion, sex, or national origin	Race, color, religion, sex, or national origin
Type of Pay Discrimination Prohibited	"for equal work on jobs the) performance of which requires equal skill, effort, and responsibility, and which are performed under similar working conditions, except where such payment is made pursuant to (i) a seniority system; (ii) a merit system; (iii) a system which measures earnings by quantity or quality of production; or (iv) a differential based on any other factor other than sex" (Equal Pay Act)	"[in] compensation, terms, conditions, or privileges of employment" (Title VII, Civil Rights Act)	"statistically significant compensation disparities between similarly situated employees . . . . after taking into account legitimate factors which influence compensation." ("Systemic Compensation Discrimination," Federal Register, June 16, 2006)
Coverage	Same as FLSA. Virtually all employers.	Employers having 15 or more employees. Those with 100 or more employees must also file annual EEO-1 reports, which report the number of employees by race, ethnicity and gender for each of nine job categories. Over 600,000 employers covered.*	Government contractors and subcontractors with $10,000 or more in government contracts. Contractors with 50 or more employees and $50,000 or more in contracts must also file annual EEO-1 reports, which report the number of employees by race, ethnicity and gender for each of nine job categories. Nearly 90,000 employers covered.**
Enforcement Agency	Equal Employment Opportunity Commission (EEOC)	Equal Employment Opportunity Commission (EEOC)	Office of Federal Contract Compliance Programs (OFCCP), Department of Labor
Primary Enforcement Action Trigger	Employee Complaint-Driven	Employee Complaint-Driven	Regular Audits

*U.S. Government Accountability Office, "Federal Agencies Should Better Monitor Their Performance in Enforcing Anti-Discrimination Laws," GAO Reports, Report Number GAO-08-799, Washington, D.C., August 2008.
**Ibid.

Many believe that this definition of valuation discrimination does not go far enough. They believe that valuation discrimination can also occur when men and women hold entirely different jobs. For example, office and clerical jobs are typically staffed by women, and craft jobs (electricians, welders) are typically staffed by men. Is it illegal to pay employees in one job group less than employees in the other if the two job groups contain work that is not equal in content or results but is, in some sense, of **comparable worth** to the employer?[39]

In this case, the proposed definition of pay discrimination hinges on the standard of *equal pay for work of comparable worth* (also called **pay equity** or **gender pay equity**). Existing federal laws in the United States do not support this standard. However, several states have enacted laws that require a comparable-worth standard for state and local government employees. For an understanding of the legal foundations for both the equal work and the comparable worth standard, let us turn to the legislation and key court cases.

THE EQUAL PAY ACT

The Equal Pay Act (EPA) of 1963 (which is part of the FLSA) forbids wage discrimination on the basis of gender if employees perform equal work in the same establishment. Jobs are considered equal if they require equal skill, effort, and responsibility and are performed under similar working conditions.

Differences in pay between men and women doing equal work are legal if these differences are based on any one of four criteria, called an *affirmative defense:*

- Seniority.
- Merit or quality of performance.
- Quality or quantity of production.
- Some factor other than sex.

These terms for comparison and permitted defenses seem deceptively simple. Yet numerous court cases have been required to clarify the act's provisions, particularly its definition of "equal."

Definition of Equal

The Supreme Court first established guidelines to define equal work in the *Schultz v. Wheaton Glass* case back in 1970. Wheaton Glass Company maintained two **job classifications** for selector-packers in its production department: male and female. The female job class carried a pay rate 10 percent below that of the male job class. The company claimed that the male job class included additional tasks such as shoveling broken glass, opening warehouse doors, and doing heavy lifting that justified the pay differential. The plaintiff claimed that the extra tasks were infrequently performed and not all men did them. Further, these extra tasks performed by some of the men were regularly performed by employees in another classification ("snap-up boys"), and these employees were paid only 2 cents an hour more than the women. Did the additional tasks sometimes performed by some members of one job class render the jobs unequal?

The Court decided they did not. It ruled that the equal work standard required only that jobs be *substantially* equal, not identical. Additionally, in several cases where the duties employees actually performed were different from those in the job descriptions, the courts held that the *actual work performed* must be used to decide whether jobs are substantially equal.

Definitions of Skill, Effort, Responsibility, Working Conditions

The Department of Labor provides these definitions of the four factors.

1. *Skill:* Experience, training, education, and ability as measured by the performance requirements of a particular job.
2. *Effort:* Mental or physical—the degree of effort (not type of effort) actually expended in the performance of a job.
3. *Responsibility:* The degree of accountability required in the performance of a job.
4. *Working conditions:* The physical surroundings and hazards of a job, including dimensions such as inside versus outside work, heat, cold, and poor ventilation.

Guidelines to clarify these definitions have evolved through court decisions. For an employer to support a claim of *unequal* work, the following conditions must be met:

1. The effort/skill/responsibility must be substantially greater in one of the jobs compared.
2. The tasks involving the extra effort/skill/responsibility must consume a *significant amount* of time for *all* employees whose additional wages are in question.
3. The extra effort/skill/responsibility must have a *value commensurate* with the questioned pay differential (as determined by the employer's own evaluation).

Time of day (e.g., working a night shift) does not constitute dissimilar working conditions. However, if a differential for working at night is paid, it must be separated from the base wage for the job.

Factors Other Than Sex

Of the four affirmative defenses for unequal pay for equal work, "a factor other than sex" has prompted the most court cases. Factors other than sex include shift differentials; temporary assignments; bona fide training programs; differences based on ability, training, or experience; and other reasons of "business necessity."

Factors other than sex have been interpreted as a broad exception that may include business reasons advanced by the employer. A practice will not automatically be prohibited simply because wage differences between men and women result. However, an employer is required to justify the business relatedness of the practice.[40] Usually a specific practice is not singled out; rather, the argument focuses on a "pattern of practices." That is what a group of female brokers at Merrill Lynch charged in their class action suit. They were concerned with how accounts from departing brokers, walk-ins, and referrals were being distributed. They felt that the top men brokers were given the most promising leads, while everyone else, including the 15 percent of brokers who were women, got the "crumbs." The women contended that Merrill Lynch discriminated against women in wages, promotions, account distributions, maternity leaves, and other areas. A negotiated settlement promised to establish a more open method for sharing leads and not to penalize brokers for time off in determining bonuses and production quotas.

Because such cases tend to be settled out of court, no legal clarification of a "factor other than sex" has ever been provided. It does seem that pay differences for equal work can be justified for demonstrably business-related reasons. But what is and is not demonstrably business-related has yet to be cataloged.

"Reverse" Discrimination

Many people dislike the term "reverse" discrimination, saying that it is still discrimination, even if the group penalized is white males. Several court cases deal with discrimination against men when pay for women is adjusted. The University of Nebraska created a model to calculate salaries based on estimated values for a faculty member's education, field of specialization, years of direct experience, years of related experience, and merit. Based on these qualifications, the university granted raises to 33 women whose salaries were less than the amount computed by the model. However, the university gave no such increases to 92 males whose salaries were also below the amount the model set for them based on their qualifications. The court found this system a violation of the Equal Pay Act. It held that, in effect, the university was using a new system to determine a salary schedule, based on specific criteria. To refuse to pay employees of one sex the minimum required by these criteria was illegal.

Viewed collectively, the courts have provided reasonably clear directions to interpret the Equal Pay Act. The design of pay systems must incorporate a policy of equal pay for substantially equal work. The determination of substantially equal work must be based on the actual work performed (the job content) and must reflect the skill, effort, responsibility, and working conditions involved. It is legal to pay men and women who perform substantially equal work differently if the pay system is designed to recognize differences in performance, seniority, quality, and quantity of results, or certain factors other than sex in a nondiscriminatory manner. Further, if a new pay system is designed, it must be equally applied to all employees.

But what does this tell us about discrimination on jobs that are *not substantially equal*—dissimilar jobs? Fifty-eight percent of all working women are not in jobs substantially equal to jobs of men, so they are not covered by the Equal Pay Act. Title VII of the Civil Rights Act extends protection to them.

TITLE VII OF THE CIVIL RIGHTS ACT OF 1964 AND RELATED LAWS

The Civil Rights Act is a far-reaching law that grew out of the civil rights movement of the 1950s and 1960s. **Title VII** of the act prohibits discrimination on the basis of sex, race, color, religion, or national origin in any employment condition, including hiring, firing, promotion, transfer, compensation, and admission to training programs. Title VII was amended in 1972, 1978, and 1990.

In addition to Title VII, the 1967 **Age Discrimination in Employment Act (ADEA)** and the 1990 **Americans with Disabilities Act (ADA)** also prohibit discrimination based on age and disability, respectively. Compliance with the ADEA is typically a key concern when companies use workforce reduction programs. The ADEA pertains not only to age-related differences in pay and employment outcomes, but in addition, it was amended in 1990 to include the Older Workers Benefit Protection Act (OWBPA), which has detailed rules regarding how separation agreements (e.g., an early retirement incentive) involving older workers are used. As one example, at least 21 days must be given to consider the agreement.

Title VII cases of pay discrimination typically focus on differences in pay, promotions, pay raises, and performance reviews. Race-based differences in these areas were at the center of litigation against Coca-Cola, which it settled for $192 million.[41] Similar issues are the basis for an ongoing sex-based discrimination lawsuit against Wal-Mart, which involves as many as 1.6 million claimants and could—if Wal-Mart does not prevail or must settle—be the first *billion-dollar plus* equal employment opportunity case settled in favor of claimants. In the meantime, of course, these cases are very costly for the company in terms of legal expenses, unfavorable publicity, employee relations, and the allocation of time away from the core business. Organizations that can successfully be proactive in maintaining compliance increase their chances of avoiding such litigation.

The passage in 2009 of the Lilly Ledbetter Fair Pay Act is expected to further increase the compliance challenge for employers. The statute of limitations for filing a claim of discrimination is within 180 days (300 days in states with their own equal employment opportunity agencies) of the date of the alleged discriminatory employment practice. Lilly Ledbetter's claim was made after she left her job as a supervisor in a tire plant and were based on the lasting effects of compensation decisions she alleged to be discriminatory that were made as much as 19 years earlier, far outside the 180 day period. In 2007, the Supreme Court ruled (*Ledbetter v. Goodyear Tire 8 Rubber Company*) that such decisions could not be litigated because they were outside the statute of limitations. However, the 2009 Act overturns this rule, instead stating that discrimination occurs—and starts the 180/300-day time period for filing a claim—"each time a discriminatory paycheck is issued, not just when the employer makes an adverse pay-setting decision."[42] According to the EEOC, "The Act restores the pre-Ledbetter position of the EEOC that each paycheck that delivers discriminatory compensation is a wrong which is actionable under the federal EEO statutes, regardless of when the discrimination began."[43] It has been argued that "employers will likely be called upon to defend against actions and decisions made by retired managers and supervisors that occurred years, and even decades, ago."[44]

Court cases have established two theories of discrimination behavior under Title VII: (1) **disparate treatment** and (2) **disparate impact.**

Disparate Treatment

Disparate or unequal treatment applies different standards to different employees: For example, asking women but not men if they plan to have children. In Japan, for example, women college students continue to report that recruiters ask them different questions than are asked of male college students. The mere fact of unequal treatment may be taken as evidence of the employer's intention to discriminate under U.S. law.

Disparate Impact

Practices that have a differential effect on members of protected groups are illegal, unless the differences are work-related. The major case that established this interpretation of Title VII is *Griggs v. Duke Power Co.,* which struck down employment tests and educational requirements that screened out a higher proportion of blacks than whites. Even though the practices were applied equally—both blacks and whites had to pass the tests—they were prohibited because (1) they had the consequence of excluding a protected group disproportionately and (2) the tests were not related to the jobs in question.

Under disparate impact, whether or not the employer intended to discriminate is irrelevant. A personnel decision can, on its face, seem neutral, but if its results are unequal, the employer must demonstrate that the decision is work-related. The two standards of discrimination—disparate treatment versus disparate impact—remain difficult to apply to pay issues, since pay differences are legal for dissimilar work. It is still not clear what constitutes pay discrimination in dissimilar jobs in the United States.[45]

EXECUTIVE ORDER 11246

Enforced by the Office of Federal Contracts Compliance Programs (OFCCP), Department of Labor, Executive Order 11246 (E.O. 11246) prohibits discrimination on the basis of race, color, religion, sex, or national origin. It requires covered government contractors to file affirmative action plans, which have three parts. First, utilization analysis compares the contractor's workforce to the available external workforce. Underutilization exists if a group (e.g., women) represent a significantly smaller percentage of the employer's workforce than of the external workforce. Second, goals and timetables are developed for achieving affirmative action. Third, action steps are developed for achieving these goals and timetables. As discussed below, the OFCCP conducts audits and seeks remedies where it finds insufficient compliance. During fiscal year 2008, for example, the OFCCP recovered a record $67,510,982 in back pay and salary and benefits for 24,508 individuals.[46] Not all of this money was obtained in compensation-related cases and not all of the OFCCP's efforts focus on compensation issues. Nevertheless, the OFCCP has increased its enforcement efforts in the area of compensation and that is our primary focus here. The OFCCP's budget is being increased for fiscal year 2010 by $25,600,000, which will be used to fund 213 new full-time employees and "enforcement and outreach efforts related to compensation."[47]

Here we focus specifically on the steps in the OFCCP's compliance review process as it applies to compensation.[48] It begins with a selection of contractors based, in part, on a mathematical model, called the Federal Contractor Selection System (FCSS), which is intended to predict the likelihood that a contractor is engaging in systemic (i.e., affecting a broad class of employees) discrimination. (Under a 1999 Memorandum of Understanding with the EEOC, individual complaints of compensation discrimination can be referred to the EEOC.) The OFCCP also selects contractors based on other factors (e.g., time since their previous review) and selects some contractors at random. In recent years, about 5 percent of all contractors have been selected for review.

If selected, the first step is a desk audit. The OFCCP will notify the employer that it is conducing an audit and will instruct the employer to provide complete information on its Affirmative Action Program and all supporting personnel activity (such as hiring, promotion decisions) and compensation data within 30 days. This is "analyzed for possible systemic discrimination indicators (i.e., a potential affected class of 10 or more applicants/workers)."[49] If such indicators are found, additional information for the desk audit will be requested. After the desk audit is completed, if the OFCCP decides the employer is in compliance, it ends the process by issuing a closure letter.

If the OFCCP believes systemic discrimination may be present, it conducts an onsite review, where it will delve deeper into statistical analyses of data (including using multiple regression analysis) and also conduct interviews with management and non-management employees for "anecdotal evidence" to consider along with statistical evidence.[50] Based on its statistical analyses and anecdotal evidence, the OFCCP will decide whether there is evidence of systemic discrimination. If so, it will issue a Notice of Violation (NOV). It will not, "except in unusual cases," rely *only* on statistical evidence.[51] If an NOV is issued, the OFCCP will seek to have the employer sign a conciliation agreement under which it agrees to stop and remedy practices identified as discriminatory. The employer may also be required to change its compensation levels for some employee groups to remedy disparities between similarly situated employees that the OFCCP judges to be the result of systemic discrimination. If the OFCCP cannot reach a settlement with the employer, it can refer the case to the Office of the Solicitor and disputes are addressed in a hearing in front of an administrative law judge. The OFCCP can also seek to disbar contractors from receiving future contracts from the government or to stop payments on current contracts.

Most companies already have their hands full managing relationships with customers, investors, and suppliers. An onsite visit by an OFCCP compliance investigator can mean that at least some HR employees will be forced to put their work in managing employee relationships on hold and instead deal with the compliance review. Outside legal counsel may be necessary, which can be costly. If an NOV is issued, the company will face further challenges. So, what can a company do to avoid running afoul of E.O. 11246 and the OFCCP?

The simple answer is: Don't discriminate. The somewhat more complex answer is don't discriminate *and* collect and analyze data to document that you are not. In fact, self-evaluation by employers is actually required. The OFCCP offers what it describes as an "incentive" do so in that it "will coordinate its compliance monitoring activities with the contractor's self-evaluation approach." If the self-evaluation approach "reasonably meets the general standards outline in the Voluntary Guidelines, OFCCP will consider the contractor's compensation practices to be in compliance with Executive Order 11246."[52] In other words, if the self-evaluation follows the standards and shows no disparities between similarly situated employee groups, the OFCCP says the employer is in compliance.

As part of the self-evaluation, the employer is required to use multiple regression analysis for any similarly situated group (SSEG) that has 30 or more total employees and at least 5 employees in each group to be compared (the 30/5 rule). An SSEG is "a grouping of employees who perform similar work, and occupy positions with similar responsibility levels and involving similar skills and qualifications."[53] The following example is similar to one given by the OFCCP:

SSEG Group	Total Employees	Female Employees	Hispanic Employees
A	34	6	10
B	32	22	4

Multiple regression would be used to make both gender-based and race-based statistical comparisons in SSEG Group A. But, in SSEG group B, only gender-based statistical comparisons could be made. The OFCCP states that the multiple regression "must include factors that are important to how the contractor in practice makes pay decisions"[54] and gives as examples: education, work experience with previous employers, seniority, time in salary grade, and performance ratings. SSEG group must also be controlled.

As with any analysis that can be seen as relevant to deciding whether an employer has engaged in or is engaging in discrimination, care must be taken to minimize legal risks. Obviously, obtaining prompt legal counsel is necessary. For the analyses to be privileged (and not open to discovery, for example, by a plaintiff's attorney in possible future litigation), they should be done under the direction of an attorney and strict communication protocols must be followed.[55]

PAY DISCRIMINATION AND DISSIMILAR JOBS

In 1981, the Supreme Court, in *Gunther v. County of Washington,* determined that pay differences for dissimilar jobs may reflect discrimination. In this case, four jail matrons in Washington County, Oregon, claimed that their work was comparable to that performed by male guards. The matrons also were assigned clerical duties, because guarding the smaller number of female prisoners did not occupy all of the work time.

Lower courts said the matrons had no grounds because the jobs did not meet the equal work requirement of the Equal Pay Act. But the Supreme Court stated that a Title VII pay case was not bound by the definitions in the Equal Pay Act. While the Supreme Court did not say that Washington County had discriminated, it did say that a claim of wage discrimination could also be brought under Title VII for situations where the jobs were not the same. Unfortunately, the Court did not say what might constitute evidence of pay discrimination in dissimilar jobs. The case was returned to a lower court for additional evidence of discrimination and was eventually settled out of court.

So if jobs are dissimilar and if no pattern of discrimination in hiring, promotion, or other personnel decisions exists, then what constitutes pay discrimination? Courts have ruled on the use of market data as well as the use of job evaluation. We will look at both of these possible standards in turn.

Proof of Discrimination: Use of Market Data

In a landmark case regarding the use of market data, Denver nurse Mary Lemons claimed that her job, held predominantly by women, was illegally paid less than the city and county of Denver paid jobs held predominantly by men (tree trimmers, sign painters, tire servicemen, etc.). Lemons claimed that the nursing job required more education and skill. Therefore, to pay the male jobs more than the nurses' jobs simply because the male jobs commanded higher rates in the local labor market was discriminatory. She argued that the market reflected historical underpayment of "women's work." The court disagreed. The situation identified by *Lemons*—pay differences in dissimilar jobs—did not by itself constitute proof of intent to discriminate.

The courts continue to uphold use of market data to justify pay differences for different jobs. *Spaulding v. University of Washington* developed the argument in greatest detail. In this case, the predominantly female faculty members of the Department of Nursing claimed that they were illegally paid less than faculty in other departments. They presented a model of faculty pay comparisons in "comparable" departments that controlled for the effects of level of education, job tenure, and other factors. They asserted that any pay difference not accounted for in their model was discrimination.

But the courts have been dubious of this statistical approach. As the late Carl Sagan used to say, "Just because it's a light doesn't make it a spaceship." Far better to define discrimination directly, rather than concluding that it is "whatever is left." The judge in the *Spaulding* case criticized the statistical model presented, saying it "unrealistically assumed the equality of all master's degrees, ignored job experience prior to university employment, and ignored detailed analysis of day-to-day responsibilities." Without such data, "we have no meaningful way of determining just how much of the proposed wage differential was due to sex and how much was due to academic discipline." "Market prices," according to the judge, "are inherently job-related."

We wish we had as much confidence in "the market" as the judge did. As you recall from Chapter 8, a lot of judgment goes into the wage survey process.[56] Which employers constitute the "relevant market"? Does the relevant market vary by occupation? Do different market definitions yield different wage patterns? Clearly, judgment is involved in answering these questions. Yet the courts have thus far neglected to examine those judgments for possible bias.

Proof of Discrimination: Jobs of Comparable Worth

A second approach to determining pay discrimination on jobs of dissimilar content hinges on finding a standard by which to compare the value of jobs. The standard must do two things. First, it must permit jobs with dissimilar content to be declared equal or "in some sense comparable."[57] Second, it must permit pay differences for dissimilar jobs that are not comparable. Job evaluation has become that standard.[58] If an employer's own job evaluation study shows that jobs of dissimilar content are of equal value to the employer (equal total job evaluation points), then isn't failure to pay them equally proof of intent to discriminate? That was the issue considered in *AFSCME v. State of Washington,* where the state commissioned a study of the concept of comparable worth (discussed later in this chapter) and its projected effect on the state's pay system. The study concluded that by basing wages on the external market, the state was paying women approximately 20 percent less than it was paying men in jobs deemed of comparable value to the state. The state took no action on this finding, alleging it could not afford to adjust wages, so the American Federation of State, County, and Municipal Employees (AFSCME) sued the state. The union alleged that since the state was aware of the adverse effect of its present policy, failure to change the policy constituted discrimination.

But an appeals court ruled that the state was not obligated to correct the disparity. Even though the state had commissioned the study, it had not agreed to implement the study's results. Therefore, the employer had not, in the court's view, admitted that the jobs were equal or established a pay system that purported to pay on the basis of comparable worth rather than markets. Rather than appeal, the parties settled out of court. The state revamped its pay system and agreed to make more than $100 million in "pay equity" adjustments.

Since this case, many public employers have undertaken "pay equity studies" to assess the "gender neutrality" of pay systems. In states and cities which enacted comparable-worth legislation for public employees, the results of these studies are used to adjust pay for jobs held predominantly by woman. In other places the results become part of the give and take of collective bargaining.

So where does this leave us? Clearly, Title VII prohibits intentional discrimination, whether or not the employees in question hold the same or different jobs. Discrimination may be proved by direct evidence of an employer's intent (e.g., an overall pattern of behavior that demonstrates disparate treatment). However, Title VII rulings also make it clear that pay discrimination is not limited only to equal jobs; it may also occur in setting different rates for different jobs. It is also clear that the use of external market rates is not illegal in the United States. Consequently, simply demonstrating pay differences on jobs that are not equal is insufficient to prove discrimination.

What additional implications for the design and administration of pay systems can be drawn? These court decisions imply that pay differentials between dissimilar jobs will not be prohibited under Title VII if the differences can be shown to be based on the content of the work, its value to the organization's objectives, and the employer's ability to attract and retain employees in competitive external labor markets. The courts appear to recognize that "the value of a particular job to an employer is but one factor influencing the rate of compensation for a job." In the absence of new legislation, comparable worth is *not* the law of the land.

EARNINGS GAPS

Exhibit 17.7 shows that women's median annual earnings compared to men's has changed from about 60 percent to 78 percent from 1980 to 2007. Exhibit 17.8 shows that Asian men's earnings compared to white men's varied between 89 and 105 percent during 1988 to 2007. Black to white men's earning ratios varied between about 68 to 74 percent, and the ratio of Hispanic to white men's earnings varied from about 55 to 64 percent. Exhibit 17.9 compares earnings of Asian, Black, and Hispanic women to white women.

Overall, note that while the gender gap has decreased (Exhibit 17.7), it still persists. Hispanics are consistently at the bottom, for both men and women. Asian women earn more than white women (Exhibit 17.9), and the gap between black and white women is less than the gap between black and white men.

EXHIBIT 17.7
Women's
Median
Earnings as a
Percentage of
Men's Median
Earnings,
Full-Time,
Year-Round
Workers,
1980–2007

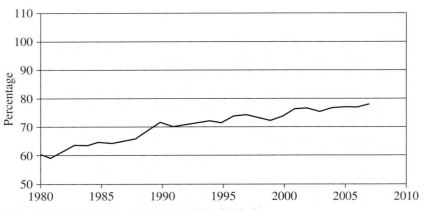

Source: U.S. Bureau of the Census, Historical Income Tables, Table P-40.

EXHIBIT 17.8
Asian, Black,
and Hispanic
Median Men's
Earnings as
a Percentage
of White,
Non-Hispanic
Median Men's
Earnings,
Full-time,
Year-Round
Workers,
1987–2007

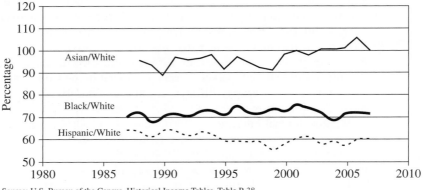

Source: U.S. Bureau of the Census, Historical Income Tables, Table P-38.

EXHIBIT 17.9
Asian, Black,
and Hispanic
Median
Women's
Earnings as
a Percentage
of White,
Non-Hispanic
Median
Women's
Earnings,
Full-Time,
Year-Round
Workers,
1987–2007

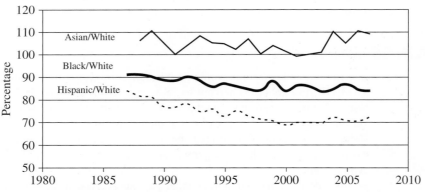

Note: median hourly earnings are derived from CPS microdata by dividing annual total earnings by the product of weeks worked during the year and hours usually worked per week. Earnings tabulations are restricted to those working at least 20 hours a week and 8 weeks a year.

Source: U.S. Bureau of the Census, Historical Income Tables, Table P-38.

EXHIBIT 17.10
Sources of
Earnings Gaps

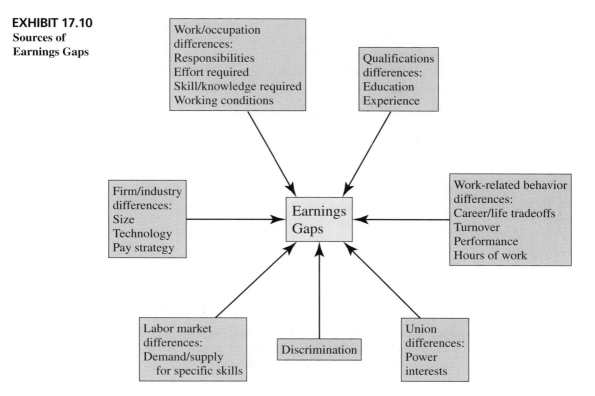

What do we know about why these gaps exist? Some of the more important sources, shown in Exhibit 17.10, include the following:

- Work/occupation differences
- Work-related behavior
- Labor market conditions
- Firm/industry differences
- Union differences
- Discrimination

Let us first examine some data and then some conflicting beliefs.

Sources of the Earnings Gaps

Considerable research has examined the factors shown in Exhibit 17.10, which are the central sources of the wage differences between men and women and the racial/ethnic groups. The issue, especially any proposed remedies, continues to generate research and debate. Our reading of the recent research is that the primary sources contributing to the gender gap differ from the primary sources for the race/ethnic gaps. It appears that differences in the work/occupation (e.g., technician vs. clerical) and differences in work-related behaviors (e.g., work-life balance challenges) are central to understanding the remaining gender wage gaps.[59] In contrast, differences in qualifications, especially educational levels and work-related experience as well as differences in occupations, are important sources of the gaps for both blacks and Hispanics compared to white men.[60]

Differences in Occupations and Qualifications

There is evidence that women of all ethnic groups are more likely than men to seek part-time and flexible work arrangements and that they are more likely than men to interrupt their careers due to family responsibilities.[61] There is also evidence that gender differences in occupational choices continue to exist.[62] For every 100 women who earn bachelor's degrees today, 73 men do.[63] However, men are more likely to enroll, graduate, and continue working in engineering and certain scientific specialties, though women's enrollment and graduation rates exceed men's in the biological sciences.

In the early 1970s, 53 percent of women workers were in administrative support (including clerical) and service occupations, compared to only 15 percent of men. At that time, less than one in five managers were women; professional women were frequently employed in traditionally female professions, such as nurse, teacher, dietitian, or librarian. Women were also underrepresented in blue-collar jobs, including higher-paying precision production and craft occupations. Today, their numbers in administrative support and service jobs are down to 41 percent, and their numbers in managerial jobs are at parity with men. In 1960, almost half of the women who graduated from college became teachers, while today less than 10 percent do so.

Evidence of increased levels of occupational attainment does not automatically mean that the wage gap will close. A study of women in science and engineering finds that even though they have already cleared the hurdles of misguided high school guidance counselors and/or lack of peer support or role models, women scientists and engineers are almost twice as likely to leave these occupations as are males.[64]

For a variety of reasons, a relatively small wage gap among younger cohorts (i.e., recent college graduates) tends to increase as the cohort ages. Perhaps women continue to be more likely to drop out of the labor force at some point for family reasons, or perhaps the barriers to continued advancement become more substantial at higher levels in the **job hierarchy.**[65]

One reviewer of all this research conjectures that some of the observed differences in wages paid in different occupations may be stuck due to inertia or, more poetically, "original sin."[66] Wage differences among occupations were determined decades ago. While a variety of reasons account for these original wage differences, an important one is the belief about gender roles and "women's work" that prevailed at the time. These pay differences have persisted and influence today's occupational wage structures even though attitudes have changed.[67]

Level of schooling and work-related experience appear to be primary sources of the pay gaps among both black and Hispanic men and women. Almost half of Hispanic men have not completed high school and only 9 percent are college graduates.[68] This may be due to the considerable differences in continuing immigration among Hispanics.

Generally, the longer Hispanic immigrants stay in the United States, the better they do educationally and financially. However, the continuing inflow of poorly educated new immigrants holds down the average wage for the whole category. Black men's high school dropout rates match those of Hispanic men. In contrast, more than half of Asian men are college graduates or hold higher degrees. All this research and discussion about sources of the earnings gaps does not mean there are not any discriminatory pay practices; it does mean that important sources of the pay gaps reside in other productivity-related factors such as level and quality of education, work-life/career tradeoffs, and occupational choices.

Differences in Industries and Firms

Other factors that affect earnings differences among men and women and among race/ethnic groups are the industries and the firms in which they are employed. A study of middle-aged lawyers revealed large differences between men and women lawyers in the types of firms that employed them. Men were much more likely than women to be in private practice and to be at large firms (over 50 lawyers). They were much *less* likely than women to be in the lower-paying nonprofit sector. Clearly, these differences are related to pay: the most highly paid legal positions are in private-practice law firms; the larger the law firm, the greater the average rate of pay.[69] There also may be different promotion opportunities among firms within the same industry.[70]

Differences in the firm's compensation policies within a specific industry is another factor that accounts for some of the earnings gap.[71] As noted in Chapters 7 and 8, some firms within an industry adopt pay strategies that place them among the leaders in their industry; other firms adopt policies that may offer more work-life balance benefits compared to cash compensation. The unknown here is whether *within an industry* some firms are more likely to attract women or minorities than other firms because of these pay-mix differences and whether this has any effect on earnings gaps.

Within a firm, differences in policies for different jobs may even exist. For example, many firms tie pay for secretaries to the pay for the manager to whom the secretary is assigned. The rationale is that the secretary and the manager function as a team. When the manager gets promoted, the secretary also takes on additional responsibilities and therefore also gets a raise. However, this traditional approach breaks down when layers of management are cut. When IBM went through a major restructuring a few years back, it cut pay by up to 36 percent for secretaries who had been assigned to managerial levels that no longer existed. IBM justified the cuts by saying the rates were way above the market.

We also know that the size of a firm is systematically related to differences in wages. Female employment is more heavily concentrated in small firms. Wages of men in large firms are 54 percent higher than wages of men in small firms. The gap was 37 percent for women in small versus large firms. Hispanic men are concentrated in construction and service firms. Other studies report that employees in some jobs can get a pay increase of about 20 percent simply by switching industries in the same geographic area while performing basically similar jobs.[72] Nevertheless, a recent study concludes that this pay premium associated with changing jobs is enjoyed primarily by white males. Women and minorities who were MBA graduates from five universities did not obtain the same pay increases as their white male classmates when they switched jobs.[73]

To the extent that these differences in job setting are the result of an individual's preference or disposition, they are not evidence of discrimination. To the extent that these differences are the result of industry and firm practices that steer women and minorities into certain occupations and industries or lower-paying parts of a profession, they may reflect discrimination.

Union Membership

Finally, we also know that belonging to a union will affect differences in earnings. Belonging to a union in the public sector seems to raise female wages more than it raises male wages. Little research has been devoted to studying the gender effect of union membership in the private sector.

Presence of Discrimination

We know that many factors affect pay and that discrimination can be one of them. Disagreement remains over what constitutes evidence of discrimination. Although the earnings gap is the most frequently cited example, closer inspection reveals the weaknesses in this statistic. Unfortunately, many studies of the earnings gap have little relevance to understanding discrimination in pay-setting practices within organizations. Some studies use aggregated data—for instance, treating all bachelor's degrees as the same, or defining an occupation too broadly (e.g., the U.S. Department of Labor categorizes Shaquille O'Neal as well as the basketball game timekeeper in the same occupation—"sports professional"). Another problem is that mere possession of a qualification or skill does not mean it is work-related. Examples of cab drivers, secretaries, and house painters with college degrees are numerous.

A standard statistical approach for determining whether discrimination explains part of the gap is to try to relate pay differences to the factors discussed above (occupation, type of work, experience, education, and the like). The procedure typically regresses some measure of earnings on those factors thought to legitimately influence earnings. If the average wage of men with a given set of values for these factors is significantly different from the average wage of women with equal factors, then the residual portion of the gap is considered discrimination. Unfortunately, in a sample limited to white males, such an approach explained only 60 to 70 percent of their earnings. So statistical studies, by themselves, are not sufficient evidence of discrimination.[74]

Cybercomp
You can track legal issues and read transcripts of Supreme Court decisions at *www.law.cornell.edu*. Many states have their own Web pages that include their compensation legislation. What information is available from your state? Compare the pay discrimination legislation in your state with another state's. What might explain these differences? Are there any unique characteristics of your state (e.g., unique industries, extent of unionization, etc.)?

Even if legitimate factors fully explain gender, ethnic, and racial group pay differences, discrimination still could have occurred. The factors shown in Exhibit 17.10 themselves may be tainted by discrimination. For example, construction laborers in California are mainly Hispanic males. A slowing of the housing market will disproportionately affect them. So, measurable factors may underestimate the effects of past discrimination. Statistical analysis needs to be treated as part of a pattern of evidence and needs to reflect the wage behaviors of specific firms.

Gaps Are Global

The gender wage gap is fairly universal. However, in a number of countries, the size of the gap is smaller than in the United States.[75] One analysis concludes that the difference can be found in narrower pay structures in European countries. In many countries, as the global guide in Chapter 16 suggests, rates negotiated by federations of employers, unions, and government agencies rather than individual companies and employees mean a narrower range of pay rates for each job, as well as smaller differences between jobs.[76]

Earlier chapters have emphasized the wide range of pay rates in the U.S. market for any job. More centralized wage decision making permits a pay gap to be closed by political/institutional fiat. Multinational companies operating in different nations face wide differences in how wages are influenced by varying social policies and regulations.

COMPARABLE WORTH

Why are jobs that are held predominantly by women, almost without exception, paid less than jobs held predominantly by men? Do job evaluation systems give adequate recognition to job-related contributions in those jobs held primarily by women? The state of Washington conducted a study that concluded that the job of a licensed practical nurse required skill, effort, and responsibility equal to that of a campus police officer. The campus police officer was paid, on average, one-and-a-half times what the state paid the licensed practical nurse.[77]

In Ontario, Canada, jobs that were deemed comparable based on numerical scores displayed a similar disparity in pay. A chief librarian made $35,050, while a dairy herd improvement manager made $38,766. A computer operations supervisor made $20,193, while a forestry project supervisor made $26,947. A typist made $10,531, while a sailor made $14,097. It is this type of wage difference between jobs judged in some sense to be comparable that is controversial. The notion of comparable worth says that if jobs require comparable skill, effort, and responsibility, the pay must be comparable, no matter how dissimilar the job content may be. (In Canada and the European Union, comparable worth is called *gender equity*.)

Comparable-worth proponents in the United States continue to lobby for either new legislation or voluntary action on the part of employers that would include the comparable-worth standard. A lot of this political activity is occurring in state and local governments. This is not surprising, since over half of all women in the workforce are employed in the public sector.

The Mechanics

Establishing a comparable-worth plan typically involves the following four basic steps:

1. *Adopt a single "gender neutral" point job evaluation plan for all jobs within a unit.* If employees are unionized, separate plans have been prepared for each bargaining unit and take precedence over previous agreements. The key to a comparable-worth system is a single job evaluation plan for jobs with dissimilar content. What a "gender neutral" point job evaluation plan is remains open to debate. Advocates of all persuasions offer often conflicting advice, and there is little research to provide guidance. Some advocates try to distinguish between "gender neutral" and "traditional" point job evaluation.[78] Close reading reveals that "traditional" refers to practices dating back 50 years that do not reflect contemporary point plan practices.

2. *All jobs with equal job evaluation results should be paid the same.* Although each factor in the job evaluation may not be equal, if the total points are equal, the wage rates must also be equal.

3. *Identify the percentages of male and female employees in each job group.* A job group is defined as a group of positions with similar duties and responsibilities that require similar qualifications, are filled by similar recruiting procedures, and are paid under the same pay schedule. Typically, a female-dominated job group is defined as having 60 percent or more female incumbents; a male-dominated job group has 70 percent or more male incumbents.

4. *The wage-to-job evaluation point ratio should be based on the wages paid for male-dominated jobs* since they are presumed to be the best estimate of nondiscriminatory wages.

These steps are based on the state of Minnesota's law that mandates comparable worth for all public-sector employees (e.g., the state, cities, school districts, libraries). Canadian federal and provincial labour departments have also published detailed guidance on procedures.[79]

To understand the mechanics more clearly, consider Exhibit 17.11. The solid dots represent jobs held predominantly by women (i.e., 60 percent or more employees are female). The circles represent jobs held predominantly by men (i.e., 70 percent or more employees are men). The policy line (solid) for the women's jobs is below the policy line (dotted) for men's jobs. A comparable-worth policy uses the results of the single job evaluation plan and prices all jobs as if they were male-dominated jobs (dotted line). Thus, all jobs with 100 job points receive $600; all those with 200 points receive $800, and so on.

Market rates for male-dominated jobs are used to convert the job evaluation points to salaries. The point-to-salaries ratio of male-dominated jobs is then applied to female-dominated jobs.

However, a mandated job evaluation, especially a single point plan that specifies a hierarchy of all jobs, seems counter to the direction in which most organizations are moving today. A partner of Hay Associates observed:

> We, ourselves, do not know of a single case where a large and diverse organization in the private sector concluded that a single job evaluation method, with the same compensable factors and weightings, was appropriate for its factory, office, professional, management, technical, and executive personnel in all profit center divisions and all staff departments.[80]

EXHIBIT 17.11
Job Evaluation Points and Salary

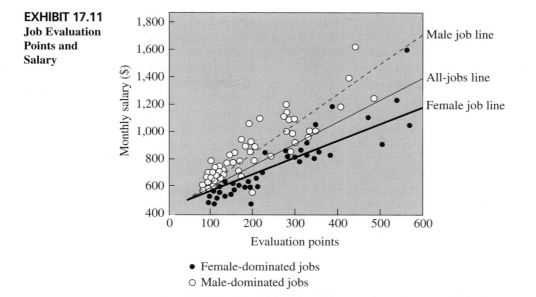

- Female-dominated jobs
- Male-dominated jobs

People who advocate a point job evaluation plan as a vehicle for comparable worth credit the technique with more explanatory power than it possesses. Nevertheless, the comparable worth debate lives on.

Anyone contemplating a pay equity study should proceed with great care—and of course, reread the relevant chapters in this book. Lest readers think this is a topic of marginal value, consider the experience of Bell Canada and its unions. After lawyers spent over a decade disputing the quality and results of a pay equity study, Bell Canada agreed to a $104 million ($91.5 million American) settlement.[81] The point job evaluation plan used in the study to determine pay equity is not being used in the contemporary workplace in Bell's operations.

Union Developments

The amount of union support for comparable worth appears to be related to its effects on the union's membership. AFSCME and the Communication Workers of America (CWA) actively support comparable worth and have negotiated comparable-worth-based pay increases, lobbied for legislation, filed legal suits, and attempted to educate their members and the public about comparable worth. The public sector faces little competition for its services and is frequently better able to absorb a wage increase, since public employees are in a better position to pressure lawmakers than are taxpayers. This probably accounts for the relative success of public employees' unions in bargaining comparable-worth pay adjustments. But tradeoffs between higher wages and fewer jobs make unions in industries facing stiff international competition (e.g., the International Ladies' Garment Workers' Union and the United Auto Workers) reluctant to aggressively support comparable worth.

The beauty of "equity adjustments," from a union's perspective, is that because they are a separate budget item, they do not appear to come at the expense of overall pay increases for all union members. Collective bargaining has produced more comparable-worth pay increases than any other approach.[82]

A Proactive Approach

Compliance with laws and regulations can be a constraint and/or an opportunity for a compensation manager. The regulatory environment certainly constrains the decisions that can be made. Once laws are passed and regulations published, employers must comply. But a proactive compensation manager can influence the nature of regulations and their interpretation. Astute professionals must be aware of legislative and judicial currents to protect both employers' and employees' interests and to ensure that compensation practices conform to judicial interpretation.

How can a compensation manager best undertake these efforts? First, join professional associations to stay informed on emerging issues and to act in concert to inform and influence public and legislative opinion. Second, constantly review compensation practices and their results. The fair treatment of all employees is the goal of a good pay system, and that is the same goal of legislation. When interpretations of what is fair treatment differ, informed public discussion is required. Such discussion cannot occur without the input of informed managers.

Your **Turn**   Self-Evaluation and Pay Discrimination

Your employer is considering whether to pursue business opportunities with the federal government. You have been asked to ". . . determine what is required to conduct a Voluntary Self-Evaluation of Compensation Practices following the June 2006 *OFCCP Guidelines*." The company needs to better understand the resources (talent, information, data access, timing, etc.) that it would need to devote to such a self-evaluation. Your boss emphasizes, "Only scope out what it will take—give me your ballpark ideas."

1. Go to *http://www.dol.gov/federalregister/PdfDisplay.aspx?Docid=11908*. Go to page 35120 and find the section with the title *Final Voluntary Guidelines-Voluntary Guidelines for Self-Evaluation of Compensation Practices for Compliance With Executive Order 11246 With Respect to Systemic Compensation Discrimination ("Voluntary Guidelines")*. There are several steps (procedures) listed. The first one, IA, deals with sorting employees into "similarly situated employee groupings." Prepare a memo that highlights the steps or procedures required in the OFCCP Self-Evaluation Guidelines.

2. Include in your memo your ideas on the resources required for your company to conduct such an evaluation: talent requirements (your estimate of number of people and skills/knowledge required), data access (type of data required for the self-evaluation), timing (your best estimate), and other resources.

3. Based on your professional judgment, discuss in the memo the factors your boss needs to consider (expected value gained, risks to manage, outsourcing, etc.) before undertaking a "Self-Evaluation" project.

Still Your **Turn**

From Barista to Manager

You work at an upscale coffee shop that is part of a nationwide chain of 200 such stores. You started as a barista, but then you moved up. Your title is now store manager. You are expected to work 55 hours per week. Your boss says you need to be in the store to get to know the customers and because, well, you are the manager. It is up to you to make sure everything runs smoothly and that there is a great customer experience, which translates into growth in store sales volume and store profit. By the way, however many hours you work, you get paid for 40 hours only (and no overtime pay) because . . . that's right, you are the manager.

However, as you think about how you spend your time at the store, you can't help but feel that a lot of your time seems to be spent on things that don't seem much like "management" to you—making coffee drinks, checking supplies, and sometimes cleaning bathrooms. So, this is the life of a manager. It seems a lot like being a barista, except that you work a lot more hours, have more responsibility, and you don't get paid all that much more. You do spend some time on training other employees and you interview job applicants. But, the district manager is around a lot and she seems to have her own ideas on who to hire most of the time and how to run the store. Plus, there are pretty clear corporate guidelines to be followed on how to run many aspects of the store.

The more you think about it, the more you think that it sure would be nice to get paid for working 55 hours. In fact, you have friends who work in other businesses and when they work over 40 hours in a week, they get time and a half for the hours beyond 40. That sounds awfully good. If you are going to spend all of your time at work, it would be nice to at least get paid for it.

Now, "switch hats" and look at it from the company point of view. Is this company running afoul of the Fair Labor Standards Act (FLSA)? Refer back to our discussion earlier in this chapter. Would this company be able to document that the store managers are exempt from the FLSA (not to mention similar state laws)? Also, what would it cost to re-classify your store managers as non-exempt? If managers feel overworked and underpaid, what do you project that they will do when the economy picks back up? Is that a concern for the company? Is the company in compliance with the FLSA? What would it cost to have a lawsuit filed against the company? Have other companies in your industry (e.g., Starbucks, Caribou, Peet's, etc.) had any FLSA issues? If so, what can you learn from their experiences? Would you advise meeting with corporate counsel? What facts and observations would you recommend be presented at such a meeting?

Summary   Governments around the world play varying roles in the workplace. Legislation in any society reflects people's expectations about the role of government. Beyond direct regulation, government affects compensation through policies and purchases that affect labor supply and demand.

In the United States, legislation reflects the changing nature of work and the workforce. In the 1930s, legislation was concerned with correcting the harsh conditions and arbitrary treatment facing employees, including children. In the 1960s, legislation turned to the issue of equal opportunity. Such legislation has had a profound impact on all of U.S. society. Nevertheless, more progress to eliminate discrimination in the workplace, including pay discrimination, is required. Contemporary issues include treatment of the recent waves of immigrants. Recent attention has shifted to increasing the transparency of compensation for executives and accounting for stock options.

Pay discrimination laws require special attention for several reasons. First, these laws regulate the design and administration of pay systems. Second, the definition of pay discrimination and thus the approaches used to defend pay practices are in a state of flux, especially as employers increase their international operations. Many of the provisions of these laws simply require sound pay practices that should have been employed in the first place. Sound practices are those with three basic features:

1. They are work-related.
2. They are related to the mission of the enterprise.
3. They include an appeals process for employees who disagree with the results.

Achieving compliance with these laws rests in large measure on the shoulders of managers of compensation. It is their responsibility to ensure that the pay system is properly designed and managed.

The earnings gaps among various ethnic and racial groups for both women and men are attributable to many factors. The sources of the gender gap appear to center on differences in work/occupational attainment and work-life challenges. The sources for blacks and Hispanics center on differences in educational levels, work-related experience, occupational attainment, and qualifications. Discrimination, whether access or valuation, is another factor. Others include market forces, industry and employer differences, and union bargaining priorities. Compensation managers need to constantly monitor pay practices to be sure that they are complying with regulations and are not discriminatory.

Is all this detail on interpretation of pay discrimination really necessary? Yes. Without understanding the interpretation of pay discrimination legislation, compensation managers risk violating the law, exposing their employers to considerable liability and expense, and losing the confidence and respect of all employees when a few are forced to turn to the courts to gain nondiscriminatory treatment.

Review Questions

1. What is the nature of government's role in compensation?
2. Explain why changes in minimum wage can affect higher-paid employees as well.
3. What is the difference between access discrimination and valuation discrimination?
4. Consider contemporary practices such as skill-competency-based plans, broad banding, market pricing, and pay-for-performance plans. Discuss how they may affect the pay discrimination debate.
5. What factors help account for the pay gap?
6. What kinds of proactive activities can an employer undertake to enhance the regulatory environment?

Endnotes

1. The job evaluation manual was introduced as evidence in *Electrical Workers (IUE) v. Westinghouse Electric Corp.,* 632 F.2d 1094, 23 FEP Cases 588 (3rd Cir. 1980), *cert. denied,* 452 U.S. 967, 25 FEP Cases 1835 (1981).

2. Philip M. Berkowitz, Anders Etgen Reitz, Thomas Müller-Bonanni, eds., *International Labor and Employment Law,* 2nd edition (Chicago, IL: American Bar Association, 2008); Organisation for Economic Co-operation and Development, "The Price of Prejudice: Labour Market Discrimination on the Grounds of Gender and Ethnicity," *OECD Employment Outlook 2008* (Paris, France: OECD, 2008), includes a survey of equal employment opportunity regulation across OECD countries; Richard A. Posthuma, Mark V. Roehling, and Michael A. Campion, "Applying U.S. Employment Discrimination Laws to International Employers: Advice for Scientists and Practitioners," *Personnel Psychology,* 59(3) (2006), pp. 705–739; The U.S. Equal Employment Opportunity Commission. "The Equal Employment Opportunity Responsibilities of Multinational Employers," *http://www.eeoc.gov/facts/multi-employers.html;* The U.S. Equal Employment Opportunity Commission. Employee Rights When Working for Multinational Employers, *http://www.eeoc.gov/facts/multi-employees.html.*

3. Bruce Kaufman, ed., *Government Regulation of the Employment Relationship* (Ithaca, NY: Cornell University Press, 1998); Arthur Gutman, *EEO Law and Personnel Practices,* 2d edition (Thousand Oaks, CA: Sage, 2000).

4. Francine D. Blau and Lawrence M. Kahn, *At Home and Abroad: U.S. Labor Market Performance in International Perspective* (Thousand Oaks, CA: Sage, 2001).

5. Michael Hodges, *Grandfather Economic Reports, mwhodges.home.att.net/state_local.html.*

6. Morris Kleiner, *Licensing Requirements: Ensuring Quality or Restricting Competition?* (Kalamazoo, MI: Upjohn, 2006).

7. George J. Borgas, Richard B. Freeman, and Lawrence F. Katz, "Searching for the Effect of Immigration on the Labor Market," *American Economic Review* 86 (1996), pp. 246–251.

8. *www.dol.gov/esa/minwage/America.htm* has an interactive map of the United States. Click on a state to find their minimum wage requirements.

9. U.S. Bureau of Labor Statistics, Characteristics of Minimum Wage Workers: 2007. *www.bls.gov.*

10. Economic Policy Institute, "Issue Guide on Minimum Wage," *www.epi.org.*

11. David Neumark and William L. Wascher, *Minimum Wages* (Cambridge, MA: MIT Press, 2008); Economic Policy Institute, "Issue Guide on Minimum Wage," 2008, *www.epi.org;* David Card and Alan Krueger, "Minimum Wages and Employment: A Case Study of the Fast-Food Industry in New Jersey and Pennsylvania," *American Economic Review,* September 1994, pp. 772–793; Lawrence F. Katz and Alan B. Krueger, "The Effect of the Minimum Wage on the Fast-Food Industry," *Industrial and Labor Relations Review* 46(1) (October 1992), pp. 6–21; K. I. Simon and R. Kaestner, "Do Minimum Wages Affect Non-Wage Job Attributes? Evidence on Fringe Benefits," *Industrial and Labor Relations Review* 58(1) (October 2004), pp. 52–70; Joseph Sabia, "Identifying Minimum Wage Effects: New Evidence From Monthly CPS Data," *Industrial Relations* 48 (2009), pp. 311–328; Hristos Doucouliagos and T. D. Stanley, "Publication Selection Bias in Minimum-Wage Research? A Meta-Regression Analysis," *British Journal of Industrial Relations* 47 (2009), pp. 406–428; "Hundreds of Economists Say: Raise the Minimum Wage," *Economic Policy Institute,* October 11, 2006.

12. Economic Policy Institute, Issue Guide on Minimum Wage. *www.epi.org,* 2008; David Neumark and William L. Wascher, *Minimum Wages* (Cambridge, MA: MIT Press, 2008); Richard V. Burkhauser and Joseph J. Sabia. "The Effectiveness of Minimum Wage Increases in Reducing Poverty: Past, Present and Future." *Contemporary Economic Policy* 25(2) (April 2007), pp. 262–281.

13. Jon Gertner, "What Is a Living Wage?" *New York Times Magazine,* January 15, 2006.

14. John G. Kilgour, "The Living Wage Ordinance Controversy," *Workspan,* First Quarter 2009, pp. 75–85.

15. David Fairris, David Runsten, Carolina Briones, and Jessica Goodheart, *Examining the Evidence: The Impact of the Los Angeles Living Wage Ordinance on Workers and Businesses, www.losangeleslivingwagestudy.org,* June 2, 2005.

16. David Neumark, "Living Wages: Protection for or Protection From Low-Wage Workers?" *Industrial and Labor Relations Review* 58(1) (October 2004), pp. 27–51

17. Dale A. Hudson, "Plaintiff's Lawyers Bullish on Merrill Lynch: Brokerage Firm Agrees to Pay $37 Million to Settle Overtime Claims by Stockbroker," *Nixon Peabody Employment Law Alert,* August 26, 2005.

18. Cindy Krischer Goodman, "Overtime Under Fire: Workday Trends Blur Overtime Rules, Clogging Courts With Lawsuits," *Wisconsin State Journal,* August 17, 2008.

19. Ibid.

20. Steven Greenhouse, "Labor Agency Is Failing Workers, Reports Says," *New York Times,* March 25, 2009.

21. Ian Rowley and Hiroko Tashiro, "Recession puts more pressure on Japan's workers," *BusinessWeek,* January 5, 2009.

22. Ibid.

23. Miguel Bustillo, "Wal-Mart to Settle 63 Suits Over Wages," Wall Street Journal, December 24, 2008.

24. *IBP, Inc. V. Alvarez,* (03-1238) No. 03–1238, 339 F.3d 894, affirmed; No. 04–66, 360 F.3d 274, affirmed in part, reversed in part, and remanded.

25. Will Parsons, "On-Call Pay Premiums and Expenses," *Culpepper Pay Trends Survey e-Bulletin,* December 2005.

26. Peter Kuhn and Fernando Lozano, *The Expanding Workweek? Understanding Trends in Long Work Hours Among U.S. Men, 1979–2004,* NBER Working Paper No. 11895, July 2006.

27. Kimberley Strassel, "Make My (Mother's) Day . . ." *The Wall Street Journal,* May 13, 2006, p. A11.

28. Douglas L. Kruse and Douglas Mahony, "Illegal Child Labor in the United States: Prevalence and Characteristics," *Industrial and Labor Relations Review* 54(1) (October 2000), pp. 17–40; Faraaz Siddiqi and Harry Anthony Patrinos, "Child Labor: Issues, Causes, and Interventions," Human Capital Development and Operations Policy Working Paper 56, *www.worldbank.org/html/extdr/hnp/hddflash/workp/wp_00056.html;* Steven Greenhouse and Michael Barbaro, "An Ugly Side of Free Trade: Sweatshops in Jordan," *New York Times,* May 3, 2006; B. Powell and D. Skarbek, "Sweatshops and Third World Living Standards: Are the Jobs Worth the Sweat?" *Journal of Labor Research* 27(2) (Spring 2006), pp. 263–279.

29. *The End of Child Labour: Within Reach* (Geneva, Switzerland: International Labor Organization, 2006).

30. *Nationwide Mutual Ins. v. Darden* (90-1802), 503 U.S. 318 (1992).

31. Dennis D. Grant (2000), "Employee or Independent Contractor? The Implications of Microsoft III," *http://library.findlaw.com/2000/Feb/1/127759.html.*

32. Bill Virgin, "Microsoft Settles 'Permatemp' Suits: Two $97 Million Cases Reshape Employment for Temps Nationwide," *Seattle Post-Intelligencer,* December 13, 2000.

33. Anne Freedman, "FedEx Agrees to Pay $27 Million in Misclassification Case," *Human Resource Executive,* January 21, 2009.

34. Ed Frauenheim, "IRS Deals Blow to Fedex on Use of Contractors," *Workforce Management,* January 14, 2008.

35. Rebecca Knight, "Politicians Shifting Blame Put Boston's Big Dig Back in News," *Financial Times,* July 16, 2006, p. 4.

36. Aaron Morris, "Prevailing-Wage Law: Noble Goal, Costly Projects," *Bluegrass Institute,* March 7, 2006, *http://www.bipps.org/ARTICLE.ASP?ID=535.*

37. *Gratz v. Bollinger,* (02-516) 539 U.S. 244 (2003).

38. *Grutter v. Bollinger,* (02-241) 539 U.S. 306 (2003).

39. Paula England, *Comparable Worth: Theories and Evidence* (Hawthorne, NY: Aldine deGruyter, 1992); Ben A. Barres, "Does Gender Matter?" *Nature* 442, July 13, 2006; Morley Gunderson, "The Evolution and Mechanics of Pay Equity in Ontario," *Canadian Public Policy* 28, suppl. 1 (2002).

40. Michael E. Gold, "Towards a Unified Theory of the Law of Employment Discrimination," *Berkeley Journal of Employment and Labor Law,* February 2001.

41. Davan Maharaj, "Coca-Cola to Settle Racial Bias Lawsuit," *Los Angeles Times,* November 17, 2000.

42. U.S. Equal Employment Opportunity Commission, "Notice Concerning the Lilly Ledbetter Fair Pay Act of 2009," *http://www.eeoc.gov/epa/ledbetter.html,* June 22, 2009.

43. Ibid.

44. Brett A. Gorovsky, "Lilly Ledbetter Fair Pay Act of 2009: What's Next for Employers?" CCH Incorporated, *http://www.cch.com/Press/news/CCHWhitePaper_LedbetterFairPayAct.pdf,* June 22, 2009.

45. Michael E. Gold, "Towards a Unified Theory of the Law of Employment Discrimination," *Berkeley Journal of Employment and Labor Law,* February 2001.

46. "OFCCP's Increased Enforcement Efforts Produce Largest Ever Financial Recovery in 2008," January 23, 2009, *www.jacksonlewis.com/legalupdates/.*

47. "OFCCP Budget Increases Announced for 2010," *Affirmative Action News,* May 8, 2009. *http://affirmativeactionnews.blogspot.com.*

48. U.S. Government Accountability Office, "Federal Agencies Should Better Monitor Their Performance in Enforcing Anti-Discrimination Laws," GAO Reports, Report Number GAO-08-799. Washington, D.C.; Debra Ann Millenson and David S. Fortney, "OFCCP Fundamentals," ABA Philadelphia Labor & Employment Conference, 2007, *http://www. abanet.org/labor/annualconference/2007/materials/data/papers/v1/009.pdf,* June 12, 2009.

49. OFCCP Directive. Transmittal Number: 285, 09/17/2008, *http://www.dol.gov/esa/ofccp/ regs/compliance/directives/dir285.htm,* June 21, 2009.

50. Office of Federal Contract Compliance Programs. Federal Contract Compliance Manual. Chapter 3—On-Site Review, *http://www.dol.gov/esa/ofccp/regs/compliance/fccm/ofcpch3. htm,* June 21, 2009.

51. "OFCCP's New Systemic Compensation Discrimination Standards and Voluntary Guidelines for Compensation Self-Evaluation," Office of Federal Contract Compliance Programs, *http://www.dol.gov/esa/ofccp/regs/compliance/faqs/comstrds.htm,* June 21, 2009.

52. Ibid.

53. Ibid.

54. Ibid.

55. Murray S. Simpson, "Analyzing Pay Equity in an Uncertain Regulatory Environment," *Compensation & Benefits Review,* November/December, pp. 29–39.

56. Sara L. Rynes and George T. Milkovich, "Wage Surveys: Dispelling Some Myths About the 'Market Wage,'" *Personnel Psychology,* Spring 1986, pp. 71–90; Charlie Trevor and Mary E. Graham, "Deriving the Market Wage: Three Decision Areas in the Compensation Survey Process," *WorldatWork Journal,* Fourth Quarter 2000, pp. 69–76; Judith K. Hellerstein, David Neumark, and Kenneth R. Troske, "Market Forces and Sex Discrimination," *Journal of Human Resources* 37(2) (Spring 2002), pp. 353–380.

57. H. Remick, ed., *Comparable Worth and Wage Discrimination* (Philadelphia: Temple University Press, 1984); B. F. Reskin and H. I. Hartmann, eds., *Women's Work, Men's Work: Segregation on the Job* (Washington, DC: National Academy Press, 1986); Morley Gunderson, *Women and the Labour Market: Transitions Towards the Future* (Toronto: ITP Nelson Publishing, 1998); Morley Gunderson and Nan Weiner, *Pay Equity: Issues, Options and Experiences* (Toronto: Butterworths, 1990).

58. *Job Evaluation: A Tool for Pay Equity* (Washington, DC: National Committee on Pay Equity, November 1987); Morley Gunderson, "The Evolution and Mechanics of Pay Equity in Ontario," *Canadian Public Policy* 28, suppl. 1 (2002).

59. U.S. Department of Labor, Bureau of Labor Statistics, "Highlights of Women's Earnings in 2007," Report 1008, October 2008; Francine D. Blau and Lawrence M. Kahn, "The Gender Pay Gap: Have Women Gone as Far as They Can?" *Academy of Management Perspectives;* D. A. Black, A. M. Haviland, S. G. Sanders, and L. J. Taylor, "Gender Wage Disparities Among the Highly Educated," *Journal of Human Resources* 42 (2008), pp. 630–659. Cheri Ostroff and Leanne Atwater, "Does Whom You Work with Matter? Effects of Referent Group Gender and Age Composition on Managers' Compensation," *Journal of Applied Psychology,* August 2003, pp. 725–740; Paula England, "The Gender System: What's Changing? What's Not?" Alice Cook Memorial Lecture, Cornell University, Ithaca, NY, March 22, 2006; Nabanita Datta Gupta, Ronald L. Oaxaca, and Nina Smith, "Swimming Upstream, Floating Downstream: Comparing Women's Relative Wage Progress In the United States and Denmark," *Industrial and Labor Relations Review,* January 2006, pp. 243–266; Warren Farrell, *Why Men Earn More: The Startling Truth Behind the Pay Gap—and What Women Can Do About It* (New York: Amacom, 2005); Gerrit Mueller and Erik Plug, "Estimating the Effect of Personality on Male and Female Earnings," *Industrial and Labor Relations Review,* October 2006, pp. 3–22.

60. June O'Neill and Dave O'Neill, *What Do Wage Differentials Tell Us About Labor Market Discrimination?* NBER Working Paper W11240, April 2005.

61. D. Anderson, M. Binder, and K. Krause, "The Motherhood Wage Penalty Revisited: Experience, Heterogeneity, Work Effort and Work-Schedule Flexibility," *Industrial and Labor Relations Review* 56(2) (January 2003), pp. 273–295; Andrew M. Gill and Duane E. Leigh, "Community College Enrollment, College Major, and the Gender Wage Gap," *Industrial and Labor Relations Review* 54(1) (October 2000), pp. 163–181; C. Brown and M. Corcoran, "Sex-Based Differences in School Content and the Male-Female Wage Gap," *Journal of Labor Economics* 15(3) (1997), pp. 431–465; M. Montgomery and I. Powell, "Does an Advanced Degree Reduce the Gender Wage Gap? Evidence From MBAs," *Industrial Relations* 42(3) (July 2003), pp. 396–418.

62. Laurie A. Morgan, "Major Matters: The Within-Major Gender Pay Gap for Early-Career College Graduates," *Industrial Relations* 47 (2008) pp. 625–650; Nicole M. Fortin, "The Gender Gap Among Young Adults in the United States: The Importance of Money Versus People," *Journal of Human Resources* 43 (2008), p. 884; C. A. Karlin, P. England, and

M. Ross, "Why Do 'Women's Jobs' Have Low Pay for Their Educational Level?" *Gender Issues* 20(4) (Fall 2002), pp. 3–22; Stephanie Boraas and William M. Rodgers III, "How Does Gender Play a Role in the Earnings Gap? An Update," *Monthly Labor Review,* March 2003, pp. 9–15.

63. Tamar Lewin, "At Colleges, Women Are Leaving Men in the Dust," *New York Times* July 9, 2006, p. 1; Francine Blau and Marianne Ferber, "Career Plans and Expectations of Young Women and Men," *Journal of Human Resources* 26(4) (1998), pp. 581–607; Greg Hundley, "Male/Female Earnings Differences in Self-Employment: The Effects of Marriage, Children, and the Household Division of Labor," *Industrial and Labor Relations Review* 54(1) (October 2000), pp. 95–114.

64. Anne E. Preston, "Why Have All the Women Gone? A Study of Exit of Women from the Science and Engineering Professions," *American Economic Review,* December 1994, pp. 1446–1462; Joy A. Schneer and Frieda Reitman, "The Importance of Gender in Mid-Career: A Longitudinal Study of MBAs," *Journal of Organizational Behavior* 15 (1994), pp. 199–207.

65. Eduardo Porter, "Stretched to Limit, Women Stall March to Work," *New York Times,* March 2, 2006, p. 1.

66. Paula England, Paul Allison, Yuxiao Wu, and Mary Ross, "Does Bad Pay Cause Occupations to Feminize, Does Feminization Reduce Pay, and How Can We Tell With Longitudinal Data?" presented at annual meeting of the American Sociological Association, August 2004, San Francisco.

67. Yet another reviewer of the same research evidence emphasizes limitations in data sources and research methods, disagreements over variables to include in the studies, and randomness. T. Tam, "Sex Segregation and Occupational Gender Inequality: Devaluation or Specialized Training," *American Journal of Sociology* 102 (1997), pp. 1652–1692.

68. June O'Neill and Dave O'Neill, *What Do Wage Differentials Tell Us About Labor Market Discrimination?* NBER Working Paper W11240, April 2005; Finis Welch, "Catching Up: Wages of Black Men," American Economic Association Papers and Proceedings, May 2003, pp. 320–322; J. Heckman, "Detecting Discrimination," *Journal of Economic Perspectives* 12(2) (1998), pp. 101–116.

69. Dan Black, Amelia Haviland, Seth Sanders, and Lowell Taylor, "Why Do Minority Men Earn Less? A Study of Wage Differentials Among the Highly Educated," *Review of Economics and Statistics,* May 2006, pp. 300–313; Robert G. Wood, Mary E. Corcoran, and Paul N. Courant, "Pay Differences Among the Highly Paid: The Male-Female Earnings Gap in Lawyers' Salaries," *Journal of Labor Economics* 11(3) (1993), pp. 417–441.

70. Barry A. Gerhart and George T. Milkovich, "Salaries, Salary Growth, and Promotions of Men and Women in a Large, Private Firm," *Pay Equity: Empirical Inquiries* (Arlington, VA: National Science Foundation, 1989); Francine Blau and Jed DeVaro, *New Evidence on Gender Difference in Promotion Rates: An Empirical Analysis of a Sample of New Hires,* NBER Working Paper No. 12321, June 2006.

71. Mary E. Graham, Julie.L. Hotchkiss, and Barry Gerhart, "Discrimination By Parts: A Fixed Effects Analysis of Starting Pay Differences Across Gender," *Eastern Economic Journal,* 26 (2000) pp. 9–27; Erica L. Groshen, "Sources of Intra-Industry Wage Dispersion: How Much Do Employers Matter?" *The Quarterly Journal of Economics,* 106 (1991) pp. 869–884; Kimberly Bayard, Judith Hellerstein, David Neumark, and Kenneth Troske, "New Evidence on Sex Segregation and Sex Differences in Wages From Matched Employee-Employer Data," *Journal of Labor Economics,* 21 (2003) pp. 887–922; George Johnson and Gary Solon, "Estimates of the Direct Effects of Comparable Worth Policy," *American Economic Review,* 76 (1986), pp. 1117–1125; Barry Gerhart, "Gender

Differences in Current and Starting Salaries: The Role of Performance, College Major, and Job Title," *Industrial and Labor Relations Review* 43 (1990), pp. 418–433.

72. George F. Dreher and Taylor H. Cox, Jr., "Labor Market Mobility and Cash Compensation: The Moderating Effects of Race and Gender," *Academy of Management Journal* 43(5) (2000), pp. 890–900; J. M. Brett and L. K. Stroh, "Jumping Ship: Who Benefits From an External Labor Market Career Strategy?" *Journal of Applied Psychology* 82 (1997), pp. 331–341; G. F. Dreher and T. H. Cox, Jr., "Race, Gender, and Opportunity: A Study of Compensation Attainment and the Establishment of Mentoring Relationships," *Journal of Applied Psychology* 81 (1996), pp. 297–308.

73. George F. Dreher and Taylor H. Cox, Jr., "Labor Market Mobility and Cash Compensation: The Moderating Effects of Race and Gender," *Academy of Management Journal* 43(5) (2000), pp. 890–900.

74. D. Weichselbaumer and R. Winter-Ebmer, "Rhetoric in Economic Research: The Case of Gender Wage Differentials," *Industrial Relations* 45(3) (2006), pp. 416–436.

75. Organisation for Economic Co-operation and Development, "The Price of Prejudice: Labour Market Discrimination on the Grounds of Gender and Ethnicity," *OECD Employment Outlook* 2008, chapter 3 (Paris: OECD, 2008).

76. Francine D. Blau and Lawrence M. Kahn, *The Sources of International Differences in Wage Inequality* (ILR Impact Brief #10), (Ithaca, NY: School of Industrial and Labor Relations, Cornell University, 2006); H. C. Jain, P. J. Sloane, and F. Horwitz, *Employment Equity and Affirmative Action: An International Comparison* (Armonk, NY: ME Sharpe, 2003); Janet C. Gornick, Marcia K. Meyers, and Katherine E. Ross, "Supporting the Employment of Mothers: Policy Variation Across Fourteen Welfare States," *Journal of European Social Policy* 7(1) (1997), pp. 45–70.

77. Sharon Toffey-Shepela and Ann T. Viviano, "Some Psychological Factors Affecting Job Segregation and Wages," in H. Remick, ed., *Comparable Worth and Wage Discrimination* (Philadelphia: Temple University Press, 1984); Helen Remick, "Beyond Equal Pay for Equal Work: Comparable Worth in the State of Washington," in Ronnie Steinber-Ratner, ed., *Equal Employment Policy for Women,* (Philadelphia: Temple University Press, 1980), pp. 405–448; "Supreme Court Decision a Victory for Pay Equity and Human Rights," press release from Public Service Alliance of Canada, June 26, 2003; Theresa Glomb, John Kammeyer-Mueller, and Maria Rotundo, "Emotional Labor Demands and Compensating Wage Differentials," *Journal of Applied Psychology* 89(4) (2004), pp. 700–714.

78. Ronnie Steinberg, "Emotional Labor in Job Evaluation: Redesigning Compensation Practices," *Annals of the American Academy of Political and Social Science* 561(1) (1999), pp. 142–157.

79. Kenneth Kovach, "An Overview and Assessment of Comparable Worth Based on a Large Scale Implementation," *Public Personnel Management* 26(1) (1997), pp. 109–122; Judith McDonald and Robert Thornton, "Private Sector Experience With Pay Equity in Ontario," *Canadian Public Policy* 24(2) (1998), pp. 227–241; Nan Weiner and Morley Gunderson, *Pay Equity: Issues, Options, and Experiences* (Toronto: Butterworths, 1990); Lynda Ames, "Fixing Women's Wages: The Effectiveness of Comparable Worth Policies," *Industrial and Labour Relations Review* 48(4) (1995), pp. 709–725.

80. Alvin O. Bellak, "Comparable Worth: A Practitioner's View," in *Comparable Worth: Issue for the 80s,* vol. 1 (Washington, DC: Equal Employment Advisory Council, 1980).

81. "Bell Canada Operators Accept Pay Equity Deal," *Canadian Employment Law Today* June 20, 2006, *www.employmentlawtoday.com;* Judy Fudge, "The Paradoxes of Pay Equity: Reflections on the Law and the Market in Bell Canada and the Public Service Alliance of Canada," *Canadian Journal of Women and the Law* 12 (2000), pp. 312–344.

82. Unions are becoming more adept at using the Web to share information. The AFSCME Web site has a section called "LaborLinks," and within that is a section called "Classification and Compensation." Here the AFSCME provides links to private wage survey sites such as *salary.com,* Wageweb, and the Executive Pay Watch, as well as links to BLS, DOT/ONET, and a few state and local government sites. In another section, it provides information on how to research companies using the Web. Unite and the SEIU provide links to the BLS. The Steelworkers Union provides information on its wage policy statement. The UAW provides detailed information on its bargaining strategies and gains, all the way down to the locals. Most unions also have newsletters that provide helpful information, and you can search the old issues to find relevant information.

Management: Making It Work

Chapter Outline

Managing, Controlling (and Sometimes Reducing) Labor Costs
Number of Employees (a.k.a.: Staffing Levels or Headcount)
Hours
Controlling Benefits
Controlling Average Cash Compensation

Control Salary Level: Top Down
Current Year's Rise
Ability to Pay
Competitive Market Pressures
Turnover Effects
Cost of Living
Rolling It All Together

Control Salary Level: Bottom Up

Ethics: Managing or Manipulating?
Where Is the Compensation Professional?

Embedded Controls
Range Maximums and Minimums

Compa-Ratios
Variable Pay
Analyzing Costs
Analyzing Value Added

Communication: Managing the Message
Say What?

Pay as Change Agent

Structuring the Compensation Function
Centralization–Decentralization
Flexibility Within Corporatewide Principles
Reengineering and Outsourcing
Balancing Flexibility and Control

Your Turn: Communication by Copier

Still Your Turn: Ethics in Compensation Decisions

This chapter is about making it work: ensuring that the right people get the right pay for achieving the right objectives in the right way. The greatest pay system design in the world is useless without competent management. So why bother with a formal system at all? If management is that important, why not simply let every manager pay whatever works best? Such total decentralization of decision making could create a chaotic array of rates. Managers could use pay to motivate behaviors that achieved their own immediate objectives, not necessarily those of the organization. Employees could be treated inconsistently and unfairly.

This was the situation in the United States in the early 1900s. The "contract system" made highly skilled workers managers as well as workers. The employer agreed to provide the "contractor" with floor space, light, power, and the necessary raw or semifinished materials. The contractor hired *and* paid labor.[1] Pay inconsistencies for the same work were common. Some contractors demanded kickbacks from employees' paychecks; many hired their relatives and friends. Dissatisfaction and grievances were widespread, eventually resulting in legislation that outlawed the arrangement.

Corruption and financial malfeasance were also part of decentralized decision making in the early 1900s. Some see parallels today. To help avoid history repeating itself and to redeem HR (and compensation) vice presidents from the image of unindicted coconspirators, the compensation system should be managed to achieve the objectives in the pay model: efficiency, fairness, and compliance.

Any discussion of managing pay must again raise the basic questions: So what is the impact of the decision or technique? Does it help the organization achieve its objectives? How?

Although many pay management issues have been discussed throughout the book, a few remain to be called out explicitly. These include (1) managing labor costs, (2) understanding embedded controls, (3) analyzing value-added returns, (4) communication, and (5) designing the compensation department.

MANAGING, CONTROLLING (AND SOMETIMES REDUCING) LABOR COSTS

Financial planning is integral to managing compensation. The cost implications of actions such as updating the pay structure, increasing merit pay, or instituting gain sharing are critical for making sound decisions. Budgets account for these costs. Creating a compensation budget requires tradeoffs, such as how much of an increase should be allocated according to employee contributions versus across-the-board increases. Tradeoffs also occur over short- versus long-term incentives, over pay increases contingent on performance versus seniority, and over cash compensation compared to benefits.

Financial planning also requires understanding the *potential returns* gained from the allocation.[2] Total compensation makes up at least 50 percent of operating expenses in many organizations. Yet, most companies have not tried to analyze the returns from their compensation decisions.[3] As we noted in Chapter 2, compensation strategy influences effectiveness not only by its influence on (labor) costs, but through its influence in helping increase revenues or returns as well. Returns might be the productivity increases expected from a new gain-sharing or profit-sharing plan, or the expected value added by boosting merit increases to the top performers.[4] In the past, financial planning in compensation was only about costs.[5] This is perhaps because costs are tangible and easy to measure, whereas the returns generated by compensation strategy may often be intangible and harder to quantify. It is important to keep in mind, however, that how easy or difficult it is to quantify something has little to do with how important it is. Fortunately, analysis of the expected returns compared to costs is becoming more common.[6] More on this later.

You already know many of the factors that affect labor costs. Exhibit 18.1 shows a simple labor cost model. Using this model, there are three main factors to control in order to manage labor costs: employment (e.g., number of workers and the hours they work), average cash compensation (e.g., wages, bonuses), and average benefit costs.

EXHIBIT 18.1
Managing
Labor Costs

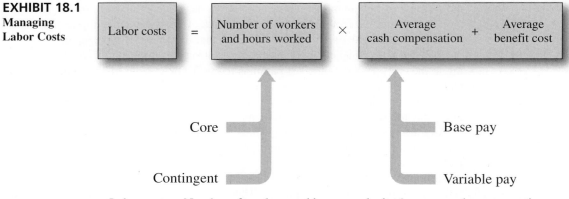

Labor costs = Number of workers and hours worked × (average cash compensation + average benefit cost)

Cash compensation and benefits have been this book's focus. However, if our objective is to better manage labor costs, then all three factors require attention.

Number of Employees (a.k.a.: Staffing Levels or Headcount)

Using information about competitors' average pay helps improve understanding of labor costs. Exhibit 18.2A shows how one organization pays its engineers relative to its competitors at each of five job levels, E5–E1. The pay for each position is the cross-hatched bar. Market pay is the shaded bar, with the average falling in the middle of the unshaded part of the bar. So the organization meets competition by paying E5, E3, and E2 engineers at about the median. But the company leads competition at E4 and lags at the entry-level E1.

Exhibit 18.2B provides more insight into the organization's labor costs. This part of the exhibit compares the organization's distribution of engineers among the five job levels to its competitors' distributions. A larger percentage of the organization's engineers are at higher levels, E4 and E5, than its competitors. So even though the organization pays above market for only one of the five job levels, its labor costs may be higher than its competitors due to its staffing pattern. So what? Looking only at total head count, as suggested in Exhibit 18.1, may mislead since the total employment level could be identical to competitors' but deployment among job levels may vary. Here, the organization differs from its competitors most at E4, where it employs a larger percent of engineering talent and also pays them more. Something is going on at E4. More information is required to better understand what underlies these differences. Are the organization's engineers more experienced and thus promoted into E4? Does the company do more sophisticated work that requires more experienced engineers? Absent some sound business-related rationale, labor costs can be reduced by redeploying staffing levels and wages at E4.[7] Obviously, paying the same wages (e.g., meeting competition) to fewer employees is less expensive. The effects on all pay objectives—efficiency and fairness—also need to be considered before taking any action.

EXHIBIT 18.2   **Staffing Analysis Identifies Reasons for Pay Variances**

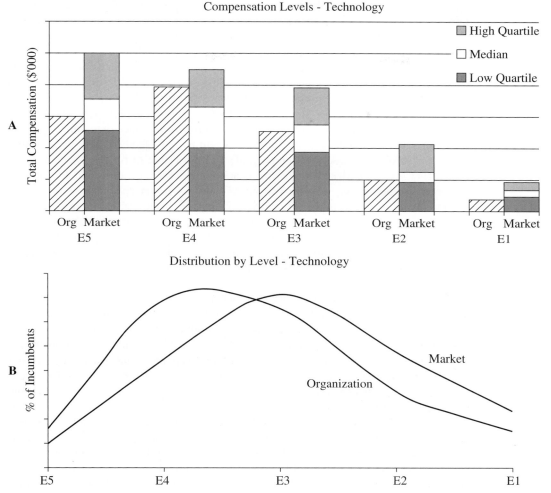

Reducing Headcount

As is apparent from following the business news during any recession, organizations often reduce headcount to cut labor costs. Such cuts may take the form of layoffs (often with severance benefits that depend on length of service) or exit incentives that are designed to encourage employees to leave "by choice." A major advantage of a reduction in force (RIF) is that it also reduces benefits costs, something that a pay cut, furlough, or reduction in hours ordinarily does not achieve. To the degree that headcount reductions can be targeted based on performance, it can also be an opportunity for an organization to re-shape its workforce in a way that creates positive sorting effects. Under such a scenario, stronger performers are unaffected (e.g., their pay is not cut) and the organization has an opportunity to maintain good employee relations with this important group.

There are, however, several potential problems with headcount reductions. First, regulatory requirements make it difficult to make targeted cuts. The Age Discrimination in Employment Act (ADEA) often comes into play if organizations target reductions among higher paid employees (to maximize labor cost savings) because higher paid employees also tend to be older employees. In addition, the Older Worker Benefits Protection Act, part of the ADEA, requires that exit incentive programs be structured in very specific ways. For example, a program must give workers 40 years old and older 21 days to consider the offer and 7 days to change their mind if they accept the offer. These and other provisions tend to make it difficult to single out high-wage and/or poor-performing workers. If exit incentives cannot be effectively targeted and all employees are eligible, which employees do you think would be most likely to take the incentive and leave? Probably those most employable and most able to find another good job, right? That is indeed what a number of organizations have experienced. Thus, you may end up, in essence, paying your top performers to leave—a very underiable sorting effect! Second, workforce reductions, especially if not handled well, can harm employee relations. Regulatory restrictions on headcount reductions can be quite stringent outside the United States. (See our discussion of works councils, for example, in Chapter 16.)[8] Third, organizations that make greater (involuntary) workforce reductions also experience greater voluntary turnover.[9] Fourth, RIFs, while reducing costs over time, are very costly in tangible terms up front due to increases in unemployment insurance tax rates, disruption of work processes and serving customers, and administrative costs of handling exits. Exit incentives, if provided, further drive up costs. Fifth, some companies have learned to run so "lean" (i.e., very few employees on manufacturing lines), and have controlled hiring so successfully, that there may be little room to cut headcount.[10] Finally, where cuts can be made, if the cuts are too deep, an organization will be poorly positioned to generate revenue if business picks up again.[11] An organization may spend a lot of money reducing headcount and then spend a lot more a short time later to hire new employees to handle increased product demand. If other firms increase hiring at the same time, costs will be even greater. Announcements of layoffs and plant closings often have favorable short-run effects on stock prices as investors anticipate improved cash flow and lower costs. However, in the longer term, adverse effects such as loss of trained employees, unrealized productivity, and lowered morale often translate into lower financial gains than anticipated. Some evidence indicates that close attention to process and employee relations during workforce reductions can help financial results.[12]

In addition, as we saw in Chapter 17, the regulatory environment differs from country to country. Many European countries have legislation as part of their social contracts that makes it very difficult to reduce headcount or wages. Managing labor costs is a greater struggle in such circumstances.

Many employers seek to buffer themselves from getting into a position where layoffs are necessary. As discussed below, use of overtime is part of this strategy. In addition, organizations establish different relationships with different groups of workers. As Exhibit 18.3 depicts, the two groups are commonly referred to as **core employees,** with whom a long-term relationship is desired, and *contingent workers,* whose employment agreements may cover only short, specific time periods. Contingent workers can be employees, but can also be independent contractors/vendors or may be

EXHIBIT 18.3
Core and
Contingent
Employees

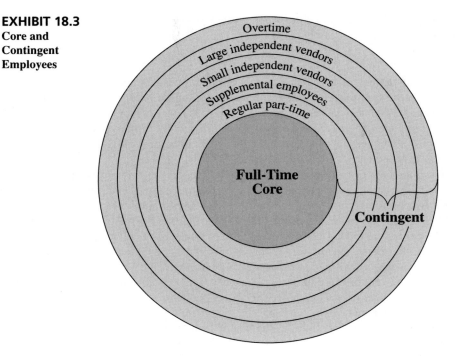

employed by staffing services firms/vendors. Rather than expand or contract the core workforce, many employers achieve flexibility and control labor costs by expanding or contracting the contingent workforce. Toyota, for example, while not cutting regular employees in either the United States or Japan during the recent recession, has cut its contract worker headcount.

The segmented supply of nurses at St. Luke's Hospital, discussed in Chapter 7 and shown in Exhibit 18.4, illustrates the variable costs from use of different sources of nurses. Regular, pool, registry, and traveler nurses are paid differently. Some have benefits from St. Luke's, others have them from the contracting agencies, and still others must purchase their own benefits (pool nurses). The tradeoffs in managing costs include

EXHIBIT 18.4
Segmented
Supplies:
St. Luke's
Labor Cost
Model

Source: © George T.
Milkovich.

Labor cost = employment × (average cash compensation + average benefits) + agency fee

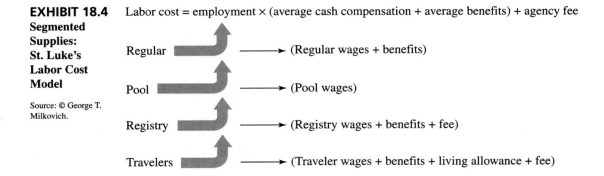

balancing patient loads, nurse-to-patient ratios, costs of alternative sources, and quality of care.[13]

Hours

Rather than define employment as number of employees, hours of work is often used. For nonexempt employees in the United States, hours over 40 per week are more expensive (one-and-a-half times regular wage). Hence, another way to manage labor costs is to examine overtime hours versus hiring more employees. St. Luke's may guarantee its regular nurses a specific number of hours, but contract nurses (pool, registry, or travelers) are "on call."

The four factors in the labor cost model—number of employees, hours worked, cash compensation, and benefit costs—are not independent. Overtime hours require higher wages but the incremental benefits cost is substantially lower than that incurred in hirng an additional regular nurse. The higher the fixed benefits costs, the more viable is the option to add overtime (even with the time and a half premium) rather than hiring another nurse. By not hiring, the organization avoids recruitment/selection costs. It also gains more flexibility to reduce labor costs if demand for its healthcare services declines in the future. In that case, rather than cuttng headcount, it can reduce hours worked, which helps avoid employee relations problems as well as the monetary costs of reducing headcount.

During the recent recession, a number of firms reduced hours and costs through the use of mandatory unpaid leave or furloughs to cut hours and thus labor costs. For example, state employees in California were required to take two furlough days off per month, resulting in a 10 percent pay cut. Wendy Roberson, one such employee, partly as a joke, founded the "Fun Furlough Fridays Club." Nobody wants a paycut, but if you are going to get some extra time off, you might as well make the best of it and enjoy it, right? Well, as it turns out, although the pay cut was real, the time off in many cases was not. The amount of work to be done did not decrease, so many "furloughed" employees found themselves at work, rather than having Fun Furlough Fridays.[14] Nevertheless, reducing hours and pay does mean that fewer headcount reductions are necessary and by avoiding these, there will be less disruption and private sector organizations should be better positioned to respond when business picks up again, at least so long as top performers don't find greener pastures in the meantime.[15]

Controlling Benefits

One of the most common approaches to reducing benefits costs recently has been for employers to suspend matching contributions (made when employees contribute) to 401(k) retirement plans. Survey data show about one in four companies either have already suspended their matching contributons or are considering doing so. Even the American Association for Retired Persons (AARP) decided it needed to suspend its 401(k) retirement plan match, a decision that was presumably not taken lightly![16] The average company match is 50 cents on the dollar up to 6 percent of pay. More companies may move to a model that makes matching contributions dependent on profits.[17]

Another action we have seen is organizations eliminating benefits such as defined benefit (pension) plans as part of seeking bankrupcy protection from creditors. Examples include several airlines (e.g., United, Delta, USAir, Northwest), automobile companies (General Motors, Chrysler), and automobile parts companies (e.g., Delphi). As noted in Chapter 13, the Pension Benefit Guaranty Corporation (PBGC) provides benefits to employees who were coverd under such plans. However, the maximum monthly retirement benefit from the PBGC is $4,500, meaning that more highly paid employees (e.g., airline pilots) can experience a significant loss in pension benefits after bankruptcy. Other, more typical, ways of controlling or reducing benefits costs have to do with efforts by companies in the area of health care (as discussed in Chapters 12 and 13).

Controlling Average Cash Compensation

Average cash compensation includes average salary level plus variable compensation payments such as bonuses, gain sharing, stock plans, and/or profit sharing. The variable component of compensation, in theory, will rise and fall in line with business performance. For example, a profit-sharing plan will ordinarily have lower than normal profit-sharing payouts in years when profits are lower than normal. If other firms are experiencing similar profit declines, then there may be less danger of losing employees through turnover when this happens and the full advantage of "automatic" labor cost flexibility can be experienced.

During the recent recession (in 2009) one in four firms froze salaries, giving no annual increase,[18] resulting in an average salary increase budget across companies of just 2.0 percent. For 2010, companies are projecting an average salary increase budget of 3.0 percent. However, they projected an increase budget for 2009 of 3.5 percent, which as we now know, was not a very accurate projection. (The often-quoted New York Yankees Hall of Fame catcher Yogi Berra is supposed to have said: "Prediction is hard, especially when you're talking about the future.")

Adjustments to average cash compensation level (here, to simplify, we focus primarily on the salary component) can be made (1) *top down,* in which top management determines the amount of money to be spent on pay and allocates it "down" to each sub-unit for the plan year, and (2) *bottom up,* in which individual employees' pay for the plan year is forecasted and summed to create an organization-wide salary budget.

CONTROL SALARY LEVEL: TOP DOWN

Top-down budgeting begins with an estimate from top management of the pay increase budget for the entire organization. Once the total budget is determined, it is then allocated to each manager, who plans how to distribute it among subordinates. There are many approaches to top-down budgeting. A typical one, **planned pay-level rise,** is simply the percentage increase in average pay for the unit that is planned to occur. Several factors influence the decision on how much to increase the average pay level for the next period: how much the average level was increased this period, ability to pay, competitive market pressures, turnover effects, and cost of living.

Current Year's Rise

This is the percentage by which the average wage changed in the past year; mathematically:

$$\text{Percent pay-level rise} =$$
$$100 \times \frac{\text{average pay at year-end} - \text{average pay at year beginning}}{\text{average pay at year beginning}}$$

Ability to Pay

Any decision to increase the average pay level is in part a function of the organization's financial circumstances. Financially healthy employers may wish to maintain their competitive positions in the labor market or share financial success through bonuses and profit sharing. Conversely, financially troubled employers may not be able to maintain competitive market positions. As noted, the conventional response has been to reduce employment. As shown earlier, by analyzing pay and staffing at each level, potential cost savings can be discovered. Other options are to reduce the rate of increase in average pay by controlling adjustments in base pay and/or variable pay. Raising employees' copays and deductibles for benefits is another. Often as a last resort, firms decrease base wages (as well as variable pay). Airline pilots and mechanics have taken highly publicized pay cuts in recent years. Other alternatives also exist. Look again at the cost model for St. Luke's and its segmented labor supply. The hospital can reduce costs by reducing the different sources of contract nurses.

Competitive Market Pressures

In Chapter 8, we discussed how managers determine an organization's competitive position in relation to its competitors. Recall that a distribution of market rates for benchmark jobs was collected and analyzed into a single average wage for each benchmark. This "average market wage" becomes the "going market rate," and this market rate changes each year in response to a variety of factors in the external market.

Turnover Effects

Sometimes referred to as **"churn"** or "slippage," the **turnover effect** recognizes the fact that when people leave (through layoffs, quitting, retiring), they typically are replaced by employees who earn a lower wage. Exhibit 18.2 illustrates where an organization is overstaffed compared to competitors. Reducing levels at E5 and E4 and replacing them with E1s and E2s will reduce labor costs. However, keep in mind the potential impact on revenues and customer satisfaction, as well as possible violation of the Age Discrimination Act.

Turnover effect can be calculated as annual turnover multiplied by the planned average increase. For example, assume that an organization whose labor costs equal $1 million a year has a turnover rate of 15 percent and a planned average increase of 6 percent. The turnover effect is $.15 \times .06 = 0.9\%$, or $9,000 ($.009 \times $1,000,000$). So instead of budgeting an additional $60,000 to fund a 6 percent increase, only $51,000 is needed. The turnover effect will also reduce benefit costs linked to base pay, such as pensions.[19]

Cost of Living

Although there is little research to support **cost of living increases,** employees undoubtedly compare their pay increases to changes in their living costs. Unions consistently argue that increasing living costs justify increasing pay.

A Distinction

It is important to distinguish among three related concepts: the *cost of living, changes in prices in the product and service markets,* and *changes in wages in labor markets.* As Exhibit 18.5 shows, changes in wages in labor markets are measured through pay surveys. These changes are incorporated into the system through market adjustments in the budget and updates of the policy line and range structure. Price changes for goods and services in the product and service markets are measured by several government indexes, one of which is the consumer price index. The third concept, the cost of living, refers to the expenditure patterns of individuals for goods and services. The cost of living is more difficult to measure because employees' expenditures depend on many things: marital status, number of dependents and ages, personal preferences, location, and so on. Different employees experience different costs of living, and the only accurate way to measure them is to examine the personal expenditures of each employee.

The three concepts are interrelated. Wages in the labor market are part of the cost of producing goods and services, and changes in wages create pressures on prices. Similarly,

EXHIBIT 18.5   **Three Distinct but Related Concepts and Their Measures**

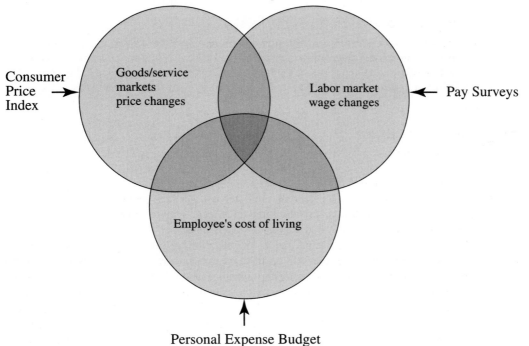

Consumer Price Index →

Goods/service markets price changes

Labor market wage changes

← Pay Surveys

Employee's cost of living

↑ Personal Expense Budget

changes in the prices of goods and services create the need for increased wages in order to maintain the same lifestyle.

The Consumer Price Index (CPI)

Many people refer to the CPI as a "cost-of-living" index, and many employers choose, as a matter of pay policy or in response to union pressures, to tie wages to it. However, the CPI does not necessarily reflect an individual employee's cost of living. Instead, it measures *changes in prices over time*. Changes in the CPI indicate only whether prices have increased more or less rapidly in an area since the base period. For example, a CPI of 110 in Chicago and 140 in Atlanta does not necessarily mean that it costs more to live in Atlanta. It does mean that prices have risen faster in Atlanta since the base year than they have in Chicago, since both cities started with bases of 100.

Cybercomp

A simple inflation calculator at *www.westegg.com/inflation/* uses the consumer price index to adjust any given amount of data from 1800 on. Most governments calculate some kind of consumer price index for their country. The Web page for the U.S. Bureau of Labor Statistics provides many of these indexes (*stats.bls.gov*). They vary on how realistically they capture actual changes in prices.

A word of caution: If you decide to use the CPI rather than labor market salary surveys to determine the merit budget, you basically are paying for inflation rather than performance or market changes.

Cybercomp

A quicker way to compare living costs is to use the "relocation salary calculator" at *www.homefair.com/homefair/calc/salcalc.html.* Enter your current city and potential new city to see what salary you need in the new city based on cost-of-living differences. How accurate is this Web site's information?

The CPI is of public interest because changes in it trigger changes in labor contracts, social security payments, federal and military pensions, and food stamp eligibility. Tying budgets or payments to the CPI is called *indexing.*

Rolling It All Together

Let us assume that the managers take into account all these factors—current year's rise, ability to pay, market adjustments, turnover effects, changes in the cost of living, and **geographic differentials**—and decide that the planned rise in average salary for the next period is 6.3 percent. This means that the organization has set a target of 6.3 percent as the increase in *average* salary that will occur in the next budget period. It does not mean that everyone's increase will be 6.3 percent. It means that at the end of the budget year, the average salary calculated to include all employees will be 6.3 percent higher than it is now.

The next question is, How do we distribute that 6.3 percent budget in a way that accomplishes management's objectives for the pay system and meets the organization's goals?

Distributing the Budget to Sub-Units

A variety of methods exist for determining what percentage of the salary budget each manager should receive. Some use a uniform percentage, in which each manager gets an equal percentage of the budget based on the salaries of each sub-unit's employees. Others vary the percentage allocated to each manager based on pay-related issues—such as turnover or performance—that have been identified in that subunit.

Once salary budgets are allocated to each sub-unit manager, they become a constraint: a limited fund of money that each manager has to allocate to subordinates. Typically, **merit increase guidelines** are used to help managers make these allocation decisions. Merit increase grids help ensure that different managers grant consistent increases to employees with similar performance ratings and in the same position in their ranges. Additionally, grids help control costs. Chapter 11 provides examples of merit increase grids. To limit the number of employees placed in high performance categories (and thus the number of employees receiving the largest merit increases), some companies used forced distribution approaches.

CONTROL SALARY LEVEL: BOTTOM UP

In contrast to top-down budgeting, where managers are told what their salary budget will be, bottom-up budgeting begins with managers' pay increase recommendations for the upcoming plan year. Exhibit 18.6 shows the process involved.

1. *Instruct managers in compensation policies and techniques.* Train managers in the concepts of a sound pay-for-performance policy and in standard company compensation techniques such as the use of pay-increase guidelines and budgeting techniques. Communicate market data and the salary ranges.

2. *Distribute forecasting instructions and worksheets.* Furnish managers with the forms and instructions necessary to preplan increases. Most firms offer managers computer software to support these analyses and to enter information and perform what-if analyses.[20] Adjustments for each individual are fed into the summary merit budget, promotion budget, equity adjustment budget, and so on, on a summary screen. These recommendations are then submitted electronically.

   The type of information available to each supervisor to guide him or her in making recommendations might include performance rating history, past raises, training background, and stock allocations are all included. Guidelines for increases based on merit, promotion, and equity adjustments are provided, and all the worksheets are linked so that the manager can model pay adjustments for employees and see the budgetary effects of those adjustments immediately.

   Some argue that providing such detailed data and recommendations to operating managers makes the process biased. How would you like your instructor to look at your overall GPA before giving you a grade in this course? Pay histories, however, ensure that managers are at least aware of this information and that pay increases for any one period are part of a continuing message to individual employees, not some ad-hoc response to short-term changes.

EXHIBIT 18.6
Compensation
Forecasting
and Budgeting
Cycle

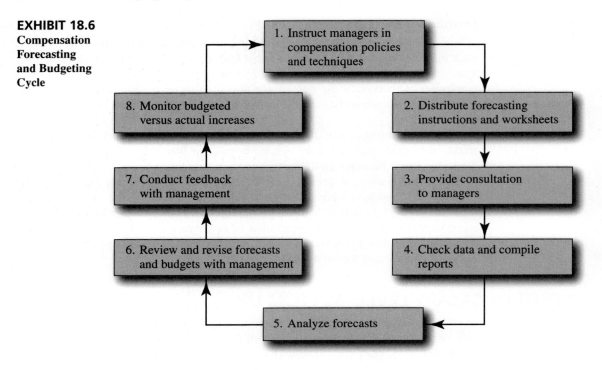

3. *Provide consultation to managers.* Offer advice and salary information services to managers upon request. Dell's online approach makes it much easier to request and apply such guidance.

4. *Check data and compile reports.* Audit the increases forecasted to ensure that they do not exceed the pay guidelines and are consistent with appropriate ranges. Then use the data to feed back the outcomes of pay forecasts and budgets.

5. *Analyze forecasts.* Examine each manager's forecast, and recommend changes based on noted inequities among different managers.

6. *Review and revise forecasts and budgets with management.* Consult with managers regarding the analysis and any recommended changes. Obtain top-management approval of forecasts.

7. *Conduct feedback with management.* Present statistical summaries of the forecasting data by department, and establish unit goals.

8. *Monitor budgeted versus actual increases.* Control the forecasted increases versus the actual increases by tracking and reporting periodic status to management.

The result of the forecasting cycle is a budget for the upcoming plan year for each organization's unit as well as estimated pay treatment for each employee. The budget does not lock in the manager to the exact pay change recommended for each employee. Rather, it represents a plan, and deviations due to unforeseen changes such as performance improvements and unanticipated promotions are common. The approach places responsibility for pay management on the managers by requiring them to plan the pay treatment for each of their employees. The compensation manager takes on the role of advisor to operating management's use of the system.[21]

ETHICS: MANAGING OR MANIPULATING?

Compensation ethics is not an oxymoron. But absent a professional code of behaviors and values, it is a challenge for compensation managers to ensure that their actions *are* ethical. The Web page for the compensation society, WorldatWork, includes the topic of ethics. Public discussion of ethics in compensation topics such as executive pay or backdating option grants benefits from the voices of informed compensation practitioners.

Managing compensation ethically is increasingly complicated for several reasons. First, pay really matters; it is important to all of us. Second is the fierce pressure to achieve results. The increased use of pay for performance, which is based on results achieved and exceeding targets, can contribute to these pressures. However, assessing results sometimes has a "smoke and mirrors" feel to it. At an organization's compensation strategy session that we attended, the chief financial officer observed that it was possible to "manage our reported earnings within several percentage points of the target. We can exceed analysts' and shareholder expectations by 1 to 10 percent." This was relatively easy for this particular company since about one-third of its earnings came from liquid investments in other companies. The remainder was revenue from its products and services. The implication of managing earnings for employees' profit-sharing payouts and executive stock valuations were not ignored. The point is that measures of financial performance do not provide an immutable gold standard. They can be "managed."[22]

Where Is the Compensation Professional?

Performance-based pay is not the only area that presents ethical dilemmas. Misusing and even failing to understand survey statistics, manipulating job evaluations, peer-company competitive data, masking overtime and pay discrimination violations, failure to understand that correlation does not mean causation, and recommending pay programs without addressing their expected costs and returns should force us to take a hard look at what we are doing.[23]

Stephen Landry, the former HR director at Sycamore Networks, reports that the company's chief financial officer pressured him to change the hiring dates of some employees to make their stock option grants worth more money. These actions were to be kept hidden from the company auditors. Instead, Landry told executives these actions were unethical and probably illegal. He was fired. Internal memos from the company reveal a "risk assessment" of the action becoming exposed. Changing the date on documents was judged a low risk since the original grant "has been deleted from the system in its entirety." Landry is suing and the SEC is investigating. If Mr. Landry's experience is not enough for the professional compensation community, over at Cable-vision, they backdated stock grants to a dead executive.[24]

A starting point to judge the ethics of our behavior may be our compensation model, presented with the advice: "Strive to achieve both efficiency and fairness."

EMBEDDED CONTROLS

Controls on managers' pay decisions come from two different aspects of the compensation process: (1) controls that are inherent in the design of the techniques, and (2) the formal **budgeting** process discussed above. Think back to the many techniques already discussed: job analysis and evaluation, skill- and competency-based plans, policy lines, **range minimums and maximums,** broad bands, performance evaluation, gain sharing, and salary-increase guidelines. In addition to their primary purposes, these techniques also regulate managers' pay decisions by guiding what managers can and cannot do. Controls are built into these techniques to direct them toward the pay system objectives. A few of these controls are examined below.

Range Maximums and Minimums

Ranges set the maximum and minimum dollars to be paid for specific work. The maximum is an important cost control. Ideally, it represents the highest value the organization places on the output of the work. With job-based structures, skills and knowledge possessed by employees may be more valuable in another job, but the range maximum represents all that the work produced in a particular job is worth to the organization. When Wal-Mart installed range maximums and minimums for its jobs, its critics accused the company of "capping wages" of its workers. Those readers who recall Chapter 8's discussion on designing ranges recognize that specific jobs may have a maximum rate (a cap) but individuals may not. They can earn beyond the job's maximum through promotions, profit sharing, and so on.[25]

Pressures to pay above the range maximum occur for a number of reasons—for example, when employees with high seniority reach the maximum or when promotion opportunities are scarce. If employees are paid above the range maximum, these rates are called **red circle rates.** Most employers "freeze" red circle rates until the ranges are shifted upward by market update adjustments so that the rate is back within the range again. If red circle rates become common throughout an organization, then the design of the ranges and the evaluation of the jobs should be reexamined.

Range minimums are just that: the minimum value placed on the work. Often rates below the minimum are used for trainees. Pay below minimum may also occur if outstanding employees receive a number of rapid promotions and pay increases have not kept up.

Broad Bands

Broad bands are intended to offer managers greater flexibility compared to a grade-range design. Usually broad bands are accompanied by external market "reference rates" and "shadow ranges" that guide managers' decisions. Bands may be more about career management than pay decisions. Rather, the control is in the salary budgets given to managers. The manager has flexibility in pay decisions, as long as the total pay comes in under the budget.

Compa-Ratios

Range midpoints reflect the pay policy line of the employer in relationship to external competition. To assess how managers actually pay employees in relation to the midpoint, an index called a **compa-ratio** is often calculated:

$$\text{Compa-ratio} = \frac{\text{average rate actual paid}}{\text{range midpoint}}$$

A compa-ratio of less than 1 means that, on average, employees in a range are paid below the midpoint. That is, managers are paying less than the intended policy. There may be several valid reasons for such a situation. The majority of employees may be new or recent hires; they may be poor performers; or promotion may be so rapid that few employees stay in the job long enough to get into the high end of the range.

A compa-ratio greater than 1 means that, on average, the rates exceed the intended policy. The reasons for this are the reverse of those mentioned above: a majority of workers with high seniority, high performance, low turnover, few new hires, or low promotion rates. Compa-ratios may be calculated for individual employees, for each range, for organization units, or for functions.

Other examples of controls designed into the pay techniques include the mutual sign-offs on job descriptions required of supervisors and subordinates. Another is slotting new jobs into the pay structure via job evaluation, which helps ensure that jobs are compared on the same factors. Similarly, an organization-wide performance management system is intended to ensure that all employees are evaluated on similar factors.

Variable Pay

The essence of variable pay is that it must be re-earned each period, in contrast to conventional merit pay increases or across-the-board increases that increase the base on which the following year's increase is calculated.

Increases added into base pay have compounding effects on costs, and these costs are significant. For example, a $15-a-week take-home pay added onto a $40,000 base compounds into a cash flow of $503,116 over 10 years. In addition, costs for some benefits also increase. By comparison, the organization could use that same $503,000 to keep base pay at $40,000 a year and pay a 26.8 percent bonus every single year. As the example shows, the greater the ratio of variable pay to base pay, the more flexible the organization's labor costs.

Apply this flexibility to the general labor cost model in Exhibit 18.1. The greater the ratios of contingent to core workers and variable to base pay, the greater the variable component of labor costs and the greater the options available to managers to control these costs. A caution: Although variability in pay and employment may be an advantage for managing labor costs, it may be less appealing from the standpoint of managing effective treatment of employees. The inherent financial insecurity built into variable plans may adversely affect employees' financial well-being, especially for lower-paid workers. Managing labor costs is only one objective for managing compensation.

Analyzing Costs

Costing out wage proposals is commonly done prior to recommending pay increases, especially for collective bargaining. For example, it is useful to bear in mind the dollar impact of a 1-cent-per-hour wage change or a 1 percent change in payroll as one goes into bargaining. Knowing these figures, negotiators can quickly compute the impact of a request for a 9 percent wage increase.

Commercial compensation software is available to analyze almost every aspect of compensation information. Software can easily compare past estimates to what actually occurred (e.g., the percentage of employees that actually did receive a merit increase and the amount). It can simulate alternate wage proposals and compare their potential effects. It can also help evaluate salary survey data and simulate the cost impact of incentive and gain-sharing options.

Analyzing Value Added

Only about one-third of 600 organizations in a recent study bothered to calculate the cost and value added by their pay programs.[26] Another survey reports that about 70 percent of the compensation specialists consider their tools "ineffective" to determine the value added. However, a handful of companies, supported by consultants and researchers, are beginning to analyze the value added (or return on investments) of pay decisions.[27] This analysis requires a shift in how compensation is viewed. Compensation becomes an investment as well as an expense. Decisions are based on analysis of the return on this investment. The hope is to answer questions such as, "So what" returns are expected from spending more on the offensive team (as do the Seattle Seahawks), or showering rewards on the top performers (as does General Electric), or on a new incentive plan based on a balanced scorecard (as does Citigroup)?[28]

Exhibit 18.7 illustrates the approach to assessing value gained. The company in this exhibit has already done an analysis that suggests that the top 10 percent of employees improve returns by about 2 to 5 percent of their average salary. Now the company is considering two actions:

1. Implement a bonus plan based on balanced scorecards for individual managers.
2. Increase the differentiation between top performers and average performers.

The exhibit shows the analysis of potential value added by these two options. The returns are grouped into four types: recruiting and retaining top talent, reducing turnover of top performers, revenue enhancement, and productivity gains. The logic, assumptions, measures, and estimates of gains are described in the exhibit. The cautious reader will immediately see that the assumptions are critical and based on research evidence, best estimates, and judgments.

The practice of analyzing the returns from compensation decisions is in its early stages. The promise is that it will direct thinking beyond treating compensation as only an expense to considering the returns gained as well. Our discussion of utility analysis in the Appendix to Chapter 7 is an example of one approach.[29] Advocates want to develop compensation managers' *analytical literacy*. Readers will recognize the similarity to topics in their finance and operations management classes. Nevertheless,

EXHIBIT 18.7 Illustration of Value-Added Analysis

Description of Value	Assumptions	Measure	Value Added	
			Low Estimate	High Estimate
Recruiting/Retaining Top Talent				
Increase pool of top people applying; Increase percent accepting offers; Decrease time to fill position	Top performers improve returns by 2% to 5% of average salary ($68,000)	Increase top talent yield ratios and turnover rates	Increases revenues by $1,400/top person	Improves revenues by $3,400/top person
Reduced Turnover/Replacement Costs				
Reduction of recruiting costs due to lower turnover of top performers	Reduction in turnover of one top performer results in a savings of $25,000 (based on an average salary of $68,000)	Savings of $25,000/top performer	$100,000 for a reduction of four "resigned" top employees	$500,000 for a reduction of 10 "resigned" top employees
		Productivity savings reflected in "loss of revenue" section		
Revenue Enhancers				
Reduced loss of revenue due to faster time to fill key customer-facing (sales, technical support) and other key positions	Revenue will increase by some percentage (e.g., 5%) Head count remains constant	Revenue increase Assume current revenue of $2 billion	2% or $40 million	5% or $100 million
Greater revenue because of focus on revenue and customer goals as driven by the balanced scorecard				
Increased revenue because of stronger and longer-lasting customer relationships due to retention of key top performers through market competitiveness and pay differentiation				
Productivity Gains				
Increased productivity by retaining top performers through significant pay differentiation and market-competitive base pay	Retaining and engaging more of the top employees results in significant productivity gains and revenue generation because top employees are 25% to 50% more productive than the average employee	Increased revenue (reflected in revenue gains-above) Head-count reduction (need fewer employees or grow slower)	A reduction in 10 head count results in a savings of $900,000 ($68,000 employee + benefit cost)	A reduction in 50 head count results in a savings of $4.5-million
Increased productivity of all employees because of greater perception of "internal alignment" and "market competitiveness" resulting from paying competitive with the market and common programs	Increasing the productivity of all results in increased revenue, customer satisfaction, or fewer head count	Head-count reduction because fewer top performers achieve the same results as more lower performers	A reduction in 1 head count results in a savings of $90,000	A reduction in 5 head count results in a savings of $450,000
	Terminating low-productivity employees and replacing them with high-productivity employees result in significant productivity gains and revenue generation			

managers still must use their heads as well as their models. Treating compensation as an investment and employees as human capital risks losing sight of them as people.[30] The fairness objective must not get lost in the search for ROI.

Making Information Useful—Compensation Enterprise Systems

A friend of ours e-mailed from Shanghai that "six months after we have acquired this operation from the government, I still cannot get an accurate headcount. I do not know how many people we actually employ or who should get paychecks!" That manager clearly needs more information. But most managers find themselves overwhelmed with too much information. The challenge is to make the information useful.

Compensation software transforms data into useful information and guides decision making. Many software packages that serve a variety of purposes are available.[31] Some of them support *employee self-service,* by which employees can access their personal information, make choices about which health care coverage they prefer, allocate savings between growth or value investment funds, access vacation schedules, or check out a list of child or elder care service providers. *Manager self-service* helps managers pay their employees appropriately. *Communication portals,* designed for employees or managers, explain compensation policies and practices, answer frequently asked questions, and explain how these systems affect their pay.[32] Other software *processes transactions.* It standardizes forms, performs some analysis, and creates reports at the click of the mouse. The advantage is that all employees at all locations are on the same system.

While compensation software is proliferating, what remains a scarcer resource is the intellectual capital: the compensation knowledge and judgment required to understand which information, analyses, and reports are useful. Part of this intellectual capital includes analytical (read "statistical and math") skills. Another part is knowledge of the business. A shortage of this knowledge among compensation managers not only limits the usefulness of compensation software but also limits the contribution of compensation management.

Computers inevitably bring up the issue of confidentiality. If personal compensation data are accessible to employees and managers, privacy and security issues as well as ethical and legal issues emerge. Regulations vary around the world. The European Union has issued the Data Privacy Directive, which is significantly stronger than U.S. regulations.[33] Unauthorized users, both inside and outside the corporation, remain a threat.

COMMUNICATION: MANAGING THE MESSAGE

Compensation communicates. It signals what is important and what is not. If you receive a pay increase for one more year of experience on your job, then one more year is important. If the pay increase is equal to any change in the CPI, then the CPI and its real meaning is important. If the increase is for moving to a bigger job or for outstanding performance, then a bigger job or outstanding performance is important. Changes in a pay system also send a powerful message. Microsoft's shift from stock options to grants tells everyone (current and future employees and stockholders) to expect lower risks and lower returns.

Earlier in this book, we stressed that employees must understand the pay system. Their understanding is shaped indirectly through the paychecks they receive and directly via formal communication about their pay, their performance, and the markets in which the organization competes. An argument for employee involvement in the design of pay systems is that it increases understanding. Two surveys are revealing. A Watson Wyatt survey of 13,000 employees reported that about only 35 percent of them understood the link between their job performance and the pay they receive. (Watson Wyatt failed to point out that some workers may simply believe that in their organizations there is no real link!)[34] WorldatWork did a second survey of 6,000 employees. Only about one-third of them said they understood how pay ranges are determined or had a reasonable idea of what their increase would be if they were promoted. Fewer than half understood how their own pay increases are calculated.[35]

Two reasons are usually given for communicating pay information. The first is that considerable resources have been devoted to designing a fair and equitable system that is intended to attract and retain qualified people and motivate performance. For managers and employees to gain an accurate view of the pay system—one that perhaps influences their attitudes about it—they need to be informed.

The second reason is that, according to some research, employees seem to misperceive the pay system. For example, they tend to overestimate the pay of those in lower-level jobs and to underestimate the pay of those in higher-level jobs. They assume that the pay structure is more compressed than it actually is. If differentials are underestimated, their motivational value is diminished.

Further, there is some evidence to suggest that the goodwill engendered by the act of being open about pay may also affect perceptions of pay equity. Interestingly, the research also shows that employees in companies with open pay communication policies are as inaccurate in estimating pay differentials as those in companies in which pay secrecy prevails.[36] (Caution: Most of this research was done over 20 years ago.) However, employers in companies with open pay policies tend to express higher satisfaction with their pay and with the pay system.[37]

In the case of benefits too, communication plays a potentially important role. We know that employees greatly underestimate the value of their benefits, which is a major concern given that benefits add roughly 40 cents on top of every dollar spent on cash compensation.[38]

WorldatWork recommends a six-stage process of communication, shown in Exhibit 18.8.[39]

Step 1 is, not surprisingly, defining the objectives of the communication program. Is it to ensure that employees fully understand all the components of the compensation system? Is it to change performance expectations? Or is it to help employees make informed health care choices? While specifying objectives as a first step seems obvious, doing so is often overlooked in the rush to design an attractive brochure, Web site, or CD.

Step 2 is to collect information from executives, managers, and employees to assess their current perceptions, attitudes, and understanding of the subject. Information may be gathered through online opinion surveys and focus groups to identify problems in understanding the compensation system.

Step 3 is a communication program that will convey the information needed to accomplish the original objectives. There is no standard approach on what to communicate to individuals about their own pay or that of their colleagues. Some organizations adopt a *marketing approach*. That includes consumer attitude surveys about the

EXHIBIT 18.8
The Compensation Communication Cycle

Source: Republished with permission. *Communicating Compensation Programs: How-To for the HR Professional.* Copyright 2004 WorldatWork.

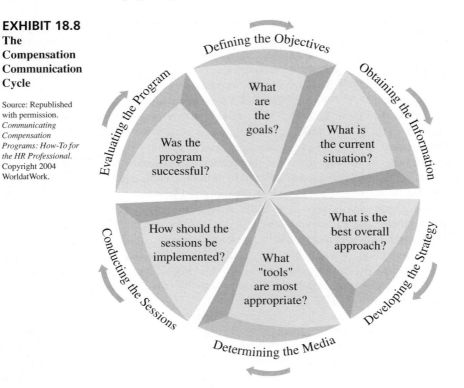

product, snappy advertising about the pay policies, and elaborate Web sites expounding policies and rationale. The objective is to manage expectations and attitudes about pay. In contrast, the *communication approach* tends to focus on explaining practices, details, and the way pay is determined. The marketing approach focuses on the strategy, values, and advantages of overall policies and may be silent on specifics such as range maximums, increase guides, and the like.

Steps 4 and 5 of the communication process are to determine the most effective media, in light of the message and the audience, and to conduct the campaign. Exhibit 18.9 recommends fine-tuning the message in terms of detail and emphasis, depending on the audience. Executives, for example, should be interested in how the compensation programs fit the business strategy. Managers need to know how to use the development and motivation aspects of the compensation program for the people they supervise. Employees may want to know the processes and policies as well as specifics about how their pay is determined. The danger is overload—information is so detailed that employees get snowed under sorting through it.

Intended and Unintended Consequences

Step 6 of the communication process suggests that the program be evaluated. Did it accomplish its goals? Pay communication often has unintended consequences.[40] For example, improving employees' knowledge about pay may cause some initial short-term

EXHIBIT 18.9   Conducting Formal Communication Sessions for Various Audiences

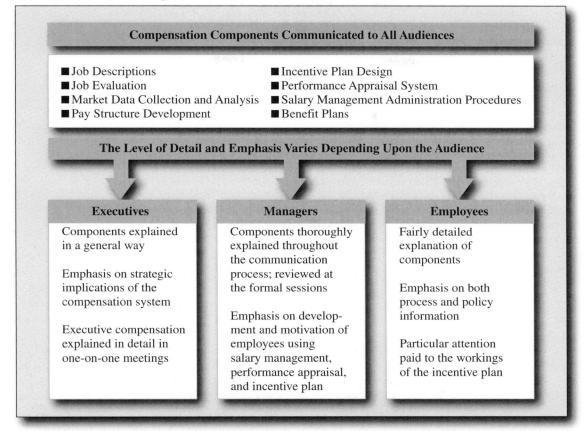

Source: Republished with permission. *Raising the Bar: Using Competencies to Enhance Employee Performance*. Copyright 1996 WorldatWork.

concerns. Over the years, employees may have rationalized a set of relationships between their pay and the perceived pay and efforts of others. Receiving accurate information may require that those perceptions be adjusted.

Cybercomp

One compensation manager reports having a great deal of difficulty with an employee who used the homefair Web site *www.homefair.com* to determine that he should receive a 30 percent pay differential to accompany his transfer from one office to another. In contrast, the manager's information showed a differential of around 12 to 15 percent. How can you judge the accuracy of information obtained on the Web? How would you deal with the unhappy employee?

EXHIBIT 18.10 Guidance from the Research on Pay Communication

Behavior	What Is It?	So What?
Persistence of beliefs	Reluctance to accept evidence that contradicts existing beliefs.	Changing existing beliefs requires actively engaging employees in pay system design and communication.
Anchoring/framing	Initial data strongly affect decisions/beliefs.	First data matters, e.g., market data swamps job-evaluation results. Previous bonus sets expectation for future bonus.
Herding	Following fashions in programs/techniques.	Benchmark selectively. Use pilot programs and test trials to guide.
Pattern recognition	People "discover" patterns in random events. They believe correlation means causation.	Higher pay may not mean higher performance; higher performance may not mean higher pay.

Say What?

If the pay system is not based on work-related or business-related logic, then the wisest course is probably to avoid formal communication until the system is put in order. However, avoiding *formal* communication is not synonymous with avoiding communication. Employees are constantly getting intended and unintended messages through the pay treatment they receive.

Many employers communicate the range for an incumbent's present job and for all the jobs in a typical career path or progression to which employees can logically aspire. Some also communicate the typical pay increases that can be expected for poor, satisfactory, and top performance. The rationale given is that employees exchange data (not always factual) and/or guess at normal treatment and that the rumor mills are probably incorrect.

How people process information and make decisions, as shown in Exhibit 18.10, offers some new ideas when contemplating compensation communications.[41]

Opening the Books

There are some who advocate sharing all financial information with employees.[42] Employees at engine rebuilder Springfield Remanufacturing receive weekly peeks at everything from revenues to labor costs. The employees, who own 31 percent of the company stock, believe that this "open-book" approach results in high commitment and an understanding of how to maintain competitiveness. Whole Foods' open-paybook approach was described in Chapter 1. Most employers don't share information with such gusto, but they are increasingly disclosing more to their employees. Some are even providing basic business and financial training to help employees better understand the information. Devotees of opening the books and providing financial training believe these methods will improve attitudes and performance, but there is no research to support this. With salary data available on the Internet (albeit often inaccurate and misleading), developing in-house compensation portals has appeal.

At the minimum, the most important information to be communicated is the work-related and business-related rationales on which pay systems are based. Some employees may not agree with these rationales or the results, but at least it will be clear that pay is determined by something other than the whims of their supervisors.

PAY AS CHANGE AGENT

Compensation often plays a singular role when organizations restructure. Strategic changes in the business strategy mean the compensation strategy must be realigned as well.

Pay is a powerful signal of change; changing people's pay captures their attention. Pay changes can play two roles in any restructuring. Pay can be a *leading catalyst* for change or a *follower* of change. Shifts from conventional across-the-board annual increases to profit sharing or from narrow job descriptions and ranges to broad roles and bands signal major change to employees. Determining the role pay plays is an important part of a strategic perspective, as you will recall from the Chapter 2 discussion of strategic mapping.

Microsoft's shift from its uniquely aggressive stock options to less risky stock awards illustrates the point. Microsoft its change in the pay mix to communicate a shift from a "workaholic—get rich quick" to a "work hard—get paid well" approach. Whether this shift acts as a catalyst or a support is open to debate. As a catalyst, it communicates change more strongly and vividly than any rhetoric could. It helps drive recruiting and retention. Yet it may be that Microsoft had already changed as an organization. Faced with murmuring employees (their options were underwater) and external conditions (an accounting rule change that required options to be treated as an expense) the shift in pay mix merely confirmed reality— that Microsoft had changed.

Whether pay is a leading catalyst for change or a follower of change, compensation managers must learn how to implement and manage change. Not only must they know the strategic and technical aspects of compensation, they also must know how to bargain, resolve disputes, empower employees, and develop teams. Being able to grab bullets in midflight doesn't hurt, either.[43]

STRUCTURING THE COMPENSATION FUNCTION

Compensation professionals seem to be constantly reevaluating where within the organization the responsibility for the design and administration of pay systems should be located. The organizational arrangements of the compensation function vary widely.[44]

Centralization–Decentralization

An important issue related to structuring the function revolves around the degree of decentralization (or centralization) in the overall organization structure. *Decentralized* refers to a management strategy of giving separate business units the responsibility of designing and administering their own systems. This contrasts with a *centralized* strategy, which locates the design and administration responsibility at corporate headquarters. A centralized compensation strategy and function is more likely to be found in smaller and/or single line of business organizations. This "one size fits all" approach is more likely to make sense when the entire company mostly competes in a single product market. Examples include Heman Miller (furniture) and McDonald's (quick service food).[45] However, in organizations (e.g., IBM) that are larger and/or compete in different product (or geographic) markets, human resource and compensation strategies are more likely to need to be tailored to fit those different contexts. In such cases, compensation professionals are increasingly likely to be embedded in each business unit. Typically, corporate will retain some number of compensation professionals, perhaps in what is known as a center for expertise. This group provides an internal consulting capability that human resource professionals in the business units, who are often human resource generalists, can be drawn on to assist in the design of compensation strategies. The mix of corporate and business unit compensation expertise is a balancing act. Too big of a corporate group risks becoming out of touch with specific business unit needs. Too many staff in the business units risks reinventing the wheel, duplication/redundancy of expertise, and higher costs. Over time, it is not unusual to see the pendulum swing within companies back and forth between more or less centralization.

Other, more decentralized organizations, such as Eaton and GE, have relatively small corporate compensation staffs. Sometimes, their primary responsibility is to manage the systems by which executives and the corporate staff are paid (although GE corporate compensation drives the salary planning process company-wide). These professionals may operate in a purely advisory capacity to other organization sub-units. The sub-units, in turn, may employ their own compensation specialists. Or the sub-units may choose to employ only personnel generalists rather than compensation specialists and may turn to outside compensation consultants to purchase the expertise required on specific compensation issues.

AES, an electric power company, has no compensation unit at all. They don't even have an HR department. Compensation functions are handled by teams of managers. Decentralizing certain aspects of pay design and administration has considerable appeal. Pushing these responsibilities (and expenses) close to the units, managers, and employees affected by them may help ensure that decisions are business-related. However, decentralization is not without dilemmas. For example, it may be difficult to transfer employees from one business unit to another. A pay system may support a sub-unit's objectives but run counter to the overall corporate objectives. Also, we have seen time and again that decentralization, which by definition includes less direct control of what managers do, can contribute to legal problems. As noted in Chapter 17, for example, Wal-Mart is facing sex-discrimination claims in what would be the largest class action discrimination suit to date (1.6 million or more claimants). Interestingly, Wal-Mart has argued that "establishing a national class is unwarranted because its store managers acted with discretion" in their decisions regarding promotion and pay of workers. So, in effect, Wal-Mart's defense is that if its managers discriminated, it was because Wal-Mart did not have centralized control over their decisions.[46]

Flexibility Within Corporatewide Principles

The answers to these and related problems of decentralization can be found in developing a set of corporatewide principles or guidelines that all must meet. The principles may differ for each major pay technique. For example, GE's business units worldwide have the flexibility to design incentive plans tailored to each unique business unit's strategies and cultures. The only guidance is to ensure that the plans adhere to GE's basic beliefs, improve financial and business objectives, and maintain or enhance GE's reputation.

Keep in mind that the pay system is one of many management systems used in the organization. Consequently, it must be congruent with these other systems. For example, it may be appealing, on paper at least, to decentralize some of the compensation functions. However, if financial data and other management systems are not also decentralized, the pay system may be at odds with other systems.

Reengineering and Outsourcing

Value chain analysis and Six Sigma are processes used to improve quality and ensure that value is added by each technique and at each stage in a process. For the compensation system, the basic question to ask is, "Does each specific activity (technique) directly contribute to our objectives?" If some added value isn't apparent, then the question is, "How should it be redesigned? Or should it be dropped?" Of those activities that do add value, the next question is, "Who should do it?" "Should the activity be done in-house, or can others do it more effectively? That is, should it be outsourced?"

Outsourcing is a viable alternative as organizations struggle with activities that do not directly contribute to objectives. These are often referred to as transactional activities, which are not unique to the organization and might be done cheaper (and perhaps also better) by an outside provider. On the other hand, more transformational or strategic activities (e.g., what pay-for-performance strategy would best align with the business strategy) are less likely to be outsourced.[47]

Cost savings are the major potential advantage of outsourcing. All those compensation pros can be laid off and/or retrained and re-assigned to other work. Sometimes, the quality of the service provided may increase also. A firm that does nothing but administer retirement benefits may be able to do a better job than a firm whose primary business is something else (e.g., making furniture or cars, selling quick service food.) Major potential disadvantages include less responsiveness to unique employee–manager problems, less control over decisions that are often critical to all employees (i.e., their pay), and information leaks to rivals and competitors. In addition, as with any contract, while an agreement may be signed stating that an outsourcing firm will provide a certain set of services and at a certain level, either side may subsequently find that their vision of the agreement and their experience of what is actually delivered may end up being different.[48]

Balancing Flexibility and Control

One of the major attacks on traditional compensation plans is that they often degenerate into bureaucratic nightmares that hinder the organization's ability to respond to competitive pressures. Some recommend reducing the controls and guidelines inherent in any pay plan. Hence, banding eliminates or at least reduces the impact of range maximums and minimums. Replacing merit grids with bonuses eliminates the link between the pay increase and the employees' salary position in the range and performance rating. Replacing job evaluation with skill- or competency-based plans permits assigning employees to a variety of work, regardless of their pay.

Such approaches are consistent with the oft-heard plea that managers should be free to manage pay. Or, as some more bluntly claim, pay decisions are too important to be left to compensation professionals. Yet, permitting managers to be free to pay employees as they judge best rests on a basic premise: Managers will use pay to achieve the organization's objectives—efficiency, fairness, and compliance with regulations—rather than their own objectives. But the ongoing leadership scandals in some corporations and public agencies casts doubt on this premise.

Clearly, some balance between hidebound controls and chaos is required to ensure that pay decisions are directed at the organization's goals yet permit sufficient flexibility to respond to unique situations. Achieving the balance becomes the art of managing compensation.

A final issue related to pay design and administration is the skills and competencies required in compensation managers. The grandest strategy and structure may seem well designed, well thought out in the abstract, but could be a disaster if people qualified to carry it out are not part of the staff. In view of the importance of a well-trained staff, both WorldatWork and the Society of Human Resource Managers (SHRM) have professional development programs to entice readers into the compensation field.

Your **Turn**   Communication by Copier

Deb Allen's life-altering discovery at work really "communicated" her company's pay practices. Swamped with work at an asset-management firm, she went into the office over the weekend and found a document abandoned on the copy machine. The document contained the base compensation, raises, performance ratings, and bonus information for 80 of her colleagues.

Ms. Allen was outraged that a noted screw-up was making $65,000 a year more than more competent colleagues, while some new hires were earning almost $200,000 more than their counterparts with more experience. The discovery led her to question why she was working weekends for less pay than others were getting. "I just couldn't stand the inequity of it," she says. Three months later she quit.

But Ms. Allen couldn't bring herself to share the information with her colleagues. "I would have been better off not knowing any of that," she explains. "I couldn't give it to people who were still working there because it would make them depressed, like it made me depressed."

1. How would you have reacted if you were Ms. Allen? Explain why.
2. Put yourself in the place of the compensation director at Ms. Allen's company. Based on the pay model and what you now know about compensation, are there any possible business- and work-related explanations for what Ms. Allen observed (i.e., the screw-up getting $65,000 more; new hires earning $200,000 more than more-experienced employees; and Ms. Allen making less pay than others)?
3. As the compensation director, what would you do if Ms. Allen had brought you this document, and asked for your help in understanding what was going on. (Firing the person who left it on the copier is not an option. It may have been you.)

Still Your **Turn**   Ethics in Compensation Decisions

Dave Dorman was CEO at AT&T for 5 years. This entitled him to an annual pension of $2.1 million, which equals about 60 percent of his salary plus bonus in his last 3 years. By contrast, former AT&T accountant Ralph Colotti's annual pension of $28,800 replaces 33 percent of his final pay. He worked at AT&T for 33 years.

Colotti's pension was held down when AT&T changed the pension formula. AT&T describes Mr. Colotti's pension as competitive in the industry. Mr. Dorman's richer deal is "reasonable, customary, and comparable to what similar sized companies offer. . . . Senior executives are provided with enhanced benefits as a way to recruit and retain the best talent and the best leadership possible."

AT&T was taken over by SBC Communications during Mr. Dorman's tenure.

What if the compensation committee of AT&T's board of directors had asked its compensation consultant and AT&T's compensation director to advise them on the questions, "What are the ethical issues here? What ethical code of conduct shall we follow when making these decisions?" What advice would you offer?

Summary

We have now completed the discussion of the pay management process. Management includes control: control of the way managers decide individual employees' pay as well as control of overall costs of labor. As we noted, some controls are designed into the fabric of the pay system (embedded controls). The salary budgeting and forecasting processes impose additional controls. The formal budgeting process focuses on controlling labor costs and generating the financial plan for the pay system. The budget sets the limits within which the rest of the system operates.

We also noted that with the continuous change in organizations, compensation managers must understand how to manage change and be knowledgeable business partners. They are responsible for communicating information about pay in a way that treats employees fairly and honestly. The basic point is that pay systems are tools, and like any tools they need to be evaluated in terms of usefulness in achieving an organization's objectives.

Review Questions

1. How can employers control labor costs?
2. How does the management of the pay system affect pay objectives?
3. Why is the structure of the compensation function important?
4. Give some examples of how employers use inherent controls.
5. What activities in managing the pay system are likely candidates to be outsourced? Why?
6. Use Exhibit 18.10 to explain how the research on individual decision making can be used in pay communication.

Endnotes

1. Sanford Jacoby, *The Embedded Corporation* (Princeton: Princeton University Press, 2005).
2. Felix Barber and Rainer Strack, "The Surprising Economics of a 'People Business'," *Harvard Business Review,* June 2005, pp. 81–90.
3. D. Scott, D. Morajda, T. McMullen, and R. Sperling, "Evaluating Pay Program Effectiveness," *WorldatWork Journal,* 15(2), Second Quarter 2006, pp. 50–59.
4. Lindsay Scott, "Managing Labor Costs Using Pay-for-Performance," Lindsay Scott & Associates, Inc., *www.npktools.com.*
5. *Reward Transformation: Turning Rewards From Costs into an Investment* (New York: Deloitte, 2006), *www.deloitte.com.*
6. Personal communication from B. Dunn, president, McLagan Partners; D. Scott, D. Morajda, T. McMullen, and R. Sperling, "Evaluating Pay Program Effectiveness," *WorldatWork Journal* 15(2), Second Quarter 2006, pp. 50–59; John Boudreau and Peter Ramstad, "From 'Professional Business Partner' to 'Strategic Talent Leader:' 'What's Next for Human Resource Management," CAHRS Working Paper 02–10, Ithaca, NY.
7. B. Dunn, president, McLagan Partners; *The Lake Wobegon Salary Survey, Lindsay Scott & Associates, Inc., www.npktools.com,* 2006.
8. Allen Smith, "Layoffs in Europe: Deal or No Deal?" *HRMagazine,* January 2009, pp. 71–73.
9. Charlie O. Trevor and Anthony J. Nyberg, "Keeping Your Headcount When All About You Are Losing Theirs: Downsizing, Voluntary Turnover Rates, and the Moderating Role of HR Practices," *Academy of Management Journal* 51 (2008), pp. 259–276.
10. Timothy Aeppel and Justin Lahart, "Lean Factories Find It Hard to Cut Jobs Even in Slump." *Wall Street Journal,* March 9, 2009, p. A1.
11. Erin White, "Retaining Employees Before an Upturn Hits," *Wall Street Journal,* May 8, 2009, *http://online.wsj.com/article/SB124178707883900633.html,* September 14, 2009; Gray Yohe, "A Delicate Balance," Human Resource Executive, March 2, 2009, *http://www. hreonline.com/HRE/story.jsp?storyId=1815633178query=morale,* September 14, 2009.
12. Clint Chadwick, Larry W. Hunter, and Stephen Walston, "Effects of Downsizing Practices on the Performance of Hospitals," *Strategic Management Journal,* 25 (2004), pp. 405–427.
13. Charles Duhigg, "Hospital Clients Nurture Firm's Scheduling Software," *Los Angeles Times,* June 21, 2006, p. C1.
14. Susan Saulny and Robbie Brown, "On a Fulough, But Never Leaving the Cubicle," *New York Times,* June 15, 2009; Jonathan Buck, "British Airways Urges Staff to Work Without Pay," *Wall Street Journal,* June 16, 2009; "The Quiet Americans: Employees Are Stoical in the Face of Pay Cuts and Compulsory Unpaid Leave," *The Economist,* June 25, 2009, *http://www. economist.com/world/unitedstates/displaystory.cfm?story_id=13915822,* September 14, 2009.
15. Riva Richmond, "How to Cut Payroll Without Layoffs," BusinessWeek, April 3, 2009, *http://www.businessweek.com/magazine/content/09_64/s0904048707309.htm,* September 14, 2009; Matthew Boyle, "Cutting Work Hours Without Cutting Staff," BusinessWeek, February 25, 2009, *http://www.businessweek.com/magazine/content/09_10/b4122055789445.htm,* September 14, 2009.
16. Ron Lieber, "Et Tu, AARP? Good Guys Cut 401(k)s, Too," *New York Times,* June 27, 2009, p. B1.
17. Sandra Block, "Companies Rethink 401(k) Plan Contributions for Employees," *USA Today,* June 24, 2009, *http://www.usatoday.com/money/perfi/retirement/2009-06-24-401k-contributions-economy_N.htm,* September 14, 2009.
18. Watson Wyatt, "2009/2010 Salary Budget Survey Results Review," *http://www. watsonwyatt.com/salarybudgetsurveypreview;* Michael Sanserino, "Pay Raises Are the Smallest in Decades, Surveys Show," *Wall Street Journal,* July 21, 2009.

19. Carlos Tejada and Gary McWilliams, "New Recipe for Cost Savings: Replace Expensive Workers," *The Wall Street Journal,* June 11, 2003, pp. 1, A12.

20. John Watson, "Delivering Total Compensation Online at Dell," *ACA News* 42(4) (April 1999), pp. 14–19.

21. Ronald T. Albright and Bridge R. Compton, *Internal Consulting Basics* (Scottsdale, AZ: American Compensation Association, 1996); John Watson, "Delivering Total Compensation Online at Dell," *ACA News* 42(4) (April 1999), pp. 14–19.

22. Flora Guidry, Andrew J. Leon, and Steve Rock, "Earnings-Based Bonus Plans and Earnings Management by Business-Unit Managers," *Journal of Accounting and Economics* 26 (1999), pp. 113–142.

23. Joseph P. O'Connor, Jr., Richard L. Priem, Joseph E. Coombs, and K. Matthew Gilley, "Do CEO Stock Options Prevent or Promote Fraudulent Financial Reporting?" Academy of Management Journal, June 2006, pp. 483–500; Frederic W. Cook, "Compensation Ethics: An Oxymoron or Valid Area for Debate?" Featured speech at ACA International Conference Workshop, 1999; Barrie Litzky, Kimberly Eddleston, and Deborah Kidder, "The Good, the Bad, and the Misguided: How Managers Inadvertently Encourage Deviant Behaviors," Academy of Management Perspectives, February 2006, pp. 91–102; Gretchen Morgenson, "Advice on Boss's Pay May Not Be So Independent," New York Times, April 10, 2006, p. B1. The WorldatWork Ethics Initiative is described on their Web site, *www.worldatwork.org.* Also see their WorldatWork Standards of Professional Practice.

24. John Hechinger and James Bandler, "In Sycamore Suite, Memo Points to Backdating Claims," *The Wall Street Journal,* July 12, 2006, p. A3. Also see C. Forelle, J. Bandler, and Steve Stecklaw, "Brocade Ex-CEO, 2 Others Charged in Options Probe," *The Wall Street Journal,* July 21, 2006, p. A1, A8; Peter Grant, James Bandler, and Charles Forelle, "Cablevision Gave Backdated Grant to Dead Official," *The Wall Street Journal,* September 22, 2006, pp. A1, A8; Della Bradshaw, "MBA Students 'Cheat the Most,'" *Financial Times,* September 21, 2006, p. 8.

25. Jennifer Hicks, an Oklahoma State University student. has coined the term "yellow circle rates" while working as a compensation specialist for FastCat. Yellow circle rates result where if you give an employee the percent raise indicated by the merit increase grid, that employee would become red circled. For Wal-Mart information. see Steven Greenhouse and Michael Barbaro, "Wal-Mart to Add Caps and Part-Timers," *The New York Times,* October 2, 2006, p. B1.

26. *Reward Transformation: Turning Rewards From Costs Into an Investment* (New York: Deloitte, 2006), *www.deloitte.com;* D. Scott, D. Morajda, T. McMullen, and R. Sperling, "Evaluating Pay Program Effectiveness," *WorldatWork Journal* 15(2) (Second Quarter 2006), pp. 50–59.

27. Wayne Cascio, *Responsible Restructuring: Creative and Profitable Alternatives to Layoffs* (San Francisco: Berrett-Koehler, 2002); John Boudreau and Peter Ramstad, "Beyond Cost per Hire and Time to Fill: Supply-Chain Measurements for Staffing," (Los Angeles: Center for Effective Organizations, 2006); Jaap deJonge, *Watson Wyatt Human Capital Index* (New York: Watson Wyatt, 2003); S. Raza, *Optimizing Human Capital Investments for Superior Shareholder Returns* (New York: Hewitt Associates, 2006); M. Huselid and B. Becker, "Improving HR Analytical Literacy: Lessons From Moneyball," chapter 32 in M. Losey, S. Meisinger, and D. Ulrich, *The Future of Human Resource Management* (Hoboken, NJ: Wiley, 2005); J. Burton and S. Pollack. "ROI of Human Capital: The United States and Europe," *Workspan,* November 2006, pp. 28–27.

28. Ibid.

29. M. C. Sturman, C. O. Trevor, J. W. Boudreau, and B. Gerhart, "Is It Worth It to Win the Talent War? Evaluating the Utility of Performance-Based Pay," *Personnel Psychology* 56 (2003), pp. 997–1035; Wayne Cascio and John Boudreau, *Investing in People* (Saddle River, NJ: Pearson Education, 2008); Mark A. Huselid, Brian E. Becker, and Richard W. Beatty, *The Workforce Scorecard* (Boston: Harvard Business School Press, 2005).

30. Peter F. Drucker, "They're Not Employees, They're People," *Harvard Business Review,* February 2002, pp. 70–77.

31. A useful guide on selecting HR software is James G. Meade, *The Human Resources Software Handbook* (San Francisco: Jossey-Bass/Pfeiffer, 2003); Mark L. Lengnick-Hall and Steve Moritz, "The Impact of e-HR on the Human Resource Management Function," *Journal of Labor Research,* Summer 2003, pp. 365–379.

32. Diane Palframan, *HR Technology Strategies* (New York: Conference Board, 2003); James H. Dulebohn and Janet H. Marler, "e-Compensation: The Potential to Transform Practice?" in H. Gueutal and D. Stone, eds., *Brave New World of e-HR : Human Resources in the Digital Age* (San Francisco: Jossey Bass, 2005), pp. 138–165.

33. Privacilla, *www.privacilla.org/business/eudirective.html.*

34. "Growing Worker Confusion About Corporate Goals Complicates Recovery, Watson Wyatt WorkUSA Study Finds," Watson Wyatt news release, September 9, 2002.

35. Robert L. Heneman, Paul W. Mulvey, and Peter V. LeBlanc, "Improve Base Pay ROI by Increasing Employee Knowledge," *WorldatWork Journal* 11(4), Fourth Quarter 2002, pp. 22–27.

36. Thomas A. Mahoney and William Weitzel. "Secrecy and Managerial Compensation," *Industrial Relations* 17(2) (1978), pp. 245–251; Julio D. Burroughs, "Pay Secrecy and Performance: The Psychological Research," *Compensation Review,* Third Quarter 1982, pp. 44–54; George Milkovich and P. H. Anderson, "Management Compensation and Secrecy Policies," *Personnel Psychology* 25 (1972), pp. 293–302.

37. Adrienne Colella, Ramona Paetzold, Asghar Zardkoohi, and Michael Wesson, "Exposing Pay Secrecy," *Academy of Management Review* 32 (2007), pp. 55–71; Renae Broderick and Barry Gerhart, "Non-Wage Compensation," in David Lewin, Daniel J. B. Mitchell, and Mahmood A. Zaidi, eds., *The Human Resource Management Handbook,* Part 3. (Greenwich, CT: JAI Press, 1997), pp. 95–135.

38. M. Wilson, G. B. Northcraft, and M. A. Neale, "The Perceived Value of Fringe Benefits," *Personnel Psychology* 38 (1985), pp. 309–320.

39. John A. Rubino, *Communicating Compensation Programs* (Scottsdale, AZ: American Compensation Association, 1997).

40. Jared Sandberg, "Why You May Regret Looking at Papers Left on the Office Copier," *The Wall Street Journal,* June 20, 2006, p. B1; John Case, "When Salaries Aren't Secret," case study, *Harvard Business Review,* May 2001.

41. A. Tversky and D. Kahneman, "The Framing of Decisions and the Psychology of Choice," *Science* 211 (1981), pp. 453–458; C. F. Camerer and U. Malmendier, "Behavioral Organizational Economics," July 8, 2006, working paper available from *www.hss.caltech. edu/ camerer/SS200/SS200.html;* Sharla A. Stewart, "Can Behavioral Economics Save Us From Ourselves?" *University of Chicago Magazine* 97(3) (February 2005), *www.magazine. uchicago.edu/0502/features/economics.shtml.*

42. "Rethinking Ways to Present Financial Information to Employees," *Employee Ownership Report,* March/April 2000, pp. 7, 10; Jack Stack and Bo Burlingham, *The Great Game of Business* (New York: Currency Doubleday, 1992); Jack Stack and Bo Burlingham, *A Stake in the Outcome* (New York: Currency Doubleday, 2002); John Case, "Opening the Books," *Harvard Business Review,* March–April, 1996, pp. 118–127.

43. Michael Beer and Mitin Nohria, "Cracking the Code of Change," *Harvard Business Review,* May–June 2000, pp. 133–141; Dave Ulrich, "A New Mandate for Human Resources," *Harvard Business Review,* January–February 1998, pp. 125–134.

44. *HR Services Delivery Research Report,* Towers Perrin, 2005, *www.towersperrin.com;* "The Psychology of Change Management," *McKinsey Quarterly,* July 2006.

45. Dave Ulrich, Jon Younger, and Wayne Brockbank, "The Next Evolution of the HR Organization," in John Storey, Patrick M. Wright, and Dave Ulrich, eds., *The Routledge Companion to Strategic Human Resource Management* (London and New York: Routledge, 2009), pp. 182–203.

46. Alexandria Sage, "Wal-Mart Sex Discrimination Case Back in Court," Reuters, March 25, 2009, *http://www.reuters.com/article/topNews/idUSTRE52O0P820090325.*

47. Stephen Miller, "Companies Continue to Selectively Outsource HR Programs," *HRMagazine* (2009), p. 76; Dave Ulrich and Wayne Brockbank, *The HR Value Proposition* (Boston, MA: Harvard Business School Press, 2005); Brian S. Klaas, "Outsourcing and the HR Function: An Examination of Trends and Developments Within North American Firms," *International Journal of Human Resource Management* 19 (2008), pp. 1500–1514.

48. Michael Skapinker, "Much to Question on Outsourcing," *Financial Times,* June 30, 2003, p. 4.

Glossary

ability   An individual's capability to engage in a specific behavior.

ability to pay   The ability of a firm to meet employee wage demands while remaining profitable; a frequent issue in contract negotiations with unions. A firm's ability to pay is constrained by its ability to compete in its product market.

access discrimination   Discrimination that focuses on the staffing and allocation decisions made by employers. It denies particular jobs, promotions, or training opportunities to qualified women or minorities. This type of discrimination is illegal under Title VII of the Civil Rights Act of 1964.

across-the-board increases   A general adjustment that provides equal increases to all employees.

Age Discrimination in Employment Act (ADEA) of 1967 (amended 1978, 1986, and 1990)   Legislation that makes nonfederal employees age 40 and over a protected class relative to their treatment in pay, benefits, and other personnel actions. The 1990 amendment is called the Older Workers Benefit Protection Act.

agency theory   A theory of motivation that depicts exchange relationships in terms of two parties: agents and principals. According to this theory, both sides of the exchange will seek the most favorable exchange possible and will act opportunistically if given a chance. As applied to executive compensation, agency theory would place part of the executive's pay at risk to motivate the executive (agent) to act in the best interests of the shareholders (principals) rather than in the executive's own self-interests.

all-salaried work force   Pay approach in which not only exempt employees (exempt from provisions of the Fair Labor Standards Act), who traditionally are paid a salary rather than an hourly rate, but also nonexempt employees receive a prescribed amount of money each pay period that does not primarily depend on the number of hours worked.

alternation ranking   A job evaluation method that involves ordering the job description alternately at each extreme. All the jobs are considered. Agreement is reached on which is the most valuable and then the least valuable. Evaluators alternate between the next most valued and next least valued and so on until the jobs have been ordered.

Americans With Disabilities Act   Legislation passed in 1990 that requires that reasonable accommodations be provided to permit employees with disabilities to perform the essential elements of a job.

appeals processes   Mechanisms are created to handle pay disagreements. They provide a forum for employees and managers to voice their complaints and receive a hearing.

balance sheet approach   A method for compensating expatriates based upon the belief that the employee should not suffer financially for accepting a foreign-based assignment. The expatriate's pay is adjusted so that the amounts of the financial responsibilities the expatriate had prior to the assignment are kept at about the same level while on assignment—the company pays for the difference.

balanced scorecard   A corporatewide, overall performance measure typically incorporating financial results, process improvements, customer service, and innovation.

base pay   *See* base wage.

base salary   *See* base wage.

base wage   The basic cash compensation that an employer pays for the work performed. Tends to reflect the value of the work itself and ignore differences in individual contributions.

Bedeaux plan   Individual incentive plan that provides a variation on straight piecework and standard hour plans. Instead of timing an entire task, a Bedeaux plan requires determination of the time required to complete each simple action of a task. Workers receive a wage incentive for completing a task in less than the standard time.

behaviorally anchored rating scales (BARS)   Variants on standard rating scales in which the various scale levels are anchored with behavioral descriptions directly applicable to jobs being evaluated.

benchmark conversion   Process of matching survey jobs by applying the employer's plan to the external jobs and then comparing the worth of the external job with its internal "match."

benchmark (key) job   A prototypical job, or group of jobs, used as a reference point for making pay comparisons within or without the organization. Benchmark jobs have well-known and stable contents; their current pay rates are generally acceptable, and the pay differentials among them are relatively stable. A group of benchmark jobs, taken together, contains the entire range of compensable factors and is accepted in the external labor market for setting wages.

benefit ceiling   A maximum payout for specific benefit claims (e.g., limiting liability for extended hospital stays to $150,000).

benefit limitation   Limit of disability income payments to some maximum percentage of income and limit of medical/dental coverage for specific procedures to a certain fixed amount.

best-pay practices   Compensation practices that allow employers to gain preferential access to superior human resource talent and competencies (i.e., valued assets), which in turn influence the strategies the organization adopts.

BLS   *See* Bureau of Labor Statistics.

bonus   A lump-sum payment to an employee in recognition of goal achievement.

bottom-up approach to pay budgeting   Approach in which individual employees' pay rates for the next plan year are forecasted and summed to create an organization's total budget.

bourse market   A market that allows haggling over terms and conditions until an agreement is reached.

branding   Establishing an image or reputation associated with a product or service. As related to total compensation systems, it seeks to establish a reputation that will influence employees' and the public's perceptions about how an organization pays its employees.

Brito v. Zia Company   Benchmark case that interpreted performance evaluation as a test, subject to validation requirements, and used these evaluations based on a rating format to lay off employees, resulting in a disproportionate of minorities being discharged.

broad banding   Collapsing a number of salary grades into a smaller number of broad grades with wide ranges.

Broad-based option plans (BBOPs)   Stock grants: A company gives employees shares of stock over a designated time period.

budgeting   A part of the organization's planning process; helps to ensure that future financial expenditures are coordinated and controlled. It involves forecasting the total expenditures required by the pay system during the next period as well as the amount of the pay increases. Bottom up and top down are the two typical approaches to the process.

Bureau of Labor Statistics (BLS)   A major source of publicly available pay data. It also calculates the consumer price index.

cafeteria (flexible) benefit plan   A benefit plan in which employees have a choice as to the benefits they receive within some dollar limit. Usually a common core benefit package is required (e.g., specific minimum levels of health, disability, retirement, and death benefits) plus elective programs from which the employee may select a set dollar amount. Additional coverage may be available through employee contributions.

capital appreciation plans   *See* long-term incentives.

career path   A progression of jobs within an organization.

cash balance plan   A defined benefit plan that looks like a defined contribution plan. Employees have a hypothetical account, such as a 401(k), into which is deposited what is typically a percentage of annual compensation. The dollar amount grows both from contributions by the employer and by some predetermined interest rate (e.g., often set equal to the rate given on 30-year treasury certificates).

central tendency   A midpoint in a group of measures.

central tendency error   A rating error that occurs when a rater consistently rates a group of employees at or close to the midpoint of a scale irrespective of the true score performance of ratees. Avoiding extremes (both high and low) in ratings across employees.

churn   *See* turnover effect.

Civil Rights Act of 1964   Legislation that prohibits, under Title VII, discrimination in terms and conditions of employment (including benefits) that is based on race, color, religion, sex, or national origin.

Civil Rights Act of 1991   Legislation that clarifies the standards for proving discrimination. Allows jury trials and damage awards.

claims processing Procedure that begins when an employee asserts that a specific event (e.g., disablement, hospitalization, unemployment) has occurred and demands that the employer fulfill a promise for payment. As such, a claims processor must first determine whether the act has, in fact, occurred.

classification Job evaluation method that involves slotting job descriptions into a series of classes or grades that cover the range of jobs and that serve as a standard against which the job descriptions are compared.

clone error A rating error that occurs when a rater gives better ratings to individuals who are like the rater in behavior or personality.

coinsurance Benefit option whereby employees share in the cost of a benefit provided to them.

commission Payment tied directly to achievement of performance standards. Commissions are directly tied to a profit index (sales, production level) and employee costs; thus, they rise and fall in line with revenues.

committee a priori judgment approach Compensable factor importance weights are assigned by a committee based on judgment.

community rating When insurance rates are based on the medical experience of that entire community. Higher use of medical facilities and services results in higher premiums.

comparable worth A policy that women performing jobs judged to be equal on some measure of inherent worth should be paid the same as men, excepting allowable differences, such as seniority, merit, production-based pay plans, and other non-sex-related factors. Objective is to eliminate use of the market in setting wages for jobs held by women.

compa-ratio An index that helps assess how managers actually pay employees in relation to the midpoint of the pay range established for jobs. It estimates how well actual practices correspond to intended policy. Calculated as average rates actually paid divided by range midpoint.

compensable factor Job attributes that provide the basis for evaluating the relative worth of jobs inside an organization. A compensable factor must be work-related, business-related, and acceptable to the parties involved.

compensating differentials Economic theory that attributes the variety of pay rates in the external labor market to differences in attractive as well as negative characteristics in jobs. Pay differences must overcome negative characteristics to attract employees.

compensation All forms of financial returns and tangible services and benefits employees receive as part of an employment relationship.

compensation at risk *See* risk sharing.

compensation differentials Differentials in pay among jobs across and within organizations, and differences among individuals in the same job in an organization.

compensation objectives The desired results of the pay system. The basic pay objectives include efficiency, fairness, and compliance with laws and regulations. Objectives shape the design of the pay system and serve as the standard against which the success of the pay system is evaluated.

competency Basic knowledge and abilities employees must acquire or demonstrate in a competency-based plan in order to successfully perform the work, satisfy customers, and achieve business objectives.

competency analysis A systematic process to identify and collect information about the competencies required for the person and the organization to be successful.

competency-based system Compensation approach that links pay to the depth and scope of competencies that are relevant to doing the work. Typically used in managerial and professional work where what is accomplished may be difficult to identify.

competitive intelligence The collection and analysis of information about external conditions and competitors that will enable an organization to be more competitive.

competitive position The comparison of the compensation offered by one employer relative to that paid by its competitors.

compliance Compliance as a pay objective means conforming to federal and state compensation laws and regulations.

compression The existence of very narrow pay differentials among jobs at different organization levels as a result of wages for jobs filled from the outside (frequently these are entry-level jobs) increasing faster than the internal pay structure.

congruency The degree of consistency or "fit" between the compensation system and other organizational components such as strategy, product-market stage, culture and values, employee needs, and union status.

Consolidated Omnibus Budget Reconciliation Act (COBRA) Legislation that provides that employees who resign or are laid off through no fault of their own are eligible to continue receiving health coverage under the employer's plan at a cost borne by the employee.

consumer-directed health care plans Costs link consumer choice of more or less expensive options to higher or lower individual costs.

consumer-driven health care benefits *See* consumer-directed health-care plans.

Consumer Price Index (CPI) A measure of the changes in prices in a fixed market basket of goods and services purchased by a hypothetical average family. *Not* an absolute measure of living costs; rather, a measure of how fast costs are changing. Published by the Bureau of Labor Statistics, U.S. Department of Labor.

content The work performed in a job and how it gets done (tasks, behaviors, knowledge required, etc.

content theories Motivation theories that focus on what motivates people rather than on how people are motivated. Maslow's need hierarchy theory and Herzberg's two-factor theory are in this category.

contingent employees A growing workforce that includes flexible workers, temporaries, part-time employees, and independent contractors whose employment is of a limited duration.

contingent workers *See* contingent employees

conventional job analysis methods Methods (e.g., functional job analysis) that typically involve an analyst using a questionnaire in conjunction with structured interviews of job incumbents and supervisors. The methods place considerable reliance on analysts' ability to understand the work performed and to accurately describe it.

coordination of benefits Process of ensuring that employer coverage of an employee does not "double pay" because of identical protection offered by the government (private pension and social security coordination) or a spouse's employer.

copay Copay requires that employees pay a fixed or percentage amount for coverage.

core employees Workers with whom a long-term, full-time work relationship is anticipated.

correlation coefficient A common measure of association that indicates how changes in one variable are related to changes in another.

cost containment An attempt made by organizations to contain benefit costs, such as imposing deductibles and coinsurance on health benefits or replacing defined benefit pension plans with defined contribution plans.

cost-cutter The cost cutter's efficiency-focused strategy stresses doing more with less by minimizing costs, encouraging productivity increases, and specifying in greater detail exactly how jobs should be performed.

cost of living Actual individual expenditures on goods and services. The only way to measure it accurately is to examine the expense budget of each employee.

cost-of-living adjustments (COLAs) Across-the-board wage and salary increases or supplemental payments based on changes in some index of prices, usually the consumer price index (CPI). If included in a union contract, COLAs are designed to increase wages automatically during the life of the contract as a function of changes in the CPI.

cost-of-living increase Same as across-the-board increase, except magnitude based on change in cost of living (e.g., as measured by the consumer price index [CPI]).

CPI *See* Consumer Price Index.

criterion contamination Allowing nonperformance factors to affect performance scores.

criterion deficiency A criterion is deficient if it fails to include all of the dimensions relevant to job performance (e.g., excluding key boarding skills for a secretary's job performance).

criterion pay structure A pay structure to be duplicated with a point plan.

culture The informal rules, rituals, and value systems that influence how people behave.

customer-driven health care Medical care package where the employer finances the cost up to a dollar maximum and the employees search for options that best fit their specific needs.

customer-focused business strategy The customer-focused business strategy stresses delighting customers and bases employee pay on how well they achieve this.

Davis-Bacon Act Legislation that requires that most federal contractors pay wage rates prevailing in the area.

deductibles   Employees cost-saving tool by which the employee pays the first x number of dollars when a benefit is used (e.g., hospitalization). The employer pays subsequent costs up to some predetermined maximum.

deferred compensation plan   Pay approach that provides income to an employee at some future time as compensation for work performed now. Types of deferred compensation programs include stock option plans and pension plans.

defined benefit plan   A benefit option or package in which the employer agrees to give the specified benefit without regard to cost maximum. Opposite of defined contribution plan.

defined contribution plan   A benefit option or package in which the employer negotiates a dollar maximum payout. Any change in benefit costs over time reduces the amount of coverage unless new dollar limits are negotiated.

delayering   Eliminating some layers or job levels in the pay structure.

differentials   Pay differences among levels within the organization, such as the difference in pay between adjacent levels in a career path, between supervisors and subordinates, between union and nonunion employees, and between executives and regular employees.

direct compensation   Pay received directly in the form of cash (e.g., wages, bonuses, incentives).

disparate impact   Discrimination theory that outlaws the application of pay practices that may appear to be neutral but have a negative effect on females or minorities unless those practices can be shown to be business-related.

disparate treatment   Discrimination theory that outlaws the application of different standards to different classes of employees unless the standards can be shown to be business-related.

distributive justice   Fairness in the amount of reward distributed to employees.

double-track system   A framework for professional employees in an organization whereby at least two general tracks of ascending compensation steps are available: (1) a managerial track to be ascended through increasing responsibility for supervision of people and (2) a professional track to be ascended through increasing contributions of a professional nature.

drive theory   A motivational theory that assumes that all behavior is induced by drives (i.e., energizers such as thirst, hunger, sex) and that present behavior is based in large part on the consequences or rewards of past behavior.

dual-career ladders   Presence of two different ways to progress in an organization, each reflecting different types of contribution to the organization's mission. The managerial ladder ascends through increasing responsibility for supervision or direction of people. The professional track ascends through increasing contributions of a professional nature that do not mainly entail the supervision of employees.

dual coverage   In families in which both spouses work, the coverage of specific claims from each spouse's employment benefit package. Employers cut costs by specifying payment limitations under such conditions.

earnings-at-risk plans   *See* risk sharing.

e-benefits   Employee benefits, from information to applications, posted on company intranet by employer, which allows employee access 24/7 and employer to update easily.

economic rent   Confusingly, rent has two different meanings for economists. The first is the commonplace definition: the income your landlord receives from your apartment. The second, also known as economic rent, is the difference between what a factor of production is paid and how much it would need to be paid to remain in its current use. If an employee is paid $10,000 a week but would be willing to work for only $1,000, that employee's economic rent is $9,000 a week.

efficiency wage theory   A theory that explains why firms are rational in offering higher-than-necessary wages.

employee benefits   The parts of the total compensation package, other than pay for time worked, provided to employees in whole or in part by employer payments (e.g., life insurance, pension, workers' compensation, vacation).

employee contributions   Comparisons among individuals doing the same job for the same organization.

employer of choice   The view that a firm's external wage competitiveness is just one facet of its overall human resource policy and that competitiveness is more properly judged on overall policies. Challenging work, great colleagues, or an organization's prestige must be factored into an overall consideration of attractiveness.

entitlement   Employee belief that returns and/or rewards are due regardless of individual or company performance.

entry jobs   Jobs that are filled from the external labor market and whose pay tends to reflect external economic factors rather than an organization's culture and traditions.

Equal Pay Act (EPA) of 1963   An amendment to the Fair Labor Standards Act of 1938 that prohibits pay differentials on jobs that are substantially equal in terms of skills, efforts, responsibility, and working conditions, except when they are the result of bona fide seniority, merit, production-based systems, or any other job-related factor other than sex.

equity theory   A theory proposing that in an exchange relationship (such as employment) the equality of outcome/input ratios between a person and a comparison other (a standard or relevant person/group) will determine fairness or equity. If the ratios diverge from each other, the person will experience reactions of unfairness and inequity.

ESOP (employee stock ownership plan)   A plan in which a company borrows money from a financial institution by using its stock as a collateral for the loan. Principal and interest loan repayments are tax-deductible. With each loan repayment, the lending institution releases a certain amount of stock being held as security. The stock is then placed into an employee stock ownership trust (ESOT) for distribution at no cost to all employees. The employees receive the stock upon retirement or separation from the company. TRASOPs and PAYSOPs are variants of ESOPs.

essay format   An open-ended performance appraisal format. The descriptors used can range from comparisons with other employees to adjectives, behaviors, and goal accomplishment.

essential elements   The parts of a job that cannot be assigned to another employee. The Americans with Disabilities Act requires that if applicants with disabilities can perform the essential elements of a job, reasonable accommodations must then be made to enable the qualified individuals to perform the job.

exchange value   The price of labor (the wage) determined in a competitive market; in other words, labor's worth (the price) is whatever the buyer and seller agree upon.

Executive Order 11246   Law signed in 1965 that prohibits discrimination by federal contractors and subcontractors in all employment practices on basis of race, sex, color, religion, or national origin.

executive perquisites (perks)   Special benefits made available to top executives (and sometimes other managerial employees). May be taxable income to the receiver. Company-related perks may include luxury offices; special parking; and company-paid membership in clubs/associations, hotels, and resorts. Personal perks include low-cost loans, personal and legal counseling, free home repairs and improvements, and so on. Since 1978, various tax and agency rulings have slowly been requiring that companies place a value on perks, thus increasing the taxable income of executives.

exempt jobs   Jobs not subject to provisions of the Fair Labor Standards Act with respect to minimum wage and overtime. Exempt employees include most executives, administrators, professionals, and outside sales representatives.

exercise period   Time during which, or after which, an individual who has been granted stock options is permitted to exercise them.

expatriate colony   A section of a large city where expatriates tend to locate and form a community that takes on some of the cultural flavor of their home country.

expatriates   Employees assigned outside their base country for any period of time in excess of one year.

expectancy (VIE) theory   A motivation theory that proposes that individuals will select an alternative based on how this choice relates to outcomes such as rewards. The choice made is based on the strength or value of the outcome and on the perceived probability that this choice will lead to the desired outcome.

experience rating   Rating system in which insurance premiums vary directly with the number of claims filed. An experience rating is applied to unemployment insurance and workers' compensation and may be applied to commercial health insurance premiums. In a *community rating system,* insurance rates are based on the medical experience of the entire community.

external competitiveness   The pay relationships among organizations; focuses attention on the competitive positions reflected in these relationships.

extrinsic rewards Rewards that a person receives from sources other than the job itself. They include compensation, supervision, promotions, vacations, friendships, and all other important outcomes apart from the job itself.

face validity The determination of the relevance of a measuring device on the basis of "appearance" only.

factor scales Measures that reflect different degrees within each compensable factor. Most commonly five to seven degrees are defined. Each degree may be anchored by typical skills, tasks and behaviors, or key job titles.

factor weights Measures that indicate the importance of each compensable factor in a job evaluation system. Weights can be derived through either a committee judgment or a statistical analysis.

Fair Labor Standards Act of 1938 (FLSA) A federal law governing minimum wage, overtime pay, equal pay for men and women in the same types of jobs, child labor, and record-keeping requirements.

Family and Medical Leave Act Legislation passed in 1993 that entitles eligible employees to receive unpaid leave up to 12 weeks per year for specified family or medical reasons, such as caring for ill family members or adopting a child.

Federal Insurance Contribution Act (FICA) The source of social security contribution withholding requirements. The FICA deduction is paid by both employer and employee.

first impression error Rating error in which the rater develops a negative (positive) opinion of an employee early in the review period and allows it to negatively (positively) color all subsequent perceptions of performance.

flat rate A single rate, rather than a range of rates, for all individuals performing a certain job. Ignores seniority and performance differences.

flexible benefit plan Benefit package in which employees are given a core of critical benefits (necessary for minimum security) and permitted to expend the remainder of their benefit allotment on options that they find most attractive.

flexible benefits *See* cafeteria (flexible) benefit plan.

flexible compensation The allocation of employee compensation in a variety of forms tailored to organization pay objectives and/or the needs of individual employees.

forms of compensation The various types of pay, which may be received directly in the form of cash (e.g., wages, bonuses, incentives) or indirectly through series and benefits (e.g., pensions, health insurance, vacations). This definition excludes other forms of rewards or returns that employees may receive, such as promotion, recognition for outstanding work behavior, and the like.

forms of pay *See* forms of compensation.

401(k) A 401(k) plan, so named for the section of the Internal Revenue Code describing the requirements, is a savings plan in which employees are allowed to defer pretax income.

gain-sharing (group incentive) plans Incentive plans that are based on some measure of group performance rather than individual performance. Taking data on a past year as a base, group incentive plans may focus on cost savings (e.g., the Scanlon, Rucker, and Improshare plans) or on profit increases (profit-sharing plans) as the standard for distributing a portion of the accrued funds among relevant employees.

Gantt plan Individual incentive plan that provides for variable incentives as a function of a standard expressed as time period per unit of production. Under this plan, a standard time for a task is purposely set at a level requiring high effort to complete.

gender pay equity *See* comparable worth.

General Schedule (GS) A job structure used by the U.S. Office of Personnel Management for white-collar employees. It has 15 "grades" (classes) plus 5 more levels on an Executive Schedule.

geographic differentials Local conditions that employees in a specific geographic area encounter, such as labor shortages and differences in housing costs.

global approach Substitution of a particular skill and experience level for job descriptions in determining external market rates. Includes rates for all individuals who possess that skill.

golden parachute A contract clause that calls for the payment of a large lump sum in specified circumstances of an executive's termination, for example, following the company's acquisition by another firm.

group incentive plans *See* gain-sharing (group incentive) plans.

halo error Rating error in which an appraiser gives favorable ratings to all job duties based on impressive performance in just one job function. For example, a rater who hates tardiness rates a prompt subordinate high across all performance dimensions exclusively because of this one characteristic.

Halsey 50–50 method   Individual incentive method that provides for variable incentives as a function of a standard expressed as time period per unit of production. This plan derives its name from the shared split between worker and employer of any savings in direct costs.

Hay job evaluation system   A point factor system that evaluates jobs with respect to know-how, problem solving, and accountability. It is used primarily for exempt (managerial/professional) jobs.

Health Maintenance Act of 1973   Legislation that requires that employers offer alternative health coverage options (e.g., health maintenance organizations) to employees.

health maintenance organization (HMO)   A nontraditional health care delivery system. HMOs offer comprehensive benefits and outpatient services, as well as hospital coverage, for a fixed monthly prepaid fee.

health reimbursement arrangements (HRAs)   The employer sets up an account for a specified amount. When an employee has qualified medical costs, they're submitted for reimbursement until the account is depleted.

health savings accounts (HSA)   An HSA is a tax-exempt account built up through contributions of the employee or the employer, or both, that can be used to pay for health care.

hierarchies (job structures)   Jobs ordered according to their relative content and/or value.

high-commitment practices   Factors such as high base pay, sharing successes only (not risks), guaranteed employment security, promotions from within, training and skill development, employee ownership, and long-term perspective. High-commitment practices are believed to attract and retain a high-committed workforce that will become the source of competitive advantage.

hit rate   The ability of a job evaluation plan to replicate a predetermined, agreed-upon job structure.

horn error   The opposite of halo error; downgrading an employee across all performance dimensions exclusively because of poor performance on one dimension.

human capital theory   An economic theory proposing that the investment one is willing to make to enter an occupation is related to the returns one expects to earn over time in the form of compensation.

human resource planning system   Put in place by the benefit administrator to make realistic estimates of human resource needs and avoid a pattern of hasty hiring and morale-breaking terminations.

Improshare (IMproved PROductivity through SHARing)   A gain-sharing plan in which a standard is developed to identify the expected hours required to produce an acceptable level of output. Any savings arising from production of agreed-upon output in fewer-than-expected hours are shared by the firm and the worker.

Incentive   Inducement offered in advance to influence future performance (e.g., sales commissions).

incentive effect   The degree to which pay influences individual and aggregate motivation among employees at any point in time.

incentive stock options (ISO)   A form of deferred compensation designed to influence long-term performance. Gives an executive the right to pay today's market price for a block of shares in the company at a future time. No tax is due until the shares are sold.

increase guidelines   Inherent compensation system controls. They specify the amount and timing of pay increases on an organizationwide basis.

indirect compensation   Noncash benefits provided to an employee.

individual incentive plans   Incentive compensation that is tied directly to objective measures of individual production (e.g., sales commissions).

individual retirement accounts (IRAs)   Tax-favored retirement savings plans that individuals can establish themselves.

Innovator   The innovator stresses new products and short response time to market trends.

instrumentality   The perceived contingency that an outcome (performing well) has another outcome (a reward such as pay).

internal alignment   The pay relationships among jobs or skill levels within a single organization; focuses attention on employee and management acceptance of those relationships. It involves establishing equal pay for jobs of equal worth and acceptable pay differentials for jobs of unequal worth.

interrater reliability The extent of agreement among raters rating the same individual, group, or phenomena.

interval scaling A particular numerical point difference has the same meaning on all parts of a scale.

inventories Questionnaires in which tasks, behaviors, and abilities are listed. The core of all quantitative job analysis.

job analysis The systematic process of collecting information related to the nature of a specific job. It provides the knowledge needed to define jobs and conduct job evaluation.

job-based structure A job-based structure relies on work content—tasks, behaviors, responsibilities.

job-based systems Systems that focus on jobs as the basic unit of analysis to determine the pay structure; hence, job analysis is required.

job class (grade) A grouping of jobs that are considered substantially similar for pay purposes.

job content Information that describes a job. May include responsibility assumed and/or the tasks performed.

job description A summary of the most important features of a job. It identifies the job and describes the general nature of the work, specific task responsibilities, outcomes, and the employee characteristics required to perform the job.

job evaluation A systematic procedure designed to aid in establishing pay differentials among jobs within a single company. It includes classification, comparison of the relative worth of jobs, blending internal and external market forces, measurement, negotiation, and judgment.

job evaluation committee Group that may be charged with the responsibility of (1) selecting a job evaluation system, (2) carrying out or at least supervising the process of job evaluation, and (3) evaluating the success with which the job evaluation has been conducted. Its role may vary among organizations, but its members usually represent all important constituencies within the organization.

job evaluation manual Handbook that contains information on the job evaluation plan and is used as a "yardstick" in evaluating jobs. It includes a description of the job evaluation method used, descriptions of all jobs, and, if relevant, a description of compensable factors, numerical degree scales, and weights; may also contain a description of the available review or appeals procedure.

job family A group of jobs involving work of the same nature but requiring different skill and responsibility levels (e.g., computing and account recording are a job family; bookkeeper, accounting clerk, and teller are jobs within that family).

job grade *See* pay grade.

job hierarchy A grouping of jobs based on their job-related similarities and differences and on their value to the organization's objectives.

job pricing The process of assigning pay to jobs, based on thorough job analysis and job evaluation.

job specifications The job specifications that can be used as a basis for hiring are knowledge, skills, and abilities required to adequately perform the tasks.

job structure Relationship among jobs inside an organization, based on work content and each job's relative contribution to achieving the organization's objectives.

just wage doctrine A theory of job value that posits a "just" or equitable wage for any occupation based on that occupation's place in the larger social hierarchy. According to this doctrine, pay structures should be designed on the basis of societal norms, customs, and tradition, not on the basis of economic and market forces.

key jobs *See* benchmark (key) job.

labor demand The employment level organizations require. An increase in wage rates will reduce the demand for labor, other factors constant. Thus, the labor demand curve (the relationship between employment levels and wage rates) is downward-sloping.

labor supply The different numbers of employees available at different pay rates.

lag pay-level policy A wage structure that is set to match market rates at the beginning of the plan year only. The rest of the plan year, internal rates will lag behind market rates. Its objective is to offset labor costs, but it may hinder a firm's ability to attract and retain quality employees.

lead pay-level policy A wage structure that is set to lead the market throughout the plan year. Its aim is to maximize a firm's ability to attract and retain quality employees and to minimize employee dissatisfaction with pay.

legally required benefits Benefits that are required by statutory law: workers' compensation, social security, and unemployment compensation are required in the United States. Required benefits vary among countries. Companies operating in foreign countries must comply with host-country compensation and benefit mandates.

leniency error   Rating error in which the rater consistently rates someone higher than is deserved.

leveling   Weighting market survey data according to the closeness of the job matches.

lifetime employment   Most prevalent in Japanese companies, the notion of employees' staying with the same company for their entire career, despite possible poor performance on the part of either an employee or the company.

line of sight   An employee's ability to see how individual performance affects incentive payout. Employees on a straight piecework pay system have a clear line of sight—their pay is a direct function of the number of units they produce; employees covered by profit sharing have a fuzzier line of sight—their payouts are a function of many forces, only one of which is individual performance.

living wage   Pay legislation in some U.S. cities that requires wages well above the federal minimum wage. Often applies only to city government employees.

local country nationals (LCNs)   Citizens of a country in which a U.S. foreign subsidiary is located. LCNs' compensation is tied either to local wage rates or to the rates of U.S. expatriates performing the same job.

long-term disability (LTD) plan   An insurance plan that provides payments to replace income lost through an inability to work that is not covered by other legally required disability income plans.

long-term incentives   Inducements offered in advance to influence longer-rate (multiyear) results. Usually offered to top managers and professionals to get them to focus on long-term organization objectives.

low-high approach   Use of the lowest- and highest-paid benchmark job in the external market to anchor an entire skill-based structure.

lump-sum award   Payment of entire increase (typically merit-based) at one time. Because amount is not factored into base pay, any benefits tied to base pay do not increase.

lump-sum bonus   *See* lump-sum award.

managed care   Steps taken to contain health care and workers' compensation costs, such as switching to preferred provider organizations for health care delivery, utilization-review procedures, and medical bill audits.

management by objectives (MBO)   An employee planning, development, and appraisal procedure in which a supervisor and a subordinate, or group of subordinates, jointly identify and establish common performance goals. Employee performance on the absolute standards is evaluated at the end of the specified period.

managing compensation   The fourth dimension in the pay model: ensuring the right people get the right pay for achieving the right objectives in the right way.

marginal product of labor   The additional output associated with the employment of one additional human resource unit, with other factors held constant.

marginal productivity theory (MPT)   In contrast to Marxist "surplus value" theory, a theory that focuses on labor demand rather than supply and argues that employers will pay a wage to a unit of labor that equals that unit's use (not exchange) value. That is, work is compensated in proportion to its contribution to the organization's production objectives.

marginal revenue of labor   The additional revenue generated when the firm employs one additional unit of human resources, with other factors held constant.

market-based health care   *See* customer-driven health care.

market pay line   Using key/benchmark jobs, a market pay policy line can be constructed that shows external market pay survey data as a function of internal job evaluation points. In many cases, the market pay policy line is obtained by using regression analysis, which yields an equation of the form "market pay = intercept + slope × job evaluation points." By plugging the job evaluation points for any job (both benchmark and non-benchmark jobs) into the equation, the predicted pay for each job can be obtained.

market pricing   Setting pay structures almost exclusively through matching pay for a very large percentage of jobs with the rates paid in the external market.

maturity curve   A plot of the empirical relationship between current pay and years since a professional has last received a degree (YSLD), thus allowing organizations to determine a competitive wage level for specific professional employees with varying levels of experience.

Medicare Prescription Drug, Improvement and Modernization Act of 2003   Seniors must choose among a variety of plans written in bureaucratic hieroglyphics.

Mental Health Act   Law passed in 1997 that stipulates that mental illness must be covered to same extent that other medical conditions are covered.

merit increase guidelines   Specifications that tie pay increases to performance. They may take one of two forms: The simplest version specifies pay increases permissible for different levels of performance. More complex guidelines tie pay not only to performance but also to position in the pay range.

merit pay   A reward that recognizes outstanding past performance. It can be given in the form of lump-sum payments or as increments to the base pay. Merit programs are commonly designed to pay different amounts (often at different times) depending on the level of performance.

Merrick plan   Individual incentive plan that provides for variable incentives as a function of units of production per time period. It works like the Taylor plan, but three piecework rates are set: (1) high—for production exceeding 100 percent of standard; (2) medium—for production between 83 and 100 percent of standard; and (3) low—for production less than 83 percent of standard.

minimum wage   A minimum-wage level for most Americans established by Congress as part of the Fair Labor Standards Act of 1938.

motivation   An individual's willingness to engage in some behavior. Primarily concerned with (1) what energizes human behavior, (2) what directs or channels such behavior, and (3) how this behavior is maintained or sustained.

multiskill systems   Systems that link pay to the number of different jobs (breadth) an employee is certified to do, regardless of the specific job he or she is doing.

National Electrical Manufacturers Association (NEMA) plan   A point factor job evaluation system that evolved into the National Position Evaluation Plan sponsored by NMTA associates.

National Metal Trades Association (NMTA) plan   A point factor job evaluation plan for production, maintenance, and service personnel.

noncontributory financing   Benefit option in which an employee benefit is fully paid for by the employer.

nonexempt employees   Employees who are subject to the provisions of the Fair Labor Standards Act.

nonexempt jobs   Jobs subject to provisions of the Fair Labor Standards Act with respect to minimum wage and overtime. Exempt employees include most executives, administrators, professionals, and outside sales representatives.

nonqualified deferred compensation plans   A plan does not qualify for tax exemption if an employer who pays high levels of deferred compensation to executives does not make proportionate contributions to lower-level employees.

nonqualified stock options   Form of compensation that gives an executive the right to purchase stock at a stipulated price; the excess over fair market value is taxed as ordinary income.

objective performance-based pay systems   Pay approach that focuses on objective performance standards (e.g., counting output) derived from organizational objectives and a thorough analysis of the job (e.g., incentive and gain-sharing plans).

occupational diseases   Diseases that arise out of the course of employment, not including "ordinary diseases of life," for which workers' compensation claims can be filed.

offshoring   Offshoring refers to the movement of jobs to locations beyond a country's borders.

on-call employees   Employees who must respond to work-related assignments/problems 24 hours a day. Firefighters, SPCA humane officers, and other emergency personnel are traditional examples. Increasingly, this group includes technical workers such as software service personnel.

organizational culture   The composite of shared values, symbols, and cognitive schemes that ties people together in the organization.

outlier   An extreme value that may distort some measures of central tendency.

outsourcing   The practice of hiring outside vendors to perform functions that do not directly contribute to business objectives and in which the organization does not have a comparative advantage.

paid time off (PTO)   Eliminates the distinction between sick days and other paid days off, thus eliminating the incentive to "fake" illness.

paired comparison ranking   A ranking job evaluation method that involves comparing all possible pairs of jobs under study.

pay discrimination   Discrimination usually defined as including (1) access discrimination, which occurs when qualified women and minorities are denied access to particular jobs, promotions, or training opportunities; and (2) valuation discrimination, which takes place when minorities or women are paid less than white males for performing substantially equal work. Both types of discrimination are illegal under Title VII of the Civil Rights Act of 1964. Some argue that valuation discrimination can also occur when men and women hold entirely different jobs (in content or results) that are of comparable worth to the employer. Existing federal laws do not support the "equal pay for work of comparable worth" standard.

pay equity (also gender pay equity)   *See* comparable worth.

pay-for-knowledge plans   A compensation practice whereby employees are paid for the number of different jobs they can adequately perform or the amount of knowledge they possess.

pay-for-performance plans   Pay that varies with some measure of individual or organizational performance, such as merit pay, lump-sum bonus plans, skill-based pay, incentive plans, variable pay plans, risk sharing, and success sharing.

pay forms   The various types of payments, or pay mix, that make up total compensation.

pay grade   One of the classes, levels, or groups into which jobs of the same or similar values are grouped for compensation purposes. All jobs in a pay grade have the same pay range—maximum, minimum, and midpoint.

pay increase guidelines   The mechanisms through which levels are translated into pay increases and, therefore, dictate the size and time of the pay reward for good performance.

pay level   An average of the array of rates paid by an employer.

pay-level policies   Decisions concerning a firm's level of pay vis-à-vis product and labor market competitors. There are three classes of pay-level policies: to lead, to match, or to follow competition.

pay-level rise   The percentage increase in the average wage rate paid. Calculated as: $100 \times$ [(Average pay-year end − average pay at year beginning)/Average pay at year beginning]

pay mix (or pay forms)   Relative emphasis among compensation components such as base pay, merit, incentives, and benefits.

pay objectives   *See* compensation objectives.

pay-policy line   Representation of the organization's pay-level policy relative to what competitors pay for similar jobs.

pay ranges   The range of pay rates from minimum to maximum set for a pay grade or class. It puts limits on the rates an employer will pay for a particular job.

pay satisfaction   A function of the discrepancy between employees' perceptions of how much pay they should receive and how much pay they do receive. If these perceptions are equal, an employee is said to experience pay satisfaction.

pay (wage) survey   The systematic process of collecting information and making judgments about the compensation paid by other employers. Pay (wage) survey data are useful in designing pay levels and structures.

pay structures   The array of pay rates for different jobs within a single organization; they focus attention on differential compensation paid for work of unequal worth.

pay techniques   Mechanisms or technologies of compensation management, such as job analysis, job descriptions, market surveys, job evaluation, and the like, that tie the four basic pay policies to the pay objectives.

pay-with-competition policy   Policy that tries to ensure that a firm's labor costs are approximately equal to those of its competitors. It seeks to avoid placing an employer at a disadvantage in pricing products or in maintaining a qualified work force.

pension benefit guaranty corporation (PBGC) Agency to which employers are required to pay insurance premiums to protect individuals from bankrupt companies (and pension plans!). In turn, the PBGC guarantees payment of vested benefits to employees formerly covered by terminated pension plans.

pension plan   A form of deferred compensation. All pension plans usually have four common characteristics: They (1) involve deferred payments to a former employee (or surviving spouse) for past services rendered; (2) specify a normal retirement age, at which time benefits begin to accrue to the employee; (3) specify a formula for calculating benefits, and (4) provide for integration with social security benefits.

performance-dimension training   Training that gives performance appraisers an understanding of the dimensions on which to evaluate employee performance.

performance evaluation (performance appraisal)   A process to determine correspondence between worker behavior/task outcomes and employer expectations (performance standards).

performance metrics   Quantitative measures of job performance.

performance share/unit plans   Cash or stock awards earned through achieving specific goals.

performance standard   An explicit statement of what work output is expected from employees in exchange for compensation.

performance-standard training   Training that gives performance appraisers a frame of reference for making ratee appraisals.

perquisites (perks)   The extras bestowed on top management, such as private dining rooms, company cars, and first-class airfare.

person-based structure   A person-based structure shifts the focus to the employee: the skills, knowledge, or competencies the employee possesses, whether or not they are used in the employee's particular job.

personal care account (PCA)   A tool used by employers to gain some control over health care costs while still providing health security to workers. The employer establishes a high deductible paid by employees but cushions the blow by setting up a PCA to cover part of the deductible cost.

phantom stock plan   Stock plan in which an increase in stock price at a fixed future date determines the cash or stock award. It is called a phantom plan because the organization in question is not publicly traded. Stock price, therefore, is an illusion. The "phantom price" is derived from standard financial accounting procedures.

planned pay-level rise   The percentage increase in average pay that is planned to occur after considering such factors as anticipated rates of change in market data, changes in cost of living, the employer's ability to pay, and the efforts of turnover and promotions. This index may be used in top-down budgeting to control compensation costs.

point (factor) method   A job evaluation method that employs (1) compensable factors, (2) factor degrees numerically scaled, and (3) weights reflecting the relative importance of each factor. Once scaled degrees and weights are established for each factor, each job is measured against each compensable factor and a total score is calculated for each job. The total points assigned to a job determine the job's relative value and hence its location in the pay structure.

point-of-service plan (POS)   A point-of-service plan is a hybrid plan combining health maintenance organization (HMO) and preferred provider organization (PPO) benefits.

policy capturing   Compensable factor importance weights are inferred using statistical methods such as regression analysis.

policy line   A pay line that reflects the organization's policy with respect to the external labor market.

portability   Transferability of pension benefits for employees moving to a new organization. ERISA does not require mandatory portability of private pensions. On a voluntary basis, the employer may agree to let an employee's pension benefit transfer to an individual retirement account (IRA) or, in a reciprocating arrangement, to the new employer.

position analysis questionnaire (PAQ)   A structured job analysis technique that classifies job information into seven basic factors: information input, mental processes, work output, relationships with other persons, job context, other job characteristics, and general dimensions. The PAQ analyzes jobs in terms of worker-oriented data.

preferred provider organization (PPO)   Health care delivery system in which there is a direct contractual relationship between and among employers, health care providers, and third-party payers. An employer is able to select providers (e.g., selected doctors) who agree to provide price discounts and submit to strict utilization controls.

Pregnancy Discrimination Act of 1978   An amendment to Title VII of the Civil Rights Act. It requires employers to extend to pregnant employees or spouses the same disability and medical benefits provided to other employees or spouses of employees.

prevailing-wage laws   Legislation that provides for a government-defined prevailing wage as the minimum wage that must be paid for work done on covered government projects or purchases. In practice, these prevailing rates have been union rates paid in various geographic areas.

probationary period   Period during which new employees are excluded from benefits coverage, usually until some term of employment (e.g., 3 months) is completed.

procedural justice/fairness   Concept concerned with the process used to make and implement decisions about pay. It suggests that the way pay decisions are made and implemented may be as important to employees as the results of the decisions.

professional employee   An employee who has specialized training of a scientific or intellectual nature and whose major duties do not entail the supervision of people.

profit-sharing plan   A plan that focuses on profitability as the standard for group incentive. These plans typically involve one of three distributions: (1) Cash or current distribution plans provide full payment to participants soon after profits have been determined (quarterly or annually); (2) deferred plans have a portion of current profits credited to employee accounts, with cash payments made at time of retirement, disability, severance, or death; and (3) combination plans that incorporate aspects of both current and deferred options.

purchasing power   The ability to buy goods and services in a certain currency, determined by exchange rates and availability of goods. Companies must determine purchasing power when allocating allowances to expatriates.

qualified deferred compensation plan   A deferred compensation program that qualities for tax exemption. It must provide contributions or benefits for employees other than executives that are proportionate to contributions provided to executives.

quantitative job analysis (QJA)   Job analysis method that relies on scaled questionnaires and inventories that produce job-related data that are documentable, can be statistically analyzed, and may be more objective than other analyses.

quoted price market   Stores that label each item's price or ads that list a job's opening starting wage are examples of quoted-price markets.

range maximums   The maximum values to be paid for a job grade, representing the top value the organization places on the output of the work.

range midpoint   The salary midway between the minimum and maximum rates of a salary range. The midpoint rate for each range is usually set to correspond to the pay-policy line and represents the rate paid for satisfactory performance on the job.

range minimums   The minimum values to be paid for a job grade, representing the minimum value the organization places on the work. Often, rates below the minimum are used for trainees.

range overlap   The degree of overlap between adjoining grade ranges is determined by the differences in midpoints among ranges and the range spread. A high degree of overlap and narrow midpoint differentials indicate small differences in the value of jobs in the adjoining grades and permit promotions without much change in the rates paid. By contrast, a small degree of overlap and wide midpoint differentials allow the manager to reinforce a promotion with a large salary increase.

ranges   *See* pay ranges.

rank and yank   Created by Jack Welch, it requires managers to force-rank employees according to some preset distribution.

ranking format   A type of performance appraisal format that requires that the rater compare employees against each other to determine the relative ordering of the group on some performance measure.

rater error training   Training that enables performance appraisers to identify and suppress psychometric errors such as leniency, severity, central tendency, and halo errors when evaluating employee performance.

rating errors   Errors in judgment that occur in a systematic manner when an individual observes and evaluates a person, group, or phenomenon. The most frequently described rating errors include halo, leniency, severity, and central tendency errors.

rating format   A type of performance appraisal format that requires that raters evaluate employees on absolute measurement scales that indicate varying levels of performance.

recency error   The opposite of first-impression error. Performance (either good or bad) at the end of the review period plays too large a role in determining an employee's rating for the entire period.

red circle rates   Pay rates that are above the maximum rate for a job or pay range for a grade.

reengineering   Making changes in the way work is designed to include external customer focus.

Usually includes organizational delayering and job restructuring.

regression   A statistical technique for relating present-pay differentials to some criterion, that is, pay rates in the external market, rates for jobs held predominantly by men, or factor weights that duplicate present rates for all jobs in the organization.

regression analysis   One output from a regression analysis is the R2. The R2 is much like a correlation in that it tells us what percentage of the variation is accounted for by the variables we are using to predict or explain.

relational returns   The nonquantifiable returns employees get from employment, such as social satisfaction, friendship, feeling of belonging, or accomplishment.

relative value of jobs   The relative contribution of jobs to organizational goals, to their external market rates, or to some other agreed-upon rates.

relevant markets   Those employers with which an organization competes for skills and products/services. Three factors commonly used to determine the relevant markets are the occupation or skills required, the geography (willingness to relocate and/or commute), and employers that compete in the product market.

reliability   The consistency of the results obtained, that is, the extent to which any measuring procedure yields the same results on repeated trials. Reliable job information does not mean that it is accurate (valid), comprehensive, or free from bias.

rent   *See* economic rent.

reopener clause   A provision in an employment contract that specifies that wages, and sometimes such nonwage items as pension/benefits, will be renegotiated under certain conditions (changes in cost of living, organization, profitability, and so on).

reservation wage   A theoretical minimum standard below which a job seeker will not accept an offer, no matter how attractive the other job attributes.

restricted stock plan   Plan that grants stock at a reduced price with the condition that it not be sold before a specified date.

reverse incentive plan   A plan where there is penalty for poor performance rather than reward for good.

reward system   The composite of all organizational mechanisms and strategies used to formally acknowledge employee behaviors and performance. It includes all forms of compensation, promotions, and assignments; nonmonetary awards and recognitions; training opportunities; job design and analysis; organizational design and working conditions; the supervisor; social networks; performance standards and reward criteria; performance evaluation; and the like.

risk sharing   An incentive plan in which employees' base wages are set below a specified level (e.g., 80 percent of the market wage) and incentive earnings are used to raise wages above the base. In good years an employee's incentive pay will more than make up for the 20 percent shortfall, giving the employee a pay premium. Because employees assume some of the risk, risk-sharing plans pay more generously than success-sharing plans in good years.

Roth IRA   For employees who meet certain requirements, all earnings are tax free when withdrawn. However, no income tax deductions are allowed for contributions.

Rowan plan   Individual incentive plan that provides for variable incentives as a function of a standard expressed as time period per unit of production. It is similar to the Halsey plan, but in this plan a worker's bonus increases as the time required to complete the task decreases.

Rucker plan   A group cost savings plan in which cost reductions due to employee efforts are shared with the employees. It involves a somewhat more complex formula than a Scanlon plan for determining employee incentivebonuses.

salary   Pay given to employees who are exempt from regulations of the Fair Labor Standards Act and hence do not receive overtime pay (e.g., managers and professionals). Exempt pay is calculated at an annual or monthly rate rather than hourly.

salary continuation plans   Benefit options that provide some form of protection for disability. Some are legally required, such as workers' compensation provisions for work-related disability and social security disability income provisions for those who qualify.

sales compensation   Any form of compensation paid to sales representatives. Sales compensation formulas usually attempt to establish direct incentives for sales outcomes.

sales value of production (SVOP)   An incentive metric that calculates the dollar value of goods produced and in inventory.

Sarbanes-Oxley Act   Legislation passed in 2002 that prohibits executives from retaining bonuses or profits from selling company stock if they mislead the public about the financial health of the company.

scaling   Determining the intervals on a measurement instrument.

Scanlon plan   A group cost-savings plan designed to lower labor costs without lowering the level of a firm's activity. Incentives are derived as the ratio between labor costs and sales value of production (SVOP).

Securities Exchange Act   Legislative act passed in 1934 that created the Securities and Exchange Commission (SEC).

segmented labor supply   A labor supply that comes from multiple markets. Some employees may come from different global locations, may receive different pay forms, and may have varied employment relationships.

self-funding plans   These plans specify that payouts only occur after the company reaches a certain profit target. Then variable payouts for individual, team, and company performance are triggered.

self-insurance compensation   System in which an organization funds its own insurance claims, for either health or life insurance or workers' compensation.

seniority increases   Pay increases tied to a progression pattern based on seniority. To the extent performance improves with time on the job, this method has the rudiments of paying for performance.

severity error   The opposite of leniency error. Rating someone consistently lower than is deserved.

shared choice   An external competitiveness policy that offers employees substantial choice among their pay forms.

shirking behavior   The propensity of employees to allow the marginal revenue product of their labor to be less than its marginal cost; to be lax.

short-term disability (STD)   *See* workers' compensation.

short-term incentives   Inducements offered in advance to influence future short-range (annual) results. Usually very specific performance standards are established.

sick leave   Paid time when an employee is not working due to illness or injury.

simplified employee pension (SEP)   A retirement income arrangement intended to markedly reduce the paperwork for regular pension plans.

single-rate pay system   A compensation policy under which all employees in a given job are paid at the same rate instead of being placed in a pay grade. Generally applies to situations in which there is little room for variation in job performance, such as an assembly line.

skill analysis   A systematic process to identify and collect information about the skills required to perform work in an organization.

skill-based pay system   *See* pay-for-knowledge plan.

skill-based structure   Skill-based structures link pay to the depth or breadth of the skills, abilities, and knowledge a person acquires that are relevant to the work.

skill-based system   Compensation approach that links pay to the depth and/or breadth of the skills, abilities, and knowledge a person acquires/demonstrates that are relevant to the work. Typically applies to operators, technicians, and office workers where the work is relatively specific and defined. The criterion chosen can influence employee behaviors by describing what is required to get higher pay.

skill blocks   Basic units of knowledge employees must master to perform the work, satisfy customers, and achieve business objectives.

skill requirement   Composite of experience, training, and ability as measured by the performance requirements of a particular job.

slippage   *See* turnover effect.

sorting effect   The effect that pay can have on the composition of the workforce. Different types of pay strategies may cause different types of people to apply to and stay with an organization.

special groups   Employee groups for whom compensation practices diverge from typical company procedures (e.g., supervisors, middle and upper management, nonsupervisory professionals, sales, and personnel in foreign subsidiaries).

spillover effect   The fact that improvements obtained in unionized firms "spill over" to nonunion firms seeking ways to lessen workers' incentives for organizing a union.

spillover error   Rating error in which the rater continues to downgrade an employee for performance errors in prior rating periods.

spot award   One-time award for exceptional performance; also called a spot bonus.

standard hour plan   Individual incentive plan in which rate determination is based on time period per unit of production and wages vary directly as a constant function of product level. In this context, the incentive rate in standard hour plans is set based on completion of a task in some expected time period.

standard rating scales   Appraisal system characterized by (1) one or more performance standards being developed and defined for the appraiser and (2) each performance standard having a measurement scale indicating varying levels of performance on that dimension. Appraisers rate the appraisee by checking the point on the scale that best represents the appraisee's performance level. Rating scales vary in the extent to which anchors along the scale are defined.

stock appreciation rights (SARs)   Rights that permit an executive to receive all the potential capital gain of a stock incentive option (ISO) without having to purchase the stock; thus, they reduce an executive's cash commitment. Payment is provided on demand for the difference between the stock option price and the current market price.

stock purchase plan (nonqualified)   A plan that is, in effect, a management stock purchase plan. It allows senior management or other key personnel to buy stock in the business. This plan has certain restrictions: (1) The stockholder must be employed for a certain period of time, (2) the business has the right to buy back the stock, and (3) stockholders cannot sell the stock for a defined period.

stock purchase plan (qualified)   A program under which employees buy shares in the company's stock, with the company contributing a specific amount for each unit of employee contribution. Also, stock may be offered at a fixed price (usually below market) and paid for in full by the employees.

straight piecework system   Individual incentive plan in which rate determination is based on units of production per time period; wages vary directly as a constant function of production level.

straight ranking procedure   A type of performance appraisal format in which the rater compares or ranks each employee relative to each other employee.

strategy   The fundamental direction of the organization. It guides the deployment of all resources, including compensation.

strategic perspective   A strategic perspective focuses on those compensation choices that help the organization gain and sustain competitive advantage.

strike price   Price an individual is permitted to buy a stock at by the company granting the stock.

subjective performance-based pay systems   Pay approach that focuses on subjective performance standards (e.g., achieving agreed-upon objectives) derived from organizational objectives and a thorough analysis of the job.

success sharing   An incentive plan (e.g., profit sharing or gain sharing) in which an employee's base wage matches the market wage and variable pay adds on during successful years. Because base pay is not reduced in bad years, employees bear little risk.

supermarket plan   *See* cafeteria (flexible) benefit plan.

supplemental unemployment benefits (SUB) plan   Employer-funded plan that supplements state unemployment insurance payments to workers during temporary periods of layoffs. Largely concentrated in the automobile, steel, and related industries.

supply chain analysis   As applied to work flow analysis, supply chain analysis looks at how an organization does its work: activities pursued to accomplish specific objectives for specific customers.

surplus value   The difference between labor's use and exchange values. According to Marx, under capitalism wages are based on labor's exchange value—which is lower than its use value—and thus provide only a subsistence wage.

survey   The systematic process of collecting and making judgments about the compensation paid by other employers.

tacit work   Complex work (as compared to transactional, or routine, work).

tally sheet   A tally sheet gives a comprehensive view on the true value of executive compensation. Add up the value of base salary, annual incentives, long-term incentives, benefits, and perks. Part of this process includes estimating the current value of stock options (using something called the Black–Scholes model), stock appreciation rights, vested and unvested pensions, and payouts upon termination.

tariff agreements   In some European countries, the wage rates negotiated by employer associations and trade union federations for all wage earners for all companies in an industry group.

task (work) data   Information on the elemental units of work (tasks), with emphasis on the purpose of each task, collected for job analysis. Work data describe the job in terms of actual tasks performed and their output.

tax equalization   A method whereby an expatriate pays neither more nor less tax than the assumed home-country tax on base remuneration.

Taylor plan   Individual incentive plan that provides for variable incentives as a function of units of production per time period. It provides two piecework rates that are established for production above and below standard, and these rates are higher and lower than the regular wage incentive level.

team incentive   Group incentive restricted to team members with payout usually based on improvements in productivity, customer satisfaction, financial performance, or quality of goods and services directly attributable to the team.

third-country nationals (TCNs)   Employees of a U.S. foreign subsidiary who maintain citizenship in a country other than the United States or the host country. TCNs' compensation is tied to comparative wages in the local country, the United States, or the country of citizenship.

360-degree feedback   A rating method that assesses employee performance from five points of view: supervisor, peer, self, customer, and subordinate.

Title VII of the Civil Rights Act of 1964   A major piece of legislation prohibiting pay discrimination. It is much broader in intent than the Equal Pay Act, forbidding discrimination on the basis of race, color, religion, sex, pregnancy, or national origin.

top-down approach to pay budgeting   Also known as *unit-level budgeting,* an approach in which a total pay budget for the organization (or unit) is determined and allocated "down" to individual employees during the plan year. There are many kinds to unit-level budgeting. They differ in the type of financial index used as a control measure. Controlling to a planned level rise and controlling to a planned compa-ratio are two typical approaches.

topping out   Situation in which employees in a skill-based compensation plan attain the top pay rate in a job category by accumulating and/or becoming certified for the top-paid skill block(s).

total cash   Base wage plus cash bonus; does not include benefits or stock options.

total compensation   The complete pay package for employees, including all forms of money, bonuses, benefits, services, and stock.

total returns   All returns to an employee, including financial compensation, benefits, opportunities for social interaction, security, status and recognition, work variety, appropriate workload, importance of work, authority/control/autonomy, advancement opportunities, feedback, hazard-free working conditions, and opportunities for personal and professional development. An effective compensation system will utilize many of these returns.

total rewards   *See* total returns.

tournament theory   The notion that larger differences in pay are more motivating than smaller differences. Like prize awards in a golf tournament, pay increases should get successively greater as one moves up the job hierarchy. Differences between the top job and the second-highest job should be the largest.

traditional time-off (TTO) plan   Paid vacations, holidays (or pay if worked), sick leave, and personal leave, tracked separately.

transactional work   Routine work.

turnover effect   The downward pressure on average wage that results from the replacement of high-wage-earning employees with workers earning a lower wage.

two-tier pay plans   Wage structures that differentiate pay for the same jobs based on hiring date. A contract is negotiated that specifies that employees hired after a stated day will receive lower wages than their higher-seniority peers working on the same or similar jobs.

underwater stock option   A stock option with a market price lower than the original offer price. Fairly common during a market downturn, these options are of no value to someone who has received them as an incentive.

unemployment benefits   *See* unemployment insurance.

unemployment compensation   *See* unemployment insurance.

unemployment insurance (UI)   State-administered program that provides financial security for workers during periods of joblessness.

unequal treatment   *See* disparate treatment.

use value   The value or price ascribed to the use or consumption of labor in the production of goods or services.

U.S. expatriates (USEs)   American citizens working for a U.S. subsidiary in a foreign country. Main compensation concerns are to "keep the expatriates whole" relative to their U.S.-based counterparts and to provide expatriates with an incentive wage for accepting the foreign assignment.

utility theory   The analysis of utility, the dollar value created by increasing revenues and/or decreasing costs by changing one or more human resource practices. It has most typically been used to analyze the payoff to making more valid employee hiring/selection decisions.

valence   The amount of positive or negative value placed on specific outcomes by an individual.

validity   The accuracy of the results obtained; that is, the extent to which any measuring device measures what it purports to measure.

value   The worth of the work; its relative contribution to organization objectives.

valuation discrimination   Discrimination that focuses on the pay women and minorities receive for the work they perform. Discrimination occurs when members of these groups are paid less than white males for performing substantially equal work. This definition of pay discrimination is based on the standard of "equal pay for equal work." Many believe that this definition is limited and that valuation discrimination can also occur when men and women hold entirely different jobs (in content or results) that are of comparable worth to the employer. Existing federal laws do not support the "equal pay for work of comparable worth" standard.

variable pay   Pay tied to productivity or some measure that can vary with the firm's profitability.

vesting   A benefit plan provision that guarantees that participants will, after meeting certain requirements, retain a right to the benefits they have accrued, or some portion of them, even if employment under their plan terminates before retirement.

wage   Pay given to employees who are covered by overtime and reporting provisions of the Fair Labor Standards Act. Nonexempts usually have their pay calculated at an hourly rate rather than a monthly or annual rate.

wage adjustment provisions   Clauses in a multilayer union contract that specify the types of wage adjustments that have to be implemented during the life of the contract. These adjustments might be specified in three major ways: (1) deferred wage increases—negotiated at the time of contract negotiation, with the time and amount specified in the contract; (2) cost-of-living adjustments (COLAs) or escalator clauses; and (3) reopener clauses.

wage and price controls   Government regulations that aim at maintaining low inflation and low levels of unemployment. They frequently focus on "cost-push" inflation, limiting the size of pay raises and the rate of increases in prices charged for goods and services. Used for limited time periods only.

wage survey   *See* pay (wage) survey.

Walsh-Healey Public Contracts Act of 1936   A federal law requiring certain employers holding federal contracts for the manufacture or provision of materials, supplies, and equipment to pay industry prevailing-wage rates.

Worker Economic Opportunity Act   Law passed in 2000 that provides that income from most stock plans need not be included in calculating overtime pay.

work flow   Work flow refers to the process by which goods and services are delivered to the customer.

zones   Ranges of pay used as controls or guidelines within pay bands that can keep the system more structurally intact. Maximums, midpoints, and minimums provide guides to appropriate pay for certain levels of work. Without zones employees may float to the maximum pay, which for many jobs in the band is higher than market value.

Name Index

Abegglen, J., 541
Abosch, K., 269, 270, 318, 521
Abowd, J., 537
Ackerman, L., 108
Adams, J., 294
Adams, S., 76
Adhikari, D., 548
Aeppel, T., 622
Ahern, E., 447
Ahlburg, D., 79
Aiman-Smith, L., 12, 319, 341, 376
Akande, A., 522
Akhtar, S., 534
Albright, R., 631
Alexander, S., 307
Allan, P., 467, 498
Allen, M., 19, 20, 24, 526
Allen, R., 303
Alliger, G., 373
Allison, P., 80, 602
Allredge, M., 176
Alvares, K., 370
Anand, V., 17
Anderson, D., 602
Anderson, P., 72, 83, 637
Anderson, R., 3
Antonioni, D., 361, 371, 372
Aoki, M., 548
Appelbaum, E., 20, 40
Armour, S., 432
Arrfelt, M., 3
Arrowsmith, J., 548
Arthur, J., 53, 319, 334, 341
Arvey, R., 108, 117, 185, 361
Ash, R., 426
Ashenfelter, O., 217
Ashforth, B., 17
Atwater, L., 371, 602
Au, K., 523
Avery, M., 534
Ayer, R., 7

Bacharach, S., 79
Backhaus, B., 307
Bacon, N., 4
Badenhausen, K., 289
Bailey, T., 20, 40
Baker, B., 15

Baker, G., 72, 76, 269, 270
Bakerman, T., 428
Balkin, D., 39, 53, 329, 339, 495
Bandler, J., 631
Banister, J., 522
Barbaro, M., 586, 632
Barber, A., 211, 218
Barber, F., 619
Barksdale, W., 341
Barnes, J., 378
Barney, J., 523
Barres, B., 591
Barrett, G., 184, 381
Barrett, L., 290
Barrick, M., 246
Barringer, M., 46, 85, 99, 422
Barsoux, J., 44, 532, 542, 558
Bart, C., 45
Bartlett, C., 175, 524
Bartol, K., 8, 381
Bartunek, J., 290
Basu, S., 522
Bates, S., 415, 426
Batt, R., 20, 40, 44, 54, 55, 78, 166, 218, 509
Bayard, K., 603
Baytos, L., 422
Bazerman, M., 17
Beam, B., 419
Bearly, W., 372
Beatty, R., 54, 373, 375, 634
Bebchuk, L., 6, 488
Bechter, B., 548
Becker, B., 21, 41, 52, 53, 54, 55, 84, 248, 287, 634
Becker, G., 213
Beer, M., 641
Belcher, D., 130, 253
Belcher, J., 329, 335, 336
Bellak, A., 606
Belman, D., 78, 110, 211
Bendix, W., 487
Bennett, M., 7
Benoit, B., 545
Benson, P., 328, 338
Berg, P., 20, 40
Bergen, C., 303
Berger, C., 231

Berger, D., 318, 480
Berger, L., 318, 339, 480
Berger, M., 557
Bergerac, M., 487
Bergey, P., 12, 376
Berkowitz, L., 294
Berkowitz, P., 574
Bernardin, H., 370, 371, 373, 375, 377
Bernhard, J., 485
Berone, P., 490
Berra, Y., 625
Betts, P., 483
Bezos, J., 6, 7
Bienstock, L., 162
Bigoness, W., 373
Binder, M., 602
Bing, S., 96
Bishop, J., 328
Björkman, I., 524
Black, D., 602, 603
Black, J., 551
Blair, D., 491
Blanchflower, D., 241
Blankfein, L., 482
Blanplain, R., 548
Blasi, J., 344, 345
Blau, F., 4, 526, 575, 602, 603, 605
Blinder, A., 4
Block, S., 455, 624
Bloom, M., 10, 44, 53, 72, 77, 81, 84, 85, 223, 245, 288, 307, 333, 521, 523, 524, 532, 533, 548, 549
Bloom, N., 55
Blumenstein, R., 415
Blumenthal, R., 11
Bobko, P., 118, 169
Bodreau, J., 182
Bogle, J., 486
Bognanno, M., 84, 537
Bond, P., 372
Borgas, G., 575
Borman, W., 108, 116, 361, 371, 373
Borowitz, A., 14
Boselie, P., 14
Bossidy, L., 50
Boswell, W., 13, 223
Bottomley, P., 147

Boudreau, J., 9, 12, 13, 19, 21, 52, 53, 113, 211, 223, 231, 233, 300, 483, 523, 533, 619, 634
Bowers, J., 182
Bowers, M., 509
Bowler, M., 46, 53
Boxall, P., 24, 40
Boyle, M., 624
Bradford, J., 2
Bradshaw, D., 631
Brannick, M., 98
Brause, A., 17
Brett, J., 603
Bretz, R., 9, 213, 218, 223, 303, 426
Brewster, C., 523
Bridgeford, L., 444
Brief, A., 285, 294, 363
Brin, D. W., 215
Briner, R., 10
Briones, C., 580
Brockbank, W., 642, 643
Brockner, J., 77, 307
Broderick, R., 637
Brogden, H., 231
Brown, C., 602
Brown, D., 540
Brown, K., 22, 23, 217, 287, 296, 299, 341
Brown, M., 43, 53, 86, 87, 106
Brown, R., 624
Brown, S., 76
Brown, S. W., 552
Brush, D., 361
Buboltz, C., 106
Buckley, J., 246
Buckley, M., 377
Buckley, R., 376
Buckman, R., 345
Budd, J., 17, 216, 529
Budhwar, P., 12
Bulkeley, W., 219
Bunkley, N., 3
Burck, C., 50
Burkhauser, R., 579
Burlingham, B., 640
Burroughs, J., 637
Burton, J., 634
Burzawa, S., 353
Buster, M., 118
Bustillo, M., 584
Buyniski, T., 344

Cable, D., 9, 212, 299, 300, 418
Cadsby, C., 9

Cafferty, T., 373, 378
Camerer, C., 640
Cameron, J., 302
Camilleri, L., 482
Campbell, C. A., 364
Campbell, C. M., 211
Campion, M., 80, 117, 131, 150, 574
Canavan, J., 166
Cannella, A., 6
Cantor, N., 375
Canyon, M., 488, 489
Cappelli, P., 211
Capwell, D., 14
Card, D., 217, 579
Cardinal, L., 514
Cardy, R., 360, 361, 373, 375, 376
Carpenter, M., 6, 274, 303, 304
Carrell, M., 300
Carroll, S., 378
Carson, K., 361
Carter, A., 76, 506, 507
Carver, B., 150
Carver, S., 432
Cascio, F., 78
Cascio, W., 8, 99, 231, 373, 377, 634
Case, J., 13, 638, 640
Catano, V., 364
Cavallini, D., 241, 250
Cayne, J., 481
Cennamo, C., 522
Certo, S., 342
Chadwick, C., 622
Chao, L., 46
Charman, R., 50
Charness, G., 78, 110, 211
Chatterjee, S., 44, 49
Chatterji, A., 49
Chauvin, K., 211
Chazan, G., 535
Chen, C., 535
Chen, G., 14
Chen, Y., 77
Chenault, K., 482
Chilton, K., 327, 344
Chiu, R., 77, 83
Christensen, C., 558
Christiansen, N., 53
Christofferson, J., 10, 11
Chu, P., 514
Chua, R., 46
Cira, D., 221, 552
Clark, G., 453
Clark, K., 498
Clegg, S., 521

Cleveland, J., 359, 360
Clifford, T., 433
Cohen, B., 82
Cohen, S., 183
Cohen, W., 447
Coil, M., 258, 552
Colbert, A., 22, 23, 217, 287, 299
Cole, N., 432
Colella, A., 12, 637
Coleman, D., 362
Collins, A., 14
Collins, C., 19, 211
Collins, D., 341
Collins, J., 148, 184
Colquitt, J., 17
Colson, K., 145
Colvin, A., 44, 55, 78, 509
Combs, J., 488
Compton, B., 631
Conlon, D., 211
Conlon, E., 298
Connell, D., 304
Conte, C., 426
Conte, M., 344
Conway, N., 10
Conyon, M., 6
Cook, A., 602
Cook, F., 18, 51, 248, 631
Cook, P., 84
Cooke, K., 371
Cooke, W., 301, 304, 341
Coombs, J., 631
Corcoran, M., 602, 603
Cornwell, L., 443
Cosier, R., 294
Courant, P., 603
Cox, T., 213, 603, 604
Craig, S., 55, 106
Crandall, N., 170, 187
Crandall, S., 105, 109, 151, 183
Crane, D., 425
Cranny, C., 370
Crepanzano, R., 150
Crumley, B., 528
Crystal, G., 483, 487, 488
Cummings, L., 376
Currall, S., 218

Dalton, D., 294, 342, 490
Daly, C., 490
Danehower, C., 418
Darbishire, O., 523
Darr, W., 364
Dash, E., 77, 490

Datta, D., 37, 54
Davenport, B., 496, 498
Davenport, T., 104
Davis, B., 377
Davis, J., 148, 284
Davis, K., 184, 417
Davis-Blake, A., 274
Day, J., 319
DeCastro, J., 13, 54, 488
Deci, E., 296, 302
Deeg, R., 523
DeGrauwe, P., 544
deJonge, J., 634
DeLay, T., 477
Delery, J., 37
deLuque, M. S., 10
Demers, R., 494
Deming, E., 361
Deming, W., 361
DeNavas-Walt, C., 4
DeNisi, A., 12, 369, 373, 375, 378, 558
Denny, A., 303, 322
Densford, L., 426
Dettrich, J., 300
DeVaro, J., 603
Devers, C., 3, 6
Deyá-Tortella, B., 13, 54, 488
Dial, K., 47
Dickens, L., 548
Dierdorff, E., 117, 169, 183
Dillon, S., 330
Dimon, J., 482
Ding, D., 83, 534
DiPrete, H., 417
Dobbins, G., 360, 361, 373, 375, 376
Doellgast, V., 55
Doerr, K., 70, 114
Dolatowski, T., 465
Dolmat-Connell, J., 480
Dong, D., 522
Donkin, R., 52, 77
Dorfman, P., 530
Dorman, D., 645
Dorman, P., 10
Dorsey, D., 108
Dorsey, S., 456
Doty, D., 37, 165
Doucouliagos, H., 579
Douma, B., 17
Doverspike, D., 183, 184
Dow Scott, K., 328
Dowling, P., 220, 522, 523, 550, 555,
        557, 558
Doyle, J., 147

Dreher, G., 213, 426, 603, 604
Drucker, P., 52, 88, 214, 636
Dubner, S., 225
Ducharme, M., 360
Duffett, A., 164, 169
Duffy, M., 12, 46, 53
Duggan, J., 269, 270
Duhigg, C., 624
Duke, A., 373
Dulebohn, J., 4, 636
Duncan, K., 23, 303, 322, 341
Dunford, B., 13, 483
Dunn, B., 619, 620
Dunnette, M., 8, 53, 76, 98, 99, 103,
        113, 118, 228, 231, 244, 299,
        303, 334, 530
Durham, C., 294
Dyer, G., 544
Dyer, L., 113, 118, 182, 302,
        303, 523, 533
Dziczek, K., 218

Earle, J., 522
Early, P., 532
Eddleston, K., 18, 631
Edwards, M., 371, 372
Edwards, P., 148
Edwards, T., 523
Efrati, A., 456
Ehrenberg, R., 84
Eidems, J., 524
Eisenberger, R., 302, 327
Eisenhardt, K., 76, 488
Eisner, M., 482, 487
El-Sa'id, H., 526
Elam, K., 15
Ellig, B., 490
Ellis, C., 142
Ellis, R., 143, 148, 185
Ellison, L., 3, 487
Ellstrand, A., 490
Elron, E., 555
Elvira, M., 375
Emerson, L., 376
Engardio, P., 220
England, P., 80, 148, 591, 602
Engle, A., 44, 182, 220, 523, 524, 532,
        550, 555, 557, 558
Erez, M., 532
Ericksen, J., 19
Eriksson, T., 84
Eskew, D., 514
Esterl, M., 202
Estrin, S., 522

Etgen Reitz, A., 574
Etter, L., 47
Evans, P., 44, 523, 532, 542, 558
Even, W., 425
Ewen, A., 371, 372

Faber, H., 47
Fabrikant, G., 521, 522
Fadel, A., 290
Fairbanks, R., 6–7
Fairris, D., 580
Fang, M., 523, 533
Fannin, T., 433
Farkas, S., 164, 169
Farr, J., 370, 371, 373, 375, 376
Farrell, W., 602
Farris, S., 482
Fay, C., 113, 138, 162, 182, 269, 270
Featherstone, L., 8
Feild, H., 381, 417
Fein, M., 339
Feldman, J., 362
Fenton-O'Creevy, M., 10
Ferber, M., 602
Feren, D., 23, 303, 322
Ferner, A., 524
Ferris, G., 39, 51, 53, 54, 55, 105, 109,
        183, 373, 376
Ferris, N., 253
Festing, M., 220, 523, 524, 550, 555,
        557, 558
Feuille, P., 508
Fey, C., 524
Feynman, R., 14
Figart, D., 184
Fink, L., 372
Finkelstein, S., 72
Fiorito, J., 505
Fischer, R., 533
Fisher, D., 319
Fishman, C., 16, 41, 246
Fishman, J., 7
Fitch, M., 303
Fitz-Enz, J., 21
Fitzens, J., 248
Flanagan, R., 506
Flint, D., 432
Floersch, R., 419, 443
Florkowski, G., 301, 341
Floyd, J., 328, 338
Foegen, J., 425
Folger, R., 80, 150, 307
Fong, M., 14, 36, 225, 522
Fong, S., 531

Ford, W., 500
Forelle, C., 631
Fortin, N., 602
Fortney, D., 595
Fossum, J., 303
Foster, A., 509
Francis, T., 453
Frank, R., 84
Frauenheim, E., 588
Fredrickson, J., 484, 486, 487
Freed, T., 70, 114
Freedman, A., 588
Freeman, R., 509, 537, 575
Freudenheim, M., 461
Fried, J., 6, 488
Fried, N., 148
Fried, Y., 290
Friedman, T., 215, 549
Fronstin, P., 463
Frost, C., 150
Frost, P., 479
Fruen, M., 417
Fry, W., 307
Fuld, D., 481
Fulmer, I. S., 6, 8, 40, 54, 284, 285, 294, 303, 328, 363

Ganzach, Y., 376
Gardner, T., 20, 24, 35, 44
Garnett, K., 193
Gastel, R., 447
Gates, S., 52
Gattiker, U., 370
Gaughan, L., 225
Gaugler, B., 375
Ge, G., 534
Geare, A., 337
Gerhart, B., 4, 6, 8, 9, 12, 14, 23, 24, 37, 39, 40, 41, 51, 53, 54, 72, 76, 78, 79, 80, 85, 166, 169, 187, 199, 203, 205, 213, 217, 218, 223, 228, 233, 244, 274, 284, 285, 287, 294, 300, 302, 303, 304, 319, 328, 334, 343, 363, 523, 533, 603, 634, 637
Gertner, J., 580
Ghoshal, S., 175, 524
Gibbons, R., 72
Gibbs, M., 19, 72, 76
Giles, C., 536
Giles, W., 417
Gill, A., 602
Gilley, K., 631
Gillis, W., 488
Gilmartin, R., 482

Gioia, D., 375, 377
Glinsky, K., 425
Glomb, T., 106, 605
Glueck, W., 428
Goethals, G., 375
Gold, M., 592, 595
Goldberg, J., 447
Goldstein, J., 76
Gomez-Mejía, L., 13, 39, 53, 54, 329, 334, 339, 486, 488, 489, 490, 495, 522, 523, 531, 533
Gonick, L., 259
Goodall, K., 83, 522
Goodheart, J., 580
Goodman, C., 581
Gopalan, S., 523
Gordy, B., 2
Gornick, J., 605
Gorovsky, B., 594
Gowani, J., 458
Graham, M., 20, 39, 51, 85, 202, 219, 241, 244, 274, 598, 603
Graham-Moore, B., 339, 515
Grams, R., 185
Grant, D., 588
Grant, P., 631
Gray, S., 114
Graybow, M., 56
Green, B., 369
Green, G., 303
Green, R., 147
Green, S., 18
Greenberg, J., 79
Greenberger, D., 514
Greenfield, J., 82
Greenhouse, S., 45, 584, 586, 632
Greenwald, M., 417
Gregerson, H., 551
Gresch, T., 544
Griffeth, R., 300
Griffith, R., 362
Grimshaw, D., 162
Groshen, E., 79, 110, 199, 211, 216, 603
Gross, S., 269, 270, 341, 555
Grossman, R., 97
Grote, D., 376
Gruenberg, M., 23, 303, 322
Guidry, F., 631
Guillard, M., 536
Gunderson, M., 143, 598, 602, 606
Gunsauley, C., 461
Gupta, N., 9, 12, 80, 83, 84, 86, 151, 162, 165, 170, 182, 602
Guthrie, J., 37, 54
Gutman, A., 575

Guzzo, R., 555
Gwynne, P., 361

Haber, W., 447
Hader, R., 12
Hall, B., 223, 342, 463
Hall, P., 523
Hallock, K., 35, 482
Hambrick, D., 3
Hammer, T., 342
Hamner, C., 375
Han, J., 211
Hand, J., 270
Hanges, P., 530
Hanna, J., 415
Hannon, J., 225
Hansen, B., 481, 482, 485, 490
Hansen, F., 423
Harding, D., 145
Hardy, C., 85
Harris, K., 376
Harris, M., 371, 372
Harrison, D., 300
Harrison, J. K., 378
Harsen, B., 344
Hartmann, H., 184, 598
Harvey, R., 98, 99
Harzing, A., 558
Hatcher, L., 334, 341
Hatfield, J., 417, 418
Haviland, A., 602, 603
Hawass, Z., 281
Hawk, E., 301, 304, 514
He, W., 535
Hechinger, J., 631
Heetderks, T., 509
Heilbroner, R., 359
Heiner, K., 307
Helbrun, I., 514
Hellerman, M., 330
Hellerstein, J., 598, 603
Henderson, A., 484, 486, 487
Hendricks, W., 19
Heneman, H., 80, 132, 142, 217, 218, 228, 300, 301, 319, 376, 377, 514, 515, 637
Heneman, R., 12, 182
Hern, D., 286
Herzberg, F., 14, 290, 291
Herzlinger, R., 462
Hicks, J., 632
Hinchcliffe, B., 265
Hippel, C., 514
Hirsch, B., 505
Hirsch, L., 487

Hirsh, E., 380
Hmurovic, B., 269
Hodges, M., 575
Hodgeson, J., 367
Hoefstede, G., 77
Hofstede, G., 530, 531, 533
Holley, W., 381
Holmstrom, B., 72, 76
Hom, P., 9, 12, 300
Honoree, A., 329
Hoover, D., 146, 148, 184
Horwitz, F., 605
Hotchkiss, J., 603
Hough, L., 8, 53, 76, 98, 99, 118, 228,
    231, 244, 299, 303, 334, 530
House, R., 10, 530
Huber, V., 105, 109, 151, 183, 296, 341
Hudson, D., 581
Hudson, K., 443
Hui, C., 10, 532, 535, 555
Hundley, G., 532
Hunter, L., 218, 622
Huntley, C., 53
Huntsman, B., 486
Hurd, M., 78
Huselid, M., 21, 40, 52, 53, 54, 55, 84,
    248, 301, 303, 634
Huseman, R., 417, 418

Iacocca, L., 487
Idson, T., 217
Iger, R., 77, 482
Ilgen, D., 362
Imelt, J., 7
Ishida, M., 521
Ivancevich, J., 377
Iyengar, S., 46

Jackson, G., 523, 548
Jackson, S., 360, 371
Jacobs, M., 4, 56
Jacoby, S., 10, 541, 548, 618
Jain, H., 605
Jaques, E., 81, 87
Jargon, J., 416
Jarrell, S., 507
Javidan, M., 10, 530
Jeffrey, T., 303
Jelf, G., 334
Jenkins, D., 12, 299
Jenkins, G., 150, 151, 165
Jenkins, H., 36
Jensen, M., 54
Jeong, H., 524
Jeter, D., 193

Jha, S., 482
Jobs, S., 487
Johnson, J., 164, 169, 221, 490
Johnson, K., 482
Johnson, L., 552
Johnson, R., 422
Jones, D., 287, 376, 482, 485, 490
Jones, E., 375
Jones, J., 372
Jones, L., 303
Joshi, M., 17
Judge, T., 9, 40, 80, 212, 217, 218, 223,
    228, 299, 300, 376, 418

Kaestner, R., 579
Kahn, L., 4, 526, 575, 602, 605
Kahneman, D., 640
Kail, J., 495
Kaiser, H., 4
Kalleberg, A., 20, 40
Kammeyer-Mueller, J., 106, 605
Kanfer, G., 14
Kanigel, R., 162
Kaplan, R., 49, 222
Kaplan, S., 6, 486
Karimi, S., 47
Karlgaard, R., 36
Karlin, C., 602
Karuza, J., 307
Karzing, A., 524
Kasparek, J., 225
Kato, T., 542, 548
Katz, H., 40, 44, 505, 509, 523, 526
Katz, J., 486
Katz, L., 537, 575, 579
Katzell, R., 322
Katzenbach, J., 327
Kaufman, B., 575
Kaufman, R., 339
Kay, I., 489
Keaveny, T., 303
Keefe, J., 44, 55, 78
Keeley, M., 370
Keillor, G., 77
Keller, W., 523
Kelley, C., 11
Kelly, K., 304
Keon, T., 299
Kernan, M., 381
Kerr, S., 12
Kersten, E., 295
Kidder, D., 18, 631
Kildreth, A., 211
Kilgour, J., 139, 580
Kim, D., 169, 337, 515

Kim, J., 532
Kim, M., 300
Kim, W., 49
Kimber, M., 329
Kimble, M., 491
King, B., 10, 11
Kinter, H., 417
Kirchoff, S., 287
Kirk, L., 494
Kirk, R., 303
Kirkpatrick, D., 74
Kirsch, A., 521, 523
Kitay, J., 521, 523
Klaas, B., 214, 218, 221, 228, 233,
    241, 643
Klasson, C., 381
Klein, M., 491
Kleiner, M., 209
Kluger, A., 369, 378
Knight, D., 162, 182, 294
Knight, R., 588
Knight, S., 329
Knowles, B., 3, 193
Kochan, T., 40, 505, 508
Kochanski, J., 175, 330
Koestner, R., 302
Kogut, B., 523
Kohn, A., 79, 299, 300, 302
Kohn, L., 218
Kono, T., 521
Konovsky, M., 80, 131, 307
Kopelman, R., 319
Koppel, N., 220
Korman, A., 106
Kostova, T., 523
Koys, D., 303
Kramer, M., 46
Krause, K., 602
Kraut, A., 106, 113
Kroumova, M., 345
Krueger, A., 211, 579
Kruse, D., 302, 304, 340, 344, 345, 586
Kühlmann, T., 522
Kuhn, P., 586
Kurdelbusch, A., 548
Kuruvilla, S., 523
Kuzmits, F., 432
Kwon, H., 55
Kwun, S., 371

Lahart, J., 622
Laird, B., 295
Lam, S., 373
Lambert, S., 426
Lan, H., 36, 535

Landes, D., 532
Landro, L., 359
Landry, S., 631
Landsbury, R., 521, 523
Landy, F., 370, 371, 373, 375, 376, 378
Lane, P., 489
Lane, W., 537, 553
Langley, M., 483, 489
Latham, G., 14, 294
Latta, G., 551, 552
Lau, C., 10, 36, 535
Lau, S., 535
Lauren, R., 7
Law, K., 169, 300
Lawler, E., 8, 12, 21, 53, 79, 83, 150,
    175, 299
Lawshe, C., 145
Lay, K., 18
Laymon, R., 142
Lazear, E., 9, 53, 84, 87, 211
Lazonick, W., 79
LeBlanc, P., 132, 142, 182, 637
Ledford, G., 165, 166, 169, 170, 176, 182
Lee, C., 10, 169, 532, 535, 555
Lee, D., 302
Lee, J., 526
Lee, K., 422
Lee, W., 526
Lefkowitz, J., 373
Leigh, D., 602
Lemons, M., 597, 598
Lengnick-Hall, M., 636
Leno, J., 193
Leon, A., 631
Leonard, D., 303
Leonard, J., 47
Letterman, D., 193
Leung, K., 77
Levenson, A., 182, 183
Levental, G., 307
Levine, D., 49, 78, 79, 110, 211, 214,
    216, 221, 223
Levine, E., 98, 106, 108, 117, 118
Levinson, H., 366
Lewellan, W., 486
Lewicki, R., 131
Lewin, D., 508, 637
Lewin, T., 602
Lewis, K., 7, 77
Li, W., 116
Liden, R., 373, 376
Lieber, R., 624
Liebman, J., 223
Lievens, F., 117

Light, P., 99
Ling, Z., 534
Lipsky, D., 184
Lister, B., 99
Litzky, B., 18, 631
Livernash, E., 80, 87, 130, 131
Lixin, W., 534
Lloyd, M., 52
Locke, E., 8, 23, 150, 294, 303, 322
Locke, R., 17, 549
Lockhart, D., 46, 53
Long, M., 218
Longnecker, C., 372, 375, 377
Loomis, C., 13
Losey, M., 21, 52, 248, 634
Louis, M., 294
Lounsbury, J., 108, 117, 185
Lozano, F., 586
Lu, X., 36, 535
Lu, Y., 36, 535
Lubben, G., 381
Lublin, J., 480, 481, 489, 491
Luk, V., 77, 83
Luria, D., 218
Lust, J., 418
Luthans, F., 12, 53

Macduffie, J., 40
Mackey, J., 42, 82
Macpherson, D., 425, 505, 506, 507
Madden, J., 21, 145
Madhani, A., 301
Madigan, R., 146, 148, 184
Madoff, B., 456
Maertz, C., 80, 131, 150
Magnan, M., 54
Maharaj, D., 594
Maher, K., 229, 508
Mahoney, C., 79
Mahoney, D., 586
Mahoney, T., 44, 69, 79, 83, 210, 637
Main, B., 487, 488
Major, B., 303
Makri, M., 489
Malm, F., 241
Malmendier, U., 640
Malos, S., 13
Mamman, A., 290
Mang, P., 319
Mani, B., 284
Marchington, M., 162
Maremont, M., 489
Markoczy, L., 532
Marler, J., 22, 35, 37, 39, 43, 99, 636

Maroney, B., 376
Marshall, F., 506, 507
Martin, D., 381
Martin, J., 509
Martocchio, J., 419, 447, 522, 535
Marx, K., 76
Maslow, A., 14, 290, 291
Masternak, R., 335
Matlioli, D., 76
Matthews, R., 443
Mattioli, D., 215
Mattle, W., 432
Mauborgne, R., 49
Maurer, T., 184
Mausner, B., 14
Mayer, R., 284
McAdams, J., 301, 304, 514
McAfee, B., 369
McCaffery, R., 414, 416, 429, 442
McCaleb, V., 23, 303, 322
McCall, B., 216
McCallion, G., 506
McClendon, A., 482, 487
McClendon, J., 218, 221, 228, 233, 241
McConkie, M., 366
McCord, N., 480
McCormick, E., 98, 103
McCoy, T., 344
McCracken, J., 47
McDaniel, M., 80, 218, 221
McDonald, J., 606
McDonaly, D., 301
McFadden, J., 419, 456
McGregor, J., 287, 381
McKenna, D., 113
McKensie, R., 302
McKenzie, F., 329, 333
McKersie, R., 505
McLellan, S., 162
McMahan, G., 41
McMullen, T., 21, 52, 54, 619, 634
McNamara, G., 3
McNamara, K., 71
McSweeney, B., 532
McWilliams, G., 52, 433, 626
Meade, J., 636
Meckler, L., 12
Meglino, B., 373
Meindl, J., 373
Meisenheimer, J., 241
Meisinger, S., 21, 52, 248, 634
Mellon, J., 47
Mendenhall, M., 44, 182, 522, 532, 549
Menefee, J., 246

Mercer, W., 173, 241, 244
Mericle, K., 169
Mero, N., 376
Mestre, C., 557
Metcalf, R., 306
Metlay, W., 377
Meyer, M., 36, 535
Meyer, P., 480
Meyers, M., 605
Michel, J., 85, 223
Mickel, A., 217
Milanowski, A., 164
Mildenbers, D., 35
Milgrom, P., 211
Milkin, M., 487
Milkovich, C., 49, 257, 301, 382
Milkovich, G., 8, 10, 12, 39, 44, 46, 49,
        53, 69, 72, 76, 77, 83, 85, 99,
        113, 117, 118, 182, 185, 199,
        203, 223, 225, 228, 244, 245,
        248, 253, 257, 273, 288, 301,
        302, 303, 304, 333, 334, 382,
        422, 495, 521, 523, 524, 532,
        533, 548, 549, 598, 603, 637
Millenson, D., 595
Miller, D., 490
Miller, G., 480
Miller, R., 15
Miller, S., 415, 443, 643
Minette, K., 4
Minton, J., 131
Mintzberg, H., 37, 43, 44
Mischel, W., 375
Mishel, L., 507
Mitani, N., 521
Mitchell, D., 637
Mitchell, O., 425
Mitchell, S., 79
Mitchell, T., 70, 114, 217, 376
Mitra, A., 10, 12, 44, 46, 53, 77, 170,
        182, 245, 521, 524, 532, 548, 549
Miyajima, H., 548
Mobley, W., 299
Mohr, R., 20
Mondy, R., 506
Monk, A., 453
Montatague, W., 375
Montemayor, E., 37, 53
Montgomery, M., 602
Moore, D., 17
Morajda, D., 21, 52, 54, 619, 634
Morgan, L., 602
Morgenson, G., 490, 631
Morgeson, F., 80, 98, 117, 131, 150

Moritz, S., 636
Morris, A., 589
Mortensen, D., 72
Moss, P., 79
Motowidlo, S., 376
Mottl, J., 433
Mount, M., 143, 148, 185, 377
Mowday, R., 290
Moynahan, J., 497
Moynihan, L., 20, 24
Muchinsky, P., 148, 184
Mueller, G., 20, 602
Müller-Bonanni, T., 574
Mulvey, P., 637
Murphy, K., 54, 232, 359, 360, 361, 378
Murray, B., 166, 169, 187
Murti, B., 490
Myers, L., 65

Nalbantian, H., 300
Napier, N., 549
Nasar, S., 452
Neale, M., 637
Nealy, S., 428
Neely, A., 362
Neil, D., 99
Nelson, R., 523
Neumark, D., 76, 509, 579, 580, 598, 603
Newman, E., 417, 418
Newman, J., 8, 81, 165, 308, 319, 339,
        376, 469
Nguyen, N., 80, 218, 221
Nicolaisen, H., 548
Nilan, K., 176
Nimps, T., 106
Nisar, T., 12
Nohria, M., 641
Nonell, R., 548
Noonan, K., 555
Nord, W., 85
Norris, F., 483
Northcraft, G., 637
Norton, D., 49
Nuti, W., 486
Nyberg, A., 6, 303, 622

O'Brien, C., 193
O'Byrne, S., 486
O'Connell, B., 497
O'Conner, J., 631
O'Donnell, S., 220
O'Neal, S., 604
O'Neill, D., 339, 340, 602
O'Neill, J., 253, 602

O'Reilly, C., 487, 488
O'Rourke, K., 523
O'Shaughnessy, K., 110
O'Sullivan, M., 79
Oaxaca, R., 602
Obama, B., 56, 488
Odden, A., 11
Oddou, G., 549
Oi, W., 217
Oler, D., 483
Oliver, C., 523
Olsen, P., 522
Olson, C., 35
Ones, D., 360, 361, 371
Ono, A., 521
Ono, H., 548
Oppler, S., 373
Ordonez, L., 17
Ornstein, S., 79
Ossinger, J., 482
Osterman, P., 20, 44, 54, 218
Ostroff, C., 40, 602
Ostrowski, J., 493
Oswald, A., 211
Oswald, R., 447
Otellini, P., 478
Oviatt, B., 294

Paauwe, J., 14, 21
Pacifici, S., 241, 250
Paetzold, R., 12, 637
Paine, T., 449
Palframan, D., 636
Palmer, D., 13
Palmisano, S., 535, 550
Pandit, V., 482
Parent, K., 301
Parker, C., 53
Parks, J., 298
Parks, L., 12, 23, 319
Parmenter, E., 420, 421, 423
Parrent, K., 169
Parsons, W., 585
Passino, E., 108, 117, 185
Patrinos, H., 586
Patten, T., 325, 338
Patterson, M., 46
Pauly, L., 523
Pearce, J., 288, 289
Pedigo, P., 113
Pencavel, J., 505
Pence, E., 377
Perlick, A., 300
Perrin, T., 108, 241, 244, 287, 641

Peters, L., 373, 378
Peterson, E., 433
Peterson, M., 509
Peterson, R., 14
Petty, M., 304
Pfeffer, J., 22, 51, 53, 274, 301
Phalen, C. C., 250
Pierson, F., 80, 87, 131
Pilarski, A., 47
Pinault, L., 51
Plug, E., 602
Podolske, A., 378
Podolsky, M., 360
Pollack, S., 634
Porter, C., 211
Porter, E., 46, 602
Porter, L., 288, 289
Porter, M., 36, 38, 39
Posner, B., 294
Poster, C., 301
Posthuma, R., 574
Powell, B., 6, 586
Powell, G., 294
Powell, I., 602
Power, S., 535
Prada, P., 220
Prager, I., 105
Pratt, N., 489
Preameaux, S., 506
Preston, A., 602
Priem, R., 631
Pritchard, R., 14
Proctor, B., 4
Prystay, C., 552
Pucik, V., 44, 523, 532, 542, 558
Pudelko, M., 521, 524, 548
Puffer, S., 373
Pulakos, E., 371, 373
Purcell, J., 24, 40, 53

Qin, F., 17
Quaid, M., 130
Quazi, H., 535
Quinn, J., 37, 72
Quinn, M., 215
Quintanilla, J., 524

Racz, J., 14, 96
Raff, D., 216
Rajagopalan, N., 39
Rajan, R., 78
Ramras, E., 117
Ramsey, M., 522
Ramstad, P., 19, 21, 52, 619, 634
Rauh, J., 486

Raza, S., 21, 52, 248, 634
Redman, T., 4
Redmon, D., 6
Reich, S., 523
Reilly, G., 6, 53, 78
Reingold, J., 451
Reinharth, L., 319
Reiter-Palmon, R., 106
Reitman, F., 602
Remick, H., 184, 598, 605
Renard, M., 378
Renaud, S., 54
Renn, R., 341
Reskin, B., 598
Reynolds, C., 551, 553
Rich, J., 250
Richmond, R., 624
Richter, A., 306, 319
Risher, H., 138, 170, 175, 187, 273, 330, 370
Rivero, J., 360, 371
Robbins, T., 378
Roberson, Q., 17, 117
Roberts, J., 211, 319
Robinson, R., 417, 418
Rock, L., 375
Rock, M., 339
Rock, S., 631
Rockell, M., 542, 548
Roderick, R., 509
Roehling, M., 574
Roengpitya, R., 342
Rogers, C., 377
Rogers, E., 377
Rogers, J., 509
Rogovsky, N., 531
Ronaldinho, 193
Rosen, C., 13
Rosen, S., 84
Ross, K., 605
Ross, M., 80, 602
Ross, R., 515
Ross, T., 334, 339, 341, 515
Rosse, R., 118
Rossier-Renaud, A., 557
Roth, K., 220, 523
Roth, P., 118
Rotundo, M., 605
Rousseau, D., 10, 22, 72, 532, 535, 555
Rowley, I., 584
Rowling, J., 24, 265
Roy, D., 12
Royer, S., 524
Rubery, J., 162
Rubino, J., 637

Ruderman, M., 307
Rudolph, A., 375
Ruggiero, L., 241
Ruh, R., 150
Runsten, D., 580
Rutt, S., 183
Ryan, R., 296, 302
Rynes, S., 4, 6, 8, 9, 12, 14, 22, 23, 37, 39, 53, 54, 72, 79, 80, 117, 185, 199, 205, 211, 213, 217, 218, 223, 228, 244, 248, 273, 274, 285, 287, 294, 299, 300, 303, 304, 319, 328, 343, 363, 598

Saari, L., 294
Saavedra, R., 371
Sabia, J., 579
Sabirianova Peter, K., 522
Sacchetti, M., 47
Sadowski, D., 548
Sagan, C., 598
Sage, A., 642
Sage, R., 14
Saitto, S., 522
Salamin, A., 9, 12
Salamin, S., 300
Sanchez, J., 105, 108, 117
Sandall, D., 106
Sandberg, J., 87, 638
Sanders, S., 602, 603
Sanders, W., 3, 304, 549
Sands, S., 498
Sanserino, M., 625
Saulny, S., 624
Sauser, W., 184
Schaubrock, S., 225
Schaubroeck, J., 12, 371, 372, 373
Schein, E., 294
Scheller, B., 425
Schellhardt, T., 375
Schenger, L., 494
Schermerhorn, J., 521
Schine, E., 304
Schlaifer, D., 467
Schloss, D., 69
Schmidt, F., 360, 361, 371
Schmidt, M., 537, 553
Schmitt, M., 548
Schneer, J., 602
Schneider, B., 9
Schriesheim, C., 70, 114, 370
Schuler, R., 360, 371, 531
Schultz, E., 453
Schulz, E., 269, 270
Schumann, P., 79

Schuster, J., 53, 170, 176, 295, 298, 304, 345
Schwab, D., 130, 185, 303, 376
Schwab, P., 302
Schwartz, B., 46
Schwartz, J., 462
Schweiger, D., 150
Schweitzer, M., 17
Scott, D., 21, 52, 54, 619, 634
Scott, K., 40, 54, 284, 334, 338
Scott, L., 52, 248, 619
Scott, W., 375
Scoville, J., 17
Scullen, S., 12, 376
Seeber, R., 184
Segal, J., 432
Senge, P., 341
Seo, M., 290
Sesil, J., 345
Shafer, R., 113
Shaffer, M., 531
Shaikin, B., 286
Shapiro, D., 290
Shapiro, K., 417, 422
Shaver, B., 433
Shaver, K., 375
Shaw, B., 46
Shaw, J., 9, 12, 46, 53, 80, 83, 84, 86, 162, 170, 182, 225
Shaw, K., 294, 303, 322
Shaw, W., 515
Sheppard, B., 131
Sherman, J., 417
Sheth, N., 220
Shethapril, N., 220
Shi, K., 116
Shilling, M., 329, 333
Shives, G., 334
Short, J., 12
Shuster, J., 300, 327
Siddiqi, F., 586
Simmering, M., 53, 86, 87
Simon, A., 484
Simon, K., 579
Simon, S., 432
Simons, J., 3
Simons, T., 117
Simpson, M., 597
Sims, H., 375, 377
Sinegal, J., 82
Singh, G., 552
Singh, P., 345, 360
Singleton, B., 304
Siskos, C., 461
Skapinker, M., 643

Skarbek, D., 6, 586
Skarlick, D., 77
Sleemi, F., 507
Sliedregt, T., 183
Sloane, P., 605
Slowik, L., 290
Smith, A., 301, 622
Smith, B., 7
Smith, D., 327, 377
Smith, E., 417
Smith, J., 4
Smith, N., 602
Smith, P., 533
Smith, S., 432, 462
Smith, W., 259
Snell, R., 508
Snell, S., 4, 41, 378
Snider, H., 433
Solis, H., 584
Solnick, L., 508
Song, F., 9
Soskice, D., 523
Southall, D., 165
Spears, B., 3
Spencer, L., 172
Spencer, S., 172
Sperling, R., 21, 52, 54, 619, 634
Spiro, R., 375
Srikanthan, S., 215
Srull, T., 375
St-Onge, S., 54
Stack, J., 640
Stadelmann, E., 544
Stahl, G., 522
Stajkovic, A., 12, 53
Stang, P., 295
Stanley, T., 507, 579
Staubus, M., 13
Stecklaw, S., 631
Steers, R., 290
Stein, N., 296
Steinberg, R., 606
Stern, R., 342
Stevens, G., 373, 375
Stevens, J., 69
Steward, J., 506, 507
Stewart, C., 386
Stewart, J., 193
Stewart, S., 640
Stewart, T., 52
Stone, K., 307
Stone, T., 18
Storey, J., 642
Strack, R., 619
Strassel, K., 586

Strauss, G., 481, 482
Streeck, W., 534
Stroh, L., 603
Strom, S., 548
Strossel, K., 47
Sturman, M., 12, 43, 53, 86, 87, 223, 225, 233, 300, 634
Sulaiman, M., 290
Surface, E., 169
Sutarso, T., 522
Sutherland, J., 79
Sutton, C., 361
Sutton, R., 22
Svejnar, J., 522
Szczesny, J., 508
Szwejczewski, M., 215

Tabuchi, H., 521
Talley, K., 12
Tam, P., 78
Tang, N., 522
Tang, T., 8, 77, 83, 522
Tanlu, L., 17
Tapon, F., 9
Tashiro, H., 584
Taylor, B., 84
Taylor, G., 80, 87, 131
Taylor, L., 602, 603
Taylor, M., 491
Taylor, P., 116
Tejada, C., 52, 626
Terhune, C., 77, 480
Terpstra, D., 329
Teschler, L., 491
Tetlock, P., 17
Thelen, K., 549
Theriault, R., 302
Thibaut, J., 307
Thierry, H., 146, 148, 183
Thompson, D., 381
Thompson, M., 162, 182
Thornton, R., 606
Timmons, H., 220
Todd, S., 376
Toffey-Shepela, S., 605
Toh, S., 558
Tolbert, P., 85
Tomita, Y., 521
Tomsho, R., 330
Toppo, G., 330
Tosi, H., 54, 486
Towler, A., 218
Trank, C., 9, 213, 303
Treacy, M., 36
Treadway, D., 373

Treiman, D., 184
Trevor, C., 9, 12, 17, 39, 51, 53, 78, 80, 83, 85, 145, 151, 202, 219, 223, 233, 241, 244, 274, 300, 598, 622, 634
Tripoli, A., 288, 289
Trogdon, J., 84
Tropman, J., 296
Troske, K., 598, 603
Tross, S., 184
Truxillo, D., 375, 376
Tsui, A., 10, 36, 288, 289, 535
Tucker, C., 76
Turban, D., 299
Turner, L., 534
Tuschke, A., 549
Tuselmann, H., 526
Tversky, A., 640
Twadell, D., 461
Tyson, J., 483

Ulrich, D., 21, 52, 248, 634, 642, 643
Ulrich, R., 485

Valtenzi, E., 373
Van der Stede, W., 182, 183
Van Reenen, J., 55
Van Sliedregt, T., 146, 148, 183
VanDeVoort, D., 269, 270
VanKirk, L., 494
Varma, A., 12, 373, 378
Vaughan-Whitehead, D., 36, 245
Villanova, P., 371
Vinnen, A., 211
Virgin, B., 588
Virick, M., 300
Visser, J., 534
Viswesvaran, C., 105, 246, 360, 361, 371
Viteles, M., 131
Viviano, A., 605
Vlasic, B., 3
Von Bergen, C., 303
von Hippel, C., 515
Vondra, A., 150
Voskuijl, O., 146, 148, 183
Vu, V., 549

Wachter, M., 509
Wade, J., 274
Wagner, L., 428
Wagner, S., 53
Wailes, N., 521, 523
Wakely, J., 150
Waldman, D., 361, 371
Waldman, M., 72

Walker, J., 549
Walker, L., 307
Walker, T., 462
Wallace, B., 290
Wallace, M., 170, 187, 486
Wallis, D., 23, 303, 322
Walsh, J., 6, 285, 294, 363
Walston, S., 622
Walters, M., 507
Walton, J., 193
Wanderer, M., 245
Wang, C., 487
Wang, L., 83
Wang, Z., 522
Ward, L., 375
Ward, S., 4
Warner, C., 496
Warner, M., 83, 522
Warren, S., 300
Wascher, W., 579
Watson, I., 411
Watson, J., 629
Watson, W., 51, 241
Waugh, S., 377, 378
Wayne, S., 373
Wazeter, D., 17, 53, 80, 83, 87
Weber, C., 117, 169, 185, 273, 301
Weber, M., 40
Wederpahn, G., 558
Weeks, B., 497
Weichselbaumer, D., 604
Weil, J., 360
Weiner, N., 598, 606
Weiss, A., 300, 334
Weiss, R., 425
Weitzel, W., 637
Welbourne, T., 145, 151, 329, 334, 531
Welch, F., 602
Welch, J., 376
Weldom, W., 485
Wells, R., 46
Welsh, R., 20
Werling, S., 4
Werner, S., 54, 486, 522, 523, 533
Wesson, M., 12, 637
Wexley, K., 376, 378
Wheller, A., 376
White, E., 622
White, L., 373
Whitley, R., 523
Whyte, W., 12
Wiarda, E., 218
Wiehoff, J., 7
Wiersma, F., 36
Wigdor, A., 12

Wilkinson, A., 4
William, S., 300
Williams, K., 373
Williams, M., 13, 80, 218, 221, 417, 418
Williamson, J., 523
Willis, C., 52
Willmott, H., 162
Wills, D., 330
Wilson, A., 105
Wilson, M., 117, 183, 637
Wilson, T., 326
Windrum, P., 526
Wingerup, P., 555
Winstanley, D., 376
Winter-Ebmer, R., 604
Wiseman, R., 3, 13, 54, 488
Wisper, L., 521
Wong, C., 300
Wood, C., 382
Wood, R., 603
Woods, T., 193, 289, 478, 500
Wright, C., 15
Wright, P., 20, 24, 37, 41, 54, 113, 182, 523, 533, 642
Wu, Y., 80, 602
Wulf, J., 78
Wyatt, W., 215, 217, 455, 625, 637
Wyer, R., 375

Yanadori, Y., 10, 22, 35, 37, 39, 43, 75, 77, 245
Yoder, M., 6
Youndt, M., 182
Young, S., 486
Younger, J., 642

Zaidi, M., 637
Zalusky, J., 515
Zardkoohi, A., 12, 637
Zatzick, C., 375
Zedeck, S., 377
Zellner, W., 343
Zenger, T., 299
Zhang, L., 535
Zhao, Z., 522
Zhou, J., 522, 535
Zhou, X., 70, 114
Zimmerman, A., 443
Zingheim, P., 53, 170, 176, 295, 298, 300, 327, 345
Zoghi, C., 20
Zucker, L., 85
Zupan, N., 522, 532

Subject Index

ACA. *See* American Compensation Association
ADA. *See* Americans With Disabilities Act
ADEA. *See* Age Discrimination in Employment Act
Affirmative action, 380–381
AFL-CIO, 77
Age Discrimination in Employment Act (ADEA), 576, 593–594, 622
Agency theory, 490
Alignment. *See* Internal alignment
Allowances, 11, 14
Alternation ranking, 135–136
Alternative reward systems, 513–514
Amazon, 6–7
American Compensation Association (ACA), 372
American Recovery and Reinvestment Act of 2009 (ARRA), 577
Americans With Disabilities Act (ADA), 104–105, 576, 593
AMO theory, 40–41
Appraisals. *See* Performance appraisals
ARRA. *See* American Recovery and Reinvestment Act of 2009

Balanced scorecard approach, 361
Balzer Tool Coating, 164–165
Bank of America, 35, 55–56, 77
BARS. *See* Behaviorally anchored rating scales
Base salary, 481–482
Base wage, 11–12
Basis of pay, 510–511
BBOPs. *See* Broad-based option plans
Bear Sterns, 3
Bedaux plans, 323
Behavioral competency indicators, 173
Behavioral-based data, 103
Behaviorally anchored rating scales (BARS), 364
Ben and Jerry's Homemade, 82
Benchmark jobs, 133–134
Benefit determination process. *See also* Employee benefits
   benefit objectives, 432
   benefit package factors, 424

Benefit determination process—*Cont.*
   benefit plan components, 423–429
   benefit survey questionnaire format, 429
   changes in benefit costs over time, 415
   claims processing, 433
   cost containment
      administrative cost containment, 433
      benefit limitations, 433
      copay, 433
      probationary periods, 433
   cost containment terminology, 434
   cost effectiveness, 417
   customer-driven health care, 422
   e-benefits, 432
   employee benefit communication, 431–433
   employee preferences, 427–429
   employer impetus, 416–417
   employer preferences
      absolute, relative compensation costs, 426–427
      benefit costs, 423–425
      compensation costs, 423
      competitor offerings, 425
      legal requirements, 426
      role of benefits, 425–426
   equity, 427–428
   ERISA and, 417
   flexible benefit plan, 428
   government impetus, 417
   growth, 416–417
   IBM, 432
   Kellogg Company, 433
   legislation impact, 427
   market-based health care, 422
   personal needs, 428–429
   planning, design, administration, 419–423
   program administration, 429–434
   Social Security, 417
   unemployment insurance, 417
   unions, 416
   value of employee benefits, 417–418
   wage, price controls, 416

Benefit determination process—*Cont.*
   Warner Brothers, employee benefit manager, 431
   workers' compensation, 417
Benefit options. *See also* Employee benefits
   benefit plans, defined, 453
   cash balance plans, 455
   CDHP, 461–462
   child care, 467
   COBRA, 452
   community rating, 459
   contingent worker benefits, 467–468
   defined contribution plans, 453–455
   dental insurance, 465
   disability, 464–465
   domestic partner benefits, 467
   elder care, 467
   employee benefit categories, 445
   employee benefits participation, 446
   employee health care costs, 459
   ERISA, 455–457
   ESOP, 454
   experience rating, 460
   FMLA, 452
   full-time *vs.* contingent employee benefits, 468
   government, private sector costs, 444
   health care, cost control, 462–464
   health care options, cost, 462
   health insurance, 4–5, 13, 460, 463
   HIPAA, 452
   historical perspective, 442–443
   HMO, 460–463
   HRAs, 461
   HSAs, 461–462
   incentive rewards, 464
   IRAs, 455
   job hopping costs, 458
   401(k) plan, 454–455
   legal insurance, 467
   legally required
      COBRA, 450–452
      FMLA, 450–452
      HIPAA, 450–452
      Social Security, 447–450
      unemployment insurance, 450–452

Benefit options.—*Cont.*
  life insurance, 458
  LTDs, 465
  McDonald's Corporation, 443
  medical payments, 458–465
  miscellaneous benefits, 465–467
  paid off time, working hours, 465
  payment, time not worked, 466–467
  PCAs, 462
  POS, 460
  PPO, 460
  profit sharing plan, 454
  PTO plans, 467
  retirement, saving plan payments,
      452–457
  retirement income provisions, 457
  Social Security, 447–450
  STD, 464–465
  TTO, 467
  unemployment insurance
      coverage, 451
      duration, 451
      financing, 450–451
      weekly benefit amount, 451
  vision care, 465
  workers' compensation, 446–447
  workers' compensation laws,
      states, 447
Benefit plan components, 423–429
Benefit program administration, 429–434
Benefits, income protection, 11, 13
Best Buy, 52
BLS. *See* Bureau of Labor Statistics
Bonuses, 482–483
Bristol-Meyers Squibb, 13
Brito v. Zia Company, 381
Broad banding, 269–272
Broad-based option plans (BBOPs),
      345–346
Bureau of Labor Statistics (BLS),
      246–247
Burger King, 480

Cafeteria-style plan, 290, 428
Capital One Bank, 6–7
Cash compensation, 11–12
CDHP. *See* Consumer Directed
      Health Plans
Certification methods, 167, 169, 180
Chaos *vs.* control, 152
Chief executive officer (CEO)
      compensation, 6–7, 77
      shareholder return, 7
China, 10

Circuit City, 52
Civil Rights Act of 1964, TItle VII,
      576, 590
  ADA and, 593
  ADEA, 593–594
  disparate impact, 595
  disparate treatment, 594
  related laws, 593–595
Civil Rights Act of 1991, 576
COBRA. *See* Consolidated Omnibus
      Budget Reconciliation Act
Coca-Cola, 480
COLAs. *See* Cost-of-living adjustments
Combination plans, individual,
      group, 346
Comparable worth, 605
  mechanics, steps, 606–607
  men *vs.* women, 605–607
Compensable factors, 139–142
Compensation
  executives
      academic research, 489–491
      agency theory, 490
      base salary, 481–482
      bonuses, 482–483
      critics, press, 485–489
      empirical data, 486
      ERISA guidelines, 484–485
      executive benefits, 484
      executive perquisites, 485
      history, 486–487
      incentive stock options, 484
      long-term incentive, capital
          appreciation plans,
          483–484
      1993 Revenue Reconciliation
          Act, 486
      nonqualified stock options, 484
      not-for-profit sector, 487
      package components, 481
      pay cuts, 487
      performance share/unit plans, 484
      phantom stock options, 484
      restricted stock plans, 484
      social comparisons, 489
      stock appreciation rights, 484
      stock options, 483–484
      Top 10, 482
  high-tech sector, 491
      dual-career ladders, 492–493
      education relative to salary, 492
  sales forces
      average salary, 495
      combination plans, 498

Compensation—*Cont.*
  compensation components, 495
  competitive practices, 497
  economic environment, 497
  market selection, 497
  organization strategy, 495–496
  plan design, 495–498
  product to be sold, 497
  sales strategy matrix, 496
  stereotypes, 495
  special groups, 478
      conflicts faced, 479
      contingent workers, 498–499
      corporate directors, 480
      executives, 480–489
      sales forces, 494–498
      scientists, engineers, 491–494
      stockholders, 481
      supervisors, 479–480
Compensation strategy
  business strategy and, 38, 44
  business units, 36
  China, 10
  choice, 46–47
  compensation implications, 43–47
  competitive dynamics, 44
  culture values, 45
  definitions, 4–10
  developing, 43–50
  employee preferences, 46
  employees, 8–10
  equity, justice, 4–5
  external competitiveness
      compensating differentials,
          209–210
      competitive advantage, 227–228
      competitive pay policy
          alternatives, 220–227
      compliance, 228
      costs control, 199–202
      decision factors, 202–209
      degree of competition, 214
      demand side modification,
          209–212
      efficiency, 227–228
      efficiency wage, 210–211
      employee groups, 223
      employee preferences, 217
      employee recruitment,
          retention, 202–205
      employer size, 216–217
      fairness, 228
      human capital, 212–213
      industry and technology, 216

Compensation strategy—*Cont.*
    labor demand, 207
    labor markets, globalization,
        219–220
    labor markets theories,
        206–207, 210
    labor supply, 209
    lag pay-level policy, 223
    lead pay-level policy, 222–223
    management perspective, 214–215
    marginal product, 207
    marginal revenue, 207–209
    match pay with competition, 221
    on-site, off-site, offshore, 215–216
    organization factors, 216–218
    organization strategy, 217–218
    pay forms, 199
    pay level, 199
    pay-mix strategies, 223–227
    people flow to work, 216
    product demand, 214
    product market factors, ability
        to pay, 213–216
    relevant markets, 218–220
    research guidance, 227–229
    reservation wage, 212–213
    revenues, 199–202
    segmented labor supplies,
        215–216
    signaling, 211–212
    supply side modifications,
        212–213
    utility analysis, 231–233
global differences, 10
Google, 34–36, 39
HR strategy and, 40–41
IBM, 39–40
implementation, 43, 50
importance, 3–4
incentive effect, 9–10
managers, 7–8
Merrill Lynch, 34–36
Microsoft, 35–36, 48–49
objectives, 15–19
pay model and, 41–43
reassessment, 43, 50
retail stores, 7–8
within same company, 36
SAS Institute, 35–36, 40–41, 48–49
social, political context, 45–46
society, 4–5
sorting effect, 9–10
stockholders, 6–7
strategy map, 43, 47–50

Compensation strategy—*Cont.*
    union preferences, 47
    Whole Foods, 41–42
Competency
    behavioral indicators, 173
    core, 170
    defined, 171–173
    Frito-Lay managers, 174
    indicators, 171
    product development, 179
    sets, 171
    structure determination, 171
    structure purpose, 174–175
    top 20, 178
    TRW human resources
        competencies, 171–172
Competitiveness
    compensation strategy alignment, 50
    compensation strategy
        differentiation, 50–51
    compensation strategy value added,
        51–53
    external, 199–205
Compliance, 17, 87
Consolidated Omnibus Budget
    Reconciliation Act
    (COBRA), 452
Consultants, 51
Consumer Directed Health Plans
    (CDHP), 461–462
Consumer Price Index (CPI), 260, 628
Content *vs.* value, 72, 74
Contingent workers, 498–499
Core competencies, 170
Costco, 7–8, 82
Cost-of-living adjustments (COLAs),
    11–12, 513
CPI. *See* Consumer Price Index
Criterion pay structure, 148
Cultures, customs, 77–78

Data collection, 99, 101–105, 176
    conventional methods, 106
    data collectors, 108
    discrepancies, 109
    quantitative methods, 106–108
    sources, 108–109
Davis-Bacon Act, 576
Delayering, 78
Delta, 3
Dental insurance, 465
Denver Classroom Teachers
    Association, 47
Denver Public Schools, 47

Disability, 464–465
Distributive justice, 80
DOL. *See* U.S. Department of Labor

Earnings gaps, 599–600
    differences in industries, firms,
        603–604
    discrimination, 604–605
    global, 605
    sources, 601–602
    union membership impact, 604
Earnings stream, present value, 14
Earnings-at-risk plans, 340–341
Eaton, 11
E-benefits, 432
ECI. *See* Employment Cost Index
Economic pressures, 75–76
Education relative to salary, 492
EEO. *See* Equal employment
    opportunity
EEOC. *See* Equal Employment
    Opportunity Commission
Efficiency, 15, 87
Employee acceptance, 80
Employee benefits, 415
    administration issues, 420–423
        full-defined contribution, 422
        health savings accounts, 422
        managed competition, 422
        menu-driven, 422
        tiered networks, 422
    cost effectiveness, 417
    customer-driven health care, 422
    employer impetus, 416–417
    ERISA, 417
    government impetus, 417
    market-based health care, 422
    planning, design, administration,
        419–423
    Social Security, 417
    unemployment insurance, 417,
        450–452
    unions, 416
    value of, 417–418
    wage, price controls, 416
    workers' compensation, 417
Employee contributions, 20
Employee data, 101–104
Employee fairness, 175
Employee Retirement Income Security
    Act (ERISA), 417, 455–457
    benefit determination
        process, 417
    benefit options, 455–457

Employee Retirement Income Security
Act (ERISA)—*Cont.*
compensation guidelines,
executives, 484–485
employee benefits, 417
employee *vs.* independent
contractor, 586, 588
Pension Benefit Guaranty
Corporation, 456
PPA, 456
requirements, 456
vesting, portability, 456
Employee selection, training, 180, 182
Employee stock ownership plans
(ESOPs), 344–345, 454, 514
Employee *vs.* independent contractor
behavior control, 587
ERISA compliance, 586, 588
financial control, 587
IRS revenue tests, 586–588
relationship type, 587
Employees, 8–10
Employment Cost Index (ECI), 241
Enron Corp., 18
Equal Employment Opportunity
Commission (EEOC), 577
Equal employment opportunity
(EEO), 380
Equal Pay Act (EPA), 76, 143, 576,
589–590
definition of equal, 591–592
factors other than sex, 592–593
reverse discrimination, 593
skill, responsibility, working
conditions, 592
Equity, justice, 4–5
Equity theory, fairness, 83
ERISA. *See* Employee Retirement
Income Security Act
ESOPs. *See* Employee stock
ownership plans
Essential job elements, 104–105
*Estrada v. FedEx Ground Package
System, Inc.,* 588
Ethics, 17–18, 631–632
European Union Working Time
Directive, 527
Evaluation forms, 147
Exchange value, 74
Executive compensation, 6
academic research, 489–491
agency theory, 490
base salary, 481–482
bonuses, 482–483
critics, press, 485–489

Executive compensation—*Cont.*
empirical data, 486
ERISA guidelines, 484–485
executive benefits, 484
executive perquisites, 485
history, 486–487
incentive stock options, 484
long-term incentive, capital
appreciation plans, 483–484
1993 Revenue Reconciliation Act, 486
nonqualified stock options, 484
not-for-profit sector, 487
package components, 481
pay cuts, 487
performance share/unit plans, 484
phantom stock options, 484
restricted stock plans, 484
SEC disclosure rule, 577
social comparisons, 489
stock appreciation rights, 484
stock options, 483–484
Top 10, 482
Executive Order 11246, 576, 595–596
Executive Pay Watch, 77
Executive perquisites, 485
Expatriate compensation, 550
allowances, premiums, 552–553
alternatives, 555–557
balance sheet approach, 554–555
compensation elements, 552–553
decreased allowances over time, 557
employee preferences, 558
expatriate selection, 551
globalization and, 559
housing, 553
LCNs, 551, 557
localization, local plus, 556
lump-sum/cafeteria approach, 557
married plus one, 556
modified balance sheet, 556–557
salary, 552–553
system objectives, 558
taxes, 553
TCNs, 551, 557
External factors, 75
external competitiveness, 19–20,
199–205
market links, 130–131
stakeholders, 76–77

Fair Labor Standards Act (FSLA),
11–12, 47, 576
administrative exemptions, 582
child labor, 586
compensatory time off, 585–586

Fair Labor Standards Act (FSLA)—*Cont.*
computer employee exemption, 583
employee *vs.* independent
contractor, 586–587
executive exemption, 582
exemptions, 581–584
highly compensation employees, 583
income covered, 585
living wage provisions, 580
minimum wage, 578–580
NOT exempt, 583
outside sales exemption, 583
overtime, hours of work, 580–586
professional exemption, 582
state laws, 583
time covered, 584–585
Fairness, 17, 87
Family and Medical Leave Act
(FMLA), 452, 576
Financial Accounting Standards Board
Statement 123 R, 577
Flexible benefit plan, 428
FMC, 166–168
FMLA. *See* Family and Medical
Leave Act
Forbes, 6
Forms of pay. *See also* Pay level design
allowances, 11, 14
base wage, 11–12
benefits, income protection, 11, 13
cash compensation, 11–12
cost-of-living adjustments, 11–12
earnings stream, present value, 14
healthcare insurance, 13
incentives, 11–13
long-term incentives, 11, 13
merit pay, 11–12
organization as network of returns,
14–15
relational returns, 10–11, 14–15
salary, 11–12
stock options, 13
total compensation, 10–11
total returns for work, 11
variable pay, 12
work/life balance, 11, 13
Fortune, 34
Four policy choices, 19–21
401(k) plan, 453–454
Frito-Lay, 174
FSLA. *See* Fair Labor Standards Act

Gain-sharing plans, 328, 336, 515
Improshare, 339
productivity standards, 335

Gain-sharing plans—*Cont.*
    Scanlon plan example, 337
    scope, formula, 335
    strength of reinforcement, 334–335
Gantt plan, individual incentive
        plans, 326
GE Healthcare, 72
General Mills, 46
General Motors (GM), 3, 13
Generic job descriptions,
        110–111
Germany, pay system
    allowance, benefits, 545
    base pay, 544
    bonuses, 544–545
    comparisons, 545–549
    tariff agreements, 544
Globalization, global perspective, 10
    competency, person-based
            structures, 178
    earnings gaps, 605
    expatriate compensation and,
            523–525, 559
    external competitiveness, labor
            markets, 219–220
    job analysis and, 114–116
GM. *See* General Motors
Google, 6
    compensation strategy, 34–36, 39
    top executives competitiveness
            strategy, 242
Government
    discrimination laws, 589–591
    employment, compensation
            interests, 575
    labor supply/demand impact, 575
    pay discrimination, dissimilar jobs,
            597–599
    pay equity, gender pay equity, 591
    prevailing wage laws, 588–589
    proof of discrimination, jobs of
            comparable worth,
            598–599
    proof of discrimination, market
            data, 597–598
    U.S. federal pay regulations,
            575–576
    value discrimination, 589
Group incentive plans, 327–333, 342
    advantages, disadvantages,
            340–341
    earnings-at-risk plans, 340–341
    profit-sharing plans,
            339–340
Gunther v. County of Washington, 597

Hay Guide Chart job evaluation
        system, 130, 143–145
Health care benefits
    customer-driven, 422
    market-based, 422
Health insurance, 4–5, 13, 460, 463
Health Insurance Portability and
        Accountability Act (HIPAA), 452
Health maintenance organizations
        (HMO), 460–463
Health reimbursement arrangements
        (HRAs), 461
Health savings accounts (HSAs),
        461–462
High-tech sector, compensation, 491, 494
    dual-career ladders, 492–493
    education relative to salary, 492
HIPAA. *See* Health Insurance Portability
        and Accountability Act
HMO. *See* Health Maintenance
        Organizations
Hofstede Culture Dimensions, 532
HRAs. *See* Health reimbursement
        arrangements
HSAs. *See* Health savings accounts
Hughes v. Microsoft, 588
Human capital, 78

IBM, 11
    benefit determination process, 432
    compensation strategy, 39–40
    job analysis, 97
    strategy execution, 40
Improshare, 339
Incentive effect, 9–10
Incentive stock options, 484
Incentives, 11–13
Individual incentive plans, 324, 327
    advantages, disadvantages, 326
    Bedaux plans, 323
    Gantt plan, 326
    group incentive plans *vs.,* 333
    Halsey 50-50 method, 325
    Merrick plan, 325
    rate determination method, 322
    reverse incentive plan, 322
    Rowan plan, 325
    simple individual-based incentive
            system, 322
    standard hour plans, 323
    straight piece-work system, 323
    Taylor plan, 325
    time study, 324
Individual Retirement Accounts
        (IRAs), 455

Individual spot awards, pay-for-
        performance plans, 321–322
Institute of Management and
        Administration (IOMA), 299
Institution modeling, 85
Insurance
    dental, 465
    health, 4–5, 13, 460, 463
    legal insurance, 467
    legally required benefits, 450–452
    life insurance, 458
    unemployment insurance, 417,
            450–452
Internal alignment
    compliance, 87
    content *vs.* value, 72, 74
    criteria, 72, 74
    cultures, customs, 77–78
    delayering, 78
    differentials, 72
    distributive justice, 80
    economic pressures, 75–76
    efficiency, 87
    egalitarian *vs.* hierarchical, 81–83
    employee acceptance, 80
    equity theory, fairness, 83
    exchange value, 74
    external factors, 75
    external stakeholders, 76–77
    fairness, 87
    HR policies, 78–79
    human capital, 78
    institution modeling, 85
    internal labor markets, 79
    job-based structure, 74
    marginal productivity, 76
    motivation, 71, 84–85
    number of levels, 72
    organization factors, 75
    organizational strategy, 70, 78
    outsourcing, 78
    pay structures change, 80–81
    pay structures consequences, 86
    performance, 84–85
    person-based structure, 74
    procedural justice, 80
    scientific research, 83–86
    structure consequences, 86–87
    tailored *vs.* loosely coupled
            structures, 81
    tournament theory, 84–85
    U.S. government and, 75–76
    use value, 74
    work design, 78
    work flow, 70–71

Internal labor markets, 79
Internal structure, 95–97, 129–130, 151–152
  bias, 184–185
  contrasting approaches, 186–187
  perfect structure, 186
  wage criteria bias, 185
International pay systems, 522
  collective bargaining, 526
  combined employer-employee tax rate on wages, 530
  cost of living, purchasing power, 537–539
  costs comparison, 536–539
  cultural diversity, 532–534
  culture and, 530–532
  employee involvement, 531
  European Union Working Time Directive, 527
  expatriate pay, 550–558
    allowances, premiums, 552–553
    balance sheet approach, 554–557
    compensation elements, 552–553
    decreased allowances over time, 557
    employee preferences, 558
    expatriate selection, 551
    globalization and, 523–525, 559
    housing, 553
    LCNs, 551, 557
    localization, local plus, 556
    lump-sum/cafeteria approach, 557
    married plus one, 556
    modified balance sheet, 556–557
    salary, 552–553
    system objectives, 558
    taxes, 553
    TCNs, 551, 557
  exporter, 549–550
  Germany, 544–548
  global context, 523–525
  globalizer, 550
  Hofstede Culture Dimensions, 532
  Japan, 540–544, 546, 548
  labor costs, productivity, 536–537
  localizer, 549
  managerial autonomy, 535
  merit pay, by country, 549
  national system compared, 540–549
  ownership, financial markets, 534–535
  regulation, 527–530
  social contract, 525–527

International pay systems—*Cont.*
  strategic mind-sets, 549–550
  systems comparison, 540
  total pay model, strategic choices, 540
  trade unions, 531
  unemployment benefits expenditures, 531
  wage determination, flexibility, 527
  worker hiring, firing, 528
International pay systems, Germany
  allowance, benefits, 545
  base pay, 544
  bonuses, 544–545
  comparisons, 545–549
  tariff agreements, 544
International pay systems, Japan, 10, 540
  base pay, 541
  benefits, allowances, 543
  bonuses, 543
  career categories, 541
  comparisons, 545–549
  salary, age matrix, 541
  skill chart, general administration work, 542
  skills, performance, 541
  years of service, 541
International Society for Performance Improvement, 295
Interval scaling, 145–147
Interview questionnaire, 107
IOMA. *See* Institute of Management and Administration
IRAs. *See* Individual Retirement Accounts

Japan, pay system, 10, 540
  base pay, 541
  benefits, allowances, 543
  bonuses, 543
  career categories, 541
  comparisons, 545–549
  overtime, 584
  salary, age matrix, 541
  skill chart, general administration work, 542
  skills, performance, 541
  years of service, 541
Japanese Trade Union Confederation, 584
Job analysis
  acceptability, 117
  across borders, 116
  ADA, 104–105
  bedrock *vs.* bureaucracy, 113–114

Job analysis—*Cont.*
  behavioral-based data, 103
  conventional procedures, 99–100
  data collection, 99, 101–105
    conventional methods, 106
    data collectors, 108
    quantitative methods, 106–108
  data collectors, 108
  data discrepancies, 109
  data sources, 108–109
  employee data, 101–104
  essential job elements, 104–105
  generic job descriptions, 110–111
  globalization and, 114–116
  IBM, 97
  internal structure, 95–97, 129–130
  interview questionnaire, 107
  job descriptions, 96, 110–113, 116
  job evaluation and, 139–140
  job family, 98
  job-based approach, 97–98
  judging, 116–118
  level of analysis, 98, 105–106
  management support, 109
  offshoring, 114–116
  O*NET, 110–111
  PAQ, 102–103
  procedures, 98–99
  QJA, 102–103, 106, 108
  reliability, 116–117
  supply chain analysis, 113
  task-based data, 102
  terminology, 98
  union support, 109
  updated job descriptions, 116–118
  usefulness, 118
  validity, 117
Job descriptions, 96, 110–113, 116
Job family, 98
Job value, 130
Job-based structures
  alternation ranking, 135–136
  appeals/review procedures, 150–151
  assumptions, 131
  based on work itself, 142
  benchmark jobs, 133–134
  chaos *vs.* control, 152
  classification, 136–139
  compensable factors, 139–142
  content, 130
  costs, 134
  criterion pay structure, 148
  defined, 129–130
  design process, 150

Job-based structures—*Cont.*
establish purpose, 132
evaluation forms, 147
existing plans, 143
external market links, 130–131
factor scaling, 145–147
factor weighting, 147
factors, 145
Hay Guide Chart job evaluation
system, 130, 143–145
internal structures and, 151–152
interval scaling, 145–147
job analysis and, 139–140
job value, 130
major decisions, 131–132
market pricing, 135
measure for measure *vs.* much ado
about nothing, 131
methods, 134–149
multinational responsibilities,
140, 142
NEMA plan, 143, 145, 147
NMTA plan, 143, 146
nonbenchmark jobs, 148
online software support, 149
organization strategy, values, 140–142
paired comparison ranking, 135–136
parties involved, 149
plan communication, 148
point methods, 139–149
ranking, 135–136
single *vs.* multiple plans, 132–134
stakeholder acceptance, 143
structure, work hierarchy, 151–152
U.S. federal government, 138
user training, 148
working conditions, 145

Kellogg Company, 433

Labor
BLS, 246–247
compensation strategy
labor demand, 207
labor markets, globalization,
219–220
labor markets theories,
206–207, 210
labor supply, 209
segmented labor supplies,
215–216
competitor labor cost, 241
costs, 7–8, 619–625
DOL, 577

Labor—*Cont.*
Fair Labor Standards Act (FSLA),
11–12, 47, 576
administrative exemptions, 582
child labor, 586
compensatory time off, 585–586
computer employee
exemption, 583
employee *vs.* independent
contractor, 586–587
executive exemption, 582
exemptions, 581–584
highly compensation
employees, 583
income covered, 585
living wage provisions, 580
minimum wage, 578–580
NOT exempt, 583
outside sales exemption, 583
overtime, hours of work, 580–586
professional exemption, 582
state laws, 583
time covered, 584–585
globalization, global perspective,
219–220
government and, 575
internal labor markets, 79
international pay systems, 536–537
labor cost model, 623
marginal product of labor, 207
marginal revenue of labor, 207
pay level design, competitor labor
cost, 241
relevant labor markets by geographic
and employee groups, 243
Large group incentive plans, 334
LCNs. *See* Local country nationals
*Ledbetter v. Goodyear Tire & Rubber
Company,* 594
Lehman Brothers, 3
Life insurance benefit options, 458
Lilly Ledbetter Fair Play Act, 577, 594
Lincoln Electric, 39, 327
Local country nationals (LCN), 551
Lockheed Martin
engineering structure, 69–70
pay structure, 73
Long-term disability plans (LTD), 465
Long-term incentive plans (LTIs), 11,
13, 342–343
BBOPs, 345–346
capital appreciation plans, 483–484
combination plans, 346
ESOPs, 344–345

LTD. *See* Long-term disability plans
Lump-sums, 320–321, 514

Management, 7–8, 20–21
cash compensation control, 625
centralization-decentralization, 641
communication, 636–637
compensation communication
cycle, 638
compensation components, 639
financial information,
640–641
intended, unintended
consequences, 638–639
research guidance, 640
compensation forecasting,
budgeting cycle, 630
compensation function structure,
641–644
core *vs.* contingent employees, 623
corporate principles, flexibility,
642–643
embedded controls
broad bands, 632
compa-ratios, 633
range maximums,
minimums, 632
value added analysis,
634–636
variable pay, 633
wage proposal costing, 634
ethics and, 631–632
flexibility *vs.* control,
643–644
hours of work control, 624
labor cost model, 623
labor costs, 619–625
number of employees, 620
pay as change agent, 641
reengineering, outsourcing, 643
salary level control: bottom up,
629–631
salary level control: top down, 625
ability to pay, 626
budget distribution, 627–628
competitive market pressures, 626
cost of living, 627–628
CPI, 628
current year's rise, 626
turnover effects, 626
staffing analysis, pay variances, 621
staffing reductions, 621–622
Management by objectives (MBO),
performance appraisals, 366–367

Management support, 109
Manufacturing sector, hourly
    compensation costs, 5–6
Marginal product of labor, 207
Marginal productivity, 76
Marginal revenue of labor, 207
Market pay line, definition, 253
MBO. *See* Management by objectives
McDonald's Corporation, 81, 443–444
Medtronic, 13
    company values, 45
    compensation strategies, 34–36, 39
    pay model, 16–17
Mental Health Act, 576
Merit pay, 11–12, 317, 319–320
Merrick, 325
Merrill Lynch, 3, 55–56
    compensation strategy, 34–36
    pay structure, 71
    work flow, 70–71
Microsoft
    compensation strategy, 35–36, 48–49
    Hughes v. Microsoft, 588
    top executives competitiveness
        strategy, 242
    Vizcaino v. Microsoft, 498, 588
Moosewood Restaurant, 72
Motivation, 71, 84–85, 175
Multinational responsibilities, 140, 142

National Electrical Manufacturers
    Association (NEMA), 143, 145
National Metal Trades Association
    (NMTA), 143, 146
Nationwide v. Darden, 588
NEMA. *See* National Electrical
    Manufacturers Association
1993 Revenue Reconciliation
    Act, 486
NMTA. *See* National Metal
    Trades Association
Nonbenchmark jobs, 148
Nonqualified stock options, 484
Not-for-profit sector, 487
Nucor Steel, 3

Occupational Information Network
    (O*NET), 110–111
Occupation-wage differentials, 511
Office of Federal Contracts Compliance
    Programs (OFCCP), 577,
    595–596
Offshoring, 114–116
Older Worker Benefits Protection
    Act, 622

O*NET. *See* Occupational Information
    Network
Online software support, 149
Oracle, 3
Organization as network of returns,
    14–15
Organization factors, 75
Organizational strategy, 70, 78
Outsourcing, 78

Paid-time-off (PTO) plans, 467
Paired comparison ranking, 135–136
PAQ. *See* Position Analysis
    Questionnaire
Pay cuts, 487
Pay differences by location, 244
Pay grades, 265–269
Pay level design
    adjustment, 240, 272–273
    bands, reference rates, 272
    benchmarks, 248
    broad banding, 269–272
    business strategy, 274
    competitive policy, 239
    competitor labor cost, 241
    external competitive levels and
        structures, 239
    flexibility control, 271
    frequency distributions, 257
    fuzzy markets, 245
    Google, 242
    grades and ranges
        bands, 270
        midpoints, minimums,
            maximums, 268
        overlap, 268–269
        promotion increase, 269
        ranges, 265–269
    job structure, 272
    major decisions, 239
    market pricing, 273–274
    measures of compensation
        advantages and
            disadvantages, 252
        survey results, 252
    Microsoft, 242
    pay grade development, 265
    pay level, 240
    pay mix, 240
    pay ranges, 266–269
    pay structure, 240, 272
    pay-policy line, 266
        choice of measure, 266
        percent of market line, 266
        updates, 266

Pay level design—*Cont.*
    range, midpoint, minimum,
        maximum, 268
    range and band contrast, 270
    range overlap, 269
    regression, 262
    regression results, market line, 262
    relevant market competitors, 241–245
    salary survey, jobs match, 249
    salary survey data, 247
    special situations, 241
    structure adjusting, 272–273
    survey, 245
        anomalies, 258
        benchmark conversion, leveling,
            249–250
        benchmark-job approach,
            248–249
        central tendency, 259
        data, 253–258
        employers, 246
        frequency distribution, 259
        information collection, 250–253
        internal structure, external
            market rates, 265
        jobs to include, 248
        low-high approach, 249
        market pay line, construct,
            261–263
        match accuracy, 257
        non-benchmark jobs, setting
            pay, 263–265
        organization data, 250
        participation, 246
        publicly available data, 246
        statistical analysis, 258–259
        total compensation data, 250, 253
        variation, 259
        word of mouse, 246–247
    survey data, 254–256
        elements, rationale, 251
        pay policy, 261
        statistical measures, 260
    survey design, 245–253
    survey purpose, 240–241
    survey results, market line
        construct, 253–265
Pay model
    compensation objectives, 15–19
    compliance, 17
    efficiency, 15
    employee contributions, 20
    ethics, 17–18
    external competitiveness, 19–20
    fairness, 17

Pay model—*Cont.*
four policy choices, 19–21
internal alignment, 19
management, 20–21
Medtronic *vs.* Whole Foods,
16–17
pay techniques, 16, 21
procedural fairness, 17
profit-sharing, 20
stock options, 20
strategic compensation and, 41–43
Pay types. *See also* Forms of pay
Pay-for-knowledge plans, 514
Pay-for-performance plans
base *vs.* variable pay, 318
BBOPs, 345–346
choice between individual, group
plans, 333
combination plans, 346
compensation at risk, 317
compliance, 307
earnings-at-risk, 317, 340–341
equity, fairness, 307
ESOPs, 344–345
gain-sharing formulas, 336
gain-sharing plans, 328, 334–339
group incentive plans, 327–334,
341–342
group *vs.* individual incentive plans,
333–334
Improshare, 339
incentive plans, 317
individual spot awards, 321–322
large group incentive plans, 334
Lincoln Electric, 327
long-term incentive plans, explosive
interest, 342–346
long-term incentives, 342–344
merit pay, 317, 319–320
performance measures
private company bonus,
330–331
sample, 330
variable pay, 319
profit-sharing plans, 339–340
Prometric Thomas Learning Call
Centers, 321
rate determination, 322–327
relative cost comparisons, 321
risk sharing, 317
risks, rewards, long-term
incentives, 343
Rucker plan, 337–339
Scanlon plan, 337–339
self-funding plan, 346

Pay-for-perfomance plans—*Cont.*
short term plans
individual incentive plans,
322–327
individual spot awards, 321–322
lump-sum bonuses, 320–321
merit pay, 319–320
standards, 306
straight piece rate plan, 324
strategy, 305–306
structure, 306
success sharing, 317
team incentive plans, 327–334,
341–342
variable pay plans, 317–318, 331–332
Xerox, 328–329
Pay-for-performance plans
evidence
cafeteria-style, flexible
compensation, 290
compensation, performance
management, 285–290
compensation, the big picture, 286
compensation and behavior,
299–305
compensation strategy,
performance
measurement, 288
compliance, 307
distributive justice, 307
employee behavior, 285
environmental obstacles, 286
equity, fairness, 307
group incentive plans, 304
incentive plans for alternative
reward plans, 305
motivation theories, 291–293
pay level
job skill development, 301
performance, 301
system acceptance, 299
turnover, 300
pay-for-performance plan
design, 305–307
plan efficiency, 305
plan standards, 306
plan strategy, 305–306
plan structure, 306
practitioners, 294–299
procedural justice, 307
scarce talent, 300
theory, behavior, 290–294
total reward system
component, 295
wage components, 297–298

Pay-for-perfomance plans—*Cont.*
individual incentive plans, 322–327
Bedaux plans, 323
method of rate determination,
322–327
reverse incentive plan, 322
simple individual-based
incentive system, 321
standard hour plans, 323
straight piece-work system, 323
time study, 324
PBGC. *See* Pension Benefit Guaranty
Corporation
PCA. *See* Personal care accounts
Pension Benefit Guaranty Corporation
(PBGC), 456
Pension Protection Act of 2006
(PPA), 456
Performance appraisals
alternation ranking, 361
American Compensation
Association, 372
appraisal formats, improvement,
361–370
appraisal process, errors, 374
balanced scorecard approach, 361
BARS, 364
Brito v. Zia Company, 381
EEO, 380
employee contribution, individual
pay, 366
employee performance, appraisal
tips, 379–380
equal employment opportunity,
performance evaluation,
380–382
errors, 373, 377
appraisal process, 374
evaluation, 376
observation, 375
storage, recall, 375–376
format evaluation, 368–370
administrative, 369
cost criterion, 369
employee development, 369
personnel research, 369
validity, 369
job performance measurement
strategies, 361–377
MBO
communications skill, 366
component success, 367
merit grids, 385
merit guidelines, design, 384–385
paired-comparison ranking, 363

Performance appraisals—*Cont.*
  pay subjective, 382, 385
    competency, customer care, 383
    performance-based guidelines,
      383–384
    salary increase matrix,
      performance rating, 384
  pay-for-performance tool,
    promotion increase, 386
  peformance-dimension training, 377
  peformance-standard training, 377
  performance evaluation process,
    377–380
  performance metrics, 360–361
  position-based guidelines, 384
  rank and yank, 376
  rate-error training, 377
  raters, 370
    customer, 372
    peers, 371
    process, 373
    self, 372
    subordinate, 372
    supervisors, 371
    training, 377
  rating process, errors, 373
  rating scale, absolute standards, 364
  ratings of managers, 374
  role in compensation decisions,
    359–361
  salary increase matrix, performance
    rating, 384
  standard rating scale, 363
    behavioral scale anchors, 365
  straight ranking, 361
  360-degree feedback, 370–373
  Workforce, 376
Performance metrics, 360–361
Performance share/unit plans, 484
Performance-based pay, 35, 54–55
Personal care accounts (PCA), 462
Person-based structures
  competency, 170–182
    analysis, 175–178
    behavior motivation, 175
    certification methods, 180
    competency indicators, 171
    competency sets, 171
    competency-based structure
      determination, 171
    competency-based structure
      purpose, 174–175
    core competencies, 170
    data collection, 176
    defining competencies, 171–173

Person-based structures—*Cont.*
    employee fairness, 175
    employee selection, training,
      180, 182
    Frito-Lay managerial
      competencies, 174
    global perspective, 178
    organizational strategy, 174
    plan objective, 175
    product development
      competency, 179
    research guidance, 182
    sample behavioral competency
      indicators, 173
    3M leadership competencies,
      176–177
    titles, high-level definitions, 181
    top 20 competencies, 178
    TRW human resources
      competencies, 171–172
    work flow, 174–175
  plan acceptability, 184
  plan administration, 183
  plan validity, 183–184
  results usefulness, 183–184
  skill plans, 162–165
    Balzer Tool Coating skill
      ladder, 164
    behavior motivation, 166, 175
    certification methods, 167, 169
    data collection, 166–167
    depth *vs.* breadth skill plans,
      162–165
    employee fairness, 165
    FMC, 166–168
    generalist/multiskill based,
      164–165
    internal structure, 163
    involved parties, 166
    research/experience, 169–170
    skill analysis, 166–169
    skill-based structures, purpose,
      165–166
    specialist, 162–164
    strategy, objectives, 165
    work flow support, 165
Phantom stock options, 484
Point methods, 139–149
Point-of-service plan (POS), 460
Position Analysis Questionnaire (PAQ),
  102–103
PPA. *See* Pension Protection Act of 2006
PPO. *See* Preferred provider
  organizations
Prax Air, 12

Preferred provider organizations (PPO),
  460–461, 463
Pregnancy Discrimination Act, 576
Price increases, 6
PricewaterhouseCoopers (PWC), 74
Procedural fairness, 17
Procedural justice, 80
Product development competency, 179
Productivity, 6
Profit-sharing, 20
  pay-for-perfomance plans, 339–340
  unions and, 515–516
Prometric Thomas Learning Call
  Centers, 321
PTO. *See* Paid-time-off plans

Quantitative job analysis (QJA),
  102–103, 106, 108

Relational returns, 10–11, 14–15
Relevant labor markets by geographic
  and employee groups, 243
Restricted stock plans, 484
Retail stores, 7–8
Reverse incentive plan, 322

Salary survey data, 247
Sales forces
  average salary, 495
  combination plans, 498
  compensation components, 495
  competitive practices, 497
  economic environment, 497
  market selection, 497
  organization strategy, 495–496
  plan design, 495–498
  product to be sold, 497
  sales strategy matrix, 496
  stereotypes, 495
Sam's Club, 7–8
Sarbanes-Oxley Act, 576
SAS Institute, 35–36, 40–41, 48–49
Schultz v. Wheaton Glass, 591
Sears, 305
Securities and Exchange Commission
  (SEC), 577
Securities Exchange Act, 576
Self-funding plan, 346
Sherman Act, 246
Short-term disability (STD),
  464–465
Simple individual-based incentive
  system, 321
Skill-based structures, 163–166
Social Security, 417, 447–450

Sorting effect, 9–10
Southwest Airlines, 39
Spaulding v. University of Washington, 598
Special groups, compensation, 478
conflicts faced, 479
contingent workers, 498–499
corporate directors, 480
executives, 480–489
sales forces, 494–498
scientists, engineers, 491–494
stockholders, 481
supervisors, 479–480
Spillover effect, unions, 509
Standard hour plans, individual incentive plans, 323
STD. *See* Short-term disability
Stock appreciation rights, 484
Stock options, 13, 20, 483–484
Stockholders, 6–7
Straight piece-work system, 323–324
Strategic choices, 46–47
best practices *vs.* fit, 53
compensation strategy, 34–41
cost cutters, 38
customer-focused, 38
innovators, 38
research evidence, 53–54
stated *vs.* unstated choices, 42–43
virtuous, vicious cycles, 54–55
Supermarket plan, 428
Supply chain analysis, 113

Tacit work, 162
TARP. *See* Troubled Asset Relief Program
Task-based data, 102
Taxes
combined employer-employee tax rate on wages, 530
expatriate compensation, 553
unemployment tax control, 451–452
TCNs. *See* Third-country nationals
Team incentive plans
gain-sharing plans, 328, 334–339
group incentive plans, 327–333
group *vs.* individual incentive plans, 328
large group incentive plans, 334
Third-country nationals (TCNs), 551
360-degree feedback, performance appraisals, 370–373

3M, 81
interview questionnaire, 107
leadership competencies, 176–177
Title VII, Civil Rights Act of 1964, 576, 590
ADA and, 593
ADEA and, 593–594
disparate impact, 595
disparate treatment, 594
related laws, 593–595
Titles, high-level definitions, 181
Top 20 competencies, 178
Total compensation, 10–11
Total returns for work, 11
Total reward system, 295
Total Well-Being Program (Medtronic), 13, 35
Tournament theory, 84–85
Traditional time-off plans (TTO), 467
Training
employee selection, 180, 182
job-based structures, 148
peformance-dimension training, 377
peformance-standard training, 377
rate-error training, 377
raters, 377
Transactional work, 162
Troubled Asset Relief Program (TARP), 4, 56, 525–526, 577
TRW human resources competencies, 171–172
TTO. *See* Traditional time-off plans

UAW. *See* United Auto Workers
Unemployment insurance, 417
coverage, 450–451
duration, 451
human resource planning, 451–452
unemployment tax control, 451–452
weekly benefit amount, 451
Unions
AFL-CIO, 77
comparable worth and, 607
earnings gaps and, 604
international pay systems and, 534
pay-for-knowledge plans and, 514
support, 109
wage impact
alternative reward systems and, 513–514
basis of pay, 510–511
COLAs, 513
employee benefits, 416
ESOPs, 514

Unions—*Cont.*
experience-merit differentials, 511–512
gain-sharing plans, 515
lump-sum awards, 514
occupation-wage differentials, 511
other differentials, 512
pay-for-knowledge plans, 514
profit-sharing plans, 515–516
spillover effect, 509
vacations, holidays, 512–513
wage adjustment provisions, 513
wage determination, 506–508
wage packages, 508–509
wages, policies and practices impact, 509–513
United Auto Workers (UAW), 47
Updated job descriptions, 116–118
U.S. Bureau of Labor Statistics, 114–115
U.S. Department of Labor (DOL), 577
U.S. Internal Revenue Service (IRS), 47
U.S. Treasury Department, 35
User training, 148

Vacations, holidays, 512–513
Variable pay, 12
Vision benefits, 465
Vizcaino v. Microsoft, 498, 588

Wagner Act, 416
Wall Street Journal, 4, 139
Wal-Mart, 4, 7–8, 11
Walsh-Health Public Contracts Act, 576
Warner Brothers, employee benefit manager, 431
Whole Foods
benefits program, 46
compensation strategy, internal alignment, 82
compensation system, 41–42
competitive advantage, 41
job evaluation, 153–157
pay model, 16–17
Work design, 78
Work flow, 70–71, 174–175
Worker Economic Opportunity Act, 576
Workers' compensation, 417, 446–447
Workforce (magazine), Performance appraisals, 376
Working conditions, 145
Work/life balance, 11, 13

Xerox Achievement Award, pay-for-perfomance plans, 328–329